Signature

Microsoft® WORD 2010

Nita Rutkosky
Pierce College at Puyallup, Puyallup, Washington

Audrey Rutkosky Roggenkamp
Pierce College at Puyallup, Puyallup, Washington

Paradigm **PUBLISHING**

St. Paul • Indianapolis

Managing Editor: Sonja Brown
Developmental Editor: Spencer Cotkin
Production Editor: Bob Dreas
Cover Designer: Leslie Anderson
Production Specialist: Desktop Solutions

Copy Editor: Lianna J. Wlasiuk
Proofreaders: Carol McLean, Crystal Bullen
Indexer: Ina Gravitz
Testers: Jeff Johnson, Pat Jarvis, Sarah Kearin

Care has been taken to verify the accuracy of information presented in this book. However, the authors, editors, and publisher cannot accept responsibility for Web, email, newsgroup, or chat room subject matter or content, or for consequences from application of the information in this book, and make no warranty, expressed or implied, with respect to its content.

Trademarks: Microsoft is a trademark or registered trademark of Microsoft Corporation in the United States and/or other countries. Some of the product names and company names included in this book have been used for identification purposes only and may be trademarks or registered trade names of their respective manufacturers and sellers. The authors, editors, and publisher disclaim any affiliation, association, or connection with, or sponsorship or endorsement by, such owners.

We have made every effort to trace the ownership of all copyrighted material and to secure permission from copyright holders. In the event of any question arising as to the use of any material, we will be pleased to make the necessary corrections in future printings. Thanks are due to the aforementioned authors, publishers, and agents for permission to use the materials indicated.

Paradigm Publishing is independent from Microsoft Corporation, and not affiliated with Microsoft in any manner. While this publication may be used in assisting individuals to prepare for a Microsoft Business Certification exam, Microsoft, its designated program administrator, and Paradigm Publishing do not warrant that use of this publication will ensure passing a Microsoft Business Certification exam.

ISBN 978-0-76384-294-9 (text)
ISBN 978-0-76384-295-6 (text and CD)

© 2011 by Paradigm Publishing, Inc.
875 Montreal Way
St. Paul, MN 55102
Email: educate@emcp.com
Website: www.emcp.com

Printed in the United States of America

19 18 17 16 15 14 13 12 11 10   1 2 3 4 5 6 7 8 9 10

Brief Contents

UNIT 1 Preparing Documents   1

Chapter 1   Creating, Printing, and Editing Documents   3

Chapter 2   Formatting Characters   35

Chapter 3   Aligning and Indenting Paragraphs   61

Chapter 4   Customizing Paragraphs   93

Chapter 5   Proofing Documents   131

UNIT 2 Formatting and Managing Documents   175

Chapter 6   Formatting Pages   177

Chapter 7   Customizing Page Formatting   211

Chapter 8   Inserting Elements and Navigating in a Document   245

Chapter 9   Maintaining Documents   273

Chapter 10   Managing and Printing Documents   307

UNIT 3 Enhancing Documents   345

Chapter 11   Inserting Images   347

Chapter 12   Inserting Shapes and WordArt   387

Chapter 13   Creating Tables   435

Chapter 14   Enhancing Tables   461

Chapter 15   Creating Charts   493

UNIT 4 Managing Data   529

Chapter 16   Merging Documents   531

Chapter 17   Sorting and Selecting   583

Chapter 18   Managing Lists   607

Chapter 19   Managing Page Numbers, Headers, and Footers   637

Chapter 20   Managing Shared Documents   669

UNIT 5 Customizing Documents and Features   711

Chapter 21   Inserting and Customizing Quick Parts   713

Chapter 22   Customizing AutoCorrect and Word Options   749

Chapter 23   Customizing Themes   787

Chapter 24   Creating and Managing Styles   809

Chapter 25   Protecting and Preparing Documents   853

UNIT 6 Referencing Data   909

Chapter 26   Inserting, Endnotes, Footnotes, and References   911

Chapter 27   Creating Indexes   941

Chapter 28   Creating Specialized Tables   963

Chapter 29   Creating Forms   995

Chapter 30   Using Outline View and Formatting with Macros   1041

Contents

Preface viii

Getting Started xiii

UNIT 1 PREPARING DOCUMENTS 1

Chapter 1
Creating, Printing, and Editing Documents

Opening Microsoft Word	6
Creating, Saving, Printing, and Closing a Document	6
Creating a New Document	13
Opening a Document	13
Pinning a Document	14
Saving a Document with Save As	15
Exiting Word	15
Editing a Document	16
Selecting Text	20
Using the Undo and Redo Buttons	24
Using Help	25
Chapter Summary	29
Commands Review	30
Key Points Review	30
Chapter Assessments	31

Chapter 2
Formatting Characters

Changing Fonts	37
Applying Styles from a Quick Styles Set	49
Applying a Theme	51
Chapter Summary	54
Commands Review	55
Key Points Review	56
Chapter Assessments	56

Chapter 3
Aligning and Indenting Paragraphs

Changing Paragraph Alignment	64
Indenting Text in Paragraphs	69
Spacing Before and After Paragraphs	73
Repeating the Last Action	73
Formatting with Format Painter	74
Changing Line Spacing	76
Changing Paragraph Spacing with the Change Styles Button	77
Applying Numbering and Bullets	78
Revealing Formatting	83
Comparing Formatting	84

Chapter Summary	86
Commands Review	86
Key Points Review	87
Chapter Assessments	88

Chapter 4
Customizing Paragraphs

Inserting Paragraph Borders and Shading	97
Sorting Text in Paragraphs	105
Manipulating Tabs on the Ruler	106
Manipulating Tabs at the Tabs Dialog Box	110
Cutting, Copying, and Pasting Text	114
Using the Clipboard	120
Using Paste Special	121
Chapter Summary	123
Commands Review	123
Key Points Review	124
Chapter Assessments	125

Chapter 5
Proofing Documents

Checking the Spelling and Grammar in a Document	135
Creating a Custom Dictionary	144
Displaying Word Count	147
Using the Thesaurus	147
Researching Information	150
Translating Text	153
Chapter Summary	158
Commands Review	159
Key Points Review	159
Chapter Assessments	160

Unit 1 Performance Assessments

Assessing Proficiencies	165
Creating Original Documents	172

UNIT 2 FORMATTING AND MANAGING DOCUMENTS 175

Chapter 6
Formatting Pages

Changing the View	181
Changing Page Setup	183
Inserting a Section Break	189
Creating Columns	191
Hyphenating Words	196
Inserting Line Numbers	197
Chapter Summary	205

Commands Review	206
Key Points Review	207
Chapter Assessments	207

Chapter 7
Customizing Page Formatting

Inserting Page Elements	215
Inserting Predesigned Page Numbering	220
Inserting Predesigned Headers and Footers	221
Finding and Replacing Text and Formatting	226
Using the Click and Type Feature	234
Vertically Aligning Text	235
Chapter Summary	237
Commands Review	238
Key Points Review	238
Chapter Assessments	239

Chapter 8
Inserting Elements and Navigating in a Document

Inserting Symbols and Special Characters	249
Creating a Drop Cap	251
Inserting the Date and Time	252
Inserting a File	253
Navigating in a Document	254
Inserting Hyperlinks	259
Creating a Cross-reference	264
Chapter Summary	266
Commands Review	266
Key Points Review	267
Chapter Assessments	267

Chapter 9
Maintaining Documents

Maintaining Documents	276
Changing Dialog Box Views	284
Sharing Documents	289
Creating a Document Using a Template	299
Chapter Summary	302
Commands Review	303
Key Points Review	303
Chapter Assessments	304

Chapter 10
Managing and Printing Documents

Working with Windows	310
Managing the Recent List	317
Previewing and Printing a Document	318
Creating and Printing Envelopes	324
Creating and Printing Labels	326
Chapter Summary	330
Commands Review	331
Key Points Review	331
Chapter Assessments	332

Unit 2 Performance Assessments

| Assessing Proficiencies | 337 |
| Creating Original Documents | 344 |

UNIT 3 ENHANCING DOCUMENTS 345

Chapter 11
Inserting Images

Inserting an Image	351
Creating SmartArt	371
Chapter Summary	379
Commands Review	380
Key Points Review	380
Chapter Assessments	381

Chapter 12
Inserting Shapes and WordArt

Creating Screenshots	391
Drawing Shapes	394
Inserting and Formatting Text Boxes	404
Linking and Unlinking Text Boxes	409
Inserting WordArt	413
Applying Character Formatting	418
Chapter Summary	424
Commands Review	425
Key Points Review	425
Chapter Assessments	426

Chapter 13
Creating Tables

Creating a Table	438
Selecting Cells	442
Changing the Table Design	445
Drawing a Table	450
Inserting a Quick Table	454
Chapter Summary	455
Commands Review	456
Key Points Review	456
Chapter Assessments	457

Chapter 14
Enhancing Tables

Changing Table Layout	464
Performing Calculations in a Table	481
Chapter Summary	486
Commands Review	486
Key Points Review	487
Chapter Assessments	488

Chapter 15
Creating Charts

Creating a Chart	496
Changing Chart Design	499
Formatting Chart Layout	503
Changing Chart Formatting	508
Chapter Summary	514
Commands Review	515
Key Points Review	515
Chapter Assessments	516

Unit 3 Performance Assessments

Assessing Proficiencies   521
Creating Original Documents   527

UNIT 4 MANAGING DATA   529

Chapter 16

Merging Documents

Completing a Merge   541
Merging Envelopes   550
Editing a Data Source File   555
Inserting Additional Fields   560
Merging with Other Data Sources   565
Using the Mail Merge Wizard   570
Chapter Summary   573
Commands Review   574
Key Points Review   575
Chapter Assessments   576

Chapter 17

Sorting and Selecting

Sorting Text   585
Sorting Records in a Data Source   592
Selecting Records   596
Finding Records   599
Chapter Summary   602
Commands Review   602
Key Points Review   603
Chapter Assessments   603

Chapter 18

Managing Lists

Inserting Custom Numbers and Bullets   610
Inserting Multilevel List Numbering   618
Inserting Special Characters   623
Finding and Replacing Special Characters   627
Chapter Summary   629
Commands Review   630
Key Points Review   630
Chapter Assessments   631

Chapter 19

Managing Page Numbers, Headers, and Footers

Customizing Page Numbers   647
Inserting Headers and Footers   651
Printing Sections   661
Keeping Text Together   662
Chapter Summary   664
Commands Review   665
Key Points Review   665
Chapter Assessments   666

Chapter 20

Managing Shared Documents

Inserting Comments   673
Tracking Changes to a Document   682

Comparing Documents   691
Combining Documents   694
Chapter Summary   697
Commands Review   698
Key Points Review   699
Chapter Assessments   699

Unit 4 Performance Assessments

Assessing Proficiencies   703
Creating Original Documents   708

UNIT 5 CUSTOMIZING DOCUMENTS AND FEATURES   711

Chapter 21

Inserting and Customizing Quick Parts

Inserting Quick Parts   718
Saving Building Block Content   722
Inserting Document Properties   736
Inserting Fields   738
Chapter Summary   741
Commands Review   742
Key Points Review   742
Chapter Assessments   743

Chapter 22

Customizing AutoCorrect and Word Options

Customizing AutoCorrect   752
Minimizing the Ribbon   760
Customizing the Quick Access Toolbar   760
Customizing the Ribbon   766
Importing/Exporting Customizations   772
Customizing Word Options   774
Chapter Summary   779
Commands Review   780
Key Points Review   780
Chapter Assessments   781

Chapter 23

Customizing Themes

Creating Themes   789
Creating Custom Theme Colors   790
Creating Custom Theme Fonts   796
Applying Theme Effects   797
Saving a Document Theme   797
Editing Custom Themes   799
Deleting Custom Themes   802
Chapter Summary   804
Commands Review   805
Key Points Review   805
Chapter Assessments   806

Chapter 24

Creating and Managing Styles

Formatting with Styles   813
Applying Styles   815
Creating Styles   818

Modifying a Style 822
Displaying All Styles 825
Revealing Style Formatting 827
Deleting a Custom Quick Styles Set 827
Creating Multilevel List and Table Styles 828
Using the Style Inspector 837
Managing Styles 839
Chapter Summary 845
Commands Review 846
Key Points Review 847
Chapter Assessments 848

Chapter 25
Protecting and Preparing Documents

Protecting Documents 857
Managing Document Properties 865
Restricting Documents 872
Inspecting a Document 878
Chapter Summary 891
Commands Review 892
Key Points Review 893
Chapter Assessments 894

Unit 5 Performance Assessments

Assessing Proficiencies 899
Creating Original Documents 906

UNIT 6 REFERENCING DATA 909

Chapter 26
Inserting Endnotes, Footnotes, and References

Creating Footnotes and Endnotes 915
Creating Citations and Bibliographies 919
Chapter Summary 933
Commands Review 933
Key Points Review 934
Chapter Assessments 934

Chapter 27
Creating Indexes

Creating an Index 943
Creating a Concordance File 952
Updating and Deleting an Index 955
Chapter Summary 956
Commands Review 956
Key Points Review 957
Chapter Assessments 957

Chapter 28
Creating Specialized Tables

Creating a Table of Contents 967
Creating a Table of Figures 977
Creating a Table of Authorities 981
Chapter Summary 986
Commands Review 987
Key Points Review 988
Chapter Assessments 988

Chapter 29
Creating Forms

Creating a Form 999
Inserting Text Controls 1004
Filling in a Form Document 1004
Editing a Form Template 1006
Inserting Instructional Text 1008
Creating Forms Using Tables 1008
Creating Drop-Down Lists 1012
Setting Properties for Content Controls 1012
Creating a Form with Legacy Tools 1018
Printing a Form 1021
Customizing Form Field Options 1022
Chapter Summary 1029
Commands Review 1030
Key Points Review 1031
Chapter Assessments 1032

Chapter 30
Using Outline View and Formatting with Macros

Creating an Outline 1046
Creating a Master Document and Subdocuments 1054
Recording a Macro 1060
Running a Macro 1063
Assigning a Macro 1066
Recording a Macro with Fill-in Fields 1057
Specifying Macro Security Settings 1070
Saving a Macro-Enabled Document or Template 1071
Recording a Macro with Fill-In Fields 1072
Chapter Summary 1076
Commands Review 1077
Key Points Review 1078
Chapter Assessments 1079

Unit 6 Performance Assessments

Assessing Proficiencies 1085
Creating Original Documents 1094

Appendix A
Proofreader Marks 1095

Appendix B
Formatting a Personal Business Letter 1096

Appendix C
Formatting a Memo 1098

Appendix D
Formatting a Business Letter 1100

Index 1103

Preface

To prepare for a successful business career, students need to acquire the skills and qualifications essential to becoming a productive member of the business community. Microcomputer systems are prevalent in business offices, and students will encounter employment opportunities that require a working knowledge of computers and computer software. Companies and organizations use microcomputers, along with the appropriate software, in a wide variety of capacities. One of the most popular uses is word processing—the creation of many different types of documents, including letters, contracts, group mailings, newsletters, and brochures.

Word processing is not only important in the business world. It is also a popular application for personal and academic use. People use word processing to write correspondence, maintain records, provide support for a home-based business or cottage industry, and to write term papers and reports for course assignments.

Signature Microsoft Word 2010 instructs students in the theories and practical applications of one of the most popular word processing programs—Microsoft Word 2010. The textbook is designed to be used in beginning through advanced word processing classes and provides approximately 80 to 120 hours of instruction. No prior knowledge of word processing is required. After successfully completing a course using this textbook, students will be able to

- Create and edit memos, letters, and reports of varying complexity
- Format and customize a range of document types and styles
- Add and modify graphics and other visual elements to enhance written communication
- Organize content into tables, lists, and other structures that promote reader understanding and efficient management in a collaborative work environment
- Plan, research, write, revise, and publish documents to meet specific information needs

To use the textbook successfully, students must have access to Microsoft Word 2010 and a microcomputer system. Word 2010 needs to be installed on the hard drive of each student computer or on a network system. To install the program properly, please refer to the Word or Microsoft Office documentation.

Textbook and Chapter Features

Signature Microsoft Word 2010 is divided into six units. Units 1–3 cover foundation, entry-level word processing skills. Units 4–6 cover intermediate- to advanced-level skills. The chapters within each unit contain the following elements:

- Performance Objectives, identifying the specific learning goals of the chapter.
- Introductory material, providing an overview of new concepts and features.
- Step-by-step exercises, organized into groups, providing students with the opportunity to practice using features immediately after they read about them.
- Model answers of intrachapter exercises, conveniently located at the beginning of each chapter.
- Chapter Summary, reviewing the main concepts of the chapter.
- Commands Review, listing the major commands learned in the chapter.
- Key Points Review, a short-answer self-check of chapter concepts.

- Chapter Assessments, offering graduated levels of performance-based exercises that students complete without step-by-step guidance. These types of Assessments include:
  - Applying Your Skills, where students demonstrate knowledge of learned features
  - Expanding Your Skills, which prompt students to learn additional skills
  - Achieving Signature Status, a set of more challenging problems

Performance Assessments at the end of each unit include the following:

- *Assessing Proficiencies:* practical computer simulation exercises that require students to make decisions about document preparation and formatting, providing ample opportunity to apply new features as well as to practice previously learned material.
- *Creating Original Documents:* writing activities that provide students with the opportunity to compose and format business documents, requiring problem-solving and creative abilities as well as hands-on computer skills.

Completing Computer Exercises

Some computer exercises in the chapters require students to access and use an existing file saved on the Student Resources CD that accompanies this textbook. The files are contained in individual folders for each chapter. A CD icon and folder name displayed on the opening page of each chapter and each set of unit assessments indicates that students need to copy a folder of files from the CD before beginning the activities. Detailed instructions on how to copy and delete folders are provided in the *Getting Started* section that follows the Preface. For added convenience, the instructions are repeated on the inside of the back cover of the book.

Student Courseware

Student Resources CD Each textbook includes a Student Resources CD that contains typed documents and files required for completing activities and exercises. The first page of each chapter provides instructions for accessing student data files from a specific folder on the Student Resources CD. The student will need to copy this folder of files from the CD to a storage medium before beginning the section activities. (See the inside back cover for instructions on copying a folder.)

Internet Resource Center Additional material for students preparing to work in the business office is available at the book-specific website at www.emcp.net/signatureword2010. Here students will find the same resources that are on the Student Resources CD along with study tools, Web links, and other information useful in education and work settings.

SNAP Training and Assessment SNAP is a Web-based program offering an interactive venue for learning Microsoft Office 2010. SNAP is composed of a learning management system, multimedia tutorials, performance skill items, document-based assessments, a concepts test bank, an online grade book, and a set of course planning tools. A CD of tutorials teaching the basics of Word is also available if instructors wish to assign additional SNAP tutorial work without using the Web-based SNAP program.

eBook For students who prefer studying with an eBook, *Signature Microsoft Word 2010* is available in an electronic form. The Web-based, password-protected eBook features dynamic navigation tools, including bookmarking, a linked table of contents, and the ability to jump to a specific page. The eBook format also supports helpful study tools, such as highlighting and note taking.

Instructor Resources

Instructor's Guide and DVD Instructor support for this text includes a printed *Instructor's Guide* packaged with an Instructor Resources DVD. The print and electronic resources include planning information, such as Lesson Blueprints, teaching hints, and sample course syllabus; presentation resources, such as PowerPoint slide shows; and assessment resources, including an overview of available assessment venues, live model answers for chapter activities, and live and PDF model answers and grading rubrics for end-of-chapter exercises. Contents of the *Instructor's Guide and Instructor Resources DVD* package are also available on the password-protected section of the Internet Resource Center for this title at www.emcp.net/signatureword2010.

Computerized Test Generator Instructors can use the **EXAM**VIEW® Assessment Suite and test banks of multiple-choice items to create customized web-based or print tests. The **EXAM**VIEW® Assessment Suite and test banks are provided on the Instructor Resources DVD.

Blackboard Cartridge This set of files allows instructors to create a personalized Blackboard website for their course and provides course content, tests, and the mechanisms for establishing communication via e-discussions and online group conferences. Available content includes a syllabus, test banks, PowerPoint presentations, and supplementary course materials. Upon request, the files can be available within 24–48 hours. Hosting the site is the responsibility of the educational institution.

Blackboard

System Requirements

This interactive text is designed for the student to complete chapter and unit work on a computer running a standard installation of Microsoft Office 2010, Standard or Professional, and the Microsoft Windows 7 operating system. To effectively run this suite and operating system, your computer should be outfitted with the following:

- 1 gigahertz (GHz) processor or faster; 1 gigabyte (GB) of RAM
- DVD drive
- 15 GB of available hard-disk space
- Computer mouse or compatible pointing device

Microsoft Office 2010 will also operate on computers running the Windows XP Service Pack 3 or the Windows Vista operating system.

Screen captures in this book were created using a screen resolution display setting of 1280 × 800. For instructions on changing the resolution for your monitor see page xxiii. Choose the resolution that best matches your computer; however, be aware that using a resolution other than 1280 × 800 means that your screens may not exactly match the illustrations in this book.

About the Authors

Nita Rutkosky began teaching business education courses at Pierce College in Puyallup, Washington, in 1978. Since then she has taught a variety of software applications to students in postsecondary Information Technology certificate and degree programs. In addition to *Signature Series Microsoft Word 2010, 2007, 2003*, and prior editions, she has co-authored *Marquee Office 2010, 2007, 2003*, and previous editions; *Benchmark Series Microsoft Office 2010, 2007, 2003*, and prior editions; and *Using Computers in the Medical Office: Microsoft Word, Excel, and PowerPoint 2007* and *2003*. She has also authored textbooks on keyboarding, WordPerfect®, desktop publishing, and voice recognition for Paradigm Publishing, Inc.

Audrey Rutkosky Roggenkamp teaches keyboarding, skill building, and Microsoft Office programs in the Business Information Technology department at Pierce College in Puyallup. In addition to this title, she has co-authored *Benchmark Series Microsoft Office 2010* and *2007*; *Marquee Office 2010* and *2007*; and *Using Computers in the Medical Office 2010* and *2003* for Paradigm Publishing, Inc.

Acknowledgements

The authors and editors are grateful to the many individuals who provided feedback on various aspects of this project. The following individuals reviewed the previous version of this book and offered valuable suggestions for *Signature Microsoft® Word 2010*:

Nisheeth Agrawal, MBA
Calhoun Community College
Huntsville, Alabama

Patty A. Anderson, MS
Florida Gateway College
Lake City, Florida

Paula Belmonte, MA
Union County College
Cranford, New Jersey

Sue Black
New Mexico Junior College
Hobbs, New Mexico

Tena Brown, MEd
National Park Community College
Hot Springs, Arkansas

Dorothy Dean, MBA, MSciEd
Illinois Central College
East Peoria, Illinois

Diane M. Goetzinger-Pena, MS
Delta College
University Center, Michigan

Michelle Hagan-Short, MA
Ivy Tech Community College
Fort Wayne, Indiana

Pat Jarvis
Truckee Meadows Community College
Reno, Nevada

Yvonne C. Leonard, MS
Coastal Carolina Community College
Jacksonville, North Carolina

Lisa Mears, MEd
Palm Beach State College
Lake Worth, Florida

Carol Mull, MS
Greenville Technical College
Greenville, South Carolina

Pamela Silvers, MAEd
Ashville-Buncombe Technical Community College
Ashville, North Carolina

Karen Weil, MEd
McLennan Community College
Waco, Texas

Jeanette White
Tyler Junior College
Tyler, Texas

The authors and editors would also like to thank the following individuals for their involvement in producing student and instructor supplements: Paula Belmonte, Union County College, Cranford, New Jersey; Janet Blum, Fanshawe College, London, Ontario; Jan Marrelli, Sault Ste. Marie, Ontario; Pat Jarvis, Truckee Meadows Community College, Reno, Nevada; Jeff Johnson, Minneapolis, Minnesota; and Joyce Zweedyk, Kalamazoo Valley Community College, Kalamazoo, Michigan.

Microsoft® Office Specialist Certification

Signature Series Microsoft Word 2010 has been approved by Microsoft as covering the objectives included in both the Microsoft Word 2010 and Microsoft Word 2010 Expert certification exams. A chart listing the objectives and where they are addressed in the book is available on the book's Internet Resource Center at www.emcp.net/signatureword2010. Posted with the chart is a section of material covering Expert objective 5.3.3, which involves using Visual Basic to link a form to a database.

What is the Microsoft Office Specialist Program?

The Microsoft Office Specialist Program enables candidates to show that they have something exceptional to offer—proven expertise in certain Microsoft programs. Recognized by businesses and schools around the world, over 4 million certifications have been obtained in over 100 different countries. The Microsoft Office Specialist Program is the only Microsoft-approved certification program of its kind.

What is the Microsoft Office Specialist Certification?

The Microsoft Office Specialist certification validates through the use of exams that you have obtained specific skill sets within the applicable Microsoft Office programs and other Microsoft programs included in the Microsoft Office Specialist Program. Candidates can choose which exam(s) they want to take according to which skills they want to validate.

The available Microsoft Office Specialist Program exams* include:

Using Windows Vista®	Using Microsoft® Office PowerPoint® 2007
Using Microsoft® Office Word 2007	Using Microsoft® Office Access® 2007
Using Microsoft® Office Word 2007 - Expert	Using Microsoft® Office Outlook® 2007
Using Microsoft® Office Excel® 2007	Using Microsoft SharePoint® 2007
Using Microsoft® Office Excel® 2007 - Expert	

The Microsoft Office Specialist Program 2010 exams* include:

Microsoft Word 2010	Microsoft PowerPoint® 2010
Microsoft Word 2010 Expert	Microsoft Access® 2010
Microsoft Excel® 2010	Microsoft Outlook® 2010
Microsoft Excel® 2010 Expert	Microsoft SharePoint® 2010

What does the Microsoft Office Specialist Approved Courseware logo represent?

The logo indicates that this courseware has been approved by Microsoft to cover the course objectives that will be included in the relevant exam. It also means that after utilizing this courseware, you may be better prepared to pass the exams required to become a certified Microsoft Office Specialist.

For more information:

To learn more about Microsoft Office Specialist exams, visit www.microsoft.com/learning/msbc. To learn about other Microsoft approved courseware from Paradigm Publishing, Inc., visit www.ParadigmCollege.com.

*The availability of Microsoft Office Specialist certification exams varies by Microsoft program, program version, and language. Visit www.microsoft.com/learning for exam availability.

Microsoft, Access, Excel, the Office Logo, Outlook, PowerPoint, SharePoint, and Windows Vista are either registered trademarks or trademarks of Microsoft Corporation in the United States and/or other countries. The Microsoft Office Specialist logo and the Microsoft Office Specialist Approved Courseware logo are used under license from Microsoft Corporation.

Getting Started

As you work your way through this textbook, you will learn functions and commands for Microsoft Office Word 2010, one of the applications included in the Microsoft Office 2010 suite. Word 2010 is a word processing program. To operate it, you will need access to a microcomputer system.

Identifying Computer Hardware

The computer equipment you will need to operate Word 2010 is referred to as **hardware**. You will need access to a microcomputer system that consists of the following six components, shown in Figure G.1: a central processing unit (CPU), monitor, keyboard, mouse, printer, and drives. Each component is described below. If you are not sure what equipment you will be operating, check with your instructor.

Figure G.1 Microcomputer System

CPU

The CPU is the intelligence of the computer. All processing occurs in it. The CPU is made up of silicon chips containing miniaturized circuitry, which are placed on boards that plug into slots within the CPU. When the computer is given an instruction, the instruction is processed through the circuitry in the CPU.

Monitor

A monitor looks like a television screen. It displays both the information of the program being run by the computer and the text being input at the keyboard. The quality of a monitor's visual display varies depending on the type of monitor and the level of resolution. Monitors can also vary in size, generally ranging from a 14-inch screen up to a 26-inch screen or larger.

Keyboard

A keyboard is used to input information into the computer. Keyboards for microcomputers vary in the number and location of the keys. Microcomputers have alphabetic and numeric keys positioned in the same location as the keys on a typewriter. The symbol keys, however, may be placed in a variety of locations, depending on the manufacturer. In addition to letters, numbers, and symbols, most microcomputer keyboards contain function keys, arrow keys, and a numeric keypad. Figure G.2 shows a keyboard.

Figure G.2 Microcomputer Keyboard

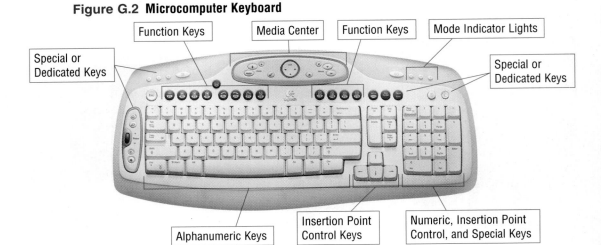

The 12 keys at the top of a keyboard, labeled with the letter F followed by a number, are called *function keys*. Use these keys to perform functions in Word. To the right (and sometimes to the left) of the regular keys is a group of *special* or *dedicated keys*. These keys are labeled with specific functions that will be performed when you press the key. Below the special keys are arrow keys. Use these keys to move the insertion point in the document screen.

In the upper right corner of the keyboard are three mode indicator lights. When you select certain modes, a light appears on the keyboard. For example, if you press the Caps Lock key, which disables the lowercase alphabet, a light appears next to Caps Lock. Similarly, pressing the Num Lock key will disable the special functions on the numeric keypad, which is located at the right side of the keyboard, and turn on the Num Lock mode indicator light.

Printer

A document you create in Word is considered ***soft copy***. If you want a hard copy of a document, you need to print it. To print documents, you will need to access a printer, which will probably be either a laser printer or an ink-jet printer. A laser printer uses a laser beam combined with heat and pressure to print documents while an ink-jet printer prints a document by spraying a fine mist of ink on the page.

Mouse

Many functions in Word are designed to operate more efficiently with a mouse. A mouse is an input device that sits on a flat surface next to the computer. You can operate a mouse with your left or right hand. When you move the mouse on the flat surface, a corresponding mouse pointer moves on the screen. Figure G.1 shows an illustration of a mouse.

Disk Drives

Depending on the computer system you are using, Microsoft Office 2010 is installed on a hard drive or as part of a network system. Whether you are using Word 2010 on a hard drive or network system, you will need to have available a digital video disc (DVD) or compact disk (CD) drive and a USB drive or other storage medium. You will insert the CD that accompanies this textbook in the DVD or CD drive and then copy folders from the CD to your storage medium. You will also save documents you complete at the computer to folders on your storage medium.

Using the Mouse

You can execute commands in Word 2010 using a keyboard or a mouse. The mouse may have two or three buttons on top, which you tap to execute specific functions and commands. To use the mouse, rest it on a flat surface or a mouse pad. Put your hand over it with your palm resting on top of the mouse and your wrist resting on the table surface.

To use the mouse, you need to understand four terms—point, click, double-click, and drag. With the mouse, you may need to *point* to a specific command, button, or icon. To point means to position the mouse pointer on the desired item. With the mouse pointer positioned on the desired item, you may need to *click* one of the buttons on the mouse. To click means to quickly tap a mouse button once. To complete two steps at one time, such as choosing and then executing a function, you may need to *double-click* a mouse button. To double-click means to tap the left mouse button twice in quick succession. To *drag* with the mouse means to press and hold the left mouse button, move the mouse pointer to a specific location, and then release the button.

Using the Mouse Pointer

The mouse pointer changes appearance depending on the function being performed or where the pointer is positioned. The mouse pointer may appear as one of the following images:

- I-beam pointer—the mouse pointer appears as an I-beam (called the I-beam pointer) in a document. It can be used to move the insertion point or select text.

- arrow pointer—the mouse pointer appears as an arrow pointing up and to the left (called the arrow pointer) when it is moved to the Title bar, Quick Access toolbar, or ribbon, or to an option in a dialog box. For example, to open a new document with the mouse, you will position the I-beam pointer on the Office button located in the upper left corner of the screen until the pointer turns into an arrow pointer, and then you will click the left mouse button. At the drop-down list that displays, you can make a selection by positioning the arrow pointer on the desired option and then clicking the left mouse button.

- double-headed arrow—the mouse pointer becomes a double-headed arrow (either pointing left and right, pointing up and down, or pointing diagonally) when you perform certain functions, such as changing the size of an object.

- four-headed arrow—in certain situations, such as when you move an object or image, the mouse pointer displays with a four-headed arrow attached. The four-headed arrow indicates that you can move the object left, right, up, or down.

- moving circle—when the computer is processing a request or when you are loading a program, the mouse pointer may appear with a moving circle beside it. The moving circle image means "please wait." When the process is completed, the moving circle image is removed.

- hand—the mouse pointer displays as a hand with a pointing index finger when you have accessed certain functions, such as the Help feature. It indicates that more information is available about the item.

Choosing Commands

In Word, you can use several methods to choose a command. A command is an instruction that tells the program to do something. You can choose a command using the mouse or the keyboard. When Word is open, the ribbon displays at the top of the screen. The ribbon contains buttons, arranged in tabs, for completing tasks. To choose a button on the Quick Access toolbar or in the ribbon, position the tip of the mouse arrow pointer on a button and then click the left mouse button.

Word provides access keys you can press to use a command in a program. Press the Alt key on the keyboard to display KeyTips that identify the access key you need to press to execute a command. For example, press the Alt key in a document and KeyTips display, as shown in Figure G.3. Continue pressing access keys until you execute the desired command. For example, if you want to begin spell checking a document, you would press the Alt key, press the R key on the keyboard to display the Review tab, and then press the S key on the keyboard.

Figure G.3 Access Key KeyTips

Choosing Commands from Drop-Down Lists

To choose a command from a drop-down list with the mouse, position the mouse pointer on the desired option and then click the left mouse button. To make a selection from a drop-down list with the keyboard, type the underlined letter in the desired option.

Some options at a drop-down list may be gray shaded (dimmed), indicating that the option is currently unavailable. If an option at a drop-down list displays preceded by a check mark, the check mark indicates that the option is currently active. If an option at a drop-down list displays followed by an ellipsis (...), a dialog box will display when that option is chosen.

Choosing Options from a Dialog Box

A dialog box contains options for applying formatting to a document or to data in a document. Some dialog boxes display with tabs along the top, which provide additional options. For example, the Font dialog box, shown in Figure G.4, contains two tabs—the Font tab and the Advanced tab. The tab that displays in front is the active tab. To make

Figure G.4 Font Dialog Box

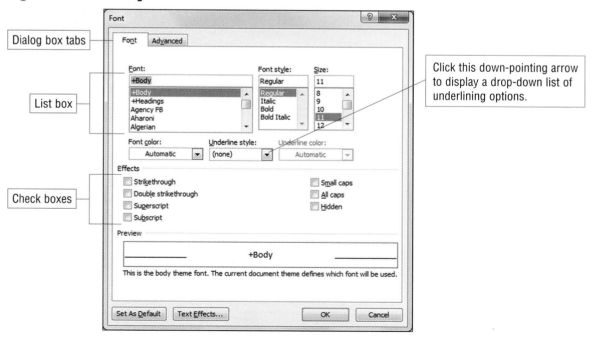

a tab active using the mouse, position the arrow pointer on the desired tab and then click the left mouse button. If you are using the keyboard, press Ctrl + Tab or press Alt + the underlined letter on the desired tab.

To choose options from a dialog box with the mouse, position the arrow pointer on the desired option and then click the left mouse button. If you are using the keyboard, press the Tab key to move the insertion point forward from option to option. Press Shift + Tab to move the insertion point backward from option to option. You can also hold down the Alt key and then press the underlined letter of the desired option. When an option is selected, it displays with a blue background or surrounded by a dashed box called a marquee. A dialog box contains one or more of the following elements: text boxes, list boxes, check boxes, option buttons, measurement boxes, and command buttons.

Text Boxes

Text boxes are options in a dialog box that require you to enter text. For example, the boxes below the *Find what* and *Replace with* options at the Find and Replace dialog box, shown in Figure G.5, are text boxes. In a text box, you type text or edit existing text. You can edit text in a text box in the same manner you would edit text in a document. (You will learn to edit text in a document in Chapter 1.) Use the Left and Right Arrow keys on the keyboard to move the insertion point without deleting text and use the Delete key or Backspace key to delete text.

Figure G.5 Find and Replace Dialog Box

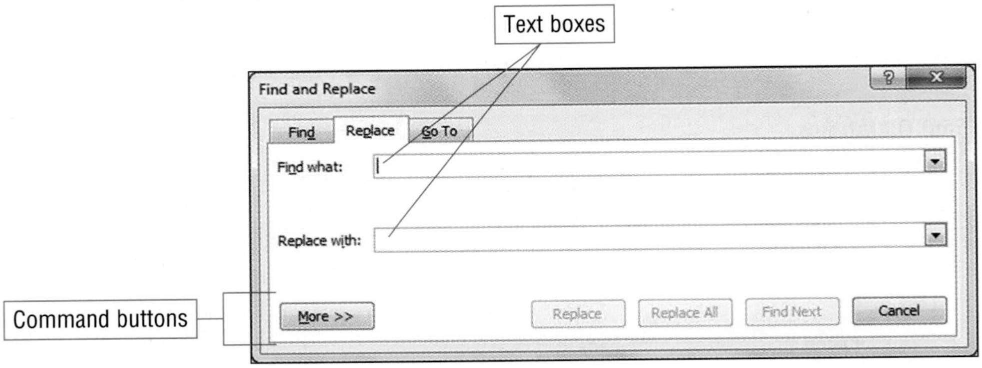

List Boxes

Some dialog boxes, such as the Font dialog box shown in Figure G.4 and the Building Blocks Organizer dialog box shown in Figure G.6, contain a list box. To make a selection from a list box with the mouse, move the arrow pointer to the desired option and then click the left mouse button.

Figure G.6 Building Blocks Organizer Dialog Box

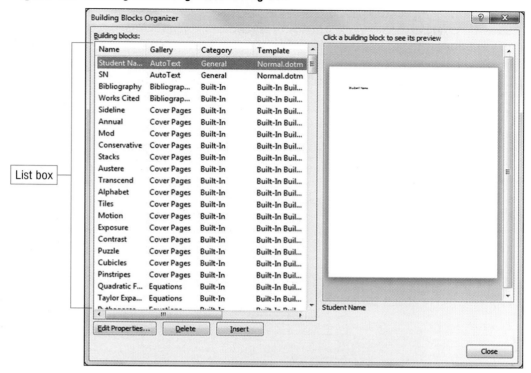

Some list boxes contain a scroll bar. This scroll bar displays at the right side of the list box (a vertical scroll bar) or at the bottom of the list box (a horizontal scroll bar). You can use a vertical scroll bar or a horizontal scroll bar to move through the list if the list is longer than the box. To move down through a list on a vertical scroll bar, position the arrow pointer on the down-pointing arrow and hold down the left mouse button. To scroll up through the list in a vertical scroll bar, position the arrow pointer on the up-pointing arrow and hold down the left mouse button. You can also move the arrow pointer above the scroll box and click the left mouse button to scroll up the list or move the arrow pointer below the scroll box and click the left mouse button to move down the list. To move through a list with a horizontal scroll bar, click the left-pointing arrow to scroll to the left of the list or click the right-pointing arrow to scroll to the right of the list.

To make a selection from a list using the keyboard, move the insertion point into the box by holding down the Alt key and pressing the underlined letter of the desired option. Press the Up and/or Down Arrow keys on the keyboard to move through the list.

In some dialog boxes, not enough room is available for a list box. In these dialog boxes, options are inserted in drop-down list boxes. Options that contain a drop-down list box display with a down-pointing arrow. For example, the *Underline style* option in the Font dialog box, shown in Figure G.4, contains a drop-down list. To display the list, click the down-pointing arrow to the right of the *Underline style* option box. If you are using the keyboard, press Alt + U.

Check Boxes

Some dialog boxes contain options preceded by a box. A check mark may or may not appear in the box. The Font dialog box, shown in Figure G.4, displays a variety of check boxes within the *Effects* section. If a check mark appears in the box, the option is active (turned on). If the check box does not contain a check mark, the option is inactive (turned off). Any number of check boxes can be active. For example, in the Font dialog box, you can insert a check mark in any or all of the boxes in the *Effects* section and these options will be active.

To make a check box active or inactive with the mouse, position the tip of the arrow pointer in the check box, and then click the left mouse button. If you are using the keyboard, press Alt + the underlined letter of the desired option.

Option Buttons

The Fill Effects dialog box with the Gradient tab selected, shown in Figure G.7, contains options in the *Colors* section as well as the *Shading styles* section preceded by option buttons. Only one option button can be selected at any time. When an option button is selected, a blue circle displays in the button. To select an option button with the mouse, position the tip of the arrow pointer inside the option button, and then click the left mouse button. To make a selection with the keyboard, hold down the Alt key, and then press the underlined letter of the desired option.

Figure G.7 Fill Effects Dialog Box

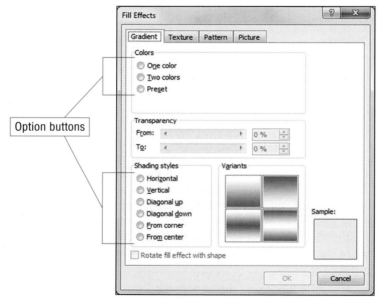

Measurement Boxes

Some options in a dialog box contain measurements or numbers you can increase or decrease. These options are generally located in a measurement box. For example, the Paragraph dialog box, shown in Figure G.8, contains the *Left*, *Right*, *Before*, and *After* measurement boxes. To increase a number in a measurement box, position the tip of the arrow pointer on the up-pointing arrow to the right of the desired option, and then click the left mouse button. To decrease the number, click the down-pointing arrow. If you are using the keyboard, press Alt + the underlined letter of the desired option, and then press the Up Arrow key to increase the number or the Down Arrow key to decrease the number.

Figure G.8 Paragraph Dialog Box

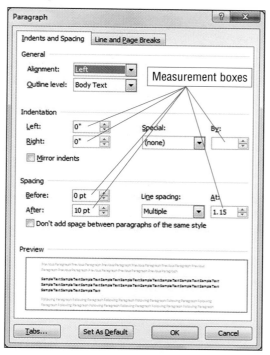

Command Buttons

In the Find and Replace dialog box, shown in Figure G.5, the boxes along the bottom of the dialog box are called command buttons. Use a command button to execute or cancel a command. Some command buttons display with an ellipsis (…). A command button that displays with an ellipsis opens another dialog box when chosen. To choose a command button with the mouse, position the arrow pointer on the desired button, and then click the left mouse button. To choose a command button with the keyboard, press the Tab key until the desired command button contains the marquee and then press the Enter key.

Choosing Commands with Keyboard Shortcuts

Word offers a variety of keyboard shortcuts you can use to executive specific commands. Keyboard shortcuts generally require two or more keys. For example, the keyboard shortcut to display the Open dialog box is Ctrl + O. To use this keyboard shortcut, hold down the Ctrl key, type the letter O on the keyboard, and then release the Ctrl key. For a list of keyboard shortcuts, refer to the Help files.

Choosing Commands with Shortcut Menus

Word includes shortcut menus that display commands and options related to the position of the mouse pointer or the insertion point. To display a shortcut menu, click the *right* mouse button or press Shift + F10. For example, if you position the mouse pointer in a paragraph of text in a document and then click the *right* mouse button, the shortcut menu shown in Figure G.9 displays in the document.

Figure G.9 Shortcut Menu

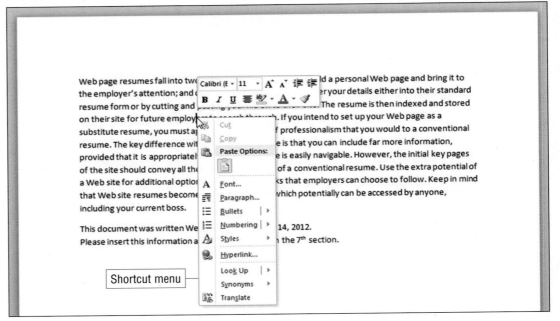

Shortcut menu

To select an option from a shortcut menu with the mouse, click the desired option. If you are using the keyboard, press the Up or Down Arrow key until the desired option is selected, and then press the Enter key. To close a shortcut menu without choosing an option, click anywhere outside the shortcut menu or press the Esc key.

Completing Computer Exercises

Some computer exercises in this textbook require you to open an existing document. These exercise documents are saved on the Student Resources CD that accompanies this textbook. The documents and files you need for each chapter are saved in individual folders. Before beginning a chapter, copy the necessary folder from the CD to your storage medium.

Copying a Folder

As you begin working in a chapter, copy the chapter folder from the CD to your storage medium using the Computer window by completing the following steps:

1. Insert the CD that accompanies this textbook in the DVD or CD drive.
2. Insert your storage medium in the appropriate drive.
3. At the Windows desktop, open the Computer window by clicking the Start button and then clicking *Computer* at the Start menu.
4. Double-click the DVD or CD drive in the Content pane (probably displays as *Signature Word 2010* followed by the drive letter) that contains the CD that accompanies this textbook.
5. Double-click the StudentDataFiles folder in the Content pane.
6. Click once on the desired chapter folder name to select it.
7. Click the Organize button on the Toolbar and then click *Copy* at the drop-down list.

8. In the Computer section in the Navigation pane, click the drive containing your storage medium. (You may need to scroll down the list box.)
9. Click the Organize button on the Toolbar and then click *Paste* at the drop-down list.
10. After the folder is copied to your storage medium, close the Computer window by clicking the Close button (the button marked with a white X on a red background) that displays in the upper right corner of the window.

Deleting a Folder

If storage is limited on your storage medium, consider deleting any previous chapter folders. Do this in the Computer window by completing the following steps:

1. Insert your storage medium in the appropriate drive.
2. At the Windows desktop, open the Computer window by clicking the Start button and then clicking *Computer* at the Start menu.
3. In the Content pane, double-click the drive where your storage medium is located.
4. Click the chapter folder in the Content pane.
5. Click the Organize button and then click *Delete* at the drop-down list.
6. At the message asking if you want to delete the folder, click the Yes button.
7. Close the Computer window by clicking the Close button that displays in the upper right corner of the window.

Customizing Settings

Before beginning computer exercises in this textbook, you may need to customize the monitor settings and turn on the display of file extensions. Exercises in the chapters in this textbook assume that the monitor display is set to 1280 × 800 pixels on a wide screen monitor and that the display of file extensions is turned on. To change the monitor display to 1280 by 800, complete the following steps:

1. At the Windows 7 desktop, right-click on any empty location on the desktop and then click *Personalize* at the shortcut menu.
2. Click the *Display* hyperlink located in the lower left corner of the window.
3. Click the *Adjust resolution* hyperlink.
4. Click the Resolution option box.
5. Use the mouse to drag the button on the slider bar up or down until *1280 × 800* displays.
6. Click the Apply button.
7. Click the OK button.
8. Close the window.

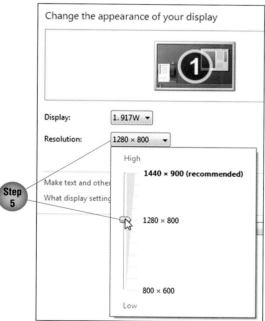

To turn on the display of file extensions, complete the following steps:

1. At the Windows 7 desktop, click the Start button and then click *Computer.*
2. At the Computer window, click the Organize button on the Toolbar and then click *Folder and search options* at the drop-down list.

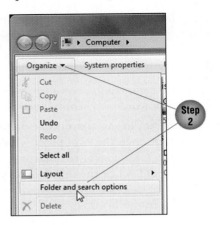

3. At the Folder Options dialog box, click the View tab.
4. Click the *Hide extensions for known file types* check box to remove the check mark.

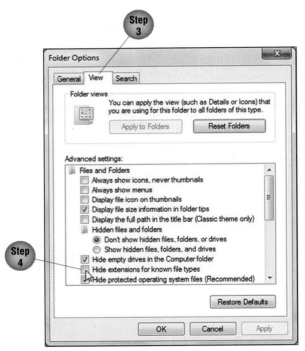

5. Click the Apply button.
6. Click the OK button.

Unit 1

Preparing Documents

Chapter 1   Creating, Printing, and Editing Documents

Chapter 2   Formatting Characters

Chapter 3   Aligning and Indenting Paragraphs

Chapter 4   Customizing Paragraphs

Chapter 5   Proofing Documents

Unit 1   Performance Assessments

Chapter 1

 **TUTORIALS**

Tutorial 1.1
Creating, Saving, and Printing a
Document
Tutorial 1.2
Editing a Document
Tutorial 1.3
Opening and Pinning a
Document
Tutorial 1.4
Using the Help Feature

Creating, Printing, and Editing Documents

Performance Objectives

Upon successful completion of Chapter 1, you will be able to:

- Open Microsoft Word
- Create, save, name, print, open, and close a Word document
- Exit Word and Windows
- Edit a document
- Move the insertion point within a document
- Scroll within a document
- Select text in a document
- Use the Undo and Redo buttons
- Use the Help feature

In this chapter, you will learn to create, save, name, print, open, close, and edit a Word document. Before continuing, make sure you read the *Getting Started* section presented at the beginning of this book. This section contains information about computer hardware and software, using the mouse, executing commands, and customizing settings.

Note: Before beginning computer exercises for this chapter, copy to your storage medium the Chapter01 folder from the CD that accompanies this textbook. Steps on how to copy a folder are presented on the inside back cover of this textbook. Do this for each chapter before starting the chapter's exercises.

In this chapter students will produce the following documents:

Exercise 1.1. C01-E01-WebResumes.docx
Exercise 1.2. C01-E02-EmailResumes.docx
Exercise 1.4. C01-E04-LtrKCC.docx
Exercise 1.5. C01-E05-SoftwareSuites.docx

Model answers for these exercises are shown on the following pages.

Exercise 1.1

C01-E01-WebResumes.docx

Web page resumes fall into two categories: individuals who build a personal web page and bring it to the employer's attention; and companies that allow you to enter your details either into their standard resume form or by cutting and pasting your file on to their site. The resume is then indexed and stored on their site for future employers to search through. If you intend to set up your web page as a substitute resume, you must apply the same level of professionalism that you would to a conventional resume. The key difference with a web page resume is that you can include far more information, provided that it is appropriately indexed and the site is easily navigable. However, the initial key pages of the site should convey all the critical information of a conventional resume. Use the extra potential of a website for additional optional information in links that employers can choose to follow. Keep in mind that website resumes become public documents, which potentially can be accessed by anyone, including your current boss.

This document was written Wednesday, November 14, 2012.
Please insert this information as the 3rd paragraph in the 7th section.

Emailing Resumes

As an alternative to mailing your resume, some employers are now happy to receive them electronically via email. This can speed up the hiring process and can save money, too. If you are applying for a job that requires some IT knowledge, sending your resume by email will demonstrate that you are comfortable with this type of technology.

As with scanned resumes, you should keep to a maximum of 70 to 80 characters per line. Any more character and you risk losing the formatting. You should send the resume as an attachment. Do not be tempted to copy and paste it into the body of the email—you will lose most of the formatting. Even though you may have a fancy email program that allows you to include formatting and graphics in the message body, the majority of email programs do not allow this, and all you will do is send an unintelligible mess to your prospective employer.

Another option to consider is to paste a text version of your resume into the body of the email. Some people advise you to do this because some recruiters may worry about opening attachments to e-mails for fear of any viruses they may contain. The pros of this are that you get your information to the recruiter. The downside is that we know that the visual appeal of the resume has a dramatic effect on the recruiter, and this type of resume is not visually appealing.

Exercise 1.2

C01-E02-EmailResumes.docx

Exercise 1.4

C01-E04-LtrKCC.docx

November 6, 2012

Dr. Avery Reynolds
Kodiak Community College
310 Northern Lights Boulevard
Anchorage, AK 99033

Dear Dr. Reynolds:

I enjoyed meeting you and discussing the implementation of a Pharmacy Tech program into the Business Information Technology curriculum. As I mentioned, we added a pharmacy tech program to our department at Cascade Community College last year.

We advertised it in our college schedule and sent brochures to all high school seniors in our district. Thirty people registered for the program, and student evaluations, which were completed last semester, were very favorable.

If you would like more information about the program, please call me at (712) 555-3400. I will be attending the National Computer Technology conference. I hope to see you there.

Sincerely,

Kerry Brown

XX
LtrKCC.docx

Software suites typically include the four most widely used applications: word processing, database management, spreadsheet, and presentation applications. Some, such as Microsoft Office, also include web page authoring programs because the development of personal web sites is becoming increasingly important to consumers. Suites are popular because buying a package is less expensive than purchasing each component program separately.

Software suites offer advantages other than price. Because the programs were developed using the same user interface, all programs in the suite function in a similar manner. A user who becomes familiar with one program can easily learn to use the others because the screen layouts, tabs, menus, buttons, icons, and toolbars are similar.

Another strong feature of suites is that they allow users to seamlessly integrate files from component programs. For example, information produced using a spreadsheet can be placed into a word processing document, or a database table can be imported into a slide show presentation.

Exercise 1.5

C01-E05-SoftwareSuites.docx

Opening Microsoft Word

Microsoft Office 2010 contains a word processing program named Word that you can use to create, save, edit, and print documents. The steps to open Word may vary depending on your system setup. Generally, to open Word, you would click the Start button on the Taskbar at the Windows desktop, point to *All Programs*, click *Microsoft Office*, and then click *Microsoft Word 2010*.

Creating, Saving, Printing, and Closing a Document

When Microsoft Word is open, a blank document displays as shown in Figure 1.1. The features of the document screen are described in Table 1.1.

Figure 1.1 Blank Document Screen

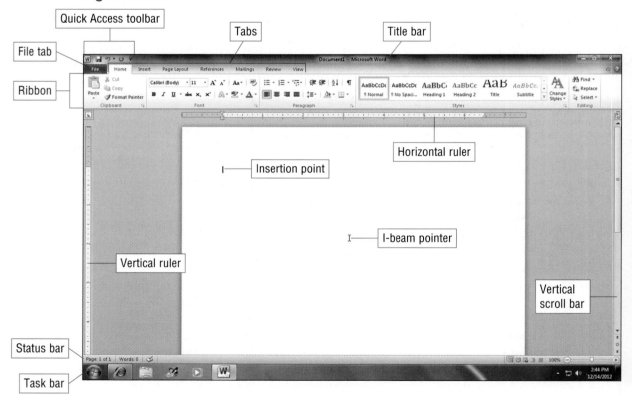

Table 1.1 Microsoft Word Screen Features

Feature	Description
Quick Access toolbar	Contains buttons for commonly used commands
File tab	Click the File tab and the Backstage view displays containing buttons and tabs for working with and managing documents
Title bar	Displays document name followed by program name
Tabs	Contain commands and features organized into groups
Ribbon	Area containing the tabs and commands divided into groups
Horizontal ruler	Used to set margins, indents, and tabs
Vertical ruler	Used to set top and bottom margins
I-beam pointer	Used to move the insertion point or to select text
Insertion point	Indicates location of next character entered at the keyboard
Vertical scroll bar	Used to view various parts of the document
Status bar	Displays number of pages and words, View buttons, and the Zoom slider bar and can be customized by right-clicking on the Status bar and then turning on or off the desired features

At a blank document, you can type information to create a document. A document is any piece of writing that conveys information—for example, a letter, report, term paper, table, and so on. As you type text, you will notice that Word contains the following helpful features:

- **Word Wrap:** You do not need to press the Enter key at the end of each line because Word wraps text from one line to the next. A word is wrapped to the next line if it begins before the right margin and continues past the right margin. You need to press the Enter key only to end a paragraph, create a blank line, or end a short line.

- **AutoCorrect:** Word automatically corrects certain words as you type them. For example, if you type *adn* instead of the word *and*, Word automatically corrects your typing when you press the spacebar after the word. AutoCorrect also superscripts the letters that follow an ordinal number. For example, if you type 2nd and then press the spacebar or Enter key, Word will convert this ordinal number to 2nd.

- **Automatic Spell Checker:** By default, Word automatically inserts a red wavy line below words that are not contained in its Spelling dictionary or automatically corrected by AutoCorrect. This underlining may include misspelled words, proper names, some terminology, and some foreign words. If you type a word that is not recognized by the Spelling dictionary, leave it as you have written it if the word is correct. However, if the word is incorrect, you have two choices—you can delete the word and then type it correctly, or you can position the I-beam pointer on the word, click the *right* mouse button, and then click the correct spelling in the pop-up list that displays.

- **Automatic Grammar Checker:** Word also includes an automatic grammar checker. If the grammar checker detects a sentence that contains a grammatical error, Word inserts a green wavy line below the sentence. You can leave the sentence as written or position the I-beam pointer on the sentence, click the *right* mouse button, and choose from the pop-up list of possible corrections.

- **Spacing Punctuation:** Typically, Word uses Calibri, a proportional typeface, as the default typeface. (You will learn more about typefaces in Chapter 2.) When you type text in a proportional typeface, space once (rather than twice) after end-of-sentence punctuation such as a period, question mark, or exclamation point, and after a colon. Because proportional typeface is set closer together, extra white space at the end of a sentence or after a colon is not needed.

- **Option Buttons:** As you insert or edit text in a document, an option button may pop up. The button that appears varies with the action you are completing. If you type a word that is corrected by AutoCorrect, if you create an automatic list, or if Word applies autoformatting to text, the AutoCorrect Options button appears. Click this button to undo the specific automatic action. If you paste text in a document, the Paste Options button appears near the text. Click this button to display the Paste Options gallery with buttons for controlling how the pasted text is formatted.

- **AutoComplete:** Microsoft Word and other Office applications include an AutoComplete feature that inserts an entire item when you type a few identifying characters. For example, type the letters *Mond* and *Monday* displays in a ScreenTip above the letters. Press the Enter key or press F3 and Word inserts *Monday* in the document.

Using the New Line Command

A Word document is based on a template that applies default formatting. Two default formats are 1.15-point line spacing and 10 points of spacing after a paragraph. Each time you press the Enter key, Word inserts 10 points of spacing and begins a new paragraph. If you want to move the insertion point down to the next line without including the additional 10 points of spacing, use the New Line command Shift + Enter.

Exercise 1.1A Creating a Document   Part 1 of 2

1. Follow the instructions in this chapter to open Microsoft Word.
2. At the blank document, type the information shown in Figure 1.2 with the following specifications:
   a. Correct any errors highlighted by the spell checker as they occur.
   b. Space once after end-of-sentence punctuation.
   c. To insert the word *Wednesday* located toward the end of the document, type Wedn and then press F3. (This illustrates the AutoComplete feature.)
   d. To insert the word *November*, type Nove and then press the Enter key. (This again illustrates the AutoComplete feature.)
   e. Press Shift + Enter after typing *November 14, 2012*. (This moves the insertion point to the next line without adding 10 points of additional spacing.)
   f. When typing the last line (the line containing the ordinal numbers), type the ordinal number text and AutoCorrect will automatically convert the letters in the ordinal numbers to superscript.
3. When you are finished typing the text, press the Enter key once.

Figure 1.2 Exercise 1.1A

Web page resumes fall into two categories: individuals who build a personal web page and bring it to the employer's attention; and companies that allow you to enter your details either into their standard resume form or by cutting and pasting your file on to their site. The resume is then indexed and stored on their site for future employers to search through. If you intend to set up your web page as a substitute resume, you must apply the same level of professionalism that you would to a conventional resume. The key difference with a web page resume is that you can include far more information, provided that it is appropriately indexed and the site is easily navigable. However, the initial key pages of the site should convey all the critical information of a conventional resume. Use the extra potential of a website for additional optional information in links that employers can choose to follow. Keep in mind that website resumes become public documents, which potentially can be accessed by anyone, including your current boss.

This document was written Wednesday, November 14, 2012.
Please insert this information as the 3rd paragraph in the 7th section.

Saving a Document

Save a document if you want to use it in the future. You can use a variety of methods to do so, such as clicking the Save button on the Quick Access toolbar, clicking the File tab and then clicking the *Save As* button in the Quick Commands area at the Backstage view, or using the keyboard shortcut Ctrl + S. Clicking the Save button on the Quick Access toolbar and clicking the File tab followed by *Save As* both display the Save As dialog box, shown in Figure 1.3. In this box, type a name for the document and then press the Enter key or click the Save button located in the lower right corner of the dialog box.

Save a Document
1. Click Save button on Quick Access toolbar.
2. Type document name.
3. Click Save button.

Save

Figure 1.3 Save As Dialog Box

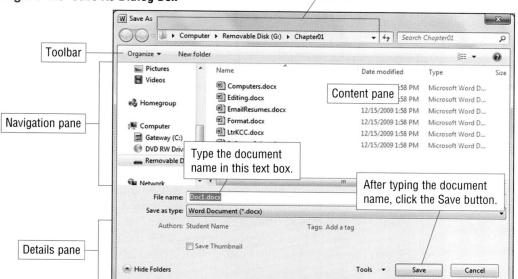

Naming a Document

Document names created in Word and other suite applications can be a maximum of 255 characters in length, including drive letter and any folder names, and may include spaces. File names cannot include any of the following characters:

forward slash (/)

backslash (\)

greater than sign (>)

less than sign (<)

asterisk (*)

question mark (?)

quotation mark (")

colon (:)

semicolon (;)

pipe symbol (|)

Printing a Document

Click the File tab and the Backstage view displays as shown in Figure 1.4. Use buttons and tabs at this view to work with and manage documents such as opening, closing, saving, and printing a document. If you want to remove the Backstage view without completing an action, click the File tab, click any other tab in the ribbon, or press the Esc key on your keyboard.

Figure 1.4 Backstage View

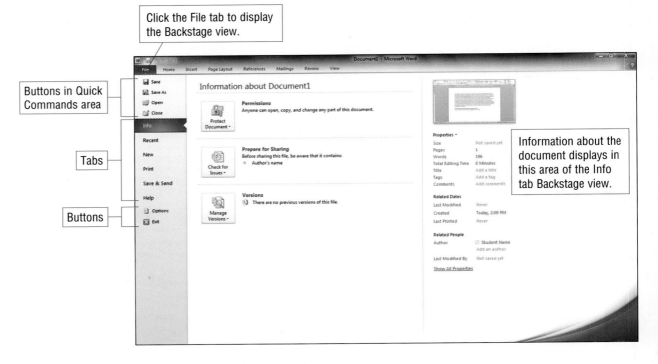

Click the File tab to display the Backstage view.

Buttons in Quick Commands area

Tabs

Buttons

Information about the document displays in this area of the Info tab Backstage view.

Many of the computer exercises you will be creating will need to be printed. A printing of a document on paper is referred to as *hard copy* and a document displayed on the screen is referred to as *soft copy*. Print a document from the Print tab of the Backstage view shown in Figure 1.5. To display this view, click the File tab and then click the Print tab. You can also display the Print tab Backstage view with the keyboard shortcut Ctrl + P.

Figure 1.5 Print Tab Backstage View

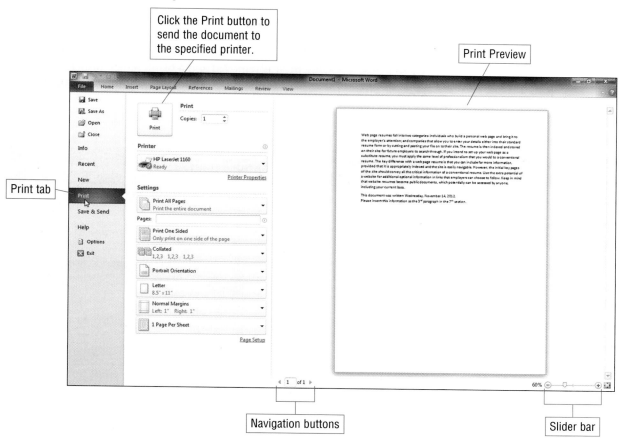

Click the Print button to send the document to the specified printer.

Print Preview

Print tab

Navigation buttons

Slider bar

The left side of the Print tab Backstage view displays three categories—*Print, Printer,* and *Settings.* Click the Print button in the *Print* category to send the document to the printer and specify the number of copies you want printed in the *Copies* option text box. Use the gallery in the *Printer* category to specify the desired printer. The *Settings* category contains a number of galleries, each with options for specifying how you want your document printed. Use the galleries to specify whether or not you want the pages collated when printed; the orientation, page size, and margins of your document; and how many pages of your document you want to print on a page.

Another method for printing a document is to insert the Quick Print button on the Quick Access toolbar and then click the button. This sends the document directly to the printer without displaying the Print tab Backstage view. To insert the button on the Quick Access toolbar, click the Customize Quick Access Toolbar button that displays at the right side of the toolbar and then click *Quick Print* at the drop-down list. To remove the Quick Print button from the Quick Access toolbar, right-click the button and then click *Remove from Quick Access Toolbar* at the drop-down list.

Print a Document
Click Quick Print button on Quick Access toolbar.
OR
1. Click File tab.
2. Click Print tab.
3. Click Print button.

Quick Print

Customize Quick Access Toolbar

Close a Document
1. Click File tab.
2. Click Close button.

Closing a Document

When you save a document, it is saved on your storage medium but remains on the document screen. To remove the document from the screen, click the File tab and then click the *Close* button in the Quick Commands area, or use the keyboard shortcut Ctrl + F4. When you close a document, it is removed and a blank screen displays. At this screen, you can open a previously saved document, create a new document, or exit the Word program.

Exercise 1.1B Saving, Printing, and Closing a Document   Part 2 of 2

1. Save the document you created in Exercise 1.1A and name it **C01-E01-WebResumes** (for Chapter 1, Exercise 1, Web resumes document) by completing the following steps:
   a. Click the Save button on the Quick Access toolbar.
   b. At the Save As dialog box, type C01-E01-WebResumes and then press the Enter key.

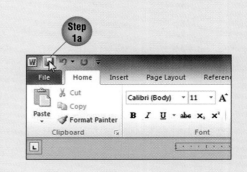

2. Print the document by clicking the File tab, clicking the Print tab at the Backstage view, and then clicking the Print button.
3. Close the document by clicking the File tab and then clicking the Close button.

Creating a New Document

When you close a document, a blank screen displays. To create a new document, first display a blank document. To do this, click the File tab, click the New tab, and then click the Create button that displays below the image of the blank document at the right side of the New tab Backstage view. You can also create a new document using the keyboard shortcut Ctrl + N, or by inserting a New button on the Quick Access toolbar. To insert the button, click the Customize Quick Access Toolbar button that displays at the right side of the toolbar and then click *New* at the drop-down list.

Opening a Document

After you save and close a document, you can open it at the Open dialog box shown in Figure 1.6. To display this dialog box, click the File tab and then click the Open button. You can also display the Open dialog box using the keyboard shortcut Ctrl + O, or by inserting an Open button on the Quick Access toolbar. To insert the button, click the Customize Quick Access Toolbar button that displays at the right side of the toolbar and then click *Open* at the drop-down list. At the Open dialog box, open a document by double-clicking the document name.

If you want to see a list of the most recently opened documents, click the File tab and then click the Recent tab. To open a document from the list, scroll down the list and then click the desired document. If you want to remove the Backstage view without completing an action (such as opening, printing, or closing a document), click the File tab, click any other tab in the ribbon, or press the Esc key on the keyboard.

Create a New Document
1. Click File tab.
2. Click New tab.
3. Click Create button.
OR
Press Ctrl + N.

Open a Document
1. Click File tab.
2. Click Open button.
3. Double-click document name.

Open

Figure 1.6 Open Dialog Box

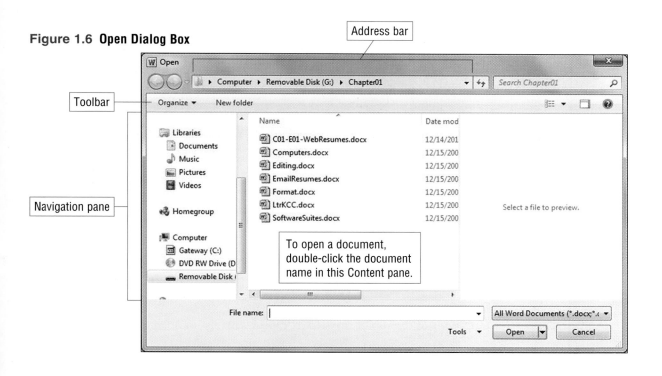

Pinning a Document

When you click the File tab and then click the Recent tab, the Recent Documents list displays with the most recently opened documents. If you want a document to remain in the list, "pin" the document to the list by clicking the Pin button that displays at the right side of the document name. This changes the dimmed gray stickpin to a blue stickpin. The next time you display the Recent Documents list, the document(s) you pinned displays at the top of the list. To "unpin" the document, click the Pin button to change it from a blue pin to a dimmed gray pin.

1. Open the **EmailResumes.docx** document by completing the following steps:
   a. Click the File tab and then click the Open button.
   b. At the Open dialog box, make sure the Chapter01 folder on your storage medium is the active folder.
   c. Double-click **EmailResumes.docx** in the Content pane.
2. Close **EmailResumes.docx**.
3. Open **Computers.docx** by completing steps similar to those in Step 1.
4. Close **Computers.docx**.
5. Pin the **EmailResumes.docx** document to the Recent Documents list by completing the following steps:
   a. Click the File tab.
   b. Click the dimmed gray stickpin that displays at the right side of the document **EmailResumes.docx**. (This moves the document to the top of the list and changes the dimmed gray stickpin to a blue stickpin.)

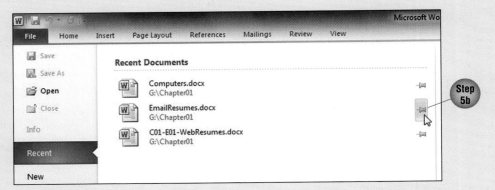

6. Click **EmailResumes.docx** at the top of the Recent Documents list to open the document.

7. With the insertion point positioned at the beginning of the document, type the text shown in Figure 1.7.
8. Unpin the **EmailResumes.docx** from the Recent Documents list by completing the following steps:
   a. Click the File tab and then click the Recent tab.
   b. At the Recent Documents list, click the blue stickpin that displays at the right of the **EmailResumes.docx** document name. (This changes the pin from a blue stickpin to a dimmed gray stickpin.)
   c. Click the File tab to return to the document.

Figure 1.7 Exercise 1.2A

Emailing Resumes

As an alternative to mailing your resume, some employers are now happy to receive them electronically via email. This can speed up the hiring process and can save money, too. If you are applying for a job that requires some IT knowledge, sending your resume by email will demonstrate that you are comfortable with this type of technology.

Saving a Document with Save As

If you open a previously saved document and want to give it a new name, use the Save As button at the Backstage view rather than the Save button. Click the File tab and then click the Save As button and the Save As dialog box displays. At this dialog box, type the new name for the document and then press the Enter key.

Exiting Word

When you are finished working with Word and have saved all necessary information, exit Word by clicking the File tab and then clicking the Exit button located below the Help tab. You can also exit the Word program by clicking the Close button located in the upper right corner of the screen.

Save a Document with Save As
1. Click File tab.
2. Click Save As button.
3. Type document name.
4. Press Enter.

Exit Word
1. Click File tab.
2. Click Exit button.
OR
Click Close button.

Close

1. With **EmailResumes.docx** open, save the document with a new name by completing the following steps:
   a. Click the File tab and then click the Save As button.
   b. At the Save As dialog box, press the Home key on your keyboard to move the insertion point to the beginning of the file name and then type C01-E02-. (Pressing the Home key saves you from having to type the entire document name.)
   c. Press the Enter key.
2. Print the document by clicking the File tab, clicking the Print tab, and then clicking the Print button in the *Print* category at the Print tab Backstage view. (If your Quick Access toolbar contains the Quick Print button, you can click the button to send the document directly to the printer.)
3. Close the document by pressing Ctrl + F4.

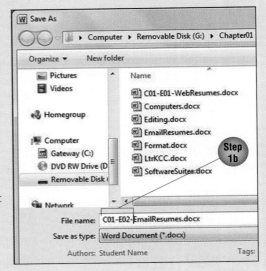

Editing a Document

You may need to change, or edit, documents that you create. To edit a document, use the mouse, the keyboard, or the mouse in combination with the keyboard to move the insertion point to specific locations in the document. To move the insertion point using the mouse, position the I-beam pointer where you want the insertion point to be located and then click the left mouse button.

In addition to moving the insertion point to a specific location, you can use the mouse to move the display of text on the document screen. Use the mouse with the ***vertical scroll bar***, located at the right side of the screen, to scroll through text in a document. Click the up scroll arrow at the top of the vertical scroll bar to scroll up through the document; click the down scroll arrow to scroll down through the document. A scroll box on the scroll bar indicates the location of the text on the document screen in relation to the remainder of the document. To scroll up one screen at a time, position the arrow pointer above the scroll box (but below the up scroll arrow) and then click the left mouse button. Position the arrow pointer below the scroll box and click the left button to scroll down a screen. If you hold down the left mouse button, the action becomes continuous. You can also position the arrow pointer on the scroll box, hold down the left mouse button, and then drag the scroll box along the scroll bar to reposition text on the document screen. As you drag the scroll box along the vertical scroll bar in a multi-page document, page numbers display in a box at the right side of the document screen. Scrolling in a document changes the text displayed but does not move the insertion point.

1. At the blank screen, open **Computers.docx**. (This document is located in the Chapter01 folder you copied to your storage medium.)
2. Save the document with Save As and name it **C01-E03-Computers**.
3. Position the I-beam pointer at the beginning of the first paragraph and then click the left mouse button.
4. Click the down scroll arrow on the vertical scroll bar several times. (This scrolls down lines of text in the document.) With the mouse pointer on the down scroll arrow, hold down the left mouse button and keep it down until the end of the document displays.

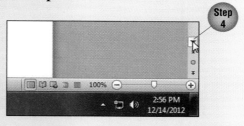

5. Position the mouse pointer on the up scroll arrow and hold down the left mouse button until the beginning of the document displays.
6. Position the mouse pointer below the scroll box and then click the left mouse button. Continue clicking the mouse button (with the mouse pointer positioned below the scroll box) until the end of the document displays.
7. Position the mouse pointer on the scroll box in the vertical scroll bar. Hold down the left mouse button, drag the scroll box to the top of the vertical scroll bar, and then release the mouse button. (Notice that the document page numbers display in a box at the right side of the document screen.)
8. Click on the title at the beginning of the document. (This moves the insertion point to the location of the mouse pointer.)

Moving the Insertion Point to a Specific Page

Along with scrolling options, Word contains navigation buttons for moving the insertion point to specific locations within a document. These buttons display toward the bottom of the vertical scroll bar and include the Previous button, the Select Browse Object button, and the Next button. The names of the Previous and Next buttons and the tasks they complete vary depending on the last navigation selected. Click the Select Browse Object button and a palette of browsing choices displays. You will learn more about the Select Browse Object button in the next section.

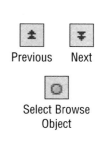

Previous   Next

Select Browse Object

Word also includes a Go To option you can use to move the insertion point to a specific page within a document. To move the insertion point to a specific page, click the Find button arrow located in the Editing group of the Home tab and then click *Go To* at the drop-down list. At the Find and Replace dialog box with the Go To tab selected, type the page number in the *Enter page number* text box and then press the Enter key. Click the Close button to close the dialog box.

Find

Browsing in a Document

As noted in the preceding section, the Select Browse Object button, located toward the bottom of the vertical scroll bar, allows you to select options for browsing through a document. Click this button and a palette of browsing choices displays. Use the options on the palette to move the insertion point to various features in a Word document. Position the arrow pointer on an option in the palette and the option name displays below the options. The options on the palette and their location vary depending on the last function performed.

Select Browse Object

Moving the Insertion Point with the Keyboard

To move the insertion point with the keyboard, use the arrow keys located to the right of the regular keyboard. You can also use the arrow keys on the numeric keypad. If you use these keys, make sure Num Lock is off. Use the arrow keys together with other keys to move the insertion point to various locations in the document, as shown in Table 1.2.

Table 1.2 Insertion Point Movement Commands

To move insertion point	Press
One character left	Left Arrow
One character right	Right Arrow
One line up	Up Arrow
One line down	Down Arrow
One word to the left	Ctrl + Left Arrow
One word to the right	Ctrl + Right Arrow
To end of a line	End
To beginning of a line	Home
To beginning of current paragraph	Ctrl + Up Arrow
To beginning of next paragraph	Ctrl + Down Arrow
Up one screen	Page Up
Down one screen	Page Down
To top of previous page	Ctrl + Page Up
To top of next page	Ctrl + Page Down
To beginning of document	Ctrl + Home
To end of document	Ctrl + End

When you move the insertion point with the keyboard, keep in mind that the Word commands use the following definitions: a word is any series of characters between spaces, a paragraph is any text that is followed by a stroke of the Enter key, and a page is text separated by a soft or hard page break. If you open a previously saved document, you can move the insertion point to where it was last located when the document was closed by pressing Shift + F5.

1. With **C01-E03-Computers.docx** open, move the insertion point to page 3 by completing the following steps:
   a. Click the Find button arrow located in the Editing group in the Home tab and then click *Go To* at the drop-down list.
   b. At the Find and Replace dialog box with the Go To tab selected, make sure *Page* is selected in the *Go to what* list box, type 3 in the *Enter page number* text box, and then press the Enter key.
   c. Click the Close button to close the Find and Replace dialog box.

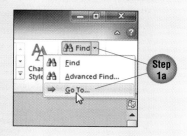

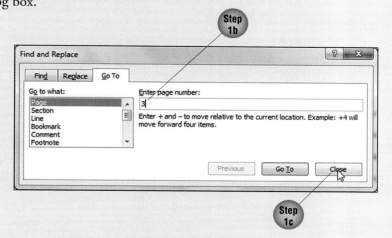

2. Click the Previous Page button located immediately above the Select Browse Object button on the vertical scroll bar. (This moves the insertion point to page 2.)
3. Click the Previous Page button again. (This moves the insertion point to page 1.)
4. Click the Next Page button located immediately below the Select Browse Object button on the vertical scroll bar. (This moves the insertion point to the beginning of page 2.)
5. Move to the beginning of page 3 by completing the following steps:
   a. Click the Select Browse Object button.
   b. At the palette of browsing choices, click the *Browse by Page* choice. (This moves the insertion point to page 3.)
6. Press Ctrl + Home to move the insertion point to the beginning of the document.
7. Practice using the keyboard commands shown in Table 1.2 to move the insertion point within the document.
8. Close **C01-E03-Computers.docx**.

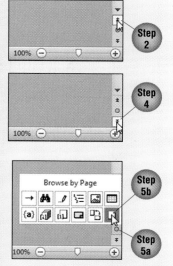

Inserting and Deleting Text

Editing a document may include inserting or deleting text. To insert text in a document, position the insertion point in the desired location and then type the text. By default, existing characters move to the right as you type the text. A number of options are available for deleting text. Some deletion commands are shown in Table 1.3.

Table 1.3 Deletion Commands

To delete	Press
Character right of insertion point	Delete key
Character left of insertion point	Backspace key
Text from insertion point to beginning of word	Ctrl + Backspace
Text from insertion point to end of word	Ctrl + Delete

If you want to type over existing text rather than have it move to the right as you insert new text, you will need to turn on the Overtype mode. With the Overtype mode on, anything you type will replace existing text. To turn on the Overtype mode, click the File tab and then click the Options button located below the Help tab. At the Word Options dialog box, click *Advanced* in the left panel. In the *Editing options* section, insert a check mark in the *Use overtype mode* check box if you want the Overtype mode always on in the document. Or, insert a check mark in the *Use the Insert key to control overtype mode* check box if you want to use the Insert key to turn Overtype mode on and off. After making your selection, click the OK button located in the lower right corner of the dialog box.

Selecting Text

You can use the mouse or the keyboard to select a specific amount of text. Once you have selected the text, you can delete it or perform other Word functions that involve it. When text is selected, it displays with a blue background as shown in Figure 1.8. The Mini toolbar also displays, in a dimmed fashion, and it contains options for performing common tasks. Move the mouse pointer over the Mini toolbar and it becomes active. (You will learn more about the Mini toolbar in Chapter 2.)

Figure 1.8 Selected Text and Mini Toolbar

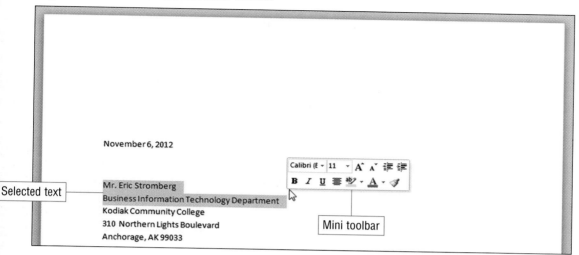

Selecting Text with the Mouse

Use the mouse to select a word, line, sentence, paragraph, or an entire document. Table 1.4 lists the steps to follow to select a specific amount of text. For example, to select a line, click in the selection bar. The selection bar is the space located toward the left side of the document screen between the left edge of the page and the text. When the mouse pointer is positioned in the selection bar, the pointer turns into an arrow pointing up and to the right.

Table 1.4 Selecting Text with the Mouse

To select	*Complete these steps using the mouse*
A word	Double-click the word.
A line of text	Click in the selection bar to the left of the line.
Multiple lines of text	Drag in the selection bar to the left of the lines.
A sentence	Hold down the Ctrl key, then click anywhere in the sentence.
A paragraph	Double-click in the selection bar next to the paragraph or triple-click anywhere in the paragraph.
Multiple paragraphs	Drag in the selection bar.
An entire document	Triple-click in the selection bar or click Select button in Editing group and then *Select All*.

To select sections of text other than a word, sentence, or paragraph, position the I-beam pointer on the first character of the text to be selected, hold down the left mouse button, drag the I-beam pointer to the last character of the text to be selected, and then release the mouse button. You can also select all text between the current insertion point and the I-beam pointer. To do this, position the insertion point where you want the selection to begin, hold down the Shift key, click the I-beam pointer at the end of the selection, and then release the Shift key. To cancel a selection using the mouse, click anywhere in the document screen outside the selected text.

Selecting Text with the Keyboard

To select a specific amount of text using the keyboard, turn on the Selection mode by pressing the F8 function key. With the Selection mode activated, use the arrow keys to select the desired text. If you want to cancel the selection, press the Esc key and then press any arrow key. You can customize the Status bar to display text indicating that the Selection mode is activated. To do this, *right* click any blank location on the Status bar and then click Selection Mode at the shortcut menu. When you press F8 to turn on the Selection mode, the words *Extend Selection* display on the Status bar. You can also select text with the commands shown in Table 1.5.

Table 1.5 Selecting Text with the Keyboard

To select	Press
One character to right	Shift + Right Arrow
One character to left	Shift + Left Arrow
To end of word	Ctrl + Shift + Right Arrow
To beginning of word	Ctrl + Shift + Left Arrow
To end of line	Shift + End
To beginning of line	Shift + Home
One line up	Shift + Up Arrow
One line down	Shift + Down Arrow
To beginning of paragraph	Ctrl + Shift + Up Arrow
To end of paragraph	Ctrl + Shift + Down Arrow
One screen up	Shift + Page Up
One screen down	Shift + Page Down
To end of document	Ctrl + Shift + End
To beginning of document	Ctrl + Shift + Home
Entire document	Ctrl + A

1. Open **LtrKCC.docx**. (This document is located in the Chapter01 folder you copied to your storage medium.)

2. Save the document with Save As and name it **C01-E04-LtrKCC**.

3. Delete the name, *Mr. Eric Stromberg*, and the department, *Business Information Technology Department*, using the mouse by completing the following steps:

   a. Position the I-beam pointer on the *M* in *Mr.* (in the address).

   b. Hold down the left mouse button and then drag the mouse down until *Mr. Eric Stromberg* and *Business Information Technology Department* are selected.

   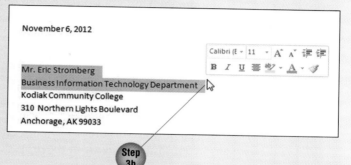

   c. Release the left mouse button.

   d. Press the Delete key.

4. Position the insertion point at the left margin of the line containing the text *Kodiak Community College*, type the name Dr. Avery Reynolds, and then press Shift + Enter.

5. Delete *Mr. Stromberg* in the salutation (after the word *Dear*) and then type Dr. Reynolds. (You choose the method for deleting.)

   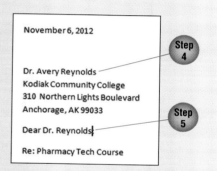

6. Delete the reference line, *Re: Pharmacy Tech Course*, using the Extend Selection key, F8, by completing the following steps:

   a. Position the insertion point on the *R* in *Re:*.

   b. Press F8 to turn on select.

   c. Press the Down Arrow key. (This selects the reference line and the spacing below it.)

   d. Press the Delete key.

7. Delete the first sentence in the first paragraph using the mouse by completing the following steps:

   a. Position the I-beam pointer anywhere in the sentence, *The North Pacific Computer Technology conference that we attended last week was very educational.*

   b. Hold down the Ctrl key and then click the left mouse button.

   c. Press the Delete key.

8. Delete the first sentence in the second paragraph (the sentence that reads, *Interest in the program has been phenomenal.*) using the keyboard by completing the following steps:

   a. Position the insertion point on the first letter of the sentence (the *I* in *Interest*).

   b. Hold down the Shift key and then press the Right Arrow key until the sentence is selected. Be sure to include the period at the end of the sentence and the space after the period.

   c. Press the Delete key.

9. Delete the third paragraph in the letter using the mouse by completing the following steps:

   a. Position the I-beam pointer anywhere in the third paragraph (the paragraph that begins, *The instructor for the Medical Coding course . . .*).

   b. Triple-click the left mouse button.

   c. Press the Delete key.

10. Save, print, and then close **C01-E04-LtrKCC.docx**.

Using the Undo and Redo Buttons

If you make a mistake and delete text that you did not intend to, or if you change your mind after deleting text and want to retrieve it, you can use the Undo or Redo buttons on the Quick Access toolbar. For example, if you type text and then click the Undo button, the text will be removed. You can undo text or commands. For example, if you add formatting such as bolding to text and then click the Undo button, the bolding is removed.

Undo

Redo

If you use the Undo button and then decide you do not want to reverse the original action, click the Redo button. For example, if you select and underline text and then decide to remove the underlining, click the Undo button. If you then decide you want the underlining back on, click the Redo button. Many Word actions can be undone or redone. Some actions, however, such as printing and saving, cannot be undone or redone.

Word maintains actions in temporary memory. If you want to undo an action performed earlier, click the Undo button arrow. This causes a drop-down list to display. To make a selection from this drop-down list, click the desired action. That action, along with any actions listed above it in the drop-down list, is undone.

Exercise 1.5   Deleting and Restoring Text with the Undo Button   Part 1 of 1

1. Open **SoftwareSuites.docx**. (This document is located in the Chapter01 folder you copied to your storage medium.)
2. Save the document with Save As and name it **C01-E05-SoftwareSuites**.
3. Make the changes indicated by the proofreaders' marks in Figure 1.9. (Proofreaders' marks are listed and described in Appendix A at the end of this textbook.)
4. Move the insertion point to the end of the document. Press the Backspace key until the last four words of the document *(or into a spreadsheet.)* are deleted. Be sure to delete the space before *or*.
5. Undo the deletion by clicking the Undo button on the Quick Access toolbar.
6. Redo the deletion by clicking the Redo button on the Quick Access toolbar.
7. Type a period after the word *presentation* to end the sentence.
8. Select the first sentence in the first paragraph and then delete it.
9. Select the second paragraph in the document and then delete it.
10. Undo the two deletions by completing the following steps:
    a. Click the down-pointing arrow to the right of the Undo button.
    b. Click the *second* Clear listed in the drop-down list. (This will redisplay the first sentence in the first paragraph and the second paragraph. The first sentence will be selected.)
11. With the first sentence of the paragraph selected, press the Delete key.
12. Save, print, and then close **C01-E05-SoftwareSuites.docx**.

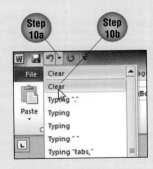

Figure 1.9 Exercise 1.5

Some commercial software vendors bundle and sell a group of software programs as a single package called a software suite, ~~also known as integrated software~~. Software suites typically include the four most widely used applications: word processing, database management, spreadsheet, and presentation ~~programs~~ *applications*. Some, such as Microsoft Office, also include Web page authoring programs because the development of personal Web sites is becoming increasingly important to consumers. Suites are popular because buying a package is ~~cheaper~~ *less expensive* than purchasing each component program separately.

Software suites offer advantages other than price. Because the programs were developed using the same user interface, all programs in the suite ~~work~~ *function* in a similar manner. A user who becomes familiar with one program can easily learn to use the others because the screen layouts, menus, *tabs,* buttons, icons, and toolbars are similar.

Another strong feature of suites is that they allow users to seamlessly integrate files from component programs. For example, information produced using a spreadsheet can be placed into a word processing document, or a database table can be imported into a slide show presentation or into a spreadsheet.

Using Help

Microsoft Word includes a Help feature that contains information about Word features and commands. This on-screen reference manual is similar to Windows Help and the Help features in Excel, PowerPoint, and Access. Click the Microsoft Word Help button (the circle with the question mark) located in the upper right corner of the screen or press the keyboard shortcut F1 to display the Word Help window. In this window, type a topic, feature, or question in the Search text box and then press the Enter key. Topics related to the search text display in the Word Help window. Click a topic that interests you. If the topic window contains a <u>Show All</u> hyperlink in the upper right corner, click this hyperlink and the topic options expand to show additional help information related to the topic. When you click the <u>Show All</u> hyperlink, it becomes the <u>Hide All</u> hyperlink.

Getting Help at the Help Tab Backstage View

The Help tab Backstage view, shown in Figure 1.10, contains an option for displaying the Word Help window as well as other options. Click the Microsoft Office Help button in the Support section to display the Word Help window and click the Getting Started button to access the Microsoft website that displays information about getting started with Word 2010. Click the Contact Us button in the Support section and the Microsoft Support website displays. Click the Options button in the Tools for Working With Office section and the Word Options dialog box displays. You will learn about this dialog box in a later chapter. Click the Check for Updates button and the Microsoft Update website displays with information on available updates. The right side of the Help tab Backstage view displays information about Office and Word.

Use Help Feature
1. Click Microsoft Word Help button.
2. Type topic or feature.
3. Press Enter.
4. Click desired topic.

Help

Figure 1.10 Help Tab Backstage View

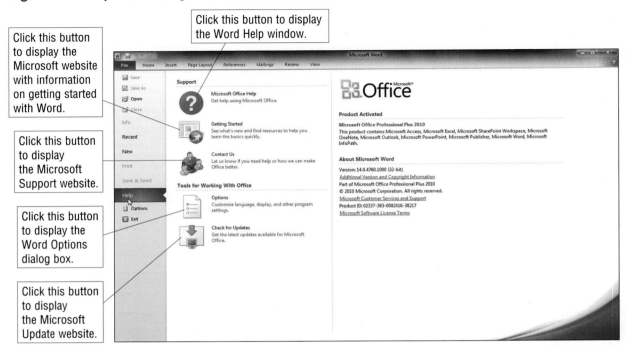

Click this button to display the Word Help window.

Click this button to display the Microsoft website with information on getting started with Word.

Click this button to display the Microsoft Support website.

Click this button to display the Word Options dialog box.

Click this button to display the Microsoft Update website.

Exercise 1.6A Using the Help Feature

Part 1 of 2

1. At a blank document, click the Microsoft Office Word Help button located in the upper right corner of the screen.

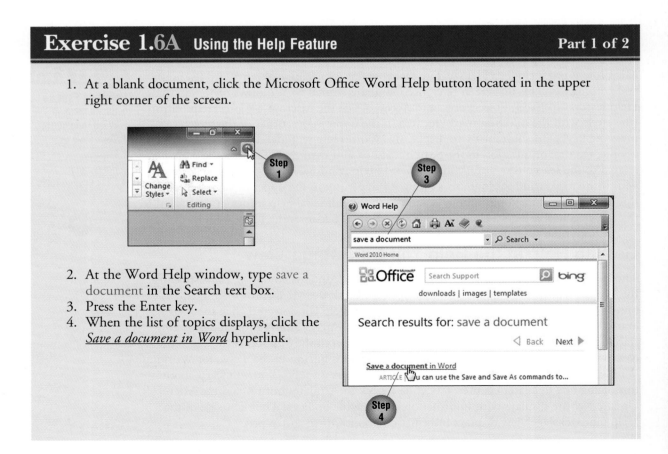

2. At the Word Help window, type *save a document* in the Search text box.
3. Press the Enter key.
4. When the list of topics displays, click the *Save a document in Word* hyperlink.

5. Click the <u>Show All</u> hyperlink that displays in the upper right corner of the window.

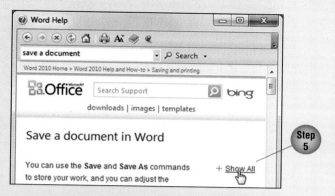

6. Read the information about saving a document.
7. Click the Close button to close the Word Help window.
8. Click the File tab and then click the Help tab.
9. Click the Getting Started button in the Support group. (You must be connected to the Internet to display the web page.)

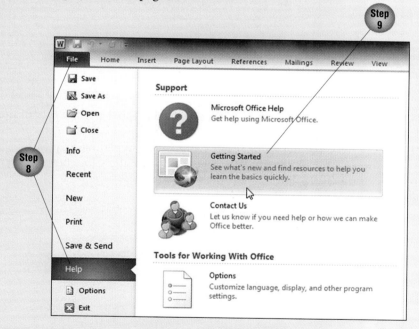

10. Look at the information that displays at the website and then click the Close button located in the upper right corner of the web page.
11. Click the File tab and then click the Help tab.
12. Click the Contact Us button, look at the information that displays at the website, and then close the web page.

Getting Help in a Dialog Box or Backstage View

Some dialog boxes, as well as the Backstage view, contain a Help button you can click to display a help window with specific information about the dialog box or Backstage view. After reading and/or printing the information, close a dialog box by clicking the Close button located in the upper right corner of the dialog box or close the Backstage view by clicking the File tab or clicking any other tab in the ribbon.

Exercise 1.6B   Getting Help in a Dialog Box and Backstage View   Part 2 of 2

1. At a blank document, click the File tab and then click the Save As button.
2. At the Save As dialog box, click the Help button located in the upper right corner of the dialog box.

3. Read the information about saving files and then click the Close button located in the upper right corner of the dialog box.
4. Close the Save As dialog box.
5. Click the File tab.
6. At the Backstage view, click the Help button located in the upper right corner of the window.
7. Click the *Introducing Backstage* hyperlink. (The name of the hyperlink may vary.)
8. After reading the information about the Backstage view, click the Close button located in the upper right corner of the dialog box.
9. Click the File tab to return to the blank document.

Chapter Summary

➤ Open Microsoft Word by clicking the Start button on the Taskbar, pointing to *All Programs*, clicking *Microsoft Office*, and then clicking *Microsoft Word 2010*.

➤ The Quick Access toolbar is located above the File tab and contains buttons for commonly used commands.

➤ Click the File tab and the Backstage view displays containing tabs and buttons for working with and managing documents.

➤ The Title bar is located to the right of the Quick Access toolbar and displays the document name followed by the program name.

➤ The Ribbon area contains tabs with commands and options divided into groups.

➤ The insertion point displays as a blinking vertical line and indicates the position of the next character to be entered in the document.

➤ The mouse displays on the screen as an I-beam pointer or as an arrow pointing up and to the left.

➤ Use the vertical scroll bar to view various parts of the document.

➤ The Status bar displays the number of pages and words, View buttons, and the Zoom slider bar.

➤ Word automatically wraps text to the next line as you type information. Press the Enter key only to end a paragraph, create a blank line, or end a short line.

➤ Word contains an AutoCorrect feature that automatically corrects certain words as they are typed.

➤ Word contains both an automatic spelling checker feature that inserts a red wavy line below words not contained in the Spelling dictionary and an automatic grammar checker that inserts a green wavy line below a sentence containing a grammatical error.

➤ The AutoComplete feature inserts an entire item when you type a few identifying characters and then press the Enter key or F3.

➤ Document names can contain a maximum of 255 characters, including the drive letter and folder names, and may include spaces.

➤ The insertion point can be moved throughout the document without interfering with text by using the mouse, the keyboard, or the mouse in combination with the keyboard.

➤ You can move the insertion point by character, word, screen, or page, and from the first to the last character in a document. Refer to Table 1.2 for keyboard insertion point movement commands.

➤ The scroll box on the vertical scroll bar indicates the location of the text in the document screen in relation to the remainder of the document.

➤ Click the Select Browse Object button located at the bottom of the vertical scroll bar to display options for browsing through a document.

➤ You can delete text by character, word, line, several lines, or partial page using specific keys or by selecting text using the mouse or the keyboard.

➤ A specific amount of text can be selected using the mouse or the keyboard. Refer to Table 1.4 for information on selecting with the mouse and refer to Table 1.5 for information on selecting with the keyboard.

➤ Use the Undo button on the Quick Access toolbar if you change your mind after typing, deleting, or formatting text and want to undo the action. Use the Redo button to redo something that has been undone with the Undo button.

➤ The Help feature in Word is an on-screen reference manual that contains information about all Word features and commands.

➤ Click the Microsoft Word Help button or press F1 to display the Word Help window. At this window, type a topic and then press the Enter key.

➤ Some dialog boxes, as well as the Backstage view, contain a Help button you can click to display information specific to the dialog box or Backstage view.

Commands Review

FEATURE	TAB, GROUP	BUTTON	FILE TAB	KEYBOARD SHORTCUT
Close document			Close	Ctrl + F4
Exit Word		X	Exit	
Find and Replace dialog box with Go To tab selected	Home, Editing	, Go To		Ctrl + G
Word Help window		?		F1
New blank document			New, Create	Ctrl + N
Open dialog box			Open	Ctrl + O
Print tab Backstage view			Print	Ctrl + P
Save document			Save	Ctr + S
Select document	Home, Editing	Select ▾		Ctrl + A
Help tab Backstage view			Help	

Key Points Review

Completion: In the space provided at the right, indicate the correct term, command, or number.

1. This toolbar contains the Save button. _____
2. Click this tab to display the Backstage view. _____
3. This is the area located toward the top of the screen that contains tabs with commands and options divided into groups. _____
4. This bar, located toward the bottom of the screen, displays number of pages and words, View buttons, and the Zoom slider bar. _____
5. This feature automatically corrects certain words as you type them. _____
6. This feature inserts an entire item when you type a few identifying characters and then press the Enter key or F3. _____
7. This is the keyboard shortcut to display the Print tab Backstage view. _____

8. This is the keyboard shortcut to close a document. _____

9. This is the keyboard shortcut to display a new blank document. _____

10. Use this keyboard command to move the insertion point to the beginning of the previous page. _____

11. Press this key on the keyboard to delete the character left of the insertion point. _____

12. Use this keyboard command to move the insertion point to the end of the document. _____

13. Using the mouse, do this to select one word. _____

14. To select various amounts of text using the mouse, you can click in this bar. _____

15. This is the keyboard shortcut to display the Word Help window. _____

Chapter *Assessments*

Applying Your Skills

Demonstrate your knowledge of features learned in this chapter by completing the following assessments.

Assessment 1.1   Type a Document

START From Scratch

1. At a blank document, type the text in Figure 1.11. (Correct any errors highlighted by the spelling checker as they occur and remember to space once after end-of-sentence punctuation.)
2. Save the document in the Chapter01 folder on your storage medium with the name **C01-A01-CoverLtrs**.
3. Print and then close **C01-A01-CoverLtrs.docx**.

Figure 1.11 Assessment 1.1

Cover letters are an essential component of your job search. During your search and transition, you will write many different letters or emails to "cover" your resume. In essence, cover letters tell your readers why you are contacting them. Often they are your very first opportunity to make an impression on a hiring decision-maker. They offer you the golden opportunity to link your unique set of skills, experiences, talents, and interests with a particular company or job opportunity. They are your formal introduction to people who can be extremely influential in your job search, and they prepare your reader for all of the details, experiences, and accomplishments you have highlighted in your resume.

Assessment 1.2   Edit a Document Containing Proofreaders' Marks

1. Open **Editing.docx**.
2. Save the document with Save As and name it **C01-A02-Editing**.
3. Make the changes indicated by the proofreaders' marks in Figure 1.12.
4. Save, print, and then close **C01-A02-Editing.docx**.

Figure 1.12 Assessment 1.2

Editing is

The process of altering the contents of an existing document is called editing. Editing occurs anytime [when] something is inserted, deleted, or modified within a document. Editing features allow users to make changes until they are satisfied with the content. Perhaps the most valued word processing editing feature is a spell checker, which matches each word in a document to a word list or dictionary. A spell checker is not context-sensitive. It will not flag words that have been spelled correctly but used incorrectly.

and

No ¶ A grammar checker checks a document for common errors in grammar, usage, and mechanics. Grammar checkers are no substitute for careful review by a knowledgeable editor, but they can be useful for identifying such problems as run-on sentences, sentence fragments, and misused apostrophes.

double negatives,

Assessment 1.3 Edit a Document Containing Proofreaders' Marks

1. Open **Format.docx**.
2. Save the document with Save As and name it **C01-A03-Format**.
3. Make the changes indicated by the proofreaders' marks in Figure 1.13.
4. Save, print, and then close **C01-A03-Format.docx**.

Figure 1.13 Assessment 1.3

which is

Word processing programs allow many different types of formatting, or the manipulation of text to change its appearance at the word, paragraph, or document level. Many word processing applications [programs] include text, paragraph, and document formatting.

the

Text formatting features include the ability to change font type, size, color, and style (such as bold, italic, or underlined). Users can also adjust the leading (the space between lines)

which is

and kerning (the amount of space that appears between letters).

which is

No ¶ Paragraph formatting changes the way a body of text flows on the page. Features related to the appearance of a paragraph include placing the text in columns or tables, aligning the text left, right, center, or justified within the margins; and double- or single-spacing lines.

spacing

No ¶ Document formatting lets users specify the form of a document as a whole, defining page numbers, headers, footers, paper size, and margin width. A style is a special shortcut feature that formats text in a single step. Styles allow users to apply text and paragraph formatting to a page, and then the styles automatically apply those same attributes to other sections of text.

Many word processing programs include

document

then

Expanding Your Skills

Explore additional feature options or use Help to learn a new skill in creating these documents.

Assessment 1.4   Compose a Document on Saving a Document

1. At a blank document, compose a paragraph explaining when you would use Save As when saving a document and the advantages of Save As.
2. Save the document with the name **C01-A04-SaveAs**.
3. Print and then close **C01-A04-SaveAs.docx**.

Assessment 1.5   Use Help to Learn About and Then Create a Document Describing Keyboard Shortcuts

1. Click the Microsoft Word Help button, type keyboard shortcuts, and then press the Enter key.
2. At the Word Help window, click the *Keyboard shortcuts for Microsoft Word* hyperlink.
3. At the keyboard shortcut window, click the *Show All* hyperlink.
4. Read through the information in the Word Help window and then close the window.
5. Create a document describing four keyboard shortcuts.
6. Save the document with the name **C01-A05-KeyboardShortcuts**.
7. Print and then close **C01-A05-KeyboardShortcuts.docx**.

Achieving Signature Status

Take your skills to the next level by completing this more challenging assessment.

Assessment 1.6   Create a Cover Letter

1. At a blank document, click the No Spacing style thumbnail located in the Styles group in the Home tab. (Clicking the No Spacing style changes the line spacing to 1 and removes the 10 points of spacing after each paragraph.)
2. Press the Enter key six times and then type the personal business letter shown in Figure 1.14. Type the current date in place of the *(Current date)* text, and type your first and last names in place of the *(Student Name)* text. Refer to Appendix B at the end of this textbook for the formatting of a block style personal business letter.
3. Save the completed document with the name **C01-A06-CoverLtr**.
4. Print and then close the **C01-A06-CoverLtr.docx**.

Figure 1.14 Assessment 1.6

3120 Magnolia Drive
Columbia, SC 29167
(Current date)

Mr. Nathaniel Jensen
Human Resources Director
Landmark Associates
4450 Seventh Avenue
Columbia, SC 29169

Dear Mr. Jensen:

In response to your advertisement on Monster.com, I would like to apply for the position of Sales Associate Trainee in the Sales and Marketing Department at your company. I have a strong interest in joining a dynamic organization such as Landmark Associates and feel I can make major contributions to the company in a short period of time.

I recently graduated from Columbia Technical College with a degree in Business Operations. For the past two years, I have been employed as an assistant in the Accounting Department at Atlantic Signs where I processed payroll and budget reports. My excellent communication skills and a strong work ethic make me a valuable asset to your training program.

I have enclosed my resume for your review. Please call me at (803) 555-3489 to schedule a meeting to discuss the Sales Associate Trainee position at Landmark Associates.

Sincerely,

(Student Name)

Enclosure

Chapter 2

TUTORIALS

Formatting Characters

Performance Objectives

Upon successful completion of Chapter 2, you will be able to:

- Change fonts and font effects
- Format selected text using buttons on the Mini toolbar
- Apply styles from Quick Styles sets
- Apply and customize themes

Tutorial 2.1
Highlighting Text
Tutorial 2.2
Formatting with the Mini Toolbar
Tutorial 2.3
Modifying the Font Using the Font Group
Tutorial 2.4
Modifying the Font Using the Font Dialog Box
Tutorial 2.5
Applying Styles and Using the Quick Styles Gallery
Tutorial 2.6
Applying Themes

Format refers to how a document looks on screen and when it is printed. As you learned in Chapter 1, Word uses a template to apply default formatting that affects the appearance of a document. Some default settings include 11-point Calibri type, 1.15-point line spacing, 10-point spacing after each paragraph, and left aligned text. In this chapter, you will learn about character formatting, including how to change the typeface, type size, and typestyle, as well as how to apply font effects such as subscripting, superscripting, and highlighting.

Chapter02

Note: Before beginning computer exercises for this chapter, copy to your storage medium the Chapter02 folder from the CD that accompanies this textbook and then make Chapter02 the active folder.

In this chapter students will produce the following documents:

Exercise 2.1. C02-E01-Terms.docx
Exercise 2.2. C02-E02-CompHardware.docx

Model answers for these exercises are shown on the following pages.

Exercise 2.1

C02-E01-Terms.docx

GLOSSARY OF TERMS

A

Active desktop: An onscreen desktop that can contain icons linked to the Web.

Android: A mobile *robot* designed to seem human.

Applet: A small computer application program, generally created using Java programming language, that performs specific functions; applets are used to extend the capabilities of Web pages.

B

Beta version: A prerelease version of a piece of software distributed so that users can test it to evaluate its features and identify any bugs.

Bluetooth: A technology that uses *infrared light signals* to send information.

Buffer: A temporary storage unit to which data can be written before being displayed, printed, or transmitted.

C

Carpal tunnel syndrome: A condition characterized by weakness, pain, or numbness of the hand(s), caused by compression of the median nerve as is passes through the wrist; the *syndrome* is associated with repetitive motion such as typing or using the computer mouse.

Cell: In a spreadsheet, the *intersection* of one row and one column into which text, numbers, formulas, links, or other elements may be entered.

Chinese abacus: Pebbles strung on a rod inside a frame. Pebbles in the upper part of an abacus correspond to 5×10^0, or 5, for the first column; 5×10^1, or 50, for the second column; 5×10^2, or 500, for the third column; and so on.

Clip art: Professionally designed graphic images sold for use in *word processing* and other types of documents; collections are sometimes included in a software program.

COMPUTER HARDWARE

A computer consists of two broad categories of components: hardware and software. Computer hardware includes all of the physical components that make up the system unit plus other devices connected to it. These connected devices are referred to as *peripheral devices* because they are outside, or peripheral to, the computer. Examples include a monitor, keyboard, mouse, hard disk drive, camera, and printer. Some peripheral devices, such as the monitor and hard disk drive, are essential components of a personal computer system. Categories of hardware devices include the system unit, input devices, output devices, storage devices, and communication devices.

System Unit

The system unit is a relatively small plastic or metal cabinet that houses the electronic components, which process data into information. Inside the cabinet, the main circuit board, called the *motherboard*, provides for the installation and connection of other electronic components. Once installed on the motherboard, the components can communicate with each other, thereby allowing the processing of data into information. The motherboard has two components, the *central processing unit* (CPU), also called the *microprocessor* (or simply *processor*), and the internal memory. The processor consists of one or more electronic chips that read, interpret, and execute instructions that operate the computer and perform specific computing tasks. When a program is executed, the processor temporarily stores the program's instructions and the data needed for the instructions into the computer's memory. *Memory*, also called *primary storage*, consists of small electronic chips that provide temporary storage for instructions and data during processing.

Input Devices

An *input device* is a hardware device that allows users to enter program instructions, data, and commands into a computer. The program or application being used determines the type of input device needed. Common input devices are the keyboard, mouse, and microphone.

Output Devices

An *output device* is a device that makes information available to the user. Popular output devices include display screens (monitors), printers, television screens, and speakers. Some output devices, such as a printer, produce output in *hard copy* (tangible) form, such as on paper or plastic. Other output devices, such as a monitor, produce output in *soft copy* (intangible) form that can be viewed but not physically handled.

Exercise 2.2

C02-E02-CompHardware.docx

Changing Fonts

The Font group in the Home tab, shown in Figure 2.1, contains a number of buttons you can use to apply character formatting to text in a document. Buttons in the top row change the font and the font size, as well as increase and decrease font size, change text case, and clear formatting. You can remove all character formatting (as well as paragraph formatting) that has been applied to text by clicking the Clear Formatting button in the top row. To remove character formatting from selected text only, press the keyboard shortcut Ctrl + spacebar. The bottom row contains buttons for applying typestyles such as bold, italic, and underlining and applying text effects, highlighting, and color.

Clear Formatting

Figure 2.1 Font Group Buttons

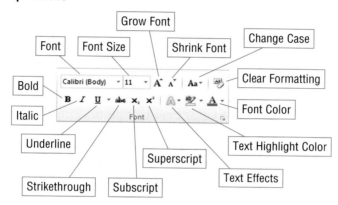

As noted earlier, 11-point Calibri type is Word's default font. You may want to change this default to some other font for reasons such as to change the mood of the document, enhance its visual appeal, or increase its readability. A font consists of three elements—typeface, type size, and typestyle.

A typeface is a set of characters with a common design and shape. It can be decorative or plain, monospaced or proportional. Word refers to typeface as **font**. A monospaced typeface allots the same amount of horizontal space for each character; a proportional typeface allots a varying amount of space for each character. Proportional typefaces are divided into two main categories: *serif* and *sans serif*. A serif is a small line at the end of a character stroke. Because serifs help move the reader's eyes across the page, serif fonts are a good choice for text-intensive documents. Sans serif typefaces are often used for headings, headlines, and advertisements.

In the previous version of Office, Microsoft added six new fonts designed for extended on-screen reading: Calibri (the default), Cambria, Candara, Consolas, Constantia, and Corbel. Calibri, Candara, and Corbel are sans serif typefaces; Cambria and Constantia are serif typefaces; and Consolas is monospaced. These six typefaces as well as some other popular typefaces are shown in Table 2.1.

Table 2.1 Serif and Sans Serif Typefaces

Serif Typefaces	Sans Serif Typefaces	Monospaced Typefaces
Cambria	Calibri	Consolas
Constantia	Candara	Courier
Times New Roman	Corbel	Letter Gothic
Bookman Old Style	Arial	

QUICK STEPS

Change Font
1. Click Font button arrow.
2. Click desired font at drop-down gallery.

Change Font Size
1. Click Font Size button arrow.
2. Click desired font size at drop-down gallery.

Calibri (Body) ▾

Font

11 ▾

Font Size

Type size is generally set in proportional size. The size of proportional type is measured vertically in units called **points**. A point is approximately ½ of an inch—the higher the point size, the larger the characters. Within a typeface, various typestyles may be available. Typestyles are divided into four main categories: regular, bold, italic, and bold italic.

Use the Font button in the Font group to change the font; use the Font Size button or the Shrink Font and Grow Font buttons to change the size. When you select text and then click the Font button arrow, a drop-down gallery displays font options. Hover your mouse pointer over a font option and the selected text in the document displays with the font applied. You can continue hovering your mouse pointer over different font options to see how the selected text displays in the specified font. The Font button drop-down gallery is an example of the **live preview** feature in Word, which allows you to see how the font formatting affects your text without having to return to the document. The live preview feature is also available when you click the Font Size button arrow.

Exercise 2.1A Changing the Font   **Part 1 of 4**

1. Open **Terms.docx**.
2. Save the document with Save As and name it **C02-E01-Terms**.
3. Change the typeface to Cambria by completing the following steps:
   a. Select the entire document by pressing Ctrl + A. (You can also select all text in the document by clicking the Select button in the Editing group and then clicking *Select All* at the drop-down list.)

b. Click the Font button arrow and then scroll down the Font drop-down gallery until *Cambria* displays. Hover the mouse pointer over *Cambria* to display a live preview of the text set in Cambria.

c. Click *Cambria*.

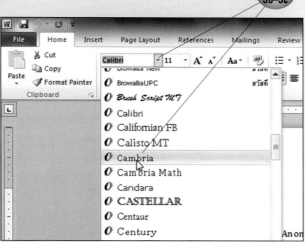

Steps
3b–3c

4. Change the type size to 14 points by completing the following steps:

   a. With the text in the document still selected, click the Font Size button arrow.

   b. At the drop-down gallery that displays, hover the mouse pointer over *14* and look at the live preview of the text in 14-point type.

   c. Click *14*.

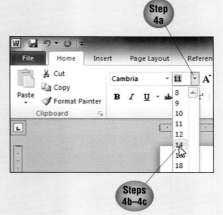

Step
4a

Steps
4b–4c

5. Deselect the text by clicking anywhere in the document.

6. Change the type size and typeface by completing the following steps:

   a. Press Ctrl + A to select the entire document.

   b. Click three times on the Shrink Font button in the Font group. (This decreases the size to 10 points.)

   c. Click twice on the Grow Font button. (This increases the size of the font to 12 points.)

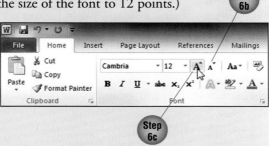

Step
6b

Step
6c

   d. Click the Font button arrow, scroll down the drop-down gallery, and then click *Constantia*. (The most recently used fonts display at the beginning of the document followed by a listing of all fonts.)

7. Save **C02-E01-Terms.docx**.

Choosing a Typestyle

B Bold   **I** Italic

U ▾ Underline

Apply a particular typestyle to text with the Bold, Italic, or Underline buttons in the bottom row in the Font group. You can apply more than one style to text. For example, you can bold and italicize the same text or apply all three styles to the same text. Click the Underline button arrow and a drop-down gallery displays with underlining options such as a double line, dashed line, and thicker underline. Click the *Underline Color* option at the Underline button drop-down gallery and a side menu displays with color options.

Exercise 2.1B   Applying Character Formatting to Text as You Type   Part 2 of 4

1. With **C02-E01-Terms.docx** open, press Ctrl + Home to move the insertion point to the beginning of the document.
2. Type a heading for the document by completing the following steps:
   a. Click the Bold button in the Font group. (This turns on bold.)
   b. Click the Underline button in the Font group. (This turns on underline.)
   c. Type Glossary of Terms.

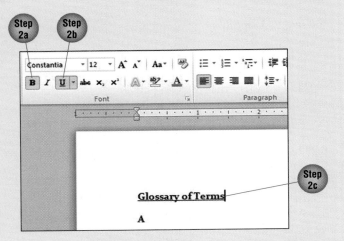

   d. Select *Glossary of Terms* and then click the Clear Formatting button in the Font group. (This removes all formatting from the text.)
   e. Return formatting to the text by clicking the Undo button on the Quick Access toolbar.
3. Press Ctrl + End to move the insertion point to the end of the document.
4. Type the text shown in Figure 2.2 with the following specifications:
   a. While typing the document, make the appropriate text bold as shown in the figure by completing the following steps:
      1) Click the Bold button in the Font group. (This turns on bold.)
      2) Type the text.
      3) Click the Bold button in the Font group. (This turns off bold.)
   b. While typing the document, italicize the appropriate text as shown in the figure by completing the following steps:
      1) Click the Italic button in the Font group.
      2) Type the text.
      3) Click the Italic button in the Font group.

5. After typing the text, press the Enter key.
6. Change the underlining below the title by completing the following steps:
   a. Select the title *Glossary of Terms*.
   b. Click the Underline button arrow and then click the third underline option from the top of the drop-down gallery.
   c. Click the Underline button arrow, point to the *Underline Color* option, and then click the Red color (second color option from the left) in the *Standard Colors* section.
7. With the title *Glossary of Terms* still selected, change the font size to 14 points.
8. Save **C02-E01-Terms.docx**.

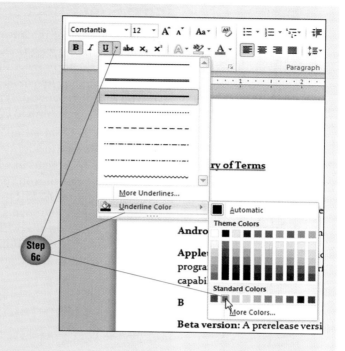

Figure 2.2 Exercise 2.1B

C

Carpal tunnel syndrome: A condition characterized by weakness, pain, or numbness of the hand(s), caused by compression of the median nerve as it passes through the wrist; the *syndrome* is associated with repetitive motion such as typing or using the computer mouse.

Cell: In a spreadsheet, the *intersection* of one row and one column into which text, numbers, formulas, links, or other elements may be entered.

Clip art: Professionally designed graphic images sold for use in *word processing* and other types of documents; collections are sometimes included in a software program.

Change Case

Strikethrough

Subscript

Superscript

Text Highlight Color

Font   Text
Color   Effects

Choosing a Font Effect

Apply font effects with some of the buttons in the top and bottom rows in the Font group. Change the case of text with the Change Case button drop-down list. Click the Change Case button in the top row of the Font group and a drop-down list displays with the options *Sentence case, lowercase, UPPERCASE, Capitalize Each Word*, and *tOGGLEcASE*. You can also change the case of selected text with the keyboard shortcut Shift + F3. Each time you press Shift + F3, selected text cycles through the case options.

The bottom row in the Font group contains buttons for applying font effects. Use the Strikethrough button to draw a line through selected text. This has a practical application in some legal documents in which deleted text must be retained in the document. Use the Subscript button to create text that is lowered slightly below the line such as the chemical formula H_2O. Use the Superscript button to create text that is raised slightly above the text line such as the mathematical equation four to the third power (written as 4^3). Click the Text Effects button in the bottom row, and a drop-down gallery displays with effect options. Use the Text Highlight Color button to highlight specific text in a document, and use the Font Color button to change the color of text.

Using Keyboard Shortcuts

Several buttons in the Font group have keyboard shortcuts. For example, you can press Ctrl + B to turn on bold, or press Ctrl + I to turn on italic. Position the mouse pointer on a button and an enhanced ScreenTip displays with the name of the button, the keyboard shortcut (if there is one), a description of the action performed by the button, and, in some cases, access to the Word Help window. Table 2.2 identifies the keyboard shortcuts available for buttons in the Font group.

Table 2.2 Font Button Keyboard Shortcuts

Font Group Button	*Keyboard Shortcut*
Font	Ctrl + Shift + F
Font Size	Ctrl + Shift + P
Grow Font	Ctrl + Shift + >
Shrink Font	Ctrl + Shift + <
Bold	Ctrl + B
Italic	Ctrl + I
Underline	Ctrl + U
Subscript	Ctrl + =
Superscript	Ctrl + Shift + +
Change Case	Shift + F3

Formatting with the Mini Toolbar

When you select text, the Mini toolbar displays in a dimmed fashion above the selected text. Hover the mouse pointer over the Mini toolbar and it becomes active. Click a button on the Mini toolbar to apply formatting to selected text.

Figure 2.3 Exercise 2.1C

Chinese abacus: Pebbles strung on a rod inside a frame. Pebbles in the upper part of an abacus correspond to 5×10^0, or 5, for the first column; 5×10^1, or 50, for the second column; 5×10^2, or 500, for the third column; and so on.

If you do not want the Mini toolbar to display when you select text, you can turn it off. To do this, click the File tab and then click the Options button. At the Word Options dialog box with the *General* option selected in the left panel, click the *Show Mini Toolbar on selection* check box to remove the check mark.

Exercise 2.1C Applying Font Effects   Part 3 of 4

1. With **C02-E01-Terms.docx** open, move the insertion point to the beginning of the term *Clip art*, press the Enter key, and then press the Up Arrow key. Type the text shown in Figure 2.3. Create the superscript numbers by clicking the Superscript button, typing the number, and then clicking the Superscript button.

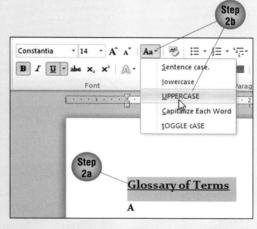

2. Change the case of text and remove underlining from the title by completing the following steps:
   a. Select the title *Glossary of Terms*.
   b. Click the Change Case button in the Font group and then click *UPPERCASE* at the drop-down list.
   c. Click the Underline button to remove the underlining.
   d. Click the Text Effects button in the Font group and then click the *Gradient Fill - Blue, Accent 1* option (fourth option from the left in the third row) at the drop-down gallery.

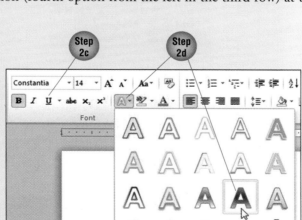

3. Strike through text by completing the following steps:
   a. Select the commas and words , *generally created using the Java programming language,* located in the *Applet* definition.
   b. Click the Strikethrough button in the Font group.

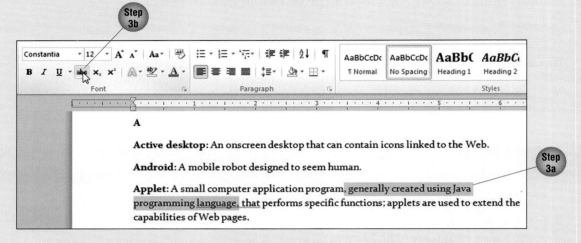

4. Change the font color by completing the following steps:
   a. Press Ctrl + A to select the entire document.
   b. Click the Font Color button arrow.
   c. Click Dark Red (the first color from the left in the *Standard Colors* section) at the drop-down gallery.

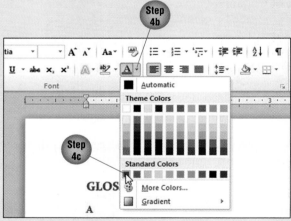

   d. Click in the document to deselect text.
5. Highlight text in the document by completing the following steps:
   a. Click the Text Highlight Color button arrow in the Font group and then click the yellow color at the drop-down palette. (This causes the mouse pointer to display as an I-beam pointer with a pen attached.)

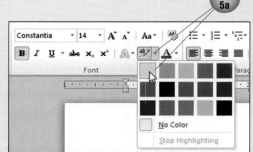

b. Select the term *Beta version* and the definition that follows.

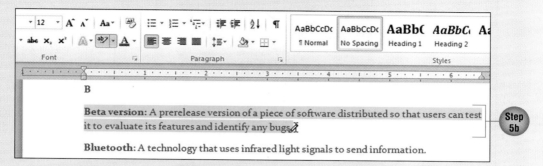

c. Click the Text Highlight Color button arrow and then click the turquoise color (third color from the left in the top row).
d. Select the term *Cell* and the definition that follows.
e. Click the Text Highlight Color button arrow and then click the yellow color at the drop-down palette.
f. Click the Text Highlight Color button to turn off highlighting.

6. Apply italic formatting using the Mini toolbar by completing the following steps:

   a. Select the word *robot* located in the *Android* definition. (When you select the word, the Mini toolbar displays.)
   b. Click the Italic button on the Mini toolbar.
   c. Select the words *infrared light signals* located in the *Bluetooth* definition and then click the Italic button on the Mini toolbar.

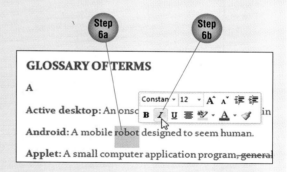

7. Save **C02-E01-Terms.docx**.

Changing Fonts at the Font Dialog Box

In addition to using the Font group buttons to apply font formatting, you can use options at the Font dialog box, shown in Figure 2.4, to change the typeface, type size, and typestyle of text as well as to apply font effects. Display the Font dialog box by clicking the Font group dialog box launcher. The dialog box launcher is a small square containing a diagonal-pointing arrow that displays in the lower right corner of the Font group.

Turning on the Display of Nonprinting Characters

The Font dialog box contains the *Hidden* option in the *Effects* section of the dialog box. With this option, you can select and then hide specific text. If you want to view the hidden text, turn on the display of nonprinting characters by clicking the Show/Hide ¶ button in the Paragraph group in the Home tab or with the keyboard shortcut Ctrl + Shift + *. When it is active, the button displays with an orange background. Hidden text displays with a dotted underline, including nonprinting characters such as paragraph symbols, tab symbols, and spacing characters. To redisplay hidden text, click the Show/Hide ¶ button to make it active, select the text, display the Font dialog box, and then remove the check mark from the *Hidden* option.

QUICK STEPS

Change Fonts
1. Click Font group dialog box launcher.
2. Choose desired options at dialog box.
3. Click OK.

Display Nonprinting Characters
Click Show/Hide ¶ button.
OR
Press Ctrl + Shift + *.

Show/Hide ¶

Figure 2.4 Font Dialog Box

Choose a typeface in this list box. Use the scroll bar at the right side of the box to view available typefaces.

Choose a typestyle in this list box. The options in the box may vary depending on the selected typeface.

Choose a type size in this list box, or select the current measurement in the top box and then type the desired measurement.

Click this button to change the default font.

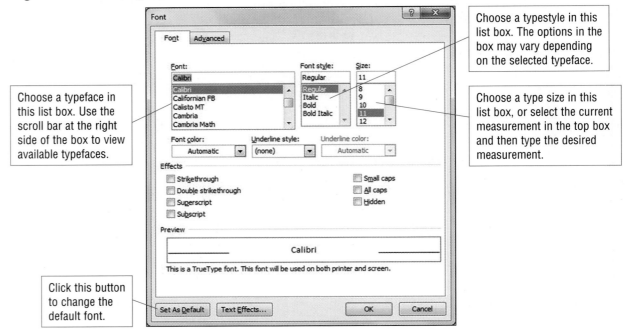

Exercise 2.1D Changing the Font at the Font Dialog Box Part 4 of 4

1. With **C02-E01-Terms.docx** open, press Ctrl + End to move the insertion point to the end of the document. (Make sure the insertion point is positioned below the last line of text.)
2. Type Submitted by Marcus Jackson and then press the Enter key.
3. Type Monday, October 15, 2012.
4. Change the font to 13-point Calibri and the font color to dark blue by completing the following steps:
   a. Press Ctrl + A to select the entire document.
   b. Click the Font group dialog box launcher.

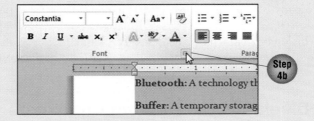

c. At the Font dialog box, click the up-pointing arrow at the right side of the *Font* list box to scroll up the list box and then click *Calibri*.
d. Click in the *Size* text box and then type 13.
e. Click the down-pointing arrow at the right side of the *Font color* list box and then click Dark Blue at the drop-down color palette (second option from the right in the *Standard Colors* section).
f. Click OK to close the dialog box.

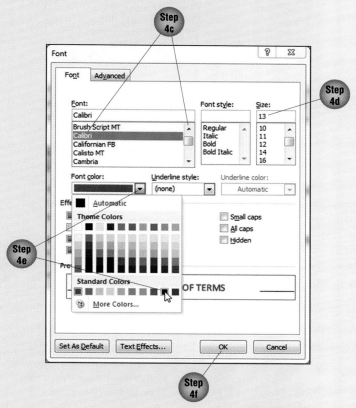

5. Double underline text by completing the following steps:
   a. Select *Monday, October 15, 2012*.
   b. Click the Font group dialog box launcher.
   c. At the Font dialog box, click the down-pointing arrow at the right side of the *Underline style* option box and then click the double-line option at the drop-down list.
   d. Click OK to close the dialog box.
6. Change text to small caps by completing the following steps:
   a. Select the text *Submitted by Marcus Jackson* and *Monday, October 15, 2012*.
   b. Display the Font dialog box.

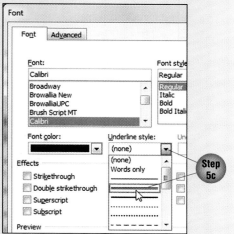

c. Click the *Small caps* option in the *Effects* section. (This inserts a check mark in the check box.)

d. Click OK to close the dialog box.

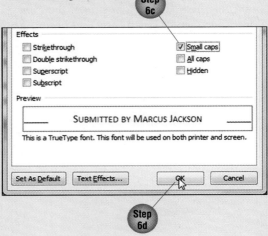

7. Hide text by completing the following steps:
   a. Select the term *Chinese abacus* and the definition that follows.
   b. Display the Font dialog box.
   c. Click the *Hidden* option in the *Effects* section. (This inserts a check mark in the check box.)
   d. Click OK to close the dialog box.

8. Click the Show/Hide ¶ button in the Paragraph group in the Home tab to turn on the display of nonprinting characters. (The hidden text is now visible and displays with a dotted underline.)

9. Redisplay the hidden text by completing the following steps:
   a. Select the term *Chinese abacus* and the definition that follows.
   b. Display the Font dialog box.
   c. Click the *Hidden* option in the *Effects* section to remove the check mark.
   d. Click OK to close the dialog box.

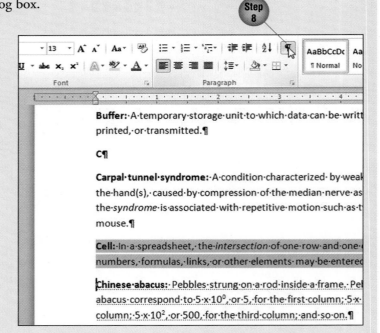

10. Click the Show/Hide ¶ button to turn off the display of nonprinting characters.

11. Save, print, and then close **C02-E01-Terms.docx**.

Applying Styles from a Quick Styles Set

Word contains a number of predesigned formats grouped into style sets called Quick Styles. Several thumbnails of the styles in the default Quick Styles set display in the Styles group in the Home tab. You can display additional styles by clicking the More button that displays at the right side of the style thumbnails. This displays a drop-down gallery of style choices. To apply a style, position the insertion point in the paragraph of text to which you want the style applied, click the More button at the right side of the style thumbnails in the Styles group, and then click the desired style at the drop-down gallery.

As noted earlier, Word applies some default formatting to documents, including 10 points of spacing after paragraphs and a line spacing of 1.15. You can remove this default formatting as well as any character formatting applied to text in your document by applying the No Spacing style to your text. This style is one of the styles that displays in the Styles group in the Home tab.

To change to a different Quick Styles set, click the Change Styles button in the Styles group in the Home tab and then point to Style Set. This displays a side menu with Quick Styles sets. Click the desired set, and the style formatting changes in the styles that display in the Styles group.

QUICK STEPS

Apply a Style
1. Position insertion point in desired paragraph of text.
2. Click More button in Styles group.
3. Click desired style.

Change Quick Styles Set
1. Click Change Styles button.
2. Point to Style Set.
3. Click desired set.

More

Change Styles

Exercise 2.2A Applying Quick Styles   Part 1 of 3

1. Open **CompHardware.docx**.
2. Save the document with Save As and name it **C02-E02-CompHardware**.
3. Remove the 10 points of spacing after paragraphs and change the line spacing to 1 by completing the following steps:
   a. Press Ctrl + A to select the entire document.
   b. Click the No Spacing style in the Styles group in the Home tab.

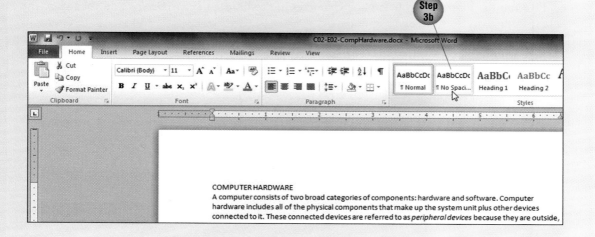

4. Position the insertion point on any character in the title *COMPUTER HARDWARE* and then click the Heading 1 style that displays in the Styles group.

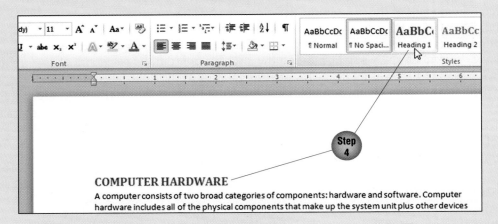

5. Position the insertion point on any character in the heading *System Unit* and then click the Heading 2 style that displays in the Styles group.

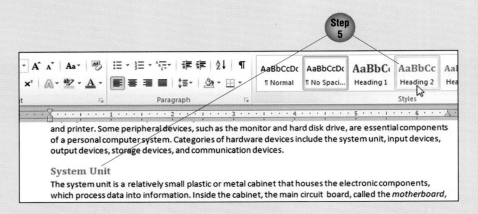

6. Position the insertion point on any character in the heading *Input Devices* and then click the Heading 2 style in the Styles group.
7. Position the insertion point on any character in the heading *Output Devices* and then click the Heading 2 style in the Styles group.

8. Click the Change Styles button in the Styles group, point to Style Set, and then click *Thatch*. (Notice how the Heading 1 and Heading 2 formatting changes.)

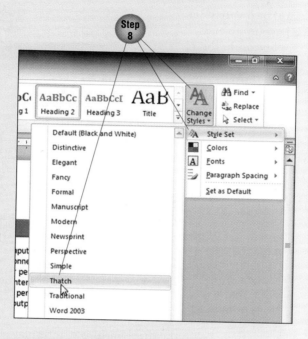

9. Save and then print **C02-E02-CompHardware.docx**.

Applying a Theme

Word provides a number of themes you can use to format text in your document. A theme is a set of formatting choices that include a color theme (a set of colors), a font theme (a set of heading and body text fonts), and an effects theme (a set of lines and fill effects). Applying a theme can give your documents a professional look. To apply a theme, click the Page Layout tab and then click the Themes button in the Themes group. At the drop-down gallery that displays, click the desired theme. You can hover the mouse pointer over a theme and the live preview feature will display your document with the theme formatting applied. With the live preview feature, you can see how the theme formatting affects your document before you make your final choice.

Apply a Theme
1. Click Page Layout tab.
2. Click Themes button.
3. Click desired theme.

Themes

1. With **C02-E02-CompHardware.docx** open, click the Page Layout tab and then click the Themes button in the Themes group.
2. At the drop-down gallery, hover your mouse pointer over each theme and notice how the text formatting changes in your document.
3. Click the *Hardcover* theme. (You will need to scroll down the drop-down gallery to display Hardcover.)
4. Save and then print **C02-E02-CompHardware.docx**.

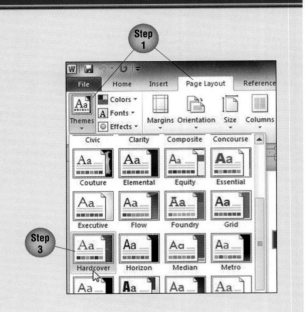

Change Theme Color
1. Click Page Layout tab.
2. Click Theme Colors button.
3. Click desired theme color.

Change Theme Fonts
1. Click Page Layout tab.
2. Click Theme Fonts button.
3. Click desired theme font.

Change Theme Effect
1. Click Page Layout tab.
2. Click Theme Effects button.
3. Click desired theme effect.

Theme Colors

Theme Fonts

You can change a theme with the three buttons that display at the right side of the Themes button. A theme contains specific color formatting, which you can change with options from the Theme Colors button in the Themes group. Click this button, and a drop-down gallery displays with named color schemes. The names of the color schemes correspond to the names of the themes. Each theme applies specific fonts, which you can change with options from the Theme Fonts button in the Themes group. Click this button and a drop-down gallery displays with font choices. Each font group in the drop-down gallery contains two choices. The first choice in the group is the font that is applied to headings and the second choice is the font that is applied to body text in the document. If you are formatting a document containing graphics with lines and fills, you can apply a specific theme of effects with options at the Theme Effects drop-down gallery.

1. With **C02-E02-CompHardware.docx** open, click the Theme Colors button in the Themes group and then click *Foundry* at the drop-down gallery. (Notice how the colors in the title and headings change.)

2. Click the Theme Fonts button, scroll down the drop-down gallery, and then click the *Elemental* option. (Notice how the document text font changes.)

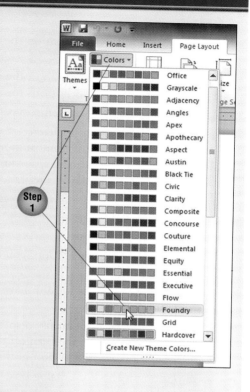

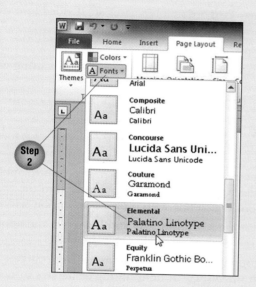

3. Save, print, and then close **C02-E02-CompHardware.docx**.

Chapter Summary

➤ The appearance of a document on the document screen and how it looks when printed is called the format.

➤ The top row in the Font group in the Home tab contains buttons for changing the font and font size. The bottom row contains buttons for applying typestyles and effects.

➤ A font consists of three elements: typeface, type size, and typestyle.

➤ A typeface (font) is a set of characters with a common design and shape. Typefaces are either monospaced, allotting the same amount of horizontal space to each character, or proportional, allotting a varying amount of space for each character. Proportional typefaces are divided into two main categories: serif and sans serif.

➤ Type size is measured in point size—the higher the point size, the larger the characters.

➤ A typestyle is a variation of style within a certain typeface. You can apply typestyle formatting with buttons in the Font group.

➤ With buttons in the Font group, you can apply font effects such as superscript, subscript, and strikethrough.

➤ Some buttons in the Font group have corresponding keyboard shortcuts. Refer to Table 2.2 for a list of these shortcuts.

➤ The Mini toolbar automatically displays above selected text. Use buttons on this toolbar to apply formatting to selected text. Turn off the Mini toolbar by removing the check mark from the *Show Mini Toolbar on selection* option in the Word Options dialog box with the *General* option selected.

➤ With options at the Font dialog box, you can change the font, font size, and font style and apply specific effects. Display this dialog box by clicking the Font group dialog box launcher.

➤ Click the Show/Hide ¶ button in the Paragraph group in the Home tab or press Ctrl + Shift + * to turn on the display of nonprinting characters. With the display of nonprinting characters turned on, hidden text will display with a dotted underline in the document.

➤ A Word document contains a number of predesigned formats grouped into style sets called Quick Styles. Change to a different Quick Styles set by clicking the Change Styles button in the Styles group in the Home tab, pointing to Style Set, and then clicking the desired set.

➤ Word provides a number of themes, which are a set of formatting choices that include a color theme (a set of colors), a font theme (a set of heading and body text fonts), and an effects theme (a set of lines and fill effects). Apply a theme and change theme colors, fonts, and effects with buttons in the Themes group in the Page Layout tab.

Commands *Review*

FEATURE	RIBBON TAB, GROUP	BUTTON	KEYBOARD SHORTCUT
Bold text	Home, Font	**B**	Ctrl + B
Change case of text	Home, Font	Aa	Shift + F3
Change Quick Styles set	Home, Styles	A	
Clear all formatting	Home, Font	Aa	
Clear character formatting			Ctrl + spacebar
Decrease font size	Home, Font	A	Ctrl + <
Display nonprinting characters	Home, Paragraph	¶	Ctrl + Shift + *
Font	Home, Font	Calibri (Body)	
Font color	Home, Font	A	
Font dialog box	Home, Font		Ctrl + Shift + F
Highlight text	Home, Font	ab	
Increase font size	Home, Font	A	Ctrl + >
Italicize text	Home, Font	*I*	Ctrl + I
Strikethrough text	Home, Font	abc	
Subscript text	Home, Font	x_2	Ctrl + =
Superscript text	Home, Font	x^2	Ctrl + Shift + +
Text Effects	Home, Font	A	
Theme Color	Page Layout, Themes		
Theme Fonts	Page Layout, Themes	A	
Themes	Page Layout, Themes	Aa	
Underline text	Home, Font	<u>U</u>	Ctrl + U

Key Points Review

Completion: In the space provided at the right, indicate the correct term, command, or number.

1. The Bold button is located in this group in the Home tab. _____

2. A font consists of a typeface, a typestyle, and this. _____

3. Proportional typefaces are divided into two main categories, serif and this. _____

4. This is the keyboard shortcut to italicize selected text. _____

5. Click this button in the Font group to remove all formatting from selected text. _____

6. This term refers to text that is raised slightly above the regular text line. _____

7. This automatically displays above selected text. _____

8. Click this to display the Font dialog box. _____

9. Click this button in the Paragraph group in the Home tab to turn on the display of nonprinting characters. _____

10. A Word document contains a number of predesigned formats grouped into style sets called this. _____

11. Apply a theme and change theme colors, fonts, and effects with buttons in the Themes group in this tab. _____

Chapter Assessments

Applying Your Skills

Demonstrate your knowledge of features learned in this chapter by completing the following assessments.

Assessment 2.1   Create and Format a Utility Program Document

START From Scratch

1. At a blank document, type the document shown in Figure 2.5.
2. Bold, italicize, and underline the text as shown.
3. Save the completed document with the name **C02-A01-UtilProgs**.
4. Print **C02-A01-UtilProgs.docx**.
5. Select the entire document and then change the font to 12-point Cambria.
6. Select *Utility Programs*, remove underlining, and change to uppercase letters.
7. Remove the bolding from the text *Antivirus software:*, *Backup utility:*, *File compression utility:*, *Device driver:*, and *Uninstaller utility:* and apply underlining instead. (Do not underline the colon [:] after each utility.)
8. Select and then hide the text *Backup utility:* and the sentence that follows it.
9. Select and then hide the last sentence in the last paragraph (the sentence that begins *Several companies produce software . . .*).
10. Turn on the display of nonprinting characters, unhide the text *Backup utility:* and the sentence that follows it.
11. Turn off the display of nonprinting characters.
12. Save, print, and then close **C02-A01-UtilProgs.docx**.

Figure 2.5 Assessment 2.1

Utility Programs

A *utility program* performs a single maintenance or repair task and is useful for correcting many of the problems that computer users are likely to encounter. Some of the most popular kinds of utility programs include the following:

Antivirus software: This type of software program protects the computer system from a virus attack.

Backup utility: This utility makes a backup copy of files on a separate disk.

File compression utility: Use this utility to reduce the size of files so they take up less disk space.

Device driver: This utility allows hardware devices, such as disk drives and printers, to work with the computer system.

Uninstaller utility: Remove programs and related system files with this utility.

An operating system typically includes several utility programs that are preinstalled at the factory. Users can also purchase and install additional utility programs of their choice. Several companies produce software suites containing a variety of utility programs.

Assessment 2.2   Format a Memo

1. Open **BookMemo.docx.**
2. Save the memo with Save As and name it **C02-A02-BookMemo**.
3. Select the book title, *Managing Network Security*, remove the underlining, and then apply italics.
4. Select the book title, *Network Management*, remove the underlining, and then apply italics.
5. Select the first occurrence of the book title, *Internet Security*, remove the underlining, and then apply italics. Select the second occurrence of the book title, remove underlining, and apply italics.
6. Select the first occurrence of the book title, *Protecting and Securing Data*, remove the underlining, and then apply italics. Select the second occurrence of the book title, remove underlining, and apply italics.
7. Select and bold the headings *DATE:*, *TO:*, *FROM:*, and *SUBJECT:*.
8. Insert your initials at the end of the document where you see the *XX*. Change the document name below your initials from **BookMemo.docx** to **C02-A02-BookMemo.docx.**
9. Select the entire document and then change to the *Cambria* font.
10. Save, print, and then close **C02-A02-BookMemo.docx**.

Assessment 2.3 Format a Training Announcement

1. Open **ManageData.docx**.
2. Save the document with Save As and name it **C02-A03-ManageData**.
3. Select the entire document.
4. Change the font to 16-point Candara bold and the font color to red.
5. Select the title MANAGING CRUCIAL DATA, change the font size to 20, and apply the *Gradient Fill - Purple, Accent 4, Reflection* text effect. ***Hint: Use the Text Effects button to apply the text effect.***
6. Save, print, and then close **C02-A03-ManageData.docx**.

Expanding Your Skills

Explore additional feature options or use Help to learn a new skill in creating these documents.

Assessment 2.4 Create and Format a Memo

1. At a blank document, type the memo shown in Figure 2.6 in appropriate memo format (refer to Appendix C at the end of this textbook for information on typing a memo). Italicize, superscript, and subscript text as shown in the memo.
2. After typing the memo, select the entire memo, and then change the font to 12-point Constantia. (If neccessary, realign the headings in the memo.)
3. Save the memo with the name **C02-A04-Memo**.
4. Print and then close **C02-A04-Memo.docx**.

Figure 2.6 Assessment 2.4

DATE: February 22, 2012; TO: Jolie Anderson; FROM: Ronald Chen; SUBJECT: Statistical Analysis

I have been running an analysis on the areas mentioned in your February 16 memo. Completing the computations has brought up the following questions:

With smaller section ratios of r^1 and r^2 (.10 to .25)^1, what will be the yield increase?

What is the interaction effect on the scores of X_1, X_2, and X_3?

Assessment 2.5 Research Text Effect Button

1. Research the options that display at the bottom of the Text Effects button drop-down gallery (*Outline, Shadow, Reflection,* and so on). Look at the various options to determine what effects are available and then write a memo to your instructor describing the options. Include in the memo at least three examples of the words *TEXT EFFECTS BUTTON OPTIONS* with various effects applied.
2. Save the completed memo and name it **C02-A05-TextEffects**.
3. Print and then close **C02-A05-TextEffects.docx**.

Achieving Signature Status

Take your skills to the next level by completing these more challenging assessments.

Assessment 2.6 Type and Format Text on Writing a Cover Letter

1. At a blank document type the text in the document shown in Figure 2.7. Apply the font and text effect formatting as shown in the figure. Apply the *Gradient Fill - Orange, Accent 6, Inner Shadow* text effect to the title, set the headings in 14-point Constantia, the subheadings in 12-point Constantia, and the remaining text in 11-point Constantia.
2. Save the completed document and name it **C02-A06-WritingCoverLtr**.
3. Print and then close **C02-A06-WritingCoverLtr.docx**.

Figure 2.7 Assessment 2.6

WRITING A COVER LETTER

Assertive vs. Aggressive

We recommend an assertive closing when writing a cover letter, but do not become too aggressive. Keep the closing of your cover letter polite, positive, and pleasant. Try using language that "requests" rather than "demands." Consider the following examples of the difference between assertive and aggressive:

Assertive:

I will call within the next few days to see if we can schedule a time to meet. I would like to share my ideas for improving the productivity of your field technicians.

Aggressive:

I will call you at 10:00 a.m. on Tuesday. Please be available to discuss my ideas for improving the productivity of your field technicians.

Assertive:

I eagerly await your ideas and suggestions. I will call on Thursday in hopes of setting up a brief meeting at a time that is convenient for you.

Aggressive:

Your support is important for my job search, and I eagerly await all the leads you can give me. I will call on Thursday to see what names you have collected thus far.

Assessment 2.7 Type a Business Letter

1. Open **NSSLtrhd.docx** and then save the document and name it **C02-A07-BCLtr**.
2. Click the No Spacing style thumbnail located in the Styles group in the Home tab and then type the text in the document shown in Figure 2.8. Refer to Appendix D at the end of this textbook for the formatting of a block style business letter. (Insert your initials instead of the *XX* located toward the end of the letter.)
3. Save the completed document and name it **C02-A07-BCLtr**.
4. Print and then close **C02-A07-BCLtr.docx**.

Figure 2.8 Assessment 2.7

February 15, 2012

Jessie Levigne, Manager
Technical Support Department
Baldwin Corporation
1590 28th Street
Springfield, IL 62126

Dear Mr. Levigne:

Based on our telephone conversation about your company data security training requirements, I suggest offering three workshops to employees at Baldwin Corporation. After attending the workshops, your employees will have the skills required to secure company data. The workshops I propose include:

Rotating Backup Process: In this workshop, participants will be briefed on the rotating backup process, which involves backing up data from specific departments on specific days of the week.

Disaster Recovery: The focus of this workshop is the development of a disaster recovery plan and will include data backup procedures, remote backup locations, and redundant systems.

Data Security: The third workshop I propose is data security and data encryption. In this workshop participants will learn about encryption schemes designed to scramble information before transferring it electronically.

I am confident that these three workshops will address your security issues. I have enclosed our standard contract for you to read. Please contact me to discuss the contract as well as the location, time, and equipment requirements for each workshop.

Sincerely,

Bryce Gyverson
Vice President

XX
C02-A07-BCLtr.docx

Enclosure

Chapter 3

Aligning and Indenting Paragraphs

Performance Objectives

Upon successful completion of Chapter 3, you will be able to:

- Change the alignment of text in paragraphs
- Indent text in paragraphs
- Increase and decrease spacing before and after paragraphs
- Repeat the last action
- Automate formatting with Format Painter
- Change line spacing in a document
- Apply numbering and bullet formatting to text
- Reveal and compare formatting

Tutorial 3.1
Aligning Text in Paragraphs
Tutorial 3.2
Changing Text Indentation
Tutorial 3.3
Setting Line and Paragraph Spacing
Tutorial 3.4
Changing Default Document Formatting
Tutorial 3.5
Repeating the Last Action and Changing Paragraph Spacing
Tutorial 3.6
Using the Format Painter
Tutorial 3.7
Creating Bulleted and Numbered Lists
Tutorial 3.8
Revealing and Comparing Formatting

As you learned previously, a paragraph in Word is any amount of text followed by the press of the Enter key. Word provides a variety of options for formatting text in a paragraph. In this chapter, you will learn to change text alignment in a paragraph, indent text, change the line spacing, and insert numbers and bullets. You will also learn how to apply formatting with Format Painter and how to reveal and compare paragraph formatting.

Note: Before beginning computer exercises for this chapter, copy to your storage medium the Chapter03 folder from the CD that accompanies this textbook and then make Chapter03 the active folder.

In this chapter students will produce the following documents:

Exercise 3.1. C03-E01-CompIndustry.docx
Exercise 3.2. C03-E02-BTAdventure.docx
Exercise 3.3. C03-E03-InternetSearch.docx
Exercise 3.4. C03-E04-CompIssues.docx

Model answers for these exercises are shown on the following pages.

COMPUTERS IN INDUSTRY

Computers were originally stand-alone devices, incapable of communicating with other computers. This changed in the 1970s and 1980s when the development of special telecommunications hardware and software led to the creation of the first private networks, allowing connected computers to exchange data. Exchanged data took the form of requests for information, replies to requests for information, and instructions on how to run programs stored on a network.

The linking of computers enables users to communicate and work together efficiently and effectively. Linked computers have become central to the communications and entertainment industries. They play a vital role in telecommunications, publishing, news services, and television and film.

Telecommunications

The industry that provi
telecommunications. The telec
phone calls automatically over
many other kinds of informatic
Data can be sent from compute
a modem. One kind of data free
be sent from person to person
innovation in telecommunicati
locations to see and hear one a

Publishing

Just twenty years ago, b
typesetting machine and then
to a computer and either a mo
as electronic publishing. Write
text. Artists and designers use
graphics, or they use inexpens
(turning them into computer-r
combine text, illustrations, and

Page 1

files to printers for production of the film and plates from which books and magazines are printed.

News Services

News providers rely on reporters located worldwide. Reporters use email to send, or upload, their stories to wire services. Increasingly, individuals get daily news reports from online services. News can also be accessed from specific providers, such as the *New York Times* or *USA Today*, via the Internet. One of the most popular Internet sites provides continuously updated weather reports.

Television and Film

Many of the spectacular graphics and special effects seen on television and in movies today are created with computers. The original *Star Wars* films, for example, relied heavily on hand-constructed models and hand-drawn graphics. Twenty years after the first release of the films, they were re-released with many new special effects, including futuristic cityscape backgrou
on computers and added to th
on special effects, Jaclyn McFa
computer simulation.

The film *Jurassic Park* b
combining puppetry an
dinosaurs. *Toy Story*, re
animated commercial r

Software products are a
Industry analysts predict that
enhance and improve the visu

Fuller, F. & Larson, B. (2010) *C
MN: Paradigm Publishi

McFadden, J. M. (2011) *The ar
Dryers Publishing Hous

Page 2

North, J. & Amundsen, R. (2010) *Computer gaming and system requirements*. Cleveland, OH: Blue Horizon Publishers.

Ziebel, K. M. & Weisenburg, H. L. (2011) *Computers and electronic publishing*. Seattle, WA: Greenlake Publishing House.

Prepared by Christian Samora
Edited by Martina Sanchez

Page 3

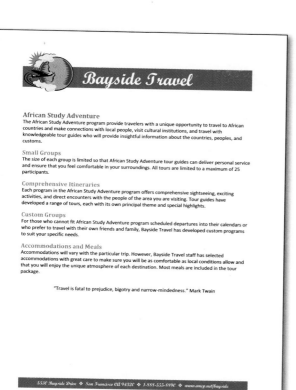

African Study Adventure

The African Study Adventure program provide travelers with a unique opportunity to travel to African countries and make connections with local people, visit cultural institutions, and travel with knowledgeable tour guides who will provide insightful information about the countries, peoples, and customs.

Small Groups

The size of each group is limited so that African Study Adventure tour guides can deliver personal service and ensure that you feel comfortable in your surroundings. All tours are limited to a maximum of 25 participants.

Comprehensive Itineraries

Each program in the African Study Adventure program offers comprehensive sightseeing, exciting activities, and direct encounters with the people of the area you are visiting. Tour guides have developed a range of tours, each with its own principal theme and special highlights.

Custom Groups

For those who cannot fit African Study Adventure program scheduled departures into their calendars or who prefer to travel with their own friends and family, Bayside Travel has developed custom programs to suit your specific needs.

Accommodations and Meals

Accommodations will vary with the particular trip. However, Bayside Travel staff has selected accommodations with great care to make sure you will be as comfortable as local conditions allow and that you will enjoy the unique atmosphere of each destination. Most meals are included in the tour package.

"Travel is fatal to prejudice, bigotry and narrow-mindedness." Mark Twain

553C Bayside Drive ❖ San Francisco CA 9432C ❖ 1-888-555-889C ❖ www.emcp.net/bayside

Exercise 3.2 C03-E02-BTAdventure.docx

Internet Research

Conduct Internet searches to find information to complete the activities described below. Write a brief report summarizing your research results. Be sure to document your sources, using the following format, which is recommended by the Modern Language Association (MLA):

- Author's name (if known)
- Title of document, in quotation marks
- Title of Internet page or online periodical, in italics (if not titled, put Home Page or give the name of the organization that created and maintains the page)
- Date of publication (for an article) or date site was last updated, if available
- Date you accessed the site
- URL, in angle brackets < >

Activities

1. Using online news sources, select a specific event that occurred in a country other than the United States within the past year. Find three separate news reports of the event and describe how each media source perceived the event.
2. Describe the kinds of information that are available on your government's website. Your summary should discuss the information available on a particular date.
3. Research the topic of high-tech stock investments as discussed in online news sources. What is the current trend as of the date of your research?
4. Robots with artificial intelligence are likely to play a large role in our future. Discuss possible applications for this new technology in the areas of manufacturing, health care, and home maintenance.

Research and Writing

1. Describe the components of a computer's central processing unit (CPU).
2. Identify at least four methods for inputting information into a computer.
3. Identify at least three methods for outputting information from a computer.
4. Explain the differences between read-only memory (ROM) and random-access memory (RAM).
5. Describe at least three types of network systems.

Technology Terms

➢ Define the terms "input" and "processing."
➢ Categorize input devices for personal computers and explain their functions.

➢ Identify the main components of the system unit and explain their functions.
➢ Explain the four basic operations of a machine cycle.
➢ Describe the different types of computer memory and their functions.

Exercise 3.3 C03-E03-InternetSearch.docx

Page 1

Page 2

Solving Problems

In groups or individually, brainstorm possible solutions to the issues presented.

Exercise 3.4

C03-E04-CompIssues.docx

- Computers currently offer both *visual* and *audio* communications. Under development are devices and technologies that will allow users to smell various types of products while looking at them on the computer screen. What are some new applications of this technology for the food industry? Can you think of other industries that could use this capability?
- Picture yourself working in the Information Technology department of a mid-sized company. Your responsibilities include evaluating employees' computer system needs and recommending equipment purchases. Recently, the company president hired a new employee and you must evaluate her computer system needs. Considering that you have a budget of $5,500 for equipping the new employee with the computer system (or systems) she needs, research possible configurations and prepare a report outlining your recommendations, including costs. Assume that for the office she needs a complete system, including a system unit, monitor, printer, speakers, keyboard, and mouse.

Changing Paragraph Alignment

QUICK STEPS

Change Paragraph Alignment
Click desired alignment button in Paragraph group.
OR
1. Click Paragraph group dialog box launcher.
2. Click *Alignment* option down-pointing arrow.
3. Click desired alignment.
4. Click OK.

The Paragraph group in the Home tab contains a number of buttons that you can use to format paragraphs in a document. The four buttons in the bottom row change the alignment of text within a paragraph. In a Word document, paragraphs are aligned at the left margin and ragged at the right margin by default. You can change this alignment to center, right, or justified alignment with the alignment buttons in the Paragraph group or with keyboard shortcuts. The keyboard shortcuts and the alignment buttons in the Paragraph group are shown in Table 3.1.

You can change the text alignment before you type a paragraph, or you can change the alignment of an existing paragraph. If you change the alignment before typing text, the alignment formatting is inserted in the paragraph mark. As you type text and press the Enter key, the paragraph formatting is continued. For example, if you click the Center button in the Paragraph group, type a paragraph of text, and then press the Enter key, the center alignment formatting is still active and the insertion point displays in the middle of the left and right margins.

To return to the default alignment (left aligned), click the Align Text Left button in the Paragraph group. You can also return all paragraph formatting to the default with the keyboard shortcut Ctrl + Q. This keyboard shortcut removes paragraph formatting

Table 3.1 Paragraph Alignment Buttons and Commands

To align text	Paragraph Group Button	Shortcut Command
At the left margin	▤	Ctrl + L
Between margins	▤	Ctrl + E
At the right margin	▤	Ctrl + R
At the left and right margins	▤	Ctrl + J

from selected text. If you want to remove all formatting—character and paragraph—from selected text, click the Clear Formatting button in the Font group.

To change the alignment of existing text in a paragraph, position the insertion point anywhere within the paragraph. You do not need to select the entire paragraph. To change the alignment of several adjacent paragraphs in a document, select a portion of the first paragraph through a portion of the last paragraph. You do not need to select all of the text in the paragraphs.

Displaying Formatting Marks

As you learned in Chapter 2, you can turn on the display of nonprinting characters by clicking the Show/Hide ¶ button in the Paragraph group in the Home tab. When you make a formatting change to a paragraph, the formatting is inserted in the paragraph mark, which is visible if the display of nonprinting characters is turned on. By default, all nonprinting characters display on the screen when you click the Show/Hide ¶ button. You can turn on the display of specific characters only by using options at the Word Options dialog box with *Display* selected, as shown in Figure 3.1. Display this dialog box by clicking the File tab, clicking the Options button located below the Help tab, and then clicking *Display* in the left panel. Insert a check mark in the check boxes in the *Always show these formatting marks on the screen* section to select those nonprinting characters that you want to display.

Show/Hide ¶

Figure 3.1 Word Options Dialog Box with Display Option Selected

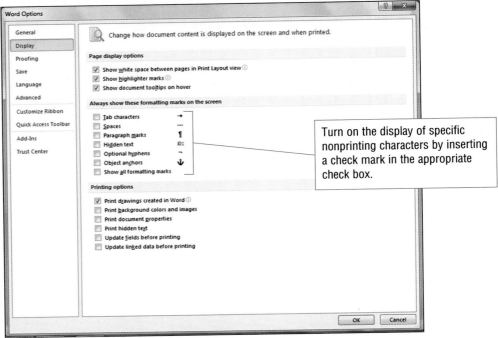

Turn on the display of specific nonprinting characters by inserting a check mark in the appropriate check box.

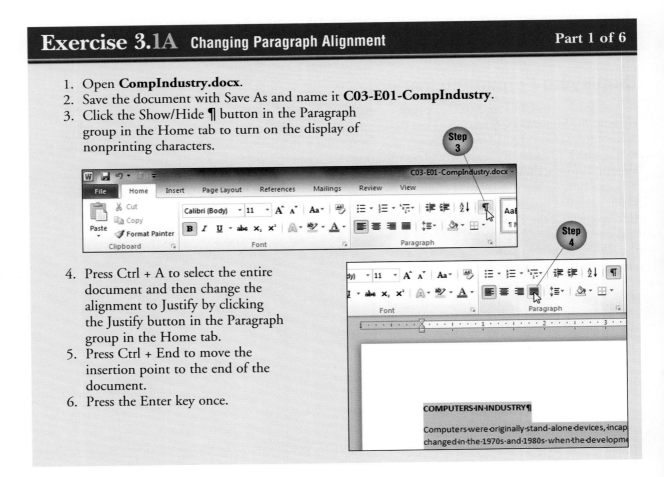

Exercise 3.1A Changing Paragraph Alignment
Part 1 of 6

1. Open **CompIndustry.docx**.
2. Save the document with Save As and name it **C03-E01-CompIndustry**.
3. Click the Show/Hide ¶ button in the Paragraph group in the Home tab to turn on the display of nonprinting characters.

Step 3

C03-E01-CompIndustry.docx

Step 4

4. Press Ctrl + A to select the entire document and then change the alignment to Justify by clicking the Justify button in the Paragraph group in the Home tab.
5. Press Ctrl + End to move the insertion point to the end of the document.
6. Press the Enter key once.

COMPUTERS·IN·INDUSTRY¶

Computers·were·originally·stand-alone·devices,·incap
changed·in·the·1970s·and·1980s·when·the·developme

7. Press Ctrl + E to center the insertion point between the left and right margins.
8. Type Prepared by Christian Samora.
9. Press Shift + Enter and then type Edited by Martina Sanchez.

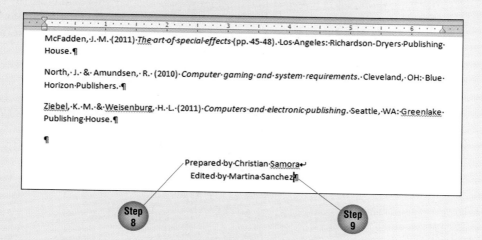

McFadden, J. M. (2011) *The art of special effects* (pp. 45-48). Los Angeles: Richardson-Dryers Publishing House. ¶

North, J. & Amundsen, R. (2010) *Computer gaming and system requirements.* Cleveland, OH: Blue Horizon Publishers. ¶

Ziebel, K. M. & Weisenburg, H. L. (2011) *Computers and electronic publishing.* Seattle, WA: Greenlake Publishing House. ¶

¶

Prepared by Christian Samora↵
Edited by Martina Sanchez¶

Step 8

Step 9

10. Click the Show/Hide ¶ button in the Paragraph group in the Home tab to turn off the display of nonprinting characters.
11. Turn on the display of paragraph marks only by completing the following steps:
    a. Click the File tab and then click the Options button.
    b. At the Word Options dialog box, click the *Display* option in the left panel.
    c. Click the *Paragraph marks* check box in the *Always show these formatting marks on the screen* section to insert a check mark.

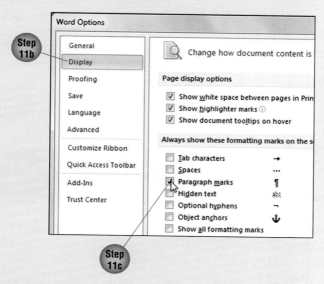

Step 11b

Step 11c

d. Click OK to close the dialog box.
12. Scroll through the document and notice how the paragraph marks display.
13. Turn off the display of the paragraph marks by completing steps similar to those in Step 11.
14. Save **C03-E01-CompIndustry.docx**.

Changing Alignment at the Paragraph Dialog Box

In addition to using the alignment buttons in the Paragraph group or keyboard shortcuts to change paragraph alignment, you can also use the *Alignment* option at the Paragraph dialog box, as shown in Figure 3.2. Display this dialog box by clicking the Paragraph group dialog box launcher. You can also display the dialog box by clicking the *right* mouse button and then clicking Paragraph at the shortcut menu that displays. At the Paragraph dialog box, click the down-pointing arrow at the right side of the *Alignment* drop-down list. At the drop-down list that displays, click the desired alignment option and then click OK to close the dialog box.

Figure 3.2 Paragraph Dialog Box with Alignment Options Displayed

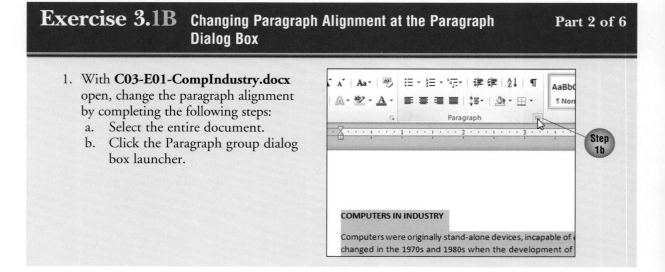

Change paragraph alignment by clicking this down-pointing arrow and then clicking the desired alignment at the drop-down list.

Use these options to specify spacing before and after paragraphs.

Exercise 3.1B Changing Paragraph Alignment at the Paragraph Dialog Box
Part 2 of 6

1. With **C03-E01-CompIndustry.docx** open, change the paragraph alignment by completing the following steps:
   a. Select the entire document.
   b. Click the Paragraph group dialog box launcher.

Step 1b

   c. At the Paragraph dialog box with the Indents and Spacing tab selected, click the down-pointing arrow at the right of the *Alignment* list box and then click *Left*.

   d. Click OK to close the dialog box.

   e. Deselect the text.

2. Change paragraph alignment by completing the following steps:

   a. Press Ctrl + End to move the insertion point to the end of the document.

   b. Position the insertion point on any character in the text *Prepared by Christian Samora*.

   c. Click the Paragraph group dialog box launcher.

   d. At the Paragraph dialog box with the Indents and Spacing tab selected, click the down-pointing arrow at the right of the *Alignment* list box and then click *Right*.

   e. Click OK. (The line of text containing the name *Christian Samora* and the line of text containing the name *Martina Sanchez* are both right-aligned because you used the New Line command, Shift + Enter, to separate the lines of text without creating a new paragraph.)

3. Save **C03-E01-CompIndustry.docx**.

Step 1c

Indenting Text in Paragraphs

By now you are familiar with the word wrap feature in Word, which ends lines and wraps the insertion point to the next line. You can indent the first line of text in a paragraph, indent all text in a paragraph, or indent the second and subsequent lines of a paragraph (called a hanging indent). You can indent text from the left margin, the right margin, or both. Several methods are available for indenting text: using buttons in the Paragraph group in either the Home tab or the Page Layout tab, using markers on the Ruler, using options at the Paragraph dialog box with the Indents and Spacing tab selected, or using keyboard shortcuts. The various methods for indenting text are shown in Table 3.2, and indent examples are shown in Table 3.3. The indent markers and Alignment button on the Ruler are shown in Figure 3.3. To display the Ruler, click the View Ruler button located at the top of the vertical scroll bar.

Figure 3.3 Ruler and Indent Markers

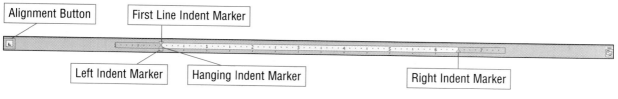

Alignment Button

First Line Indent Marker

Left Indent Marker

Hanging Indent Marker

Right Indent Marker

Table 3.2 Methods for Indenting Text

Indent	*Methods for Indenting*
First line of paragraph	• Press the Tab key. • Display Paragraph dialog box, click the down-pointing arrow to the right of the *Special* list box, click *First line*, and then click OK. • Drag the first line indent marker on the Ruler. • Click the Alignment button located at the left side of the Ruler until the First Line Indent button displays and then click on the Ruler at the desired location.
Text from left margin	• Click the Increase Indent button in the Paragraph group in the Home tab to increase the indent or click the Decrease Indent button to decrease the indent. • Display the Paragraph dialog box, type the desired indent measurement in the *Left* measurement box, and then click OK. • Drag the left indent marker on the Ruler. • Press Ctrl + M to increase the indent or press Ctrl + Shift + M to decrease the indent. • Insert a measurement in the Indent Left measurement box in the Paragraph group in the Page Layout tab.
Text from right margin	• Display the Paragraph dialog box, type the desired indent measurement in the *Right* measurement box, and then click OK. • Drag the right indent marker on the Ruler. • Insert a measurement in the Indent Right measurement box in the Paragraph group in the Page Layout tab.
All lines of text except the first (called a hanging indent)	• Display the Paragraph dialog box, click the down-pointing arrow at the right side of the *Special* list box, click *Hanging*, and then click OK. • Press Ctrl + T. (Press Ctrl + Shift + T to remove hanging indent.) • Click the Alignment button located at the left side of the Ruler until the Hanging Indent button displays and then click on the Ruler at the desired location.

Table 3.3 Paragraph Indent Examples

First line indent example:

This is an example of text with the first line of text indented. You can create the first line indent with the Tab key, options at the Paragraph dialog box, and with the first line indent marker on the Ruler.

Left indent example:

This is an example of text indented 0.5 inch from the left margin. You can create left indented text with the Increase Indent button in the Paragraph group in the Home tab, options at the Paragraph dialog box, the Indent Left measurement box in the Paragraph group in the Page Layout tab, the left indent marker on the Ruler, and with the keyboard shortcut Ctrl + M.

Right indent example:

This is an example of text indented 0.5 inch from the right margin. You can create right indented text with options at the Paragraph dialog box, the right indent marker on the Ruler, and with the Indent Right measurement box in the Paragraph group in the Page Layout tab.

Hanging indent example:

This paragraph is an example of a hanging indent. This style of indenting is generally used in works cited and reference pages to identify sources. Create a hanging indent with options at the Paragraph dialog box, the hanging indent button on the Ruler, and the keyboard shortcut Ctrl + T.

This is another example of a paragraph indented with a hanging indent. When creating a hanging indent, make sure you let text wrap within the paragraph.

Exercise 3.1C Indenting Paragraphs

1. With **C03-E01-CompIndustry.docx** open, indent the first line of text in paragraphs by completing the following steps:
   a. Select the first two paragraphs of text in the document (the two paragraphs of text after the title *COMPUTERS IN INDUSTRY* and before the heading *Telecommunications*).
   b. Make sure the Ruler displays. If it does not, click the View Ruler button 🔲 located at the top of the vertical scroll bar.
   c. Position the mouse pointer on the First Line Indent marker on the Ruler, hold down the left mouse button, drag the marker to the 0.5-inch mark, and then release the mouse button.

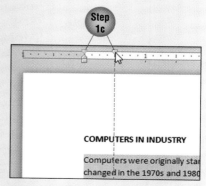

Step 1c

COMPUTERS IN INDUSTRY

Computers were originally star
changed in the 1970s and 1980

    d. Position the insertion point on any character in the paragraph below the *Telecommunications* heading and then drag the First Line Indent marker on the Ruler to the 0.5-inch mark.

    e. Indent the first line of the paragraph below the *Publishing* heading and the *News Services* heading.

    f. Indent the first line of the first paragraph and the first line of the third paragraph in the *Television and Film* heading.

2. The second paragraph in the *Television and Film* section is a quote and needs to be indented from the left and right margins by completing the following steps:

    a. Position the insertion point anywhere within the second paragraph in the *Television and Film* section (the paragraph that begins *The film* Jurassic Park *brought . . .*).

    b. Click the Paragraph group dialog box launcher.

    c. At the Paragraph dialog box, with the Indents and Spacing tab selected, select the current measurement in the *Left* measurement box, and then type 0.5.

    d. Select the current measurement in the *Right* measurement box and then type 0.5.

    e. Click OK or press the Enter key.

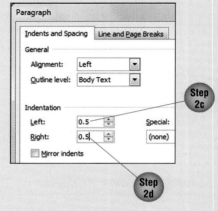

3. Create a hanging indent for the first paragraph in the *REFERENCES* section by positioning the insertion point anywhere in the first paragraph below *REFERENCES* and then pressing Ctrl + T.

4. Create a hanging indent for the second paragraph in the *REFERENCES* section by completing the following steps:

    a. Position the insertion point anywhere in the second paragraph in the *REFERENCES* section.

    b. Click the Alignment button located at the left side of the Ruler until the Hanging Indent button displays.

    c. Click on the 0.5-inch mark on the Ruler.

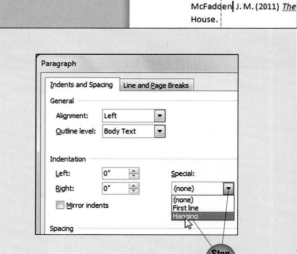

5. Create a hanging indent for the third and fourth paragraphs in the REFERENCES section by completing the following steps:

    a. Select a portion of the third and fourth paragraphs.

    b. Click the Paragraph group dialog box launcher.

    c. At the Paragraph dialog box with the Indents and Spacing tab selected, click the down-pointing arrow at the right side of the *Special* list box and then click *Hanging* at the drop-down list.

    d. Click OK or press the Enter key.

6. Save **C03-E01-CompIndustry.docx**.

Spacing Before and After Paragraphs

As you learned earlier, the insertion of 10 points of spacing after a paragraph is one of the default settings in Word. You can remove this spacing, increase it, or decrease it. You can also insert spacing before a paragraph. To change spacing before or after a paragraph, use the Spacing Before and Spacing After measurement boxes located in the Paragraph group in the Page Layout tab or the *Before* and/or *After* options at the Paragraph dialog box with the Indents and Spacing tab selected.

You can also add or remove paragraph spacing with the bottom two options from the Line and Paragraph Spacing button drop-down gallery. The two options will vary depending on the paragraph spacing where the insertion point is positioned. For example, if you position the insertion point in a paragraph of text with the default spacing, the options display as *Add Space Before Paragraph* and *Remove Space After Paragraph*. Click the *Add Space Before Paragraph* option and Word adds 12 points of spacing before the paragraph.

Spacing before or after a paragraph is part of that paragraph, and it will be moved, copied, or deleted with the paragraph. If a paragraph, such as a heading, contains spacing before it and the paragraph falls at the top of a page, Word ignores the spacing.

Spacing before or after paragraphs is added in points. A vertical inch contains approximately 72 points. To add spacing before or after a paragraph, click the Page Layout tab, select the current measurement in the Spacing Before or the Spacing After measurement box, and then type the desired number of points. You can also click the up- or down-pointing arrows at the right side of the Spacing Before and Spacing After measurement boxes to increase or decrease the amount of spacing.

QUICK STEPS

Change Paragraph Spacing
1. Click Page Layout tab.
2. Change spacing with Spacing Before and/or Spacing After measurement boxes.

OR

1. Click Home tab or Page Layout tab.
2. Click Paragraph group dialog box launcher.
3. Insert measurement in *Before* and/or *After* measurement box.
4. Click OK.

Repeat Last Action
Press F4
OR
Press Ctrl + Y.

Repeating the Last Action

If you apply formatting to a selection of text and then want to apply the same formatting to other text in the document, consider using the Repeat command. To use this command, apply the desired formatting, move the insertion point to the next location where you want the formatting applied, and press the F4 function key or press Ctrl + Y.

Exercise 3.1D Spacing Before and After Paragraphs and Repeating Last Action   Part 4 of 6

1. With **C03-E01-CompIndustry.docx** open, change the spacing after paragraphs to 6 points by completing the following steps:
   a. Select the entire document.
   b. Click the Page Layout tab.
   c. Click once on the down-pointing arrow at the right side of the Spacing After measurement box in the Paragraph group (this inserts *6 pt* in the box).

2. Add 18 points of spacing above and 12 points of spacing below the two titles by completing the following steps:
   a. Position the insertion point on any character in the title *COMPUTERS IN INDUSTRY*.
   b. Click three times on the up-pointing arrow at the right side of the Spacing Before measurement box (this changes the measurement to *18 pt*).
   c. Click once on the up-pointing arrow at the right side of the Spacing After measurement box (this changes the measurement to *12 pt*).

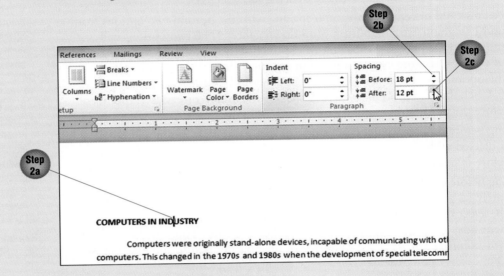

   d. Position the insertion point on any character in the title *REFERENCES* and then press F4 (this is the Repeat command).
3. Save **C03-E01-CompIndustry.docx**.

Formatting with Format Painter

Format Painter

The Clipboard group in the Home tab contains a button for copying character formatting to different locations in the document. This button, called Format Painter, displays as a paintbrush. To use the Format Painter button, position the insertion point on a character containing the desired character formatting, click the Format Painter button, and then select text to which you want the character formatting applied. When you click the Format Painter button, the mouse I-beam pointer displays with a paintbrush attached. If you want to apply character formatting a single time, click the Format Painter button once. If you want to apply the character formatting in more than one location in the document, double-click the Format Painter button. After selecting and applying formatting, click the Format Painter button to turn it off or press the Esc key.

1. With **C03-E01-CompIndustry.docx** open, click the Home tab.
2. Select the entire document and then change the font to 12-point Cambria.
3. Select the title *COMPUTERS IN INDUSTRY*, click the Center button in the Paragraph group, and then change the font to 16-point Candara bold.
4. Apply 16-point Candara bold formatting to the *REFERENCES* heading by completing the following steps:
    a. Click on any character in the title *COMPUTERS IN INDUSTRY*.
    b. Click once on the Format Painter button in the Clipboard group.

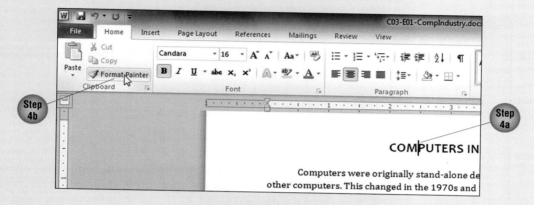

    c. Press Ctrl + End to move the insertion point to the end of the document and then click on any character in the heading *REFERENCES*. (This applies the 16-point Candara bold formatting and centers the text.)
5. Select the heading *Telecommunications* and then change the font to 14-point Candara bold.
6. Use the Format Painter button and apply 14-point Candara bold formatting to the other headings by completing the following steps:
    a. Position the insertion point on any character in the heading *Telecommunications*.
    b. Double-click the Format Painter button in the Clipboard group.
    c. Using the mouse, click on any character in the heading *Publishing*.
    d. Using the mouse, select the heading *News Services*.
    e. Using the mouse, select the heading *Television and Film*.
    f. Click once on the Format Painter button in the Clipboard group. (This turns off the feature.)
    g. Deselect the heading.
7. Save **C03-E01-CompIndustry.docx**.

Change Line Spacing
1. Click Line and Paragraph Spacing button in Paragraph group.
2. Click *Spacing* option at drop-down list.
OR
Enter keyboard shortcut.
OR
1. Click Paragraph group dialog box launcher.
2. Click *Line Spacing* option down-pointing arrow.
3. Click desired line spacing option.
4. Click OK.
OR
1. Click Paragraph group dialog box launcher.
2. Type line measurement in *At* text box.
3. Click OK.

Changing Line Spacing

The default line spacing in a Word document is 1.15. In some documents, you may want to change to another line spacing such as single, 1.5 spacing, or double spacing. Change line spacing by using the Line and Paragraph Spacing button in the Paragraph group in the Home tab, keyboard shortcuts, or options at the Paragraph dialog box. The keyboard shortcuts for changing line spacing are shown in Table 3.4.

Table 3.4 Line Spacing Keyboard Shortcuts

Press	*To change line spacing to*
Ctrl + 1	single spacing
Ctrl + 2	double spacing
Ctrl + 5	1.5 line spacing

To change line spacing at the Paragraph dialog box, use the *Line spacing* option or the *At* option. If you click the down-pointing arrow at the right side of the *Line spacing* option, a drop-down list displays with a variety of spacing options. To change the line spacing to double, click *Double* at the drop-down list. You can type a specific line spacing measurement in the *At* text box. For example, to change the line spacing to 1.75, type 1.75 in the *At* text box.

Line and Paragraph Spacing

Exercise 3.1F Changing Line Spacing   Part 6 of 6

1. With **C03-E01-CompIndustry.docx** open, change the line spacing for all paragraphs to double spacing by completing the following steps:
   a. Select the entire document.
   b. Click the Line and Paragraph Spacing button in the Paragraph group in the Home tab.
   c. Click *2.0* at the drop-down list.
2. With the entire document still selected, press Ctrl + 5. (This changes the line spacing to 1.5.)

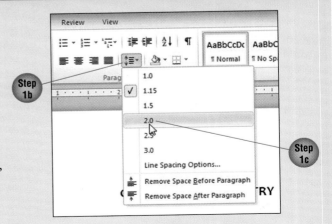

3. Change the line spacing to 1.3 using the Paragraph dialog box by completing the following steps:
   a. With the document still selected, click the Paragraph group dialog box launcher.
   b. At the Paragraph dialog box with the Indents and Spacing tab selected, click inside the *At* text box, and then type 1.3. (This text box is located to the right of the *Line spacing* list box.)
   c. Click OK or press the Enter key.
   d. Deselect the text.
4. Save, print, and then close **C03-E01-CompIndustry.docx**.

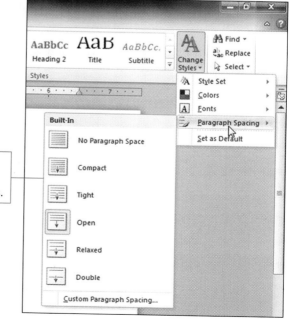

Changing Paragraph Spacing with the Change Styles Button

In Chapter 2, you learned how to apply a Quick Style set to a document with the Change Styles button in the Styles group in the Home tab. The Change Styles button drop-down list also contains a *Paragraph Spacing* option you can use to apply predesigned paragraph spacing to text in a document. Click the Change Styles button and then point to *Paragraph Spacing* and a side menu displays as shown in Figure 3.4. Hover your mouse over an option at the side menu and, after a moment, a ScreenTip displays with information about the formatting applied by the option. For example, if you hover the mouse over the *Compact* option at the side menu, a ScreenTip displays telling you that the Compact option will change the spacing before paragraphs to zero points, the spacing after paragraphs to four points, and the line spacing to one. Use options at the *Paragraph Spacing* side menu to quickly apply paragraph spacing to text in your document.

Figure 3.4 Change Styles Button Paragraph Spacing Side Menu

This side menu displays a list of predesigned paragraph spacing options.

1. Open **BTAdventure.docx**.
2. Save the document with Save As and name it **C03-E02-BTAdventure**.
3. Change the paragraph spacing using the Change Styles button by completing the following steps:
   a. Click the Change Styles button in the Styles group in the Home tab.
   b. Point to *Paragraph Spacing* at the drop-down list.
   c. Hover the mouse over each of the paragraph spacing options beginning with *Compact* and read the ScreenTip that displays for each option explaining the paragraph spacing applied by the option.
   d. Click the *Double* option at the side menu.
4. Scroll through the document and notice the paragraph spacing.
5. Change the paragraph spacing by clicking the Change Styles button, pointing to *Paragraph Spacing*, and then clicking *Compact* at the side menu.
6. Save, print, and then close **C03-E02-BTAdventure.docx**.

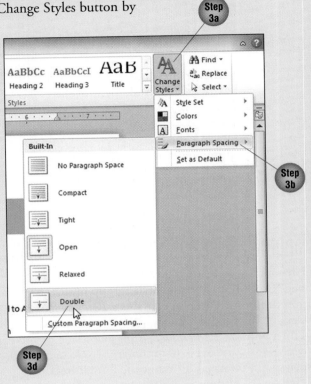

Step 3a

Step 3b

Step 3d

Bullets

Numbering

Applying Numbering and Bullets

Use buttons in the Paragraph group to automatically number paragraphs or insert bullets before them. Use the Bullets button to insert bullets before specific paragraphs, and use the Numbering button to insert numbers.

Numbering Paragraphs

Type Numbered Paragraphs
1. Type 1.
2. Press spacebar.
3. Type text.
4. Press Enter.

If you type 1., press the spacebar, type a paragraph of text, and then press the Enter key, Word indents the number approximately 0.25 inch and then hang indents the text in the paragraph approximately 0.5 inch from the left margin. In addition, Word insets 2. at the beginning of the next paragraph, indented 0.25 inch from the left margin. Continue typing items, and Word inserts the next number in the list. To turn off numbering, press the Enter key twice or click the Numbering button in the Paragraph group. (You can also remove all paragraph formatting from a paragraph, including automatic numbering, with the keyboard shortcut Ctrl + Q. Remove all formatting including character and paragraph formatting from selected text by clicking the Clear Formatting button in the Font group.)

If you press the Enter key twice between numbered paragraphs, the automatic number is removed. To turn it back on, type the next number in the list (and the period) followed by a space, type the paragraph of text, and then press the Enter key. Word will automatically indent the number and hang indent the text.

When the AutoFormat feature inserts numbering and indents text, the AutoCorrect Options button displays. Click this button and a drop-down list displays with options for undoing and/or stopping the automatic numbering. An AutoCorrect Options button also displays when AutoFormat inserts automatic bulleting in a document.

Exercise 3.3A Typing Numbered Paragraphs   Part 1 of 4

1. Open **InternetSearch.docx**.
2. Save the document with Save As and name it **C03-E03-InternetSearch**.
3. Press Ctrl + End to move the insertion point to the end of the document and then type the text shown in Figure 3.5. When you type the numbered paragraphs, complete the following steps:
   a. Type 1. and then press the spacebar. (This indents the number and the period 0.25 inch from the left margin and moves the insertion point 0.5 inch from the left margin. Also, the AutoCorrect Options button displays. Use this button if you want to undo or stop automatic numbering.)
   b. Type the paragraph of text and then press the Enter key. (This moves the insertion point down to the next line, inserts 2. indented 0.25 inch from the left margin, and indents the insertion point 0.5 inch from the left margin.
   c. Continue typing the remaining text. (Remember, you do not need to type the paragraph number and period—these are automatically inserted.)
   d. After typing the last question, press the Enter key twice. (This turns off paragraph numbering.)
4. Save **C03-E03-InternetSearch.docx**.

Figure 3.5 Exercise 3.3A

Research and Writing

1. Describe the components of a computer's central processing unit (CPU).
2. Identify at least four methods for inputting information into a computer.
3. Identify at least three methods for outputting information from a computer.
4. Explain the difference between read-only memory (ROM) and random-access memory (RAM).
5. Describe at least three types of network systems.

If you do not want automatic numbering in a document, turn off the feature at the AutoCorrect dialog box with the AutoFormat As You Type tab selected, as shown in Figure 3.6. To display this dialog box, click the File tab and then click the Options button. At the Word Options dialog box, click *Proofing* in the left panel and then click the AutoCorrect Options button that displays in the *AutoCorrect options* section of the dialog box. At the AutoCorrect dialog box, click the AutoFormat As You Type tab and then click the *Automatic numbered lists* check box to remove the check mark. Click OK to close the AutoCorrect dialog box and then click OK to close the Word Options dialog box.

Create Numbered Paragraphs
1. Select text.
2. Click Numbering button in Paragraph group in Home tab.

Figure 3.6 AutoCorrect Dialog Box with the AutoFormat As You Type Tab Selected

Remove the check mark from this check box to turn off automatic bulleting.

Remove the check mark from this check box to turn off automatic numbering.

You can also automate the creation of numbered paragraphs with the Numbering button in the Paragraph group. To use this button, type the text (do not type the number) for each paragraph to be numbered, select the paragraphs to be numbered, and then click the Numbering button in the Paragraph group. You can insert or delete numbered paragraphs in a document.

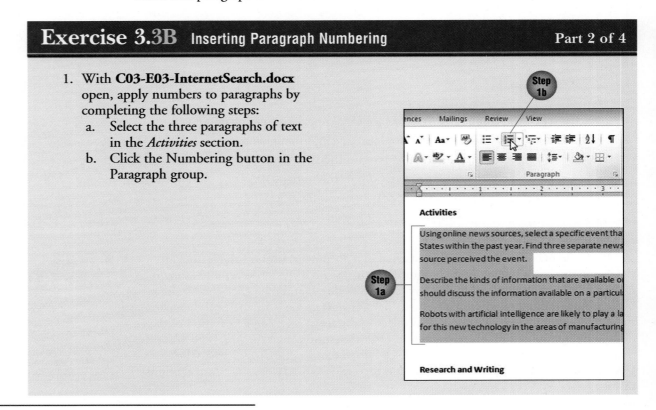

Exercise 3.3B Inserting Paragraph Numbering   Part 2 of 4

1. With **C03-E03-InternetSearch.docx** open, apply numbers to paragraphs by completing the following steps:
   a. Select the three paragraphs of text in the *Activities* section.
   b. Click the Numbering button in the Paragraph group.

Step 1b

Step 1a

2. Add the paragraph shown in Figure 3.7 between paragraphs 2 and 3 in the *Activities* section by completing the following steps:
   a. Position the insertion point immediately to the right of the period at the end of the second paragraph.
   b. Press the Enter key.
   c. Type the paragraph shown in Figure 3.7.

Activities

1. Using online news sources, select a specific event that occurred in a country other than the United States within the past year. Find three separate news reports of the event and describe how each media source perceived the event.
2. Describe the kinds of information that are available on your government's website. Your summary should discuss the information available on a particular date.
3. Research the topic of high-tech stock investments as discussed in online news sources. What is the current trend as of the date of your research?
4. Robots with artificial intelligence are likely to play a large role in our future. Discuss possible applications for this new technology in the areas of manufacturing, health care, and home maintenance.

Step 2c

3. Save **C03-E03-InternetSearch.docx**.

Figure 3.7 Exercise 3.3B

Research the topic of high-tech stock investments as discussed in online news sources. What is the current trend as of the date of your research?

Bulleting Paragraphs

Type Bulleted Paragraphs
1. Type *, >, or - symbol.
2. Press spacebar.
3. Type text.
4. Press Enter.

In addition to automatically numbering paragraphs, the AutoFormat feature in Word creates bulleted paragraphs. Figure 3.8 shows an example of bulleted paragraphs. Word automatically creates bulleted lists with hanging indents when you begin a paragraph with one of the following symbols: *, >, or -. Type one of the symbols, press the spacebar, type text, and then press the Enter key. The AutoFormat feature inserts a bullet approximately 0.25 inch from the left margin and indents the text following the bullet another 0.25 inch. The type of bullet inserted depends on the type of character entered. For example, if you use the asterisk (*) symbol, a round bullet is inserted, and an arrow bullet is inserted if you type the greater than symbol (>). The automatic bulleting feature, like the automatic numbering feature, can be turned off at the AutoCorrect dialog box with the AutoFormat As You Type tab selected.

Figure 3.8 Bulleted Paragraphs

- This is a paragraph preceded by a bullet. A bullet indicates a list of items or topics.
- This is another paragraph preceded by a bullet. You can easily create bulleted paragraphs by typing certain symbols before the text or with the Bullets button in the Paragraph group.

When typing bulleted text, pressing the Tab key will demote the bullet and text to the next tab and change the bullet to a hollow circle. Press Shift + Tab when typing bulleted text and the text is promoted to the previous tab and the bullet is changes to the previous level bullet.

Exercise 3.3C Typing Bulleted Paragraphs   Part 3 of 4

1. With **C03-E03-InternetSearch.docx** open, press Ctrl + End to move the insertion point to the end of the document and then press the Enter key once.
2. Type the heading *Technology Objectives* in bold as shown in Figure 3.9 and then press the Enter key.
3. Type a greater than symbol (>), press the spacebar, type the text of the first bulleted paragraph in Figure 3.9, and then press the Enter key.
4. Type the text of the second bulleted paragraph and then press the Enter key.
5. Press the Tab key (this demotes the bullet to a hollow circle) and then type the bulleted text.
6. Press the Enter key (this displays another hollow circle bullet), type the bulleted text, and then press the Enter key.
7. Press Shift + Tab (this promotes the bullet to an arrow), type the bulleted text, and then press the Enter key twice (this turns off bullets).
8. Promote bulleted text by positioning the insertion point at the beginning of the text *Identify the main components...* and then pressing Shift + Tab. Promote the other hollow circle bullet to an arrow. (The five paragraphs of text should be preceded by an arrow bullet.)
9. Save **C03-E03-InternetSearch.docx**.

Figure 3.9 Exercise 3.3C

Technology Objectives

> ➢ Define the terms "input" and "processing."
> ➢ Categorize input devices for personal computers and explain their functions.
>   o Identify the main components of the system unit and explain their functions.
>   o Explain the four basic operations of a machine cycle.
> ➢ Describe the different types of computer memory and their functions.

Another way to create bulleted paragraphs is with the Bullets button in the Paragraph group. To create bulleted paragraphs using the Bullets button, type the text (do not type the bullet) of the paragraphs, select the paragraphs, and then click the Bullets button in the Paragraph group.

Create Bulleted Paragraphs
1. Select text.
2. Click Bullets button in Paragraph group in Home tab.

Exercise 3.3D Inserting Bullets Using the Bullets Button   Part 4 of 4

1. With **C03-E03-InternetSearch.docx** open, insert bullets before the six paragraphs of text below the paragraph in the *Internet Research* section by completing the following steps:
   a. Select the paragraphs of text in the *Internet Research* section from *Author's name (if known)* through *URL, in angle brackets < >*.
   b. Click the Bullets button in the Paragraph group. (Because the last bullet you inserted was an arrow bullet, an arrow is inserted before the selected text.)
2. Save, print, and then close **C03-E03-InternetSearch.docx**.

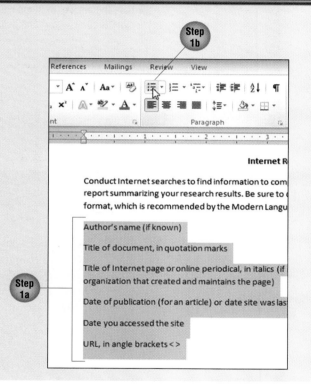

Revealing Formatting

To identify formatting that has been applied to specific text in a document, access the Reveal Formatting task pane, shown in Figure 3.10. The Reveal Formatting task pane displays font, paragraph, and section formatting applied to text where the insertion point is positioned or to selected text. Display the Reveal Formatting task pane with the keyboard shortcut Shift + F1. Generally, a minus symbol precedes *Font* and *Paragraph* and a plus symbol precedes *Section* in the *Formatting of selected text* section of the Reveal Formatting task pane. Click the minus symbol to hide any items below a heading and click the plus symbol to reveal items. Some of the items below headings in the *Formatting of selected text* section are hyperlinks. Click a hyperlink and a dialog box displays with the specific option.

Figure 3.10 Reveal Formatting Task Pane

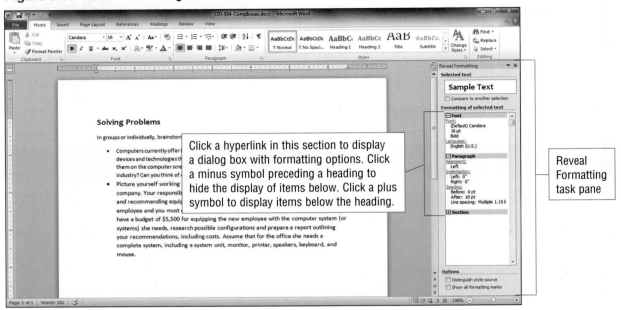

Click a hyperlink in this section to display a dialog box with formatting options. Click a minus symbol preceding a heading to hide the display of items below. Click a plus symbol to display items below the heading.

Reveal Formatting task pane

Exercise 3.4A Revealing Formatting   Part 1 of 2

1. Open **CompIssues.docx**.
2. Save the document with Save As and name it **C03-E04-CompIssues**.
3. Press Shift + F1 to display the Reveal Formatting task pane.
4. Click anywhere in the heading *Solving Problems* and then notice the formatting information that displays in the Reveal Formatting task pane.
5. Click in the bulleted paragraph and notice the formatting information that displays in the Reveal Formatting task pane.

QUICK STEPS

Compare Formatting
1. Display Reveal Formatting task pane.
2. Click or select text.
3. Click *Compare to another selection* check box.
4. Click or select text.

Comparing Formatting

In addition to using the Reveal Formatting task pane to identify formatting, you can use it to compare the formatting of two text selections to identify differences. To compare formatting, select the first text sample to be compared, click the *Compare to another selection* check box, and then select the second text sample. Any differences between the two selections display in the *Formatting differences* list box.

1. With **C03-E04-CompIssues.docx** open, make sure the Reveal Formatting task pane displays. If it does not, turn it on by pressing Shift + F1.
2. Select the first bulleted paragraph (the paragraph that begins *Computers currently offer both . . .*).
3. Click the *Compare to another selection* check box to insert a check mark.
4. Select the second bulleted paragraph (the paragraph that begins *Picture yourself working in the . . .*).
5. Determine the formatting differences by reading the information in the *Formatting differences* list box. (The list box displays *11 pt -> 12 pt* below the <u>Font</u> hyperlink, indicating that the difference is point size.)

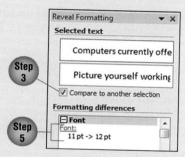

6. Format the second bulleted paragraph so the text is set in 11-point size.
7. Click the *Compare to another selection* check box to remove the check mark.
8. Select the word *visual* that displays in the first sentence in the first bulleted paragraph.
9. Click the *Compare to another selection* check box to insert a check mark.
10. Select the word *audio* that displays in the first sentence of the first bulleted paragraph.
11. Determine the formatting differences by reading the information in the *Formatting differences* list box.

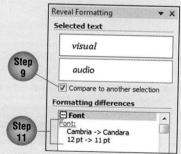

12. Format the word *audio* so it matches the formatting of the word *visual*.
13. Click the *Compare to another selection* check box to remove the check mark.
14. Close the Reveal Formatting task pane by clicking the Close button (contains an X) that displays in the upper right corner of the task pane.
15. Save, print, and then close **C03-E04-CompIssues.docx**.

Chapter Summary

➤ In Word, a paragraph is any amount of text followed by a paragraph mark (a stroke of the Enter key). Word inserts into the paragraph mark any paragraph formatting that is turned on.

➤ By default, paragraphs in a Word document are aligned at the left margin and ragged at the right margin. Change this default alignment with buttons in the Paragraph group, at the Paragraph dialog box, or with keyboard shortcuts for left, center, right, or fully aligned.

➤ To turn on or off the display of nonprinting characters such as paragraph marks, click the Show/Hide ¶ button in the Paragraph group in the Home tab.

➤ Indent text in paragraphs with indent buttons in the Paragraph group in the Home tab, indent buttons in the Paragraph group in the Page Layout tab, keyboard shortcuts, options at the Paragraph dialog box, markers on the Ruler, or use the Alignment button on the Ruler. Refer to Table 3.2 for a description of the various methods for indenting text, and refer to Table 3.3 for paragraph indent examples.

➤ Increase or decrease spacing before and after paragraphs using the Spacing Before and Spacing After measurement boxes in the Paragraph group in the Page Layout tab, the *Before* and/or *After* options at the Paragraph dialog box, or the bottom two options at the Line and Paragraph Spacing button drop-down gallery.

➤ Repeat the last action by pressing the F4 function key or pressing Ctrl + Y.

➤ Use the Format Painter button in the Clipboard group in the Home tab to copy character formatting that you have already applied to text to different locations in the document.

➤ Change line spacing with the Line and Paragraph Spacing button in the Paragraph group in the Home tab, keyboard shortcuts, or options at the Paragraph dialog box.

➤ Number paragraphs with the Numbering button in the Paragraph group in the Home tab, and insert bullets before paragraphs with the Bullets button.

➤ Display the Reveal Formatting task pane to display formatting applied to text. Use the *Compare to another selection* option in the task pane to compare the formatting of two text selections to determine how the formatting differs.

Commands Review

FEATURE	RIBBON TAB, GROUP	BUTTON, OPTION	KEYBOARD SHORTCUT
Bullets	Home, Paragraph		
Center align text	Home, Paragraph		Ctrl + E
Clear all formatting	Home, Font		
Clear paragraph formatting			Ctrl + Q
Format Painter	Home, Clipboard		Ctrl + Shift + C
Justify align text	Home, Paragraph		Ctrl + J

FEATURE	RIBBON TAB, GROUP	BUTTON, OPTION	KEYBOARD SHORTCUT
Left align text	Home, Paragraph	▤	Ctrl + L
Line spacing	Home, Paragraph	▤▼	Ctrl + 1 (single) Ctrl + 2 (double) Ctrl + 5 (1.5)
Numbering	Home, Paragraph	▤▼	
Paragraph dialog box	Home, Paragraph Page Layout, Paragraph	▣	
Paragraph spacing	Home, Styles	AA , Paragraph Spacing	
Repeat last action			F4 or Ctrl + Y
Reveal Formatting task pane			Shift + F1
Right align text	Home, Paragraph	▤	Ctrl + R
Spacing after paragraph	Page Layout, Paragraph	After: 0 pt	
Spacing before paragraph	Page Layout, Paragraph	Before: 0 pt	

Key Points Review

Completion: In the space provided at the right, indicate the correct term, command, or number.

1. Click this button in the Paragraph group to turn on the display of nonprinting characters.

2. This is the default paragraph alignment.

3. Return all paragraph formatting to normal with this keyboard shortcut.

4. Click this button in the Paragraph group in the Home tab to align text at the right margin.

5. In this type of paragraph, the first line of text remains at the left margin and the remaining lines of text are indented to the first tab.

6. Use this button in the Clipboard group in the Home tab to copy character formatting already applied to text to different locations in the document.

7. Repeat the last action by pressing F4 or with this keyboard shortcut.

8. Change line spacing to 1.5 with this keyboard shortcut.

9. The Numbering button is located in this group in the Home tab.

10. Automate the creation of bulleted paragraphs with this button in the Home tab. _____

11. This button displays when the AutoFormat feature inserts numbers. _____

12. Bulleted lists with hanging indents are automatically created when you begin a paragraph with the asterisk symbol (*), the hypen (-), or this symbol. _____

13. You can turn off automatic numbering and bullets at the AutoCorrect dialog box with this tab selected. _____

14. Press these keys to display the Reveal Formatting task pane. _____

Chapter *Assessments*

Applying Your Skills

Demonstrate your knowledge of features learned in this chapter by completing the following assessments.

Assessment 3.1   Create and Format a Training Announcement

START From Scratch

1. At a blank document, click the No Spacing style in the Styles group and then type the text shown in Figure 3.11 with the following specifications:
   a. Center and right align text as indicated.
   b. After typing the text, select the centered text and change the font to 18-point Constantia bold.
   c. Select the right aligned text and change the font to 10-point Constantia bold.
   d. Increase paragraph spacing after each line of centered text by 12 points.
2. Save the document and name it **C03-A01-DataTraining**.
3. Print and then close **C03-A01-DataTraining.docx**.

Figure 3.11 Assessment 3.1

DATA SECURITY
Technical Support Training
Building C, Room 250
Thursday, April 26, 2012
3:00 to 5:30 p.m.

Technical Support Department
Support and Services Team

Assessment 3.2 Format a Document on Buying a Handheld Computer

1. Open **HandheldComp.docx**.
2. Save the document with Save As and name it **C03-A02-HandheldComp**.
3. Select the second through the fifth paragraphs of text below the title and then indent the left and right margins 0.5 inch.
4. Select the first sentence of each of the indented paragraphs and apply bold formatting.
5. Apply the Heading 2 style to the title of the document.
6. Change the style set to Modern.
7. Apply the Elemental theme.
8. Center the title.
9. Save and then print **C03-A02-HandheldComp.docx**.
10. Select the indented paragraphs of text and then click the Bullets button.
11. Display the Paragraph dialog box, change the *Left* indent to *0.25"*, make sure the hanging indent is set at *0.25"*, and then close the dialog box.
12. Save, print, and then close **C03-A02-HandheldComp.docx**.

Assessment 3.3 Create and Format a Bibliography

1. At a blank document, create the document shown in Figure 3.12 with the following specifications:
   a. Click the No Spacing style.
   b. Change the line spacing to double.
   c. Center, bold, and italicize text as indicated.
   d. Create hanging paragraphs as indicated. (Make sure you let text wrap within paragraphs to create the hanging paragraphs correctly.)
   e. Change the alignment of paragraphs to justified.
2. Save the document and name it **C03-A03-Biblio**.
3. Print and then close **C03-A03-Biblio.docx**.

Figure 3.12 Assessment 3.3

BIBLIOGRAPHY

Albright, A. A. (2011). *Managing telecommunications* (2nd ed.) (pp. 24-33). Salt Lake City, UT: Blue

   Ridge Publishing Company.

Brown-Smythe, L. N. (2012). *Creating and maintaining local area networks* (pp. 19-22). Boston:

   Northhampton Publishers.

Lopez, V. C. (2010). *The future of nanotechnology* (pp. 43-51). Philadelphia: Graystone and

   Hampton Publishing House.

Okada, D. G. (2011). *Electronic commerce* (2nd ed.) (pp. 38-42). New Orleans, LA: Pontchartrain

   Publishing, Inc.

Assessment 3.4   Format a Travel Document

1. Open **TravelAdv.docx**.
2. Save the document with Save As and name it **C03-A04-TravelAdv**.
3. Move the insertion point to the end of the document and then type the text shown in Figure 3.13.
4. Select the entire document and then add 6 points of spacing after paragraphs.
5. Apply the Heading 1 style to the title *Hawaiian Adventures* and apply the Heading 2 style to the three headings in the document (*Rainy Day Activities*, *Kauai Sights*, and *Photo Opportunities*).
6. Change the style set to *Thatch*.
7. Apply the *Flow* theme.
8. Select the second through the fifth paragraphs of text in the *Rainy Day* section and then apply bullet formatting.
9. Bold the first word (and the colon) that begins each of the four bulleted paragraphs.
10. Select the paragraphs of text in the *Kauai Sights* section and then apply bullet formatting.
11. Insert the following paragraph of text between paragraphs 2 and 3 in the *Kauai Sights* section:
    Tree tunnel: Fragrant eucalyptus trees provide a canopy of green en route to Koloa and Poipu.
12. Bold the text followed by a colon that begins each bulleted paragraph in the *Kauai Sights* section.
13. Select the bulleted text below the *Photo Opportunities* heading and then increase the left paragraph indentation to 2.1 inch.
14. Center the title.
15. Save, print, and then close **C03-A04-TravelAdv.docx**.

Figure 3.13 Assessment 3.4

Photo Opportunities
> Hanalei Pier and Bay
> Green Waioli Huiia Church
> Lumahai Beach
> Coconut Grove
> Fern Grotto
> Sleeping Giant

Expanding Your Skills

Explore additional feature options or use Help to learn a new skill in creating this document.

Assessment 3.5   Insert Symbol Bullets

1. At a blank document, click the Bullets button arrow, click the *Define New Bullet* option that displays at the bottom of the drop-down list, and then experiment with creating a symbol bullet.
2. Open **PlanResume.docx** and then save the document and name it **C03-A05-PlanResume**.
3. Select the paragraphs of text in the document and then apply a new symbol bullet of your choosing.
4. After inserting the symbol bullets, move the insertion point to the end of the document. Type an explanation of the steps you followed to insert the new symbol bullet and then number the steps.
5. Save, print, and then close the **C03-A05-PlanResume.docx**.

Achieving Signature Status

Take your skills to the next level by completing these more challenging assessments.

Assessment 3.6   Format a Document on Resume Strategies

1. Open **ResumeStrategies.docx** and then save the document and name it **C03-A06-ResumeStrategies**.
2. Apply character and paragraph formatting so your document appears as shown in Figure 3.14.
3. Save, print, and then close **C03-A06-ResumeStrategies.docx**.

Figure 3.14 Assessment 3.6

NINE STRATEGIES FOR AN EFFECTIVE RESUME

Following are the nine core strategies for writing an effective and successful resume:

1. Who are you and how do you want to be perceived?
2. Sell it to me ... don't tell it to me.
3. Use keywords.
4. Use the "big" and save the "little."
5. Make your resume "interviewable."
6. Eliminate confusion with structure and content.
7. Use function to demonstrate achievement.
8. Remain in the realm of reality.
9. Be confident.

Writing Style

Always write in the first person, dropping the word "I" from the front of each sentence. This style gives your resume a more aggressive and more professional tone than the passive third person voice. Here are some examples:

First Person

    Manage 22-person team responsible for design and marketing of a new portfolio of PC-based applications for Landmark's consumer-sales division.

Third Person

    Ms. Sanderson manages a 22-person team responsible for design and marketing of a new portfolio of PC-based application for Landmark's consumer-sales division.

REFERENCES

Kurzweil, M. J. & Middleton, C. A. (2011). *Designing a sure-fire resume* (pp. 6-10). Indianapolis, IN: Rushton-Jansen Publishing House.

Perreault, R. M. & Engstrom, E. L. (2010). *Writing resumes and cover pages* (pp. 31-34). Los Angeles: Pacific Blue Printing.

Assessment 3.7   Type a Business Letter

1. Open **BGLtrhd.docx** and then save the document and name it **C03-A07-PSPLetter**.
2. Type the text in the document shown in Figure 3.15 with the following specifications:
   - Insert bullets as shown in the figure.
   - Indent the bulleted paragraphs of text 0.5 inch from the right margin.
   - Change the alignment to Justified for the paragraphs of text in the body of the letter.
   - Insert your initials instead of the *XX* located toward the end of the letter.
3. Save, print, and then close **C03-A07-PSPLetter.docx**.

Figure 3.15   Assessment 3.7

 BARRINGTON & GATES

January 11, 2012

Ms. Cameron Silvana
Pioneer Square Properties
19332 South 122nd Street
Austin, TX 73302

Dear Ms. Silvana:

RE: Residential Lease Agreement

During our telephone conversation today, you asked me to review the standard contract your company, Pioneer Square Properties, uses for residential rental properties. I was able to download the residential lease agreement from your website and suggest that you add/change the following items:

- **Rent:** The total rent for the term is the sum of _____ *DOLLARS* ($_____) payable on the _____ day of each month of the term.
- **Condition of Premises:** Lessee stipulates, represents, and warrants that Lessee has examined the Premises, and that they are at the time of this Agreement in good order, repair, and in a safe, clean, and tenantable condition.
- **Damage to Premises:** In the event Premises are destroyed or rendered wholly unlivable, by fire, storm, earthquake, or other casualty not caused by the negligence of Lessee, this Agreement shall terminate.

After reviewing the proposed changes, call or email me so we can schedule an appointment to finalize the agreement. During our meeting I would like to discuss the development of additional forms for your company.

Sincerely,

Grace MacIntyre
Attorney at Law

XX
C03-A07-PSPLetter.docx

200 TENTH STREET • SUITE 100 • AUSTIN, TX 73341 • 512–555–2000

Chapter 4

SNAP TUTORIALS

Tutorial 4.1
Adding a Border and Shading
to Selected Text
Tutorial 4.2
Applying Custom Borders and
Shading
Tutorial 4.3
Sorting Text in Paragraphs
Tutorial 4.4
Setting Tabs Using the Ruler
Tutorial 4.5
Setting Tabs Using the Tabs
Dialog Box
Tutorial 4.6
Cutting, Copying, and Pasting
Text
Tutorial 4.7
Using the Office Clipboard
Tutorial 4.8
Using Paste Special

Customizing Paragraphs

Performance Objectives

Upon successful completion of Chapter 4, you will be able to:

- Insert paragraph borders and shading
- Apply custom borders and shading
- Sort paragraph text
- Set, clear, and move tabs on the Ruler and at the Tabs dialog box
- Cut, copy, and paste text in a document
- Copy and paste text between documents

In the last chapter, you learned some of the options Word provides for formatting text in a paragraph. In this chapter, you will learn additional options, including how to apply borders and shading, sort paragraphs, and manipulate tabs both on the Ruler and at the Tabs dialog box. You will also learn to perform edits, such as selecting and then deleting, moving, or copying text, using buttons in the Home tab or keyboard shortcuts.

Chapter04

Note: Before beginning computer exercises for this chapter, copy to your storage medium the Chapter04 folder from the CD that accompanies this textbook and then make Chapter04 the active folder.

In this chapter students will produce the following documents:

Exercise 4.1. C04-E01-Quiz.docx
Exercise 4.2. C04-E02-IntlCorres.docx
Exercise 4.3. C04-E03-Tabs.docx
Exercise 4.4. C04-E04-LtrFormat.docx
Exercise 4.5. C04-E05-ManageData.docx
Exercise 4.6. C04-E06-FinalAgrmnt.docx

Model answers for these exercises are shown on the following pages.

Exercise 4.1

C04-E01-Quiz.docx

CHAPTER 10 QUIZ

Directions: For each item, circle the letter of the best answer from those provided.

1. Processed data that can be used immediately or stored in computer-usable form for later use is called
   a. Input
   b. Output
   c. Data retrieval
   d. Manipulated data

2. A tiny single point in anything being displayed on a screen is called a
   a. Dot
   b. Screen point
   c. Pixel
   d. Microsync

3. A term that describes the number of pixels in the display, or the quality of the text and graphics being displayed, is
   a. Resolution
   b. Density
   c. Coordination
   d. Element filtering

4. The component that converts digital signals into text so it can be displayed on a monitor is called a(n)
   a. Hypertext card
   b. RAM chip
   c. Graphics adapter
   d. Analog adapter

5. The most common type of device for producing hardcopy output is the
   a. Monitor
   b. Printer
   c. Plotter
   d. Speaker

International Correspondence

With the increased number of firms conducting business worldwide, international written communication has assumed new importance. Follow these guidelines when corresponding internationally, especially with people for whom English is not the primary language:

- Avoid slang, jargon, and idioms.
- Develop an awareness of cultural differences that may interfere with the communication process.
- Use a direct writing style and clear, precise words.

International Addresses

Use the company's letterhead or a business card as a guide for spelling and other information. Include the following when addressing international correspondences:

Line 1: Addressee's Name, Title
Line 2: Company Name
Line 3: Street Address
Line 4: City and Codes
Line 5: COUNTRY NAME (capitalized)

Canadian Codes and Provinces

AB – Alberta
BC – British Columbia
MB – Manitoba
NB – New Brunswick
NL – Newfoundland and Labrador
NS – Nova Scotia
ON – Ontario
PE – Prince Edward Island
QC – Quebec
SK – Saskatchewan

Canadian Codes and Territories

NT – Northwest Territories
NU – Nunavut
YT – Yukon

Exercise 4.2

C04-E02-IntlCorres.docx

TRAINING

Title	Date	Time
Producing Documents	March 7	10:00 a.m. to 3:30 p.m.
Preparing Spreadsheets	March 12	9:00 a.m. to Noon
Designing Newsletters	March 26	1:00 to 5:00 p.m.
Managing Databases	April 5	9:00 a.m. to 5:00 p.m.
Preparing Presentations	April 10	1:30 to 4:30 p.m.
Managing Clients Records	April 18	2:00 to 5:00 p.m.

NEW EMPLOYEE TRAINING

January 5	February 2
January 12	February 7
January 17	February 9
January 19	February 21

CONTENTS

The Writing Process 1
Editing and Proofreading 3
Grammar 5
Punctuation 12
Capitalization 15
Abbreviations and Symbols 19
Spelling and Word Division 24

Employee	Hire Date	Department
Marilyn Cameron	July 1, 2012	Administration
Hayden St. Germaine	July 1, 2012	Research & Development
Gene Docherty	July 1, 2012	Maintenance Services
Charles Metzger	August 1, 2012	Public Relations
Victoria Peterson	August 1, 2012	Technical Services

Exercise 4.3 C04-E03-Tabs.docx

Letter Formatting

Achieving a balanced overall appearance to enhance readability is the primary goal of letter formatting. When you prepare business letters, consider the following formatting guidelines:

Spacing: Generally, single space lines in business letters but double space between paragraphs.

Justification: A ragged right edge aids readability because no unnecessary spacing appears within lines of text. Use left justification (ragged right edge) for business letters.

Adjusting for Letter Length: To achieve a balanced appearance, exceptionally long or short letters may require one or more of the following margin or spacing adjustments:

- Place the date higher or lower on the page.
- Delete space between the date and the inside address.
- Adjust side margins from three-quarters of an inch as a minimum and one and a half inches as a maximum.
- Delete space between the complimentary close and the writer's signature line, leaving enough space for the signature.
- Allow long letters to go beyond a single page.

When a letter goes beyond a single page, use a header on all pages after the first to avoid confusion if the pages become separated. In addition, make sure isolated words or lines of text (often called *widows* and *orphans*) do not begin or end a page.

Margins: To achieve a balanced appearance, use equal margins on the left and right and approximately equal margins at the top and bottom, with the bottom margin two or three spaces greater than the top.

Attention Line: Use the attention line when you want a specific person to receive a letter containing a message intended for an entire company or group within a company. The attention line appears as the first line of the inside address and may include a person's name or simply a job title or department name.

Date Line: Include the month, day, and year with no abbreviations.

Adjusting for Letter Length: To achieve a balanced appearance, exceptionally long or short letters may require one or more of the following margin or spacing adjustments:

- Place the date higher or lower on the page.
- Delete space between the date and the inside address.

Exercise 4.4 C04-E04-LtrFormat.docx   Page 1

- Adjust side margins from three-quarters of an inch as a minimum and one and one-half inches as a maximum.
- Delete space between the complimentary close and the writer's signature line, leaving enough space for the signature.
- Allow long letters to go beyond a single page.

When a letter goes beyond a single page, use a header on all pages after the first to avoid confusion if the pages become separated. In addition, make sure isolated words or lines of text (often called *widows* and *orphans*) do not begin or end a page.

Page 2

Exercise 4.5

C04-E05-ManageData.docx

MANAGING CRUCIAL DATA
Technical Support Training
Building C, Room 250
Tuesday, April 10, 2012
9:00 a.m. to 11:30 a.m.

MANAGING CRUCIAL DATA
Technical Support Training
Building C, Room 250
Tuesday, April 10, 2012
9:00 a.m. to 11:30 a.m.

MANAGING CRUCIAL DATA
Technical Support Training
Building C, Room 250
Tuesday, April 10, 2012
9:00 a.m. to 11:30 a.m.

MANAGING CRUCIAL DATA
Technical Support Training
Building C, Room 250
Tuesday, April 10, 2012
9:00 a.m. to 11:30 a.m.

MANAGING CRUCIAL DATA
Technical Support Training
Building C, Room 250
Tuesday, April 10, 2012
9:00 a.m. to 11:30 a.m.

MANAGING CRUCIAL DATA
Technical Support Training
Building C, Room 250
Tuesday, April 10, 2012
9:00 a.m. to 11:30 a.m.

CONTRACT NEGOTIATION ITEMS

1. The Employer agrees that, during the term of this Agreement, it shall not cause or initiate any lockout of Employees.

2. During the term of this Agreement, the **TWU** agrees not to engage in, authorize, sanction, or support any strike, slowdown, or other acts of curtailment or work stoppage.

3. A differential of one dollar and seventy cents ($1.70) will be paid for work performed on Shift 3.

4. MBP agrees to negotiate with TWU for wage rates for jobs that may be established in the future and which are not included in said minimum wage schedule.

5. No MBP employee shall be compelled to work more than five (5) hours without being permitted to have a lunch period.

6. Payroll calculations are based on the week beginning 12:01 a.m. Sunday and ending noon Saturday. The payroll day runs from midnight to midnight.

NEGOTIATING TEAM

- Max Tillman, Chief Negotiator
- Jill Monahan
- William Nordyke
- Candace Rutledge
- Anthony Ceriotti
- Luanne Hayes

Exercise 4.6

C04-E06-FinalAgrmnt.docx

Inserting Paragraph Borders and Shading

Every paragraph you create in Word is surrounded by an invisible frame. You can apply a border to that frame. You can apply the border to a specific side of the paragraph or to all sides. You can also customize the type of border line and add shading to fill the border. Two methods are available for adding borders and shading to paragraphs: you can use the Borders and Shading buttons in the Paragraph group, or you can use options from the Borders and Shading dialog box.

Borders

Shading

Inserting Paragraph Borders

When you add a border to a paragraph of text, the border expands and contracts as you insert or delete text from the paragraph. You can create a border around a single paragraph or around multiple paragraphs. One method for creating a border is to use options from the Borders button in the Paragraph group. The name of the button changes depending on the last border option selected. Click the Borders button arrow, and a drop-down list displays as shown in Figure 4.1.

QUICK STEPS

Insert Paragraph Border
1. Select text.
2. Click Borders button arrow.
3. Click desired border at drop-down list.

Figure 4.1 Borders Button Drop-down List

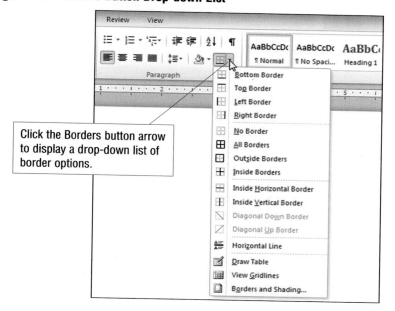

Click the Borders button arrow to display a drop-down list of border options.

At the drop-down list, click the option that will insert the desired border. For example, to insert a border at the bottom of the paragraph, click the *Bottom Border* option. Clicking an option adds the border to the paragraph where the insertion point is located. To add a border to more than one paragraph, select the paragraphs first and then click the desired border option.

1. Open **Quiz.docx** and save the document with the name **C04-E01-Quiz**.
2. Make the following changes to the document.
   a. Select the entire document, change the font to 12-point Cambria, and then deselect the text.
   b. Center the title *CHAPTER 10 QUIZ*.
3. Insert a border above and below the title by completing the following steps:
   a. Position the insertion point on any character in the title *CHAPTER 10 QUIZ*.
   b. Click the Borders button arrow and then click *Bottom Border* at the drop-down list.
   c. Click the Borders button arrow and then click *Top Border* at the drop-down list.
4. Insert an outside border to specific text by completing the following steps:
   a. Select the text (including the multiple-choice options) for the first item.
   b. Click the Borders button arrow and then click *Outside Borders* at the drop-down list.

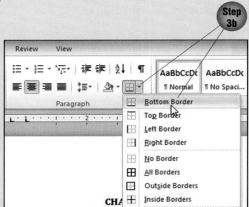

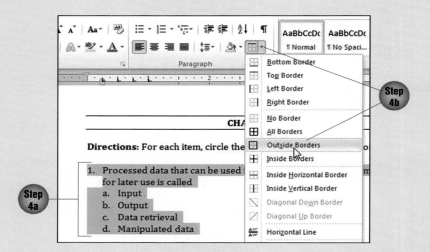

5. Select the text (including the multiple-choice options) for the second item and then press the Repeat command, F4. (This command repeats the last function.)
6. Select each of the remaining items and multiple-choice options and press F4.
7. Save **C04-E01-Quiz.docx**.

Adding Paragraph Shading

Use the Shading button in the Paragraph group to add shading behind a paragraph or behind selected text. If you want shading applied behind specific text, select the text, click the Shading button arrow, and then click the desired color at the drop-down gallery shown in Figure 4.2. If you want shading applied behind the entire paragraph, position the insertion point in the paragraph without selecting text, click the Shading button arrow, and then click the desired color at the drop-down gallery.

Apply Paragraph Shading
1. Select text or click in desired paragraph.
2. Click Shading button arrow.
3. Click desired shade in drop-down gallery.

Figure 4.2 Shading Button Drop-down Gallery

Click the Shading button arrow to display a drop-down gallery of shading options.

Click the More Colors option to display the Colors dialog box containing additional color options.

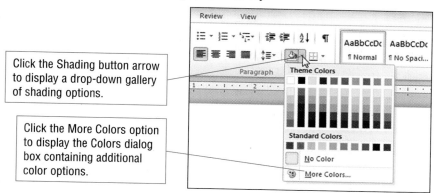

The shading colors are arranged in color themes. Choose one of the theme colors or one of the standard colors that display at the bottom of the gallery, or click the *More Colors* option to display the Colors dialog box. At this dialog box with the Standard tab selected, click the desired color or click the Custom tab and then specify a custom color.

Exercise 4.1B   Applying Shading to Paragraphs   Part 2 of 2

1. With **C04-E01-Quiz.docx** open, apply paragraph shading by completing the following steps:
   a. Position the insertion point on any character in the title *CHAPTER 10 QUIZ*.
   b. Click the Shading button arrow and then click the *Olive Green, Accent 3, Lighter 40%* option.
2. Apply shading to the number 1. item text by completing the following steps:
   a. Position the insertion point on any character in the number 1. text.

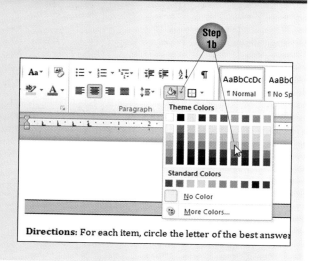

b. Click the Shading button arrow and then click the *Olive Green, Accent 3, Lighter 60%* option. (Clicking this option applies shading to the number 1. text but not to the multiple-choice options.)

3. Use the Repeat command, F4, to apply the same formatting to the remaining numbered items (not the multiple-choice options).

4. Save, print, and then close **C04-E01-Quiz.docx**.

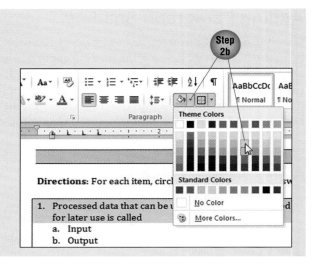

Customizing Borders and Shading

QUICK STEPS

Customize Borders
1. Click Borders button arrow.
2. Click *Borders and Shading* at drop-down list.
3. Specify desired border, style, color, and width.
4. Click OK.

Customize Shading
1. Click Borders button arrow.
2. Click *Borders and Shading* at drop-down list.
3. Click Shading tab.
4. Specify desired shading.
5. Click OK.

If you want to further customize paragraph borders and shading, use options at the Borders and Shading dialog box. Display this dialog box by clicking the Borders button arrow and then clicking *Borders and Shading* at the drop-down list. With the Borders tab selected, as shown in Figure 4.3, the Borders and Shading dialog box contains options for specifying the border style, color, and width. Click the Shading tab, and the dialog box displays as shown in Figure 4.4 with options for applying a fill color and pattern.

Figure 4.3 Borders and Shading Dialog Box with the Borders Tab Selected

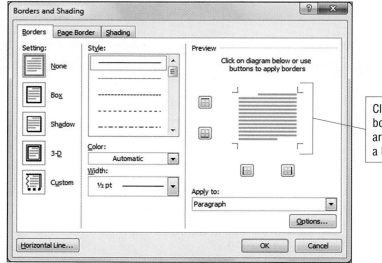

Click the sides, top, or bottom of this preview area to insert or remove a border.

Figure 4.4 Borders and Shading Dialog Box with the Shading Tab Selected

Click this down-pointing arrow to display a drop-down list of shading options.

Borders and Shading

Borders | Page Border | Shading

Fill
No Color

Patterns
Style: Clear
Color: Automatic

Preview

If you selected text in a document, this option displays as *Text*. If you do not have text selected, this option displays as *Paragraph*.

Apply to:
Paragraph

Horizontal Line...   OK   Cancel

Exercise 4.2A   Adding a Customized Border and Shading to a Document   Part 1 of 3

1. Open **IntlCorres.docx** and then save the document with the name **C04-E02-IntlCorres**.
2. Insert a custom border and add shading to a heading by completing the following steps:
   a. Move the insertion point to any character in the heading *International Correspondence*.
   b. Click the Borders button arrow and then click *Borders and Shading* at the drop-down list.
   c. At the Borders and Shading dialog box with the Borders tab selected, click the down-pointing arrow at the right side of the *Color* option box and then click Dark Blue in the *Standard Colors* section.

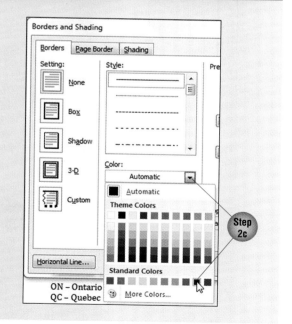

d. Click the down-pointing arrow at the right of the *Width* option box and then click *1 pt* at the drop-down list.

e. Click the top border of the box in the *Preview* section of the dialog box.

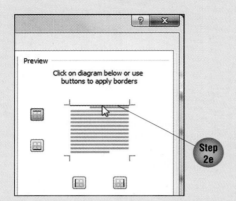

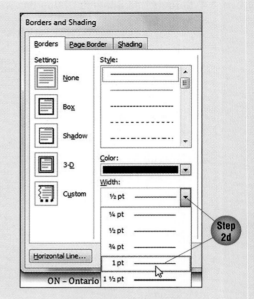

f. Click the down scroll arrow in the *Style* list box and then click the first thick-thin line combination.

g. Click the down-pointing arrow at the right side of the *Color* option box and then click Dark Blue in the *Standard Colors* section.

h. Click the bottom border of the box in the *Preview* section of the dialog box.

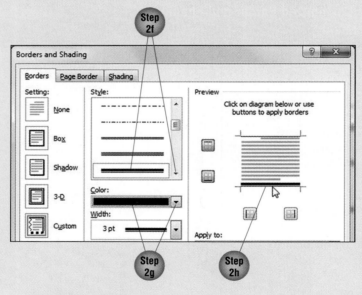

i. Click the Shading tab.

j. Click the down-pointing arrow at the right side of the *Fill* option box and then click *Olive Green, Accent 3, Lighter 60%*.

k. Click OK to close the dialog box.

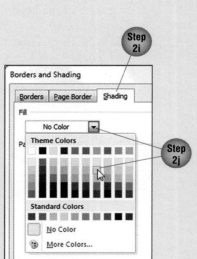

3. Use Format Painter to apply the same border and shading formatting to the remaining headings by completing the following steps:
   a. Position the insertion point on any character in the heading *International Correspondence*.
   b. Double-click the Format Painter button in the Clipboard group in the Home tab.
   c. Select the heading *International Addresses*.
   d. Select the heading *Canadian Codes and Provinces*.
   e. Select the heading *Canadian Codes and Territories*.
   f. Click the Format Painter button once.
4. Save **C04-E02-IntlCorres.docx**.

Changing Borders and Shading Options

By default, a paragraph border displays and prints with one point of spacing from the text to the top and bottom borders and four points of spacing from the text to the left and right borders. You can change these defaults with options at the Border and Shading Options dialog box shown in Figure 4.5. Display this dialog box by clicking the Options button at the Borders and Shading dialog box with the Borders tab selected. To increase the amount of spacing between text and a paragraph border, increase the number in the appropriate measurement box in the dialog box.

Figure 4.5 Border and Shading Options Dialog Box

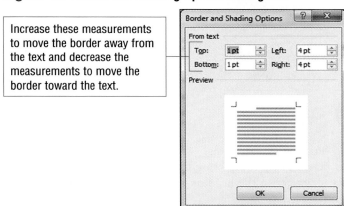

If you apply shading to a paragraph of text but not a paragraph border, changing the measurements at the Border and Shading Options dialog box will not affect shading. However, if the paragraph contains borders as well as shading, changes to measurements at the Border and Shading Options dialog box will affect the borders as well as the shading.

1. With **C04-E02-IntlCorres.docx** open, increase the spacing above and below the border and shading applied to the heading *International Correspondence* by completing the following steps:
   a. Position the insertion point on any character in the heading *International Correspondence*.
   b. Click the Borders button arrow and then click *Borders and Shading* at the drop-down list.
   c. At the Borders and Shading dialog box with the Borders tab selected, click the Options button that displays in the lower right corner.
   d. At the Border and Shading Options dialog box, click the up-pointing arrow at the right side of the *Top* measurement box until *6 pt* displays.
   e. Select the current measurement in the *Bottom* measurement box and then type 6.
   f. Click OK to close the Border and Shading Options dialog box.

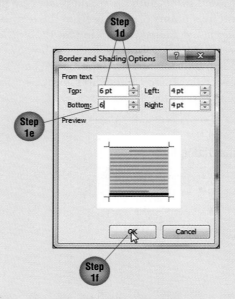

   g. Click OK to close the Borders and Shading dialog box.
2. Apply the same formatting to the other headings by completing the following steps:
   a. Position the insertion point on any character in the heading *International Addresses* and then press F4 (the Repeat command).
   b. Position the insertion point on any character in the heading *Canadian Codes and Provinces* and then press F4.
   c. Position the insertion point on any character in the heading *Canadian Codes and Territories* and then press F4.
3. Save **C04-Ex02-IntlCorres.docx**.

Sorting Text in Paragraphs

You can sort text that is arranged in paragraphs alphabetically by the first character. This character can be a number, symbol (such as $ or #), or letter. You can type the paragraphs you want to sort at the left margin or indent them to a tab stop. Unless you select specific paragraphs to be sorted, Word sorts the entire document.

Sort Text in Paragraphs
1. Select desired paragraphs.
2. Click Sort button.
3. Make any needed changes at Sort Text dialog box.
4. Click OK.

Sort

To sort text in paragraphs, open the document. If the document contains text you do not want sorted, select the specific paragraphs you do want sorted. Click the Sort button in the Paragraph group, and the Sort Text dialog box displays as shown in Figure 4.6. At this dialog box, click OK. If you select text and then display the dialog box, the *Sort by* option is set at *Paragraphs*. If the text you select is numbers, then *Numbers* displays in the Sort Text dialog box.

Figure 4.6 Sort Text Dialog Box

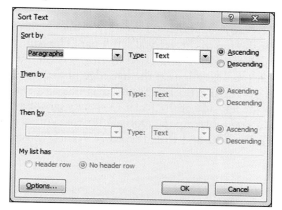

Exercise 4.2C Sorting Paragraphs

Part 3 of 3

1. With **C04-E02-IntlCorres.docx** open, sort the bulleted text alphabetically by completing the following steps:

   a. Select the bulleted paragraphs in the *International Correspondence* section.

   b. Click the Sort button in the Paragraph group.

   c. At the Sort Text dialog box, make sure *Paragraphs* displays in the *Sort by* option box and the *Ascending* option is selected.

   d. Click OK.

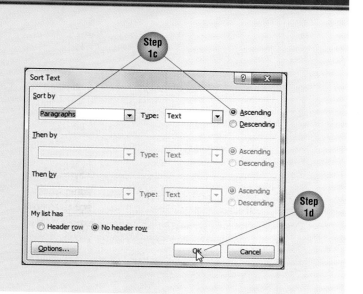

Step 1c

Step 1d

2. Sort the numbered paragraphs by completing the following steps:
   a. Select the numbered paragraphs in the *International Addresses* section.
   b. Click the Sort button in the Paragraph group.
   c. Click OK at the Sort Text dialog box.
3. Follow the steps outlined above to sort alphabetically the Canadian provinces and then the Canadian territories.
4. Save, print, and then close **C04-E02-IntlCorres.docx**.

Manipulating Tabs on the Ruler

When you work with a document, Word offers a variety of default settings. One of these defaults is a left tab set every 0.5 inch. For some documents, these default tabs are appropriate; for others, you may want to create your own tabs. You can set tabs on the Ruler or at the Tabs dialog box.

Use the Ruler to set, move, and delete tabs. If the Ruler is not visible, click the View Ruler button located at the top of the vertical scroll bar. The Ruler displays left tabs set every 0.5 inch. These default tabs are indicated by tiny vertical lines along the bottom of the Ruler. With a left tab, text aligns at the left edge of the tab. The other types of tabs that can be set on the Ruler are center, right, decimal, and bar. Use the Alignment button that displays at the left side of the Ruler to specify tabs. Each time you click the Alignment button, a different tab or paragraph alignment symbol displays. Table 4.1 shows the tab alignment buttons and which type of tab each will set.

Table 4.1 Tab Alignment Symbols

Alignment Button	Type of Tab
⌐	Left tab
⊥	Center tab
⌐	Right tab
⊥	Decimal tab
ι	Bar tab

Setting Tabs

To set a left tab on the Ruler, make sure the left alignment symbol (see Table 4.1) displays in the Alignment button. Position the arrow pointer just below the tick mark (on the Ruler) where you want the tab symbol to appear and then click the left mouse button once. When you set a tab on the Ruler, Word automatically deletes any default tabs to the left. You can set a center, right, decimal, or bar tab on the Ruler in a similar manner. When you set tabs on the Ruler, a dotted guideline displays to help align tabs.

Before setting a tab on the Ruler, click the Alignment button at the left side of the Ruler until the appropriate tab symbol is displayed and then set the tab. If you change the tab symbol in the Alignment button, the symbol remains until you change it again or you exit Word. If you exit and then reenter Word, the tab symbol returns to the default of left tab.

If you want to set a tab at a specific measurement on the Ruler, hold down the Alt key, position the arrow pointer at the desired position, and then hold down the left mouse button. This displays two measurements on the Ruler. The first measurement displays the location of the arrow pointer on the Ruler in relation to the left edge of the page. The second measurement is the distance from the location of the arrow pointer on the Ruler to the right margin. With the left mouse button held down, position the tab symbol at the desired location, and then release the mouse button and the Alt key.

If you change tab settings and then type tabbed text using the New Line command, Shift + Enter, the tab formatting is stored in the paragraph mark at the end of the typed text. If you want to make changes to the tab settings for text in the columns, position the insertion point anywhere within the columns (all of the text in the columns does not have to be selected) and then make the changes. If you want to make changes to tab settings for text in columns that you created by pressing the Enter key at the end of each line (rather than the New Line command, Shift + Enter), you need to select all lines of text in columns and then make the changes.

QUICK STEPS

Set Tabs on Ruler
1. Click Alignment button on Ruler.
2. Click desired location on Ruler.

Exercise 4.3A **Setting Left, Center, and Right Tabs on the Ruler** **Part 1 of 5**

1. At a blank document, type TRAINING centered and bolded as shown in Figure 4.7.
2. Press the Enter key and then return the paragraph alignment back to left and turn off bold.
3. Set a left tab at the 0.5-inch mark, a center tab at the 3.25-inch mark, and a right tab at the 6-inch mark by completing the following steps:
   a. Click the Show/Hide ¶ button in the Paragraph group in the Home tab to turn on the display of nonprinting characters.
   b. Make sure the Ruler is displayed. (If not, click the View Ruler button located at the top of the vertical scroll bar.)

c. Make sure the left tab symbol displays in the Alignment button at the left side of the Ruler.

d. Position the arrow pointer on the 0.5-inch mark on the Ruler and then click the left mouse button.

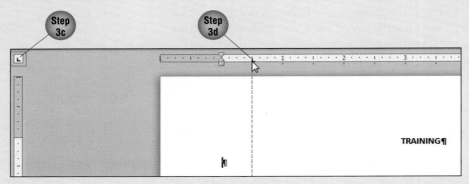

e. Position the arrow pointer on the Alignment button at the left side of the Ruler and then click the left mouse button to display the center tab symbol (see Table 4.1).

f. Position the arrow pointer below the 3.25-inch mark on the Ruler. Hold down the Alt key and then the left mouse button. Make sure the first measurement on the Ruler displays as 3.25″ and then release the mouse button and the Alt key.

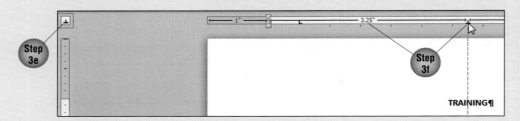

g. Position the arrow pointer on the Alignment button at the left side of the Ruler and then click the left mouse button to display the right tab symbol (see Table 4.1).

h. Position the arrow pointer below the 6-inch mark on the Ruler. Hold down the Alt key and then the left mouse button. Make sure the first measurement on the Ruler displays as 6″ and then release the mouse button and the Alt key.

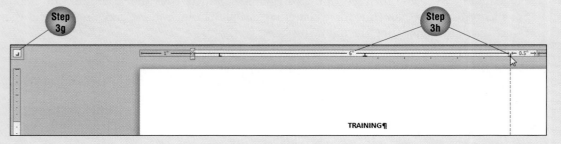

4. Type the text in columns as shown in Figure 4.7. Press the Tab key before typing each column entry and press Shift + Enter after typing the text in the third column.

5. After typing the last column entry, press the Enter key twice.

6. Press Ctrl + Q to remove paragraph formatting (tab settings).

7. Click the Show/Hide ¶ button to turn off the display of nonprinting characters.

8. Save the document and name it **C04-E03-Tabs**.

Figure 4.7 Exercise 4.3A

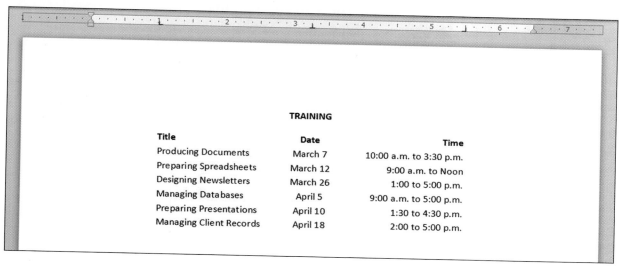

TRAINING		
Title	**Date**	**Time**
Producing Documents	March 7	10:00 a.m. to 3:30 p.m.
Preparing Spreadsheets	March 12	9:00 a.m. to Noon
Designing Newsletters	March 26	1:00 to 5:00 p.m.
Managing Databases	April 5	9:00 a.m. to 5:00 p.m.
Preparing Presentations	April 10	1:30 to 4:30 p.m.
Managing Client Records	April 18	2:00 to 5:00 p.m.

Moving Tabs

After a tab has been set on the Ruler, it can be moved to a new location. To move a tab, position the arrow pointer on the tab symbol on the Ruler, hold down the left mouse button, drag the symbol to the new location on the Ruler, and then release the mouse button.

Deleting Tabs

To delete a tab from the Ruler, position the arrow pointer on the tab symbol you want deleted, hold down the left mouse button, drag the symbol down into the document, and then release the mouse button.

Exercise 4.3B Moving Tabs   **Part 2 of 5**

1. With **C04-E03-Tabs.docx** open, position the insertion point on any character in the first entry in the tabbed text.
2. Position the arrow pointer on the left tab symbol at the 0.5-inch mark, hold down the left mouse button, drag the left tab symbol to the 1-inch mark on the Ruler, and then release the mouse button. *Hint: Use the Alt key to help you precisely position the tab symbol.*

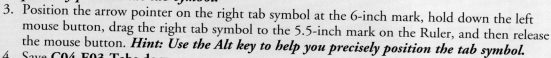

3. Position the arrow pointer on the right tab symbol at the 6-inch mark, hold down the left mouse button, drag the right tab symbol to the 5.5-inch mark on the Ruler, and then release the mouse button. *Hint: Use the Alt key to help you precisely position the tab symbol.*
4. Save **C04-E03-Tabs.docx**.

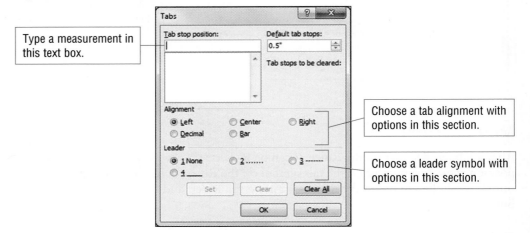

Manipulating Tabs at the Tabs Dialog Box

QUICK STEPS

Set Tabs at Tabs Dialog Box
1. Click Paragraph group dialog box launcher.
2. Click Tabs button.
3. Specify tab positions, alignments, and leader options.
4. Click OK.

Use the Tabs dialog box, shown in Figure 4.8, to set tabs at a specific measurement. You can also use the Tabs dialog box to set tabs with preceding leaders and to clear one tab or all tabs. To display the Tabs dialog box, click the Paragraph group dialog box launcher. At the Paragraph dialog box, click the Tabs button located in the bottom left corner of the dialog box.

Figure 4.8 Tabs Dialog Box

Type a measurement in this text box.

Choose a tab alignment with options in this section.

Choose a leader symbol with options in this section.

Clearing Tabs

At the Tabs dialog box, you can clear an individual tab or all tabs. To clear all tabs, click the Clear All button. To clear an individual tab, specify the tab position and then click the Clear button.

Setting Tabs

At the Tabs dialog box, you can set a left, right, center, or decimal tab as well as a bar tab. (For an example of a bar tab, refer to Figure 4.9.) You can also set a left, right, center, or decimal tab with preceding leaders. To change the type of tab using the Tabs dialog box, display the dialog box and then click the desired tab in the *Alignment* section. Type the desired measurement for the tab in the *Tab stop position* measurement box.

1. With **C04-E03-Tabs.docx** open, press Ctrl + End to move the insertion point to the end of the document.
2. Type the title NEW EMPLOYEE TRAINING bolded and centered as shown in Figure 4.9, press the Enter key, change the paragraph alignment back to left, and turn off bold.
3. Display the Tabs dialog box and then set left tabs and a bar tab by completing the following steps:
    a. Click the Paragraph group dialog box launcher.
    b. At the Paragraph dialog box, click the Tabs button located in the lower left corner of the dialog box.
    c. Make sure *Left* is selected in the *Alignment* section of the dialog box.
    d. Type 1.75 in the *Tab stop position* measurement box.
    e. Click the Set button.
    f. Type 4 in the *Tab stop position* text box and then click the Set button.
    g. Type 3.25 in the *Tab stop position* text box, click *Bar* in the *Alignment* section, and then click the Set button.
    h. Click OK to close the Tabs dialog box.

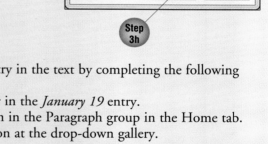

4. Type the text in columns as shown in Figure 4.9. Press the Tab key before typing each column entry and press Shift + Enter to end each line.
5. After typing *February 21*, complete the following steps:
    a. Press the Enter key.
    b. Clear tabs by displaying the Tabs dialog box, clicking the Clear All button, and then clicking OK.
    c. Press the Enter key.
6. Remove the 10 points of spacing after the last entry in the text by completing the following steps:
    a. Position the insertion point on any character in the *January 19* entry.
    b. Click the Line and Paragraph Spacing button in the Paragraph group in the Home tab.
    c. Click the *Remove Space After Paragraph* option at the drop-down gallery.
7. Save **C04-E03-Tabs.docx**.

Figure 4.9 Exercise 4.3C

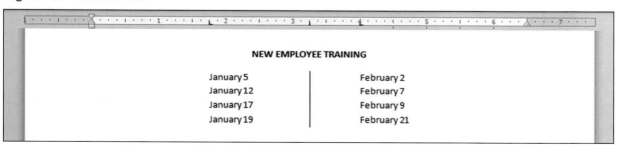

Setting Leader Tabs

The four types of tabs can also be set with leaders (only at the Tabs dialog box, not on the Ruler). Leaders are useful in a table of contents or other material where you want to direct the reader's eyes across the page. Figure 4.10 shows an example of leaders. Leaders can be periods (.), hyphens (-), or underlines (_). To add leaders to a tab, click the type of leader desired in the *Leader* section of the Tabs dialog box.

Exercise 4.3D Setting a Left Tab and a Right Tab with Dot Leaders   **Part 4 of 5**

1. With **C04-E03-Tabs.docx** open, press Ctrl + End to move the insertion point to the end of the document.
2. Type the title CONTENTS bolded and centered as shown in Figure 4.10.
3. Press the Enter key and then return the paragraph alignment back to left and turn off bold.
4. Set a left tab and then a right tab with dot leaders by completing the following steps:
   a. Click the Paragraph group dialog box launcher.
   b. Click the Tabs button located in the lower left corner of the Paragraph dialog box.
   c. At the Tabs dialog box, make sure *Left* is selected in the *Alignment* section of the dialog box.
   d. With the insertion point positioned in the *Tab stop position* measurement box, type 1 and then click the Set button.
   e. Type 5.5 in the *Tab stop position* measurement box.
   f. Click *Right* in the *Alignment* section of the dialog box.
   g. Click *2 ......* in the *Leader* section of the dialog box and then click the Set button.
   h. Click OK to close the dialog box. 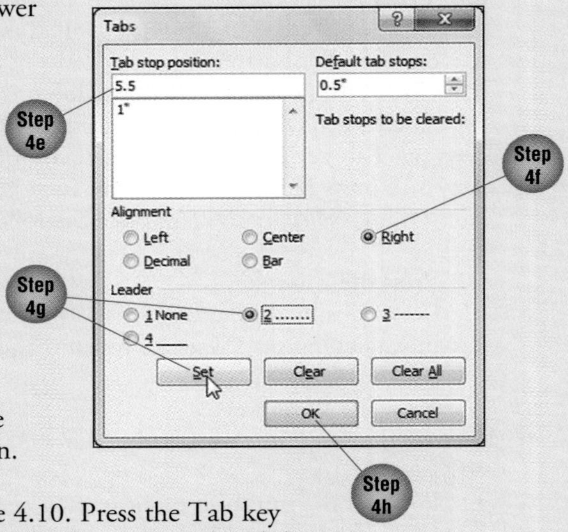
5. Type the text in columns as shown in Figure 4.10. Press the Tab key before typing each column entry and press Shift + Enter to end each line.
6. After typing the last column of text, press the Enter key twice and then press Ctrl + Q to remove paragraph formatting.
7. Save **C04-E03-Tabs.docx**.

Step 4e · Step 4f · Step 4g · Step 4h

Figure 4.10 Exercise 4.3D

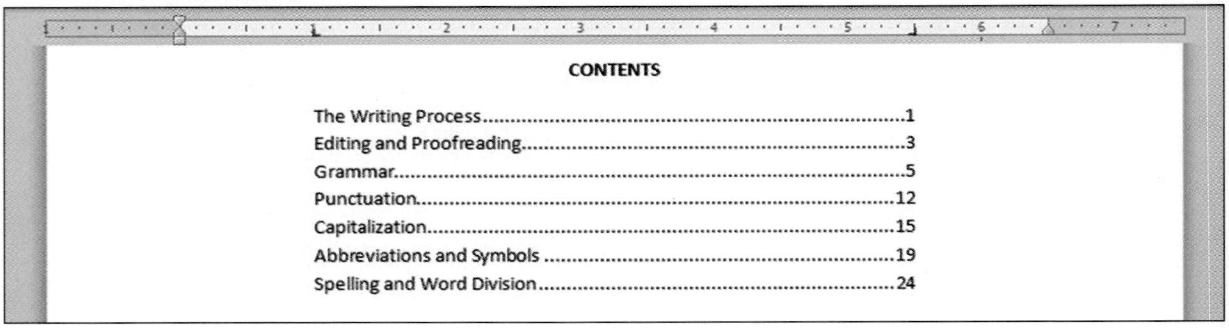

CONTENTS

The Writing Process...1
Editing and Proofreading...3
Grammar...5
Punctuation...12
Capitalization..15
Abbreviations and Symbols 19
Spelling and Word Division...24

Determining Tab Settings

When you are setting tabs for typing column text, try to balance the columns on the page. To do this, leave the same amount of space between columns and the same amount of space from the left margin to the first column and from the right margin to the end of text in the last column. For example, if the first column of text begins at the 1-inch mark on the Ruler, you would want the text in the last column to end at the 5.5-inch mark on the Ruler, which is one inch from the right margin. To do this, set tabs at approximate locations for each column and then type the text. After typing the text in columns, select the text and then move the tab markers on the Ruler until the columns appear balanced.

In Figure 4.11, notice that the columns are set so the space from the left edge of the page to the first column of text is approximately the same amount of space from the right edge of the page to the end of text in the third column. Also, notice that the first and second columns of text are separated by approximately the same amount of space as between the second and third columns.

Exercise 4.3E Determining Tab Settings

Part 5 of 5

1. With **C04-E03-Tabs.docx** open, press Ctrl + End to move the insertion point to the end of the document.
2. Click the *No Spacing* style in the Styles group in the Home tab. (This changes the line spacing to single and the spacing after paragraphs to *0 pt*.)
3. Looking at the columns of text in Figure 4.11, determine the approximate locations on the Ruler to set a left tab (for the first column of text), a center tab (for the middle column of text), and a right tab (for the third column of text).
4. Type the text in columns as shown in Figure 4.11. Press the Enter key after typing each line of text. (Do not use the New Line command, Shift + Enter.)
5. Select the lines of text you just typed and then drag the tab markers on the Ruler until the three columns are balanced on the page. Make sure that the first column begins at about the same distance from the left margin as the last column ends before the right margin.
6. Save, print, and then close **C04-E03-Tabs.docx**.

Figure 4.11 Exercise 4.3E

Employee	Hire Date	Department
Marilyn Cameron	July 1, 2012	Administration
Hayden St. Germaine	July 1, 2012	Research & Development
Gene Docherty	July 1, 2012	Maintenance Services
Charles Metzger	August 1, 2012	Public Relations
Victoria Peterson	August 1, 2012	Technical Services

Cutting, Copying, and Pasting Text

When you edit a document, you may need to delete specific text, move it to a different location, or copy it to various locations in the document. You can complete these activities using buttons in the Clipboard group in the Home tab.

Deleting Selected Text

Cut

Word offers several methods for deleting text from a document. To delete a single character, you can use either the Delete key or the Backspace key. To delete more than a single character, select the text and then press the Delete key on the keyboard, or click the Cut button in the Clipboard group. If you press the Delete key, the text is deleted permanently. (You can restore deleted text with the Undo button on the Quick Access toolbar.) The Cut button in the Clipboard group removes the selected text from the document and inserts it in the ***Clipboard***. The Clipboard feature in Word is a temporary area of memory. The Clipboard holds text while it is being moved or copied to a new location in the document or to a different document.

Cutting and Pasting Text

Move Selected Text
1. Select text.
2. Click Cut button.
3. Move to desired location.
4. Click Paste button.

Paste

To move text to a different location in the document, select the text, click the Cut button in the Clipboard group, position the insertion point at the location where you want the text inserted, and then click the Paste button in the Clipboard group.

You can also move selected text with a shortcut menu. To do this, select the text and then position the I-beam pointer inside the selected text until it turns into an arrow pointer. Click the *right* mouse button and then click *Cut* at the shortcut menu. Position the insertion point where you want the text inserted, click the *right* mouse button, and then click *Paste* at the shortcut menu. Keyboard shortcuts are also available for cutting and pasting text. Use Ctrl + X to cut text and Ctrl + V to paste text.

When selected text is cut from a document and inserted in the Clipboard, it stays in the Clipboard until other text is inserted in the Clipboard. For this reason, you can paste text from the Clipboard more than just once. For example, if you cut text to the Clipboard, you can paste this text in different locations within the document or other documents as many times as desired.

1. Open **LtrFormat.docx** and save the document with the name **C04-E04-LtrFormat**.
2. Move a paragraph by completing the following steps:
   a. Select the *Spacing:* paragraph.
   b. Click the Cut button in the Clipboard group in the Home tab.

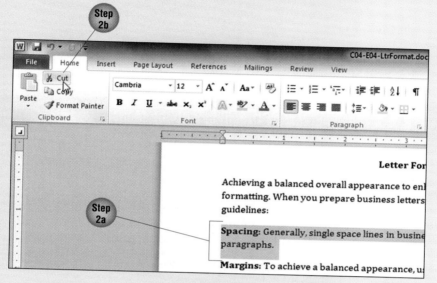

   c. Position the insertion point at the beginning of the *Justification:* paragraph.
   d. Click the Paste button in the Clipboard group.

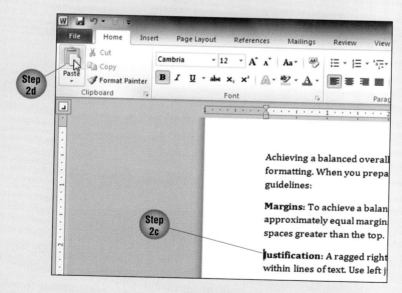

3. Following the steps outlined above, move the *Margins:* paragraph before the *Date Line:* paragraph.
4. Save **C04-E04-LtrFormat.docx**.

QUICK STEPS

Move Text with Mouse
1. Select text.
2. Position mouse pointer in selected text.
3. Hold down left mouse button and drag to desired location.

Moving Text by Dragging with the Mouse

You can also use the mouse to move text. To do this, select text to be moved and then position the I-beam pointer inside the selected text until it turns into an arrow pointer. Hold down the left mouse button, drag the arrow pointer (which displays as an arrow with a gray box attached) to the location where you want to insert the selected text, and then release the button.

Exercise 4.4B Moving Text by Dragging with the Mouse Part 2 of 3

1. With **C04-E04-LtrFormat.docx** open, use the mouse to select the *Date Line:* paragraph.
2. Move the I-beam pointer inside the selected text until it becomes an arrow pointer.
3. Hold down the left mouse button, drag the arrow pointer (which displays with a small gray box attached) so that the insertion point, which displays as a grayed vertical bar, is positioned below the *Attention Line:* paragraph, and then release the mouse button.

> **Margins:** To achieve a balanced appearance, use equal margins on the left and right and approximately equal margins at the top and bottom, with the bottom margin two or three spaces greater than the top.
>
> **Date Line:** Include the month, day, and year with no abbreviations.
>
> **Attention Line:** Use the attention line when you want a specific person to receive a letter containing a message intended for an entire company or group within a company. The attention line appears as the first line of the inside address and may include a person's name or simply a job title or department name.

Step 3

4. Deselect the text.
5. Save **C04-E04-LtrFormat.docx**.

Using the Paste Options Button

Paste Options

When selected text is pasted, the Paste Options button displays in the lower right corner of the text. Click this button (or press the Ctrl key on the keyboard) and the Paste Options gallery displays as shown in Figure 4.12. Use options from this gallery to specify how you want information pasted in the document. Hover the mouse over a button in the gallery and the Live Preview displays the text in the document as it will appear when pasted. By default, pasted text retains the formatting of the selected text. You can choose to match the formatting of the pasted text with the formatting of the destination text or paste only the text without retaining formatting. To determine the

Figure 4.12 Paste Options Button Drop-Down List

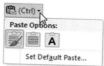

Click the option that specifies the formatting you desire for the pasted text.

function of a button in the Paste Options gallery, hover the mouse over a button and a ScreenTip displays with an explanation of the button function as well as the keyboard shortcut. For example, hover the mouse pointer over the first button from the left in the Paste Options gallery, and the ScreenTip displays with the information *Keep Source Formatting (K)*. Click this button or press the letter *K* on the keyboard, and the pasted text keeps its original formatting.

Exercise 4.4C Using the Paste Options Button

Part 3 of 3

1. With **C04-E04-LtrFormat.docx** open, open **LtrLength.docx**.
2. Press Ctrl + A to select the entire document and then click the Cut button in the Clipboard group.
3. Close **LtrLength.docx** without saving the changes.
4. Move the insertion point to the end of **C04-E04-LtrFormat.docx**.
5. Click the Paste button in the Clipboard group.
6. Click the Paste Options button that displays at the end of the paragraph and then click the middle button in the Paste Options gallery (Merge Formatting (M) button). (This changes the font so it matches the paragraphs before the pasted paragraphs.)

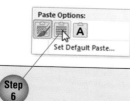

Step 6

7. Apply paragraph shading of your choosing to the title of the document. (Make sure the title is readable through the shading.)
8. Save, print, and then close **C04-E04-LtrFormat.docx**.

Copying and Pasting Text

Copying selected text can be useful in documents that contain repetitive portions of text. You can use this function to insert duplicate portions of text in a document instead of retyping the text. After you have selected text, copy it to a different location with the Copy and Paste buttons in the Clipboard group in the Home tab or by using the mouse. You can also use the keyboard shortcut Ctrl + C to copy text.

Copy

Exercise 4.5A Copying Text   Part 1 of 2

1. Open **ManageData.docx** and save the document with the name **C04-E05-ManageData**.
2. Make the following changes to the document:
   a. Press Ctrl + A to select the entire document.
   b. Change the line spacing to single.
   c. Change the spacing after paragraphs from *10 pt* to *3 pt*. (You will need to select *10 pt* in the measurement box and then type 3.)
   d. Change the font to 12-point Candara bold.
   e. Press Ctrl + End to move the insertion point to the end of the document and then press the Enter key.
3. Copy the text in the document to the end of the document by completing the following steps:
   a. Press Ctrl + A to select the entire document.
   b. Click the Copy button in the Clipboard group.

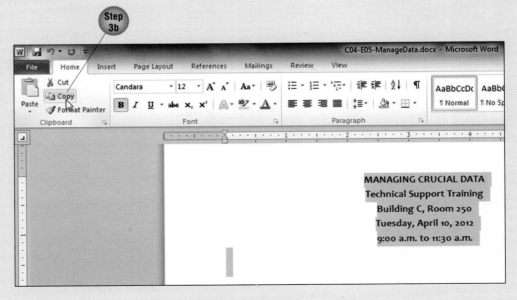

   c. Move the insertion point to the end of the document.
   d. Click the Paste button in the Clipboard group.

---

4. Copy the text again at the end of the document. To do this, position the insertion point at the end of the document, and then click the Paste button in the Clipboard group. (This inserts a copy of the text from the Clipboard.)
5. Save **C04-E05-ManageData.docx**.

To use the mouse to copy text, select the text and then position the I-beam pointer inside the selected text until it becomes an arrow pointer. Hold down the left mouse button and hold down the Ctrl key. Drag the arrow pointer (displays with both a small gray box and a box containing a plus symbol) to the location where you want to insert the copied text (make sure the insertion point, which displays as a grayed vertical bar, is positioned in the desired location), and then release the mouse button and then the Ctrl key.

Exercise 4.5B Copying Selected Text Using the Mouse   Part 2 of 2

1. With **C04-E05-ManageData.docx** open, select all of the text in the document using the mouse.
2. Move the I-beam pointer inside the selected text until it becomes an arrow pointer.
3. Hold down the Ctrl key and then the left mouse button. Drag the arrow pointer (displays with a box with a plus symbol inside) to the end of the document, release the mouse button, and then the Ctrl key.

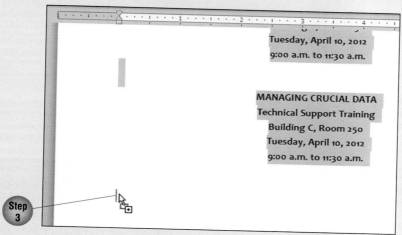

4. Deselect the text.
5. Make sure all text fits on one page. If not, consider deleting any extra blank lines.
6. Save, print, and then close **C04-E05-ManageData.docx**.

QUICK STEPS

Use Clipboard

1. Click Clipboard group dialog box launcher.
2. Select and copy desired text.
3. Move to desired location.
4. Click desired option in Clipboard task pane.

Using the Clipboard

Use the Clipboard to collect and paste multiple items. You can collect up to 24 different items and then paste them in various locations. To display the Clipboard task pane, click the Clipboard group dialog box launcher located in the lower right corner of the Clipboard group. The Clipboard task pane displays at the left side of the screen in a manner similar to that shown in Figure 4.13.

Select text or an object you want to copy and then click the Copy button in the Clipboard group. Continue selecting text or items and clicking the Copy button. To insert an item, position the insertion point in the desired location and then click the button in the Clipboard task pane representing the item. If the copied item is text, the first 50 characters display beside the button in the Clipboard task pane. When all desired items are inserted, click the Clear All button to remove any remaining items. As noted previously, the Clipboard provides temporary storage. When you turn off your computer, any items remaining in the Clipboard are deleted. To save Clipboard content permanently, save it as a separate document.

Figure 4.13 Clipboard Task Pane

Click this button to paste all of the Clipboard items into the document.

Click this button to clear all items from the Clipboard.

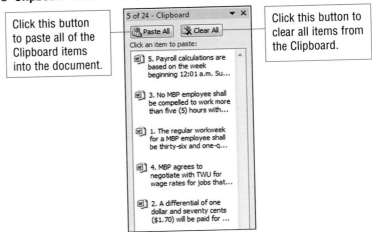

Exercise 4.6A Collecting and Pasting Paragraphs of Text   Part 1 of 2

1. Open **ContItems.docx.**
2. Turn on the display of the Clipboard task pane by clicking the Clipboard group dialog box launcher. (If the Clipboard task pane list box contains any text, click the Clear All button located toward the top of the task pane.)
3. Select paragraph 1 in the document (the *1.* is not selected) and then click the Copy button in the Clipboard group.
4. Select paragraph 3 in the document (the *3.* is not selected) and then click the Copy button in the Clipboard group.
5. Close **ContItems.docx.**

Step 2

6. Paste the paragraphs by completing the following steps:
   a. Press Ctrl + N to display a new blank document. (If the Clipboard task pane does not display, click the Clipboard group dialog box launcher.)
   b. Type CONTRACT NEGOTIATION ITEMS centered and bolded.
   c. Press the Enter key, turn off bold, and return the paragraph alignment to left.
   d. Click the Paste All button in the Clipboard task pane to paste both paragraphs in the document.
   e. Click the Clear All button in the Clipboard task pane.

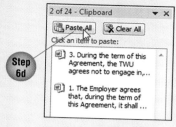

7. Open **UnionAgrmnt.docx.**
8. Select and then copy each of the following paragraphs:
   a. Paragraph *2* in the *Wages* section.
   b. Paragraph *4* in the *Wages* section.
   c. Paragraph *1* in the *Workweek* section.
   d. Paragraph *3* in the *Workweek* section.
   e. Paragraph *5* in the *Workweek* section.
9. Close **UnionAgrmnt.docx.**
10. Make sure the insertion point is positioned at the end of the document and then paste the paragraphs by completing the following steps:
    a. Click the button in the Clipboard task pane representing paragraph 2. (When the paragraph is inserted in the document, the paragraph number changes to *3*.)
    b. Click the button in the Clipboard task pane representing paragraph *4*.
    c. Click the button in the Clipboard task pane representing paragraph *3*.
    d. Click the button in the Clipboard task pane representing paragraph *5*.

11. Click the Clear All button located toward the top of the Clipboard task pane.
12. Close the Clipboard task pane.
13. Save the document and name it **C04-E06-FinalAgrmnt.**

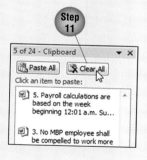

Using Paste Special

Use options at the Paste Special dialog box, shown in Figure 4.14, to specify the format for pasted text. Display this dialog box by clicking the Paste button arrow in the Clipboard group and then clicking *Paste Special* at the drop-down list. The options in the *As* list box vary depending on the cut or copied text or object and the source application. For example, in Exercise 4.6B you will select and copy text from one document and paste the text into another document without the formatting.

Figure 4.14 Paste Special Dialog Box

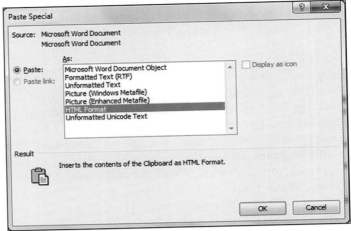

Exercise 4.6B Copying Text Using the Paste Special Dialog Box   Part 2 of 2

1. With **C04-E06-FinalAgrmnt.docx** open, press Ctrl + End to move the insertion point to the end of the document and then press the Enter key once.
2. Open the document named **TeamMembers.docx**.
3. Press Ctrl + A to select the entire document and then click the Copy button.
4. Close **TeamMembers.docx**.
5. At the **C04-E06-FinalAgrmnt.docx** document, click the Paste button arrow and then click *Paste Special* at the drop-down list.
6. At the Paste Special dialog box, click *Unformatted Text* in the *As* list box.
7. Click OK to close the dialog box.

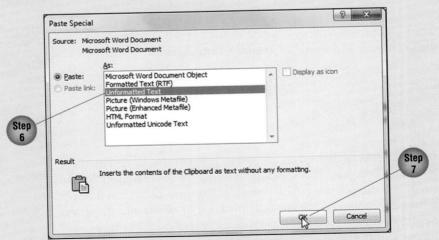

8. Select and then bold the title *Negotiating Team*.
9. Select the names below the title and then click the Bullets button.
10. Save, print, and then close **C04-E06-FinalAgrmnt.docx**.

Chapter Summary

➤ A paragraph created in Word contains an invisible frame, and you can insert a border around this frame. Click the Borders button arrow to display a drop-down list of border choices.

➤ Apply shading to text by clicking the Shading button arrow and then clicking the desired color at the drop-down gallery.

➤ Use options at the Borders and Shading dialog box with the Borders tab selected to add a customized border to a paragraph or selected paragraphs, and use options with the Shading tab selected to add shading or a pattern to a paragraph or selected paragraphs.

➤ Use options at the Border and Shading Options dialog box to move a paragraph border closer to or farther away from the paragraph text.

➤ Use the Sort button in the Paragraph group in the Home tab to sort text arranged in paragraphs alphabetically by the first character, which includes numbers, symbols, or letters.

➤ By default, tabs are set every 0.5 inch. You can change these defaults using the Ruler or with options at the Tabs dialog box.

➤ Use the Alignment button at the left side of the Ruler to select a left, right, center, decimal, or bar tab. When you set a tab on the Ruler, any default tabs to the left are automatically deleted.

➤ After a tab has been set on the Ruler, you can move or delete the tab.

➤ At the Tabs dialog box, you can set any of the four types of tabs as well as a bar at a specific measurement. You can also set tabs with preceding leaders and clear one tab or all tabs. Preceding leaders can be periods, hyphens, or underlines.

➤ Cut, copy, and paste text using buttons in the Clipboard group or with keyboard shortcuts.

➤ When selected text is pasted, the Paste Options button displays in the lower right corner of the text. Click the button and the Paste Options gallery displays with buttons for specifying how you want information pasted in the document.

➤ With the Clipboard, you can collect up to 24 items and then paste them in various locations in a document.

Commands Review

FEATURE	RIBBON TAB, GROUP	BUTTON, OPTION	KEYBOARD SHORTCUT
Borders	Home, Paragraph	⊞ ▾	
Borders and Shading dialog box	Home, Paragraph	⊞ ▾ , Borders and Shading	
Border and Shading Options dialog box	Home, Paragraph	⊞ ▾ , Borders and Shading, Options	
Clear character and paragraph formatting	Home, Font	⮺	
Clear paragraph formatting			Ctrl + Q

FEATURE	RIBBON TAB, GROUP	BUTTON, OPTION	KEYBOARD SHORTCUT
Clipboard task pane	Home, Clipboard		
Copy text	Home, Clipboard		Ctrl + C
Cut text	Home, Clipboard		Ctrl + X
New Line command			Shift + Enter
Paragraph dialog box	Home, Paragraph or Page Layout, Paragraph		
Paste text	Home, Clipboard		Ctrl + V
Shading	Home, Paragraph		
Sort Text dialog box	Home, Paragraph		
Tabs dialog box	Home, Paragraph	, Tabs	

Key Points Review

Completion: In the space provided at the right, indicate the correct term, symbol, or command.

1. The Borders button is located in this group in the Home tab. _____

2. Use options at this dialog box with the Borders tab selected to add a customized border to a paragraph or selected paragraphs. _____

3. Sort text arranged in paragraphs alphabetically by the first character, which includes numbers, symbols, or this. _____

4. By default, each tab is set apart from the other by this measurement. _____

5. This is the default tab type. _____

6. When setting tabs on the Ruler, choose the tab type with this button. _____

7. Press these keys to end a line with the New Line command. _____

8. Tabs can be set on the Ruler or here. _____

9. This group in the Home tab contains the Cut, Copy, and Paste buttons. _____

10. This is the keyboard shortcut to paste text. _____

11. To copy selected text with the mouse, hold down this key while dragging selected text. _____

12. With this task pane, you can collect up to 24 items and then paste the items in various locations in the document. _____

Chapter Assessments

Applying Your Skills

Demonstrate your knowledge of features learned in this chapter by completing the following assessments.

Assessment 4.1 Format an Abbreviations Document

1. Open **Abbre.docx** and save the document with the name **C04-A01-Abbre**.
2. Type the text shown in Figure 4.15 immediately below the *R.N. Registered Nurse* text. Make sure you tab to the correct tab stop and press the Enter key to end each line.
3. Apply the Heading 1 style to the title *Abbreviations* and apply the Heading 2 style to the two headings *Personal Names* and *Academic, Professional, and Religious Designations*.
4. Change the style set to Formal.
5. Apply the Module theme.
6. Select the columns of text in the *PERSONAL NAMES* section and then drag the left tab at the 1-inch mark on the Ruler to the 0.5-inch mark and drag the left tab at the 3.5-inch mark on the Ruler to the 1.5-inch mark.
7. Select the columns of text in the *ACADEMIC, PROFESSIONAL, AND RELIGIOUS DESIGNATIONS* section and then complete the following:
   a. Sort the text alphabetically.
   b. Drag the left tab at the 1-inch mark on the Ruler to the 0.5-inch mark.
   c. Drag the left tab at the 3.5-inch mark on the Ruler to the 1.5-inch mark.
8. Apply a top border to the title *ABBREVIATIONS* (in the same color as the bottom border) and apply shading of your choosing.
9. Apply shading to the other two headings in the document.
10. Save, print, and then close **C04-A01-Abbre.docx**.

Figure 4.15 Assessment 4.1

M.D.	Doctor of Medicine
Ed.D.	Doctor of Education
D.D.S.	Doctor of Dental Science
D.D.	Doctor of Divinity

Assessment 4.2 Type and Format a Table of Contents Document

1. At a blank document, type the document shown in Figure 4.16 with the following specifications:
   a. Change the font to 11-point Cambria.
   b. Bold and center the title as shown.
   c. Before typing the text in columns, display the Tabs dialog box, and then set left tabs at the 1-inch mark and the 1.5-inch mark, and a right tab with dot leaders at the 5.5-inch mark.
2. Save the document with the name **C04-A02-TofC**.
3. Print **C04-A02-TofC.docx**.

4. Select the text in columns and then move the tab symbols on the Ruler as follows:
   a. Delete the left tab symbol that displays at the 1.5-inch mark.
   b. Set a new left tab at the 0.5-inch mark.
   c. Move the right tab at the 5.5-inch mark to the 6-inch mark.
   d. Deselect the text.
5. Apply paragraph borders and shading of your choosing to enhance the visual appeal of the document.
6. Save, print, and then close **C04-A02-TofC.docx**.

Figure 4.16 Assessment 4.2

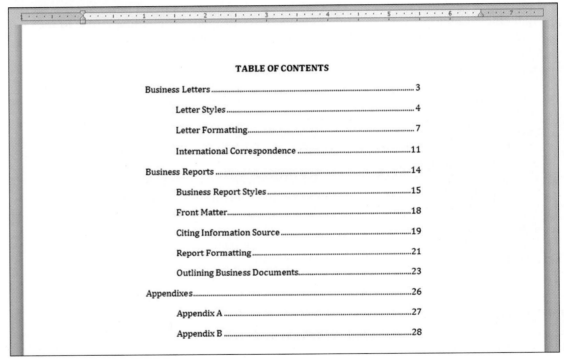

TABLE OF CONTENTS

Business Letters 3

    Letter Styles 4

    Letter Formatting 7

    International Correspondence 11

Business Reports 14

    Business Report Styles 15

    Front Matter 18

    Citing Information Source 19

    Report Formatting 21

    Outlining Business Documents 23

Appendixes 26

    Appendix A 27

    Appendix B 28

Assessment 4.3   Type an Employee List

1. At a blank document, create the document shown in Figure 4.17 with the following specifications:
   a. Click the No Spacing style in the Styles group in the Home tab.
   b. Change the font to 12-point Candara.
   c. Bold text as shown in the figure.
   d. When typing the text in columns, set a left tab for the first column, a center tab for the second column, and a right tab for the third column.
   e. Apply shading as shown in the figure.
2. Save the document and name it **C04-A03-NewEmp**.
3. Print and then close **C04-A03-NewEmp.docx**.

Figure 4.17 Assessment 4.3

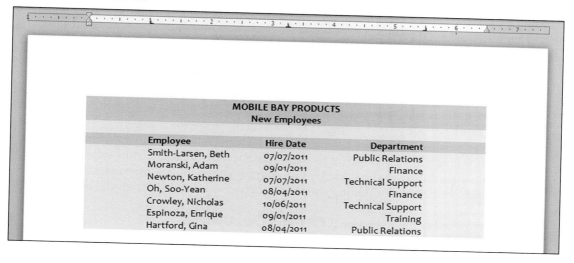

MOBILE BAY PRODUCTS New Employees		
Employee	**Hire Date**	**Department**
Smith-Larsen, Beth	07/07/2011	Public Relations
Moranski, Adam	09/01/2011	Finance
Newton, Katherine	07/07/2011	Technical Support
Oh, Soo-Yean	08/04/2011	Finance
Crowley, Nicholas	10/06/2011	Technical Support
Espinoza, Enrique	09/01/2011	Training
Hartford, Gina	08/04/2011	Public Relations

Assessment 4.4 Format a Beta Testing Agreement Document

1. Open **BetaTestAgrmnt.docx** and save the document with the name **C04-A04-BetaTestAgrmnt**.
2. Select and then delete the paragraph that begins *Licensee agrees that Software includes . . . .*
3. Move the paragraph that begins *This Agreement shall be governed, construed and . . .* above the paragraph that begins *In consideration of the mutual covenants . . . .*
4. Open **AgrmntItems.docx**.
5. Turn on the display of the Clipboard task pane. (If necessary, clear the contents.)
6. Select and then copy the first paragraph.
7. Select and then copy the second paragraph.
8. Select and then copy the third paragraph.
9. Select and then copy the fifth paragraph.
10. Close **AgrmntItems.docx**.
11. With **C04-A04-BetaTestAgrmnt.docx** open, turn on the display of the Clipboard task pane.
12. Paste the paragraph that begins *Licensee shall comply with . . .* above the paragraph that begins *In consideration of the mutual . . . .*
13. Paste the paragraph that begins *This Agreement constitutes the entire . . .* above the paragraph that begins *Stylus Enterprises:.*
14. Paste the paragraph that begins *IN WITNESS WHEREOF, parties hereto . . .* above the paragraph that begins *Stylus Enterprises:.*
15. Clear all items from the Clipboard task pane and then close it.
16. Apply border and shading to enhance the visual appeal of the agreement.
17. Save, print, and then close **C04-A04-BetaTestAgrmnt.docx**.

Expanding Your Skills

Explore additional feature options or use Help to learn a new skill in creating this document.

Assessment 4.5 Write a Letter on Changing the Paste Options Default

START From Scratch

1. As you learned in this chapter, the Paste Options button displays when you paste text in a document. When you click the Paste Options button, the Paste Options gallery displays with three buttons. By default, the first button from the left (Keep

Source Formatting) is active. You can change this default with options at the Word Options dialog box with *Advanced* selected in the left panel. Display this dialog box by pasting text, clicking the Paste Options button, and then clicking the *Set Default Paste* option at the bottom of the Paste Options gallery. (You can also display this dialog box by clicking the File tab, clicking the Options button below the Help tab, and then clicking the *Advanced* option in the left panel.)

   At a blank document, open the Word Options dialog box. Figure out how to change the default paste options when pasting text within and between documents from the default *Keep Source Formatting* to *Merge Formatting*. (Do not actually make the change.)

2. After learning how to change the paste options default, write a letter to your instructor using the personal business letter style (refer to Appendix B). Include in the letter information on the three buttons that display in the Paste Options button gallery. In addition, include steps on how to change the default for pasting within and between documents from the default to *Merge Formatting*.

3. Save the completed letter and name it **C04-A05-PasteOptions**.

4. Print and then close **C04-A05-PasteOptions.docx**.

Achieving Signature Status

Take your skills to the next level by completing these more challenging assessments.

Assessment 4.6   Create an Open House Notice

1. At a blank document, create the document shown in Figure 4.18 with the following specifications:
   - Change the font to Candara, the line spacing to single, and the spacing after paragraphs to 4 points.
   - Press the Enter key once and then type the text shown in the top box in Figure 4.18.
   - Apply character and paragraph formatting to text and set tabs so the text in your document appears similar to the text in the document in Figure 4.18. Press the Enter key three times after typing the text *Refreshments available*.
   - Select the text in your document from the beginning of the document to the blank line below *Refreshments available.* (do not include the last two blank lines in the document) and then apply the border shown in Figure 4.18 using the third option from the bottom of the list in the *Styles* list box, applying a dark red color, and changing the width to *4 1/2 pt*. Apply the light aqua shading to the text as shown in the figure.
   - After creating the first box, copy it and paste it two times in the document so your document contains a total of three boxes as shown in Figure 4.18.

2. Save the document and name it **C04-A06-OpenHouse**.

3. Print and then close **C04-A06-Openhouse.docx**.

Figure 4.18 Assessment 4.6

OPEN HOUSE
Sponsored by the Marketing Department

Location.. Room 100

Date ....Friday, May 11

Time..1:00 to 3:30 p.m.

Refreshments available.

OPEN HOUSE
Sponsored by the Marketing Department

Location.. Room 100

Date ....Friday, May 11

Time..1:00 to 3:30 p.m.

Refreshments available.

OPEN HOUSE
Sponsored by the Marketing Department

Location.. Room 100

Date ....Friday, May 11

Time..1:00 to 3:30 p.m.

Refreshments available.

Assessment 4.7 Create and Format a Table of Contents Document

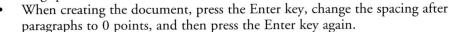

1. At a blank document, create the table of contents document in Figure 4.19 with the following specifications:
   - When creating the document, press the Enter key, change the spacing after paragraphs to 0 points, and then press the Enter key again.
   - Type the title and subtitle, press the Enter key three times, and then change the spacing after paragraphs back to 10 points.
   - Apply the borders and shading and set tabs as shown in the figure.
2. Save the completed document and name it **C04-A07-Ch01TofC**.
3. Print and then close **C04-A07-Ch01TofC.docx**.

Figure 4.19 Assessment 4.7

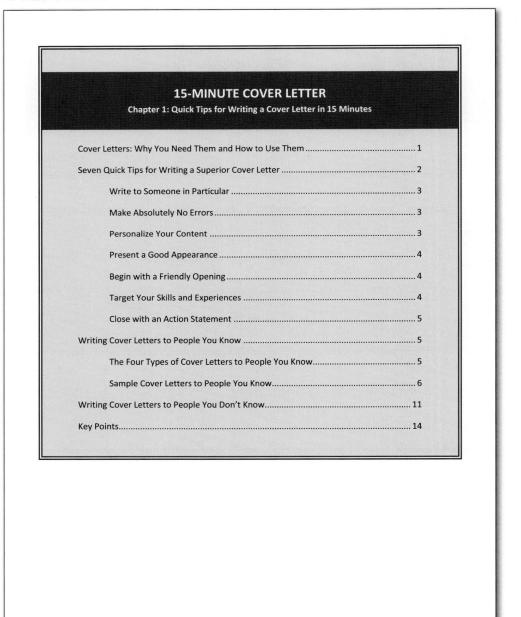

15-MINUTE COVER LETTER
Chapter 1: Quick Tips for Writing a Cover Letter in 15 Minutes

Cover Letters: Why You Need Them and How to Use Them 1

Seven Quick Tips for Writing a Superior Cover Letter 2

    Write to Someone in Particular 3

    Make Absolutely No Errors 3

    Personalize Your Content 3

    Present a Good Appearance 4

    Begin with a Friendly Opening 4

    Target Your Skills and Experiences 4

    Close with an Action Statement 5

Writing Cover Letters to People You Know 5

    The Four Types of Cover Letters to People You Know 5

    Sample Cover Letters to People You Know 6

Writing Cover Letters to People You Don't Know 11

Key Points 14

Chapter 5

 **TUTORIALS**

Tutorial 5.1
Using the Spelling and Grammar Feature
Tutorial 5.2
Creating a Custom Dictionary
Tutorial 5.3
Changing Spelling and Grammar Checking Options
Tutorial 5.4
Display document word, paragraph, and character counts
Tutorial 5.5
Displaying Readability Statistics
Tutorial 5.6
Using the Thesaurus
Tutorial 5.7
Using translation features
Tutorial 5.8
Search for and request specific information from online sources

Proofing Documents

Performance Objectives

Upon successful completion of Chapter 5, you will be able to:

- Complete a spelling and grammar check on text in a document
- Create a custom dictionary and change the default dictionary
- Display synonyms and antonyms for specific words using the Thesaurus
- Display document word, paragraph, and character counts
- Use the translation feature to translate words from English to other languages
- Research information online

Word includes a number of proofing tools to help create thoughtful and well-written documents. In addition to using a spell checker, grammar checker, and Thesaurus, you can display information about a document's readability. With options at the Research task pane, you can translate words from English to other languages and search for and request specific information from online sources. In this chapter you will learn how to use these proofing tools as well as how to create a custom dictionary.

Note: Before beginning computer exercises for this chapter, copy to your storage medium the Chapter05 folder from the CD that accompanies this textbook and then make Chapter05 the active folder.

In this chapter students will produce the following documents:

Exercise 5.1. C05-E01-VacAdventure.docx
Exercise 5.2. C05-E02-Interfaces.docx
Exercise 5.3. C05-E03-NanoTech.docx
Exercise 5.5. C05-E05-ResumeStyles.docx
Exercise 5.5. C05-E05-TranslateTerms.docx

Model answers for these exercises are shown on the following pages.

Exercise 5.1

C05-E01-VacAdventure.docx

VACATION ADVENTURES – "FUN2012"

Hurry and book now for one of our special FUN2012 vacation packages. Book within the next two weeks and you will be eligible for our special discount savings as well as earn a complimentary $100 gift card you can use at any of the resorts in our FUN2012 plan.

FUN2012 Disneyland Adventure

Round-trip air fare into Los Angeles, California
Three-night hotel accommodations and hotel taxes
Three-day Resort Ticket
24-hour traveler assistance

FUN2012 Florida Adventure

Round-trip airfare to Orlando, Florida
Seven-night hotel accommodations and hotel taxes
Four-day Resort Ticket
Two-day Bonus Ticket
Free transportation to some sites

FUN2012 Cancun Adventure

Round-trip airfare to Cancun, Mexico
Five-night hotel accommodations and hotel taxes
Free shuttle to and from the airport
Two excursion tickets

Book a complete air/hotel FUN2012 vacation package and SAVE on fall travel! Bookings must be made by October 29, 2012, for travel October 30 through December 19, 2012 (blackout dates apply). Take advantage of these fantastic savings!

Sophisticated Natural Interfaces

As computers continue to shrink in size and grow in power, it only makes sense that we will eventually be wearing our PCs. Wearing our computers, however, will require one critical difference in the type of interface used. Keyboards, mice, and monitors are far too cumbersome to hang from a person's body. This is where artificial intelligence (AI) comes in. Wearable computers will require a natural interface to operate. The most natural and easily foreseeable new interface would be speech-based.

Imagine a full PC system the size of a watch that weighs only a few ounces and could be strapped on a wrist. Any style and color would be available, of course. How could you control such a computer? Perhaps it would come with a tiny ear-bud that users could use to hear whatever their PC had to say. Other systems might allow users to wear an acoustical system that rests on the person's inner ear. When the computer speaks, only the wearer could hear it.

Another type of natural interface could be a ballpoint pen. Someone might want to talk to his or her computer during a meeting when silence is required. What if a pen were part of the computer system, and the computer could read what the user was writing and then take commands or dictation as the user wrote notes on a notepad? This means a computer could listen to the meeting, transcribe what was said, and at the same time, take commands and notes from the user as additional input.

Exercise 5.2

C05-E02-Interfaces.docx

Exercise 5.3
C05-E03-NanoTech.docx

Nanotechnology

Researchers in such fields as physics, chemistry, materials science, and computer science are using nanotechnology, which involves manipulating materials at the atomic or molecular level to build machines, including microscopic, massively parallel computers that will be more powerful than the supercomputers of today. Scientists could program these computers to replicate themselves. Doctors could then inject them into a human body to hunt down and destroy deadly viruses or cancers. Scientists have already used the technology to create carbon nanotubes that are 100 times stronger and 100 times lighter than steel. Using various ways to interweave the nanotubes, computer manufacturers can mold them into insulators, conductors, or semiconductors.

In late 2001, IBM announced that its scientists had built a computer circuit made of nanotubes, the first logic circuit consisting of a single molecule. Although the circuit can execute only one simple operation (true/false), the development was nevertheless seen as a giant advancement in the field of computer circuitry because it could eventually lead to the creation of processors that hold up to 10,000 times more transistors in the same amount of space. In 2003, a Woburn, Massachusetts, company called Nantero Inc. introduced a nonvolatile random-access memory (NRAM) chip that uses single-walled carbon nanotubules only 20 billionths of a meter wide. The miniscule tubules are arranged in a grid that holds 5 billion bits of data in one square centimeter, which is several times the density of current high-capacity memory chips. Because the NRAM chips are about five times faster than today's speediest memory chips and they are nonvolatile, the chips are considered an exciting development for use as flash memory in digital cameras and cell phones. The federal government predicts that by the year 2015, nanotubes and the field of nanotechnology will be a trillion-dollar-a-year industry and that one in four jobs will be nano-related.

Résumé Styles

The traditional chronological résumé lists your work experience in reverse-chronological order (starting with your current or most recent position). The functional style deemphasizes the "where and "when" of your career and instead groups similar experience, talents, and qualifications regardless of when they occurred. Today, however, most résumés follow neither a strictly chronological nor strictly functional format; rather, they are an effective mixture of the two styles usually known as a "combination" or "hybrid" format.

El resumen cronológico tradicional enumera su experiencia profesional en orden reverso-cronológica (comenzando con su corriente o la mayoría de la posición reciente). El estilo funcional deemphasizes "sin importar donde y "cuando" de su carrera y en lugar de otro agrupa experiencia, talentos, y calificaciones similares cuando ocurrieron. Hoy, sin embargo, la mayoría de los resúmenes siguen ni un formato terminantemente cronológico ni terminantemente funcional; algo, son una mezcla eficaz de los dos estilos conocidos generalmente como "combinación" o formato "híbrido".

Exercise 5.5
C05-E05-ResumeStyles.docx

Exercise 5.5

C05-E05-TranslateTerms.docx

	TRANSLATION	
	English to Spanish	
	English to French	
Term	**Spanish**	**French**
Central	centrico	centre
Data	datos	donnees
Directory	directorio	repertoire
External	externo	exterieur

Checking the Spelling and Grammar in a Document

Check Spelling and Grammar
1. Click Review tab.
2. Click Spelling & Grammar button.
3. Change or ignore error.
4. Click OK.

Spelling & Grammar

Two tools for creating professional, polished-looking documents are a spell checker and a grammar checker. The spell checker in Word finds misspelled words and offers replacement words. It also finds duplicate words and irregular capitalizations. When you spell check a document, the spell checker compares the words in your document to the words in its dictionary. If the spell checker finds a match, it passes over the word. If it does not find a match, the spell checker stops and selects the following:

- a misspelled word, when the misspelling does not match another word that exists in the dictionary
- typographical errors (such as transposed letters)
- double word occurrences (such as *and and*)
- irregular capitalization
- some proper names
- jargon and some technical terms

The grammar checker in Word searchs a document for errors in grammar, punctuation, and word usage. Word's spell checker and the grammar checker can help you create a well-written document, but they do not replace the need for proofreading.

To check the spelling or grammar of a document you are working in, save the document first; or, open a saved document and then complete these basic steps:

1. Click the Review tab.
2. Click the Spelling and Grammar button. (You can also press the keyboard shortcut F7.)
3. If the spell checker detects an error, it selects the misspelled word and displays a Spelling and Grammar dialog box, similar to the one shown in Figure 5.1. The sentence that contains the misspelled word displays in the *Not in Dictionary:* text box. If the grammar checker detects a grammatical error, it selects the sentence with the error and displays a Spelling and Grammar dialog box, similar to the one shown in Figure 5.2.

Figure 5.1 Spelling and Grammar Dialog Box with Spelling Error Selected

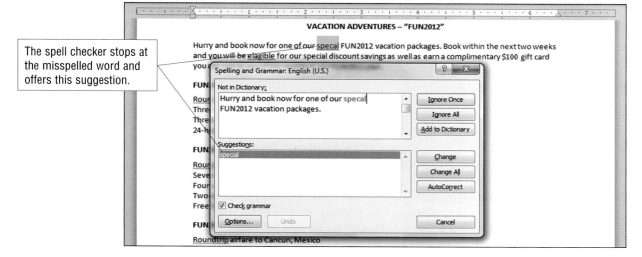

Figure 5.2 Spelling and Grammar Dialog Box with Grammar Error Selected

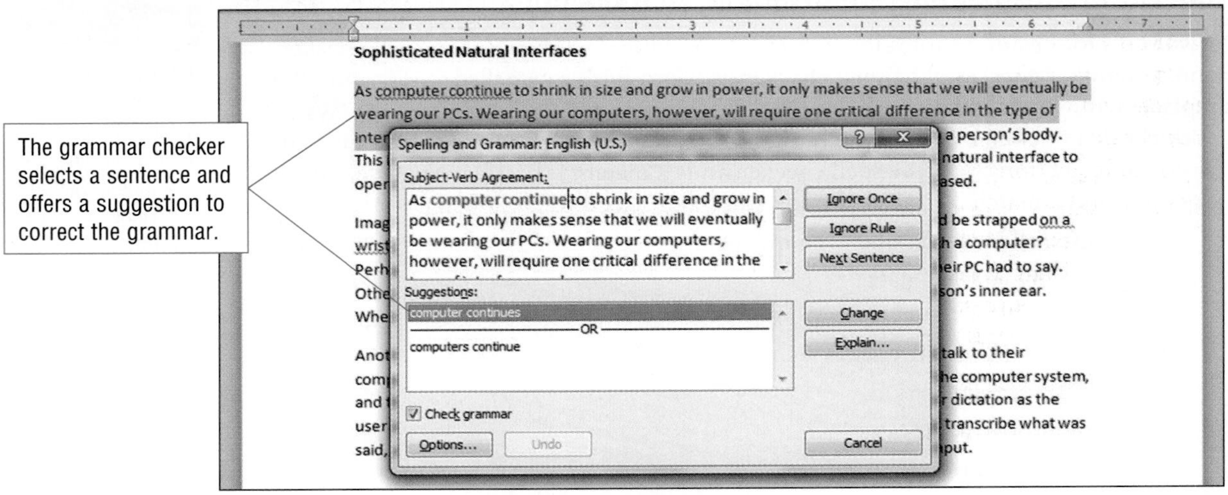

The grammar checker selects a sentence and offers a suggestion to correct the grammar.

4. If a misspelled word is selected, replace the word with the correct spelling, tell Word to ignore it and continue checking the document, or add the word to a custom dictionary. If a sentence containing a grammatical error is selected, it displays in the top text box in the Spelling and Grammar dialog box. Choose to ignore or change errors found by the grammar checker.

5. When the spelling and grammar check is complete, the message *The spelling and grammar check is complete* displays. Click OK to close the message box or press the Enter key.

When a word or sentence is selected during a spelling or grammar check, you need to determine if the word or sentence should be corrected or ignored. Word provides buttons at the right side and bottom of the Spelling and Grammar dialog box to help you make decisions. The buttons that display vary depending on the type of error selected. These buttons and their functions are described in Table 5.1.

Spell Checking a Document

Word completes both a spelling check and grammar check on a document by default. If you want to check only the spelling in a document and not the grammar, remove the check mark from the *Check grammar* check box located in the lower left corner of the Spelling and Grammar dialog box. If you want to complete a spelling and grammar check on only a portion of a document, first select the text you want checked and then click the Spelling and Grammar button.

Editing While Spell Checking

While you are spell checking a document, you can temporarily leave the Spelling and Grammar dialog box to make corrections in the document and then resume spell checking. For example, suppose while spell checking you notice a sentence that you want to change. To correct the sentence, you would move the mouse pointer to the location in the sentence where you want to make the change, click the left mouse button, and make the change. To resume spell checking, you would click the Resume button, which formerly displayed as the Ignore Once button.

Table 5.1 Spelling and Grammar Dialog Box Buttons

Button	Function
Ignore Once	During spell checking, skips that occurrence of the word; during grammar checking, leaves currently selected text as written.
Ignore All	During spell checking, skips that occurrence of the word and all other occurrences of the word in the document.
Ignore Rule	During grammar checking, leaves currently selected text as written and ignores the current rule for remainder of the grammar check.
Add to Dictionary	Adds selected word to the main spell check dictionary.
Delete	Deletes the currently selected word(s).
Change	Replaces selected word in sentence with selected word in *Suggestions* list box.
Change All	Replaces selected word in sentence with selected word in *Suggestions* list box and all other occurrences of the word.
AutoCorrect	Inserts selected word and correct spelling of word in AutoCorrect dialog box.
Explain	During grammar checking, displays grammar rule information about the selected text.
Undo	Reverses most recent spelling and grammar action.
Next Sentence	Accepts manual changes made to sentence and then continues grammar checking.
Options	Displays a dialog box with options for customizing a spelling and grammar check.

Changing Spelling Options

Click the Options button at the Spelling and Grammar dialog box, and the Word Options dialog box displays with the *Proofing* option selected, as shown in Figure 5.3. (You can also display the Word Options dialog box by clicking the File tab, clicking the Options button located below the Help tab, and then clicking *Proofing* in the left panel of the dialog box.) Use options at this dialog box to customize spell checking by identifying what you want the spell checker to check or ignore. You can also create or edit a custom dictionary.

Change Spelling Options
1. Click File tab.
2. Click Options button.
3. Click *Proofing*.
4. Specify options.
5. Click OK.

Figure 5.3 Word Options Dialog Box with Proofing Selected

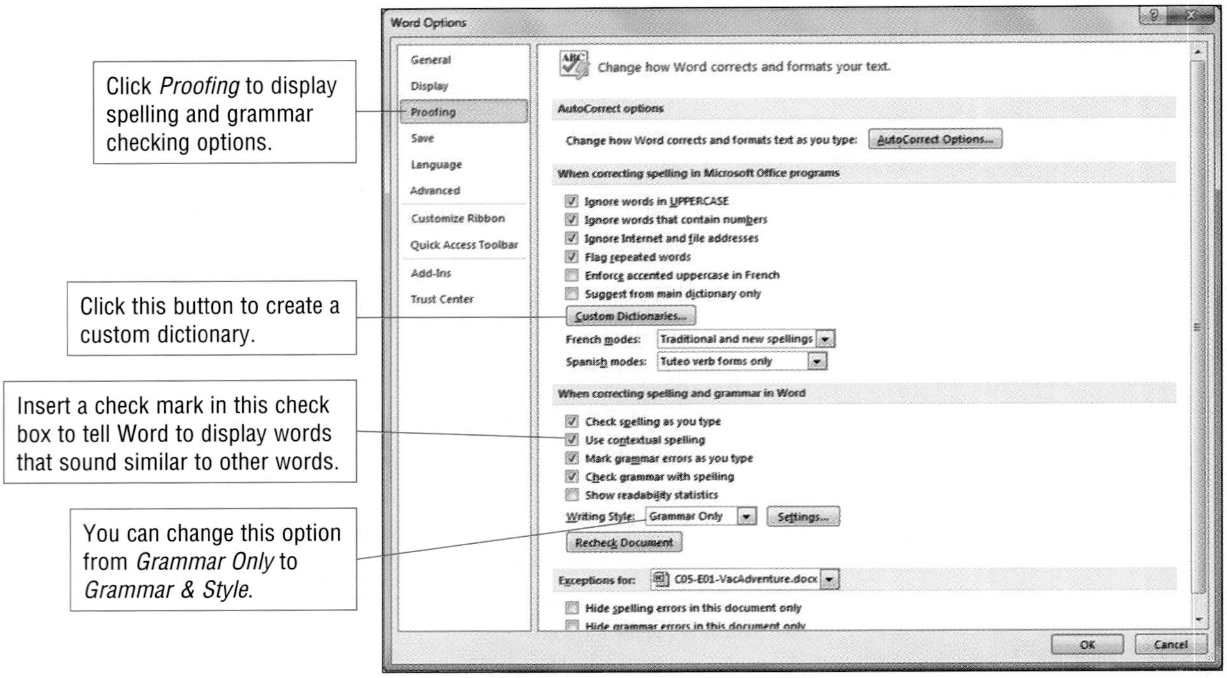

Click *Proofing* to display spelling and grammar checking options.

Click this button to create a custom dictionary.

Insert a check mark in this check box to tell Word to display words that sound similar to other words.

You can change this option from *Grammar Only* to *Grammar & Style*.

Exercise 5.1 Spell Checking a Document with Words in Uppercase and with Numbers

Part 1 of 1

1. Open **VacAdventure.docx** and save the document with the name **C05-E01-VacAdventure**.
2. Check spell checking options by completing the following steps:
   a. Click the File tab.
   b. Click the Options button.
   c. At the Word Options dialog box, click the *Proofing* option in the left panel.

   Step 2c

   d. Make sure the *Ignore words in UPPERCASE* check box and the *Ignore words that contain numbers* check box each contain a check mark.

   Step 2d

   e. Click OK to close the dialog box. 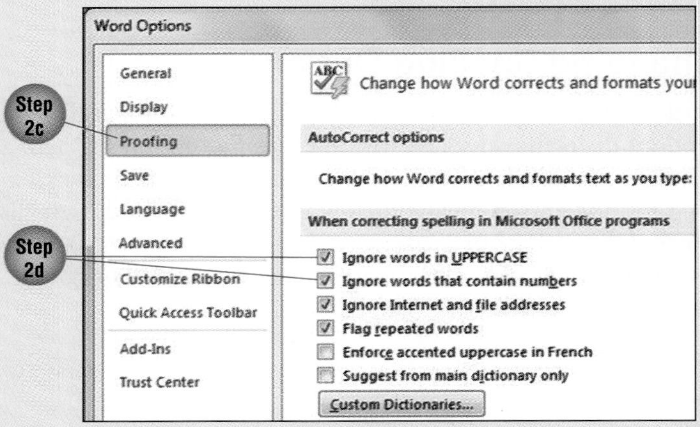
3. Complete a spelling check on the document by completing the following steps:
   a. Click the Review tab.
   b. Click the Spelling & Grammar button in the Proofing group.

---

c. When the spell checker selects the word *specal,* the proper spelling is selected in the *Suggestions* list box. Click the Change button (or Change All button) to correct the misspelling.

d. When the spell checker selects the word *elagible,* the proper spelling is selected in the *Suggestions* list box. Click the Change button.

e. When the spell checker selects *Roundtrip* and suggests *Round-trip,* click the Change All button. (Make sure you click the Change All button and not the Change button since *Roundtrip* appears in multiple locations in the document.)

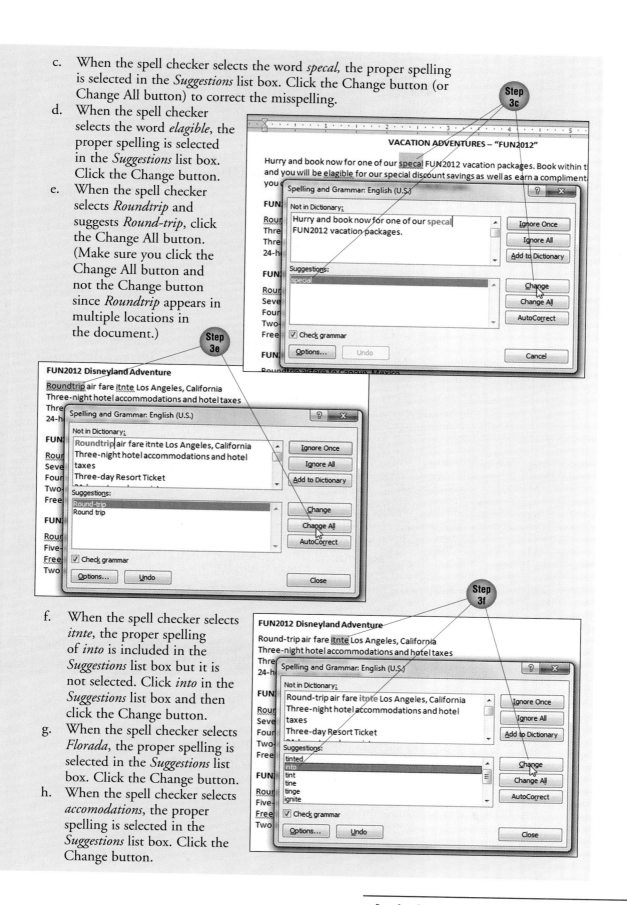

f. When the spell checker selects *itnte,* the proper spelling of *into* is included in the *Suggestions* list box but it is not selected. Click *into* in the *Suggestions* list box and then click the Change button.

g. When the spell checker selects *Florada,* the proper spelling is selected in the *Suggestions* list box. Click the Change button.

h. When the spell checker selects *accomodations,* the proper spelling is selected in the *Suggestions* list box. Click the Change button.

   i.   When the grammar checker selects the word *Free*, click the Ignore Rule button.

   j.   When the message displays telling you that the spelling and grammar check is complete, click the OK button.

4. Save, print, and then close **C05-E01-VacAdventure.docx**.

Checking the Grammar in a Document

The grammar checking feature in Word allows you to search a document for errors in grammar, style, punctuation, and word usage. Like the spell checker, the grammar checker does not find every error in a document and may stop at correct phrases. The grammar checker can help you create a well-written document, but it does not replace the need for proofreading.

To complete a grammar check on a document, click the Review tab and then click the Spelling and Grammar button in the Proofing group. The grammar checker selects the first sentence that contains a grammatical error and displays the sentence in the top text box in the dialog box. A suggested correction displays in the *Suggestions* text box. You can choose to ignore or change errors found by the grammar checker. When the grammar checker is finished, the open document displays with the changes made during the check inserted in it. By default, a spelling check is completed on a document during a grammar check.

The grammar checker checks a document for a variety of grammar and style errors. In some situations, you may want the grammar checker to ignore a particular grammar or style rule. To tell the grammar checker to ignore a rule, click the Ignore Rule button the first time the text breaking that particular grammar or style rule displays. If the grammar checker selects a sentence that contains a grammar or style error and you want the sentence left as written, click the Next Sentence button. This tells the grammar checker to leave the current sentence unchanged and move to the next sentence.

When a sentence with a grammar error displays in the Spelling and Grammar dialog box, click the Explain button and the Word Help window displays with information about the specific grammar rule. Read this information carefully. Some suggestions may not be valid, and a problem identified by the grammar checker may not be a problem. After reading the information in the Word Help window, click the Close button located in the upper right corner of the window.

Exercise 5.2A   Checking Grammar in a Document   Part 1 of 3

1. Open **Interfaces.docx** and save the document with the name **C05-E02-Interfaces**.
2. Check the grammar in the document by completing the following steps:
   a.   Click the Review tab.
   b.   Click the Spelling & Grammar button in the Proofing group.
   c.   When the grammar checker selects the sentence that begins *As computer continue to . . .* and displays *computer continues* and *computers continue* in the *Suggestions* text box, click the Explain button.
   d.   Read the information about Subject-Verb Agreement that displays in the Word Help window and then click the Close button located in the upper right corner of the window.

e. Click *computers continue* in the *Suggestions* list box and then click the Change button.

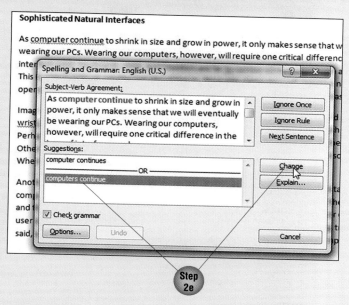

Step
2e

f. The grammar checker selects the sentence that begins *Keyboards, mice, and monitors are . . .* and displays *too* in the *Suggestions* list box.

g. Click the Explain button, read the information about commonly confused words that displays in the Word Help window, and then close the window.

h. With *too* selected in the *Suggestions* list box, click the Change button.

i. When the grammar checker selects the sentence that begins *Imagine a full PC system the size . . .*, click *on a wrist* in the *Suggestions* list box and then click the Change button.

j. At the message telling you that the spelling and grammar check is complete, click OK.

3. Save **C05-E02-Interfaces.docx**.

Changing Grammar Checking Options

You can customize the type of grammar checking you complete on a document by using options in the *When correcting spelling and grammar in Word* section of the Word Options dialog box with *Proofing* selected. Insert a check mark in the check box preceding those options you want active in a document and remove the check mark from the check boxes preceding those you want inactive.

Consider making active the *Use contextual spelling* option when you are proofing a document that contains words that sound similar but have different meanings, such as *to* and *too* and *there* and *their*. When this feature is active, Word inserts a wavy blue line below words that sound similar to other words.

By default, the grammar checker checks only the grammar in a document. The *Writing Style* option in the Word Options dialog box with *Proofing* selected has a default setting of *Grammar Only*. You can change this default setting to *Grammar and Style*. To determine what style issues the grammar checker will select, click the Settings button and the Grammar Settings dialog box displays with grammar options. Insert a check mark for those options you want active and remove the check mark from those options you want inactive during a grammar check.

Change Grammar Checking Options
1. Click File tab.
2. Click Options button.
3. Click *Proofing*.
4. Specify options.
5. Click OK.

1. With **C05-E02-Interfaces.docx** open, change grammar settings by completing the following steps:

    a. Click the File tab.

    b. Click the Options button.

    c. At the Word Options dialog box, click the *Proofing* option in the left panel.

    d. Make sure the *Use contextual spelling* check box contains a check mark.

    e. Click the down-pointing arrow at the right side of the *Writing Style* option box and then click *Grammar & Style* at the drop-down list.

    f. Click the Recheck Document button.

    g. At the message that displays, click Yes.

    h. Click OK to close the Word Options dialog box.

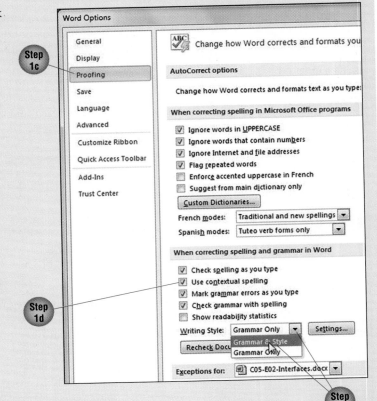

2. Complete grammar and style check on the document by completing the following steps:

    a. Press Ctrl + Home to move the insertion point to the beginning of the document.

    b. Make sure the Review tab is selected.

    c. Click the Spelling & Grammar button in the Proofing group.

    d. When the grammar checker selects the sentence that begins *Imagine a full PC system the size . . .* , click the Explain button. Read the information on verb use that displays in the Word Help window, close the window, and then click the Ignore Once button.

    e. When the grammar checker selects the sentence that begins *When the computer speaks only . . .* and inserts *speaks* in the *Suggestions* list box, click the Change button.

    f. When the grammar checker selects the sentence that begins *Someone might want to talk to their . . .* and inserts *his or her* in the *Suggestions* list box, click the Change button.

    g. At the message telling you that the spelling and grammar check is complete, click OK.

3. Save and then print **C05-E02-Interfaces.docx**.

Displaying Readability Statistics

After you have completed a spelling and grammar check, you can display a document's readability statistics at the Readability Statistics dialog box. Figure 5.4 shows the dialog box and the readability statistics for **C05-E02-Interfaces.docx**. Readability statistics provide useful information about the level of writing in a document, including the number of words, characters, paragraphs, and sentences in the document; the average number of sentences per paragraph, words per sentence, and characters per word. Readability statistics also include other information about a document's readability, such as the percentage of passive sentences, the Flesch Reading Ease score, and the Flesch-Kincaid grade-level rating, which are described in Table 5.2. You can control the display of readability statistics with the *Show readability statistics* check box in the Word Options dialog box with *Proofing* selected.

Show Readability Statistics
1. Click File tab.
2. Click Options button.
3. Click *Proofing*.
4. Click *Show readability statistics* check box.
5. Click OK.
6. Complete spelling and grammar check.

Figure 5.4 Readability Statistics Dialog Box

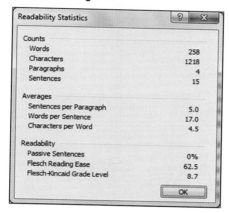

Table 5.2 Readability Statistics

Flesch Reading Ease	This score is based on the average number of syllables per word and the average number of words per sentence. The higher the score, the greater the number of people who will be able to understand the text in the document. Standard writing generally scores in the 60-70 range.
Flesch-Kincaid Grade Level	This rating is based on the average number of syllables per word and the average number of words per sentence. The score indicates a grade level. Standard writing is generally written at the seventh or eighth grade level.

1. With **C05-E02-Interfaces.docx** open, display readability statistics for the document by completing the following steps:

   a. Click the File tab and then click the Options button.

   b. At the Word Options dialog box, click *Proofing* in the left panel.

   c. Click the *Show readability statistics* check box to insert a check mark.

   d. Click OK to close the Word Options dialog box.

   e. Make sure the Review tab is selected and then click the Spelling & Grammar button.

   f. Look at the readability statistics that display in the Readability Statistics dialog box and then click OK to close the dialog box.

2. Change the grammar options back to the default by completing the following steps:

   a. Click the File tab and then click the Options button.

   b. At the Word Options dialog box, click *Proofing* in the left panel.

   c. Click the *Show readability statistics* check box to remove the check mark.

   d. Click the down-pointing arrow at the right side of the *Writing Style* option box and then click *Grammar Only* at the drop-down list.

   e. Click OK to close the Word Options dialog box.

3. Save and then close **C05-E02-Interfaces.docx**.

Create Custom Dictionary

1. Click File tab.
2. Click Options button.
3. Click *Proofing*.
4. Click Custom Dictionaries button.
5. Click New button.
6. Type name for dictionary, press Enter.

Creating a Custom Dictionary

When Word completes a spelling check on a document, it uses the default CUSTOM.DIC custom dictionary. You can add or remove words from this default dictionary. In a multiple-user environment, you might also consider creating your own custom dictionary and then selecting it as the default. In this way, multiple users can create their own dictionaries to use when spell checking a document.

To create a custom dictionary, display the Word Options dialog box with *Proofing* selected, and then click the Custom Dictionaries button. Clicking this button displays the Custom Dictionaries dialog box, shown in Figure 5.5. At this dialog box, click the New button to display the Create Custom Dictionary dialog box. Type a name for the dictionary in the *File name* text box and then press the Enter key. The new dictionary name will display in the *Dictionary List* box in the Custom Dictionaries dialog box. You can use more than one dictionary when spell checking a document. Insert a check mark in the check box next to any dictionary you want to use.

Figure 5.5 Custom Dictionaries Dialog Box

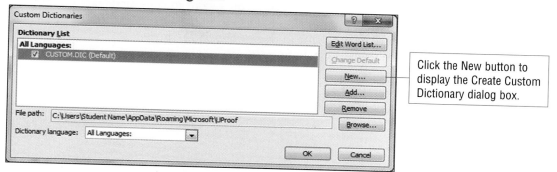

Click the New button to display the Create Custom Dictionary dialog box.

Changing the Default Dictionary

At the Custom Dictionaries dialog box, the default dictionary displays in the *Dictionary List* box followed by *(Default)*. You can change this default by clicking the desired dictionary name in the list box and then clicking the Change Default button.

Removing a Dictionary

Remove a custom dictionary with the Remove button at the Custom Dictionaries dialog box. To do this, display the Custom Dictionaries dialog box, click the dictionary name in the *Dictionary List* box, and then click the Remove button. You are not prompted to confirm the removal of the dictionary so make sure you select the correct name before clicking the Remove button.

QUICK STEPS

Remove Custom Dictionary
1. Click File tab.
2. Click Options button.
3. Click *Proofing*.
4. Click Custom Dictionaries button.
5. Click custom dictionary name.
6. Click Remove.
7. Click OK.

Exercise 5.3A Creating a Custom Dictionary and Changing the Default Dictionary Part 1 of 3

1. Open **NanoTech.docx**, notice the wavy red lines indicating words that are not recognized by the spell checker (that is, words not in the custom dictionary) and then close the document.
2. At a blank document, create a custom dictionary, add words to it, and then change the default dictionary by completing the following steps:
   a. Click the File tab and then click the Options button.
   b. At the Word Options dialog box, click *Proofing* in the left panel.
   c. Click the Custom Dictionaries button.
   d. At the Custom Dictionaries dialog box, click the New button.
   e. At the Create Custom Dictionary dialog box, type your first and last names (without a space between) in the *File name* text box and then press the Enter key.

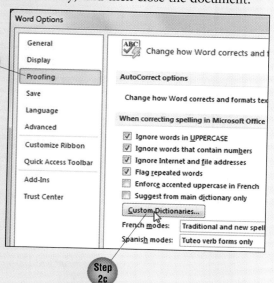

f. At the Custom Dictionaries dialog box, add a word to your dictionary by completing the following steps:
   1) Click your dictionary name in the *Dictionary List* box.
   2) Click the Edit Word List button.

3) At your custom dictionary dialog box, type nano in the *Word(s)* text box.
4) Click the Add button.

g. Complete the steps outlined in 2f3 and 2f4 to add the following words:

   nanotubes
   nanotubules
   Nantero

h. When you have added the words, click the OK button to close the dialog box.

i. At the Custom Dictionaries dialog box with your dictionary name selected in the *Dictionary List* box, click the Change Default button. (Notice that the word *(Default)* displays after your custom dictionary.)

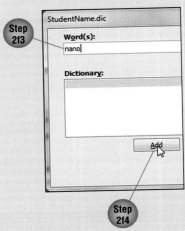

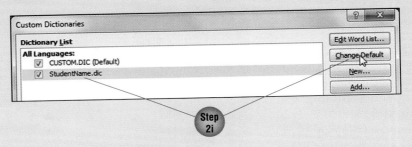

j. Click OK to close the Custom Dictionaries dialog box.
k. Click OK to close the Word Options dialog box.
3. Open **NanoTech.docx** and then save the document and name it **C05-E03-NanoTech**.
4. Complete a spelling and grammar check on your document. (The spell checker will not stop at the words you added to your custom dictionary.)
5. Save and then print **C05-E03-NanoTech.docx**.
6. Change the default dictionary and then remove your custom dictionary by completing the following steps:
   a. Click the File tab and then click the Options button.
   b. At the Word Options dialog box, click *Proofing* in the left panel.
   c. Click the Custom Dictionaries button.
   d. At the Custom Dictionaries dialog box, click CUSTOM.DIC in the *Dictionary List* box.

e. Click the Change Default button. (This changes the default back to the CUSTOM. DIC dictionary.)
f. Click your dictionary name in the *Dictionary List* box.
g. Click the Remove button.
h. Click OK to close the Custom Dictionaries dialog box.
i. Click OK to close the Word Options dialog box.

Displaying Word Count

The Status bar displays the total number of words in your document. If you want to display more information, such as the number of pages, paragraphs, and lines, display the Word Count dialog box, shown in Figure 5.6. Display this dialog box by clicking the word count section of the Status bar or by clicking the Review tab and then clicking the Word Count button in the Proofing group. If you want to count the words in a portion of the document only, select the text first.

Figure 5.6 Word Count Dialog Box

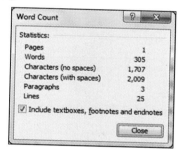

Using the Thesaurus

With the Thesaurus feature in Word you can find synonyms, antonyms, and related words for a particular word. Synonyms are words that have the same or nearly the same meaning; antonyms are words that have opposite meanings. Word may display antonyms as well as synonyms for some words. With Thesaurus, you can improve the clarity of business documents.

To use Thesaurus, click the Review tab and then click the Thesaurus button in the Proofing group. (You can also use the keyboard shortcut Shift +F7.) This displays the Research task pane. Click in the *Search for* text box located toward the top of the Research task pane, type the word for which you want to find synonyms or antonyms, and then press the Enter key or click the Start searching button (the button marked with a white arrow on a green background). A list of synonyms and antonyms displays in the task pane list box. Figure 5.7 shows the Research task pane with synonyms for the word *twist* displayed.

Figure 5.7 Research Task Pane

Type a word in this text box and press Enter. Synonyms and antonyms for the word display in the list box below.

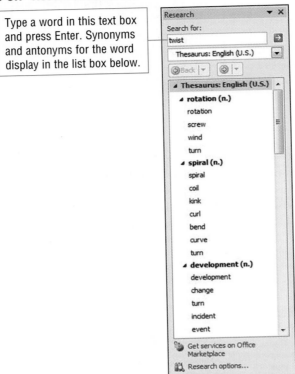

Depending on the word you are looking up, the words that display in the Research task pane list box may be followed by *(n.)* for *noun*, *(adj.)* for *adjective*, or *(adv.)* for *adverb*. When antonyms display, they are at the end of the list of related synonyms and they are followed by the word *(Antonym)*.

Thesaurus provides synonyms for the selected word along with a list of related synonyms. For example, the task pane list box shown in Figure 5.7 displays several main synonyms for *twist,* and each is preceded by a triangle symbol. The triangle symbol indicates that the list of related synonyms is expanded. Click the triangle symbol again and the list of related synonyms collapses.

As you look up synonyms and antonyms for various words, you can display the list for previous words by clicking the Previous search button (contains a left arrow and the word *Back*) located above the Research task pane list box (see Figure 5.7). Click the Next search button to display the next search in the sequence. You can also click the down-pointing arrow at the right side of the Next search button to display a list of words for which you have looked up synonyms and antonyms.

1. With **C05-E03-NanoTech.docx** open, click the word count section of the Status bar.

Step 1

2. After reading the statistics in the Word Count dialog box, click the Close button.
3. Redisplay the Word Count dialog box by clicking the Review tab and then clicking the Word Count button in the Proofing group.

Step 3

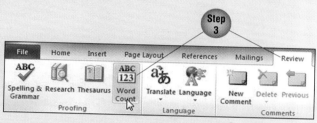

4. Click the Close button to close the Word Count dialog box.
5. Change the word *twist* in the first paragraph to *interweave* using Thesaurus by completing the following steps:
    a. Select the word *twist* located in the last sentence of the first paragraph.
    b. Click the Review tab.
    c. Click the Thesaurus button in the Proofing group.
    d. At the Research task pane, scroll down the list box to display the synonyms below *wind*, hover the mouse pointer over the synonym *interweave*, click the down-pointing arrow that displays at the right of the word, and then click *Insert* at the drop-down list.

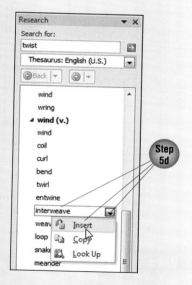

Step 5d

6. Find synonyms for the word *fashion* by completing the following steps:
    a. Click on any character in the word *fashion* located in the last sentence in the first paragraph.
    b. Click the Thesaurus button in the Proofing group in the Review tab.
    c. Hover the mouse pointer over the synonym *mold* in the Research task pane list box, click the down-pointing arrow at the right of the word, and then click *Insert* at the drop-down list.
7. Complete steps similar to those in Step 6 to change *perform* in the second sentence of the second paragraph to *execute*.
8. Close the Research task pane by clicking the Close button located in the upper right corner of the task pane.
9. Save **C05-E03-NanoTech.docx**.

Another method for displaying synonyms for a word is to use a shortcut menu. To do this, position the mouse pointer on the word and then click the *right* mouse button. At the shortcut menu that displays, point to Synonyms and then click the desired synonym at the side menu. Click the Thesaurus option located toward the bottom of the side menu to display synonyms and antonyms for the word in the Research task pane.

Exercise 5.3C **Replacing Synonyms Using a Shortcut Menu** **Part 3 of 3**

1. With **C05-E03-NanoTech.docx** open, position the mouse pointer on the word *thrilling* located in the second sentence from the end of the document.
2. Click the *right* mouse button.
3. At the shortcut menu that displays, point to Synonyms and then click *exciting* at the side menu.

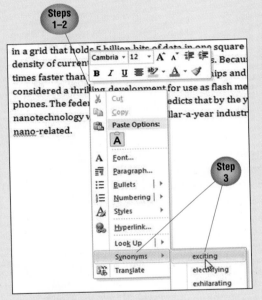

4. Change the word *a* that displays before *exciting* to *an*.
5. Save, print, and then close **C05-E03-NanoTech.docx**.

QUICK STEPS

Request Information from Online Sources
1. Click Review tab.
2. Click Research button.
3. Type word or topic.
4. Specify resources.
5. Click Start searching button.

Researching Information

Along with Thesaurus, the Research task pane offers options that you can use to search for and request specific information from online sources. The online resources available to you depend on the locale to which your system is set, authorization information indicating that you are allowed to download the information, and your Internet service provider.

Display the Research task pane by clicking the Review tab and then clicking the Research button in the Proofing group. You can also display the Research task pane by holding down the Alt key and then clicking anywhere in the open document. Determine which resources are available by clicking the down-pointing arrow at the right of the resources option box (the option box located below the *Search for* text box). The drop-down list includes reference books, research sites, business and financial sites, and other services. If you want to use a specific reference in your search, click it at the drop-down list, type the desired word or topic in the *Search for* text box, and then press the Enter key. Items matching your word or topic display in the task pane list box. Depending on the item, the list box may contain hyperlinks you can click to access additional information on the Internet.

You can control the available research options by clicking the <u>Research options</u> hyperlink located at the bottom of the Research task pane. Clicking this link displays the Research Options dialog box where you can insert a check mark before those items you want available and remove the check mark from those items you do not want available.

Research

Exercise 5.4 Researching Information
Part 1 of 1

Note: Your computer must be connected to the Internet to complete this exercise.

1. At a blank document, display the Research task pane by clicking the Review tab and then clicking the Research button in the Proofing group.
2. Search for information in a dictionary on the term *avatar* by completing the following steps:
   a. Click in the *Search for* text box or select any text that displays in the text box and then type avatar.
   b. Click the down-pointing arrow to the right of the resources option box (the down-pointing arrow located immediately below the Start searching button).
   c. At the drop-down list of resources, click *Encarta Dictionary: English (North America)*. If this reference is not available, click any other dictionary available to you.

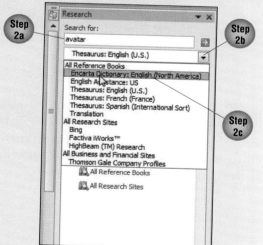

   d. Read the dictionary definitions for avatar.
3. Search for information on the term *avatar* in an encyclopedia by completing the following steps:
   a. Make sure *avatar* displays in the *Search for* text box.

b. Click the down-pointing arrow at the right of the resources option box and then click *Bing* in the *All Research Sites* section of the list box.

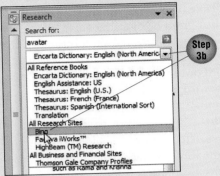

c. Look at the information that displays in the task pane list box and then click the hyperlink for Wikipedia.
d. After reading the information that displays in your Web browser, close the browser window.

4. Search for information on the term *netiquette* in an encyclopedia by completing the following steps:
   a. Select *avatar* that displays in the *Search for* text box and then type **netiquette**.
   b. Click the Start searching button that displays at the right side of the *Search for* text box.

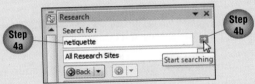

c. Look at the information that displays in the task pane list box and then click the hyperlink for Wikipedia.
d. After reading the information that displays in your Web browser, close the browser window.

5. At the blank Word document, close the Research task pane by clicking the Close button that displays in the upper right corner of the task pane.

Translating Text

Word provides features you can use to translate text from one language into another. You can translate words at the Research task pane or with options from the Translate button in the language group in the Review tab.

Translating Text at the Research Task Pane

To translate a word using the Research task pane, type the word in the *Search for* text box, click the down-pointing arrow at the right of the resources option box, and then click *Translation* at the drop-down list. In the *Translation* list box, specify the languages you are translating to and from.

Translate Text
1. Click Review tab.
2. Click Research button.
3. Type word in *Search for* text box.
4. Click down-pointing arrow at right of resources option box.
5. Click *Translation*.
6. If necessary, specify *From* language and *To* language.

Exercise 5.5A Translating Words   Part 1 of 2

1. At a blank document, click the Review tab and then click the Research button in the Proofing group.
2. Click in the *Search for* text box (or select any text that appears in the text box) and then type document.
3. Click the down-pointing arrow at the right of the resources option box and then click *Translation* at the drop-down list.
4. Make sure that *English (U.S.)* displays in the *From* option box. (If it does not, click the down-pointing arrow at the right of the *From* option and then click *English (U.S.)* at the drop-down list.)
5. Click the down-pointing arrow at the right of the *To* option and then click *Spanish (International Sort)* at the drop-down list.
6. Read the Spanish translation of *document* in the Research task pane.
7. Click the down-pointing arrow at the right of the *To* option and then click *French (France)* at the drop-down list.
8. Read the French translation of *document* in the Research task pane.
9. Close the Research task pane.

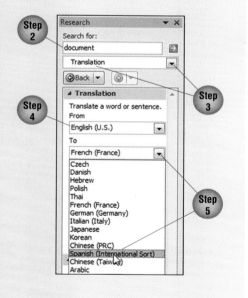

Translating Text with the Translate Button

QUICK STEPS

Translate Entire Document
1. Open document.
2. Click Review tab.
3. Click Translate button.
4. Click *Translate Document* at drop-down list.
5. At message, click Send button.

Translate Selected Text
1. Select text.
2. Click Review tab.
3. Click Translate button.
4. Click *Translate Selected Text*.

Turn on Mini Translator
1. Click Review tab.
2. Click Translate button.
3. Click *Mini Translator*.

In addition to the Research task pane, you can use the Translate button in the Language group in the Review tab to translate text. The Translate button contains options for translating with a mini translator as well as accessing online the Microsoft® Translator. Click the Translate button and a drop-down list displays with four options. Click the top option, *Translate Document,* and Word will send your document for translation by Microsoft® Translator. When you click the option, a message displays telling you that Word is about to send your document for translation in unencrypted HTML format and asking if you want to continue. To continue to the translator, click the Send button. With the second option, *Translate Selected Text*, Microsoft® Translator will translate the selected text in a document and insert the translation in the Research task pane.

Click the third option *Mini Translator*, to turn this feature on. With the mini translator turned on, point to a word or select a phrase in your document and the translation of the text displays in a box above the text. To turn off the mini translator, click the Translate button in the Language group in the Review tab and then click the *Mini Translator* option. If the mini translator is turned on, the icon that displays to the left of the *Mini Translator* option displays with an orange background.

Use the fourth option from the Translate button, *Choose Translation Language*, to specify the language from which you want to translate and the language to which you want to translate. When you click the option, the Translation Language Options dialog box displays as shown in Figure 5.8. At this dialog box, specify the translation language and whether you want to translate the entire document or turn on the mini translator.

Translate

Figure 5.8 Translation Language Options Dialog Box

Use this option to choose the translation language for the Mini Translator.

Choose translation languages with these options.

Note: Check with your instructor before completing this exercise.

1. Open **ResumeStyles.docx** and then save the document and name it **C05-E05-ResumeStyles**.
2. Change the translation language to Spanish by completing the following steps:
   a. Click the Review tab.
   b. Click the Translate button in the Language group and then click the *Choose Translation Language* option at the drop-down list.

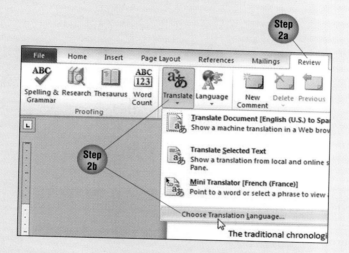

   c. At the Translation Language Options dialog box, make sure that *English (U.S.)* displays in the *Translate from* option box.
   d. Click the down-pointing arrow at the right of the *Translate to* option box in the *Choose document translation languages* section and then click *Spanish (International Sort)* at the drop-down list. (Skip this step if *Spanish (International Sort)* is already selected.)

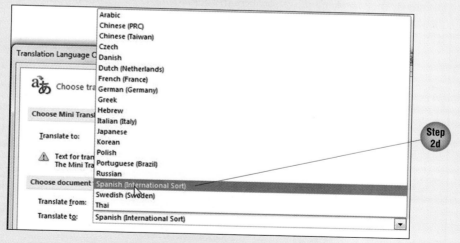

   e. Click OK to close the dialog box.

3. Translate the entire document to Spanish by completing the following steps:
   a. Click the Translate button and then click the *Translate Document [English (U.S.) to Spanish (International Sort)]* option.

Step
3a

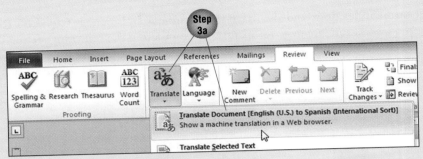

   b. At the message telling you that Word is about to send the document for translation over the Internet in unencrypted HTML format, click the Send button.
   c. In a few moments the Microsoft® Translator window will open. (If the window does not display, check the Status bar and click the button on the bar representing the translator.)
   d. Select the translated text.
   e. Press Ctrl + C to copy the text.
   f. Close the Microsoft® Translator window.
   g. At the **C05-E05-ResumeStyles.docx** document, press Ctrl + End to move the insertion point to the end of the document and then press Ctrl + V to insert the copied text.
4. Save, print, and then close **C05-E05-ResumeStyles.docx**.
5. Open **TranslateTerms.docx** and then save the document and name it **C05-E05-TranslateTerms**.
6. Translate the word *Central* into Spanish by completing the following steps:
   a. Click the Review tab.
   b. Click the Translate button and then click the *Choose Translation Language* option at the drop-down list.
   c. At the Translation Language Options dialog box, click the down-pointing arrow at the right of the *Translate to* option box in the *Choose Mini Translator Language* section and then click *Spanish (International Sort)* at the drop-down list. Skip this step if Spanish International Sort is already selected.
   d. Click OK to close the dialog box.
   e. Click the Translate button and then click *Mini Translator [Spanish (International Sort)]* at the drop-down list. (This turns on the mini translator.)

Step
6e

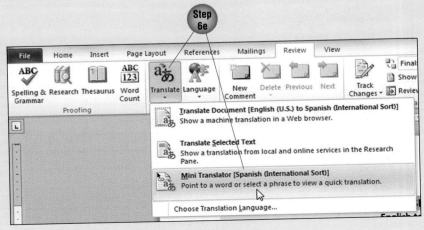

f. Hover the mouse over the word *Central* in the table. Look at the translation that displays in the box above the word. Type one of the Spanish terms in the Spanish column.

g. Complete steps similar to those in Step 6f to display Spanish translations for the remaining terms. For each term, type one of the Spanish terms in the appropriate location in the table. Type the terms without any accents or special symbols.

7. Use the mini translator to translate terms into French by completing the following steps:

a. Click the Translate button and then click the *Choose Translation Language* option at the drop-down list.

b. At the Translation Language Options dialog box, click the down-pointing arrow at the right of the *Translate to* option box and then click *French (France)* at the drop-down list.

c. Click OK to close the dialog box.

d. With the mini translator turned on, hover the mouse over the word *Central* in the table (the mini translator displays dimmed above the word).

e. Move the mouse pointer to the mini translator and then choose one of the French terms and type it in the French column.

f. Complete steps similar to those in Steps 7d and 7e to display French translations for the remaining terms. Type one of the French terms in the appropriate locations in the table and type the terms without any accents or special symbols.

8. Turn off the mini translator by clicking the Translate button and then clicking *Mini Translator [French (France)]* at the drop-down list.

9. Save, print, and then close **C05-E05-TranslateTerms.docx**.

Chapter Summary

- The spell checker matches the words in your document with the words in its dictionary. If a match is not found, the word is selected and possible corrections are suggested.

- When checking the spelling or grammar in a document, you can temporarily leave the Spelling and Grammar dialog box, make corrections in the document, and then resume checking.

- Customize spell checking options at the Word Options dialog box with *Proofing* selected in the left panel.

- With the grammar checker, you can search a document for correct grammar, style, punctuation, and word usage.

- When the grammar checker detects a grammar error, you can display information about the error by clicking the Explain button at the Spelling and Grammar dialog box.

- Customize grammar checking with options in the *When correcting spelling and grammar in Word* section of the Word Options dialog box with *Proofing* selected.

- Turn on the *Use contextual spelling* option if you want Word to insert a wavy blue line below words that sound similar to other words. During a spelling and grammar check, Word will stop at a word with a wavy blue line and offer alternate words.

- To display readability statistics on a document, insert a check mark in the *Show readability statistics* check box in the Word Options dialog box with *Proofing* selected and then complete a spelling and grammar check.

- Word uses the CUSTOM.DIC custom dictionary when spell checking a document. Add your own custom dictionary at the Custom Dictionaries dialog box. Display this dialog box by clicking the Custom Dictionaries button at the Word Options dialog box with *Proofing* selected.

- The Word Count dialog box displays the number of pages, words, characters, paragraphs, and lines in a document. Display this dialog box by clicking the word count section of the Status bar or clicking the Word Count button in the Proofing group in the Review tab.

- Use Thesaurus to find synonyms and antonyms for words in your document. Display synonyms and antonyms at the Research task pane or by right-clicking a word and then pointing to Synonyms at the shortcut menu.

- Use options at the Research task pane to search for specific information from online sources.

- Use the Translate button in the Language group in the Review tab to translate a document, selected text, or a word from one language to another.

Commands *Review*

FEATURE	RIBBON TAB, GROUP	BUTTON	KEYBOARD SHORTCUT
Spelling and Grammar dialog box	Review, Proofing	ABC✓	F7
Word Options dialog box	File, Options		
Word Count dialog box	Review, Proofing	ABC 123	
Research task pane	Review, Proofing		
Research task pane for synonyms and antonyms	Review, Proofing		Shift + F7
Translate text in document	Review, Language	aあ, Translate Document	
Translate selected text	Review, Language	aあ, Translate Selected Text	
Translation Language Options dialog box	Review, Language	aあ, Choose Translation Language	
Mini Translator	Review, Language	aあ, Mini Translator	

Key Points *Review*

Completion: In the space provided at the right, indicate the correct term, symbol, or command.

1. Click this tab to display the Proofing group.

2. Click this button in the Spelling and Grammar dialog box to replace the selected word with the word in the *Suggestions* list box.

3. Click this button in the Spelling and Grammar dialog box to display the Word Help window with information about the selected text.

4. During spelling check of a document, click this button to skip the occurrence of the word and all other occurrences of the word in the document.

5. This is the keyboard shortcut to display the Spelling and Grammar dialog box.

6. To display options for customizing spelling and grammar checking, click the File tab, click the Options button located below the Help tab, and then click this option in the left panel.

7. Consider making this option active in the Word Options dialog box when correcting a document that contains words that sound similar but have different meanings.

8. This is the default setting for the *Writing Style* option at the Word Options dialog box with *Proofing* selected. _____

9. This readability score is based on the average number of syllables per word and average number of words per sentence. _____

10. When completing a spelling check on a document, Word uses this custom dictionary by default. _____

11. The Research task pane displays when you click the Research button or this button. _____

12. Click the Translate button and then click the Translate Document option and this online service translates the text in the document. _____

13. Turn this feature on to point to a word or selected text and view a quick translation. _____

Chapter *Assessments*

Applying Your Skills

Demonstrate your knowledge of features learned in this chapter by completing the following assessments.

Assessment 5.1 Complete a Spelling and Grammar Check and Format a Style Document on Numbers

1. Open **Numbers.docx** and save the document with the name **C05-A01-Numbers**.
2. Complete a spelling and grammar check on the document.
3. Apply the Heading 1 style to the title *NUMBERS* and apply the Heading 2 style to the two headings *Time Expressions* and *Dates*.
4. Change the style set to *Formal*.
5. Select the indented text in the *Time Expressions* section and then apply bullets.
6. Select the indented text in the *Dates* section and then apply bullets.
7. Save, print, and then close **C05-A01-Numbers.docx**.

Assessment 5.2 Complete a Spelling and Grammar Check and Proofread a Document

1. Open **PrepareResume.docx** and save the document with the name **C05-A02-PrepareResume**.
2. Sort the numbered paragraphs in ascending order (lowest number to highest number).
3. Complete a spelling and grammar check on the document.
4. Proofread the document and make necessary changes. (The document contains mistakes that the spelling and grammar checker will not find.)
5. Apply the Heading 1 style to the title and apply the Heading 2 style to the two headings in the document.
6. Change the style set to *Perspective*.
7. Apply the *Hardcover* theme and change the theme colors to Clarity.
8. Apply the *Brown, Accent 2, Lighter 80%* shading (located in the sixth column in the drop-down color palette) to the two headings in the document.
9. Center the title PREPARING A RESUME.
10. Save, print, and then close **C05-A02-PrepareResume.docx**.

Assessment 5.3 Complete a Spelling, Grammar, and Style Check on a Document Using Contextual Spelling

1. Open **CyberScenario.docx** and save the document with the name **C05-A03-CyberScenario**.
2. Display the Word Options dialog box with *Proofing* selected, insert a check mark in the *Use contextual spelling* check box, change the *Writing Style* option to *Grammar & Style*, and then close the dialog box.
3. Complete a spelling and grammar check on the document.
4. Proofread the document and make necessary changes.
5. Apply formatting to enhance the visual appeal of the document.
6. Display the Word Options dialog box with *Proofing* selected, remove the check mark from the *Use contextual spelling* check box, change the *Writing Style* option to *Grammar Only*, and then close the dialog box.
7. Save, print, and then close **C05-A03-CyberScenario.docx**.

Assessment 5.4 Create and Format a Document Featuring Translated Terms

1. At a blank document, use the translation feature to find the Spanish and French translations for the following terms:
   Memory
   Logic
   Navigate
   Register
   System
   Utility
   Voice
2. Type the English words followed by the Spanish and French translations. Set the text in columns and then apply formatting to enhance the visual appeal of the document.
3. Save the document with the name **C05-A04-Translations**.
4. Print and then close **C05-A04-Translations.docx**.

Expanding Your Skills

Explore additional feature options or use Help to learn a new skill in creating this document.

Assessment 5.5 Write and Translate Steps for Customizing the Grammar Check

1. At a blank document, display the Word Options dialog box with *Proofing* selected in the left panel and then experiment with the options in each section.
2. Write a paragraph of text that briefly describes the options in the Word Options dialog box with *Proofing* selected.
3. Create an appropriate title for the document.
4. Translate the entire document into a language other than French or Spanish. ***Hint: Make sure you change the translation language at the Translation Language Options dialog box and then use the Translate Document option from the Translate button drop-down list.***
5. Copy the translated text from the website to your document.
6. Save the document and name it **C05-A05-OptionsTranslate**.
7. Print and then close **C05-A05-OptionsTranslate.docx**.

Achieving Signature Status

Take your skills to the next level by completing these more challenging assessments.

Assessment 5.6　Format a Document on Resume Writing

1. Open the document named **WriteResume.docx** and then save the document and name it **C05-A06-WriteResume**.
2. Complete a spelling and grammar check and apply character and paragraph formatting so your document appears as shown in Figure 5.9. (The text is set in the Cambria font.)
3. Proofread the document and make any additional edits so that your document contains the same text as the document in Figure 5.9.
4. Save, print, and then close **C05-A06-WriteResume.docx**.

Figure 5.9 Assessment 5.6

WRITING YOUR RESUME

Contact Information

Before getting into the major sections of the resume, let's briefly address the very top section: your name and contact information.

Name

You would think that writing your name would be the easiest part of writing your resume but you should consider the following factors:

- Although most people choose to use their full, formal name at the top of a resume, using the name by which you prefer to be called is becoming more acceptable.

- Keep in mind that it is to your advantage that readers feel comfortable when calling you for an interview. Their comfort level may decrease if your name is gender-neutral, difficult to pronounce, or very unusual; they don't know how to ask for you. You can make it easier for them by following these examples:

> Lynn T. Cowles (Mr.)
>
> (Ms.) Michael Murray
>
> Tzirina (Irene) Kahn
>
> Ndege "Nick" Vernon

Address

You should always include your home address on your resume. If you use a post office box for mail, include both your mailing address and your physical residence address. An exception to this is when you are posting your resume on the Internet. For security purposes, include just your phone and email contact as well as possibly your city and state with no street address.

Telephone Number(s)

Your home telephone number must be included so that people can pick up the phone and call you immediately. In addition, you can also include a cell phone number.

Email Address

Without question, if you have an email address, include it on your resume. Email is now often the preferred method of communication while job searching, particularly in the early stages of each contact. If you do not have an email account, you can obtain a free, accessible-anywhere address from a provider such as www.yahoo.com, www.microsoft.com, or www.gmail.com.

Assessment 5.7   Type a Business Letter

1. Open **NSSLtrhd.docx** and then save the document and name it **C05-A07-MtgLtr**.
2. Type the text in the document shown in Figure 5.10 with the following specifications:
    *   Insert the bullet before the bulleted paragraphs of text as shown in the figure.
    *   Change the alignment to justify for the body of the letter.
    *   Insert your initials instead of the *XX* located toward the end of the letter.
3. Check the spelling and grammar in the document.
4. Save, print, and then close **C05-A07-MtgLtr.docx**.

Figure 5.10 Assessment 5.7

January 11, 2012

Dr. Gene Krezel
2310 North 122nd Street
Peoria, IL 61612

Dear Dr. Krezel:

RE: Shareholder's Annual General Meeting

You are cordially invited to attend the 2012 annual general meeting of shareholders of Northland Security Systems. The meeting will be held at the Evergreen Auditorium at the principal executive offices of Northland Security Systems. During the meeting, the Board will ask for your vote on the following issues:

*   The election of four directors.
*   The approval of an amendment to the company's long-term incentive plan to reduce the number of shares authorized for issuance under the plan.
*   The ratification of the appointment by the audit committee of the company's independent auditor.
*   The transaction of such other business as may be properly brought before the meeting or any adjournment or postponement of the meeting.

As an owner of shares, you can vote one of four ways. You can vote by attending the annual general meeting, by registering your vote at the company's website, by calling the company's toll-free telephone number and registering your vote, or by mailing your official ballot. If you need assistance or further information, please contact one of our support representatives available at our company website or by calling our support line.

Sincerely,

Faith Isenberg
Chief Executive Officer

XX
C05-A07-MtgLtr.docx

Performance Assessments

U N I T 1

Preparing Documents

ASSESSING PROFICIENCIES

In this unit, you have learned to create, edit, save, and print Word documents; use writing tools such as the spelling checker, grammar checker, and Thesaurus; and format characters and paragraphs.

Note: Before beginning computer assessments, copy to your storage medium the Unit01PA folder from the CD that accompanies this textbook and then make Unit01PA the active folder.

Assessment U1.1   Format an Online Shopping Document

1. Open **ShopOnline.docx** and save the document with the name **U1-PA01-ShopOnline**.
2. Select the entire document and then change the font to 12-point Cambria.
3. Apply 14-point Calibri bold formatting to the two titles (*ONLINE SHOPPING* and *REFERENCES*) and the three headings (*Advantages of Online Shopping*, *Online Shopping Venues*, and *Online Shopping Safety Tips*).
4. Center the titles *ONLINE SHOPPING* and *REFERENCES*.
5. Select the second through the fifth paragraphs in the *Advantages of Online Shopping* section and then apply bullet formatting.
6. Select the first sentence of each of the bulleted paragraphs and apply bold formatting.
7. Select and then sort in ascending order the numbered paragraphs in the *Online Shopping Safety Tips* section.
8. Apply a hanging indent to the paragraphs of text below the *REFERENCES* title.
9. Apply *Aqua, Accent 5, Lighter 60%* paragraph shading and a bottom border line to the two titles.
10. Apply *Aqua, Accent 5, Lighter 80%* paragraph shading and a bottom border line to the three headings in the document.
11. Move the insertion point to the REFERENCES title and then add 18 points of spacing before the title.
12. Save, print, and then close **U1-PA01-ShopOnline.docx**.

Assessment U1.2   Format a Corporate Report

1. Open **ComReport.docx** and save the document with the name **U1-PA02-ComReport**.
2. Make the following changes to the document:
   a. Change the bullets in the *Compensation Philosophy* section to custom bullets of your choosing.
   b. Apply the Heading 1 style to the title *Compensation Committee Report*.
   c. Select the heading *Compensation Philosophy* and then apply the Emphasis style. Select the heading *Competitive Compensation* and then apply the Emphasis style.
   d. Change the style set to Thatch.
   e. Apply the Paper theme.

f. Apply the Equity theme colors.

g. Center the title.

3. Save, print, and then close **U1-PA02-ComReport.docx**.

Assessment U1.3   Create, Format, and Copy a Training Announcement

1. At a blank document, click the No Spacing style in the Styles group in the Home tab, press the Enter key, and then type the text shown in Figure U1.1 with the following specifications:

   a. Center and right-align text as indicated.

   b. After typing the text, press the Enter key four times.

   c. Set the centered text in 16-point Candara and change the font color to dark blue.

   d. Set the right-aligned text in 10-point Candara and change the font color to dark blue.

   e. Select from the blank line at the beginning of the document through one blank line below the right-aligned text, apply a thick-thin paragraph border and change the border color to *Blue, Accent 1, Darker 25%*, and then apply the *Olive Green, Accent 3, Lighter 80%* shading.

   f. Copy the text (including the borders and shading) and paste it two times in the document. (The document should have a total of three announcements that fit on one page and are evenly distributed.)

2. Save the document and name it **U1-PA03-ManageData**.

3. Print and then close **U1-PA03-ManageData.docx**.

Figure U1.1 Assessment U1.3

> Managing Data
> Tuesday, March 6, 2012
> Corporate Headquarters
> Conference Room A
> 8:30 to 10:30 a.m.
>
> Training Department
> Technical Support Team

Assessment U1.4   Format a Software Document

1. Open **ProdSoftware.docx** and save the document with the name **U1-PA04-ProdSoftware**.

2. Select the entire document and then make the following changes:

   a. Change the spacing after paragraphs to zero points.

   b.   Change the line spacing to 1.5.

   c.   Change the font to 12-point Constantia.

3. Indent the paragraphs that begin with bold text 0.5 inch from the left and right margins.

4. Select the title and then change the font to 14-point Constantia bold.

5. Center the title and then apply *Olive Green, Accent 3, Lighter 60%* paragraph shading to the title.

6. Insert a double border line above the title and a single border line below the title.

7. Insert 6 points of spacing before the first paragraph of text below the title.

8. Save, print, and then close **U1-PA04-ProdSoftware.docx**.

Assessment U1.5 Format a Travel Document

1. Open **CedarMeadows.docx** and save the document with the name **U1-PA05-CedarMeadows**.

2. Move the insertion point to the end of the document and then type the text shown in Figure U1.2.

3. Select the entire document and then add 6 points of spacing after paragraphs.

4. Apply the Heading 1 style to the title.

5. Apply the Heading 2 style to the two headings *Fast Facts* and *Special Highlights*.

6. Change the style set to Traditional.

7. Apply the Solstice theme.

8. Select the paragraphs of text in the *Fast Facts* section and then apply paragraph numbering.

9. Insert the following paragraph between paragraphs 3 and 4: Ski School: The Cedar Meadows Ski School employs over 225 certified ski instructors and offers a variety of programs.

10. Bold the words (and the colon) that begin the six numbered paragraphs.

11. Save, print, and then close **U1-PA05-CedarMeadows.docx**.

Figure U1.2 Assessment U1.5

Special Highlights
- 4,800 acres
- 79 trails
- 25 lifts
- Largest bi-state ski resort
- 3,500-foot vertical drop and 5.5-mile mountain descent
- 250 inches annual snowfall

Assessment U1.6 Set Tabs and Create a Training Costs Document

START From Scratch

1. At a blank document, create the document shown in Figure U1.3. Set a left tab for the text in the first column and set right tabs for the text in the second and third columns.

2. After typing the text, make the following changes:

   a.   Select the title and subtitle and change the font size to 14 points.

   b.   Apply *Purple, Accent 4, Lighter 60%* paragraph shading to the title.

   c.   Apply *Purple, Accent 4, Lighter 80%* paragraph shading to the subtitle.

    d. Move the insertion point to the end of the document on the line below the text and then apply the *Purple, Accent 4, Lighter 80%* paragraph shading.

3. Save the document with the name **U1-PA06-TrainCosts**.
4. Print and then close **U1-PA06-TrainCosts.docx**.

Figure U1.3 Assessment U1.6

SMITH-ALLEN ENTERPRISES

Training Costs

Human Resources	$20,250	$23,500
Production	21,230	18,075
Ancillary Services	1,950	3,400
Sales and Marketing	10,375	9,500
Finances	15,300	17,200

START From Scratch

Assessment U1.7 Set Tabs and Create a Vacation Packages Document

1. At a blank document, create the document shown in Figure U1.4. Set a left tab for the text in the first column and set a right tab with leaders for the text in the second column.
2. After typing the text, make the following changes:
    a. Apply the Heading 1 style to the title *Rates and Packages*.
    b. Apply the Heading 2 style to the headings *Value Season*, *Peak Season*, and *Holiday Season*.
    c. Change the style set to Traditional.
    d. Change the theme fonts to Aspect. (Change the theme *fonts*, not the theme.)
    e. Center the title, *Rates and Packages*, insert a top single-line border, apply *Blue, Accent 1, Lighter 80%* paragraph shading, and change the spacing from the title text to the top paragraph border to *3 pt* and change the spacing from the title text to the bottom paragraph border to *4 pt*.
       Hint: Do this at the Border and Shading Options dialog box.
    f. Change the paragraph spacing after the three headings in the document to 12 points.
3. Save the document with the name **U1-PA07-Rates**.
4. Print and then close **U1-PA07-Rates.docx**.

Rates and Packages

Value Season

Hotel Room. . . . . $90 to $115

One-Bedroom Suite . . . . $115 to $140

Two-Bedroom Suite . . . . $145 to $170

Peak Season

Hotel Room. . . . . $100 to $130

One-Bedroom Suite . . . . $130 to $160

Two-Bedroom Suite . . . . $165 to $195

Holiday Season

Hotel Room. . . . . $140 to $150

One-Bedroom Suite . . . . $160 to $175

Two-Bedroom Suite . . . . $180 to $200

Assessment U1.8 Customize Grammar Checking and Check Spelling and Grammar in a Document

1. Open **Activities.docx** and save the document with the name **U1-PA08-Activities**.
2. Display the Word Options dialog box with *Proofing* selected, insert a check mark in the *Use contextual spelling* check box, change the *Writing Style* option to *Grammar & Style*, and then close the dialog box.
3. Complete a spelling and grammar check on the document.
4. Proofread the document and make any necessary changes.
5. Apply formatting to enhance the visual appeal of the document.
6. Display the Word Options dialog box with *Proofing* selected, remove the check mark from the *Use contextual spelling* check box, change the *Writing Style* option to *Grammar Only*, and then close the dialog box.
7. Save, print, and then close **U1-PA08-Activities.docx**.

Assessment U1.9   Format Resume Formats

1. At a blank document, create the document shown in Figure U1.5. Apply character and paragraph formatting so the document appears as shown in the figure.
2. Save the completed document and name it **U1-PA09-ResumeFormat**.
3. Print and then close **U1-PA09-ResumeFormat.docx**.

Figure U1.5 Assessment U1.9

Executive Education Format

EDUCATION

Executive Leadership Program... STANFORD UNIVERSITY
Executive Development Program .... NORTHWESTERN UNIVERSITY
Master of Business Administration degree... HARVARD UNIVERSITY
Bachelor of Science degree..UNIVERSITY OF PENNSYLVANIA

Certification Format

TECHNICAL CERTIFICATIONS & DEGREES

Registered Nurse, University of Maryland, 2008
Certified Nursing Assistant, University of Maryland, 2006
Certified Nursing Aide, State of Maryland, 2002
Bachelor of Science in Nursing (BSN), University of Maryland, 2008

Assessment U1.10 Format a Job Announcement

1. Open the document named **JobAnnounce.docx** and then save the document and name it **U1-PA10-JobAnnounce**. (The medical center letterhead appears in a header.)
2. Apply formatting so the document appears as shown in Figure U1.6. *Hint: Change the spacing from the text in the title JOB ANNOUNCEMENT to the top and bottom paragraph borders to 4 pt with measurements at the Border and Shading Options dialog box.*
3. Save, print, and then close **U1-PA10-JobAnnounce.docx**.

Figure U1.6 Assessment U1.10

Green Lake Medical Center
100 Ninth Avenue Southeast
Newark, NJ 07102
(201) 555-1000

JOB ANNOUNCEMENT

JOB TITLE.. Medical Office Assistant
STATUS ....Full-time employment
SALARY ....Depending on experience
CLOSING DATE .... February 1, 2012

JOB SUMMARY

- Register new patients; assist with form completion
- Retrieve charts
- Enter patient data into computer database
- Maintain and file medical records
- Schedule patients
- Call patients with appointment reminders
- Answer telephones and route messages
- Call and/or fax pharmacy for prescription order refills
- Mail lab test results to patients
- Perform other clerical duties as required

REQUIRED SKILLS

- Keyboarding (35+ wpm)
- Knowledge of Microsoft Word, Excel, and PowerPoint
- Thorough understanding of medical terms
- Excellent grammar and spelling skills
- Excellent customer service skills

EDUCATION

- High school diploma
- Post-secondary training as a medical office assistant, CMA or RMA preferred
- CPR certification

For further information, contact Olivia Summers (201) 555-1057.

CREATING ORIGINAL DOCUMENTS

The activities in Assessments U1.11, U1.12, and U1.13 give you the opportunity to practice your writing skills as well as demonstrate your mastery of the important Word features presented in this unit. Use correct grammar, precise word choices, and clear sentence construction. Follow the steps below to improve your writing skills.

THE WRITING PROCESS

Plan: Gather ideas, select the information to include, and choose the order in which to present it.

> **Checkpoints**
> - What is the purpose?
> - What information do readers need to reach your intended conclusion?

Write: Keeping the reader in mind and following the information plan, draft the document using clear, direct sentences that say what you mean.

> **Checkpoints**
> - What are the subpoints for each main thought?
> - How can you connect paragraphs so the reader moves smoothly from one idea to the next?

Revise: Improve what you have written by changing, deleting, rearranging, or adding words, sentences, and paragraphs.

> **Checkpoints**
> - Is the meaning clear?
> - Do the ideas follow a logical order?
> - Have you included any unnecessary information?
> - Have you built your sentences around strong verbs and nouns?

Edit: Check spelling, sentence construction, word use, punctuation, and capitalization.

> **Checkpoints**
> - Can you spot any redundancies or clichés?
> - Can you reduce any phrases to an effective word (for example, change *the fact that* to *because*)?
> - Have you used commas only where there is a strong reason for doing so?
> - Did you proofread the document for errors that your spelling checker cannot identify?

Publish: Prepare a final copy that could be reproduced and shared with others.

> **Checkpoints**
> - Which design elements, for example, bolding and different fonts, would help highlight important ideas or sections?
> - Would charts or other graphics help clarify meaning?

Assessment U1.11   Create and Format an Announcement

Situation: You work in the public relations department at Coleman Development Corporation, and your supervisor has asked you to prepare an announcement about the appointment of the new corporate president using the following information:

- The Board of Trustees has appointed Stephanie Branson as president of Coleman Development Corporation.

- She has 25 years of experience in the land management field and has spent the past 11 years as president of Lancaster, Inc.

- The selection process began over six months ago and included several interviews with board members and visitations by board members to Lancaster. An open house is planned for Friday, August 10, 2012, from 1:30 to 5:00 p.m., in the corporation's conference room.

Include a title for the announcement. Save the announcement and name it **U1-PA11-Announce**. Print and then close **U1-PA11-Announce.docx**.

Assessment U1.12   Create and Format a Word Commands Document

Situation: You work in the training department at Crossroads Industries, and your supervisor has asked you to prepare a brief summary of some Word commands for use in Microsoft Word training classes. She has asked you to include the following information:

- A brief explanation of how to move the insertion point to a specific page.

- Keyboard commands to move the insertion point to the beginning and to the end of a line and to the beginning and end of a document.

- Commands to delete text from the insertion point to the beginning of a word and from the insertion point to the end of a word.

- Steps to select a word, a sentence, a paragraph, and an entire document using the mouse.

- Keyboard command to select the entire document.

Save the document with the name **U1-PA12-WordCommands**. Print and then close **U1-PA12-WordCommands.docx**.

Assessment U1.13   Prepare a Memo Illustrating Font Use

Situation: You work as the assistant to the public relations manager at your local chamber of commerce. The manager, Makenzie Keenan, wants to maintain a consistent style for articles published in the chamber's monthly newsletter. She wants you to explore the use of various handwriting, decorative, and plain fonts. She would like you to choose two handwriting fonts, two decorative fonts, and two plain fonts and then prepare a memo to her illustrating the use of each of these fonts. (Refer to Appendix C for information on formatting a memo.) When typing information about a font, set the text in the font you are describing. Save the completed memo and name it **U1-PA13-Fonts**. Print and then close **U1-PA13-Fonts.docx**.

Unit 2

Formatting and Managing Documents

Chapter 6   Formatting Pages

Chapter 7   Customizing Page Formatting

Chapter 8   Inserting Elements and Navigating in a Document

Chapter 9   Maintaining Documents

Chapter 10   Managing and Printing Documents

Unit 2   Performance Assessments

Chapter 6

 **TUTORIALS**

Formatting Pages

Performance Objectives

Upon successful completion of Chapter 6, you will be able to:

- Change document views
- Change margins, page orientation, and paper size in a document
- Format pages at the Page Setup dialog box
- Insert section breaks
- Create and format text in columns
- Hyphenate words automatically and manually
- Insert line numbers in a document
- Insert a watermark, page color, and page border

Tutorial 6.1
Organizing the Document View
Tutorial 6.2
Changing Page Setup
Tutorial 6.3
Modifying Page Orientation and
Changing Margins
Tutorial 6.4
Inserting Section Breaks
Tutorial 6.5
Applying Columns
Tutorial 6.6
Hyphenating Words
Tutorial 6.7
Adding Borders, Shading, and
Watermarks to Pages
Tutorial 6.8
Inserting Line Numbers

A Word document generally displays in Print Layout view. You can change this default view with buttons in the view area on the Status bar or with options in the View tab. A Word document also has default top, bottom, left, and right margins of 1 inch. You can change these default margins with the Margins button in the Page Setup group in the Page Layout tab or with options at the Page Setup dialog box. To apply formatting to a specific portion of a document, insert a continuous section break or a section break that begins a new page. Inserting a section break is useful when you want to arrange text in columns. With the hyphenation feature in Word, you can hyphenate words at the end of lines to create a less ragged right margin. You can also insert a variety of page formatting elements in your documents, including a watermark, page background color, and page borders.

Note: Before beginning computer exercises for this chapter, copy to your storage medium the Chapter06 folder from the CD that accompanies this textbook and then make Chapter06 the active folder.

In this chapter students will produce the following documents:

Exercise 6.1. C06-E01-Computers.docx
Exercise 6.2. C06-E02-BestFitResume.docx
Exercise 6.3. C06-E03-CompCommunications.docx
Exercise 6.4. C06-E04-CompSecurity.docx

Model answers for these exercises are shown on the following pages.

Exercise 6.1

C06-E01-Computers.docx

THE COMPUTER ADVANTAGE

Before the early 1980s, computers were unknown to the average person. Many people had never even seen a computer, let alone used one. The few computers that existed were relatively large, bulky devices confined to secure computer centers in corporate or government facilities. Referred to as mainframes, these computers were maintenance intensive, requiring special climate-controlled conditions and several full-time operators for each machine. Because early mainframes were expensive and difficult to operate, usage was restricted to computer programmers and scientists, who used them to perform complex operations, such as processing payrolls and designing sophisticated military weaponry.

Beginning in the early 1980s, the computer world changed dramatically with the introduction of microcomputers, also called personal computers (PCs). These relatively small computers were considerably more affordable and much easier to use than their mainframe ancestors. Within a few years, ownership of personal computers became widespread in the workplace, and today, the personal computer is a standard appliance in homes and schools.

Today's computers come in a variety of shapes and sizes and differ significantly in computing capability, price, and speed. Whatever their size, cost, or power, all computers offer advantages over manual technologies in the areas of speed, accuracy, versatility, storage capabilities, and communications capabilities.

Speed

Computers operate with lightening-like speed, and processing speeds are increasing as computer manufacturers introduce new and improved models. Contemporary personal computers are capable of executing billions of program instructions in one second. Some larger computers, such as supercomputers, can execute trillions of instructions per second, a rate important for processing huge amounts of data involved in forecasting weather, monitoring space shuttle flights, and managing other data-intensive applications.

Accuracy

People sometimes blame human errors on a computer. In truth, if a computer user enters correct data and uses accurate programs, computers are extremely accurate. A popular expression among computer professionals is "garbage in—garbage out" (GIGO), which means that if inaccurate programs and/or data are entered into a computer for processing, the resulting output will also be inaccurate. The computer user is responsible for entering data correctly and making certain that programs are correct.

Versatility

Computers are perhaps the most versatile of all machines or devices. They can perform a variety of personal, business, and scientific applications. Families use computers for entertainment, communications, budgeting, online shopping, completing homework assignments, playing games, and listening to music. Banks conduct money transfers, account withdrawals, and the payment of checks via computer. Retailers use computers to process sales transactions and to check on the availability of products. Manufacturers can manage their entire production, warehousing, and selling processes with computerized systems. Schools access computers for keeping records, conducting distance learning classes, scheduling events, and analyzing budgets. Universities, government agencies, hospitals, and scientific organizations conduct life-enhancing research using computers. Perhaps the most ambitious such computer-based scientific research of all time is the Human Genome Project. Completed in April of 2003, this program was more than two years ahead of schedule and at a cost considerably lower than originally forecast. This project represented an international effort to sequence three billion DNA (deoxyribonucleic acid) letters in the human genome, which is the collection of gene types that comprise every person. Scientists from all over the world can now access the genome database and use the information to research ways to improve human health and fight disease.

Storage

Storage is a defining computer characteristic and is one of the features that revolutionized early computing, for it made computers incredibly flexible. A computer is capable of accepting and storing programs and data. Once stored in the computer, a user can access a program again and again to process different data. [...] of data in comparably tiny physical spaces. For example, one compact disk [...] agazine text, and the capacities of internal storage devices are many times

[...] ntain special equipment and programs that allow them to communicate [...] hone lines, cable connections, and satellites. A structure in which

computers are linked together using special programs and equipment is a network. Newer communications technologies allow users to exchange information over wireless networks using wireless devices such as personal digital assistants (PDAs), notebook computers, cell phones, and pagers.

A network can be relatively small or quite large. A local area network (LAN) is one confined to a relatively small geographical area, such as a building, factory, or college campus. A wide area network (WAN) spans a large geographical area and might connect a company's manufacturing plants dispersed throughout North America. Constant, quick connections along with other computer technologies have helped boost productivity for manufacturers.

BEST FIT RESUME

The Right Fit

Recruitment consultants often talk about the job "fit." The way they see recruitment and the way many firms think about it is in terms of getting a good fit between the employer and the employee. Merely putting your life history on a resume is highly unlikely to demonstrate the best fit. This is why tailoring your resume to the particular position is so important.

Fit is all about matching a candidate to a particular job. The best candidate for the job will be the one that best matches all of the requirements of the job. Employers tend to think about fit in terms of four different qualities:

- **Knowledge:** The experience and qualifications you possess and the ability to demonstrate knowledge.
- **Skills:** The skills you have demonstrated (perhaps evidenced by your qualifications).
- **Abilities:** Potential to carry out a range of different tasks beyond your immediate skills or knowledge.
- **Attitudes:** The degree to which you are enthusiastic, flexible, and positive in approach.

Preparing the "Best Fit" Resume

To produce the best fitting resume, you need to know about yourself and about the job to which you are applying. Before you do anything else, ask yourself why you are preparing a resume. The answer to this question is going to vary from one person to the next. Here are nine reasons for writing a resume:

1. You have seen a job advertised in the paper that appeals to you.
2. You have seen a job on an Internet job site that appeals to you.
3. Your friends or family told you of a job opening at a local company.
4. You want to work for the local company and thought that sending a resume to the company might get their attention.
5. You have seen a job advertised internally at work.
6. You are going for a promotion.
7. You want to market yourself to win a contract or a proposal or be elected to a committee or organization.
8. You are about to be downsized and want to update your resume to be ready for any good opportunities.
9. You are feeling fed up and writing down all your achievements will cheer you up and might motivate you to look for a better job.

All of these certainly are good reasons to write a resume, but the resume serves many different purposes. One way of seeing the differences is to identify who is going to read the resume.

The Right Mix

In some situations you will have a good idea of what the employer is looking for because you have a job advertisement in front of you and can tailor you resume accordingly. For others, you have no idea what the employer might want to see. Updating your resume from time to time is a good idea so you do not forget important details. Note that the result of such a process will not be a winning resume but a useful list of tasks and achievements.

Exercise 6.2 C06-E02-BestFitResume.docx

COMPUTERS IN COMMUNICATIONS

Computers were originally stand-alone devices, incapable of communicating with other computers. This changed in the 1970s and 1980s when the development of special telecommunications hardware and software led to the creation of the first private networks, allowing connected computers to exchange data. Exchanged data took the form of requests for information, replies to requests for information, or instructions on how to run programs stored on the network.

The ability to link computers enables users to communicate and work together efficiently and effectively. Linked computers have become central to the communications industry. They play a vital role in telecommunications, publishing, and news services.

Telecommunications

The industry that provides for communication across distances is called telecommunications. The telephone industry uses computers to switch and route phone calls automatically over telephone lines. In addition to the spoken word, many other kinds of information move over such lines, including faxes and computer data. Data can be sent from computer to computer over telephone lines using a device known as a modem. One kind of data frequently sent by modem is electronic mail, or email, which can be sent from person to

person via the Internet or an online service. A more recent innovation in telecommunications is teleconferencing, which allows people in various locations to see and hear one another and thus hold virtual meetings.

Publishing

Just twenty years ago, book manuscripts were typeset mechanically on a typesetting machine and then reproduced on a printing press. Now anyone who has access to a computer and either a modem or a printer can undertake what has come to be known as electronic publishing. Writers and editors use word processing applications to produce text. Artists and designers use drawing and painting applications to created original graphics, or they use inexpensive scanners to digitize illustrations and photographs (turn them into computer-readable files). Typesetters use personal computers to combine text, illustrations, and photographs. Publishers typically send computer-generated files to printers for production of the film and plates from which books and magazines are printed.

News Services

News providers rely on reporters located worldwide. Reporters use email to send, or upload, their stories to wire services. Increasingly, individuals get daily news reports from online services. News can

also be accessed from specific providers, such as the *New York Times* or *USA Today*, via the Internet. One of the most popular Internet sites provides continuously updated weather reports.

Exercise 6.3 C06-E03-CompCommunications.docx

Page 1

Page 2

Exercise 6.4

C06-E04-CompSecurity.docx

SECTION 1: UNAUTHORIZED ACCESS

Like uncharted wilderness, the Internet lacks borders. This inherent openness is what makes the Internet so valuable and yet so vulnerable. Over its short life, the Internet has grown so quickly that the legal system has not been able to keep pace. The security risks posed by networks and the Internet can be grouped into three categories: unauthorized access, information theft, and denial of service.

Hackers, individuals who gain access to computers and networks illegally, are responsible for most cases of unauthorized access. Hackers tend to exploit sites and programs that have poor security measures in place. However, they also gain access to more challenging sites by using sophisticated programs and strategies. Many hackers claim they hack merely because they like the challenge of trying to defeat security measures. They rarely have a more malicious motive, and they generally do not aim to destroy or damage the sites that they invade. In fact, hackers dislike being identified with those who seek to cause damage. They refer to hackers with malicious or criminal intent as *crackers*.

USER IDS AND PASSWORDS

To gain entry over the Internet to a secure computer system, most hackers focus on finding a working user ID and password combination. User IDs are easy to come by and are generally not secure information. Sending an email, for example, displays the sender's user ID in the return address, making it very public. The only missing element is the password. Hackers know from experience which passwords are common; they have programs that generate thousands of likely passwords and they try them systematically over a period of hours or days.

SYSTEM BACKDOORS

Programmers can sometimes inadvertently aid hackers by providing unintentional entrance to networks and information systems. One such unintentional entrance is a system "backdoor," which is a user ID and password that provides the highest level of authorization. Programmers innocently create a "backdoor" in the early days of system development to allow other programmers and team members to access the system to fix problems. Through negligence or by design, the user ID and password are sometimes left behind in the final version of the system. People who know about them can then enter the system, bypassing the security perhaps years later, when the backdoor has been forgotten.

SPOOFING

o a network via the Internet involves spoofing, which is the process
pretending to send information from a legitimate source. It works
ystem automatically puts on every message sent. The address is
g computer is programmed to accept as a trusted source of

SPYWARE

Spyware is a type of software that allows an intruder to spy upon someone else's computer. This alarming technology takes advantage of loopholes in the computer's security systems and allows a stranger to witness and record another person's every mouse click or keystroke on the monitor as it occurs. The spy can record activities and gain access to passwords and credit card information. Spyware generally requires the user to install it on the machine that is being spied upon, so it is highly unlikely that random strangers on the Internet could simply begin watching your computer. In the workplace, however, someone might be able to install the software without the victim's knowledge. Disguised as an email greeting, for example, the program can operate like a virus that gets the unwary user to install the spyware unknowingly.

SECTION 2: INFORMATION THEFT

Information can be a company's most valuable possession. Stealing corporate information, a crime included in the category of industrial espionage, is unfortunately both easy to do and difficult to detect. This is due in part to the invisible nature of software and data. If a cracker breaks into a company network and manages to download the company database from the network onto a disk, there is no visible sign to the company that anything is amiss. The original database is still in place, working the same way it always has.

WIRELESS DEVICE SECURITY

The growing number of wireless devices has created a new opportunity for data theft. Wireless devices such as cameras, Web phones, networked computers, PDAs, and input and output peripherals are inherently less secure than wired devices. Security is quite lax, and in some cases nonexistent, in new wireless technologies for handheld computers and cell phone systems. In a rush to match competition, manufacturers have tended to sacrifice security to move a product to the marketplace faster. Already, viruses are appearing in emails for cell phones and PDAs. With little protection available for these new systems, hackers and spies are enjoying a free hand with the new technology. One of the few available security protocols for wireless networks is Wired Equivalent Privacy (WEP), developed in conjunction with the standard for wireless local area networks. Newer versions of WEP with enhanced security features make it more difficult for hackers to intercept and modify data transmissions sent by radio waves or infrared signals.

DATA BROWSING

Data browsing is a less damaging form of information theft that involves an invasion of privacy. Workers in many organizations have access to networked databases that contain private information about people. Accessing this information without an official reason is against the law. The IRS had a particularly large problem with data browsing in the late 1990s. Some employees were fired and the rest were given specialized training in appropriate conduct.

Changing the View

By default, a Word document displays in Print Layout view. In this view, the document displays on the screen as it will appear when printed. Other views are available such as Draft, Web Layout, and Full Screen Reading. Change views with buttons in the view area on the Status bar or with options in the View tab. Figure 6.1 identifies the buttons in the view area on the Status bar. Along with the View buttons, the Status bar also contains a Zoom slider bar (see Figure 6.1). Drag the button on the Zoom slider bar to increase or decrease the display size or click the Zoom Out button to decrease size and click the Zoom In to increase size.

Zoom Out

Zoom In

Figure 6.1 Viewing Buttons and Zoom Slider Bar

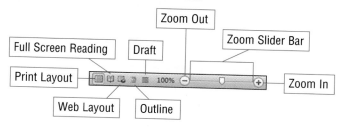

Displaying a Document in Draft View

Change to Draft view and the document displays in a format for efficient editing and formatting. In this view, margins and features such as headers and footers do not display on the screen. Change to Draft view by clicking the Draft button in the view area on the Status bar or click the View tab and then click the Draft button in the Document Views group.

Draft (Status bar)

Draft

Displaying a Document in Web Layout View

Use Web Layout view to see how the document displays as a web page. In Web Layout view, text is wrapped to fit the window, backgrounds are visible, and graphics appear as they would display in a browser. Display a document in Web Layout view by clicking the View tab and then clicking the Web Layout button in the Document Views group or by clicking the Web Layout button in the view area on the Status bar.

Web

Web (Status bar)

Displaying a Document in Full Screen Reading View

The Full Screen Reading view displays a document in a format for easy viewing and reading. Change to Full Screen Reading view by clicking the Full Screen Reading button in the view area on the Status bar or by clicking the View tab and then clicking the Full Screen Reading button in the Document Views group.

You can navigate in Full Screen Reading view using the keys on the keyboard, as shown in Table 6.1. You can also navigate in Full Screen Reading view with options from the View Options button that displays toward the top right of the screen or with the Next Screen and Previous Screen buttons located at the top of the window and also located at the bottom of each page. You can customize the Full Screen Reading view with options from the View Options drop-down list. Display this list by clicking the View Options button located in the upper right corner of the Full Screen Reading window.

Display Document in Full Screen Reading View
Click Full Screen Reading button in view area on Status bar.
OR
1. Click View tab.
2. Click Full Screen Reading button.

Full Screen Reading (Status bar)

Full Screen Reading

Table 6.1 Keyboard Commands in Full Screen Reading View

Press this key . . .	to complete this action
Page Down key or spacebar	Move to the next page or section
Page Up key or Backspace key	Move to the previous page or section
Right Arrow key	Move to next page
Left Arrow key	Move to previous page
Home	Move to first page in document
End	Move to last page in document
Esc	Return to previous view

Exercise 6.1A Changing Views

Part 1 of 5

1. Open **Computers.docx** and save the document with the name **C06-E01-Computers**.
2. Click the Draft button located in the view area on the Status bar.
3. Using the mouse, drag the Zoom slider bar button to the left to decrease the size of the document display to approximately 60%. (The percentage displays at the left side of the Zoom Out button.)
4. Drag the Zoom slider bar button back to the middle until *100%* displays at the left side of the Zoom Out button.
5. Click the Web Layout button in the view area on the Status bar. Scroll through the document and notice the wider margins and that the document does not contain page breaks.
6. Click the Print Layout button in the view area on the Status bar.
7. Click the Full Screen Reading button located in the view area on the Status bar.
8. Click the View Options button located toward the top right of the viewing window and then click *Show Two Pages* at the drop-down list.

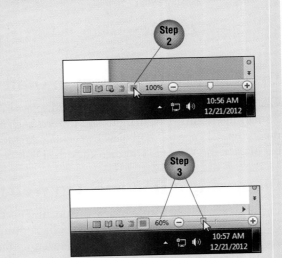

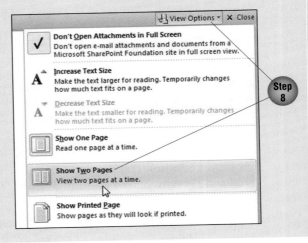

9. Click the Next Screen button to display the next two pages in the viewing window.

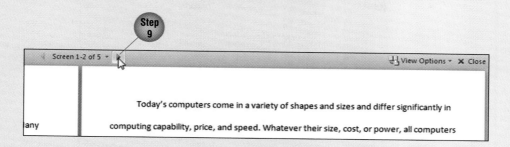

10. Click the Previous Screen button to display the previous two pages.
11. Click the View Options button located toward the top right of the viewing window and then click *Show One Page* at the drop-down list.
12. Practice navigating using the keyboard commands shown in Table 6.1.
13. Increase the size of the text by clicking the View Options button and then clicking the *Increase Text Size* option.

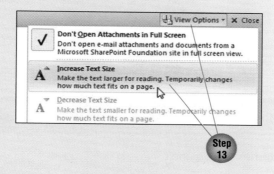

14. Press the Home key to display the first viewing page.
15. Decrease the size of the text by clicking the View Options button and then clicking the *Decrease Text Size* option.
16. Click the Close button located in the upper right corner of the screen.

Changing Page Setup

The Page Setup group in the Page Layout tab contains a number of buttons that you can use to change the setup of pages in a document. With these buttons, you can perform actions such as changing the margins, page orientation, page size, and inserting page breaks. As you will learn in the next chapter, you can also use the three buttons in the Pages group in the Insert tab to insert a page break, a blank page, or a cover page.

Changing Margins

Change page margins with options at the Margins drop-down list, shown in Figure 6.2. To display this list, click the Page Layout tab and then click the Margins button in the Page Setup group. To change the margins, click one of the preset options that displays in the drop-down list.

Change Margins
1. Click Page Layout tab.
2. Click Margins button.
3. Click desired margin option.

Margins

Figure 6.2 Margins Drop-down List

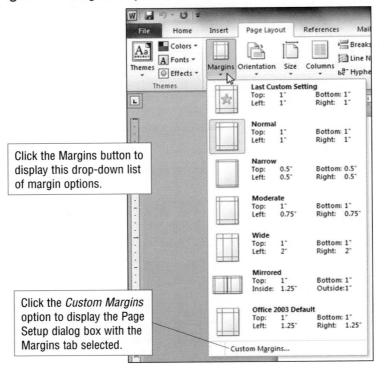

Click the Margins button to display this drop-down list of margin options.

Click the *Custom Margins* option to display the Page Setup dialog box with the Margins tab selected.

Exercise 6.1B Changing Margins

1. With **C06-E01-Computers.docx** open, make the following changes to the document:
   a. Center the title *THE COMPUTER ADVANTAGE.*
   b. Select the entire document, change the line spacing to single, and then deselect the text.
2. Click the Page Layout tab.
3. Click the Margins button in the Page Setup group and then click the *Office 2003 Default* option.
4. Save **C06-E01-Computers.docx**.

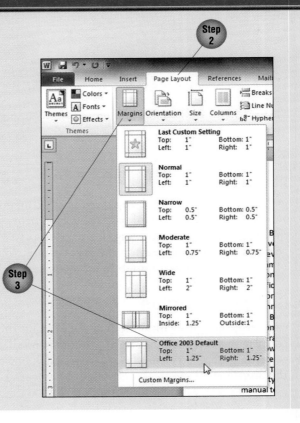

Step 2

Step 3

Chapter Six

Changing Page Orientation

Click the Orientation button in the Page Setup group in the Page Layout tab, and two options for orienting pages in a document display—*Portrait* and *Landscape*. In Portrait orientation, which is the default, the page is 11 inches tall and 8.5 inches wide. In Landscape orientation, the page is 8.5 inches tall and 11 inches wide. When you change the page orientation, the page margins change automatically.

Can you imagine some instances in which you might use a landscape orientation? Suppose you are preparing a company's annual report and you need to include a couple of tables that have several columns of text. If you use the default portrait orientation, the columns would need to be quite narrow, possibly so narrow that reading becomes difficult. Changing the orientation to landscape results in three more inches of usable space. Also, you are not committed to using landscape orientation for the entire document. You can use portrait and landscape in the same document. To do this, select the text, display the Page Setup dialog box, click the desired orientation, and change the *Apply to* option to *Selected text*.

Change Page Orientation
1. Click Page Layout tab.
2. Click Orientation button.
3. Click desired orientation.

Orientation

Exercise 6.1C   Changing Page Orientation   Part 3 of 5

1. With **C06-E01-Computers.docx** open, make sure the Page Layout tab is selected.
2. Click the Orientation button in the Page Setup group.
3. Click *Landscape* at the drop-down list.
4. Scroll through the document and notice how the text displays on the page in Landscape orientation.
5. Save **C06-E01-Computers.docx**.

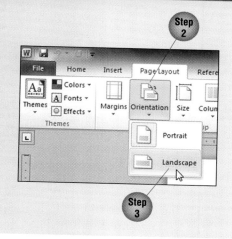

Changing Page Size

The template Word uses to apply default formatting is based on a page size of 8.5 inches wide and 11 inches tall. You can change this default setting with options at the Size drop-down list, shown in Figure 6.3. Display this drop-down list by clicking the Size button in the Page Setup group in the Page Layout tab.

Change Page Size
1. Click Page Layout tab.
2. Click Size button.
3. Click desired size option.

Size

Figure 6.3 Size Drop-down List

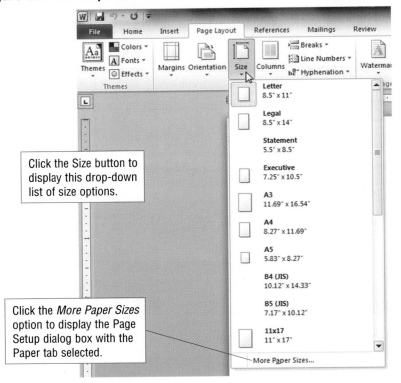

Click the Size button to display this drop-down list of size options.

Click the *More Paper Sizes* option to display the Page Setup dialog box with the Paper tab selected.

Exercise 6.1D Changing Page Size

Part 4 of 5

1. With **C06-E01-Computers.docx** open, make sure the Page Layout tab is selected.
2. Click the Orientation button in the Page Setup group and then click *Portrait* at the drop-down list. (This changes the orientation back to the default.)
3. Click the Size button in the Page Setup group.
4. Click the *A5* option (displays with *5.83" × 8.27"* below *A5*). If this option is not available, choose an option with a similar size.
5. Scroll through the document and notice how the text displays on the page.

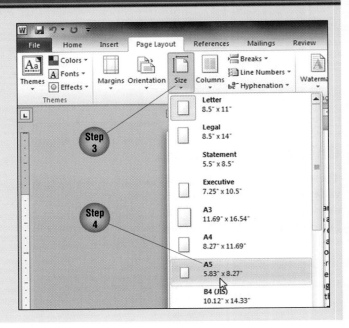

6. Click the Size button and then click *Legal* (displays with *8.5" × 14"* below *Legal*).
7. Scroll through the document and notice how the text displays on the page.
8. Click the Size button and then click *Letter* (displays with *8.5" × 11"* below *Letter*). (This returns the size back to the default.)
9. Save **C06-E01-Computers.docx**.

Changing Margins at the Page Setup Dialog Box

The Margins button drop-down list provides you with a number of preset margins. If these margins do not fit your needs, you can set specific margins at the Page Setup dialog box with the Margins tab selected, as shown in Figure 6.4. Display this dialog box by clicking the Page Setup group dialog box launcher or by clicking the Margins button and then clicking *Custom Margins* at the bottom of the drop-down list.

To change margins, select the current measurement in the *Top*, *Bottom*, *Left*, or *Right* measurement box and then type the new measurement. You can also increase a measurement by clicking the up-pointing arrow at the right of the measurement box. Decrease a measurement by clicking the down-pointing arrow. As you change the margin measurements at the Page Setup dialog box, the sample page in the *Preview* section illustrates the effects of the margin changes.

Change Margins at Page Setup Dialog Box
1. Click Page Layout tab.
2. Click Page Setup group dialog box launcher.
3. Specify desired margins.
4. Click OK.

Figure 6.4 Page Setup Dialog Box with Margins Tab Selected

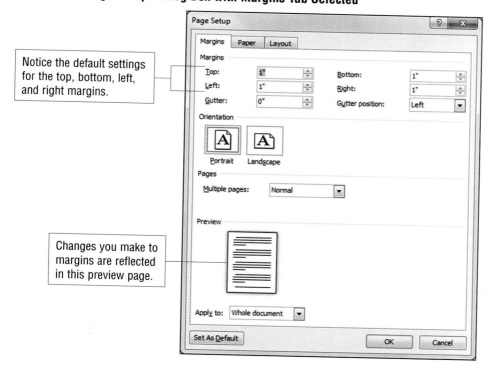

Notice the default settings for the top, bottom, left, and right margins.

Changes you make to margins are reflected in this preview page.

Changing Paper Size at the Page Setup Dialog Box

Change Page Size at Page Setup Dialog Box

1. Click Page Layout tab.
2. Click Size button.
3. Click *More Paper Sizes* at drop-down list.
4. Specify desired size.
5. Click OK.

The Size button drop-down list contains a number of preset page sizes. If these sizes do not fit your needs, you can specify page size at the Page Setup dialog box with the Paper tab selected. Display this dialog box by clicking the Size button in the Page Setup group and then clicking *More Paper Sizes,* which displays at the bottom of the drop-down list.

Exercise 6.1E Changing Margins at the Page Setup Dialog Box   Part 5 of 5

1. With **C06-E01-Computers.docx** open, make sure the Page Layout tab is selected.
2. Click the Page Setup group dialog box launcher.
3. At the Page Setup dialog box with the Margins tab selected, click the down-pointing arrow at the right side of the *Top* measurement box until *0.5"* displays.
4. Click the down-pointing arrow at the right side of the *Bottom* measurement box until *0.5"* displays.
5. Select the current measurement in the *Left* measurement box and then type 0.75.
6. Select the current measurement in the *Right* measurement box and then type 0.75.

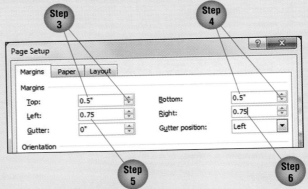

7. Click OK to close the dialog box.
8. Click the Size button in the Page Setup group and then click *More Paper Sizes* at the drop-down list.
9. At the Page Setup dialog box with the Paper tab selected, click the down-pointing arrow at the right side of the *Paper size* option and then click *A4* at the drop-down list.
10. Click OK to close the dialog box.
11. Scroll through the document and notice how the text displays on the page.
12. Click the Size button in the Page Setup group and then click *Letter* at the drop-down list.
13. Save, print, and then close **C06-E01-Computers.docx**.

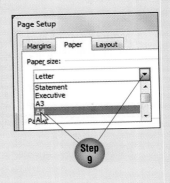

Inserting a Section Break

You can change the layout and formatting of specific portions of a document by inserting section breaks. For example, you can insert section breaks and then change margins for the text between the section breaks. If you want to format specific text in a document into columns, insert a section break.

Insert a section break in a document by clicking the Page Layout tab, clicking the Breaks button in the Page Setup group, and then clicking the desired option in the *Section Breaks* section of the drop-down list, shown in Figure 6.5. You can insert a section break that begins a new page or a continuous section break that does not insert a page break. A continuous section break separates the document into sections but does not insert a page break. Click one of the other three options in the *Section Breaks* section of the Breaks drop-down list if you want to insert a section break that begins a new page.

Insert Section Break
1. Click Page Layout tab.
2. Click Breaks button.
3. Click section break type at drop-down list.

Breaks

Figure 6.5 Breaks Button Drop-down List

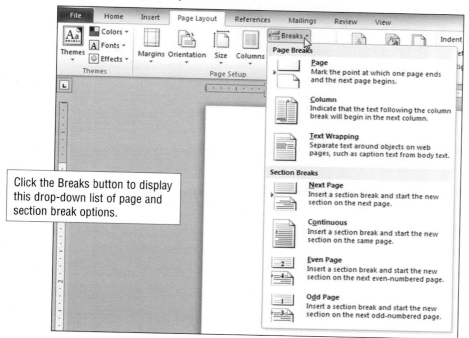

Click the Breaks button to display this drop-down list of page and section break options.

A section break inserted in a document is not visible in Print Layout view. Click the Draft button and a section break displays in the document as a double row of dots with the words *Section Break* in the middle. Depending on the type of section break you insert, text follows *Section Break*. For example, if you insert a continuous section break, the words *Section Break (Continuous)* display in the middle of the row of dots. If you delete a section break, the text that follows the section break takes on the formatting of the text preceding the break. To delete a section break, click the View tab and then click the Draft button in the Document Views group. In Draft view, click on the section break (this moves the insertion point to the left margin on the section break) and then press the Delete key.

Delete a Section Break
1. Click View tab.
2. Click Draft button.
3. Click on section break.
4. Press Delete key.

1. Open **BestFitResume.docx** and save the document and name it **C06-E02-BestFitResume**.
2. Select the entire document and then change the font size to *12*.
3. Insert an odd page section break in the document by completing the following steps:
   a. With the insertion point positioned at the beginning of the document (at the beginning of the title), click the Page Layout tab.
   b. Click the Breaks button in the Page Setup group and then click *Odd Page* at the drop-down list.

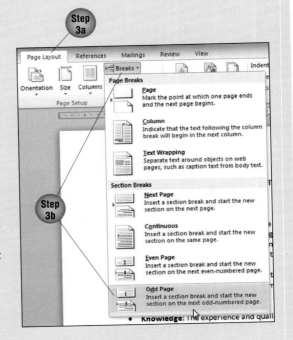

4. Move the insertion point to the beginning of the heading *The Right Mix* and then insert an even page break by clicking the Breaks button in the Page Setup group and then clicking *Even Page* at the drop-down list.
5. Move the insertion point to the beginning of the document and notice that the blank page at the beginning of the document is identified at the left side of the Status bar as *Page 1 of 6*. Scroll through the other pages and notice that the last page of the document is identified as *Page 6 of 6*.
6. Move the insertion point to the beginning of the document and then delete the section break by completing the following steps:
   a. Click the Draft button in the view area on the Status bar.
   b. Position the insertion point on the section break above the title (displays as a double row of dots across the screen with the text *Section Break (Odd Page)*.

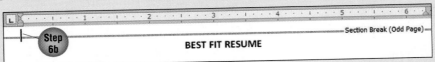

   c. Press the Delete key.
   d. Position the insertion point on the section break above the heading *The Right Mix* and then delete the even page section break.
7. Select the entire document and then change the font size to *11*.
8. Click the Print Layout button in the view area on the Status bar.
9. Move the insertion point to the beginning of the heading *Preparing the "Best Fit" Resume* and then insert a continuous section break by clicking the Page Layout tab, clicking the Breaks button, and then clicking *Continuous* at the drop-down list.
10. Move the insertion point to the beginning of the heading *The Right Mix* and then insert a continuous section break.
11. Click in the first paragraph of text below the heading *Preparing the "Best Fit" Resume* and then change the left and right margins to 1.25 inches.
12. Scroll through the document and notice that the margin changes affect only the text between the two continuous section breaks.
13. Save and then print **C06-E02-BestFitResume.docx**.

Creating Columns

When you are preparing any document that contains text, the readability of the document is an important consideration. As you learned in the last chapter, readability refers to the ease with which a person can read and understand groups of words. Line length in a document can enhance or detract from the readability of the text. If the length is too long, the reader may lose his or her place on the line and have a difficult time moving to the next line below. To improve the readability of documents such as newsletters or reports, you may want to set the text in columns. One commonly used type of column is the newspaper column, which is typically used for text in newspapers, newsletters, and magazines. In newspaper columns, text flows up and down in the document.

You can set text in columns with the Columns button in the Page Setup group in the Page Layout tab or with options from the Columns dialog box. The Columns button creates columns of equal width. To create columns with varying widths, use the Columns dialog box. A document can include as many columns as space permits on the page. Word determines how many columns can be included based on page width, margin width, and the size and spacing of the columns. Columns must be at least 0.5 inch in width. Changes in column width affect the entire document or the section of the document in which the insertion point is positioned.

Exercise 6.2B   Formatting Text into Columns   Part 2 of 3

1. With **C06-E02-BestFitResume.docx** open, delete the section breaks by completing the following steps:
   a. Click the Draft button in the view area on the Status bar.
   b. Position the insertion point on the section break above the heading *Preparing the "Best Fit" Resume*.

> - **Abilities:** Potential to carry out a range of different tasks beyond your immediate skills or knowledge.
> - **Attitudes:** The degree to which you are enthusiastic, flexible, and positive in approach.
>
> ==Section Break (Continuous)======
>
> **Preparing the "Best Fit" Resume**
>
> To produce the best fitting resume, you need to know about yourself and about the job to which you are applying. Before you do anything else, ask yourself why you are preparing a

Step 1b

   c. Press the Delete key.
   d. Position the insertion point on the section break above the heading *The Right Mix* and then press the Delete key.
   e. Click the Print Layout button in the view area on the Status bar.
2. Move the insertion point to the beginning of the heading *The Right Fit* (located immediately below the title of the document) and then insert a continuous section break.
3. Format the text (except the title) into two columns by completing the following steps:
   a. Make sure the insertion point is positioned below the section break.

b. With the Page Layout tab active, click the Columns button in the Page Setup group and then click *Two* at the drop-down list.
4. Scroll through the document and notice the text set in two columns.
5. Save **C06-E02-BestFitResume.docx**.

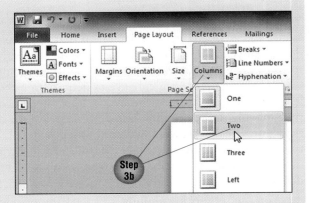

By inserting section breaks in a document, you can format specific text in a document into columns. In Exercise 6.2B, you inserted a section break and then formatted the text into two columns from the section break to the end of the document. You can also create columns within text by inserting a continuous section break at the beginning of the text you want to format into columns and inserting a continuous section break at the location where you want the columns of text to end.

Exercise 6.2C Formatting Text into Columns within a Document Part 3 of 3

1. With **C06-E02-BestFitResume.docx** open, delete the continuous section break and return text to one column by completing the following steps:
   a. Click the Draft button in the view area on the Status bar.
   b. Position the insertion point on the continuous section break above the heading *The Right Fit* and then press the Delete key.
   c. With the Page Layout tab active, click the Columns button and then click *One* at the drop-down list. (This returns the document text to one column and also changes the document view to the Print Layout view.)
2. Format the bulleted text into two columns by completing the following steps:
   a. Position the insertion point at the beginning of the word *Knowledge* that displays after the first bullet in the bulleted paragraphs of text and then insert a continuous section break.
   b. Insert a continuous section break at the blank line below the last bulleted paragraph of text.
   c. Move the insertion point to any character in the bulleted text.
   d. With the Page Layout tab active, click the Columns buttons and then click *Two* at the drop-down list.
3. Completing steps similar to those in Step 2, format the numbered paragraphs into two columns. ***Hint: Insert a continuous section break at the beginning of the first numbered paragraph and insert a continuous section break at the blank line below the last numbered paragraph of text.***
4. Select the entire document and then change the font to Cambria.
5. Move the insertion point to title *BEST FIT RESUME* and then change the bottom margin to 0.8 inch. ***Hint: Do this at the Page Setup dialog box with the Margins tab selected.***
6. Save, print, and then close **C06-E02-BestFitResume.docx**.

Creating Columns with the Columns Dialog Box

You can use the Columns dialog box to create newspaper columns that are equal or unequal in width. To display the Columns dialog box, shown in Figure 6.6, click the Columns button in the Page Setup group in the Page Layout tab and then click *More Columns* at the drop-down list.

Figure 6.6 Columns Dialog box

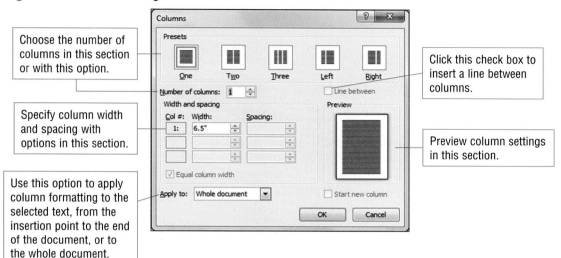

Choose the number of columns in this section or with this option.

Specify column width and spacing with options in this section.

Use this option to apply column formatting to the selected text, from the insertion point to the end of the document, or to the whole document.

Click this check box to insert a line between columns.

Preview column settings in this section.

Using options at the Columns dialog box, you can specify the style and number of columns, enter your own column measurements, and create unequal columns. You can also insert a line between columns. By default, column formatting is applied to the whole document. With the *Apply to* option at the bottom of the Columns dialog box, you can change this from *Whole document* to *This point forward*. With the *This point forward* option, a section break is inserted and the column formatting is applied to text from the location of the insertion point to the end of the document or until other column formatting is encountered. The *Preview* section of the dialog box displays an example of how the columns will appear in your document.

Removing Column Formatting

To remove column formatting using the Columns button, position the insertion point in the section containing columns, click the Page Layout tab, click the Columns button, and then click *One* at the drop-down list. You can also remove column formatting at the Columns dialog box by selecting the *One* option in the *Presets* section.

Create Columns at Columns Dialog Box
1. Click Page Layout tab.
2. Click Columns button.
3. Click *More Columns* at drop-down list.
4. Specify columns options.
5. Click OK.

Insert Column Break

1. Position insertion point at desired location.
2. Click Page Layout tab.
3. Click Breaks button.
4. Click *Column* at drop-down list.

Inserting a Column Break

When Word formats text into columns, it automatically breaks the columns to fit the page. At times, column breaks may appear in an undesirable location. You can insert a column break by positioning the insertion point where you want the column to end, clicking the Page Layout tab, clicking the Breaks button, and then clicking *Column* at the drop-down list. You can also insert a column break with the keyboard shortcut Ctrl + Shift + Enter.

Exercise 6.3A   Formatting Columns at the Columns Dialog Box   Part 1 of 4

1. Open **CompCommunications.docx** and then save the document and name it **C06-E03-CompCommunications**.
2. Format text in columns by completing the following steps:
   a. Position the insertion point at the beginning of the first paragraph of text in the document.
   b. Click the Page Layout tab.
   c. Click the Columns button in the Page Setup group and then click *More Columns* at the drop-down list.
   d. At the Columns dialog box, click *Two* in the *Presets* section.
   e. Click the up-pointing arrow at the right of the *Spacing* option box to display *0.6"*.
   f. Click the *Line between* check box to insert a check mark.
   g. Click the down-pointing arrow at the right side of the *Apply to* option box and then click *This point forward* at the drop-down list.
   h. Click OK to close the dialog box.

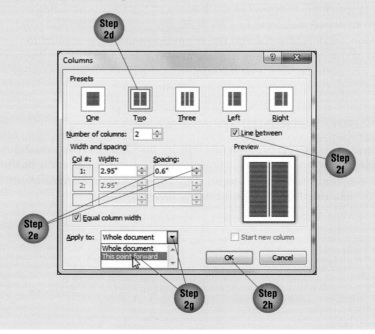

3. Insert a column break by completing the following steps:
   a. Position the insertion point at the beginning of the *News Services* heading.
   b. Click the Breaks button in the Page Setup group and then click *Column* at the drop-down list.
4. Save and then print **C06-E03-CompCommunications.docx**.

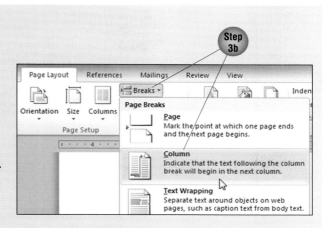

Balancing Columns on a Page

In documents that contain text formatted into columns, Word automatically lines up (balances) the last line of text at the bottom of each column, except on the last page. Text in the first column of the last page may flow to the end of the page, while the text in the second column may end far short of the end of the page. You can balance columns by inserting a continuous section break at the end of the text.

Exercise 6.3B Formatting and Balancing Columns of Text   Part 2 of 4

1. With **C06-E03-CompCommunications.docx** open, delete the column break by completing the following steps:
   a. Position the insertion point at the beginning of the *News Services* heading.
   b. Click the Draft button in the view area on the Status bar.
   c. Position the insertion point on the column break.

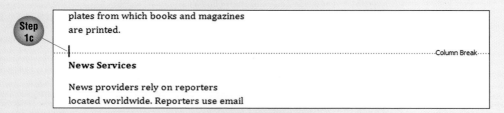

   d. Press the Delete key.
   e. Click the Print Layout button in the view area on the Status bar.
2. Select the entire document and then change the font to Constantia.
3. Move the insertion point to the end of the document and then balance the columns by clicking the Page Layout tab, clicking the Breaks button, and then clicking *Continuous* at the drop-down list.
4. Apply the *Red, Accent 2, Lighter 60%* paragraph shading to the title *COMPUTERS IN COMMUNICATIONS*.
5. Apply the *Red, Accent 2, Lighter 80%* paragraph shading to each of the headings in the document.
6. Save **C06-E03-CompCommunications.docx**.

QUICK STEPS

Automatic Hyphenation
1. Click Page Layout tab.
2. Click Hyphenation button.
3. Click *Automatic* at drop-down list.

Manual Hyphenation
1. Click Page Layout tab.
2. Click Hyphenation button.
3. Click *Manual* at drop-down list.
4. Click Yes or No to hyphenate indicated words.
5. When complete, click OK.

Hyphenation

Hyphenating Words

In some Word documents, especially documents that have left and right margins wider than 1 inch or text set in columns, the right margin may appear quite ragged. To improve the display of line text, consider hyphenating long words that fall at the end of the text line. With the hyphenation feature in Word, you can hyphenate words in a document automatically or manually.

Automatically Hyphenating Words

To hyphenate words automatically, click the Page Layout tab, click the Hyphenation button in the Page Setup group, and then click *Automatic* at the drop-down list. Scroll through the document and check to see if hyphens display in appropriate locations within the words. If after hyphenating words in a document you want to remove all hyphens, immediately click the Undo button on the Quick Access toolbar.

Manually Hyphenating Words

If you want to control where a hyphen appears in a word, choose manual hyphenation. To do this, click the Page Layout tab, click the Hyphenation button in the Page Setup group, and then click *Manual* at the drop-down list. This displays the Manual Hyphenation dialog box, shown in Figure 6.7. (The word in the *Hyphenate at* text box will vary.) At this dialog box, click Yes to hyphenate the word as indicated in the *Hyphenate at* text box, click No if you do not want the word hyphenated, or click Cancel to cancel hyphenation. Continue clicking Yes or No at the Manual Hyphenation dialog box. At the message indicating hyphenation is complete, click OK.

Figure 6.7 Manual Hyphenation Dialog Box

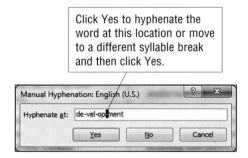

Click Yes to hyphenate the word at this location or move to a different syllable break and then click Yes.

At the Manual Hyphenation dialog box, you can reposition the hyphen in the *Hyphenate at* text box. Word displays the word with syllable breaks indicated by a hyphen. The position at which the word will be hyphenated displays as a blinking bar. If you want to hyphenate at a different location in the word, position the blinking bar where you want the hyphen and then click Yes.

1. With **C06-E03-CompCommunications.docx** open, press Ctrl + Home and then hyphenate words automatically by completing the following steps:
   a. Click the Page Layout tab.
   b. Click the Hyphenation button in the Page Setup group and then click *Automatic* at the drop-down list.
2. Scroll through the document and notice the automatic hyphenation.
3. Click the Undo button to remove the hyphens.
4. Manually hyphenate words by completing the following steps:
   a. Click the Hyphenation button in the Page Setup group and then click *Manual* at the drop-down list.

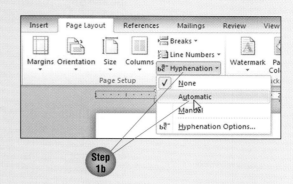

Step 1b

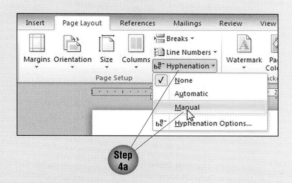

Step 4a

   b. At the Manual Hyphenation dialog box, make one of the following choices:
      • Click Yes to hyphenate the word as indicated in the *Hyphenate at* text box.
      • Move the hyphen in the word to a more desirable location and then click Yes.
      • Click No if you do not want the word hyphenated.
   c. Continue clicking Yes or No at the Manual Hyphenation dialog box.
   d. At the hyphenation complete message, click OK.
5. Save **C06-E03-CompCommunications.docx**.

Inserting Line Numbers

You can use the Line Numbers button in the Page Setup group in the Page Layout tab to insert line numbers in a document. Numbering lines has practical applications for certain legal papers and for reference purposes. To number lines in a document, click the Page Layout tab, click the Line Numbers button in the Page Setup group, and then click the desired line number option at the drop-down list.

Insert Line Numbers

1. Click Page Layout tab.
2. Click Line Numbers button.
3. Click desired line number option.

OR

1. Click Page Layout tab.
2. Click Line Numbers button.
3. Click *Line Numbering Options* at drop-down list.
4. Click Line Numbers button.
5. Specify line numbering options at dialog box.
6. Click OK.
7. Click OK.

Line Numbers

If you want more control over inserting line numbers in a document, click the Line Numbers button and then click *Line Numbering Options* at the drop-down list. At the Page Setup dialog box with the Layout tab selected, click the Line Numbers button that displays at the bottom of the dialog box. This displays the Line Numbers dialog box, shown in Figure 6.8. Use options at this dialog box to insert line numbering and to specify the starting number, where line numbers are printed, the interval between printed line numbers, and whether line numbers are consecutive or start over at the beginning of each page.

Figure 6.8 Line Numbers Dialog Box

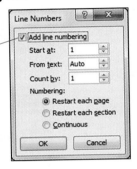

Click this check box to turn on line numbering and make the remaining options active. Use options at this dialog box to customize how line numbers appear in the document.

Exercise 6.3D Inserting Line Numbers   Part 4 of 4

1. With **C06-E03-CompCommunications.docx** open, insert line numbers by completing the following steps:
   a. Position the insertion point at the beginning of the first paragraph below the title *COMPUTERS IN COMMUNICATIONS*.
   b. Make sure Page Layout is the active tab.
   c. Click the Line Numbers button in the Page Setup group.
   d. Click *Continuous* at the drop-down list.
   e. Scroll through the document and notice how the numbers appear in the document.
   f. Turn off line numbering by clicking the Line Numbers button and then clicking *None*.

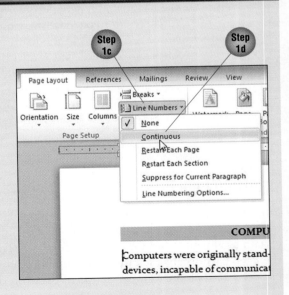

---

2. Insert line numbers at the Line Numbers dialog box by completing the following steps:
   a. With the insertion point positioned at the beginning of the first paragraph below the title *COMPUTERS IN COMMUNICATIONS*, click the Line Numbers button and then click *Line Numbering Options* at the drop-down list.
   b. At the Page Setup dialog box with the Layout tab selected, click the Line Numbers button that displays at the bottom of the dialog box.
   c. At the Line Numbers dialog box, click the *Add line numbering* option.
   d. Click the up-pointing arrow at the right side of the *Count by* option to display *2* in the text box.
   e. Click OK to close the Line Numbers dialog box.
   f. Click OK to close the Page Setup dialog box.
3. Scroll through the document and notice the appearance of the line numbers.
4. Remove line numbering by clicking the Line Numbers button and then clicking *None*.
5. Save, print, and then close **C06-E03-CompCommunications.docx**.

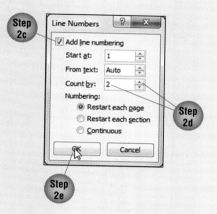

Formatting the Page Background

The Page Background group in the Page Layout tab contains three buttons for customizing a page background. Click the Watermark button and choose a predesigned watermark from a drop-down list. If a document is going to be viewed on-screen or on the Web, consider adding a page color. In Chapter 4, you learned how to apply borders and shading to text at the Borders and Shading dialog box. This dialog box also contains options for inserting a page border.

Inserting a Watermark

A watermark is a lightened image that displays behind text in a document. Word provides a number of predesigned watermarks that you can insert in a document. Display these watermarks by clicking the Watermark button in the Page Background group in the Page Layout tab. Scroll through the list of watermarks and then click the desired option.

Changing Page Color

Use the Page Color button in the Page Background group to apply background color to a document. This background color is intended for viewing a document on screen or on the Web. The color is visible on the screen but does not print. Insert a page color by clicking the Page Color button and then clicking the desired color at the color palette.

Insert Watermark
1. Click Page Layout tab.
2. Click Watermark button.
3. Click desired option at drop-down list.

Change Page Color
1. Click Page Layout tab.
2. Click Page Color button.
3. Click desired option at color palette.

Watermark   Page Color

1. Open **CompSecurity.docx** and save the document with the name **C06-E04-CompSecurity**.
2. Make the following changes to the document:
   a. Apply the Heading 1 style to the two titles in the document *SECTION 1: UNAUTHORIZED ACCESS* and *SECTION 2: INFORMATION THEFT*.
   b. Apply the Heading 2 style to all of the headings in the document.
   c. Change the style set to Formal.
3. Insert a watermark by completing the following steps:
   a. Move the insertion point to the beginning of the document.
   b. Click the Page Layout tab.
   c. Click the Watermark button in the Page Background group.
   d. At the drop-down list, click the *CONFIDENTIAL 1* option.

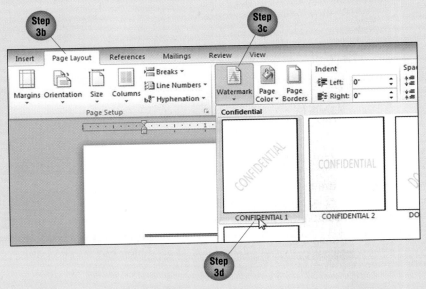

4. Scroll through the document and notice how the watermark displays behind the text.
5. Remove the watermark and insert a different one by completing the following steps:
   a. Click the Watermark button in the Page Background group and then click *Remove Watermark* at the drop-down list.
   b. Click the Watermark button and then click *DO NOT COPY 1* at the drop-down list.
6. Scroll through the document and notice how the watermark displays.
7. Move the insertion point to the beginning of the document.

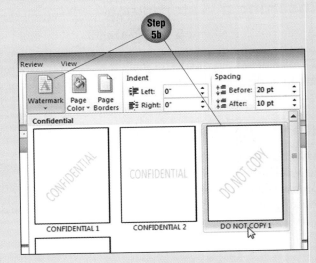

8. Click the Page Color button in the Page Background group and then click *Aqua, Accent 5, Lighter 80%* at the color palette.

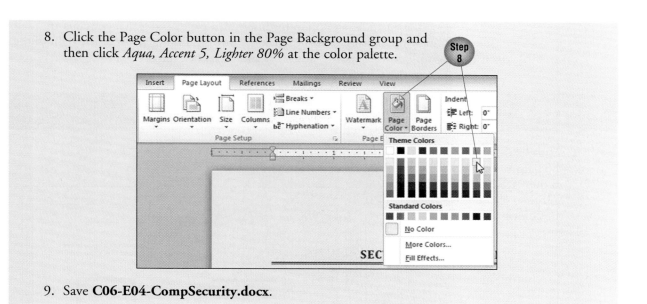

Step 8

9. Save **C06-E04-CompSecurity.docx**.

Inserting a Page Border

To improve the visual appeal of a document, consider inserting a page border. When you insert a page border in a multiple-page document, the border prints on each page. To insert a page border, click the Page Borders button in the Page Background group in the Page Layout tab. This displays the Borders and Shading dialog box with the Page Border tab selected, as shown in Figure 6.9. At this dialog box, you can specify the border style, color, and width.

Insert Page Border
1. Click Page Layout tab.
2. Click Page Borders button.
3. Specify desired options at dialog box.

Page Borders

Figure 6.9 Borders and Shading Dialog Box with Page Border Tab Selected

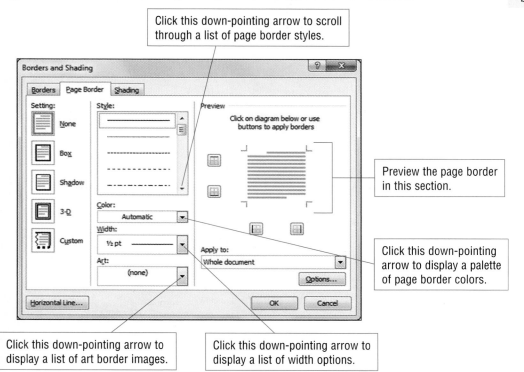

Click this down-pointing arrow to scroll through a list of page border styles.

Preview the page border in this section.

Click this down-pointing arrow to display a palette of page border colors.

Click this down-pointing arrow to display a list of art border images.

Click this down-pointing arrow to display a list of width options.

The dialog box includes an option for inserting a page border that contains an image. To display the images available, click the down-pointing arrow at the right of the *Art* list box. Scroll down the drop-down list and then click the desired image.

1. With **C06-E04-CompSecurity.docx** open, remove the page color by clicking the Page Color button in the Page Background group and then clicking *No Color* at the color palette.
2. Insert a page border by completing the following steps:
   a. Click the Page Borders button in the Page Background group in the Page Layout tab.
   b. Click the *Box* option in the *Setting* section.
   c. Scroll down the list of line styles in the *Style* list box until the end of the list displays and then click the third line from the end.
   d. Click the down-pointing arrow at the right of the *Color* list box and then click *Red, Accent 2, Darker 50%* at the color palette.
   e. Click OK to close the dialog box.
3. Save and then print **C06-E04-CompSecurity.docx**.
4. Insert an image page border by completing the following steps:
   a. Click the Page Borders button in the Page Background group.
   b. Click the down-pointing arrow at the right side of the *Art* list box and then click the border image shown at the right.
   c. Click OK to close the dialog box.
5. Save **C06-E04-CompSecurity.docx**.

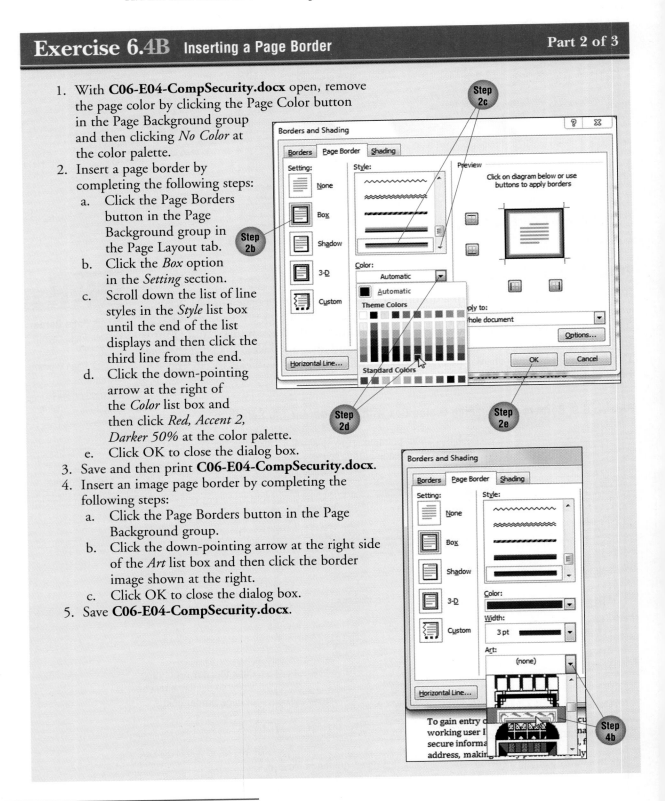

By default, a page border displays and prints 24 points from the top, left, right, and bottom edges of the page. Some printers, particularly inkjet printers, have a nonprinting area around the outside edges of the page that can interfere with the printing of a border. Before printing a document with a page border, click the File tab and then click the Print tab. Look at the preview of the page at the right side of the Print tab Backstage view and determine whether the entire border is visible. If a portion of the border is not visible in the preview page (generally at the bottom and right side of the page), consider changing measurements at the Border and Shading Options dialog box shown in Figure 6.10. You can also change measurements at the Border and Shading Options dialog box to control the location of the page border on the page.

Figure 6.10 Border and Shading Options Dialog Box

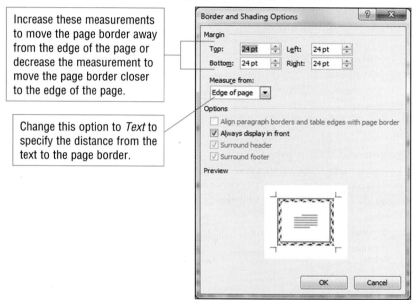

Increase these measurements to move the page border away from the edge of the page or decrease the measurement to move the page border closer to the edge of the page.

Change this option to *Text* to specify the distance from the text to the page border.

To display the Border and Shading Options dialog box, click the Page Layout tab and then click the Page Borders button. At the Borders and Shading dialog box with the Page Border tab selected, click the Options button that displays in the lower right corner of the dialog box. The options at the Border and Shading Options dialog box change depending on whether you click the Options button at the Borders and Shading dialog box with the Borders tab selected or the Page Border tab selected. In Chapter 4, you learned about changing measurements for paragraph borders at the Border and Shading Options dialog box. At the Border and Shading Options dialog box for page borders, increase and/or decrease the spacing between the page border and the edge of the page with the measurement boxes in the *Margin* section.

If your printer contains a nonprinting area and the entire page border will not print, consider increasing the spacing from the page border to the edge of the page. For example, if you insert a page border and then display the document in the Print tab Backstage view and notice that not all of the bottom and right borders print, increase the measurement in the *Right* and the *Bottom* measurement boxes at the Border and Shading Options dialog box.

The *Measure from* option box at the Border and Shading Options dialog box has the default setting of *Edge of page*. You can change this option to *Text*, which changes the top and bottom measurements to *1 pt* and the left and right measurements to *4 pt* and moves the page border into the page. Use the measurement boxes to specify the distance you want the page border displayed and printed from the text in the document.

1. With **C06-E04-CompSecurity.docx** open, increase the spacing from the page border to the edges of the page by completing the following steps:
   a. Click the Page Layout tab and then click the Page Borders button.
   b. At the Borders and Shading dialog box with the Page Border tab selected, click the Options button located in the lower right corner.
   c. At the Border and Shading Options dialog box, click the up-pointing arrow at the right side of the *Top* measurement box until *31 pt* displays. (This is the maximum measurement allowed.)
   d. Increase the measurement for the *Left, Bottom,* and *Right* measurement boxes to *31 pt*.
   e. Click OK to close the Border and Shading Options dialog box.
   f. Click OK to close the Borders and Shading dialog box.
2. Save **C06-04-CompSecurity.docx** and then print only page 1.
3. Change the page border and page border options by completing the following steps:
   a. With the Page Layout tab active, click the Page Borders button.
   b. At the Borders and Shading dialog box, scroll down the *Style* list box and then click the third line option from the bottom.
   c. Click the down-pointing arrow at the right of the *Color* option box and then make sure the *Red, Accent 2, Darker 50%* option is selected at the color palette.
   d. Click the Options button.
   e. At the Border and Shading Options dialog box, click the down-pointing arrow at the right of the *Measure from* option box and then click *Text* at the drop-down list.
   f. Click the up-pointing arrow at the right of the *Top* measurement box until *10 pt* displays.
   g. Increase the measurement for the *Bottom* measurement box to *10 pt* and the measurement in the *Left* and *Right* measurement boxes to *14 pt*.
   h. Click the *Surround header* check box to remove the check mark.
   i. Click the *Surround footer* check box to remove the check mark.
   j. Click OK to close the Border and Shading Options dialog box.
   k. Click OK to close the Borders and Shading dialog box.
4. Save **C06-04-CompSecurity.docx** and then print only page 1.
5. Close **C06-E04-CompSecurity.docx**.

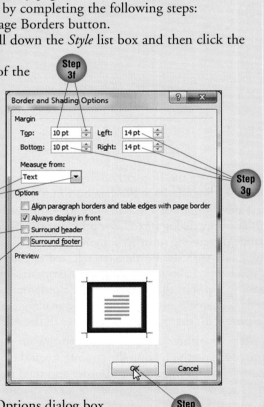

Chapter *Summary*

- ➤ You can change the document view with buttons in the view area on the Status bar or with options in the View tab.
- ➤ Print Layout is the default view, which you can change to other views such as Draft view or Full Screen Reading view.
- ➤ The Draft view displays the document in a format for efficient editing and formatting.
- ➤ Use the Zoom slider bar to change the percentage of the display.
- ➤ Full Screen Reading view displays a document in a format for easy viewing and reading.
- ➤ Navigate in Full Screen Reading view using keys on the keyboard or with the Next and Previous buttons.
- ➤ By default, a Word document contains 1-inch top, bottom, left, and right margins. Change margins with preset margin settings at the Margins button drop-down list or with options at the Page Setup dialog box with the Margins tab selected.
- ➤ The default page orientation is Portrait, which you can change to Landscape with the Orientation button in the Page Setup group in the Page Layout tab.
- ➤ The default page size is 8.5 by 11 inches, which can be changed with options at the Size button drop-down list or options at the Page Setup dialog box with the Paper tab selected.
- ➤ Insert a section break in a document to apply formatting to a portion of a document. You can insert a continuous section break or a section break that begins a new page. View and/or delete a section break in Draft view because section breaks are not visible in Print Layout view.
- ➤ Set text in columns to improve readability of documents such as newsletters or reports. Format text in columns using the Columns button in the Page Setup group in the Page Layout tab or with options at the Columns dialog box.
- ➤ Remove column formatting with the Columns button in the Page Layout tab or at the Columns dialog box. Balance column text on the last page of a document by inserting a continuous section break at the end of the text.
- ➤ Improve the display of text lines by hyphenating long words that fall at the end of the line. You can automatically or manually hyphenate words in a document.
- ➤ Number lines in a document with options from the Line Numbers button drop-down list or with options at the Line Numbers dialog box.
- ➤ A watermark is a lightened image that displays behind text in a document. Use the Watermark button in the Page Background group in the Page Layout tab to insert a watermark.
- ➤ Insert page color in a document with the Page Color button in the Page Background group. Page color is designed for viewing a document on screen and does not print.
- ➤ Click the Page Borders button in the Page Background group and the Borders and Shading dialog box displays with the Page Border tab selected. Use options at this dialog box to insert a page border or an image page border in a document.
- ➤ By default, a page border displays and prints 24 points from the top, left, right, and bottom edges of the page. You can change this default spacing at the Border and Shading Options dialog box.
- ➤ At the Border and Shading Options dialog box, select *Text* at the *Measure from* option box and then you can specify the distance from text in a document to the page border.

Commands *Review*

FEATURE	RIBBON TAB, GROUP	BUTTON, OPTION
Borders and Shading dialog box with Page Border tab selected	Page Layout, Page Background	
Border and Shading Options dialog box	Page Layout, Page Background	, Options
Columns	Page Layout, Page Setup	
Columns dialog box	Page Layout, Page Setup	, More Columns
Continuous section break	Page Layout, Page Setup	, Continuous
Draft view	View, Document Views	
Full Screen Reading view	View, Document Views	
Hyphenate words automatically	Page Layout, Page Setup	, Automatic
Hyphenate words manually	Page Layout, Page Setup	, Manual
Line numbers	Page Layout, Page Setup	
Margins	Page Layout, Page Setup	
Orientation	Page Layout, Page Setup	
Page color	Page Layout, Page Background	
Page Setup dialog box with Margins tab selected	Page Layout, Page Setup	, Custom Margins; or Page Setup group dialog box launcher
Page Setup dialog box with Paper tab selected	Page Layout, Page Setup	, More Paper Sizes
Page size	Page Layout, Page Setup	
Print Layout view	View, Document Views	
Section break	Page Layout, Page Setup	
Watermark	Page Layout, Page Background	

Key Points *Review*

Completion: In the space provided at the right, indicate the correct term, symbol, or command.

1. This view displays a document in a format for efficient editing and formatting. _____

2. This view displays a document in a format for easy viewing and reading. _____

3. This is the default measurement for the top, bottom, left, and right margins. _____

4. This is the default page orientation. _____

5. Set specific margins at this dialog box with the Margins tab selected. _____

6. View a section break in this view. _____

7. Format text into columns with the Columns button located in this group in the Page Layout tab. _____

8. Balance column text on the last page of a document by inserting this type of break at the end of the text. _____

9. If you hyphenate words in a document and then decide to remove the hyphens, immediately click this button. _____

10. A lightened image that displays behind text in a document is called this. _____

11. The Page Borders button displays in this group in the Page Layout tab. _____

12. Change the position of the page border from the edge of the page with options at this dialog box. _____

Chapter *Assessments*

Applying Your Skills

Demonstrate your knowledge of features learned in this chapter by completing the following assessments.

Assessment 6.1   Apply Formatting to a Computers in Industry Report

1. Open **CompIndustry.docx** and save the document with the name **C06-A01-CompIndustry**.
2. Apply the Heading 1 style to the titles *COMPUTERS IN INDUSTRY* and *REFERENCES*.
3. Apply the Heading 2 style to the headings in the report.
4. Change the style set to Formal.
5. Hang indent the paragraphs of text below the *REFERENCES* title.
6. Change the top, left, and right margins to 1.25 inches.
7. Manually hyphenate the text in the document. (Do not hyphenate proper nouns.)
8. Insert the SAMPLE 1 watermark in the document. (You will need to scroll down the list box to display this watermark.)
9. Insert a page border of your choosing.

10. Display the Border and Shading Options dialog box and then change the top, left, bottom, and right measurements to *31 pt*. **Hint: Display the Border and Shading Options dialog box by clicking the Options button at the Borders and Shading dialog box with the Page Border tab selected.**
11. Save, print, and then close **C06-A01-CompIndustry.docx**.

Assessment 6.2   Apply Formatting to a Data Security Training Notice

1. Open **DataTraining.docx** and save the document with the name **C06-A02-DataTraining**.
2. Change the font for the entire document to 12-point Candara.
3. Set the title in 14-point Candara bold and center it.
4. Change the page orientation to *Landscape*.
5. Change the left and right margins to 1.8 inches and the top margin to 2.3 inches.
6. Insert the ASAP 1 watermark in the document.
7. Insert a page border of your choosing. (Display the document in Print tab Backstage view and determine whether the entire page border will print. If the entire page border is not visible, display the Border and Shading Options dialog box and change the top, left, bottom, and right measurements to *31 pt*.)
8. Save, print, and then close **C06-A02-DataTraining.docx**.

Assessment 6.3   Apply Formatting to a Computer Viruses and Security Report

1. Open **CompViruses.docx** and save the document with the name **C06-A03-CompViruses**.
2. Select text from the title *SECTION 4: HARDWARE AND SOFTWARE SECURITY RISKS* to the end of the document and then press the Delete key.
3. Select the entire document, change the font to 12-point Cambria, and then deselect the text.
4. Change the top margin to 1.5 inches.
5. Format the text from the first paragraph to the end of the document into two columns with 0.6 inch spacing and a line between columns.
6. Manually hyphenate the text in the document.
7. Balance the columns on the second page.
8. Center the title and change the font size of the title to 14 points. Add shading to the title and insert a double-line bottom border and a single-line top border.
9. Apply shading to the headings in the document and apply a single-line bottom border to each heading.
10. Save, print, and then close **C06-A03-CompViruses.docx**.

Expanding Your Skills

Explore additional feature options or use Help to learn a new skill in creating this document.

Assessment 6.4   Apply a Picture Watermark

1. Open **BGClientLtr.docx** and then save it and name it **C06-A04-BGClientLtr**.
2. Click the Page Layout tab, click the Watermark button, and then click *Custom Watermark* at the drop-down list.
3. At the Printed Watermark dialog box, learn how to insert a picture as a watermark into a document.
4. Insert the picture named **BG.jpg** (located in the Chapter06 folder) as a watermark.
5. Save, print, and then close **C06-A04-BGClientLtr.docx**.

Achieving Signature Status

Take your skills to the next level by completing these more challenging assessments.

Assessment 6.5   Create and Format an Announcement

1. At a blank document, create the announcement shown in Figure 6.11. Set the text in Constantia, change to landscape orientation, change the left and right margins to 2 inches, and set appropriate tabs for the tabbed text. Insert the watermark as shown and insert the page border. (The page border is an art border located approximately two-thirds of the way down the *Art* option drop-down list.) Change the page border color to dark red and the text color to dark blue.
2. Display the document in Print tab Backstage view and determine whether the entire page border will print. If the entire page border is not visible, display the Border and Shading Options dialog box and change the top, left, bottom, and right measurements to *31 pt*.
3. Save the completed document and name it **C06-A05-Announce**.
4. Print and then close **C06-A05-Announce.docx**.

Figure 6.11 Assessment 6.5

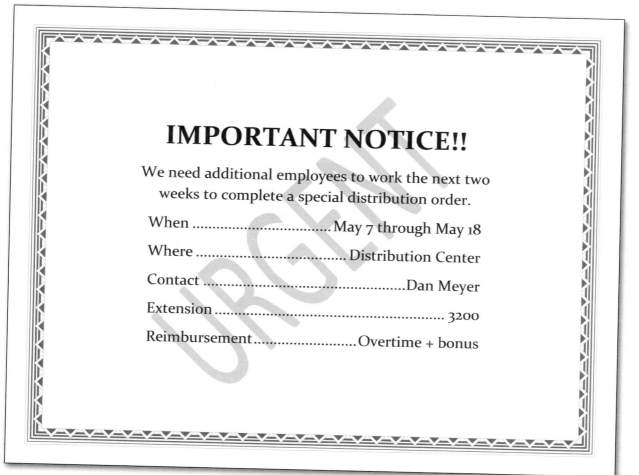

IMPORTANT NOTICE!!

We need additional employees to work the next two
weeks to complete a special distribution order.

When .... May 7 through May 18

Where .... Distribution Center

Contact .... Dan Meyer

Extension 3200

Reimbursement.......................Overtime + bonus

Assessment 6.6   Format a Report on Delivering a Presentation

1. Open **DeliverPres.docx** and then save it and name it **C06-A06-DeliverPres**.
2. Apply character formatting to the title and headings (set the title in 16-point Constantia bold and the headings in 12-point Constantia bold and italic) and insert bullets as shown in Figure 6.12.
3. Change the left and right margins to 0.8″.
4. Set the text from the beginning of the first paragraph of text to the end of the document in two columns with a line between.
5. Apply the paragraph shading and border to the title as shown in the figure.
6. Apply the page border and change the page border color to *Purple, Accent 4, Darker 50%*. (The page border is an art border located approximately three-quarters of the way down the *Art* option drop-down list—approximately the twentieth border option from the bottom of the list.)
7. Display the document in Print tab Backstage view and determine whether the entire page border will print. If the entire page border is not visible, display the Border and Shading Options dialog box and change the top, left, bottom, and right measurements to *31 pt*.
8. Save, print, and then close **C06-A06-DeliverPres.docx**.

Figure 6.12 Assessment 6.6

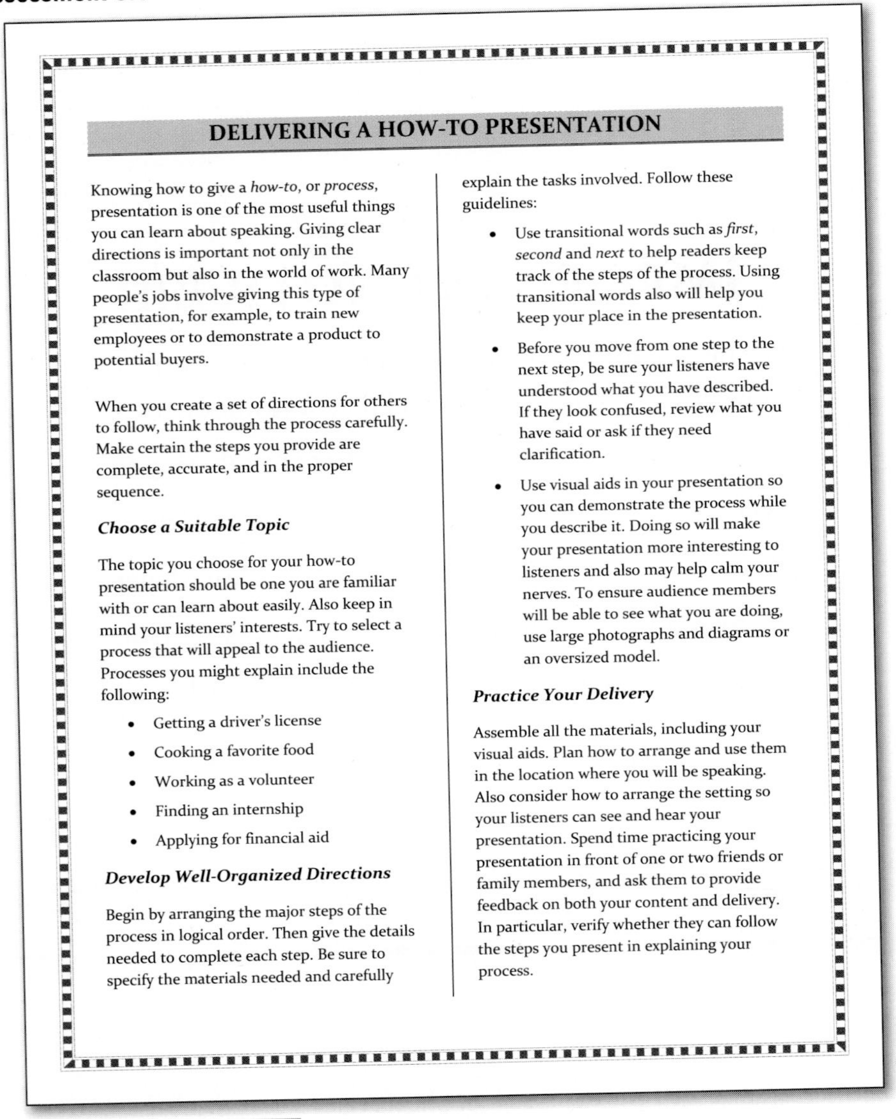

DELIVERING A HOW-TO PRESENTATION

Knowing how to give a *how-to*, or *process*, presentation is one of the most useful things you can learn about speaking. Giving clear directions is important not only in the classroom but also in the world of work. Many people's jobs involve giving this type of presentation, for example, to train new employees or to demonstrate a product to potential buyers.

When you create a set of directions for others to follow, think through the process carefully. Make certain the steps you provide are complete, accurate, and in the proper sequence.

Choose a Suitable Topic

The topic you choose for your how-to presentation should be one you are familiar with or can learn about easily. Also keep in mind your listeners' interests. Try to select a process that will appeal to the audience. Processes you might explain include the following:

- Getting a driver's license
- Cooking a favorite food
- Working as a volunteer
- Finding an internship
- Applying for financial aid

Develop Well-Organized Directions

Begin by arranging the major steps of the process in logical order. Then give the details needed to complete each step. Be sure to specify the materials needed and carefully explain the tasks involved. Follow these guidelines:

- Use transitional words such as *first*, *second* and *next* to help readers keep track of the steps of the process. Using transitional words also will help you keep your place in the presentation.

- Before you move from one step to the next step, be sure your listeners have understood what you have described. If they look confused, review what you have said or ask if they need clarification.

- Use visual aids in your presentation so you can demonstrate the process while you describe it. Doing so will make your presentation more interesting to listeners and also may help calm your nerves. To ensure audience members will be able to see what you are doing, use large photographs and diagrams or an oversized model.

Practice Your Delivery

Assemble all the materials, including your visual aids. Plan how to arrange and use them in the location where you will be speaking. Also consider how to arrange the setting so your listeners can see and hear your presentation. Spend time practicing your presentation in front of one or two friends or family members, and ask them to provide feedback on both your content and delivery. In particular, verify whether they can follow the steps you present in explaining your process.

Chapter 7

SNAP TUTORIALS

Tutorial 7.1
Inserting Page Elements
Tutorial 7.2
Inserting Page Numbers and
Page Breaks
Tutorial 7.3
Creating Headers and Footers
Tutorial 7.4
Modifying Headers and Footers
Tutorial 7.5
Finding and Replacing Text
Tutorial 7.6
Finding and Replacing
Formatting
Tutorial 7.7
Using Click and Type
Tutorial 7.8
Using Vertical Alignment

Customizing Page Formatting

Performance Objectives

Upon successful completion of Chapter 7, you will be able to:

- Insert a page break, blank page, and cover page
- Insert page numbering
- Insert and edit predesigned headers and footers
- Use the Click and Type feature
- Vertically align text

In Chapter 6, you learned how to format pages in a Word document by changing margin sizes, page orientation, and paper size; setting text in columns; hyphenating words; and inserting graphic elements. In this chapter, you will learn how to insert other elements such as cover pages, blank pages, page breaks, page numbers, and headers and footers. You will also learn how to align text vertically; how to use the Click and Type feature, which allows you to insert text in specific locations in a document; and how to use the Find and Replace feature, which allows you to search for specific text or formatting and replace it with other text or formatting.

Note: Before beginning computer exercises for this chapter, copy to your storage medium the Chapter07 folder from the CD that accompanies this textbook and then make Chapter07 the active folder.

In this chapter students will produce the following documents:

Exercise 7.1. C07-E01-CompSecurity.docx
Exercise 7.2. C07-E02-Computers.docx
Exercise 7.3. C07-E03-Lease.docx
Exercise 7.4. C07-E04-WordTrain.docx

Model answers for these exercises are shown on the following pages.

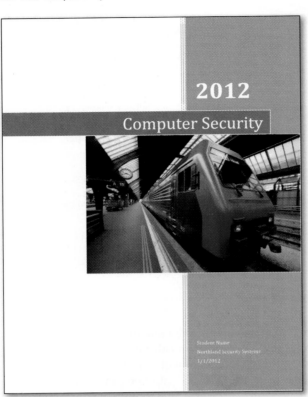

Exercise 7.1

C07-E01-CompSecurity.docx

2012

Computer Security

Student Name
Northland Security Systems
1/1/2012

Page 1

SECTION 1: UNAUTHORIZED ACCESS

Like uncharted wilderness, the Internet lacks borders. This inherent openness is what makes the Internet so valuable and yet so vulnerable. Over its short life, the Internet has grown so quickly that the legal system has not been able to keep pace. The security risks posed by networks and the Internet can be grouped into three categories: unauthorized access, information theft, and denial of service.

Hackers, individuals who gain access to computers and networks illegally, are responsible for most cases of unauthorized access. Hackers tend to exploit sites and programs that have poor security measures in place. However, they also gain access to more challenging sites by using sophisticated programs and strategies. Many hackers claim they hack merely because they like the challenge of trying to defeat security measures. They rarely have a more malicious motive, and they generally do not aim to destroy or damage the sites that they invade. In fact, hackers dislike being identified with those who seek to cause damage. They refer to hackers with malicious or criminal intent as crackers.

USER IDS AND PASSWORDS

To gain entry over the Internet to a secure computer system, most hackers focus on finding a working user ID and password combination. User IDs are easy to come by and are generally not secure information. Sending an email, for example, displays the sender's user ID in the return address, making it very public. The only missing element is the password. Hackers know from experience which passwords are common; they have programs that generate thousands of likely passwords and they try them systematically over a period of hours or days.

SYSTEM BACKDOORS

Programmers can sometimes inadvertently aid hackers by providing unintentional entrance to networks and information systems. One such unintentional entrance is a system "backdoor," which is a user ID and password that provides the highest level of authorization. Programmers innocently create a "backdoor" in the early days of system development to allow other programmers and team members to access the system to fix problems. Through negligence or by design, the user ID and password are sometimes left behind in the final version of the system. People who know about them can then enter the system, bypassing the security, perhaps years later, when the backdoor has been forgotten.

SPOOFING

A sophisticated way to break into a network via the Internet involves spoofing, which is the process of fooling another computer by pretending to send information from a legitimate source. It works by altering the address that the system automatically puts on every message sent. The address is changed to one that the receiving computer is programmed to accept as a trusted source of information.

1

Page 2

SPYWARE

Spyware is a type of software that allows an intruder to spy upon someone else's computer. This alarming technology takes advantage of loopholes in the computer's security systems and allows a stranger to witness and record another person's every mouse click or keystroke on the monitor as it occurs. The spy can record activities and gain access to passwords and credit card information. Spyware generally requires the user to install it on the machine that is being spied upon, so it is highly unlikely that random strangers on the Internet could simply begin watching your computer. In the workplace, however, someone might be able to install the software without the victim's knowledge. Disguised as an email greeting, for example, the program can operate like a virus that gets the unwary user to install the spyware unknowingly.

2

Page 3

SECTION 2: INFORMATION THEFT

Information can be a company's most valuable possession. Stealing corporate information, a crime included in the category of industrial espionage, is unfortunately both easy to do and difficult to detect. This is due in part to the invisible nature of software and data. If a cracker breaks into a company network and manages to download the company database from the network onto a disk, there is no visible sign to the company that anything is amiss. The original database is still in place, working the same way it always has.

WIRELESS DEVICE SECURITY

The growing number of wireless devices has created a new opportunity for data theft. Wireless devices such as cameras, Web phones, networked computers, PDAs, and input and output peripherals are inherently less secure than wired devices. Security is quite lax, and in some cases nonexistent, in new wireless technologies for handheld computers and cell phone systems. In a rush to match competition, manufacturers have tended to sacrifice security to move a product to the marketplace faster. Already, viruses are appearing in emails for cell phones and PDAs. With little protection available for these new systems, hackers and spies are enjoying a free hand with the new technology. One of the few available security protocols for wireless networks is Wired Equivalent Privacy (WEP), developed in conjunction with the standard for wireless local area networks. Newer versions of WEP with enhanced security features make it more difficult for hackers to intercept and modify data transmissions sent by radio waves or infrared signals.

DATA BROWSING

Data browsing is a less damaging form of information theft that involves an invasion of privacy. Workers in many organizations have access to networked databases that contain private information about people. Accessing this information without an official reason is against the law. The IRS had a particularly large problem with data browsing in the late 1990s. Some employees were fired and the rest were given specialized training in appropriate conduct.

3

Page 4

THE COMPUTER ADVANTAGE

Before the early 1980s, computers were unknown to the average person. Many people had never even seen a computer, let alone used one. The few computers that existed were relatively large, bulky devices confined to secure computer centers in corporate or government facilities. Referred to as mainframes, these computers were maintenance intensive, requiring special climate-controlled conditions and several full-time operators for each machine. Because early mainframes were expensive and difficult to operate, usage was restricted to computer programmers and scientists, who used them to perform complex operations, such as processing payrolls and designing sophisticated military weaponry.

Beginning in the early 1980s, the computer world changed dramatically with the introduction of microcomputers, also called personal computers (PCs). These relatively small computers were considerably more affordable and much easier to use than their mainframe ancestors. Within a few years, ownership of personal computers became widespread in the workplace, and today, the personal computer is a standard appliance in homes and schools.

Today's computers come in a variety of shapes and sizes and differ significantly in computing capability, price, and speed. Whatever their size, cost, or power, all computers offer advantages over manual technologies in the areas of speed, accuracy, versatility, storage capabilities, and communications capabilities.

The Computer Advantage

Page 1

SPEED

Computers operate with lightening-like speed, and processing speeds are increasing as computer manufacturers introduce new and improved models. Contemporary personal computers are capable of executing billions of program instructions in one second. Some larger computers, such as supercomputers, can execute trillions of instructions per second, a rate important for processing huge amounts of data involved in forecasting weather, monitoring space shuttle flights, and managing other data-intensive applications.

ACCURACY

People sometimes blame human errors on a computer. In truth, if a computer user enters correct data and uses accurate programs, computers are extremely accurate. A popular expression among computers professionals is "garbage in—garbage out" (GIGO), which means that if inaccurate programs and/or data are entered into a computer for processing, the resulting output will also be inaccurate. The computer user is responsible for entering data correctly and making certain that programs are correct.

VERSATILITY

Computers are perhaps the most versatile of all machines or devices. They can perform a variety of personal, business, and scientific applications. Families use computers for entertainment, communications, budgeting, online shopping, completing homework assignments, playing games, and listening to music. Banks conduct money transfers, account withdrawals, and the payment of checks via computer. Retailers use computers to process sales transactions and to check on the availability of products. Manufacturers can manage their entire production, warehousing, and selling processes with computerized systems. Schools access computers for keeping records,

The Computer Advantage

Page 2

conducting distance learning classes, scheduling events, and analyzing budgets. Universities, government agencies, hospitals, and scientific organizations conduct life-enhancing research using computers. Perhaps the most ambitious such computer-based scientific research of all time is the Human Genome Project. Completed in April of 2003, this program was more than two years ahead of schedule and at a cost considerably lower than originally forecast. This project represented an international effort to sequence three billion DNA (deoxyribonucleic acid) letters in the human genome, which is the collection of gene types that comprise every person. Scientists from all over the world can now access the genome database and use the information to research ways to improve human health and fight disease.

STORAGE

Storage is a defining computer characteristic and is one of the features that revolutionized early computing, for it made computers incredibly flexible. A computer is capable of accepting and storing programs and data. Once stored in the computer, a user can access a program again and again to process different data. Computers can store huge amounts of data in comparably tiny physical spaces. For example, one compact disk can store about 109,000 pages of magazine text, and the capacities of internal storage devices are many times larger.

The Computer Advantage

Page 3

COMMUNICATIONS

Most modern computers contain special equipment and programs that allow them to communicate with other computers through telephone lines, cable connections, and satellites. A structure in which computers are linked together using special programs and equipment is a network. Newer communications technologies allow users to exchange information over wireless networks using wireless devices such as personal digital assistants (PDAs), notebook computers, cell phones, and pagers.

A network can be relatively small or quite large. A local area network (LAN) is one confined to a relatively small geographical area, such as a building, factory, or college campus. A wide area network (WAN) spans a large geographical area and might connect a company's manufacturing plants dispersed throughout North America. Constant, quick connections along with other computer technologies have helped boost productivity for manufacturers.

The Computer Advantage

Page 4

Model Answers

Exercise 7.3

C07-E03-Lease.docx

RENT AGREEMENT

THIS RENT AGREEMENT (hereinafter referred to as the "Agreement") made and entered into this DAY of MONTH, YEAR, by and between Maggie Branson and Lee Gardella.

WITNESSETH:

WHEREAS, Maggie Branson is the owner of real property and is desirous of renting the Premises to Lee Gardella upon the terms and conditions as contained herein.

NOW, THEREFORE, for and in consideration of the covenants and obligations contained herein and other good and valuable consideration, the receipt and sufficiency of which is hereby acknowledged, the parties hereto agree as follows:

1. **TERM.** Maggie Branson rents to Lee Gardella and Lee Gardella rents from Maggie Branson the Premises.
2. **RENT.** The total rent for the premise is RENT due on the first day of each month minus any set off for approved repairs.
3. **DAMAGE DEPOSIT.** Upon the due execution of this Agreement, Lee Gardella shall deposit with Maggie Branson the sum of DEPOSIT receipt of which is hereby acknowledged by Maggie Branson, as security for any damage caused to the Premises during the term hereof. Such deposit shall be returned to Lee Gardella, without interest, and minus any set off for damages to the Premises upon the termination of this Agreement.
4. **USE OF PREMISES.** The Premises shall be used and occupied by Lee Gardella and Lee Gardella's immediate family, exclusively, as a private single family dwelling, and no part of the Premises shall be used at any time during the term of this Agreement by Lee Gardella for the purpose of carrying on any business, profession, or trade of any kind, or for any purpose other than as a private single family dwelling. Lee Gardella shall not allow any other person, other than Lee Gardella's immediate family, to occupy the Premises.
5. **CONDITION OF PREMISES.** Lee Gardella stipulates, represents, and warrants that Lee Gardella has examined the Premises, and that they are in good order, repair, and in a safe, clean and tenantable condition.
6. **ALTERATIONS AND IMPROVEMENTS.** Lee Gardella shall make no alterations or improvements on the Premises or construct any building or make any other improvements on the Premises without the prior written consent of Maggie Branson.
7. **NON-DELIVERY OF POSSESSION.** In the event Maggie Branson cannot deliver [...] mises to Lee Gardella upon the commencement of the term, [...] aggie Branson or its agents, then Maggie Branson or its agents [...] but the rental herein provided shall abate until possession is [...] n or its agents shall have thirty (30) days in which to give [...] ssession is tendered within such time, Lee Gardella agrees to

Page 1

accept the demised Premises and pay the rental herein provided from that date. In the event possession cannot be delivered within such time, through no fault of Maggie Branson or its agents, then this Agreement and all rights hereunder shall terminate.

8. **UTILITIES.** Lee Gardella shall be responsible for arranging for and paying for all utility services required on the Premises.

IN WITNESS WHEREOF the parties have reviewed the information above and certify, to the best of their knowledge, that the information provided by the signatory is true and accurate.

_____

Maggie Branson

_____

Lee Gardella

Page 2

Chapter Seven

MICROSOFT WORD TRAINING

Formatting Company Documents

Thursday, January 19, 2012

Technology Department Training Center

8:30 a.m. to 11:30 a.m.

Sponsored by
Culver Training Services

Inserting Page Elements

The Pages group in the Insert tab contains three buttons that you can use to insert and then format or modify elements in a document. With these buttons, you can insert a page break, a blank page, and a predesigned cover page.

Inserting a Page Break

Word assumes that you are using standard-sized paper, which is 8.5 inches wide and 11 inches long. With default top and bottom margins of 1 inch, a Word document contains approximately 9 inches of text on a page. At approximately the 10-inch mark, Word automatically inserts a page break. You can insert your own page break in a document with the keyboard shortcut Ctrl + Enter or with the Page Break button in the Pages group in the Insert tab.

A page break automatically inserted by Word is considered a *soft* page break; a page break that you insert is considered a *hard* page break. A soft page break adjusts automatically when you add or delete text from a document. A hard page break does not adjust and is therefore less flexible than a soft page break. If you add or delete text from a document with a hard page break, check the break to determine whether it is still in a desirable location. If you are working in Draft view, a hard page break displays as a row

Insert Page Break
1. Click Insert tab.
2. Click Page Break button

OR

Press Ctrl + Enter.

Page Break

of dots with the words Page Break in the center. To delete a page break, position the insertion point immediately below the page break and then press the Backspace key or position the insertion point above the page break and then press the Delete key. In Draft view, position the insertion point on the page break and then press the Delete key.

Exercise 7.1A Inserting Page Breaks   Part 1 of 3

1. Open **CompSecurity.docx** and save the document with the name **C07-E01-CompSecurity**.
2. Make the following formatting changes:
   a. Apply the Heading 1 style to the two titles: *SECTION 1: UNAUTHORIZED ACCESS* and *SECTION 2: INFORMATION THEFT*.
   b. Apply the Heading 2 style to the six headings: *User IDs and Passwords, System Backdoors, Spoofing, Spyware, Wireless Device Security*, and *Data Browsing*.
   c. Change the style set to Simple.
      Hint: Use the Change Styles *button in* the Styles group in the Home tab.
3. Insert a page break by completing the following steps:
   a. Position the insertion point at the beginning of the title *SECTION 2: INFORMATION THEFT* (located on page 2).
   b. Click the Insert tab and then click the Page Break button in the Pages group.

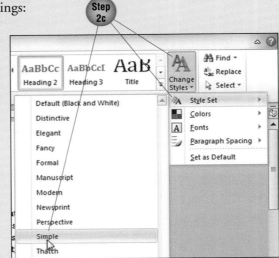

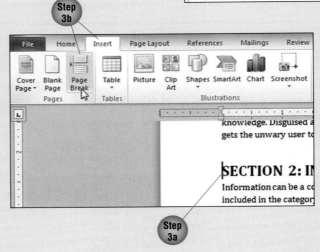

4. Move the insertion point to the beginning of the heading *Spyware* and then press Ctrl + Enter to insert a page break.
5. Scroll through the document and notice the page breaks. Delete the page break above *Spyware* by positioning the insertion point at the immediate right of the period that ends the paragraph in the *Spoofing* paragraph and then pressing the Delete key twice.
6. Save **C07-E01-CompSecurity.docx**.

Inserting a Blank Page

Click the Blank Page button in the Pages group in the Insert tab to insert a blank page at the position of the insertion point. Inserting a blank page can be useful as a spaceholder in a document when you want to insert an illustration, graphic, or figure.

Inserting a Cover Page

If you are preparing a document for distribution to others, or if you simply want to improve a document's visual appeal, consider inserting a cover page. With the Cover Page button in the Pages group in the Insert tab, you can insert a predesigned, formatted cover page and then type text in specific locations on the page to personalize it. Click the Cover Page button and a drop-down list displays, similar to the one shown in Figure 7.1. The drop-down list provides a visual representation of each cover page option. Scroll through the list and then click the cover page you want to use.

These predesigned cover pages contain location placeholders where you can enter specific information. For example, a cover page might contain the placeholder *[Type the document title]*. Click anywhere in the placeholder and then type the desired text. The first time you click placeholder text, all of the text is selected. If you have typed text in a placeholder, clicking in the text will position the insertion point at that location. If you want to delete the entire placeholder, click the placeholder tab and then press the Delete key. To delete the text but not the placeholder, select only the text in the placeholder and then press the Delete key.

Blank Page   Cover Page

Figure 7.1 Cover Page Drop-down List

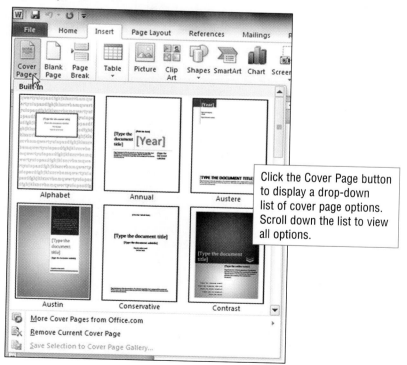

Click the Cover Page button to display a drop-down list of cover page options. Scroll down the list to view all options.

1. With **C07-E01-CompSecurity.docx** open, create a blank page by completing the following steps:
   a. Move the insertion point to the beginning of the heading *Spoofing* (located on the first page).
   b. Click the Insert tab.
   c. Click the Blank Page button in the Pages group.

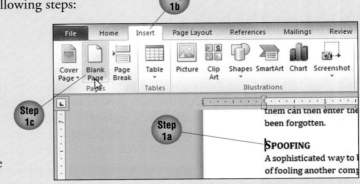

2. Insert a cover page by completing the following steps:
   a. Press Ctrl + Home to move the insertion point to the beginning of the document.
   b. Click the Cover Page button in the Pages group in the Insert tab.
   c. At the drop-down list, scroll down and then click the *Motion* cover page.
   d. Click anywhere in the placeholder text [Year], click the down-pointing arrow that displays at the right of the placeholder, and then click the Today button that displays at the bottom of the drop-down calendar.

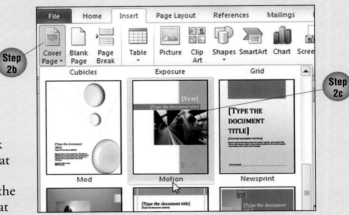

e. Click anywhere in the placeholder text *[Type the document title]* and then type Computer Security.

f. Scroll down the page and then click the placeholder text *[Student name]* and then type your first and last names. If a name already displays, select the name and then type your first and last names.

g. Click the placeholder text *[Type the company name]* and then type Northland Security Systems. If a name already displays, select the name and then type Northland Security Systems.

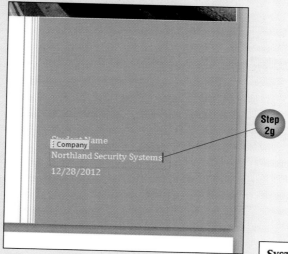

3. Remove the blank page you created in Step 1 by completing the following steps:
   a. Move the insertion point to the end of the paragraph in the *System Backdoors* section.
   b. Press the Delete key until the *Spoofing* heading displays below the paragraph.
4. Save **C07-E01-CompSecurity.docx**.

SYSTEM BACKDOORS
Programmers can sometimes in networks and information syste is a user ID and password that p create a "backdoor" in the early members to access the system t password are sometimes left be them can then enter the system been forgotten.

SPOOFING
A sophisticated way to break in of fooling another computer by

Inserting Predesigned Page Numbering

Insert Page Numbering
1. Click Insert tab.
2. Click Page Number button.
3. Click desired option at drop-down list.

Word, by default, does not print page numbers on document pages. If you want to insert page numbers in a document, use the Page Number button in the Header & Footer group in the Insert tab. When you click the Page Number button, a drop-down list displays with options for specifying where on the page you want the page number inserted. Point to an option at this list, and a drop-down list displays of predesigned page formats. Scroll through the options in the drop-down list and then click the desired option. You can remove page numbering from a document by clicking the Page Number button and then clicking *Remove Page Numbers* at the drop-down list.

Page Number

Exercise 7.1C   Inserting Predesigned Page Numbering   Part 3 of 3

1. With **C07-E01-CompSecurity.docx** open, insert page numbering by completing the following steps:
   a. Move the insertion point to the beginning of the title *SECTION 1: UNAUTHORIZED ACCESS*.
   b. Click the Insert tab.
   c. Click the Page Number button in the Header & Footer group and then point to *Top of Page*.
   d. Scroll down the drop-down list and then click the *Brackets 2* option.

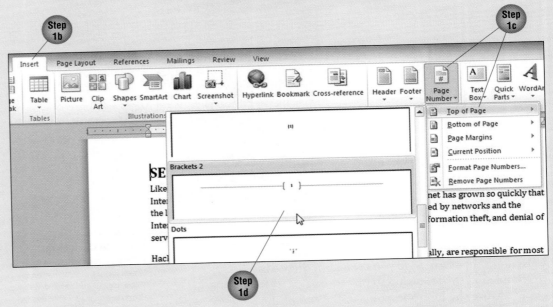

2. Double-click in the document and then scroll through it to view the page numbering that displays at the top of each page except the cover page.
3. Remove the page numbering by clicking the Insert tab, clicking the Page Number button, and then clicking *Remove Page Numbers* at the drop-down list.

4. Click the Page Number button, point to *Bottom of Page*, scroll down the drop-down list, and then click the *Thin Line* option.

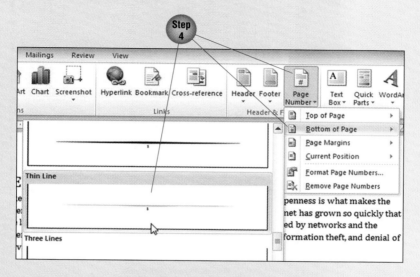

5. Double-click in the document and view page numbering.
6. Insert a page break at the beginning of the heading *SPYWARE*.
7. Save, print, and then close **C07-E01-CompSecurity.docx**.

Inserting Predesigned Headers and Footers

Text that appears at the top of every page of a multipage document is called a ***header***; text that appears at the bottom of every page is referred to as a ***footer***. Headers and footers are common in manuscripts, textbooks, reports, and other publications. You can insert a predesigned header in a document by clicking the Insert tab and then clicking the Header button in the Header & Footer group. This displays the drop-down list, shown in Figure 7.2. At this list, click the predesigned header you want to use, and the header is inserted in the document. The header is visible in Print Layout view but not in Draft view.

A predesigned header or footer, like a predesigned cover page, may contain location placeholders where you can enter specific information. For example, a header might contain the placeholder *[Type the document title]*. Click anywhere in the placeholder and then type the desired text. The first time you click placeholder text, all of the text is selected. If you have typed text in a placeholder, clicking in the text will position the insertion point at that location. If you want to delete the entire placeholder, click the placeholder tab and then press the Delete key. To delete the text but not the placeholder, select only the text in the placeholder and then press the Delete key.

Figure 7.2 Header Button Drop-down List

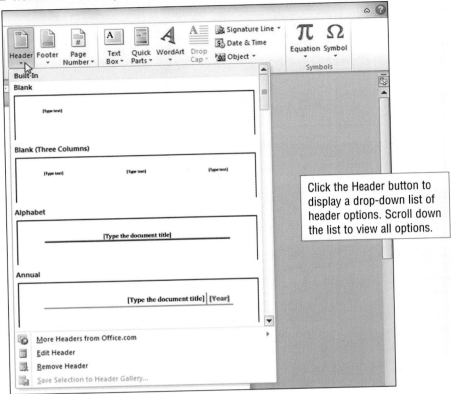

Click the Header button to display a drop-down list of header options. Scroll down the list to view all options.

Exercise 7.2A Inserting a Predesigned Header in a Document   Part 1 of 3

1. Open **Computers.docx** and save the document with the name **C07-E02-Computers**.
2. Change the top margin by completing the following steps:
   a. Click the Page Layout tab.
   b. Click the Margins button in the Page Setup group and then click *Custom Margins* at the drop-down list.
   c. Type 1.5 in the *Top* measurement box.

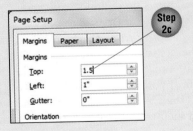

   d. Click OK.
3. Make the following changes to the document:
   a. Apply the Heading 1 style to the title *THE COMPUTER ADVANTAGE*.
   b. Apply the Heading 2 style to the five headings: *Speed, Accuracy, Versatility, Storage,* and *Communications*.

   c. Change the style set to Formal.

   d. Move the insertion point to the beginning of the heading *Speed* (located at the bottom of page 1) and then insert a page break by clicking the Insert tab and then clicking the Page Break button in the Pages group.

   e. Move the insertion point to the beginning of the heading *Communications* (located at the bottom of page 3) and then insert a page break by pressing Ctrl + Enter.

4. Press Ctrl + Home to move the insertion point to the beginning of the document and then insert a header by completing the following steps:

   a. Click the Insert tab.

   b. Click the Header button in the Header & Footer group.

   c. Scroll to the bottom of the drop-down list that displays and then click *Tiles*.

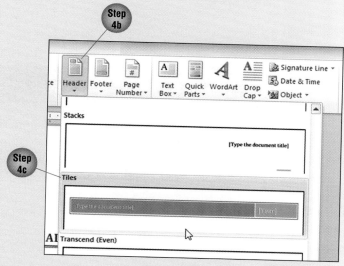

   d. Click anywhere in the placeholder text *[Type the document title]* and then type The Computer Advantage.

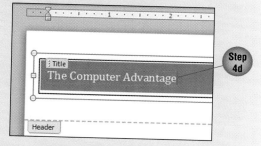

   e. Click anywhere in the placeholder text *[Year]* and then type the current year.

   f. Double-click in the document text. (This makes the document text active and dims the header.)

5. Scroll through the document to see how the header will print.

6. Save and then print **C07-E02-Computers.docx**.

Footer

Insert a predesigned footer in the same way you would insert a header. Click the Footer button in the Header & Footer group in the Insert tab, and a drop-down list displays similar to the Header button drop-down list shown in Figure 7.2. Click the desired footer, and the predesigned footer formatting is applied to the document.

Removing a Header or Footer

Remove a header from a document by clicking the Insert tab and then clicking the Header button in the Header & Footer group. At the drop-down list that displays, click the *Remove Header* option. Complete similar steps to remove a footer.

Exercise 7.2B   Removing a Header and Inserting a Predesigned Footer   Part 2 of 3

1. With **C07-E02-Computers.docx** open, press Ctrl + Home to move the insertion point to the beginning of the document.
2. Remove the header by clicking the Insert tab, clicking the Header button in the Header & Footer group, and then clicking the *Remove Header* option at the drop-down list.

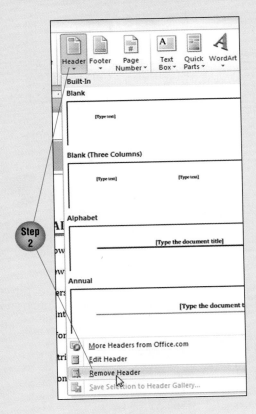

3. Insert a footer in the document by completing the following steps:
   a. Click the Footer button in the Header & Footer group.
   b. Click *Alphabet* at the drop-down list.

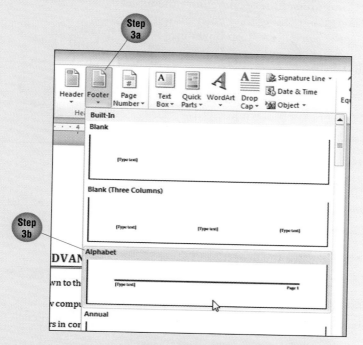

c. Click anywhere in the placeholder text *[Type text]* and then type The Computer Advantage.

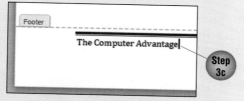

d. Double-click in the document text. (This makes the document text active and dims the footer.)
4. Scroll through the document to see how the footer will print.
5. Save and then print **C07-E02-Computers.docx**.

Editing a Predesigned Header or Footer

Predesigned headers and footers contain elements such as page numbers and the document title. You can change the formatting of an element by clicking it and then applying the desired formatting. You can also select and then delete an element. In Print Layout view, you can display the header or footer pane for editing by double-clicking a header or footer. You can also display the header pane for editing by clicking the Insert tab, clicking the Header button, and then clicking the *Edit Header* option. To edit a footer, click the Footer button in the Insert tab and then click *Edit Footer* at the drop-down list.

1. With **C07-E02-Computers.docx** open, remove the footer by clicking the Insert tab, clicking the Footer button, and then clicking *Remove Footer* at the drop-down list.

2. Insert and then format a header by completing the following steps:

   a. Click the Header button in the Header & Footer group in the Insert tab, scroll down the drop-down list, and then click *Motion (Odd Page)*. (This header inserts the document title as well as the page number.)

   b. Delete the document title from the header by clicking anywhere in the text *The Computer Advantage*, selecting the text, and then pressing the Delete key.

   c. Double-click in the document text.

3. Insert and then format a footer by completing the following steps:

   a. Click the Insert tab.

   b. Click the Footer button, scroll down the drop-down list, and then click *Motion (Odd Page)*.

   c. Select the date that displays in the footer and then type The Computer Advantage. (If the placeholder *[Pick the date]* displays instead of the date, click in the placeholder and then type The Computer Advantage.)

   d. Select the text you just typed (*The Computer Advantage*) and then click the Home tab.

   e. Turn on bold and change the font size to 12.

   f. Double-click in the document text.

4. Scroll through the document to see how the header and footer will print.

5. Save, print, and then close **C07-E02-Computers.docx**.

Finding and Replacing Text and Formatting

With the Find feature in Word you can search in a document for specific characters or types of formatting. With the Find and Replace feature, you can search for specific characters or types of formatting and replace them with other characters or formatting. The Find button and the Replace button are located in the Editing group in the Home tab.

Finding Text

Click the Find button in the Editing group in the Home tab (or press the keyboard shortcut Ctrl + F) and the Navigation pane displays at the left side of the screen with the third tab selected. Hover the mouse over the third tab and a ScreenTip displays with the information *Browse the results from your current search*. With this tab selected, type search text in the search text box and any occurrence of the text in the document is highlighted and a fragment of the text surrounding the search text displays in a thumbnail in the

Navigation pane. For example, search for *Lessee* in the **Lease.docx** document and the screen displays as shown in Figure 7.3. Notice that any occurrence of *Lessee* displays highlighted in yellow in the document and the Navigation pane displays thumbnails of text surrounding the occurrences of *Lessee*.

Click a text thumbnail in the Navigation pane and the occurrence of the search text is selected in the document. If you hover your mouse over a text thumbnail in the Navigation pane, the page number location displays in a small box near the mouse pointer. You can also move to the next occurrence of the search text by clicking the Next Search Result button located toward the upper right of the Navigation pane. Click the Previous Search Result button to move to the previous occurrence of the search text.

Figure 7.3 Navigation Pane Showing Search Results

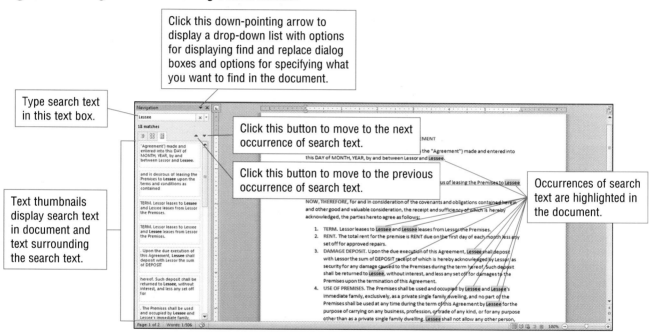

Click this down-pointing arrow to display a drop-down list with options for displaying find and replace dialog boxes and options for specifying what you want to find in the document.

Type search text in this text box.

Click this button to move to the next occurrence of search text.

Click this button to move to the previous occurrence of search text.

Text thumbnails display search text in document and text surrounding the search text.

Occurrences of search text are highlighted in the document.

Click the down-pointing arrow at the right of the search text box and a drop-down list displays with options for displaying dialog boxes, such as the Find Options dialog box or the Find and Replace dialog box, and also options for specifying what you want to find in the document such as figures, tables, and equations.

You can also highlight search text in a document with options at the Find and Replace dialog box with the Find tab selected. Display this dialog box by clicking the Find button arrow in the Editing group in the Home tab and then clicking the *Advanced Find* option at the drop-down list. You can also display the Find and Replace dialog box with the Find tab selected by clicking the down-pointing arrow at the right of the search text box in the Navigation pane and then clicking the *Advanced Find* option at the drop-down list. To highlight search text, type the search text in the *Find what* text box, click the Reading Highlight button, and then click *Highlight All* at the drop-down list. All occurrences of the text in the document are highlighted. To remove highlighting, click the Reading Highlight button and then click *Clear Highlighting* at the drop-down list.

1. Open **Lease.docx** and then save the document and name it **C07-E03-Lease**.
2. Find all occurrences of *lease* by completing the following steps:
   a. Click the Find button in the Editing group in the Home tab.
   b. Type lease in the search text box in the Navigation pane.
   c. After a moment, all occurrences of *lease* in the document are highlighted and text thumbnails display in the Navigation pane. Click a couple of the text thumbnails in the Navigation pane to select the text in the document.
   d. Click the Previous Search Result button to select the previous occurrence of *lease* in the document.
3. Use the Find and Replace dialog box with the Find tab selected to highlight all occurrences of *Premises* in the document by completing the following steps:
   a. Press Ctrl + Home to move the insertion point to the beginning of the document.
   b. Click the down-pointing arrow at the right of the search text box in the Navigation pane and then click *Advanced Find* at the drop-down list.
   c. At the Find and Replace dialog box with the Find tab selected (and *lease* selected in the *Find what* text box), type Premises.
   d. Click the Reading Highlight button and then click *Highlight All* at the drop-down list.
   e. Click in the document to make it active and then scroll through the document and notice the occurrences of highlighted text.
   f. Click in the dialog box to make it active.
   g. Click the Reading Highlight button and then click *Clear Highlighting* at the drop-down list.
   h. Click the Close button to close the Find and Replace dialog box.
4. Close the Navigation pane by clicking the Close button that displays in the upper right corner of the pane.

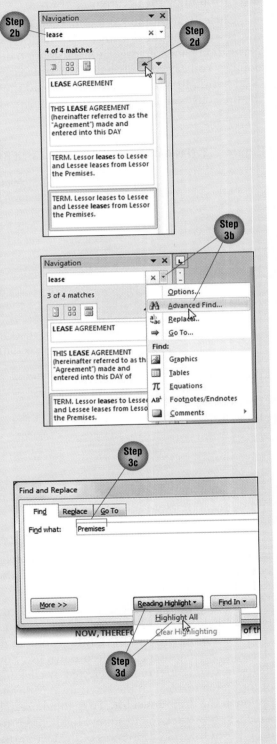

Finding and Replacing Text

To find and replace text, click the Replace button in the Editing group in the Home tab or use the keyboard shortcut Ctrl + H. Either action displays the Find and Replace dialog box with the Replace tab selected, as shown in Figure 7.4. Type the text you want to find in the *Find what* text box, press the Tab key, and then type the replacement text.

The Find and Replace dialog box contains several command buttons. Click the Find Next button to tell Word to find the next occurrence of the characters. Click the Replace button to replace the characters and find the next occurrence. If you know that you want all occurrences of the characters in the *Find what* text box replaced with the characters in the *Replace with* text box, click the Replace All button. This replaces every occurrence from the location of the insertion point to the beginning or end of the document (depending on the search direction). Click the Cancel button to close the Find and Replace dialog box. If you make a mistake when replacing text, close the Find and Replace dialog box and then click the Undo button on the Quick Access toolbar.

Figure 7.4 Find and Replace Dialog Box with the Replace Tab Selected

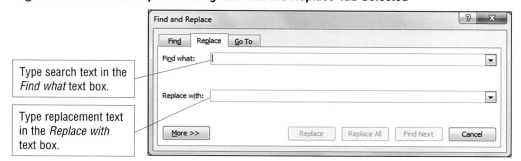

Type search text in the *Find what* text box.

Type replacement text in the *Replace with* text box.

Exercise 7.3B Finding and Replacing Text

Part 2 of 4

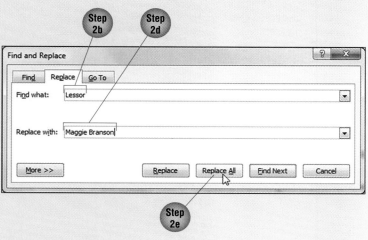

1. With **C07-E03-Lease.docx** open, make sure the insertion point is positioned at the beginning of the document.
2. Find all occurrences of *Lessor* and replace with *Maggie Branson* by completing the following steps:
   a. Click the Replace button in the Editing group in the Home tab.
   b. At the Find and Replace dialog box with the Replace tab selected, type Lessor in the *Find what* text box.
   c. Press the Tab key to move the insertion point to the *Replace with* text box.
   d. Type Maggie Branson.
   e. Click the Replace All button.

f. At the message *Word has completed its search of the document and has made 13 replacements*, click OK. (Do not close the Find and Replace dialog box.)

3. With the Find and Replace dialog box still open, complete the steps outlined in Step 2 to find all occurrences of *Lessee* and replace with *Lee Gardella*. (Word should make 18 replacements.)

4. Close the Find and Replace dialog box.

5. Save **C07-E03-Lease.docx**.

Choosing Check Box Options

The Find and Replace dialog box contains a variety of search option check boxes that you can choose to complete a search. To display these options, click the More button located at the bottom of the dialog box. Clicking the More button expands the Find and Replace dialog box, as shown in Figure 7.5. Table 7.1 describes each option in the expanded dialog box and what the result of clicking that option will be. To remove the display of options, click the Less button. (The Less button was previously the More button.)

Figure 7.5 Expanded Find and Replace Dialog Box

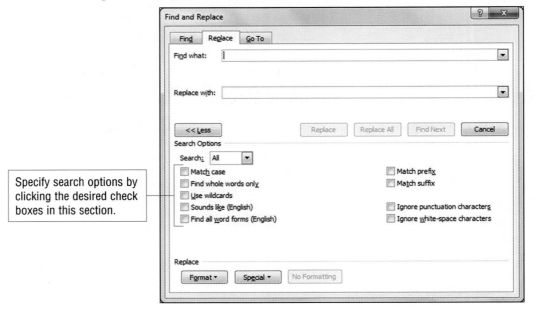

Specify search options by clicking the desired check boxes in this section.

Table 7.1 Options Available at the Expanded Find and Replace Dialog Box

Choose this option	To
Match case	Exactly match the case of the search text. For example, if you search for *Book* and select the *Match case* option, Word will stop at *Book* but not *book* or *BOOK*.
Find whole words only	Find a whole word, not a part of a word. For example, if you search for *her* and do not select *Find whole words only*, Word will stop at *there*, *here*, *hers*, etc.
Use wildcards	Search for wildcards, special characters, or special search operators.
Sounds like	Match words that sound alike but are spelled differently such as *know* and *no*.
Find all word forms	Find all forms of the word entered in the *Find what* text box. For example, if you enter *hold*, Word will stop at *held* and *holding*.
Match prefix	Find only those words that begin with the letters in the *Find what* text box. For example, if you enter *per*, Word will stop at words such as *perform* and *perfect* but skip words such as *super* and *hyperlink*.
Match suffix	Find only those words that end with the letters in the *Find what* text box. For example, if you enter *ly*, Word will stop at words such as *accurately* and *quietly* but skip over words such *catalyst* and *lyre*.
Ignore punctuation characters	Ignore punctuation within characters. For example, if you enter *US* in the *Find what* text box, Word will stop at *U.S.*
Ignore white-space characters	Ignore spaces between letters. For example, if you enter *F B I* in the *Find what* text box, Word will stop at *FBI*.

Exercise 7.3C Finding and Replacing Word Forms and Suffixes   Part 3 of 4

1. With **C07-E03-Lease.docx** open, make sure the insertion point is positioned at the beginning of the document.
2. Find all word forms of the word *lease* and replace with *rent* by completing the following steps:
   a. Click the Replace button in the Editing group in the Home tab.
   b. At the Find and Replace dialog box with the Replace tab selected, type lease in the *Find what* text box.
   c. Press the Tab key and then type rent in the *Replace with* text box.
   d. Click the More button.
   e. Click the *Find all word forms* option. (This inserts a check mark in the check box.)
   f. Click the Replace All button.

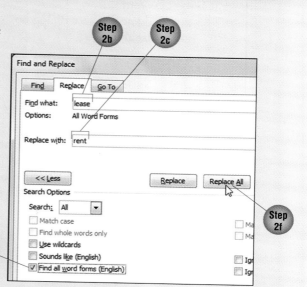

g. At the message telling you that Replace All is not recommended with Find All Word Forms, click OK.

h. At the message *Word has completed its search of the document and has made 5 replacements*, click OK.

i. Click the *Find all word forms* option to remove the check mark.

3. Find the word *less* and replace with the word *minus* and specify that you want Word to find only those words that end in *less* by completing the following steps:

a. At the expanded Find and Replace dialog box, select the text in the *Find what* text box and then type less.

b. Select the text in the *Replace with* text box and then type minus.

c. Click the *Match suffix* check box to insert a check mark and tell Word to find only words that end in *less*.

d. Click the Replace All button.

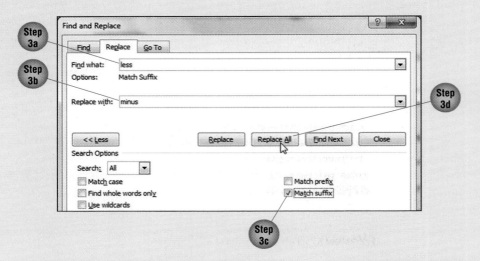

e. At the message telling you that two replacements were made, click OK.

f. Click the *Match suffix* check box to remove the check mark.

g. Click the Less button.

h. Close the Find and Replace dialog box.

4. Save **C07-E03-Lease.docx**.

Finding and Replacing Formatting

At the Find and Replace dialog box with the Replace tab selected, you can select options to search for characters with specific formatting and replace them with other characters or formatting. To specify formatting in the Find and Replace dialog box, click the More button and then click the Format button that displays toward the bottom of the dialog box. At the pop-up list that displays, identify the type of formatting you want to find.

1. With **C07-E03-Lease.docx** open, make sure the insertion point is positioned at the beginning of the document.
2. Find text set in 11-point Calibri bold dark orange and replace it with text set in 12-point Cambria bold dark blue by completing the following steps:

   a. Click the Replace button in the Editing group.

   b. At the Find and Replace dialog box, press the Delete key. (This deletes any text that displays in the *Find what* text box.)

   c. Click the More button. (If a check mark displays in any of the check boxes, click the option to remove the check mark.)

   d. With the insertion point positioned in the *Find what* text box, click the Format button located toward the bottom of the dialog box and then click *Font* at the drop-down list.

   e. At the Find Font dialog box, click *Calibri* in the Font list box, *Bold* in the Font style list box, *11* in the Size list box, and change the Font color to dark orange (*Orange, Accent 6, Darker 50%*).

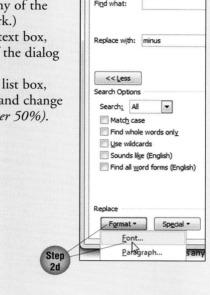

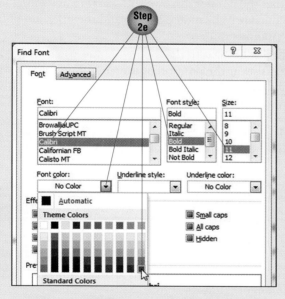

   f. Click OK to close the Find Font dialog box.

   g. At the Find and Replace dialog box, select any text in the *Replace with* text box and then press the Delete key.

   h. Click the Format button located toward the bottom of the dialog box and then click *Font* at the drop-down list.

   i. At the Replace Font dialog box, click *Cambria* in the Font list box, *Bold* in the Font style list box, *12* in the Size list box, and change the font color to *Dark Blue* (second color option from the right in the Standard Colors section).

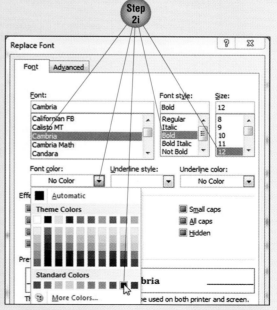

    j.   Click OK to close the Replace Font dialog box.
    k.   At the Find and Replace dialog box, click the Replace All button.
    l.   At the message telling you that the search of the document is complete and 13
        replacements were made, click OK.
3. Clear formatting from the Find and Replace dialog box by completing the following steps:
    a.   Click in the *Find what* text box and then click the No Formatting button.
    b.   Click in the *Replace with* text box and then click the No Formatting button.
    c.   Click the Less button and then close the Find and Replace dialog box.
4. Save, print, and then close **C07-E03-Lease.docx**.

Using the Click and Type Feature

QUICK STEPS

Use Click and Type
1. Hover mouse at left margin, between left and right margin, or at right margin.
2. Double-click left mouse button.

Word contains a Click and Type feature that you can use to position the insertion point at a specific location and alignment in the document. To use Click and Type, make sure the document displays in Print Layout view and then hover the mouse pointer at the location where you want the insertion point positioned. As you move the mouse pointer, you will notice that the pointer displays with varying horizontal lines representing the alignment. Double-click the mouse button and the insertion point is positioned at the location of the mouse pointer.

If the horizontal lines do not display next to the mouse pointer when you double-click the mouse button, a left tab is set at the position of the insertion point. If you want to change the alignment and not set a tab, make sure the horizontal lines display near the mouse pointer before double-clicking the mouse. You can turn off the Click and Type feature by clicking the File tab and then clicking the Options button located below the Help tab. Click the *Advanced* option in the left panel, click the *Enable click and type* check box to remove the check mark, and then click OK.

Exercise 7.4A Using Click and Type   Part 1 of 2

1. At a blank document, create the centered text shown in Figure 7.6 by completing the following steps:
    a.   Position the I-beam pointer between the left and right margins at about the 3.25-inch mark on the horizontal ruler and the top of the vertical ruler.
    b.   When the center alignment lines display below the I-beam pointer, double-click the left mouse button.

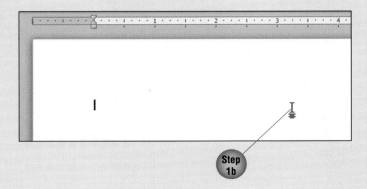

Step 1b

    c.   Type the centered text shown in Figure 7.6. Press Shift + Enter to end each text line.

2. Change to right alignment by completing the following steps:

    a.   Position the I-beam pointer near the right margin at approximately the 1.5-inch mark on the vertical ruler until the right alignment lines display at the left side of the I-beam pointer.

    b.   Double-click the left mouse button.

    c.   Type the right-aligned text shown in Figure 7.6. Press Shift + Enter to end the text line.

3. Select the centered text and then change the font to 14-point Constantia bold and the line spacing to double.

4. Select the right-aligned text, change the font to 10-point Constantia bold, and then deselect the text.

5. Save the document and name it **C07-E04-WordTrain.**

Figure 7.6 Exercise 7.4A

MICROSOFT WORD TRAINING
Formatting Company Documents
Thursday, January 19, 2012
Technology Department Training Center
8:30 a.m. to 11:30 a.m.

Sponsored by
Culver Training Services

Vertically Aligning Text

Text in a Word document is aligned at the top of the page by default. You can change this alignment with the *Vertical alignment* option at the Page Setup dialog box with the Layout tab selected, as shown in Figure 7.7. Display this dialog box by clicking the Page Layout tab, clicking the Page Setup group dialog box launcher, and then clicking the Layout tab at the Page Setup dialog box.

The *Vertical alignment* option box in the Page Setup dialog box contains four choices: *Top, Center, Justified,* and *Bottom.* The default setting is *Top,* which aligns text at the top of the page. Choose *Center* if you want text centered vertically on the page. The *Justified* option aligns text between the top and the bottom margins. The *Center* option positions text in the middle of the page vertically, while the *Justified* option adds space between paragraphs of text (not within) to fill the page from the top to bottom margins. If you center or justify text, it does not display as centered or justified on the screen in Draft view, but it does display centered or justified in Print Layout view. Choose the *Bottom* option to align text in the document vertically along the bottom of the page.

QUICK STEPS

Vertically Align Text
1. Click Page Layout tab.
2. Click Page Setup group dialog box launcher.
3. Click Layout tab.
4. Click down-pointing arrow at right of Vertical alignment option.
5. Click desired alignment.
6. Click OK.

Figure 7.7 Page Setup Dialog Box with Layout Tab Selected

Click this down-pointing arrow to display a list of vertical alignment options.

Exercise 7.4B Vertically Centering Text

Part 2 of 2

1. With **C07-E04-WordTrain.docx** open, click the Page Layout tab and then click the Page Setup group dialog box launcher.
2. At the Page Setup dialog box, click the Layout tab.
3. Click the down-pointing arrow at the right of the *Vertical alignment* option box and then click *Center* at the drop-down list.
4. Click OK to close the dialog box.
5. Save, print, and then close **C07-E04-WordTrain.docx**.

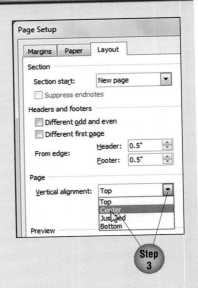

Step 3

Chapter *Summary*

➤ The page break that Word inserts automatically is a soft page break. A page break that you insert is a hard page break. Insert a hard page break by clicking the Page Break button in the Pages group in the Insert tab or by pressing Ctrl + Enter.

➤ Insert a blank page in a document by clicking the Blank Page button in the Pages group in the Insert tab.

➤ Insert a predesigned and formatted cover page by clicking the Cover Page button in the Pages group in the Insert tab and then clicking the desired option at the drop-down list.

➤ Insert predesigned and formatted page numbering by clicking the Page Number button in the Header & Footer group in the Insert tab, specifying the desired location of the page numbers, and then clicking the desired page numbering option.

➤ Text that appears at the top of every page is called a header; text that appears at the bottom of every page is called a footer.

➤ You can insert predesigned headers and footers in a document with the Header button and the Footer button in the Header & Footer group in the Insert tab.

➤ A header or footer displays in Print Layout view but will not display in Draft view.

➤ You can remove or edit predesigned headers and footers.

➤ Use the Navigation pane to search for specific characters or formatting. Use the Find and Replace feature to search for specific characters or formatting and replace the items found with other characters or formatting.

➤ Display the Navigation pane by clicking the Find button in the Editing group in the Home tab or by pressing Ctrl + F.

➤ Type search text in the search text box in the Navigation pane, and any occurrence of the text is highlighted in the document and thumbnails of the search text display in the Navigation pane.

➤ At the Find and Replace dialog box, click the Find Next button to find the next occurrence of specific characters or formatting. Click the Replace button to replace the characters or formatting and find the next occurrence; click the Replace All button to replace all occurrences of the characters or formatting.

➤ Click the More button at the Find and Replace dialog box to display additional options for completing a search.

➤ Use the Click and Type feature to center, right-align, and left-align text.

➤ Vertically align text in a document with the *Vertical alignment* option at the Page Setup dialog box with the Layout tab selected.

Commands Review

FEATURE	RIBBON TAB, GROUP	BUTTON	KEYBOARD SHORTCUT
Blank page	Insert, Pages		
Cover page	Insert, Pages		
Find and Replace dialog box with Find tab selected	Home, Editing	Find ▾ , Advanced Find	
Find and Replace dialog box with Replace tab selected	Home, Editing		Ctrl + H
Footer	Insert, Header & Footer		
Header	Insert, Header & Footer		
Navigation pane	View, Show		Ctrl + F
Page break	Insert, Pages		Ctrl + Enter
Page numbering	Insert, Header & Footer		
Page Setup dialog box	Page Layout, Page Setup		

Key Points Review

Completion: In the space provided at the right, indicate the correct term, symbol, or command.

1. Press these keys on the keyboard to insert a page break. _____

2. The Cover Page button is located in the Pages group in this tab. _____

3. A predesigned cover page generally contains these, which are locations where you can enter specific information. _____

4. The Page Number button is located in this group in the Insert tab. _____

5. Text that appears at the top of every page is called this. _____

6. A footer displays in Print Layout view, but not this view. _____

7. Click this button in the Editing group in the Home tab to display the Navigation pane. _____

8. This is the keyboard shortcut to display the Find and Replace dialog box with the Replace tab selected. _____

9. If you want to replace every occurrence of what you are searching for in a document, click this button at the Find and Replace dialog box. _____

10. Click this option at the Find and Replace dialog box if you are searching for a word and all of its forms.

    _____

11. Use this feature to position the insertion point at a specific location and alignment in a document.

    _____

12. Vertically align text with the *Vertical alignment* option at the Page Setup dialog box with this tab selected.

    _____

Chapter *Assessments*

Applying Your Skills

Demonstrate your knowledge of features learned in this chapter by completing the following assessments.

Assessment 7.1   Format and Insert a Cover Page in a Document

1. Open **CompIndustry.docx** and save the document with the name **C07-A01-CompIndustry**.
2. Select text from the beginning of the title *REFERENCES* (located on the second page) to the end of the document and then delete the selected text.
3. Apply the Heading 1 style to the title of the document and apply the Heading 2 style to the headings in the document.
4. Change the style set to Modern.
5. Change the theme colors to Concourse.
6. Insert a page break at the beginning of the heading *News Services*.
7. Move the insertion point to the beginning of the document and then insert the *Mod* cover page.
8. Insert the following text in the specified placeholders:
    a. Type *Computers in Industry* in the *[Type the document title]* placeholder.
    b. Delete the *[Type the document subtitle]* placeholder. **Hint: To delete a placeholder, click in the placeholder text, click the placeholder tab, and then press the Delete key.**
    c. Delete the *[Abstract]* placeholder.
    d. Type your first and last names in the *[Type the author name]* placeholder.
    e. Insert the date in the *[Pick the date]* placeholder.
9. Move the insertion point to any character in the title *COMPUTERS IN INDUSTRY* in the main document (not in the cover page) and then insert the *Outline Circle 3* page numbering at the bottom of the pages (the page numbering will not appear on the cover page).
10. Save, print, and then close **C07-A01-CompIndustry.docx**.

Assessment 7.2   Format and Insert a Header and Footer in a Report

1. Open **CompViruses.docx** and save the document with the name **C07-A02-CompViruses**.
2. Insert a page break at the beginning of the title *SECTION 4: HARDWARE AND SOFTWARE SECURITY RISKS*.
3. Apply the Heading 1 style to the two titles in the document and apply the Heading 2 style to the five headings in the document.
4. Change the style set to Fancy.
5. Select the entire document and then remove the italic formatting.
6. Apply the Apex theme.
7. Move the insertion point to the beginning of the document and then insert the Pinstripes header. Type Computer Security in the *[Type the document title]* placeholder.
8. Insert the Pinstripes footer and type your first and last names in the *[Type text]* placeholder.
9. Change the theme colors to Oriel (make sure you change the theme colors and not the theme).

10. Save and then print **C07-A02-CompViruses.docx**.
11. Remove the header and footer.
12. Insert the Austere (Odd Page) footer and then make the following changes:
    a. Select and then delete the *[Type the company name]* placeholder.
    b. Select the text and page number in the footer and then change the font to 10-point Constantia bold.
13. Insert the *DRAFT 1* watermark in the document.
14. Insert a page border of your choosing in the document. Make sure that the entire page border prints on the page and does not display over the footer. If the entire page border is not visible, change measurements at the Border and Shading Options dialog box.
15. Save, print, and then close **C07-A02-CompViruses.docx**.

Assessment 7.3   Find and Replace Text in a Real Estate Agreement

1. Open **REAgrmnt.docx** and save the document with the name **C07-A03-REAgrmnt**.
2. Find all occurrences of BUYER (matching the case) and replace with Craig Metzner. (If the *Find what* and/or *Replace with* options contain any formatting, delete the formatting.)
3. Find all occurrences of SELLER (matching the case) and replace with Carol Winters.
4. Find all word forms of the word *buy* and replace with *purchase*.
5. Search for 14-point Tahoma bold formatting in dark red and replace with 12-point Constantia bold formatting in black.
6. Clear the formatting from the Find and Replace dialog box.
7. Insert page numbers at the bottom of each page.
8. Save, print, and then close **C07-A03-REAgrmnt.docx**.

Assessment 7.4   Create a Notice Using Click and Type

1. At a blank document, use the Click and Type feature to create the document shown in Figure 7.8.
2. Select the centered text and then change the font to 16-point Candara bold in dark blue.
3. Select the right-aligned text and then change the font to 12-point Candara bold in dark blue.
4. Change the vertical alignment of the text to *Center*.
5. Save the document and name it **C07-A04-CoData**.
6. Print and then close **C07-A04-CoData.docx**.

Figure 7.8 Assessment 7.4

Securing Company Data

Systems for Backing up Crucial Data

Tuesday, February 7, 2012

Corporate Training Center

1:30 to 4:00 p.m.

Sponsored by

Madison Security Systems

Expanding Your Skills

Explore additional feature options or use Help to learn a new skill in creating these documents.

Assessment 7.5   Find and Replace Using a Wildcard

1. Open **ComLease.docx** and then save it and name it **C07-A05-ComLease**.
2. One of the options available at the expanded Find and Replace dialog box is *Use wildcards*. You can use wildcard characters to specify characters or a range of characters when searching for text. Click the *Use wildcards* check box and then click the Special button at the bottom of the expanded Find and Replace dialog box and a pop-up list displays. The top items in the pop-up list are wildcard characters you can use when finding specific text. You can click the desired wildcard character at the pop-up list or type the wildcard character on the keyboard. Click the Replace button in the Editing group in the Home tab to display the Find and Replace dialog box and then click the More button to expand the dialog box. Click the *Use wildcards* check box to insert a check mark. Click the Special button and then look at the information that displays in the pop-up list.
3. The name *Arigalason* is spelled a variety of ways in the document. The name is spelled *Arigalason, Aragalason, Aragalasen,* and *Arigalasen*. The correct spelling is *Arigalason*, so you decide to use a wildcard character to search for all versions of the spelling and replace with the correct spelling. To begin, click in the *Find what* text box and then type Ar?galas?n. (The question mark wildcard character represents one character in the search text.)
4. Click in the *Replace with* text box and then type Arigalason (which is the correct spelling).
5. Click the Replace All button. (Word will make 23 replacements.)
6. Remove the check mark from the *Use wildcards* check box, click the Less button, and then close the dialog box.
7. Click the Find button to display the Navigation pane, type leas* in the Search text box and then press the Enter key. (The asterisk is the wildcard character indicating any characters, not just one character.) Word highlights any occurrence of text that begins with *leas*.
8. Scroll through the document and notice the highlighted occurrences and then close the Navigation pane.
9. Apply the Heading 1 style to the title and the Heading 2 style to the headings in the document.
10. Change the style set to Thatch and change the theme colors to Clarity (make sure you change the theme colors and not the theme).
11. Center the title in the document.
12. Apply the Conservative footer to the document.
13. Save and print **C07-A05-ComLease.docx**.

Assessment 7.6   Insert a Cover Page from Office.com

1. With **C07-A05-ComLease.docx** open, save it and name it **C07-A06-ComLease**.
2. Click the Insert tab, click the Cover Page button, and then click the *More Cover Pages from Office.com* option. Look at the additional cover pages and then insert a cover page of your choice. Insert the appropriate text in the cover page placeholders. (Consider deleting some placeholders if they are not pertinent to the lease agreement.)
3. Print only the cover page of the document.
4. Save and then close **C07-A06-ComLease.docx**.

Achieving Signature Status

Take your skills to the next level by completing this more challenging assessment.

Assessment 7.7   Format a Resume Document

1. Open **ResumeInfo.docx** and then save it and name it **C07-A07-ResumeInfo**.
2. Format the document so it appears as shown in Figure 7.9 with the following specifications:
   - Apply the Heading 1 style to the title and the Heading 3 style to the headings and then change the Quick Styles set to Thatch.
   - Change the paragraph spacing to *Relaxed*. ***Hint: Do this with the Change Styles button in the Home tab.***
   - Apply the Apex theme and change the theme colors to Elemental.
   - Insert the page border on the second and third pages only. (To determine how to do this, display the Borders and Shading dialog box with the Page Border tab selected and then experiment with the *Apply to* option.) Change the border color to *Blue, Accent 1, Darker 25%* (located in the fifth column from the left). Make sure the entire page border prints on the page. If not, change measurements at the Border and Shading Options dialog box.
   - Insert the *Accent Bar 2* page number at the top of the page.
   - Insert the *Stacks* footer. Type your first and last names in the *[Type the company name]* placeholder, select your name and then change the font color to black. With the insertion point positioned on any character in your name, display the Borders and Shading dialog box with the Borders tab selected, change the color to *Blue, Accent 1, Darker 25%*, click the top border of the preview diagram (this changes the blue-gray border line to blue), and then close the dialog box.
   - Apply any other formatting required so your document appears as shown in Figure 7.9.
3. Save, print, and then close **C07-A07-ResumeInfo.docx**.

Figure 7.9 Assessment 7.7

Becoming a Job Detective

Imagine the scene: an office in the city, but there is someone missing from one desk. Witnesses say the missing person is dynamic, well qualified, and pays exceptional attention to detail. Every employer has a "prime suspect" in mind when they advertise a position, and they tend to leave clues to that person's identity in their job description. In this chapter, we teach you to become a job detective, so that you can pick up all the clues and solve the mystery—what would the ideal candidate for this job look like?

To produce the best "fitting" resume, you need to know about yourself and the job you are applying for. Before you do anything else, ask yourself why you are preparing a resume. The answer to this question is going to vary from one person to the next, and here are our top ten reasons for writing a resume:

1. You have seen a job tha
2. You want to market yo
   or organization.
3. You have seen a job tha
4. Your friends or family
5. You want to work for t
   company might get its
6. You have seen a job ad
7. You are going for a pro
8. You are about to be do
   good opportunities.
9. You are feeling fed up,
   might motivate you to
10. You are thinking "Oh,
    remember what I've be

All of these certainly are good r
purposes. One way of understar
resume in each case.

INFORMATION ABOU

You should tailor the informati
sounds fine, but how do you do
can. The main sources of inform

- A job advertisement
- A job description
- A friend in the compa
- The media
- Gossip and rumor
- Someone already doin

There is no substitute for experi
to apply for in the same compa
like. Bear in mind, of course, th
differently than the way that pe
be very different than yours. H
opportunity. Make sure you do

Resumes 1 through 5 will be read by potential employers who probably do not know you. Resume 6 and 7 are likely to be read by your boss or other people who know you. Resumes 8 through 10 are really for your own benefit and should not be considered as suitable for sending out to employers.

THE RIGHT MIX

Think about the list of reasons again. How else can you divide up these reasons? A most important difference is that, in some cases, you will have a good idea of what the employer is looking for because you have a job advertisement in front of you and can tailor your resume accordingly. For others, you have no idea what the reader might want to see. Updating your resume from time to time is a good idea so you do not forget important details, but remember that the result of such a process will not be a winning resume. It will be a useful list of tasks and achievements.

Writing a resume is like baking
on. It is what you do with the in
and failure. Keeping your resu
potentially very useful, but do

INFORMATION ABOUT
You should tailor the informati
sounds fine, but how do you do
can. The main sources of inform

INFORMATION ABOUT THE COMPANY
The main sources of information about an employer are normally the following:

- The media
- Annual reports/company brochures
- Industry/trade magazines or journals
- The Internet—on the company's own site or at general sites
- Industry directories

GOSSIP AND RUMOR

Other sources of information about companies are available; if you are serious about wanting to know more about a potential employer (and you should be), it is worth a visit to your local library. Ask a reference librarian to help you with your search. It will help if you explain to the librarian that you are looking for information on a specific company to help with your job search.

Student Name

Chapter 8

Tutorial 8.1
Inserting Symbols and Special Characters
Tutorial 8.2
Creating a Drop Cap and Inserting the Date and Time
Tutorial 8.3
Inserting a File
Tutorial 8.4
Navigating Using the Navigation Pane
Tutorial 8.5
Navigating with Bookmarks
Tutorial 8.6
Creating and Editing Hyperlinks
Tutorial 8.7
Linking to a File in Another Program, a New Document, and an E-mail Address
Tutorial 8.6
Creating a Cross-Reference

Inserting Elements and Navigating in a Document

Performance Objectives

Upon successful completion of Chapter 8, you will be able to:

- Insert symbols and special characters
- Insert a drop cap
- Insert the date and time
- Insert a file into an open document
- Navigate in a document using the Navigation pane, thumbnails, bookmarks, hyperlinks, and cross-references
- Insert hyperlinks to a location in the same document, a different document, and a file in another program

You can insert a variety of elements into a Word document to serve a variety of purposes. In this chapter, you will learn to insert symbols, special characters, and drop caps to add visual appeal. You will learn to insert the date and/or time in a number of formats to identify when a document was created and automatically update the information to reflect when a document was revised. You will learn how to insert one file into another to efficiently combine the content of two documents, and you will learn how to insert hyperlinks, bookmarks, and cross-references to provide additional information for readers and to allow for more efficient navigation within a document.

Note: Before beginning computer exercises for this chapter, copy to your storage medium the Chapter08 folder from the CD that accompanies this textbook and then make Chapter08 the active folder.

In this chapter students will produce the following documents:

Exercise 8.1. C08-E01-ProdSoftware.docx
Exercise 8.2. C08-E02-CompSecurity.docx

Model answers for these exercises are shown on the following pages.

Exercise 8.1

C08-E01-ProdSoftware.docx

PRODUCTIVITY SOFTWARE

Productivity software is designed to improve efficiency and performance on the job and at home. It is the largest category of application software for individual use. Employment notices appearing in newspapers and magazines often list required computer skills, such as word processing or spreadsheet expertise. Some employment notices even specify that an applicant must be certified in a particular application.

In-depth knowledge of productivity software applications and skill in using them can make a potential employee more valuable to a business, organization, or agency. Productivity software includes the following categories:

Word processing: Used to write, format, and print letters, memos, reports, and other documents.

Desktop publishing: Used to produce newsletters, advertisements, and other high-quality documents.

Spreadsheet: Used to produce spreadsheets and manipulate financial and other numerical data.

Project management: Used to schedule and manage projects.

Presentation graphics: Used to create and display slide shows.

Computer-aided design: Used to create and edit detailed designs of products.

PERSONAL-USE SOFTWARE

Shoppers browsing in computer stores are likely to see numerous software applications designed for home and personal use. Among the many products available are applications for writing letters, making out wills, designing a new home, landscaping a lawn, preparing and filing tax returns, and managing finances. Software suites are also available for home and personal use, although sometimes the suites available for home use do not contain all the features found in business versions.

More than one-half of U.S. homes now include a personal computer on which a variety of software applications have been installed. Most application software programs are relatively inexpensive. Some vendors advertise popular word processing programs for as little as $99. includes the following categories:

ware: Assists users with paying bills, balancing checkbooks, and expenses, and maintaining investment records.
are: Designed to aid in analyzing federal and state tax status, as ansmit tax returns.

1

Page 1

- **Legal documents software:** Designed to help analyze, plan, and prepare a variety of legal documents, including will and trusts.
- **Games and entertainment software:** Designed to provide fun as well as challenges to users and include interactive games, videos, and music.

Created by: Rueben Cedeño
Northland Security Systems®
May 6, 2012
11:45:13 AM

2

Page 2

Computer Security

2/28/2012
Northland Security Systems
Student Name

Page 1

1

SECTION 1: UNAUTHORIZED ACCESS

Like uncharted wilderness, the Internet lacks borders. This inherent openness is what makes the Internet so valuable and yet so vulnerable. Over its short life, the Internet has grown so quickly that the legal system has not been able to keep pace. The security risks posed by networks and the Internet can be grouped into three categories: unauthorized access, information theft, and denial of service.

Hackers, individuals who gain access to computers and networks illegally, are responsible for most cases of unauthorized access. Hackers tend to exploit sites and programs that have poor security measures in place. However, they also gain access to more challenging sites by using sophisticated programs and strategies. Many hackers claim they hack merely because they like the challenge of trying to defeat security measures. They rarely have a more malicious motive, and they generally do not aim to destroy or damage the sites that they invade. In fact, hackers dislike being identified with those who seek to cause damage. They refer to hackers with malicious or criminal intent as crackers. Types of Viruses

USER IDS AND PASSWORDS

To gain entry over the Inter[...]
a working user ID and passw[...]
generally not secure informa[...]
ID in the return address, ma[...]
Hackers know from experien[...]
generate thousands of likely[...]
hours or days.Password Sug[...]

Programmers can sometimes[...]
entrance to networks and inf[...]
system "backdoor," which is [...]
authorization. Programmers[...]
development to allow other p[...]
problems. Through negligenc[...]
behind in the final version of[...]
system, bypassing the securi[...]

A sophisticated way to break[...]
process of fooling another co[...]
source. It works by altering t[...]

Page 2

2

message sent. The address is changed to one that the receiving computer is programmed to accept as a trusted source of information.

SPYWARE

Spyware is a type of software that allows an intruder to spy upon someone else's computer. This alarming technology takes advantage of loopholes in the computer's security systems and allows a stranger to witness and record another person's every mouse click or keystroke on the monitor as it occurs. The spy can record activities and gain access to passwords and credit card information. Spyware generally requires the user to install it on the machine that is being spied upon, so it is highly unlikely that random strangers on the Internet could simply begin watching your computer. In the workplace, however, someone might be able to install the software without the victim's knowledge. Disguised as an email greeting, for example, the program can operate like a virus that gets the unwary user to install the spyware unknowingly.

SECTION 2: INFORMATION THEFT

Information can be a company's most valuable possession. Stealing corporate information, a crime included in the category of industrial espionage, is unfortunately both easy to do and difficult to detect. This is due in part to the invisible nature of software and data. If a cracker breaks into a company network and manages to download the company database from the network onto a disk, there is no visible sign to the company that anything is amiss. The original database is still in place, working the same way it always has.

WIRELESS DEVICE SECURITY

The growing number of wireless devices has created a new opportunity for data theft. Wireless devices such as cameras, Web phones, networked computers, PDAs, and input and output peripherals are inherently less secure than wired devices. Security is quite lax, and in some cases nonexistent, in new wireless technologies for handheld computers and cell phone systems. In a rush to match competition, manufacturers have tended to sacrifice security to move a product to the marketplace faster. Already, viruses are appearing in emails for cell phones and PDAs. With little protection available for these new systems, hackers and spies are enjoying a free hand with the new technology. One of the few available security protocols for wireless networks is Wired Equivalent Privacy (WEP), developed in conjunction with the standard for wireless local area networks. Newer versions of WEP with enhanced security features make it more difficult for hackers to intercept and modify data transmissions sent by radio waves or infrared signals.

Northland Security Systems | Confidential

Page 3

3

DATA BROWSING

Data browsing is a less damaging form of information theft that involves an invasion of privacy. Workers in many organizations have access to networked databases that contain private information about people. Accessing this information without an official reason is against the law. The IRS had a particularly large problem with data browsing in the late 1990s. Some employees were fired and the rest were given specialized training in appropriate conduct.

SECTION 3: COMPUTER VIRUSES

One of the most familiar forms of risk to computer security is the computer virus. A computer virus is a program written by a hacker or cracker designed to perform some kind of trick upon an unsuspecting victim. The trick performed in some cases is mild, such as drawing an offensive image on the screen, or changing all of the characters in a document to another language. Sometimes the trick is much more severe, such as reformatting the hard drive and erasing all the data, or damaging the motherboard so that it cannot operate properly. Computer Virus Presentation

Viruses can be categorized by
espionage, and hardware-des
rather just an inconvenience.
the hard drive. The installed
the heart of a personal compu
Some viruses are designed to
espionage viruses, they do no
system later for the purpose
rarely, a virus is created that
itself. Called hardware-destr
destroy chips, drives, and oth

Data Browsing.)

METI

Viruses can create effects tha
are operated and transmitted
transmitted as an attachmen
the victim to click on the atta
transmission is by a macro, a
automate certain functions. A
then becomes infected when

4

sector of a floppy disk or hard disk contains a variety of information, including how the disk is organized and whether it is capable of loading an operating system. When a disk is left in a drive and the computer reboots, the operating system automatically reads the boot sector to learn about that disk and to attempt to start any operating system on that disk. A boot sector virus is designed to alter the boot sector of a disk, so that whenever the operating system reads the boot sector, the computer will automatically become infected.

Other methods of virus infection include the Trojan horse virus, which hides inside another legitimate program or data file, and the stealth virus, which is designed to hide itself from detection software. Polymorphic viruses alter themselves to prevent antivirus software from detecting them by examining familiar patterns. Polymorphic viruses alter themselves randomly as they move from computer to computer, making detection more difficult. Multipartite viruses alter their form of attack. Their name derives from their ability to attack in several different ways. They may first infect the boot sector and then later move on to become a Trojan horse type by infecting a disk file. These viruses are more sophisticated, and therefore more difficult to guard against. Another type of virus is the logic bomb, which generally sits quietly dormant waiting for a specific event or set of conditions to occur. A famous logic bomb was the widely publicized Michelangelo virus, which infected personal computers and caused them to display a message on the artist's birthday.

SECTION 4: HAI

Although hackers, crackers,
company faces a variety of ot
these risks involve types of s
copying. Click to view types

A fundamental element in m
protecting the electrical powe
brownouts have very adverse
called a surge protector can
extension cord and splitter. A
uninterruptible power supply
a power strip, but much mor
steady spike-free power, but

Although accurate estimates
dollars a year in stolen comp

5

such theft goes unnoticed or unreported. Someone takes a hard drive or a scanner home for legitimate use, then leaves the job sometime later, and keeps the machine. Sometimes, employees take components to add to their home PC systems or a thief breaks into a business and hauls away computers. Such thefts cost far more than the price of the stolen computers because they also involve the cost of replacing the lost data, the cost of the time lost while the machines are gone, and the cost of installing new machines and training people to use them.

CRACKING SOFTWARE FOR COPYING

A common goal of hackers is to crack a software protection scheme. A crack is a method of circumventing a security scheme that prevents a user from copying a program. A common protection scheme for software is to require that the installation CD be resident in the drive whenever the program runs. Making copies of the CD with a burner, however, easily fools this protection scheme. Some game companies are taking the extra step of making duplication difficult by scrambling some of the data on the original CDs, which CD burners will automatically correct when copying. When the copied and corrected CD is used, the software checks for the scrambled track information. If the error is not found, the software will not run.

Hold down the Ctrl key and then click the logo shown below to display a list of training courses offered by Northland Security Systems

Click to send an email

Northland Security Systems | Confidential

Page 4

Page 5

Inserting Symbols and Special Characters

You can use the Symbol button in the Symbols group in the Insert tab to insert special symbols in a document. Click the button to display a drop-down list with the most recently inserted symbols and a *More Symbols* option. Click one of the symbols that displays in the list to insert it in the document or click the *More Symbols* option to display the Symbol dialog box, shown in Figure 8.1. At the Symbol dialog box, double-click the symbol you want to insert and then click Close; or, click the symbol you want to insert, click the Insert button, and then click Close.

Figure 8.1 Symbol Dialog Box with Symbols Tab Selected

Use the *Font* option to select the desired set of characters.

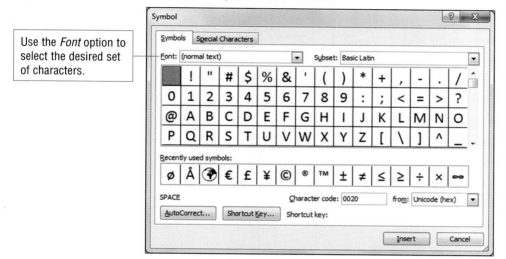

Insert a Symbol
1. Click Insert tab.
2. Click Symbol button.
3. Click desired symbol at drop-down list.
OR
1. Click Insert tab.
2. Click Symbol button.
3. Click *More Symbols*.
4. Select desired font.
5. Double-click desired symbol.
6. Click Close.

Symbol

At the Symbol dialog box with the Symbols tab selected, you can change the font by using the *Font* option. When you change the font, different symbols display in the dialog box. Click the Special Characters tab, and a list of special characters display along with the keyboard shortcuts to create them.

Exercise 8.1A Inserting Symbols and Special Characters   Part 1 of 4

1. Open **ProdSoftware.docx** and save the document with the name **C08-E01-ProdSoftware**.
2. Press Ctrl + End to move the insertion point to the end of the document.
3. Type Created by:, and then press the spacebar once.
4. Type the first name Rueben and then press the spacebar.
5. Insert the last name *Cedeño* by completing the following steps:
   a. Type Cede.
   b. Click the Insert tab.
   c. Click the Symbol button in the Symbols group.
   d. Click *More Symbols* at the drop-down list.

e.   At the Symbol dialog box, make sure the *Font* option displays as *(normal text)* and then double-click the ñ symbol (located in approximately the tenth, eleventh, or twelfth row).

f.   Click the Close button.

g.   Type o.

6.   Press Shift + Enter.

7.   Insert the computer laptop symbol (💻) by completing the following steps:

a.   Click the Symbol button and then click *More Symbols*.

b.   At the Symbol dialog box, click the down-pointing arrow at the right of the *Font* option and then click *Wingdings* at the drop-down list. (You will need to scroll down the list to display this option.)

c.   Double-click 💻 (located in approximately the second row).

d.   Click the Close button.

8.   Type Northland Security Systems.

9.   Insert the registered trademark symbol (®) by completing the following steps:

a.   Click the Symbol button and then click *More Symbols*.

b.   At the Symbol dialog box, click the Special Characters tab.

c.   Double-click the ® symbol (tenth option from the top).

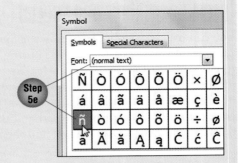

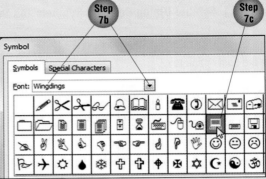

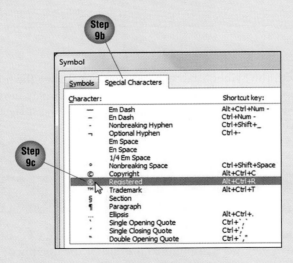

d.   Click the Close button.

e.   Press Shift + Enter.

10. Select the computer laptop symbol (💻) and then change the font size to 18.

11. Save **C08-E01-ProdSoftware.docx**.

Creating a Drop Cap

A drop cap is a design element often used to enhance the appearance of text. A drop cap is the first letter of the first word of a paragraph enlarged and set into the paragraph to extend (drop) more than one line space. Drop caps identify the beginning of major sections or parts of a document. They generally look best when they are used in paragraphs that contain text set in a proportional font. You can create a drop cap with the Drop Cap button in the Text group in the Insert tab. You can choose to set the drop cap in the paragraph or in the margin. At the Drop Cap dialog box, you can specify the font, the number of lines you want the letter to drop, and the distance you want the letter positioned from the text of the paragraph. To drop cap the first letter in a paragraph, select the word and then click the Drop Cap button.

QUICK STEPS

Create Drop Cap
1. Click Insert tab.
2. Click Drop Cap button.
3. Click desired type at drop-down list.

Drop Cap

Exercise 8.1B Inserting a Drop Cap   Part 2 of 4

1. With **C08-E01-ProdSoftware.docx** open, create a drop cap by completing the following steps:
   a. Position the insertion point on the first word of the first paragraph of text (*Productivity*).
   b. Click the Insert tab.
   c. Click the Drop Cap button in the Text group.
   d. Click *In margin* at the drop-down gallery.
2. To see how the size and location of a drop cap affect the visual appeal of the document, make the drop smaller and change its location by completing the following steps:
   a. With the *P* selected in the word *Productivity*, click the Drop Cap button in the Text group and then click *None* at the drop-down gallery.
   b. Click the Drop Cap button and then click *Drop Cap Options* at the drop-down gallery.
   c. At the Drop Cap dialog box, click *Dropped* in the *Position* section.
   d. Change the font to Cambria.
   e. Change the *Lines to drop* option to 2.
   f. Click OK to close the dialog box.
   g. Click outside the drop cap to deselect it.
3. Save **C08-E01-ProdSoftware.docx**.

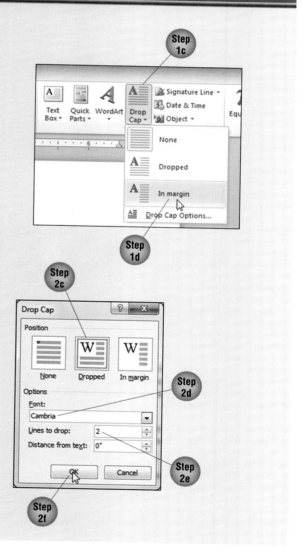

Inserting the Date and Time

Insert Date and Time
1. Click Insert tab.
2. Click Date and Time button.
3. Click option in list box.
4. Click OK.

Use the Date and Time button in the Text group in the Insert tab to insert the current date and time into a document. Click this button and the Date and Time dialog box displays, as shown in Figure 8.2 (the date that displays on your screen will vary from the one you see in the figure). At the Date and Time dialog box, click the desired date and/or time format in the *Available formats* list box.

Date & Time

Figure 8.2 Date and Time Dialog Box

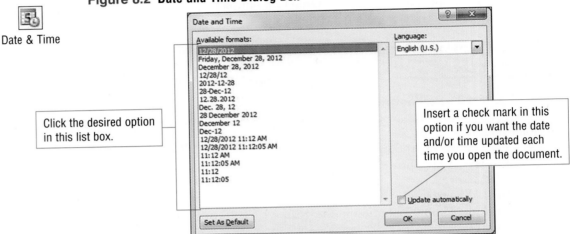

Click the desired option in this list box.

Insert a check mark in this option if you want the date and/or time updated each time you open the document.

If the *Update automatically* check box at the bottom of the dialog box does not contain a check mark, the date and/or time that you click are inserted in the document as normal text that can be edited in the usual manner. You can also insert the date and/or time as a field. The advantage to inserting the date or time as a field is that you can update the field with the keyboard shortcut F9. Insert a check mark in the *Update automatically* check box to insert the date and/or time as a field. You can also insert the date as a field using the keyboard shortcut Alt + Shift + D, and insert the time as a field with the keyboard shortcut Alt + Shift + T.

1. With **C08-E01-ProdSoftware.docx** open, press Ctrl + End and make sure the insertion point is positioned below the company name.

2. Insert the current date by completing the following steps:
   a. Click the Date & Time button in the Text group in the Insert tab.
   b. At the Date and Time dialog box, click the third option from the top in the *Available formats* group.
   c. Click in the *Update automatically* check box to insert a check mark.
   d. Click OK to close the dialog box.

3. Press Shift + Enter.

4. Insert the current time by completing the following steps:
   a. Click the Date & Time button.
   b. At the Date and Time dialog box, click the third option from the *bottom* in the *Available formats* list box.
   c. Click OK to close the dialog box.

5. Save **C08-E01-ProdSoftware.docx**.

6. Update the time by clicking the time and then pressing F9.

7. Save and then print **C08-E01-ProdSoftware.docx**.

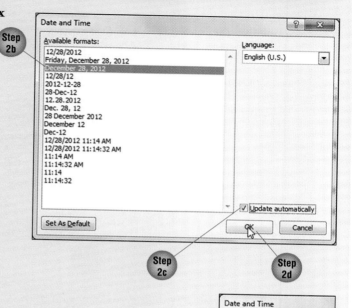

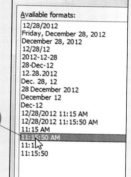

Inserting a File

If you want to insert the contents of one document into another, use the Object button in the Text group in the Insert tab. With the document into which you are inserting content open, click the Object button arrow and then click *Text from File* to display the Insert File dialog box. This dialog box is similar to the Open dialog box. Navigate to the desired folder and then double-click the document you want to insert in the open document.

Insert a File
1. Open document.
2. Click Insert tab.
3. Click Object button arrow.
4. Click *Text from File*.
5. Navigate to desired folder.
6. Double-click document name.

Object

1. With **C08-E01-ProdSoftware.docx** open, insert a file into the open document by completing the following steps:
   a. Move the insertion point to the blank line above the text *Created by: Rueben Cedeño*.
   b. Click the Insert tab.
   c. Click the Object button arrow in the Text group.
   d. Click *Text from File* at the drop-down list.

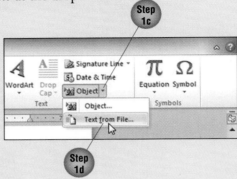

   e. At the Insert File dialog box, navigate to the Chapter08 folder and then double-click **PersSoftware.docx**.
2. Make the following changes to the document:
   a. Apply the Heading 2 style to the two headings in the document.
   b. Select the four paragraphs of text in the *Personal-use Software* section that each begin with bolded text and then click the Bullets button in the Paragraph group.
   c. Change the top margin to 1.5 inch.
   d. Change the style set to Formal.
   e. Apply the Pushpin theme.
   f. Insert page numbering centered at the bottom of each page.
3. Save, print, and then close **C08-E01-ProdSoftware.docx**.

Display Navigation Pane
1. Click View tab.
2. Click *Navigation Pane* check box.

Navigating in a Document

Word includes a number of features you can use to navigate in a document. Along with the navigating features you have already learned, you can also navigate using the Navigation pane and by inserting bookmarks, cross-references, and hyperlinks.

Navigating Using the Navigation Pane

To navigate using the Navigation pane shown in Figure 8.3, click the View tab and then click the *Navigation Pane* check box in the Show tab. The Navigation pane displays at the left side of the screen and includes a Search text box and a pane with three tabs. Click the first tab and titles and headings with styles applied display in the Navigation pane. Click a title or heading in the pane and the insertion point moves to that title or heading. Click the second tab and thumbnails of each page display in the pane. Click a thumbnail to move the insertion point to the specific page. Click the third tab to browse the current search results in the document. Close the Navigation pane by clicking the *Navigation Pane* check in the Show group in the View tab or by clicking the Close button located in the upper right corner of the pane.

Figure 8.3 **Navigation Pane**

Click this tab to display thumbnails of each page in the Navigation pane.

Click this tab to browse the current search results in the document.

Click this tab and titles and headings with styles applied display in the Navigation pane.

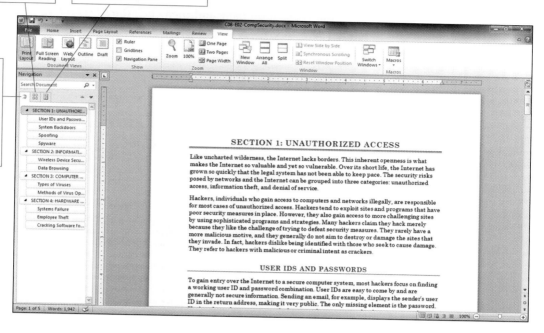

1. Open **CompSecurity.docx** and save the document with the name **C08-E02-CompSecurity**.
2. Press Ctrl + End and then insert a file by completing the following steps:
   a. Click the Insert tab.
   b. Click the Object button arrow in the Text group.
   c. Click *Text from File* at the drop-down list.
   d. At the Insert File dialog box, navigate to the Chapter08 folder and then double-click **CompViruses.docx**.
3. Make the following changes to the document:
   a. Apply the Heading 1 style to the four section titles in the document.
   b. Apply the Heading 2 style to all of the headings in the document.
   c. Change the style set to Formal.
   d. Apply the Oriel theme to the document.

4. Navigate in the document using the Navigation pane by completing the following steps:
   a. Click the View tab.
   b. Click the Navigation Pane check box in the Show group to insert a check mark. (This displays the Navigation pane at the left side of the screen.)
   c. Click the left tab in the Navigation pane and then click the *SECTION 2: INFORMATION THEFT* title.

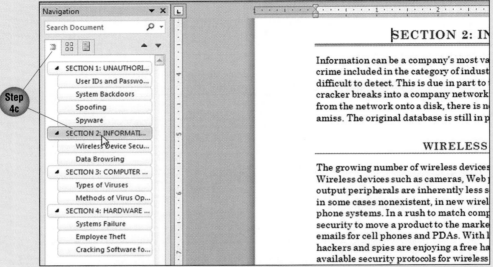

   d. Click the *SECTION 4: HARDWARE AND SOFTWARE SECURITY RISKS* title in the Navigation pane.
   e. Click *Spoofing* in the Navigation pane.
5. Navigate in the document using thumbnails by completing the following steps:
   a. Click the middle tab in the Navigation pane. (This displays page thumbnails in the pane.)
   b. Click the number 3 thumbnail in the Navigation pane.
   c. Click the number 1 thumbnail in the Navigation pane.
6. Close the Navigation pane by clicking the Close button located in the upper right corner of the Navigation pane.
7. Save **C08-E02-CompSecurity.docx**.

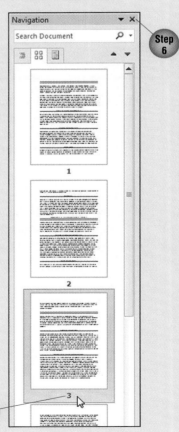

Navigating with Bookmarks

In a long document, you may find it useful to mark a specific location to allow you to quickly move the insertion point to that location. Use the Bookmark button to create bookmarks for locations in a document. To create a bookmark, position the insertion point at the desired location, click the Insert tab, and then click the Bookmark button in the Links group. This displays the Bookmark dialog box, shown in Figure 8.4. Type a name for the bookmark in the *Bookmark name* text box and then click the Add button. Repeat these steps as many times as needed to insert the desired bookmarks. Give each bookmark a unique and meaningful name. A bookmark name must begin with a letter; it can contain numbers but not spaces. Use the underscore character if you want to separate words in a bookmark name.

Figure 8.4 Bookmark Dialog Box

Type a name for the bookmark in this text box.

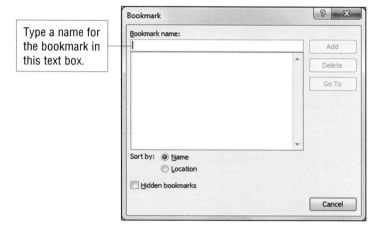

Create a Bookmark
1. Position insertion point at desired location.
2. Click Insert tab.
3. Click Bookmark button.
4. Type name for bookmark.
5. Click Add button.

Navigate with Bookmarks
1. Click Insert tab.
2. Click Bookmark button.
3. Double-click desired bookmark name.
OR
1. Click Insert tab.
2. Click Bookmark button.
3. Click bookmark name.
4. Click Go To button.

Bookmark

By default, bookmarks that you insert are not visible in the document. You can turn on the display of bookmarks at the Word Options dialog box with *Advanced* selected. Display this dialog box by clicking the File tab and then clicking the Options button. At the Word Options dialog box, click the *Advanced* option in the left panel. Click the *Show bookmarks* check box in the *Show document content* section to insert a check mark. Complete similar steps to turn off the display of bookmarks. A bookmark displays in the document as an I-beam marker.

You can also create a bookmark for selected text. To do this, select the text first and then complete the steps to create a bookmark. When you create a bookmark for selected text, a left bracket ([) indicates the beginning of the selected text and a right bracket (]) indicates the end of selected text. The bookmark brackets do not print.

After you have inserted bookmarks in a document, you can move the insertion point to a specific bookmark. To do this, display the Bookmark dialog box and then double-click the bookmark name. You can also click the Bookmark name and then click the Go To button. When Word stops at the location of the bookmark, click the Close button to close the dialog box. If you move the insertion point to a bookmark created with selected text, Word moves the insertion point to the bookmark and selects the text. You can delete bookmarks in the Bookmark dialog box by clicking the bookmark name in the list box and then clicking the Delete button.

1. With **C08-E02-CompSecurity.docx** open, turn on the display of bookmarks by completing the following steps:

    a. Click the File tab and then click the Options button.

    b. At the Word Options dialog box, click *Advanced* in the left panel.

    c. Click the *Show bookmarks* check box in the *Show document content* section to insert a check mark. (You will need to scroll down the dialog box to see this option.)

    d. Click OK to close the dialog box.

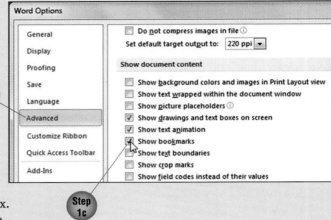

2. Insert a bookmark by completing the following steps:

    a. Move the insertion point to the beginning of the first paragraph in the document (below the title SECTION 1: UNAUTHORIZED ACCESS).

    b. Click the Insert tab.

    c. Click the Bookmark button in the Links group.

    d. At the Bookmark dialog box, type Access in the *Bookmark name* text box.

    e. Click the Add button.

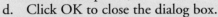

3. Insert a bookmark named *Viruses* at the beginning of the first paragraph in the TYPES OF VIRUSES section (located on page 3).

4. Insert a bookmark named *Electrical* at the beginning of the first paragraph in the SYSTEMS FAILURE section (located on page 4).

5. Navigate to the Viruses bookmark by completing the following steps:

    a. Click the Bookmark button in the Links group.

    b. At the Bookmark dialog box, click *Viruses* in the list box.

    c. Click the Go To button.

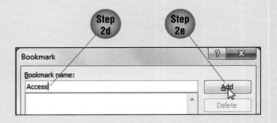

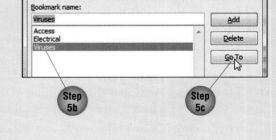

6. With the Bookmark dialog box open, navigate to the Access bookmark by double-clicking *Access* in the list box.

7. With the Bookmark dialog box open, delete the *Electrical* bookmark by clicking *Electrical* in the list box and then clicking the Delete button.

8. Click the Close button to close the Bookmark dialog box.

9. Save **C08-E02-CompSecurity.docx**.

Inserting Hyperlinks

A hyperlink in a document can serve a number of purposes: Click it to navigate to a specific location in the document, to display a different document, to open a file in a different program, to create a new document, or to link to an email address. Insert a hyperlink by clicking the Hyperlink button located in the Links group in the Insert tab. This displays the Insert Hyperlink dialog box, shown in Figure 8.5. You can also display the Insert Hyperlink dialog box by pressing Ctrl + K. At this dialog box, identify what you want to link to and the location of the link. Click the ScreenTip button to customize the hyperlink ScreenTip.

Insert Hyperlink
1. Click Insert tab.
2. Click Hyperlink button.
3. Make desired changes at Insert Hyperlink dialog box.
4. Click OK.

Hyperlink

Figure 8.5 Insert Hyperlink Dialog Box

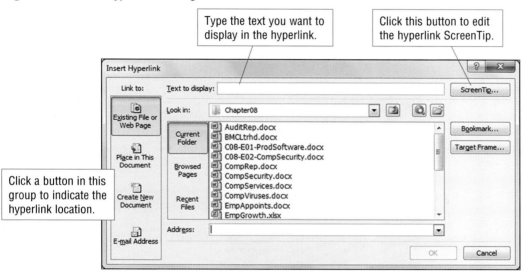

Type the text you want to display in the hyperlink.

Click this button to edit the hyperlink ScreenTip.

Click a button in this group to indicate the hyperlink location.

Linking to a Place in the Document

To create a hyperlink to another location in the document, you need to mark the location either by applying heading styles to text or by inserting bookmarks. To hyperlink to a heading or bookmark in a document, display the Insert Hyperlink dialog box and then click the Place in This Document button in the *Link to* group. This displays text with heading styles applied and bookmarks in the *Select a place in this document* list box. Click the desired heading style or bookmark name, and the heading or bookmark name displays in the *Text to display* text box. You can leave the text as displayed or you can select the text and then type the text you want to appear in the document.

Navigating Using Hyperlinks

Navigate to a hyperlink by hovering the mouse over the hyperlink text, holding down the Ctrl key, and then clicking the left mouse button. When you hover the mouse over hyperlink text, a ScreenTip displays with the name of the heading or bookmark. If you want specific information to display in the ScreenTip, click the ScreenTip button in the Insert Hyperlink dialog box, type the desired text in the Set Hyperlink ScreenTip dialog box, and then click OK.

1. With **C08-E02-CompSecurity.docx** open, insert a hyperlink to a bookmark in the document by completing the following steps:
   a. Position the insertion point at the immediate right of the period that ends the first paragraph of text in the *SECTION 4: HARDWARE AND SOFTWARE SECURITY RISKS* section (located on page 4).
   b. Press the spacebar once.
   c. If necessary, click the Insert tab.
   d. Click the Hyperlink button in the Links group.
   e. At the Insert Hyperlink dialog box, click the Place in This Document button in the *Link to* group.
   f. Scroll down the *Select a place in this document* list box and then click *Access,* which displays below *Bookmarks* in the list box.
   g. Select the text that displays in the *Text to display* text box and then type Click to view types of unauthorized access.
   h. Click the ScreenTip button located in the upper right corner of the dialog box. At the Set Hyperlink ScreenTip dialog box, type View types of unauthorized access to computers and then click OK.
   i. Click OK to close the Insert Hyperlink dialog box.

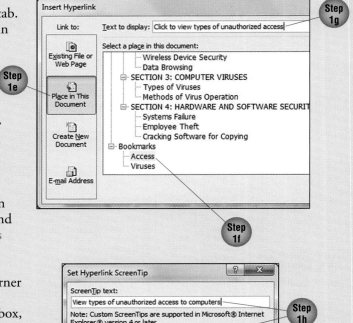

2. Navigate to the hyperlinked location by hovering the mouse over the <u>Click to view types of unauthorized access</u> hyperlink, holding down the Ctrl key, and then clicking the left mouse button.
3. Insert a hyperlink to a heading in the document by completing the following steps:
   a. Press Ctrl + Home to move the insertion point to the beginning of the document.
   b. Move the insertion point to the immediate right of the period that ends the second paragraph in the document and then press the spacebar.
   c. Click the Hyperlink button in the Insert tab.
   d. At the Insert Hyperlink dialog box with the Place in This Document button selected in the *Link to* group, click the *Types of Viruses* heading in the *Select a place in this document* list box.
   e. Click OK to close the Insert Hyperlink dialog box.
4. Navigate to the hyperlinked heading by hovering the mouse over the <u>Types of Viruses</u> hyperlink, holding down the Ctrl key, and then clicking the left mouse button.
5. Save **C08-E02-CompSecurity.docx**.

Linking to a File in Another Program

In some situations, you may want to provide information to your readers from a variety of sources. You may want to provide information in a Word document, an Excel spreadsheet, or a PowerPoint presentation. To link a Word document to a file in another application, display the Insert Hyperlink dialog box and then click the Existing File or Web Page button in the *Link to* group. Use the *Look in* option to navigate to the folder containing the desired file and then click the file. Make other changes in the Insert Hyperlink dialog box as needed and then click OK.

Linking to a New Document

In addition to linking to an existing document, you can create a hyperlink to a new document. To do this, display the Insert Hyperlink dialog box and then click the Create New Document button in the *Link to* group. Type a name for the new document in the *Name of new document* text box and then specify if you want to edit the document now or later.

Linking Using a Graphic

You can use a graphic such as a clip art image, picture, or text box, to hyperlink to file or website. To hyperlink with a graphic, select the graphic, click the Insert tab, and then click the Hyperlink button. (You can also right-click the graphic and then click *Hyperlink* at the shortcut menu.) At the Insert Hyperlink dialog box, specify where you want to link to and text you want to display in the hyperlink.

Linking to an Email Address

You can insert a hyperlink to an email address at the Insert Hyperlink dialog box. To do this, click the E-Mail Address button in the *Link to* group, type the desired address in the *E-mail address* text box, and type a subject for the email in the *Subject* text box. Click in the *Text to display* text box and then type the text you want to display in the document. To use this feature, the email address you use must be set up in Outlook 2010.

Exercise 8.2D Inserting a Hyperlink to Another Program, a New Document, and Using a Graphic   **Part 4 of 5**

1. The file **C08-E02-CompSecurity.docx** contains information used by Northland Security Systems. The company also has a PowerPoint presentation that contains similar information. Link the document with the presentation by completing the following steps:
   a. Move the insertion point to the immediate right of the period that ends the paragraph in the SECTION 3: COMPUTER VIRUSES section and then press the spacebar.
   b. If necessary, click the Insert tab.
   c. Click the Hyperlink button in the Links group.

d. At the Insert Hyperlink dialog box, click the Existing File or Web Page button in the *Link to* group.
e. Click the down-pointing arrow at the right side of the *Look in* list box and then navigate to the Chapter08 folder on your storage medium.
f. Click the presentation named **NSSPres.pptx** in the list box.
g. Select the text in the *Text to display* text box in the dialog box and then type Computer Virus Presentation.

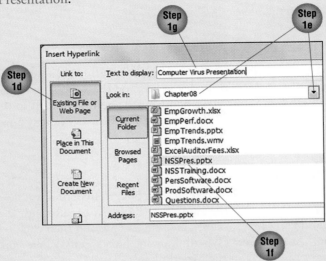

h. Click OK to close the Insert Hyperlink dialog box.
2. View the PowerPoint presentation by completing the following steps:
    a. Position the mouse pointer over the Computer Virus Presentation hyperlink, hold down the Ctrl key, and then click the left mouse button.
    b. At the PowerPoint presentation, click the Slide Show button in the view area on the Status bar.
    c. Click the left mouse button to advance each slide.
    d. Click the left mouse button at the black screen that displays the message *End of slide show, click to exit.*
    e. Close the presentation and PowerPoint by clicking the Close button (contains an X) that displays in the upper right corner of the screen.

3. Insert a hyperlink with a graphic by completing the following steps:
    a. Press Ctrl + End to move the insertion point to the end of the document.
    b. Click the compass image to select it.
    c. Click the Hyperlink button in the Insert tab.
    d. At the Insert Hyperlink dialog box, make sure the Existing File or Web Page button is selected in the *Link to* group.
    e. Navigate to the Chapter08 folder on your storage medium and then double-click the document named **NSSTraining.docx**. (This selects the document name and closes the dialog box.)
4. Navigate to the NSSTraining.docx document by hovering the mouse pointer over the compass image, holding down the Ctrl key, and then clicking the left mouse button.
5. Close the document by clicking the File tab and then clicking the Close button.

6. Insert a hyperlink to a new document by completing the following steps:
   a. Move the insertion point to the immediate right of the period that ends the paragraph in the *USER IDS AND PASSWORDS* section and then press the spacebar.
   b. Click the Hyperlink button in the Insert tab.
   c. Click the Create New Document button in the *Link to* group.
   d. In the *Name of new document* text box, type X:\Chapter08\PasswordSuggestions (type the letter of the drive where your storage medium is located in place of the *X*).
   e. Edit the text in the *Text to display* text box so it displays as *Password Suggestions*.
   f. Make sure the *Edit the new document now* option is selected and then click OK.

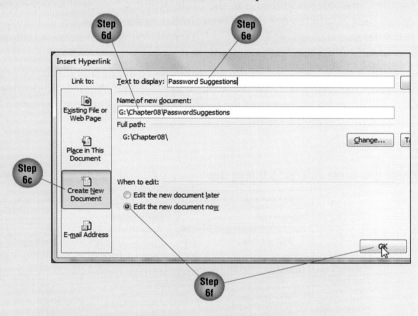

   g. At the blank document, turn on bold, type Please type any suggestions you have for creating secure passwords:, turn off bold and then press the Enter key.
   h. Save and then close the document.
7. Press Ctrl + End to move the insertion point to the end of the document and then press the Enter key four times.
8. Insert a hyperlink to your email or your instructor's email address by completing the following steps:
   a. Click the Hyperlink button.
   b. At the Insert Hyperlink dialog box, click the E-mail Address button in the *Link to* group.
   c. Type your email address or your instructor's email address in the *E-mail address* text box.
   d. Select the current text in the *Text to display* text box and then type Click to send an email.
   e. Click OK to close the dialog box.
      Optional: If you have Outlook setup, click the <u>Click to send an email</u> hyperlink and then send a message indicating that you have completed inserting hyperlinks in the C08-E02-ComSecurity.docx document.
9. Save **C08-E02-CompSecurity.docx**.

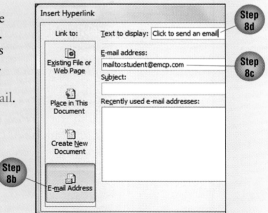

Creating a Cross-reference

A cross-reference in a Word document refers the reader to another location within the document. Cross-referencing is useful in a long document or in a document that contains related information. You can insert a reference to an item such as a heading, figure, or table. For example, you can insert a cross-reference that refers readers to another location with more information about the topic or that refers readers to a specific table or page. Cross-references are inserted in a document as hyperlinks.

To insert a cross-reference, type introductory text, click the Insert tab, and then click the Cross-reference button in the Links group. Clicking the Cross-reference button displays the Cross-reference dialog box, similar to the one shown in Figure 8.6. At the Cross-reference dialog box, identify the reference type (what you are referencing), where the reader should refer, and the specific text.

The reference identified in the Cross-reference dialog box displays immediately after the introductory text. To move to the specified reference, hold down the Ctrl key, position the mouse pointer over the introductory text (pointer turns into a hand), and then click the left mouse button.

Figure 8.6 Cross-reference Dialog Box

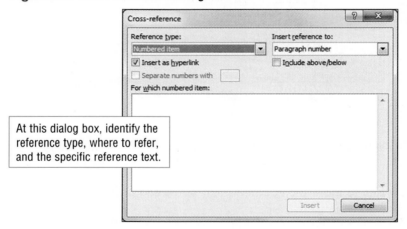

At this dialog box, identify the reference type, where to refer, and the specific reference text.

Exercise 8.2E Inserting and Navigating with Cross-references   **Part 5 of 5**

1. With **C08-E02-CompSecurity.docx** open, insert a cross-reference in the document by completing the following steps:
   a. Move the insertion point so it is positioned at the immediate right of the period that ends the paragraph in the *TYPES OF VIRUSES* section (located on page 2).
   b. Press the spacebar once and then type (For more information, refer to.
   c. Press the spacebar once.
   d. If necessary, click the Insert tab.
   e. Click the Cross-reference button in the Links group.

f. At the Cross-reference dialog box, click the down-pointing arrow at the right of the *Reference type* list box and then click *Heading* at the drop-down list.

g. Click *Data Browsing* in the *For which heading* list box.

h. Click the Insert button.

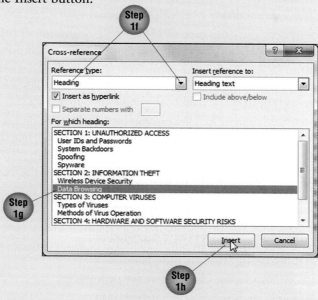

i. Click the Close button to close the dialog box.

j. At the document, type a period followed by the right parenthesis.

2. Move to the reference text by holding down the Ctrl key, positioning the mouse pointer over *Data Browsing* until the pointer turns into a hand, and then clicking the left mouse button.

3. Save **C08-E02-CompSecurity.docx**.

4. Apply the following formatting to the document:

   a. Insert page numbering that prints at the top of each page at the right margin.

   b. Insert the Puzzle [Odd Page] footer. Click the *[Type the company name]* placeholder and then type Northland Security Systems.

   c. Insert the Pinstripes cover page and insert the following in the specified placeholders:

   [Type the document title] = Computer Security
   [Type the document subtitle] = (Delete this placeholder)
   [Pick the date] = Insert today's date.
   [Type the author name] = Your first and last names

5. Check the page breaks in the document and if a heading displays at the bottom of a page and the paragraph of text that follows displays on the next page, insert a page break at the beginning of the heading.

6. Save and then print **C08-E02-CompSecurity.docx**.

7. Turn off the display of bookmarks by completing the following steps:

   a. Click the File tab and then click the Options button.

   b. At the Word Options dialog box, click *Advanced* in the left panel.

   c. Click the *Show bookmarks* check box in the *Show document content* section to remove the check mark.

   d. Click OK to close the dialog box.

8. Close **C08-E02-CompSecurity.docx**.

Chapter Summary

➤ Insert symbols with options at the Symbol dialog box with the Symbols tab selected; insert special characters with options at the Symbol dialog box with the Special Characters tab selected.

➤ To enhance the appearance of text, use drop caps to identify the beginning of major sections or parts of a paragraph. Create drop caps with the Drop Cap button in the Text group in the Insert tab.

➤ Click the Date & Time button in the Text group in the Insert tab to display the Date and Time dialog box. Insert the date or time with options at this dialog box or with keyboard shortcuts. If the date or time is inserted as a field, update the field with the Update Field key, F9.

➤ Insert a document into an open document by clicking the Insert tab, clicking the Object button arrow, and then clicking *Text from File* at the drop-down list. At the Insert File dialog box, double-click the desired document.

➤ Navigate in a document with the Navigation pane or by inserting bookmarks, hyperlinks, or cross-references.

➤ Insert bookmarks with options at the Bookmark dialog box.

➤ Insert hyperlinks in a document with options at the Insert Hyperlink dialog box. You can insert a hyperlink to an existing file or web page, a location in the current document, a new document, or an email. You can also use a graphic to link to a file or website.

➤ Create a cross-reference with options at the Cross-reference dialog box.

Commands Review

FEATURE	RIBBON TAB, GROUP	BUTTON	KEYBOARD SHORTCUT
Symbol dialog box	Insert, Symbols	Ω	
Drop cap	Insert, Text	🅰	
Date and Time dialog box	Insert, Text	📅	
Insert date			Alt + Shift + D
Insert time			Alt + Shift + T
Update field			F9
Insert file	Insert, Text	📄	
Navigation pane	View, Show	Navigation Pane	
Bookmark dialog box	Insert, Links	📄	
Insert Hyperlink dialog box	Insert, Links	🌐	Ctrl + K
Cross-reference dialog box	Insert, Links	📑	

Key Points Review

Completion: In the space provided at the right, indicate the correct term, symbol, or command.

1. The Symbol button is located in this tab.
2. Click this option at the Symbol button drop-down list to display the Symbol dialog box.
3. The first letter of the first word of a paragraph that is set into a paragraph is called this.
4. This is the keyboard shortcut to insert the current date.
5. This is the keyboard shortcut to insert the current time.
6. The Date & Time button is located in this group in the Insert tab.
7. This is the Update Field keyboard shortcut.
8. Display the Insert File dialog box by clicking the Object button arrow in the Insert tab and then clicking this option.
9. The Navigation Pane check box is located in the Show group in this tab.
10. Turn on the display of bookmarks in a document with the *Show bookmarks* check box in this dialog box with *Advanced* selected.
11. The Bookmark button is located in this group in the Insert tab.
12. Navigate to a hyperlink by hovering the mouse over the hyperlink text, holding down this key, and then clicking the left mouse button.
13. To link a Word document to a file in another application, click this button in the *Link to* group in the Insert Hyperlink dialog box.
14. By default, cross-references are inserted in a document as this.

Chapter Assessments

Applying Your Skills

Demonstrate your knowledge of features learned in this chapter by completing the following assessments.

Assessment 8.1   Apply Headers and Footers to Employee Orientation Documents

1. Open **EmpAppoints.docx** and save the document with the name **C08-A01-EmpAppoints**.
2. Press Ctrl + End to move the insertion point to the end of the document and then insert the file named **EmpPerf.docx**.
3. Press Ctrl + End to move the insertion point to the end of the document and then type Séverin Technologies®.
4. Press Shift + Enter and then insert the current date.

5. Press Shift + Enter and then insert the current time.
6. Create a drop cap with the first letter of the first paragraph of text (the word *Acceptance*) and specify that the drop cap is dropped two lines.
7. Make the following changes to the document:
   a. Insert a page break at the beginning of the title *EMPLOYEE PERFORMANCE* located on the second page.
   b. Apply the Heading 1 style to the two titles in the document *EMPLOYMENT APPOINTMENTS* and *EMPLOYEE PERFORMANCE*.
   c. Apply the Heading 2 style to the four headings *Types of Appointments*, *Work Performance Standards*, *Performance Evaluation*, and *Employment Records*.
   d. Change the style set to Simple.
   e. Apply the Apothecary theme.
   f. Center the two titles.
   g. Add 12 points of space after the first title (*EMPLOYMENT APPOINTMENTS*).
   h. Insert the Pinstripes header and type Employee Handbook in the *[Type the document title]* placeholder.
   i. Insert the Pinstripes footer and type Séverin Technologies in the *[Type text]* placeholder.
8. Save, print, and then close **C08-A01-EmpAppoints.docx**.

Assessment 8.2   Format and Navigate in Corporate Report Documents

1. Open **AuditRep.docx** and save the document with the name **C08-A02-AuditRep**.
2. Move the insertion point to the end of the document and then insert the document named **CompRep.docx**.
3. Apply the following formatting (you choose the specific formatting):
   a. Apply heading styles of your choosing to the titles and headings.
   b. Apply a style set.
   c. Apply a theme.
   d. Insert a header and/or footer.
   e. Insert a cover page.
4. Check the pages breaks in the document and if a heading displays at the bottom of the page with the text following the heading displaying at the top of the next page, keep the heading with the text. To do this, move the insertion point to the heading, display the Paragraph group with the Line and Page Breaks tab selected, insert a check mark in the *Keep with next* check box, and then close the dialog box.
5. Turn on the display of bookmarks.
6. Move the insertion point to the end of the third paragraph in the document (the paragraph that begins *The audit committee selects . . .*) and then insert a bookmark named Audit.
7. Move the insertion point to the end of the first paragraph in the *Fees to Independent Auditor* section, following the *(Excel Worksheet)* text, and then insert a bookmark named Audit_Fees.
8. Move the insertion point to the end of the last paragraph of text in the document and then insert a bookmark named Compensation.
9. Navigate in the document using the bookmarks.
10. Move the insertion point to the end of the first paragraph in the *Committee Responsibilities* section and then insert a hyperlink to the *Audit_Fees* bookmark.
11. Select the text *(Excel Worksheet)* that displays at the end of the first paragraph in the *Fees to Independent Auditor* section and then insert a hyperlink to the Excel file named **ExcelAuditorFees.xlsx** that is located in the Chapter08 folder on your storage medium.
12. Click the *(Excel Worksheet)* hyperlink and then print the Excel worksheet that displays by clicking the File tab, clicking the Print tab, and then clicking the Print button in the Print tab Backstage view.
13. Close the Excel program without saving the workbook.
14. Save, print, and then close **C08-A02-AuditRep.docx**.

Expanding Your Skills

Explore additional feature options or use Help to learn a new skill in creating these documents.

Assessment 8.3 Customize Drop Cap Options

1. Open **CompServices.docx** and then save the document and name it **C08-A03-CompServices**.
2. Display the Drop Cap dialog box and then determine how to change the drop cap font and the distance from the text.
3. Create a drop cap for the first letter below the title and each of the headings in the document with the following specifications:
    - Drop the cap within the text.
    - Change the drop cap font to Castellar.
    - Drop the cap two lines.
    - Change the *Distance from text* option to 0.1".
    - With the drop cap selected, change the font color to *Orange, Accent 6, Darker 50%*.
4. Save, print, and then close **C08-A03-CompServices.docx**.
5. At a blank document, write a memo to your instructor describing the steps you took to create the drop caps in **C08-A03-CompServices.docx**. (Refer to Appendix C for the proper formatting of a memo.)
6. Save the completed memo and name it **C08-A03-DropCapMemo**.
7. Print and then close **C08-A03-DropCapMemo.docx**.

Assessment 8.4 Determine Symbol Keyboard Shortcuts and Write a Letter

1. You work for a computer services and training company, and your boss has asked you to send a letter to a client regarding symbols and keyboard shortcuts. To begin, open **BMCLtrhd.docx** and then save the document and name it **C08-A04-BMCClientLtr**.
2. You can insert some symbols in a document using a keyboard shortcut. If a symbol contains a keyboard shortcut, it will display in the Symbol dialog box when the symbol is selected. Go to the Symbol dialog box with the *(normal text)* font selected and then click the cent symbol (¢) (located in approximately the sixth row). Notice that the *Shortcut key:* option located toward the bottom of the dialog box is followed by *Ctrl + /, C*. This keyboard shortcut indicates that to insert a cent symbol in a document you would hold down the Ctrl key, press the / key on the keyboard, release the Ctrl key, and then type the letter c. If you click the Japanese Yen symbol (¥), *Shortcut key: Alt + 0165* displays toward the bottom of the Symbol dialog box. To insert the Yen symbol using the keyboard, press the Num Lock key on the numeric keypad if it is not active, hold down the Alt key, type 0165, and then release the Alt key. At the Symbol dialog box, identify and write down the keyboard shortcuts for the following symbols:
    - Cent symbol (¢)
    - Yen symbol (¥)
    - British pound symbol (£)
    - Copyright symbol (©)
    - Registered symbol (®)
    - Paragraph symbol (¶)
3. Your boss has asked you to type a letter to a client that describes the steps to follow to insert a symbol from the Symbol dialog box and also includes information on how to insert the symbols listed above using keyboard shortcuts. Address the letter to the following name and address using the block-style business letter style (refer to Appendix D):

Patrick Shaughnessy, President
A-line Manufacturing
4512 Northeast 18th Avenue
Casper, WY 82605

4. After typing the letter, save, print, and then close **C08-A04-BMCClientLtr.docx**.

Achieving Signature Status

Take your skills to the next level by completing this more challenging assessment.

Assessment 8.5   Create and Format a Document on Résumés for Career Changers

1. At a blank document, create the document shown in Figure 8.7 with the following specifications:
   a. The bulleted paragraphs of text are saved in a file named **Questions.docx**. Insert that file into your document instead of typing the bulleted text.
   b. Apply character formatting as indicated in Figure 8.7.
   c. Apply the Heading 1 style to the title and the Heading 3 style to the headings.
   d. Change the Quick Styles set to Thatch.
   e. Apply the Origin theme and change the theme colors to Concourse.
   f. Insert the Conservative footer.
   g. Select the text *(Top Ten Growth Industries)* and then create a hyperlink that links to the Excel workbook named **EmpGrowth.xlsx**.
   h. Select the text *(Employment Trends)* and then create a hyperlink that links to the PowerPoint presentation named **EmpTrends.pptx**.
   i. Apply any other formatting required to ensure that your document appears the same as the document in Figure 8.7.
2. Click the hyperlink to display the **EmpGrowth.xlsx** Excel workbook. After viewing the workbook exit Excel without saving the workbook.
3. Click the hyperlink to display the **EmpTrends.pptx** PowerPoint presentation. Run the presentation by clicking the Slide Show button that displays in the view area on the Status bar. Click the left mouse button to advance each slide. After viewing the presentation, exit PowerPoint.
4. Save the document and name it **C08-A05-CareerChangers**.
5. Print and then close **C08-A05-CareerChangers.docx**.

Figure 8.7 Assessment 8.5

RÉSUMÉS FOR CAREER CHANGERS

The fact that you are seeking to change careers will dictate almost everything that you write in your résumé, how you write it, and where it is positioned. Your goal is to paint a picture of the "new" you and not simply reiterate what you have done in the past, expecting a prospective employer to figure out that you can do the "new" thing just as well. If you fall into the career-changer category, the critical questions you must ask yourself about your résumé and your job search are the following:

- ***How are you going to paint a picture of the "new" you?*** What are you going to highlight about your past experience that ties directly to your current objectives? What accomplishments, skills, and qualifications are you going to "sell" in your résumé to support your "new" career objective?
- ***What résumé format are you going to use?*** Is a chronological, functional, or hybrid résumé format going to work best for you? Which format will give you the greatest flexibility to highlight the skills you want to bring to the forefront in support of your career change?
- ***Where are you going to look for a job?*** Assuming you know the type of position and industry you want to enter at this point in your career, how are you going to identify and approach those companies?

When you can answer the how, what, and where, you will be prepared to write your résumé and launch your search campaign. Your résumé should focus on your skills, achievements, and qualifications, demonstrating the value and benefit you bring to a prospective employer as they relate to your current career goals. The focus is on the "new" you and not necessarily what you have done professionally in the past.

CAREER OBJECTIVES

Before you begin writing your résumé, you will need to begin by defining your career or job objectives such as the types of positions, companies, and industries in which you are interested. This is critical because a haphazard, unfocused job search will lead you nowhere.

EMPLOYMENT TRENDS

One of the best ways to begin identifying your career objectives is to look at what opportunities are available today, in the immediate future, and in the longer-term future. A useful tool is the U.S. Department of Labor's Bureau of Labor Statistics. (Top-ten Growth Industries)

Numerous employment opportunities across diverse sectors within our economy, from advanced technology positions to hourly wage jobs in construction and home health care are available. Some of the most interesting findings that you will discover when investigating potential industry and job targets are listed in a PowerPoint presentation. (Employment Trends)

Figure 8.7 Assessment 8.5 (continued)

JOB SEARCH AND YOUR CAREER

To take advantage of these opportunities, you must be an educated job seeker. This means you must know what you want in your career, where the hiring action is, what qualifications and credentials you need to attain your desired career goals, and how best to market your qualifications.

The employment market has changed dramatically from only a few years ago. According to the U.S. Department of Labor, you should expect to hold between 10 and 20 different jobs during your career. No longer is stability the status quo. Today, the norm is movement, onward and upward, in a fast-paced and intense employment market where many opportunities are available for career changers. To take advantage of all of the opportunities, every job seeker must proactively control and manage his/her career.

Page 2

Chapter Eight

Chapter 9

Tutorial 9.1
Maintaining Documents
Tutorial 9.2
Managing Folders
Tutorial 9.3
Managing Documents
Tutorial 9.4
Changing Dialog Box Views
Tutorial 9.5
Creating Documents Using a
Word Template
Tutorial 9.6
Sharing Documents
Tutorial 9.7
Viewing and Sharing
Documents
Tutorial 9.8
Saving a Document as a
Web Page

Maintaining Documents

Performance Objectives

Upon successful completion of Chapter 9, you will be able to:

- Create and rename a folder
- Select, delete, copy, move, rename, and print documents
- Move a document from one folder into another
- Create a document using a Word template

Nearly every company that conducts business maintains a filing system. The system may consist of paper documents, folders, and file cabinets, or it may consist of electronic files and folders stored on a computer hard drive or other storage medium. Whatever type of system a business uses, the daily maintenance of files is important to the company's operations. In this chapter, you will learn to maintain files (documents) in Word, including how to create folders and copy, move, and rename documents. You will also learn how to create a document using a Word template.

Note: Before beginning computer exercises for this chapter, copy to your storage medium the Chapter09 folder from the CD that accompanies this textbook and then make Chapter09 the active folder.

In this chapter students will produce the following documents:

Chapter 9 Optional Exercise. C09-Optl-WWTravel.docx
Exercise 9.2. C09-E02-IntlCorres.docx
Exercise 9.2. C09-E02-IntlCorres-RichTxt.rtf
Exercise 9.2. C09-E02-IntlCorres-Word97-2003.doc
Exercise 9.2. C09-E02-IntlCorres-PlainTxt.txt
Exercise 9.3. C09-E03-LtrLuncheon.docx

Model answers for these exercises are shown on the following pages.

Chapter 9 Optional Exercise

C09-Optl-WWTravel.docx

World Wide Travel

2400 International Drive
Las Vegas, NV 77534
1-800-555-3445
www.emcp.net/worldwide

At World Wide Travel, we offer a variety of services for meeting your travel needs. We will:

- Plan vacations
- Schedule flights
- Make hotel reservations
- Prepare a travel itinerary
- Locate tour companies
- Book tours
- Provide passport assistance

Connect to the Northwest Airlines website and discover a wide range of travel opportunities and experiences.

World Wide Travel
Great Vacations!
Great Fun!
Great Savings!

International Correspondence

With the increased number of firms conducting business worldwide, international written communication has assumed new importance. Follow these guidelines when corresponding internationally, especially with people for whom English is not the primary language:

- Use a direct writing style and clear, precise words.
- Avoid slang, jargon, and idioms.
- Develop an awareness of cultural differences that may interfere with the communication process.

International Addresses

Use the company's letterhead or a business card as a guide for spelling and other information. Include the following when addressing international correspondences:

Line 3: Street Address
Line 1: Addressee's Name, Title
Line 5: COUNTRY NAME (capitalized)
Line 2: Company Name
Line 4: City and Codes

Canadian Codes and Provinces

ON – Ontario
QC – Quebec
NS – Nova Scotia
NB – New Brunswick
MB – Manitoba
BC – British Columbia
PE – Prince Edward Island
SK – Saskatchewan
AB – Alberta
NL – Newfoundland and Labrador

Canadian Codes and Territories

NT – Northwest Territories
YT – Yukon
NU – Nunavut

Exercise 9.2

C09-E02-IntlCorres.docx
C09-E02-IntlCorres-RichTxt.rtf
C09-E02-IntlCorres-Word97-2003.doc

Exercise 9.2

C09-E02-IntlCorres-PlainTxt.txt

C09-E02-IntlCorres-PlainTxt.txt
International Correspondence
With the increased number of firms conducting business worldwide, international
written communication has assumed new importance. Follow these guidelines when
corresponding internationally, especially with people for whom English is not the
primary language:
* Use a direct writing style and clear, precise words.
* Avoid slang, jargon, and idioms.
* Develop an awareness of cultural differences that may interfere with the
communication process.

International Addresses
Use the company's letterhead or a business card as a guide for spelling and other
information. Include the following when addressing international correspondences:
Line 3: Street Address
Line 1: Addressee's Name, Title
Line 5: COUNTRY NAME (capitalized)
Line 2: Company Name
Line 4: City and Codes

Canadian Codes and Provinces
ON – Ontario
QC – Quebec
NS – Nova Scotia
NB – New Brunswick
MB – Manitoba
BC – British Columbia
PE – Prince Edward Island
SK – Saskatchewan
AB – Alberta
NL – Newfoundland and Labrador

Canadian Codes and Territories
NT – Northwest Territories
YT – Yukon
NU – Nunavut

12/28/2012

Student Name
Franklin Securities
210 Benton Boulevard
Kansas City, MO 64111

Ms. Rebecca Brunson
21220 N.E. 100th St.
Kansas City, MO 64112

Dear Ms. Brunson:

I am pleased you can join me for lunch Wednesday, October 10, from 11:30 a.m. to 1:00 p.m. This event will be held at the company corporate headquarters. The attached map shows the location of the corporate headquarters building.

Franklin Securities is continually involved in a strategic planning process that attempts to respond to the needs of the community we serve. We are hosting a series of luncheons to tell community leaders about our work and to discuss how we can work together to strengthen our community.

I look forward to seeing you Wednesday and hearing your views on future community planning. If you have any questions, please call me at 816-555-8550.

Sincerely,

Student Name
Vice President
Franklin Securities

Exercise 9.3

C09-E03-LtrLuncheon.docx

Maintaining Documents

Many file (document) management tasks in Word can be completed at either the Open or the Save As dialog box. These tasks include copying, moving, printing, and renaming documents; opening multiple documents; and creating new folders and renaming existing folders.

Using Print Screen

Keyboards contain a Print Screen button that you can use to capture the contents of the screen into a file. That file can then be inserted in a Word document. The Print Screen feature is useful for file management in that you can print folder contents that help you keep track of documents and folders. To use the Print Screen key, display the desired information on the screen and then press the Print Screen key on your keyboard (generally located in the top row). When you press the Print Screen key, nothing seems to happen but, in fact, the screen image is captured in a file that is inserted in the Clipboard. To insert this file in a document, click the Paste button in the Clipboard group in the Home tab. You can also paste the file by right-clicking in a blank location in a document and then clicking the *Paste* option at the shortcut menu or by pressing the keyboard shortcut Ctrl + V. If you want to capture only the active dialog box, hold down the Alt key while pressing the Print Screen key.

QUICK STEPS

Create a Folder
1. Display Open dialog box.
2. Click New folder button.
3. Type folder name.
4. Press Enter.

New folder

Creating a Folder

Word documents, like paper documents, should be grouped logically and placed in *folders*. The main folder on a storage medium is called the *root* folder, and you can create additional folders within the root folder. At both the Open and Save As dialog boxes, documents display in the Content pane preceded by the document icon ; folders display preceded by the folder icon . You can create a new folder by clicking the New folder button located on either dialog box toolbar. This inserts a folder in the Content pane that contains the text *New folder*. Type a name for the folder (the name you type replaces *New folder*) and then press the Enter key. A folder name can contain a maximum of 255 characters. Numbers, spaces, and symbols (except those symbols listed in Chapter 1 in the "Naming a Document" section) can be used in the folder name.

To make the new folder active, double-click the folder name in the Open dialog box Content pane. The current folder path displays in the Address bar in the Open dialog box as shown in Figure 9.1. The path includes the current folder as well as any previous folders. If the folder is located in an external storage device, the drive letter and name may display in the path. For example, if you create a folder named Contracts in the Chapter09 folder on your storage medium, the Address bar will display Chapter09 followed by a right-pointing triangle and then Contracts. Two left-pointing arrows display before Chapter09. These arrows indicate that Chapter09 is a subfolder within a folder or in a drive. Click the two left-pointing arrows and a drop-down list displays with the folder name or drive letter that is up one level from Chapter09. The drop-down list also includes other common folders and locations.

Figure 9.1 Open Dialog Box

Address bar

Preview pane

Toolbar

Navigation pane

> Computer ▶ Removable Disk (G:) ▶ Chapter09

Organize ▾   New folder

Recent Places

Libraries
- Documents
- Music
- Pictures
- Videos

Homegroup

Computer
- Gateway (C:)
- DVD RW Drive (D:)
- Removable Disk (G

BetaTestAgrmnt.docx
BGClientLtr.docx
CompComm.docx
CompHardware.docx
CompIndustry.docx
CompSecurity.docx
GrammarCheck01.docx
GrammarCheck02.docx
IntlCorres.docx
InviteLtr.docx
LeaseAgrmnt.docx
LtrFormat.docx
LtrGenMtg.docx
LtrKCC.docx

LtrLuncheon.docx
SpellCheck01.docx
SpellCheck02.docx
TravelAdv.docx
UnionAgrmnt.docx
WWTravel.docx

Select a file to preview.

To open a document, double-click the document name in this Content pane.

File name: [   ]   All Word Documents (*.docx;*.c ▾

Tools ▾   Open ▾   Cancel

Exercise 9.1A Creating a Folder

Part 1 of 7

1. Display the Open dialog box and open the Chapter09 folder on your storage medium.
2. Click the New folder button located on the dialog box toolbar.
3. Type Document and then press the Enter key.
4. Capture the screen contents as an image and insert the image in a document by completing the following steps:
   a. With the Open dialog box displayed, press the Print Screen key on your keyboard (generally located in the top row of your keyboard).
   b. Close the Open dialog box.
   c. At a blank document, click the Paste button in the Clipboard group in the Home tab. (If a blank document does not display on your screen, press Ctrl + N to open a blank document.)
   d. With the screen contents image inserted in the document, print the document by clicking the File tab, clicking the Print tab, and then clicking the Print button at the Print tab Backstage view.
5. Close the document without saving it.

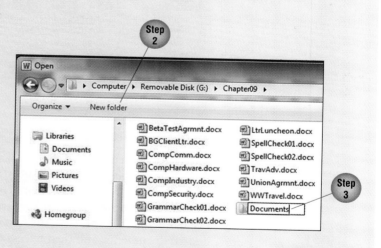

Step 2

> Computer ▶ Removable Disk (G:) ▶ Chapter09 ▶

Organize ▾   New folder

Libraries
- Documents
- Music
- Pictures
- Videos

Homegroup

BetaTestAgrmnt.docx
BGClientLtr.docx
CompComm.docx
CompHardware.docx
CompIndustry.docx
CompSecurity.docx
GrammarCheck01.docx
GrammarCheck02.docx

LtrLuncheon.docx
SpellCheck01.docx
SpellCheck02.docx
TravAdv.docx
UnionAgrmnt.docx
WWTravel.docx
Documents

Step 3

QUICK
STEPS

Rename a Folder
1. Display Open dialog box.
2. Right-click folder.
3. Click *Rename*.
4. Type new name.
5. Press Enter.

Renaming a Folder

As you organize files and folders, you may decide to rename a folder. You can rename a folder using the Organize button in the Open or Save As dialog box or using a shortcut menu. To rename a folder using the Organize button, display the Open or the Save As dialog box, click the folder you want to rename, click the Organize button located on the dialog box toolbar, and then click *Rename* at the drop-down list. Clicking *Rename* selects the folder name and inserts a border around it. Type the new name for the folder and then press the Enter key. To rename a folder using a shortcut menu, display the Open or Save As dialog box, right-click the folder you want to rename, and then click *Rename* at the shortcut menu. Type a new name for the folder and then press the Enter key.

Exercise 9.1B   Renaming a Folder   Part 2 of 7

1. Display the Open dialog box and then right-click the *Document* folder name in the list box.
2. Click *Rename* at the shortcut menu.
3. Type Letters and then press the Enter key.

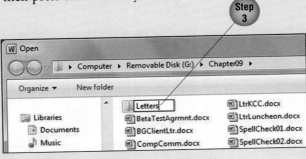

Selecting Documents

You can complete document management tasks on one or more selected documents. To select one document, display the Open dialog box and then click the desired document. To select several adjacent documents (documents that display next to each other), click the first document, hold down the Shift key, and then click the last document. To select documents that are not adjacent, click the first document, hold down the Ctrl key, click any other desired documents, and then release the Ctrl key.

QUICK
STEPS

Delete a Document
1. Display Open dialog box.
2. Click document name.
3. Click Organize button.
4. Click *Delete* at drop-down list.
5. Click Yes.

Deleting Documents

At some point, you may want to delete certain documents from your storage medium or from any other drive or folder in which you may be working. To delete a document, display the Open or Save As dialog box, click the document, click the Organize button on the toolbar, and then click *Delete* at the drop-down list. At the dialog box asking you to confirm the deletion, click Yes. To delete a document using a shortcut menu, right-click the document name in the Content pane, click *Delete* at the shortcut menu, and then click Yes at the confirmation dialog box.

Deleting to the Recycle Bin

When you delete a document from your storage medium, it is deleted permanently. (Recovery programs are available, however, that will help you recover deleted text. If you accidentally delete a document or documents from a storage medium such as a USB flash drive, do not do anything more with the drive until you can run a recovery program.) In contrast, documents deleted from the hard drive are automatically sent to the Windows Recycle Bin. If you accidentally delete a document to the Recycle Bin, it can be easily restored. To free space on the drive, empty the Recycle Bin periodically. Restoring a document from or emptying the contents of the Recycle Bin is completed at the Windows desktop (not in Word). To empty the Recycle Bin, complete the following steps:

1. Display the Windows desktop. If necessary, turn on the computer and Windows will open. If you are currently working in Word, click the Minimize button at the right side of the Title bar. The Minimize button is marked with a single underline symbol (_).

2. At the Windows desktop, double-click the *Recycle Bin* icon (usually located at the left side of the desktop).

3. At the Recycle Bin window, click the Empty the Recycle Bin button.

4. At the question asking if you are sure you want to empty the Recycle Bin, click Yes.

If you want to empty only specific documents from the Recycle Bin, hold down the Ctrl key while clicking the documents to be emptied. Position the mouse pointer on one of the selected documents, click the right mouse button, and then click *Delete* at the shortcut menu. At the question asking if you want to delete the selected documents, click Yes.

A document or selected documents can also be restored from the Recycle Bin. To do this, complete the following steps:

1. At the Windows desktop, double-click the *Recycle Bin* icon.

2. At the Recycle Bin window, click the document to be restored. (If you are restoring more than one document, hold down the Ctrl key while clicking the desired documents.)

3. Click the Restore this item button. (If more than one document is selected, the button name changes to Restore the selected items.)

At the Recycle Bin window, you can also restore a document by positioning the mouse pointer on the document to be restored, clicking the right mouse button, and then clicking *Restore* at the shortcut menu.

If you minimized the Word program by clicking the Minimize button, you can maximize (display the Word screen) the Word program on the desktop by clicking the Word button located on the Taskbar (at the bottom of the screen).

1. Open **CompIndustry.docx** and save the document with the name **C09-E01-CompIndustry**.
2. Close **C09-E01-CompIndustry.docx**.
3. Delete **C09-E01-CompIndustry.docx** by completing the following steps:
   a. Display the Open dialog box.
   b. Click **C09-E01-CompIndustry.docx** to select it.
   c. Click the Organize button on the toolbar and then click *Delete* at the drop-down list.
   d. At the question asking if you want to delete **C09-E01-CompIndustry.docx**, click Yes.

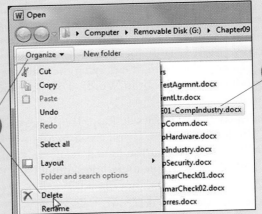

4. Delete selected documents by completing the following steps:
   a. At the Open dialog box, click **CompComm.docx**.
   b. Hold down the Shift key and then click **CompSecurity.docx**.
   c. Position the mouse pointer on a selected document and then click the right mouse button.
   d. At the shortcut menu that displays, click *Delete*.
   e. At the question asking if you want to delete the items, click Yes.
5. Open **LtrKCC.docx** and save the document with the name **C09-E01-LtrKCC**.
6. Save a copy of the **C09-E01-LtrKCC.docx** document in the Letters folder by completing the following steps:
   a. With **C09-E01-LtrKCC.docx** open, click the File tab and then click the Save As button.
   b. At the Save As dialog box, double-click the Letters folder located at the beginning of the Chapter09 Content pane (folders are listed before documents).
   c. Click the Save button located in the lower right corner of the dialog box.
7. Close **C09-E01-LtrKCC.docx**.
8. Display the Open dialog box and then click *Chapter09* in the Address bar.

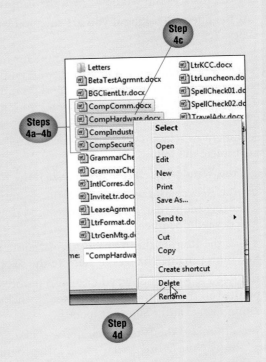

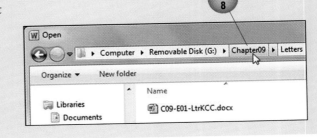

Copying and Moving Documents

You can copy a document to another folder without opening the document first. To do this, use the *Copy* and *Paste* options from the Organize button drop-down list or the shortcut menu at the Open or Save As dialog box. You can copy a document or selected documents into the same folder. When you do this, Word inserts a hyphen followed by the word *Copy* to the document name.

You can also remove a document from one folder and insert it in another folder using the *Cut* and *Paste* options from the Organize button drop-down list or the shortcut menu at the Open dialog box. To do this with the Organize button, display the Open dialog box, select the desired document, click the Organize button, and then click *Cut* at the drop-down list. Navigate to the desired folder, click the Organize button, and then click *Paste* at the drop-down list. To do this with the shortcut menu, display the Open dialog box, position the arrow pointer on the document to be removed (cut), click the right mouse button, and then click *Cut* at the shortcut menu. Navigate to the desired folder, position the arrow pointer in a white area in the Content pane, click the right mouse button, and then click *Paste* at the shortcut menu.

Copy or Move a Document
1. Display Open dialog box.
2. Right-click document name.
3. Click *Copy* or *Cut*.
4. Navigate to desired folder.
5. Right-click blank area.
6. Click *Paste*.

Exercise 9.1D Copying Documents   Part 4 of 7

1. At the Open dialog box with *Chapter09* the active folder, copy a document to another folder by completing the following steps:
   a. Click **LtrGenMtg.docx** in the Content pane, click the Organize button, and then click *Copy* at the drop-down list.
   b. Navigate to the Letters folder by double-clicking *Letters* at the beginning of the Content pane.
   c. Click the Organize button and then click *Paste* at the drop-down list.
2. Go back to the Chapter09 folder by clicking *Chapter09* in the Address bar.
3. Copy several documents to the Letters folder by completing the following steps:
   a. Click once on **LtrFormat.docx**. (This selects the document.)
   b. Hold down the Ctrl key, click **LtrKCC.docx**, click **LtrLuncheon.docx**, and then release the Ctrl key.
   c. Position the arrow pointer on one of the selected documents, click the right mouse button, and then click *Copy* at the shortcut menu.
   d. Double-click the Letters folder.
   e. Position the arrow pointer in any white area in the Content pane, click the right mouse button, and then click *Paste* at the shortcut menu.
4. Click *Chapter09* in the Address bar.
5. Move **TravelAdv.docx** to the Letters folder by completing the following steps:
   a. Position the arrow pointer on **TravelAdv.docx**, click the right mouse button, and then click *Cut* at the shortcut menu.
   b. Double-click Letters to make it the active folder.

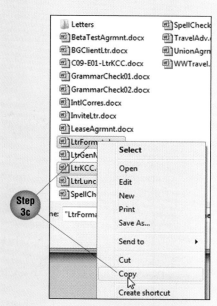

c. Position the arrow pointer in the white area in the Content pane, click the right mouse button, and then click *Paste* at the shortcut menu.

6. Capture the Open dialog box as an image and insert the image in a document by completing the following steps:
   a. With the Open dialog box displayed, hold down the Alt key and then press the Print Screen key on your keyboard.
   b. Close the Open dialog box.
   c. At a blank document, click the Paste button in the Clipboard group in the Home tab. (If a blank document does not display on your screen, press Ctrl + N to open a blank document.)
   d. With the dialog box image inserted in the document, print the document by clicking the File tab, clicking the Print tab, and then clicking the Print button at the Print tab Backstage view.

7. Close the document without saving it.
8. Display the Open dialog box and make *Chapter09* the active folder.

QUICK STEPS

Rename a Document
1. Display Open dialog box.
2. Click document name.
3. Click Organize button, *Rename*.
4. Type new name.
5. Press Enter.

Renaming Documents

At the Open dialog box, you can use the *Rename* option from the Organize button drop-down list to give a document a different name. The *Rename* option changes the name of the document but keeps it in the same folder. To use *Rename*, display the Open dialog box, click once on the document to be renamed, click the Organize button, and then click *Rename* at the drop-down list. When you click *Rename*, a black border surrounds the document name and the name is selected. Type the new name and then press the Enter key. You can also rename a document by right-clicking the document name at the Open dialog box and then clicking *Rename* at the shortcut menu. Type the desired name for the document and then press the Enter key.

Organize ▼

Exercise 9.1E Renaming Documents   Part 5 of 7

1. Rename a document located in the Letters folder by completing the following steps:
   a. At the Open dialog box with the *Chapter09* folder active, double-click the *Letters* folder to make it active.
   b. Click once on **LtrKCC.docx** to select it.
   c. Click the Organize button on the toolbar.
   d. Click *Rename* at the drop-down list.
   e. Type LtrPharmacyTech and then press the Enter key.

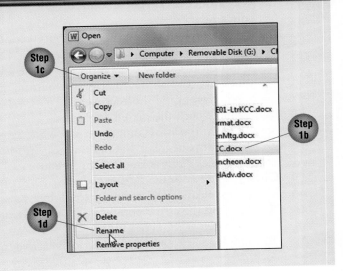

2. Capture the Open dialog box as an image and insert the image in a document by completing the following steps:
   a. Hold down the Alt key and then press the Print Screen key on your keyboard.
   b. Close the Open dialog box.
   c. At a blank document, click the Paste button in the Clipboard group in the Home tab. (If a blank document does not display on your screen, press Ctrl + N to open a blank document.)
   d. With the dialog box image inserted in the document, print the document.
3. Close the document without saving it.
4. Display the Open dialog box and make *Chapter09* the active folder.

Deleting a Folder

As you learned earlier in this chapter, you can delete a selected document or documents. You can also delete a folder and all its contents in the same manner.

Using Open Button Options

Click the Open button arrow in the Open dialog box and a drop-down list displays with options for specifying how you want to open the document. Click the *Open Read-Only* option to open a document that cannot be edited and then saved with the same name. This option is useful in a situation where you do not want the original document modified. With some of the other options at the drop-down list, you can open a document as a copy, open the document in a web browser, and open and repair the document.

Opening Multiple Documents

To open more than one document, select the documents in the Open dialog box and then click the Open button. You can also open multiple documents by positioning the arrow pointer on one of the selected documents, clicking the right mouse button, and then clicking *Open* at the shortcut menu.

QUICK STEPS

Delete a Folder
1. Display Open dialog box.
2. Click folder name.
3. Click Organize button, *Delete*.
4. Click Yes.

Open Multiple Documents
1. Display Open dialog box.
2. Select desired documents.
3. Click Open button.

Exercise 9.1F Deleting a Folder and Opening Multiple Documents   Part 6 of 7

1. At the Open dialog box, click the *Letters* folder to select it.
2. Click the Organize button and then click *Delete* at the drop-down list.
3. At the question asking if you want to remove the folder and its contents, click Yes.
4. Open a document as read-only by completing the following steps:
   a. At the Open dialog box, click **LtrFormat.docx** in the Content pane to select it.

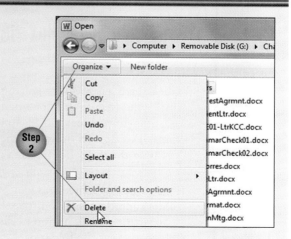

Step 2

b. Click the Open button arrow (located toward the lower right corner of the dialog box) and then click *Open Read-Only* at the drop-down list.

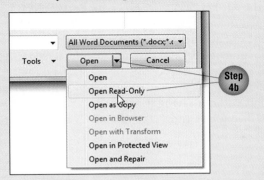

c. Notice the title bar displays the name *LtrFormat.docx [Read-Only]*.
d. Click the Save button on the Quick Access toolbar and notice that the Save As dialog box displays. (This is because you cannot save a read-only document with the original name.)
e. Click the Cancel button to close the Save As dialog box.
f. Close the **LtrFormat.docx [Read-Only]** document.

5. Open a document as a copy by completing the following steps:
   a. Display the Open dialog box and then click **LtrGenMtg.docx** in the Content pane to select it.
   b. Click the Open button arrow and then click *Open as Copy* at the drop-down list.
   c. Notice the title bar displays the name *Copy (1)LtrGenMtg.docx*.
   d. Close the **Copy (1)LtrGenMtg.docx** document.

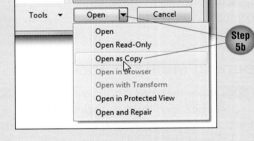

6. Open multiple documents by completing the following steps:
   a. Display the Open dialog box and then select **LtrFormat.docx, LtrGenMtg.docx,** and **LtrKCC.docx.**
   b. Click the Open button located toward the lower right corner of the dialog box.
   c. Close the open documents.

Change Dialog Box View
1. Display Open or Save As dialog box.
2. Click Change your view button arrow.
3. Click desired view at drop-down list.

Change your view

Changing Dialog Box Views

With options in the Change your view button drop-down list at the Open or Save As dialog box, you can customize the display of folders and documents in the Content pane. Click the Change your view button arrow and a drop-down list displays with options for displaying folders and documents as extra large, large, medium, or small icons, as well as displaying folders and documents in a list, with specific details, as tiles, or in content form. To select an option in the drop-down list, you can click the desired option, or you can drag the slider bar (located at the left of the list) to the desired option button.

Choose one of the icon options (extra large, large, medium, or small) to display folders and documents as icons in the Content pane. With the *List* option selected, folders and documents display in the Content pane listed in alphabetical order by name. Choose the *Details* option to display additional information about documents and folders such as the folder or document type and modification date as well as document size. With the *Tiles* option selected, folders and documents display as icons along with information on folder or document type and size. Choose the *Content* option and the document name displays along with the author's name, date the document was modified, and the document size.

You can cycle through the various views by clicking the Change your view button. Each time you click the button, the next view displays. Continue clicking the Change your view button until the desired view is selected.

Displaying Document Properties

If you want to learn more about a specific document such as the document location, size, creation date, any modification dates and the date the document was last accessed, display the document properties. You can do this with the *Properties* option at the Organize button drop-down list in the Open dialog box or the Save As dialog box. Figure 9.2 displays the properties dialog box for UnionAgrmnt.docx (the dates and times in the dialog box will vary).

Display Document Properties
1. Display Open dialog box.
2. Click desired document.
3. Click Organize button.
4. Click Properties.

Figure 9.2 **Properties Dialog Box**

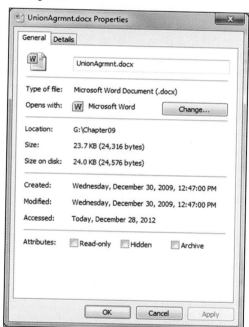

If you display document properties for a document saved on an external storage medium, such as a USB flash drive, the properties dialog box will display with two tabs—General and Details. If you display document properties for a document saved in a folder on the computer's hard drive, the properties dialog box displays with five tabs—General, Security, Custom, Details, and Previous Versions. Each tab displays additional information about the document.

Changing Dialog Box Layout

Generally, the Open dialog box displays with the Navigation pane at the left and the Content pane at the right. You can customize this layout with options at the Organize button *Layout* side menu. Click the Organize button in the Open dialog box, point to *Layout*, and a side menu displays with options for turning on or off the display of the Navigation pane, the Details pane, the Preview pane, and the Library pane. Click the Organize button in the Save As dialog box, point to *Layout,* and the side menu displays with options for turning on or off the display of the Navigation pane and the Library pane. If an option is on, a check mark displays before the option.

Exercise 9.1G Changing Views, Displaying Properties, and Changing Layout   Part 7 of 7

1. Display the Open dialog box.
2. Change the views at the Open dialog box by completing the following steps:
   a. Click the Change your view button arrow on the toolbar. (When you hover the mouse pointer over the down-pointing arrow at the right of the Change your view button, a ScreenTip displays with the text *More options*.)
   b. At the drop-down list that displays, drag the button on the slider bar that displays at the left of the list to the *Extra Large Icons* option. (This displays the folders and documents in the Content pane as large icons.)

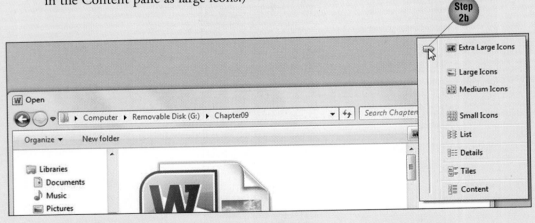

   c. Scroll through the Content pane to view the folders and documents as extra large icons.
   d. Click the Change your view button arrow and then click *Medium Icons* at the drop-down list.

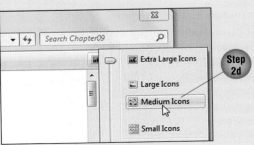

e. Scroll through the Content pane to view the folders and documents as medium-sized icons.

f. Click the Change your view button arrow and then drag the button on the slider bar to the *Details* option.

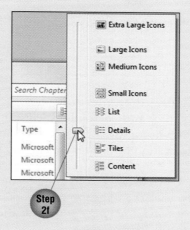

Step 2f

g. Scroll through the list of documents in the Content pane and view the information on the size and type of documents and the last modification date.

h. Click the Change your view button until the documents in the Content pane display as a list.

3. Display document properties for specific documents by completing the following steps:

a. At the Open dialog box, click **UnionAgrmnt.docx.**

b. Click the Organize button and then click *Properties* at the drop-down list.

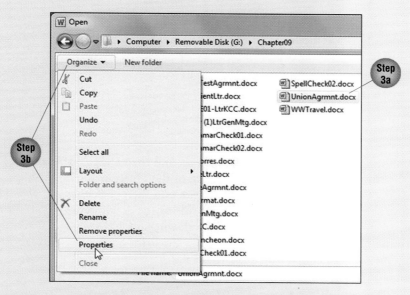

Step 3b

Step 3a

c. At the UnionAgrmnt.docx Properties dialog box, read the properties information that displays in the dialog box with the General tab selected.

d. Click the Details tab and then read the information that displays in the dialog box.

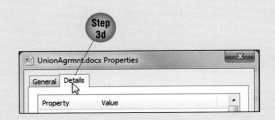

e. Close the UnionAgrmnt.docx Properties dialog box.
f. At the Open dialog box, click **IntlCorres.docx**, click the Organize button, and then click *Properties* at the drop-down list.
g. Read the properties information for the document and then close the properties dialog box.
4. Customize the layout of the Open dialog box by completing the following steps:
    a. At the Open dialog box, click the Organize button, point to *Layout* at the drop-down list, and then click *Navigation pane* at the side menu. (This should remove the Navigation pane from the dialog box.)

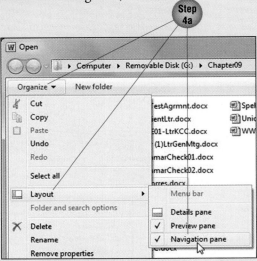

    b. Click the Organize button, point to *Layout*, and then click *Details pane*. (This should display the Details pane along the bottom of the Open dialog box.)
    c. Click the Organize button, point to *Layout*, and then click *Preview pane*. (This should remove the Preview pane from the right side of the dialog box.)
5. Print the screen contents by completing the following steps:
    a. With the Open dialog box displayed, press the Print Screen key on your keyboard.
    b. Close the Open dialog box.
    c. At a blank document, click the Paste button.
    d. Print the document.
    e. Close the document without saving it.
6. Return the display of the Open dialog box back to the default by completing the following steps:
    a. Display the Open dialog box, click the Organize button, point to *Layout* at the drop-down list, and then click *Navigation pane* at the side menu. (This should display the Navigation pane at the left side of the dialog box.)

b. Click the Organize button, point to *Layout,* and then click *Details pane.* (This should remove the display of the Details pane.)

c. Click the Organize button, point to *Layout,* and then click *Preview pane.* (This should display the Preview pane at the right side of the dialog box.)

7. Close the Open dialog box.

Sharing Documents

Click the File tab and then click the Save & Send tab and the Save & Send tab Backstage view displays as shown in Figure 9.3. With options at this view, you can share documents by sending them as an email attachment or a fax, save your document as a different file type, and post your document to a special location such as a blog.

Figure 9.3 Save & Send Tab Backstage View

With the Send Using E-mail option selected, this section displays options for sending the document as an e-mail attachment, as a PDF or XPS attachment, or as an Internet fax.

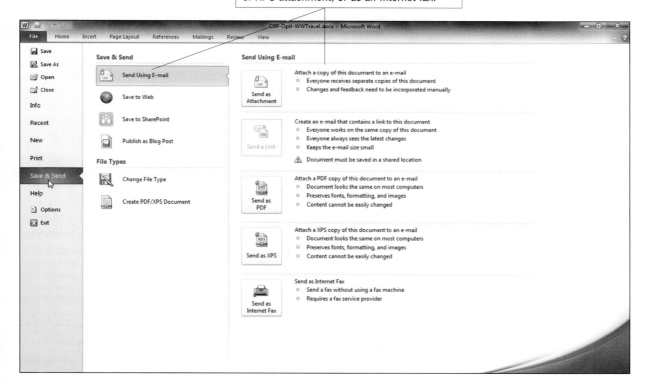

Sending a Document Using E-mail

With the Send Using E-mail option selected in the *Save & Send* category, options for sending a document display such as sending a copy of the document as an attachment to an email, creating an email that contains a link to the document, attaching a PDF or XPS copy of the open document to an email, and sending an email as an Internet fax. To send the document as an attachment, you need to set up an Outlook email account. If you want to create an email that contains a link to the document, you need to save the document to a web server. Use the last option, Send as Internet Fax, to fax the current document without using a fax machine. To use this button, you must be signed up with a fax service provider. If you have not previously signed up for a service, you will be prompted to do so.

With the remaining two options in the *Send Using E-mail* category of the Save & Send tab Backstage view, you can send the document in PDF or XPS format. The letters PDF stand for *portable document format*, which is a document format developed by Adobe Systems® that captures all of the elements of a document as an electronic image. An XPS document is a Microsoft document format for publishing content in an easily viewable format. The letters XPS stand for *XML paper specification*, and the letters XML stand for *extensible markup language*, which is a set of rules for encoding documents electronically. The options listed below, Attach a PDF copy of this document to an email and Attach a XPS copy of this document to an email, describe the format and the advantages of saving in the PDF or XPS format.

Saving to SkyDrive

If you want to share documents with others, consider saving documents to SkyDrive, which is a file storage and sharing service that allows you to upload files that can be accessed from a web browser. To save a document to SkyDrive, you need a Windows Live ID account. If you have a Hotmail, Messenger, or Xbox LIVE account, you have a Windows Live ID account. To save a document to SkyDrive, open the document, click the File tab, click the Save & Send tab, and then click the Save to Web button in the Save & Send category. In the *Save to Windows Live* section, click the Sign In button. At the connecting dialog box, type your email address, press the tab key, type your password, and then press Enter. Once you are connected to your Windows Live ID account, specify whether you want the file saved to your personal folder or saved to your shared folder, and then click the Save As button. At the Save As dialog box, click the Save button or type a new name in the *File name* text box and then click the Save button. One method for accessing your file from SkyDrive is to log into your Windows Live ID account and then look for the SkyDrive hyperlink. Click this hyperlink and your personal and shared folder contents display.

Saving to SharePoint

Microsoft SharePoint is a collection of products and software that includes a number of components. If your company or organization uses SharePoint, you can save a document in a library on your organization's SharePoint site so you and your colleagues have a central location for accessing documents. To save a document to a SharePoint library, open the document, click the File tab, click the Save & Send tab, and then click the Save to SharePoint button.

Saving a Document as a Blog Post

You can save a Word document as a blog post with the Publish as Blog Post button in the Save & Send tab Backstage view. To save a blog post, you must have a blog site established. Click the Publish as Blog Post button and information about supported blog sites displays at the right side of the Save & Send tab Backstage view. To publish a document as a blog post, open the document, click the File tab, click the Save & Send tab, click the Publish as Blog Post button in the Save & Send category, and then click the Publish as Blog Post button in the Publish as Blog Post category. If you do not have a blog site established, click the Register Now button and then complete the blog registration wizard steps. If you have a blog site established, the document will open in a new window. Type a title for the blog post and then click the Publish button that displays in the Blog group in the Blog Post tab.

Chapter 9 Optional Exercise Sending a Document as an Email Attachment, Saving to SkyDrive, and Publishing as a Blog Post Part 1 of 1

Before completing this optional exercise, check with your instructor to determine if you have Outlook set up as your email provider, if you have a Windows Live ID account, and if you have a blog site established.

1. Open **WWTravel.docx** and then save the document and name it **C09-Optl-WWTravel**.
2. Send the document as an email attachment by completing the following steps:
   a. Click the File tab and then click the Save & Send tab.
   b. At the Save & Send tab Backstage view, click the Send as Attachment button in the *Send Using E-mail* category.

   c. At the Outlook window, type your instructor's email address in the *To* text box.
   d. Click the Send button.

3. With **C09-Optl-WWTravel.docx** open, save the document to SkyDrive by completing the following steps:
   a. Click the File tab, click the Save & Send tab, and then click the Save to Web button in the Save & Send category.
   b. In the *Save to Windows Live* section, click the Sign In button.

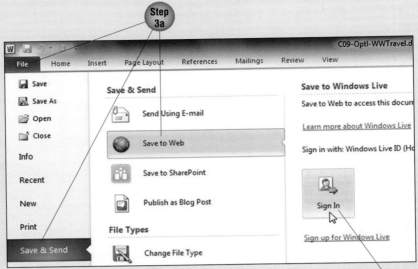

   c. At the connecting dialog box, type your email address, press the Tab key, type your password, and then press Enter.
   d. Once you are connected to your Windows Live ID account, specify whether you want the file saved to your personal folder or saved to your shared folder, and then click the Save As button.
   e. At the Save As dialog box, click the Save button.
   f. Close **C09-Optl-WWTravel.docx**.
4. If you have a blog site established, save the travel document as a blog post by completing the following steps:
   a. Open the **C09-Optl-WWTravel.docx** document from the Chapter09 folder on your storage medium.
   b. Click the File tab, click the Save & Send tab, and then click the Publish as Blog Post button in the Save & Send category.
   c. Click the Publish as Blog Post button in the Publish as Blog Post category.
   d. If you have a blog site established, the document will open in a new window. If you do not have a blog site established, click the Register Now button and then complete the blog registration wizard steps. Type a title for the blog post and then click the Publish button that displays in the Blog group in the Blog Post tab.
   e. Close the blog post document.
5. Close **C09-Optl-WWTravel.docx**.

Saving a Document in a Different Format

When you save a document, the document is automatically saved as a Word document. If you need to share a document with someone who is using a different word processing program or a different version of Word, you may want to save the document in another format. At the Save & Send tab Backstage view, click the Change File Type option in the *File Types* category and the view displays as shown in Figure 9.4.

Figure 9.4 Save & Send Tab Backstage View with Change File Type Option Selected

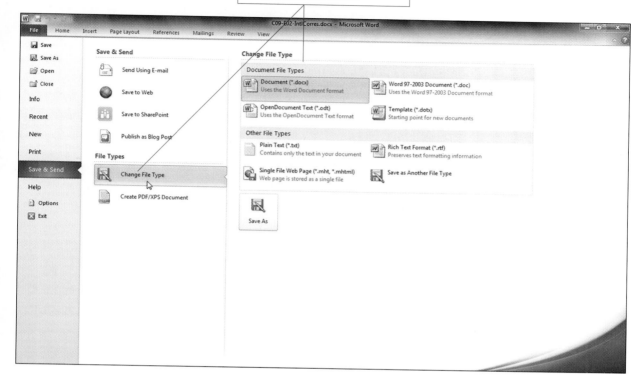

Click the Change File Type option to display options for saving a file in a different format.

With options in the *Document File Types* section, you can choose to save a Word document with the default file format, save the document in a previous version of Word, save the document in OpenDocument text format, or save the document as a template. The OpenDocument text format is an XML-based file format for displaying, storing, and editing files such as word processing, spreadsheet, or presentation files. OpenDocument format is free from any licensing, royalty payments or other restrictions, and, since technology changes at a rapid pace, saving a document in OpenDocument text format ensures that the information in the file can be accessed, retrieved, and used now and in the future.

Additional file types are available in the *Other File Types* section. If you need to send your document to another user who does not have access to Microsoft Word, consider saving the document in plain text or rich text file format. Use the *Plain Text (*.txt)* option to save the document with all formatting stripped, which is good for universal file exchange. Use the *Rich Text Format (*.rtf)* option to save the document with most of the character formatting applied to text in the document such as bold, italic, underline, bullets, and fonts as well as some paragraph formatting such as justification. Before the widespread use of Adobe's portable document format (PDF), rich text format was the most portable file format used to exchange files. With the *Single File Web Page (*.mht, *.mhtml)* option, you can save your document as a single page web document. Click the *Save as Another File Type* option and the Save As dialog box displays. Click the Save as type option button and a drop-down list displays with a variety of available file type options.

QUICK STEPS

Save Document in Different Format
1. Click File tab.
2. Click Save & Send tab.
3. Click Change File Type option in *File Types* category.
4. Click desired format in *Change File Type* category.

1. Open **IntlCorres.docx** and save the document and name it **C09-E02-IntlCorres**.
2. Apply the following formatting to the document.
   a. Apply the Heading 2 style to the four headings in the document.
   b. Change the style set to Traditional.
   c. Change the theme to Solstice.
3. Click the Save button on the Quick Access toolbar to save the document.
4. Save the document in Word 97-2003 format by completing the following steps:
   a. Click the File tab and then click the Save & Send tab.
   b. At the Save & Send tab Backstage view, click the *Change File Type* option in the *File Types* category.
   c. Click the *Word 97-2003 Document (*.doc)* option in the *Document File Types* section and then click the Save As button.

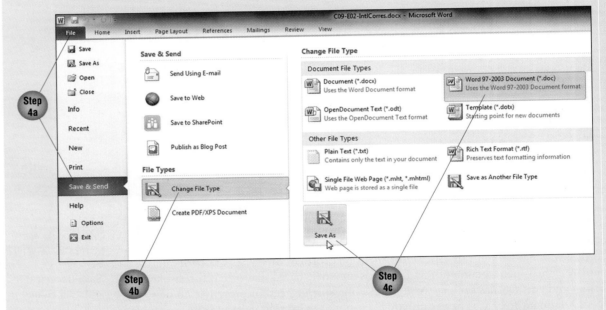

d. At the Save As dialog box with the *Save as type* option button changed to *Word 97-2003 Document (*.doc)*, type C09-E02-IntlCorres-Word97-2003 and then press the Enter key.

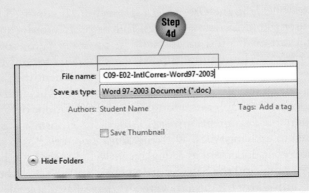

5. At the document, notice the title bar displays the words *[Compatibility Mode]* after the document name.
6. Click the Page Layout tab and notice the buttons in the Themes group are dimmed. (This is because the themes features were not available in Word 97 through 2003.)
7. Close **C09-E02-IntlCorres-Word97-2003.doc**.
8. Open **C09-E02-IntlCorres.docx**.
9. Save the document in plain text format by completing the following steps:
   a. Click the File tab and then click the Save & Send tab.
   b. At the Save & Send tab Backstage view, click the Change File Type option in the *File Types* category.
   c. Click the *Plain Text (*.txt)* option in the *Other File Types* section and then click the Save As button.

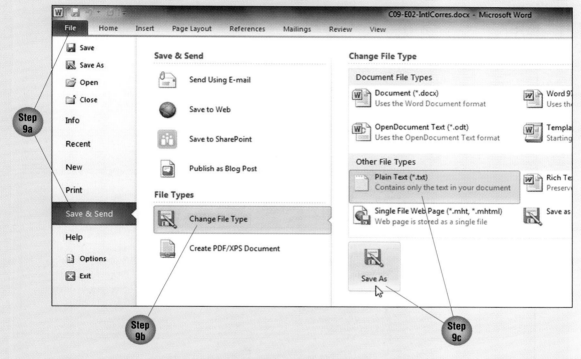

   d. At the Save As dialog box, type C09-E02-IntlCorres-PlainTxt and then press the Enter key.
   e. At the File Conversion dialog box, click OK.
10. Close **C09-E02-IntlCorres-PlainTxt.txt**.
11. Display the Open dialog box and, if necessary, display all files. To do this, click the file type button at the right of the *File name* text box and then click *All Files (*.*)* at the drop-down list.

12. Double-click **C09-E02-IntlCorres-PlainTxt.txt**. (If a File Conversion dialog box displays, click OK. Notice that the character and paragraph formatting has been removed from the document.)
13. Close **C09-E02-IntlCorres-PlainTxt.txt**.

Save Document in Different Format at Save As Dialog Box
1. Open document.
2. Click File tab, click Save As button.
3. Type document name.
4. Click Save as type button.
5. Click desired format at drop-down list.
6. Click Save button.

In addition to options in the Save & Send tab Backstage view with the Change File Type option selected, you can save a document in a different format using the Save as type option button at the Save As dialog box. Click the Save as type option button and a drop-down list displays as shown in Figure 9.5. The drop-down list contains all available file formats for saving a document.

Figure 9.5 Save As Dialog Box with Save as type Option Button Drop-down List

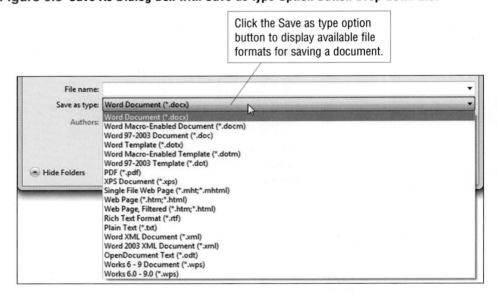

Click the Save as type option button to display available file formats for saving a document.

File name:
Save as type: Word Document (*.docx)
Authors:

Word Document (*.docx)
Word Macro-Enabled Document (*.docm)
Word 97-2003 Document (*.doc)
Word Template (*.dotx)
Word Macro-Enabled Template (*.dotm)
Word 97-2003 Template (*.dot)
PDF (*.pdf)
XPS Document (*.xps)
Single File Web Page (*.mht;*.mhtml)
Web Page (*.htm;*.html)
Web Page, Filtered (*.htm;*.html)
Rich Text Format (*.rtf)
Plain Text (*.txt)
Word XML Document (*.xml)
Word 2003 XML Document (*.xml)
OpenDocument Text (*.odt)
Works 6 - 9 Document (*.wps)
Works 6.0 - 9.0 (*.wps)

Hide Folders

Exercise 9.2B Saving a Document in a Different Format Using the Save as type Option Button   Part 2 of 3

1. Open **C09-E02-IntlCorres.docx**.
2. Save the document in rich text format by completing the following steps:
   a. Click the File tab and then click the Save As button.

b. At the Save As dialog box, type C09-E02-IntlCorres-RichTxt in the *File name* text box.
c. Click the Save as type option button.
d. Scroll down the drop-down list and then click *Rich Text Format (*.rtf)*.

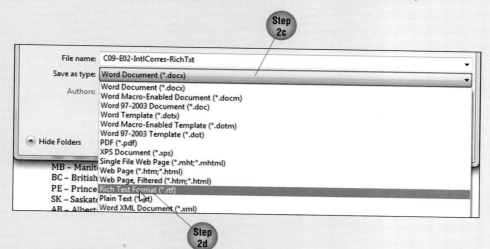

e. Click the Save button.
3. Close the document.
4. Display the Open dialog box and, if necessary, display all files.
5. Double-click **C09-E02-IntlCorres-RichText.rtf**. (Notice that the formatting was retained in the document.)
6. Close the document.

Saving in PDF/XPS Format

As you learned earlier, the portable document format (PDF) captures all of the elements of a document as an electronic image, and the XPS document format is used for publishing content in an easily viewable format. To save a document in PDF or XPS format, click the File tab, click the Save & Send tab, click the Create PDF/XPS Document option in the *File Types* category, and then click the Create a PDF/XPS button in the *Create a PDF/ XPS Document* category of the Backstage view. This displays the Publish as PDF or XPS dialog box with the *PDF (*.pdf)* option selected in the Save as type option button. If you want to save the document in XPS format, click the Save as type option button and then click *XPS Document (*.xps)* at the drop-down list. At the Save As dialog box, type a name in the *File name* text box and then click the Publish button. If you save the document in PDF format, the document opens in Adobe Reader and if you save the document in XPS format, the document opens the XPS Viewer window.

You can open a PDF file in Adobe Reader or in your web browser, and you can open an XPS file in your web browser. To open a PDF file or XPS file in your web browser, click the File option in the browser menu bar and then click *Open* at the drop-down list. At the Open dialog box, click the Browse button. At the browser window open dialog box, change the files of type to *All Files (*.*)*, navigate to the desired folder, and then double-click the document.

Save Document in PDF/XPS Format
1. Open document.
2. Click File tab.
3. Click Save & Send tab.
4. Click Create PDF/ XPS Document option.
5. Click Create a PDF/ XPS button.
6. At Publish as PDF or XPS dialog box, specify if you want to save in PDF or XPS format.
7. Click Publish button.

1. Open **WWTravel.docx**.
2. Save the document in PDF file format by completing the following steps:
   a. Click the File tab and then click the Save & Send tab.
   b. At the Save & Send tab Backstage view, click the Create PDF/XPS Document option in the *File Types* category.
   c. Click the Create a PDF/XPS button.

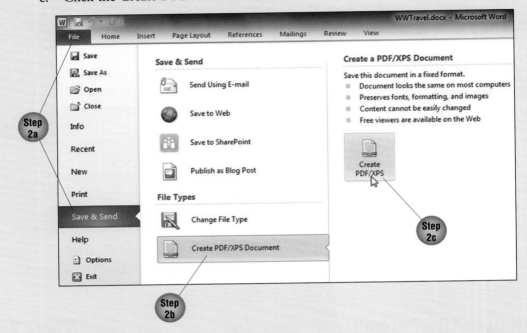

   d. At the Publish as PDF or XPS dialog box, make sure *PDF (*.pdf)* is selected in the Save as type option button and then click the Publish button.

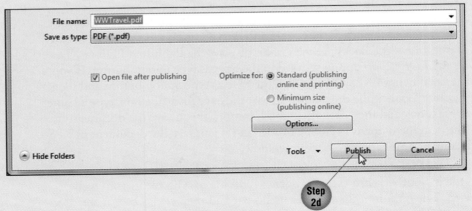

3. Scroll through the document in Adobe Reader.
4. Click the Close button located in the upper right corner of the window to close Adobe Reader.
5. Close **WWTravel.docx**.

6. Capture the contents of the Chapter09 folder as an image by completing the following steps:
   a. Press Ctrl + N to open a blank document and then display the Open dialog box with the *Chapter09* folder active.
   b. Make sure the files of type displays as *All Files (*.*)*.
   c. Check to make sure the documents display in List view. If not, click the Change your view button arrow and then click *List* at the drop-down list.
   d. Hold down the Alt key and then press the Print Screen key.
   e. Close the Open dialog box.
   f. At the blank document, click the Paste button.
   g. Print the document and then close the document without saving it.

Creating a Document Using a Template

Word includes a number of template documents formatted for specific uses. Each Word document is based on a template document, with the *Normal* template the default. With Word templates, you can easily create a variety of documents such as letters, faxes, and awards, with specialized formatting. Display templates by clicking the File tab and then clicking the New tab. This displays the New tab Backstage view as shown in Figure 9.6.

Create Document using a Template
1. Click File tab.
2. Click New tab.
3. Click Sample templates button.
4. Double-click desired template.

Figure 9.6 New Tab Backstage View

Click this button to display installed templates.

Use this option to search for templates at the Office.com site.

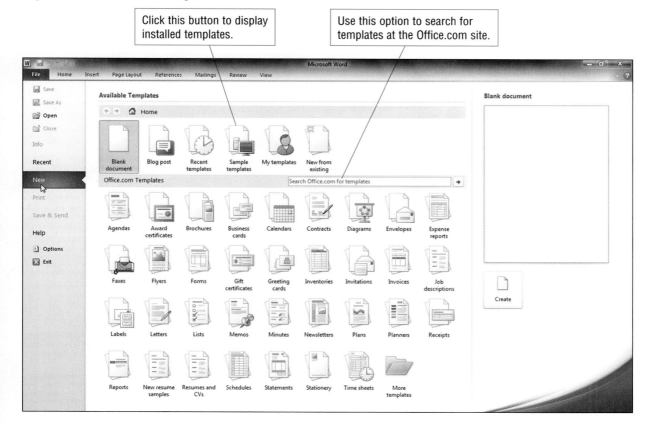

Click the Sample templates button in the *Available Templates* category and installed templates display. Click the desired template in the Sample templates list box and a preview of the template displays at the right side of the screen. With options below the template preview, you can choose to open the template as a document or as a template. Click the Create button and the template opens and displays on the screen. Locations for personalized text display in placeholders in the template document. Select the placeholder text and then type the personalized text.

If you are connected to the Internet, you can download a number of predesigned templates that Microsoft offers. Templates are grouped into categories and the category names display in the *Office.com Templates* section of the New tab Backstage view. Click the desired template category and available templates display. Click the desired template and then click the Download button.

Exercise 9.3   Creating a Letter Using a Template   Part 1 of 1

1. Click the File tab and then click the New tab.
2. At the New tab Backstage view, click the Sample templates button in the *Available Templates* category.

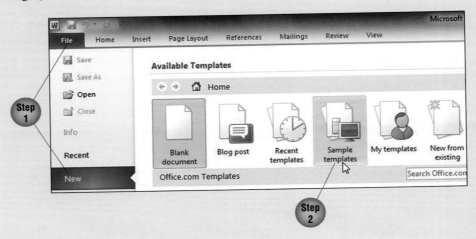

3. Double-click the *Equity Letter* template.

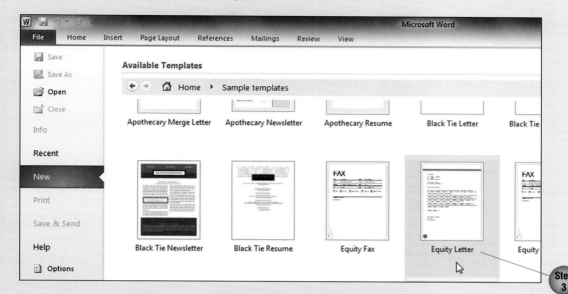

4. Click the placeholder text *[Pick the date]*, click the down-pointing arrow at the right of the placeholder, and then click the Today button located at the bottom of the calendar.
5. Click in the name that displays below the date, select the name, and then type your first and last names.
6. Click the placeholder text *[Type the sender company name]* and then type Franklin Securities.
7. Click the placeholder text *[Type the sender company address]*, type 210 Benton Boulevard, press the Enter key, and then type Kansas City, MO 64111.
8. Click the placeholder text *[Type the recipient name]* and then type Ms. Rebecca Brunson.
9. Click the placeholder text *[Type the recipient address]*, type 21220 N.E. 100th St., press the Enter key, and then type Kansas City, MO 64112.

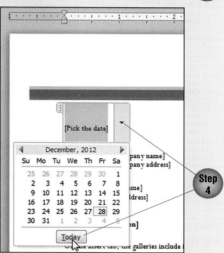

10. Click the placeholder text *[Type the salutation]* and then type Dear Ms. Brunson:. Select the text you just typed and then remove bold formatting.
11. Insert a file in the document by completing the following steps:
    a. Click anywhere in the three paragraphs of text in the body of the letter and then click the Delete key.
    b. Click the Insert tab.
    c. Click the Object button arrow in the Text group and then click *Text from File* at the drop-down list.
    d. At the Insert File dialog box, navigate to the Chapter09 folder on your storage medium and then double-click **LtrLuncheon.docx**.
    e. Press the Delete key once to remove the blank space above the complimentary close.
12. Click the placeholder text *[Type the closing]* and then type Sincerely,.
13. Click the placeholder text *[Type the sender title]* and then type Vice President.
14. Save the document with the name **C09-E03-LtrLuncheon**.
15. Print and then close **C09-E03-LtrLuncheon.docx**.

Chapter *Summary*

➤ Group Word documents logically into folders. Create a new folder with the New folder button at the Open or Save As dialog box.

➤ You can select one or several documents at the Open dialog box. Copy, move, rename, delete, print, or open a document or selected documents.

➤ Delete documents and/or folders with the *Delete* option at the Organize button drop-down list at the Open or Save As dialog box or with the *Delete* option from the shortcut menu.

➤ Documents deleted from the hard drive are sent to the Windows Recycle Bin. You can empty or recover documents from the Recycle Bin.

➤ Use the *Cut, Copy*, and *Paste* options from the Organize button drop-down list or the Open or Save As dialog box shortcut menu to move or copy a document from one folder to another.

➤ Rename documents with the *Rename* option from the Open dialog box Organize button drop-down list or shortcut menu.

➤ Use options from the Open button arrow in the Open dialog box to open a document in a different format such as read-only or as a copy.

➤ You can open multiple documents from the Open dialog box.

➤ Change views in the Open dialog box or Save As dialog box with options from the Change your view button arrow drop-down list.

➤ Use the *Properties* option at the Organize button drop-down list to display information about the currently selected document in the Content pane.

➤ Customize the layout of the Open or Save As dialog box with layout options from the Organize button *Layout* side menu.

➤ With options at the Save & Send tab Backstage view, you can send a document as an email attachment or fax, save your document to SkyDrive and SharePoint, save your document in a different file format, and post your document to a special location such as a blog.

➤ With options in the *Send Using E-mail* category of the Save & Send tab Backstage view, you can send a document in PDF or XPS format. The letters PDF stand for *portable document format*, which is a format that captures all elements of a document as an electronic image. The letters XPS stand for *XML paper specification*, which is a Microsoft format for publishing content in an easily viewable format.

➤ Click the Change File Type option in the *File Types* category at the Save & Send tab Backstage view, and options display for saving the document in a different file format such as OpenDocument Text, Plain Text, Rich Text Format, and Single File Web Page; you can also save as a previous version of Word and as a template.

➤ You can also save documents in a different file format with the Save as type option button at the Save As dialog box.

➤ Save a document in PDF or XPS format with the Create PDF/XPS Document option in the *File Types* category in the Save & Send tab Backstage view.

➤ Word includes a number of template documents you can use to create a variety of documents. Display the list of template documents by clicking the File tab, clicking the New tab, and then clicking the Sample templates button.

Commands *Review*

FEATURE	RIBBON TAB, GROUP	BUTTON, OPTION	KEYBOARD SHORTCUT
Open dialog box	File	Open	Ctrl + O
Save As dialog box	File	Save As	Shift + F12
New tab Backstage view	File	New	
Save & Send tab Backstage view	File	Save & Send	
Recycle Bin			

Key Points *Review*

Completion: In the space provided at the right, indicate the correct term, command, or number.

1. Create a new folder with this button at the Open or Save As dialog box.

2. To make the previous folder active, click the folder name in this bar in the Open or Save As dialog box.

3. Using the mouse, select adjacent documents at the Open dialog box by holding down this key while clicking the desired documents.

4. Using the mouse, select nonadjacent documents at the Open dialog box by holding down this key while clicking the desired documents.

5. Documents deleted from the hard drive are automatically sent to this bin.

6. Use this option from the Open dialog box Organize button drop-down list to give a document a different name.

7. Choose this view at the Open dialog box Change your view button arrow drop-down list to display information about folders and documents such as size, type, and modification date.

8. Choose this view at the Open dialog box Change your view button drop-down list to display folders and documents alphabetized by name.

9. Copy a document to another folder without opening the document with the *Copy* option and this option from the Open dialog box shortcut menu.

10. With this option selected in the *Save & Send* category at the Save & Send tab Backstage view, options for sending a document display.

11. The letters PDF stand for this.

12. Saving a document in this file format strips out all formatting. _____

13. You can save a document in a different file format with this option button at the Save As dialog box. _____

14. To save a document in PDF format, click this option at the Save & Send tab Backstage view and then click the Create PDF/XPS button. _____

15. Display installed templates by clicking this button in the *Available Templates* category of the New tab Backstage view. _____

Chapter Assessments

Applying Your Skills

Demonstrate your knowledge of features learned in this chapter by completing the following assessments.

Assessment 9.1   Create a Folder and Copy and Rename Documents

1. Display the Open dialog box with *Chapter09* the active folder and then create a new folder named CheckingTools.
2. Copy (be sure to copy and not cut) all documents that begin with *SpellCheck* and *GrammarCheck* into the CheckingTools folder.
3. With the CheckingTools folder active, rename **SpellCheck01.docx** to **VacationAdventures.docx**.
4. Rename **GrammarCheck01.docx** to **NaturalInterfaces.docx**.
5. Click the Print Screen key to capture in a file an image of the Open dialog box, close the Open dialog box, insert the file in a blank document, print the document, and then close it without saving it.
6. Display the Open dialog box and make *Chapter09* the active folder.
7. Delete the CheckingTools folder and all documents contained within it.

Assessment 9.2   Save a Document in Different Formats

1. Open **LeaseAgrmnt.docx** and save the document with the name **C09-A02-LeaseAgrmnt**.
2. Make the following changes to the document:
   a. Apply the Heading 2 style to the title *LEASE AGREEMENT*.
   b. Change the style set to Simple.
   c. Apply the Oriel theme.
   d. Center the title.
   e. Add 12 points of spacing after the title.
3. Save and then print **C09-A02-LeaseAgrmnt.docx**.
4. With **C09-A02-LeaseAgrmnt.docx** open, save the document in the Word 97-2003 format with the name **C09-A02-LeaseAgrmnt-W97-2003**.
5. Close **C09-A02-LeaseAgrmnt-W97-2003.doc**.
6. Open **C09-A02-LeaseAgrmnt.docx** and then save the document in the plain-text format with the name **C09-A02-LeaseAgrmnt-PlainTxt**.
7. Print and then close **C09-A02-LeaseAgrmnt-PlainTxt.txt**.
8. Open **C09-A02-LeaseAgrmnt.docx** and then save the document in PDF format with the name **C09-A02-LeaseAgrmnt-PDF**. After viewing the document in Adobe Reader, click the Close button located in the upper right corner of the screen.
9. Close **C09-A02-LeaseAgrmnt.docx** without saving changes.

Assessment 9.3 Use a Template to Create a Fax Document

1. Open the Equity fax template from the New tab Backstage view with the Sample templates button selected and then insert the following information in the specified fields.

   > To: Charlene Renquist
   > From: (your first and last names)
   > Fax: (816) 555-9010
   > Pages: 3
   > Phone: (816) 555-9005
   > Date: (insert current date)
   > Re: Financial Contract
   > CC: Eric Young
   > Insert an *X* in the *For Review* check box
   > Comments: Please review the Financial Contract and advise me of any legal issues.

2. Save the fax document with the name **C09-A03-Fax**.
3. Print and then close **C09-A03-Fax.docx**.

Expanding Your Skills

Explore additional feature options or use Help to learn a new skill in creating this document.

Assessment 9.4 Create a Calendar and Write a Memo

1. Use a calendar template from the *Office.com Templates* section of the New tab Backstage view and create a calendar of your choosing.
2. When the calendar is complete, print only the first page of the calendar.
3. Save the document and name it **C09-A04-Calendar**.
4. Close **C09-A04-Calendar.docx**.
5. At a blank document, write a memo to your instructor describing the steps you followed to create the calendar in **C09-A04-Calendar.docx**.
6. Save the completed memo and name it **C09-A04-Memo**.
7. Print and then close **C09-A04-Memo.docx**.

Achieving Signature Status

Take your skills to the next level by completing these more challenging assessments.

Assessment 9.5 Create a Folder and Save Documents in Different Formats

1. Look at the Open dialog box shown in Figure 9.7. Create a new folder named FileFormats as shown in the figure. Open documents from the Chapter09 folder on your storage medium and then save them into the FileFormats folder you created in the four file formats shown in the Content pane in the figure. ***Hint: Look at the file extension of the documents and the information in the*** Type ***column to determine the document format in which you need to save the document.***
2. When you have completed saving the documents in the appropriate file formats, display the Open dialog box with the *FileFormats* folder active, change the view to *Details*, and then hold down the Alt key and press the Print Screen key to capture an image of your Open dialog box. Paste the image into a blank document, print the document, and then close the document without saving it.

Figure 9.7 Assessment 9.5

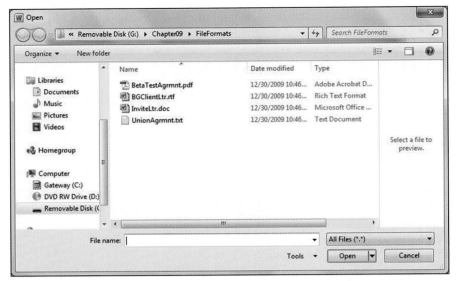

Assessment 9.6   Create an Invitation

1. Create the company annual picnic invitation shown in Figure 9.8 with the following specifications:

   - Use the company picnic invitation flyer. Find this flyer in the *Office.com Templates* section of the New tab Backstage view by clicking the *Invitations* folder and then clicking the *Business invitations* folder.

   - Edit the information so it displays as shown in the figure. (Type your first and last names in place of *(Student Name)* located toward the bottom of the invitation.)

Figure 9.8 Assessment 9.6

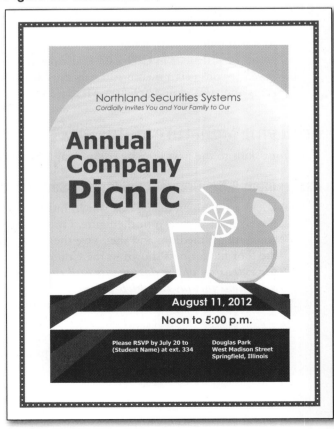

   - Insert the page border with the following specifications:

     - Use the art border that is approximately the eighteenth border from the bottom of the Art button drop-down list.

     - Change the *Width* to *10 pt*.

     - Change the color to dark red.

     - Check the invitation in the Print tab Backstage view, and if the entire page border is not visible, change the measurements at the Border and Shading Options dialog box.

2. Save the completed invitation and name it **C09-A06-Invitation**.

3. Print and then close **C09-A06-Invitation.docx**.

Chapter 10

Managing and Printing Documents

Tutorial 10.1
Working with Windows
Tutorial 10.2
Changing Document Zoom and
Hiding/Showing White Space
Tutorial 10.3
Managing the Recent List
Tutorial 10.4
Managing Versions
Tutorial 10.5
Previewing and Printing
Documents
Tutorial 10.6
Creating and Printing Envelopes
Tutorial 10.7
Creating and Printing Labels

Performance Objectives

Upon successful completion of Chapter 10, you will be able to:

- Open, close, arrange, split, maximize, minimize, and restore documents
- Print specific pages or sections of a document
- Print multiple copies of a document
- Create and print envelopes and labels

When you work in Word, you can view a single document on the screen or multiple documents. You can open and close windows; arrange windows; and maximize, minimize, and restore documents. In this chapter, you will learn how to complete these tasks and how to customize printing and print envelopes and labels.

Note: Before beginning computer exercises for this chapter, copy to your storage medium the Chapter10 folder from the CD that accompanies this textbook and then make Chapter10 the active folder.

In this chapter students will produce the following documents:

Exercise 10.1. C10-E01-CompComm.docx
Exercise 10.2. C10-E02-Env.docx
Exercise 10.3. C10-E03-LtrPharmTech.docx
Exercise 10.4. C10-E04-Labels.docx

Model answers for these exercises are shown on the following pages.

COMPUTERS IN ENTERTAINMENT

Possibilities in the television and film industries have soared with computer technology, especially in production. Computer games have captured the public imagination and created enormous growth in the computer game market.

TELEVISION AND FILM

Many of the spectacular graphics and special effects seen on television and in movies today are created with computers. The original *Star Wars* films, for example, relied heavily on hand-constructed models and hand-drawn graphics. Twenty years after the first release of the films, they were re-released with many new special effects, including futuristic cityscape backgrounds, new alien creatures, and new sounds that were created on computers and added to the films by means of computerized video editing. In an article on special effects, Jaclyn McFadden, an industry expert talked about the evolution of computer simulation.

The film *Jurassic Park* brought computer simulation to a new level by combining puppetry and computer animation to simulate realistic looking dinosaurs. *Toy Story*, released in 1996, was the first wholly computer-animated commercial movie.

Software products are available that automatically format scripts of various kinds. Industry analysts predict that the improvements in computer technology will continue to enhance and improve the visual appeal of television and film media.

HOME ENTERTAINMENT

The advent of powe...
complexity. In the 1...
the computer game...
arcade-style compu...

Exercise 10.1
C10-E01-CompComm.docx

Page 1

Other computer games make use of television or of small, independent, hand-held devices. Games are now able to take advantage of three-dimensional graphics that create virtual environments.

COMPUTERS IN COMMUNICATIONS

Computers were originally stand-alone devices, incapable of communicating with other computers. This changed in the 1970s and 1980s when the development of special telecommunications hardware and software led to the creation of the first private networks, allowing connected computers to exchange data. Exchanged data took the form of requests for information, replies to requests for information, or instructions on how to run programs stored on the network.

The ability to link computers enables users to communicate and work together efficiently and effectively. Linked computers have become central to the communications industry. They play a vital role in telecommunications, publishing, and news services.

TELECOMMUNICATIONS

The industry that provides for communication across distances is called telecommunications. The telephone industry uses computers to switch and route phone calls automatically over telephone lines. In addition to the spoken word, many other kinds of information move over such lines, including faxes and computer data. Data can be sent from computer to computer over telephone lines using a device known as a modem. One kind of data frequently sent by modem is electronic mail, or email, which can be sent from person to person via the Internet or an online service. A more recent innovation in telecommunications is teleconferencing, which allows people in various locations to see and hear one another and thus hold virtual meetings.

Just twenty years ag...
has access to a com...
word processing ap...
inexpensive scanne...

Page 2

text, illustrations, and photographs. Publishers typically send computer-generated files to printers for production of the film and plates from which books and magazines are printed.

NEWS SERVICES

News providers rely on reporters located worldwide. Reporters use email to send, or upload, their stories to wire services. Increasingly, individuals get daily news reports from online services. News can also be accessed from specific providers, such as the *New York Times* or *USA Today*, via the Internet. One of the most popular Internet sites provides continuously updated weather reports.

Page 3

Chapter Ten

JOSEPH DEROUSSE
1005 E 102 AVE
KANSAS CITY MO 64110-2089

CRYSTAL BERGMAN
8975 N 32 ST
KANSAS CITY MO 64119-4201

Exercise 10.2

C10-E02-Env.docx

Mrs. Amanda Hargrove
Business Technology Department
Clearwater Community College
5500 Mountain Drive
Boise, ID 83706

Mrs. Amanda Hargrove
Business Technology Department
Clearwater Community College
5500 Mountain Drive
Boise, ID 83706

Mrs. Amanda Hargrove
Business Technology Department
Clearwater Community College
5500 Mountain Drive
Boise, ID 83706

Mrs. Amanda Hargrove
Business Technology Department
Clearwater Community College
5500 Mountain Drive
Boise, ID 83706

Mrs. Amanda Hargrove
Business Technology Department
Clearwater Community College
5500 Mountain Drive
Boise, ID 83706

Mrs. Amanda Hargrove
Business Technology Department
Clearwater Community College
5500 Mountain Drive
Boise, ID 83706

Mrs. Amanda Hargrove
Business Technology Department
Clearwater Community College
5500 Mountain Drive
Boise, ID 83706

Mrs. Amanda Hargrove
Business Technology Department
Clearwater Community College
5500 Mountain Drive
Boise, ID 83706

Mrs. Amanda Hargrove
Business Technology Department
Clearwater Community College
5500 Mountain Drive
Boise, ID 83706

Mrs. Amanda Hargrove
Business Technology Department
Clearwater Community College
5500 Mountain Drive
Boise, ID 83706

Mrs. Amanda Hargrove
Business Technology Department
Clearwater Community College
5500 Mountain Drive
Boise, ID 83706

Mrs. Amanda Hargrove
Business Technology Department
Clearwater Community College
5500 Mountain Drive
Boise, ID 83706

Mrs. Amanda Hargrove
Business Technology Department
Clearwater Community College
5500 Mountain Drive
Boise, ID 83706

Mrs. Amanda Hargrove
Business Technology Department
Clearwater Community College
5500 Mountain Drive
Boise, ID 83706

Mrs. Amanda Hargrove
Business Technology Department
Clearwater Community College
5500 Mountain Drive
Boise, ID 83706

Mrs. Amanda Hargrove
Business Technology Department
Clearwater Community College
5500 Mountain Drive
Boise, ID 83706

Mrs. An
Busines
Clearwa
5500 M
Boise, I

Mrs. An
Busines
Clearwa
5500 M
Boise, I

Mrs. An
Busines
Clearwa
5500 M
Boise, I

Mrs. An
Busines
Clearwa
5500 M
Boise, I

Mrs. An
Busines
Clearwa
5500 M
Boise, I

Exercise 10.3

C10-E03-LtrPharmTech.docx

DEBRA FOSTER
9054 N 23 ST
BOISE ID 83709

CHARLES MOZONNE
12003 203 ST SE
BOISE ID 83799

CASSANDRA REID
9045 VISTA AVE
BOISE ID 83719

BEN AND JILL NYE
6013 FAIRVIEW AVE
BOISE ID 83720

MARK CHAVEZ
805 ORCHARD ST
BOISE ID 83720

KARL KNOWLES
23102 HARRISON BLVD
BOISE ID 83722

Exercise 10.4

C10-E04-Labels.docx

Working with Windows

In Word, you can open multiple documents and move the insertion point among them. You can move and copy information between documents or compare content between documents. The maximum number of documents you can have open at one time depends on the memory capacity of your computer system and the amount of data in each document. When you open a new window, it displays on top of any previously opened window(s) that you have not closed. Once you have multiple windows open, you can resize them to see all of one document or a portion of each on the screen.

When a document is open, a Word button displays on the Taskbar. Hover the mouse over this button and a thumbnail of the document displays above the button. If you have more than one document open, the Word button on the Taskbar displays another layer in a cascaded manner. The layer behind the Word button displays only a portion of the edge at the right of the button. If you have multiple documents open, hovering the mouse over the Word button on the Taskbar will cause thumbnails of all of the documents to display above the button. To change to the desired document, click the thumbnail that represents the document.

Another method for determining which documents are open is to click the View tab and then click the Switch Windows button in the Window group. The document name that displays in the list with the check mark in front of it is the *active* document. The active document contains the insertion point. To make one of the other documents active, click the document name. If you are using the keyboard, type the number shown in front of the desired document.

Switch Windows

New Window

Opening a New Window

Open a document, click the New Window button in the Window group, and Word opens a new window that contains the same document. The document name in the Title bar displays and is followed by :2. Changes you make to one document are reflected in the other document.

Arrange Windows
1. Open documents.
2. Click View tab.
3. Click Arrange All.

Arranging Windows

If you have more than one document open, you can arrange them on the screen so that a portion of each is visible. To do this, click the View tab and then click the Arrange All button in the Window group. Figure 10.1 shows a document screen with four open documents that have been arranged to make a portion of each visible.

Arrange All

Maximize

Minimize

Restore Down

Maximizing, Restoring, and Minimizing Documents

Use the Maximize and Minimize buttons in the active document window to change the size of the window. The Maximize button is located in the upper right corner of the active document window, immediately to the left of the Close button. (The Close button is marked with an *X*.) The Minimize button is located immediately to the left of the Maximize button.

If you arrange all open documents and then click the Maximize button in the active document, the active document expands to fill the document screen. In addition, the Maximize button becomes the Restore Down button. To return the active document back to the size it was before being maximized, click the Restore Down button. If you click the Minimize button in the active document, the document is reduced and displays as a layer behind the Word button on the Taskbar. To maximize a document that has been minimized, click the Word button on the Taskbar and then click the thumbnail representing the document.

Figure 10.1 Arranged Documents

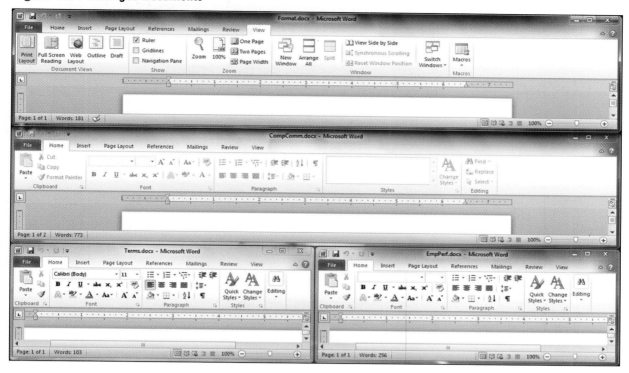

Note: If you are using Word on a network system that contains a virus checker, you may not be able to open multiple documents at once. Continue by opening each document individually.

1. Open the following documents: **Terms.docx**, **Format.docx**, **EmpPerf.docx**, and **CompComm.docx**.
2. Arrange the windows by clicking the View tab and then clicking the Arrange All button in the Window group.
3. Make sure **Format.docx** is the active document by clicking the Switch Windows button and then clicking Format.doc at the drop-down list.
4. Close **Format.docx** by clicking the Close button in the upper right corner of the Format.docx document.
5. Make **EmpPerf.docx** active and then close it.
6. Make **CompComm.docx** active and then minimize it by clicking the Minimize button in the upper right corner of the window.

Step 4

Step 6

7. Maximize **Terms.docx** by clicking the Maximize button at the right side of the title bar. (The Maximize button is the button at the right of the title bar, immediately left of the Close button.)
8. Close **Terms.docx**.
9. Restore **CompComm.docx** by clicking the Word button on the Taskbar.

Step 9

10. Maximize **CompComm.docx**.
11. Open a new window with the **CompComm.docx** document by clicking the New Window button in the Window group in the View tab. (Notice the document name in the Title bar displays and is followed by *:2*.)
12. Close the second version of the document by hovering the mouse pointer over the Word button on the Taskbar and then clicking the close button in the upper right corner of the *CompComm.docx:2* document thumbnail (the thumbnail that displays above the Word button on the Taskbar).

Split Window
1. Open document.
2. Click View tab.
3. Click Split button.
OR
Drag split bar.

Split

Remove Split

Splitting a Window

You can divide a window into two ***panes*** when you want to view different parts of a document at the same time. You may want to display an outline for a report in one pane, for example, and the portion of the report that you are editing in the other. The original window is split into two panes that extend horizontally across the screen.

To split a window, click the View tab and then click the Split button in the Window group. A wide gray line displays in the middle of the screen, and the mouse pointer becomes a double-headed arrow pointing up and down with a small double line between the heads. Move this double-headed arrow pointer up or down, if desired, by dragging the mouse or by pressing the up- and/or down-pointing arrow keys on the keyboard. When the double-headed arrow is positioned at the desired location in the document, click the left mouse button or press the Enter key.

You can also split a window with the split bar. The split bar is the small, black horizontal bar above the View Ruler button at the top of the vertical scroll bar. To split the window with the split bar, position the arrow pointer on the split bar until it turns into a short double line with an up- and down-pointing arrow. Hold down the left mouse button, drag the double-headed arrow into the document screen to the location where you want the window split, and then release the mouse button.

When a window is split, the insertion point is positioned in the bottom pane. To move it to the other pane with the mouse, position the I-beam pointer in the other pane and then click the left mouse button. To remove the split line from the document, click the View tab and then click the Remove Split button in the Window group. You can also remove the split line by double-clicking the split bar or dragging the split bar to the top or bottom of the screen.

1. With **CompComm.docx** open, save the document with Save As, and name it **C10-E01-CompComm**.
2. Click the View tab and then click the Split button in the Window group.

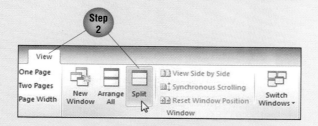

3. With the split line displayed in the middle of the document screen, click the left mouse button.
4. Scroll down the document in the bottom pane, select text from the title *REFERENCES* to the end of the document, and then delete the selected text.
5. Move the first section below the second section by completing the following steps:
   a. Click the Home tab and then click in the top pane.
   b. Select the *COMPUTERS IN COMMUNICATION* section from the title to right above *COMPUTERS IN ENTERTAINMENT*.
   c. Click the Cut button in the Clipboard group in the Home tab.
   d. Position the arrow pointer at the end of the document in the bottom window pane, click the left mouse button, and then press the Enter key.
   e. Click the Paste button in the Clipboard group in the Home tab.
6. Remove the split from the window by clicking the View tab and then clicking the Remove Split button in the Window group.
7. Apply the Heading 1 style to the two titles and the Heading 2 style to the five headings in the document.
8. Change the style set to Formal.
9. Move the insertion point to the beginning of the document and then save **C10-E01-CompComm.docx**.

Viewing Documents Side by Side

If you want to compare the contents of two documents, open both, click the View tab, and then click the View Side by Side button in the Window group. Both documents display on the screen arranged side by side, as shown in Figure 10.2. By default, synchronous scrolling is active. With this feature active, scrolling in one document results in the same scrolling in the other. This feature is useful when you want to compare text, formatting, or other features between documents. If you want to scroll in one document and not the other, click the Window group button in the View tab and then click the Synchronous Scrolling button to turn it off.

View Side by Side
1. Open two documents.
2. Click View tab.
3. Click View Side by Side button.

View Side   Synchronous
by Side   Scrolling

Figure 10.2 **Viewing Documents Side by Side**

Use View Side by Side to compare the formatting of two different documents.

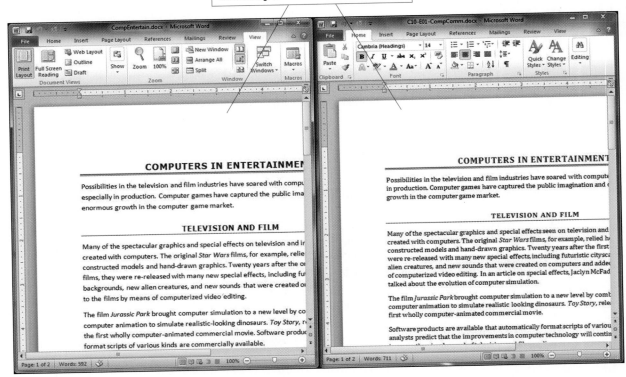

When you have arranged documents on the screen or are viewing documents side by side, you can drag the document window borders to increase or decrease the size of any document. To change the size of a document window, position the mouse pointer on a window border until the pointer displays as a two-headed arrow, hold down the left mouse button, and then drag the border to the desired location. If you change the size of documents you are viewing side by side, click the Reset Window Position button in the Window group in the View tab to reset the document windows so that both display equally on the divided screen.

Reset Window
Position

Exercise 10.1C Viewing Documents Side by Side   Part 3 of 7

1. With **C10-E01-CompComm.docx** open, open **CompEntertain.docx**.
2. Click the View tab and then click the View Side by Side button in the Window group.
3. Scroll through both documents simultaneously and notice the difference between the two documents. Change the formatting of the titles and headings in the **C10-E01-CompComm.docx** document so the font and font color match the titles and headings in the **CompEntertain.docx** document.
4. Make **C10-E01-CompComm.docx** active and then click the Save button on the Quick Access toolbar.

5. Turn off synchronous scrolling by clicking the View tab and then clicking the Synchronous Scrolling button in the Window group. (If the Synchronous Scrolling button is not visible, you may need to click the Window group button and then click the Synchronous Scrolling button.)

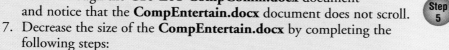

Step 5

6. Scroll through the **C10-E01-CompComm.docx** document and notice that the **CompEntertain.docx** document does not scroll.

7. Decrease the size of the **CompEntertain.docx** by completing the following steps:

    a. Position the mouse pointer on the right edge of the **CompEntertain.docx** document until the mouse pointer turns into a double-headed arrow.

    b. Hold down the left mouse button, drag to the left approximately one inch, and then release the mouse button.

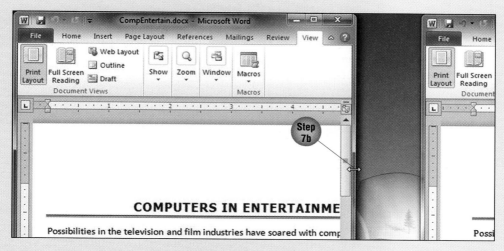

8. Increase the size of the **C10-E01-CompComm.docx** document by completing the following steps:

    a. Position the mouse pointer on the left edge of the **C10-E01-CompComm.docx** document until the pointer turns into a double-headed arrow.

    b. Hold down the left mouse button and drag to the left until the left edge of the **C10-E01-CompComm.docx** document border lines up with the right border of the **CompEntertain.docx** document.

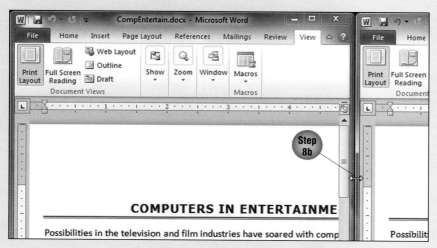

9. Reset the windows by clicking the View tab and then clicking the Reset Window Position button in the Window group. (If the Reset Window Position button is not visible, you may need to click the Window group button and then click the Reset Window Position button.)

Step 9

10. Make **CompEntertain.docx** the active document and then close it.

Zoom

100%

One Page

Two Pages

Page Width

Changing Document Zoom

In Chapter 6, you learned to increase or decrease the visual display of a document with buttons on the Zoom slider bar. You can also increase or decrease a document's visual display with buttons in the Zoom group in the View tab. Click the Zoom button and the Zoom dialog box displays. This is the same dialog box that displays when you click the percentage number on the Status bar. Use options at the Zoom dialog box to change the percentage of display. If you change the document display, you can return it to the normal display (100%) by clicking the 100% button in the Zoom group. Use the remaining buttons in the Zoom group to change the display to one page or two pages, or to change the page width. If you click the Page Width button, the document expands across the screen.

Hiding/Showing White Space

In Chapter 6, you also learned that a document page displays in Print Layout view as it will appear when printed, showing the white space at the top and bottom of the page determined by the default margins. To save space on the screen in Print Layout view, you can remove the white space by positioning the mouse pointer at the top edge or bottom edge of a page or between pages until the pointer displays as the *Hide White Space* icon and then double-clicking the left mouse button. To redisplay the white space, position the mouse pointer on the thin, gray line separating pages until the pointer turns into the *Show White Space* icon and then double-click the left mouse button.

Exercise 10.1D Zooming in a Document and Hiding/Showing White Space   Part 4 of 7

1. With **C10-E01-CompComm.docx** open, press Ctrl + Home.
2. Click the View tab.
3. Click the Zoom button in the Zoom group.
4. At the Zoom dialog box, click the *Text width* option.
5. Click OK to close the dialog box.

Step 4

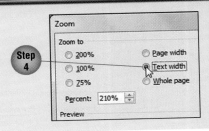

6. After viewing the document in *Text width*, click the 100% button in the Zoom group.
7. Click the Zoom button, click *200%* at the Zoom dialog box, and then click OK to close the dialog box.
8. After viewing the document in 200%, click the 100% button in the Zoom group.
9. Click the Two Pages button in the Zoom group.
10. Click the Page Width button.
11. Click the 100% button.
12. Press Ctrl + Home to move the insertion point to the beginning of the document.
13. Hide the white spaces at the top and bottom of the document pages by positioning the mouse pointer at the top edge of a page until the pointer turns into the *Hide White Space* icon and then double-clicking the left mouse button.

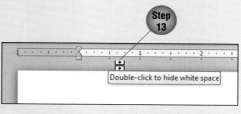

14. Scroll through the document and notice how the pages display.
15. Redisplay the white spaces at the top and bottom of pages by positioning the mouse pointer on any thin, gray, horizontal line separating pages until the pointer turns into the *Show White Space* icon and then double-clicking the left mouse button.

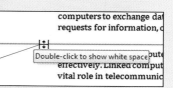

16. Save **C10-E01-CompComm.docx**.

Managing the Recent List

Word keeps a list of the most recently opened documents in the Recent tab Backstage view as shown in Figure 10.3 (the names and recent places may vary from what you see in the figure). The most recently opened document names display in the *Recent*

Figure 10.3 Recent Tab Backstage View

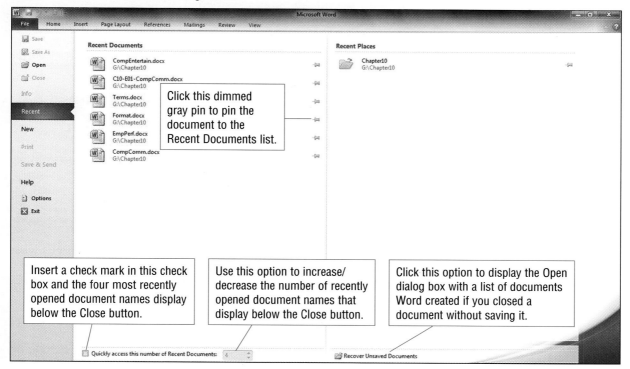

Documents list and the most recently access folder names display in the *Recent Places* list. Generally, the twenty most recently opened document names display in the *Recent Documents* list. As you learned in Chapter 1, you can pin and unpin document names from the *Recent Documents* list.

The Recent tab Backstage view contains the option *Quickly access this number of Recent Documents* located below the *Recent Documents* list. Insert a check mark in this option and the names of the four most recently opened documents display in the Backstage navigation bar (the panel at the left) below the Close button. You can increase or decrease the number of displayed document names by increasing or decreasing the number that displays at the right side of the *Quickly Access this number of Recent Documents* option.

If you close a document without saving it, you can recover it with the *Recover Unsaved Documents* option located below the *Recent Places* list. Click this option and the Open dialog box displays with document names that Word automatically saved. At this dialog box, double-click the desired document name to open the document.

You can clear the contents (except pinned documents) of the *Recent Documents* list by right-clicking a document name in the list and then clicking *Clear unpinned Documents* at the shortcut menu. At the message asking if you are sure you want to remove the items, click the Yes button. To clear the *Recent Places* list, right-click a folder in the list and then click *Clear unpinned Places* at the shortcut menu. Click Yes at the message asking if you are sure you want to remove the items.

Exercise 10.1E   Managing Documents at the Recent Tab Backstage View   Part 5 of 7

1. Close **C10-E01-CompComm.docx**.
2. Click the File tab. (This displays the Recent tab Backstage view.)
3. Click the dimmed, gray pin that displays at the right side of *C10-E01-CompComm.docx*. (This pins the document to the *Recent Documents* list.)
4. Click the *Quickly access this number of Recent Documents* option to insert a check mark.
5. Click the down-pointing arrow at the right side of the number *4*. (This changes *4* to *3*.)
6. Click the *Recover Unsaved Documents* option located below the *Recent Places* list.
7. At the Open dialog box that displays, look at any unsaved document names that display in the list box and then click the Cancel button.
8. Open **C10-E01-CompComm.docx** by clicking the File tab and then clicking **C10-E01-CompComm.docx** that displays below the Close button.

Preview a Document
1. Click File tab.
2. Click Print tab.

Previewing and Printing a Document

With options at the Print tab Backstage view shown in Figure 10.4, you can specify what you want to print and also preview the pages before printing. To display the Print tab Backstage view, click the File tab and then click the Print tab.

Figure 10.4 Print Tab Backstage View

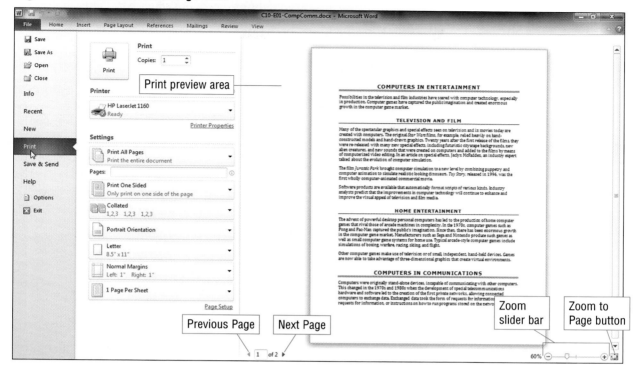

Previewing Pages in a Document

When you display the Print tab Backstage view, a preview of the page where the insertion point is positioned displays at the right side (see Figure 10.4). Click the Next Page button (right-pointing arrow), located below and at the left of the page, to view the next page in the document and click the Previous Page button (left-pointing arrow) to display the previous page in the document. Use the Zoom slider bar to increase/decrease the size of the page, and click the Zoom to Page button to fit the page in the viewing area in the Print tab Backstage view.

Exercise 10.1F   Previewing the Document   Part 6 of 7

1. With **C10-E01-CompComm.docx** open, press Ctrl + Home to move the insertion point to the beginning of the document.
2. Preview the document by clicking the File tab and then clicking the Print tab.
3. At the Print tab Backstage view, click the Next Page button located below and at the left of the preview page. (This displays page 2 in the preview area.)

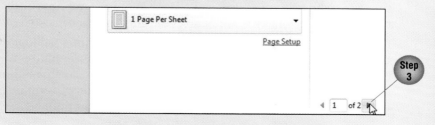

---

4. Click twice on the plus symbol that displays at the right of the Zoom slider bar. (This increases the size of the preview page.)
5. Click three times on the minus symbol that displays at the left of the Zoom slider bar until two pages display in the preview area.
6. Change the zoom at the Zoom dialog box by completing the following steps:
   a. Click the percentage number that displays at the left of the Zoom slider bar.
   b. At the Zoom dialog box, click the *Many pages* option in the *Zoom to* section.
   c. Click OK to close the dialog box. (Notice that the two pages in the document display as thumbnails in the preview area.)
7. Click the Zoom to Page button that displays at the right of the Zoom slider bar. (This returns the page to the default size.)
8. Click the File tab to return to the document.

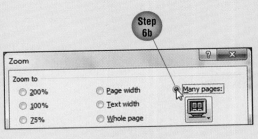

Printing Pages in a Document

If you want control over what prints in a document, use options at the Print tab Backstage view. Click the first gallery in the *Settings* category, and a drop-down list displays with options for printing all pages in the document, selected text, the current page, or a custom range of pages in the document. If you want to select and then print a portion of the document, choose the *Print Selection* option. With this option, only the text that you have selected in the current document prints. (This option is dimmed unless text is selected in the document.) Click the *Print Current Page* option to print only the page on which the insertion point is located. With the *Print Custom Range* option, you can identify a specific page, multiple pages, or a range of pages to print. If you want specific pages printed, use a comma (,) to indicate *and*, and use a hyphen (-) to indicate *through*. For example, to print pages 2 and 5, you would type 2,5 in the *Pages* text box. To print pages 6 through 10, you would type 6-10.

With the other galleries available in the *Settings* category of the Print tab Backstage view, you can specify on which sides of the pages you want to print, change the page orientation (portrait or landscape), specify how you want the pages collated, choose a page size, specify margins, and specify how many pages you want to print on a page.

If you want to print more than one copy of a document, use the *Copies* text box located to the right of the Print button. If you print several copies of a document that has multiple pages, Word collates the pages as they print. For example, if you print two copies of a three-page document, pages 1, 2, and 3 print, and then the pages print a second time. Printing collated pages is helpful for assembly but takes more printing time. To reduce printing time, you can tell Word *not* to print collated pages. To do this, click the *Collated* gallery in the *Settings* category and then click *Uncollated*.

If you want to send a document directly to the printer without displaying the Print tab Backstage view, consider adding the Quick Print button to the Quick Access toolbar. To do this, click the Customize Quick Access Toolbar button located at the right of the toolbar and then click *Quick Print* at the drop-down gallery. Click the Quick Print button and all pages of the open document print.

1. With **C10-E01-CompComm.docx** open, print selected text by completing the following steps:
   a. Select the heading *Television and Film* and the three paragraphs of text that follow it.
   b. Click the File tab and then click the Print tab.
   c. At the Print tab Backstage view, click the first gallery in the *Settings* category and then click *Print Selection* at the drop-down list.
   d. Click the Print button.

2. Change the margins and page orientation and then print only the first page by completing the following steps:
   a. Press Ctrl + Home to move the insertion point to the beginning of the document.
   b. Click the File tab and then click the Print tab.
   c. At the Print tab Backstage view, click the *Portrait Orientation* gallery in the *Settings* category and then click *Landscape Orientation* at the drop-down list.
   d. Click the *Normal Margins* gallery in the *Settings* category and then click *Narrow Margins* at the drop-down list.
   e. Click the *Print All Pages* gallery in the *Settings* category and then click *Print Current Page* at the drop-down list.
   f. Click the Print button. (The first page of the document prints in landscape orientation with 0.5-inch margins.)

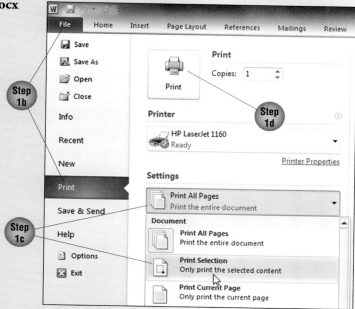

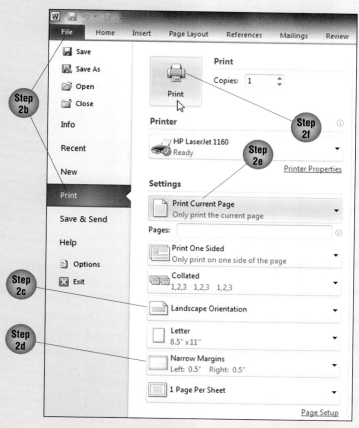

3. Select the entire document and then change the line spacing to *1.5*.
4. Print all of the pages on one page by completing the following steps:
   a. Click the File tab and then click the Print tab.
   b. At the Print tab Backstage view, click the *1 Page Per Sheet* gallery in the *Settings* category and then click *2 Pages Per Sheet* at the drop-down list.
   c. Click the Print button.

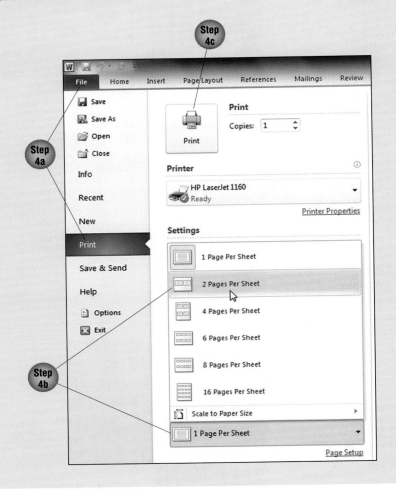

5. Print two copies of specific pages by completing the following steps:
    a. Click the File tab and then click the Print tab.
    b. Click in the *Pages* text box (located below the *Print Custom Range* gallery in the *Settings* category and then type 1,3.
    c. Click the up-pointing arrow at the right side of the *Copies* text box (located to the right of the Print button) to display 2.
    d. Click the *Collated* gallery in the *Settings* category and then click *Uncollated* at the drop-down list.
    e. Click the Print button. (The first page of the document will print twice and then the third page will print twice.)

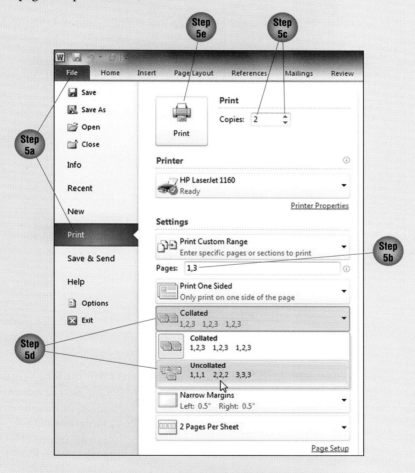

6. Save and then close **C10-E01-CompComm.docx**.
7. Make the following changes to the Recent tab Backstage view.
    a. Click the File tab.
    b. Change the number to the right of *Quickly access this number of Recent Documents* from 3 to 4.
    c. Click the *Quickly access this number of Recent Documents* option to remove the check mark.
    d. Unpin the *C10-E01-CompComm.docx* document name from the *Recent Documents* list by clicking the blue pin that displays at the right side of *C10-E01-CompComm.docx*.
    e. Click the File tab to remove the Recent tab Backstage view.

QUICK STEPS

Create Envelope
1. Click Mailings tab.
2. Click Envelopes button.
3. Type delivery address.
4. Click in *Return address* text box.
5. Type return address.
6. Click Add to Document button or Print button.

Envelopes

Creating and Printing Envelopes

Word provides options to automate the creation of envelopes. To create an envelope, display the Envelopes and Labels dialog box with the Envelopes tab selected, as shown in Figure 10.5. Display this dialog box by clicking the Mailings tab and then clicking the Envelopes button in the Create group. At the dialog box, type the delivery address in the *Delivery address* text box and the return address in the *Return address* text box. You can send the envelope directly to the printer by clicking the Print button or insert the envelope in an open document by clicking the Add to Document button.

Figure 10.5 Envelopes and Labels Dialog Box with Envelopes Tab Selected

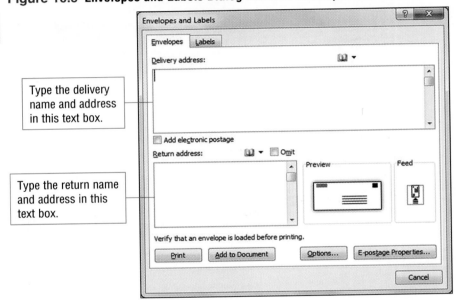

If you enter a return address and then click the Print button, Word displays the question *Do you want to save the new return address as the default return address?* Click Yes if you want the current return address available for future envelopes. Click No if you do not want the current return address used as the default. If a default return address displays in the *Return address* section of the dialog box, you can tell Word to omit the return address when printing the envelope by clicking the *Omit* check box to insert a check mark.

The Envelopes and Labels dialog box contains a *Preview* sample box and a *Feed* sample box. The *Preview* sample box shows how the envelope will appear when printed, and the *Feed* sample box shows how to insert the envelope into the printer.

When you address envelopes, consider following the general guidelines issued by the United States Postal Service (USPS). The USPS guidelines suggest using all capital letters with no commas or periods for return and delivery addresses. USPS guidelines also suggest using abbreviations for street designations (such as *ST* for *Street* and *AVE* for *Avenue*). Figure 10.6 shows a delivery and return address following the USPS guidelines. For a complete list of address abbreviations, visit the USPS website.

1. At a blank document, create an envelope that prints the delivery address and return address shown in Figure 10.6. Begin by clicking the Mailings tab.
2. Click the Envelopes button in the Create group.
3. At the Envelopes and Labels dialog box with the Envelopes tab selected, click in the *Delivery Address* text box and then type the delivery address shown in Figure 10.6 (the one containing the name *CRYSTAL BERGMAN*). (Press the Enter key to end each line in the name and address.)
4. Click in the *Return address* text box. (If any text displays in the *Return address* text box, select and then delete it.)
5. Type the return address shown in Figure 10.6 (the one containing the name *JOSEPH DEROUSSE*). (Press the Enter key to end each line in the name and address.)
6. Click the Add to Document button.
7. At the message *Do you want to save the new return address as the default return address?*, click No.
8. Save the document with the name **C10-E02-Env**.
9. Print and then close **C10-E02-Env.docx**. *Note: Manual feed of the envelope may be required. Please check with your instructor.*

Step 3

Step 5

Step 6

Envelopes and Labels

Envelopes | Labels

Delivery address:

CRYSTAL BERGMAN
8975 N 32 ST
KANSAS CITY MO 64119-4201

☐ Add electronic postage

Return address: ☐ Omit

JOSEPH DEROUSSE
1005 E 102 AVE
KANSAS CITY MO 64110-2089

Preview   Feed

Verify that an envelope is loaded before printing.

Print | Add to Document | Options... | E-postage Properties...

Cancel

Figure 10.6 Exercise 10.2

JOSEPH DEROUSSE
1005 E 102 AVE
KANSAS CITY MO 64110-2089

CRYSTAL BERGMAN
8975 N 32 ST
KANSAS CITY MO 64119-4201

If you open the Envelopes and Labels dialog box in a document that contains a name and address with each line ending with a press of the Enter key (not Shift + Enter), Word automatically inserts the name and address in the *Delivery address* text box of the dialog box. To automatically insert a delivery address, open a document containing a name and address and then display the Envelopes and Labels dialog box. The name and address are inserted in the *Delivery address* text box as they appear in the letter and may not conform to the USPS guidelines. The USPS guidelines for addressing envelopes are only suggestions, not requirements.

Exercise 10.3A   Creating an Envelope in an Existing Document   Part 1 of 2

1. Open **LtrPharmTech.docx**.
2. Click the Mailings tab.
3. Click the Envelopes button in the Create group.
4. At the Envelopes and Labels dialog box with the Envelopes tab selected, make sure the delivery address contained in LtrPharmTech.docx displays properly in the *Delivery address* text box.
5. If any text displays in the *Return address* text box, insert a check mark in the *Omit* check box (located at the right of the *Return address* option). (This tells Word not to print the return address on the envelope.)
6. Click the Print button.

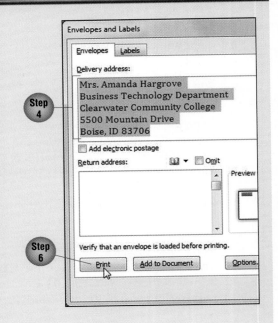

QUICK STEPS

Create Labels
1. Click Mailings tab.
2. Click Labels button.
3. Type desired address(es).
4. Click New Document button or Print button.

Labels

Creating and Printing Labels

Use the labels feature in Word to print text on mailing labels, file labels, disk labels, or other types of labels. The feature includes a variety of predefined labels you can purchase at an office supply store. To create a sheet of mailing labels with the same name and address using the default options, click the Labels button in the Create group in the Mailings tab. At the Envelopes and Labels dialog box with the Labels tab selected as shown in Figure 10.7, type the desired address in the *Address* text box. Click the New Document button to insert the mailing label in a new document, or click the Print button to send the mailing label directly to the printer. If you open the Envelopes and Labels dialog box with the Labels tab selected in a document that contains a name and address with each line ending with a press of the Enter key (not Shift + Enter), Word automatically inserts the name and address in the *Address* text box of the dialog box.

Figure 10.7 Envelopes and Labels Dialog Box with Labels Tab Selected

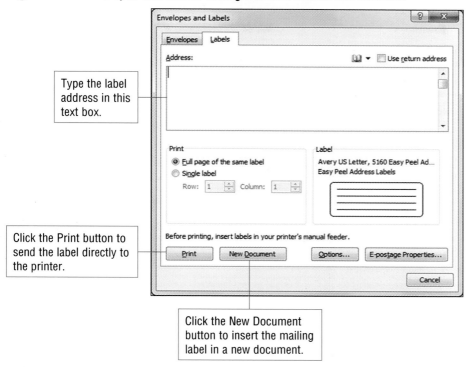

Type the label address in this text box.

Click the Print button to send the label directly to the printer.

Click the New Document button to insert the mailing label in a new document.

Click the Options button at the Envelopes and Labels dialog box with the Labels tab selected, and the Label Options dialog box displays, as shown in Figure 10.8. At the Label Options dialog box, choose the type of printer, the desired label product, and the product number. This dialog box also displays information about the selected label such as type, height, width, and paper size. When you select a label, Word automatically determines label margins. If, however, you want to customize these default settings, click the Details button.

Figure 10.8 Label Options Dialog Box

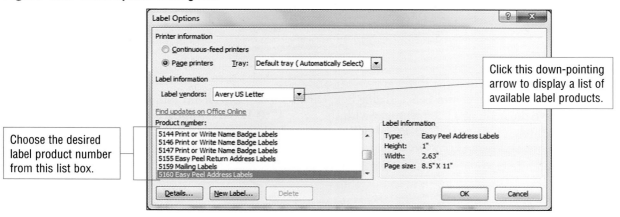

Click this down-pointing arrow to display a list of available label products.

Choose the desired label product number from this list box.

1. With **LtrPharmTech.docx** open, create mailing labels with the delivery address. Begin by clicking the Mailings tab.
2. Click the Labels button in the Create group.
3. At the Envelopes and Labels dialog box with the Labels tab selected, make sure the delivery address displays properly in the *Address* text box.
4. Click the Options button.
5. At the Label Options dialog box, click the down-pointing arrow at the right of the *Label vendors* option and then click *Avery US Letter* at the drop-down list.
6. Scroll down the *Product number* list box and then click *5160 Easy Peel Address Labels*.

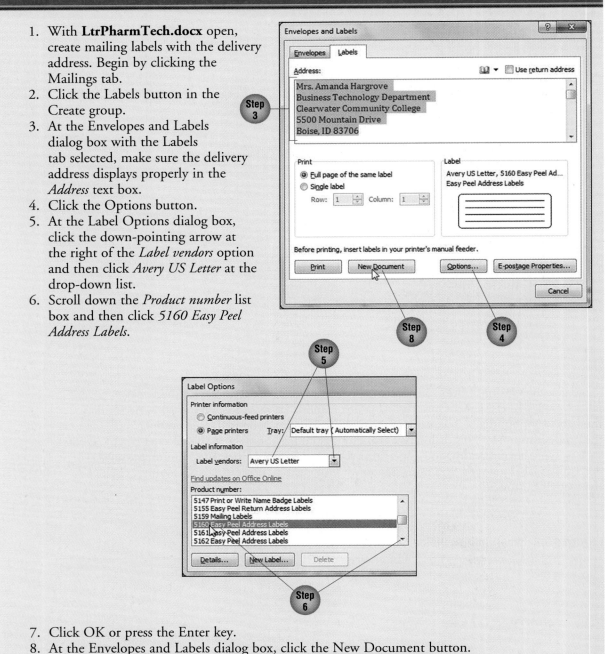

7. Click OK or press the Enter key.
8. At the Envelopes and Labels dialog box, click the New Document button.
9. Save the mailing label document with the name **C10-E03-LtrPharmTech**.
10. Print and then close **C10-E03-LtrPharmTech.docx**.
11. Close **LtrPharmTech.docx**.

To create a sheet of mailing labels with a different name and address in each label, start with a blank document, display the Envelopes and Labels dialog box with the Labels tab selected, and then click the New Document button. The Envelopes and

Labels dialog box is removed from the screen and the document displays with label forms. The insertion point is positioned in the first label form. Type the name and address in this label and then press the Tab key to move the insertion point to the next label. Pressing Shift + Tab moves the insertion point back to the preceding label.

Exercise 10.4   Creating Customized Mailing Labels   Part 1 of 1

1. At a blank document, click the Mailings tab.
2. Click the Labels button in the Create group.
3. At the Envelopes and Labels dialog box with the Labels tab selected, click the Options button.
4. At the Label Options dialog box, make sure *Avery US Letter* is selected. If not, click the down-pointing arrow at the right of the *Label vendors* option and then click *Avery US Letter* at the drop-down list.
5. Scroll down the *Product number* list box and then click *5810 Address Labels*.
6. Click OK or press the Enter key.
7. At the Envelopes and Labels dialog box, click the New Document button.
8. At the document, type in the first label the first name and address shown in Figure 10.9 (the name and address for Charles Mozonne).
9. Press the Tab key twice to move the insertion point to the next label and then type the second name and address shown in Figure 10.9.
10. Press the Tab key twice to move the insertion point to the next label and then type the third name and address shown in Figure 10.9.
11. Press the Tab key once (this moves the insertion point to the label below the label containing the name *DEBRA FOSTER*).
12. Type the fourth name and address shown in Figure 10.9. Continue in this manner until you have typed all of the names and addresses.
13. Save the document and name it **C10-E04-Labels**.
14. Print and then close **C10-E04-Labels.docx**.
15. At the blank document, close the document without saving changes.

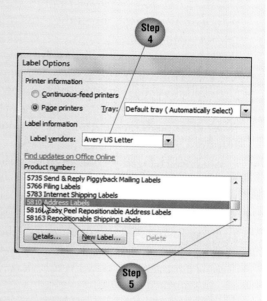

Step 4

Step 5

Figure 10.9 Exercise 10.4

DEBRA FOSTER 9054 N 23 ST BOISE ID 83709	CHARLES MOZONNE 12003 203 ST SE BOISE ID 83799	CASSANDRA REID 9045 VISTA AVE BOISE ID 83719
BEN AND JILL NYE 6013 FAIRVIEW AVE BOISE ID 83720	MARK CHAVEZ 805 ORCHARD ST BOISE ID 83720	KARL KNOWLES 23102 HARRISON BLVD BOISE ID 83722

Chapter Summary

➤ Move among open documents on your screen by clicking the Word button on the Taskbar and then clicking the thumbnail representing the desired document or by clicking the View tab, clicking the Switch Windows button in the Window group, and then clicking the desired document name.

➤ View a portion of all open documents by clicking the View tab and then clicking the Arrange All button in the Window group.

➤ Use the Minimize, Maximize, and Restore Down buttons in the upper right corner of the window to reduce or increase the size of the active window.

➤ Divide a window into two panes by clicking the View tab and then clicking the Split button in the Window group. This enables you to view different parts of the same document at one time.

➤ View the contents of two open documents side by side by clicking the View tab and then clicking the View Side by Side button in the Window group.

➤ By default, synchronous scrolling is turned on when you view documents side by side. If you want to scroll through each document individually, click the Synchronous Scrolling button to turn off the feature.

➤ If you have changed the size of side-by-side document windows, click the Reset Window Position button to reset the document windows so they are displayed equally on the divided screen.

➤ Use buttons in the Zoom group in the View tab to increase or decrease the visual display of a document.

➤ In Print Layout view, you can remove the white spaces at the top and bottom of pages.

➤ Recently opened document names, as well as recently accessed location names, display in the Recent tab Backstage view. At this view, you can display below the Close button the four most recently opened document names, recover unsaved documents, and clear the contents of the Recent Documents and Recent Places lists.

➤ Preview a document at the Print tab Backstage view. Scroll through the pages in the document with the Next Page and Previous Page buttons that display below the preview page. Use the Zoom slider bar to increase/decrease the display size of the preview page.

➤ At the Print tab Backstage view you can customize the print job by changing the page orientation, size, and margins; specify how many pages you want to print on one page; specify the number of copies and whether to collate the pages; and specify the printer.

➤ At the Envelopes and Labels dialog box with the Envelope tab selected, you can use the envelope feature to create and print an envelope.

➤ If you open the Envelopes and Labels dialog box in a document that contains a name and address with each line ending with a press of the Enter key (not Shift + Enter), that information is automatically inserted in the *Delivery address* text box in the dialog box.

➤ Use the labels feature to print text on mailing labels, file labels, disk labels, or other types of labels.

Commands *Review*

FEATURE	RIBBON TAB, GROUP	BUTTON, OPTION	KEYBOARD SHORTCUT
Arrange all documents	View, Window		
Minimize document			
Maximize document			
Restore down			
Split window	View, Window		
View documents side by side	View, Window		
Synchronous scrolling	View, Window		
Reset window position	View, Window		
Zoom dialog box	View, Zoom		
100% display	View, Zoom		
One Page view	View, Zoom		
Two Pages view	View, Zoom		
Page Width view	View, Zoom		
Print tab Backstage view	File, Print		Ctrl + P
Envelopes and Labels dialog box with Envelopes tab selected	Mailings, Create		
Envelopes and Labels dialog box with Labels tab selected	Mailings, Create		

Key Points *Review*

Completion: In the space provided at the right, indicate the correct term, command, or number.

1. To determine which documents are open, click the View tab and then click this button in the Window group. _____

2. Click this button in the Window group in the View tab to arrange all open documents so a portion of each document displays. _____

3. Click this button and the active document fills the editing window. _____

4. Click this button and the active document reduces to the Word button on the Taskbar. _____

5. The split bar is the small black horizontal bar located above this button at the top of the vertical scroll bar. _____

6. To display documents side by side, click this button in the Window group in the View tab. _____

7. If you are viewing documents side by side and decide you want to scroll in one and not the other, click this button in the Window group in the View tab. _____

8. When viewing documents side by side, click this button in the Window group in the View tab to reset document windows so they display equally on the divided screen. _____

9. This group in the View tab contains options for changing the display of the document to one page or two pages. _____

10. To remove white space on the document from the top and bottom of pages, double-click this icon. _____

11. Type this in the *Pages* text box in the *Settings* category at the Print tab Backstage view to print pages 3 through 6 of the open document. _____

12. Type this in the *Pages* text box in the *Settings* category at the Print tab Backstage view to print pages 4 and 9 of the open document. _____

13. The Envelopes button is located in the Create group in this tab. _____

14. If you open the Envelopes and Labels dialog box in a document containing a name and address, the name and address are automatically inserted in this text box of the dialog box. _____

Chapter Assessments

Applying Your Skills

Demonstrate your knowledge of features learned in this chapter by completing the following assessments.

Assessment 10.1   Arrange Documents

1. Open **BetaTestAgrmnt.docx**, **CompHardware.docx**, and **CompSecurity.docx**.
2. Make **CompHardware.docx** the active document.
3. Make **BetaTestAgrmnt.docx** the active document.
4. Arrange all of the windows.
5. Make **CompSecurity.docx** the active document and then minimize it.
6. Minimize the remaining documents.
7. Restore **BetaTestAgrmnt.docx**.
8. Restore **CompHardware.docx**.

9. Restore **CompSecurity.docx**.
10. Maximize and then close **BetaTestAgrmnt.docx** and then maximize and close **CompSecurity.docx**.
11. Maximize **CompHardware.docx** and then save the document and name it **C10-A01-CompHardware**.
12. Open **Hardware.docx**.
13. View the **C10-A01-CompHardware.docx** document and **Hardware.docx** document side by side.
14. Scroll through both documents simultaneously. Notice the formatting differences between the two documents. Change the font, font size, and paragraph shading in **C10-A01-CompHardware.docx** so they match the formatting in **Hardware.docx**.
15. Make **Hardware.docx** active and then close it.
16. Save, print, and then close **C10-A01-CompHardware.docx**.

Assessment 10.2 Create an Envelope

1. At a blank document, create an envelope with the text shown in Figure 10.10.
2. Save the envelope document with the name **C10-A02-Envelope**.
3. Print and then close **C10-A02-Envelope.docx**.

Figure 10.10 Assessment 10.2

SHAWN FINNEGAN
3078 SIXTH AVE
SALT LAKE CITY UT 84119

DR DAVID TOMOLLA
12039 CHAMBER ST
SALT LAKE CITY UT 84110

Expanding Your Skills

Explore additional feature options or use Help to learn a new skill in creating these documents.

Assessment 10.3 Create Mailing Labels

1. Create mailing labels with the names and addresses shown in Figure 10.11. Use a label option of your choosing. (You may need to check with your instructor before choosing an option.)
2. Save the document with the name **C10-A03-Labels**.
3. Print and then close **C10-A03-Labels.docx**.
4. At the blank document, close the document without saving changes.

Figure 10.11 Assessment 10.3

LINDA GOULD
3210 CRANSTON ST
PROVIDENCE RI 02903

ROBERT ALBRIGHT
10228 123 ST NE
PROVIDENCE RI 02908

TRAVIS KANE
5532 S BROAD ST
PROVIDENCE RI 02905

CHARLES WHITE
887 N 42 ST
PROVIDENCE RI 02903

RAY PETROVICH
12309 45 AVE N
PROVIDENCE RI 02904

BLAINE ISHAM
12110 141 ST SE
PROVIDENCE RI 02907

Assessment 10.4   Create and Format Labels

1. At a blank document, display the Envelopes and Labels dialog box with the Labels tab selected.
2. Type the following name and address in the *Address* text box:
    Barrington & Gates
    200 Tenth Street, Suite 100
    Austin, TX 73341
3. Click the New Document button.
4. In a previous chapter, you learned how to indent paragraphs of text using the Left Indent marker on the Ruler. You can also use this marker to increase the indent of text within labels. Increase the indent of the labels text by completing the following steps:
    a. Press Ctrl + A to select all of the labels.
    b. Drag the Left Indent marker on the Ruler to the 0.5-inch marker on the Ruler.
    c. Click in any label to deselect the text.
5. With the insertion point positioned in a label, the Table Tools tab displays in the Ribbon. With options at the Table Tools Layout tab, you can adjust the vertical alignment of text within labels. You decide that the label text would look better in the labels if it was centered vertically in each label. To do this, complete the following steps:
    a. Click the Table Tools Layout tab.
    b. Click the Select button at the left side of the Table Tools Layout tab and then click *Select Table* at the drop-down list.
    c. With the text in all of the labels selected, click the Align Center Left button located in the Alignment group in the Table Tools Layout tab.
    d. Click in any label to deselect the text.
6. Save the label document and name it **C10-A04-BGLabels**.
7. Print and then close **C10-A04-BGLabels.docx**.

Achieving Signature Status

Take your skills to the next level by completing these more challenging assessments.

Assessment 10.5   Create Custom Labels

1. You can create a sheet of labels with the same information in each label either by typing the information in the *Address* text box at the Envelopes and Labels dialog box or by typing the desired information, selecting it, and then creating the label. Using this technique, create the sheet of labels shown in Figure 10.12 with the following specifications:
    *   At a blank document, type the company name and address (shown in the first label in Figure 10.12).

- Set the text in 14-point Harlow Solid Italic and set the "S" in "Southland" and the "A" in "Aviation" in 20-point size. Change the font color to blue.
- Select the company name and address and then create the labels by displaying the Envelopes and Labels dialog box with the Labels tab selected and then clicking the New Document button. Use the Avery US Letter label, product number 5160 when creating the labels.
- At the labels document, select the entire document and then click the Center button. (This centers all of the names and addresses in each label.)

2. Save the completed labels document and name it **C10-A05-SALabels**.
3. Print and then close the document.

Figure 10.12 Assessment 10.5

Assessment 10.6   Create Personal Labels

1. At a blank document, type your name and address and then apply formatting to enhance the appeal of the text (you determine the font, font size, and font color).
2. Create labels with your name and address (you determine the label vendor and product number).
3. Save the label document and name it **C10-A06-PersonalLabels**.
4. Print and then close the document.

Performance Assessments

Formatting and Managing Documents

ASSESSING PROFICIENCIES

In this unit, you have learned to format the pages of a document by changing page margins, orientation, and size. You have learned to improve the visual display of a document by inserting a cover page, page color, page border, drop cap, and watermark. You have learned to insert other elements such as special symbols and characters, page numbers, headers and footers, and the date and time. You have also learned how to hyphenate words, navigate within a document, insert hyperlinks, and maintain and print documents.

Note: Before beginning computer assessments, copy to your storage medium the Unit02PA folder from the CD that accompanies this textbook and then make Unit02PA the active folder.

Assessment U2.1 Format a Corporate Report

1. Open **Terra.docx** and save the document with the name **U2-PA01-Terra**.
2. Move the insertion point to the beginning of the heading *Manufacturing* and then insert the file named **R&D.docx**.
3. Apply the Heading 1 style to the title and the Heading 2 style to the headings in the document.
4. Change the style set to Thatch. Center the title TERRA ENERGY CORPORATION.
5. Apply the Executive theme.
6. Insert a continuous section break at the beginning of the first paragraph (the paragraph that begins *Terra Energy Corporation is a . . .*).
7. Format the text below the section break into two columns.
8. Balance the columns on the second page.
9. Create a drop cap with the first letter of the first word *Terra* that begins the first paragraph of text and make the drop cap two lines in height.
10. Manually hyphenate words in the document.
11. Insert page numbering that prints at the bottom center of each page.
12. Insert the Motion cover page and type the appropriate text in the text placeholders.
13. Save, print, and then close **U2-PA01-Terra.docx**.

Assessment U2.2 Create and Format an Announcement

1. At a blank document, use the Click and Type feature to create the document shown in Figure U2.1.
2. Select the centered text and then change the font to 20-point Cambria and the font color to dark orange (*Orange, Accent 6, Darker 50%*).
3. Select the right-aligned text and then change the font to 14-point Cambria and the font color to dark orange (*Orange, Accent 6, Darker 50%*).
4. Change the vertical alignment of the text to *Center*.
5. Insert a page border and, if possible, change the color of the border to dark orange (*Orange, Accent 6, Darker 50%*).

6. Save the document with the name **U2-PA02-InvestDisc**.
7. Print **U2-PA02-InvestDisc.docx**.
8. Change the page orientation to landscape.
9. Save, print, and then close **U2-PA02-InvestDisc.docx**.

Figure U2.1 **Assessment U2.2**

INVESTMENT SERVICES PANEL DISCUSSIONS

Fiduciary Responsibility in Retirement Plans

Best Practices in Technology

Redefining Investment Advice

Small Business Succession Planning

Sponsored by
Qualité Group®

Assessment U2.3   Format a Computer Security Report

1. Open **CompViruses.docx** and save the document with the name
   U2-PA03-CompViruses.
2. Apply the following formatting:
   a. Apply the Heading 1 style to the two titles and the Heading 2 style to the
      five headings.
   b. Change the style set to Modern.
   c. Apply the Concourse theme.
   d. Insert the Conservative footer.
3. Move to the end of the paragraph in the *Types of Viruses* section, press the
   spacebar, and then type (Pie Chart).
4. If necessary, turn on the display of bookmarks. (Do this at the Word Options
   dialog box with *Advanced* selected in the left panel.)
5. Move the insertion point to the end of the paragraph in the *Types of Viruses*
   section (following the *(Pie Chart)* text), press the spacebar, and then insert a
   bookmark named Types.
6. Move the insertion point to the end of the first paragraph in the *Methods of
   Virus Operation* section and then insert a bookmark named Effects.
7. Move the insertion point to the end of the second paragraph in the *Methods of
   Virus Operation* section and then insert a bookmark named Infection.
8. Navigate in the document using the bookmarks.
9. Move the insertion point to the end of the first paragraph in the *SECTION 4:
   HARDWARE AND SOFTWARE SECURITY RISKS* section and then insert a
   hyperlink to the Effects bookmark with the display text *Click to display virus
   effects*.
10. Select the text *(Pie Chart)* that you inserted at the end of the paragraph in the
    Types of Viruses section and then insert a hyperlink to the Excel file named
    Viruses.xlsx, located in the Unit02PA folder on your storage medium.

11. Hold down the Ctrl key, click the (Pie Chart) hyperlink, and then print the Excel worksheet that displays by clicking the File tab, clicking the Print tab, and then clicking the Print button. Close the Excel program.
12. Insert the DRAFT1 watermark in the document.
13. Save, print, and then close **U2-PA03-CompViruses.docx**.

Assessment U2.4   Create a Business Letter Using a Template

1. Open the *Equity Letter* template at the New Document dialog box and then type the following information in the specified fields:

[Pick the date]	(Insert today's date)
Name	Click in the name that displays below the date, select the name, and then type your first and last names.
Sender company name	Mobile Bay Products
Sender company address	700 Michigan Avenue
	Mobile, AL 36606
Recipient name	Dr. Erin Sutton
Recipient address	5110 Third Avenue
	Prichard, AL 36610
Salutation	Dear Dr. Sutton:

2. Select the salutation text and remove the bold formatting.
3. Delete the three paragraphs of text in the body of the letter and then insert **AnnualMtg.docx.** (Press the Delete key once to remove the blank space above the complimentary close.)
4. Type the following information in the specified fields:

Closing	Sincerely,
Sender title	President

5. Save the document with the name **U2-PA04-AnnualMtg**.
6. Print and then close **U2-PA04-AnnualMtg.docx**.

Assessment U2.5   Format an Employment Document

1. Open **EmpAppoints.docx** and save the document with the name **U2-PA05-EmpAppoints**.
2. Change the top, left, and right margins to 1.25 inches.
3. Apply the Heading 1 style to the title *EMPLOYMENT APPOINTMENTS* and the Heading 2 style to the heading *Types of Appointments*.
4. Change the style set to Simple.
5. Insert a page break at the beginning of the text *Reappointment*.
6. Move the insertion point to the end of the document and then insert the current date and time.
7. Insert the Alphabet header and type Employee Handbook for the document title.
8. Insert the Alphabet footer and type Employment Appointments in the *[Type text]* placeholder.
9. Save, print, and then close **U2-PA05-EmpAppoints.docx**.

Assessment U2.6   Create an Envelope

1. At a blank document, create an envelope with the text shown in Figure U2.2.
2. Save the envelope document with the name **U2-PA06-Env**.
3. Print and then close **U2-PA06-Env.docx**.

Figure U2.2 Assessment U2.6

DR ERIN SUTTON
5110 THIRD AVE
PRICHARD AL 36610

MRS VIOLET KOHLBERG
12032 145TH ST E
MOBILE AL 36607

Assessment U2.7   Create Mailing Labels

1. Create mailing labels with the name and address for Dr. Erin Sutton shown in Figure U2.2, using the label vendor and product of your choosing.
2. Save the document with the name **U2-PA07-Labels**.
3. Print and then close **U2-PA07-Labels.docx**.

Assessment U2.8   Format a Report

1. Open **VisualAids.docx** and then save it and name it **U2-PA08-VisualAids**.
2. Format the report so it appears as shown in Figure U2.3 with the following specifications:
    - Change the top margin to 1.5 inch.
    - Set the text in 12-point Cambria and set the title in 16-point Cambria.
    - Set the text in columns as shown in the figure.
    - Apply bullets to the text as shown in the figure and then decrease the indent so the bullets display at the left margin.
    - Insert the Pinstripes header and the Pinstripes footer.
    - Apply other character and paragraph formatting so the report displays as shown in the figure.
    - Use the hyphenation feature and manually hyphenate text in the report. (Figure U2.3 does not show manual hyphenations.)
3. Save, print, and then close **U2-PA08-VisualAids.docx**.

Figure U2.3 Assessment U2.8

they arrive. To ensure your presentation will go smoothly, practice with your visual aids:

- If possible, practice in the room where you will speak with the equipment you will use.

- Perhaps ask a classmate to operate the projector while you concentrate on delivery.
- Coordinate using your notes with your visual aids. Your notes should indicate when each particular visual should be displayed.

Page 2

ENHANCING A PRESENTATION

Many oral presentations can be enhanced with the use of visual aids: illustrations, diagrams, models, and other materials listeners can see. Selecting appropriate visual aids and handling them purposefully are the keys to their effective use.

Using Visual Aids

Using visuals is a good idea if doing so will help support the audience's understanding of your message. Here are some tips on deciding whether and how to include visual aids:

- For some subjects, such as art and travel, the value of using visual aids is obvious.
- Using visuals also makes sense in a how-to speech in which you demonstrate a process.
- Visuals are useful, as well, for topics that involve statistics and other numbers, which lend themselves to charts and graphs. In any case, avoid using visual aids as filler for your presentation.
- Choose a reasonable number and variety of visual aids. What matters is the appropriateness, not the quantity, of items. In fact, having too many visuals may interfere with your delivery and make your presentation run over the allotted time.

Locating Visual Aids

There are many sources of visual aids. Photographs, reproductions of artwork, and charts and diagrams are available in magazines, newspapers, and books and on the Internet. Some libraries have folders containing pamphlets, illustrations, and similar materials. If you photocopy printed materials or download items from the Internet, be sure you follow copyright law. For assistance, check with your teacher or librarian. Another option is to create visual aids, such as charts of statistics. Prepare each chart on a large piece of cardboard or tag board using felt-tip pens. Ensure that all type and graphics are legible. At the bottom of the chart, in smaller type, provide the source of the information.

Practicing Your Presentation

If you plan to use an overhead or PowerPoint projector, make sure the display can be viewed clearly from all areas of the room. Likewise, ensure that everyone will be able to see any photograph, chart, or diagram you display. Audience members will lose interest and become distracted if you use visuals they cannot see. Passing materials among audience members may distract their attention from your presentation. If you need to distribute materials, place them on audience members' seats before

Page 1

START From Scratch

Assessment U2.9   Prepare a Gift Certificate

1. Create the gift certificates shown in Figure U2.4 with the following specifications:
   - Use the *Gift certificate (Summer Santa design)* template in the *Gift certificates* option in the Office.com Templates section of the New tab Backstage view.
   - Insert the appropriate information in the certificates as shown in the figure.
   - Change the font size to *28* and the color to dark blue for the company name *World Wide Travel* in all three certificates.
   - Delete the text *Cut along dotted line* that displays above each certificate. (To do this, click in the text, click the dashed border surrounding the text, and then press the Delete key.)
2. Save the gift certificate document and name it **U2-PA09-GiftCert**.
3. Print and then close **U2-PA09-GiftCert.docx**.

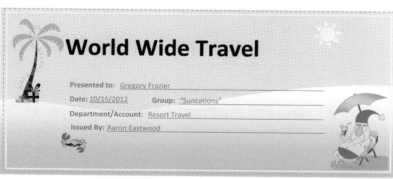

CREATING ORIGINAL DOCUMENTS

The activities in Assessments 10, 11, and 12 give you the opportunity to practice your writing skills as well as demonstrate your mastery of some of the important Word features presented in this unit. When composing the documents, use correct grammar, precise word choices, and clear sentence construction.

Assessment U2.10   Format a Computer Guidelines Company Document

Situation: You work in the technology support department at Mobile Bay Products, and your supervisor has asked you to format a document providing computer use guidelines. Open **CompGuidelines.docx**, save the document with the name **U2-PA10-CompGuidelines,** and then format it by applying or inserting at least the following elements: a style set; a heading style; a header, footer, and/or page numbers; and a cover page. Save, print, and then close **U2-PA10-CompGuidelines.docx**. Use one of the Word letter templates and write a letter to your instructor describing how you formatted the U2-PA10-CompGuidelines.docx document, including the reasons you chose specific formatting. Save the completed letter with the name **U2-PA10-Ltr**. Print and then close **U2-PA10-Ltr.docx**.

Assessment U2.11   Create a Calendar Using a Calendar Template

Situation: You are responsible for monitoring employee vacation days and decide to use a Word calendar template to record the information. Download a calendar for the next year that allows you to enter information. In the appropriate calendar months (use months for the next year), enter the following data on employee vacation days:

- Mariah Brown, first two weeks of June
- Jaden Holland, second week of July
- Maddie O'Hara, last two weeks of July
- Evan Noland, first week of August

Save the completed calendar document with the name **U2-PA11-Calendar**. Print only those pages containing the months of June, July, and August and then close **U2-PA11-Calendar.docx**.

Assessment U2.12   Research and Prepare a Netiquette Report

Situation: Your supervisor at Mobile Bay Products wants to provide employees with a document that describes *netiquette* ("Internet etiquette" rules). She has asked you to research the topic and then create a document that will be distributed to employees. Use the Internet (or any other resource available to you) and search for information on "rules of netiquette." Locate at least two sources that provide information on netiquette. Using the information you locate, create a document that describes netiquette rules and apply formatting to enhance the document's visual appeal. Use your own words when describing netiquette rules; cutting and pasting text from the Internet is plagiarism. At the end of the document, type the web addresses for the sites you used as references. Save the document with the name **U2-PA12-Netiquette**. Print and then close **U2-PA12-Netiquette.docx**.

Unit 3

Enhancing Documents

Chapter 11   Inserting Images

Chapter 12   Inserting Shapes and WordArt

Chapter 13   Creating Tables

Chapter 14   Enhancing Tables

Chapter 15   Creating Charts

Unit 3   Performance Assessments

Inserting Images

 **TUTORIALS**

Tutorial 11.1
Inserting, Sizing, and Moving Images
Tutorial 11.2
Customizing and Formatting an Image
Tutorial 11.3
Applying Advanced Formatting to Images
Tutorial 11.4
Creating SmartArt
Tutorial 11.5
Arranging and Moving a SmartArt Diagram
Tutorial 11.6
Creating an Organizational Chart with SmartArt

Performance Objectives

Upon successful completion of Chapter 11, you will be able to:

- Insert, format, and customize pictures
- Insert, format, and customize clip art images
- Create and format SmartArt diagrams
- Create and format SmartArt organizational charts

Inserting images into your documents can further increase their visual appeal and attract readers' attention. In this chapter, you will learn to insert these elements and display data in a more visual way by creating a SmartArt graphic. The SmartArt feature provides a number of predesigned diagrams and organizational charts.

Note: Before beginning computer exercises for this chapter, copy to your storage medium the Chapter11 folder from the CD that accompanies this textbook and then make Chapter11 the active folder.

In this chapter students will produce the following documents:

Exercise 11.1. C11-E01-EditedPictures.docx
Exercise 11.2. C11-E02-SummerRates.docx
Exercise 11.3. C11-E03-WtrLuncheon.docx
Exercise 11.4. C11-E04-CompSecurity.docx
Exercise 11.5. C11-E05-CompCommunications.docx
Exercise 11.6. C11-E06-Diagrams.docx
Exercise 11.7. C11-E07-OrgDiagram.docx

Model answers for these exercises are shown on the following pages.

Exercise 11.1
C11-E01-EditedPictures.docx

Figure 1 Olympic Mountains

Exercise 11.2
C11-E02-SummerRates.docx

Windmill Garden Nursery

Winter Luncheon

Wonderland Lanai

Saturday, November 17

Admission $20

Exercise 11.3 C11-E03-WtrLuncheon.docx

SECTION 1: UNAUTHORIZED ACCESS

Like uncharted wilderness, the Internet lacks borders. This inherent openness is what makes the Internet so valuable and yet so vulnerable. Over its short life, the Internet has grown so quickly that the legal system has not been able to keep pace. The security risks posed by networks and the Internet can be grouped into three categories: unauthorized access, information theft, and denial of service.

Hackers, individuals who gain access to computers and networks illegally, are responsible for most cases of unauthorized access. Hackers tend to exploit sites and programs that have poor security measures in place. However, they also gain access to more challenging sites by using sophisticated programs and strategies. Many hackers claim they hack merely because they like the challenge of trying to defeat security measures. They rarely have a more malicious motive, and they generally do not aim to destroy or damage the sites that they invade. In fact, hackers dislike being identified with those who seek to cause damage. They refer to hackers with malicious or criminal intent as *crackers*.

USER IDS AND PASSWORDS

To gain entry over the Internet to a secure computer system, most hackers focus on finding a working user ID and password combination. User IDs are easy to come by and are generally not secure information. Sending an email, for example, displays the sender's user ID in the return address, making it very public. The only missing element is the password. Hackers know from experience which passwords are common; they have programs that generate thousands of likely passwords and they try them systematically over a period of hours or days.

SYSTEM BACKDOORS

Programmers can sometimes inadvertently aid hackers by providing unintentional entrance to networks and information systems. One such unintentional entrance is a system "backdoor," which is a user ID and password that provides the highest level of authorization. Programmers innocently create a "backdoor" in the early days of system development to allow other programmers and team members to access the system to fix problems. Through negligence or by design, the user ID and password are sometimes left behind in the final version of the system. People who know about them can then enter the system, bypassing the security perhaps years later, when the backdoor has been forgotten.

SPOOFING

A sophisticated way to break into a network via the Internet involves spoofing, which is the process of fooling another computer by pretending to send information from a legitimate source. It works by altering the address that the system automatically puts on every message sent. The address is changed to one that the receiving computer is programmed to accept as a trusted source of information.

SPYWARE

Spyware is a type of software that allows an intruder to spy upon someone else's computer. This alarming technology takes advantage of loopholes in the computer's security systems and allows a stranger to witness and

Exercise 11.4 C11-E04-CompSecurity.docx

Page 1

---

record another person's every mouse click or keystroke on the monitor as it occurs. The spy can record activities and gain access to passwords and credit card information. Spyware generally requires the user to install it on the machine that is being spied upon, so it is highly unlikely that random strangers on the Internet could simply begin watching your computer. In the workplace, however, someone might be able to install the software without the victim's knowledge. Disguised as an email greeting, for example, the program can operate like a virus that gets the unwary user to install the spyware unknowingly.

SECTION 2: INFORMATION THEFT

Information can be a company's most valuable possession. Stealing corporate information, a crime included in the category of industrial espionage, is unfortunately both easy to do and difficult to detect. This is due in part to the invisible nature of software and data. If a cracker breaks into a company network and manages to download the company database from the network onto a disk, there is no visible sign to the company that anything is amiss. The original database is still in place, working the same way it always has.

WIRELESS DEVICE SECURITY

The growing number of wireless devices has created a new opportunity for data theft. Wireless devices such as cameras, Web phones, networked computers, PDAs, and input and output peripherals are inherently less secure than wired devices. Security is quite lax, and in some cases nonexistent, in new wireless technologies for handheld computers and cell phone systems. In a rush to match competition, manufacturers have tended to sacrifice security to move a product to the marketplace faster. Already, viruses are appearing in emails for cell phones and PDAs. With little protection available for these new systems, hackers and spies are enjoying a free hand with the new technology. One of the few available security protocols for wireless networks is Wired Equivalent Privacy (WEP), developed in conjunction with the standard for wireless local area networks. Newer versions of WEP with enhanced security features make it more difficult for hackers to intercept and modify data transmissions sent by radio waves or infrared signals.

DATA BROWSING

Data browsing is a less damaging form of information theft that involves an invasion of privacy. Workers in many organizations have access to networked databases that contain private information about people. Accessing this information without an official reason is against the law. The IRS had a particularly large problem with data browsing in the late 1990s. Some employees were fired and the rest were given specialized training in appropriate conduct.

Exercise 11.4 C11-E04-CompSecurity.docx

Page 2

COMPUTERS IN COMMUNICATIONS

Computers were originally stand-alone devices, incapable of communicating with other computers. This changed in the 1970s and 1980s when the development of special telecommunications hardware and software led to the creation of the first private networks, allowing connected computers to exchange data. Exchanged data took the form of requests for information, replies to requests for information, or instructions on how to run programs stored on the network. The ability to link computers enables users to communicate and work together efficiently and effectively. Linked computers have become central to the communications industry. They play a vital role in telecommunications, publishing, and news services.

TELECOMMUNICATIONS

The industry that provides for communication across distances is called telecommunications. The telephone industry uses computers to switch and route phone calls automatically over telephone lines. In addition to the spoken word, many other kinds of information move over such lines, including faxes and computer data. Data can be sent from computer to computer over telephone lines using a device known as a modem. One kind of data frequently sent by modem is electronic mail, or email, which can be sent from person to person via the Internet or an online service. A more recent innovation in telecommunications is teleconferencing, which allows people in various locations to see and hear one another and thus hold virtual meetings.

PUBLISHING

Just twenty years ago, book manuscripts were typeset mechanically on a typesetting machine and then reproduced on a printing press. Now anyone who has access to a computer and either a modem or a printer can undertake what has come to be known as electronic publishing. Writers and editors use word processing applications to produce text. Artists and designers use drawing and painting applications to created original graphics, or they use inexpensive scanners to digitize illustrations and photographs (turn them into computer-readable files). Typesetters use personal computers to combine text, illustrations, and photographs. Publishers typically send computer-generated files to printers for production of the film and plates from which books and magazines are printed.

NEWS SERVICES

News providers rely on reporters located worldwide. Reporters use email to send, or upload, their stories to wire services. Increasingly, individuals get daily news reports from online services. News can also be accessed from specific providers, such as the *New York Times* or *USA Today*, via the Internet. One of the most popular Internet sites provides continuously updated weather reports.

Exercise 11.5 C11-E05-CompCommunications.docx

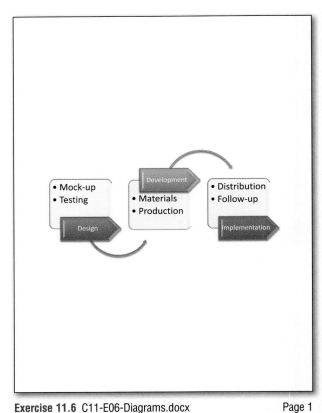

Exercise 11.6 C11-E06-Diagrams.docx   Page 1

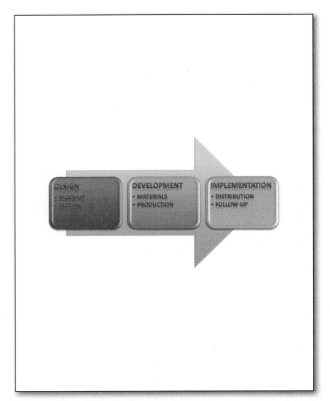

Exercise 11.6 C11-E06-Diagrams.docx   Page 2

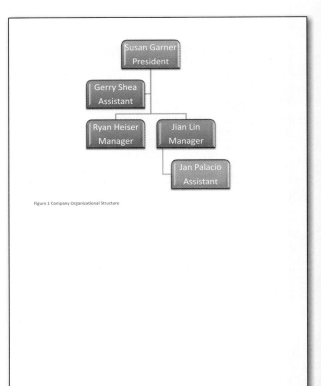

Figure 1 Company Organizational Structure

Exercise 11.7 C11-E07-OrgDiagram.docx

Inserting an Image

You can insert a picture or clip art image into a Word document by using buttons in the Illustrations group in the Insert tab, shown in Figure 11.1. Click the Picture button to display the Insert Picture dialog box where you can specify the desired picture file you want to insert, or click the Clip Art button to display the Clip Art task pane where you can choose from a variety of available images.

Figure 11.1 Insert Tab Illustrations Group Buttons

Use buttons in this group in the Insert tab to insert images in a document.

Inserting a Picture

To insert a picture in a document, click the Insert tab and then click the Picture button in the Illustrations group. At the Insert Picture dialog box, navigate to the folder that contains the picture you want to insert and then double-click the picture. After you have inserted the picture, you can use buttons in the Picture Tools Format tab to format and customize it. In addition to inserting a picture you have saved to your storage medium, you can insert a picture from a web page. To do this, open the web page, open the document you want to insert the picture into, and then drag the picture from the web page to the document. If the picture is linked, the link displays in your document rather than the image.

Customizing and Formatting an Image

When you insert an image in a document, the image is selected and the Picture Tools Format tab, shown in Figure 11.2, becomes active. Use buttons in this tab to format the image. With buttons in the Adjust group, you can recolor the picture or clip art image, correct its brightness and contrast, and apply artistic effects. You can reset the picture or clip art back to its original color or change to a different image. You can also compress the size of the image file with the Compress Pictures button. Compressing the size of an image is a good idea because it reduces the amount of space the image requires on your storage medium.

With buttons in the Picture Styles group, you can apply a predesigned style to your image, change the image border, or apply other effects to the image. Use the Remove Background button to remove unwanted portions of the picture. With options in the Arrange group, you can position the image on the page, specify how text will wrap around it, align the image with other elements in the document, and rotate the image. With the Crop button in the Size group, you can remove any unnecessary parts of the image and specify the image size with the Shape Height and Shape Width measurement boxes.

In addition to the options in the Picture Tools Format tab, you can format an image with options at the shortcut menu. Display this menu by right-clicking the image. One of the options at this shortcut menu is *Insert Caption*. Click this option and the Caption dialog box displays. At this dialog box, type the caption you want to display below the image and then click OK. You can also display the Caption dialog box by clicking the References tab and then clicking the Insert Caption button in the Captions group.

Insert Picture
1. Click Insert tab.
2. Click Picture button.
3. Navigate to desired folder.
4. Double-click desired picture in Insert Picture dialog box.

Picture

Figure 11.2 Picture Tools Format Tab

Exercise 11.1   Inserting a Picture

1. At a blank document, click the Insert tab and then click the Picture button in the Illustrations group.
2. At the Insert Picture dialog box, navigate to the Chapter11 folder on your storage medium and then double-click *Olympics.jpg*.
3. Click the Artistic Effects button in the Adjust group and then click the *Cutout* option at the drop-down gallery (first option from the left in the fifth row).

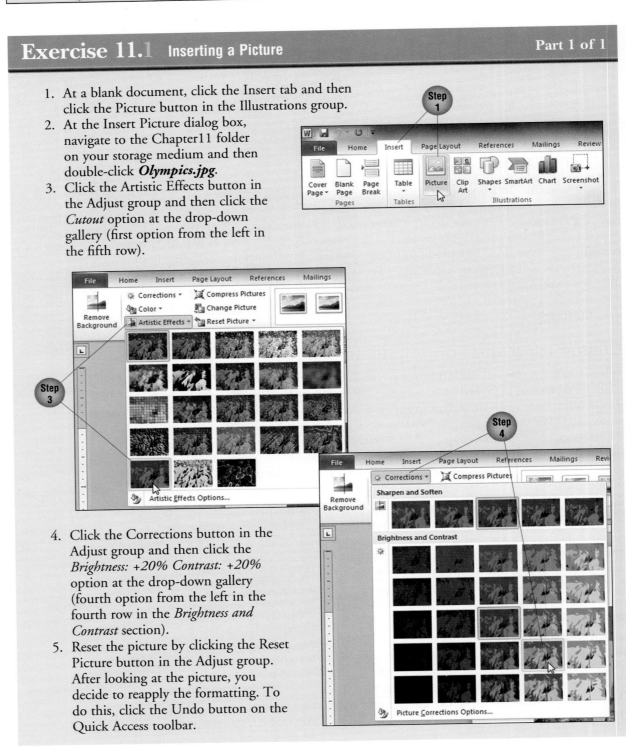

4. Click the Corrections button in the Adjust group and then click the *Brightness: +20% Contrast: +20%* option at the drop-down gallery (fourth option from the left in the fourth row in the *Brightness and Contrast* section).
5. Reset the picture by clicking the Reset Picture button in the Adjust group. After looking at the picture, you decide to reapply the formatting. To do this, click the Undo button on the Quick Access toolbar.

Chapter Eleven

6. Click the Corrections button in the Adjust group and then click the *Sharpen: 50%* option at the drop-down gallery (last option in the *Sharpen and Soften* section).

7. Click the More button at the right of the picture style thumbnails in the Picture Styles group and then click the *Perspective Shadow, White* option at the drop-down gallery (see image below).

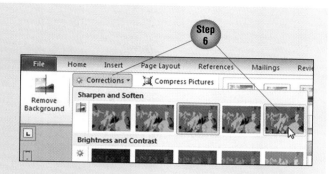

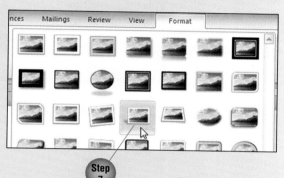

8. Click the Picture Border button arrow in the Picture Styles group and then click the *Blue, Accent 1, Lighter 40%* color (located in the fifth column).

9. Insert a caption by right-clicking the picture image and then clicking *Insert Caption*. At the Caption dialog box (with the insertion point positioned in the *Caption* text box), press the spacebar once, type Olympic Mountains and then click OK. (The caption *Figure 1 Olympic Mountains* is inserted below and to the left of the picture.)

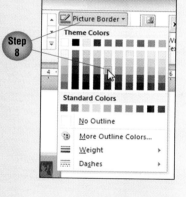

10. Press Ctrl + End and then press the Enter key twice.
11. Click the Insert tab and then click the Picture button.
12. At the Insert Picture dialog box, make sure the Chapter11 folder on your storage medium is active and then double-click *Ship.jpg*.

13. With the ship picture selected, remove some of the background by completing the following steps:

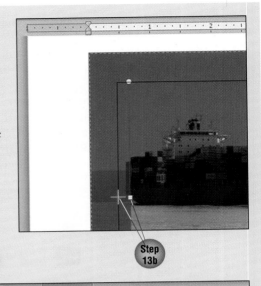

Step 13b

a. Click the Remove Background button in the Adjust group in the Picture Tools Format tab.

b. Using the left middle sizing handle, drag the border to the left to include the back of the ship (see image at the right).

c. Click the Mark Areas to Remove button in the Refine group in the Background Removal tab. (The mouse pointer displays as a pencil.)

d. Click anywhere in the water that displays below the ship. (This removes the water from the picture. If all of the water is not removed, click in the remaining water to remove it.)

e. Using the right middle sizing handle, drag the border to the left so the border is near the front of the ship.

Step 13c

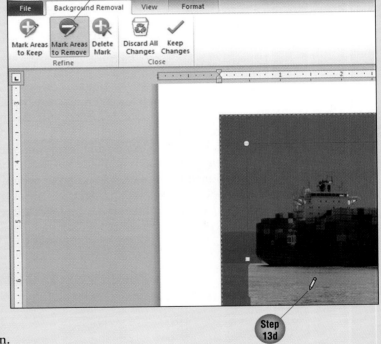

Step 13d

f. You notice that part of the structure above the front of the ship has been removed, and you want to include it in the picture. To begin, click the Mark Areas to Keep button in the Refine group in the Background Removal tab. (The mouse pointer displays as a pencil.)

g. Using the mouse, position the pencil at the top of the structure (as shown at the right), drag down to the top of the containers on the ship, and then release the mouse button.

h. Click the Keep Changes button in the Close group in the Background Removal tab.

14. Click the Corrections button in the Adjust group and then click the *Brightness: +40% Contrast: +20%* option at the drop-down gallery (last option in the fourth row in the *Brightness and Contrast* section).

15. Click the Corrections button in the Adjust group and then click the *Sharpen: 50%* option at the drop-down gallery (last option in the *Sharpen and Soften* section).

16. Click outside the picture to deselect it.

17. Save the document and name it **C11-E01-EditedPictures**.

18. Print and then close **C11-E01-EditedPictures.docx**.

Step 13g

Sizing an Image

You can change the size of an image with the Shape Height and Shape Width measurement boxes in the Size group in the Picture Tools Format tab or with the sizing handles that display around a selected image, as shown in Figure 11.3. To increase or decrease an image's size with a sizing handle, position the mouse pointer on a handle until the pointer turns into a double-headed arrow and then hold down the left mouse button. Drag the sizing handle in to decrease or out to increase the size of the image and then release the mouse button. Use the middle sizing handles at the left or right side of the image to make the image wider or thinner. Use the middle sizing handles at the top or bottom of the image to make the image taller or shorter. Use the sizing handles at the corners of the image to change both the width and height at the same time.

Drag the rotation handle to rotate the image.

Figure 11.3 Selected Image

![Selected image with sizing handles and rotation handle]

Moving an Image

Move an image to a specific location on the page with options from the Position button drop-down gallery. The Position button is located in the Arrange group in the Picture Tools Format tab. When you choose an option at the Position button drop-down gallery, the image is moved to the specified location on the page and the text wraps around the image.

Position

You can also move an image by dragging it to the desired location. Before dragging an image, however, you must first choose how the text will wrap around it by clicking the Wrap Text button in the Arrange group and then clicking the desired wrapping style at the drop-down list. After choosing a wrapping style, move the image by positioning the mouse pointer on the image border until the arrow pointer turns into a four-headed arrow. Hold down the left mouse button, drag the image to the desired position, and then release the mouse button.

Wrap Text

A third way to move an image is with the arrow keys on the keyboard. To move the image in small increments (called *nudging*), hold down the Ctrl key while pressing an arrow key. To help precisely position an image, consider turning on gridlines. Do this by clicking the Align button in the Arrange group in the Picture Tools Format tab and then clicking View Gridlines.

To rotate an image, use the rotation handle (see Figure 11.3) or the Rotate button in the Arrange group. To use the rotation handle, position the mouse pointer on the round, green rotation handle until the pointer displays as a circular arrow. Hold down the left mouse button, drag in the desired direction, and then release the mouse button.

Figure 11.4 Exercise 11.2

BLUE MOUNTAIN SPA AND RESORT

Special Summer Rates

Complimentary Breakfast Buffet

June 1 through August 31

Exercise 11.2 Inserting and Customizing a Picture   Part 1 of 1

1. At a blank document, press the Enter key two times and then type the text and center it as shown in Figure 11.4.
2. Select the text and then change the font to 18-point Franklin Gothic Heavy and the text color to dark blue.
3. Press Ctrl + Home to move the insertion point to the beginning of the document.
4. Insert a picture by completing the following steps:
   a. Click the Insert tab.
   b. Click the Picture button in the Illustrations group.
   c. At the Insert Picture dialog box, navigate to your Chapter11 folder.
   d. Double-click ***Mountain.jpg*** in the list box.
5. Crop the picture by completing the following steps:
   a. Click the Crop button in the Size group.
   b. Position the mouse pointer on the bottom middle crop handle (which displays as a short black line) until the pointer turns into the crop tool (which displays as a small, black T).
   c. Hold down the left mouse button, drag up to just below the mountain as shown at the right, and then release the mouse button.
   d. Click the Crop button in the Size group to turn off the feature.

Step 5c

6. Increase the size of the picture by selecting the current measurement in the Shape Width measurement box, typing 6, and then pressing the Enter key.
7. Position the picture by clicking the Position button in the Arrange group and then clicking the middle option in the top row in the *With Text Wrapping* section (*Position in Top Center with Square Text Wrapping*).

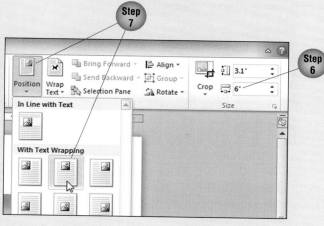

8. Move the picture behind the text by clicking the Wrap Text button in the Arrange group and then clicking *Behind Text* at the drop-down list.
9. Rotate the image by clicking the Rotate button in the Arrange group and then clicking *Flip Horizontal* at the drop-down list.

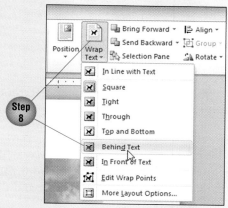

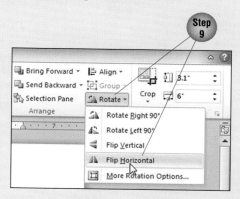

10. Click the Corrections button in the Adjust group and then click the *Brightness: 0% (Normal) Contrast: 40%* option at the drop-down gallery (third option from the left in the bottom row in the *Brightness and Contrast* section).
11. Click the Color button in the Adjust group and then click the *Temperature: 4700 K* option (first option in the *Color Tone* section).

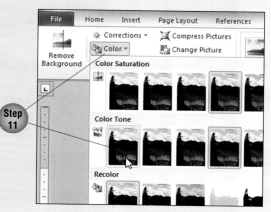

12. Click the Artistic Effects button in the Adjust group and then click the *Paint Brush* option at the drop-down gallery (third option from the left in the second row).

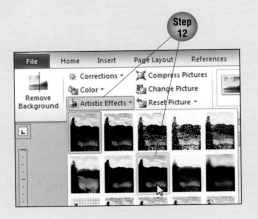

13. Click the More button at the right of the picture style thumbnails in the Picture Styles group and then click the *Drop Shadow Rectangle* option at the drop-down gallery (fourth option in the top row).
14. Save the document and name it **C11-E02-SummerRates**.
15. Close **C11-E02-SummerRates.docx**.
16. Display the Open dialog box, *right*-click the **C11-E01-SummerRates.docx** document, and then click *Properties* at the shortcut menu.
17. At the Properties dialog box with the General tab selected, notice the size information that displays after *Size* and *Size on disk* and then close the Properties dialog box.
18. Open **C11-E02-SummerRates.docx**.
19. Compress the picture by completing the following steps:
    a. Click just inside the picture to select it (make sure sizing handles display around the image).
    b. Click the Picture Tools Format tab.
    c. Click the Compress Pictures button in the Adjust group in the Picture Tools Format tab.

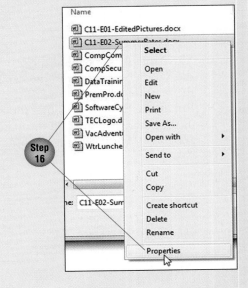

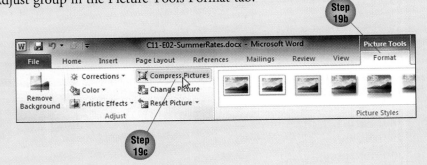

d. At the Compress Pictures dialog box, make sure the *Apply only to this picture* check box and the *Delete cropped areas of pictures* check box each contain a check mark.

e. Make sure the *Use document resolution* option is selected in the *Target output* section.

f. Click OK to close the dialog box.

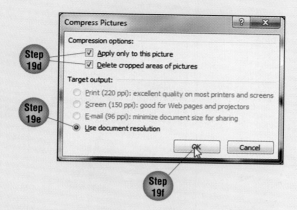

20. Click outside the picture to deselect it.
21. Save, print, and then close **C11-E02-SummerRates.docx**.
22. Display the Open dialog box, *right*-click the **C11-E02-SummerRates.docx** document, and then click *Properties* at the shortcut menu.
23. At the Properties dialog box with the General tab selected, notice the size information that displays after *Size* and *Size on disk* (the numbers are less than the original numbers).
24. Close the Properties dialog box.
25. Close the Open dialog box.

Inserting a Clip Art Image

Microsoft Office includes a gallery of media images you can insert in a document. The gallery includes clip art, photographs, and movie images, as well as sound clips. To insert an image in a Word document, click the Insert tab and then click the Clip Art button in the Illustrations group. This displays the Clip Art task pane at the right side of the screen, as shown in Figure 11.5.

To view all picture, sound, and motion files available in the gallery, make sure the *Search for* text box in the Clip Art task pane does not contain any text and then click the Go button. Scroll through the images that display until you find one you want to use and then click the image to insert it in the document. Use buttons in the Picture Tools Format tab (see Figure 11.2) to format and customize the clip art image.

If you are searching for a specific type of image, click in the *Search for* text box, type a category, and then click the Go button. For example, if you want to find images related to business, click in the *Search for* text box, type business, and then click the Go button. Clip art images related to business display in the viewing area of the task pane. If you are connected to the Internet, Word will search for images matching the word or topic at the Microsoft Office Online website. You can drag a clip art image from the Clip Art task pane to your document.

Insert Clip Art Image
1. Click Insert tab.
2. Click Clip Art button.
3. Type search word or topic.
4. Press Enter.
5. Click desired image.

Clip Art

Figure 11.5 Clip Art Task Pane

Type a search word or topic in this text box.

Use this option to specify the type of files for which you are searching.

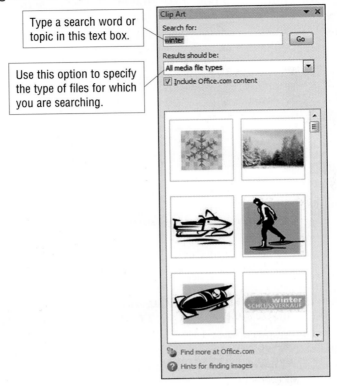

Exercise 11.3 Inserting and Formatting a Clip Art Image   **Part 1 of 1**

1. Open **WtrLuncheon.docx** and save the document with the name **C11-E03-WtrLuncheon**.
2. Select the text and then change the font to 20-point Harrington bold and the text color to purple.
3. Press Ctrl + Home to move the insertion point to the beginning of the document.
4. Insert a clip art image by completing the following steps:
   a. Click the Insert tab and then click the Clip Art button in the Illustrations group.
   b. At the Clip Art task pane, select any text that displays in the *Search for* text box, type winter, and then press the Enter key.
   c. Click the snowflake image in the list box as shown at the right.
   d. Close the Clip Art task pane by clicking the Close button (the button marked with an X) located in the upper right corner of the task pane.
5. Click the Wrap Text button in the Arrange group and then click *Square* at the drop-down list.

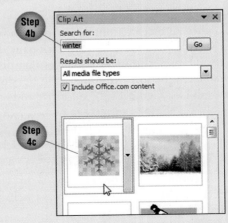

6. Click in the Shape Height measurement box, type 2.3, and then press the Enter key.

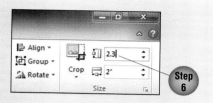
Step 6

7. With the clip art image selected, press the right arrow key on the keyboard until the left edge of the image aligns at approximately the 0.5-inch mark on the Ruler.
8. Click outside the image to deselect it.
9. Save, print, and then close **C11-E03-WtrLuncheon.docx**.

Unless the Clip Art task pane default setting has been customized, the task pane displays all illustrations, photographs, videos, and audio files. The *Results should be* option has a default setting of *Selected media file types*. Click the down-pointing arrow at the right of this option to display media types. To search for a specific media type, remove the check mark before all options at the drop-down list except for the desired type. For example, if you are searching only for photograph images, remove the check mark before Illustrations, Videos, and Audio.

Exercise 11.4   Inserting an Image

Part 1 of 1

1. Open **CompSecurity.docx** and save the document with the name **C11-E04-CompSecurity**.
2. Apply the Heading 1 style to the two titles and apply the Heading 2 style to the six headings in the document.
3. Change the style set to Modern. ***Hint: Do this with the Change Styles button in the Styles group in the Home tab.***
4. Insert a clip art image by completing the following steps:
   a. Move the insertion point so it is positioned at the beginning of the first paragraph of text (the sentence that begins *Like uncharted wilderness . . .*).
   b. Click the Insert tab.
   c. Click the Clip Art button in the Illustrations group.
   d. At the Clip Art task pane, click the down-pointing arrow at the right of the *Results should be* option box and then click in the *Photographs, Videos,* and *Audio* check boxes to remove the check marks. (The *Illustrations* check box should be the only one with a check mark.)

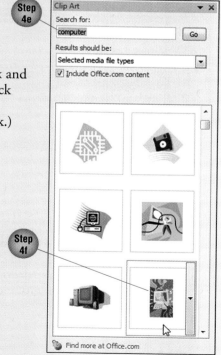
Step 4e

Step 4f

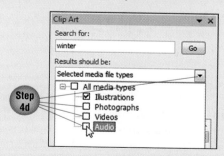
Step 4d

   e. Select any text that displays in the *Search for* text box, type computer, and then press the Enter key.
   f. Click the computer image in the list box as shown at the right.

g. Click the down-pointing arrow at the right of the *Results should be* option box and then click in the *All media types* check box to insert a check mark.

h. Close the Clip Art task pane by clicking the Close button (the button marked with an X) located in the upper right corner of the task pane.

5. Crop the clip art image by completing the following steps:
   a. Click the Crop button in the Size group.
   b. Position the mouse pointer on the top middle crop handle (which displays as a short black line) until the pointer turns into the crop tool.
   c. Hold down the left mouse button, drag down to just above the top of the computer as shown at the right, and then release the mouse button.
   d. Click the Crop button in the Size group to turn off the feature.

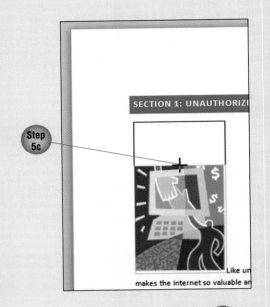

Step 5c

6. Decrease the size of the picture by clicking in the Shape Height measurement box, typing 1.5, and then pressing the Enter key.

7. Change the text wrapping by clicking the Wrap Text button in the Arrange group and then clicking *Square* at the drop-down list.

8. Rotate the image by clicking the Rotate button in the Arrange group and then clicking *Flip Horizontal* at the drop-down list.

9. Click the Corrections button in the Adjust group and then click the *Brightness: 0% (Normal) Contrast: +40%* option (third option from the left in the bottom row).

10. Click the Picture Effects button in the Picture Styles group, point to *Shadow*, and then click the *Offset Right* option (first option from the left in the second row in the *Outer* section).

11. Click outside the clip art image to deselect it.

12. Save, print, and then close **C11-E04-CompSecurity.docx**.

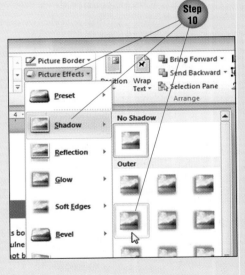

Step 10

Applying Advanced Formatting to Images

The Picture Tools Format tab contains a number of buttons and options you can use to format pictures and clip art images. Additional formatting options are available at the Format Picture dialog box shown in Figure 11.6. Display this dialog box by clicking the Picture Styles group dialog box launcher in the Picture Tools Format tab.

Formatting categories display at the left side of the dialog box. Click a formatting category and the options at the right side of the dialog box change to reflect formatting options related to the category. Many of the options available at the Format Picture dialog box are also available on the Picture Tools Format tab. The dialog box is a central location for formatting options and also includes some additional advanced formatting options.

In addition to the Format Picture dialog box, you can customize the layout of images with options at the Layout dialog box. Display the Layout dialog box by clicking the Size group dialog box launcher in the Picture Tools Format tab. The Layout dialog box has three tabs. Click the Position tab and the dialog box displays as shown in Figure 11.7.

Figure 11.6 Format Picture Dialog Box

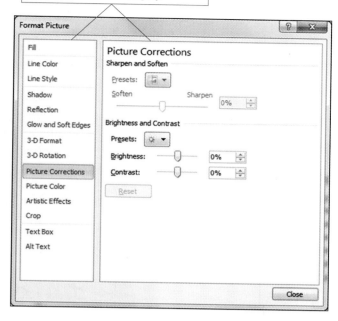

Figure 11.7 Layout Dialog Box with Position Tab Selected

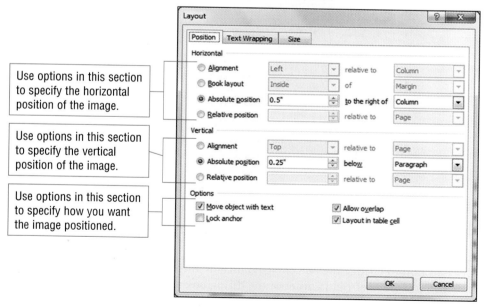

Use options in this section to specify the horizontal position of the image.

Use options in this section to specify the vertical position of the image.

Use options in this section to specify how you want the image positioned.

Use options at the Layout dialog box with the Position tab selected to specify horizontal and vertical layout options. In the *Horizontal* section, choose the *Alignment* option to specify whether you want the image horizontally left-, center-, or right-aligned relative to the margin, page, column, or character. Choose the *Book layout* option if you want to align the image with inside or outside margins on the page. Use the *Absolute position* option to align the image horizontally with the specified amount of space between the left edge of the image and the left edge of the page, column, left margin, or character. In the *Vertical* section of the dialog box, use the *Alignment* option to align the image at the top, bottom, center, inside, or outside relative to the page, margin, or line. In the *Options* section, you can attach (anchor) the image to a paragraph so that the image and paragraph move together. Choose the *Move object with text* option if you want the image to move up or down on the page with the paragraph to which it is anchored. Keep the image anchored in the same place on the page by choosing the *Lock anchor* option. Choose the *Allow overlap* option if you want images with the same wrapping style to overlap.

Use options at the Layout dialog box with the Text Wrapping tab selected as shown in Figure 11.8 to specify the wrapping style for the image. You can also specify which sides you want text to wrap around, and you can specify the amount of space you want between the text and the top, bottom, left, and right edges of the image.

Figure 11.8 Layout Dialog Box with Text Wrapping Tab Selected

Choose options in this dialog box to specify text wrapping around the image as well as the distance from the image to text.

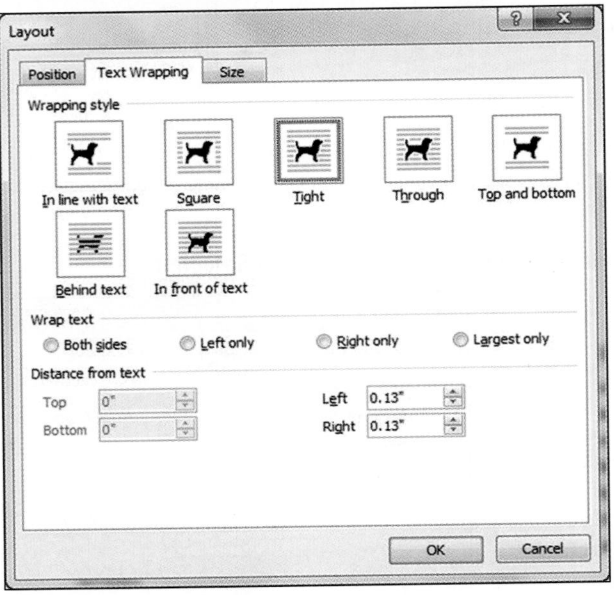

Click the Size tab at the Layout dialog box and it displays as shown in Figure 11.9. Use options in the *Height* and *Width* sections to specify the height and width measurements of the image relative to the margin, page, top margin, bottom margin, inside margin, or outside margin. Use the *Rotation* option to rotate the image by degrees and use options in the *Scale* section to change the percentage of height and width scale. Click the Reset button located in the lower right corner of the dialog box to reset the image size.

Figure 11.9 Layout Dialog Box with Size Tab Selected

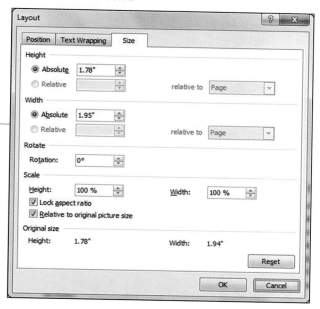

Specify the image height, width, rotation, and scale and also reset the size of the image with options in this dialog box.

Exercise 11.5A   Applying Advanced Formatting to a Clip Art Image   Part 1 of 2

1. Open **CompCommunications.docx** and save the document and name it **C11-E05-CompCommunications**.
2. Insert an image of a computer in the Publishing section in the document as shown in Figure 11.10 (shown on page 369) by completing the following steps:
   a. Click the Insert tab and then click the Clip Art button in the Illustrations group.
   b. At the Clip Art task pane, select any text that displays in the *Search for* text box, type computer, and then press the Enter key.
   c. Click once on the computer image shown in Figure 11.10. (If this clip art image is not available, choose another computer image.)
   d. Close the Clip Art task pane.
3. Change the image formatting by completing the following steps:
   a. With the clip art image selected and the Picture Tools Format tab active, click the Picture Styles group dialog box launcher.

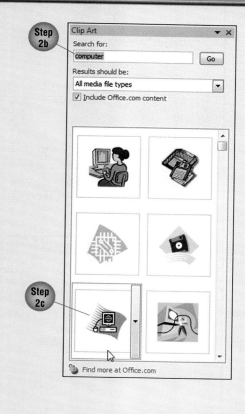

Step 2b

Step 2c

b. At the Format Picture dialog box, click the *Fill* option at the left side of the dialog box.
c. Click the *Gradient fill* option.
d. Click the Preset colors button and then click the *Fog* option at the drop-down list.
e. Click the *Line Color* option at the left side of the dialog box.
f. Click the *Solid line* option.
g. Click the *Color* button and then click the dark blue color in the *Standard Colors* section of the drop-down list.

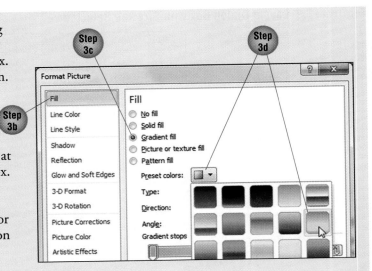

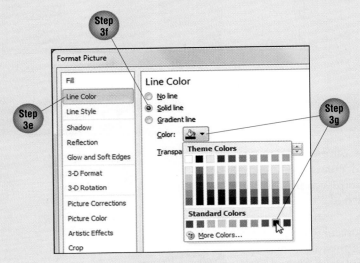

h. Click the *Glow and Soft Edges* option at the left side of the dialog box.
i. Click the Color button in the *Glow* section and then click the *Blue, Accent 1, Lighter 80%* color option.
j. Drag the Size slider bar in the *Glow* section to the left until *5 pt* displays in the point measurement box.

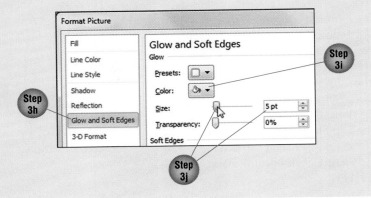

k. Click the *Shadow* option at the left side of the dialog box.
l. Click the Presets button and then click the *Offset Bottom* option at the drop-down list.

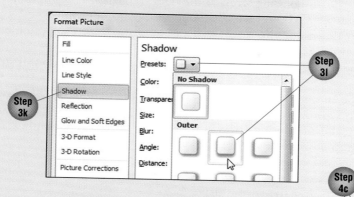

m. Click the Close button to close the Format Picture dialog box.
4. Change the size, wrapping, and position of the image by completing the following steps:
  a. With the clip art image selected and the Picture Tools Format tab active, click the Size group dialog box launcher.
  b. At the Layout dialog box with the Size tab selected, click the *Lock aspect ratio* check box to remove the check mark.
  c. Click the down-pointing arrow at the right of the *Absolute* measurement box in the *Height* section until *1.28"* displays in the measurement box. (This measurement may vary slightly.)
  d. Click the down-pointing arrow at the right of the *Absolute* measurement box in the *Width* section until *1.45"* displays in the measurement box. (This measurement may vary slightly.)
  e. Click the Text Wrapping tab.
  f. Click the *Tight* option in the *Wrapping style* section.
  g. Click once on the down-pointing arrow at the right of the *Left* option in the *Distance from text* section to display *0.1"* in the measurement box.
  h. Click once on the down-pointing arrow at the right of the *Right* option to display *0.1"* in the measurement box.

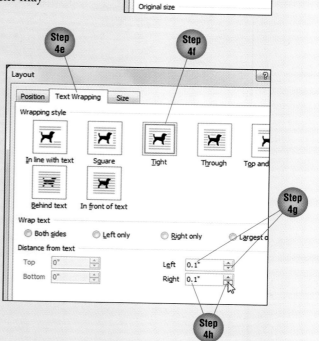

i.   Click the Position tab.
j.   Click the *Alignment* option in the *Horizontal* section.
k.   Click the down-pointing arrow at the right of the *Alignment* option box (in the *Horizontal* section) and then click *Right* at the drop-down list.
l.   Click the down-pointing arrow at the right of the *relative to* option box and then click *Margin* at the drop-down list.
m.   Click the *Absolute position* option in the *Vertical* section. (Skip this step if it is already selected.)
n.   Select the current measurement in the box to the right of the *Absolute position* option and then type 6.6.
o.   Click the down-pointing arrow at the right of the *below* option box and then click *Page* at the drop-down list.
p.   Click the *Lock anchor* check box to insert a check mark.
q.   Remove the check marks from all other options in the *Options* section.
r.   Click OK to close the Layout dialog box.

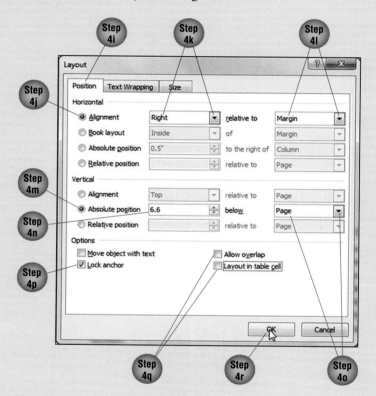

5.   Click outside the image to deselect it.
6.   Manually hyphenate text in the document.
     (The text in Figure 11.10 does not display hyphenation.)
7.   Save **C11-E05-CompCommunications.docx**.

Figure 11.10 Exercises 11.5A and 11.5B

> ### COMPUTERS IN COMMUNICATIONS
>
> Computers were originally stand-alone devices, incapable of communicating with other computers. This changed in the 1970s and 1980s when the development of special telecommunications hardware and software led to the creation of the first private networks, allowing connected computers to exchange data. Exchanged data took the form of requests for information, replies to requests for information, or instructions on how to run programs stored on the network. The ability to link computers enables users to communicate and work together efficiently and effectively. Linked computers have become central to the communications industry. They play a vital role in telecommunications, publishing, and news services.
>
> #### TELECOMMUNICATIONS
>
> The industry that provides for communication across distances is called telecommunications. The telephone industry uses computers to switch and route phone calls automatically over telephone lines. In addition to the spoken word, many other kinds of information move over such lines, including faxes and computer data. Data can be sent from computer to computer over telephone lines using a device known as a modem. One kind of data frequently sent by modem is electronic mail, or email, which can be sent from person to person via the Internet or an online service. A more recent innovation in telecommunications is teleconferencing, which allows people in various locations to see and hear one another and thus hold virtual meetings.
>
> #### PUBLISHING
>
> Just twenty years ago, book manuscripts were typeset mechanically on a typesetting machine and then reproduced on a printing press. Now anyone who has access to a computer and either a modem or a printer can undertake what has come to be known as electronic publishing. Writers and editors use word processing applications to produce text. Artists and designers use drawing and painting applications to created original graphics, or they use inexpensive scanners to digitize illustrations and photographs (turn them into computer-readable files). Typesetters use personal computers to combine text, illustrations, and photographs. Publishers typically send computer-generated files to printers for production of the film and plates from which books and magazines are printed.
>
> #### NEWS SERVICES
>
> News providers rely on reporters located worldwide. Reporters use email to send, or upload, their stories to wire services. Increasingly, individuals get daily news reports from online services. News can also be accessed from specific providers, such as the *New York Times* or *USA Today*, via the Internet. One of the most popular Internet sites provides continuously updated weather reports.

Ungrouping Images

If you want to edit individual components of a clip art image, ungroup the image. To do this, click the clip art image to make it active, click the Group button in the Arrange group in the Picture Tools Format tab, and then click *Ungroup* at the drop-down list. A dialog box will display telling you that the image is an imported picture and not a group and asks if you want to convert it to a Microsoft Office drawing object. At this message, click the Yes button. With the image ungrouped, the Drawing Tools Format tab displays at the top of the ribbon but it is not active. Click the Drawing Tools Format tab to make it active, click the specific component of the image you want to format, and then use buttons on the tab to apply formatting.

1. With **C11-E05-CompCommunications.docx** open, press Ctrl + N to open a new blank document. (You will ungroup and format an image in the blank document and then copy it to the **C11-E05-CompCommunications.docx** document.)

2. Insert a clip art image from the Chapter11 folder you copied to your storage medium by completing the following steps:

   a. Click the Insert tab and then click the Picture button in the Illustrations group.

   b. At the Insert Picture dialog box, navigate to the Chapter11 folder on your storage medium and then double-click **laptop.wmf**.

   c. With the image inserted in the document and the Picture Tools Format tab active, click the Group button in the Arrange group and then click *Ungroup* at the drop-down list.

   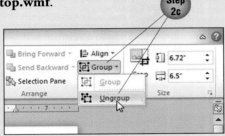

   d. At the message telling you the image is an imported picture and not a group and asking if you want to convert it to a Microsoft Office drawing object, click the Yes button.

3. Format specific components of the image by completing the following steps:

   a. Click the Drawing Tools Format tab to make it active.

   b. Click on the yellow color that displays behind the laptop computer.

   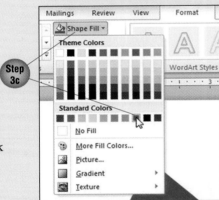

   c. Click the Shape Fill button arrow in the Shape Styles group and then click the blue color in the *Standard Colors* section of the drop-down palette.

   d. Click the gray color inside the laptop monitor, click the Shape Fill button arrow in the Shape Styles group, and then click the light blue color that displays in the *Standard Colors* section.

   e. Click the light teal color that displays behind the keys on the laptop and then click the Shape Fill button. (This applies the light blue fill color since that was the last color you selected.)

   f. Click the red color that displays inside the laptop monitor, click the Shape Fill button arrow, and then click the light green color in the *Standard Colors* section.

4. Change the text wrapping and size then copy and paste the image by completing the following steps:

   a. Click on the border of the image. (This selects the entire image, not just a component of the image.)

   b. Click the Wrap Text button and then click *Tight* at the drop-down list.

   c. Click in the *Shape Height* measurement box, type 1.4, and then press the Enter key.

   d. Click the Home tab and then click the Copy button in the Clipboard group.

   e. Click the Word button on the Taskbar and then click the thumbnail representing *C11-E05-CompCommunications.docx*.

   f. Click the Paste button in the Illustrations group in the Home tab.

   g. With the image inserted in the document, drag the image so it is positioned as shown in Figure 11.10. (When dragging the image, make sure you use the gray border around the entire image.)

h. Drag the computer image you inserted in the document in Exercise 11.5A so it is positioned as shown in Figure 11.10.

5. Save, print, and then close **C11-E05-CompCommunications.docx**.

6. Close the document containing the laptop image without saving the document.

Creating SmartArt

With the SmartArt feature in Word you can insert diagrams and organizational charts in a document. SmartArt offers a variety of predesigned diagrams and organizational charts that are available at the Choose a SmartArt Graphic dialog box, shown in Figure 11.11. At this dialog box, *All* is selected in the left panel, and all available predesigned diagrams display in the middle panel.

Figure 11.11 **Choose a SmartArt Graphic Dialog Box**

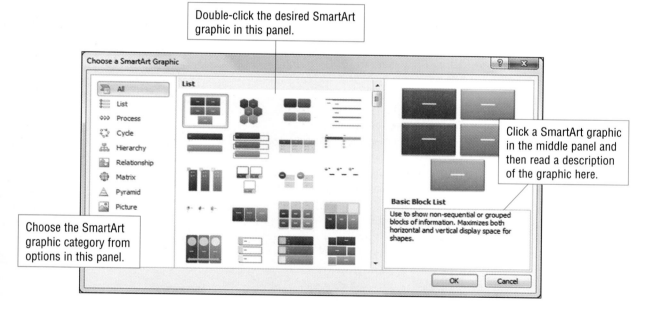

Double-click the desired SmartArt graphic in this panel.

Click a SmartArt graphic in the middle panel and then read a description of the graphic here.

Choose the SmartArt graphic category from options in this panel.

Inserting and Formatting a SmartArt Diagram

Predesigned diagrams display in the middle panel of the Choose a SmartArt Graphic dialog box. Use the scroll bar at the right of the middle panel to scroll down the list of diagram choices. Click a diagram in the middle panel, and the name of the diagram displays in the right panel along with a description of the diagram type. SmartArt includes diagrams for presenting a list of data; showing data processes, cycles, and relationships; and presenting data in a matrix or pyramid. Double-click a diagram in the middle panel of the dialog box and the diagram is inserted in the document.

When the diagram is inserted in the document, a text pane may display at the left of the diagram. You can insert text in the diagram by typing in the text pane or directly in the diagram. Apply design formatting to a diagram with options in the SmartArt Tools Design tab, shown in Figure 11.12. This tab is active when the diagram is inserted in the document. With options and buttons in this tab, you can add objects, change the diagram layout, apply a style to the diagram, and reset the diagram back to the original formatting.

Insert a SmartArt Diagram
1. Click Insert tab.
2. Click SmartArt button.
3. Double-click desired diagram.

SmartArt

Figure 11.12 SmartArt Tools Design Tab

Exercise 11.6A   Inserting and Formatting a Diagram   Part 1 of 2

1. At a blank document, insert the diagram shown in Figure 11.13 by completing the following steps:
   a. Click the Insert tab.
   b. Click the SmartArt button in the Illustrations group.
   c. At the Choose a SmartArt Graphic dialog box, click *Process* in the left panel and then double-click the *Alternating Flow* diagram (see image at right).
   d. If a *Type your text here* text pane does not display at the left side of the diagram, click the Text Pane button in the Create Graphic group to display the pane.
   e. With the insertion point positioned after the top bullet in the *Type your text here* text pane, type Design.
   f. Click *[Text]* that displays below *Design* and then type Mock-up.
   g. Continue clicking occurrences of *[Text]* and typing text so the text pane displays as shown at the right.
   h. Close the text pane by clicking the Close button (marked with an X) that displays in the upper right corner of the pane. (You can also click the Text Pane button in the Create Graphic group.)
   i. Click inside the diagram border but outside any shape. (This deselects any shapes but keeps the diagram selected.)
2. Change the diagram colors by clicking the Change Colors button in the SmartArt Styles group and then clicking the first option in the *Colorful* section (*Colorful - Accent Colors*).

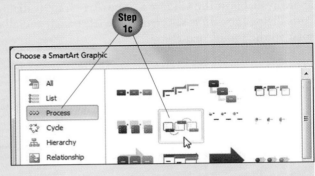

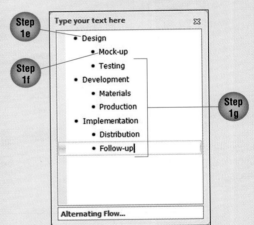

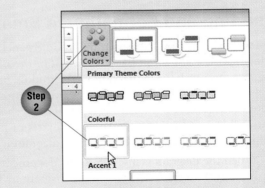

3. Apply a style by clicking the More button that displays at the right of the thumbnails in the SmartArt Styles group and then clicking the second option from the left in the top row of the *3-D* section (*Inset*).

4. Copy the diagram and then change the layout by completing the following steps:
   a. Click the Home tab.
   b. Click the Copy button in the Clipboard group.
   c. Press Ctrl + End, press the Enter key once, and then press Ctrl + Enter to insert a page break.
   d. Click the Paste button in the Clipboard group.
   e. Click the bottom diagram in the document.
   f. Click the SmartArt Tools Design tab.
   g. Click the More button that displays at the right of the thumbnails in the Layouts group and then click the *Continuous Block Process* layout.
   h. Click outside the diagram to deselect it.

5. Save the document and name it **C11-E06-Diagrams**.

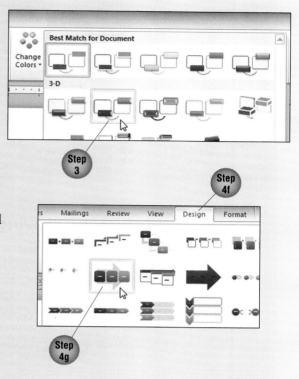

Figure 11.13 Exercise 11.6A

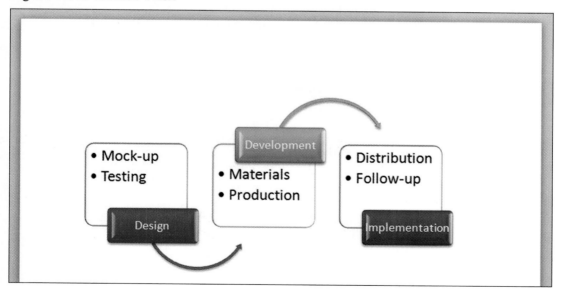

Apply formatting to a diagram with options in the SmartArt Tools Format tab, shown in Figure 11.14. With options and buttons in this tab, you can change the size and shape of objects in the diagram; apply shape styles and WordArt styles; change the shape fill, outline, and effects; and arrange and size the diagram.

Figure 11.14 SmartArt Tools Format Tab

Arranging and Moving a SmartArt Diagram

Before moving a SmartArt diagram, you must select a text wrapping style. Select a text wrapping style with the Position or Wrap Text buttons in the SmartArt Tools Format tab. Click the Position button, and then click the desired position at the drop-down gallery or click the Wrap Text button and then click the desired wrapping style at the drop-down list. Move the diagram by positioning the arrow pointer on the diagram border until the pointer turns into a four-headed arrow, holding down the left mouse button, and then dragging the diagram to the desired location.

Exercise 11.6B Formatting Diagrams   Part 2 of 2

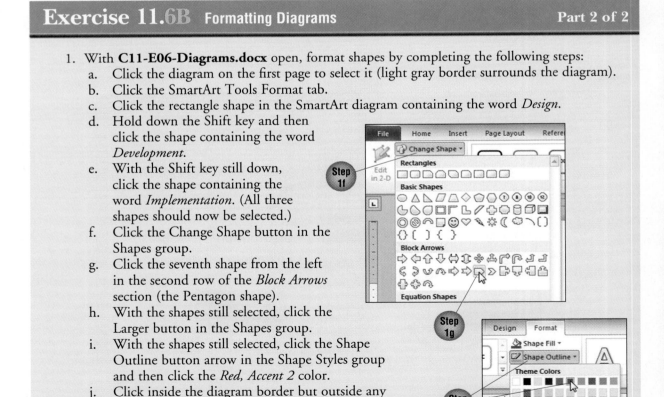

1. With **C11-E06-Diagrams.docx** open, format shapes by completing the following steps:
   a. Click the diagram on the first page to select it (light gray border surrounds the diagram).
   b. Click the SmartArt Tools Format tab.
   c. Click the rectangle shape in the SmartArt diagram containing the word *Design*.
   d. Hold down the Shift key and then click the shape containing the word *Development*.
   e. With the Shift key still down, click the shape containing the word *Implementation*. (All three shapes should now be selected.)
   f. Click the Change Shape button in the Shapes group.
   g. Click the seventh shape from the left in the second row of the *Block Arrows* section (the Pentagon shape).
   h. With the shapes still selected, click the Larger button in the Shapes group.
   i. With the shapes still selected, click the Shape Outline button arrow in the Shape Styles group and then click the *Red, Accent 2* color.
   j. Click inside the diagram border but outside any shape. (This deselects the shapes but keeps the diagram selected.)

2. Change the size of the diagram by completing the
   following steps:
   a. Click the Size button located at the right side of the tab.
   b. Select the current measurement in the Shape Height
       measurement box, type 4, and then press the Enter key.
3. Click the Position button and then click the middle option
   in the second row of the *With Text Wrapping* section (the
   Position in Middle Center with Square Text Wrapping option).

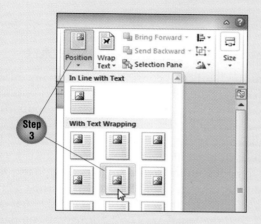

4. Format the bottom diagram by completing
   the following steps:
   a. Press Ctrl + End to move to the end
       of the document and then click in the
       bottom diagram to select it.
   b. Hold down the Shift key and then click
       each of the three shapes.
   c. Click the More button at the right of
       the style thumbnails in the WordArt
       Styles group.
   d. Click the last WordArt style in the
       lower right corner of the drop-down
       gallery (*Fill - Blue, Accent 1, Metal
       Bevel, Reflection*).
   e. Click the Text Outline button arrow
       in the WordArt Styles group and
       then click the light blue color in the
       Standard Colors section (the seventh
       color from the left).
   f. Click the Text Effects button in
       the WordArt Styles group, point to
       Glow at the drop-down list, and then
       click the last option in the top row
       (*Orange, 5 pt glow, Accent color 6*).
   g. Click inside the diagram border but
       outside any shape.

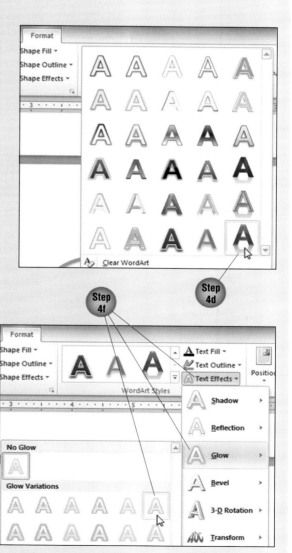

h. Click the third shape (containing the title *Implementation*) and then change the fill color by clicking the Shape Fill button arrow and then clicking the *Purple, Accent 4, Lighter 40%* color.

i. Click inside the diagram border but outside the shape.

5. Arrange the diagram by clicking the Position button and then clicking the middle option in the second row of the *With Text Wrapping* section (the *Position in Middle Center with Square Text Wrapping* option).

6. Save, print, and then close **C11-E06-Diagrams.docx**.

Creating an Organizational Chart with SmartArt

QUICK STEPS

Insert an Organizational Chart
1. Click Insert tab.
2. Click SmartArt button.
3. Click *Hierarchy*.
4. Double-click desired organizational chart.

If you need to visually illustrate hierarchical data, consider creating an organizational chart with a SmartArt option. To display organizational chart SmartArt options, click the Insert tab and then click the SmartArt button in the Illustrations group. At the Choose a SmartArt Graphic dialog box, click *Hierarchy* in the left panel. Organizational chart options display in the middle panel of the dialog box. Double-click the desired organizational chart, and the chart is inserted in the document. Type text in a chart by selecting the shape and then typing text in the shape, or you can type text in the *Type your text here* window that displays at the left of the diagram. Format a SmartArt organizational chart with options and buttons in the SmartArt Tools Design tab, similar to the one shown in Figure 11.12, and the SmartArt Tools Format tab, similar to the one shown in Figure 11.14.

Exercise 11.7 Creating and Formatting an Organizational Chart   Part 1 of 1

1. At a blank document, create the organizational chart shown in Figure 11.15. To begin, click the Insert tab.

2. Click the SmartArt button in the Illustrations group.

3. At the Choose a SmartArt Graphic dialog box, click *Hierarchy* in the left panel of the dialog box and then double-click the first option in the middle panel, *Organization Chart*.

4. If a *Type your text here* pane displays at the left side of the organizational chart, close the pane by clicking the Text Pane button in the Create Graphic group.

5. Delete one of the boxes in the organizational chart by clicking the border of the box in the lower right corner to select it and then pressing the Delete key. (Make sure that the selection border that surrounds the box is a solid line and not a dashed line. If a dashed line displays, click the box border again. This should change it to a solid line.)

6. With the bottom right box selected, click the Add Shape button arrow and then click the *Add Shape Below* option.

7. Click *[Text]* in the top box, type Susan Garner, press the Enter key, and then type President. Click in each of the remaining boxes and type the text as shown in Figure 11.15.

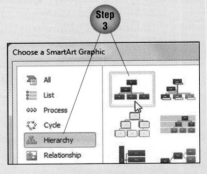

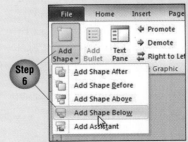

8. Click the More button located at the right of the style thumbnails in the SmartArt Styles group and then click the *Inset* style in the *3-D* section (second option from the left in the top row of the *3-D* section).

9. Click the Change Colors button in the SmartArt Styles group and then click the *Colorful Range - Accent Colors 4 to 5* in the *Colorful* section (fourth option from the left in the *Colorful* section).

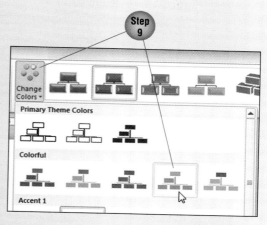

10. Click the SmartArt Tools Format tab.

11. Click the tab (displays with a right- and left-pointing triangle) that displays at the left side of the diagram border. (This displays the *Type your text here* window.)

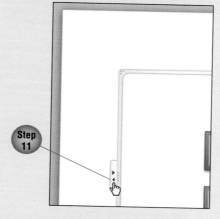

12. Using the mouse, select the text that displays in the *Type your text here* window.

13. Click the Change Shape button in the Shapes group and then click the *Round Same Side Corner Rectangle* option (second option from the right in the top row).

14. Click the Shape Outline button in the Shape Styles group and then click the dark blue color (second color from the right in the *Standard Colors* section).

15. Close the *Type your text here* window by clicking the Close button (marked with an X) located in the upper right corner of the window.

16. Click inside the organizational chart border but outside any shape.

17. Click the Size button, click the Shape Height measurement box, and type 4.

18. Click the Size button, click in the Shape Width measurement box, type 6.5, and then press the Enter key.

19. Insert a caption by clicking the References tab and then clicking the Insert Caption button in the Captions group. At the Caption dialog box, press the spacebar once, type Company Organizational Structure, and then click OK.

20. Save the document with the name **C11-E07-OrgDiagram**.

21. Print and then close the **C11-E07-OrgDiagram.docx**.

Figure 11.15 Exercise 11.7

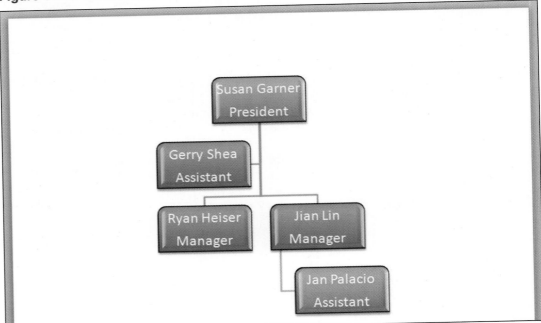

Chapter Eleven

Chapter *Summary*

- Insert an image such as a picture or clip art with buttons in the Illustrations group in the Insert tab.
- To insert a picture, click the Insert tab, click the Picture button, navigate to the desired folder at the Insert Picture dialog box, and then double-click the picture.
- Customize and format an image with options and buttons in the Picture Tools Format tab or with options at the shortcut menu. Display the shortcut menu by right-clicking on the image.
- Size an image with the Shape Height and Shape Width measurement boxes in the Picture Tools Format tab or with the sizing handles that display around a selected image.
- Move an image with options from the Position button drop-down gallery located in the Picture Tools Format tab or by choosing a text wrapping style and then moving the image by dragging it with the mouse.
- You can also move an image using the arrow keys on the keyboard. Hold down the Ctrl key while pressing an arrow key on the keyboard to move the image in small increments.
- To insert a clip art image, click the Insert tab, click the Clip Art button, and then click the desired image in the Clip Art task pane.
- To search for specific types of clip art images, type the desired topic in the *Search for* text box in the Clip Art task pane.
- By default, the Clip Art task pane displays all available media images. Narrow the search to specific locations by clicking the down-pointing arrow at the right of the *Results should be* option and then removing the check mark from any option you do not want searched.
- Use options at the Format Picture dialog box to format an image such as a picture or clip art image. Display this dialog box by clicking the Picture Styles group dialog box launcher in the Picture Tools Format tab.
- At the Format Picture dialog box, click the desired category at the left side of the dialog box and the options at the right side of the dialog box change to reflect the category.
- Customize the layout of images with options at the Layout dialog box. Display this dialog box by clicking the Size group dialog box launcher in the Picture Tools Format tab.
- The Layout dialog box contains three tabs. Click the Position tab to specify the position of the image in the document, click the Text Wrapping tab to specify a wrapping style for the image, and click the Size tab to display options for specifying the height and width of the image.
- To edit individual components of a clip art image, ungroup the image. To do this, click the clip art image to select it, click the Group button in the Arrange group in the Picture Tools Format tab, and then click *Ungroup* at the drop-down list. At the message that displays, click the Yes button.
- Use the SmartArt feature to insert predesigned diagrams and organizational charts in a document.
- Choose a SmartArt diagram at the Choose a SmartArt Graphic dialog box. Display this dialog box by clicking the Insert tab and then clicking the SmartArt button in the Illustrations group.
- Format a SmartArt diagram or organizational chart with options and buttons in the SmartArt Tools Design tab and the SmartArt Tools Format tab.
- To move a SmartArt diagram, first choose a text wrapping style with the Position or Wrap Text buttons in the SmartArt Tools Format tab. After applying a wrapping style, move the diagram by positioning the arrow pointer on the diagram border until the pointer turns into a four-headed arrow, holding down the left mouse button, and then dragging the diagram to the desired location.

Commands *Review*

FEATURE	RIBBON TAB, GROUP	BUTTON
Insert Picture dialog box	Insert, Illustrations	
Clip Art task pane	Insert, Illustrations	
Choose a SmartArt Graphic dialog box	Insert, Illustrations	
Format Picture dialog box	Picture Tools Format, Picture Styles	
Layout dialog box	Picture Tools Format, Style	

Key Points *Review*

Completion: In the space provided at the right, indicate the correct term, symbol, or command.

1. Insert an image in a document with buttons in this group in the Insert tab. _____

2. Click the Picture button in the Insert tab, and this dialog box displays. _____

3. Customize and format an image with options and buttons in this tab. _____

4. Size an image with the sizing handles that display around the selected image or with these boxes in the Picture Tools Format tab. _____

5. To move an image in small increments, hold down this key while pressing an arrow key on the keyboard. _____

6. Click the Clip Art button in the Insert tab, and this displays at the right side of the screen. _____

7. Click this dialog box launcher at the Picture Tools Format tab to display the Format Picture dialog box. _____

8. The Layout dialog box contains three tabs: Position, Size, and this. _____

9. With options in the Layout dialog box with this tab selected, you can specify horizontal and vertical layout options. _____

10. If you want to edit individual components of a clip art image, do this to the image. _____

11. The SmartArt button is located in this tab. _____

12. Click the SmartArt button and this dialog box displays. _____

13. Insert a SmartArt diagram in a document and this tab is active. _____

14. If you need to visually illustrate hierarchical data, consider creating this with the SmartArt feature. _____

Chapter *Assessments*

Applying Your Skills

Demonstrate your knowledge of features learned in this chapter by completing the following assessments.

Assessment 11.1   Create a Flyer with a Picture and Text

1. At a blank document, press the Enter key three times, type Ocean View Condominiums, press the Enter key, and then type 1-888-555-6570.
2. Press Ctrl + Home and then insert the picture **Ocean.jpg** with the following specifications:
   a. Change the position to *Position in Top Center with Square Text Wrapping*.
   b. Change the text wrapping to *Behind Text*.
   c. Change the width to 4.5 inches.
   d. Correct the brightness and contrast to Brightness: *-20%* Contrast: *+20%*.
3. Select the text, change the font to 26-point Script MT Bold and the text color to white, and then center the text.
4. Save the document with the name **C11-A01-OVC**.
5. Print and then close **C11-A01-OVC.docx**.

Assessment 11.2   Insert and Format a Clip Art Image

1. Open **PremPro.docx** and save the document with the name **C11-A02-PremPro**.
2. Insert in the document a clip art image related to fruits or vegetables. Format, size, and position the clip art image attractively on the page.
3. Save, print, and then close **C11-A02-PremPro.docx**.

Assessment 11.3   Insert and Format a Clip Art Image in a Data Security Training Notice

1. Open **DataTraining.docx** and save the document with the name **C11-A03-DataTraining**.
2. Insert the clip art image shown in Figure 11.16 using the search word *computer*. (The original clip art image contains white lines on a blue background.)
3. Display the Format Picture dialog box and make the following changes:
   a. Click *Fill* at the left side of the dialog box, click the *Gradient fill* option, click the Preset colors button, and then click the *Moss* option.
   b. Click *Shadow* at the left side of the dialog box, click the Presets button, and then click the *Inside Top* option (in the *Inner* section).
   c. Click *Reflection* at the left side of the dialog box, click the Presets button, and then click the *Tight Reflection, touching* option.
4. Change the text wrapping to *Square*.
5. Change the shape height measurement to *2"*.
6. Display the Layout dialog box with the Position tab selected and then change the horizontal absolute position to *4.5"* and the vertical absolute position to *1.1"*. **Hint: Display the Layout dialog box by clicking the Size group dialog box launcher in the Picture Tools Format tab.**
7. Apply green paragraph shading to the title as shown in Figure 11.16 and change the title text color to white.
8. Save, print, and then close **C11-A03-DataTraining.docx**.

Figure 11.16 Assessment 11.3

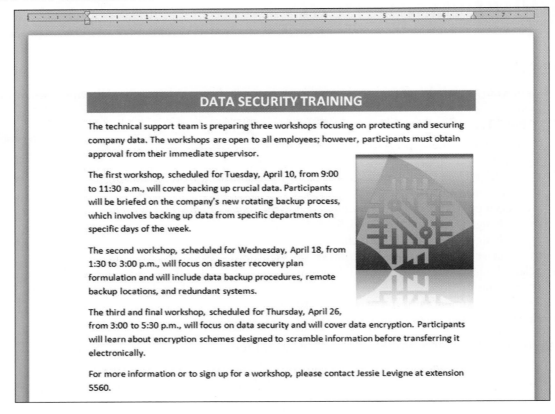

DATA SECURITY TRAINING

The technical support team is preparing three workshops focusing on protecting and securing company data. The workshops are open to all employees; however, participants must obtain approval from their immediate supervisor.

The first workshop, scheduled for Tuesday, April 10, from 9:00 to 11:30 a.m., will cover backing up crucial data. Participants will be briefed on the company's new rotating backup process, which involves backing up data from specific departments on specific days of the week.

The second workshop, scheduled for Wednesday, April 18, from 1:30 to 3:00 p.m., will focus on disaster recovery plan formulation and will include data backup procedures, remote backup locations, and redundant systems.

The third and final workshop, scheduled for Thursday, April 26, from 3:00 to 5:30 p.m., will focus on data security and will cover data encryption. Participants will learn about encryption schemes designed to scramble information before transferring it electronically.

For more information or to sign up for a workshop, please contact Jessie Levigne at extension 5560.

Assessment 11.4   Insert, Ungroup, and Recolor a Clip Art Image in a Vacation Document

1. Open **VacAdventure.docx** and save the document with the name **C11-A04-VacAdventure**.
2. Complete a grammar and spelling check on the document. (Be sure to proofread the document after completing the grammar and spelling check since some mistakes will be passed over.)
3. Insert the clip art image shown in Figure 11.17 with the following specifications:
   a. Use the word *travel* to search for the clip art image.
   b. Change the text wrapping of the clip art image to *Square*.
   c. Change the height measurement to *2.7"*.
   d. Ungroup the clip art image.
   e. Recolor individual components in the clip art so it appears as shown in Figure 11.17.
   f. Move the clip art image so it is positioned as shown in Figure 11.17.
4. Save, print, and then close **C11-A04-VacAdventure.docx**.

Assessment 11.5   Create and Format a Cycle Design

1. At a blank document, create the SmartArt cycle diagram shown in Figure 11.18 with the following specifications:
   a. Use the *Basic Radial* cycle diagram.
   b. Add a shape.
   c. Apply the *Polished* SmartArt style.
   d. Change the colors to *Colorful Range – Accent Colors 3 to 4*.
   e. Change the height of the SmartArt diagram to *5.5"* and the width to *6.5"*.
   f. Type the text in the shapes as shown in Figure 11.18.
2. Save the completed document and name it **C11-A05-TECDiagram**.
3. Print and then close **C11-A05-TECDiagram.docx**.

Figure 11.17 Assessment 11.4

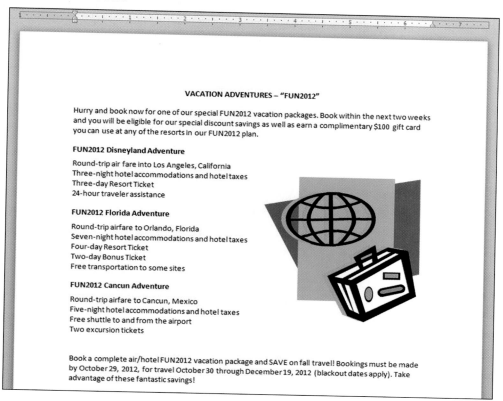

Figure 11.18 Assessment 11.5

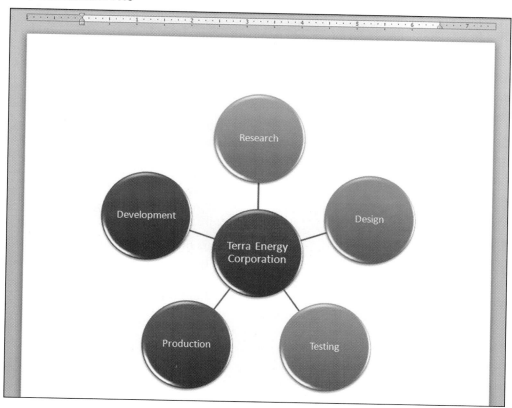

Assessment 11.6   Create and Format a SmartArt Organizational Chart

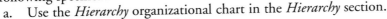

1. At a blank document, create the organizational chart shown in Figure 11.19 with the following specifications:
   a. Use the *Hierarchy* organizational chart in the *Hierarchy* section.
   b. Select the top text box and insert a shape above.
   c. Select the top right text box and then add a shape below.
   d. Apply the *Colorful Range - Accent Colors 2 to 3* option.
   e. Increase the height to 4.5 inches and the width to 6.5 inches.
   f. Type the text in each text box as shown in Figure 11.19.
   g. Position the organizational chart in the middle of the page.
2. Save the document with the name **C11-A06-OrgChart**.
3. Print and then close **C11-A06-OrgChart.docx**.

Figure 11.19 Assessment 11.6

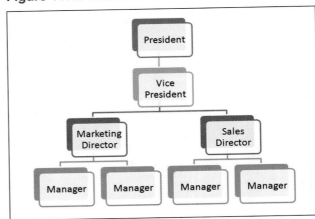

Expanding Your Skills

Explore additional feature options or use Help to learn a new skill in creating this document.

Assessment 11.7   Create a Flyer

1. Create the flyer shown in Figure 11.20 with the following specifications:
   - Set the text in Comic Sans MS (you determine the point size).
   - Insert and format the paragraph borders and page border as shown in the figure. (Create the border below the title as a bottom border of the title *Pugs on Parade*. At the Borders and Shading dialog box, choose the third line style from the end of the *Style* list box and change the color to dark red.)
   - Insert the ***Pug.jpg*** picture (use the Picture button in the Insert tab).
   - Click the Remove Background button in the Picture Tools Format tab and then experiment with the options for marking areas to keep and marking areas to remove. Learn how to use the Delete Mark, Discard All Changes, and Keep Changes buttons. Remove and/or keep backgrounds so your picture displays as shown in Figure 11.20. (This may take some practice to be able to remove and/or keep the necessary backgrounds for the picture.)
   - Change the text wrapping for the picture to *Behind Text* and then size and position the picture as shown in the figure.
   - Make any other changes so your document appears the same as Figure 11.20.
2. Check to make sure the entire page border will print. If it will not, increase the measurements at the Border and Shading Options dialog box.
3. Save the completed document and name it **C11-A07-PugFlyer**.
4. Print and then close **C11-A07-PugFlyer.docx**.

Figure 11.20 Assessment 11.7

Pugs on Parade!

Come join us for the fifth annual "Pugs on Parade"
party, Saturday, July 7, at Mercer Way Park
from 1:00 to 3:00 p.m.

Admission is free!

Prizes will be awarded for the best costumes.

Achieving Signature Status

Take your skills to the next level by completing these more challenging assessments.

Assessment 11.8   Ungroup and Recolor a Clip Art Image

1. At a blank document, create the document shown in Figure 11.21 with the
   following specifications:
   a. Insert the clip art image by opening the document named **TECLogo.docx** and
      then copying the clip art image from the **TECLogo.docx** document and pasting
      it into the blank document. (Do not use the Clip Art button to do this.)
   b. Flip the clip art image, ungroup the image, and recolor components so your clip art image
      displays the same as the image in Figure 11.21.
   c. Type the text in the document as shown in Figure 11.21.
   d. Set the title in Copperplate Gothic bold. Make any other formatting changes so your
      document is formatted the same as the document in Figure 11.21.

2. Save the completed document and name it **C11-A08-TECRevs**.
3. Print and then close **C11-A08-TECRevs.docx**.
4. Close **TECLogo.docx** without saving changes.

Figure 11.21 Assessment 11.8

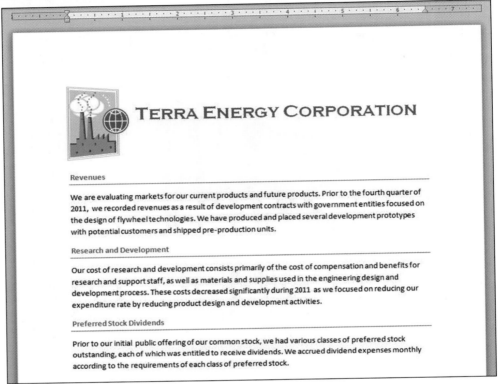

Assessment 11.9   Create and Format a SmartArt Diagram

START From Scratch

1. At a blank document, create the SmartArt diagram shown in Figure 11.22 with the following specifications:
   a. Use the *Pyramid List* diagram.
   b. Apply the *Inset* SmartArt style.
   c. Change the color to purple (*Colorful Range - Accent Colors 4 to 5*).
   d. Apply light green shape-fill color to the bottom shape, light blue fill color to the middle shape, and red fill color to the top shape.
   e. Type the text in each shape as shown in Figure 11.22.
2. Save the document with the name **C11-A09-Levels**.
3. Print and then close **C11-A09-Levels.docx**.

Figure 11.22 Assessment 11.9

Red Level
$150,000+

Blue Level
$100,000 - $149,999

Green Level
$75,000 - $99,999

Chapter 12

SNAP TUTORIALS

Tutorial 12.1
Creating and Inserting a
Screenshot
Tutorial 12.2
Inserting and Formatting a
Shape
Tutorial 12.3
Inserting and Formatting Text
Boxes
Tutorial 12.4
Inserting and Customizing a
Pull Quote
Tutorial 12.5
Inserting and Modifying
WordArt
Tutorial 12.6
Applying Character Formatting
Tutorial 12.7
Using OpenType Features
Tutorial 12.8
Applying Text Effects

Inserting Shapes and WordArt

Performance Objectives

Upon successful completion of Chapter 12, you will be able to:

- Insert and format screenshot images
- Draw and format shapes
- Select and align objects
- Insert predesigned pull quote text boxes
- Draw and format text boxes
- Link text boxes
- Insert, format, and customize WordArt
- Apply character spacing, OpenType features, and text effects

In the previous chapter, you learned to use buttons in the Illustrations group such as the Picture, Clip Art, and SmartArt buttons. The Illustrations group also contains a Screenshot button you can use to capture the contents of a screen as an image or capture a portion of the screen. In this chapter, you will learn how to create and insert screenshot images in a document as well as other elements. In earlier chapters you learned to insert symbols, special characters, drop caps, and images to enhance the visual appeal of your documents. Other elements you can use to improve a document's visual appeal include shapes, text boxes, and WordArt. With the Shapes button in the Illustrations group in the Insert tab, you can draw a variety of shapes. You can then customize those shapes with options in the Drawing Tools Format tab. You can use the Text Box button, also in the Insert tab, to draw and insert a text box in your document, and you can customize the text box with options in the Drawing Tools Format tab. With the WordArt feature you can distort or modify text to conform to a variety of shapes. Use options at the Font dialog box with the Advanced tab selected to apply character spacing to text; apply OpenType features such as ligatures, number styles, and stylistic sets; and apply text effects.

Note: Before beginning computer exercises for this chapter, copy to your storage medium the Chapter12 folder from the CD that accompanies this textbook and then make Chapter12 the active folder.

In this chapter students will produce the following documents:

Exercise 12.1. C12-E01-BackstageViews.docx
Exercise 12.1. C12-E01-TECCoverPages.docx
Exercise 12.2. C12-E02-LelandFS.docx
Exercise 12.3. C12-E03-Hawaii.docx
Exercise 12.4. C12-E04-PRDonorApp.docx

Model answers for these exercises are shown on the following pages.

Save & Send Backstage View

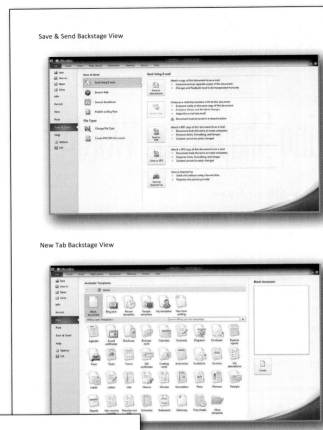

Exercise 12.1

C12-E01-BackstageViews.docx

New Tab Backstage View

TERRA ENERGY CORPORATION

SAMPLE COVER PAGES

Exercise 12.1

C12-E01-TECCoverPages.docx

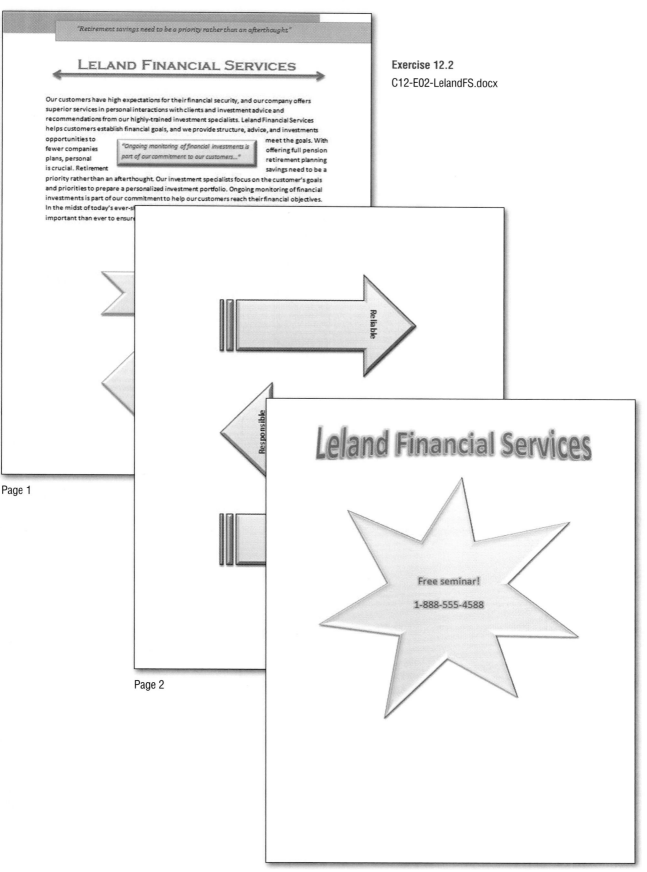

Page 1

Page 2

Page 3

Exercise 12.3

C12-E03-Hawaii.docx

HAWAII

RAINY DAY ACTIVITIES

Expect to have a rainy day or two during your vacation, especially in the winter months between November and March. With a little planning, you can have just as much fun indoors as outdoors. To make the most of a rainy day, enjoy one of the activities listed below.

- **Movies:** Take advantage of matinee prices. The Sunshine Marketplace Theaters offer discount tickets and current feature films.
- **Shopping:** Most of the area shopping centers are "open-air" complexes with some roof covering, ideal havens from the rain. Visit the Coconut Grove Shopping Center or the Kukui Shopping Village.
- **Museums:** Learn about the history of Hawaii through murals, artifacts, and artwork by visiting one of several museums located throughout the islands. Most museums offer special family activities the first Saturday of each month.
- **Theater:** Several local community performing arts centers offer annual productions for children and adults. Admission prices are very affordable, and most theaters have special matinee prices.

KAUAI SIGHTS

- **Na Pali Coast:** Unless you are a rugged hiker, you can see this fifteen-mile, spectacular landmark only by air or boat.
- **North Shore:** Find shadowy mountains, lush valleys, and spectacular coastlines along a string of one-lane bridges.
- **Hanalei Valley Lookout:** Pull over to see wetland taro fields with a backdrop of purple mountains.
- **Kilauea Point:** This National Wildlife Refuge is home to nesting seabirds and an original lighthouse.
- **Sleeping Giant:** Nounou Mountain provides the "man in repose" profile best seen from Kuhio Highway 56 in Kapaa.
- **Coconut Coast:** You will know when you are here because palm trees line Kuhio Highway 56 on the island's east side.

Phoenix Rising

Donor Appreciation

*Enjoy the "flavor of Tanzania"
and an evening of cultural entertainment...*

We want to show our appreciation to all of our donors by offering an evening of fine foods, cultural entertainment, and a presentation by our international advocate. Your evening begins at 6:00 p.m. and includes:

- ✦ Social hour from 6:00 to 7:00 p.m.
- ✦ Opening remarks by the president of Phoenix Rising
- ✦ Five-course meal of traditional Tanzanian dishes
- ✦ Tanzanian music and entertainment
- ✦ Presentation by Renate Santorini, the international advocate for Phoenix Rising

Donation Goal for 2013 – 2014
$3,500,000

Please call the Phoenix Rising office to let us know if you will be joining us.

1500 Frontier Avenue ✦ Eugene, OR 97440 ✦ 541-555-4110

Exercise 12.4

C12-E04-PRDonorApp.docx

Creating Screenshots

The Illustrations group in the Insert tab contains a Screenshot button, which you can use to capture the contents of a screen as an image or capture a portion of a screen. If you want to capture the entire screen, open a new document, click the Insert tab, click the Screenshot button, and then click the desired screen thumbnail at the drop-down list. The currently active document does not display as a thumbnail at the drop-down list, only any other file or program you have open. If you do not have another file or program open, the Windows desktop displays. When you click the desired thumbnail, the screenshot is inserted as an image in the open document, the image is selected, and the Picture Tools Format tab is active. Use buttons in this tab to customize the screenshot image.

QUICK STEPS

Insert Screenshot
1. Open blank document.
2. Open another document.
3. Display desired information in document.
4. Make blank document active.
5. Click Insert tab.
6. Click Screenshot button.
7. Click desired window at drop-down list.

Screenshot

Exercise 12.1A   **Inserting and Formatting a Screenshot**   **Part 1 of 2**

1. Open a blank document.
2. Open a second blank document, type Save & Send Tab Backstage View at the left margin, and then press the Enter key.
3. Save the document and name it **C12-E01-BackstageViews**.
4. Click the Word button on the Taskbar and then click the thumbnail representing the blank document.

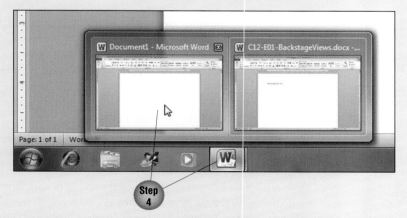

5. Display the Save & Send tab Backstage view by clicking the File tab and then clicking the Save & Send tab.
6. Click the Word button on the Taskbar and then click the **C12-E01-BackstageViews.docx** thumbnail.
7. Insert and format a screenshot of the Save & Send tab Backstage view by completing the following steps:

a. Click the Insert tab.

b. Click the Screenshot button in the Illustrations group and then click the thumbnail that displays in the drop-down list. (This inserts a screenshot of the Save & Send tab Backstage view in the document.)

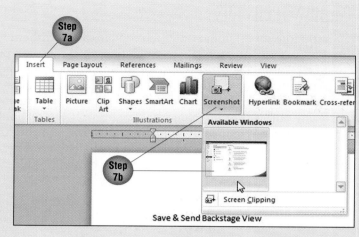

c. With the screenshot image selected, click the More button that displays at the right side of the thumbnails in the Picture Styles group and then click the *Drop Shadow Rectangle* option (approximately the fourth option from the left in the top row).

d. Select the measurement in the *Shape Width* text box, type 5.5, and then press the Enter key.

8. Press Ctrl + End and then press the Enter key. (This moves the insertion point below the screenshot image.)

9. Type New Tab Backstage View at the left margin and then press the Enter key.

10. Click the Word button on the Taskbar and then click the thumbnail representing the blank document (contains the image of the Save & Send tab Backstage view).

11. At the Backstage view, click the New tab. (This displays the New tab Backstage view.)

12. Click the Word button on the Taskbar and then click the **C12-E01-BackstageViews.docx** thumbnail.

13. Insert and format a screenshot of the New tab Backstage view by completing Step 7.

14. Decrease the size of both screenshots so they both fit on one page.

15. Press Ctrl + Home to move the insertion point to the beginning of the document.

16. Save, print, and then close **C12-E01-BackstageViews.docx**.

17. At the New tab Backstage view, click the File tab and then close the document without saving it.

Insert Screen Clipping

1. Open blank document.
2. Open another document.
3. Display desired information in document.
4. Make blank document active.
5. Click Insert tab.
6. Click Screenshot button.
7. Click *Screen Clipping*.
8. Drag to specify area in document to capture.

In addition to making a screenshot of an entire screen, you can make a screenshot of a specific portion of the screen by clicking the *Screen Clipping* option at the Screenshot button drop-down list. When you click this option, the other open document, file, or Windows desktop displays in a dimmed manner and the mouse pointer displays as a crosshair. Using the mouse, draw a border around the specific area of the screen you want to capture. The specific area you identified is inserted in the other document as an image, the image is selected, and the Picture Tools Format tab is active. If you have only one document or file open when you click the Screenshot tab, clicking the *Screen Clipping* option will cause the Windows desktop to display.

In Chapter 9, you learned how to create a screen capture with the Print Screen button on your keyboard. The advantage of using the Print Screen button is that you can capture an open dialog box, which you cannot do with the Screenshot button. If you use the Print Screen button to create a screen capture and then paste the image in a document, the image is selected and the Picture Tools Format tab is active. Use buttons in this tab to customize the image. The advantage of using the Screenshot button in the Insert tab rather than the Print Screen button is that you can use the *Screen Clipping* option to identify a specific area of the screen that you want to capture.

1. Open **TECLtrhd.docx**, save it, and name it **C12-E01-TECCoverPages**.
2. Type the text Sample Cover Pages and then press the Enter key twice.
3. Select the text you just typed, change the font to 18-point Copperplate Gothic Bold, and then center the text.
4. Press Ctrl + End to move the insertion point below the text.
5. Open the document named **TECCoverPg01.docx**.
6. Click the Word button on the Taskbar and then click the **C12-E01-TECCoverPages.docx** thumbnail.
7. Create and format a screenshot screen clipping by completing the following steps:
   a. Click the Insert tab.
   b. Click the Screenshot button in the Illustrations group and then click *Screen Clipping*.

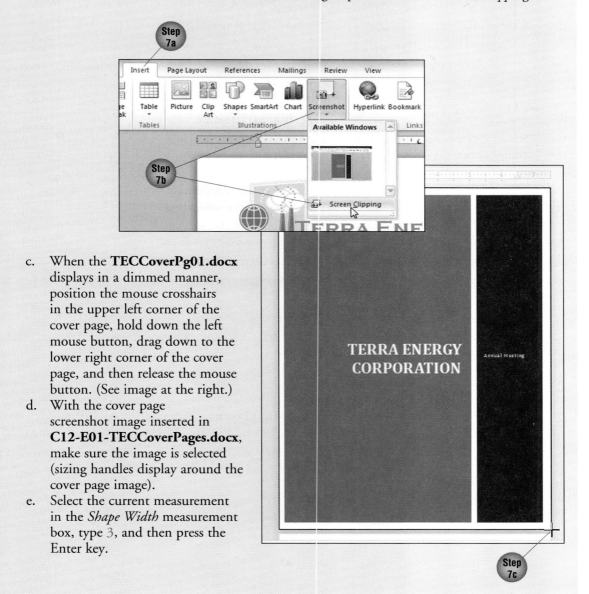

   c. When the **TECCoverPg01.docx** displays in a dimmed manner, position the mouse crosshairs in the upper left corner of the cover page, hold down the left mouse button, drag down to the lower right corner of the cover page, and then release the mouse button. (See image at the right.)
   d. With the cover page screenshot image inserted in **C12-E01-TECCoverPages.docx**, make sure the image is selected (sizing handles display around the cover page image).
   e. Select the current measurement in the *Shape Width* measurement box, type 3, and then press the Enter key.

    f.   Click the Wrap Text button in the Arrange group in the Picture Tools Format tab and then click *Square* at the drop-down gallery.

8. Click the Word button on the Taskbar and then click the **TECCoverPg01.docx** thumbnail.

9. Close **TECCoverPg01.docx**.

10. Open **TECCoverPg02.docx**.

11. Click the Word button on the Taskbar and then click the **C12-E01-TECCoverPages.docx** thumbnail.

12. Create and format a screenshot by completing steps similar to those in Step 7.

13. Position the two cover page screenshot images so they are side by side in the document with some space between the cover pages.

14. Save, print, and then close **C12-E01-TECCoverPages.docx**.

15. Close **TECCoverPg02.docx**.

QUICK STEPS

Draw a Shape
1. Click Insert tab.
2. Click Shapes button.
3. Click desired shape in drop-down list.
4. Drag in document to create shape.

Shapes

Drawing Shapes

With the Shapes button in the Insert tab, you can draw a variety of objects such as lines, basic geometric shapes, block arrows, flowchart shapes, callouts, stars, and banners. When you click a shape at the drop-down list, the mouse pointer displays as a crosshair (plus sign). Click in the document to insert the shape or position the crosshairs where you want the shape to begin, hold down the left mouse button, drag to create the shape, and then release the mouse button. This inserts the shape in the document and also displays the Drawing Tools Format tab, shown in Figure 12.1. Use buttons in this tab to replace the shape with another shape, apply a style to the shape, position or arrange the shape, or change the size of the shape. This tab contains many of the same options and buttons contained in the Picture Tools Format tab.

Figure 12.1 Drawing Tools Format Tab

Drawing Lines

The Shapes button drop-down list includes lines and enclosed shapes. To draw a line, click an option in the *Lines* group. When the mouse pointer changes to a crosshair, position the crosshair in the document and then drag to draw the line. If you want to draw a straight horizontal or vertical line, hold down the Shift key while dragging with the mouse.

1. Open **LelandFS.docx** and then save the document and name it **C12-E02-LelandFS**.
2. Type and format the text shown in Figure 12.2 by completing the following steps:
   a. Press the Enter key and then type Leland Financial Services.
   b. Select the text, change the font to 24-point Copperplate Gothic Bold, the font color to olive green (*Olive Green, Accent 3, Darker 25%*), and then center the text.
   c. Deselect the text.
3. Insert and format the line below the text as shown in Figure 12.2 by completing the following steps:
   a. Click the Insert tab.
   b. Click the Shapes button and then click the third option from the left in the *Lines* section (*Double Arrow*).
   c. Hold down the Shift key and then drag to create a horizontal line that is approximately 6.5 inches in length (see Figure 12.2).
   d. With the line selected, click the More button at the right of the thumbnails in the Shape Styles group and then click the *Intense Line - Accent 3* option.

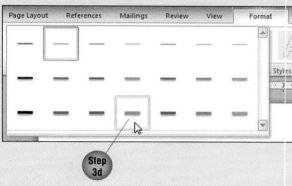

   e. Click the Shape Outline button in the Shadow Styles group and then click the same olive green color you selected for the text (*Olive Green, Accent 3, Darker 25%*).
   f. Click the Shape Effects button in the Shadow Styles group, point to *Shadow*, and then click the *Offset Bottom* option in the *Outer* section.
4. Click outside the line to deselect it.
5. Save **C12-E02-LelandFS.docx**.

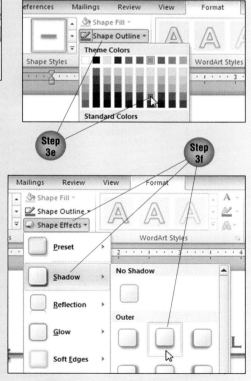

Figure 12.2 Exercise 12.2A

LELAND FINANCIAL SERVICES

Drawing Enclosed Shapes

If you choose a shape in the *Lines* section of the Shapes button drop-down list, the shape you draw is considered a **line drawing.** If you choose an option in one of the other sections of the drop-down list, the shape you draw is considered an **enclosed shape.** When you draw an enclosed shape, you can maintain the shape's proportions by holding down the Shift key while dragging to create the shape. For example, to draw a square, choose the *Rectangle* shape and then hold down the Shift key while drawing the shape. To draw a circle, choose the *Oval* shape and then hold down the Shift key while drawing the shape.

Exercise 12.2B **Drawing and Formatting an Arrow Shape**   Part 2 of 10

1. With **C12-E02-LelandFS.docx** open, press Ctrl + End to move the insertion point to the end of the document.
2. Press Ctrl + Enter to insert a page break.
3. Make sure the horizontal and vertical rulers are visible. If not, click the View Ruler button that displays at the top of the vertical scroll bar.

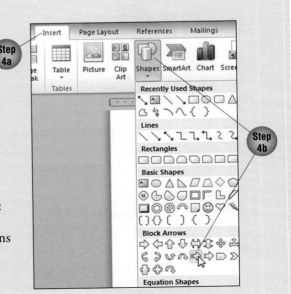

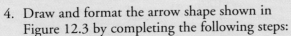

4. Draw and format the arrow shape shown in Figure 12.3 by completing the following steps:
   a. Click the Insert tab.
   b. Click the Shapes button in the Illustrations group and then click the *Striped Right Arrow* shape in the *Block Arrows* section.

c. Position the mouse pointer (which displays as a crosshair) in the document at approximately the 1-inch mark on the horizontal ruler and the 0.5-inch mark on the vertical ruler.

d. Hold down the Shift key and the left mouse button, drag to the right until the tip of the arrow is positioned at approximately the 5.5-inch mark on the horizontal ruler, and then release the mouse button and the Shift key.

5. Format the arrow by completing the following steps:

a. Click in the Shape Height measurement box in the Size group and then type 2.4.

b. Click in the Shape Width measurement box in the Size group, type 4.5, and then press the Enter key.

c. Click the More button at the right of the thumbnails in the Shape Styles group and then click the *Subtle Effect - Olive Green, Accent 3* option at the drop-down gallery.

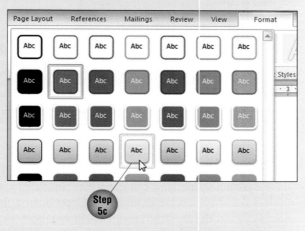

Step 5c

d. Click the Shape Effects button, point to *Bevel*, and then click the *Angle* option in the *Bevel* section.

e. Click the Shape Outline button arrow and then click the dark blue color in the *Standard Colors* section.

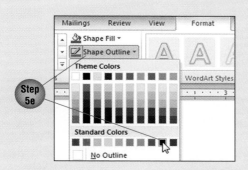

Step 5e

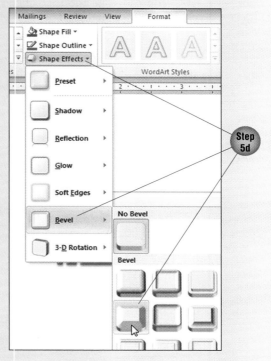

Step 5d

6. Save **C12-E02-LelandFS.docx**.

Figure 12.3 Exercise 12.2B

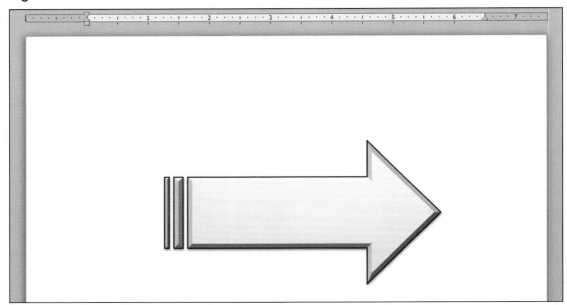

Copy a Shape
1. Select desired shape.
2. Click Copy button.
3. Position insertion point at desired location.
4. Click Paste button.
OR
1. Select desired shape.
2. Hold down Ctrl key.
3. Drag shape to desired location.

Copying Shapes

Once you have drawn a shape, you can copy it to another location in the document. To do this, select the shape and then click the Copy button in the Clipboard group in the Home tab. Position the insertion point at the location where you want to insert the copied image and then click the Paste button. You can also copy a selected shape by holding down the Ctrl key while dragging the shape to the desired location.

Exercise 12.2C Copying a Shape   Part 3 of 10

1. With **C12-E02-LelandFS.docx** open, copy the arrow by completing the following steps:
   a. With the arrow selected, position the mouse pointer on the arrow border until the mouse pointer displays with a four-headed arrow attached and then hold down the Ctrl key.
   b. Drag down until the outline of the copied arrow displays just below the top (original) arrow, release the mouse button, and then release the Ctrl key.

c. Copy the arrow again by holding down the Ctrl key and then dragging the outline of the copied arrow just below the second arrow.
2. Flip the middle arrow by completing the following steps:
   a. Click the middle arrow to select it.
   b. If necessary, click the Drawing Tools Format tab.
   c. Click the Rotate button in the Arrange group and then click *Flip Horizontal* at the drop-down gallery.
3. Save **C12-E02-LelandFS.docx**.

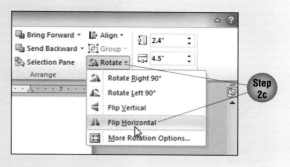

Selecting and Aligning Shapes

If you are working with multiple shapes, you can select the shapes and then apply formatting to the shapes. To select multiple shapes, hold down the Shift key, click each shape you want to select, and then release the Shift key. You can also hold down the Ctrl key and then click the desired shapes.

The Align button in the Arrange group in the Drawing Tools Format tab contains options for aligning multiple shapes in a document. To align shapes, click the desired shapes, click the Align button in the Arrange group, and then click the desired alignment option at the drop-down list. For example, if you want to align all of the shapes at the left side of the page, click the *Align Left* option at the Align button drop-down list. If you want to distribute the selected shapes horizontally on the page, click the *Distribute Horizontally* option at the Align button drop-down list.

Exercise 12.2D   Selecting and Aligning Arrow Shapes   Part 4 of 10

1. With **C12-E02-LelandFS.docx** open, display the arrows on the second page.
2. Select and align the arrows by completing the following steps:
   a. Click the top arrow to select it.
   b. Hold down the Shift key.
   c. Click the middle arrow and then click the bottom arrow.
   d. Release the Shift key.
   e. With the three arrows selected, click the Align button in the Arrange group in the Drawing Tools format tab and then click *Align Left* at the drop-down list.

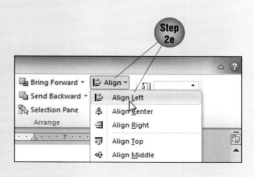

3. Distribute the arrows vertically by clicking the Align button and then clicking *Distribute Vertically* at the drop-down list.
4. Save **C12-E02-LelandFS.docx**.

Inserting Text in a Shape

When you draw a shape in a document, you can type text directly in the shape. Select the text and then use options in the WordArt Styles group in the Drawing Tools Format tab to format text. You can also apply formatting to text in a shape with options available at other tabs such as the Home tab.

Editing a Shape and Points in a Shape

Edit Shape

The Drawing Tools Format tab contains an Edit Shape button in the Insert Shapes group. Click this button and a drop-down list displays with options to change the shape and customize the shape with edit points. Click the Edit Shape button and then point to the *Change Shape* option and a side menu displays with shape options. Click the desired shape option and the shape in the document conforms to the chosen shape. Click the *Edit Points* option at the Edit Shape button drop-down list and the selected shape displays with edit points around the shape. The edit points display as small, black squares at each intersecting point in the shape. To use an edit point, position the mouse pointer on the desired edit point until the pointer displays as a small square surrounded by an up-pointing, right-pointing, down-pointing, and left-pointing triangle. Hold down the left mouse button, drag to the desired position, and then release the mouse button.

Exercise 12.2E   Inserting Text in a Shape and Editing Shape Points   **Part 5 of 10**

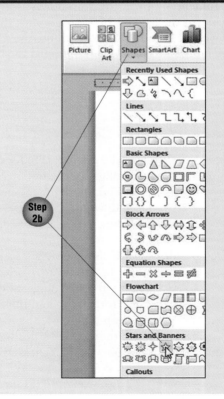

1. With **C12-E02-LelandFS.docx** open, press Ctrl + End to move the insertion point to the end of the document (the insertion point will display above the shapes) and then press Ctrl + Enter to insert a page break. (The shapes will remain on the previous page.)
2. Insert a shape by completing the following steps:
   a. Click the Insert tab.
   b. Click the Shapes button in the Illustrations group and then click the *5-Point Star* shape in the *Stars and Banners* section.
   c. Hold down the Shift key, drag in the document to create a star shape that is approximately 4 inches in height and width, and then release the mouse button and then the Shift key.
   d. With the Drawing Tools Format tab active, click the Shape Height measurement box and then type 4.
   e. Click in the Shape Width measurement box, type 4, and then press the Enter key.

---

3. Change the shape by clicking the Edit Shape button in the Insert Shapes group in the Drawing Tools Format tab, pointing to *Change Shape*, and then click the *7-Point Star* shape in the *Stars and Banners* section in the shapes side menu.

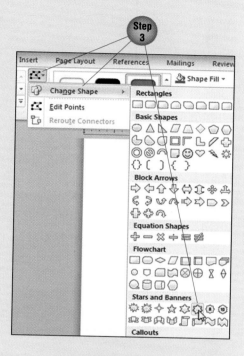

4. Format the shape by completing the following steps:
   a. Click the More button at the right of the thumbnails in the Shape Styles group and then click the *Subtle Effect – Olive Green, Accent 3* option.

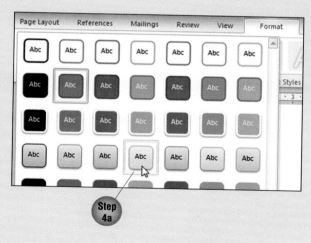

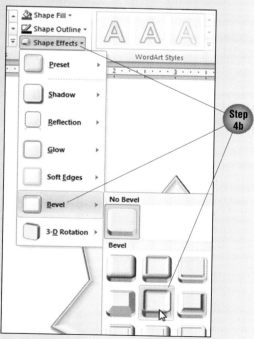

   b. Click the Shape Effects button in the Shape Styles group, point to *Bevel*, and then click the *Soft Round* option in the *Bevel* section.

5. Edit points in the shape by completing the following steps:
   a. Click the Edit Shape button and then click *Edit Points* at the drop-down list.
   b. Using the mouse, position the mouse pointer on the edit point at the outside of the top left point, drag up and out as shown in the image at the right, and then release the mouse button.

   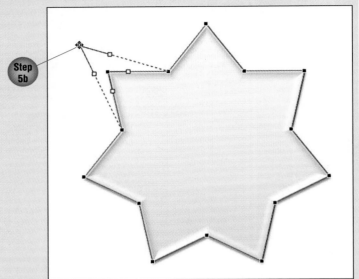

   c. Using the mouse, position the mouse pointer on the edit point at the outside of the top right point, drag down and out as shown in the image below, and then release the mouse button.

   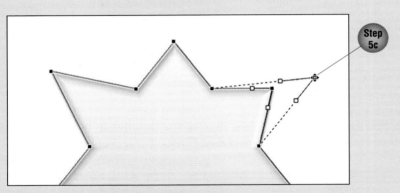

   d. Continue dragging edit points until your image displays in a manner similar to the image shown in Figure 12.4.
   e. Click outside the shape to remove the edit points.
6. Insert and format text in the shape by completing the following steps:
   a. Click in the shape to select it.
   b. Make sure the Drawing Tools Format tab is active.
   c. Type Free seminar!, press the Enter key, and then type 1-888-555-4588. (This text will appear in the middle of the shape.)
   d. Select the text you just typed.
   e. Click the Text Fill button arrow in the WordArt Styles group in the Drawing Tools Format tab and then click *Olive Green, Accent 3, Darker 50%* at the drop-down palette.

   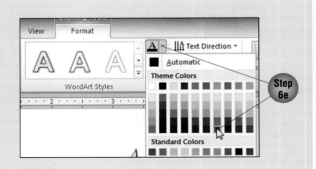

f. Click the Text Effects button, point to *Glow*, and then click the *Aqua, 8 pt glow, Accent color 5* option in the *Glow Variations* section.

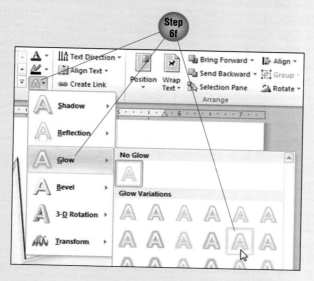

g. Click the Home tab.
h. Click the Font Size button arrow and then click *18* at the drop-down gallery. (Your text and shape should appear similar to what you see in Figure 12.4.)
7. Save **C12-E02-LelandFS.docx**.

Figure 12.4 Exercise 12.2E

QUICK STEPS

Draw a Text Box
1. Click Insert tab.
2. Click Text Box button in Text group.
3. Click *Draw Text Box.*
4. Drag in document to create box.

Text Box

Inserting and Formatting Text Boxes

With the Text Box button in the Text group in the Insert tab, you can insert a predesigned text box or draw a text box and then apply formatting with options at the Drawing Tools Format tab (see Figure 12.1). Click the Text Box button and a drop-down list displays with a variety of predesigned text boxes. Click one of the text boxes to insert it in the document or click the *Draw Text Box* button and then drag in the document to create a text box.

Inserting a Predesigned Text Box

By inserting a predesigned text box in a document, you can insert a pull quote in a document, which is a quote that is "pulled" from an article, enlarged, and displayed in a strategic or attractive location on the page. Use a pull quote in an article to attract readers' attention. Some advantages of using pull quotes are that they reinforce important concepts, summarize the message, and break up blocks of text to make them easier to read.

Insert a pull quote in a document by clicking the Insert tab, clicking the Text Box button, and then clicking the desired pull quote text box at the drop-down list. Type the quote you have selected inside the text box and then format the text and/or customize the text box with buttons in the Drawing Tools Format tab.

Exercise 12.2F   Inserting and Formatting a Pull Quote Text Box   **Part 6 of 10**

1. With **C12-E02-LelandFS.docx** open, press Ctrl + Home to move the insertion point to the beginning of the document.
2. Insert and format the pull quote text box shown in Figure 12.5 by completing the following steps:
   a. Click the Insert tab.
   b. Click the Text Box button in the Text group, scroll down the drop-down list, and then click the *Tiles Sidebar* pull quote text box.
   c. With the insertion point positioned in the text box, type "Retirement savings need to be a priority rather than an afterthought."
   d. Click the Shape Fill button arrow in the Shapes Styles group and then click the *Olive Green, Accent 3, Lighter 40%* color at the drop-down palette.
   e. Select the text in the pull quote text box, click the Home tab, click the Font Size button arrow, and then click *12* at the drop-down list.
   f. With the text still selected, click the Font Color button arrow and then click the *Olive Green, Accent 3 Darker 50%* color.
3. Save **C12-E02-LelandFS.docx**.

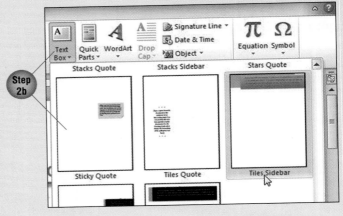

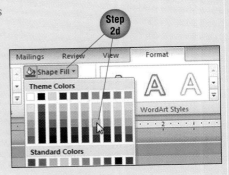

Figure 12.5 Exercise 12.2F

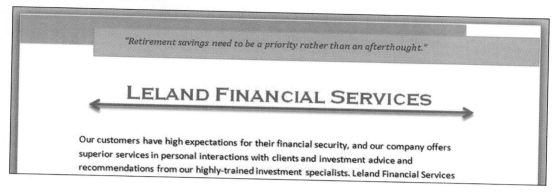

"Retirement savings need to be a priority rather than an afterthought."

LELAND FINANCIAL SERVICES

Our customers have high expectations for their financial security, and our company offers superior services in personal interactions with clients and investment advice and recommendations from our highly-trained investment specialists. Leland Financial Services

Drawing and Formatting a Text Box

Along with inserting predesigned pull quote text boxes, you can use the Text Box button to draw a text box in a document. To draw a text box, click the Insert tab, click the Text box button, and then click *Draw Text Box* at the drop-down list. Position the mouse pointer, which displays as a crosshair, in the document and then drag to create the text box. You can also just click in the document. This inserts a small text box in the document with the insertion point inside.

Exercise 12.2G Inserting and Formatting Text Boxes   Part 7 of 10

1. With **C12-E02-LelandFS.docx** open, press Ctrl + Home.
2. Create and format the text box shown in Figure 12.6. Begin by clicking the Insert tab.
3. Click the Text Box button in the Text group and then click the *Draw Text Box* option at the drop-down list.
4. Click at the left side of the middle of the paragraph of text. (This inserts a text box in the document.)
5. Type "Ongoing monitoring of financial investments is part of our commitment to our customers…".

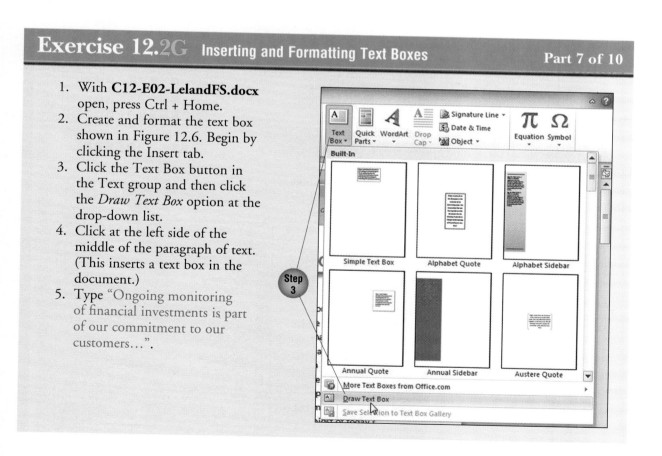

6. Customize the text box by completing the following steps:

   a. With the Drawing Tools Format tab active, click in the Shape Height measurement box and then type 0.6.

   b. Click in the Shape Width measurement box, type 3.2, and then press the Enter key.

   c. Click the Shape Effects button, point to *Shadow*, and then click the *Offset Diagonal Bottom Right* option at the side menu (first option in the *Outer* section).

   d. Click the Shape Effects button, point to *3-D Rotation*, and then click *Perspective Left* at the side menu (second option from the left in the top row of the *Perspective* section).

   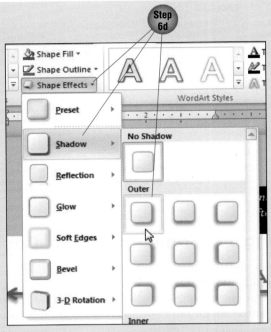

   e. Click the More button at the right of the style thumbnails in the Shape Styles group, and then click *Subtle Effect – Olive Green, Accent 3* at the drop-down gallery.

   f. Click the Shape Effects button, point to *Bevel*, and then click the *Cool Slant* option (last option in the top row in the *Bevel* section).

   g. Click the Wrap Text button in the Arrange group and then click *Tight* at the drop-down list.

7. Customize the text in the text box by completing the following steps:

   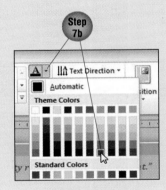

   a. Click the border of the text box. (Make sure you do not see the insertion point in the text box.)

   b. Click the Text Fill button arrow and then click *Olive Green, Accent 5, Darker 50%* at the drop-down palette.

   c. Click the Text Effects button, point to *Glow*, and then click the *Olive Green, 5 pt glow, Accent color 3* option (located in the top row in the *Glow Variations* section).

   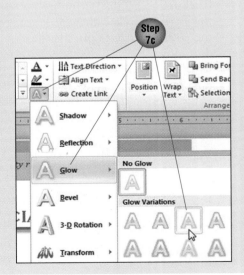

   d. Click the Home tab and then click the Italic button in the Font group.

8. Drag the text box so it is positioned as shown in Figure 12.6.

9. Save **C12-E02-LelandFS.docx**.

Figure 12.6 Exercise 12.2G

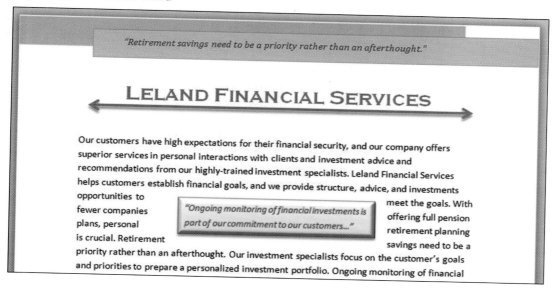

Inserting a Text Box in a Shape

In addition to typing text directly in a shape, you can draw a text box in a shape, type text in the text box, and then customize the text box as well as the text with options at the Drawing Tools Format tab. When you draw a text box in a shape, the text box is actually layered on top of the shape. If you want to move the shape and the text box, you will need to select both objects. To select a shape and a text box inside a shape, click the text box, hold down the Shift key, and then click the shape.

Exercise 12.2H Inserting and Copying Text Boxes Part 8 of 10

1. With **C12-E02-LelandFS.docx** open, display page two (the page containing the three arrows).
2. Insert text boxes in the tips of the arrows as shown in Figure 12.7. Begin by inserting a text box in the top arrow by completing the following steps:

   a. Click the Insert tab, click the Text Box button in the Text group, and then click *Draw Text Box* at the drop-down list.

   b. Click in the top arrow. (This inserts a small text box on top of the shape.)

   c. Press Ctrl + E to change the alignment to center and then type Reliable.

   d. Click the Text Direction button and then click *Rotate all text 90°* at the drop-down list.

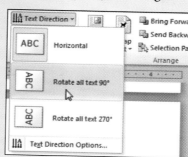

e. Click in the Shape Height measurement box and then type 0.4.

f. Click in the Shape Width measurement box, type 1.4, and then press the Enter key.

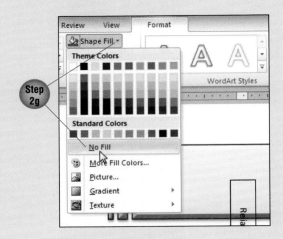

g. Click the Shape Fill button arrow in the Shape Styles group and then click *No Fill* at the drop-down gallery.

h. Click the Shape Outline button arrow in the Shape Styles group and then click *No Outline* at the drop-down gallery.

i. Click the border to make the border a solid line.

j. Drag the text box so it is positioned in the tip of the arrow. (Refer to Figure 12.7.)

k. Click on any character in the word *Reliable*.

l. Select *Reliable*.

m. Click the Home tab.

n. Change the font size to 16, turn on bold, and then change the font color to *Olive Green, Accent 3, Darker 50%*.

o. Click outside the text box.

3. Complete steps similar to those in Step 2 to insert the word *Responsible* in the middle arrow *except* click *Rotate all text 270°* in Step 2d.

4. Complete steps similar to those in Step 2 to insert the word *Committed* in the bottom arrow.

5. Save **C12-E02-LelandFS.docx**.

Figure 12.7 Exercise 12.2H

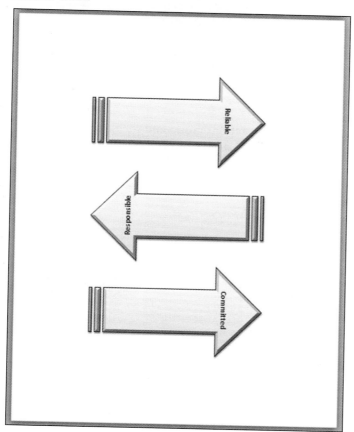

Linking and Unlinking Text Boxes

You can create several text boxes and then have text flow from one text box to another by linking the text boxes. To do this, draw the desired text boxes and then select the first text box you want in the link. Click the Create Link button in the Text group in the Drawing Tools Format tab, and the mouse pointer displays with a link image attached. Click an empty text box to link it with the selected text box. To break a link between two boxes, select the first text box in the link and then click the Break Link button in the Text group. When you break a link, all of the text is placed in the selected text box.

QUICK STEPS

Link Text Boxes
1. Select first text box.
2. Click Create Link button.
3. Click empty text box.

Create Link

Break Link

1. With **C12-E02-LelandFS.docx** open, press Ctrl + Home to move the insertion point to the beginning of the document.
2. Create the arrows and text boxes as shown in Figure 12.8. Begin by drawing and formatting an arrow below the paragraph of text on page one by completing the following steps:
   a. Click the Insert tab.
   b. Click the Shapes button in the Illustrations group and then click the sixth option from the left in the second row of the *Block Arrows* section (*Notched Right Arrow*).

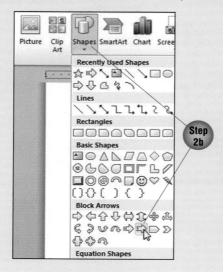

Figure 12.8 Exercise 12.2I

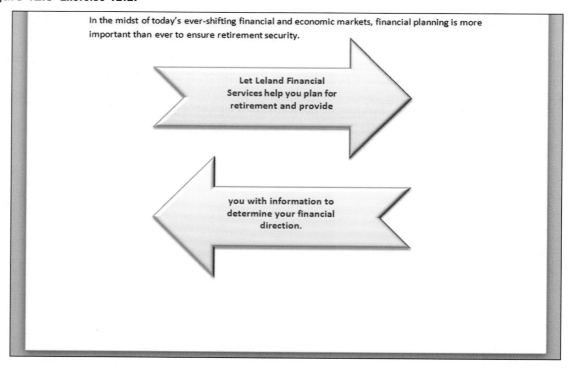

c. Drag in the document screen to create an arrow that is approximately 4 inches wide and 2 inches tall.

d. Click the More button at the right of the thumbnails in the Shape Styles group and then click the *Subtle Effect - Olive Green, Accent 3* option.

e. Click the Shape Effects button, point to *Bevel*, and then click the *Circle* option in the *Bevel* section.

f. Click in the Shape Height measurement box in the Size group and then type 2.

g. Click in the Shape Width measurement box in the Size group, type 4, and then press the Enter key.

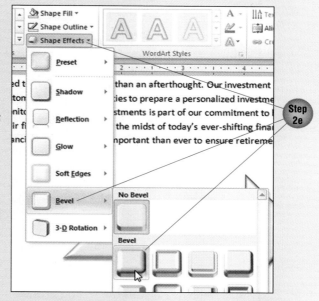

3. With the arrow selected, copy it by holding down the Ctrl key, dragging the arrow below the original arrow, and releasing the mouse button and then the Ctrl key.

4. With the bottom arrow selected, click the Rotate button in the Arrange group and then click *Flip Horizontal* at the drop-down list.

5. Make sure both arrows fit on page one. If not, move the arrows so they are positioned on page one.

6. Insert a text box inside the top arrow and format the text box by completing the following steps:

a. Click in the top arrow to select it.

b. Click the Insert tab.

c. Click the Text Box button in the Text group and then click *Draw Text Box* at the drop-down list.

d. Draw a text box inside the arrow as shown below.

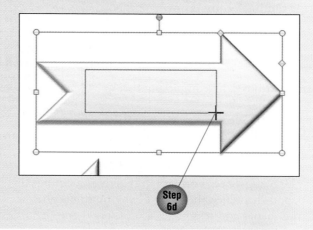

7. Format the text box by completing the following steps:
   a. Change the height measurement to 0.8 inch and the width measurement to 2 inches.
   b. Click the Shape Fill button arrow and then click *No Fill*.
   c. Make sure the text box is visually centered in the arrow. (If you need to move the text box, click the text box border so it turns into a solid line border and then use the mouse to drag the text box to the desired position.)

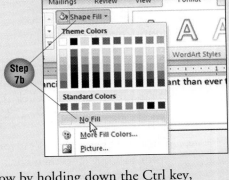

8. With the text box selected, copy it to the bottom arrow by holding down the Ctrl key, dragging the text box inside the bottom arrow, releasing the mouse button, and then releasing the Ctrl key.

9. Link the text boxes by completing the following steps:
   a. Click in the text box in the top arrow to select it.
   b. Click the Create Link button in the Text group.
   c. Click the text box in the second arrow.

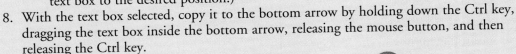

10. With the top text box selected, make the following changes:
    a. Click the Home tab.
    b. Change the font size to 12 points, the font color to *Olive Green, Accent 3, Darker 50%*, and turn on bold.
    c. Change the line spacing to single.
    d. Click the Center button in the Paragraph group.
    e. Type Let Leland Financial Services help you plan for retirement and provide you with information to determine your financial direction. (The text will flow to the text box in the bottom arrow.)

11. Remove the border around the text boxes by completing the following steps:
    a. Click in the text box in the top arrow.
    b. With the top text box selected, click the Drawing Tools Format tab.
    c. Click the Shape Outline button arrow and then click *No Outline*.
    d. Click the bottom text box.
    e. Click the Shape Outline button arrow and then click *No Outline*.

12. Align the shapes and text boxes by completing the following steps:
    a. Click the top arrow to select it.
    b. Hold down the Shift key and then click the text box in the top arrow, click the bottom arrow, and then click the text box in the bottom arrow.
    c. Release the mouse button and then the Shift key.
    d. Make sure the Drawing Tools Format tab is active, click the Align button in the Arrange group, and then click the *Align Center* option at the drop-down list.
    e. Click outside the shapes and text boxes to deselect them. (Your arrows and text boxes should appear as shown in Figure 12.8.)

13. Save **C12-E02-LelandFS.docx**.

14. Break the link between the text boxes by completing the following steps:
    a. Click in the text in the top arrow. (This inserts a dashed border around the text box.)

b. Click the Drawing Tools Format tab.
c. Click the Break Link button in the Text group. (Notice that the text in the bottom arrow moves up into the text box in the top arrow.)
15. Link the text boxes again by clicking the Create Link button in the Text group and then clicking in the bottom arrow.
16. Click in a white portion of the document to deselect the text box and then save **C12-E02-LelandFS.docx**.

Inserting WordArt

With the WordArt feature, you can distort or modify text to conform to a variety of shapes. This is useful for creating company logos, letterhead, flyer titles, or headings. To insert WordArt in a document, click the Insert tab and then click the WordArt button in the Text group. This displays the WordArt drop-down list shown in Figure 12.9. Select the desired option at the drop-down list and a WordArt text box is inserted in the document containing the words *Your text here* and the Drawing Tools Format tab is active. Type the desired WordArt text and then format the WordArt with options in the Drawing Tools Format tab.

QUICK STEPS

Insert WordArt Text
1. Click Insert tab.
2. Click WordArt button.
3. Click desired WordArt option at drop-down list.
4. Type desired WordArt text.

WordArt

Figure 12.9 WordArt Drop-down List

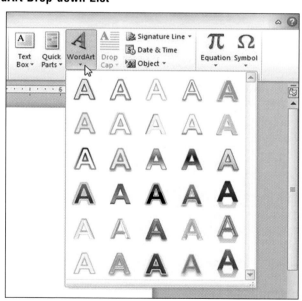

Formatting WordArt Text

With options in the WordArt Styles group in the Drawing Tools Format tab, you can apply formatting to the WordArt text. You can apply a predesigned WordArt style, change the WordArt text color or text outline color, and apply a text effect such as shadow, reflection, glow, bevel, 3-D rotation, and transform. With the transform option, you can conform the WordArt text to a specific shape. To do this, click the Text Effects button, point to *Transform*, and then click the desired shape at the drop-down gallery. Use options in the Arrange group to specify the position, alignment, and rotation of the WordArt text, and specify the size of the WordArt with options in the Size group.

1. With **C12-E02-LelandFS.docx** open, press Ctrl + End to move the insertion point to the end of the document. (The insertion point should be positioned above the shape on the third page.)
2. Insert WordArt text by completing the following steps:
   a. Click the Insert tab.
   b. Click the WordArt button in the Text group and then click the *Fill – Olive Green, Accent 3, Outline – Text 2* option.

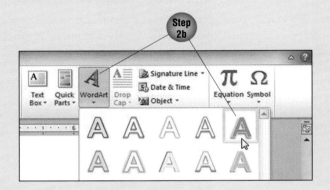

   c. Type Leland Financial Services.
3. Format the WordArt text by completing the following steps:
   a. Click the outside border of the WordArt text box so the border displays as a solid line instead of a dashed line.
   b. Click the Text Fill button arrow in the WordArt Styles group in the Drawing Tools Format tab and then click the *Olive Green, Accent 3, Darker 25%* option.
   c. Click the Text Effects button, point to *Glow*, and then click the *Aqua, 5 pt glow, Accent color 5* option in the *Glow Variations* section.

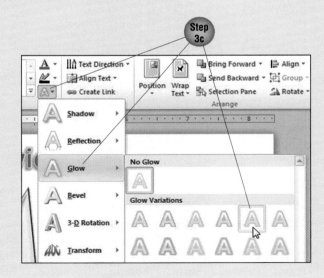

d. Click the Text Effects button, point to *3-D Rotation*, and then click the *Perspective Above* option in the *Perspective* section.

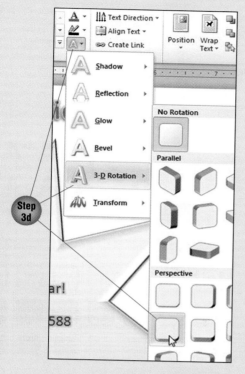

e. Click in the Shape Height measurement box and then type 1.
f. Click in the Shape Width measurement box, type 6.5, and then press the Enter key.
g. Click the Text Effects button, point to *Transform*, and then click the *Deflate* option in the *Warp* section.
h. Click the star shape and then move it down the page to make room for the WordArt text at the top of the third page.
i. Make sure the WordArt text box is positioned at the beginning of the third page between the left and right margins.
j. Click outside the WordArt text box to deselect it.
4. Save, print, and then close **C12-E02-LelandFS.docx**.

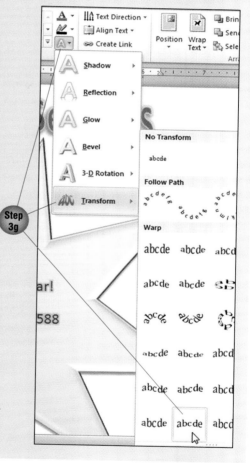

Formatting the WordArt Text Box

WordArt text is inserted in a text box, and this text box can be customized with options in the Shape Styles group in the Drawing Tools Format tab. Use options in this group to apply a predesigned style to the WordArt text box, change the text box fill color and outline color, and apply an effect to the WordArt text box such as shadow, reflection, glow, soft edges, bevel, and 3-D rotation.

1. Open **Hawaii.docx** and then save the document and name it **C12-E03-Hawaii**.
2. Create and customize the WordArt text shown in Figure 12.10. Begin by clicking the Insert tab.
3. Click the WordArt button in the Text group and then click the *Gradient Fill – Turquoise, Accent 1, Outline – White, Glow – Accent 2* option.
4. Type HAWAII.
5. Click the outside border of the WordArt text box so the border displays as a solid line.
6. Click the More button at the right of the thumbnails in the Shape Styles group and then click *Subtle Effect – Turquoise, Accent 1* at the drop-down gallery.
7. Click the Text Outline button arrow and then click the dark blue color in the *Standard Colors* section.
8. Click the Text Effects button, point to *Glow*, and then click the *Turquoise, 8 pt glow, Accent color 1* option in the *Glow Variations* section.

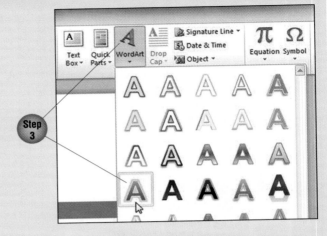

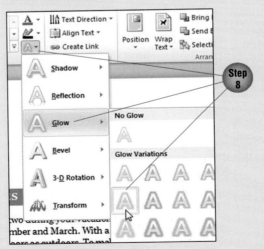

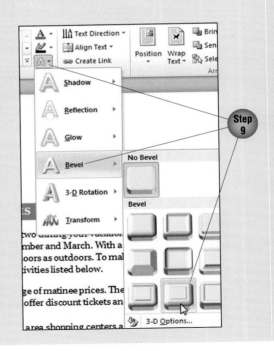

9. Click the Text Effects button, point to *Bevel*, and then click the *Riblet* option.
10. Click the Wrap Text button and then click *Tight* at the drop-down list.

11. Click the Rotate button and then click *Rotate Left 90°* at the drop-down list.
12. Click in the Shape Height measurement box and then type 1.3.
13. Click in the Shape Width measurement box and then type 7.2.
14. Click the Text Effects button, point to *Transform*, and then click the *Square* option (first option in the *Warp* section).
15. Using the mouse, drag the WordArt so it is positioned as shown in Figure 12.10.
16. Save, print, and then close **C12-E03-Hawaii.docx**.

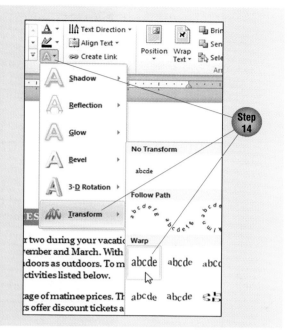

Figure 12.10 Exercise 12.3

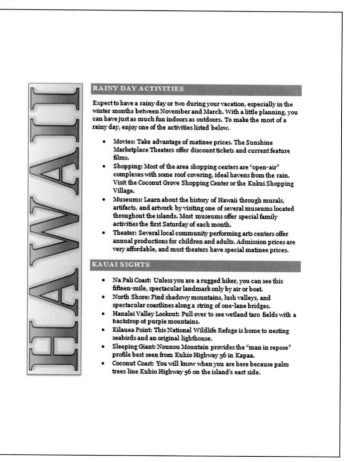

Applying Character Formatting

With the WordArt feature, you format text to improve the visual appeal of the text. You can also format text by applying a specific font and choosing font options at the Font dialog box with the Advanced tab selected. At this dialog box, you can specify character spacing for characters in a font, apply OpenType features, and apply text effects to selected text.

Adjusting Character Spacing

Each typeface is designed with a specific amount of space between characters. You can change this character spacing with options in the Character Spacing section of the Font dialog box with the Advanced tab selected as shown in Figure 12.11. Display this dialog box by clicking the Font group dialog box launcher in the Home tab and then clicking the Advanced tab at the dialog box.

Figure 12.11 Font Dialog Box with Advanced Tab Selected

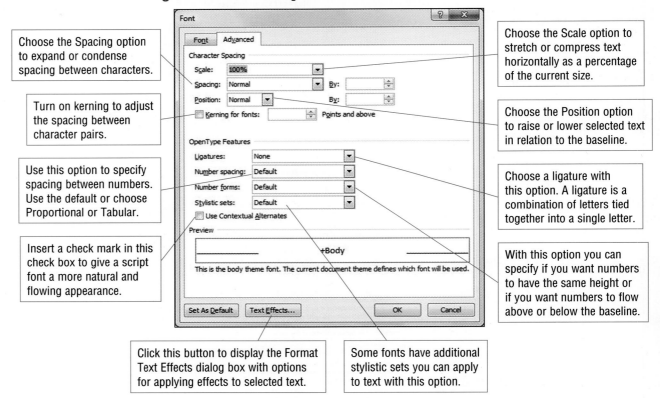

Choose the Spacing option to expand or condense spacing between characters.

Turn on kerning to adjust the spacing between character pairs.

Use this option to specify spacing between numbers. Use the default or choose Proportional or Tabular.

Insert a check mark in this check box to give a script font a more natural and flowing appearance.

Choose the Scale option to stretch or compress text horizontally as a percentage of the current size.

Choose the Position option to raise or lower selected text in relation to the baseline.

Choose a ligature with this option. A ligature is a combination of letters tied together into a single letter.

With this option you can specify if you want numbers to have the same height or if you want numbers to flow above or below the baseline.

Click this button to display the Format Text Effects dialog box with options for applying effects to selected text.

Some fonts have additional stylistic sets you can apply to text with this option.

Choose the *Scale* option to stretch or compress text horizontally as a percentage of the current size. You can choose a percentage from 1 to 600. Expand or condense the spacing between characters with the *Spacing* option. Choose either the *Expanded* or *Condensed* option and then enter the desired point size in the *By* text box. Raise or lower selected text in relation to the baseline with the *Position* option. Choose either the *Raised* or *Lowered* option and then enter the point size in the *By* text box.

Insert a check mark in the *Kerning* check box to apply kerning to selected text in a document. **Kerning** refers to the adjustment of spacing between certain character combinations by positioning two characters closer together than normal and uses the shape and slope of characters to improve their appearance. Kerning allows more text in a specific amount of space and also looks more natural and helps the eye move along the text. Consider kerning text in larger font sizes, such as 14 points or higher, and text set in italics. Figure 12.12 displays text without and with kerning applied. Notice how the letters *Te* and *Va* are closer together in the kerned text in Figure 12.12 compared to the text that is not kerned. Turn on automatic kerning by displaying the font dialog box with the Advanced tab selected and then inserting a check mark in the *Kerning for fonts* check box. Specify the beginning point size that you want kerned in the *Points and above* text box.

Figure 12.12 Text Without and With Kerning Applied

Tennison Valley (not kerned)
Tennison Valley (kerned)

Exercise 12.4A Adjusting Character Spacing and Kerning Text **Part 1 of 4**

1. Open **PRDonorApp.docx**, save the document, and name it **C12-E04-PRDonorApp**.
2. Select the title *Donor Appreciation*.
3. At the Home tab, click the Font group dialog box launcher.
4. At the Font dialog box, click the Advanced tab.
5. Click the down-pointing arrow at the right of the *Scale* option box and then click *150%* at the drop-down list.
6. Click the down-pointing arrow at the right of the *Spacing* option box and then click *Condensed* at the drop-down list.
7. Click the *Kerning for fonts* check box to insert a check mark.
8. Click OK to close the dialog box.
9. Select the text *Enjoy the "flavor of Tanzania" and an evening of cultural entertainment...*
10. Click the Font group dialog box launcher to display the Font dialog box with the Advanced tab selected.
11. Click the *Kerning for fonts* check box to insert a check mark and then click OK to close the dialog box.
12. Save **C12-E04-PRDonorApp.docx**.

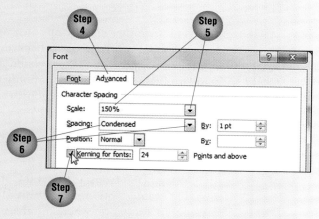

Using OpenType Features

The OpenType font file format is a format developed by Adobe and Microsoft to work on both Macintosh and Windows computers. The benefits of the OpenType format are the cross-platform compatibility, meaning you can move font files between Macintosh and Windows computers; the ability to support expanded character sets and layout figures; and the capability for Web page designers to create high-quality on-screen fonts for online documents.

Word 2010 offers some advanced OpenType features in the Font dialog box with the Advanced tab selected (see Figure 12.11) that desktop publishers and Web and graphic designers can use to enhance the visual appeal of text. At the Font dialog box with the Advanced tab selected, *Ligatures* is the first option in the *OpenType Features* section. A ligature is a combination of characters tied together into a single letter. The OpenType standard specifies four categories of ligatures—*Standard Only, Standard and Contextual, Historical and Discretionary*, and *All*. The font designer decides which category to support and in which group to put combinations of characters.

With the *Standard Only* option selected, the standard set of ligatures that most typographers and font designers determine are appropriate for the font are applied to text. Common ligatures include letter combinations with the letter "f," as shown in Figure 12.13. Notice how the *fi* and *fl* letter combinations are combined when ligatures are applied.

Figure 12.13 Ligature Combination Examples

final flavor (not using ligatures)
final flavor (using ligatures)

With the other ligature options, you can specify contextual ligatures, which are ligatures that the font designer believes are appropriate for use with the font, but are not standard ligatures. Historical and discretionary ligatures are ligatures that were once standard but are no longer commonly used, but are available to create a historical or "period" effect. You can also choose the *All* ligatures option, which applies all ligature combinations to selected text.

The *Number spacing* option in the *OpenType Features* section is set at *Default*, which means that spacing between numbers is determined by the font designer. You can choose *Proportional*, which spaces numbers with varying widths. Three Microsoft fonts—Candara, Constantial, and Corbel—use proportional number spacing by default. Use the *Tabular* option if you want to specify that each number is the same width. This is useful in a situation where numbers are set in columns and you want all numbers the same width so they align vertically. The Cambria, Calibri, and Consolas fonts use tabular spacing by default.

Like the *Number spacing* option, the *Number forms* option is set at *Default*, which means the font designer determines the number form. Change this to *Lining* if you want all numbers to have the same height and not to extend below the baseline of the text. Generally, lining numbers are easier to read in tables and forms. The Cambria, Calibri, and Consolas fonts use lining number forms by default. Choose the *Old-style* option and the lines of the numbers can flow above or below the baseline of the text. For some fonts, changing the *Number forms* option to *Old-style* would result in numbers such as *3* and *5* extending below the baseline or centered higher on the line. Three fonts that use *Old-style* number forms include Candara, Constantia, and Corbel.

Exercise 12.4B Applying a Ligature and a Number Form Part 2 of 4

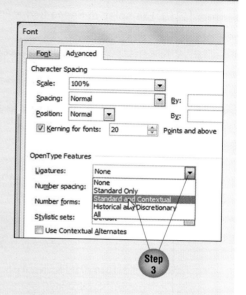

1. With **C12-E04-PRDonorApp.docx** open, select the text *Enjoy the "flavor of Tanzania" and an evening of cultural entertainment....*
2. Click the Font group dialog box launcher. (If necessary, click the Advanced tab.)
3. At the Font dialog box with the Advanced tab selected, click the down-pointing arrow at the right of the *Ligatures* option box and then click *Standard and Contextual* at the drop-down list.
4. Click OK to close the dialog box.
5. Select the text *2013 – 2014* and *$3,500,000*.
6. Display the Font dialog box with the Advanced tab selected.
7. Click the down-pointing arrow at the right side of the *Number forms* option box and then click *Old-style* at the drop-down list.
8. Click OK to close the dialog box.
9. Save **C12-E04-PRDonorApp.docx**.

A font designer may include a number of stylistic sets for a specific font. A different stylistic set may apply additional formatting to the characters in a font. For example, the sentences in Figure 12.14 are set in 16-point Gabriola. Notice the slight variations in characters in some of the stylistic sets. Choose a stylistic set and the *Preview* section of the dialog box displays a visual representation of the characters with the stylistic set applied.

Figure 12.14 Examples of Gabriola Font Stylistic Sets

Typography refers to the appearance of printed characters on the page. (Default set)

Typography refers to the appearance of printed characters on the page. (Stylistic set 4)

Typography refers to the appearance of printed characters on the page. (Stylistic set 5)

Typography refers to the appearance of printed characters on the page. (Stylistic set 6)

Insert a check mark in the *Use Contextual Alternates* option in the Font dialog box with the Advanced tab selected and letter combinations are fine-tuned based on the surrounding characters. Use this feature to give your script font a more natural and flowing appearance. Figure 12.15 shows text set in 12-point Segoe Script. The first line of text is the default and the second line of text has the contextual alternate option selected. Notice the slight differences in letters such as *t*, *n*, *s*, and *h*.

Figure 12.15 Examples of Segoe Script Font with and without Contextual Alternate Selected

A font designer determines the appearance of each character in a font.

A font designer determines the appearance of each character in a font.

Not all fonts contain ligature combinations, number spacing and forms, stylistic sets, or contextual alternates. Experiment with fonts using the options in the Font dialog box with the Advanced tab selected to find the font and font options for your document.

Exercise 12.4C Applying a Stylistic Set and Contextual Alternate   Part 3 of 4

1. With **C12-E04-PRDonorApp.docx** open, select the bulleted text.
2. Display the Font dialog box with the Advanced tab selected.
3. Click the down-pointing arrow at the right of the *Stylistic sets* option box and then click *4* at the drop-down list.
4. Click OK to close the dialog box.
5. Select the text *Please call the Phoenix Rising office to let us know if you will be joining us.*
6. Display the Font dialog box with the Advanced tab selected.
7. Click the *Use Contextual Alternates* check box to insert a check mark.
8. Click OK to close the Font dialog box.
9. Save **C12-E04-PRDonorApp.docx**.

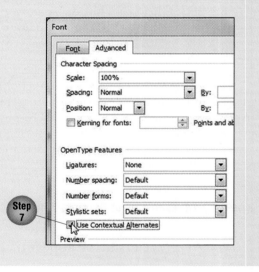

Applying Text Effects

Click the Text Effects button that displays at the bottom of the Font dialog box with the Advanced tab selected and the Format Text Effects dialog box displays as shown in Figure 12.16. Formatting categories display at the left of the dialog box. Click a formatting category and the options at the right of the dialog box change to reflect the category. Many of the options available at the dialog box also are available by clicking the Text Effects button in the Font group in the Home tab.

Figure 12.16 Format Text Effects Dialog Box

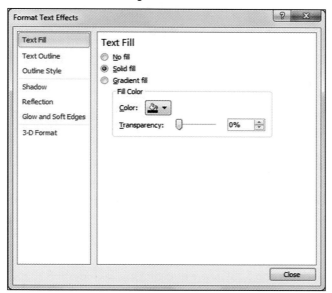

Exercise 12.4D Applying Text Effects   Part 4 of 4

1. With **C12-E04-PRDonorApp.docx** open, select the title *Donor Appreciation*.
2. Display the Font dialog box with the Advanced tab selected.
3. Click the Text Effects button located in the lower left corner of the dialog box.
4. At the Format Text Effects dialog box, make sure *Text Fill* is selected at the left of the dialog box.
5. Click the *Gradient fill* option.
6. Click the Preset colors button and then click *Mahogany* at the drop-down list (last option in the third row).
7. Click the *Text Outline* option at the left of the dialog box.
8. Click the *Solid line* option.
9. Click the Color button and then click the *Orange, Accent 6, Darker 50%* color (located in the last column).
10. Click the *Shadow* option at the left of the dialog box.
11. Click the Presets button and then click *Offset Left* at the drop-down list (located in the *Outer* section).

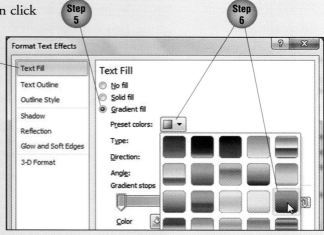

12. Click the *Glow and Soft Edges* option at the left of the dialog box.
13. Click the Presets button in the *Glow* section and then click *Orange, 5 pt glow, Accent color 6* at the drop-down list (last option in the first row in the *Glow Variations* section).
14. Click the Close button to close the Format Text Effects dialog box.
15. Click OK to close the Font dialog box and then deselect the title.
16. Save, print, and then close **C12-E04-PRDonorApp.docx**.

Chapter Summary

- ➤ Use the Screenshot button in the Illustrations group in the Insert tab to capture the contents of a screen or capture a portion of a screen.
- ➤ Use buttons in the Picture Tools Format tab to customize a screenshot image.
- ➤ Draw shapes in a document by clicking the Shapes button in the Illustrations group in the Insert tab, clicking the desired shape at the drop-down list, and then dragging in the document to draw the shape.
- ➤ With shape options at the Shapes button drop-down list, you can draw lines or enclosed shapes.
- ➤ When you draw a line, hold down the Shift key to draw a straight horizontal or vertical line. When you draw an enclosed shape, maintain the proportions of the shape by holding down the Shift key while dragging in the document to create the shape.
- ➤ Copy a shape by holding down the Ctrl key while dragging the selected shape.
- ➤ Customize a shape with options in the Drawing Tools Format tab.
- ➤ Select multiple shapes by holding down the Shift key while clicking each desired shape.
- ➤ Use the Align button in the Arrange group in the Drawing Tools Format tab to align multiple shapes in a document.
- ➤ Insert text in a shape by clicking in the shape and then typing the desired text.
- ➤ Change the shape of the selected shape by clicking the Edit Shape button in the Drawing Tools Format tab, pointing to the *Change Shape* option, and then clicking the desired shape at the side menu.
- ➤ Modify a shape by dragging edit points. Display edit points by clicking the Edit Shape button in the Drawing Tools Format tab and then clicking *Edit Points* at the drop-down list.
- ➤ Insert a pull quote in a document with a predesigned text box by clicking the Insert tab, clicking the Text Box button, and then clicking the desired predesigned text box at the drop-down list.
- ➤ Format a pull quote text box with options in the Drawing Tools Format tab.
- ➤ Draw a text box by clicking the Text Box button in the Text group in the Insert tab, clicking *Draw Text Box* at the drop-down list, and then clicking in the document or dragging in the document.
- ➤ Format and customize a text box with buttons in the Drawing Tools Format tab.
- ➤ Link drawn text boxes with the Create Link button in the Text group in the Drawing Tools Format tab. Break a link with the Break Link button in the Text group.
- ➤ Use WordArt to distort or modify text to conform to a variety of shapes.
- ➤ Insert WordArt text by clicking the Insert tab, clicking the WordArt button in the Text group, clicking the desired WordArt option at the drop-down list, and then typing the desired text.
- ➤ Customize WordArt with options in the Drawing Tools Format tab.
- ➤ Use options in the Character Spacing section of the Font dialog box with the Advanced tab selected to adjust character spacing and turn on kerning.
- ➤ The OpenType Features section of the Font dialog box with the Advanced tab selected includes options for choosing a ligature style, specifying number spacing and form, and applying stylistic sets.
- ➤ Click the Text Effects button at the Font dialog box to display the Format Text Effects dialog box. Use options at this dialog box to apply effects to selected text.

Commands *Review*

FEATURE	RIBBON TAB, GROUP	BUTTON	OPTION
Screenshot	Insert, Illustrations		
Shapes	Insert, Illustrations		
Edit shape	Drawing Tools Format, Insert Shapes		
Predesigned text box	Insert, Text		
Draw text box	Insert, Text		Draw Text Box
Create text box link	Drawing Tools Format, Text		
Break text box link	Drawing Tools Format, Text		
WordArt	Insert, Text		
Font dialog box	Home, Font		

Key Points *Review*

Completion: In the space provided at the right, indicate the correct term, symbol, or command.

1. To capture a portion of a screen, click the Screenshot button in the Illustrations group in the Insert tab and then click this option at the drop-down list.

2. The Shapes button is located in this tab.

3. With options at the Shapes button drop-down list, you can draw lines or these.

4. To draw a straight horizontal or vertical line, hold down this key while dragging in the document.

5. To copy a selected shape, hold down this key while dragging the shape.

6. Select multiple shapes by holding down the Ctrl key or this key while clicking shapes.

7. The Align button is located in this group in the Drawing Tools Format tab.

8. Change the shape of the selected shape by clicking this button in the Drawing Tools Format tab, pointing to *Change Shape*, and then clicking the desired shape at the side menu.

9. Modify a shape by dragging these points.

10. Display available predesigned pull quote text boxes by clicking the Insert tab and then clicking this button in the Text group.

11. Format a pull quote text box with options in this tab. _____

12. Link text boxes with this button in the Text group in the Drawing Tools Format tab. _____

13. The WordArt button is located in this group in the Insert tab. _____

14. This group in the Drawing Tools Format tab contains buttons for spacing WordArt text and specifying the vertical and horizontal height of text. _____

15. Use this button in the Drawing Tools Format tab to change the WordArt fill color. _____

16. Turn on kerning with the *Kerning for fonts* check box located in this section of the Font dialog box with the Advanced tab selected. _____

17. This term refers to a combination of characters tied together into a single letter. _____

18. Use this option at the Font dialog box with the Advanced tab selected to specify if you want numbers to have the same height or to flow above or below the baseline. _____

19. Click this button at the Font dialog box to display the Format Text Effects dialog box. _____

Chapter Assessments

Applying Your Skills

Demonstrate your knowledge of features learned in this chapter by completing the following assessments.

Assessment 12.1 Create a Screenshot

1. Open **C12-E02-LelandFS.docx** and then open **ScreenshotMemo.docx**.
2. Type the current date after the *DATE:* heading, type your instructor's name after the *TO:* heading, and type your name after the *FROM:* heading.
3. With **ScreenshotMemo.docx** the active document, move the insertion point to the end of the document and then insert a screenshot of the screen containing the **C12-E02-LelandFS.docx** document.
4. Change the text wrapping of the screenshot image to *Top and Bottom*.
5. Move the insertion point below the screenshot image, type XX, press Shift + Enter, and then type C12-A01-ScreenshotMemo.docx (where you insert your initials in place of the *XX*).
6. Save the document and name it **C12-A01-ScreenshotMemo**.
7. Print and then close **C12-A01-ScreenshotMemo.docx**.
8. Close **C12-E02-LelandFS.docx**.

Assessment 12.2 Create a Letterhead with Text and a Drawn Line

1. At a blank document, type the text *Blue Water Charters* shown in Figure 12.17 with the following specifications:
   a. Change the font to 56-point Freestyle Script bold and the font color to blue. (To change the font size to 56 points, you will need to select the current point size in the Font Size text box and then type 56.)
   b. Center the text.

2. Select the text *Blue Water Charters*, display the Format Text Effects dialog box (display this dialog box by clicking the Text Effects button at the Font dialog box) and then apply the following effects:
   a. With Text Fill selected at the left of the dialog box, click the *Gradient fill* option, click the Preset colors button, and then click *Ocean* at the drop-down list.
   b. Click the Text Outline option, click the *Solid line* option, click the Color button, and then click the dark blue color (second color from the right in the *Standard Colors* section).
   c. Click the Shadow option, click the Presets button, and then click the *Offset Diagonal Bottom Right* option (located in the *Outer* section).
   d. Click the 3-D Format option, click the Top button in the *Bevel* section, and then click the *Circle* option in the *Bevel* section.
3. Draw the line below the text with the *Line* option at the Shapes drop-down list and then apply the following formatting:
   a. Apply the *Intense Line - Accent 1* shape style.
   b. Apply the *Offset Bottom* shadow effect.
4. Save the document with the name **C12-A02-BWC**.
5. Print and then close **C12-A02-BWC.docx**.

Figure 12.17 Assessment 12.2

Assessment 12.3   Create an Announcement with a Shape and Text Box

1. At a blank document, create the shape shown in Figure 12.18 with the following specifications:
   a. Use the *Bevel* shape (located in the *Basic Shapes* section of the drop-down list).
   b. Change the height to 3.3 inches and the width to 5.7 inches.
   c. Apply the *Subtle Effect – Orange, Accent 6* shape style.
   d. Apply the *Offset Diagonal Top Right* shadow effect.
   e. Apply the *Orange, 5 pt glow, Accent color 6* glow effect.
   f. Change the position of the text box to *Position in Top Center with Square Text Wrapping*. **Hint: Use the Position button in the Arrange group in the Drawing Tools Format tab.**
2. Type the text inside the shape as shown in Figure 12.18. After typing the text, select the text and then change the font to 36-point Monotype Corsiva bold and the font color to *Orange, Accent 6, Darker 50%*.
3. Save the document and name it **C12-A03-EmpofMonth**.
4. Print and then close **C12-A03-EmpofMonth.docx**.

Figure 12.18 Assessment 12.3

Assessment 12.4 Format Columns and Insert a Pull Quote in a Document

1. Open **SoftwareCycle.docx** and save the document with the name **C12-A04-SoftwareCycle**.
2. Apply the Heading 1 style to the title of the report and apply the Heading 2 style to the five headings in the report.
3. Change the style set to Traditional.
4. Change the theme colors to Newsprint. (Make sure you change the theme colors and not the theme.)
5. Format the text into two columns from the first paragraph of text to the end of the document.
6. Select the title *COMMERCIAL LIFE CYCLE*, increase the spacing after the title to 12 points, and then center the title.
7. Insert the *Contrast Sidebar* predesigned text box in the document and then type the following text in the text box: "The commercial software life cycle is repeated every time a new version of a program is needed."
8. Apply the *Dark Red, Accent 6, Darker 25%* shape fill color.
9. Select the text in the text box and then change the font size to 12.
10. Click the Drawing Tools Format tab and then change the shape height to 1.3".
11. Move the insertion point to the end of the document and then insert a continuous section break. (This balances the two columns.)
12. Save, print, and then close **C12-A04-SoftwareCycle.docx**.

Assessment 12.5 Create a Flyer with Shapes and a Text Box

1. At a blank document, create the left circular arrow shown in Figure 12.19 with the following specifications:
   a. Draw the shape using the *Curved Right Arrow* shape (located in the *Block Arrows* section of the drop-down list).
   b. Change the height of the arrow to 4.8 inches and the width of the arrow to 3 inches.
   c. Apply the *Light 1 Outline, Colored Fill – Red, Accent 2* shape style.
   d. Change the shape outline color to dark blue.
2. Copy the arrow shape to the right and then flip the arrow horizontally and then flip it vertically.
3. Select only the right arrow and then move it up slightly so it is positioned as shown in Figure 12.19.

4. Draw a text box between the arrows that is 1.3 inches tall and 4 inches wide and then change the shape outline to *No Outline*.
5. Type the text inside the text box with the following specifications:
   a. Change the line spacing to single.
   b. Change the paragraph alignment to Center.
   c. Change the font to 28-point Franklin Gothic Heavy and the font color to dark blue.
6. Drag the text box so the text is positioned between the arrows as shown in Figure 12.19.
7. Save the document and name it **C12-A05-TeamBuildFlyer**.
8. Print and then close **C12-A05-TeamBuildFlyer.docx**.

Figure 12.19 Assessment 12.5

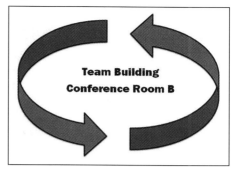

Assessment 12.6   Create a Banner with WordArt Text

1. At a blank document, create the document shown in Figure 12.20. Insert the WordArt text (Mountain Adventures) with the following specifications:
   a. Use the *Fill – Red, Accent 2, Matte Bevel* WordArt style. (This WordArt style contains red text. You will change this text color to blue.)
   b. Click the border of the WordArt text box to change the border to a solid line and then apply the *Dark Blue, Text 2, Lighter 40%* text fill color.
   c. Apply the *Olive Green, 5 pt glow, Accent color 3* glow text effect. **Hint: Make sure you use the Text Effects button and not the Shape Effects button.**
   d. Apply the *Perspective Relaxed Moderately* 3-D rotation text effect. (Make sure you use the Text Effects button.)
   e. Change the height to 1.3 inches and the width to 6.5 inches.
   f. Apply the *Inflate Top* transform text effect.
2. Save the document and name it **C12-A06-MABanner**.
3. Print and then close **C12-A06-MABanner.docx**.

Figure 12.20 Assessment 12.6

Assessment 12.7   Apply Character Spacing and OpenType Features

1. Open **PRDonations.docx** and then save the document and name it **C12-A07-PRDonations**.
2. Select the quote text *"In every community there is work to be done. In every nation there are wounds to heal. In every heart there is the power to do it."* and then change the stylistic set to *4*. (Do this at the Font dialog box with the Advanced tab selected.)

3. Select the heading *Domestic Donations*, change the scale to *90%* and the spacing to *Expanded*. (Do this at the Font dialog box with the Advanced tab selected.)
4. Apply the same formatting in Step 3 to the heading *International Donations*.
5. Select the numbers in the *Domestic Donations* section. **Hint: To select just the numbers, position the mouse pointer at the beginning of $450,000, hold down the Alt key, and then use the mouse to drag and select the four numbers in the second column.** With the numbers selected, change the number spacing to *Tabular*. (Do this at the Font dialog box with the Advanced tab selected.)
6. Select the numbers in the International Donations section and then change the number spacing to *Tabular*.
7. Select the text *We are dedicated to working toward a more just and peaceful world.* and then insert a check mark in the *Use Contextual Alternates* check box at the Font dialog box with the Advanced tab selected.
8. Save, print, and then close **C12-A07-PRDonations.docx**.

Expanding Your Skills

Explore additional feature options or use Help to learn a new skill in creating these documents.

Assessment 12.8   Edit a Drawn Line

1. Open **C12-A02-BWC.docx** and save the document and name it **C12-A08-BWC**.
2. Click the horizontal line to select it, click the Drawing Tools Format tab, and then click the Shape Styles group dialog box launcher. This displays the Format Shape dialog box with additional options for customizing the shape.
3. Click *Line Style* at the left side of the dialog box and then look over the options. Change the line style width to 4 points and change the beginning and ending arrow style to *Diamond Arrow*. **Hint: Do this with the Begin type and End type buttons in the Arrow settings section.**
4. Click *Glow and Soft Edges* at the left side of the dialog box, click the Color button in the *Glow* section, and then click the *Aqua Accent 5, Lighter 40%* color. Change the size to *3 pt* and then close the dialog box.
5. Save, print, and then close **C12-A08-BWC.docx**.

Assessment 12.9   Format and Insert WordArt Text in a Travel Document

1. Open **CedarMeadows.docx** and then save the document with the name **C12-A09-CedarMeadows**.
2. Make the following changes to the document:
   a. Apply the Heading 1 style to the title and the Heading 2 style to the one heading in the document.
   b. Select the paragraphs of text below the *Fast Facts* heading and then apply bullets.
   c. Change the style set to Traditional.
   d. Change the left and right margins to 1.5 inches.
3. Insert the WordArt text as shown in Figure 12.21 using the *Gradient Fill – Blue, Accent 1* WordArt style.
4. Click the WordArt text box border to make it a solid line and then click the WordArt Styles group dialog box launcher. Explore the options available at this dialog box with each of the options selected at the left side of the dialog box. After exploring the dialog box, make the following changes:
   a. Click *Text Fill* at the left side of the dialog box and then change the gradient fill direction to *Linear Up*. **Hint: Use the Direction button.**
   b. Click *Shadow* at the left side of the dialog box and then apply the *Offset Diagonal Top Left* shadow effect. **Hint: Use the Presets button.** Change the shadow color to blue.
   c. Click *Reflection* at the left side of the dialog box and then apply the *Tight Reflection, touching* reflection. **Hint: Use the Presets button.**
   d. Click *3-D Format* at the left side of the dialog box and then apply the Slope bevel format. **Hint: Use the Top button in the Bevel section.**

e. Close the dialog box.
5. With the WordArt text box selected (solid line), make the following changes:
    a. Change the height to 1 inch and the width to 5.5 inches.
    b. Change the text wrapping to *Square*.
    c. Apply the *Square* transform text effect.
    d. If necessary, drag the WordArt text so it is positioned as shown in Figure 12.21.
6. Save, print, and then close **C12-A09-CedarMeadows.docx**.

Figure 12.21 Assessment 12.9

Ski Resorts

Cedar Meadows

A typical day at Cedar Meadows begins with a ride up the Alpine Express. At the top, the air is crisp and cool, and the view is unlike anything you have ever seen: The deep, dark blue of the sky provides a stark contrast to the line of white at the horizon, where snow divides the lake and the sky.

You push off and begin your descent, trailing a wake of powder. The snow beneath your skis is so dry it squeaks. You do not really care where you are going or how you get there. The important thing is that you are here. Cedar Meadows is a destination where pleasures abound. Here you can feed your spirit with endless excitement and relaxation.

Fast Facts

- Terrain: The Cedar Meadows terrain includes 20 percent beginner slopes, 45 percent intermediate slopes, and 35 percent advanced slopes.

- Lifts: Cedar Meadows resort has one aerial tram, three high-speed quads, eight triple chairs, seven double chairs, and six surface lifts.

- Elevations: The base elevation is 6,540 feet; the summit, 10,040 feet; the vertical drop, 3,500 feet; and the longest run is 5.5 miles.

- Ski School: With over 225 certified ski instructors, the Cedar Meadows Ski School offers a variety of programs.

- Children's Services: Children ages 4 through 12 can take advantage of the Snow Explorers program, which offers young skiers an exciting adventure in alpine skiing and snowboarding.

- Ski Shuttles: Free ski shuttles travel the Cedar Meadows resort seven days a week.

Achieving Signature Status

Take your skills to the next level by completing these more challenging assessments.

Assessment 12.10   Create an Announcement

1. At a blank document, create the announcement shown in Figure 12.22. Insert the WordArt text with the following specifications:
    a. Use the *Gradient Fill – Blue, Accent 1* WordArt style.

b. Apply the *Inside Diagonal Top Left* shadow text effect. ***Hint: Use the Text Effects button.***

c. Apply the *Subtle Effect – Blue, Accent 1* shape style.

d. Apply the *Offset Top* shadow shape effect. ***Hint: Use the Shape Effects button.***

e. Apply the *Square* transform text effect. ***Hint: Use the Text Effects button.***

2. Insert the caduceus clip art image as shown in the figure with the following specifications:

- Use the word *medicine* to locate the clip art image.
- Change the text wrapping to *Tight*.
- Apply the *Blue, Accent color 1 Dark* clip art image color.
- Correct the brightness and contrast to *Brightness: +20% Contrast: -20%*.
- Size and move the clip art image as shown in the figure.

3. Apply character (set the text in the Candara font), paragraph, and page formatting so your document appears similar to the document in Figure 12.22.

4. Check to make sure the entire page border will print. If it will not, increase the measurements in the Border and Shading Options dialog box.

5. Save the completed announcement and name it **C12-A10-FirstAidCourse**.

6. Print and then close **C12-A10-FirstAidCourse.docx**.

Figure 12.22 Assessment 12.10

First Aid at Work

The Safety Committee is offering a two-day first aid course for employees. The objective of the course is to equip employees with the essential knowledge and practical experience to enable them to carry out first aid in the workplace. Course content includes health and safety administration, handling an incident and developing an action plan, recognizing and treating injuries and illnesses, and cardio-pulmonary resuscitation (CPR).

Dates .... March 8 and 9

Times .... 9:00 a.m. to 4:00 p.m.

Location .... Administration Building

Room .... Conference Room 200

Registration is available from February 15 until the course begins on March 8. Before registering, please check with your immediate supervisor to ensure that you can be excused from your normal duties for the two days.

For more information, contact Maxwell Singh at extension 3505.

Assessment 12.11   Insert Screenshots in a Memo

1. Open **FirstAidMemo.docx** and then save it and name it **C12-A11-FirstAidMemo**.
2. Insert screenshots so your document appears as shown in Figure 12.23. Use the **FirstAidAnnounce.docx** to create the first screenshot and use the document **C12-A10-FirstAidCourse.docx** you created in Assessment 12.10 for the second screenshot. Before making either screenshot, make sure the entire announcement page displays on the screen. If you cannot see the entire page, adjust the zoom.
3. Save, print, and then close **C12-A11-FirstAidMemo.docx**.

Figure 12.23 Assessment 12.11

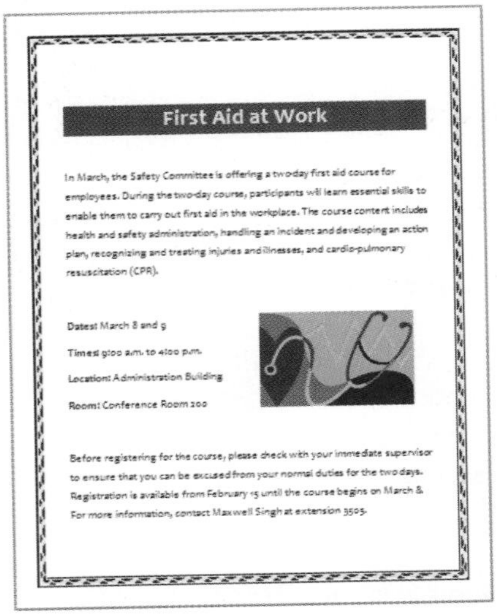

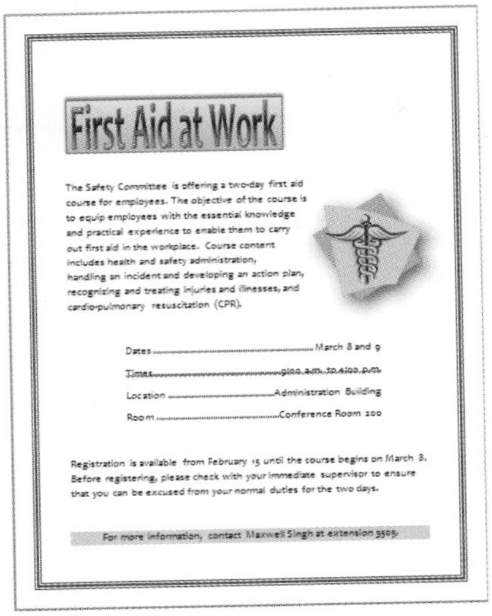

Chapter 13

 **TUTORIALS**

Tutorial 13.1
Creating a Table
Tutorial 13.2
Modifying a Table
Tutorial 13.3
Applying Shading and Borders
to a Table
Tutorial 13.4
Drawing a Table
Tutorial 13.5
Inserting a Quick Table

Creating Tables

Performance Objectives

Upon successful completion of Chapter 13, you will be able to:

- Create and format a table
- Change the table design
- Draw a table
- Insert an Excel spreadsheet
- Insert a Quick Table

Tables provide a systematic way to organize and display data in a document. With the Tables feature in Word, you can organize data such as text, numbers, or formulas into columns and rows to create a variety of tables. In this chapter you will learn to create tables using several different methods, including inserting a Quick Table. You will also learn how to format data in a table and apply table styles.

Note: Before beginning computer exercises for this chapter, copy to your storage medium the Chapter13 folder from the CD that accompanies this textbook and then make Chapter13 the active folder.

In this chapter students will produce the following documents:

Exercise 13.1. C13-E01-Tables.docx
Exercise 13.2. C13-E02-YrlySales.docx
Exercise 13.3. C13-E03-WMExecs.docx
Exercise 13.4. C13-E04-Worksheet.docx
Exercise 13.5. C13-E05-Calendar.docx

Model answers for these exercises are shown on the following pages.

TECHNICAL SUPPORT PERSONNEL

Name	Title	Telephone Number
Alan Hubbard	Manager	555-3203 Ext. 5401
Debbie Morrissey	Assistant Manager	555-3312 Ext. 5320
Christopher Sorenson	Technician	555-3938 Ext. 5327
Donna Grabowski	Technician	555-3894 Ext. 5411
William Koehler	Technician	555-3809 Ext. 5388

HUMAN RESOURCES PERSONNEL

Name	Title	Telephone Number
Melissa Clemensen	Manager	555-7463 Ext. 2100
Joseph Reeves	Assistant	555-7601 Ext. 2311
Stephanie Tomasi	Assistant	555-7548 Ext. 2408
Myong Han	Assistant Manager	555-7487 Ext. 2105
David Hoover	Assistant	555-7444 Ext. 2238

Exercise 13.1

C13-E01-Tables.docx

WOODRIDGE MANUFACTURING

YEARLY SALES

State	First Quarter	Second Quarter	Third Quarter	Fourth Quarter
Maine	$100,340	$105,249	$110,985	$123,679
New Hampshire	$105,674	$101,563	$100,257	$110,947
Massachusetts	$152,491	$162,490	$153,276	$160,054
Connecticut	$104,239	$97,639	$100,574	$106,379
New York	$203,549	$211,574	$199,548	$225,340
Pennsylvania	$189,542	$192,438	$200,459	$221,398
New Jersey	$175,463	$188,390	$173,429	$200,118

Exercise 13.2

C13-E02-YrlySales.docx

Exercise 13.3

C13-E03-WMExecs.docx

WOODRIDGE MANUFACTURING	
Ethan Sanchez	President
Shawna Richards	Vice President
Jennifer Powell	Director
Chase Selden	Director
Lee Kazlowski	Director

Exercise 13.4

C13-E04-Worksheet.docx

National Sales		
Division	Amount	2% Inc.
North	$1,683,000	$171,666,000
South	$1,552,000	$158,304,000
Central	$1,024,000	$104,448,000
East	$1,778,000	$181,356,000
West	$1,299,000	$132,498,000

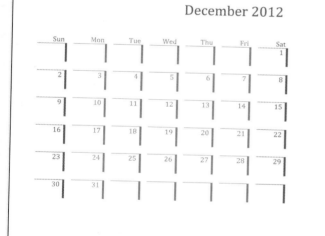

December 2012

Sun	Mon	Tue	Wed	Thu	Fri	Sat
						1
2	3	4	5	6	7	8
9	10	11	12	13	14	15
16	17	18	19	20	21	22
23	24	25	26	27	28	29
30	31					

Exercise 13.5

C13-E05-Calendar.docx

QUICK STEPS

Create a Table
1. Click Insert tab.
2. Click Table button.
3. Drag to create desired number of columns and rows.
4. Click mouse button.
OR
1. Click Insert tab.
2. Click Table button.
3. Click *Insert Table*.
4. Specify number of columns and rows.
5. Click OK.

Table

Creating a Table

A table is made up of information boxes called **cells**. A cell is the intersection between a column and a row. Cells can contain text, numbers, characters, graphics, or formulas. You can use the Tables feature to create cells and organize data in columns and rows. To create a table, click the Insert tab, click the Table button in the Tables group, drag down and to the right until the correct number of columns and rows display, and then click the mouse button.

Figure 13.1 shows a sample table with four columns and three rows. Various features of a Word table are identified in the figure, such as gridlines, end-of-cell markers, end-of-row markers, move table column markers, and the resize handle. In a Word table, nonprinting characters identify the end of a cell and the end of a row. The end-of-cell marker displays inside each cell, and the end-of-row marker displays at the end of each row of cells. To view these characters, click the Show/Hide ¶ button in the Paragraph group in the Home tab.

Figure 13.1 Table

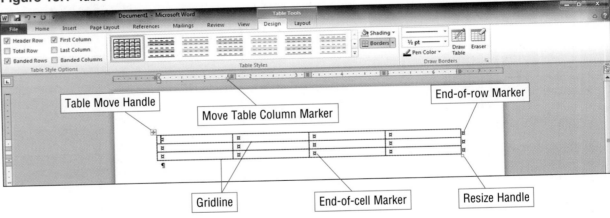

Cells in a table have a cell designation. The columns in a table are lettered from left to right, beginning with *A*; the rows in a table are numbered from top to bottom beginning with *1*. The cell in the upper left corner of the table is cell A1. The cell to the right of A1 is B1, the cell to the right of B1 is C1, and so on. When you create a table, the insertion point displays in cell A1 (in the upper left corner of the table).

When the insertion point is positioned in a cell in the table, the move table column markers display on the horizontal ruler (see Figure 13.1). If the horizontal ruler is not displayed, you can display it—and the markers—by clicking the View Ruler button located toward the top of the vertical scroll bar. These markers represent the end of a column and are useful when changing the width of columns.

Entering Text in Cells

With the insertion point positioned in a cell, type or edit the cell's contents. If the text you type does not fit on one line, it wraps to the next line within the same cell. Or, if you press the Enter key within a cell, the insertion point moves to the next line within that cell. The cell lengthens vertically to accommodate the text, and all cells in that row also lengthen.

Moving the Insertion Point within a Table

To move the insertion point to a different cell within a table using the mouse, click in the desired cell. To move the insertion point to different cells within a table using the keyboard, use the keyboard commands shown in Table 13.1.

Table 13.1 Insertion Point Movement within a Table Using the Keyboard

To move the insertion point	Press these keys
To next cell	Tab
To preceding cell	Shift + Tab
Forward one character	Right Arrow key
Backward one character	Left Arrow key
To previous row	Up Arrow key
To next row	Down Arrow key
To first cell in the row	Alt + Home
To last cell in the row	Alt + End
To top cell in the column	Alt + Page Up
To bottom cell in the column	Alt + Page Down

If you want to move the insertion point to a tab stop within a cell, press Ctrl + Tab. If the insertion point is located in the last cell of the table and you press the Tab key, Word adds another row to the table. You can insert a page break within a table by pressing Ctrl + Enter. The page break is inserted between rows, not within.

1. At a blank document, turn on bold, and then type the title TECHNICAL SUPPORT PERSONNEL shown in Figure 13.2.
2. Turn off bold and then press the Enter key.
3. Create the table shown in Figure 13.2 by completing the following steps:
   a. Click the Insert tab.
   b. Click the Table button in the Tables group.
   c. Move the mouse pointer down and to the right until the number above the grid displays as *3×6* and then click the mouse button.

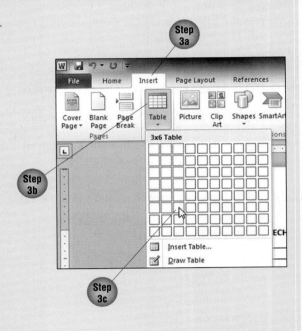

4. Type the text in the cells as indicated in Figure 13.2. Press the Tab key to move to the next cell or press Shift + Tab to move to the preceding cell. To indent the text in the cells in the middle column, press Ctrl + Tab to move the insertion point to a tab within the cells, and then type the text. (If you accidentally press the Enter key within a cell, immediately press the Backspace key. Do not press the Tab key after typing the text in the last cell. If you do, another row is inserted in the table. If this happens, immediately click the Undo button on the Quick Access toolbar.)
5. Save the table in the Chapter13 folder on your storage medium with the name **C13-E01-Tables**.

Figure 13.2 Exercise 13.1A

TECHNICAL SUPPORT PERSONNEL

Name	Title	Telephone Number
Alan Hubbard	Manager	555-3203 Ext. 5401
Debbie Morrissey	Assistant Manager	555-3312 Ext. 5320
Christopher Sorenson	Technician	555-3938 Ext. 5327
Donna Grabowski	Technician	555-3894 Ext. 5411
William Koehler	Technician	555-3809 Ext. 5388

You can also create a table with options at the Insert Table dialog box, shown in Figure 13.3. To display this dialog box, click the Insert tab, click the Table button in the Tables group, and then click *Insert Table* at the drop-down list. At the Insert Table dialog box, enter the desired number of columns and rows and then click OK.

Figure 13.3 Insert Table Dialog Box

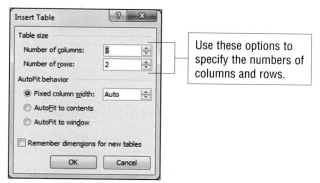

Use these options to specify the numbers of columns and rows.

Exercise 13.1B Creating a Table with the Insert Table Dialog Box   Part 2 of 3

1. With **C13-E01-Tables.docx** open, press Ctrl + End to move the insertion point below the table.
2. Press the Enter key twice.
3. Turn on bold and then type the title HUMAN RESOURCES PERSONNEL shown in Figure 13.4.
4. Turn off bold and then press the Enter key.
5. Insert the table by completing the following steps:
   a. Click the Insert tab.
   b. Click the Table button in the Tables group and then click *Insert Table* at the drop-down list.
   c. At the Insert Table dialog box, type 3 in the *Number of columns* text box. (The insertion point is automatically positioned in this text box.)
   d. Press the Tab key (this moves the insertion point to the *Number of rows* option).
   e. Type 6.
   f. Click OK.

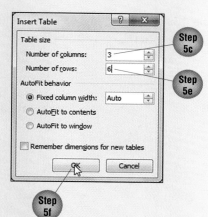

6. Type the text in the cells as indicated in Figure 13.4. Press the Tab key to move to the next cell or press Shift + Tab to move to the preceding cell. To indent the text in cells B1 through B6, press Ctrl + Tab to move the insertion point to a tab within cells and then type the text.
7. Save **C13-E01-Tables.docx**.

Figure 13.4 Exercise 13.1B

HUMAN RESOURCES PERSONNEL

Name	Title	Telephone Number
Melissa Clemensen	Manager	555-7463 Ext. 2100
Myong Han	Assistant Manager	555-7487 Ext. 2105
David Hoover	Assistant	555-7444 Ext. 2238
Joseph Reeves	Assistant	555-7601 Ext. 2311
Stephanie Tomasi	Assistant	555-7548 Ext. 2408

Selecting Cells

You can format data within a table in several ways. For example, you can change the alignment of text within cells or rows, select and then move rows or columns, or you can add character formatting such as bold, italic, and underlining. To format specific cells, rows, or columns, you must first select them.

Selecting in a Table with the Mouse

Use the mouse pointer to select a cell, column, row, or an entire table. Table 13.2 provides instructions for selecting specific portions of a table or the entire table with the mouse. The left edge of each cell, between the left column border and the end-of-cell marker or first character in the cell, is called the *cell selection bar.* When you position the mouse pointer in the cell selection bar, it turns into a black arrow pointing up and to the right (instead of the left). Each row in a table contains a *row selection bar,* which is the space just to the left of the left edge of the table. When you position the mouse pointer in the row selection bar, the mouse pointer turns into an arrow pointing up and to the right.

Table 13.2 Selecting in a Table with the Mouse

To select this	Do this
A cell	Position the mouse pointer in the cell selection bar at the left edge of the cell until it turns into a black arrow pointing up and to the right and then click the left mouse button.
A row	Position the mouse pointer in the row selection bar at the left edge of the table until it turns into an arrow pointing up and to the right and then click the left mouse button. To select nonadjacent rows, hold down the Ctrl key while selecting rows.
A column	Position the mouse pointer on the uppermost horizontal gridline of the table in the appropriate column until it turns into a short, down-pointing arrow and then click the left mouse button. To select nonadjacent columns, hold down the Ctrl key while selecting columns.
Adjacent cells	Position the mouse pointer in the first cell to be selected, hold down the left mouse button, drag the mouse pointer to the last cell to be selected, and then release the mouse button.
All cells in a table	Click the table move handle, or position the mouse pointer in any cell in the table, hold down the Alt key, and then double-click the left mouse button. You can also position the mouse pointer in the row selection bar for the first row at the left edge of the table until it turns into an arrow pointing up and to the right, hold down the left mouse button, drag down to select all rows in the table, and then release the left mouse button.
Text within a cell	Position the mouse pointer at the beginning of the text and then hold down the left mouse button as you drag the mouse across the text. (When a cell is selected, the cell background color changes to blue. When text within a cell is selected, only those lines containing text are selected.)

Selecting in a Table with the Keyboard

Another way to select specific cells within a table is to use the keyboard. Table 13.3 presents the commands for selecting specific portions of a table.

Table 13.3 Selecting in a Table with the Keyboard

To select	Press
The next cell's contents	Tab
The preceding cell's contents	Shift + Tab
The entire table	Alt + 5 (on numeric keypad with Num Lock off)
Adjacent cells	Hold down Shift key, then press an arrow key repeatedly.
A column	Position insertion point in top cell of column, hold down Shift key, then press down-pointing arrow key until column is selected.

If you want to select only the text within a cell rather than the entire cell, press F8 to turn on the *Extend* mode, and then move the insertion point with an arrow key. When a cell is selected, the cell background color changes to blue. When text within a cell is selected, only those lines containing text are selected. You can move text to a different cell by selecting the text and then dragging the selected text to a different cell.

Exercise 13.1C Selecting Cells, Applying Formatting, and Moving Rows   **Part 3 of 3**

1. With **C13-E01-Tables.docx** open, select the heading *TECHNICAL SUPPORT PERSONNEL*, change the font to 14-point Candara, and then center the text.
2. Apply the same formatting to the heading *HUMAN RESOURCES PERSONNEL*.
3. Change the formatting for the entire top table by completing the following steps:
   a. Hover the mouse pointer over any cell in the top table until the table move handle displays in the upper left corner of the table.
   b. Position the mouse pointer over the table move handle until the pointer displays as a four-headed arrow and then click the left mouse button. (This selects the entire table.)
   c. Click the Home tab.
   d. Click the Font button arrow and then click *Candara* at the drop-down gallery.
   e. Deselect the table by clicking in any cell in the table.

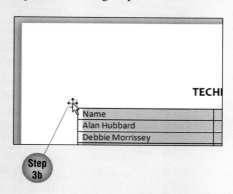

Step 3b

4. Center text in cells in the third column of the top table by completing the following steps:
   a. Position the mouse pointer in the cell below the heading Telephone Number (555-3203 Ext. 5401).
   b. Hold down the left mouse button, drag down to the bottom cell in the table (the cell containing the telephone number 555-3809 Ext. 5388).
   c. Make sure the Home tab is active and then click the Center button in the Paragraph group.

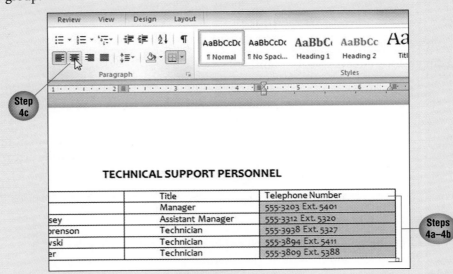

5. Apply formatting to the first row in the top table by completing the following steps:
   a. Position the mouse pointer in the row selection bar at the left side of the first row until the pointer turns into an arrow pointing up and to the right and then click the left mouse button. (This selects the entire first row of the top table.)
   b. Make sure the Home tab is active.
   c. Click the Bold button in the Font group.
   d. Click the Center button in the Paragraph group.
   e. Click the Shading button arrow and then click the dark red color (*Red, Accent 2, Darker 50%*). (This automatically changes the font color to white.)

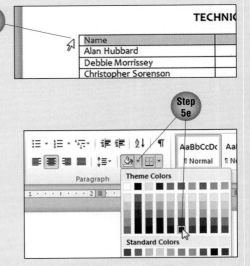

6. Apply paragraph shading to rows in the top table by completing the following steps:
   a. Click immediately right of the name *Alan Hubbard*.
   b. Hold down the Shift key and then press the Right Arrow key on the keyboard until the entire row is selected.
   c. Click the Shading button arrow and then click the light red color (*Red, Accent 2, Lighter 80%*).
   d. Select the fourth row in the table (begins with the name *Christopher Sorenson*) by positioning the mouse pointer in the row selection bar at the left edge of the fourth row until the pointer turns into an arrow pointing up and to the right and then click the left mouse button.

e. Press F4. (This is the Repeat command that repeats the last action.)
   f. Select the sixth row (begins with the name *William Koehler*) and then press F4.
7. Complete steps similar to those in Steps 6b–6c to apply red color (*Red, Accent 2, Lighter 60%*) to rows 3 and 5.
8. Complete steps similar to those in Steps 3 through 6 to apply formatting and shading to the bottom table *except* use purple colors for shading.
9. Move two rows in the bottom table by completing the following steps:
   a. Position the mouse pointer in the row selection bar at the left side of the row containing the name *Joseph Reeves*, hold down the left mouse button, drag down to select two rows (the *Joseph Reeves* row and the *Stephanie Tomasi* row).
   b. Click the Home tab and then click the Cut button in the Clipboard group.
   c. Move the insertion point so it is positioned at the beginning of the name *Myong Han* and then click the Paste button in the Clipboard group.
10. Save, print, and then close **C13-E01-Tables.docx**.

Changing the Table Design

When you insert a table, the Table Tools Design tab, shown in Figure 13.5, becomes active. This tab contains options for applying and changing table styles. The tab also contains a button for applying borders, a button for applying shading, and a button for drawing a table.

Figure 13.5 Table Tools Design Tab

Applying Table Styles

Word provides a number of predesigned table styles that you can use to format your tables and add visual appeal. The Table Styles group in the Table Tools Design tab displays several styles. Word provides additional styles that you can view by clicking the More button that displays at the right of the styles. Clicking the More button displays a drop-down gallery of style options. Hover the mouse pointer over an option, and the table in the document displays with the formatting applied.

With options in the Table Style Options group, also in the Table Tools Design tab, you can further refine predesigned style formatting that you have applied to your table. For example, if your table contains a total column, you can insert a check mark in the *Total Row* option. If your table contains data in the first column that you would like set off from the other columns of data, you can insert a check mark in the *First Column* check box. If you make a mistake while formatting a table, immediately click the Undo button on the Quick Access toolbar.

1. At a blank document, create the table shown in Figure 13.6 by completing the following steps:
    a. Type the heading *WOODRIDGE MANUFACTURING* centered and in bold.
    b. Type the subheading *YEARLY SALES* centered and in bold.
    c. Press the Enter key once after typing the subheading, change the paragraph alignment back to left, turn off bold, and then click the Insert tab.
    d. Click the Table button in the Tables group in the Insert tab, drag down and to the right until *5×8* displays above the grid.
    e. Type the text in the cells as shown in Figure 13.6.
2. Center the text in all of the columns except the first column by completing the following steps:
    a. Position the mouse pointer at the top of the second column until the pointer displays as a down-pointing black arrow, hold down the left mouse button, drag to the fifth column, and then release the mouse button.
    b. Press Ctrl + E.
3. Apply a table style by completing the following steps:
    a. Make sure the insertion point is positioned in a cell in the table and that the Table Tools Design tab is active.
    b. In the Table Styles Options group, make sure the *Header Row* and *Banded Rows* check boxes are checked and that all other check boxes are unchecked.

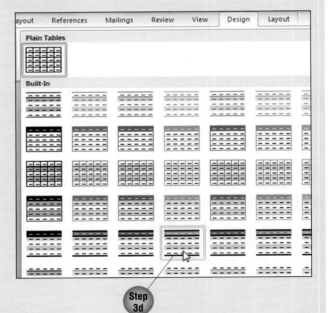

    c. Click the More button that displays at the right side of the table styles in the Table Styles group.
    d. Click the fourth option from the left in the fifth row from the top in the *Built-In* section (*Medium Shading 2 - Accent 3*).
4. Save the document with the name **C13-E02-YrlySales**.
5. Print **C13-E02-YrlySales.docx**.
6. With the document open, make the following changes:
    a. Make sure the Table Tools Design tab is active.
    b. Remove the check mark from the *Banded Rows* check box in the Table Style Options group.
    c. Insert a check mark in the *First Column* check box and in the *Banded Columns* check box.
    d. Make sure the *Header Row* check box contains a check mark.
7. Save **C13-E02-YrlySales.docx**.

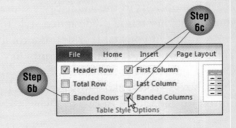

Figure 13.6 Exercise 13.2A

		WOODRIDGE MANUFACTURING		
		YEARLY SALES		
State	First Quarter	Second Quarter	Third Quarter	Fourth Quarter
Maine	$100,340	$105,249	$110,985	$123,679
New Hampshire	$105,674	$101,563	$100,257	$110,947
Massachusetts	$152,491	$162,490	$153,276	$160,054
Connecticut	$104,239	$97,639	$100,574	$106,379
New York	$203,549	$211,574	$199,548	$225,340
Pennsylvania	$189,542	$192,438	$200,459	$221,398
New Jersey	$175,463	$188,390	$173,429	$200,118

Applying Shading and Borders

Apply shading to a table by clicking the Shading button arrow in the Table Styles group and then clicking the desired shading color at the drop-down gallery. Apply borders by clicking the Borders button arrow and then clicking the desired border at the drop-down list. If you want more control over shading and borders, click the *Borders and Shading* option at the Borders button drop-down gallery. This displays the Borders and Shading dialog box with the Borders tab selected, as shown in Figure 13.7.

Another method for inserting borders is to draw them with the pen pointer. To do this, click the Draw Table button in the Draw Borders group in the Table Tools Design tab, and then draw along the table gridlines. When you click the Draw Table button, the mouse pointer displays as a pen pointer. Use the Line Style, Line Weight, and Pen Color buttons in the Draw Borders group to specify the type of border line you want to draw.

Figure 13.7 Borders and Shading Dialog Box with Borders Tab Selected

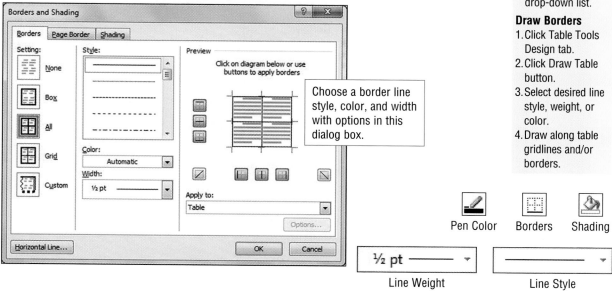

QUICK STEPS

Apply Shading to Table
1. Click Table Tools Design tab.
2. Click Shading button arrow.
3. Click desired shading color.

Apply Borders to Table
1. Click Table Tools Design tab.
2. Click Borders button arrow.
3. Click desired border option at drop-down list.

Draw Borders
1. Click Table Tools Design tab.
2. Click Draw Table button.
3. Select desired line style, weight, or color.
4. Draw along table gridlines and/or borders.

Pen Color Borders Shading

½ pt ——— Line Weight

——— Line Style

1. With **C13-E02-YrlySales.docx** open, change cell shading by completing the following steps:
   a. Make sure the Table Tools Design tab is active.
   b. Select the cells in the second column *except* the first cell.
   c. Click the Shading button arrow in the Table Styles group.
   d. Click the light purple color (*Purple, Accent 4, Lighter 80%*) at the drop-down gallery.
   e. Select the cells in the fourth column *except* the first cell and then press F4.
   f. Select the cells in the third column *except* the first cell.
   g. Click the Shading button arrow in the Table Styles group.
   h. Click the light green color (*Olive Green, Accent 3, Lighter 80%*) at the drop-down gallery.
   i. Select the cells in the fifth column *except* the first cell and then press F4.

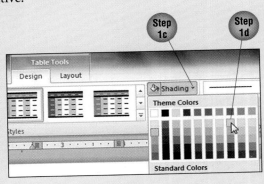

2. Change cell borders by completing the following steps:
   a. Select the first column in the table.
   b. Click the Borders button arrow in the Table Styles group and then click the *Left Border* option at the drop-down list.
   c. Select the fifth column in the table.
   d. Click the Borders button arrow in the Table Styles group and then click the *Right Border* option at the drop-down list.

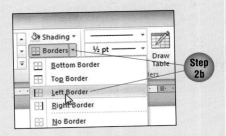

3. Customize cell borders by completing the following steps:
   a. Select the entire table by hovering the mouse pointer over the table and then clicking the table move handle.
   b. Click the Borders button arrow in the Table Styles group and then click the *Borders and Shading* option located at the bottom of the drop-down list.
   c. At the Borders and Shading dialog box with the Borders tab selected, click the down-pointing arrow at the right of the *Color* option.
   d. Click the purple color at the drop-down list (*Purple, Accent 4, Darker 25%*).
   e. Click the *Box* option in the *Setting* section.
   f. Click OK to close the dialog box.
   g. Select the first row of the table.
   h. Click the Borders button arrow and then click *Bottom Border* at the drop-down list.

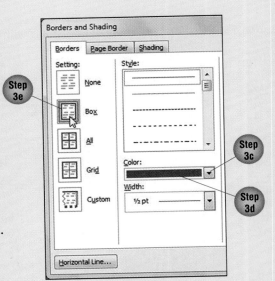

4. Draw a double-line border by completing the following steps:

a. Click the Line Style button arrow in the Draw Borders group and then click the first double-line option at the drop-down list. (This turns on the Draw Table button and changes the mouse pointer to a pen.)

b. Click the Line Weight button arrow and then click *¾ pt* at the drop-down list.

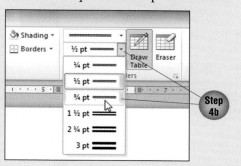

c. Click the Pen Color button arrow and then click the purple color (*Purple, Accent 4, Darker 50%*) at the drop-down palette.

d. Drag with the pen pointer along the bottom border of the first row from the first cell to the last cell in the row.

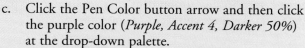

State	First Quarter	Second Quarter	Third Quarter	Fourth Quarter
			WOODRIDGE MANUFACTURING	
			YEARLY SALES	
Maine	$100,340	$105,249	$110,985	$123,679
New Hampshire	$105,674	$101,563	$100,257	$110,947
Massachusetts	$152,491	$162,490	$153,276	$160,054

5. Draw a single-line border between columns by completing the following steps:

a. Click the Line Style button arrow and then click the single-line option that displays toward the top of the drop-down list.

b. Click the Line Weight button arrow and then click *¼ pt* at the drop-down list.

c. Leave the pen color at *Purple, Accent 4, Darker 50%*.

d. Draw along the right side of the cells in the second column from the bottom of the first row to the last row.

e. Draw along the right side of the cells in the third column from the bottom of the top row to the last row.

f. Draw along the right side of the cells in the fourth column from the bottom of the top row to the last row.

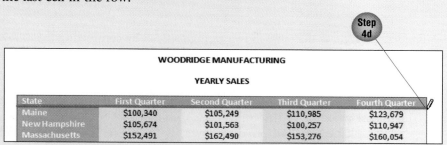

State	First Quarter	Second Quarter
Maine	$100,340	$105,249
New Hampshire	$105,674	$101,563
Massachusetts	$152,491	$162,490
Connecticut	$104,239	$97,639
New York	$203,549	$211,574
Pennsylvania	$189,542	$192,438
New Jersey	$175,463	$188,390

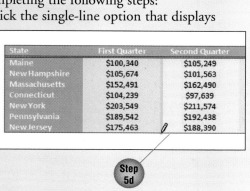

g. Click the Draw Table button to deactivate it.
6. Select the heading and subheading in the document (*WOODRIDGE MANUFACTURING* and *YEARLY SALES*) and then change the font color to dark purple (*Purple, Accent 4, Darker 50%*). (Do this with the Font Color button in the Home tab.)
7. Save, print, and then close **C13-E02-YrlySales.docx**.

QUICK STEPS

Draw a Table
1. Click Insert tab.
2. Click Table button.
3. Click *Draw Table* at drop-down list.
4. Drag pen pointer in document to create table.

Eraser

Drawing a Table

In Exercise 13.2B, you used options in the Draw Borders group to draw borders in and around an existing table. You can also use these options to draw an entire table. To draw a table, click the Insert tab, click the Table button in the Tables group, and then click *Draw Table* at the drop-down list. This turns the mouse pointer into a pen and also displays guidelines on the horizontal and vertical rulers that identify the location of the pen in the document. Drag the pen pointer in the document screen to create the table using the guidelines as a reference.

The first time you release the mouse button when drawing a table, the Table Tools Design tab becomes active. Use buttons in this tab to customize the table as well as to apply table styles, shading, and borders. If you make a mistake while drawing a table, click the Eraser button in the Draw Borders group (this changes the mouse pointer to an eraser) and then drag over any border lines you want to erase.

Exercise 13.3 Drawing a Table   Part 1 of 1

1. At a blank document, draw the table shown in Figure 13.8 by completing the following steps:
   a. Click the Insert tab.
   b. Click the Table button in the Tables group and then click *Draw Table* at the drop-down list.
   c. Move the pen pointer to approximately the 2-inch marker on the horizontal ruler and the 1-inch marker on the vertical ruler. (Use the guidelines to position the pen.)
   d. Hold down the left mouse button, drag down and to the right until the guideline displays at approximately the 4.5-inch marker on the horizontal ruler and the 3-inch marker on the vertical ruler, and then release the mouse button.

Step 1d

e. Click the Line Style button arrow and then click the first thick/thin line option at the drop-down list.

f. Drag over each border of the table to change the border to a thick/thin line.

g. Click the Line Style button arrow and then click the first double-line option at the drop-down list.

h. Drag to create the first row with the double-line border.

i. Click the Line Style button arrow and then click the single-line option.

j. Drag in the table to create the remaining rows and columns as shown in Figure 13.8. If you are not satisfied with a table border, click the Eraser button in the Draw Borders group and then drag across the border line you want to remove.

k. Click the Draw Table button to deactivate it.

2. Type the text in the table as shown in Figure 13.8.

3. Apply a table style by completing the following steps:

a. In the Table Style Options group, insert a check mark in the *Header Row* and *Banded Rows* options and remove the check marks (if any) from the other options in the group.

b. Click the More button that displays at the right side of the table styles in the Table Styles group.

c. Click the second option from the left in the fifth row from the top in the *Built-In* section (*Medium Shading 2 - Accent 1*).

d. Center the title in Row 1.

4. Save the document with the name **C13-E03-WMExecs**.

5. Print and then close **C13-E03-WMExecs.docx**.

Figure 13.8 Exercise 13.3

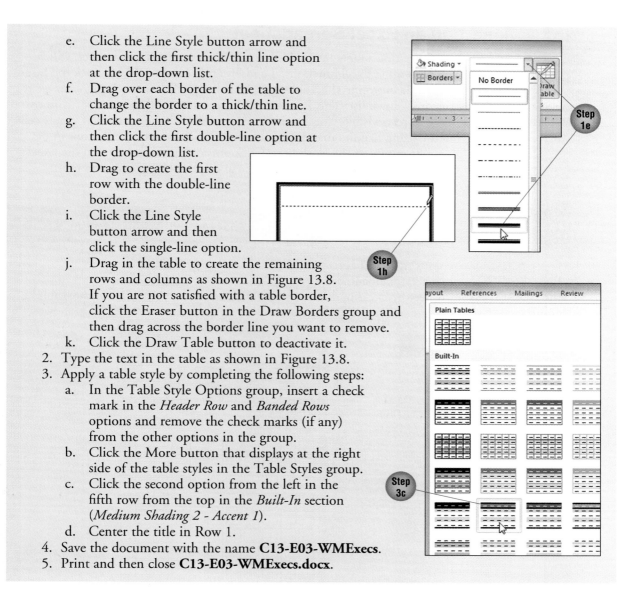

WOODRIDGE MANUFACTURING	
Ethan Sanchez	President
Shawna Richards	Vice President
Jennifer Powell	Director
Chase Selden	Director
Lee Kazlowski	Director

Insert Excel Spreadsheet
1. Click Insert tab.
2. Click Table button.
3. Click Excel Spreadsheet.

Inserting an Excel Spreadsheet

In addition to inserting a table in a slide, you can insert an Excel spreadsheet, which provides you with some Excel functions. To insert an Excel spreadsheet, click the Insert tab, click the Table button in the Tables group, and then click the *Excel Spreadsheet* option at the drop-down list. This inserts a small worksheet in the document with two columns and two rows visible. You can increase and decrease the number of visible cells by dragging the sizing handles that display around the worksheet. Use buttons in the Excel ribbon tabs to format the worksheet. Click outside the worksheet and the Excel ribbon tabs are removed. Double-click the table to display the Excel ribbon tabs.

Exercise 13.4 Inserting and Formatting an Excel Spreadsheet   Part 1 of 1

1. Open **SalesIncrease.docx** in the Chapter13 folder on your storage medium.
2. Press Ctrl + N to open a blank document.
3. Insert an Excel spreadsheet by clicking the Insert tab, clicking the Table button in the Tables group, and then clicking *Excel Spreadsheet* at the drop-down list.

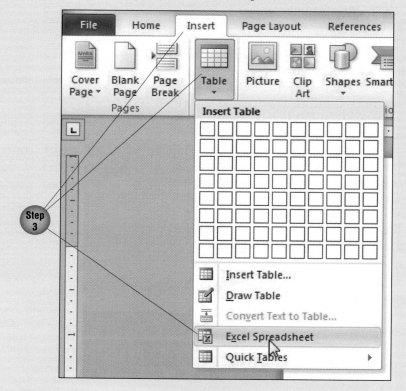

4. Decrease the size of the worksheet by completing the following steps:
   a. Position the mouse pointer on the sizing handle (small, black square) located in the lower right corner of the worksheet until the pointer displays as a black, diagonal, two-headed arrow.
   b. Hold down the left mouse button, drag up and to the left, and release mouse button. Continue dragging the sizing handles until columns A, B, and C and rows 1 through 7 are visible.

5. Copy a table into the Excel worksheet by completing the following steps:
   a. Hover the mouse pointer over the Word button on the Taskbar and then click the thumbnail representing **SalesIncrease.docx**.
   b. Hover your mouse pointer over the table and then click the table move handle (small square containing a four-headed arrow) that displays in the upper left corner of the table. (This selects all cells in the table.)
   c. Click the Copy button in the Clipboard group in the Home tab.
   d. Close **SalesIncrease.docx**.
   e. With the first cell in the worksheet active, click the Paste button in the Clipboard group.

6. Format the worksheet and insert a formula by completing the following steps:
   a. Increase the width of the second column by positioning the mouse pointer on the column boundary between columns B and C and double-clicking the left mouse button.
   b. Click in cell C3, type the formula =**B3*102**, and then press Enter.

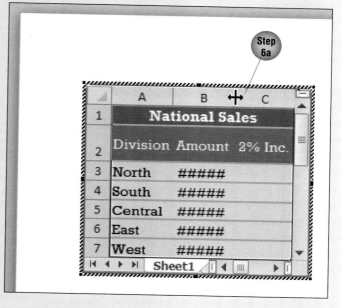

7. Copy the formula in C3 to cells C4 through C7 by completing the following steps:
   a. Position the mouse pointer (white plus symbol) in cell C3, hold down the left mouse button, drag down to cell C7, and then release the mouse button.
   b. Click the Fill button in the Editing group in the Home tab and then click *Down* at the drop-down list.

8. Click outside the worksheet to remove the Excel ribbon tabs.
9. Click in the table, click the Page Layout tab, click the Wrap Text button in the Arrange group, and then click *Tight* at the drop-down list.
10. Drag the worksheet so it is centered between the left and right margins and then click outside the worksheet to deselect it.
11. Save the document and name it **C13-E04-Worksheet**.
12. Print and then close **C13-E04-Worksheet.docx**

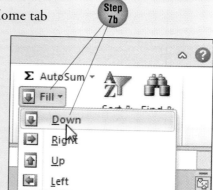

Inserting a Quick Table

Word includes a Quick Tables feature you can use to insert predesigned tables in a document. To insert a quick table, click the Insert tab, click the Table button, point to *Quick Tables,* and then click the desired table at the side menu. When the quick table is inserted in the document, the Table Tools Design tab becomes active. Use options in this tab to further customize the table.

Insert a Quick Table
1. Click Insert tab.
2. Click Table button.
3. Point to *Quick Tables* in drop-down list.
4. Click desired table at side menu.

Exercise 13.5 Inserting a Quick Table   Part 1 of 1

1. At a blank document, click the Insert tab.
2. Click the Table button, point to *Quick Tables*, and then click *Calendar 3* at the side menu.

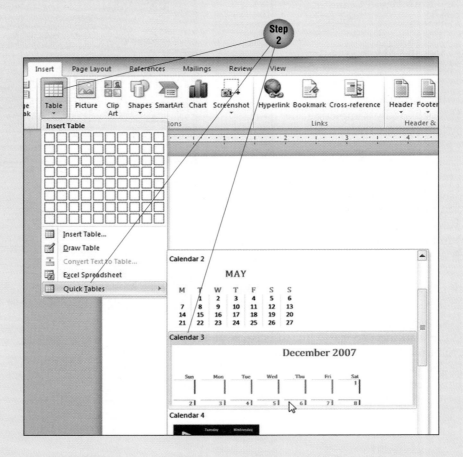

3. Edit text in each of the cells so the month, year, and days reflect the current date.
4. Save the completed monthly calendar with the name **C13-E05-Calendar**.
5. Print and then close **C13-E05-Calendar.docx**.

Chapter Summary

➤ Use the Tables feature to create columns and rows of information. A cell is the intersection between a column and a row.

➤ A table can contain text, characters, numbers, data, graphics, or formulas.

➤ Create a table by clicking the Insert tab, clicking the Table button in the Tables group, dragging the mouse pointer down and to the right until the desired number of columns and rows display in the grid, and then releasing the mouse button. You can also create a table with options at the Insert Table dialog box.

➤ Columns in a table are lettered from left to right beginning with A. Rows are numbered from top to bottom beginning with 1.

➤ The lines that form the cells of the table are called gridlines.

➤ To move the insertion point to different cells within the table using the mouse, click in the desired cell.

➤ To move the insertion point to different cells within the table using the keyboard, refer to Table 13.1.

➤ Position the mouse pointer on the cell selection bar, the row selection bar, or the top gridline of a column to select a cell, row, or column. Click the table move-handle to select the entire table.

➤ Refer to Table 13.3 for a list of keyboard commands for selecting specific cells within a table.

➤ When you insert a table in a document, the Table Tools Design tab becomes active.

➤ Apply formatting to a table with the table styles available in the Table Styles group in the Table Tools Design tab.

➤ Further refine predesigned style formatting applied to columns and rows with options in the Table Style Options group in the Table Tools Design tab.

➤ Use the Shading button in the Table Styles group in the Table Tools Design tab to apply shading to a cell or selected cells and use the Borders button to apply borders.

➤ Customize shading and borders with options at the Borders and Shading dialog box. Display this dialog box by clicking the Borders button arrow and then clicking *Borders and Shading*.

➤ Draw a table in a document by clicking the Insert tab, clicking the Table button, and then clicking *Draw Table*. Using the mouse, drag in the document to create the table.

➤ With options in the Draw Borders group, you can change the border line style, weight, and color and turn the eraser on or off.

➤ Insert an Excel spreadsheet to provide Excel functions by clicking the Insert tab, clicking the Table button in the Tables group, and then clicking *Excel Spreadsheet* at the drop-down list.

➤ Quick Tables are predesigned tables you can insert in a document by clicking the Insert tab, clicking the Table button, pointing to *Quick Tables*, and then clicking the desired option at the side menu.

Commands *Review*

FEATURE	RIBBON TAB, GROUP	BUTTON, OPTION	KEYBOARD SHORTCUT
Create table	Insert, Tables	▦ , drag in grid	
Insert Table dialog box	Insert, Tables	▦ , Insert Table	
Move insertion point to next cell			Tab
Move insertion point to previous cell			Shift + Tab
Move insertion point to tab stop within cell			Ctrl + Tab
Insert page break within a table			Ctrl + Enter
Draw a table	Insert, Tables	▦ , Draw Table	
Insert Quick Table	Insert, Tables	▦ , Quick Tables	

Key Points *Review*

Completion: In the space provided at the right, indicate the correct term, symbol, or command.

1. The Table button is located in this tab. _____

2. This term refers to the intersection between a row and a column. _____

3. When you hover the mouse pointer over a table, this displays in the upper left corner of the table. _____

4. Press this key to move the insertion point to the next cell. _____

5. Press these keys to move the insertion point to the previous cell. _____

6. The space just to the left of the left edge of the table is referred to as this. _____

7. When you insert a table in a document, this tab is active. _____

8. Click the Borders button arrow and then click *Borders and Shading,* and the Borders and Shading dialog box displays with this tab active. _____

9. To draw borders in a table using the mouse, click this button in the Draw Borders group. _____

10. To remove a border line, click this button in the Draw Borders group and then drag across the border. _____

11. Use this feature to insert predesigned tables in a document. _____

Chapter *Assessments*

Applying Your Skills

Demonstrate your knowledge of features learned in this chapter by completing the following assessments.

Assessment 13.1   Create and Format a Table in a Letter

1. Open **LtrCofC.docx** and save the document with the name **C13-A01-LtrCofC**.
2. Move the insertion point to the blank line between the two paragraphs of text in the body of the letter and then create the table shown in Figure 13.9 with the following specifications:
   a. Create a table with three columns and eight rows.
   b. Center, bold, and italicize the text in the first row.
   c. Bold the text in the cells below the *Name* heading.
   d. Apply blue fill to the first row (*Blue, Accent 1, Darker 50%*).
   e. Apply green fill to the second, fourth, sixth, and eighth rows (*Olive Green, Accent 3, Lighter 80%*).
   f. Apply blue fill to the third, fifth, and seventh rows (*Blue, Accent 1, Lighter 80%*).
3. Save, print, and then close **C13-A01-LtrCofC.docx**.

Figure 13.9 Assessment 13.1

Name	*Title*	*Department*
Shawn Kilpatrick	Chief Executive Officer	Administration
Gerald Palmer	President	Administration
Emily Higgins	Vice President	Administration
Ryan Keaton	Finances Manager	Finances
Jim Everson	Resources Coordinator	Purchasing
Isabelle Brown	Training Coordinator	Support and Training Services
Sandy Romano-Ellison	Public Relations Manager	Public Relations

Assessment 13.2   Create and Format a Tour Package Table

1. At a blank document, create the text and table shown in Figure 13.10 with the following specifications:
   a. Set the title *BAYSIDE TRAVEL TOUR PACKAGES* in 16-point size.
   b. Create a table with four columns and five rows.
   c. Type the text in the cells as shown in Figure 13.10.
   d. Insert check marks in the *Header Row* and *Banded Rows* check boxes in the Table Style Options group in the Table Tools Design tab and remove the check mark from any other check boxes in the group.
   e. Apply the *Medium Shading 1 - Accent 5* table style.
   f. Apply the *Orange, Accent 6, Lighter 80%* orange fill to rows three and five.
2. Save the document with the name **C13-A02-TourPkgs**.
3. Print and then close **C13-A02-TourPkgs.docx**.

Figure 13.10 Assessment 13.2

BAYSIDE TRAVEL TOUR PACKAGES

Name	Duration	Costs	Discount
Hawaiian Fun in the Sun	5 days and 4 nights	From $709 to $1049	20% in March
Hawaiian Nights	8 days and 7 nights	From $1079 to $1729	10% in March and April
Hawaiian Fun Tours	10 days and 9 nights	From $1999 to $2229	15% in April and May
Hawaiian Island Tours	14 days and 13 nights	From $2499 to $3099	10% in May and June

Assessment 13.3 Format a Contact List Table

1. Open **Contacts.docx** and save the document with the name **C13-A03-Contacts**.
2. Select the entire document and then change the font to Candara.
3. Apply the *Light List – Accent 4* table style to the table. Remove the check mark from the *First Column* check box in the Table Style Options group in the Table Tools Design tab and make sure the *Header Row* check box contains a check mark.
4. Select the title, *CONTACT LIST*, change the point size to 16, change the font color to purple, and center the title.
5. Save, print, and then close **C13-A03-Contacts.docx**.

Expanding Your Skills

Explore additional feature options or use Help to learn a new skill in creating these documents.

Assessment 13.4 Draw and Format an Employment Information Table

1. At a blank document, type the title JOBS IN DEMAND, press the Enter key, draw a table and then, in the table, type the text shown below.
2. Apply formatting to enhance the visual appeal of the table.
3. Save the document with the name **C13-A04-Jobs**.
4. Print and then close **C13-A04-Jobs.docx**.

JOBS IN DEMAND

Position	Weekly Income	Yearly Openings
Accountants/Auditors	$975	852
Financial Managers	$895	343
Loan Officers	$875	301
Registered Nurses	$852	1,550
Teachers, Elementary	$780	1,112
Teachers, Secondary	$750	1,258

Assessment 13.5 Create a Monthly Calendar with a Quick Table

1. Use Quick Table to create a monthly calendar for next month.
2. Apply any additional formatting to enhance the visual appeal of the calendar.
3. Save the document with the name **C13-A05-MoCalendar**.
4. Print and then close **C13-A05-MoCalendar.docx**.

Achieving Signature Status

Take your skills to the next level by completing this more challenging assessment.

Assessment 13.6   Create and Format Tables

1. At a blank document create the document shown in Figure 13.11 with the following specifications:
   * Set the headings in 16-point size.
   * Apply the *Light Grid - Accent 5* table style to the two tables and remove the check marks from the *Header Row* and *First Column* check boxes in the Table Style Options group in the Table Tools Design tab.
   * Vertically center the text on the page.
2. Save the completed document and name it **C13-A06-ResumeWords**.
3. Print and then close the document.

Figure 13.11 Assessment 13.6

Résumé Writing: Positive Verbs

Overcame	Achieved	Developed	Discovered	Controlled
Managed	Delivered	Reorganized	Won	Applied
Defeated	Created	Engineered	Overhauled	Presented
Founded	Instigated	Established	Succeeded	Contributed
Modified	Specialized	Expanded	Repaired	Improved
Analyzed	Coordinated	Trained	Accomplished	Investigated
Persuaded	Helped	Proved	Utilized	Simplified

Résumé Writing: Powerful Adjectives

Quickly	Successfully	Rapidly	Carefully	Decisively
Competently	Capably	Resourcefully	Efficiently	Consistently
Effectively	Positively	Cooperatively	Selectively	Creatively
Assertively	Energetically	Enthusiastically	Responsibly	Diligently

Chapter 14

TUTORIALS

Tutorial 14.1
Changing the Table Design
Tutorial 14.2
Sorting Text in a Table and
Performing Calculations
Tutorial 14.3
Merging and Splitting Cells and
Tables
Tutorial 14.4
Changing Column Width and
Height and Cell Margins
Tutorial 14.5
Converting Text to a Table and
a Table to Text

Enhancing Tables

Performance Objectives

Upon successful completion of Chapter 14, you will be able to:

- Edit and format a table
- Change the table design and layout
- Sort text in a table
- Perform calculations on data in a table

In Chapter 13, you learned to create tables and format them by applying table styles, borders, and shading. In this chapter, you will learn how to enhance tables by changing the table layout; inserting and deleting columns and rows; merging and splitting cells; and changing cell size, cell alignment, and cell margins. You will also learn to sort text in a table and perform calculations on data in a table.

Note: Before beginning computer exercises for this chapter, copy to your storage medium the Chapter14 folder from the CD that accompanies this textbook and then make Chapter14 the active folder.

In this chapter students will produce the following documents:

Exercise 14.1. C14-E01-LoanTables.docx
Exercise 14.2. C14-E02-EmpTable.docx
Exercise 14.3. C14-E03-SalesDivTable.docx
Exercise 14.4. C14-E04-Sales&Support.docx

Model answers for these exercises are shown on the following pages.

MORTGAGE BANKERS

Mortgage Banker	Mortgage Loans	Home Equity Loans
Brittany Stevens	$2,490,520	$1,101,340
Vernon Rosenfeld	$1,905,348	$1,003,265
Janelle Fisher	$2,005,476	$1,057,422
Joseph Lundeen	$2,315,380	$1,320,341
Marilyn Luo	$1,058,394	$1,429,554
William Morrisette	$2,409,822	$1,539,588

CONTACT INFORMATION, NORTH

Name	Title	Company	Telephone	
Kimberly Gibson	Vice President	First Financial Trust	(412) 555-3948	Ext. 231
Neville Lewis	Loan Officer	Prime One Savings	(503) 555-9986	
Chandra Hall	Manager	Horizon Mutual	(712) 555-0331	

CONTACT INFORMATION, SOUTH

Name	Title	Company	Telephone	
Harrison Brooks	Vice President	Mainland Bank	(313) 555-8555	
Richard Osaka	President	Meridian Savings	(603) 555-9002	Ext. 782
Julio Rivas	Loan Officer	Mountain Bank	(206) 555-1048	

Waiting Period	Plan 2012 Employees	Basic Plan Employees
30 days	0.85%	0.81%
60 days	0.79%	0.67%
90 days	0.59%	0.49%
120 days	0.35%	0.30%
180 days	0.26%	0.23%

CONTACT INFORMATION, NORTH

Name	Title	Company	Telephone
Donna Gould	President	Freestone Bank	(206) 555-9002
John DePaolo	Vice President	North Sound Bank	(253) 555-5300
Dean Zuniga	President	Cornerstone Savings	(425) 555-1048
Joaquin Morgan	Loan Officer	Miles Bank	(206) 555-2102
Maureen Grand	Vice President	National Savings	(253) 555-4215
Noel Nielsen	Loan Officer	Hill Savings and Loan	(253) 555-0033

Exercise 14.1 C14-E01-LoanTables.docx   Page 1

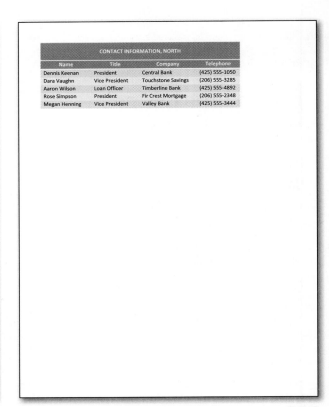

CONTACT INFORMATION, NORTH

Name	Title	Company	Telephone
Dennis Keenan	President	Central Bank	(425) 555-1050
Dara Vaughn	Vice President	Touchstone Savings	(206) 555-3285
Aaron Wilson	Loan Officer	Timberline Bank	(425) 555-4892
Rose Simpson	President	Fir Crest Mortgage	(206) 555-2348
Megan Henning	Vice President	Valley Bank	(425) 555-3444

Page 2

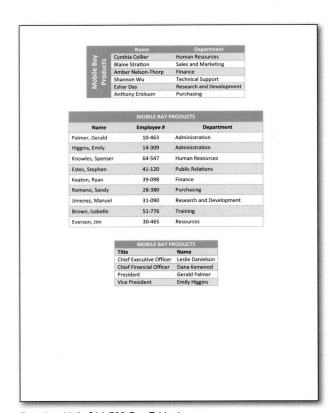

	Name	Department
Mobile Bay Products	Cynthia Collier	Human Resources
	Blaine Stratton	Sales and Marketing
	Amber Nelson-Thorp	Finance
	Shannon Wu	Technical Support
	Eshar Das	Research and Development
	Anthony Erickson	Purchasing

MOBILE BAY PRODUCTS

Name	Employee #	Department
Palmer, Gerald	10-463	Administration
Higgins, Emily	14-309	Administration
Knowles, Spenser	64-547	Human Resources
Estes, Stephen	41-120	Public Relations
Keaton, Ryan	39-098	Finance
Romano, Sandy	28-380	Purchasing
Jimenez, Manuel	31-090	Research and Development
Brown, Isabelle	51-776	Training
Everson, Jim	30-465	Resources

MOBILE BAY PRODUCTS

Title	Name
Chief Executive Officer	Leslie Danielson
Chief Financial Officer	Dana Kenwood
President	Gerald Palmer
Vice President	Emily Higgins

Exercise 14.2 C14-E02-EmpTable.docx

Exercise 14.3

C14-E03-SalesDivTable.docx

MOBILE BAY PRODUCTS
Sales Division

Salesperson	Sales, 2010	Sales, 2011
Hubbard, Christopher	$320,348	$400,570
Washington, Isaac	$395,675	$402,530
Barclay, Kurt	$400,394	$425,304
Tanaka, Diana	$428,528	$399,511
Coulter, Jolene	$600,340	$597,288
Kohler, Roger	$610,476	$700,387
Owens, Kendra	$700,328	$675,329
Total	$3,456,089	$3,600,919
Average	$493,727	$514,417
Top Sales	$700,328	$700,387

Region	First Qtr.	Second Qtr.	Third Qtr.	Fourth Qtr.	Total
Northwest	$225,430	$157,090	$239,239	$220,340	$842,099
Southwest	$133,450	$143,103	$153,780	$142,498	$572,831
Northeast	$275,340	$299,342	$278,098	$266,593	$1,119,373
Southeast	$211,349	$222,330	$201,849	$239,432	$874,960
Total	$845,569	$821,865	$872,966	$868,863	$3,409,263
Average	$211,392	$205,466	$218,242	$217,216	$852,316

FIRST QUARTER DIVISION SALES			
Customer	Actual	Planned	Difference
JR Systems	$20,450.75	$20,000.00	$450.75
Linden Production	$94,375.50	$70,000.00	$24,375.50
Danner Designs	$14,540.00	$12,000.00	$2,540.00
Valley Supplies	$68,947.00	$70,000.00	($1,053.00)
Sunset Enterprises	$58,390.00	$65,000.00	($6,610.00)

TECHNICAL SUPPORT – EMPLOYEE HOURS			
Name	Hours	Rate	Salary
Jessie Levigne	40	$45.00	$1800.00
Eduardo Quintana	30	$40.00	$1200.00
Carol Runyon	40	$39.50	$1580.00
Chad Mahoney	40	$35.00	$1400.00
Kyung Shin	25	$35.00	$875.00

Exercise 14.4

C14-E04-Sales&Support.docx

Changing Table Layout

When you insert a table in a document, the Table Tools Design tab becomes active. In Chapter 13, you learned how to use options in this tab to format tables. You can also format a table with options in the Table Tools Layout tab. To display the Table Tools Layout tab, shown in Figure 14.1, position the insertion point in a table and click the tab. Use options and buttons in the tab to select specific cells within the table, delete and insert rows and columns, merge and split cells, specify the height and width of cells, sort data in cells, and insert formulas. Some of these table layout options are also available at a shortcut menu that can be viewed by right-clicking a table.

Figure 14.1 Table Tools Layout Tab

Selecting in a Table with the Select Button

Select

As you learned in Chapter 13, you can select a specific cell, column, or row in a table using either the mouse or the keyboard. You can also select in a table with the Select button, located in the Table group in the Table Tools Layout tab. To select with this button, position the insertion point in the desired cell, column, or row and then click the Select button. At the drop-down list that displays, specify what you want to select—the entire table or a column, row, or cell.

Insert   Insert
Above   Below

Inserting and Deleting Rows and Columns

Insert   Insert
Left   Right

Delete

With buttons in the Rows & Columns group in the Table Tools Layout tab, you can insert rows or columns and delete rows or columns. Click the button in the group that inserts the row or column in the desired location, such as above, below, to the left, or to the right of a row or column that you have selected. To delete a row, column, or the entire table, click the Delete button and then click the option specifying what you want to delete.

Exercise 14.1A Inserting and Deleting Columns, Rows, and a Table   Part 1 of 4

1. Open **LoanTables.docx** and save the document with the name **C14-E01-LoanTables**.
2. Insert a new row in the top table and type text in the new cells by completing the following steps:
   a. Click in the cell containing the name *Joseph Lundeen*.
   b. Click the Table Tools Layout tab.

c. Click the Insert Above button in the Rows & Columns group.
d. Type Janelle Fisher in the first cell of the new row, press the Tab key, and then type $2,005,476 in the middle cell of the new row. Press the Tab key and then type $1,057,422 in the third cell of the new row.

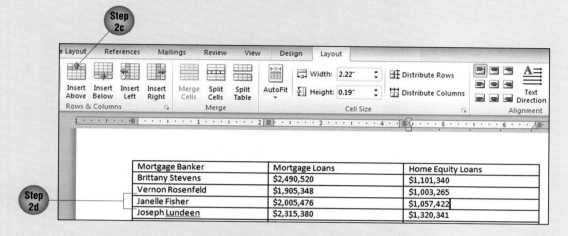

3. Insert three new rows in the middle table and type text in the new cells by completing the following steps:
   a. Select the three rows of cells that begin with the names *Kimberly Gibson*, *Neville Lewis*, and *Ivy Talmadge*.
   b. Click the Insert Below button in the Rows & Columns group.
   c. Type the following text in the new cells:

Chandra Hall	Horizon Mutual	(712) 555-0331
Harrison Brooks	Mainland Bank	(313) 555-8555
Richard Osaka	Meridian Savings	(603) 555-9002

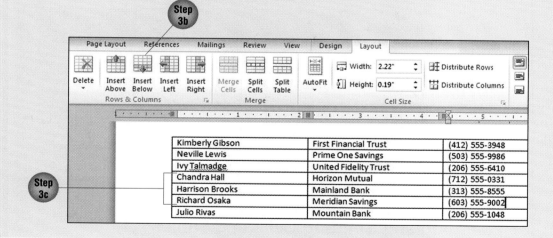

4. Delete a row in the middle table by completing the following steps:
   a. Click in the cell containing the name *Ivy Talmadge*.
   b. Click the Delete button in the Rows & Columns group and then click *Delete Rows* at the drop-down list.
5. Insert a new column in the middle table and type text in the new cells by completing the following steps:
   a. Click in the cell containing the text *First Financial Trust*.
   b. Click the Insert Left button in the Rows & Columns group.
   c. Type the following text in the new cells:

B1	=	Vice President
B2	=	Loan Officer
B3	=	Manager
B4	=	Vice President
B5	=	President
B6	=	Loan Officer

6. Delete the bottom table by completing the following steps:
   a. Click in any cell in the bottom table.
   b. Make sure the Table Tools Layout tab is active.
   c. Click the Delete button in the Rows & Columns group and then click *Delete Table* at the drop-down list.
7. After deleting the table, you decide you want the table back in the document. To do this, click the Undo button on the Quick Access toolbar.
8. Save **C14-E01-LoanTables.docx**.

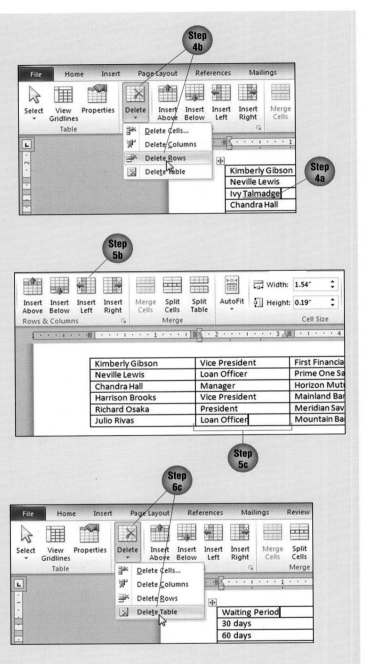

Merging and Splitting Cells and Tables

Merge
Cells

Split
Cells

Split
Table

Click the Merge Cells button in the Merge group in the Table Tools Layout tab to merge selected cells and click the Split Cells button to split the currently active cell. When you click the Split Cells button, the Split Cells dialog box displays. At this dialog box, specify the number of columns or rows you want to split the active cell into. If you want to split one table into two tables, position the insertion point in a cell in the row that you want to be the first row in the new table and then click the Split Table button.

1. With **C14-E01-LoanTables.docx** open, insert a new row in the top table and merge cells in the row by completing the following steps:
   a. Click in the cell containing the text *Mortgage Banker.*
   b. Click the Insert Above button in the Rows & Columns group in the Table Tools Layout tab.
   c. With all of the cells in the new row selected, click the Merge Cells button in the Merge group.
   d. Type MORTGAGE BANKERS and then press Ctrl + E to center-align the text in the cell.

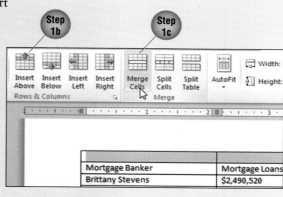

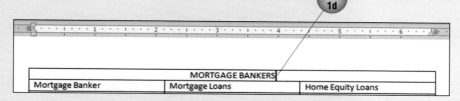

2. Insert rows and text in the middle table and merge cells by completing the following steps:
   a. Click in the cell containing the text *Kimberly Gibson.*
   b. Make sure the Table Tools Layout tab is active.
   c. Click the Insert Above button twice. (This inserts two rows at the top of the table.)
   d. With the cells in the top row selected, click the Merge Cells button in the Merge group.
   e. Type CONTACT INFORMATION, NORTH and then press Ctrl + E to change the paragraph alignment to center.
   f. Type the following text in the four cells in the new second row.

   Name   Title   Company   Telephone

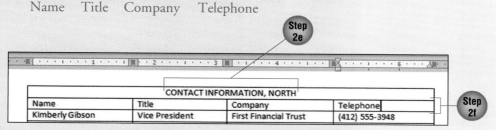

3. Split a cell by completing the following steps:
   a. Click in the cell containing the telephone number (412) 555-3948.
   b. Click the Table Tools Layout tab.
   c. Click the Split Cells button in the Merge group.
   d. At the Split Cells dialog box, click OK. (The telephone number will wrap to a new line. You will change this in the next exercise.)
   e. Click in the new cell.
   f. Type Ext. 231 in the new cell.

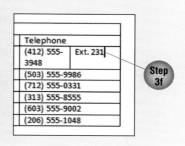

4. Split the cell containing the telephone number (603) 555-9002 and then type Ext. 782 in the new cell.

5. Split the middle table into two tables by completing the following steps:
   a. Click in the cell containing the name *Harrison Brooks*.
   b. Click the Split Table button in the Merge group.
   c. Click in the cell containing the name *Harrison Brooks* (in the first row of the new table) and then click the Table Tools Layout tab.
   d. Click the Insert Above button.
   e. With the new row selected, click the Merge Cells button.
   f. Type CONTACT INFORMATION, SOUTH in the new row and then press Ctrl + E to center-align the text.

6. Insert a new row in the third table and type text in the new cells by completing the following steps:
   a. Click in the cell containing the name *Harrison Brooks*.
   b. Make sure the Table Tools Layout tab is active.
   c. Click the Insert Above button in the Rows & Columns group.
   d. Type Name in the first cell, type Title in the second cell, type Company in the third cell, and type Telephone in the fourth cell.

7. Save **C14-E01-LoanTables.docx**.

Changing Column Width and Height

Distribute Rows

Distribute Columns

When you create a table, the column width and row height are equal. You can customize the width of columns and the height of rows with buttons in the Cell Size group in the Table Tools Layout tab. Use the Table Row Height measurement box to increase or decrease the height of rows and use the Table Column Width measurement box to increase or decrease the width of columns. The Distribute Rows button distributes equally the height of selected rows, and the Distribute Columns button distributes equally the width of selected columns.

You can also change column width using the move table column markers on the horizontal ruler or by using the table gridlines. To change column width using the move table column markers, position the mouse pointer on a marker until it turns into a left and right arrow and then drag the marker to the desired position. Hold down the Shift key and then drag a table column marker, and the horizontal ruler remains stationary while the table column marker moves. Hold down the Alt key and then drag a table column marker, and measurements display on the horizontal ruler. To change column width using gridlines, position the arrow pointer on the gridline separating columns until the insertion point turns into a left and right arrow with a vertical line between and then drag the gridline to the desired position. If you want to see the column measurements on the horizontal ruler as you drag a gridline, hold down the Alt key.

Adjust row height in a manner similar to that used to adjust column width. You can drag the adjust table row marker on the vertical ruler or drag the gridline separating rows. Hold down the Alt key while dragging the adjust table row marker or the row gridline, and measurements display on the vertical ruler.

AutoFit

Use the AutoFit button in the Cell Size group to make the column widths in a table automatically fit the contents. To do this, position the insertion point in any cell in the table, click the AutoFit button in the Cell Size group, and then click *AutoFit Contents* at the drop-down list.

In addition to changing column width and row height with measurement boxes in the Cell Size group in the Table Tools Layout tab, you can use options at the Properties dialog box for changing measurements. To change the width of a column, click in a cell in the column and then click the Properties button in the Table group in the Table Tools Layout tab. At the Table Properties dialog box, click the Column tab, insert the desired measurement in the *Preferred width* measurement box, and then click OK to close the dialog box. To change row height, click in a cell in the row and then click the Properties button. At the Table Properties dialog box, click the Row tab, insert the desired measurement in the *Specify height* measurement box, and then click OK to close the dialog box.

Exercise 14.1C Changing Column Width and Row Height   Part 3 of 4

1. With **C14-E01-LoanTables.docx** open, change the width of the first column in the second table by completing the following steps:
    a. Click in the cell containing the name *Kimberly Gibson*.
    b. Position the mouse pointer on the move table column marker that displays just right of the 1.5-inch mark on the horizontal ruler until the pointer turns into an arrow pointing left and right.
    c. Hold down the Shift key and then the left mouse button.
    d. Drag the marker to the 1.25-inch mark, release the Shift key, and then release the mouse button.

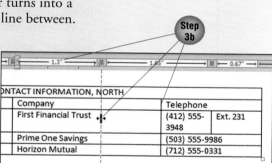

2. Complete steps similar to those in Step 1 to drag the move table column marker that displays just right of the 3-inch mark on the horizontal ruler to the 2.5-inch mark. (Make sure you hold down the Shift key and then drag the marker.)
3. Change the width of the third column in the second table by completing the following steps:
    a. Position the mouse pointer on the gridline separating the third and fourth columns until the pointer turns into a left and right arrow with a vertical double line between.
    b. Hold down the Alt key and then the left mouse button, drag the gridline to the left until the measurement for the third column on the horizontal ruler displays as *1.3″*, release the Alt key, and then release the mouse button. (If the Research task pane displays, click the Close button in the upper right corner of the task pane to close it.)

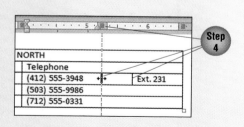

4. Position the mouse pointer on the gridline that separates the telephone number *(412) 555-3948* from the extension *Ext. 231* and then drag the gridline to the 5.25-inch mark on the horizontal ruler.
5. Click in the cell containing the text *Ext. 231* and then drag the right border of the second table to the 6-inch mark on the horizontal ruler.
6. Click in any cell in the third table and then drag the column boundaries so they match the column boundaries in the second table. ***Hint: Use the guidelines that display when dragging boundaries to help you position the column boundaries.***

7. AutoFit the columns in the top table by completing the following steps:
   a. Click in any cell in the top table.
   b. Click the AutoFit button in the Cell Size group and then click *AutoFit Contents* at the drop-down list.

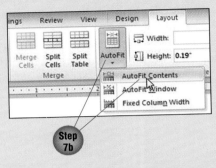

Step 7b

8. Increase the height of the first row in the top table by completing the following steps:
   a. Make sure the insertion point is located in one of the cells in the top table.
   b. Position the mouse pointer on the top adjust table-row marker on the vertical ruler.
   c. Hold down the left mouse button and hold down the Alt key.
   d. Drag the adjust table row marker down until the first row measurement on the vertical ruler displays as *0.4″*, release the mouse button, and then release the Alt key.

Step 8d

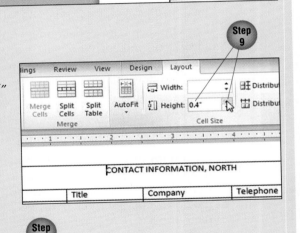

9. Click in the cell containing the text *CONTACT INFORMATION, NORTH* located in the second table and then click the up-pointing arrow at the right of the *Table Row Height* measurement box in the Cell Size group in the Table Tools Layout tab until *0.4″* displays in the box.

Step 9

10. Change the height of the top row in the third table by completing the following steps:
    a. Click in the cell containing the text *CONTACT INFORMATION, SOUTH* located in the third table.
    b. Click the Properties button in the Table group in the Table Tools Layout tab.
    c. At the Table Properties dialog box, click the Row tab.
    d. Click the *Specify height* check box to insert a check mark.
    e. Click the up-pointing arrow at the right of the *Specify height* measurement box until *0.4″* displays in the box.
    f. Click OK to close the dialog box.

Step 10c

Step 10d

Step 10e

11. Change the width of the first and second columns in the bottom table by completing the following steps:
    a. Click in the cell containing the text *Waiting Period* (located in the bottom table).
    b. Click in the *Table Column Width* measurement box in the Cell Size group in the Table Tools Layout tab, type 1.3, and then press the Enter key.

Step 11b

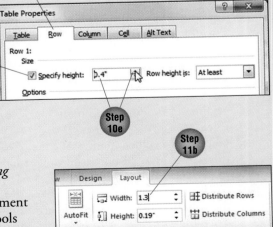

c. Click in the cell containing the text *Plan 2012 Employees* and then click the down-pointing arrow at the right of the *Table Column Width* measurement box until *1.6"* displays in the box.

12. Change the width of the third column in the bottom table by completing the following steps:
    a. Click in the cell containing the text *Basic Plan Employees*.
    b. Click the Properties button in the Table group in the Table Tools Layout tab.
    c. At the Table Properties dialog box, click the Column tab.
    d. Click the down-pointing arrow at the right of the *Preferred width* measurement box until *1.8"* displays in the box.

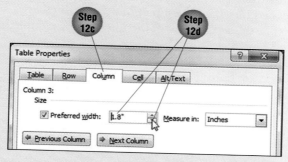

    e. Click OK to close the dialog box.
13. Save **C14-E01-LoanTables.docx**.

Changing Cell Alignment

The Alignment group in the Table Tools Layout tab includes a number of buttons for specifying the horizontal and vertical alignment of text in cells. The buttons contain a visual representation of the alignment; you can also hover the mouse pointer over a button to determine the alignment.

You can also change the alignment of text in a cell with options at the Table Properties dialog box, with the Cell tab selected. Display this dialog box by clicking the Properties button in the Table group in the Table Tools Layout tab. Click the Cell tab, and the *Vertical alignment* section of the dialog box displays options to align text at the top, center, or bottom of cells.

Properties

Viewing Gridlines

When you create a table, cell borders are identified by horizontal and vertical thin, black gridlines. You can remove a cell border gridline but maintain the cell border. If you remove cell border gridlines or apply a table style that removes gridlines, the gridlines display as dashed lines. You can turn on or off the display of these dashed gridlines with the View Gridlines button in the Table group in the Table Tools Layout tab.

Repeating a Header Row

If a table is divided between pages, consider adding the header row at the beginning of the table that extends to the next page. This helps the reader understand the data that displays in each column. To repeat a header row, click in the header row, and then click the Repeat Header Rows button in the Data group in the Table Tools Layout tab. If you want to repeat more than one header row, select the rows and then click the Repeat Header Rows button.

1. With **C14-E01-LoanTables.docx** open, vertically align text in the top cell in the top table by completing the following steps:
   a. Click in the top cell in the top table (the cell containing the title *MORTGAGE BANKERS*).
   b. Click the Align Center button in the Alignment group in the Table Tools Layout tab.
2. Complete steps similar to those in Step 1 to vertically align text in the top cell in the second table and the top cell in the third table.
3. Format and align text in the second row in the top table by completing the following steps:
   a. Select the second row in the top table.
   b. Press Ctrl + B.
   c. Click the Align Center button in the Alignment group.
4. Complete steps similar to those in Step 3 to format and align text in the second row in the second table and the second row in the third table.
5. Apply a table style by completing the following steps:
   a. Click in any cell in the top table.
   b. Click the Table Tools Design tab.
   c. Insert or remove check marks from the options in the Table Style Options group so only *Header Row* and *Banded Rows* contain check marks in the check boxes.
   d. Click the More button that displays at the right of the table style thumbnails in the Table Styles group.
   e. Scroll down the drop-down gallery and then click *Colorful List* (the first option from the left in the thirteenth row in the *Built-In* section).
   f. Click in the top row in the table, click the Table Tools Layout tab, and then click the Align Center button in the Alignment group.
6. Complete steps similar to those in Step 5 to apply the *Colorful List - Accent 1* table style and change cell alignment in the second table.
7. Complete steps similar to those in Step 5 to apply the *Colorful List - Accent 2* table style and change cell alignment in the third table.
8. Complete steps similar to those in Step 5 to apply the *Colorful List - Accent 3* table style and change cell alignment in the bottom table.
9. Select all cells in the bottom table and then center the text in the cells.
10. Select the cells below the *Mortgage Loans* heading and the *Home Equity Loans* heading in the top table and then center the text in the cells.
11. Some of the table styles removed border gridlines. If you do not see dashed gridlines in the tables, turn on the display of these gridlines by positioning your insertion point in a table and then clicking the View Gridlines button in the Table group in the Table Tools Layout tab.
12. Press Ctrl + End to move the insertion point to the end of the document, press the Enter key, and then insert a table into the current document by completing the following steps:
    a. Click the Insert tab.
    b. Click the Object button arrow in the Text group and then click *Text from File* at the drop-down list.
    c. At the Insert File dialog box, navigate to the Chapter14 folder on your storage medium and then double-click **ContactsNorth.docx**.
13. Repeat the header row by completing the following steps:
    a. Select the first two rows in the table you just inserted.
    b. Click the Table Tools Layout tab.
    c. Click the Repeat Header Rows button in the Data group.
14. Save, print, and then close **C14-E01-LoanTables.docx**.

Changing Cell Margin Measurements

Cells in a Word table have specific default margin settings. Top and bottom margins in a cell have a default measurement of 0 inches and left and right margins have a default setting of .08 inch. You can change these default settings with options at the Table Options dialog box, shown in Figure 14.2. Display this dialog box by clicking the Cell Margins button in the Alignment group in the Table Tools Layout tab. Use the options in the *Default cell margins* section to change the top, bottom, left, or right cell margin measurements.

Cell Margins

Changing the cell margins affects all cells in a table. If you want to change the cell margin measurements for one cell or for selected cells, position the insertion point in the cell or select the desired cells and then click the Properties button in the Table group in the Table Tools Layout tab. (You can also click the Cell Size group dialog box launcher.) At the Table Properties dialog box, click the Cell tab and then click the Options button that displays in the lower right corner of the dialog box. This displays the Cell Options dialog box, shown in Figure 14.3.

Figure 14.2 Table Options Dialog Box

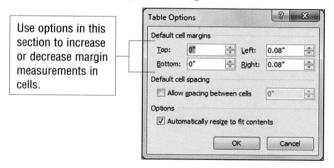

Use options in this section to increase or decrease margin measurements in cells.

Figure 14.3 Cell Options Dialog Box

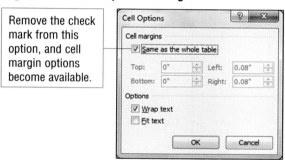

Remove the check mark from this option, and cell margin options become available.

Before you can set new cell margin measurements, you must remove the check mark from the *Same as the whole table* option. When the check mark is removed from this option, the cell margin options become available. Specify the new cell margin measurements and then click OK to close the dialog box.

Exercise 14.2A   Changing Cell Margin Measurements   Part 1 of 4

1. Open **EmpTable.docx** and save the document with the name **C14-E02-EmpTable**.
2. Change the top and bottom margins for all cells in the table by completing the following steps:
    a. Position the insertion point in any cell in the table and then click the Table Tools Layout tab.
    b. Click the Cell Margins button in the Alignment group.
    c. At the Table Options dialog box, change the *Top* and *Bottom* measurements to *0.05"*.
    d. Click OK to close the Table Options dialog box.

Step 2c

Step 2d

3. Change the top and bottom cell margin measurements for the first row of cells by completing the following steps:
   a. Select the first row of cells (the cells containing *Name* and *Department*).
   b. Click the Properties button in the Table group.
   c. At the Table Properties dialog box, click the Cell tab.
   d. Click the Options button.
   e. At the Cell Options dialog box, remove the check mark from the *Same as the whole table* option.
   f. Change the *Top* and *Bottom* measurements to *0.1″*.
   g. Click OK to close the Cell Options dialog box.
   h. Click OK to close the Table Properties dialog box.
4. Change the left cell margin measurement for specific cells by completing the following steps:
   a. Select all rows in the table *except* the top row.
   b. Click the Cell Size group dialog box launcher.
   c. At the Table Properties dialog box, click the Cell tab.
   d. Click the Options button.
   e. At the Cell Options dialog box, remove the check mark from the *Same as the whole table* option.
   f. Change the *Left* measurement to *0.3″*.
   g. Click OK to close the Cell Options dialog box.
   h. Click OK to close the Table Properties dialog box.
5. Save **C14-E02-EmpTable.docx**.

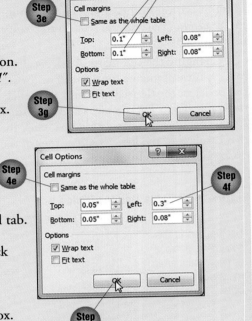

QUICK STEPS

Change Cell Direction
1. Click in desired cell.
2. Click Table Tools Layout tab.
3. Click Text Direction button until text is in desired position.

Change Table Alignment
1. Click in table.
2. Click Table Tools Layout tab.
3. Click Properties button.
4. Click Table tab.
5. Click desired alignment option.

Text Direction

Changing Cell Direction

You can change the direction of text in a cell with the Text Direction button in the Alignment group in the Table Tools Layout tab. Each time you click the Text Direction button, the text in the cell rotates 90 degrees.

Changing Table Alignment

By default, a table aligns at the left margin. Change this alignment with options at the Table Properties dialog box, with the Table tab selected, as shown in Figure 14.4. To change the alignment, click the desired alignment option in the Alignment section of the dialog box.

Figure 14.4 Table Properties Dialog Box with Table Tab Selected

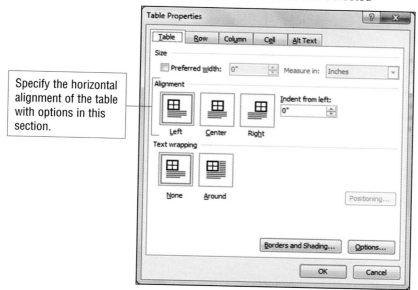

Specify the horizontal alignment of the table with options in this section.

Exercise 14.2B Changing Table Alignment

Part 2 of 4

1. With **C14-E02-EmpTable.docx** open, insert a new column and change text direction by completing the following steps:
   a. Click in any cell in the first column and then click the Table Tools Layout tab.
   b. Click the Insert Left button in the Rows & Columns group.
   c. With the cells in the new column selected, click the Merge Cells button in the Merge group.
   d. Type Mobile Bay Products.
   e. Click the Align Center button in the Alignment group.
   f. Click twice on the Text Direction button in the Alignment group.
   g. With Mobile Bay Products selected, click the Home tab, increase the font size to *14*, and, if necessary, turn on bold.

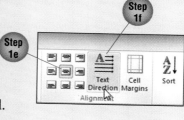

Step 1f

Step 1e

2. AutoFit the contents by completing the following steps:
   a. Click in any cell in the table.
   b. Click the Table Tools Layout tab.
   c. Click the AutoFit button in the Cell Size group and then click the *AutoFit Contents* at the drop-down list.
3. Change the table alignment by completing the following steps:
   a. Click the Properties button in the Table group in the Table Tools Layout tab.
   b. At the Table Properties dialog box, click the Table tab.
   c. Click the *Center* option in the *Alignment* section.
   d. Click OK.

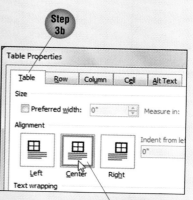

Step 3b

Step 3c

4. Select the two cells containing the text *Name* and *Department* and then click the Align Center button in the Alignment group.
5. Save **C14-E02-EmpTable.docx**.

Changing Table Size with the Resize Handle

When you hover the mouse pointer over a table, a resize handle displays as a small, white square in the lower right corner of the table. Drag this resize handle to increase or decrease the size and proportion of the table.

Moving a Table

Position the mouse pointer in a table, and a table move handle displays in the upper left corner. Use this handle to move the table in the document. To move a table, position the mouse pointer on the table move handle until the pointer turns into a four-headed arrow, hold down the left mouse button, drag the table to the desired position, and then release the mouse button.

Exercise 14.2C   Resizing and Moving Tables   Part 3 of 4

1. With **C14-E02-EmpTable.docx** open, insert a table into the current document by completing the following steps:
   a. Press Ctrl + End to move the insertion point to the end of the document and then press the Enter key.
   b. Click the Insert tab.
   c. Click the Object button arrow in the Text group and then click *Text from File* at the drop-down list.
   d. At the Insert File dialog box, navigate to the Chapter14 folder and then double-click **EmpDept.docx.**
2. AutoFit the bottom table by completing the following steps:
   a. Click in any cell in the bottom table.
   b. Click the Table Tools Layout tab.
   c. Click the AutoFit button in the Cell Size group and then click *AutoFit Contents* at the drop-down list.
3. Format the bottom table by completing the following steps:
   a. Click the Table Tools Design tab.

b. Click the More button that displays at the right of the Table Styles group and then click the *Medium Shading 1 - Accent 5* style (sixth style from the left in the fourth row of the *Built-In* section).

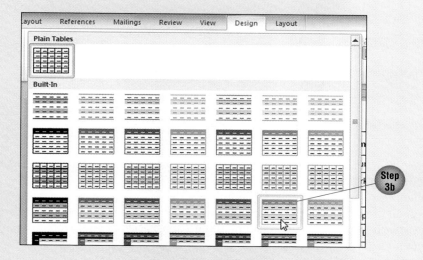

Step 3b

c. Click the *First Column* check box to remove the check mark.
d. Select the first and second rows, click the Table Tools Layout tab, and then click the Align Center button in the Alignment group.
e. Select the second row and then press Ctrl + B to turn on bold.
4. Resize the bottom table by completing the following steps:
    a. Position the mouse pointer on the resize handle located in the lower right corner of the bottom table.
    b. Hold down the left mouse button, drag down and to the right until the width and height of the table increase approximately 1 inch, and then release the mouse button.

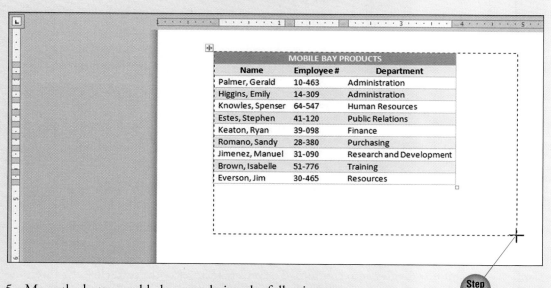

MOBILE BAY PRODUCTS		
Name	**Employee #**	**Department**
Palmer, Gerald	10-463	Administration
Higgins, Emily	14-309	Administration
Knowles, Spenser	64-547	Human Resources
Estes, Stephen	41-120	Public Relations
Keaton, Ryan	39-098	Finance
Romano, Sandy	28-380	Purchasing
Jimenez, Manuel	31-090	Research and Development
Brown, Isabelle	51-776	Training
Everson, Jim	30-465	Resources

Step 4b

5. Move the bottom table by completing the following steps:
    a. Hover the mouse pointer over the bottom table.
    b. Position the mouse pointer on the table move handle until the pointer displays with a four-headed arrow attached.

c. Hold down the left mouse button, drag the table so it is positioned equally between the left and right margins, and then release the mouse button.

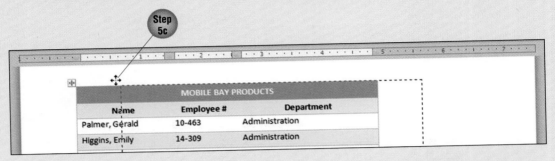

Step 5c

6. Select the cells in the column below the heading *Employee #* and then click the Align Top Center button in the Alignment group.
7. Center align text vertically in cells by completing the following steps:
   a. Select all of the cells in the three columns below the headings *Name, Employee #,* and *Department* (begin with the cell containing *Palmer, Gerald* and select through the cell containing *Resources*).
   b. Click the Properties button in the Table group.
   c. At the Table Properties dialog box, click the Cell tab.
   d. Click the *Center* option in the *Vertical alignment* section.

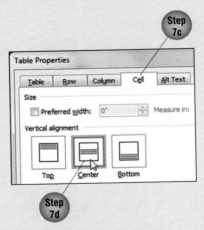

Step 7c

Step 7d

   e. Click OK to close the dialog box.
8. Save **C14-E02-EmpTable.docx**.

Converting Text to a Table

QUICK STEPS

Convert Text to Table
1. Select text.
2. Click Insert tab.
3. Click Table button.
4. Click *Convert Text to Table*.

You can create a table and then enter data in the cells, or you can create data and then convert it to a table. To convert text to a table, type the text and separate it with a separator character such as a comma or tab. The separator character identifies where you want text divided into columns. To convert text, select the text, click the Insert tab, click the Table button in the Tables group, and then click *Convert Text to Table* at the drop-down list.

Converting a Table to Text

You can convert a table to text by positioning the insertion point in any cell of the table, clicking the Table Tools Layout tab, and then clicking the Convert to Text button in the Data group. At the Convert Table to Text dialog box, specify the desired separator and then click OK.

Convert Table to Text

1. Position insertion point in any cell of table.
2. Click Table Tools Layout tab.
3. Click Convert to Text button.
4. Specify desired separator at Convert Table to Text dialog box.
5. Click OK.

Convert to Text

Exercise 14.2D Converting Text to a Table

Part 4 of 4

1. With **C14-E02-EmpTable.docx** open, press Ctrl + End to move the insertion point to the end of the document. (Make sure the insertion point is positioned approximately a double space below the bottom table.)
2. Insert the document named **MBExecs.docx** into the current document.
3. Convert the text to a table by completing the following steps:
   a. Select the text you just inserted.
   b. Click the Insert tab.
   c. Click the Table button in the Tables group and then click *Convert Text to Table* at the drop-down list.
   d. At the Convert Text to Table dialog box, type 2 in the *Number of columns* text box.
   e. Click the *AutoFit to contents* option in the *AutoFit behavior* section.
   f. Click the *Commas* option in the *Separate text at* section.
   g. Click OK.

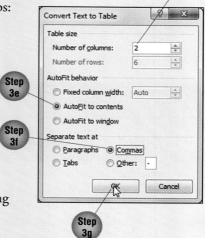

4. Select and merge the cells in the top row (the row containing the title *MOBILE BAY PRODUCTS)* and then change the alignment to Center.
5. Apply the *Medium Shading 1 - Accent 5* table style (sixth style from the left in the fourth row of the *Built-In* section) and remove the check mark from the *First Column* check box in the Table Style Options group in the Table Tools Design tab.
6. Drag the table so it is centered and positioned below the table above.
7. Apply the *Medium Shading 1 - Accent 5* style to the top table. Increase the width of the columns so the text *MOBILE BAY PRODUCTS* is visible and the text in the second and third columns displays on one line.
8. If necessary, drag the table so it is centered and positioned above the middle table. Make sure the three tables fit on one page.

9. Save and then print **C14-E02-EmpTable.docx**.
10. Convert a table to text by completing the following steps:
    a. Select the middle table.
    b. Click the Copy button in the Clipboard group in the Home tab.
    c. Press Ctrl + N (this displays a blank document).
    d. Click the Paste button in the Clipboard group.
    e. Select the table and then click the Table Tools Layout tab.
    f. Click the Convert to Text button in the Data group.
    g. At the Convert Table to Text dialog box, click the *Tabs* option in the *Separate text with* section, and then click OK.
    h. Select and then bold the title *MOBILE BAY PRODUCTS*.
    i. Print the document.
    j. Close the document without saving it.
11. Save and then close **C14-E02-EmpTable.docx**.

Step 10g

Sort Text in Tables
1. Select desired rows in table.
2. Click Sort button in Table Tools Layout tab.
3. Specify the column containing text to sort.
4. Click OK.

Sorting Text in a Table

With the Sort button in the Data group in the Table Tools Layout tab, you can sort text in selected cells in a table in ascending or descending alphabetic or numeric order and also by date. To sort text, select the desired rows in the table and then click the Sort button in the Data group. At the Sort dialog box, specify the column containing the text on which you want to sort, and then click OK.

Sort

Exercise 14.3A   Sorting Text in a Table   Part 1 of 2

1. Open **SalesDivTable.docx** and save the document with the name **C14-E03-SalesDivTable**.
2. Sort text in the top table by completing the following steps:
   a. Select all of the rows containing names (from *Kohler, Roger* through *Washington, Isaac*).
   b. Click the Table Tools Layout tab.
   c. Click the Sort button in the Data group.
   d. At the Sort dialog box, click OK. (This sorts the last names in the first column in alphabetical order.)

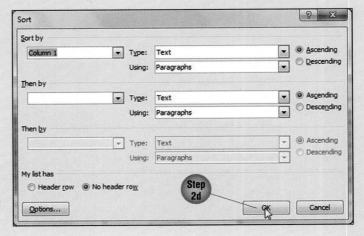

Step 2d

3. Re-sort the table by 2010 Sales by completing the following steps:
   a. With the rows still selected, click the Sort button in the Data group.
   b. At the Sort dialog box, click the down-pointing arrow at the right side of the *Sort by* option box and then click *Column 2* at the drop-down list.
   c. Click OK.
   d. Deselect the rows.
4. Save **C14-E03-SalesDivTable.docx**.

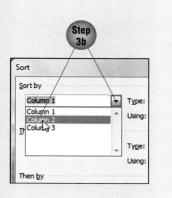

Performing Calculations in a Table

You can use the Formula button in the Data group in the Table Tools Layout tab to insert formulas that calculate data in a table. Numbers in the cells of a table can be added, subtracted, multiplied, and divided. In addition, you can calculate averages, percentages, and minimum and maximum values. Although you can calculate data in a Word table, an Excel worksheet is more suitable for complex calculations.

Formula

To perform a calculation on data in a table, position the insertion point in the cell where you want the result of the calculation inserted and then click the Formula button in the Data group in the Table Tools Layout tab. This displays the Formula dialog box, shown in Figure 14.5. At this dialog box, accept the default formula that displays in the *Formula* text box or type the desired calculation and then click OK.

Figure 14.5 Formula Dialog Box

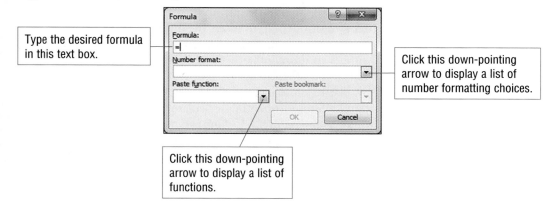

In the default formula, the **SUM** part of the formula is called a ***function.*** Word provides other functions you can use to write a formula. These functions are available at the *Paste function* drop-down list in the Formula dialog box. For example, you can use the AVERAGE function to average numbers in cells. Specify the numbering format at the *Number format* drop-down list in the Formula dialog box. For example, if you are calculating money amounts, you can specify that the calculated numbers display with no numbers or two numbers following the decimal point.

1. With **C14-E03-SalesDivTable.docx** open, insert a formula by completing the following steps:
   a. In the top table, click in cell B9 (the empty cell located immediately below the cell containing the amount *$700,328*).
   b. Click the Table Tools Layout tab.
   c. Click the Formula button in the Data group.
   d. At the Formula dialog box, make sure *=SUM(ABOVE)* displays in the *Formula* option box.
   e. Click the down-pointing arrow at the right side of the *Number format* option box and then click *#,##0* at the drop-down list (top option in the list).
   f. Click OK to close the Formula dialog box.

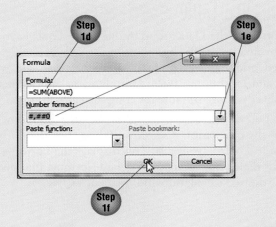

   g. In the table, type a dollar sign ($) before the number just inserted in cell B9.
2. Complete steps similar to those in Steps 1c through 1g to insert the Sum formula in cell C9 (the empty cell located immediately below the cell containing the amount *$675,329*).
3. In the bottom table, complete steps similar to those in Steps 1c through 1g to insert Sum formulas that calculate totals in the cells in the *Total* row.
4. In the bottom table, complete steps similar to those in Steps 1c through 1g to insert in cell F2 (the cell below the *Total* heading) a Sum formula that calculates the total of cells in the row. (The Formula dialog box will display *=SUM(LEFT)* instead of *=SUM(ABOVE)*.)
5. Insert a formula in the second cell below the *Total* heading (cell F3) by completing the following steps:
   a. Click in cell F3.
   b. Click the Formula button in the Data group.
   c. At the Formula dialog box, press the Backspace key to delete *ABOVE)*.
   d. Type LEFT).
   e. Click the down-pointing arrow at the right side of the *Number format* option box and then click *#,##0* at the drop-down list (top option in the list).
   f. Click OK to close the Formula dialog box.
   g. In the table, type a dollar sign ($) before the number just inserted in cell F3.

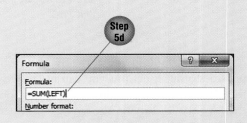

6. In the bottom table, complete steps similar to those in Steps 5b through 5g to insert Sum formulas that calculate totals of cells in the rows in the *Total* column.

7. Insert a formula that calculates the average of amounts by completing the following steps:
   a. Click in cell B10 in the top table. (Cell B10 is the empty cell immediately right of the cell containing the word *Average*.)
   b. Click the Formula button in the Data group.
   c. At the Formula dialog box, delete the formula in the *Formula* text box *except* the equals sign.
   d. With the insertion point positioned immediately right of the equals sign, click the down-pointing arrow at the right side of the *Paste function* option box and then click *AVERAGE* at the drop-down list.
   e. With the insertion point positioned between the left and right parentheses, type B2:B8.
   f. Click the down-pointing arrow at the right side of the *Number format* option box and then click *#,##0* at the drop-down list (top option in the list).
   g. Click OK to close the Formula dialog box.
   h. Type a dollar sign ($) before the number just inserted in cell B10.

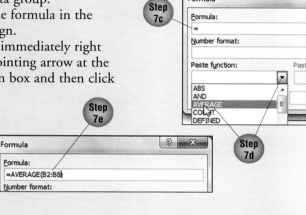

8. Complete steps similar to those in Steps 7b through 7h to insert in the top and bottom tables formulas that calculate averages. Insert formulas in the *Average* rows of both tables. (When inserting an average formula in a cell in the bottom table, identify only those amounts in row 2 through row 5.)

9. Insert a formula that calculates the maximum number by completing the following steps:
   a. Click in cell B11 (the empty cell immediately right of the cell containing the words *Top Sales*).
   b. Click the Formula button in the Data group.
   c. At the Formula dialog box, delete the formula in the *Formula* text box *except* the equals sign.
   d. With the insertion point positioned immediately right of the equals sign, click the down-pointing arrow at the right side of the *Paste function* option box and then click *MAX* at the drop-down list. (You will need to scroll down the list to display the *MAX* option.)
   e. With the insertion point positioned between the left and right parentheses, type B2:B8.
   f. Click the down-pointing arrow at the right side of the *Number format* option box and then click *#,##0* at the drop-down list (top option in the list).
   g. Click OK to close the Formula dialog box.
   h. Type a dollar sign ($) before the number just inserted in cell B10.

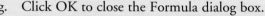

10. Complete steps similar to those in Steps 9b through 9h to insert the maximum number in cell C11.

11. Apply formatting to each table to enhance the visual appeal of the tables.

12. Save, print, and then close **C14-E03-SalesDivTable.docx**.

Writing Formulas

In addition to using the functions provided in the Formula dialog box, you can write your own formulas. Use the four basic operators when you write a formula, including the plus sign (+) for addition, the minus sign (hyphen) for subtraction, the asterisk (*) for multiplication, and the forward slash (/) for division. If a calculation contains two or more operators, Word calculates from left to right. If you want to change the order of the calculations, use parentheses around the part of the calculation to be performed first.

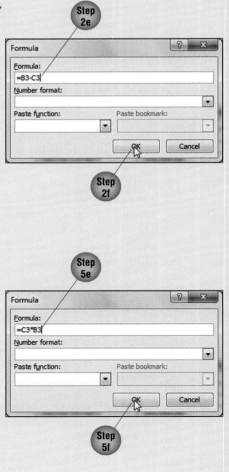

Exercise 14.4A   Writing Formulas in Tables   Part 1 of 2

1. Open **Sales&Support.docx** and save the document with the name **C14-E04-Sales&Support**.
2. Write a formula in the top table that calculates the difference in amounts by completing the following steps:
   a. Click in cell D3 (the empty cell located immediately below the cell containing the heading *Difference*).
   b. Click the Table Tools Layout tab.
   c. Click the Formula button in the Data group.
   d. At the Formula dialog box, press the Backspace key to delete *SUM(LEFT)* that displays in the *Formula* option box. (Do not delete the equals sign.)
   e. Type B3-C3.
   f. Click OK to close the Formula dialog box.
3. Click in cell D4 and then complete steps similar to those in Steps 2c through 2f, except type B4-C4 in the *Formula* text box in the Formula dialog box. (Amounts enclosed in parentheses indicate a negative amount.)
4. Insert the correct formula in the remaining cells in column D. (Make sure you change the cell designation for each formula. For example, type B5-C5 when inserting the formula in cell D5.)
5. Write a formula in the bottom table that calculates the salary amounts by completing the following steps:
   a. Click in cell D3 (the empty cell located immediately below the cell containing the heading *Salary*).
   b. Click the Table Tools Layout tab.
   c. Click the Formula button in the Data group.
   d. At the Formula dialog box, press the Backspace key to delete *SUM(LEFT)* that displays in the *Formula* option box. (Do not delete the equals sign.)
   e. Type C3*B3.
   f. Click OK to close the Formula dialog box.
6. Click in cell D4 and then complete steps similar to those in Steps 5c through 5f, except type C4*B4 in the *Formula* text box in the Formula dialog box.

7. Insert the correct formula in the remaining cells in column D. (Make sure you change the cell designation for each formula. For example, type C5*B5 when inserting the formula in cell D5.)
8. Make the following changes to the top table:
    a. AutoFit the contents of the table.
    b. Apply the *Medium Shading 2 - Accent 5* table style.
    c. Remove the check mark from the *First Column* check box in the Table Style Options group in the Table Tools Design tab.
    d. Select all of the cells containing amounts, click the Table Tools Layout tab, and then click the Align Top Right button in the Alignment group.
9. Make the following changes to the bottom table:
    a. AutoFit the contents of the table.
    b. Apply the *Medium Shading 2 - Accent 5* table style.
    c. Remove the check mark from the *First Column* check box in the Table Style Options group in the Table Tools Design tab.
    d. Select the cells containing amounts in the *Rate* and *Salary* columns, click the Table Tools Layout tab, and then click the Align Top Right button in the Alignment group.
    e. Select the hour numbers below the *Hours* heading and then click the Align Top Center button in the Alignment group.
10. Center each table between the left and right margins.
11. Save and then print **C14-E04-Sales&Support.docx**.

Recalculating a Formula

If you change numbers in cells that are part of a formula, recalculate the formula. To do this, select the result of the formula and then press the F9 function key. This recalculates the formula and inserts the new result in the cell. You can recalculate adjacent cells by selecting the cells and then pressing F9. You can also recalculate by selecting the result of the formula, clicking the Formula button in the Table Tools Layout tab, and then clicking OK at the Formula dialog box.

Exercise 14.4B   **Recalculating Formulas**   **Part 2 of 2**

1. With **C14-E04-Sales&Support.docx** open, make the following changes to amounts in the top table:
    a. Change the amount in cell B4 from *$65,375.50* to *$94,375.50*.
    b. Change the amount in cell B6 from *$75,328.20* to *$68,947.00*.
2. Recalculate the amounts in cells D4 and D6 in the top table by completing the following steps:
    a. Click the number in cell D4 and then press the F9 function key.
    b. Click the number in cell D6 and then press the F9 function key.
3. Make the following changes to numbers in the bottom table:
    a. Change the number in cell B4 from *40* to *30*.
    b. Change the amount in cell C5 from *$38.00* to *$39.50*.
4. Recalculate the amounts in cells D4 and D5 in the bottom table by selecting cells D4 and D5 and then pressing the F9 function key.
5. Save, print, and then close **C14-E04-Sales&Support.docx**.

Chapter Summary

➤ Change the layout of a table with options and buttons in the Table Tools Layout tab.

➤ You can select a cell, row, column, or table using the Select button in the Table group in the Table Tools Layout tab.

➤ Insert and delete columns and rows with buttons in the Rows & Columns group in the Table Tools Layout tab.

➤ Merge selected cells with the Merge Cells button and split cells with the Split Cells button, both located in the Merge group in the Table Tools Layout tab.

➤ Change column width and row height using the height and width measurement boxes in the Cell Size group in the Table Tools Layout tab; by dragging move table column markers on the horizontal ruler, adjust table row markers on the vertical ruler, or gridlines in the table; or with the AutoFit button in the Cell Size group.

➤ Change alignment of text in cells with buttons in the Alignment group in the Table Tools Layout tab.

➤ If a table spans two pages, you can insert a header row at the beginning of the rows that extend to the next page. To do this, click in the header row, or select the desired header rows, and then click the Repeat Header Rows button in the Data group in the Table Tools Layout tab.

➤ Change cell margins with options at the Table Options dialog box.

➤ Change text direction in a cell with the Text Direction button in the Alignment group.

➤ Change the table alignment at the Table Properties dialog box with the Table tab selected.

➤ Use the resize handle to change the size of the table and use the table move handle to move the table.

➤ Convert text to a table with the *Convert Text to Table* option at the Table button drop-down list. Convert a table to text with the Convert to Text button in the Data group in the Table Tools Layout tab.

➤ Sort selected rows in a table with the Sort button in the Data group.

➤ Perform calculations on data in a table by clicking the Formula button in the Data group in the Table Tools Layout tab and then specifying the formula and number format at the Formula dialog box.

➤ Write a formula with basic operators including the plus sign for addition, the minus sign for subtraction, the asterisk for multiplication, and the forward slash for division.

➤ Recalculate a formula by clicking in the cell containing the result of the formula and then pressing the F9 function key or by clicking the Formula button in the Table Tools Layout tab and then clicking OK at the Formula dialog box.

Commands Review

FEATURE	RIBBON TAB, GROUP	BUTTON	OPTION
Select table	Table Tools Layout, Table		
Insert column left	Table Tools Layout, Rows & Columns		
Insert column right	Table Tools Layout, Rows & Columns		
Insert row above	Table Tools Layout, Rows & Columns		

FEATURE	RIBBON TAB, GROUP	BUTTON	OPTION
Insert row below	Table Tools Layout, Rows & Columns		
Delete table	Table Tools Layout, Rows & Columns		Delete Table
Delete row	Table Tools Layout, Rows & Columns		Delete Rows
Delete column	Table Tools Layout, Rows & Columns		Delete Columns
Merge cells	Table Tools Layout, Merge		
Split Cells dialog box	Table Tools Layout, Merge		
Split table	Table Tools Layout, Merge		
Distribute rows	Table Tools Layout, Cell Size		
Distribute columns	Table Tools Layout, Cell Size		
AutoFit table contents	Table Tools Layout, Cell Size		
Table Properties dialog box	Table Tools Layout, Table		
Cell alignment	Table Tools Layout, Alignment		
View gridlines	Table Tools Layout, Table		
Repeat header row	Table Tools Layout, Data		
Table Options dialog box	Table Tools Layout, Alignment		
Cell direction	Table Tools Layout, Alignment		
Convert text to table	Insert, Tables		Convert Text to Table
Convert table to text	Table Tools Layout, Data		
Sort text in table	Table Tools Layout, Data		
Formula dialog box	Table Tools Layout, Data		

Key Points *Review*

Completion: In the space provided at the right, indicate the correct term, command, or number.

1. Click this button in the Table Tools Layout tab to insert a column at the left of the column containing the insertion point.

2. One method for changing column width is dragging this on the horizontal ruler.

3. Insert and delete columns and rows with buttons in this group in the Table Tools Layout tab.

4. Click this button in the Table Tools Layout tab to merge the selected cell. _____

5. Use this measurement box in the Table Tools Layout tab to increase or decrease the height of rows. _____

6. Hold down this key while dragging a table column marker, and measurements display on the horizontal ruler. _____

7. Use this button in the Cell Size group in the Table Tools Layout tab to make the column widths in a table automatically fit the contents. _____

8. This is the default setting for the left and right margins in a cell. _____

9. Change the table alignment at this dialog box with the Table tab selected. _____

10. Hover the mouse pointer over a table, and this displays in the lower right corner of the table. _____

11. Position the mouse pointer in a table, and this displays in the upper left corner. _____

12. Click this button to display the *Convert Text to Table* option. _____

13. The Sort button is located in this group in the Table Tools Layout tab. _____

14. When writing a formula, this symbol indicates multiplication. _____

15. When writing a formula, this symbol indicates division. _____

Chapter Assessments

Applying Your Skills

Demonstrate your knowledge of features learned in this chapter by completing the following assessments.

Assessment 14.1   Create and Format a Supply Request Form Table

1. At a blank document, create the table shown in Figure 14.6 with the following specifications:
   a. Create a table with five columns and eight rows.
   b. Insert three additional rows in the table.
   c. Merge the cells in the first row.
   d. Type the text in the cells as shown in Figure 14.6.
   e. Change the row height of the first row to *0.58* inch.
   f. Select the text in the first row and then change the font size to 22 points.
   g. Select rows 2 through 11 and then change the row height for the selected cells to 0.3 inch.
   h. Apply the *Medium Shading 2 - Accent 2* table style.
   i. Remove the check mark from the *First Column* option in the Table Style Options group.
   j. Change the alignment of the text in the first row to Align Center.
   k. Change the alignment of the text in the second row to Align Center and turn on bold.
2. Save the document with the name **C14-A01-SupplyForm.**
3. Print and then close **C14-A01-SupplyForm.docx.**

Figure 14.6 Assessment 14.1

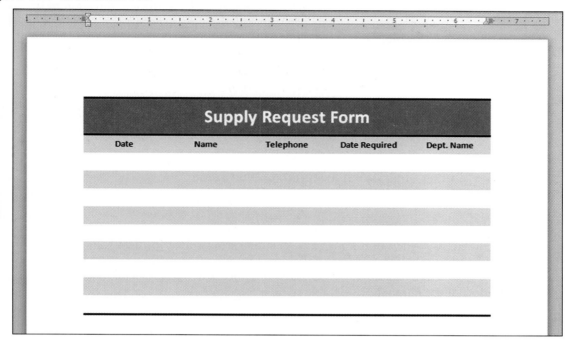

Assessment 14.2   Format a Transportation Services Table

1. Open **Services.docx** and save the document with the name **C14-A02-Services**.
2. Format the table so it appears as shown in Figure 14.7 with the following specifications:
   a. Delete the row that begins with *City Travel 24-hour customer service*.
   b. Click in the cell containing the text *Edgewood City Transit*, insert four new rows above, and then type the following text in the new rows:

Valley Rail Road	
Railway information	*(208) 555-8775*
Status hotline	*(208) 555-8740*
Travel information	*(208) 555-8442*

   c. Select the cells containing the text *Railway information*, *Status hotline*, and *Travel information* and then change the left cell margin measurement to *0.3″*. ***Hint: Refer to Exercise 14.2A, Step 4.***
   d. Select the two cells below *City Travel Card* (the cells containing indented text) and then change the left cell margin measurement to 0.3 inch.
   e. Select the three cells below *Edgewood City Transit* (the cells containing indented text) and then change the left cell margin measurement to 0.3 inch.
   f. Select the three cells below *Mainline Bus* (the cells containing indented text) and then change the left cell margin measurement to 0.3 inch.

Figure 14.7 Assessment 14.2

	Service	Telephone
Edgewood Area Transportation Services	***City Travel Card***	
	City Travel office	(208) 555-6500
	Card inquiries	(208) 555-9005
	Valley Rail Road	
	Railway information	(208) 555-8775
	Status hotline	(208) 555-8740
	Travel information	(208) 555-8442
	Edgewood City Transit	
	Subway and bus information	(208) 555-5475
	Service status hotline	(208) 555-1194
	Travel information	(208) 555-9043
	Mainline Bus	
	Bus routes	(208) 555-4355
	Emergency hotline	(208) 555-5121
	Travel information	(208) 555-4550

g. Insert a column at the left of the first column and then merge the cells in the new column. Type the text Edgewood Area Transportation Services, change the text direction so it displays as shown in Figure 14.7, and then change the alignment to Align Center. With the text selected, change the font size to 18.

h. Use the move table column marker to change the width of the first column to 1 inch.

i. Change the width of the second column to 2.2 inches, and then change the width of the third column to approximately 1.1 inch.

j. Apply bold and italic to text as shown in Figure 14.7.

k. Apply shading to cells as shown in Figure 14.7.

3. Center the table between the left and right margins.

4. Save, print, and then close **C14-A02-Services.docx**.

Assessment 14.3   Create and Format a Training Costs Table

START From Scratch

1. At a blank document, create the table shown in Figure 14.8 with the following specifications:

   a. Create a table with two columns and eight rows.

   b. Merge the cells in the top row and then change the alignment to Align Center.

   c. Type the text in the cells as shown in Figure 14.8.

   d. Right-align the cells containing the money amounts as well as the blank line below the last amount (cells B2 through B8).

   e. AutoFit the contents of the cells.

   f. Apply the *Medium Shading 2 - Accent 4* table style.

   g. Change the font size to 14 for the text in cell A1.

   h. Use the resize handle located in the lower right corner of the table and increase the width and height of the table by approximately 1 inch.

2. Insert a formula in cell B8 that sums the amounts in cells B2 through B7. (Type a dollar sign before the number inserted by the formula.)

3. Select the entire table and then change the vertical cell alignment to Center. ***Hint: Refer to Exercise 14.2C, Step 7.***

4. Save the document with the name **C14-A03-TrainCosts**.

5. Print and then close **C14-A03-TrainCosts.docx**.

Figure 14.8 Assessment 14.3

TRAINING COSTS	
Human Resource	$23,150
Research and Development	$78,455
Public Relations	$10,348
Purchasing	$22,349
Administration	$64,352
Sales and Marketing	$18,450
Total	

Assessment 14.4   Insert Formulas and Format a Training Department Table

1. Open **TrainDept.docx** and save the document with the name **C14-A04-TrainDept**.
2. Insert formulas in the cells below the *Average* heading that calculate the averages of the numbers in the modules columns. Change the *Number format* to *0* at the Formula dialog box.
3. Change the number in cell B6 from *78* to *90* and change the number in cell B7 from *76* to *90*. Recalculate the averages in cells E6 and E7.
4. Apply the *Medium Shading 2 - Accent 5* table style. Remove the check mark from the *First Column* check box in the Table Style Options group in the Table Tools Design tab.
5. Save, print, and then close **C14-A04-TrainDept.docx**.

Assessment 14.5   Insert Formulas and Format a Financial Analysis Table

1. Open **FinAnalysis.docx** and save the document with the name **C14-A05-FinAnalysis**.
2. Insert a formula in cell B13 that sums the amounts in cells B6 through B12.
3. Insert a formula in cell C13 that sums the amounts in cells C6 through C12.
4. Insert a formula in cell B14 that subtracts the amount in B13 from the amount in B4. **Hint: The formula should look like this: =B4-B13**.
5. Insert a formula in cell C14 that subtracts the amount in C13 from the amount in C4. **Hint: The formula should look like this: =C4-C13**. (Make sure you insert dollar signs before the numbers inserted by the formulas.)
6. Apply the *Medium Shading 2 - Accent 5* table style. Remove the check mark from the *First Column* check box in the Table Style Options group in the Table Tools Design tab.
7. Select the top two rows in the table and then change the alignment to Align Center.
8. Select the third row in the table and then change the alignment to Align Top Right.
9. Save, print, and then close **C14-A05-FinAnalysis.docx**.

Expanding Your Skills

Explore additional feature options or use Help to learn a new skill in creating these documents.

Assessment 14.6   Insert an Average Formula

1. Open **NSSQuizAverages.docx** and then save the document with the name **C14-A06-NSSQuizAverages**.
2. Position the insertion point in the last cell in the *Average* column containing data (the cell containing *67%*). Display the Formula dialog box, determine how the formula was written to calculate the quiz averages, determine the number format, and then close the dialog box.
3. Move the insertion point to the empty cell below *67%* and then insert a formula to calculate the averages. Click in the next empty cell in the *Average* column and then press F4 to repeat the last function (which was inserting the formula). Continue moving the insertion point to the next empty cell in the *Average* column and pressing F4.
4. Center align the table.
5. Save and then close **C14-A06-NSSQuizAverages.docx**.

Assessment 14.7   Insert a Table in a Document and Repeat a Header Row

1. Open **NSSQuizAveLtr.docx** and then save the document with the name **C14-A07-NSSQuizAveLtr**.
2. Move the insertion point to the beginning of the second paragraph in the letter and then insert the **C14-A06-NSSQuizAverages.docx** document into the letter. **Hint: Do this with the Object button arrow in the Text group in the Insert tab.**
3. Specify that you want the first row in the table to display at the top of the table on the second page as a header row.
4. Insert your initials at the end of the letter in place of the *XX*.
5. Save, print, and then close **C14-A07-NSSQuizAveLtr.docx**.

Achieving Signature Status

Take your skills to the next level by completing this more challenging assessment.

Assessment 14.8 Create a Cover Letter Containing a Table

1. At a blank document, create the document shown in Figure 14.9. Create and format the table as shown in the figure.
2. Save the completed document and name it **C14-A08-CoverLtr.**
3. Print and then close **C14-A08-CoverLtr.docx.**

Figure 14.9 Assessment 14.8

4523 Parkland Road
Indianapolis, IN 46211
March 3, 2012

Mr. Alan Lundgren
Orion News Tribune
211 South 42nd Street
Indianapolis, IN 46204

Dear Mr. Lundgren:

Your advertised opening for a corporate communications staff writer describes interesting challenges. As you can see from the table below, my skills and experience are excellent matches for the position.

QUALIFICATIONS AND SKILLS	
Your Requirements	**My Experience, Skills, and Value Offered**
Two years of business writing experience	Four years of experience creating diverse business messages, from corporate communications to feature articles and radio broadcast material.
Ability to complete projects on deadline	Proven project coordination skills and tight deadline focus. My current role as producer of a daily, three-hour, talk-radio program requires planning, coordination, and execution of many detailed tasks, always in the face of inflexible deadlines.
Oral presentation skills	Unusually broad experience, including high-profile roles as an on-air radio presence and "the voice" for an on-hold telephone message company.
Relevant education (BA or BS)	BA in Mass Communications; one year post-graduate study in Multimedia Communications.

As you will note from the enclosed résumé, my experience encompasses corporate, print media, and multimedia environments. I offer a diverse and proven skill set that can help your company create and deliver its message to various audiences to build image, market presence, and revenue. I look forward to meeting with you to discuss the value I can offer your company.

Sincerely,

Justine Brock

Enclosure: Résumé

Chapter 15

 **TUTORIALS**

Tutorial 15.1
Creating Charts
Tutorial 15.2
Changing Chart Design, Layout,
and Formatting
Tutorial 15.3
Inserting a Picture and Shape
in a Chart
Tutorial 15.4
Arranging and Sizing a Chart

Creating Charts

Performance Objectives

Upon successful completion of Chapter 15, you will be able to:

- Create charts
- Change chart design
- Edit chart data
- Change chart layout and style
- Select and format chart elements
- Insert objects in charts
- Apply shapes and styles
- Position and size charts

In Chapters 13 and 14, you learned to create tables to organize data. Although tables provide an adequate way to present and display data, a chart can provide a more visual representation. Sometimes referred to as a ***graph***, a chart is a picture of numeric data. If you have Microsoft Excel installed on your computer, you can create a chart in a Word document and use the chart design, formatting, and layout options provided in Excel. If you do not have Excel installed on your computer, Word uses the Microsoft Graph feature to create your chart. Exercises and assessments in this chapter assume that you have Excel installed on your computer.

 Note: Before beginning computer exercises for this chapter, copy to your storage medium the Chapter15 folder from the CD that accompanies this textbook and then make Chapter15 the active folder.

In this chapter students will produce the following documents:

Exercise 15.1. C15-E01-SalesChart.docx
Exercise 15.2. C15-E02-BudgetChart.docx
Exercise 15.3. C15-E03-PopChart.docx
Exercise 15.4. C15-E04-TourChart.docx

Model answers for these exercises are shown on the following pages.

Exercise 15.1
C15-E01-SalesChart.docx

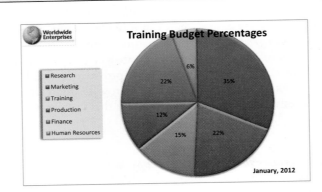

Exercise 15.2
C15-E02-BudgetChart.docx

Chapter Fifteen

Exercise 15.3
C15-E03-PopChart.docx

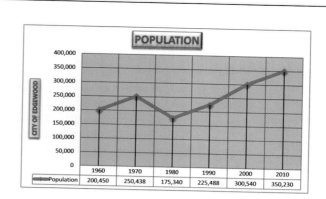

Exercise 15.4
C15-E04-TourChart.docx

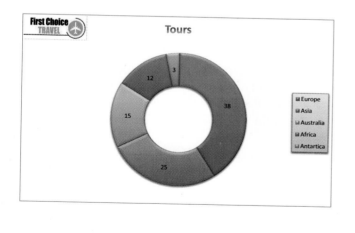

Creating Charts

495

Insert a Chart
1. Click Insert tab.
2. Click Chart button.
3. Click desired chart type and style.
4. Enter data in Excel spreadsheet.
5. Close Excel.

Creating a Chart

In Word, you can create a variety of charts, including bar and column charts, pie charts, area charts, and much more. Table 15.1 describes the eleven basic chart types you can create in Word. To create a chart, click the Insert tab and then click the Chart button in the Illustrations group. This displays the Insert Chart dialog box, shown in Figure 15.1. At this dialog box, choose the type of chart you want to create from the list at the left side of the dialog box, click the chart style, and then click OK.

Chart

Table 15.1 Types of Charts

Area	An area chart emphasizes the magnitude of change, rather than the rate of change, over time. It also shows the relationship of parts to a whole by displaying the sum of the plotted values.
Bar	A bar chart shows individual figures at a specific time, or shows variations between components but not in relationship to the whole.
Bubble	A bubble chart compares sets of three values in a manner similar to a scatter chart, with the third value displayed as the size of the bubble marker.
Column	A column chart compares separate (noncontinuous) items as they vary over time.
Doughnut	A doughnut chart shows the relationship of parts of the whole.
Line	A line chart shows trends and change over time at even intervals. It emphasizes the rate of change over time rather than the magnitude of change.
Pie	A pie chart shows proportions and relationships of parts to the whole.
Radar	A radar chart emphasizes differences, amounts of change over time, and variations and trends. Each category has its own value axis radiating from the center point. Lines connect all values in the same series.
Stock	A stock chart shows five values for a stock—open, high, low, volume, and close.
Surface	A surface chart shows trends in values across two dimensions in a continuous curve.
XY (Scatter)	A scatter chart shows either the relationships among numeric values in several data series or plots the interception points between x and y values. It shows uneven intervals of data and is commonly used in scientific data.

Figure 15.1 Insert Chart Dialog Box

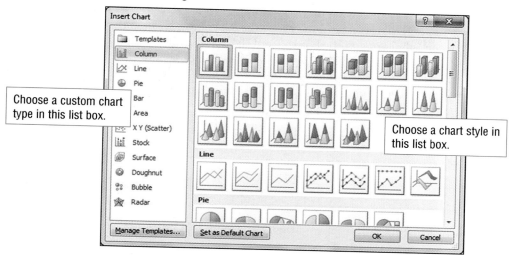

Choose a custom chart type in this list box.

Choose a chart style in this list box.

When you click OK, a sample chart is inserted in your Word document, and Excel opens with sample data, as shown in Figure 15.2. Type the desired data in the Excel worksheet cells over the existing data. To type data in the Excel worksheet, click in the desired cell, type the data, and then press the Tab key to make the next cell active. Press Shift + Tab to make the previous cell active or press the Enter key to make the cell below active. As you type data in the Excel worksheet, the entries are reflected in the chart in the Word document.

Enter data in cells in the Excel worksheet. The data entered is reflected in the Word document chart.

Figure 15.2 Sample Chart

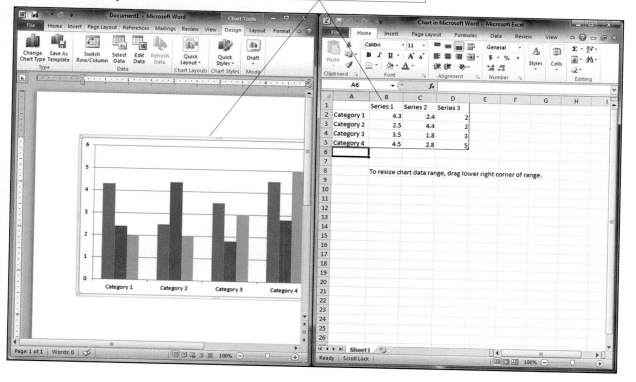

The Excel cells that you use to create the chart are surrounded by a blue border. Below that border, the following message displays: "To resize chart data range, drag lower right corner of range." If you need to change the data range, position the mouse pointer on the bottom right corner of the border until the mouse pointer displays as a double-headed arrow pointing diagonally. Hold down the left mouse button and then drag up, down, left, or right until the border is in the desired location. You can also click in a cell immediately outside the border, and, when you insert data in the cell, the border expands.

Close

When you have entered all the data in the worksheet, click the Close button that displays in the upper right corner of the screen (the top Close button). This closes the Excel window, expands the Word document window, and displays the chart in the document.

Exercise 15.1A Creating a Column Chart   Part 1 of 4

1. At a blank document, click the Insert tab and then click the Chart button in the Illustrations group.
2. At the Insert Chart dialog box with the first column chart selected, click OK.
3. In the Excel worksheet, position the mouse pointer on the bottom right corner of the border until the mouse pointer displays as a double-headed arrow pointing diagonally. Hold down the left mouse button, drag to the left until the border displays at the right side of column C, and then release the mouse button.
4. Type the text in the cells as shown in Figure 15.3 by completing the following steps:
   a. Click in cell B1 in the Excel worksheet and then type 1st Half.
   b. Press the Tab key and then type 2nd Half in cell C1.
   c. Press the Tab key.
   d. Continue typing the remaining data in the cells as indicated in Figure 15.3.
5. When you have entered all the data, click the Close button that displays in the upper right corner of the Excel window.
6. Save the document in the Chapter15 folder on your storage medium with the name **C15-E01-SalesChart**.

	A	B	C	D	E
1		Series 1	Series 2		
2	Category 1	4.3	2.4		
3	Category 2	2.5	4.4		
4	Category 3	3.5	1.8		
5	Category 4	4.5	2.8		
6					
7					
8		To resize chart data range, drag lower right			

Step 3

Step 5

Figure 15.3 Exercise 15.1A

	A	B	C	D	E	F	G
1		1st Half	2nd Half	Series 3			
2	Northeast	$320,540	$475,235	2			
3	Northwest	$210,568	$250,455	2			
4	Southeast	$175,450	$190,400	3			
5	Southwest	$120,406	$130,245	5			
6							
7							
8		To resize chart data range, drag lower right corner of range.					

Changing Chart Design

When you insert a chart in a document, the Chart Tools Design tab, shown in Figure 15.4, becomes active. Use options in this tab to change the chart type, edit chart data, change the chart layout, or apply a chart style.

Figure 15.4 Chart Tools Design Tab

Changing the Chart Type

After you create a chart, you can change the chart type by clicking the Change Chart Type button in the Type group in the Chart Tools Design tab. This displays the Change Chart Type dialog box. This dialog box and the Insert Chart dialog box, shown in Figure 15.1, contain the same options. At the Change Chart Type dialog box, click the desired chart type in the panel at the left and click the desired chart style at the right.

Saving a Chart as a Template

If you consistently create the same type of chart, you can save the formatting and layout of that chart type as a template. To do this, click the Save As Template button in the Type group in the Chart Tools Design tab. At the Save Chart Template dialog box, type a name for the template and then click Save. To use a default template, click the Insert tab and then click the Chart button. At the Insert Chart dialog box, click *Template* in the left panel and then double-click the desired template in the list box. Chart templates are saved in the Templates folder on the hard drive. You can delete a chart template at the Templates folder.

Change Chart Type and Style
1. Make the chart active.
2. Click Chart Tools Design tab.
3. Click Change Chart Type button.
4. Click desired chart type.
5. Click desired chart style.
6. Click OK.

Change Chart Type   Save As Template

Exercise 15.1B Changing the Chart Type   Part 2 of 4

1. Make sure **C15-E01-SalesChart.docx** is open.
2. Click in the chart outside of any chart elements. (This displays a light gray border around the chart.)
3. Change the chart type by completing the following steps:
   a. Click the Chart Tools Design tab.
   b. Click the Change Chart Type button in the Type group.
   c. At the Change Chart Type dialog box, click the *Bar* option in the left panel.
   d. Click the *Clustered Bar in 3-D* option in the Styles group.

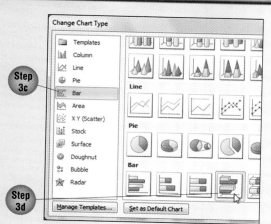

Step 3c

Step 3d

e. Click OK to close the dialog box.
4. Save and then print **C15-E01-SalesChart.docx**.
5. Return to a column chart by completing the following steps:
   a. Make sure the chart is active and then click the Change Chart Type button in the Type group.
   b. At the Change Chart Type dialog box, click the *Column* option in the left panel.
   c. Click the *3-D Clustered Column* option in the Styles group.

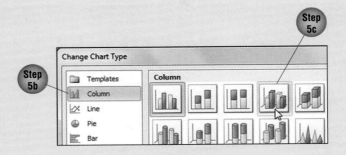

   d. Click OK to close the dialog box.
6. Save **C15-E01-SalesChart.docx**.
7. Save the chart as a template by completing the following steps:
   a. With the chart selected, click the Save as Template button in the Type group in the Chart Tools Design tab.
   b. At the Save Chart Template dialog box, type your initials followed by **ChartTemplate** and then press Enter.

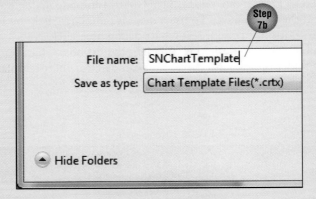

8. Create a chart with the template by completing the following steps:
   a. Press Ctrl + N to display a new blank document.
   b. Click the Insert tab and then click the Chart button in the Illustrations group.

c. Click *Templates* in the left panel of the dialog box and then double-click the chart template that begins with your initials. (Notice that the chart contains the formatting you applied to the chart but does not include the data in the chart you used to save the chart template.)

d. Close the Excel window by clicking the Close button located in the upper right corner of the window.

9. Print the chart by pressing Ctrl + P to display the Print tab Backstage view and then clicking the Print button.

10. Delete the chart template you created by completing the following steps:

   a. Display the Open dialog box.
   b. Scroll up the navigation pane located at the left side of the dialog box and then click the *Templates* folder.
   c. Double-click the Charts folder located in the Open dialog box content pane.
   d. Right-click the chart template that begins with your initials and then click the *Delete* option at the shortcut menu.
   e. Click Yes at the message asking if you want to move the file to the Recycle Bin.
   f. Click the Cancel button to close the Open dialog box.

11. Close the document without saving it.

Managing Data

Use options in the Data group in the Chart Tools Design tab to change the order of data in the chart, select specific data, edit data, or refresh the data. When you create a chart, the cells in the Excel worksheet are linked to the chart in the Word document. If you need to edit data in the chart, click the Edit Data button, and the Excel worksheet opens. Make the desired changes to cells in the Excel worksheet and then click the Close Window button.

Edit Data

Exercise 15.1C Managing Data in a Chart   Part 3 of 4

1. With **C15-E01-SalesChart.docx** open, edit the data and switch the rows and columns by completing the following steps:
   a. Make sure the chart and the Chart Tools Design tab are active.
   b. Click the Edit Data button in the Data group.
   c. Click in cell B2 (the cell containing the amount *$320,540*), type 357975, and then press the Enter key. (When you press the Enter key, a dollar sign is automatically inserted in front of the number, and a thousands separator comma is inserted between 7 and 9.)
   d. With cell B3 active (the cell containing the amount *$210,568*), type 270568, and then press the Enter key.

e. Click in the Word document to make it active.

f. In the Word document, click the Switch Row/Column button in the Data group.

2. Click the Close button that displays in the upper right corner of the Excel window.

3. Save **C15-E01-SalesChart.docx**.

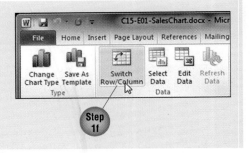

Changing the Chart Layout and Style

The Chart feature in Word provides a number of predesigned chart layouts and chart styles that you can apply to your chart. The Chart Layouts group displays three chart layouts. Click one of these layouts or click the More button and then click a layout at the drop-down list of additional layout options. The Chart Styles group displays four chart styles. Click one of these to apply a predesigned style to a chart or click the More button and then click a style at the drop-down list of additional style options.

Exercise 15.1D   **Changing the Chart Layout and Style**   **Part 4 of 4**

1. With **C15-E01-SalesChart.docx** open, change the chart layout by completing the following steps:
   a. Make sure the chart and the Chart Tools Design tab are active.
   b. Click the first layout option in the Chart Layouts group (*Layout 1*).
   c. Click the text *Chart Title* that displays toward the top of the chart and then type Division Sales.

2. Change the chart style by completing the following steps:
   a. Click the More button that displays at the right of the thumbnails in the Chart Styles group.
   b. Click the second option from the left in the bottom row (*Style 42*).

3. Save, print, and then close **C15-E01-SalesChart.docx**.

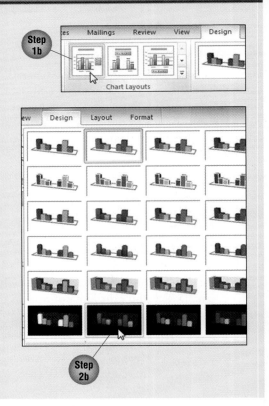

Formatting Chart Layout

Click the Chart Tools Layout tab, shown in Figure 15.5, and options display for changing and customizing chart elements. With options in this tab, you can format or modify specific chart elements, insert elements, add labels to the chart, customize the chart background, and add analysis items to the chart.

Figure 15.5 Chart Tools Layout Tab

Selecting Elements

To format or modify a specific element in a chart, select the element first. You can select an element by clicking it or by clicking the Chart Elements button in the Current Selection group in the Chart Tools Layout tab. With the element selected, apply the desired formatting. Click the Format Selection button in the Current Selection group, and a dialog box displays with options for formatting the selected element.

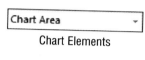

Chart Elements

Format Selection

Exercise 15.2A Creating a Pie Chart

Part 1 of 3

1. At a blank document, create a pie chart by completing the following steps:
   a. Click the Insert tab.
   b. Click the Chart button in the Illustrations group.
   c. At the Insert Chart dialog box, click the *Pie* option in the left panel and then click OK.
2. In the Excel worksheet, position the mouse pointer on the bottom right corner of the border until the mouse pointer displays as a double-headed arrow pointing diagonally. Hold down the left mouse button, drag down until the border displays at the bottom of row 7, and then release the mouse button.
3. Type the text in the cells as shown in Figure 15.6.
4. When all data is entered, click the Close button that displays in the upper right corner of the Excel window.
5. With the Chart Tools Design tab selected, click the More button at the right of the thumbnails in the Chart Styles group and then click the second option from the left in the fourth row (*Style 26*).

6. Customize the chart title by completing the following steps:
   a. Click the Chart Tools Layout tab.
   b. Click the Chart Elements button arrow in the Current Selection group and then click *Chart Title* at the drop-down list.
   c. Type Training Budget Percentages.
   d. Click the Chart Elements button arrow in the Current Selection group and then click *Legend* at the drop-down list.
   e. Click the Format Selection button in the Current Selection group.
   f. At the Format Legend dialog box, click the *Fill* option at the left side of the dialog box.
   g. Click the *Solid fill* option in the *Fill* section of the dialog box.
   h. Click the Color button in the *Fill* section and then click the blue color (*Blue, Accent 1, Lighter 80%*).
   i. Click the *Shadow* option at the left side of the dialog box.
   j. Click the *Presets* button in the *Shadow* group and then click the third option from the left in the second row in the *Outer* section (*Offset Left*).

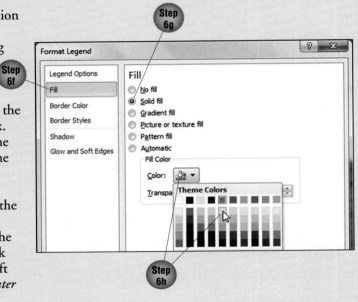

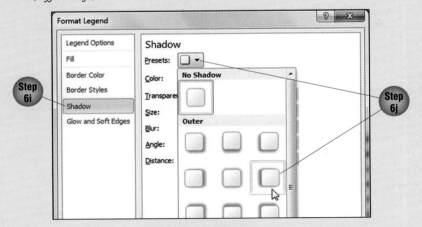

   k. Click the Close button to close the Format Legend dialog box.
7. Save the document with the name **C15-E02-BudgetChart**.

Figure 15.6 Exercise 15.2A

▲	A	B	C
1		Sales	
2	Research	35%	
3	Marketing	22%	
4	Training	15%	
5	Production	12%	
6	Finance	22%	
7	Human Resources	6%	
8		To resize chart da	

QUICK STEPS

Insert Picture in Chart
1. Click Chart Tools Layout tab.
2. Click Picture button.
3. Navigate to desired folder.
4. Double-click desired picture.

Inserting Elements

Insert elements, such as pictures or shapes, in a chart with buttons in the Insert group in the Chart Tools Layout tab. Click the Picture button, and the Insert Picture dialog box displays. At this dialog box, navigate to the folder that contains the picture you want to insert and then double-click the picture. Click the Shapes button to draw a shape in the chart, and click the Draw Text Box button to insert a text box in the chart.

Picture   Shapes

Draw Text Box

Exercise 15.2B Inserting a Picture and Shape   Part 2 of 3

1. With **C15-E02-BudgetChart.docx** open, insert a picture by completing the following steps:
   a. With the Chart Tools Layout tab active, click the Picture button in the Insert group.
   b. At the Insert Picture dialog box, navigate to the Chapter15 folder on your storage medium and then double-click **WELogo.jpg**.
   c. With the logo selected, decrease the size of the logo so it displays in the upper left corner of the chart as shown at the right.
   d. Click in the chart outside of any chart elements to deselect the logo.
2. Insert a text box by completing the following steps:
   a. Make sure the chart is active and then click the Chart Tools Layout tab.
   b. Click the Draw Text Box button in the Insert group.
   c. Drag in the chart and draw a text box as shown below.
   d. Press Ctrl + B to turn on bold and then type January, 2012.
   e. Click in the chart outside the text box.
3. Save **C15-E02-BudgetChart.docx**.

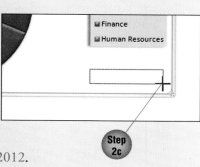

Step 1c

Step 2c

Positioning Labels

QUICK STEPS

Position Labels
1. Make the chart active.
2. Click Chart Tools Layout tab.
3. Click desired labels button.
4. Choose desired option at drop-down list.

Use options in the Labels group in the Chart Tools Layout tab to insert and position labels in your chart. For example, click the Chart Title button, and a drop-down list displays with options for removing the chart title, centering the title and overlaying it on the chart, and displaying the title above the chart. You can also position a label by dragging it. To do this, select the label, position the mouse pointer over the selected label or over the label border until the pointer displays with a four-headed arrow attached, hold down the left mouse button, and then drag the label to the desired location.

Chart Title

Exercise 15.2C Inserting and Positioning Elements   Part 3 of 3

1. With **C15-E02-BudgetChart.docx** open, change the position of chart elements by completing the following steps:
   a. Make sure the chart and the Chart Tools Layout tab are active.
   b. Click the Chart Title button in the Labels group and then click *Centered Overlay Title* at the drop-down list.
   c. Click the Legend button in the Labels group and then click *Show Legend at Left* at the drop-down list.
   d. Click the Data Labels button and then click *Center* at the drop-down list.

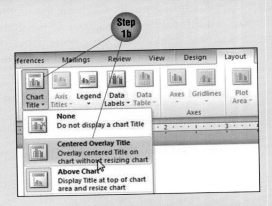

2. Drag the title so it is centered over the pie by completing the following steps:
   a. Click the title to select it.
   b. Position the mouse pointer on the title border until the pointer displays with a four-headed arrow attached.
   c. Hold down the left mouse button and then drag to the right until the title border is positioned as shown below.

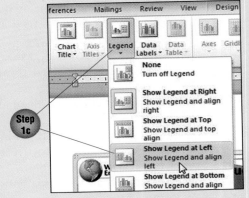

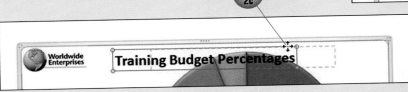

3. Complete steps similar to those in Step 2 to drag the legend so it is centered between the left edge of the chart border and the pie.
4. Save, print, and then close **C15-E02-BudgetChart.docx**.

Customizing Chart Backgrounds

You can further customize a chart with buttons in the Axes, Background, and Analysis groups. Use buttons in the Axes group to specify whether you want major and/or minor horizontal and vertical lines in the chart. With buttons in the Background group, you can format the chart wall and floor and rotate the chart. Depending on the type of chart you are customizing, some of the buttons in the Background group may not be active. Use buttons in the Analysis group to add analysis elements such as trend lines, up and down bars, and error bars.

Exercise 15.3A   Creating and Formatting a Line Chart   Part 1 of 2

1. At a blank document, create a line chart by completing the following steps:
   a. Click the Insert tab.
   b. Click the Chart button in the Illustrations group.
   c. At the Insert Chart dialog box, click the *Line* option in the left panel.
   d. Click the fourth option from the left in the *Line* section (*Line with Markers*).
   e. Click OK to close the dialog box.
2. In the Excel worksheet, position the mouse pointer on the bottom right corner of the border until the mouse pointer displays as a double-headed arrow pointing diagonally. Hold down the left mouse button, drag left until the border displays at the right side of column B, and then release the mouse button.
3. Drag the bottom right corner down until the border displays at the bottom of row 7.
4. Type the text in cells as shown in Figure 15.7.
5. When you have entered all the data, click the Close button that displays in the upper right corner of the Excel window.
6. With the Chart Tools Design tab active, click the More button at the right of the thumbnails in the Chart Layouts group and then click the second option from the left in the second row (*Layout 5*).
7. Click the More button at the right of the thumbnails in the Chart Styles group and then click the third option from the left in the third row (*Style 19*).
8. Click the text *Axis Title* that displays at the left side of the chart and then type City of Edgewood.
9. Customize the chart title by completing the following steps:
   a. Click the Chart Tools Layout tab.
   b. Click the Chart Elements button arrow in the Current Selection group and then click *Chart Title* at the drop-down list.
   c. Click the Format Selection button in the Current Selection group.

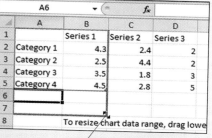

Step 3

Step 9b

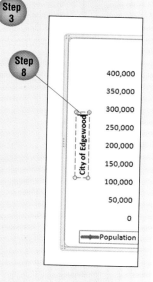

Step 8

---

d. At the Format Chart Title dialog box, make sure the *Fill* option at the left side of the dialog box is selected.
e. Click the *Solid fill* option in the *Fill* section of the dialog box.
f. Click the Color button in the *Fill* section and then click the blue color (*Blue, Accent 1, Lighter 80%*).
g. Click the *Shadow* option at the left side of the dialog box.
h. Click the *Presets* button in the *Shadow* group and then click the first option from the left in the first row in the *Outer* section (*Offset Diagonal Bottom Right*).
i. Click the Close button to close the Format Chart Title dialog box.

10. Click the Gridlines button in the Axes group, point to *Primary Vertical Gridlines*, and then click *Major Gridlines* at the side menu.
11. Click the Lines button in the Analysis group and then click *Drop Lines* at the drop-down list.
12. Save the document with the name **C15-E03-PopChart**.

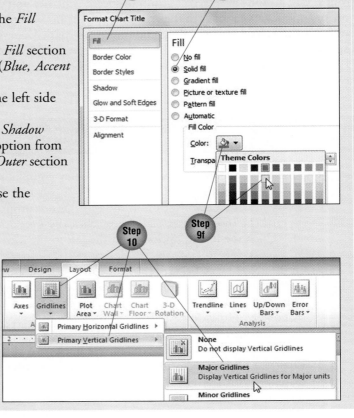

Figure 15.7 Exercise 15.3A

◢	A	B	C	D
1		Population	Series 2	Series 3
2	1960	200,450	2.4	2
3	1970	250,438	4.4	2
4	1980	175,340	1.8	3
5	1990	225,488	2.8	5
6	2000	300,540		
7	2010	350,230		
8		To resize chart data range, drag lowe

Changing Chart Formatting

Customize the format of a chart and chart elements with options in the Chart Tools Format tab, shown in Figure 15.8. This tab and the Chart Tools Layout tab both contain the same Current Selection group. With the other options in the tab, you can apply a predesigned style to a shape, a predesigned WordArt style to text, or arrange and size the chart.

Figure 15.8 Chart Tools Format Tab

Applying Shape and WordArt Styles

The Shape Styles group in the Chart Tools Format tab contains buttons that you can use to apply predesigned styles to shapes inserted in your chart. Click the More button at the right of the styles in the group, and a drop-down gallery of shape styles displays. Use the buttons that display at the right of the Shape Styles group to apply fill, an outline, and an effect to a selected shape. The WordArt Styles group contains predesigned styles you can apply to text in a chart. Use the buttons that display at the right of the WordArt Styles group to apply fill, an outline, or an effect to text in a chart.

Exercise 15.3B Applying Styles to a Chart   **Part 2 of 2**

1. With **C15-E03-PopChart.docx** open, apply a style to the axis title by completing the following steps:
   a. Make sure the chart is selected and then click the Chart Tools Format tab.
   b. Click the Chart Elements button arrow in the Current Selection group and then click the *Vertical (Value) Axis Title* option at the drop-down list.
   c. With the axis title selected, click the More button at the right of the shapes in the Shape Styles group and then click *Subtle Effect - Purple, Accent 4* at the drop-down gallery.
   d. Click the More button that displays at the right of the thumbnails in the WordArt Styles group and then click the fifth option from the left in the fourth row (*Gradient Fill - Purple, Accent 4, Reflection*).

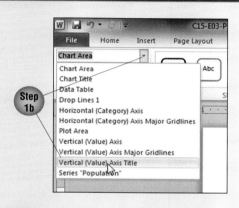

Step 1b

Step 1c

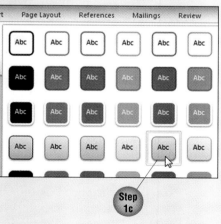

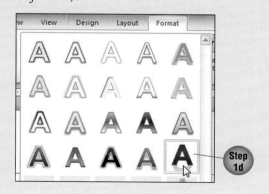

Step 1d

e. Click the Text Effects button that displays at the right of the WordArt Styles group, point to *Glow*, and then click the third option from the left in the third row (*Olive Green, 11 pt glow, Accent color 3*).

2. Apply a style and style effect to the chart title by completing the following steps:
   a. Click the chart title to select it.
   b. Click the *Subtle Effect - Purple, Accent 4* style that displays in the Shape Styles group.

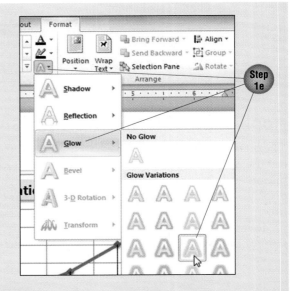

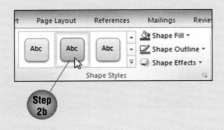

c. Click the Shape Effects button arrow that displays at the right of the Shape Styles group, point to *Bevel*, and then click *Circle* at the side menu.
d. Click the More button that displays at the right of the WordArt Styles group and then click the fifth option from the left in the fourth row (*Gradient Fill - Purple, Accent 4, Reflection*).
e. Click the Text Effects button that displays at the right of the WordArt Styles group, point to *Glow*, and then click the third option from the left in the third row (*Olive Green, 11 pt glow, Accent color 3*).

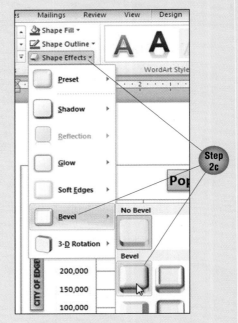

3. Apply a style outline to the data table by completing the following steps:
   a. Click the Chart Elements button arrow and then click *Data Table* at the drop-down list.
   b. Click the Shape Outline button arrow that displays at the right of the Shape Styles group.
   c. Click the purple color in the *Standard Colors* section.
4. Apply a style outline to the vertical axis by completing the following steps:
   a. Click the Chart Elements button arrow and then click *Vertical (Value) Axis* at the drop-down list.
   b. Click the Shape Outline button arrow and then click the purple color in the *Standard Colors* section.
5. Apply a shape fill to the plot area by completing the following steps:
   a. Click the Chart Elements button arrow and then click *Plot Area* at the drop-down list.
   b. Click the Shape Fill button arrow and then click the light green color that displays in the *Standard Colors* section.
6. Save, print, and then close **C15-E03-PopChart.docx**.

Arranging a Chart

With buttons and options in the Arrange group in the Chart Tools Format tab, you can change the location of a chart in a document and change the chart's position relative to other elements. If you want to move a chart in a document, you must first specify how you want text to wrap around the chart in its new location. To do this, click the Position button and then click a position option or click the Wrap Text button and then click a wrapping style. With the other buttons in the Arrange group, you can send the chart behind other elements, move it in front of other elements, specify the alignment, or rotate the chart.

Sizing a Chart

You can increase or decrease the size of a chart by selecting the chart and then dragging a sizing handle. You can also size a chart to specific measurements with the Shape Height and Shape Width measurement boxes in the Size group in the Chart Tools Format tab. Change the height or width by clicking the up- or down-pointing arrows that display at the right of the measurement box or click the current measurement in the box and then type a specific measurement.

QUICK STEPS

Change Chart Height and/or Width
1. Make the chart active.
2. Click Chart Tools Format tab.
3. Insert desired height and width in the Shape Height and Shape Width measurement boxes.

Position   Wrap Text

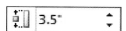

Shape Height

Shape Width

Exercise 15.4 Creating and Formatting a Doughnut Chart   Part 1 of 1

1. At a blank document, create a doughnut chart by completing the following steps:
   a. Click the Insert tab.
   b. Click the Chart button in the Illustrations group.
   c. At the Insert Chart dialog box, click the *Doughnut* option in the left panel and then click OK.
2. In the Excel worksheet, type the text in cells as shown in Figure 15.9.
3. When you have entered all of the data, click the Close button that displays in the upper right corner of the Excel window.
4. With the Table Tools Design tab selected, click the More button at the right of the thumbnails in the Chart Styles group and then click the second option from the left in the fourth row (*Style 26*).
5. Insert a picture logo by completing the following steps:
   a. Click the Chart Tools Layout tab.
   b. Click the Picture button in the Insert group.
   c. At the Insert Picture dialog box, navigate to the Chapter15 folder on your storage medium and then double-click the ***FCTLogo.jpg*** file.
   d. With the logo selected, decrease the size of the logo so it displays in the upper left corner of the chart as shown at the right.
   e. Deselect the logo.

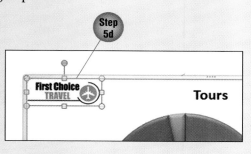

6. Insert data labels by clicking the Data Labels button in the Labels group in the Chart Tools Layout tab and then clicking *Show* at the drop-down list.

7. Apply a WordArt style to the chart title by completing the following steps:
   a. Click the Chart Tools Format tab.
   b. Click the chart title to select it.
   c. Click the More button at the right of the thumbnails in the WordArt Styles group and then click the fourth option from the left in the third row (*Gradient Fill - Blue, Accent 1*).

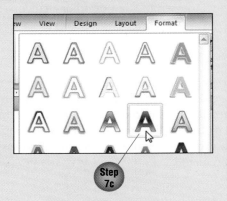

Step 7c

8. Add a shape style to the legend by completing the following steps:
   a. Click the legend to select it.
   b. Click the More button at the right of the thumbnails in the Shape Styles group and then click the second option from the left in the fourth row (*Subtle Effect - Blue, Accent 1*).

9. Increase the size of the doughnut by completing the following steps:
   a. Click the Chart Elements button arrow and then click *Plot Area* at the drop-down list.
   b. Drag the lower right sizing handle to increase the size of the doughnut.
   c. Drag the doughnut so it is better centered in the chart area.

10. Select the chart area and then change text wrapping by clicking the Wrap Text button in the Arrange group and then clicking *Square* at the drop-down list.

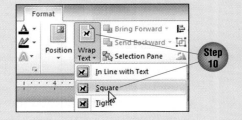

Step 10

11. Increase the height of the chart by clicking in the Shape Height measurement box in the Size group, typing 4, and then pressing the Enter key.

12. Increase the width of the chart by clicking in the Shape Width measurement box, typing 6.5, and then pressing the Enter key.

Step 11

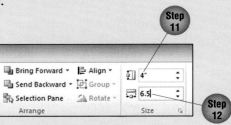

Step 12

13. Position the chart by clicking the Position button in the Arrange group and then clicking the second option from the left in the second row of the *With Text Wrapping* section (*Position in Middle Center with Square Text Wrapping*).

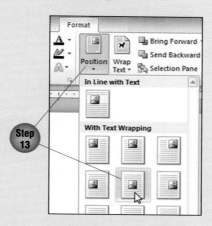

14. Save the document with the name **C15-E04-TourChart**.
15. Print and then close **C15-E04-TourChart.docx**.

Figure 15.9 Exercise 15.4

▲	A	B	C
1		Tours	
2	Europe	38	
3	Asia	25	
4	Australia	15	
5	Africa	12	
6	Antartica	3	
7			
8		To resize chart data ra	

Chapter Summary

➤ A chart is a visual presentation of data. You can create a chart with the Chart button in the Insert tab.

➤ At the Insert Chart dialog box, choose one of eleven available chart types: area, bar, bubble, column, doughnut, line, pie, radar, stock, surface, or XY scatter charts.

➤ Enter data for a chart in an Excel worksheet. As you enter data, press the Tab key to make the next cell active, press Shift + Tab to make the previous cell active, and press the Enter key to make the cell below active.

➤ Use the Change Chart Type button in the Chart Tools Design tab to change the type of the existing chart.

➤ Cells in the Excel worksheet that are used to create a chart are linked to the chart in the Word document. Click the Edit Data button in the Chart Tools Design tab, make changes to text in the Excel worksheet, and the changes are reflected in the chart in the Word document.

➤ Select and modify chart elements with options in the Current Selection group in the Chart Tools Layout tab.

➤ Insert elements in a chart, such as pictures, shapes, and text boxes, with buttons in the Insert group in the Chart Tools Layout tab.

➤ Use options in the Labels group in the Chart Tools Layout tab to insert and position labels such as chart and axis tables, a legend, and data labels.

➤ Insert major and/or minor horizontal and vertical gridlines with buttons in the Axes group in the Chart Tools Layout tab.

➤ The Shape Styles group in the Chart Tools Format tab contains predesigned styles you can apply to shapes in a chart. The group also contains buttons for applying shape fill, outline, and effects. Use options in the WordArt Styles group to apply styles to text in a chart. Use buttons in the group to apply fill, outline, and effects to text.

➤ Use options in the Arrange group in the Chart Tools Format tab to position and arrange a chart in the document. To move a chart, choose a text wrapping style, and then drag the chart to the desired location.

➤ Change the height and width of the chart with buttons in the Size group in the Chart Tools Format tab.

Commands *Review*

FEATURE	RIBBON TAB, GROUP	BUTTON, OPTION	KEYBOARD SHORTCUT
Insert Chart dialog box	Insert, Illustrations		
Make next cell active			Tab
Make previous cell active			Shift + Tab
Make cell below active			Enter
Change Chart Type dialog box	Chart Tools Design, Type		
Save Chart Template dialog box	Chart Tools Design, Type		
Edit chart data	Chart Tools Design, Data		
Select chart elements	Chart Tools Layout, Current Selection	Chart Area	
Format selection	Chart Tools Layout, Current Selection		
Chart title	Chart Tools Layout, Labels		

Key Points *Review*

Completion: In the space provided at the right, indicate the correct term, symbol, or command.

1. When creating a chart, enter data in this.

2. This is the number of chart types available at the Insert Chart dialog box.

3. Use this type of chart to show proportions and relationships of parts to the whole.

4. Use this type of chart to compare separate items as they vary over time.

5. When a chart is first inserted in a document, this tab is active.

6. Click this button to open the Excel worksheet containing the chart data.

7. The Chart Elements button is located in this group in the Chart Tools Layout tab.

8. Click the Picture button in the Insert group in the Chart Tools Layout tab, and this dialog box displays.

9. This group in the Chart Tools Format tab contains predesigned styles you can apply to shapes in a chart.

10. This group in the Chart Tools Format tab contains predesigned styles you can apply to chart text. _____

11. Control the position of a chart in a document with options and buttons in this group in the Chart Tools Format tab. _____

Chapter *Assessments*

Applying Your Skills

Demonstrate your knowledge of features learned in this chapter by completing the following assessments.

Assessment 15.1   Create and Format a Column Chart

1. At a blank document, use the data in Figure 15.10 to create a column chart with the following specifications:
   a. Apply the *Layout 1* chart layout.
   b. Apply the *Style 16* chart style.
   c. Select the chart title text and then type Sales by State.
   d. Insert the **WELogo.jpg** logo picture in the chart and then size and move the logo so it is positioned in the upper right corner of the chart. (Make sure the logo is small enough that it does not overlap any chart elements.)
   e. Show the legend at the bottom of the chart. ***Hint: Do this with the Legend button in the Labels group in the Chart Tools Layout tab.***
   f. Insert major and minor vertical primary gridlines.
   g. Select the legend and then apply the *Aqua, Accent 5, Lighter 80%* shape fill.
   h. Select the chart title, apply the *Aqua, Accent 5, Lighter 80%* shape fill, and then apply the *Gradient Fill - Orange, Accent 6, Inner Shadow* WordArt style.
2. Save the document with the name **C15-A01-StSalesChart**.
3. Print and then close **C15-A01-StSalesChart.docx**.

Figure 15.10 Assessment 15.1

	Sales 2009	Sales 2010	Sales 2011
Florida	$356,750	$400,790	$325,490
Georgia	$475,230	$385,675	$425,450
Alabama	$225,545	$300,245	$312,680

Assessment 15.2   Create and Format a Pie Chart

1. At a blank document, use the data in Figure 15.11 to create a pie chart with the following specifications:
   a. Apply the *Layout 6* chart layout.
   b. Apply the *Style 10* chart style.
   c. Select the chart title text and then type Department Expenses.
   d. Move the legend to the left side of the chart. (Select and then drag the legend so it is positioned between the left edge of the chart border and the pie.)
   e. Apply *Olive Green, Accent 3, Lighter 80%* shape fill to the chart area.

    f. Apply the glow shape effect *Olive Green, 5 pt. glow, Accent color 3* to the chart area.
    g. Apply the WordArt style *Gradient Fill - Blue, Accent 1* to the chart title text.
    h. Change the chart height to 3 inches and the chart width to 4 inches.
    i. Select the plot area and then drag the pie so it is centered below the title. (Make sure the legend and pie do not overlap.)
    j. Position the chart centered at the top of the page. ***Hint: Do this with the Position button in the Arrange group in the Chart Tools Format tab.***
2. Save the document with the name **C15-A02-ExpChart**.
3. Print **C15-A02-ExpChart.docx**.
4. With the chart selected, display the Excel worksheet and edit the data in the worksheet by changing the following:
    a. Change the *Salaries* percentage from *67%* to *62%*.
    b. Change the *Travel* percentage from *15%* to *17%*.
    c. Change the *Equipment* percentage from *11%* to *14%*.
5. Save, print, and then close **C15-A02-ExpChart.docx**.

Figure 15.11 Assessment 15.2

Category	Percentage
Salaries	67%
Travel	15%
Equipment	11%
Supplies	7%

Assessment 15.3   Create and Format a Bar Chart

1. At a blank document, use the data in Figure 15.12 to create a bar chart with the following specifications:
    a. Change the bar chart type to *Clustered Bar in 3-D*.
    b. Apply the *Layout 9* chart layout.
    c. Apply the *Style 40* chart style.
    d. Show the data labels.
    e. Insert major primary horizontal gridlines.
    f. Increase the height of the chart to 4 inches and the width to 6.5 inches.
    g. Position the chart in the middle of the page.
2. Save the document with the name **C15-A03-CoSalesChart**.
3. Print and then close **C15-A03-CoSalesChart.docx**.

Figure 15.12 Assessment 15.3

	Sales in Millions
Africa	2.8
Asia	7.5
Europe	10.3
North America	12.2
South America	4.8

Assessment 15.4   Create and Format a Line Chart

1. At a blank document, use the data in Figure 15.13 to create a line chart with the following specifications:
   a. Choose the *Line with Markers* line chart type.
   b. Click the Switch Row/Column button. (The Excel chart must be open to switch the rows and columns.)
   c. Apply the *Layout 5* chart layout.
   d. Apply the *Style 26* chart style.
   e. Delete the *Axis Title* text that displays at the left side of the chart.
   f. Select the chart title text and then type Population Comparison.
   g. Insert major primary vertical gridlines.
   h. Insert drop lines. ***Hint: Do this with the Lines button in the Analysis group.***
   i. Select the data table and then apply a blue shape outline.
   j. Select the plot area and then apply *Olive Green, Accent 3, Lighter 80%* shape fill.
   k. Select the chart area and then apply *Aqua, Accent 5, Lighter 60%* shape fill.
   l. With the chart area still selected, apply the *Cool Slant* bevel shape effect.
   m. Select the chart title and then apply the *Gradient Fill - Blue, Accent 1* WordArt style.
   n. Change the chart height to 4.5 inches and the chart width to 6.5 inches.
   o. Position the chart in the middle of the page.
2. Save the document with the name **C15-A04-PopCompChart**.
3. Print and then close **C15-A04-PopCompChart.docx**.

Figure 15.13 Assessment 15.4

	1970	1980	1990	2000	2010
Lanville	58,980	61,248	65,320	53,120	78,340
Mill Creek	68,458	70,538	55,309	64,328	70,537

Expanding Your Skills

Explore additional feature options or use Help to learn a new skill in creating these documents.

Assessment 15.5   Create and Format a Chart

1. At a blank document, create a chart and chart type of your choosing with the data shown in Figure 15.14. You determine the design, layout, and format of the chart and chart elements. Insert a chart title with the text *Taxes*.
2. Save the document with the name **C15-A05-TaxesChart**.
3. Print and then close **C15-A05-TaxesChart.docx**.

Figure 15.14 Assessment 15.5

	Budgeted	Actual
City	$15,000	$17,350
County	$22,000	$24,100
Federal	$53,500	$48,750

Assessment 15.6 Type a Business Letter Containing a Column Chart

1. Open **BMCLtrhd.docx** and then save the document with the name **C15-A06-LtrtoCP**.
2. Type the letter shown in Figure 15.15 and insert and format the chart as shown in Figure 15.15. *Hint: After applying the chart style, you will need to select the title and change to a smaller font size.*
3. Save, print, and then close **C15-A06-LtrtoCP.docx**.

Figure 15.15 Assessment 15.6

Blue Mountain Computer Services and Training
502 East 33rd Street ☐ Casper, WY 82607 ☐ 307-555-2218 ☐ www.emcp.net/bmc

July 10, 2012

Ms. Olivia Sullivan
Cashmere Products
3120 Jackson Street
Casper, WY 82645

Dear Ms. Sullivan:

We are confident that the computer training your employees have received at Blue Mountain Computer Services and Training enables them to perform their computer-related job duties more quickly and efficiently. The information below specifies the number of employees at Cashmere Products who have participated in the three sessions of training we offer on Office 2010.

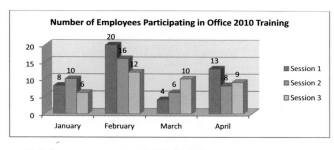

We have established our computer training schedule for the second half of 2012, which is enclosed with this letter. For the second half of 2012, we are offering a number of advanced courses on Word 2010, Excel 2010, and PowerPoint 2010. If you have additional computer training needs, please let me know.

Sincerely,

Patricia Callaway
Training Coordinator

XX
C15-A06-LtrtoCP.docx

Enclosure

"Let our five-star customer service team provide all of your computer support and training needs."

Achieving Signature Status

Take your skills to the next level by completing this more challenging assessment.

Assessment 15.7 Create and Format a Pie Chart

1. Open **TECLtrhd.docx** and then save the document and name it **C15-A07-ExpChart**.
2. Create and format the pie chart shown in Figure 15.16 with the following specifications:
   - Use the *Pie in 3-D* pie chart option.
   - Set the title in 20-point Copperplate Gothic Bold and change the font color to blue.
   - Insert the data labels at the inside end of each pie piece.
   - Remove the shape outline from the chart.
   - Move the legend as shown in the figure.
3. Save, print, and then close **C15-A07-ExpChart.docx**.

Figure 15.16 Assessment 15.7

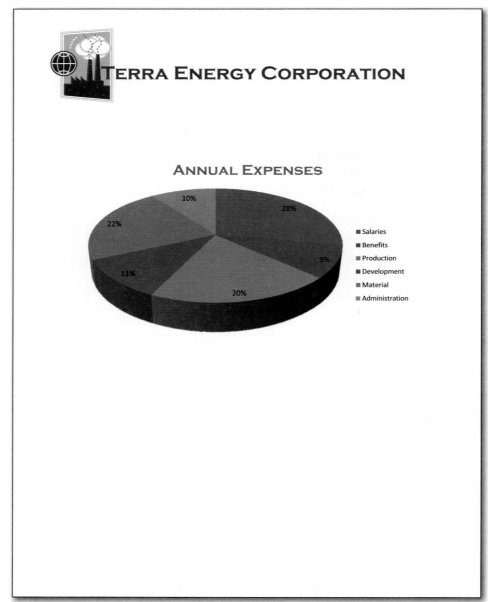

Performance *Assessments*

Enhancing Documents

ASSESSING PROFICIENCIES

In this unit, you have learned to improve the visual appeal of documents by inserting, customizing, and formatting pictures, clip art images, screen images, shapes, text boxes, and WordArt. You learned how to present data visually in SmartArt diagrams and charts. You also learned how to create, format, and customize tables and how to calculate data in tables.

Note: Before beginning computer assessments, copy to your storage medium the Unit03PA folder from the CD that accompanies this textbook and then make Unit03PA the active folder.

Assessment U3.1   **Format a Computers Report**

1. Open **CompComm.docx** and save the document with the name **U3-PA01-CompComm**.
2. Make the following changes to the document:
   a. Select text from the beginning of the title *COMPUTERS IN ENTERTAINMENT* (located at the bottom of page one) to the end of the document and then press the Delete key.
   b. Apply the Heading 1 style to the title of the report and apply the Heading 2 style to the three headings in the report.
   c. Change the style set to Simple.
   d. Apply the Civic theme.
3. Format the text from the first paragraph to the end of the document into two columns.
4. Center the title *COMPUTERS IN COMMUNICATIONS* and change the spacing before to 6 points and the spacing after to 12 points.
5. Insert the Transcend Sidebar built-in text box and then make the following customizations:
   a. Type the following text in the text box: "The linking of computers enables users to communicate and work together efficiently and effectively . . . "
   b. Apply the *Orange, Accent 6, Darker 50%* shape fill.
6. Save, print, and then close **U3-PA01-CompComm.docx**.

Assessment U3.2   **Create a Flyer with WordArt and a Clip Art Image**

START From Scratch

1. Create the flyer shown in Figure U3.1 with the following specifications:
   a. Create the WordArt with the following specifications:
      • Use the *Fill – Tan, Text 2, Outline – Background 2* option (first option from the left in the top row) at the WordArt button drop-down gallery.
      • Change the width to 6.5 inches and the height to 1 inch.
      • Apply the *Deflate* text effect transform shape.
      • Apply the *Olive Green, Accent 3, Lighter 40%* text fill color.
      • Change the shape outline to *No Outline*.
   b. Type the text shown in the figure in 22-point Calibri and bold and center the text. Change the text color to *Olive Green, Accent 3, Darker 50%*.

c. Insert the clip art image shown in the figure (use the keyword *buildings* to find the clip art) and then change the wrapping style to *Square*. Position and size the image as shown in the figure.

2. Save the document with the name **U3-PA02-Flyer**.

3. Print and then close **U3-PA02-Flyer.docx**.

Figure U3.1 Assessment U3.2

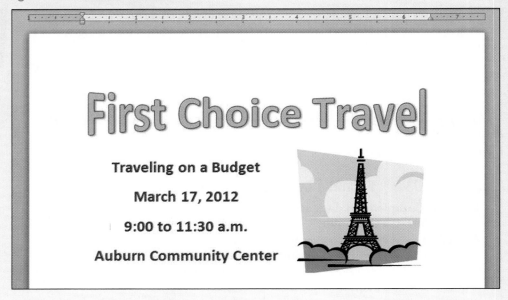

 Assessment U3.3   Create and Format an Organizational Chart

1. Use SmartArt to create an organizational chart for the following text (in the order displayed). Apply formatting to enhance the chart's visual appeal.

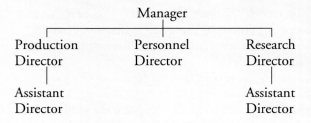

2. Save the completed document with the name **U3-PA03-OrgChart**.

3. Print and then close **U3-PA03-OrgChart.docx**.

 Assessment U3.4   Create and Format a Radial Diagram

1. At a blank document, create the diagram shown in Figure U3.2 with the following specifications:
   a. Create the cycle diagram using the *Basic Radial* diagram, insert two additional shapes, and then type text (turn on bold) in the shapes as shown in the figure.
   b. Change the color to *Colorful Range - Accent Colors 3 to 4*.
   c. Apply the *Intense Effect* SmartArt style.

     d. Increase the height to 4.5 inches and the width to 6.5 inches.

     e. Position the chart in the middle of the page.

2. Save the document with the name **U3-PA04-ServerDiagram**.

3. Print and then close **U3-PA04-ServerDiagram.docx**.

Figure U3.2 Assessment U3.4

Assessment U3.5   Create and Format a Training Announcement

1. Create the announcement shown in Figure U3.3 with the following specifications:

     a. Use the *Bevel* shape in the *Basic Shapes* section of the Shapes drop-down list to create the shape.

     b. Apply the *Moderate Effect - Olive Green, Accent 3* style to the shape.

     c. Change the shape outline to white.

     d. Apply the *Offset Diagonal Top Left* shadow to the shape.

     e. Change the shape height to 2.8 inches and the shape width to 6 inches.

     f. Type the text inside the bevel shape as shown in the figure. Set the text in 20-point Candara bold, change the font color to dark blue, and center the text.

2. Save the completed document with the name **U3-PA05-NetworkTrain**.

3. Print and then close **U3-PA05-NetworkTrain.docx**.

Figure U3.3 Assessment U3.5

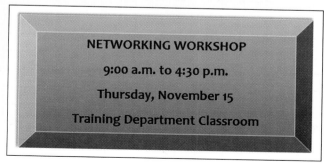

Assessment U3.6   Create an Announcement with a Picture and Text

1. At a blank document, insert the picture **River.jpg** located in the Unit03PA folder on your storage medium. ***Hint: Insert the picture using the Picture button.***
2. Crop out a portion of the trees at the left and at the right and a portion of the hill at the top.
3. Correct the brightness and contrast to *Brightness: 0% Normal Contrast: +40%.*
4. Specify that the picture should wrap behind text.
5. Insert the text *Riverside Apartments* on one line and *1-888-555-8800* on the second line. Change the font color of the text to white and turn on bold.
6. Increase the size of the picture so it is easier to see and the size of the text so it is easier to read. Center the text and position it on the picture on top of the river so it is readable.
7. Save the document with the name **U3-PA06-RAFlyer**.
8. Print and then close **U3-PA06-RAFlyer.docx**.

Assessment U3.7   Create and Format a Table

1. At a blank document, create the table shown in Figure U3.4 with the following specifications:
   a. Merge and center cells as shown in the figure and then type the text as shown.
   b. Change the height of row 1 to 0.7 inch, the height of row 2 to 0.4 inch, and the height of the remaining rows to 0.3 inch.
   c. Change the font size to 16 points for the text in the first row.
   d. Align, center, and bold the text in the first three rows.
   e. Apply the shading as shown (use *Aqua, Accent 5, Lighter 40%* for the first and third rows and use *Aqua, Accent 5, Lighter 80%* for the second row).
2. Save the document with the name **U3-PA07-ComMembers**.
3. Print and then close **U3-PA07-ComMembers.docx**.

Figure U3.4 Assessment U3.7

COLEMAN DEVELOPMENT CORPORATION		
Community Development Committee Members		
Name	**Company**	**Address**

Assessment U3.8   Format a Travel Table

1. Open **TravelPkgs.docx** and save the document with the name **U3-PA08-TravelPkgs**.
2. Format the table so it displays as shown in Figure U3.5 with the following specifications:
   a. Select the entire table and then change the font to 12-point Candara.
   b. Change the column widths so the columns display as shown in the figure.
   c. Apply the *Medium Shading 2 - Accent 1* table style. Remove the check mark from the *First Column* option in the Table Style Options group.
   d. Align and center the text in the first two rows.
   e. Increase the font size of the text in row 1 to 18 points.
   f. Bold the text in rows 2 and 3.
   g. Slightly increase the height of rows 1 and 2 as shown in Figure U3.5.
   h. Center the text in row 3.
   i. Center the cells in the columns below the headings *Length* and *Estimated Cost*.
3. Save the document with the name **U3-PA08-TravelPkgs**.
4. With **U3-PA08-TravelPkgs.docx** open, open the document named **BTLtrtoMA.docx** and then save the document with the name **U3-PA08-BTLtrtoMA**.
5. Select the table and the blank line below the table and then click the Copy button in the Home tab. Make **U3-PA08-BTLtrtoMA.docx** active, position the insertion point at the beginning of the second paragraph in the letter, and then click the Paste button in the Home tab.
6. Replace the initials *XX* that display toward the end of the document with your initials.
7. Save, print, and then close **U03-PA08-BTLtrtoMA.docx**.
8. Close **U03-PA08-TravelPkgs.docx**.

Figure U3.5 Assessment U3.8

BAYSIDE TRAVEL		
Family Fun Ski and Snowboard Vacations		
Package	**Length**	**Estimated Cost**
Lake Tahoe, Nevada	3 days, 2 nights	$229 to $259
Lake Tahoe, Nevada	7 days, 6 nights	$459 to $599
Sun Valley, Idaho	3 days, 2 nights	$249 to $279
Sun Valley, Idaho	7 days, 6 nights	$499 to $629
Jackson Hole, Wyoming	3 days, 2 nights	$239 to $269
Jackson Hole, Wyoming	7 days, 6 nights	$469 to $629

Assessment U3.9   Calculate Averages in a Table

1. Open **EmpOrient.docx** and save the document with the name **U3-PA09-Quiz**.
2. Insert formulas in the appropriate cells that calculate the averages of the quizzes. (Change the *Number Format* option at the Formula dialog box to *0*.)
3. AutoFit the contents of the table.

4. Apply a table style of your choosing to the table.
5. Apply any other formatting to improve the visual appeal of the table.
6. Save, print, and then close **U3-PA09-Quiz.docx**.

Assessment U3.10   Calculate Quantities and Totals in a Table

1. Open **PurOrder.docx** and save the document with the name **U3-PA10-PurOrder**.
2. Insert, in the appropriate cells, formulas that multiply the quantity by the unit price. In the bottom cell in the fourth column, insert a formula that totals the amounts in the cells above.
3. Save, print, and then close **U3-PA10-PurOrder.docx**.

Assessment U3.11   Create and Format a Column Chart

1. At a blank document, use the data in Figure U3.6 to create a column chart with the following specifications:
   a. Change the chart type to *3-D Clustered Column*.
   b. Apply the *Layout 3* chart layout.
   c. Apply the *Style 35* chart style.
   d. Select the chart title text and then type 2011 Sales.
   e. Insert a small text box in the lower left corner of the chart and then type your first and last names.
   f. Insert major primary vertical gridlines.
   g. Select the chart area, apply *Orange, Accent 6, Lighter 60%* shape fill, and apply the *Offset Bottom* shadow shape effect.
   h. Select the chart title and then apply the *Gradient Fill - Blue, Accent 1* WordArt style.
   i. Change the chart height to 4 inches and the chart width to 6.5 inches.
   j. Position the chart in the middle of the page.
2. Save the document with the name **U3-PA11-SalesChart**.
3. Print **U3-PA11-SalesChart.docx**.
4. With the chart selected, display the Excel worksheet and edit the data in the worksheet by changing the following:
   a. Change the amount in cell C2 from *$285,450* to *$302,500*.
   b. Change the amount in cell C4 from *$180,210* to *$190,150*.
5. Save, print, and then close **U3-PA11-SalesChart.docx**.

Figure U3.6 Assessment U3.11

Salesperson	First Half	Second Half
Bratton	$235,500	$285,450
Daniels	$300,570	$250,700
Hughes	$170,200	$180,210
Marez	$358,520	$376,400

Assessment U3.12　Create and Format a Pie Chart

START From Scratch

1. At a blank document, use the data in Figure U3.7 to create a pie chart with the following specifications:
   a. Apply the *Layout 6* chart layout.
   b. Apply the *Style 26* chart style.
   c. Select the chart title text and then type District Expenditures.
   d. Move the legend to the left side of the chart.
   e. Select the chart area, apply *Purple, Accent 4, Lighter 80%* shape fill, and apply the *Purple, 5 pt glow, Accent color 4* glow shape effect.
   f. Select the legend, apply *Purple, Accent 4, Lighter 40%* shape fill, and apply the *Offset Left* shadow shape effect.
   g. Apply the WordArt style *Gradient Fill - Purple, Accent 4, Reflection* to the chart title text.
   h. Select the plot area and then increase the size of the pie so it better fills the chart area. (You may need to move the pie.)
   i. Select the legend and then move it so it is centered between the left edge of the chart border and the pie.
   j. Position the chart centered at the top of the page.
2. Save the document with the name **U3-PA12-ExpendChart**.
3. Print and then close **U3-PA12-ExpendChart.docx**.

Figure U3.7　Assessment U3.12

	Percentage
Basic Education	42%
Special Needs	20%
Support Services	19%
Vocational	11%
Compensatory	8%

CREATING ORIGINAL DOCUMENTS

The activities in Assessments U3.13–U3.16 give you the opportunity to practice your writing skills as well as demonstrate your mastery of the important Word features presented in this unit. When you compose the documents, use correct grammar, precise word choices, and clear sentence construction.

Assessment U3.13　Write Steps Describing How to Use SmartArt

Situation: You work in the training department of Coleman Development Corporation, and you are responsible for preparing a training document on how to use Word 2010. Create a document that describes the SmartArt feature and the types of diagrams a user can create with it. Provide specific steps describing how to create an organizational chart using the *Organizational Chart* diagram and specific steps describing how to create a *Radial Cycle* diagram. Save the completed document with the name **U3-PA13-SmartArt**. Print and then close **U3-PA13-SmartArt.docx**.

Assessment U3.14   Create an Expenditures Table

Situation: You are the vice president of Coleman Development Corporation, and you need to prepare a table showing the equipment expenditures for each department, as shown below:

COLEMAN DEVELOPMENT CORPORATION
Equipment Expenditures

Department	Amount
Personnel	$20,400
Research	$58,300
Finance	$14,900
Production	$90,100
Sales	$51,000
Marketing	$52,600

Create a table with the data and apply appropriate formatting to it. Save the document with the name **U3-PA14-EquipExpend**. Print and then close **U3-PA14-EquipExpend.docx**.

Assessment U3.15   Create a Column Chart

Situation: You decide that the data in the table you created in Assessment U3.14 would be easier to visualize if it were inserted in a chart. Using the information from the table, create a column chart and apply formatting to enhance its visual appeal. Save the completed document with the name **U3-PA15-EquipExpChart**. Print and then close **U3-PA15-EquipExpChart.docx**.

Assessment U3.16   Create a Store Letterhead

Situation: You work for Evergreen Sports, a sports equipment store that specializes in hiking gear. You have been asked to design letterhead for the store. When designing the letterhead, include an appropriate clip art image along with the following information:

Evergreen Sports
4500 Lowell Avenue
Portland, OR 99821
(503) 555-8220

Save the completed letterhead document with the name **U3-PA16-ESLtrhd**. Print and then close **U3-PA16-ESLtrhd.docx**.

Unit 4

Managing Data

Chapter 16   Merging Documents

Chapter 17   Sorting and Selecting

Chapter 18   Managing Lists

Chapter 19   Managing Page Numbers, Headers, and Footers

Chapter 20   Managing Shared Documents

Unit 4   Performance Assessments

Chapter 16

Tutorial 16.1
Creating a Main Document
Tutorial 16.2
Creating a Data Source File
Tutorial 16.3
Creating Form Letters Using
Mail Merge
Tutorial 16.4
Merging Envelopes
Tutorial 16.5
Editing a Data Source File
Tutorial 16.6
Comparing and Merging
Documents

Merging Documents

Performance Objectives

Upon successful completion of Chapter 16, you will be able to:

- Create and merge letters, envelopes, labels, and directories
- Create custom fields for a merge
- Edit main documents and data source files
- Input text during a merge
- Insert a Merge Record # field and an If…Then…Else… field in a main document
- Use the Mail Merge wizard to merge documents

Word includes a Mail Merge feature that you can use to create customized letters, envelopes, labels, directories, email messages, and faxes. The Mail Merge feature is useful when you need to send the same letter to a number of people, but you want to personalize it and create an envelope or mailing label for each person. Mail Merge allows you to merge a main document, such as a letter, with a data source file, such as a database of names and addresses. In this chapter, you will use Mail Merge to create customized letters, envelopes, labels, and directories.

Note: Before beginning computer exercises for this chapter, copy to your storage medium the Chapter16 folder from the CD that accompanies this textbook and then make Chapter16 the active folder.

In this chapter, students will produce the following documents:

Exercise 16.1. C16-E01-CofELtrs.docx
Exercise 16.2. C16-E02-CofEEnvs.docx
Exercise 16.3. C16-E03-CofELabels.docx
Exercise 16.4. C16-E04-CofEDirectory.docx
Exercise 16.5. C16-E05-Labels.docx
Exercise 16.6. C16-E06-Directory.docx
Exercise 16.7. C16-E07-CofELetters.docx
Exercise 16.8. C16-E08-BTToursLtrs.docx
Exercise 16.9. C16-E09-BTToursLtrs.docx
Exercise 16.10. C16-E10-BTToursLtrs.docx
Exercise 16.12. C16-E12-PRLtrs.docx

Model answers for these exercises are shown on the following pages.

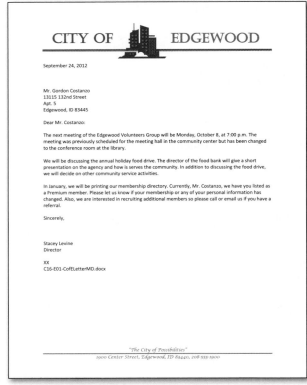

Chapter Sixteen

Exercise 16.2

C16-E02-CofEEnvs.docx

Mrs. Barbara Colburn
12309 Second Street
Apt. B-205
Edgewood, ID 83447

Mr. Brian Kosel
345 Rosewood Avenue
Edgewood, ID 83445

Model Answers

Mrs. Barbara Colburn
12309 Second Street
Apt. B-205
Edgewood, ID 83447

Mr. Brian Kosel
345 Rosewood Avenue
Edgewood, ID 83445

Mr. Gordon Costanzo
13115 132nd Street
Apt. 5
Edgewood, ID 83445

Dr. Tracy Malone
7485 North Collins
Edgewood, ID 83447

Exercise 16.3
C16-E03-CofELabels.docx

Last Name	First Name	Membership
Colburn	Barbara	Gold
Kosel	Brian	Platinum
Costanzo	Gordon	Premium
Malone	Tracy	Platinum

Exercise 16.4
C16-E04-CofEDirectory.docx

Mrs. Claudia Levinson
1521 North 32nd Street
Lexington, KY 40511

Ms. Laurel Kittner
12303 North 141st
Apt. 3-B
Lexington, KY 40507

Dr. Miguel Trivelas
5840 North 132nd
P.O. Box 9045
Lexington, KY 40517

Mr. Ryan Wright
10291 South 41st
Lexington, KY 40511

Mr. Arthur Washbaugh
1203 24th Street
Lexington, KY 40511

Mrs. Kayla Stuben
450 Madison Street
P.O. Box 3643
Lexington, KY 40526

Exercise 16.5
C16-E05-Labels.docx

Name	Home Phone	Cell Phone
Levinson, Claudia	859-555-5579	859-555-5879
Diaz, Jeffrey	859-555-2386	859-555-9902
Kittner, Laurel	859-555-5889	859-555-8349
Hershey, Karl	859-555-1214	859-555-5611
Pirone, Mary	859-555-5540	859-555-1200
Trivelas, Miguel	859-555-4585	859-555-7522
Wright, Ryan	859-555-0899	859-555-1233
Carmichael, Dale	859-555-7900	859-555-5628
Novak, Marianne	859-555-3499	859-555-5890
Washbaugh, Arthur	859-555-4523	859-555-2903
Stuben, Kayla	859-555-8891	859-555-9703
Montague, Amanda	859-555-2047	859-555-5563

Exercise 16.6
C16-E06-Directory.docx

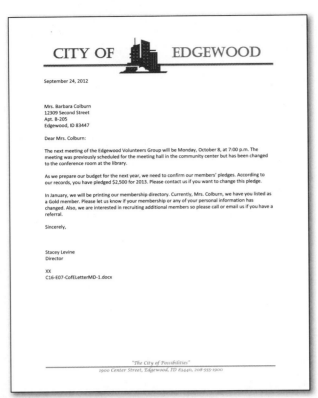

Exercise 16.7 C16-E07-CofELetters.docx

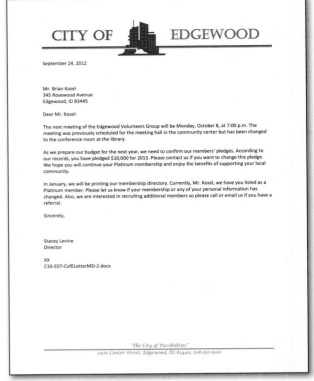

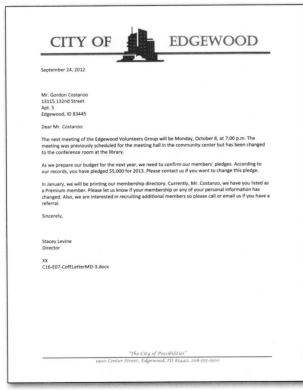

Chapter Sixteen

Exercise 16.8

C16-E08-BTTourLtrs.docx

April 10, 2012

Mr. Jeremiah Roberts
5532 Logan Street
San Francisco, CA 94122

Dear Mr. Roberts:

At Bayside Travel, we strive to provide our clients with fun- and adventure-filled travel vacations. We have created an exciting new vacation tour that you do not want to miss! Our tour explores the beauty, culture, and history of Slovenia, Croatia, Albania, and Greece—all countries located in the Balkans region along the Adriatic Sea.

Bayside Travel is offering a 13-night, 14-day travel tour that combines all types of transportation—from airplanes to all-terrain vehicles. The tour begins in Slovenia, ends in Greece, and includes the following countries and activities:

- Days 1 through 3: Travel to Slovenia and tour the country by boat and bus.
- Days 4 through 6: Travel to Croatia and tour the country by boat, bus, and all-terrain vehicle.
- Days 7 through 9: Travel to Montenegro and tour the country by all-terrain vehicle.
- Days 10 through 11: Travel to Albania and tour the country by bus.
- Days 12 through 14: Travel to Greece and tour the country by ferry, bus, and all-terrain vehicle.

We are offering this exciting adventure only one time this year, so don't miss this opportunity to visit these beautiful countries along the Adriatic Sea. Visit our website or call one of our travel consultants for more information on this tour.

Sincerely,

Mandy Takada
Travel Consultant

XX
BTTourLtr.docx

can Francisco CA 94320 ❖ 1-888-555-8890 ❖ www.emcp.net/bayside

April 10, 2012

Mrs. Carrie Chen
10233 North 52nd Avenue
Daly City, CA 94015

Dear Mrs. Chen:

At Bayside Travel, we strive to provide our clients with fun- and adventure-filled travel vacations. We have created an exciting new vacation tour that you do not want to miss! Our tour explores the beauty, culture, and history of Slovenia, Croatia, Albania, and Greece—all countries located in the Balkans region along the Adriatic Sea.

Bayside Travel is offering a 13-night, 14-day travel tour that combines all types of transportation—from airplanes to all-terrain vehicles. The tour begins in Slovenia, ends in Greece, and includes the following countries and activities:

- Days 1 through 3: Travel to Slovenia and tour the country by boat and bus.
- Days 4 through 6: Travel to Croatia and tour the country by boat, bus, and all-terrain vehicle.
- Days 7 through 9: Travel to Montenegro and tour the country by all-terrain vehicle.
- Days 10 through 11: Travel to Albania and tour the country by bus.
- Days 12 through 14: Travel to Greece and tour the country by ferry, bus, and all-terrain vehicle.

We are offering this exciting adventure only one time this year, so don't miss this opportunity to visit these beautiful countries along the Adriatic Sea. Visit our website or call one of our travel consultants for more information on this tour.

Sincerely,

Mandy Takada
Travel Consultant

XX
BTTourLtr.docx

5530 Bayside Drive ❖ San Francisco CA 94320 ❖ 1-888-555-8890 ❖ www.emcp.net/bayside

Exercise 16.9

C16-E09-BTTourLtrs.docx

Bayside Travel

April 10, 2012

Mrs. Leanne Blaylock
18872 West 78th
San Francisco, CA 94127

Dear Mrs. Blaylock:

At Bayside Travel, we strive to provide our clients with fun- and adventure-filled travel vacations. We have created an exciting new vacation tour that you do not want to miss! Our tour explores the beauty, culture, and history of Slovenia, Croatia, Albania, and Greece—all countries located in the Balkans region along the Adriatic Sea.

Bayside Travel is offering a 13-night, 14-day travel tour that combines all types of transportation—from airplanes to all-terrain vehicles. The tour begins in Slovenia, ends in Greece, and includes the following countries and activities:

- Days 1 through 3: Travel to Slovenia and tour the country by boat and bus.
- Days 4 through 6: Travel to Croatia and tour the country by boat, bus, and all-terrain vehicle.
- Days 7 through 9: Travel to Montenegro and tour the country by all-terrain vehicle.
- Days 10 through 11: Travel to Albania and tour the country by bus.
- Days 12 through 14: Travel to Greece and tour the country by ferry, bus, and all-terrain vehicle.

We are offering this exciting adventure only one time this year, so don't miss this opportunity to visit these beautiful countries along the Adriatic Sea. Visit our website or call one of our travel consultants for more information on this tour.

Sincerely,

Mandy Takada
Travel Consultant

XX
BTTourLtr.docx

San Francisco CA 94320 ❖ 1-888-555-8890 ❖ www.emcp.net/bayside

Page 1

Bayside Travel

April 10, 2012

Mr. Issac Cousineau
4500 Williams Road
Daly City, CA 94015

Dear Mr. Cousineau:

At Bayside Travel, we strive to provide our clients with fun- and adventure-filled travel vacations. We have created an exciting new vacation tour that you do not want to miss! Our tour explores the beauty, culture, and history of Slovenia, Croatia, Albania, and Greece—all countries located in the Balkans region along the Adriatic Sea.

Bayside Travel is offering a 13-night, 14-day travel tour that combines all types of transportation—from airplanes to all-terrain vehicles. The tour begins in Slovenia, ends in Greece, and includes the following countries and activities:

- Days 1 through 3: Travel to Slovenia and tour the country by boat and bus.
- Days 4 through 6: Travel to Croatia and tour the country by boat, bus, and all-terrain vehicle.
- Days 7 through 9: Travel to Montenegro and tour the country by all-terrain vehicle.
- Days 10 through 11: Travel to Albania and tour the country by bus.
- Days 12 through 14: Travel to Greece and tour the country by ferry, bus, and all-terrain vehicle.

We are offering this exciting adventure only one time this year, so don't miss this opportunity to visit these beautiful countries along the Adriatic Sea. Visit our website or call one of our travel consultants for more information on this tour.

Sincerely,

Mandy Takada
Travel Consultant

XX
BTTourLtr.docx

5530 Bayside Drive ❖ San Francisco CA 94320 ❖ 1-888-555-8890 ❖ www.emcp.net/bayside

Page 2

Exercise 16.10

C16-E10-BTTourLtrs.docx

Bayside Travel

April 10, 2012

Donald Rutledge
3730 Rodesco Drive
Oakland, CA 94604

Dear Donald Rutledge:

At Bayside Travel, we strive to provide our clients with fun- and adventure-filled travel vacations. We have created an exciting new vacation tour that you do not want to miss! Our tour explores the beauty, culture, and history of Slovenia, Croatia, Albania, and Greece—all countries located in the Balkans region along the Adriatic Sea.

Bayside Travel is offering a 13-night, 14-day travel tour that combines all types of transportation—from airplanes to all-terrain vehicles. The tour begins in Slovenia, ends in Greece, and includes the following countries and activities:

- Days 1 through 3: Travel to Slovenia and tour the country by boat and bus.
- Days 4 through 6: Travel to Croatia and tour the country by boat, bus, and all-terrain vehicle.
- Days 7 through 9: Travel to Montenegro and tour the country by all-terrain vehicle.
- Days 10 through 11: Travel to Albania and tour the country by bus.
- Days 12 through 14: Travel to Greece and tour the country by ferry, bus, and all-terrain vehicle.

We are offering this exciting adventure only one time this year, so don't miss this opportunity to visit these beautiful countries along the Adriatic Sea. Visit our website or call one of our travel consultants for more information on this tour.

Sincerely,

Mandy Takada
Travel Consultant

XX
BTTourLtr.docx

San Francisco CA 94320 ❖ 1-888-555-8890 ❖ www.emcp.net/bayside

Page 1

Bayside Travel

April 10, 2012

Patricia Kaelin
4818 Cedar Boulevard
Oakland, CA 94618

Dear Patricia Kaelin:

At Bayside Travel, we strive to provide our clients with fun- and adventure-filled travel vacations. We have created an exciting new vacation tour that you do not want to miss! Our tour explores the beauty, culture, and history of Slovenia, Croatia, Albania, and Greece—all countries located in the Balkans region along the Adriatic Sea.

Bayside Travel is offering a 13-night, 14-day travel tour that combines all types of transportation—from airplanes to all-terrain vehicles. The tour begins in Slovenia, ends in Greece, and includes the following countries and activities:

- Days 1 through 3: Travel to Slovenia and tour the country by boat and bus.
- Days 4 through 6: Travel to Croatia and tour the country by boat, bus, and all-terrain vehicle.
- Days 7 through 9: Travel to Montenegro and tour the country by all-terrain vehicle.
- Days 10 through 11: Travel to Albania and tour the country by bus.
- Days 12 through 14: Travel to Greece and tour the country by ferry, bus, and all-terrain vehicle.

We are offering this exciting adventure only one time this year, so don't miss this opportunity to visit these beautiful countries along the Adriatic Sea. Visit our website or call one of our travel consultants for more information on this tour.

Sincerely,

Mandy Takada
Travel Consultant

XX
BTTourLtr.docx

5530 Bayside Drive ❖ San Francisco CA 94320 ❖ 1-888-555-8890 ❖ www.emcp.net/bayside

Page 2

Exercise 16.12

C16-E12-PRLtrs.docx

December 2, 2012

Mr. Donald Reyes
14332 150th Street East
Eugene, OR 97408

Dear Mr. Reyes:

Phoenix Rising is a global community supporting individuals in more than twenty countries who are survivors of war and violence and who are rebuilding their lives. Our organization includes dedicated staff, dedicated volunteers, and generous donors like you. For more than three decades, Phoenix Rising has provided direct financial and emotional support to individuals living on the edge of hope.

Your generosity makes economic independence possible for people while we provide vocational skills training, small business development, and income-generation support. All of these things are needed for long-term peace, stability, and security.

As we look to the new year, we ask you to continue to support those individuals we serve by making a monetary contribution. With your ongoing support, Phoenix Rising can continue to address their immediate and long-term needs, work to improve their status and opportunities, and work toward a more just and peaceful world.

Sincerely,

Neela Shamae
Executive Director

XX
C16-E08-PRLtrs.docx

Page 1

December 2, 2012

Ms. Hannah Devereaux
9005 Fifth Street
Springfield, OR 97478

Dear Ms. Devereaux:

Phoenix Rising is a global community supporting individuals in more than twenty countries who are survivors of war and violence and who are rebuilding their lives. Our organization includes dedicated staff, dedicated volunteers, and generous donors like you. For more than three decades, Phoenix Rising has provided direct financial and emotional support to individuals living on the edge of hope.

Your generosity makes economic independence possible for people while we provide vocational skills training, small business development, and income-generation support. All of these things are needed for long-term peace, stability, and security.

As we look to the new year, we ask you to continue to support those individuals we serve by making a monetary contribution. With your ongoing support, Phoenix Rising can continue to address their immediate and long-term needs, work to improve their status and opportunities, and work toward a more just and peaceful world.

Sincerely,

Neela Shamae
Executive Director

XX
C16-E08-PRLtrs.docx

1500 Frontier Avenue • Eugene, OR 97440 • 541-555-4110

Page 2

Completing a Merge

A merge generally takes two files: a ***main document*** and a ***data source file***. The main document contains the standard text and/or the fields that identify where variable information will be inserted during the merge. The data source file contains the variable information that will be inserted into the main document.

Use the Start Mail Merge button in the Mailings tab, shown in Figure 16.1, to specify the type of main document you want to create; use the Select Recipients button to create a data source file or to choose an existing data source file.

Figure 16.1 Mailings Tab

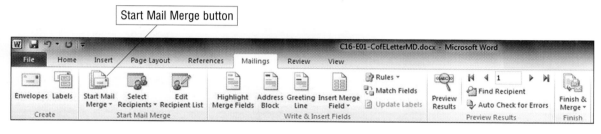

Creating a Data Source File

You begin a mail merge by clicking the Mailings tab, clicking the Start Mail Merge button, and selecting the type of main document that you want to create from the drop-down list. Before you actually create the main document though, you must determine the type of variable information you will need to insert into that document and create a data source file. Word provides predetermined field names for this purpose. Use these field names if they represent the data you are creating. Variable information in a data source file is saved as a ***record.*** A record is a series of fields, and each record contains all of the information for one unit (for example, a person, family, customer, client, or business). A data source file is a series of records.

Create a data source file by clicking the Select Recipients button in the Start Mail Merge group in the Mailings tab and then clicking *Type New List* at the drop-down list. At the New Address List dialog box, shown in Figure 16.2, use the predesigned fields offered by Word and type the required data, or edit the fields by deleting and/or inserting custom fields and then typing the data. When you have entered all the records, click OK. At the Save Address List dialog box, navigate to the desired folder, type a name for the data source file, and then click OK. Word saves a data source file as an Access database. You do not need Access on your computer to complete a merge with a data source file.

Create Data Source File
1. Click Mailings tab.
2. Click Select Recipients button.
3. Click *Type New List* at drop-down list.
4. Type data in predesigned or custom fields.
5. Click OK.

Start Mail Merge

Select Recipients

Figure 16.2 New Address List Dialog Box

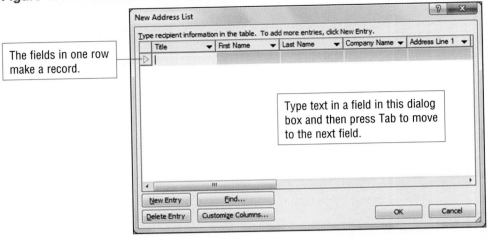

The fields in one row make a record.

Type text in a field in this dialog box and then press Tab to move to the next field.

Exercise 16.1A Creating a Data Source File   Part 1 of 3

1. Open **CofELtrhd.docx** from the Chapter16 folder on your storage medium and then save the document with the name **C16-E01-CofELetterMD.docx**.
2. Click the Mailings tab.
3. Click the Start Mail Merge button in the Start Mail Merge group and then click *Letters* at the drop-down list.
4. Click the Select Recipients button in the Start Mail Merge group and then click *Type New List* at the drop-down list.
5. At the New Address List dialog box, predesigned fields display in the list box. Delete the fields you do not need by completing the following steps:
    a. Click the Customize Columns button.
    b. At the Customize Address List dialog box, click *Company Name* to select it, and then click the Delete button.

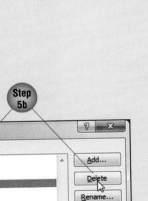

   c. At the message asking if you are sure that you want to delete the field, click Yes.

d. Complete steps similar to those in Steps 5b and 5c to delete the following fields:

> *Country or Region*
> *Home Phone*
> *Work Phone*
> *E-mail Address*

6. Insert a custom field by completing the following steps:

a. At the Customize Address List dialog box, click the Add button.

b   At the Add Field dialog box, type Membership and then click OK.

c. Click the OK button to close the Customize Address List dialog box.

7. At the New Address List dialog box, enter the following information for the first client by completing the following steps:

a. Make sure the insertion point is positioned in the *Title* text box.

b. Type Mrs. and then press the Tab key. (This moves the insertion point to the *First Name* field. You can also press Shift + Tab to move to the previous field.)

c. Type Barbara and then press the Tab key.

d. Type Colburn and then press the Tab key.

e. Type 12309 Second Street and then press the Tab key.

f. Type Apt. B-205 and then press the Tab key.

g. Type Edgewood and then press the Tab key.

h. Type ID and then press the Tab key.

i. Type 83447and then press the Tab key.

j. Type Gold and then press the Tab key.

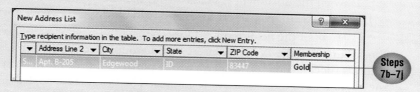

k. With the insertion point positioned in the *Title* field, complete steps similar to those in Steps 7b through 7j to enter the information for the three clients shown in Figure 16.3.

8. After entering all of the information for the last client in Figure 16.3 (Dr. Tracy Malone), click the OK button located in the bottom right corner of the New Address List dialog box.

9. At the Save Address List dialog box, navigate to the *Chapter16* folder on your storage medium, type C16-E01-CofEDS in the *File name* text box, and then click the Save button.

Figure 16.3 Exercise 16.1A

Title	=	Mr.
First Name	=	Brian
Last Name	=	Kosel
Address Line 1	=	345 Rosewood Avenue
Address Line 2	=	(leave this blank)
City	=	Edgewood
State	=	ID
ZIP Code	=	83445
Membership	=	Platinum

Title	=	Mr.
First Name	=	Gordon
Last Name	=	Costanzo
Address Line 1	=	13115 132nd Street
Address Line 2	=	Apt. 5
City	=	Edgewood
State	=	ID
ZIP Code	=	83445
Membership	=	Premium

Title	=	Dr.
First Name	=	Tracy
Last Name	=	Malone
Address Line 1	=	7485 North Collins
Address Line 2	=	(leave this blank)
City	=	Edgewood
State	=	ID
ZIP Code	=	83447
Membership	=	Platinum

Creating a Main Document

Address Block   Greeting Line

Insert Merge Field

After creating and typing records in the data source file, you can type the main document. As you type, insert fields identifying where you want variable information to appear when the document is merged with the data source file. Use buttons in the Write & Insert Fields group to insert fields and field blocks in the main document.

Insert all of the fields required for the inside address of a letter with the Address Block button in the Write & Insert Fields group. Click this button, and the Insert Address Block dialog box displays with a preview of how the fields will be inserted in the document to create the inside address. The Insert Address dialog box also contains buttons and options for customizing the fields. Click OK and «AddressBlock» is inserted in the document. The «AddressBlock» field is an example of a composite field that groups a number of fields together.

Click the Greeting Line button, and the Insert Greeting Line dialog box displays with options for customizing how the fields are inserted in the document to create the greeting line. When you click OK at the dialog box, the «GreetingLine» composite field is inserted in the document.

If you want to insert an individual field from the data source file, click the Insert Merge Field button arrow and then click the desired field at the drop-down list containing the fields in the data source file. You can also click the Insert Merge Field button and then click the desired field at the Insert Merge Field dialog box.

Note: If a message displays while you are completing exercises that indicates opening a document will run the SQL command, click Yes.

1. With **C16-E01-CofELetterMD** open, type the date September 24, 2012, as shown in Figure 16.4, and then press the Enter key four times.
2. Insert address fields by completing the following steps:
   a. Click the Mailings tab and then click the Address Block button in the Write & Insert Fields group.
   b. At the Insert Address Block dialog box, click the OK button.
   c. Press the Enter key twice.

3. Insert greeting line fields by completing the following steps:
   a. Click the Greeting Line button in the Write & Insert Fields group.
   b. At the Insert Greeting Line dialog box, click the down-pointing arrow at the right of the option box containing the comma (the box to the right of the box containing *Mr. Randall*).
   c. At the drop-down list that displays, click the colon.
   d. Click OK to close the Insert Greeting Line dialog box.
   e. Press the Enter key twice.

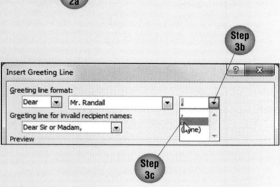

4. Type the letter text shown in Figure 16.4. When you reach the «Title» field, insert the field by clicking the Insert Merge Field button arrow and then clicking *Title* at the drop-down list.

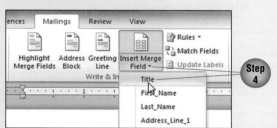

5. Press the spacebar and then insert the «Last_Name» field by clicking the Insert Merge Field button arrow and then clicking *Last_Name* at the drop-down list.
6. When you reach the «Membership» field, insert the field by clicking the Insert Merge Field button arrow and then clicking *Membership* at the drop-down list.
7. Type the remainder of the letter text shown in Figure 16.4. (Insert your initials instead of the *XX* at the end of the letter.)
8. Save **C16-E01-CofELetterMD.docx**.

Figure 16.4 Exercise 16.1B

September 24, 2012

«AddressBlock»

«GreetingLine»

The next meeting of the Edgewood Volunteers Group will be Monday, October 8, at 7:00 p.m. The meeting was previously scheduled for the meeting hall in the community center but has been changed to the conference room at the library.

We will be discussing the annual holiday food drive. The director of the food bank will give a short presentation on the agency and how it serves the community. In addition to discussing the food drive, we will decide on other community service activities.

In January, we will be printing our membership directory. Currently, «Title» «Last_Name», we have you listed as a «Membership» member. Please let us know if your membership or any of your personal information has changed. Also, we are interested in recruiting additional members so please call or email us if you have a referral.

Sincerely,

Stacey Levine
Director

XX
C16-E01-CofELetterMD.docx

Previewing a Merge

Preview Results

First   Previous
Record   Record

Next   Last
Record   Record

Find Recipient

To view the main document as it will appear when merged with the first record in the data source file, click the Preview Results button in the Mailings tab. To view the main document merged with other records, use the navigation buttons in the Preview Results group. This group contains five buttons: First Record, Previous Record, Go to Record, Next Record, and Last Record. Click the button that will display the main document merged with the record you want to view. To use the Go to Record button, click the button, type the number of the desired record, and then press the Enter key. You can turn off the preview feature by clicking the Preview Results button.

The Preview Results group in the Mailings tab also includes a Find Recipient button. If you want to search for and preview merged documents with specific entries, click the Preview Results button and then click the Find Recipient button. This displays the Find Entry dialog box shown in Figure 16.5. At this dialog box, type the specific field entry for which you are searching in the *Find* text box and then click the Find Next button. Continue clicking the Find Next button until Word displays a message telling you that there are no more entries that contain the text you typed. At this message, click OK.

Figure 16.5 Find Entry Dialog Box

Checking for Errors

Before merging documents, you can check for errors using the Auto Check for Errors button in the Preview Results group in the Mailings tab. Click this button and the Checking and Reporting Errors dialog box shown in Figure 16.6 displays containing three options. Click the first option *Simulate the merge and report errors in a new document* to tell Word to test the merge, not make any changes, and report errors in a new document. Choose the second option *Complete the merge, pausing to report each error as it occurs* and Word will merge the documents and display errors as they occur during the merge. Choose the third option *Complete the merge without pausing. Report errors in a new document* and Word will complete the merge without pausing and insert any errors in a new document.

Auto Check
for Errors

Figure 16.6 Checking and Reporting Errors Dialog Box

Choose an option at this dialog box to tell Word to simulate the merge and then check for errors; or complete the merge and then pause to report errors; or report errors without pausing.

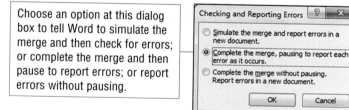

Merging Documents

To complete the merge, click the Finish & Merge button in the Finish group in the Mailings tab. At the drop-down list that displays, you can choose to merge the records and create a new document, send the merged documents directly to the printer, or send the merged documents by email.

To merge the documents and create a new document with the merged records, click the Finish & Merge button and then click *Edit Individual Documents* at the drop-down list. At the Merge to New Document dialog box, make sure *All* is selected in the *Merge records* section and then click OK. This merges the records in the data source file with the main document and inserts the merged documents in a new document.

You can identify specific records you want merged with options at the Merge to New Document dialog box shown in Figure 16.7. Display this dialog box by clicking

Merge Documents
1. Click Finish & Merge button.
2. Click *Edit Individual Documents* at drop-down list.
3. Make sure *All* is selected in Merge to New Document dialog box.
4. Click OK.

Finish & Merge

the Finish & Merge button in the Mailings tab and then clicking the *Edit Individual Documents* option at the drop-down list. Click the *All* option to merge all records in the data source. Click the *Current record* option if you want to merge only the current record. If you have not previewed the merge and changed record numbers, the *Current record* option will merge only the first record in the data source. If you want to merge a different record, click the Preview Results to turn it on and then click the Next Record button until the desired merged record displays. Click the Finish & Merge button, click the *Edit Individual Documents* option, click *Current record* at the Merge to New Document dialog box, and then click OK. Use the *From* and *To* text boxes to specify a range of records. For example, if you want to merge only records 1 through 3, you would type 1 in the *From* text box and 3 in the *To* text box and then click OK.

Figure 16.7 Merge to New Document Dialog Box

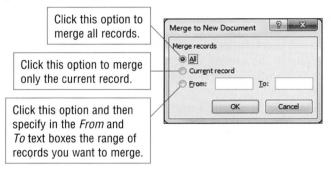

Click this option to merge all records.

Click this option to merge only the current record.

Click this option and then specify in the *From* and *To* text boxes the range of records you want to merge.

Exercise 16.1C Merging the Main Document with the Data Source File   Part 3 of 3

1. With **C16-E01-CofELetterMD.docx** open, preview the main document merged with the first record in the data source file by clicking the Preview Results button in the Mailings tab.
2. Click the Next Record button to view the main document merged with the second record in the data source file.

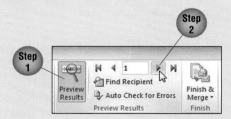

3. Click the Last Record button to view the main document merged with the last record in the data source file.
4. Click the First Record button to view the first record merged.

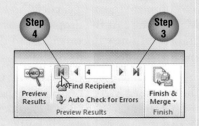

5. Find records with the ZIP code *83445* by completing the following steps:
   a. Click the Find Recipient button in the Preview Results group.
   b. At the Find Entry dialog box, type *83445* in the *Find* text box and then click the Find Next button.

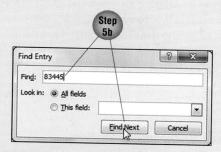

Step 5b

   c. Continue clicking the Find Next button (noticing the merged letters that display) until a message displays telling you that there are no more entries that contain the text you typed. At this message, click OK.
   d. Click the Cancel button to close the Find Entry dialog box.
6. Click the Preview Results button to turn off the preview feature.
7. Automatically check for errors by completing the following steps:

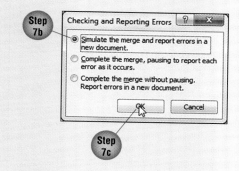

Step 7b

Step 7c

   a. Click the Auto Check for Errors button in the Preview Results group in the Mailings tab.
   b. At the Checking and Reporting Errors dialog box, click the first option *Simulate the merge and report errors in a new document.*
   c. Click OK.
   d. If a new document displays with any errors, print the document and then close it without saving it. If a message displays telling you that no errors were found, click OK.
8. Click the Finish & Merge button in the Finish group and then click *Edit Individual Documents* at the drop-down list.

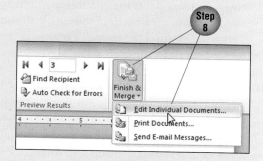

Step 8

9. At the Merge to New Document dialog box, make sure *All* is selected and then click OK.
10. Save the merged letters document with the name **C16-E01-CofELtrs**.
11. Print **C16-E01-CofELtrs.docx**. (This document will print four letters.)
12. Close **C16-E01-CofELtrs.docx**.
13. Save and then close **C16-E01-CofELettersMD.docx**.

Merging Envelopes

If you create a letter as your main document and then merge it with a data source file, you will likely need properly addressed envelopes in which to send the letters. To create customized envelopes, prepare an envelope main document to be merged with the data source file. To do this, click the Mailings tab, click the Start Mail Merge button, and then click *Envelopes* at the drop-down list. This displays the Envelope Options dialog box, shown in Figure 16.8. At this dialog box, specify the desired envelope size, make any other changes, and then click OK.

Figure 16.8 Envelope Options Dialog Box

Click this down-pointing arrow to display a list of available envelope options.

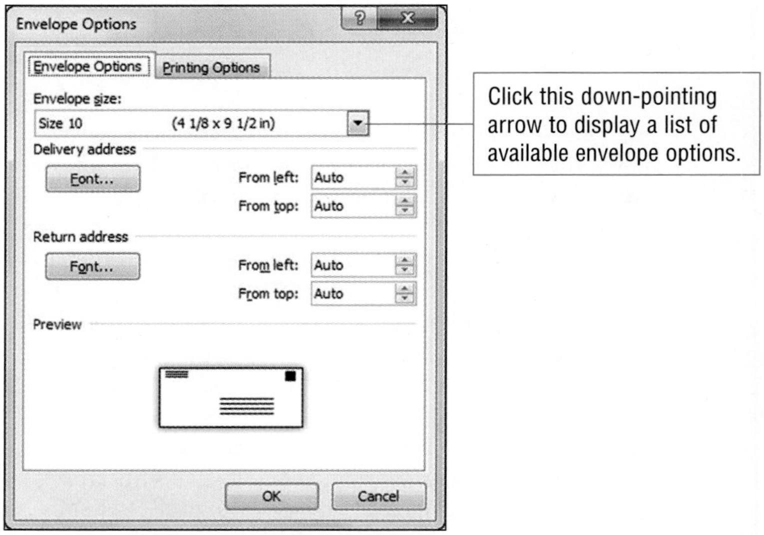

After selecting an envelope as the main document type, the next step in the envelope merge process is to create a data source file to merge with the envelope document or identify an existing file to use. To identify an existing data source file, click the Select Recipients button in the Start Mail Merge group, and then click *Use Existing List* at the drop-down list. At the Select Data Source dialog box, navigate to the folder that contains the data source file you want to use and then double-click the file.

With the data source file attached to the envelope main document, insert the appropriate fields. Click in the envelope approximately where the recipient's address should appear and a box with a dashed blue border displays. Click the Address Block button in the Write & Insert Fields group and then click OK at the Insert Address Block dialog box.

1. At a blank document, click the Mailings tab.
2. Click the Start Mail Merge button in the Start Mail Merge group and then click *Envelopes* at the drop-down list.

Step 1

Step 2

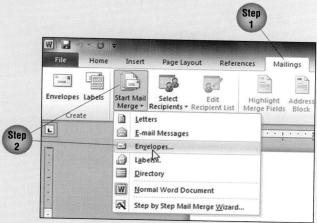

3. At the Envelope Options dialog box, make sure the envelope size is 10 and then click OK.
4. Click the Select Recipients button in the Start Mail Merge group and then click *Use Existing List* at the drop-down list.
5. At the Select Data Source dialog box, navigate to the Chapter16 folder on your storage medium and then double-click the data source file named **C16-E01-CofEDS.mdb**.

Step 4

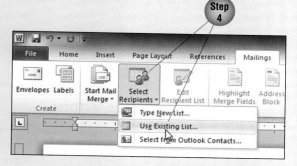

6. In the envelope document click in the approximate location where the recipient's address will appear. (This causes a box with a dashed blue border to display. If you do not see this box, try clicking in a different location on the envelope.)

Step 6

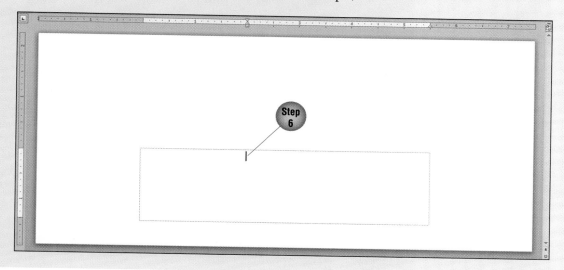

7. Click the Address Block button in the Write & Insert Fields group.
8. At the Insert Address Block dialog box, click the OK button.
9. Click the Preview Results button to view the envelope merged with the first record in the data source file.
10. Click the Preview Results button to turn it off.
11. Click the Finish & Merge button in the Finish group and then click *Edit Individual Documents* at the drop-down list.
12. At the Merge to New Document dialog box, specify that you want only the first two records to merge by completing the following steps:
    a. Click in the *From* text box and then type 1.
    b. Click in the *To* text box and then type 2.
    c. Click OK. (This merges only the first two records and opens a document with two merged envelopes.)
13. Save the merged envelopes document with the name **C16-E02-CofEEnvs**.
14. Print **C16-E02-CofEEnvs.docx**. (This document will print two envelopes. Manual feed of the envelopes may be required. Please check with your instructor.)
15. Close **C16-E02-CofEEnvs.docx**.
16. Save the envelope main document with the name **C16-E02-EnvMD**.
17. Close **C16-E02-EnvMD.docx**.

Merging Labels

You can create mailing labels for records in a data source file in much the same way that you create envelopes. Click the Start Mail Merge button and then click *Labels* at the drop-down list. This displays the Label Options dialog box, shown in Figure 16.9. Make sure the label that you want to use is selected and then click OK to close the dialog box. Next, create the data source file or identify an existing data source file to use. With the data source file attached to the label main document, insert the appropriate fields and then complete the merge.

Figure 16.9 Label Options Dialog Box

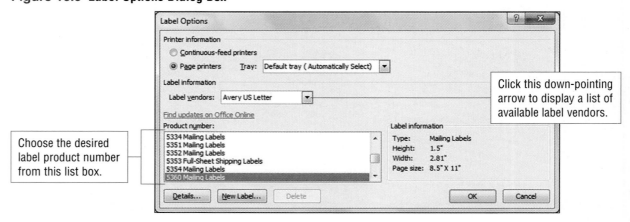

Choose the desired label product number from this list box.

Click this down-pointing arrow to display a list of available label vendors.

1. At a blank document, click the Mailings tab.
2. Click the Start Mail Merge button in the Start Mail Merge group and then click *Labels* at the drop-down list.
3. At the Label Options dialog box, complete the following steps:

   a. If necessary, click the down-pointing arrow at the right of the *Label vendors* option and then click *Avery US Letter* at the drop-down list. (If this product vendor is not available, choose a vendor that offers labels that print on a full page.)

   b. Scroll in the *Product number* list box and then click *5360 Mailing Labels*. (If this option is not available, choose a label number that prints labels in two or three columns down a full page.)

   c. Click OK to close the dialog box.

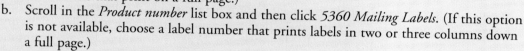

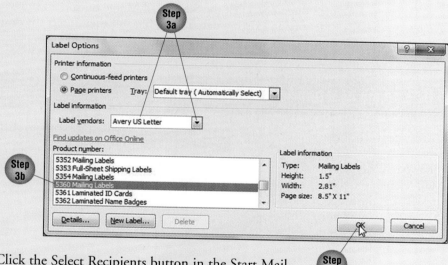

4. Click the Select Recipients button in the Start Mail Merge group and then click *Use Existing List* at the drop-down list.
5. At the Select Data Source dialog box, navigate to the Chapter16 folder on your storage medium and then double-click the data source file named **C16-E01-CofEDS.mdb**.
6. At the labels document, click the Address Block button in the Write & Insert Fields group.
7. At the Insert Address Block dialog box, click the OK button. (This inserts «AddressBlock» in the first label. The other labels contain the «Next Record» field.)
8. Click the Update Labels button in the Write & Insert Fields group. (This adds the «AddressBlock» field after each «Next Record» field in the second and subsequent labels.)

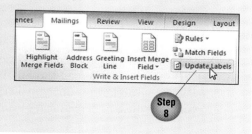

9. Click the Preview Results button to view the labels merged with the records in the data source file.
10. Click the Preview Results button to turn it off.
11. Click the Finish & Merge button in the Finish group and then click *Edit Individual Documents* at the drop-down list.
12. At the Merge to New Document dialog box, make sure *All* is selected and then click OK.
13. Save the merged labels document with the name **C16-E03-CofELabels**.
14. Print and then close **C16-E03-CofELabels.docx**.
15. Save the label main document with the name **C16-E03-CofELabelsMD**.
16. Close **C16-E03-CofELabelsMD.docx**.

Merging a Directory

When you merge letters, envelopes, or mailing labels, a new form is created for each record. For example, if the data source file merged with a letter contains eight records, eight letters are created. If the data source file merged with a mailing label contains twenty records, twenty labels are created. In some situations, you may want merged information to remain on the same page. This is useful, for example, when you want to create a list such as a directory or address list.

To create a merged directory, click the Start Mail Merge button and then click *Directory*. Create or identify an existing data source file and then insert the desired fields in the directory document. Set tabs if you want to insert text in columns.

Exercise 16.4   Merging a Directory   **Part 1 of 1**

1. At a blank document, click the Mailings tab.
2. Click the Start Mail Merge button in the Start Mail Merge group and then click *Directory* at the drop-down list.
3. Click the Select Recipients button in the Start Mail Merge group and then click *Use Existing List* at the drop-down list.
4. At the Select Data Source dialog box, navigate to the Chapter16 folder on your storage medium and then double-click the data source file named **C16-E01-CofEDS.mdb**.

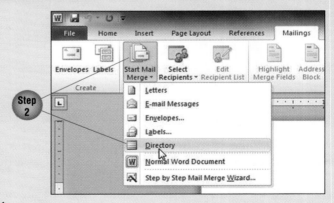

5. At the document, set left tabs on the Ruler at the 1-inch mark, the 2.5-inch mark, and the 4-inch mark and then press the Tab key. (This moves the insertion point to the tab set at the 1-inch mark.)
6. Click the Insert Merge Field button arrow and then click *Last_Name* at the drop-down list.
7. Press the Tab key to move the insertion point to the 2.5-inch mark.
8. Click the Insert Merge Field button arrow and then click *First_Name* at the drop-down list.
9. Press the Tab key to move the insertion point to the 4-inch mark.
10. Click the Insert Merge Field button arrow and then click *Membership* at the drop-down list.

11. Press the Enter key once.
12. Click the Finish & Merge button in the Finish group and then click *Edit Individual Documents* at the drop-down list.
13. At the Merge to New Document dialog box, make sure *All* is selected and then click OK. (This merges the fields in the document.)
14. Press Ctrl + Home, press the Enter key once, and then press the Up Arrow key once.
15. Press the Tab key, turn on bold, and then type Last Name.
16. Press the Tab key and then type First Name.
17. Press the Tab key and then type Membership.

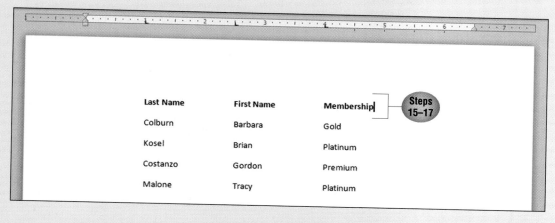

Last Name	First Name	Membership	Steps 15–17
Colburn	Barbara	Gold	
Kosel	Brian	Platinum	
Costanzo	Gordon	Premium	
Malone	Tracy	Platinum	

18. Save the directory document with the name **C16-E04-CofEDirectory**.
19. Print and then close **C16-E04-CofEDirectory.docx**.
20. Close the directory main document without saving it.

Editing a Data Source File

If you need to edit a main document, do so in the usual manner: open it, make the required changes, and then save the document. Because a data source file is actually an Access database file, you cannot open it in the usual manner. To open a data source file for editing, use the Edit Recipient List button in the Start Mail Merge group in the Mailings tab. When you click the Edit Recipient List button, the Mail Merge Recipients dialog box, shown in Figure 16.10, displays. Select or edit records at this dialog box.

Edit Data Source File
1. Open main document.
2. Click Mailings tab.
3. Click Edit Recipient List button.
4. Make desired changes at Mail Merge Recipients dialog box.
5. Click OK.

Edit Recipient List

Figure 16.10 Mail Merge Recipients Dialog Box

Select specific records by removing the check marks from those records you do not want included in the merge.

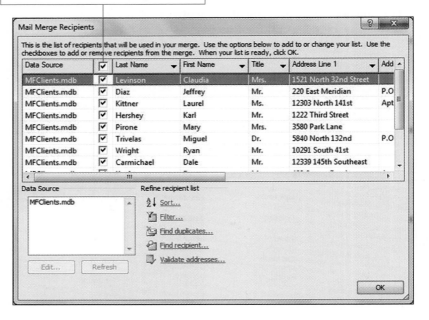

Selecting Specific Records

At the Mail Merge Recipients dialog box, the first field of each record is preceded by a check mark. If you do not want a specific record included in a merge, remove the check mark. In this way, you can select and then merge specific records in the data source file with the main document.

Exercise 16.5 Selecting Records and Merging Mailing Labels   Part 1 of 1

1. At a blank document, create mailing labels for clients living in Lexington. Begin by clicking the Mailings tab.
2. Click the Start Mail Merge button in the Start Mail Merge group and then click *Labels* at the drop-down list.
3. At the Label Options dialog box, make sure *Avery US Letter* displays in the *Label products* option box, and *5360 Mailing Labels* displays in the *Product number* list box, and then click OK.
4. Click the Select Recipients button in the Start Mail Merge group and then click *Use Existing List* at the drop-down list.
5. At the Select Data Source dialog box, navigate to the Chapter16 folder on your storage medium and then double-click the data source file named **MFClients.mdb**.
6. Click the Edit Recipient List button in the Start Mail Merge group.

---

7. At the Mail Merge Recipients dialog box, complete the
   following steps:
   a. Click the check box located immediately left of the
      Last Name field to remove the check mark. (This
      removes all of the check marks from the check boxes.)
   b. Click the check box immediately left of each of the
      following last names: *Levinson, Kittner, Trivelas,
      Wright, Washbaugh,* and *Stuben.* (These are the clients
      who live in Lexington.)
   c. Click OK to close the dialog box.
8. At the labels document, click the Address Block button in
   the Write & Insert Fields group.
9. At the Insert Address Block dialog box, click the OK button.
10. Click the Update Labels button in the Write & Insert Fields group.
11. Click the Finish & Merge button in the Finish group and then click *Edit Individual
    Documents* at the drop-down list.
12. At the Merge to New Document dialog box, make sure *All* is selected and then click OK.
13. Save the merged labels document with the name **C16-E05-Labels**.
14. Print and then close **C16-E05-Labels.docx**.
15. Close the main labels document without saving it.

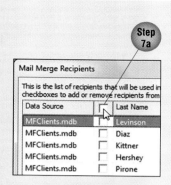

Editing Records

A data source file may need periodic editing to add or delete customer names, update
fields, insert new fields, or delete existing fields. To edit a data source file, click the Edit
Recipient List button in the Start Mail Merge group. At the Mail Merge Recipients
dialog box, click the data source file name in the *Data Source* list box and then click the
Edit button that displays below the list box. This displays the Edit Data Source dialog
box, shown in Figure 16.11. At this dialog box, you can add a new entry, delete an
entry, find a particular entry, and customize columns.

Figure 16.11 Edit Data Source Dialog Box

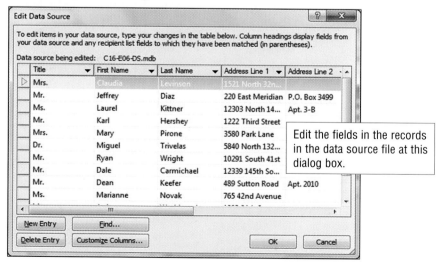

1. Make a copy of the **MFClients.mdb** file by completing the following steps:
   a. Display the Open dialog box and make Chapter16 on your storage medium the active folder.
   b. If necessary, change the file type button to *All Files (*.*)*.
   c. Right-click the **MFClients.mdb** file and then click *Copy* at the shortcut menu.
   d. Position the mouse pointer in an empty area in the Content pane of the Open dialog box (outside of any file name), click the *right* mouse button, and then click *Paste* at the shortcut menu. (This inserts a copy of the file in the dialog box Content pane and names the file **MFClients - Copy.mdb**.)
   e. Right-click the file name **MFClients - Copy.mdb** and then click *Rename* at the shortcut menu.
   f. Type C16-E06-DS and then press the Enter key.
   g. Close the Open dialog box.
2. At a blank document, click the Mailings tab.
3. Click the Select Recipients button and then click *Use Existing List* from the drop-down list.
4. At the Select Data Source dialog box, navigate to the Chapter16 folder on your storage medium and then double-click the data source file named **C16-E06-DS.mdb**.
5. Click the Edit Recipient List button in the Start Mail Merge group.
6. At the Mail Merge Recipients dialog box, click *C16-E06-DS.mdb* that displays in the *Data Source* list box (located in the lower left of the dialog box) and then click the Edit button.
7. Delete the record for Dean Keefer by completing the following steps:
   a. Click the square that displays at the beginning of the row for Mr. Dean Keefer.
   b. Click the Delete Entry button.
   c. At the message asking if you want to delete the entry, click the Yes button.
8. Insert a new record by completing the following steps:
   a. Click the New Entry button in the dialog box.
   b. Type the following text in the new record in the specified fields:
      - Title = Mrs.
      - First Name = Amanda
      - Last Name = Montague
      - Address Line 1 = 632 Tenth Street
      - Address Line 2 = (none)
      - City = Lexington
      - State = KY
      - ZIP Code = 40506
      - Home Phone = 859-555-2047

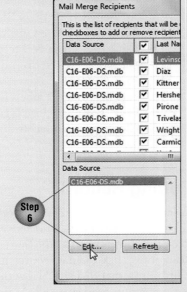

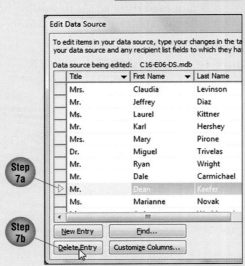

9. Insert a new field and type text in the field by completing the following steps:
   a. At the Edit Data Source dialog box, click the Customize Columns button.
   b. At the message asking if you want to save the changes made to the data source file, click Yes.
   c. At the Customize Address List dialog box, click *ZIP Code* in the *Field Names* list box.
   d. Click the Add button.
   e. At the Add Field dialog box, type Cell Phone and then click OK.
   f. Change the order of the fields so the *Cell Phone* field displays after the *Home Phone* field. To move the *Cell Phone* field, make sure it is selected and then click the Move Down button.
   g. Click OK to close the Customize Address List dialog box.
   h. At the Edit Data Source file, scroll to the right to display the *Cell Phone* field (last field in the file) and then type the following cell phone numbers (after typing each cell phone number, except the last number, press the Down Arrow key to make the next cell below active):

   Step 9d

   Step 9c

   Step 9e

   Record 1 = 859-555-5879
   Record 2 = 859-555-9902
   Record 3 = 859-555-8349
   Record 4 = 859-555-5611
   Record 5 = 859-555-1200
   Record 6 = 859-555-7522
   Record 7 = 859-555-1233
   Record 8 = 859-555-5628
   Record 9 = 859-555-5890
   Record 10 = 859-555-2903
   Record 11 = 859-555-9703
   Record 12 = 859-555-5563

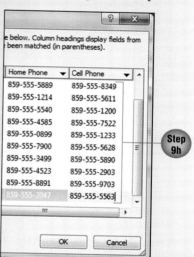

   Step 9h

   i. Click OK to close the Edit Data Source dialog box.
   j. At the message asking if you want to update the recipient list and save changes, click Yes.
   k. At the Mail Merge Recipients dialog box, click OK.
10. Create a directory by completing the following steps:
    a. Click the Start Mail Merge button and then click *Directory* at the drop-down list.
    b. At the blank document, set left tabs on the horizontal ruler at the 1-inch mark, the 3-inch mark, and the 4.5-inch mark.
    c. Press the Tab key (this moves the insertion point to the first tab set at the 1-inch mark).
    d. Click the Insert Merge Field button arrow and then click *Last_Name* at the drop-down list.
    e. Type a comma and then press the spacebar.
    f. Click the Insert Merge Field button arrow and then click *First_Name* at the drop-down list.
    g. Press the Tab key, click the Insert Merge Field button arrow, and then click *Home_Phone* at the drop-down list.
    h. Press the Tab key, click the Insert Merge Field button arrow, and then click *Cell_Phone* at the drop-down list.
    i. Press the Enter key once.

j. Click the Finish & Merge button in the Finish group and then click *Edit Individual Documents* at the drop-down list.

k. At the Merge to New Document dialog box, make sure *All* is selected and then click OK. (This merges the fields in the document.)

11. Press Ctrl + Home, press the Enter key once, and then press the Up Arrow key once.
12. Press the Tab key, turn on bold, and then type Name.
13. Press the Tab key and then type Home Phone.
14. Press the Tab key and then type Cell Phone.

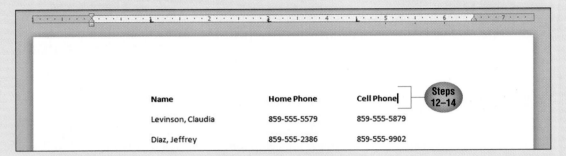

Name	Home Phone	Cell Phone
Levinson, Claudia	859-555-5579	859-555-5879
Diaz, Jeffrey	859-555-2386	859-555-9902

Steps 12–14

15. Save the directory document with the name **C16-E06-Directory**.
16. Print and then close **C16-E06-Directory.docx**.
17. Close the directory main document without saving it.

Inserting Additional Fields

The Mail Merge feature provides a number of methods for inserting fields in a main document. In addition to the methods you have used so far, you can also insert fields with the Rules button in the Write & Insert Fields group in the Mailings tab. Click the Rules button to display a drop-down list of additional fields.

Rules

Inputting Text during a Merge

Word's Merge feature contains a large number of fields that you can insert in a main document. One such field, the *Fill-in* field, is used to input information with the keyboard during a merge.

In some situations you may not need to keep all variable information in a data source file. For example, you may not need to keep variable information that changes regularly, such as a customer's monthly balance, a product price, and so on. Insert a Fill-in field in a main document to input variable information into a document during the merge using the keyboard. A Fill-in field is inserted in a main document by clicking the Rules button in the Write & Insert Fields group in the Mailings tab and then clicking *Fill-in* at the drop-down list. This displays the Insert Word Field: Fill-in dialog box, shown in Figure 16.12. At this dialog box, type a short message indicating what should be entered with the keyboard and then click OK. At the Microsoft Word dialog box, the message you entered displays in the upper left corner. Type the text you want to display in the document and then click OK. When you have added a Fill-in field or fields, save the main document in the normal manner. A document can contain any number of Fill-in fields.

Figure 16.12 Insert Word Field: Fill-in Dialog Box

In this text box, type a short message indicating what should be entered at the keyboard.

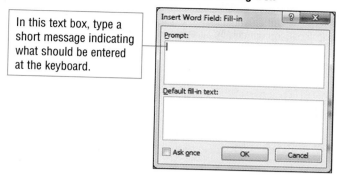

When you merge the main document with the data source file, the first record is merged and the Microsoft Word dialog box displays with the message you entered displayed in the upper left corner. Type the required information for the first record in the data source file and then click OK. Word displays the dialog box again. Type the required information for the second record in the data source file and then click OK. Continue in this manner until you have entered the required information for each record in the data source file. Word then completes the merge.

Inserting a Record Number

If you are merging a small number of records, you can look at each merged document to determine if all records merged and printed. If you have a large number of records in a data source and want to ensure that each document merges and prints, consider inserting a Merge Record # field in the document. This field will insert a record number in each merged document. For example, if you are merging letters, the code will insert number 1 in the first merged letter, number 2 in the second, and so on. With the merge record number in each letter, you can ensure that all letters print. To insert a Merge Record # field, click the Rules button in the Write & Insert Fields group in the Mailings tab and then click *Merge Record #* at the drop-down list. This inserts the field «Merge Record #» in the document.

Inserting an If...Then...Else... Field

Use an If...Then...Else... field to tell Word to compare two values and then, depending on what is determined, enter one set of text or another. When you click *If...Then...Else...* at the Rules button drop-down list, the Insert Word Field: IF dialog box displays as shown in Figure 16.13.

Figure 16.13 Insert Word Field: IF Dialog Box

Click the down-pointing arrow at the right of the Field name option box and then click the field name you want Word to compare.

Click the down-pointing arrow at the right of the Comparison option box and then click the desired value option you want Word to use when comparing the specified field.

Type in this text box the specific field value you want Word to use when comparing text in the specified field.

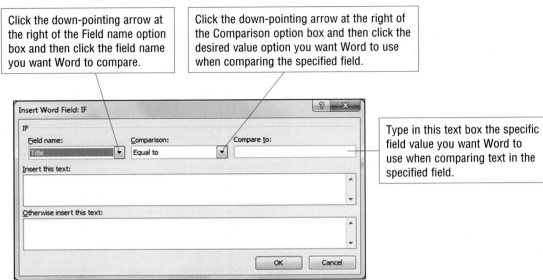

Specify the field you want Word to compare with the *Field name* option. Click the down-pointing arrow at the right of the *Field name* option box and then click the desired field at the drop-down list. The drop-down list displays all of the fields you specified when creating the data source. Use the *Comparison* option to identify how you want Word to compare values. By default, *Equal to* displays in the *Comparison* option box. Click the down-pointing arrow at the right of the option box and a drop-down list displays with a variety of value options such as *Not equal to*, *Less than*, *Greater than*, and so on. In the *Compare to* text box, type in the specific field value you want Word to use. For example, if you want to include a statement in a letter for all customers with the ZIP code 98405, you would click the down-pointing arrow at the right of the *Field name* option box and then click *ZIP_Code* at the drop-down list. You would then click in the *Compare to* text box and type 98405.

Once you have established the field name and specific field entry, you then type in the *Insert this text* text box the text you want inserted if the field entry matches, and type in the *Otherwise insert this text* text box the text you want inserted if the field entry is not matched. You can also leave the *Otherwise insert this text* text box empty. This tells Word to not insert any text if the specific entry value is not met.

By default, an If…Then…Else… field does not display in the document. If you want to make the field visible, press Alt + F9. To turn off the display, press Alt + F9 again. Turning on the display of field codes also expands other merge codes.

Figure 16.14 Exercise 16.7

As we prepare our budget for the next year, we need to confirm our members' pledges. According to our records, you have pledged (pledge) for 2013. Please contact us if you want to change this pledge.

Exercise 16.7 Adding Fill-in Fields to a Main Document

Part 1 of 1

1. Open the document named **C16-E01-CofELetterMD.docx** and save it with the name **C16-E07-CofELetterMD**. (At the message indicating that opening the document will run the SQL command, click Yes.)
2. Change the second paragraph in the body of the letter to the paragraph shown in Figure 16.14. Insert the Fill-in field (pledge) by completing the following steps:

   a. Click the Mailings tab.

   b. Click the Rules button in the Write & Insert Fields group and then click *Fill-in* at the drop-down list.

   c. At the Insert Word Field: Fill-in dialog box, type Insert pledge amount in the *Prompt* text box and then click OK.

   d. At the Microsoft Word dialog box with *Insert pledge amount* displayed in the upper left corner, type (pledge) and then click OK.

   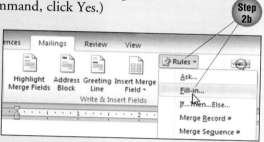

   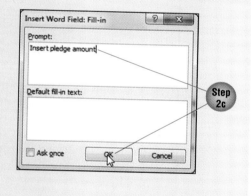

   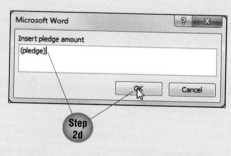

   e. Continue typing the remaining text shown in Figure 16.14.
3. Insert an If...Then...Else... field that tells Word to add text if the Membership code is equal to *Platinum* by completing the following steps:

   a. Position the insertion point one space to the right of the period that ends the new second paragraph you just typed.

   b. Click the Rules button in the Write & Insert Fields group and then click *If...Then...Else...* at the drop-down list.

   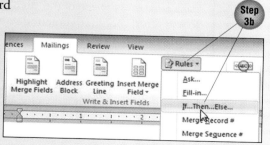

c. At the Insert Word Field: IF dialog box, click the down-pointing arrow at the right of the *Field name* option box and then click *Membership* at the drop-down list. (You will need to scroll down the list box to display this field.)

d. Click in the *Compare to* text box and then type Platinum.

e. Click in the *Insert this text* text box and then type We hope you will continue your Platinum membership and enjoy the benefits of supporting your local community.

f. Click OK to close the dialog box.

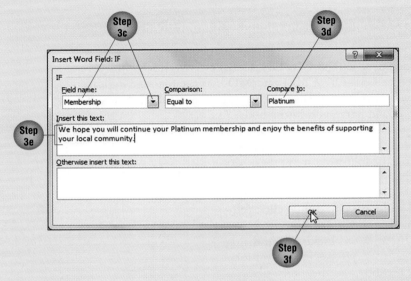

g. View the If...Then...Else... field code (as well as expand the other merge codes) by pressing Alt + F9.

h. After viewing the expanded fields, press Alt + F9 again to turn off the display.

4. Change the file name after your initials toward the bottom of the letter to *C16-E07-CofELetterMD*.

5. Insert a Merge Record # field by completing the following steps:
    a. Position the insertion point immediately right of the letters *MD* in the document name *C16-E07-CofELetterMD.docx*.
    b. Type a hyphen.
    c. Click the Rules button in the Write & Insert Fields group and then click *Merge Record #* at the drop-down list.

6. Save **C16-E07-CofELetterMD.docx**.

7. Merge the main document with the data source file by completing the following steps:
    a. Click the Finish & Merge button and then click *Edit Individual Documents* at the drop-down list.
    b. At the Merge to New Document dialog box, make sure *All* is selected and then click OK.
    c. When Word merges the main document with the first record, a dialog box displays with the message *Insert pledge amount* and the text *(pledge)* selected. At this dialog box, type $2,500 and then click OK.

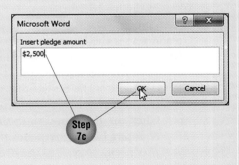

    d. At the dialog box with the message *Insert pledge amount*, type $10,000 (over *$2,500*) and then click OK.

e. At the dialog box with the message *Insert pledge amount*, type $5,000 (over *$10,000*) and then click OK.

f. At the dialog box with the message *Insert pledge amount*, type $10,000 (over *$5,000*) and then click OK.

8. Save the merged document with the name **C16-E07-CofELetters**.
9. Print and then close **C16-E07-CofELetters.docx**.
10. Save and then close **C16-E07-CofELetterMD.docx**.

Merging with Other Data Sources

In this chapter you have merged a main document with a data source. Word saves a data source as an Access database with the .mdb file extension. (In Access 2010, a database file is saved with the .accdb file extension.) You can merge a main document with other data sources, such as a Word document containing data in a table, an Excel worksheet, an Access database table, and an Outlook contacts list.

Exercise 16.8 — Merging a Main Document with a Word Table Data Source — Part 1 of 1

1. Open **BTTourLtr.docx** located in the Chapter16 folder on your storage medium.
2. Save the document with Save As and name it **C16-E08-BTTourLtrMD**.
3. Identify a Word table as the data source by completing the following steps:
   a. Click the Mailings tab.
   b. Click the Select Recipients button in the Start Mail Merge group and then click *Use Existing List* at the drop-down list.
   c. At the Select Data Source dialog box, navigate to the Chapter16 folder on your storage medium and then double-click **BTClientTable.docx**.
4. Press the Down Arrow key four times and then click the Address Block button in the Write & Insert Fields group.
5. At the Insert Address Block dialog box, click OK.
6. Press the Enter key twice.
7. Insert the greeting line fields by completing the following steps:
   a. Click the Greeting Line button in the Write & Insert Fields group.
   b. At the Insert Greeting Line dialog box, click the down-pointing arrow at the right of the option box containing the comma (the box to the right of the box containing *Mr. Randall*).
   c. At the drop-down list that displays, click the colon.
   d. Click OK to close the Insert Greeting Line dialog box.
8. Scroll to the end of the letter. Delete the *XX* and replace with your initials.
9. Merge the document by clicking the Finish & Merge button in the Finish group and then clicking *Edit Individual Documents* at the drop-down list. At the Merge to New Document dialog box, click OK.
10. Save the merged letters with the name **C16-E08-BTTourLtrs**.
11. Print the first two pages (letters) of the document and then close the document.
12. Save and then close **C16-E08-BTTourLtrMD.docx**.

If the fields in a data source do not match the fields in the address block, you can use options at the Match Fields dialog box to match the field names in the data source with the field names in the address block. Display the Match Fields dialog box by clicking the Match Fields button in the Write & Insert group or by clicking the Match Fields button in the Insert Address Block dialog box or the Greeting Line dialog box. To match fields, click the down-pointing arrow at the right side of the field you want to match and then click the desired field at the drop-down list of fields in the data source. For example, in Exercise 16.9, you will use an Excel worksheet as a data source. One of the fields, Mailing Address, does not have a match in the address block, so you will use the Match Fields button to match the *Address 1* field in the address block to the *MailingAddress* field in the Excel worksheet.

Exercise 16.9 Merging a Main Document with an Excel Worksheet Data Source — Part 1 of 1

1. Open **BTTourLtr.docx** and then save the document with Save As and name it **C16-E09-BTTourLtrMD**.
2. Identify an Excel worksheet as the data source by completing the following steps:
   a. Click the Mailings tab.
   b. Click the Select Recipients button in the Start Mail Merge group and then click *Use Existing List* at the drop-down list.
   c. At the Select Data Source dialog box, navigate to the Chapter16 folder on your storage medium and then double-click **BTClientsExcel.docx**.
   d. At the Select Table dialog box, click OK.

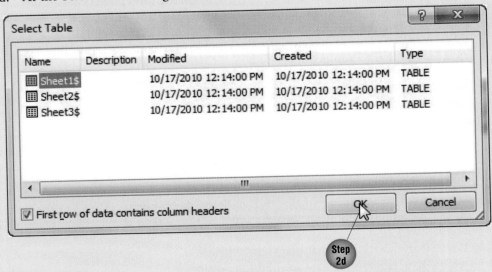

3. Press the Down Arrow key four times and then insert the address block by completing the following steps:
   a. Click the Address Block button in the Write & Insert Fields group.

b. At the Insert Address Block dialog box, click the Match Fields button.

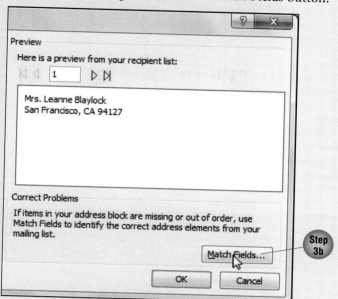

Step
3b

c. At the Match Fields dialog box, click the down-pointing arrow at the right side of the *Address 1* field and then click *MailingAddress* at the drop-down list.
d. Click OK to close the Match Fields dialog box.
e. Click OK to close the Insert Address Block dialog box.

4. Press the Enter key twice.
5. Insert the greeting line fields by completing the following steps:
    a. Click the Greeting Line button in the Write & Insert Fields group.
    b. At the Insert Greeting Line dialog box, click the down-pointing arrow at the right of the option box containing the comma (the box to the right of the box containing *Mr. Randall*).

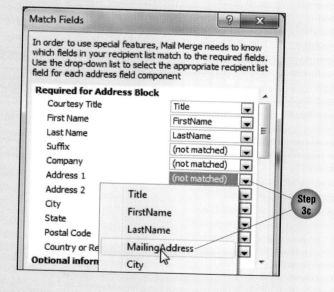

Step
3c

    c. At the drop-down list that displays, click the colon.
    d. Click OK to close the Insert Greeting Line dialog box.
6. Scroll to the end of the letter. Delete the *XX* and replace with your initials.

7. Merge the document by clicking the Finish & Merge button in the Finish group and then clicking *Edit Individual Documents* at the drop-down list. At the Merge to New Document dialog box, click OK.
8. Save the merged letters with the name **C16-E09-BTTourLtrs**.
9. Print the first two pages (letters) of the document and then close the document.
10. Save and then close **C16-E09-BTTourLtrMD.docx**.

In addition to a Word table and an Excel worksheet, you can use an Access database table as a data source. To choose an Access database table, display the Select Data Source dialog box, navigate to the desired folder, and then double-click the desired database. At the Select Table dialog box, select the desired table and then click OK.

Exercise 16.10 Merging a Main Document with an Access Database Table Data Source   Part 1 of 1

1. Open **BTTourLtr.docx** and then save the document with Save As and name it **C16-E10-BTTourLtrMD**.
2. Identify an Access table as the data source by completing the following steps:
   a. Click the Mailings tab.
   b. Click the Select Recipients button in the Start Mail Merge group and then click *Use Existing List* at the drop-down list.
   c. At the Select Data Source dialog box, navigate to the Chapter16 folder on your storage medium and then double-click **BaysideTravel.accdb**.
   d. At the Select Table dialog box, click the *Clients* table and then click OK.

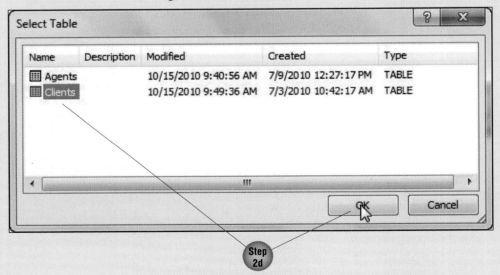

3. Press the Down Arrow key four times.
4. Click the Address Block button in the Write & Insert Fields group and then click OK at the Insert Address Block dialog box.
5. Press the Enter key twice.

6. Insert the greeting line fields by completing the following steps:
   a. Click the Greeting Line button in the Write & Insert Fields group.
   b. At the Insert Greeting Line dialog box, click the down-pointing arrow at the right of the option box containing the comma (the box to the right of the box containing *Mr. Randall*).
   c. At the drop-down list that displays, click the colon.
   d. Click OK to close the Insert Greeting Line dialog box.
7. Scroll to the end of the letter. Delete the *XX* and replace with your initials.
8. Merge the document by clicking the Finish & Merge button in the Finish group and then clicking *Edit Individual Documents* at the drop-down list. At the Merge to New Document dialog box, click OK.
9. Save the merged letters with the name **C16-E10-BTTourLtrs**.
10. Print the first two pages (letters) of the document and then close the document.
11. Save and then close **C16-E10-BTTourLtrMD.docx**.

If you use Outlook to send emails, you can use an Outlook contact list as a data source. You can create the email message in a Word document, identify it as an email message, and then send the email message to contacts in the contact list. To do this, open the document containing the email message or type the email message in a blank document. Click the Mailings tab, click the Start Mail Merge button in the Start Mail Merge group, and then click *E-mail Messages* at the drop-down list. This changes the display of the document on the screen. Click the Select Recipients button in the Start Mail Merge group and then click *Select from Outlook Contacts* at the drop-down list. Complete steps to identify the specific Outlook contact list and then merge the email message with the names in the list.

Exercise 16.11 Merging a Main Document with an Outlook Contact List Data Source   Part 1 of 1

1. Open **BTTourLtr.docx** and then save the document with Save As and name it **C16-E11-BTTourLtrMD**.
2. Identify the main document as an email by completing the following steps:
   a. Click the Mailings tab.
   b. Click the Start Mail Merge button in the Start Mail Merge group and then click *E-mail Messages* at the drop-down list.

3. Identify an Outlook Contacts list as the data source by completing the following steps:
   a. Click the Select Recipients button in the Start Mail Merge group and then click *Select from Outlook Contacts* at the drop-down list.
   b. If a Choose Profile dialog box displays, click OK.
   c. At the Select Contacts dialog box, click the desired contact list name in the list box and then click OK.
   d. At the Mail Merge Recipients dialog box, make sure the desired contact names are selected and then click OK.

4. Press the Down Arrow key four times.

5. Insert the greeting line fields by completing the following steps:
   a. Click the Greeting Line button in the Write & Insert Fields group.
   b. At the Insert Greeting Line dialog box, click the down-pointing arrow at the right of the option box containing the comma (the box to the right of the box containing *Mr. Randall*).
   c. At the drop-down list that displays, click the colon.
   d. Click OK to close the Insert Greeting Line dialog box.

6. Scroll to the end of the email. Delete the *XX* and replace with your initials.

7. Merge the emails by completing the following steps:
   a. Click the Finish & Merge button in the Finish group.
   b. Click *Send E-mail Messages* at the drop-down list.
   c. At the Merge to E-mail dialog box, click in the *Subject line* text box and then type Adriatic Tour.
   d. Click OK.

8. Save and then close **C16-E11-BTTourLtrMD.docx**.

Using the Mail Merge Wizard

The Mail Merge feature includes a Mail Merge wizard that guides you through the merge process. To access the Wizard, click the Mailings tab, click the Start Mail Merge button, and then click the *Step by Step Mail Merge Wizard* at the drop-down list. The first of six Mail Merge task panes displays at the right side of the screen. Completing the tasks at one task pane displays the next task pane. The options in each task pane may vary depending on the type of merge you are performing. Generally, you complete one of the following steps at each task pane:

Step 1:   Select the type of document you want to create (letter, email message, envelope, label, or directory).

Step 2:   Specify whether you want to use the current document window to create the main document, start from a template, or start from an existing document.

Step 3:   Specify whether you are typing a new list (for the variable information), using an existing list, or selecting from an Outlook contacts list. Depending on the choice you make, you may need to select a specific data source file or create a new data source file.

Step 4:   Use the items in this task pane to help you prepare the main document. For example, if you are creating a letter, click the Address Block button in the Write & Insert Fields group in the Mailings tab, and the Wizard inserts the required codes in the main document for merging names and addresses. Click the Greeting Line button in the Write & Insert Fields group, and the Wizard inserts codes for a greeting. You can also click the More Fields button to display a list of fields that can be inserted in the document.

Step 5:   Preview the merged documents.

Step 6:   Complete the merge. At this step, you can send the merged document to the printer and/or edit the merged document.

Exercise 16.12 Preparing Form Letters Using the Mail Merge Wizard   Part 1 of 1

1. At a blank document, click the Mailings tab, click the Start Mail Merge button in the Start Mail Merge group, and then click *Step by Step Mail Merge Wizard* at the drop-down list.
2. At the first Mail Merge task pane, make sure *Letters* is selected in the *Select document type* section and then click the <u>Next: Starting document</u> hyperlink located toward the bottom of the task pane.
3. At the second Mail Merge task pane, click the *Start from existing document* option in the *Select starting document* section.
4. Click the Open button in the *Start from existing* section of the task pane.
5. At the Open dialog box, navigate to the Chapter16 folder on your storage medium and then double-click *PRLtrMD.docx*.
6. Click the <u>Next: Select recipients</u> hyperlink located toward the bottom of the task pane.
7. At the third Mail Merge task pane, click the <u>Browse</u> hyperlink that displays in the *Use an existing list* section of the task pane.
8. At the Select Data Source dialog box, navigate to the Chapter16 folder on your storage medium and then double-click *PRClients.mdb*.
9. At the Mail Merge Recipients dialog box, click OK.
10. Click the <u>Next: Write your letter</u> hyperlink that displays toward the bottom of the task pane.
11. At the fourth Mail Merge task pane, enter fields in the form letter by completing the following steps:
    a. Position the insertion point a double-space above the first paragraph of text in the letter.

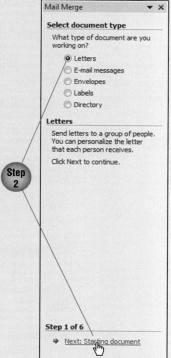

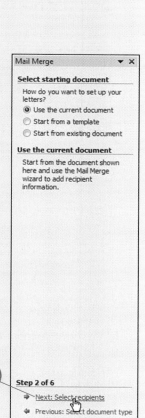

b. Click the Address block hyperlink located in the *Write your letter* section of the task pane.

c. At the Insert Address Block dialog box, click the OK button.

d. Press the Enter key twice and then click the Greeting line hyperlink located in the *Write your letter* section of the task pane.

e. At the Insert Greeting Line dialog box, click the down-pointing arrow at the right of the option box containing the comma (the box to the right of the box containing *Mr. Randall*).

f. At the drop-down list that displays, click the colon.

g. Click OK to close the Insert Greeting Line dialog box.

12. Click the Next: Preview your letters hyperlink located toward the bottom of the task pane.

13. At the fifth Mail Merge task pane, look over the letter that displays in the document window and make sure the information merged properly. If you want to see the letters for the other recipients, click the button in the Mail Merge task pane containing the right-pointing arrow.

14. Click the Preview Results button in the Preview Results group to turn off the preview feature.

15. Click the Next: Complete the merge hyperlink that displays toward the bottom of the task pane.

16. At the sixth Mail Merge task pane, click the Edit individual letters hyperlink that displays in the *Merge* section of the task pane.

17. At the Merge to New Document dialog box, make sure *All* is selected and then click the OK button.

18. Save the merged letters document with the name **C16-E12-PRLtrs**.

19. Print only the first two pages of **C16-E12-PRLtrs.docx**. (This document contains seven pages.)

20. Close **C16-E12-PRLtrs.docx**.

21. At the sixth Mail Merge task pane, close the letter main document without saving it.

Chapter *Summary*

➤ Use the Mail Merge feature to create letters, envelopes, labels, directories, email messages, and faxes for multiple recipients, all with personalized information.

➤ A merge generally takes two documents—the data source file, which contains information that varies for each recipient, and the main document, which contains standard text (text intended for all recipients) along with fields identifying where the variable information will be inserted during the merge process.

➤ Variable information in a data source file is saved as a record. A record contains all of the information for one unit. A series of fields makes one record, and a series of records makes a data source file.

➤ A data source file is saved as an Access database, but you do not need Access on your computer to complete a merge with a data source file.

➤ You can use predesigned fields when creating a data source file, or you can create your own custom fields at the Customize Address List dialog box.

➤ Use the Address Block button in the Write & Insert Fields group in the Mailings tab to insert all of the fields required for the inside address of a letter. This inserts the «AddressBlock» field, which is considered a composite field because it groups a number of fields together.

➤ Click the Greeting Line button in the Write & Insert Fields group in the Mailings tab to insert the «GreetingLine» composite field in the document.

➤ Click the Insert Merge Field button arrow in the Write & Insert Fields group in the Mailings tab to display a drop-down list of fields contained in the data source file.

➤ Click the Preview Results button in the Mailings tab to view the main document merged with the first record in the data source. Use the navigation buttons in the Preview Results group in the Mailings tab to display the main document merged with other records.

➤ Click the Find Recipient button in the Preview Results group in the Mailings tab to search for and preview merged documents with specific entries. Click the Find Recipient button and the Find Entry dialog box displays.

➤ Before merging documents, check for errors by clicking the Auto Check for Errors button in the Preview Results group in the Mailings tab. This displays the Checking and Reporting Errors dialog box with three options for checking errors.

➤ Click the Finish & Merge button in the Mailings tab to complete the merge.

➤ Select specific records for merging by inserting or removing check marks preceding the desired records at the Mail Merge Recipients dialog box. Display this dialog box by clicking the Edit Recipient List button in the Mailings tab.

➤ Edit specific records in a data source file at the Edit Data Source dialog box. Display this dialog box by clicking the Edit Recipient List button in the Mailings tab, clicking the desired data source file name in the *Data Source* list box, and then clicking the Edit button.

➤ Use a Fill-in field in a main document to insert variable information with the keyboard during a merge.

➤ Insert a Merge Record # field in a main document to insert a record number in each merged document. To insert this field, click the Rules button in the Write & Insert Fields group in the Mailings tab and then click *Merge Record #* at the drop-down list.

➤ Use an If…Then…Else… field to compare two values and then, depending on what is determined, enter one set of text or another. To insert this field, click the Rules button in the Write & Insert Fields group in the Mailings tab and then click *If…Then…Else…* at the drop-down list. At the Insert Word Field: IF dialog box that displays, make the desired changes and then click OK.

- You can merge a main document with a Word table, Excel worksheet, Access table, or Outlook contact list data source.
- If fields in a data source do not match the fields used in the address block, use options at the Match Fields dialog box to match fields.
- Word includes a Mail Merge wizard you can use to guide you through the process of creating letters, envelopes, labels, directories, and email messages with personalized information.

Commands Review

FEATURE	RIBBON TAB, GROUP	BUTTON, OPTION
New Address List dialog box	Mailings, Start Mail Merge	, Type New List
Letter main document	Mailings, Start Mail Merge	, Letters
Find Entry dialog box	Mailings, Preview Results	
Checking and Reporting Errors dialog box	Mailings, Preview Results	
Envelopes main document	Mailings, Start Mail Merge	, Envelopes
Labels main document	Mailings, Start Mail Merge	, Labels
Directory main document	Mailings, Start Mail Merge	, Directory
Preview merge results	Mailings, Preview Results	
Mail Merge Recipients dialog box	Mailings, Start Mail Merge	
Address Block field	Mailings, Write & Insert Fields	
Greeting Line field	Mailings, Write & Insert Fields	
Insert merge fields	Mailings, Write & Insert Fields	
Fill-in merge field	Mailings, Write & Insert Fields	, Fill-in
Merge Record # field	Mailings, Write & Insert Fields	, Merge Record #
Insert Word Field: IF dialog box	Mailings, Write & Insert Fields	, If…Then…Else
Match Fields dialog box	Mailings, Start Mail Merge	
Mail Merge wizard	Mailings, Start Mail Merge	, Step by Step Mail Merge Wizard

Key Points Review

Completion: In the space provided at the right, indicate the correct term, command, or number.

1. A merge generally takes two files, a data source file and this. _____

2. This term refers to all of the information for one unit in a data source file. _____

3. Create a data source file by clicking this button in the Mailings tab and then clicking *Type New List* at the drop-down list. _____

4. A data source file is saved as this type of file. _____

5. Create your own custom fields in a data source file with options at this dialog box. _____

6. Use this button in the Mailings tab to insert all of the required fields for the inside address in a letter. _____

7. The «GreetingLine» field is considered this type of field because it includes all of the fields required for the greeting line. _____

8. Click this button in the Mailings tab to display the first record merged with the main document. _____

9. Click this button in the Preview Results group in the Mailings tab to display the Find Entry dialog box. _____

10. Before merging a document, check for errors using this button in the Preview Results group in the Mailings tab. _____

11. To complete a merge, click this button in the Finish group in the Mailings tab. _____

12. Select specific records in a data source file by inserting or removing check marks from the records in this dialog box. _____

13. Use this field to insert variable information with the keyboard during a merge. _____

14. Insert this field in a main document to insert a record number in each merged document. _____

15. Insert this field in a main document to tell Word to compare two values and then enter one set of text or another. _____

16. Click this option at the Start Mail Merge button drop-down list to begin the Mail Merge wizard. _____

Chapter *Assessments*

Applying Your Skills

Demonstrate your knowledge of features learned in this chapter by completing the following assessments.

Assessment 16.1   Use Mail Merge to Create Letters

1. Open **BTLtrhd.docx** and then save the document with the name **C16-A01-BTLtrMD**.
2. Look at the information shown in Figure 16.15 and Figure 16.16. Use the Mail Merge feature to prepare four letters using the information shown in the figures (refer to Appendix D at the end of this textbook for information on formatting a business letter).
3. Name the data source file **C16-A01-BT-DS** and name the merged letters document **C16-A01-BTLtrs**.
4. Print and then close **C16-A01-BTLtrs.docx**.
5. Save and then close **C16-A01-BTLtrMD.docx**.

Figure 16.15 Assessment 16.1

Mrs. Tina Cardoza
2314 Magnolia Drive
P.O. Box 231
San Francisco, CA 94120

Mr. Lucas Yarborough
12110 South 142nd Street
(leave this blank)
Daly City, CA 94015

Mrs. Lucille Alvarez
2554 Country Drive
(leave this blank)
Daly City, CA 94017

Mr. Daryl Gillette
120 Second Street
(leave this blank)
San Francisco, CA 94128

Assessment 16.2   Use Mail Merge to Create Envelopes

1. Create an envelope main document and merge it with the **C16-A01-BT-DS.mdb** data source file.
2. Save the merged envelopes document with the name **C16-A02-BTEnvs**.
3. Print and then close **C16-A02-BTEnvs.docx**. Close the envelope main document without saving it. (Manual feed of envelopes may be required. Check with your instuctor.)

Assessment 16.3   Use Mail Merge to Create Labels

1. Use the Mail Merge feature to prepare mailing labels for the names and addresses in the **C16-A01-BT-DS.mdb** file.
2. Save the merged labels document with the name **C16-A03-BTLabels**.
3. Print and then close **C16-A03-BTLabels.docx**. Close the label main document without saving it.

Figure 16.16 Assessment 16.1

April 4, 2012

«AddressBlock»

«GreetingLine»

Now is the time to sign up for a sun-filled, fun-filled family vacation. We are offering three-day, seven-day, and ten-day fun-and-sun vacation packages to several southern destinations, including Los Angeles, Orlando, Miami, New Orleans, and Maui. Limited by a budget? No problem. We can find the perfect vacation for you and your family that fits within your budget.

We know we can create a vacation package that is as exciting and adventurous as your previous vacation. Right now, you can spend seven days and six nights in beautiful and tropical Maui, Hawaii, at the Pacific Beach Cabanas for under $700 per person including airfare! We also have a four-day, three-night vacation package to Orlando, Florida, for less than $400 per person. To find out about these fabulous and affordable vacations, stop by our office and talk to a travel consultant or give us a call to book your next fun-and-sun family vacation.

Sincerely,

Mandy Takada
Travel Consultant

XX
C16-A01-BTLtrMD.docx

Assessment 16.4   Edit Records and then Merge Letters with Fill-in Field

1. Open **C16-A01-BTLtrMD.docx** (at the message telling you that the document will run an SQL command, click Yes) and save the main document with the name **C16-A04-BTLtrMD**.
2. Edit the **C16-A01-BT-DS.mdb** data source file by making the following changes:
   a. Display the record for Mrs. Tina Cardoza and then change the last name from *Cardoza* to *Cordova*.
   b. Display the record for Mr. Daryl Gillette, change the street address from *120 Second Street* to *9843 22nd Southwest*, and change the ZIP code from *94128* to *94102*.
   c. Delete the record for Mr. Lucas Yarborough.

d. Insert three new records with the following information:

Mr. Curtis Jackson	Ms. Tanya Forrester	Mr. Joshua Mercado
13201 North Fourth Street	575 Taylor Street	7650 Union Street
(leave blank)	Apt. 120	(leave blank)
Daly City, CA 94017	San Francisco, CA 94127	San Francisco, CA 94123

3. At the main document, add the following sentence at the beginning of the second paragraph in the letter (insert a Fill-in field for *(vacation)* shown in the sentence below [you determine the prompt]):

   Last summer we booked a fabulous (vacation) for you and your entire family.

4. Move the insertion point immediately below the document name, type Letter, press the space bar once, and then insert a Merge Record # field.

5. Press the Enter key twice and then insert an If…Then…Else… field with the following specifications:
   a. At the Insert Word Field: IF dialog box, specify the *City* field in the *Field name* option box.
   b. Type Daly City in the *Compare to* text box.
   c. In the *Insert this text* text box, type the text shown below and then close the dialog box.

      P.S. A representative from Wildlife Eco-Tours will present information on upcoming tours at our Daly City branch office the first Saturday of next month. Come by and hear about exciting and adventurous eco-tours.

6. Change the file name below your reference initials to *C16-A04-BTLtrMD.docx*.

7. Merge the main document with the data source file and type the following text for each of the records:

Record 1	=	Ocean Vista Mexican cruise
Record 2	=	Disneyland California vacation
Record 3	=	Ocean Vista Caribbean cruise
Record 4	=	River Rafting Adventure vacation
Record 5	=	Australia Down Under vacation
Record 6	=	DisneyWorld Florida vacation

8. Save the merged document with the name **C16-A04-BTLtrs**.

9. Print and then close **C16-A04-BTLtrs.docx**.

10. Save and then close **C16-A04-BTLtrMD.docx**.

Assessment 16.5   Use the Mail Merge Wizard to Create Envelopes

1. At a blank document, use the Mail Merge wizard to merge the records in the **PRClients.mdb** data source with an envelope main document. (Use the standard Size 10 envelope.)
2. Save the merged envelopes document with the name **C16-A05-PREnvs**.
3. Print only the first two envelopes in the document and then close **C16-A05-PREnvs.docx**.
4. Close the envelope main document without saving it.

Expanding Your Skills

Explore additional feature options or use Help to learn a new skill in creating these documents.

Assessment 16.6   Create a Client Directory

1. Make a copy of the **PRClients.mdb** file located in the Chapter16 folder on your storage medium and insert the copy into the same folder. Rename the copied file **C16-A06-PRClients.mdb**.
2. At a blank document, create a directory main document and specify **C16-A06-PRClients.mdb** as the data source file.
3. Add a new field named *Telephone* to the **C16-A06-PRClients.mdb** data source file. *Hint: To do this, click the Edit Recipient List button, click the **C16-A06-PRClients.mdb** file name in*

the **Data Source** *list box and then click the* **Edit** *button. At the Edit Data Source dialog box, click the* **Customize Columns** *button. Add the new* **Telephone** *field and then move it so it displays after the* **ZIP Code** *field.*

4. Insert the following telephone numbers in the specified fields:

Reyes	=	541-555-3904
Devereaux	=	541-555-6675
Heaton	=	541-555-4982
LeBlanc	=	541-555-0012
Seydell	=	541-555-6599
Pena	=	541-555-2189
Morrisey	=	541-555-9922

5. Add the following records to the data source (in the appropriate fields):

Mr. Greg Parker
3411 45th Street
Eugene, OR 97405
541-555-4188

Dr. Jane Takahara
10293 Mountain Drive
Springfield, OR 97477
541-555-9441

Mrs. Karen Jennings
1302 Washington Avenue
Eugene, OR 97402
541-555-6817

Mr. Chris Martinez
109 Voss Drive
Springfield, OR 97478
541-555-4045

6. At the blank directory document, set a left tab at the 1-inch mark and the 4-inch mark.
7. Insert the «Last_Name» field at the 1-inch tab, type a comma, press the space bar, and then insert the «First_Name» field. Press the tab key, insert the «Telephone» field, and then press the Enter key.
8. Merge the directory main document with the data source.
9. Insert the heading *Name* in bold above the column containing the last and first names and insert the heading *Telephone* in bold above the column containing the telephone numbers.
10. Save the directory and name it **C16-A06-PRDirectory**.
11. Print **C16-A06-PRDirectory.docx**.
12. Select the text in the document and then convert it to a table. ***Hint: Use the Table button in the Tables group in the Insert tab.***
13. With the text converted to a table, delete the first column (which is empty), autofit the contents in the table, and then apply a table style of your choosing. Make any other formatting changes to enhance the display of the table.
14. Save, print, and then close **C16-A06-PRDirectory.docx**.
15. Close the directory main document without saving it.

Assessment 16.7   Merge Specific Records

1. Open **PRLtrMD.docx** and save it with the name **C16-A07-PRLtrMD**.
2. Identify **C16-A06-PRClients.mdb** as the data source file.
3. Insert the appropriate fields in the letter main document.
4. Change the file name below the reference initials at the bottom of the letter to **C16-A07-PRLtrMD.docx**.
5. Merge only records 8 through 11. ***Hint: Do this at the Merge to New Document dialog box.***
6. Save the merged letters document and name it **C16-A07-PRLtrs8-11**.
7. Print and then close the **C16-A07-PRLtrs8-11.docx** document.
8. Save and then close the **C16-A07-PRLtrMD.docx** document.

Assessment 16.8   Merge Labels with an Excel Worksheet

1. Use the Mail Merge feature to prepare name badges with the following specifications:
   a. Click the Start Mail Merge button in the Mailings tab and then click *Labels* at the drop-down list. At the Label Options dialog box, change the *Label vendors* option to *Avery US Letter* and then click the *42395 EcoFriendly Name Badges* option in the *Product number* list box. Click OK to close the dialog box.
   b. Specify the **BTClientsExcel.xlsx** workbook as the data source. Click OK at the Select table dialog box.
   c. Use the Insert Merge Field button in the Mailings tab to insert the *FirstName* field. Press the spacebar and then insert the *LastName* field. Press the Enter key, insert the *City* field, type a comma, press the spacebar, and then insert the *State* field.
   d. Update the labels and then merge the labels.
2. At the labels document, click the table move handle (displays in the upper left corner of the table) to select the entire table. Click the Home tab and then change the font size to 20. Click the Table Tools Layout tab and then click the Align Center button in the Alignment group.
3. Save the name badge document and name it **C16-A08-BTNameBadges**.
4. Print and then close **C16-A08-BTNameBadges.docx**.
5. Close the label main document without saving it.

Achieving Signature Status

Take your skills to the next level by completing this more challenging assessment.

Assessment 16.9   Create and Merge a Data Source and Main Document

1. Open **NSSLtrhd.docx** and then save the document with the name **C16-A09-NSSLtrMD**.
2. Look at the information shown in Figure 16.17 and Figure 16.18. Use the Mail Merge feature to prepare six letters using the information shown in the figures. Name the data source file **C16-A09-NSS-DS.mdb**. (When creating the records in the data source file, make sure to add a *Department* field.)
3. Prepare the main document with the following specifications:
   a. Insert the current date at the beginning of the letter.
   b. Since the «AddressBlock» composite field will not insert the *Department* field, you need to insert each individual field required for the inside address. To do this, use the Insert Merge Field button to insert the fields so they appear as follows (make sure you insert spaces where necessary):

   «Title» «First_Name» «Last_Name»
   «Department»
   «Company_Name»
   «Address_Line_1»
   «City», «State» «ZIP_Code»

Figure 16.17 Assessment 16.9

Mrs. Sylvia Patterson
Human Resources Department
Rolling Hills Manufacturing
31203 33rd Street South
Springfield, IL 62133
217-555-3310

Mr. Russell Navarro
Technology Department
Woodmark Products
8844 South 24th Street
Peoria, IL 61623
309-555-1800

Mr. Wade Townsend
IT Department
Keystone Technologies
145 South 95th Street
Springfield, IL 62129
217-555-7770

Mr. Dale Marshall
Training Department
Providence Care
2712 Martin Luther King, Jr. Way
Peoria, IL 61639
217-555-0775

Ms. Amanda Sperring
Human Resources Department
Frontier Steel
310 Riddell Avenue
Decatur, IL 62524
217-555-9742

Mrs. Emma Battner
Training Department
Franklin Services
2010 Patterson Court East
Peoria, IL 61618
309-555-3153

   c. Insert the appropriate greeting line field.
   d. Type the appropriate complimentary close and type your first and last names in the complimentary close.
   e. Type your initials and the document name in the appropriate location in the letter.
   f. After typing the letter, insert a Merge Record # field toward the bottom of the letter (you determine the location).
   g. Insert an If…Then…Else field at the beginning of the last paragraph of text in the letter (the paragraph that begins *As a valued client…*). Specify the *City* field in the *Field name* option box, type Peoria in the *Compare to* text box, and type the following information in the *Insert this text* text box (make sure you press the space bar once after typing the text): At our Peoria NSS Training Academy, we are offering two additional courses including *Network Security* and *Web Applications Security*. Please call for more information about these courses.
4. Before merging the letters, check for errors.
5. Complete the merge and then save the merged letters document and name it **C16-A09-NSSCoursesLtrs**.
6. Print and then close **C16-A09-NSSCoursesLtrs.docx**.
7. Save and then close **C16-A09-NSSLtrMD.docx**.

Figure 16.18 Assessment 16.9

We have scheduled the Springfield NSS Training Academy course offerings for next month. If you have additional data security training needs, please give us a call and we can customize a training course for your company. Courses next month at the Springfield NSS Training Academy include:

Course Title	Total Hours	Cost
Securing Windows	8 hours	$375
Intrusion Detection	3 hours	$250
Basic Security Essentials	6 hours	$350
Advanced Security Essentials	4 hours	$295
Perimeter Protection	3 hours	$195

As a valued client of Northland Security Systems, we are offering your company a 10 percent discount on all courses offered next month. To qualify for the discount, participants must be signed up before the first of the month. You can register employees at our website or by calling us at 1-888-555-2200.

Chapter 17

TUTORIALS

Tutorial 17.1
Sort text in paragraphs, columns, and tables
Tutorial 17.2
Sort records in a data source file
Tutorial 17.3
Select specific records for merging

Sorting and Selecting

Performance Objectives

Upon successful completion of Chapter 17, you will be able to:

- Sort text in paragraphs, columns, and tables
- Sort on more than one field
- Sort records in a data source file
- Select specific records in a data source file for merging

Word is primarily a word processing program, but it includes some basic database functions. For example, you can sort text that is set in paragraphs, columns, or a table; you can sort records in a data source file; and you can select specific records from a data source file to be merged with a main document.

Note: Before beginning computer exercises for this chapter, copy to your storage medium the Chapter17 folder from the CD that accompanies this textbook and then make Chapter17 the active folder.

In this chapter, students will produce the following documents:

Exercise 17.1. C17-E01-MBSortDoc.docx
Exercise 17.2B. C17-E02-MFLabels-01.docx
Exercise 17.2C. C17-E02-MFLabels-02.docx
Exercise 17.2D. C17-E02-MFLabels-03.docx
Exercise 17.2E. C17-E02-MFLabels-04.docx

Model answers for these exercises are shown on the following pages.

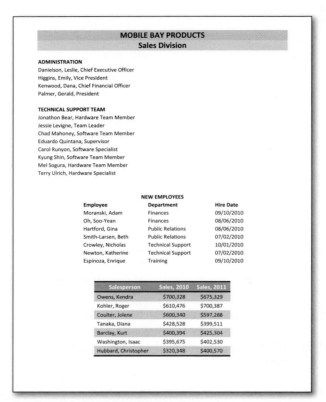

MOBILE BAY PRODUCTS
Sales Division

ADMINISTRATION
Danielson, Leslie, Chief Executive Officer
Higgins, Emily, Vice President
Kenwood, Dana, Chief Financial Officer
Palmer, Gerald, President

TECHNICAL SUPPORT TEAM
Jonathon Bear, Hardware Team Member
Jessie Levigne, Team Leader
Chad Mahoney, Software Team Member
Eduardo Quintana, Supervisor
Carol Runyon, Software Specialist
Kyung Shin, Software Team Member
Mel Sogura, Hardware Team Member
Terry Ulrich, Hardware Specialist

NEW EMPLOYEES

Employee	Department	Hire Date
Moranski, Adam	Finances	09/10/2010
Oh, Soo-Yean	Finances	08/06/2010
Hartford, Gina	Public Relations	08/06/2010
Smith-Larsen, Beth	Public Relations	07/02/2010
Crowley, Nicholas	Technical Support	10/01/2010
Newton, Katherine	Technical Support	07/02/2010
Espinoza, Enrique	Training	09/10/2010

Salesperson	Sales, 2010	Sales, 2011
Owens, Kendra	$700,328	$675,329
Kohler, Roger	$610,476	$700,387
Coulter, Jolene	$600,340	$597,288
Tanaka, Diana	$428,528	$399,511
Barclay, Kurt	$400,394	$425,304
Washington, Isaac	$395,675	$402,530
Hubbard, Christopher	$320,348	$400,570

Exercise 17.1 C17-E01-MBSortDoc.docx

Mr. Dale Carmichael	Mr. Karl Hershey	Mr. Dean Keefer
12339 145th Southeast	1222 Third Street	489 Sutton Road
Paris, KY 40361	Paris, KY 40361	Apt. 2010
		Paris, KY 40361

Mr. Jeffrey Diaz	Ms. Marianne Novak	Mrs. Mary Pirone
220 East Meridian	765 42nd Avenue	3580 Park Lane
P.O. Box 3499	Winchester, KY 40391	Winchester, KY 40391
Winchester, KY 40391		

Ms. Laurel Kittner	Mrs. Claudia Levinson	Mr. Arthur Washbaugh
12303 North 141st	1521 North 32nd Street	1203 24th Street
Apt. 3-B	Lexington, KY 40511	Lexington, KY 40511
Lexington, KY 40507		

Mr. Ryan Wright	Dr. Miguel Trivelas	Mrs. Kayla Stuben
10291 South 41st	5840 North 132nd	450 Madison Street
Lexington, KY 40511	P.O. Box 9045	P.O. Box 3643
	Lexington, KY 40517	Lexington, KY 40526

Exercise 17.2B C17-E02-MFLabels-01.docx

Ms. Laurel Kittner	Mrs. Claudia Levinson	Mr. Arthur Washbaugh
12303 North 141st	1521 North 32nd Street	1203 24th Street
Apt. 3-B	Lexington, KY 40511	Lexington, KY 40511
Lexington, KY 40507		

Mr. Ryan Wright	Dr. Miguel Trivelas	Mrs. Kayla Stuben
10291 South 41st	5840 North 132nd	450 Madison Street
Lexington, KY 40511	P.O. Box 9045	P.O. Box 3643
	Lexington, KY 40517	Lexington, KY 40526

Exercise 17.2C C17-E02-MFLabels-02.docx

Mr. Dale Carmichael	Mr. Karl Hershey	Mr. Dean Keefer
12339 145th Southeast	1222 Third Street	489 Sutton Road
Paris, KY 40361	Paris, KY 40361	Apt. 2010
		Paris, KY 40361
Mr. Jeffrey Diaz	Ms. Marianne Novak	Mrs. Mary Pirone
220 East Meridian	765 42nd Avenue	3580 Park Lane
P.O. Box 3499	Winchester, KY 40391	Winchester, KY 40391
Winchester, KY 40391		

Mrs. Claudia Levinson	Mr. Arthur Washbaugh	Mr. Ryan Wright
1521 North 32nd Street	1203 24th Street	10291 South 41st
Lexington, KY 40511	Lexington, KY 40511	Lexington, KY 40511

Exercise 17.2D C17-E02-MFLabels-03.docx   **Exercise 17.2E** C17-E02-MFLabels-04.docx

Sorting Text

In Word, you can sort text in paragraphs, text in columns within a table, or records in a data source file. As Table 17.1 shows, Word can perform three types of sorts: text, numbers, and date.

Sorting Text in Paragraphs

As you learned in Chapter 4, you can sort text arranged in paragraphs by the first character of the paragraph. This character can be a number or a symbol (such as $ or #). In an alphanumeric sort, Word sorts paragraphs beginning with a punctuation mark or special symbol first, followed by paragraphs beginning with a number, and then paragraphs beginning with a letter. Remember, in Word, a paragraph can be a single word or line followed by a press of the Enter key. If you sort paragraphs alphanumerically or numerically, Word treats dates as regular text. Unless you select specific paragraphs to be sorted, Word sorts an entire document.

To sort text arranged in paragraphs, select the text and then click the Sort button in the Paragraph group in the Home tab. This displays the Sort Text dialog box, shown in Figure 17.1, which contains sorting options. The default setting for the *Sort by* option is *Paragraphs*. This default setting changes depending on the text in the document. For example, if you are sorting text in a table, the *Sort by* option has a default setting of *Column 1*.

Sort Text in Paragraphs
1. Select text.
2. Click Sort button.
3. Make any needed changes at the Sort Text dialog box.
4. Click OK.

Sort

Figure 17.1 Sort Text Dialog Box

Use options in this dialog box to specify the text on which you want to sort, the type of sort, and the sort order.

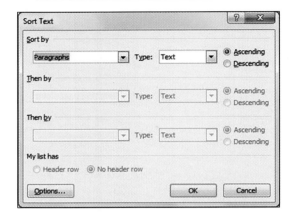

The *Type* option at the Sort Text dialog box has a default setting of *Text*. You can change this to *Number* or *Date*. Table 17.1 describes how Word sorts numbers and dates. When Word sorts paragraphs that are separated by more than a single space, the extra hard returns (a stroke of the Enter key) are removed and inserted at the beginning of the paragraphs selected for the sort.

Table 17.1 Types of Sorts

Text	In a text sort, Word arranges text in the following order: text beginning with a special symbol, such as $ and #, first; text preceded by numbers second; and alphabetic by letter third. Word can also sort letters by case: text beginning with uppercase letters first, followed by text beginning with lowercase letters.
Number	In a number sort, Word arranges text in numeric order and ignores any alphabetic text. Only the numbers 0 through 9 and symbols pertaining to numbers are recognized. These symbols include $, %, ( ), a decimal point, a comma, and the symbols for the four basic operations: + (addition), - (subtraction), * (multiplication), and / (division). Word can sort numbers in ascending or descending order.
Date	In a date sort, Word chronologically sorts dates that are expressed in a common date format, such as 06-01-2012; 06/01/2012; June 1, 2012; or 1 June 2012. Word does not sort dates that include abbreviated month names without periods. Word does not sort dates that are expressed as a month, day, or year only. Like numeric sorts, date sorts can be in ascending or descending order.

1. Open **MBSortDoc.docx** and save the document with the name **C17-E01-MBSortDoc**.
2. Sort the names under the ADMINISTRATION heading alphabetically by last name by completing the following steps:
   a. Select the four lines of text below the ADMINISTRATION heading.
   b. Click the Sort button in the Paragraph group in the Home tab.
   c. At the Sort Text dialog box, click OK.
3. Save **C17-E01-MBSortDoc.docx**.

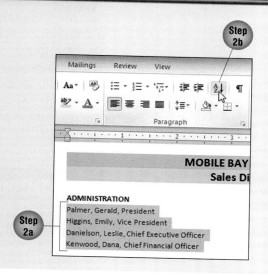

Step 2b

Step 2a

Changing Sort Options

The *Sort by* options at the Sort Text dialog box will vary depending on the options selected in the Sort Options dialog box, shown in Figure 17.2. To display this dialog box, click the Options button at the Sort Text dialog box.

Figure 17.2 Sort Options Dialog Box

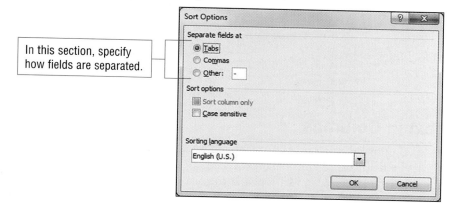

In this section, specify how fields are separated.

The *Separate fields at* section of the dialog box contains three options. The first option, *Tabs*, is the default setting. At this setting, Word assumes that the text to be sorted is divided by tabs. You can change this setting to *Commas* or *Other*. With the *Other* setting, you can specify which character that divides text to sort by. For example, suppose a document contains first and last names in paragraphs separated by a space and you want to sort by the last name. To do this, you would click *Other* at the Sort Options dialog box and then press the spacebar. This inserts a space, which is not visible, in the *Other* text box. If names are separated by a comma, click the *Commas* option.

The Sort Options dialog box contains two choices in the *Sort options* section. The first choice, *Sort column only*, sorts only the selected column. This choice is dimmed unless a column of text is selected. If a check mark appears in the *Case sensitive* check box, Word will sort text so that a word whose first letter is a capital letter is sorted before any word with the same first letter in lowercase. This option is available only if *Text* is selected in the *Type* option box at the Sort Text dialog box.

When you make changes at the Sort Options dialog box, those changes are reflected in the choices available with the *Sort by* option at the Sort Text dialog box. For example, if you click *Other* at the Sort Options dialog box and then press the spacebar, the choices for *Sort by* at the Sort Text dialog box will include *Word 1*, *Word 2*, *Word 3*, and so on.

Exercise 17.1B Sorting Text Separated by Spaces   Part 2 of 6

1. With **C17-E01-MBSortDoc.docx** open, sort the names of the technical support team alphabetically by last name by completing the following steps:
   a. Select the eight lines of text below the TECHNICAL SUPPORT TEAM heading.
   b. Click the Sort button.
   c. At the Sort Text dialog box, click the Options button.
   d. At the Sort Options dialog box, click *Other* and then press the spacebar. (This indicates the first and last names are separated by a space.)
   e. Click OK.
   f. At the Sort Text dialog box, click the down-pointing arrow at the right of the *Sort by* option and then click *Word 2* at the drop-down list.
   g. Click OK.
2. Save **C17-E01-MBSortDoc.docx**.

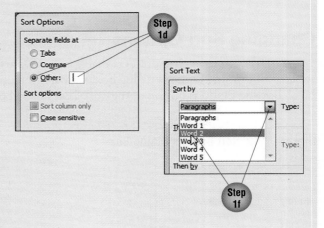

QUICK STEPS

Sort Text in Columns

1. Select specific text.
2. Click Sort button.
3. Click Options button.
4. Specify *Tabs* as separator.
5. Click OK.
6. Make any needed changes at Sort Text dialog box.
7. Click OK.

Sorting Text in Columns

To sort text set in columns, the text must be separated by tabs. When Word sorts text in columns, it sorts by field. Word considers text typed at the left margin to be *Field 1*, text typed at the first tab stop *Field 2*, text typed at the second tab stop *Field 3*, and so on. To sort text arranged in columns, display the Sort Text dialog box and then click the Options button. At the Sort Options dialog box, make sure *Tabs* is selected in the *Separate fields at* section of the dialog box and then click OK. At the Sort Text dialog box, display the appropriate field number in the *Sort by* option box and then click OK.

When you sort text in columns, make sure the columns are separated by one tab only. If you press the Tab key more than once between columns, Word recognizes each tab as a separate column. In this case, the field number you specify may correspond to an empty column rather than the desired column.

1. With **C17-E01-MBSortDoc.docx** open, sort text in columns by completing the following steps:
   a. Select the seven lines of text set in columns that display below the headings *Employee*, *Department*, and *Hire Date*.
   b. Click the Sort button.
   c. Click the Options button.
   d. At the Sort Options dialog box, make sure the *Separate fields at* option is set at *Tabs* and then click OK to close the dialog box.

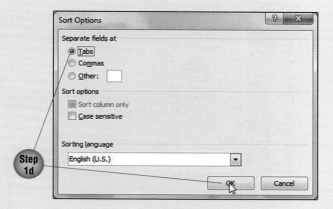

   e. At the Sort Text dialog box, make sure *Field 2* displays in the *Sort by* option box. (If not, click the down-pointing arrow at the right of the *Sort by* option and then click *Field 2* at the drop-down list.)
   f. Click OK.
2. With the columns of text still selected, sort by the third column of text by date by completing the following steps:
   a. Click the Sort button.
   b. Click the down-pointing arrow at the right of the *Sort by* option and then click *Field 4* at the drop-down list.
   c. Click OK.
3. Save **C17-E01-MBSortDoc.docx**.

Specifying a Header Row

In Exercise 17.1C, you identified columns by field numbers. You can also identify columns by heading. If the columns of text you are sorting contain column headings, you can specify this at the Sort Text dialog box by clicking the *Header row* option in the *My list has* section. Clicking the *Header row* option changes the sort options from field numbers to the column heading names. For example, in Exercise 17.1D, you will sort column text by department. To do this, you will select the columns of text including the header row, display the Sort Text dialog box, and then click the *Header row* option in the *My list has* section. When you click the down-pointing arrow at the right of the *Sort by* option, the drop-down list displays the options *Employee*, *Department*, and *Hire Date* instead of field numbers. (The drop-down list will also contain the option *(Field 1)*, which identifies the left margin.)

1. With **C17-E01-MBSortDoc.docx** open, sort text in columns by department by completing the following steps:
   a. Select the eight lines of text set in columns beginning with the row containing the column headings *Employee*, *Department*, and *Hire Date*.
   b. Click the Sort button.
   c. At the Sort Text dialog box, click the *Header row* option in the *My list has* section.
   d. Click the Options button.
   e. At the Sort Options dialog box, make sure the *Separate fields at* option is set at *Tabs* and then click OK to close the dialog box.
   f. At the Sort Text dialog box, click the down-pointing arrow at the right of the *Sort by* option and then click *Department* at the drop-down list.
   g. Click OK.

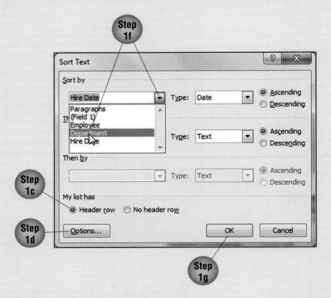

2. With the columns of text still selected, sort by the first column alphabetically by completing the following steps:
   a. Click the Sort button.
   b. At the Sort Text dialog box, click the *Header row* option in the *My list has* section.
   c. Click the down-pointing arrow at the right side of the *Sort by* option and then click *Employee* at the drop-down list.
   d. Click OK.
3. Save **C17-E01-MBSortDoc.docx**.

Sorting on More than One Field

When sorting text, you can sort on more than one field. For example, in Exercise 17.1E you will sort the department entries alphabetically and then sort the employee names alphabetically within the departments. To do this, you specify the department column in the *Sort by* option and then specify the employee column in the *Then by* option.

1. With **C17-E01-MBSortDoc.docx**
   open, sort two columns by
   completing the following steps:
   a. Make sure the eight lines of text
      set in columns are still selected
      (including the header row).
   b. Click the Sort button.
   c. At the Sort Text dialog box,
      click the *Header row* option in
      the *My list has* section of the
      dialog box.
   d. Click the down-pointing arrow
      at the right of the *Sort by* option
      and then click *Department*.
   e. Click the down-pointing arrow
      at the right of the *Then by*
      option and then click *Employee*
      at the drop-down list.
   f. Click OK.
2. Save **C17-E01-MBSortDoc.docx**.

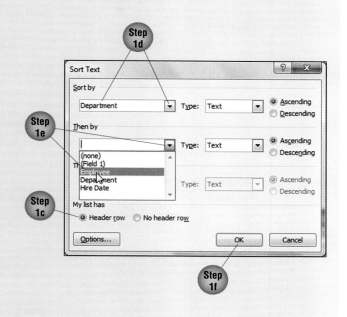

Sorting Text in Tables

You can sort text in columns within a table in much the same way that you sort columns
of text separated by tabs. If a table contains a header, click the *Header row* option at the
Sort dialog box. The Sort Text dialog box becomes the Sort dialog box when you are
sorting in a table. If you want to sort only specific cells in a table, select the cells and
then complete the sort.

Sort Text in Table
1. Position insertion
   point in table.
2. Click Sort button.
3. Make any needed
   changes at Sort
   dialog box.
4. Click OK.

1. With **C17-E01-MBSortDoc.docx** open, sort text in the first column of the table that
   displays toward the bottom of the page by completing the following steps:
   a. Position the insertion point in any cell in the table.
   b. Click the Sort button.

c. At the Sort dialog box, make sure the *Header row* option is selected in the *My list has* section.

d. Click the down-pointing arrow at the right of the *Sort by* option and then click *Salesperson* at the drop-down list.

e. Click OK.

2. Sort the numbers in the second column in descending order by completing the following steps:

a. Select all of the cells in the table except the cells in the first row.

b. Click the Sort button.

c. At the Sort dialog box, click the down-pointing arrow at the right of the *Sort by* option and then click *Column 2* at the drop-down list.

d. Click *Descending*.

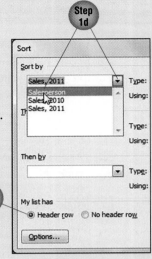

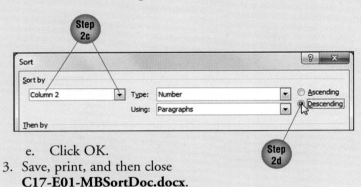

e. Click OK.

3. Save, print, and then close **C17-E01-MBSortDoc.docx**.

Sorting Records in a Data Source

To sort records in a data source file, click the Mailings tab, click the Select Recipients button, and then click *Use Existing List*. At the Select Data Source dialog box, navigate to the folder that contains the data source file you want to use and then double-click the file. Click the Edit Recipient List button in the Start Mail Merge group in the Mailings tab, and the Mail Merge Recipients dialog box, shown in Figure 17.3 with data for Exercise 17.2A, displays.

Click the field column heading to sort data in ascending order in a specific field. To perform additional sorts, click the down-pointing arrow at the right of the field column heading and then click the desired sort order.

Select Recipients

Edit Recipient List

Figure 17.3 Mail Merge Recipients Dialog Box

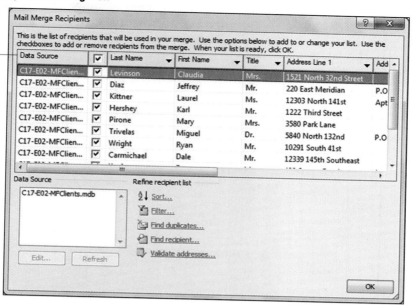

To sort on a specific field, click on the column heading.

Exercise 17.2A Sorting Data in a Data Source

Part 1 of 5

1. Make a copy of the **MFClients.mdb** file by completing the following steps:
   a. Display the Open dialog box and make Chapter17 the active folder.
   b. If necessary, change the file type button to *All Files (*.*)*.
   c. Right-click on the ***MFClients.mdb*** file and then click *Copy* at the shortcut menu.
   d. Position the mouse pointer in a white portion of the Open dialog box Content pane (outside of any file name), click the *right* mouse button, and then click *Paste* at the shortcut menu. (This inserts a copy of the file in the dialog box Content pane and names the file **MFClients - Copy.mdb**.)
   e. Right-click on the file name ***MFClients - Copy.mdb*** and then click *Rename* at the shortcut menu.
   f. Type C17-E02-MFClients and then press the Enter key.
   g. Close the Open dialog box.
2. At a blank document, click the Mailings tab, click the Start Mail Merge button in the Start Mail Merge group, and then click *Labels* at the drop-down list.

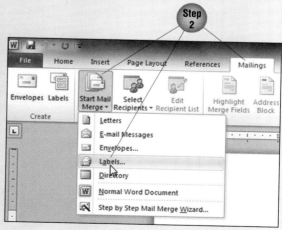

3. At the Label Options dialog box, click the down-pointing arrow at the right of the *Label vendors* option and then click *Avery US Letter* at the drop-down list.
4. Scroll down the *Product number* list box, click *5360 Mailing Labels*, and then click OK.

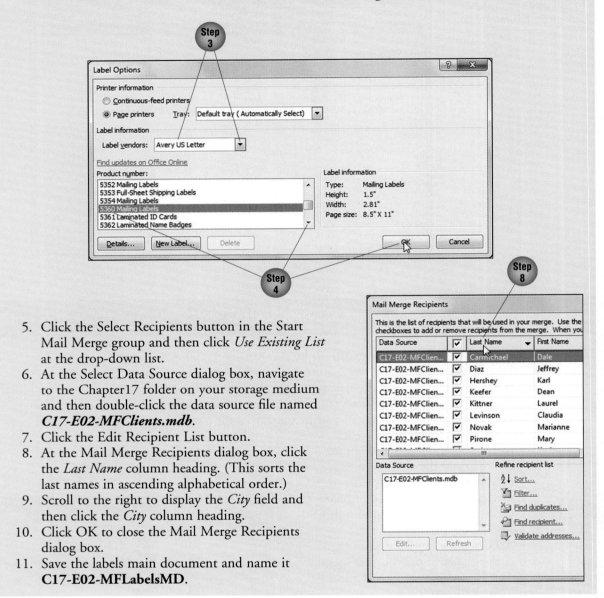

5. Click the Select Recipients button in the Start Mail Merge group and then click *Use Existing List* at the drop-down list.
6. At the Select Data Source dialog box, navigate to the Chapter17 folder on your storage medium and then double-click the data source file named **C17-E02-MFClients.mdb**.
7. Click the Edit Recipient List button.
8. At the Mail Merge Recipients dialog box, click the *Last Name* column heading. (This sorts the last names in ascending alphabetical order.)
9. Scroll to the right to display the *City* field and then click the *City* column heading.
10. Click OK to close the Mail Merge Recipients dialog box.
11. Save the labels main document and name it **C17-E02-MFLabelsMD**.

If you want more control over the sort or if you want to sort on more than one field, click the <u>Sort</u> hyperlink located in the *Refine recipient list* section of the Mail Merge Recipients dialog box. Clicking this hyperlink displays the Filter and Sort dialog box with the Sort Records tab selected, as shown in Figure 17.4. The options at the dialog box are similar to the options available at the Sort Text (and Sort) dialog box.

Figure 17.4 Filter and Sort Dialog Box with Sort Records Tab Selected

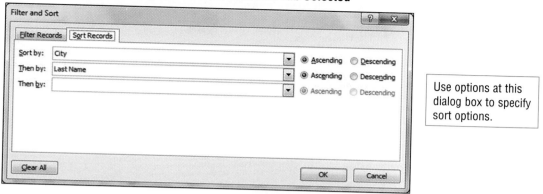

Use options at this dialog box to specify sort options.

Exercise 17.2B   Refining a Sort

1. With **C17-E02-MFLabelsMD.docx** open, sort records by ZIP codes and then by last name by completing the following steps:
    a. Click the Edit Recipient List button.
    b. At the Mail Merge Recipients dialog box, click the <u>Sort</u> hyperlink located in the *Refine recipient list* section.
    c. At the Filter and Sort dialog box with the Sort Records tab selected, click the down-pointing arrow at the right of the *Sort by* option box and then click *ZIP Code* at the drop-down list. (You will need to scroll down the list to display the *ZIP Code* field.)
    d. Make sure *Last Name* displays in the *Then by* option box.
    e. Click OK to close the Filter and Sort dialog box.

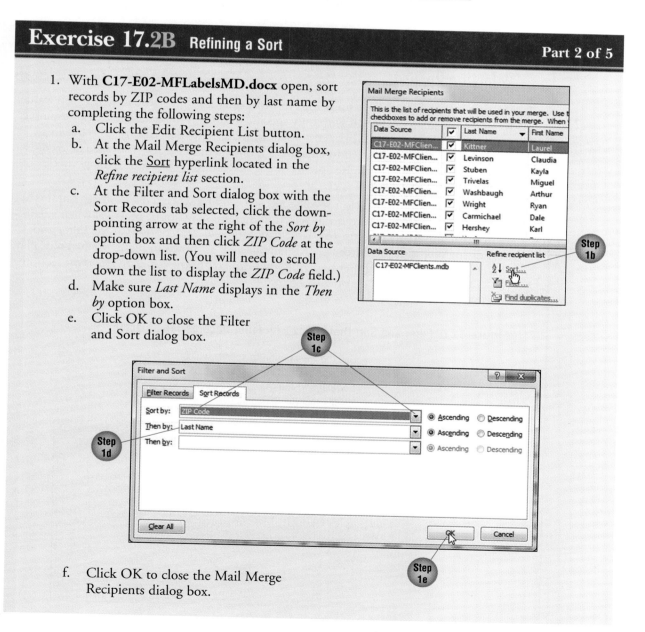

    f. Click OK to close the Mail Merge Recipients dialog box.

2. At the labels document, click the Address Block button in the Write & Insert Fields group.
3. At the Insert Address Block dialog box, click OK.
4. Click the Update Labels button in the Write & Insert Fields group.
5. Click the Finish & Merge button in the Finish group and then click *Edit Individual Documents* at the drop-down list.
6. At the Merge to New Document dialog box, make sure *All* is selected and then click OK.
7. Save the merged labels and name the document **C17-E02-MFLabels-01**.
8. Print and then close **C17-E02-MFLabels-01.docx**.
9. Save **C17-E02-MFLabelsMD.docx**.

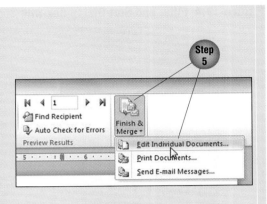

Selecting Records

If a data source file contains numerous records, situations may arise in which you want to merge the main document with only specific records in the data source. For example, you may want to send a letter to customers with a specific ZIP code or who live in a particular city. As you learned in Chapter 16, one method for selecting specific records is to display the Mail Merge Recipients dialog box and then insert or remove check marks from specific records.

Using check boxes to select specific records is useful when a data source contains a limited number of records, but this selection method may not be practical when a data source contains many records. In a large data source file, use options at the Filter and Sort dialog box with the Filter Records tab selected, as shown in Figure 17.5. To display this dialog box, click the Filter hyperlink that displays in the *Refine recipient list* section of the Mail Merge Recipients dialog box.

Figure 17.5 Filter and Sort Dialog Box with Filter Records Tab Selected

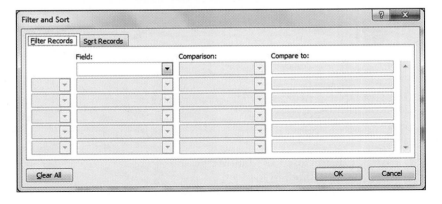

When you select a field from the *Field* drop-down list, Word automatically inserts *Equal to* in the *Comparison* option box. To make other comparisons, click the down-pointing arrow to the right of the *Comparison* option box. A drop-down list displays with these additional options: *Not equal to, Less than, Greater than, Less than or equal, Greater than or equal, Is blank,* and *Is not blank.* Use one of these options to create a select equation.

Exercise 17.2C Selecting Records

1. With **C17-E02-MFLabelsMD.docx** open, find records with a ZIP code greater than *40400* by completing the following steps:
   a. Click the Edit Recipient List button.
   b. At the Mail Merge Recipients dialog box, click the <u>Filter</u> hyperlink in the *Refine recipient list* section of the dialog box.
   c. At the Filter and Sort dialog box, click the down-pointing arrow at the right of the *Field* option and then click *ZIP Code* at the drop-down list. (You will need to scroll down the list to display *ZIP Code.* When *ZIP Code* is inserted in the *Field* option box, *Equal to* is inserted in the *Comparison* option box, and the insertion point is positioned in the *Compare to* text box.)
   d. Type *40400* in the *Compare to* text box.
   e. Click the down-pointing arrow at the right of the *Comparison* option box and then click *Greater than* at the drop-down list.

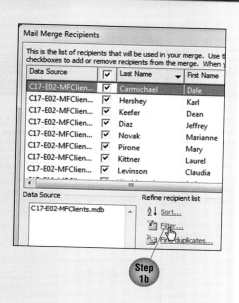

Step 1b

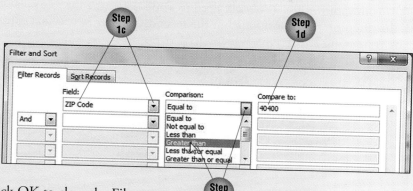

Step 1c   Step 1d

Step 1e

   f. Click OK to close the Filter and Sort dialog box.
   g. Click OK to close the Mail Merge Recipients dialog box.
2. At the labels document, click the Finish & Merge button in the Finish group and then click *Edit Individual Documents* at the drop-down list.
3. At the Merge to New Document dialog box, make sure *All* is selected and then click OK.
4. Save the merged labels and name the document **C17-E02-MFLabels-02**.
5. Print and then close **C17-E02-MFLabels-02.docx**.
6. Save **C17-E02-MFLabelsMD.docx**.

When you select a field from the *Field* option box, Word automatically inserts *And* in the first box at the left side of the dialog box. You can change this, if needed, to *Or*. With the *And* and *Or* options, you can specify more than one condition for selecting records. For example, in Exercise 17.2D, you will select all records for clients living in the cities of Paris or Winchester. If the data source file contained another field such as a specific financial plan for each customer, you could select all customers in a specific city who subscribe to a specific financial plan. For this situation, you would use the *And* option.

If you want to clear the current options at the Filter and Sort dialog box with the Filter Records tab selected, click the Clear All button. This clears any text from text boxes and leaves the dialog box on the screen. Click the Cancel button if you want to close the Filter and Sort dialog box without specifying any records.

Exercise 17.2D   Selecting Records with Specific Cities   Part 4 of 5

1. With **C17-E02-MFLabelsMD.docx** open, find all records for recipients who live in the cities of *Paris* and *Winchester* by completing the following steps:
   a. Click the Edit Recipient List button.
   b. At the Mail Merge Recipients dialog box, click the <u>Filter</u> hyperlink in the *Refine recipient list* section of the dialog box.
   c. At the Filter and Sort dialog box, click the Clear All button that displays in the lower left corner of the dialog box.
   d. Click the down-pointing arrow at the right of the *Field* option and then click *City* at the drop-down list. (You will need to scroll down the list to display this field.)
   e. Type Paris in the *Compare to* text box.
   f. Click the down-pointing arrow to the right of the option box containing the word *And* (at the left side of the dialog box) and then click *Or* at the drop-down list.
   g. Click the down-pointing arrow at the right of the second *Field* option box and then click *City* at the drop-down list. (You will need to scroll down the list to display this field.)
   h. With the insertion point positioned in the second *Compare to* text box (the one below the box containing *Paris*), type Winchester.
   i. Click OK to close the Filter and Sort dialog box.

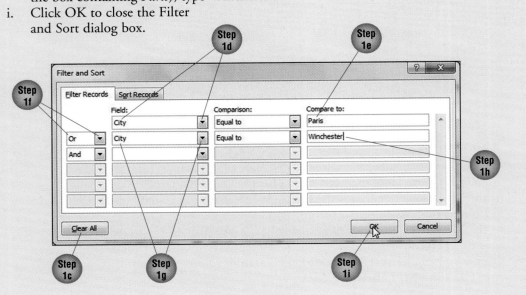

j. Click OK to close the Mail Merge Recipients dialog box.
2. At the labels document, click the Finish & Merge button in the Finish group and then click *Edit Individual Documents* at the drop-down list.
3. At the Merge to New Document dialog box, make sure *All* is selected and then click OK.
4. Save the merged labels and name the document **C17-E02-MFLabels-03**.
5. Print and then close **C17-E02-MFLabels-03.docx**.
6. Save **C17-E02-MFLabelsMD.docx**.

Finding Records

The <u>Find duplicates</u> and <u>Find recipient</u> hyperlinks in the *Refine recipient list* section of the Mail Merge Recipients dialog box can be very useful for finding records in an extensive data source file. Use the <u>Find duplicates</u> hyperlink if you want to locate any duplicate records that appear in the data source file. If you need to find a specific record or records that meet a specific criterion, use the <u>Find recipient</u> hyperlink. The <u>Validate addresses</u> hyperlink in the *Refine recipient list* section is available only if you have installed address validation software. (Visit the Microsoft Office website to find more information about address validation add-ins.)

When you click the <u>Find duplicates</u> hyperlink, any duplicate records display in the Find Duplicates dialog box. At this dialog box, remove the check mark from the duplicate record you do not want to include in the merge. To find a specific record in a data source file, click the <u>Find recipient</u> hyperlink. At the Find Entry dialog box, type the text you want to find and then click the Find Next button. Continue clicking the Find Next button until a message displays telling you that there are no more entries that contain the text you typed. By default, Word searches for the specified text in all fields of all records in the data source file. You can limit the search by clicking the down-pointing arrow at the right of the *This field* option box and then clicking the specific field. Type the text to find in the *Find* text box and then click OK.

Exercise 17.2E Finding Records

Part 5 of 5

1. With **C17-E02-MFLabelsMD.docx** open, remove the filter by completing the following steps:
   a. Click the Edit Recipient List button.
   b. At the Mail Merge Recipients dialog box, click the <u>Filter</u> hyperlink in the *Refine recipient list* section.
   c. At the Filter and Sort dialog box, click the Clear All button that displays in the lower left corner of the dialog box.
   d. Click OK to close the Filter and Sort dialog box.
   e. At the Mail Merge Recipients dialog box, click the <u>Find duplicates</u> hyperlink in the *Refine recipient list* section.

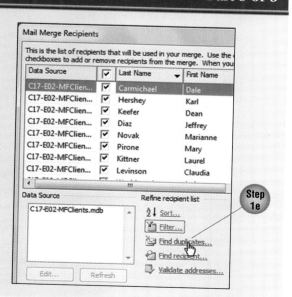

f. At the Find Duplicates dialog box, which indicates that there are no duplicate items, click OK.

2. Find all records containing the ZIP code *40511* by completing the following steps:

   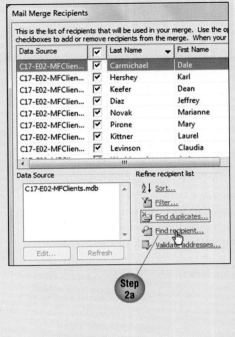

   a. At the Mail Merge Recipients dialog box, click the <u>Find recipient</u> hyperlink in the *Refine recipient list* section.

   b. At the Find Entry dialog box, click the down-pointing arrow at the right of the *This field* option box and then click *ZIP Code* at the drop-down list. (You will need to scroll down the list to display this option.)

   c. Click in the *Find* text box and then type 40511.

   d. Click the Find Next button.

   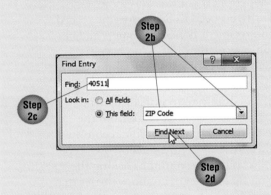

   e. When the first record is selected containing the ZIP code *40511*, click the Find Next button.

   f. Continue clicking the Find Next button until a message displays telling you that there are no more entries that contain the text you typed. At this message, click OK.

   g. Click the Cancel button to close the Find Entry dialog box.

3. Select and then merge records of those clients with a ZIP code of 40511 by completing the following steps:

   a. At the Mail Merge Recipients dialog box, click the <u>Filter</u> hyperlink in the *Refine recipient list* section of the dialog box.

   b. At the Filter and Sort dialog box, click the down-pointing arrow at the right of the *Field* option and then click *ZIP Code* at the drop-down list. (You will need to scroll down the list to display this field.)

   c. Type 40511 in the *Compare to* text box.

   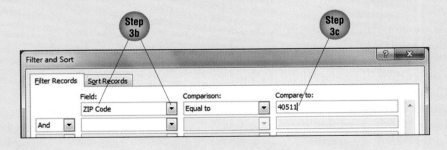

    d.   Click OK to close the Filter and Sort dialog box.

    e.   Click OK to close the Mail Merge Recipients dialog box.

4. At the labels document, click the Finish & Merge button in the Finish group and then click *Edit Individual Documents* at the drop-down list.

5. At the Merge to New Document dialog box, make sure *All* is selected and then click OK.

6. Save the merged labels and name the document **C17-E02-MFLabels-04**.

7. Print and then close **C17-E02-MFLabels-04.docx**.

8. Save and then close **C17-E02-MFLabelsMD.docx**.

Chapter Summary

➤ Word is a word processing program that includes some basic database functions that you can use to alphabetize information, arrange numbers numerically, or select specific records from a data source.

➤ You can sort text in paragraphs, columns, or tables. You can also sort records in a data source file and select specific records for merging with a main document.

➤ Word can perform three types of sorts: text, number, and date.

➤ Unless specific text is selected, Word sorts text in the entire document.

➤ Use the Sort button in the Paragraph group in the Home tab to sort text in paragraphs, columns, and tables.

➤ The *Sort by* option at the Sort Text dialog box has a default setting of *Paragraphs*. This default setting changes depending on the text in the document.

➤ Click the Options button in the Sort Text dialog box to display the Sort Options dialog box. Use the *Separate fields at* section to specify the character that divides text to be sorted.

➤ To sort text in columns, the text must be separated with tabs. When Word sorts text set in columns, it considers the left margin *Field 1*, the first column *Field 2*, and so on.

➤ Use the *Header row* option in the *My list has* option in the Sort Text dialog box to sort all text in columns except the first row.

➤ You can sort on more than one field with the *Sort by* and *Then by* options at the Sort dialog box.

➤ You can sort text in the columns of a table much the same way you sort columns of text. The Sort Text dialog box becomes the Sort dialog box when you sort in a table.

➤ Sort records in a data source file at the Mail Merge Recipients dialog box. Sort by clicking the column heading. You can also sort by clicking the Sort hyperlink in the *Refine recipient list* section of the Mail Merge Recipients dialog box. This displays the Filter and Sort dialog box with the Sort Records tab selected.

➤ Select specific records in a data source file by inserting or removing check marks from the check boxes preceding records or with options at the Filter and Sort dialog box with the Filter Records tab selected. Display the dialog box by clicking the Filter hyperlink that displays in the *Refine recipient list* section.

➤ Use the *Comparison* option box in the Filter and Sort dialog box to refine your search to records that meet specific criteria.

➤ Use the Find duplicates hyperlink in the *Refine recipient list* section of the Mail Merge Recipients dialog box to find duplicate records in a data source file and use the Find recipient hyperlink to search for records that match a specific criterion.

Commands Review

FEATURE	RIBBON TAB, GROUP	BUTTON
Sort Text dialog box	Home, Paragraph	![A-Z sort]
Sort Options dialog box	Home, Paragraph	![A-Z sort], Options
Filter and Sort dialog box with Sort Records tab selected	Mailings, Start Mail Merge	![icon], Sort
Filter and Sort dialog box with Select Records tab selected	Mailings, Start Mail Merge	![icon], Filter

Key Points Review

Completion: In the space provided at the right, indicate the correct term, symbol, or command.

1. You can sort text in paragraphs, columns, or this.
2. The three types of sorts you can perform in a document include text, number, and this.
3. The Sort button is located in this group in the Home tab.
4. Click the Sort button with paragraphs of text selected, and this dialog box displays.
5. This is the default setting for the *Separate at* option at the Sort Options dialog box.
6. When you sort text in columns, Word considers the left margin this field number.
7. If you select column text, including the column headings, click this option in the *My list has* section of the Sort Text dialog box.
8. With the insertion point positioned in a table, clicking the Sort button displays this dialog box.
9. Click this at the Mail Merge Recipients dialog box to sort data in a specific column.
10. Click this hyperlink at the Mail Merge Recipients dialog box, and the Filter and Sort dialog box displays with the Sort Records tab selected.
11. Click this button at the Filter and Sort dialog box with the Filter Records tab selected to clear any text from text boxes.
12. Click this hyperlink in the Mail Merge Recipients dialog box to search for records that match a specific criterion.

Chapter Assessments

Applying Your Skills

Demonstrate your knowledge of features learned in this chapter by completing the following assessments.

Assessment 17.1   Sort Text in a McCormack Funds Document

1. Open **McFSortDoc.docx** and save the document with the name **C17-A01-McFSortDoc**.
2. Sort the nine lines of text below the *Executive Team* heading in ascending alphabetic order by last name.
3. Select the columns of text below the *New Employees* heading and then sort the columns alphabetically by last name in the first column.
4. Sort by the *Salesperson* column in the table located toward the bottom of the document in ascending order.
5. Save, print, and then close **C17-A01-McFSortDoc.docx**.

Assessment 17.2   Sort Text in a Medical Health Services Document

1. Open **MHSSortDoc.docx** and save the document with the name **C17-A02-MHSSortDoc**.
2. Sort the columns of text below the *MEDICAL HEALTH SERVICES* title by clinic name in ascending order.
3. Sort the columns of text below the *EXECUTIVE TEAM* heading by last name in ascending order.
4. Sort by the *Second Half Expenses* column in the table located toward the bottom of the document in descending order.
5. Save, print, and then close **C17-A02-MHSSortDoc.docx**.

Assessment 17.3   Create Labels for Key Life Customers

1. Make a copy of the **KLCustomers.mdb** file by completing the following steps:
   a. Display the Open dialog box and make Chapter17 the active folder.
   b. If necessary, change the file type button to *All Files (*.*)*.
   c. Right-click on the **KLCustomers.mdb** file and then click *Copy* at the shortcut menu.
   d. Position the mouse pointer in a white portion of the Open dialog box Content pane (outside of any file name), click the *right* mouse button, and then click *Paste* at the shortcut menu. (This inserts a copy of the file in the dialog box Content pane and names the file **KLCustomers - Copy.mdb**.)
   e. Right-click on the file name **KLCustomers - Copy.mdb** and then click *Rename* at the shortcut menu.
   f. Type C17-A03-KLCustomersDS and then press the Enter key.
   g. Close the Open dialog box.
2. Use the Mail Merge feature to create mailing labels with the *Avery US Letter 5360* label product. Use the existing data source **C17-A03-KLCustomersDS.mdb** for the labels.
3. Display the Mail Merge Recipients dialog box, sort records by ZIP code in ascending order and then by last name in ascending order, and then save the labels document with the name **C17-A03-KLLabels**.
4. Print and then close **C17-A03-KLLabels.docx**.
5. Close the labels main document without saving it.

Assessment 17.4   Create Labels for Key Life Boston Customers

1. Use the Mail Merge feature to create mailing labels with the *Avery US Letter 5360* label product. Use the existing data source **C17-A03-KLCustomersDS.mdb** for the labels.
2. Display the Mail Merge Recipients dialog box, display the Filter and Sort dialog box with the Filter Records tab selected, and then select only those customers living in Boston.
3. Complete the merge and then save the labels document with the name **C17-A04-KLLabelsBoston**.
4. Print and then close **C17-A04-KLLabelsBoston.docx**.
5. Close the labels main document without saving it.

Expanding Your Skills

Explore additional feature options or use Help to learn a new skill in creating this document.

Assessment 17.5   Create Name Tag Labels for Contacts in New York

1. At a blank document, click the Mailings tab, click the Start Mail Merge button, and then click *Labels* at the drop-down list.
2. At the Label Options dialog box, make sure the *Label vendors* option displays with *Avery US Letter*, click *45395 EcoFriendly Name Badges* in the list box (you will need to scroll up or down the list box), and then click OK.

3. Click the document to make it active, click the Select New Recipients button, and then click *Type New List* at the drop-down list.
4. Create and customize a data source file so it appears as shown in Figure 17.6. Type the information in the appropriate fields for the 14 records shown in the figure.
5. Name the data source file **ContactsDS**.
6. At the main document, insert the fields in the first label as shown below:
   «First_Name» «Last_Name»
   «Company_Name»
   «State»
   «Work_Phone»
7. Update the labels.
8. Edit **ContactsDS.mdb** and then sort by company name in ascending order and then filter by the state of New York.
9. Merge the name tag labels.
10. With the name tag labels displayed, complete the following steps:
    a. Click in any label in the document and then click the Table Tools Layout tab.
    b. Select the entire table. ***Hint: Use the Select button in the Table Tools Layout tab.***
    c. Click the Table Tools Design tab and then apply the *Light Shading – Accent 3* table style.
    d. Click the Table Tools Layout tab and then change the alignment to *Align Center*.
    e. With the table selected, change the font to 16-point Lucida Calligraphy bold.
11. Save the name tag labels document and name it **C17-A05-NYNameTags**.
12. Print and then close **C17-A05-NYNameTags.docx**.
13. Close the name tag labels main document without saving it.

Figure 17.6 Assessment 17.5

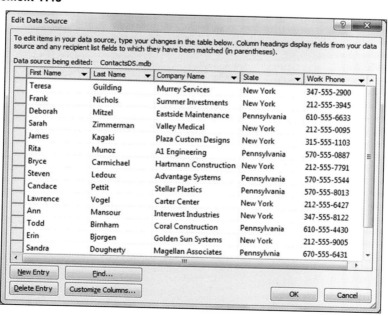

Achieving Signature Status

Take your skills to the next level by completing this more challenging assessment.

Assessment 17.6   Create a Contacts Table

1. Open **Contacts.docx** and then save the document with the name **C17-A06-Contacts**.
2. Sort the text in ascending order by the state and then by the company name.
3. After sorting the text, select it and then convert it to a table.
4. Apply formatting so your table(s) display as shown in Figure 17.7.
5. Save, print, and then close **C17-A06-Contacts.docx**.

Figure 17.7 Assessment 17.6

CORPORATE CONTACTS

Company	Contact	State	Telephone
Carter Center	Lawrence Vogel	New York	212-555-6427
Golden Sun Systems	Erin Bjorgen	New York	212-555-9005
Hartmann Construction	Bryce Carmichael	New York	212-555-7791
Interwest Industries	Ann Mansour	New York	347-555-8122
Murrey Services	Teresa Guilding	New York	347-555-2900
Plaza Custom Designs	James Kagaki	New York	315-555-1103
Summer Investments	Frank Nichols	New York	212-555-3945
Valley Medical	Sarah Zimmerman	New York	212-555-0095

Company	Contact	State	Telephone
A1 Engineering	Rita Munoz	Pennsylvania	570-555-0887
Advantage Systems	Steven Ledoux	Pennsylvania	570-555-5544
Coral Construction	Todd Birnham	Pennsylvania	610-555-4430
Eastside Maintenance	Deborah Mitzel	Pennsylvania	610-555-6633
Magellan Associates	Sandra Dougherty	Pennsylvania	670-555-6431
Stellar Plastics	Candace Pettit	Pennsylvania	570-555-8013

Chapter 18

Tutorial 18.1
Inserting Custom Numbers and Bullets
Tutorial 18.2
Inserting Multilevel Lists
Tutorial 18.3
Inserting Intellectual Property Symbols
Tutorial 18.4
Insert Hyphens and Nonbreaking Characters
Tutorial 18.5
Find and Replace Special Characters

Managing Lists

Performance Objectives

Upon successful completion of Chapter 18, you will be able to:

- Insert custom numbers and bullets
- Define numbering formatting
- Define custom bullets
- Insert multilevel list numbering
- Define multilevel list numbering
- Insert special characters, hyphens, and nonbreaking spaces
- Find and replace special characters

Inserting a bullet before each item in a list draws a reader's attention to the list. Similarly, inserting numbers before a list of items in sequence emphasizes their order. You can insert numbers and bullets and create multiple-level bulleted or numbered paragraphs with buttons in the Paragraph group in the Home tab. Use options from these buttons' drop-down lists to customize bullets and numbers and to create customized multilevel numbering. In this chapter, you will learn how to create and insert customized bullets and numbering; how to insert special characters such as intellectual property protection symbols, hyphens, and nonbreaking spaces; and how to search for and replace special characters.

Note: Before beginning computer exercises for this chapter, copy to your storage medium the Chapter18 folder from the CD that accompanies this textbook and then make Chapter18 the active folder.

In this chapter, students will produce the following documents:

Exercise 18.1. C18-E01-TDAgenda.docx
Exercise 18.2. C18-E02-TravelAdv.docx
Exercise 18.3. C18-E03-CSList.docx
Exercise 18.4. C18-E04-SpecialCharacters.docx

Model answers for these exercises are shown on the following pages.

TRAINING DEPARTMENT AGENDA

I)	Approval of Minutes
II)	Introductions
III)	Organizational Overview
IV)	Review of Goals
V)	Expenses
VI)	Technology
VII)	Future Goals
VIII)	Proposals
IX)	Adjournment

RESEARCH DEPARTMENT AGENDA

I)	Approval of Minutes
II)	Introductions
III)	Review of Goals
IV)	Current Projects
V)	Materials
VI)	Staffing
VII)	Future Projects
VIII)	Adjournment

Exercise 18.1

C18-E01-TDAgenda.docx

HAWAIIAN ADVENTURES

RAINY DAY ACTIVITIES

Expect to have a rainy day or two during your vacation, especially in the winter months between November and March. With a little planning, you can have just as much fun indoors as outdoors. To make the most of a rainy day, enjoy one of the activities listed below.

- Movies: Take advantage of matinee prices. The Sunshine Marketplace Theaters offer discount tickets and current feature films.
- Shopping: Most of the area shopping centers are "open-air" complexes with some roof covering, ideal havens from the rain. Visit the Coconut Grove Shopping Center or the Kukui Shopping Village.
- Museums: Learn about the history of Hawaii through murals, artifacts, and artwork by visiting one of several museums located throughout the island. Most museums offer special family activities the first Saturday of each month.
- Theater: Several local community performing arts centers offer annual productions for children and adults. Admission prices are very affordable, and most theaters have special matinee prices.

KAUAI SIGHTS

- Na Pali Coast: Unless you are a rugged hiker, you can see this fifteen-mile, spectacular landmark only by air or boat.
- North Shore: Find shadowy mountains, lush valleys, and spectacular coastlines along a string of one-lane bridges.
- Hanalei Valley Lookout: Pull over to see wetland taro fields with a backdrop of purple mountains.
- Kilauea Point: This national wildlife refuge is home to nesting seabirds and an original lighthouse.
- Sleeping Giant: Nounou Mountain provides the "man in repose" profile best seen from Kuhio Highway 56 in Kapaa.
- Coconut Coast: You will know when you are here because palm trees line Kuhio Highway 56 on the island's east side.

Exercise 18.2

C18-E02-TravelAdv.docx

Exercise 18.3

C18-E03-CSList.docx

COMPUTER SECURITY

A. Security Issues
  1. Network Security Risks
    a) Unauthorized Access
    b) Information Theft
    c) Denial of Service Attacks
  2. Computer Viruses
    a) Virus Types
    b) Virus Methods
    c) Virus Symptoms
B. Security Strategies
  1. Computer Protection
    a) Anti-virus Software
    b) Firewalls
  2. Security Strategies
    a) Data Backup
    b) Data Encryption
    c) Passwords
    d) User ID

NETWORKS

A. Networking over the Web
  1. Data Transmission
    a) Bandwidth
    b) Analog and Digital Transmission
    c) Parallel and Serial Transmission
  2. Communications Media
    a) Wired Communications Media
    b) Wireless Communications Media
B. Network Design
  1. Network Topologies
    a) Bus Topologies
    b) Star Topologies
    c) Ring Topologies
    d) Hybrid Topologies
  2. Network Hardware
    a) Hubs
    b) Repeaters
    c) Routers
    d) Gateways
    e) Bridges

INTELLECTUAL PROPERTY PROTECTION

A copyright protects original works in areas such as publishing, music, literature, and drama. Use the © symbol to identify copyrighted intellectual property. Create this symbol by typing (c), using the keyboard shortcut Alt + Ctrl + C, or by clicking the symbol in the Symbol dialog box with the Special Characters tab selected.

A trademark identifies a word, symbol, device or name such as a brand name. Use the ™ symbol to identify a trademarked name or product. Create this symbol by typing (tm), using keyboard shortcut Alt + Ctrl + T, or by clicking the symbol in the Symbol dialog box with the Special Character tab selected.

A registered trademark is a trademark that has been registered with the U.S. Patent & Trademark Office. Use the ® symbol to identify a registered trademark. Create this symbol by typing (r), using the keyboard shortcut Alt + Ctrl + R, or by clicking the symbol button in the Symbol dialog box with the Special Characters tab selected.

SOFTWARE TRAINING

The Microsoft® Office Word training is scheduled for Thursday, March 2, from 9:00–10:30 a.m. Additional training for other applications in the Office suite—Excel, PowerPoint, and Access—will be available during the month of April. Contact the Training Department for additional information. All Tri-State employees are eligible for the training.

KEYBOARD SHORTCUTS

Microsoft Word includes a number of keyboard shortcuts you can use to access features and commands. The ScreenTip for some buttons displays the keyboard shortcut you can use to execute the command. For example, hovering the mouse over the Font button causes the ScreenTip to display Ctrl + Shift + F as the keyboard shortcut. Additional Home tab Font group keyboard shortcuts include Ctrl + B to bold text, Ctrl + I to italicize text, and Ctrl + U to underline text. You can also press Ctrl + Shift + + to turn on superscript and press Ctrl + = to turn on subscript.

Exercise 18.4

C18-E04-SpecialCharacters.docx

Inserting Custom Numbers and Bullets

Numbering

Bullets

In Chapter 3, you learned to number paragraphs and insert bullets automatically using the Numbering button and the Bullets button in the Paragraph group in the Home tab. After you insert numbers or bullets, you can customize them by clicking the Numbering button arrow or the Bullets button arrow and then choosing an option from the drop-down gallery.

Inserting Custom Numbers

As you learned earlier, you can insert numbers as you type text, or you can type text, select it, and then apply numbering formatting. Whether you insert numbers as you type text or click the Numbering button in the Paragraph group to apply number formatting after you type text, Word inserts Arabic numbers (1., 2., 3., and so on) in the document by default. You can change this default numbering by clicking the Numbering button arrow and then clicking the option you desire at the Numbering drop-down gallery, shown in Figure 18.1.

To change list levels, click the Numbering button arrow, point to the *Change List Level* option located toward the bottom of the drop-down gallery, and then click the desired list level at the side menu. You can set the numbering value with options at the Set Numbering Value dialog box. Display this dialog box by clicking the Numbering button arrow and then clicking the *Set Numbering Value* option located at the bottom of the drop-down gallery.

Figure 18.1 Numbering Gallery

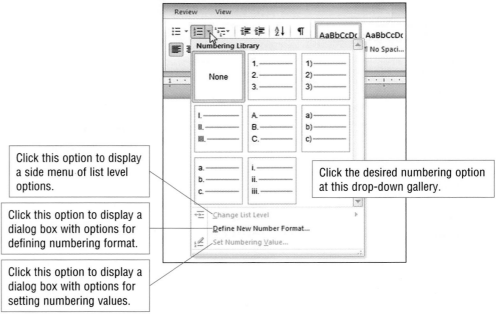

Click this option to display a side menu of list level options.

Click this option to display a dialog box with options for defining numbering format.

Click this option to display a dialog box with options for setting numbering values.

Click the desired numbering option at this drop-down gallery.

1. Open **TDAgenda.docx** and save the document with the name **C18-E01-TDAgenda**.
2. Restart the numbering for the list to 1 by completing the following steps:
   a. Select the numbered paragraphs.
   b. Click the Numbering button arrow and then click *Set Numbering Value* at the side menu.
   c. At the Set Numbering Value dialog box, select the number in the *Set value to* option box, type 1, and then press the Enter key.

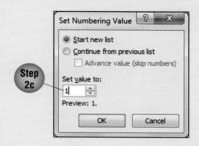

Step 2c

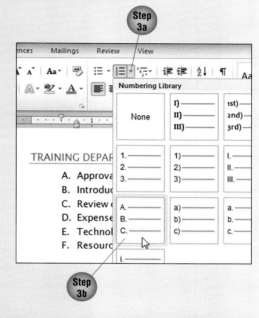

Step 3a

Step 3b

3. Change the numbering of the paragraphs to letters by completing the following steps:
   a. With the numbered paragraphs selected, click the Numbering button arrow.
   b. At the Numbering drop-down gallery, click the option that uses capital letters as shown at the right (the location of the option may vary).
4. Add text to the agenda by positioning the insertion point immediately to the right of the text *Introductions*, pressing the Enter key, and then typing Organizational Overview.
5. Demote the lettered list by completing the following steps:
   a. Select the lettered paragraphs.
   b. Click the Numbering button arrow, point to the *Change List Level* option and then click the *a.* option at the side menu.

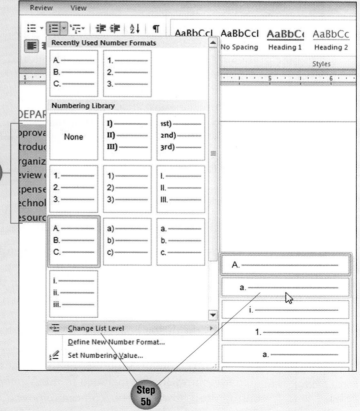

Step 5a

Step 5b

6. With the paragraphs still selected, promote the list by clicking the Decrease Indent button in the Paragraph group in the Home tab. (The changes back to capital letters.)

7. Move the insertion point to the end of the document and then type The meeting will stop for lunch, which is catered and will be held in the main conference center from 12:15 to 1:30.

8. Press the Enter key twice and then click the Numbering button.

9. Click the AutoCorrect Options button that displays next to the A. inserted in the document and then click the *Continue Numbering* option at the drop-down list. (This change the letter from *A.* to *H.*)

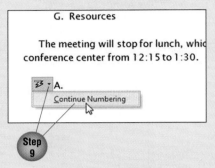

10. Type Future Goals, press the Enter key, type Proposals, press the Enter key, and then type Adjournment.

11. Press the Enter key and the letter *K.* is inserted in the document. Turn off the list creation by clicking the Numbering button arrow and then click the *None* option at the drop-down gallery.

12. Save and then print **C18-E01-TDAgenda.docx**.

13. Select and then delete the paragraph of text in the middle of the list, including the blank lines above and below the text. (All of the lettered items should be listed consecutively with the same spacing between.)

14. Select the lettered paragraphs, click the Numbering button arrow, and then clicking the option that uses numbers followed by a right parenthesis (*1), 2), 3)*, and so on).

15. Save **C18-E01-TDAgenda.docx**.

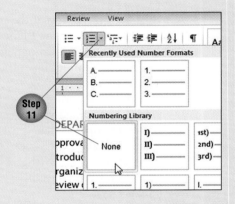

Define Numbering Formatting
1. Click Numbering button arrow.
2. Click *Define New Number Format* at drop-down gallery.
3. Choose the desired number formatting option.
4. Click OK.

Defining a Numbering Format

In addition to using the default numbering format or a custom numbering format in the *Numbering Library* section in the Numbering button drop-down gallery, you can define your own numbering format with options at the Define New Number Format dialog box, shown in Figure 18.2. Display this dialog box by clicking the Numbering button arrow and then clicking *Define New Number Format* at the drop-down gallery. With options at the dialog box, you can specify the number style, font, and alignment and preview the formatting in the *Preview* section.

When you define a numbering format at the Define New Number Format dialog box, it is automatically included in the *Numbering Library* section in the Numbering button drop-down gallery. You can remove a numbering format from the drop-down gallery by right-clicking it and then clicking *Remove* at the shortcut menu.

Figure 18.2 Define New Number Format Dialog Box

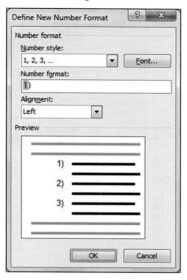

Use options at this dialog box to specify the number style, font, format, and alignment and to preview the formatting.

Exercise 18.1B   Defining a Numbering Format   Part 2 of 2

1. With **C18-E01-TDAgenda.docx** open, define a new number format by completing the following steps:
   a. Position the insertion point on any character in the numbered text.
   b. Click the Numbering button arrow.
   c. Click *Define New Number Format* at the drop-down gallery.
   d. At the Define New Number Format dialog box, click the down-pointing arrow at the right of the *Number style* option and then click the *1st, 2nd, 3rd ...* option.
   e. Click the Font button that displays at the right of the *Number style* list box.

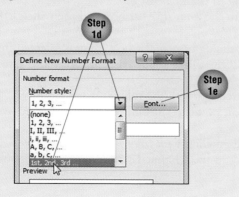

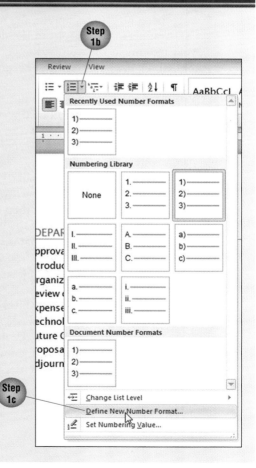

f. At the Font dialog box, scroll down the *Font* list box and then click *Candara*.

g. Click *Bold* in the *Font style* list box.

h. Click OK to close the Font dialog box.

i. Click the down-pointing arrow at the right of the *Alignment* option box and then click *Right* at the drop-down list.

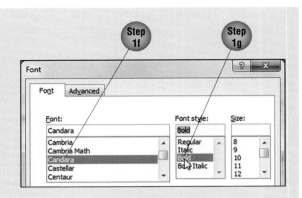

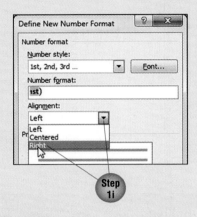

j. Click OK to close the Define New Number Format dialog box. (This applies the new formatting to the numbered paragraphs in the document.)

2. After looking at the numbering with the new formatting applied, define another number format by completing the following steps:

a. With the insertion point positioned on any character in the numbered text, click the Numbering button arrow.

b. Click *Define New Number Format* at the drop-down gallery.

c. At the Define New Number Format dialog box, click the down-pointing arrow at the right of the *Number style* option and then click the *I, II, III, …* option.

d. Click the Font button that displays at the right of the *Number style* list box.

e. At the Font dialog box, click *Cambria* in the *Font* list box.

f. Check to make sure *Bold* is selected in the *Font style* list box and then click OK to close the Font dialog box.

g. At the Define New Number Format dialog box, make sure *Right* is selected in the *Alignment* option box and then click OK. (This applies the new formatting to the numbered paragraphs in the document.)

3. Insert a file into the current document by completing the following steps:

a. Press Ctrl + End to move the insertion point to the end of the document.

b. Click the Insert tab.

c. Click the Object button arrow and then click *Text from File* at the drop-down list.

d. At the Insert File dialog box, navigate to the Chapter18 folder and then double-click **RDAgenda.docx**.

4. Position the insertion point on any character in the title *RESEARCH DEPARTMENT AGENDA*, click the Home tab, and then click the *Heading 2* style in the Styles group.
5. Select the text below the title *RESEARCH DEPARTMENT AGENDA*, click the Numbering button arrow, and then click the Roman numeral style that you defined.
6. Save, print, and then close **C18-E01-TDAgenda.docx**.

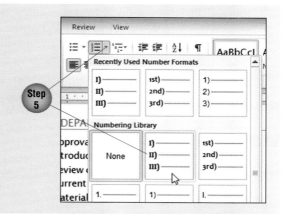

Defining and Inserting Custom Bullets

When you click the Bullets button in the Paragraph group, a round bullet is inserted in the document. You can insert custom bullets by clicking the Bullets button arrow and then clicking the desired bullet at the drop-down gallery. This drop-down gallery displays the most recently used bullets along with an option for defining new bullets. Click the *Define New Bullet* option, and the Define New Bullet dialog box displays, as shown in Figure 18.3. With options at this dialog box, you can choose a symbol or picture bullet, change the font size of the bullet, and specify the alignment of the bullet. When you choose a custom bullet, consider matching the theme or mood of the document to maintain a consistent look, or create a picture bullet to add visual interest.

Figure 18.3 Define New Bullet Dialog Box

Use options at this dialog box to choose a symbol or picture bullet and change the font size and alignment of the bullet.

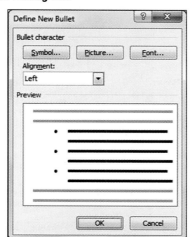

When you define a new bullet at the Define New Bullet dialog box, it is automatically included in the *Bullet Library* section in the Bullets button drop-down gallery. You can remove a bullet from the drop-down gallery by right-clicking the bullet and then clicking *Remove* at the shortcut menu.

As with a numbered list, you can change the level of a bulleted list. To do this, click the item or select the items you want to change, click the Bullets button arrow, and then point to *Change List Level*. At the side menu of bullet options that displays, click the desired bullet. With the *Change List Level* option, you can change a single-level list into a multilevel list. If you want to insert a line break in the list while the automatic bullets feature is on without inserting a bullet, press Shift + Enter. (You can also insert a line break in a numbered list without inserting a number by pressing Shift + Enter.)

Exercise 18.2 Defining and Inserting Custom Bullets — Part 1 of 1

1. Open **TravelAdv.docx** and save the document with the name **C18-E02-TravelAdv**.
2. Make the following changes to the document:
   a. Select the entire document and then change the line spacing to 1.15.
   b. Apply the Heading 1 style to the title *Hawaiian Adventures*.
   c. Apply the Heading 2 style to the two headings *Rainy Day Activities* and *Kauai Sights*.
   d. Change the style set to Distinctive.
   e. Change the theme to Flow.
3. Define and insert a picture bullet by completing the following steps:
   a. Select text in the *Rainy Day Activities* section from the paragraph that begins with *Movies* through the paragraph that begins with *Theater*.
   b. Click the Home tab.
   c. Click the Bullets button arrow and then click *Define New Bullet* at the drop-down gallery.

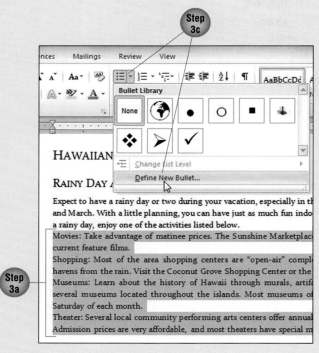

d. At the Define New Bullet dialog box, click the Picture button.

e. At the Picture Bullet dialog box, click the round, green bullet shown at the right. (You may need to scroll down the list box to display this bullet.)

f. Click OK to close the Picture Bullet dialog box.

g. Click OK to close the Define New Bullet dialog box. (This applies the new bullet to the selected paragraphs.)

4. Define and insert a symbol bullet by completing the following steps:

a. Select the paragraphs of text below the heading *Kauai Sights*.

b. Click the Bullets button arrow and then click *Define New Bullet* at the drop-down gallery.

c. At the Define New Bullet dialog box, click the Symbol button.

d. At the Symbol dialog box, click the down-pointing arrow at the right of the *Font* option, scroll down the drop-down list, and then click *Wingdings*.

e. Click the flower symbol shown at the right.

f. Click OK to close the Symbol dialog box.

g. At the Define New Bullet dialog box, click the Font button.

h. At the Font dialog box, click *14* in the *Size* list box.

i. Click the down-pointing arrow at the right of the *Font color* option and then click the color *Green, Accent 5, Darker 50%*, shown at the right.

j. Click OK to close the Font dialog box.

k. At the Define New Bullet dialog box, click OK.

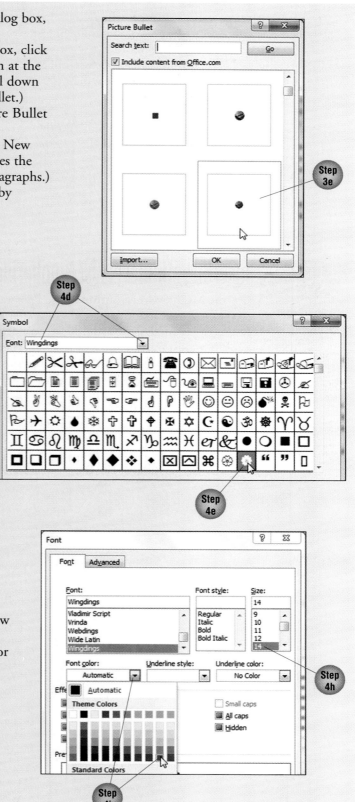

5. Remove from the Bullet Library the two bullets you have just defined by completing the following steps:
   a. Click the Bullets button arrow.
   b. Right-click the round, green picture bullet in the *Bullet Library* section and then click *Remove* at the shortcut menu.
   c. Click the Bullets button arrow.
   d. Right-click the flower symbol bullet in the *Bullet Library* section and then click *Remove* at the shortcut menu.
6. Save, print, and then close **C18-E02-TravelAdv.docx**.

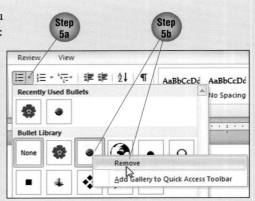

Inserting Multilevel List Numbering

Use the Multilevel List button in the Paragraph group in the Home tab to specify the type of numbering for paragraphs of text at the left margin, first tab, second tab, and so on. Apply predesigned multilevel numbering to text in a document by clicking the Multilevel List button and then clicking the desired numbering style at the drop-down gallery, shown in Figure 18.4. Some options at the Multilevel List drop-down gallery display with *Heading 1*, *Heading 2*, and so on, after the number. Click one of these options, and Word inserts the numbering and applies the heading styles to the text.

Figure 18.4 Multilevel List Drop-down Gallery

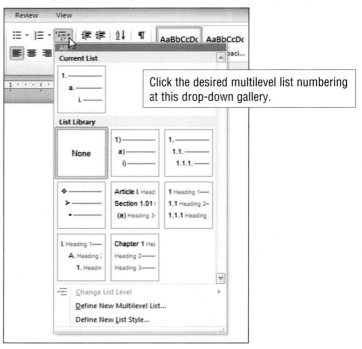

Click the desired multilevel list numbering at this drop-down gallery.

1. Open **CSList.docx** and save the document with the name **C18-E03-CSList**.
2. Change tab settings by completing the following steps:
    a. Select the paragraphs of text below the title.
    b. Click the Paragraph group dialog box launcher.
    c. At the Paragraph dialog box, click the Tabs button located in the lower left corner of the dialog box.
    d. At the Tabs dialog box, select the *0.5"* measurement in the *Default tab stops* box and then type 0.25.

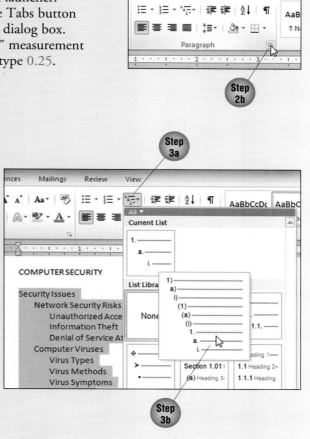

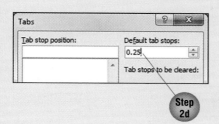

    e. Click OK to close the Tabs dialog box.
3. With the text still selected, apply multilevel numbering by completing the following steps:
    a. Click the Multilevel List button in the Paragraph group in the Home tab.
    b. At the drop-down gallery, click the middle option in the top row of the *List Library* section.
    c. Deselect the text.
4. Save and then print **C18-E03-CSList.docx**.

Defining a Multilevel List

The Multilevel List button drop-down gallery contains predesigned multiple-level numbering options. If the gallery does not contain the type of numbering you want to use, you can define your own. To do this, click the Multilevel List button and then click *Define New Multilevel List*. This displays the Define new Multilevel list dialog box, shown in Figure 18.5. At this dialog box, click a level in the *Click level to modify* option box and then specify the number format, style, position, and alignment. When you define a multilevel list style, you can mix numbers and bullets in the same list.

Define Multilevel List
1. Click Multilevel List button.
2. Click *Define New Multilevel List* at drop-down gallery.
3. Click desired level, number format, and/or position.
4. Click OK.

Figure 18.5 Define New Multilevel List Dialog Box

Click a level in this option box and then specify the number format, style, position, and alignment.

Exercise 18.3B Defining a New Multilevel List   Part 2 of 3

1. With **C18-E03-CSList.docx** open, define a multilevel list by completing the following steps:
   a. Select the paragraphs of text below the title.
   b. Click the Multilevel List button in the Paragraph group in the Home tab.
   c. Click the *Define New Multilevel List* option at the drop-down gallery.
   d. At the Define new Multilevel list dialog box, make sure *1* is selected in the *Click level to modify* list box.
   e. Click the down-pointing arrow at the right of the *Number style for this level* option and then click *A, B, C, …* at the drop-down list.
   f. Click in the *Enter formatting for number* text box, delete any text that displays after *A*, and then type a period (.). (The entry in the text box should now display as *A.*)
   g. Click the up-pointing arrow at the right of the *Aligned at* measurement box until *0.3″* displays in the measurement box.
   h. Click the up-pointing arrow at the right of the *Text indent at* measurement box until *0.6″* displays in the measurement box.

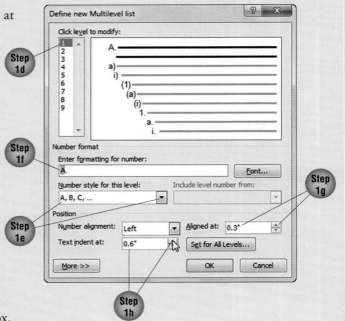

Step 1d

Step 1f

Step 1e

Step 1g

Step 1h

i.   Click *2* in the *Click level to modify* list box.

j.   Click the down-pointing arrow at the right of the *Number style for this level* option and then click *1, 2, 3, …* at the drop-down list.

k.   Click in the *Enter formatting for number* text box, delete any text that displays after the *1*, and then type a period (.).

l.   Click the up-pointing arrow at the right of the *Aligned at* measurement box until *0.6″* displays in the measurement box.

m.   Click the up-pointing arrow at the right of the *Text indent at* measurement box until *0.9″* displays in the measurement box.

n.   Click *3* in the *Click level to modify* list box.

o.   Click the down-pointing arrow at the right of the *Number style for this level* option and then click *a, b, c, …* at the drop-down list.

p.   Make sure *a)* displays in the *Enter formatting for number* text box. (If not, delete any text that displays after the *a* and then type a right parenthesis.)

q.   Click the up-pointing arrow at the right of the *Aligned at* measurement box until *0.9″* displays in the measurement box.

r.   Click the up-pointing arrow at the right of the *Text indent at* measurement box until *1.2″* displays in the measurement box.

s.   Click OK to close the dialog box. (This applies the new multilevel numbering to the selected text.)

t.   Deselect the text.

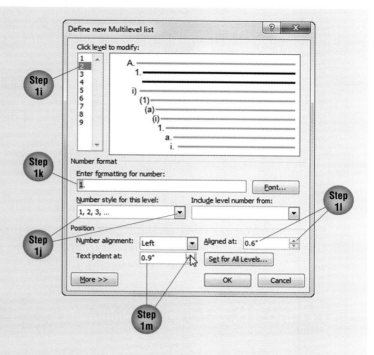

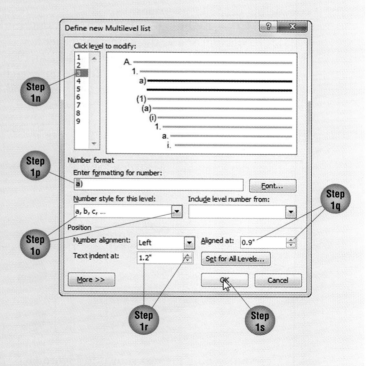

2. Make the following formatting changes to the document:
   a. Apply the Heading 1 style to the title *COMPUTER SECURITY*.
   b. Change the style set to Formal.
   c. Apply the Solstice theme.
3. With the document still open, make the following changes:
   a. Select and then delete *Network Sniffers* in the *Computer Protection* section.
   b. Move the insertion point immediately right of the text *Data Encryption*, press the Enter key, and then type Passwords.
4. Save **C18-E03-CSList.docx**.

Typing a Multilevel List

You can select text and apply a multilevel list to it, or you can apply the list and then type the text. As you type text, press the Tab key to move to the next level or press Shift + Tab to move to the previous level.

Exercise 18.3C   Typing a Multilevel List   Part 3 of 3

---

1. With **C18-E03-CSList.docx** open, type the text shown in Figure 18.6 in a multilevel list by completing the following steps:
   a. Press Ctrl + End to move the insertion point to the end of the document and then press the Enter key.
   b. Type NETWORKS and then press the Enter key twice.
   c. Turn on the multilevel list you defined in Exercise 18.3B by clicking the Multilevel List button and then clicking the list (displays in the *Lists in Current Documents* section of the drop-down gallery).
   d. Type Networking over the Web as shown in Figure 18.6.
   e. Press the Enter key, press the Tab key, and then type Data Transmission as shown in Figure 18.6.

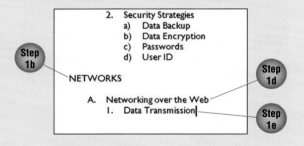
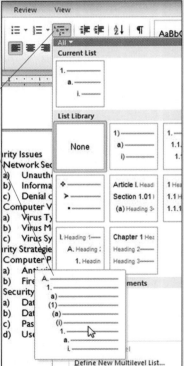

   f. Continue typing the text shown in Figure 18.6. Press the Tab key to indent text to the next level or press Shift + Tab to decrease the indent to the previous level. (The multilevel list will apply letter and number formatting.)
   g. Apply the Heading 1 style to the title *NETWORKS*.
2. Save, print, and then close **C18-E03-CSList.docx**.

Figure 18.6 Exercise 18.3C

NETWORKS

Networking over the Web
     Data Transmission
          Bandwidth
          Analog and Digital Transmission
          Parallel and Serial Transmission
     Communications Media
          Wired Communications Media
          Wireless Communications Media
Network Design
     Network Topologies
          Bus Topologies
          Star Topologies
          Ring Topologies
          Hybrid Topologies
     Network Hardware
          Hubs
          Repeaters
          Routers
          Gateways
          Bridges

Inserting Special Characters

In Chapter 8, you learned how to insert symbols and special characters with options at the Symbol dialog box with the Symbols tab or the Special Characters tab selected. You can also insert special symbols and characters by typing a sequence of characters or by using keyboard shortcuts. Word creates some special characters automatically as you type text.

Inserting Intellectual Property Symbols

Among the symbols you can insert in Word are three intellectual property protection symbols: ©, ™, and ®. Insert the © symbol to identify copyrighted intellectual property, use the ™ symbol to identify a trademark, and use the ® symbol to identify a registered trademark. You can insert these symbols with options at the Symbol dialog box with the Special Characters tab selected, by typing a sequence of characters, or by using a keyboard shortcut. Insert a © symbol by typing (c) or pressing Alt + Ctrl + C, insert a ™ symbol by typing (tm) or pressing Alt + Ctrl + T, and insert a ® symbol by typing (r) or pressing Alt + Ctrl + R.

Exercise 18.4A Inserting Intellectual Property Symbols — Part 1 of 4

1. At a blank document, type the text shown in Figure 18.7. Insert the intellectual property symbols using the sequence of characters or the keyboard shortcuts. To insert (c), (tm), and (r) rather than the actual symbol, type the sequence of characters and then immediately click the Undo button. This changes the symbol back to the sequence of characters.
2. Save the document with the name **C18-E04-SpecialCharacters.**

Figure 18.7 Exercise 18.4A

INTELLECTUAL PROPERTY PROTECTION

A copyright protects original works in areas such as publishing, music, literature, and drama. Use the © symbol to identify copyrighted intellectual property. Create this symbol by typing (c), using the keyboard shortcut Alt + Ctrl + C, or by clicking the symbol in the Symbol dialog box with the Special Characters tab selected.

A trademark identifies a word, symbol, device, or name such as a brand name. Use the ™ symbol to identify a trademarked name or product. Create this symbol by typing (tm), using the keyboard shortcut Alt + Ctrl + T, or by clicking the symbol in the Symbol dialog box with the Special Characters tab selected.

A registered trademark is a trademark that has been registered with the U.S. Patent & Trademark Office. Use the ® symbol to identify a registered trademark. Create this symbol by typing (r), using the keyboard shortcut Alt + Ctrl + R, or by clicking the symbol in the Symbol dialog box with the Special Characters tab selected.

Inserting Hyphens

In Chapter 6, you learned how to use the Hyphenation button in the Page Setup group in the Page Layout tab to hyphenate words automatically or manually. In addition to inserting a regular hyphen in a document, you can insert an optional hyphen and a nonbreaking hyphen, as well as an en dash and an em dash. One method for inserting a regular hyphen is to press the hyphen key on the keyboard and use it to create compound words such as *fresh-looking* and *sister-in-law*. An optional hyphen is one inserted by Word when you automatically hyphenate a document. An optional hyphen will display only if the word falls at the end of the line and the word is divided between lines. Word removes the optional hyphen if the word is not divided between two lines. Optional hyphens display as a hyphen if you turn on the display of nonprinting characters.

You may not want some hyphenated text divided between lines. For example, you may not want a company name such as *Knowles-Myers Corporation* divided between *Knowles* and *Myers* on two lines. To avoid a break like this, you would insert a nonbreaking hyphen by clicking the *Nonbreaking Hyphen* option at the Symbol dialog box with the Special Characters tab selected or with the keyboard shortcut Ctrl + Shift + -.

In a written piece, an em dash is used to indicate a break in a thought or a shift in tone. It is particularly useful in long sentences or sentences with a number of commas. For example, the sentence "The main focus of this document is on general-purpose, single-user computers—personal computers—that enable users to complete a variety of computing tasks." contains two em dashes surrounding the words *personal computers*. To create an em dash in a Word document, type the word, type two hyphens, type the next word, and then press the spacebar. When you press the spacebar, Word automatically converts the two hyphens to an em dash. If automatic formatting of em dashes is turned off, you can insert an em dash with the *Em Dash* option at the Symbol dialog box with the Special Characters tab selected or with the keyboard shortcut Alt + Ctrl + - (on the numeric keypad). (You must use the hyphen key on the numeric keypad rather than the hyphen key that is located between the zero key and the = key.)

An en dash is used in a written piece to indicate inclusive dates, times, or numbers. For example, in the text 9:30–11:00 a.m., the numbers should be separated by an en dash rather than a regular hyphen. Unlike em dashes, Word does not automatically convert a hyphen to an en dash. To create an en dash, click the *En Dash* option at the Symbol dialog box with the Special Characters tab selected or with the keyboard shortcut Ctrl + - (on the numeric keypad).

Exercise 18.4B Inserting Hyphens   Part 2 of 4

1. With **C18-E04-SpecialCharacters.docx** open, press Ctrl + End, press the Enter key, and then type the text in Figure 18.8 with the following specifications:
   a. Type the en dash between the times *9:00–10:30 a.m.* by pressing Ctrl + - (on the numeric keypad).
   b. Create the em dashes before and after *Excel, PowerPoint, and Access* by typing two hyphens.
   c. Insert a nonbreaking hyphen for *Tri-State* by pressing Ctrl + Shift + -.
2. Save **C18-E04-SpecialCharacters.docx**.

Figure 18.8 Exercise 18.4B

SOFTWARE TRAINING

The Microsoft® Office Word training is scheduled for Thursday, March 2, from 9:00–10:30 a.m. Additional training for other applications in the Office suite—Excel, PowerPoint, and Access—will be available during the month of April. Contact the Training Department for additional information. All Tri-State employees are eligible for the training.

QUICK
STEPS

Insert Nonbreaking Spaces
1. Click Insert tab.
2. Click Symbol button, *More Symbols*.
3. Click Special Characters tab.
4. Double-click *Nonbreaking Space* option.
5. Click Close.
OR
Press Ctrl + Shift + spacebar.

Inserting Nonbreaking Spaces

As you type text in a document, Word makes line-end decisions and automatically wraps text to the next line. In some situations, word wrap may break on two separate lines words or phrases that should remain together. To control where text is wrapped to the next line, consider inserting a nonbreaking space between words. Insert a nonbreaking space with the *Nonbreaking Space* option at the Symbol dialog box with the Special Characters tab selected or with the keyboard shortcut Ctrl + Shift + spacebar. If nonprinting characters are turned on, a normal space displays as a dot and a nonbreaking space displays as a degree symbol.

Exercise 18.4C Inserting Nonbreaking Spaces   Part 3 of 4

1. With **C18-E04-SpecialCharacters.docx** open, click the Show/Hide ¶ button in the Paragraph group in the Home tab.
2. Press Ctrl + End, press the Enter key, and then type the text in Figure 18.9. Insert nonbreaking spaces in the keyboard shortcuts by pressing Ctrl + Shift + spacebar before and after the plus symbol in the keyboard shortcuts.
3. Turn off the display of nonprinting characters.
4. Save and then print **C18-E04-SpecialCharacters.docx**.

Figure 18.9 Exercise 18.4C

KEYBOARD SHORTCUTS

Microsoft Word includes a number of keyboard shortcuts you can use to access features and commands. The ScreenTip for some buttons displays the keyboard shortcut you can use to execute the command. For example, hovering the mouse over the Font button causes the ScreenTip to display Ctrl + Shift + F as the keyboard shortcut. Additional Home tab Font group keyboard shortcuts include Ctrl + B to bold text, Ctrl + I to italicize text, and Ctrl + U to underline text. You can also press Ctrl + Shift + + to turn on superscript and press Ctrl + = to turn on subscript.

Finding and Replacing Special Characters

You can use the Find and Replace feature to find special text and replace it with other text. You can also use this feature to find special formatting, characters, or nonprinting elements in a document. To display a list of special characters and nonprinting elements, display the Find and Replace dialog box with either the Find or Replace tab selected, expand the dialog box, and then click the Special button. This displays a pop-up list similar to the one shown in Figure 18.10.

QUICK STEPS

Find and Replace Special Character
1. Click Replace button.
2. Click More button.
3. Click in *Find what* text box.
4. Click Special button.
5. Click desired character.
6. Click in *Replace with* text box.
7. Click Special button.
8. Click desired character.
9. Click *Replace All*.

Figure 18.10 Special Button Pop-up List

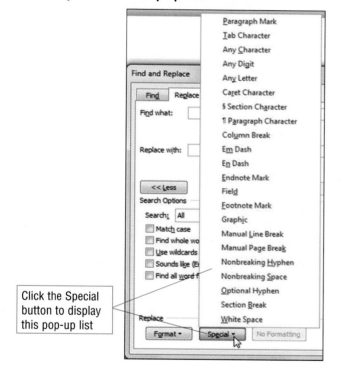

Click the Special button to display this pop-up list

Exercise 18.4D Finding and Replacing Nonbreaking Spaces   Part 4 of 4

1. With **C18-E04-SpecialCharacters.docx** open, find all occurrences of nonbreaking spaces and replace them with regular spaces by completing the following steps:
   a. Press Ctrl + Home to move the insertion point to the beginning of the document.
   b. Click the Replace button in the Editing group in the Home tab.
   c. At the Find and Replace dialog box with the Replace tab selected, click the More button.

d. Click in the *Find what* text box and then click the Special button that displays toward the bottom of the dialog box.

e. At the pop-up list that displays, click Nonbreaking Space. (This inserts ^s in the *Find what* text box.)

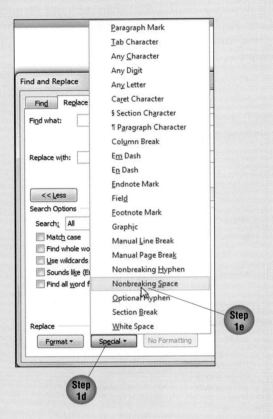

f. Click in the *Replace with* text box (make sure the text box does not contain any text) and then press the spacebar once. (This tells Word to find a nonbreaking space and replace it with a regular space.)

g. Click the Replace All button.

h. At the message telling you that Word completed the search and made the replacements, click OK.

i. Click the Less button.

j. Click the Close button to close the Find and Replace dialog box.

2. Save, print, and then close **C18-E04-SpecialCharacters.docx**.

Chapter Summary

➤ Use the Bullets button to insert bullets before specific paragraphs of text and use the Numbering button to insert numbers.

➤ Insert custom numbers or letters by clicking the Numbering button arrow and then clicking the desired option at the drop-down gallery.

➤ Set the numbering value with options at the Set Numbering Value dialog box. Display this dialog box by clicking the Numbering button arrow and then clicking *Set Numbering Value* at the drop-down gallery.

➤ Define your own numbering format with options at the Define New Number Format dialog box. Display this dialog box by clicking the Numbering button arrow and then clicking *Define New Number Format* at the drop-down gallery.

➤ Insert custom bullets by clicking the Bullets button arrow and then clicking the desired option at the drop-down gallery.

➤ Define your own custom bullet with options at the Define New Bullet dialog box. Display this dialog box by clicking the Bullets button arrow and then clicking *Define New Bullet* at the drop-down gallery.

➤ Apply multilevel numbering to paragraphs of text by clicking the Multilevel List button in the Paragraph group in the Home tab.

➤ Define your own multilevel list numbering format with options at the Define new Multilevel list dialog box. Display this dialog box by clicking the Multilevel List button and then clicking *Define New Multilevel List* at the drop-down gallery.

➤ When you type a multilevel list, press the Tab key to move to the next level and press Shift + Tab to move to the previous level.

➤ Insert special characters and symbols with options at the Symbol dialog box with the Special Characters tab selected, by typing a sequence of characters, or with keyboard shortcuts.

➤ Use the © symbol to identify copyrighted intellectual property, use the ™ symbol to identify a trademark, and use the ® symbol to identify a registered trademark.

➤ You can insert regular, optional, and nonbreaking hyphens in a document, as well as en dashes and em dashes.

➤ Insert a nonbreaking hyphen by clicking the *Nonbreaking Hyphen* option at the Symbol dialog box with the Special Characters tab selected or with the keyboard shortcut Ctrl + Shift + -.

➤ Use an em dash to indicate a break in a thought or a shift in tone in a sentence. To insert an em dash, type a word, type two hyphens, type the next word, and press the spacebar. You can also insert an em dash with the keyboard shortcut Alt + Ctrl + - (on the numeric keypad) or at the Symbol dialog box with the Special Characters tab selected.

➤ Use an en dash to indicate inclusive dates, times, or numbers. To insert an en dash, click the *En Dash* option at the Symbol dialog box with the Special Characters tab selected or with the keyboard shortcut Ctrl + - (on the numeric keypad).

➤ Insert a nonbreaking space between words that you do not want separated on two lines. Insert a nonbreaking space by clicking the *Nonbreaking Space* option at the Symbol dialog box with the Special Characters tab selected or with the keyboard shortcut Ctrl + Shift + spacebar.

➤ Use the Find and Replace feature to find special characters and replace them with other characters or text. Click the Special button at the Find and Replace dialog box to display a pop-up list of special characters.

Commands *Review*

FEATURE	RIBBON TAB, GROUP	BUTTON, OPTION	KEYBOARD SHORTCUT
Numbering	Home, Paragraph		
Bullets	Home, Paragraph		
Multilevel List	Home, Paragraph		
Define New Number Format dialog box	Home, Paragraph	, Define New Number Format	
Define New Bullet dialog box	Home, Paragraph	, Define New Bullet	
Define new Multilevel list dialog box	Home, Paragraph	, Define New Multilevel List	
Symbol dialog box	Insert, Symbols	Ω, More Symbols	
Copyright symbol ©			Alt + Ctrl + C
Trademark symbol ™			Alt + Ctrl + T
Registered symbol ®			Alt + Ctrl + R
Nonbreaking hyphen			Ctrl + Shift + -
Em dash			Alt + Ctrl + - (on numeric keypad)
En dash			Ctrl + - (on numeric keypad)
Nonbreaking space			Ctrl + Shift + spacebar
Find and Replace dialog box with Replace tab selected	Home, Editing	ab↵ac	Ctrl + H

Key Points *Review*

Completion: In the space provided at the right, indicate the correct term, symbol, or command.

1. The Numbering button is located in this group in the Home tab. _____

2. Define your own numbering format with options at this dialog box. _____

3. A bullet that you define at the Define New Bullet dialog box is automatically included in this section in the Bullets button drop-down gallery. _____

4. Click this button to number paragraphs of text at the left margin, first tab, second tab, and so on.

   _____

5. As you type a multilevel list, press these keys to move to the previous level.

   _____

6. Type this sequence of characters on the keyboard to insert a copyright symbol.

   _____

7. This is the keyboard shortcut to insert the ® symbol.

   _____

8. Use this type of hyphen in a sentence to indicate a break in a thought or a shift in tone.

   _____

9. Use this type of hyphen to indicate inclusive dates, times, and numbers.

   _____

10. This is the keyboard shortcut for inserting a nonbreaking space.

    _____

11. Click this button in the expanded Find and Replace dialog box to display a list of special characters.

    _____

Chapter Assessments

Applying Your Skills

Demonstrate your knowledge of features learned in this chapter by completing the following assessments.

Assessment 18.1   Insert Custom Bullets and Numbering in a Technology Document

1. Open **ElecTech.docx** and save the document with the name **C18-A01-ElecTech**.
2. Apply the following formatting to the document.
   a. Apply the Heading 1 style to the title *ELECTRONIC TECHNOLOGY*.
   b. Apply the Heading 2 style to the headings *Technology Information Questions, Technology Timeline: Storage Devices and Media, Information Systems and Commerce* (located on page two), and *Internet* (located on page three).
   c. Change the style set to Formal.
   d. Change the theme to Paper and the theme colors to Flow.
3. Select the questions below the *TECHNOLOGY INFORMATION QUESTIONS* heading and then insert check mark (✔) bullets.
4. Create a computer disk symbol bullet in 14-point font size and then apply the symbol bullet to the six paragraphs of text below the *TECHNOLOGY TIMELINE: STORAGE DEVICES AND MEDIA* heading. **Hint: You can find the disk symbol in the Wingdings font (located in approximately the second row).**
5. Select the paragraphs of text below the heading *INFORMATION SYSTEMS AND COMMERCE*, click the Multilevel List button, and then click the middle option in the top row of the *List Library* section.
6. Select the paragraphs of text below the heading *INTERNET* and then apply the same multilevel list numbering.
7. Save and then print **C18-A01-ElecTech.docx**.
8. Select the paragraphs of text below the heading *INFORMATION SYSTEMS AND COMMERCE* and then define a new multilevel list with the following specifications:
   a. Level 1 that inserts Arabic numbers (1, 2, 3) followed by a period and is aligned at 0 inch and indented at 0.25 inch.
   b. Level 2 that inserts capital letters (A, B, C) followed by a period and is aligned at 0.25 inch and indented at 0.5 inch.

    c. Level 3 that inserts Arabic numbers (1, 2, 3) followed by a right parenthesis and is aligned at 0.5 inch and indented at 0.75 inch.

    d. Make sure the new multilevel list numbering is applied to the selected paragraphs.

9. Select the paragraphs of text below the heading *INTERNET* and then apply the new multilevel list numbering.

10. Save, print, and then close **C18-A01-ElecTech.docx**.

Assessment 18.2   Type a Corporate Report Document with Special Characters

1. At a blank document, type the text shown in Figure 18.11. Insert nonbreaking hyphens in the corporate name (*Perez-Lin-Hyatt*), insert en dashes in the money amount (*$20–25 million*) and the meeting times (in the *Department Meetings*

Figure 18.11 Assessment 18.2

Corporate Report

During 2012, Perez-Lin-Hyatt Industrial invested $28 million on capital expenditures and an additional $20–25 million on research and engineering. All major projects undergo a rigorous financial analysis to ensure they meet all investment return objectives. Employees completed two major projects at Perez-Lin-Hyatt including expansion of Asian and northern Europe markets. Major effort at Perez-Lin-Hyatt centered on development of product line extensions of our Tubular™ and ReedBit™ drill technology. The outlook for 2013 is encouraging. The backlog for our products—an important indicator of current demand—grew to a record $265 million at year-end 2012.

Perez-Lin-Hyatt Industrial Corporate Report©

Department Meetings

Finance: Tuesday, 9:30–11:00 a.m.

Purchasing: Wednesday, 3:00–4:30 p.m.

Training: Thursday, 8:30–9:30 a.m.

Keyboard Shortcuts

Word includes keyboard shortcuts you can use for creating, viewing, and saving documents. Press Ctrl + N to display a new blank document, or press Ctrl + O to open a document. Use the shortcut Ctrl + W to close the currently open document. Additional keyboard shortcuts include pressing Alt + Ctrl + S to split the document window and pressing Alt + Shift + C to remove the document window split.

---

section), insert em dashes around *an important indicator of current demand*, insert the ™ and © symbols correctly, and insert nonbreaking spaces within keyboard shortcuts.

2. Save the document with the name **C18-A02-CorpReport**.
3. Print and then close **C18-A02-CorpReport.docx**.

Expanding Your Skills

Explore additional feature options or use Help to learn a new skill in creating this document.

Assessment 18.3 Create and Insert a Picture Bullet in a Document

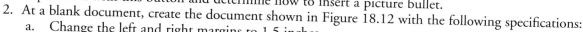

1. In this chapter you learned to insert custom bullets in a document. In addition to symbols and pictures provided by Microsoft, you can also create bullets with your own pictures. Display the Define New Bullet dialog box, click the Picture button, and notice the Import button that displays in the lower left corner of the dialog box. Experiment with this button and determine how to insert a picture bullet.
2. At a blank document, create the document shown in Figure 18.12 with the following specifications:
   a. Change the left and right margins to 1.5 inches.

Figure 18.12 Assessment 18.3

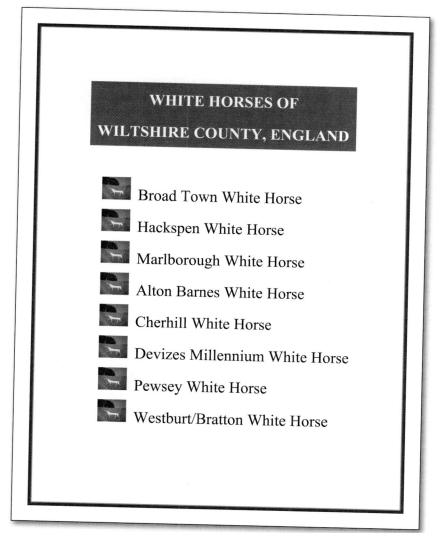

   b. Set the text in 36-point Angsana New. (If this typeface is not available, choose a similar typeface.)

   c. Import as a picture bullet the picture named ***WhiteHorse.jpg*** located in the Chapter18 folder on your storage medium. Apply the bullet to the text as shown in Figure 18.12.

   d. Apply *Olive Green, Accent 3, Darker 50%* shading to the title as shown in the figure and change the title text font color to white.

   e. Insert the page border as shown in the figure. ***Hint: Use the third option from the bottom in the*** **Style** ***list box at the Borders and Shading dialog box with the Page Border tab selected and change the color to*** **Olive Green, Accent 3, Darker 50%**.

   f. Make any other formatting changes so your document appears as shown in Figure 18.12.

3. Save the document and name it **C18-A03-WhiteHorses**.

4. Print and then close the document.

Achieving Signature Status

Take your skills to the next level by completing these more challenging assessments.

Assessment 18.4   Type a Business Letter

1. Open **NSSLtrhd.docx** and then save the document with the name **C18-A04-TrainingLtr**.

2. Type the letter shown in Figure 18.13 with the following specifications:

   a. Insert the current date in place of *(Current date)* in the letter.

   b. Insert the appropriate symbols as shown in the figure.

   c. Insert a nonbreaking space between the words *Mont* and *Tremblant* in the company name.

   d. Insert en dashes between the times in the third column in the table.

   e. Format the table as shown. ***Hint: Apply the*** **Light Grid – Accent 3** ***table style, center the table, and make any other changes so your table appears as shown in Figure 18.13***.

   f. Type your first and last names in place of *(Student Name)* in the letter.

3. Save, print, and then close **C18-A04-TrainingLtr.docx**.

Figure 18.13 Assessment 18.4

Northland Security Systems
3200 North 22nd Street ✦ Springfield ✦ IL ✦ 62102

(Current date)

Ms. Chloë St. Jérôme
Mont Tremblant-Broughton
4500-320 St. Laurent
Montréal, QC H3Y 1C4
CANADA

Dear Ms. St. Jérôme:

Thank you for contracting with Northland Security Systems to provide training to employees at Mont Tremblant-Broughton. As our agreement states, we will be providing the following on-site software training for employees at your company:

Software	Date	Times
Adobe® InDesign	Tuesday, March 6	9:00–11:30 a.m. and 1:00–5:00 p.m.
	Thursday, March 8	9:00–11:30 a.m. and 1:00–3:00 p.m.
Microsoft® Word 2010	Wednesday, March 7	8:00–11:30 a.m. and 1:00–5:00 p.m.
Microsoft® Excel 2010	Tuesday, March 13	8:00–11:30 a.m. and 1:00–3:00 p.m.
	Thursday, March 15	9:00–11:30 a.m. and 1:00–3:00 p.m.
Intuit® QuickBooks	Wednesday, March 14	8:00–11:30 a.m. and 1:00–5:00 p.m.

Our training coordinator, Barbara Goodwin, will contact you this week to confirm the number of employees that will be attending each training session, the training location, and equipment needs. Ms. Goodwin, as well as three instructors, will be staying in Montréal during the two weeks of training. She may contact you for a referral on lodging near your company headquarters.

We look forward to conducting the training sessions and are confident that employees of Mont Tremblant-Broughton will acquire the skills they need to manage the software applications they use on the job. If you need to contact me or Ms. Goodwin, please give us a call at 1-888-555-2200.

Sincerely,

(Student Name)

XX
C18-A04-TrainingLtr.docx

1-888-555-2200 ✦ www.emcp.com/nss

Chapter 19

TUTORIALS

Tutorial 19.1
Customizing Page Numbers
Tutorial 19.2
Customizing Headers and Footers
Tutorial 19.3
Print sections of a document
Tutorial 19.4
Keeping text together

Managing Page Numbers, Headers, and Footers

Performance Objectives

Upon successful completion of Chapter 19, you will be able to:
- Insert, format, and remove page numbers
- Insert, format, edit, and remove headers and footers
- Print sections of a document
- Control widows and orphans and keep text together on a page

As you learned earlier, Word provides predesigned page numbers, headers, and footers you can insert in a document. You can customize page numbers with options at the Page Number Format dialog box, and you can create and edit your own headers and footers with options in the Header & Footer Tools Design tab. In this chapter, you will learn how to customize page numbers, create and customize headers and footers, print sections of a document, and control text flow on pages.

Note: Before beginning computer exercises for this chapter, copy to your storage medium the Chapter19 folder from the CD that accompanies this textbook and then make Chapter19 the active folder.

In this chapter, students will produce the following documents:

Exercise 19.1. C19-E01-CompSecurity.docx
Exercise 19.2. C19-E02-CompComm.docx
Exercise 19.3. C19-E03-EmpHandbook.docx
Exercise 19.4. C19-E04-EmpHandbook.docx
Exercise 19.5. C19-E05-EmpHandbook.docx
Exercise 19.6. C19-E06-EmpHandbook.docx
Exercise 19.7. C19-E07-OnlineShop.docx

Model answers for these exercises are shown on the following pages.

Exercise 19.1
C19-E01-CompSecurity.docx

TABLE OF CONTENTS

SECTION 1: UNAUTHORIZED ACCESS 1

    User IDs and Passwords 1

    System Backdoors 1

    Spoofing 2

    Spyware 2

SECTION 2: INFORMATION THEFT

    Wireless Device Security 3

    Data Browsing 3

i

Page 1

SECTION 1: UNAUTHORIZED ACCESS

Like uncharted wilderness, the Internet lacks borders. This inherent openness is what makes the Internet so valuable and yet so vulnerable. Over its short life, the Internet has grown so quickly that the legal system has not been able to keep pace. The security risks posed by networks and the Internet can be grouped into three categories: unauthorized access, information theft, and denial of service.

Hackers, individuals who gain access to computers and networks illegally, are responsible for most cases of unauthorized access. Hackers tend to exploit sites and programs that have poor security measures in place. However, they also gain access to more challenging sites by using sophisticated programs and strategies. Many hackers claim they hack merely because they like the challenge of trying to defeat security measures. They rarely have a more malicious motive, and they generally do not aim to destroy or damage the sites that they invade. In fact, hackers dislike being identified with those who seek to cause damage. They refer to hackers with malicious or criminal intent as *crackers*.

User IDs and Passwords

To gain entry over the Internet to a secure computer system, most hackers focus on finding a working user ID and password combination. User IDs are easy to come by and are generally not secure information. Sending an email, for example, displays the sender's user ID in the return address, making it very public. The only missing element is the password. Hackers know from experience which passwords are common; they have programs that generate thousands of likely passwords and they try them systematically over a period of hours or days.

System Backdoors

Programmers can sometimes inadvertently aid hackers by providing unintentional entrance to networks and information systems. One such unintentional entrance is a system "backdoor," which is a

1

Page 2

Chapter Nineteen

Page 3

user ID and password that provides the highest level of authorization. Programmers innocently create a "backdoor" in the early days of system development to allow other programmers and team members to access the system to fix problems. Through negligence or by design, the user ID and password are sometimes left behind in the final version of the system. People who know about them can then enter the system, bypassing the security, perhaps years later, when the backdoor has been forgotten.

Spoofing

A sophisticated way to break into a network via the Internet involves spoofing, which is the process of fooling another computer by pretending to send information from a legitimate source. It works by altering the address that the system automatically puts on every message sent. The address is changed to one that the receiving computer is programmed to accept as a trusted source of information.

Spyware

Spyware is a type of software t
alarming technology takes advanta
stranger to witness and record and
occurs. The spy can record activitie
generally requires the user to insta
that random strangers on the Inter
however, someone might be able t
email greeting, for example, the pr
spyware unknowingly.

Page 4

SECTION 2: INFORMATION THEFT

Information can be a company's most valuable possession. Stealing corporate information, a crime included in the category of industrial espionage, is unfortunately both easy to do and difficult to detect. This is due in part to the invisible nature of software and data. If a cracker breaks into a company network and manages to download the company database from the network onto a disk, there is no visible sign to the company that anything is amiss. The original database is still in place, working the same way it always has.

Wireless Device Security

The growing number of wireless devices has created a new opportunity for data theft. Wireless devices such as cameras, Web pho
are inherently less secure than wir
new wireless technologies for han
competition, manufacturers have
faster. Already, viruses are appeari
for these new systems, hackers an
few available security protocols fo
conjunction with the standard for
security features make it more dif
radio waves or infrared signals.

Data Browsing

Data browsing is a less damagi
Workers in many organizations ha

Page 5

about people. Accessing this information without an official reason is against the law. The IRS had a particularly large problem with data browsing in the late 1990s. Some employees were fired and the rest were given specialized training in appropriate conduct.

4

Chapter 1 Computers in Communications

Computers were originally stand-alone devices, incapable of communicating with other computers. This changed in the 1970s and 1980s when the development of special telecommunications hardware and software led to the creation of the first private networks, allowing connected computers to exchange data. Exchanged data took the form of requests for information, replies to requests for information, or instructions on how to run programs stored on the network.

The ability to link computers enables users to communicate and work together efficiently and effectively. Linked computers have become central to the communications industry. They play a vital role in telecommunications, publishing, and news services.

Telecommunications

The industry that provides for communication across distances is called telecommunications. The telephone industry uses computers to switch and route phone calls automatically over telephone lines. In addition to the spoken word, many other kinds of information move over such lines, including faxes and computer data. Data can be sent from computer to computer over telephone lines using a device known as a modem. One kind of data frequently sent by modem is electronic mail, or email, which can be sent from person to person via the Internet or an online service. A more recent innovation in telecommunications is teleconferencing, which allows people in various locations to see and hear one another and thus hold virtual meetings.

Publishing

Just twenty years ago, book manuscripts were typeset mechanically on a typesetting machine and then reproduced on a printing press. Now, anyone who has access to a computer and either a modem or

Exercise 19.2 C19-E02-CompComm.docx

a printer can undertake what has come to be known as electronic publishing. Writers and editors use word processing applications to produce text. Artists and designers use drawing and painting applications to created original graphics, or they use inexpensive scanners to digitize illustrations and photographs (turn them into computer-readable files). Typesetters use personal computers to combine text, illustrations, and photographs. Publishers typically send computer-generated files to printers for production of the film and plates from which books and magazines are printed.

News Services

News providers rely on reporters located worldwide. Reporters use email to send, or upload, their stories to wire services. Increasingly, individuals get daily news reports from online services. News can also be accessed from specific providers, such as the *New York Times* or *USA Today*, via the Internet. One of the most popular Internet sites provides continuously updated weather reports.

Chapter 2 Computers in Entertainment

Possibilities in the television and film industries have soared with computer technology, especially in production. Computer games have captured the public imagination and created enormous growth in the computer game market.

Television and Film

Many of the spectacular graphics and special effects seen on television and in movies today are created with computers. The original *Star Wars* films, for example, relied heavily on hand-constructed models and hand-drawn graphics. Twenty years after the first release of the films, they were re-released with many new special effects, including futuristic cityscape backgrounds, new alien creatures, and new sounds that were created on computers and added to the films by means of computerized video editing. In an article on special effects, Jaclyn McFadden, an industry expert talked about the evolution of computer simulation.

The film *Jurassic Park* brought computer simulation to a new level by combining puppetry and computer animation to simulate realistic looking dinosaurs. *Toy Story*, released in 1996, was the first wholly computer-animated commercial movie.

Software products are available that automatically format scripts of various kinds. Industry analysts predict that the improvements in computer technology will continue to enhance and improve the visual appeal of television and film media.

Home Entertainment

The advent of powerful desktop personal computers has led to the production of home computer games that rival those of arcade machines in complexity. In the 1970s, computer games such as Pong

and Pac-Man captured the public's imagination. Since then, there has been enormous growth in the computer game market. Manufacturers such as Sega and Nintendo produce such games as well as small computer game systems for home use. Typical arcade-style computer games include simulations of boxing, warfare, racing, skiing, and flight.

Other computer games make use of television or of small, independent, hand-held devices. Games are now able to take advantage of three-dimensional graphics that create virtual environments.

Page 1 Document

 Worldwide Enterprises   4/2/2010 11:24 AM

PROBATIONARY PERIODS

Acceptance by an applicant of an offer of employment by an appointing authority and their mutual agreement to the date of hire is known as an appointment.

TYPES OF APPOINTMENTS

New Hire: When you initially accept an appointment, you are considered a new hire. As a new hire, you will be required to serve a probationary period of either six months or one year.

Reemployment: Reemployment is a type of appointment that does not result in a break in service. The following are types of reemployment:

1. Military reemployment: Any remaining portion of a probationary period must be completed upon return to the company.
2. Reemployment of a permanent employee who has been laid off: Completion of a new probationary period is required if you are reemployed in a different class or in a different department.
3. Reemployment due to reclassification of a position to a lower class.
4. Reemployment of seasonal employees.
5. Reemployment due to a permanent disability arising from an injury sustained at work.

Further information on this subject can be obtained by contacting your personnel representative or a representative in the human resources department.

Reinstatement: If you have resigned from company service as a permanent employee in good standing, you may be reinstated to the same or a similar class within a two-year period following termination.

The probationary period following reinstatement may be waived, but you will not be eligible to compete in promotional examinations until you have completed six months of permanent service. You cannot be reinstated to a position that is at grade 20 or above if the position is allocated at a higher grade level than the position you held at the time of termination.

Reappointment: You may be reappointed to a class that you formerly held or to a comparable class if you meet the current minimum qualifications and receive the appointing authority's approval. If you are a probationary employee, you must complete a new probationary period. You cannot be reappointed to a position at grade 20 or above if the position is allocated at a higher level than the position you formerly held.

Demotion: An employee may request or accept a demotion to a position in a class with a lower grade level if the employee meets the minimum qualifications and if the appointing authority approves. You may not demote through non-competitive means to a position at

Student Name   Page | 1   C19-E03-EmpHandbook.docx

Page 2 Document

 Worldwide Enterprises   4/2/2010 11:24 AM

grade 20 or higher if the position is allocated to a higher grade level than the position you currently hold.

Promotion: Promotion is advancement to a vacant position in a class that has a higher grade than the class previously held. As an employee of the company, you may compete in recruitments for promotional openings when you have served six months (full-time equivalent) of consecutive service. When you accept a promotion, you will be required to serve a trial period of either six months or one year. If you fail to attain permanent status in a vacant position to which you were promoted, you shall be restored to your former position.

EMPLOYEE PERFORMANCE

WORK PERFORMANCE STANDARDS

Work performance standards are written statements of the results and/or behavior expected of an employee when his or her job elements are satisfactorily performed under existing working conditions. Each employee in a permanent position must be provided with a current set of work performance standards for his or her position.

PERFORMANCE EVALUATION

If you are serving a six-month (full-time equivalent) probationary period, your supervisor will evaluate your performance at the end of the second and fifth months. If you are completing a one-year (full-time equivalent) probationary period, your evaluations will be conducted at the end of the third, seventh, and eleventh months. You will receive a copy of each performance report. Once you have attained permanent status, your performance will be evaluated annually during the month prior to your pay progression date.

Each evaluation will include a discussion between you and your supervisor to review and clarify goals and methods to achieve them. The evaluation will also include a written report of your progress in the job. Evaluations will be made with reference to established work performance standards.

EMPLOYMENT RECORDS

Your official personnel file is maintained in the human resources department. The human resources department maintains a working file with copies of the documentation in your specific department. Your file includes personnel action documents, mandatory employment forms, your performance evaluations, and documentation of disciplinary action. Your file may include letters of commendation, training certificates, or other work-related documents that you or your supervisor has requested to be included in your file.

COMPENSATION

Student Name   Page | 2   C19-E03-EmpHandbook.docx

Page 3 Document

 Worldwide Enterprises   4/2/2010 11:24 AM

RATE OF PAY

The compensation schedule for employees consists of pay ranges for each grade. Within each grade are ten steps. As an employee of the company, your pay will be set at one of the steps within the grade for the class to which you are appointed. Your pay is further determined by the compensation schedule applicable to your participation in the company's retirement system.

DIRECT DEPOSIT OPTION

You have the option to forward your paycheck directly to a checking or savings account in a bank of your choice. The company payroll center representative can provide you with a direct deposit authorization card.

PAY PROGRESSION

You will receive a merit salary increase annually on your pay progression date if your last performance evaluation was standard or better, and you have not reached the top step in your grade. The maximum merit salary increase is an adjustment of one step annually.

If your date of promotion coincides with your pay progression date, the merit salary increase will be computed first and the promotional increase applied to your new pay rate. If you continue to do satisfactory work, you will remain eligible for annual merit salary increases until you have reached the maximum step within your grade. In addition to merit salary increases, your salary may be adjusted by general salary increases granted by the company.

OVERTIME

Under state law, overtime is any time worked in excess of eight hours a day, eight hours in a 16-hour period, or 40 hours in a week. Employees who choose and are approved for variable/innovative workday schedules earn overtime after 40 hours in a week.

Cash payment is the principal method of compensation for overtime. Payments are computed based on the employee/employer-paid salary schedule. Agreements may be reached with your employer to provide for compensatory time off in lieu of cash payments. Compensatory time must be taken within a reasonable time after accrual at the direction of the appointing authority. If you request compensatory time off and give at least two weeks' notice, it cannot be unreasonably denied.

LONGEVITY PAY

When you have completed eight years of continuous service and have standard or better performance, you will be entitled to longevity pay based on a longevity chart. (Click to display Longevity Schedule.)

Student Name   Page | 3   C19-E03-EmpHandbook.docx

Page 4 Document

 Worldwide Enterprises   4/2/2010 11:24 AM

Eligible full-time or part-time employees who work less than full-time for a portion of the 6-month qualifying period are entitled to a prorated amount based on the semi-annual payment. Longevity payments are issued in July and December.

PAYMENT FOR HOLIDAYS

Nonexempt employees are entitled to receive payment for eleven holidays per year when they are in "paid status" during any portion of the shift immediately preceding the holiday. In addition, a nonexempt employee who works on a holiday is entitled to earn time and one-half cash payment or time and one-half compensatory time for the hours worked on the holiday. Exempt employees who work on a holiday do not receive additional compensation, but may have their schedule adjusted during the week in which the holiday occurs or in a subsequent week to recognize the holiday or additional time worked.

SHIFT DIFFERENTIAL

Shift differential is an adjustment in pay equivalent to an additional 5 percent of an employee's normal rate of pay. To qualify, a nonexempt employee must work in a unit requiring multiple shifts in a 24-hour period and be assigned to a period of work of at least 8 hours of which at least four hours fall between 6:00 p.m. and 7:00 a.m. Employees working a qualifying shift that is reduced due to daylight savings time will still receive shift differential pay for that shift.

Student Name   Page | 4   C19-E03-EmpHandbook.docx

Exercise 19.3 C19-E03-EmpHandbook.docx   Page 1

Page 2

Page 3

Page 4

Model Answers

Page 1

PROBATIONARY PERIODS

Acceptance by an applicant of an offer of employment by an appointing authority and their mutual agreement to the date of hire is known as an appointment.

TYPES OF APPOINTMENTS

New Hire: When you initially accept an appointment, you are considered a new hire. As a new hire, you will be required to serve a probationary period of either six months or one year.

Reemployment: Reemployment is a type of appointment that does not result in a break in service. The following are types of reemployment:

1. Military reemployment: Any remaining portion of a probationary period must be completed upon return to the company.
2. Reemployment of a permanent employee who has been laid off: Completion of a new probationary period is required if you are reemployed in a different class or in a different department.
3. Reemployment due to reclassification of a position to a lower class.
4. Reemployment of seasonal employees.
5. Reemployment due to a permanent disability arising from an injury sustained at work.

Further information on this subject can be obtained by contacting your personnel representative or a representative in the human resources department.

Reinstatement: If you have resigned from company service as a permanent employee in good standing, you may be reinstated to the same or a similar class within a two-year period following termination.

The probationary period following reinstatement may be waived, but you will not be eligible to compete in promotional examinations until you have completed six months of permanent service. You cannot be reinstated to a position that is at grade 20 or above if the position is allocated at a higher grade level than the position you held at the time of termination.

Reappointment: You may be reappointed to a class that you formerly held or to a comparable class if you meet the current minimum qualifications and receive the appointing authority's approval. If you are a probationary employee, you must complete a new probationary period. You cannot be reappointed to a position at grade 20 or above if the position is allocated at a higher level than the position you formerly held.

Demotion: An employee may request or accept a demotion to a position in a class with a lower grade level if the employee meets the minimum qualifications and if the appointing authority approves. You may not demote through non-competitive means to a position at

Page 2

grade 20 or higher if the position is allocated to a higher grade level than the position you currently hold.

Promotion: Promotion is advancement to a vacant position in a class that has a higher grade than the class previously held. As an employee of the company, you may compete in recruitments for promotional openings when you have served six months (full-time equivalent) of consecutive service. When you accept a promotion, you will be required to serve a trial period of either six months or one year. If you fail to attain permanent status in a vacant position to which you were promoted, you shall be restored to your former position.

EMPLOYEE PERFORMANCE

WORK PERFORMANCE STANDARDS

Work performance standards are written statements of the results and/or behavior expected of an employee when his or her job elements are satisfactorily performed under existing working conditions. Each employee in a permanent position must be provided with a current set of work performance standards for his or her position.

PERFORMANCE EVALUATION

If you are serving a six-month (full-time equivalent) probationary period, your supervisor will evaluate your performance at the end of the second and fifth months. If you are completing a one-year (full-time equivalent) probationary period, your evaluations will be conducted at the end of the third, seventh, and eleventh months. You will receive a copy of each performance report. Once you have attained permanent status, your performance will be evaluated annually during the month prior to your pay progression date.

Each evaluation will include a discussion between you and your supervisor to review and clarify goals and methods to achieve them. The evaluation will also include a written report of your progress in the job. Evaluations will be made with reference to established work performance standards.

EMPLOYMENT RECORDS

Your official personnel file is maintained in the human resources department. The human resources department maintains a working file with copies of the documentation in your specific department. Your file includes personnel action documents, mandatory employment forms, your performance evaluations, and documentation of disciplinary action. Your file may include letters of commendation, training certificates, or other work-related documents that you or your supervisor has requested to be included in your file.

COMPENSATION

Page 3

RATE OF PAY

The compensation schedule for employees consists of pay ranges for each grade. Within each grade are ten steps. As an employee of the company, your pay will be set at one of the steps within the grade for the class to which you are appointed. Your pay is further determined by the compensation schedule applicable to your participation in the company's retirement system.

DIRECT DEPOSIT OPTION

You have the option to forward your paycheck directly to a checking or savings account in a bank of your choice. The company payroll center representative can provide you with a direct deposit authorization card.

PAY PROGRESSION

You will receive a merit salary increase annually on your pay progression date if your last performance evaluation was standard or better, and you have not reached the top step in your grade. The maximum merit salary increase is an adjustment of one step annually.

If your date of promotion coincides with your pay progression date, the merit salary increase will be computed first and the promotional increase applied to your new pay rate. If you continue to do satisfactory work, you will remain eligible for annual merit salary increases until you have reached the maximum step within your grade. In addition to merit salary increases, your salary may be adjusted by general salary increases granted by the company.

OVERTIME

Under state law, overtime is any time worked in excess of eight hours a day, eight hours in a 16-hour period, or 40 hours in a week. Employees who choose and are approved for variable/innovative workday schedules earn overtime after 40 hours in a week.

Cash payment is the principal method of compensation for overtime. Payments are computed based on the employee/employer-paid salary schedule. Agreements may be reached with your employer to provide for compensatory time off in lieu of cash payments. Compensatory time must be taken within a reasonable time after accrual at the direction of the appointing authority. If you request compensatory time off and give at least two weeks' notice, it cannot be unreasonably denied.

LONGEVITY PAY

When you have completed eight years of continuous service and have standard or better performance, you will be entitled to longevity pay based on a longevity chart. (Click to display Longevity Schedule.)

Page 4

Eligible full-time or part-time employees who work less than full-time for a portion of the 6-month qualifying period are entitled to a prorated amount based on the semi-annual payment. Longevity payments are issued in July and December.

PAYMENT FOR HOLIDAYS

Nonexempt employees are entitled to receive payment for eleven holidays per year when they are in "paid status" during any portion of the shift immediately preceding the holiday. In addition, a nonexempt employee who works on a holiday is entitled to earn time and one-half cash payment or time and one-half compensatory time for the hours worked on the holiday. Exempt employees who work on a holiday do not receive additional compensation, but may have their schedule adjusted during the week in which the holiday occurs or in a subsequent week to recognize the holiday or additional time worked.

SHIFT DIFFERENTIAL

Shift differential is an adjustment in pay equivalent to an additional 5 percent of an employee's normal rate of pay. To qualify, a nonexempt employee must work in a unit requiring multiple shifts in a 24-hour period and be assigned to a period of work of at least 8 hours of which at least four hours fall between 6:00 p.m. and 7:00 a.m. Employees working a qualifying shift that is reduced due to daylight savings time will still receive shift differential pay for that shift.

PROBATIONARY PERIODS

Acceptance by an applicant of an offer of employment by an appointing authority and their mutual agreement to the date of hire is known as an appointment.

TYPES OF APPOINTMENTS

New Hire: When you initially accept an appointment, you are considered a new hire. As a new hire, you will be required to serve a probationary period of either six months or one year.

Reemployment: Reemployment is a type of appointment that does not result in a break in service. The following are types of reemployment:

1. Military reemployment: Any remaining portion of a probationary period must be completed upon return to the company.
2. Reemployment of a permanent employee who has been laid off: Completion of a new probationary period is required if you are reemployed in a different class or in a different department.
3. Reemployment due to reclassification of a position to a lower class.
4. Reemployment of seasonal employees.
5. Reemployment due to a permanent disability arising from an injury sustained at work.

Further information on this subject can be obtained by contacting your personnel representative or a representative in the human resources department.

Reinstatement: If you have resigned from company service as a permanent employee in good standing, you may be reinstated to the same or a similar class within a two-year period following termination.

The probationary period following reinstatement may be waived, but you will not be eligible to compete in promotional examinations until you have completed six months of permanent service. You cannot be reinstated to a position that is at grade 20 or above if the position is allocated at a higher grade level than the position you held at the time of termination.

Reappointment: You may be reappointed to a class that you formerly held or to a comparable class if you meet the current minimum qualifications and receive the appointing authority's approval. If you are a probationary employee, you must complete a new probationary period. You cannot be reappointed to a position at grade 20 or above if the position is allocated at a higher level than the position you formerly held.

Demotion: An employee may request or accept a demotion to a position in a class with a lower grade level if the employee meets the minimum qualifications and if the appointing authority approves. You may not demote through non-competitive means to a position at

---

grade 20 or higher if the position is allocated to a higher grade level than the position you currently hold.

Promotion: Promotion is advancement to a vacant position in a class that has a higher grade than the class previously held. As an employee of the company, you may compete in recruitments for promotional openings when you have served six months (full-time equivalent) of consecutive service. When you accept a promotion, you will be required to serve a trial period of either six months or one year. If you fail to attain permanent status in a vacant position to which you were promoted, you shall be restored to your former position.

EMPLOYEE PERFORMANCE

WORK PERFORMANCE STANDARDS

Work performance standards are written statements of the results and/or behavior expected of an employee when his or her job elements are satisfactorily performed under existing working conditions. Each employee in a permanent position must be provided with a current set of work performance standards for his or her position.

PERFORMANCE EVALUATION

If you are serving a six-month (full-time equivalent) probationary period, your supervisor will evaluate your performance at the end of the second and fifth months. If you are completing a one-year (full-time equivalent) probationary period, your evaluations will be conducted at the end of the third, seventh, and eleventh months. You will receive a copy of each performance report. Once you have attained permanent status, your performance will be evaluated annually during the month prior to your pay progression date.

Each evaluation will include a discussion between you and your supervisor to review and clarify goals and methods to achieve them. The evaluation will also include a written report of your progress in the job. Evaluations will be made with reference to established work performance standards.

EMPLOYMENT RECORDS

Your official personnel file is maintained in the human resources department. The human resources department maintains a working file with copies of the documentation in your specific department. Your file includes personnel action documents, mandatory employment forms, your performance evaluations, and documentation of disciplinary action. Your file may include letters of commendation, training certificates, or other work-related documents that you or your supervisor has requested to be included in your file.

COMPENSATION

Model Answers

RATE OF PAY

The compensation schedule for employees consists of pay ranges for each grade. Within each grade are ten steps. As an employee of the company, your pay will be set at one of the steps within the grade for the class to which you are appointed. Your pay is further determined by the compensation schedule applicable to your participation in the company's retirement system.

DIRECT DEPOSIT OPTION

You have the option to forward your paycheck directly to a checking or savings account in a bank of your choice. The company payroll center representative can provide you with a direct deposit authorization card.

PAY PROGRESSION

You will receive a merit salary increase annually on your pay progression date if your last performance evaluation was standard or better, and you have not reached the top step in your grade. The maximum merit salary increase is an adjustment of one step annually.

If your date of promotion coincides with your pay progression date, the merit salary increase will be computed first and the promotional increase applied to your new pay rate. If you continue to do satisfactory work, you will remain eligible for annual merit salary increases until you have reached the maximum step within your grade. In addition to merit salary increases, your salary may be adjusted by general salary increases granted by the company.

OVERTIME

Under state law, overtime is any time worked in excess of eight hours a day, eight hours in a 16-hour period, or 40 hours in a week. Employees who choose and are approved for variable/innovative workday schedules earn overtime after 40 hours in a week.

Cash payment is the principal method of compensation for overtime. Payments are computed based on the employee/employer-paid salary schedule. Agreements may be reached with your employer to provide for compensatory time off in lieu of cash payments. Compensatory time must be taken within a reasonable time after accrual at the direction of the appointing authority. If you request compensatory time off and give at least two weeks' notice, it cannot be unreasonably denied.

LONGEVITY PAY

When you have completed eight years of continuous service and have standard or better performance, you will be entitled to longevity pay based on a longevity chart. (Click to display Longevity Schedule.)

Eligible full-time or part-time employees who work less than full-time for a portion of the 6-month qualifying period are entitled to a prorated amount based on the semi-annual payment. Longevity payments are issued in July and December.

PAYMENT FOR HOLIDAYS

Nonexempt employees are entitled to receive payment for eleven holidays per year when they are in "paid status" during any portion of the shift immediately preceding the holiday. In addition, a nonexempt employee who works on a holiday is entitled to earn time and one-half cash payment or time and one-half compensatory time for the hours worked on the holiday. Exempt employees who work on a holiday do not receive additional compensation, but may have their schedule adjusted during the week in which the holiday occurs or in a subsequent week to recognize the holiday or additional time worked.

SHIFT DIFFERENTIAL

Shift differential is an adjustment in pay equivalent to an additional 5 percent of an employee's normal rate of pay. To qualify, a nonexempt employee must work in a unit requiring multiple shifts in a 24-hour period and be assigned to a period of work of at least 8 hours of which at least four hours fall between 6:00 p.m. and 7:00 a.m. Employees working a qualifying shift that is reduced due to daylight savings time will still receive shift differential pay for that shift.

Exercise 19.6

C19-E06-EmpHandbook.docx

PROBATIONARY PERIODS

Acceptance by an applicant of an offer of employment by an appointing authority and their mutual agreement to the date of hire is known as an appointment.

TYPES OF APPOINTMENTS

New Hire: When you initially accept an appointment, you are considered a new hire. As a new hire, you will be required to serve a probationary period of either six months or one year.

Reemployment: Reemployment is a type of appointment that does not result in a break in service. The following are types of reemployment:

1. Military reemployment: Any remaining portion of a probationary period must be completed upon return to the company.
2. Reemployment of a permanent employee who has been laid off: Completion of a new probationary period is required if you are reemployed in a different class or in a different department.
3. Reemployment due to reclassification of a position to a lower class.
4. Reemployment of seasonal employees.
5. Reemployment due to a permanent disability arising from an injury sustained at work.

Further information on this subject can be obtained by contacting your personnel representative or a representative in the human resources department.

Reinstatement: If you have resigned from company service as a permanent employee in good standing, you may be reinstated to the same or a similar class within a two-year period following termination.

The probationary period following reinstatement may be waived, but you will not be eligible to compete in promotional examinations until you have completed six months of permanent service. You cannot be reinstated to a position that is at grade 20 or above if the position is allocated at a higher grade level than the position you held at the time of termination.

Reappointment: You may be reappointed to a class that you formerly held or to a comparable class if you meet the current minimum qualifications and receive the appointing authority's approval. If you are a probationary employee, you must complete a new probationary period. You cannot be reappointed to a position at ...sition is allocated at a higher level than the position you

Page 1

Page 1

Demotion: An employee may request or accept a demotion to a position in a class with a lower grade level if the employee meets the minimum qualifications and if the appointing authority approves. You may not demote through non-competitive means to a position at grade 20 or higher if the position is allocated to a higher grade level than the position you currently hold.

Promotion: Promotion is advancement to a vacant position in a class that has a higher grade than the class previously held. As an employee of the company, you may compete in recruitments for promotional openings when you have served six months (full-time equivalent) of consecutive service. When you accept a promotion, you will be required to serve a trial period of either six months or one year. If you fail to attain permanent status in a vacant position to which you were promoted, you shall be restored to your former position.

Section 1   Page 2

Page 2

Page 3

EMPLOYEE PERFORMANCE

WORK PERFORMANCE STANDARDS

Work performance standards are written statements of the results and/or behavior expected of an employee when his or her job elements are satisfactorily performed under existing working conditions. Each employee in a permanent position must be provided with a current set of work performance standards for his or her position.

PERFORMANCE EVALUATION

If you are serving a six-month (full-time equivalent) probationary period, your supervisor will evaluate your performance at the end of the second and fifth months. If you are completing a one-year (full-time equivalent) probationary period, your evaluations will be conducted at the end of the third, seventh, and eleventh months. You will receive a copy of each performance report. Once you have attained permanent status, your performance will be evaluated annually during the month prior to your pay progressi...

Each evaluation will include...
and clarify goals and metho...
written report of your prog...
established work performa...

Your official personnel file...
human resources departme...
documentation in your spe...
documents, mandatory em...
documentation of disciplina...
training certificates, or othe...
requested to be included i...

Section 2

Page 4

COMPENSATION

RATE OF PAY

The compensation schedule for employees consists of pay ranges for each grade. Within each grade are ten steps. As an employee of the company, your pay will be set at one of the steps within the grade for the class to which you are appointed. Your pay is further determined by the compensation schedule applicable to your participation in the company's retirement system.

DIRECT DEPOSIT OPTION

You have the option to forward your paycheck directly to a checking or savings account in a bank of your choice. The company payroll center representative can provide you with a direct deposit authorization card.

PAY PROGRESSION

You will receive a merit sal...
your last performance eval...
the top step in your grade....
one step annually.

If your date of promotion c...
increase will be computed...
pay rate. If you continue to...
merit salary increases until...
In addition to merit salary i...
increases granted by the c...

Under state law, overtime i...
hours in a 16-hour period, ...
approved for variable/inno...
a week.

Cash payment is the princi...
computed based on the em...
be reached with your empl...
payments. Compensatory t...
at the direction of the appo...
give at least two weeks' no...

Section 3

Page 5

LONGEVITY PAY

When you have completed eight years of continuous service and have standard or better performance, you will be entitled to longevity pay based on a longevity chart. (Click to display Longevity Schedule.)

Eligible full-time or part-time employees who work less than full-time for a portion of the 6-month qualifying period are entitled to a prorated amount based on the semi-annual payment. Longevity payments are issued in July and December.

PAYMENT FOR HOLIDAYS

Nonexempt employees are entitled to receive payment for eleven holidays per year when they are in "paid status" during any portion of the shift immediately preceding the holiday. In addition, a nonexempt employee who works on a holiday is entitled to earn time and one-half cash payment or time and one-half compensatory time for the hours worked on the holiday. Exempt employees who work on a holiday do not receive additional compensation, but may have their schedule adjusted during the week in which the holiday occurs or in a subsequent week to recognize the holiday or additional time worked.

SHIFT DIFFERENTIAL

Shift differential is an adjustment in pay equivalent to an additional 5 percent of an employee's normal rate of pay. To qualify, a nonexempt employee must work in a unit requiring multiple shifts in a 24-hour period and be assigned to a period of work of at least 8 hours of which at least four hours fall between 6:00 p.m. and 7:00 a.m. Employees working a qualifying shift that is reduced due to daylight savings time will still receive shift differential pay for that shift.

Section 3

Page 2

ONLINE SHOPPING

Online shopping, also called electronic shopping or e-shopping, is shopping that involves the use of a computer, modem, browser, and the Internet to locate, examine, select, and pay for products.

Many businesses encourage consumers to shop online because it saves employee time, thus reducing staffing needs and saving money for the company. For example, some major airlines offer special discounts to travelers who purchase their tickets over the Internet, and most are eliminating paper tickets altogether.

ADVANTAGES OF ONLINE SHOPPING

For the consumer, online shoppi[ng]
methods. These advantages inclu[de]

- More product informatio[n]
  wide variety of products,
- Ease of comparison shopp[ing]
  similar stores and locate t[he]
- Convenience. With e-shop[ping]
  you want from the privac[y]
- Greater selection. Becaus[e]
  offer you an almost unlim[ited]

Like brick-and-mortar superstor[es]
candy bars to household applian[ces]
tailer superstores have proved e[s]

When shopping malls were intro[duced]
of being able to shop in a wide va[riety]
concept, an online shopping mall
businesses, in fact, do not have i[n]
only at an online shopping mall.

C19-E07-OnlineShop.docx

Page 1

ONLINE SHOPPING VENUES

Just as consumers can visit a variety of brick-and-mortar retail outlets, such as stores and shopping malls, Internet shoppers can browse several types of online shopping venues, including online stores, superstores, and shopping malls.

ONLINE STORES

An online store, also called a virtual store, is a seller's website where customers can view and purchase a merchant's products and services. The site, or storefront, groups its products or services in categories that link to a list of merchandise within each category. The user clicks a desired category to view pictures, descriptions, and prices of available products.

C19-E07-OnlineShop.docx

Page 2

ONLINE SHOPPING SAFETY TIPS

The number one concern consumers have about shopping online is security. The truth, however, is that shopping online is safe and secure if you know what to look for. Following these guidelines can help you avoid trouble.

- Never provide your social security number.
- Find out the privacy policy of shopping sites before you buy.
- Keep current on the latest Internet scams.
- Look for sites that follow privacy rules from a privacy watchdog such as TRUSTe.
- Answer only the minimum questions when filling out forms.
- Only buy at secure sites.

C19-E07-OnlineShop.docx   Page 3

Page 3

Customizing Page Numbers

In Chapter 7, you learned to use the Page Number button in the Header & Footer group in the Insert tab to insert page numbers in a document. You inserted the numbers by clicking the Page Number button, pointing to the desired position on the page at the drop-down list, and then clicking a predesigned page number option. You removed page numbering from a document by clicking the Page Number button and then clicking the *Remove Page Numbers* option at the drop-down list.

When you insert page numbers, Word inserts Arabic numbers (1, 2, 3, and so on) by default and numbers pages sequentially beginning with number 1. You can customize these default settings with options at the Page Number Format dialog box, shown in Figure 19.1. To display this dialog box, click the Insert tab, click the Page Number button in the Header & Footer group, and then click *Format Page Numbers* at the drop-down list.

QUICK STEPS

Insert Page Numbers
1. Click Insert tab.
2. Click Page Number button.
3. Point to desired position.
4. Click desired predesigned page number option.

Remove Page Numbers
1. Click Insert tab.
2. Click Page Number button.
3. Click *Remove Page Numbers* at drop-down list.

Page Number

Figure 19.1 Page Number Format Dialog Box

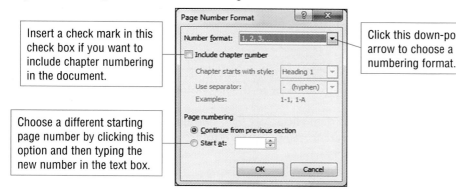

Insert a check mark in this check box if you want to include chapter numbering in the document.

Choose a different starting page number by clicking this option and then typing the new number in the text box.

Click this down-pointing arrow to choose a numbering format.

Click the *Number format* option in the Page Number Format dialog box to change numbering from Arabic numbers to one of the following options: Arabic numbers preceded and followed by hyphens (- 1 -, - 2 -, - 3 -, and so on), lowercase letters (a, b, c, and so on), uppercase letters (A, B, C, and so on), lowercase Roman numerals (i, ii, iii, and so on), or uppercase Roman numerals (I, II, III, and so on).

By default, page numbering begins with 1 and continues sequentially from 1 through all of the pages and sections in a document. You can change the beginning page number with the *Start at* option at the Page Number Format dialog box. To do this, click the *Start at* option and then type the desired beginning page number in the text box.

1. Open **CompSecurity.docx** and save the document with the name **C19-E01-CompSecurity**.
2. Insert section breaks that begin new pages by completing the following steps:

   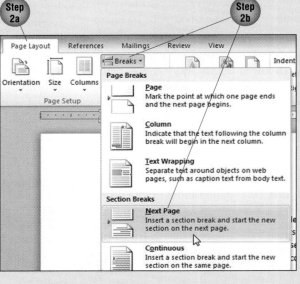

   a. With the insertion point positioned at the beginning of the *SECTION 1: UNAUTHORIZED ACCESS* title, click the Page Layout tab.
   b. Click the Breaks button in the Page Setup group and then click *Next Page* in the *Section Breaks* section of the drop-down list.
   c. Move the insertion point to the beginning of the title *SECTION 2: INFORMATION THEFT*.
   d. Click the Breaks button in the Page Setup group and then click *Next Page* in the *Section Breaks* section of the drop-down list.
3. Insert a file by completing the following steps:
   a. Press Ctrl + Home to move the insertion point to the beginning of the document.
   b. Click the Insert tab.
   c. Click the Object button arrow and then click *Text from File* at the drop-down list.
   d. At the Insert File dialog box, navigate to the Chapter19 folder and then double-click **TableofContents.docx**.
4. Make the following changes to the document:
   a. Apply the Heading 1 style to the following titles in the body of the report (not the titles in the Table of Contents):

      TABLE OF CONTENTS
      SECTION 1: UNAUTHORIZED ACCESS
      SECTION 2: INFORMATION THEFT
   b. Apply the Heading 2 style to the following headings in the body of the report (not the headings in the Table of Contents):

      User IDs and Passwords
      System Backdoors
      Spoofing
      Spyware
      Wireless Device Security
      Data Browsing

   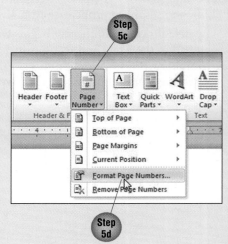

   c. Change the style set to Manuscript.
5. Insert lowercase Roman numeral page numbering for the table of contents page by completing the following steps:
   a. Press Ctrl + Home.
   b. Click the Insert tab.
   c. Click the Page Number button in the Header & Footer group.
   d. Click *Format Page Numbers* at the drop-down list.

e. At the Page Number Format dialog box, click the down-pointing arrow at the right of the *Number format* option and then click *i, ii, iii, …* at the drop-down list.

f. Click OK to close the dialog box.

g. Click the Page Number button in the Header & Footer group, point to *Bottom of Page*, and then click the *Plain Number 2* option at the side menu.

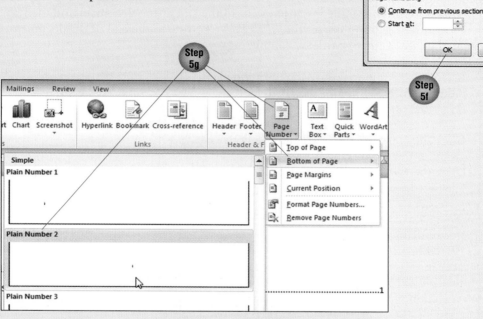

6. Start numbering beginning with 1 by completing the following steps:

   a. Double-click in the document to make the document active.

   b. Position the insertion point on any character in the title *SECTION 1: UNAUTHORIZED ACCESS* (located on page two).

   c. Click the Insert tab.

   d. Click the Page Number button in the Header & Footer group and then click *Format Page Numbers* at the drop-down list.

   e. At the Page Number Format dialog box, click the *Start at* option in the *Page numbering* section. (This inserts a number 1 in the *Start at* text box.)

   f. Click OK to close the dialog box.

7. Save, print, and then close **C19-E01-CompSecurity.docx.**

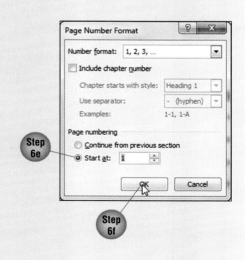

You can number chapters in a document with an option at the Multilevel List button drop-down list in the Home tab and then apply chapter numbering to the document. To do this, click the *Include chapter number* check box at the Page Number Format dialog box and then specify with what style the chapter starts and what separator you want to use for the page number.

Exercise 19.2 Inserting Chapter Numbering   Part 1 of 1

1. Open **CompComm.docx** and save the document with the name **C19-E02-CompComm**.
2. Press Ctrl + End to move the insertion point to the end of the document and then select and delete text from the beginning of the *REFERENCES* title to the end of the document.
3. Change the case of the first title by completing the following steps:
   a. Press Ctrl + Home to move the insertion point to the beginning of the document.
   b. Select the title *COMPUTERS IN COMMUNICATIONS*.
   c. Click the Change Case button in the Font group in the Home tab.
   d. Click the *Capitalize Each Word* option.
   e. Change the word *In* to *in*.
4. Complete steps similar to those in Step 3 to change the case of the other title in the document, *COMPUTERS IN ENTERTAINMENT*.
5. Move the insertion point to the beginning of the title *Computers in Entertainment* and then insert a section break that begins a new page.
6. Apply the Heading 1 style to the two titles in the document and apply the Heading 2 style to the five headings in the document.
7. Change the style set to Manuscript.
8. Apply chapter multilevel list numbering by completing the following steps:
   a. Press Ctrl + Home to move the insertion point to the beginning of the document.
   b. If necessary, click the Home tab.
   c. Click the Multilevel List button in the Paragraph group.
   d. Click the last option in the *List Library* section of the drop-down gallery. (This inserts *Chapter 1* before the first title and *Chapter 2* before the second title.)
9. Insert chapter numbering in the document by completing the following steps:
   a. With the insertion point positioned at the beginning of the document, click the Insert tab.

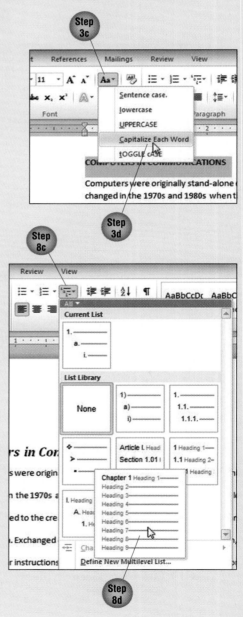

b. Click the Page Number button in the Header & Footer group and then click *Format Page Numbers* at the drop-down list.

c. At the Page Number Format dialog box, click the *Include chapter number* check box to insert a check mark.

d. Click OK.

e. Click the Page Number button in the Header & Footer group, point to *Bottom of Page*, and then click the *Plain Number 2* option.

f. Double-click in the document.

g. Move the insertion point so it is positioned on any character in the second title *Chapter 2 Computers in Entertainment*.

h. Click the Insert tab.

i. Click the Page Number button in the Header & Footer group and then click *Format Page Numbers*.

j. At the Page Number Format dialog box, click the *Include chapter number* check box to insert a check mark.

k. Click OK to close the dialog box.

10. Scroll through the document and notice the chapter numbering. (The page number for the first page displays as *1-1* indicating page 1 of chapter 1. The numbering preceding the page number changes to *2* for the pages in the chapter 2 section.)

11. Save, print, and then close **C19-E02-CompComm.docx**.

Inserting Headers and Footers

In Chapter 7, you learned to insert predesigned headers with the Header button in the Insert tab and predesigned footers with the Footer button. If the predesigned headers and footers provided by Word do not meet your needs, you can create your own. To create a header, click the Insert tab, click the Header button in the Header & Footer group, and then click *Edit Header* at the drop-down list. This displays a Header pane in the document and also displays the Header & Footer Tools Design tab, shown in Figure 19.2. With options in this tab you can insert elements such as page numbers, pictures, and clip art; navigate to other headers or footers in the document; and position headers and footers on different pages in a document.

Header   Footer

Figure 19.2 Header & Footer Tools Design Tab

Inserting Elements in Headers and Footers

Use buttons in the Insert group in the Header & Footer Tools Design tab to insert elements in the header or footer such as the date and time, Quick Parts, pictures, and clip art images. Click the Date & Time button, and the Date and Time dialog box displays with options for inserting the current date as well as the current time. Click the Quick Parts button, and a drop-down list displays with options for inserting predesigned building blocks and fields. Click the Picture button, and the Insert Picture dialog box displays. At this dialog box, navigate to the desired folder and double-click the picture file. Click the Clip Art button, and the Clip Art task pane displays. At this task pane, you can search for and then insert an image into a header or footer.

Date & Time

Picture

Clip Art

Exercise 19.3A   Inserting Elements in a Header and Footer   Part 1 of 2

1. Open **EmpHandbook.docx** and save the document with the name **C19-E03-EmpHandbook**.
2. Make the following changes to the document:
   a. Apply the Heading 1 style to the following titles:
      PROBATIONARY PERIODS
      EMPLOYEE PERFORMANCE
      COMPENSATION
   b. Apply the Heading 2 style to the following titles:
      Types of Appointments
      Work Performance Standards
      Performance Evaluation
      Employment Records
      Rate of Pay
      Direct Deposit Option
      Pay Progression
      Overtime
      Longevity Pay
      Payment for Holidays
      Shift Differential
   c. Change the style set to Formal.
   d. Change the left and right margins to 1.25 inches.

---

3. Insert a header by completing the following steps:
   a. Click the Insert tab.
   b. Click the Header button in the Header & Footer group.
   c. Click *Edit Header* at the drop-down list.
   d. With the insertion point positioned in the Header pane, click the Picture button in the Insert group in the Header & Footer Tools Design tab.

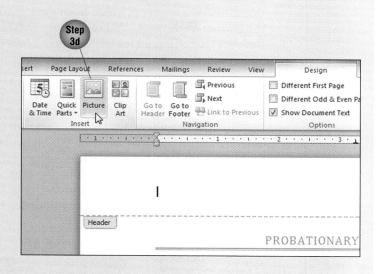

Step 3d

   e. At the Insert Picture dialog box, navigate to the Chapter19 folder on your storage medium and then double-click **WELogo.jpeg**.
   f. With the image selected, click in the Shape Height measurement box, type 0.6, and then press the Enter key.

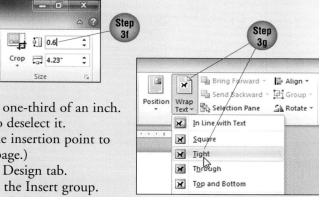

Step 3f

Step 3g

   g. Click the Wrap Text button and then click *Tight* at the drop-down list.
   h. Drag the image up approximately one-third of an inch.
   i. Click to the right of the picture to deselect it.
   j. Press the Tab key. (This moves the insertion point to approximately the middle of the page.)
   k. Click the Header & Footer Tools Design tab.
   l. Click the Date & Time button in the Insert group.
   m. At the Date and Time dialog box, click the twelfth option from the top (the option that displays the date in numbers and the time in hours and minutes) and then click OK to close the dialog box.
   n. Select the date and time text, click the Home tab, and then click the Bold button. Click the Font Size button arrow and then click *10* at the drop-down gallery.
   o. Double-click in the document to make the document active and dim the header.
4. Save **C19-E03-EmpHandbook.docx**.

Navigating in Headers and Footers

If a document contains a header and footer or is divided into sections, use the buttons in the Navigation group in the Header & Footer Tools Design tab to navigate to various headers or footers. If a header pane is open, clicking the Go to Footer button will make active the footer on the same page. If a document is divided into sections, click the Previous or Next buttons to navigate between headers and footers.

Go to Footer

Previous   Next

Positioning a Header or Footer

Word inserts a header 0.5 inch from the top edge of the page and a footer 0.5 inch from the bottom of the page. You can change these default positions with buttons in the Position group in the Header & Footer Tools Design tab. Use the Header from Top and Footer from Bottom measurement boxes to adjust the position of the header or footer on the page.

By default, headers and footers contain two tab settings. A center tab is set at 3.25 inches, and a right tab is set at 6.5 inches. If the document contains default left and right margin settings of 1 inch, the center tab set at 3.25 inches is the center of the document, and the right tab set at 6.5 inches is at the right margin. If you make changes to the default margins, you may need to move the default tabs before inserting header or footer text at the center or right tabs. You can also set and position tabs with the Insert Alignment Tab button in the Position group. Click this button, and the Alignment Tab dialog box displays. Use options at this dialog box to change tab alignment and set tabs with leaders.

Exercise 19.3B Positioning Headers and Footers   Part 2 of 2

1. With **C19-E03-EmpHandbook.docx** open, create a footer by completing the following steps:
   a. Click the Insert tab.
   b. Click the Footer button in the Header & Footer group and then click *Edit Footer* at the drop-down list.
   c. With the insertion point positioned in the footer pane, type your first and last names at the left margin.
   d. Press the Tab key. (This moves the insertion point to the center tab position.)
   e. Click the Page Number button in the Header & Footer group, point to *Current Position*, and then click *Accent Bar 2* at the side menu.

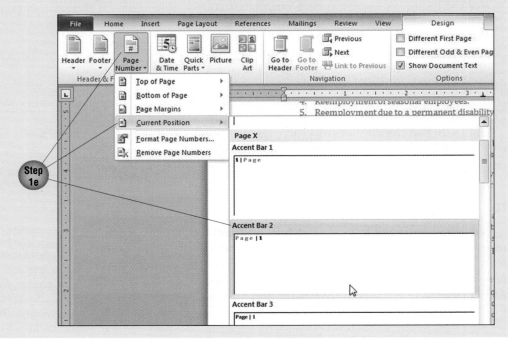

f. Press the Tab key and then type C19-E03-EmpHandbook.docx.

g. Notice that the center tab and the right tab are off slightly because the left and right margins in the document are set at 1.25 inches instead of 1 inch. To correctly align the text, drag the Center tab marker to the 3-inch mark on the Ruler and drag the Right tab marker to the 6-inch mark on the Ruler. (If the Ruler is not visible, turn on its display by clicking the View Ruler button located at the top of the vertical scroll bar.)

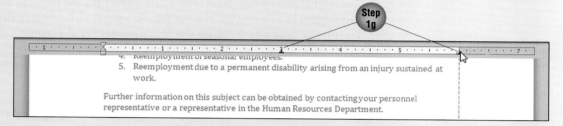

h. Select all of the footer text and then change the font to 10-point Cambria bold.

2. Edit the header by completing the following steps:

a. Click the Header & Footer Tools Design tab.

b. Click the Go to Header button in the Navigation group.

c. Move the insertion point to the beginning of the date and then press the Tab key. (This right-aligns the text at the right margin.)

d. Drag the Right tab marker to the 6-inch mark on the ruler.

3. Change the position of the header and footer by completing the following steps:

a. With the Header & Footer Tools Design tab active, click once on the down-pointing arrow at the right of the Header from Top measurement box to display 0.4".

b. Click in the Footer from Bottom measurement box, type 0.8, and then press the Enter key.

c. Click the Close Header and Footer button.

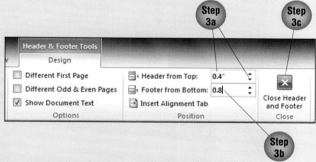

4. Save and then print **C19-E03-EmpHandbook.docx**.

QUICK
STEPS

Create Different
First Page Header
or Footer
1. Click Insert tab.
2. Click Header or
   Footer button.
3. Click *Edit Header* or
   Edit Footer at drop-
   down list.
4. Click *Different First
   Page* check box.
5. Insert desired
   elements and/or
   text for the first
   page.
6. Click Next button.
7. Insert desired
   elements and/
   or text for the
   remaining pages.

Creating a Different First Page Header or Footer

By default, Word inserts a header or footer on every page in the document. You can create different headers or footers within one document. For example, you can create a unique header or footer for the first page and then insert a different header or footer on subsequent pages.

To create a different first page header, click the Insert tab, click the Header button, and then click *Edit Header* at the drop-down list. Click the *Different First Page* check box to insert a check mark, and the First Page Header pane displays with the insertion point inside. Insert elements or type text to create the first page header and then click the Next button in the Navigation group. This displays the Header pane with the insertion point positioned inside. Insert elements and/or type text to create the header. Complete similar steps to create a different first page footer.

In some situations you may want the first page header or footer to be blank. This is particularly useful if a document contains a title page and you do not want the header or footer to print at the top or bottom of the first page.

Exercise 19.4   Creating a Header That Prints on all Pages Except the First Page   Part 1 of 1

1. With **C19-E03-EmpHandbook.docx** open, save the document with Save As and name it
   C19-E04-EmpHandbook.
2. Remove the header and footer by completing the following steps:
   a. Click the Insert tab.
   b. Click the Header button in the Header & Footer group and then click *Remove Header*
      at the drop-down list.
   c. Click the Footer button in the Header & Footer group and then click *Remove Footer* at
      the drop-down list.
3. Press Ctrl + Home and then create a header
   that prints on all pages except the first page by
   completing the following steps:
   a. With the Insert tab active, click the Header
      button in the Header & Footer group.
   b. Click *Edit Header* at the drop-down list.
   c. Click the *Different First Page* check box
      located in the Options group.
   d. With the insertion point positioned in the
      First Page Header pane, click the Next
      button in the Navigation group. (This tells
      Word that you want the first page header
      to be blank.)

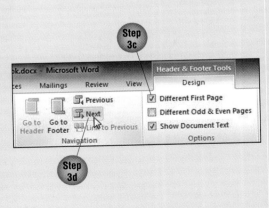

e. With the insertion point positioned in the Header pane, click the Page Number button, point to *Top of Page*, and then click *Accent Bar 2* at the drop-down side menu.

f. Click the Close Header & Footer button.

4. Scroll through the document and observe that the header appears on the second through fourth pages.

5. Save and then print **C19-E04-EmpHandbook.docx**.

Creating Odd and Even Page Headers or Footers

If your document will be read in book form with facing pages, consider inserting odd and even page headers or footers. When a document in book form has facing pages, the outside margin is the left side of the left page and the right side of the right page. In addition, the page at the right side is generally numbered with odd page numbers, and the page at the left side is generally numbered with even page numbers. You can create even and odd headers or footers to insert this type of page numbering. Use the *Different Odd & Even Pages* check box in the Options group in the Header & Footer Tools Design tab to create odd and even headers and/or footers.

Create Odd and Even Page Headers or Footers

1. Click Insert tab.
2. Click Header or Footer button.
3. Click *Edit Header* or *Edit Footer* at drop-down list.
4. Click *Different Odd & Even Pages* check box.
5. Insert desired elements and/or text.

Exercise 19.5   Creating an Even Page and Odd Page Footer   Part 1 of 1

1. With **C19-E04-EmpHandbook.docx** open, save the document with Save As and name it **C19-E05-EmpHandbook**.

2. Remove headers from the document by completing the following steps:
   a. Click the Insert tab.
   b. Click the Header button in the Header & Footer group and then click *Edit Header* at the drop-down list.
   c. Click the *Different First Page* check box in the Options group to remove the check mark.
   d. Click the Header button in the Header & Footer group in the Header & Footer Tools Design tab and then click *Remove Header* at the drop-down list. (This displays the insertion point in an empty Header pane.)

3. Create a footer that prints on odd pages and another that prints on even pages by completing the following steps:
   a. Click the Go to Footer button in the Navigation group in the Header & Footer Tools Design tab.
   b. Click the *Different Odd & Even Pages* check box in the Options group. (This displays the Odd Page Footer pane with the insertion point inside.)

c. Click the Footer button in the Header & Footer group.

d. Scroll down the list of predesigned footers and then click the *Mod (Odd Page)* option.

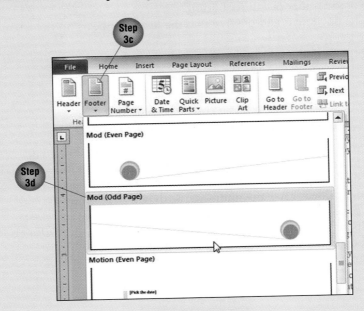

e. Click the Next button in the Navigation group. (This displays the Even Page Footer pane with the insertion point inside.)

f. Click the Footer button in the Header & Footer group.

g. Scroll down the list of predesigned footers and then click the *Mod (Even Page)* option.

h. Click the Close Header and Footer button.

4. Scroll through the document and view the odd page and even page footers. After looking at the footers, change the color of the titles and headings in the document to match the color of the circles by completing the following steps:

a. Click the Page Layout tab.

b. Click the Theme Colors button in the Themes group.

c. Click the Elemental option at the drop-down gallery.

5. Save and then print **C19-E05-EmpHandbook.docx**.

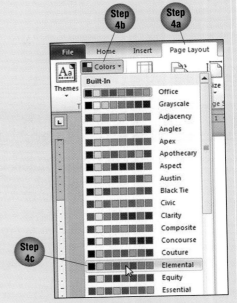

Creating Headers and Footers for Different Sections

You can divide a document into sections and then apply different formatting in each section. You can insert a section break that begins a new page or insert a continuous section break. If you want different headers and/or footers for pages in a document, divide the document into sections.

For example, if a document contains several chapters, you can create a section for each chapter and then create a different header or footer for each section. When you divide a document into sections by chapter, insert a section break for each chapter that also begins a new page.

When a header or footer is created for a specific section in a document, the header or footer can be created for all previous and next sections or just for next sections. By default, each section in a document is linked to the other sections. If you want a header or footer to print on only specific pages in a section and not the previous or next sections, you must deactivate the Link to Previous button. This tells Word not to print the header or footer on previous sections. Word will, however, print the header or footer on the following sections. If you do not want the header or footer to print on the following sections, create a blank header or footer at the next section. When creating a header or footer for a specific section in a document, preview the document to determine if the header or footer appears on the correct pages.

QUICK STEPS

Create Header/ Footer for Different Sections
1. Insert section break in desired location.
2. Click Insert tab.
3. Click Header or Footer button.
4. Click *Edit Header* or *Edit Footer* at drop-down list.
5. Click Link to Previous to deactivate.
6. Insert desired elements and/or text.
7. Click Next button.
8. Insert desired elements and/or text.

Link to Previous

Exercise 19.6A   Creating Footers for Different Sections   Part 1 of 2

1. With **C19-E05-EmpHandbook.docx** open, save the document with Save As and name it **C19-E06-EmpHandbook**.
2. Remove the odd and even page footers by completing the following steps:
   a. Click the Insert tab.
   b. Click the Footer button and then click *Edit Footer* at the drop-down list.
   c. Click the *Different Odd & Even Pages* check box to remove the check mark.
   d. Click the Footer button and then click *Remove Footer* at the drop-down list.
   e. Click the Close Header and Footer button.
3. Insert a section break that begins a new page by completing the following steps:
   a. Move the insertion point to the beginning of the title *EMPLOYEE PERFORMANCE*.
   b. Click the Page Layout tab.
   c. Click the Breaks button in the Page Setup group and then click *Next Page* in the *Section Breaks* section of the drop-down list.

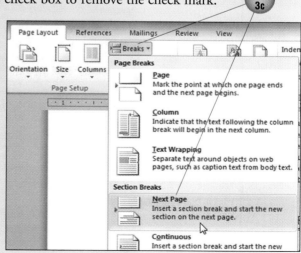

---

4. Insert a section break that begins a new page at the beginning of the title *COMPENSATION*.
5. Create section and page numbering footers for the three sections by completing the following steps:
   a. Position the insertion point at the beginning of the document.
   b. Click the Insert tab.
   c. Click the Footer button in the Header & Footer group and then click *Edit Footer* at the drop-down list.
   d. At the Footer -Section 1- pane, turn on bold, type Section 1, and then press the Tab key twice. (This moves the insertion point to the right margin.)
   e. Type Page and then press the spacebar.
   f. Click the Header & Footer Tools Design tab.
   g. Click the Page Number button in the Header & Footer group, point to *Current Position*, and then click *Plain Number* at the side menu.
   h. Click the Next button in the Navigation group.
   i. Click the Link to Previous button to deactivate it. (This removes the message *Same as Previous* from the top right side of the footer pane.)
   j. Change the text *Section 1* to *Section 2* in the footer.

   k. Click the Next button in the Navigation group.
   l. Click the Link to Previous button to deactivate it. (This removes the message *Same as Previous* from the top right side of the footer pane.)
   m. Change the text *Section 2* to *Section 3* in the footer.
   n. Click the Close Header and Footer button.
6. Begin page numbering with number 1 at the beginning of the second section by completing the following steps:
   a. Position the insertion point on any character in the title *EMPLOYEE PERFORMANCE*.
   b. Click the Insert tab.
   c. Click the Page Number button in the Header & Footer group and then click *Format Page Numbers*.
   d. At the Page Number Format dialog box, click the *Start at* option (this inserts *1* in the *Start at* text box).
   e. Click OK.
7. Begin page numbering with number 1 at the beginning of the *COMPENSATION* title by completing steps similar to those in Step 6.
8. Apply the Foundry theme.
9. Save **C19-E06-EmpHandbook.docx**.

Printing Sections

You can print specific pages in a document by inserting page numbers in the *Pages* text box at the Print tab Backstage view. When entering page numbers in this text box, use a hyphen to indicate a range of consecutive pages for printing or a comma to specify nonconsecutive pages. If a document contains sections, use the *Pages* text box at the Print tab Backstage view to specify the section and pages within the section that you want printed. For example, if a document is divided into three sections and you want to print only section two, you would type s2 in the *Pages* text box. If a document contains six sections and you want to print sections three through five, you would type s3-s5 in the *Pages* text box.

You can also identify specific pages within or between sections for printing. For example, to print pages two through five of section four, you would type p2s4-p5s4; to print from page three of section one through page five of section four, you would type p3s1-p5s4; to print page one of section three, page four of section five, and page six of section eight, you would type p1s3,p4s5,p6s8.

Exercise 19.6B · **Printing Sections**   **Part 2 of 2**

1. With **C19-E06-EmpHandbook.docx** open, click the File tab and then click the Print tab.
2. At the Print tab Backstage view, specify that you want to print page one of section one, page one of section two, and page one of section three by clicking in the *Pages* text box and then typing p1s1,p1s2,p1s3.
3. Click the Print button.

4. Save and then close **C19-E06-EmpHandbook.docx**.

Keeping Text Together

Keep Text Together
1. Click Paragraph group dialog box launcher.
2. Click Line and Page Breaks tab.
3. Click *Keep with next, Keep lines together,* and/or *Page break before.*
4. Click OK.

In a multiple-page document, soft page breaks inserted by Word can occur in undesirable locations. For example, a soft page break may cause a heading to display at the bottom of a page while the text connected to the heading displays at the beginning of the next page. A soft page break can also create a *widow* or *orphan.* A widow is a short, last line of text in a paragraph that appears at the top of a page, and an orphan is the first line of text in a paragraph that appears at the bottom of a page. Use options at the Paragraph dialog box with the Line and Page Breaks tab selected, as shown in Figure 19.3, to control widows and orphans as well as to keep a paragraph, a group of paragraphs, or a group of lines together.

By default, the *Widow/Orphan control* option is active, and Word tries to avoid creating a widow or orphan when inserting a soft page break. The other three options in the *Pagination* section of the dialog box are not active by default. Use the *Keep with next* option if you want to keep a line together with the next line. This is useful for keeping a heading together with the first line below it. If you want to keep a group of selected lines together, use the *Keep lines together* option. Use the *Page break before* option to tell Word to insert a page break before selected text.

Figure 19.3 Paragraph Dialog Box with Line and Page Breaks Tab Selected

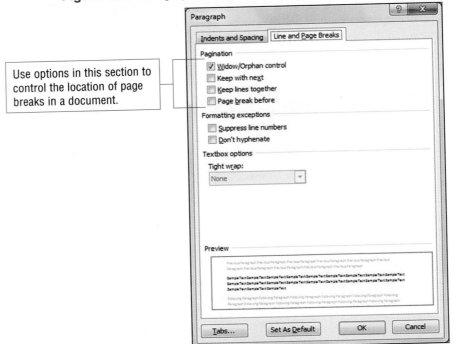

Use options in this section to control the location of page breaks in a document.

1. Open **OnlineShop.docx** and save the document with the name **C19-E07-OnlineShop**.
2. Select the entire document and then change the line spacing to 2.0.
3. Keep a heading together with the paragraph of text that follows it by completing the following steps:
   a. Move the insertion point to the beginning of the heading *ONLINE SHOPPING VENUES*.
   b. Click the Paragraph group dialog box launcher.
   c. At the Paragraph dialog box, click the Line and Page Breaks tab.
   d. Click the *Keep with next* check box to insert a check mark.

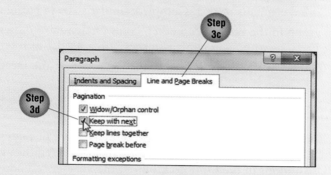

   e. Click OK to close the dialog box.
4. Insert a soft page break before text by completing the following steps:
   a. Move the insertion point to the end of the second page.
   b. Move the insertion point to the beginning of the heading *ONLINE SHOPPING SAFETY TIPS*.
   c. Click the Paragraph group dialog box launcher.
   d. At the Paragraph dialog box with the Line and Page Breaks tab selected, click the *Page break before* check box to insert a check mark.

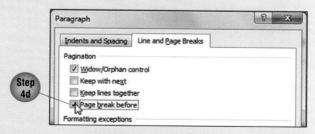

   e. Click OK to close the dialog box.
5. Insert a predesigned footer in the document by completing the following steps:
   a. Move the insertion point to the beginning of the document.
   b. Click the Insert tab.
   c. Click the Footer button in the Header & Footer group.
   d. Click the *Alphabet* option at the drop-down list.
   e. Click the placeholder text *[Type text]* and then type C19-E07-OnlineShop.docx.
   f. Double-click in the document to close the footer pane.
6. Save, print, and then close **C19-E07-OnlineShop.docx**.

Chapter Summary

- By default, Word inserts Arabic numbers (1, 2, 3, and so on) as page numbers and numbers the pages in a document sequentially beginning with number 1. You can change these default settings with options at the Page Number Format dialog box.

- You can number chapters in a document with an option at the Multilevel List button drop-down gallery and then apply chapter numbering with the *Include chapter number* option at the Page Number Format dialog box.

- You can insert predesigned headers and footers in a document or create your own.

- To create a header, click the Insert tab, click the Header button, and then click *Edit Header*. At the Header pane, insert the desired elements or text. Complete similar steps to create a footer.

- Use buttons in the Insert group in the Header & Footer Tools Design tab to insert elements such as the date and time, Quick Parts, pictures, and clip art images into a header or footer.

- Navigate to headers and footers with buttons in the Navigation group in the Header & Footer Tools Design tab.

- Word inserts a header or footer 0.5 inch from the edge of the page. Reposition a header or footer with buttons in the Position group in the Header & Footer Tools Design tab.

- You can create a unique header or footer on the first page; omit a header or footer on the first page; create different headers or footers for odd and even pages; or create different headers or footers for sections in a document. Use options in the Options group in the Header & Footer Tools Design tab to specify the type of header or footer you want to create.

- To print sections or specific pages within a section, use the *Pages* option at the Print dialog box. When specifying sections and pages, use the letter *s* before the section number and the letter *p* before the page number.

- Word attempts to avoid creating a widow or orphan when inserting soft page breaks. Turn the widow/orphan feature on or off at the Paragraph dialog box with the Line and Page Breaks tab selected. This dialog box also contains options for controlling the location of page breaks in a document keeping a paragraph, a group of paragraphs, or a group of lines together.

Commands *Review*

FEATURE	RIBBON TAB, GROUP	BUTTON, OPTION
Page Number	Insert, Header & Footer	⊞
Page Number Format dialog box	Insert, Header & Footer	⊞ , Format Page Numbers
Header	Insert, Header & Footer	⊞
Footer	Insert, Header & Footer	⊞
Create header	Insert, Header & Footer	⊞ , Edit Header
Create footer	Insert, Header & Footer	⊞ , Edit Footer
Paragraph dialog box	Insert, Paragraph	⊡

Key Points *Review*

Completion: In the space provided at the right, indicate the correct term, symbol, or command.

1. If you insert page numbers in a document, by default, Word uses this type of number.

2. Customize page numbering with options at this dialog box.

3. To create your own header, click the Insert tab, click the Header button in the Header & Footer group, and then click this option at the drop-down list.

4. This group in the Header & Footer Tools Design tab contains the Picture and Clip Art buttons.

5. By default, a header is positioned this distance from the top of the page.

6. By default a header and footer contain two tab settings, a center tab and this type of tab.

7. When you create a header, clicking the *Different First Page* check box causes this pane to display.

8. Type this in the *Pages* text box at the Print tab Backstage view to print section five.

9. Type this in the *Pages* text box at the Print tab Backstage view to print page two of section four and page five of section eight.

10. The *Keep lines together* option is available at the Paragraph dialog box with this tab selected.

Chapter Assessments

Applying Your Skills

Demonstrate your knowledge of features learned in this chapter by completing the following assessments.

Assessment 19.1   Insert and Customize Page Numbering in a Computer Report

1. Open **CompViruses.docx** and save the document with the name **C19-A01-CompViruses**.
2. Make the following changes to the document:
   a. Delete *SECTION 3:* in the first title in the document so the title displays as *COMPUTER VIRUSES*.
   b. Delete *SECTION 4:* in the second title in the document so the title displays as *HARDWARE AND SOFTWARE SECURITY RISKS*.
   c. Apply the Heading 1 style to the two titles and the Heading 2 style to the five headings.
   d. Insert at the beginning of the title *HARDWARE AND SOFTWARE SECURITY RISKS* a section break that begins a new page.
   e. Change the style set to Modern.
   f. Apply the Concourse theme.
   g. Apply chapter multilevel list numbering.
   h. Insert chapter numbering at the bottom of each page in both sections in the document. ***Hint: Refer to Exercise 19.2, Step 9.***
3. Save, print, and then close **C19-A01-CompViruses.docx**.

Assessment 19.2   Create Odd and Even Page Footers in a Robot Report

1. Open **Robots.docx** and save the document with the name **C19-A02-Robots**.
2. Make the following changes to the document:
   a. Apply the Heading 2 style to the title *ROBOTS AS ANDROIDS*.
   b. Apply the Heading 3 style to the headings *Visual Perception, Audio Perception, Tactile Perception, Locomotion,* and *Navigation*.
   c. Change the style set to Manuscript.
   d. Center the title *ROBOTS AS ANDROIDS*.
   e. Keep the heading *Audio Perception* together with the following paragraph of text.
3. Create an odd page footer that includes the following:
   a. Insert the current date at the left margin. (Choose the date option that displays the month spelled out, such as *January 1, 2012*.)
   b. Insert a clip art image related to robots in the middle of the footer. Change the height of the robot image to approximately 0.6 inch and apply *Tight* text wrapping. (If you do not have robot images available, choose another clip art image related to computers or technology.)
   c. At the right margin, type Page, press the spacebar, and then insert a page number at the current position.
4. Create an even page footer that includes the following:
   a. At the left margin, type Page, press the spacebar, and then insert a page number at the current position.
   b. In the middle of the footer, insert the same clip art image you inserted in the odd page footer.
   c. Insert the current date at the right margin in the same format you chose for the odd page footer.
5. Save, print, and then close **C19-A02-Robots.docx**.

Assessment 19.3   Create and Edit Footers in a Computer Virus and Security Report

1. Open **CompChapters.docx** and save the document with the name **C19-A03-CompChapters**.
2. Make the following changes to the document:
   a. Change the theme to Origin.
   b. Change the top margin to 1.5 inches.
   c. At the beginning of the title CHAPTER 2: SECURITY RISKS, insert a section break that begins a new page.
   d. Keep the heading *CRACKING SOFTWARE FOR COPYING* together with the paragraph following it.
3. Create a footer for the first section in the document that prints *Chapter 1* at the left margin, the page number in the middle, and your first and last names at the right margin.
4. Edit the footer for the second section so it prints *Chapter 2* instead of *Chapter 1*.
5. Begin page numbering with number 1 at the beginning of the second section.
6. Print page one of section one and page one of section two.
7. Save and then close **C19-A03-CompChapters.docx**.

Expanding Your Skills

Explore additional feature options or use Help to learn a new skill in creating this document.

Assessment 19.4   Insert a Horizontal Line in a Footer in an Online Shopping Report

1. Word includes a horizontal line feature you can use to insert a graphic line in a document or header or footer. At a blank document, look at the horizontal line options that are available at the Horizontal Line dialog box. Display this dialog box by clicking the Borders button arrow in the Paragraph group in the Home tab and then clicking *Borders and Shading* at the drop-down list. At the Borders and Shading dialog box, click the Horizontal Line button that displays at the bottom left side of the dialog box. Experiment inserting horizontal lines in a document and then close the document.
2. Open **OnlineShop.docx** and save the document with the name **C19-A04-OnlineShop**.
3. Keep the heading *ONLINE SHOPPING MALLS* together with the paragraph following it.
4. Create a footer that prints a horizontal line of your choosing on each page. After inserting the horizontal line, press the Enter key, press the Tab key, and then insert the current date.
5. The Header & Footer Tools Design tab contains a number of buttons you can use to insert data in a header or footer. With the Quick Parts button in the Insert group, you can insert pieces of content such as fields and document properties. Click the Quick Parts button and then hover your mouse over or click the options at the drop-down list to determine what options are available.
6. Close the footer pane.
7. Create a header that inserts an author document property. To do this, display the header pane, click the Quick Parts button, point to *Document Property*, and then click *Author* at the side menu. This inserts the Author placeholder that contains a name. If the name is not your name, click the Author placeholder tab (this selects the text in the placeholder) and then type your first and last names.
8. Press the Right Arrow key to move the insertion point to the right of the Author placeholder and then press the Tab key twice.
9. Insert the file name as a field. To do this, click the Quick Parts button and then click *Field* at the drop-down list. At the Field dialog box, click *FileName* in the *Field names* list box (you will need to scroll down the list box) and then click OK.
10. Make the document active.
11. Save, print, and then close **C19-A04-OnlineShop.docx**.

Achieving Signature Status

Take your skills to the next level by completing this more challenging assessment.

Assessment 19.5   Format a Document with Headers, Footers, and Page Numbering

1. Open **InternetChapters.docx** and save the document with the name **C19-A05-InternetChapters**.
2. Make the following changes to the document:
    a. Insert a section break that begins a new page at the beginning of the centered title *Online Content* and at the beginning of the centered title *E-Commerce*.
    b. Apply the Heading 1 style to the three centered titles (*Navigating and Searching the Web*, *Online Content*, and *E-Commerce*).
    c. Apply the Heading 2 style to the ten headings in the document.
    d. Change the style set to Thatch.
    e. Apply the Flow theme and change the theme colors to Clarity.
    f. Apply chapter multilevel list numbering. (This will insert the word *Chapter* followed by the chapter number before each of the three titles with the Heading 1 style applied.)
    g. Move the insertion point to the beginning of the document and then create an odd page header that prints your name at the left margin and the current date at the right margin. Insert a border line below the text. Create an even page header that prints the current date at the left and your name at the right margin. Insert a border line below the text.
    h. Create an odd page footer that inserts page numbering at the bottom right margin of each page and includes chapter page numbering. Insert a border line above the page number (the border line will span from the left to the right margin). Create an even page footer that inserts page numbering at the bottom left margin of each page and includes chapter page numbering. Insert a border line above the page number.
    i. Move the insertion point to the chapter 2 title and then change the page numbering so it starts with 1 and includes chapter page numbering.
    j. Move the insertion point to the chapter 3 title and then change the page numbering so it starts with 1 and includes chapter page numbering.
3. Scroll through the document. Odd pages should have your name displayed at the top of the page at the left margin and the current date at the right margin with a border line below, along with the page number (including the chapter number) at the bottom of the page at the right margin with a border line above. Even pages should have the current date displayed at the top of the page at the left margin and your name at the right margin with a border line below, along with the page number (including the chapter number) at the bottom of the page at the left margin with a border line above. The page numbers for the first two pages should display 1-1 and 1-2. The third and fourth pages should display 2-1 and 2-2. (This is because you specified that you wanted chapter numbering included and that you wanted to start with page 1.) The fifth and sixth pages should display 3-1 and 3-2.
4. Save **C19-A05-InternetChapters.docx**.
5. Print only the first page of sections one and two and both pages of section three.
6. Close **C19-A05-InternetChapters.docx**.
7. If a message displays asking if you want to save your building blocks, click the Don't Save button.

Chapter 20

SNAP TUTORIALS

Managing Shared Documents

Performance Objectives

Upon successful completion of Chapter 20, you will be able to:

- Insert, edit, and delete comments
- Track changes to a document and customize tracking
- Compare documents
- Combine documents

Tutorial 20.1
Inserting and Editing Comments

Tutorial 20.2
Inserting Coments in the Reviewing Pane and Distinguishing Comments from Other Users

Tutorial 20.3
Tracking Changes to a Document

Tutorial 20.4
Displaying for Review and Showing Markup

Tutorial 20.5
Customizing Track Changing and Compare Options

Tutorial 20.6
Comparing Documents

Tutorial 20.7
Combining Documents

In a company environment, you may need to work with other employees to create documents. You may be part of a work group, or team of employees, whose computers are networked to facilitate the sharing of files, printers, and other resources. As a member of a work group, you can use a number of Word features to help you collaborate with group members to review and revise shared documents. In this chapter, you will use these features to perform work group activities such as inserting comments into a document, tracking changes made by multiple users, comparing documents, and combining documents from multiple users.

If a Word 2010 document (in the .docx format) is located on a server running Microsoft SharePoint Server 2010, multiple users can edit the document concurrently. Concurrent editing allows a group of users to work on a document at the same time or a single user to work on the same document from different computers. If a document is not located on a server running SharePoint Server 2010, Word 2010 supports only single-user editing. Exercises and assessments in this chapter assume that the files you are editing are not located on a server running SharePoint Server 2010.

Note: Before beginning computer exercises for this chapter, copy to your storage medium the Chapter20 folder from the CD that accompanies this textbook and then make Chapter20 the active folder.

In this chapter, students will produce the following documents:

Exercise 20.1. C20-E01-CompComm.docx
Exercise 20.2. C20-E02-BldgAgrmnt.docx
Exercise 20.4. C20-E04-CombinedLease.docx

Model answers for these exercises are shown on the following pages.

Exercise 20.1

C20-E01-CompComm.docx

COMPUTERS IN COMMUNICATIONS

Computers were originally stand-alone devices, incapable of communicating with other computers. This changed in the 1970s and 1980s when the development of special telecommunications hardware and software led to the creation of the first private networks, allowing connected computers to exchange data. Exchanged data took the form of requests for information, replies to requests for information, or instructions on how to run programs stored on the network.

The ability to link computers enables users to communicate and work together efficiently and effectively. Linked computers have become central to the communications industry. They play a vital role in telecommunications, publishing, and news services.

Telecommunications

The industry that provides for communication across distances is called telecommunications. The telephone industry uses computers to switch and route phone calls automatically over telephone lines. In addition to the spoken word, many other kinds of information move over such lines, including faxes and computer data. Data can be sent from computer to computer over telephone lines using a device known as a modem. One kind of data frequently sent by modem is electronic mail, or email, which can be sent from person to person via the Internet or an online service. A more recent innovation in telecommunications is teleconferencing, which allows people in various locations to see and hear one another and thus hold virtual meetings. Source?

Comment [SN1]: Please add the source for the information in this paragraph.

Publishing

Just twenty years ago, book manuscripts were typeset mechanically on a typesetting machine and then reproduced on a printing press. Now, anyone who has access to a computer and either a modem or a printer can undertake what has come to be known as electronic publishing. Writers and editors use word processing applications to produce text. Artists and designers use drawing and painting applications to created original graphics, or they use inexpensive scanners to digitize illustrations and photographs (turn them into computer-readable files). Typesetters use personal computers to combine text, illustrations, and photographs. Publishers typically send computer-generated files to printers for production of the film and plates from which books and magazines are printed. Images and/or pictures.

News Services

News providers rely on reporters located worldwide. Reporters use email to send, or upload, their stories to wire services. Increasingly, individuals get daily news reports from online services. News can also be accessed from specific providers, such as the *New York Times* or *USA Today*, via the Internet. One of the most popular Internet sites provides continuously updated weather reports.

COMPUTERS IN ENTERTAINMENT

Page 1

Possibilities in the television and film industries have soared with computer technology, especially in production. Computer games have captured the public imagination and created enormous growth in the computer game market.

Television and Film

Many of the spectacular graphics and special effects seen on television and in movies today are created with computers. The original *Star Wars* films, for example, relied heavily on hand-constructed models and hand-drawn graphics. Twenty years after the first release of the films, they were re-released with many new special effects, including futuristic cityscape backgrounds, new alien creatures, and new sounds that were created on computers and added to the films by means of computerized video editing. In an article on special effects, Jaclyn McFadden, an industry expert talked about the evolution of computer simulation. Websites?

Comment [SN2]: Include hyperlinks related to websites and include any pertinent websites.

The film *Jurassic Park* brought computer simulation to a new level by combining puppetry and computer animation to simulate realistic looking dinosaurs. *Toy Story*, released in 1996, was the first wholly computer-animated commercial movie.

Software products are available that automatically format scripts of various kinds. Industry analysts predict that the improvements in computer technology will continue to enhance and improve the visual appeal of television and film media.

Home Entertainment

The advent of powerful desktop personal computers has led to the production of home computer games that rival those of arcade machines in complexity. In the 1970s, computer games such as Pong and Pac-Man captured the public's imagination. Since then, there has been enormous growth in the computer game market. Manufacturers such as Sega and Nintendo produce such games as well as small computer game systems for home use. Typical arcade-style computer games include simulations of boxing, warfare, racing, skiing, and flight. Examples?

Comment [RJ3]: Provide pictures of gaming systems.

Other computer games make use of television or of small, independent, hand-held devices. Games are now able to take advantage of three-dimensional graphics that create virtual environments.

REFERENCES

Fuller, F. & Larson, B. (2005). *Computers: understanding technology* (pp. 121-125). St. Paul, MN: Paradigm Publishing.

McFadden, J. M. (2010). *The art of special effects* (pp. 45-48). Los Angeles: Richardson-Dryers Publishing House.

North, J. & Amundsen, R. (2009). *Computer gaming*. Cleveland, OH: Blue Horizon Publishers.

Ziebel, K. M. & Weisenburg, H. L. (2010). *Computers and publishing*. Seattle, WA: Greenlake Publishing House.

Page 2

Chapter Twenty

Exercise 20.2

C20-E02-BldgAgrmnt.docx

BUILDING CONSTRUCTION AGREEMENT

THIS AGREEMENT made this ____day of_____, 20___ by and between _____, hereinafter referred to as "builder," and _____, hereinafter referred to as "owner," the builder and the owner, for the considerations hereinafter named, agrees as follows:

Construction Loan and Financing Arrangements: The owner either has or will obtain a construction loan to finance the work to be performed under this Agreement. If adequate financing has not been arranged within sixty (60) days of the date of this Agreement, or the owner cannot provide evidence to the builder of other financial ability to pay the full amount of the contract, then the builder at his option may treat this Agreement as null and void and retain the down payment made on the execution of this Agreement.

Supervision of Work: Owner agrees that the direction and supervision of the working force, including subcontractors, rests exclusively with the builder, or his/her duly designated agent, and owner agrees not to issue any instructions to, or otherwise interfere with, same.

Start of Construction: The builder shall commence construction of the residence as soon as practical after the signing of this Agreement and adequate financial arrangements satisfactory to the builder have been made.

Changes, Alterations, and Extras: All changes in or departures from the plans and/or specifications shall be in writing. When changes in, or departure from, plans and specifications requested in writing by owner will result in furnishing of additional labor and materials, the owner shall pay the builder for such extras at a price agreed upon in writing before commencement of said change. Where such change results in the omitting of any labor or materials, the builder shall allow the owner a credit at a price agreed to in writing before commencement of said changes.

Possession of Residence upon Completion: On final payment by owner, and upon owner's request, builder will provide owner with affidavit stating that all labor, materials and equipment used in the construction have been paid for or will be paid for in full by the builder unless otherwise noted. Builder shall not be required to give possession of the residence to the owner before final payment by owner. Final payment constitutes acceptance of the residence as being satisfactorily completed unless a separate escrow agreement is executed between the parties stipulating the unfinished items.

Exclusions: The owner is solely responsible for the purchase and installation of any septic tank or other individual subsurface sewage disposal system that may be required on the property.

Builder's Right to Terminate the Contract: Should the work be stopped by any public authority for a period of sixty (60) days or more, through no fault of the builder, or should the work be stopped through act or neglect of the owner for a period of seven (7) days, or should the owner fail to pay the builder any

---

payment within seven (7) days after it is due, then the builder may stop wor[...] and recover from the owner payment for all work executed and any loss sus[...] and damages.

The Owner acknowledges that he/she has read and fully understands the provisions of this Agreement.

IN WITNESS WHEREOF, the builder and owner have hereunto set their hands this _____day of _____, 20____.

_____   _____
BUILDER   OWNER

Exercise 20.4

C20-E04-CombinedLease.docx

LEASE AGREEMENT

THIS LEASE AGREEMENT (hereinafter referred to as the "Agreement") is made and entered into this ___ day of _____, 2012, by and between Lessor and Lessee.

Term

Lessor leases to Lessee and Lessee leases from Lessor the described Premises together with any and all appurtenances thereto, for a term of ____ year(s), such term beginning on _____, and ending at midnight on _____.

Damage Deposit

Upon the signing of this Agreement, Lessee shall deposit with Lessor the sum of _____ DOLLARS ($_____) receipt of which is hereby acknowledged by Lessor, as security for any damage caused to the Premises during the leasing term. Such deposit shall be returned to Lessee, without interest ,upon the termination of this leasing Agreement.

Rent

The total rent for the term hereof is the sum of _____ DOLLARS ($_____) less any reimbursements and payable on the _____ day of each month of the term. All such payments shall be made to Lessor at Lessor's address on or before the due date and without demand.

Use of Premises

The Premises shall be used and occupied by Lessee and Lessee's immediate family, exclusively, as a private, single-family dwelling, and no part of the Premises shall be used at any time during the term of this Agreement by Lessee for the purpose of carrying on any business, profession, or trade of any kind, or for any purpose other than as a private, single-family dwelling. Lessee shall not allow any other person, other than Lessee's immediate family or transient relatives and friends who are guests of Lessee, to use or occupy the Premises without first obtaining Lessor's written consent to such use.

Condition of Premises

Lessee stipulates, represents, and warrants that Lessee has examined the Premises, and that they are at the time of this Agreement in good order, repair, and in a safe, clean, and tenantable condition.

Alterations and Improvements

 to or improvements on the Premises without the prior written terations, changes, and/or improvements built, constructed, or e shall be and become the property of the Lessor and remain on the lier termination of this Agreement.

Page 1

Damage to Premises

In the event Premises are destroyed or rendered wholly unlivable by fire, storm, earthquake, or other casualty not caused by the negligence of Lessee, this Agreement shall terminate from such time except for the purpose of enforcing rights that may have accrued hereunder.

_____
LESSEE

_____
LESSOR

Page 2

Inserting Comments

You can provide feedback and suggest changes to a document that someone else has written by inserting comments into it. Similarly, you can obtain feedback on a document that you have written by distributing it electronically to work group members and having them insert their comments into it. To insert a comment in a document, select the text or item you would like to comment on or position the insertion point at the end of that text, click the Review tab, and then click the New Comment button in the Comments group. Generally, clicking the New Comment button displays a comment balloon at the right margin, as shown in Figure 20.1.

QUICK STEPS

Insert Comment in Balloon
1. Select text.
2. Click Review tab.
3. Click the New Comment button.
4. Type comment in balloon.

New Comment

Figure 20.1 Comment Balloon

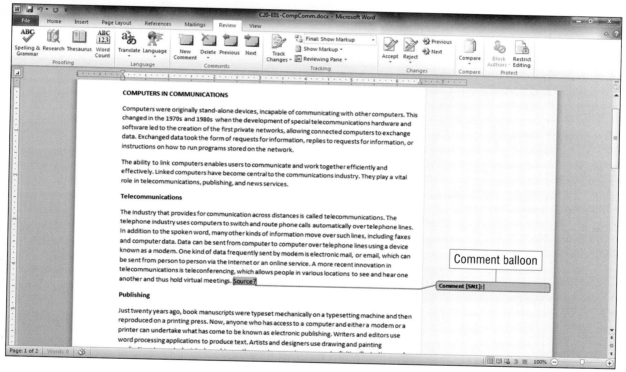

If default settings have been changed, clicking the New Comment button may display the Reviewing pane at the left side of the document rather than a comment balloon at the right margin. If this happens, click the Show Markup button in the Tracking group in the Review tab, point to *Balloons*, and then click *Show Only Comments and Formatting in Balloons* at the side menu. An advantage to using comment balloons is that you can easily view and respond to viewer comments. In addition, if the *Markup Area Highlight* option, which you will learn about later in this chapter, is active, the margin area where all balloons appear is highlighted.

Show Markup

1. Open **CompComm.docx** and save the document with the name **C20-E01-CompComm**.
2. Insert a comment by completing the following steps:
   a. Position the insertion point at the end of the paragraph in the *Telecommunications* section.
   b. Press the spacebar once and then type Source?.
   c. Select *Source?*.
   d. Click the Review tab.
   e. Click the New Comment button in the Comments group. (If the insertion point does not display in a comment balloon, click the Show Markup button in the Tracking group, point to *Balloons*, and then click *Show Only Comments and Formatting in Balloons* at the side menu. If the Reviewing pane displays, turn it off by clicking the Reviewing Pane button in the Tracking group.)
   f. Type Please add the source for the information in this paragraph. in the comment balloon.

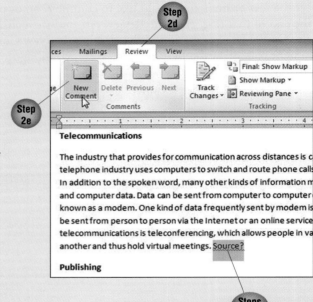

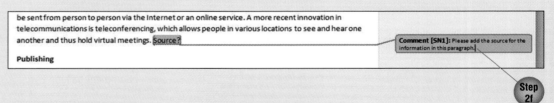

3. Insert another comment by completing the following steps:
   a. Move the insertion point to the end of the paragraph in the *Publishing* section.
   b. Press the spacebar once, type Images and/or pictures., and then select *Images and/or pictures.*
   c. Click the New Comment button in the Comments group.
   d. Type Include several images and/or pictures of publishing equipment. in the comment balloon.

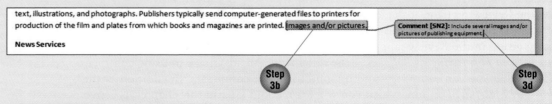

4. Save **C20-E01-CompComm.docx**.

Inserting Comments in the Reviewing Pane

You can insert comments in the Reviewing pane rather than in comment balloons, if you prefer. The Reviewing pane displays inserted comments as well as changes tracked with the Track Changes feature. (You will learn about tracking changes later in this chapter.) To insert a comment in the Reviewing pane, click the Show Markup button in the Tracking group in the Review tab, point to *Balloons*, and then click *Show All Revisions Inline* at the side menu. The Reviewing pane displays at the left side of the screen, as shown in Figure 20.2. Click the New Comment button in the Comments group and then type your comment in the Reviewing pane. If the pane does not display, turn it on by clicking the Reviewing Pane button in the Tracking group. (The Reviewing pane might display along the bottom of the screen rather than at the left side. To specify where you want the pane to display, click the Reviewing Pane button arrow in the Tracking group in the Review tab and then click *Reviewing Pane Vertical* or *Reviewing Pane Horizontal*.)

Insert Comment in Reviewing Pane
1. Click Review tab.
2. Click Show Markup button.
3. Point to *Balloons*.
4. Click *Show All Revisions Inline* at side menu.
5. Click the New Comment button.
6. Type comment in Reviewing pane.

Reviewing Pane

Figure 20.2 Vertical Reviewing Pane

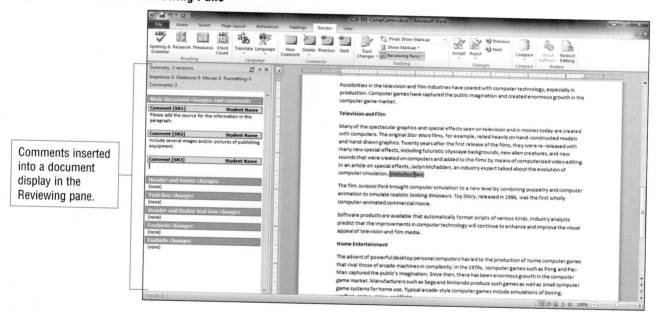

Comments inserted into a document display in the Reviewing pane.

The summary section at the top of the Reviewing pane provides a count of the number of comments inserted and a count of various types of changes that have been made to the document. After typing your comment in the Reviewing pane, close the pane by clicking the Reviewing Pane button in the Tracking group or clicking the Close button (the button marked with an X) located in the upper right corner of the pane.

1. With **C20-E01-CompComm.docx** open, show comments in the Reviewing pane rather than in comment balloons by completing the following steps:
   a. If necessary, click the Review tab.
   b. Click the Show Markup button.
   c. Point to *Balloons* at the drop-down list.
   d. Click *Show All Revisions Inline* at the side menu.

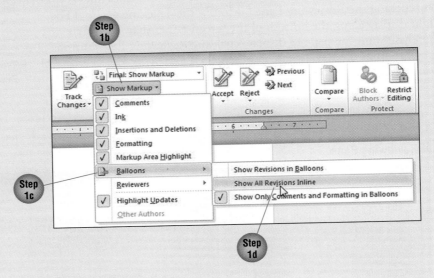

2. Insert a comment by completing the following steps:
   a. Move the insertion point to the end of the first paragraph of text in the *Television and Film* section.
   b. Press the spacebar once, type Websites?, and then select *Websites?*.
   c. Click the New Comment button in the Comments group in the Review tab.
   d. With the insertion point positioned in the Reviewing pane, type Include hyperlinks related to websites.

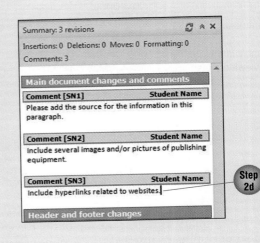

3. Click the Reviewing Pane button in the Tracking group to turn off the display of the Reviewing pane.
4. Save **C20-E01-CompComm.docx**.

Navigating between Comments

When you are working in a long document with many inserted comments, the Previous and Next buttons in the Comments group in the Review tab can be useful. Click the Next button to move the insertion point to the next comment or click the Previous button to move the insertion point to the preceding comment.

Editing a Comment

You can edit a comment in the Reviewing pane or in a comment balloon. To edit a comment in the Reviewing pane, click the Reviewing Pane button to turn on the pane and then click in the comment that you want to edit. Make the desired changes to the comment and then close the Reviewing pane. To edit a comment in a comment balloon, turn on the display of comment balloons, click in the comment balloon, and then make the desired changes.

Edit a Comment
1. Click Review tab.
2. Click the Reviewing Pane button.
3. Click in desired comment in pane.
4. Make desired changes.
OR
1. Click Review tab.
2. Turn on display of comment balloons.
3. Click in comment balloon.
4. Make desired changes.

Previous   Next

Exercise 20.1C   Editing Comments   Part 3 of 4

1. With **C20-E01-CompComm.docx** open, navigate from one comment to another by completing the following steps:
   a. Press Ctrl + Home to move the insertion point to the beginning of the document.
   b. If necessary, click the Review tab.
   c. Click the Next button in the Comments group. (This moves the insertion point to the first comment reference, opens the Reviewing pane, and inserts the insertion point in the pane.)

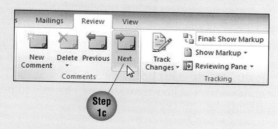

   d. Click the Next button to display the second comment.
   e. Click the Next button to display the third comment.
   f. Click the Previous button to display the second comment.
2. With the insertion point positioned in the Reviewing pane, edit the second comment to read *Include several clip art images, photos, or other images of publishing equipment.*
3. Click the Reviewing Pane button to close the pane.
4. Edit a comment in a comment balloon by completing the following steps:
   a. Click the Show Markup button, point to *Balloons,* and then click *Show Only Comments and Formatting in Balloons* at the side menu.

b. Move the insertion point to the first paragraph in the *Television and Film* section and then click in the comment balloon that displays at the right.

c. Move the insertion point immediately left of the period at the end of the sentence and then type and include any pertinent websites.

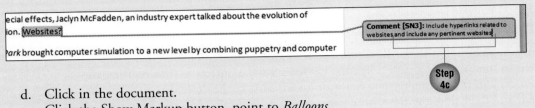

ecial effects, Jaclyn McFadden, an industry expert talked about the evolution of ion. Websites?

Comment [SN3]: Include hyperlinks related to websites and include any pertinent websites

ark brought computer simulation to a new level by combining puppetry and computer

Step 4c

d. Click in the document.

e. Click the Show Markup button, point to *Balloons*, and then click *Show All Revisions Inline*.

5. Save **C20-E01-CompComm.docx**.

Change User Name and Initials
1. Click File tab.
2. Click Options button.
3. Type desired name in *User name* text box.
4. Type desired initials in *Initials* text box.

Print Document with Comments
1. Click File tab, Print tab.
2. Click first gallery in Settings category.
3. If necessary, click *Print Markup* to insert check mark.
4. Click Print button.

Print Only Comments
1. Click File tab, Print tab.
2. Click first gallery in Settings category.
3. Click *List of Markup* in drop-down list box.
4. Click Print button.

Distinguishing Comments from Other Users

More than one user can make comments in a document. Word uses color to distinguish comments made by different users, generally displaying the first user's comments in red and the second user's comments in blue (these colors may vary). You can change the user name and initials at the Word Options dialog box with *General* selected, as shown in Figure 20.3. To change the user name, select the name that displays in the *User name* text box and then type the desired name. Complete similar steps to change the user initials in the *Initials* text box.

Printing Comments

To print a document with the comments, display the Print tab Backstage view, and then click the first gallery in the *Settings* category (this is the gallery containing the text *Print All Pages*). A drop-down list displays with a list box as well as options below the list box. The option *Print Markup* is one of the options that displays below the drop-down list box. Insert a check mark before this option if you want the document to print with the comments. If you want to print the document without the comments, remove the check mark from the *Print Markup* option at the Print tab Backstage view gallery drop-down list. If you want to print only the comments and not the document, click the first gallery in the *Settings* category in the Print tab Backstage view and then click *List of Markup* in the drop-down list box. This prints the contents of the Reviewing Pane, which may include comments, tracked changes, and changes to headers, footers, text boxes, footnotes, and endnotes.

Figure 20.3 Word Options Dialog Box with General Selected

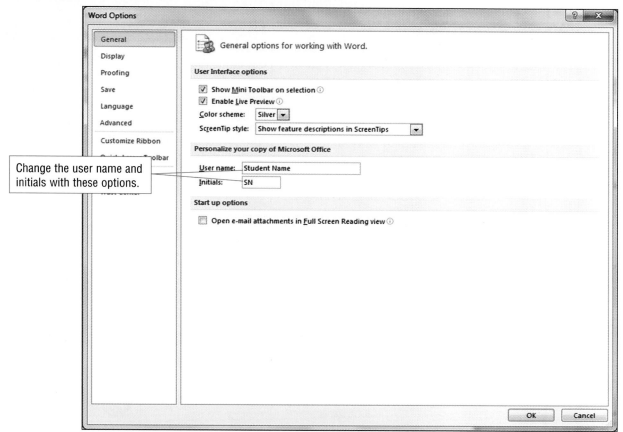

Change the user name and initials with these options.

Deleting a Comment

You can delete a comment by clicking the Next button in the Comments group in the Review tab until the desired comment is selected and then clicking the Delete button. If you want to delete all comments in a document, click the Delete button arrow and then click *Delete All Comments in Document* at the drop-down list.

QUICK STEPS

Print Document without Comments
1. Click File tab, Print tab.
2. Click first gallery in Settings category.
3. If necessary, click *Print Markup* to remove check mark.
4. Click Print button.

Delete a Comment
1. Click Review tab.
2. Click Next button until desired comment is selected.
3. Click Delete button.

Delete

1. With **C20-E01-CompComm.docx** open, change the user information by completing the following steps:
   a. Click the File tab.
   b. Click the Options button located below the Help tab.
   c. At the Word Options dialog box, make sure *General* is selected in the left panel.
   d. Make a note of the current name and initials in the *Personalize your copy of Microsoft Office* section.
   e. Select the name displayed in the *User name* text box and then type Rene Johnson.
   f. Select the initials displayed in the *Initials* text box and then type RJ.

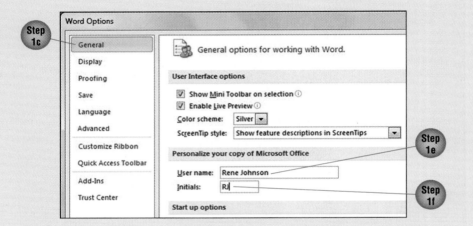

   g. Click OK to close the Word Options dialog box.
2. Insert a comment by completing the following steps:
   a. Move the insertion point to the end of the first paragraph of text in the *Home Entertainment* section.
   b. Press the spacebar once and then type Examples?.
   c. Make sure the Review tab is active and then select *Examples?*.
   d. Click the New Comment button in the Comments group.
   e. Type Provide pictures of gaming systems. in the Reviewing pane.
   f. Click the Reviewing Pane button to close the pane.

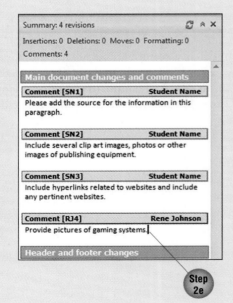

3. Print only the information in the Reviewing pane by completing the following steps:
   a. Click the File tab and then click the Print tab. (You can also display the Print tab Backstage view by pressing Ctrl + P.)
   b. At the Print tab Backstage view, click the first gallery in the *Settings* category and then click *List of Markup* in the drop-down list box.
   c. Click the Print button.

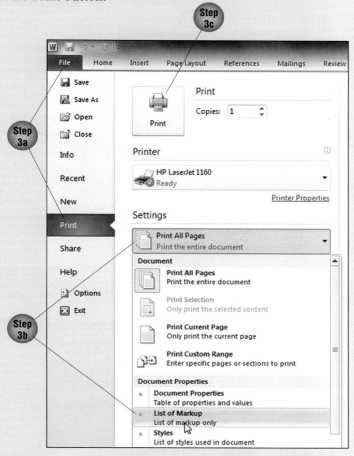

4. Delete a comment by completing the following steps:
   a. Press Ctrl + Home.
   b. If necessary, click the Review tab.
   c. Click the Next button in the Comments group.
   d. Click the Next button again.
   e. Click the Delete button in the Comments group.

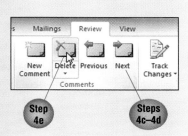

5. Print only the information in the Reviewing pane by completing Step 3.
6. Close the Reviewing pane.
7. Change the user information back to the default by completing the following steps:
   a. Click the File tab and then click the Options button.
   b. At the Word Options dialog box with *General* selected, select *Rene Johnson* in the *User name* text box and then type the original name.
   c. Select the initials *RJ* in the *Initials* text box and then type the original initials.
   d. Click OK to close the dialog box.
8. Save and then close **C20-E01-CompComm.docx**.

Turn on Tracking
1. Click Review tab.
2. Click Track Changes button.
OR
Press Ctrl + Shift + E.

Track Changes

Tracking Changes to a Document

If more than one person in a work group needs to review and edit a document, consider using the Track Changes feature in Word. When Track Changes is turned on, Word tracks each deletion, insertion, or formatting change made to a document. For example, when you delete text, it is not removed from the document. Instead, it displays in a different color with a line through it. Word uses a different color (up to eight) for each person who makes changes to the document. In this way, anyone looking at the document can identify which user made which changes.

Turn on tracking by clicking the Review tab and then clicking the Track Changes button in the Tracking group. You can also turn on tracking by pressing Ctrl + Shift + E. Turn off tracking by completing the same steps. By default, Word displays changes such as deletions and insertions in the document. Word displays formatting changes, such as a change of font or font size, in the text and also inserts a vertical line at the left margin to indicate where a formatting change has been made.

You can specify what tracking information displays in a document with options at the Balloons side menu. To show all revisions in balloons at the right margin, click the Show Markup button, point to *Balloons*, and then click *Show Revisions in Balloons* at the side menu. Click the *Show Only Comments and Formatting in Balloons* option at the side menu, and insertions and deletions display in the text while comments and formatting changes display in balloons at the right margin.

Exercise 20.2A   Tracking Changes in a Document   Part 1 of 5

1. Open **BldgAgrmnt.docx** and save the document with the name **C20-E02-BldgAgrmnt**.
2. Turn on tracking by clicking the Review tab and then clicking the Track Changes button in the Tracking group.
3. Type BUILDING between *THIS* and *AGREEMENT* in the first paragraph of text. (The text you type displays in the document underlined and in red.)
4. Delete *thirty (30)* in the second paragraph. (The deleted text displays in the document as strikethrough text.)
5. Type sixty (60).

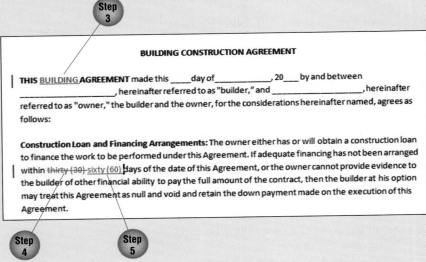

6. Move a paragraph of text by completing the following steps:
   a. Select the paragraph of text that begins with *Supervision of Work:* including the blank line below the paragraph.
   b. Press Ctrl + X to cut the text. (The text stays in the document and displays in red with strikethrough characters.)
   c. Position the insertion point at the beginning of the word *Start* (in the paragraph that begins *Start of Construction and Completion:*).
   d. Press Ctrl + V to insert the cut text. (This inserts the text in green with a double underline in the new location and also changes the text in the original location to green with double-strikethrough characters.)
7. Turn off tracking by clicking the Track Changes button in the Tracking group.
8. Display revisions in balloons by clicking the Show Markup button, pointing to *Balloons*, and then clicking *Show Revisions in Balloons* at the side menu.
9. After looking at the revisions in balloons, click the Show Markup button, point to *Balloons*, and then click *Show All Revisions Inline* at the side menu.
10. Save **C20-E02-BldgAgrmnt.docx**.

You can display information about tracked changes by positioning the mouse pointer on a change. After approximately one second, a box displays above the change listing the author of the change, the date, time, and type of change (for example, whether it was a deletion or insertion). You can also display information about tracked changes by displaying the Reviewing pane. Each change is listed separately in the pane. Use the up and down scroll arrows at the right of the Reviewing pane to scroll through and view each change.

Changing User Information

In the "Distinguishing Comments from Other Users" section earlier in this chapter, you learned how to change the user name and initials at the Word Options dialog box. You can also display the Word Options dialog box with *General* selected by clicking the Track Changes button arrow and then clicking *Change User Name* at the drop-down list.

QUICK STEPS

Change User Information
1. Click Review tab.
2. Click Track Changes button arrow.
3. Click *Change User Name*.
4. Type desired name in *User name* text box.
5. Type desired initials in *Initials* text box.

Exercise 20.2B   Changing User Information and Tracking Changes   Part 2 of 5

---

1. With **C20-E02-BldgAgrmnt.docx** open, change the user information by completing the following steps:
   a. If necessary, click the Review tab.
   b. Click the Track Changes button arrow and then click *Change User Name*.

c. At the Word Options dialog box with *General* selected, select the name in the *User name* text box and then type Lorrie Carter.

d. Select the initials in the *Initials* text box and then type LC.

e. Click OK to close the dialog box.

2. Make additional changes to the contract and track the changes by completing the following steps:

a. Click the Track Changes button to turn on tracking.

b. Select the title *BUILDING CONSTRUCTION AGREEMENT* and then change the font size to 14.

c. Delete the text *at his option* located in the second sentence in the second paragraph. (Your tracking color may vary from what you see below.)

d. Delete the text *and Completion* that displays in the beginning text in the fourth paragraph.

Construction Loan and Financing Arrangements: The owner either has or will obtain a construction loan to finance the work to be performed under this Agreement. If adequate financing has not been arranged within ~~thirty (30)~~ sixty (60) days of the date of this Agreement, or the owner cannot provide evidence to the builder of other financial ability to pay the full amount of the contract, then the builder ~~at his option~~ may treat this Agreement as null and void and retain the down payment made on the execution of this Agreement.

Step 2c

Supervision of Work: Owner agrees that the direction and supervision of the working force, including subcontractors, rests exclusively with the builder, or his/her duly designated agent, and owner agrees not to issue any instructions to, or otherwise interfere with, same.

Step 2d

Start of Construction ~~and Completion~~: The builder shall commence construction of the residence as soon as practical after the signing of this Agreement and adequate financial arrangements satisfactory to the builder have been made.

e. Delete *thirty (30)* in the paragraph that begins *Builder's Right to Terminate the Contract:* (located on the second page).

f. Type sixty (60).

g. Select the text *IN WITNESS WHEREOF* that displays toward the bottom of the document and then turn on bold.

3. Click the Review tab and then click the Track Changes button to turn off tracking.

4. Click the Reviewing Pane button to turn on the display of the pane and then use the up- and down-pointing arrow at the right side of the Reviewing pane to review the changes.

5. View the changes in balloons by clicking the Show Markup button, pointing to *Balloons*, and then clicking *Show Revisions in Balloons*.

6. Close the Reviewing pane and then scroll through the document and view the changes in the balloons.

7. Click the Show Markup button, point to *Balloons*, and then click *Show All Revisions Inline* at the drop-down list.

8. Change the user information back to the information that displayed before you typed *Lorrie Carter* and the initials *LC* by completing the following steps:

a. Click the Track Changes button arrow and then click *Change User Name*.

b. At the Word Options dialog box, select *Lorrie Carter* in the *User name* text box and then type the original name.

c. Select the initials *LC* in the *Initials* text box and then type the original initials.

d. Click OK to close the dialog box.

9. Print the document with the markups by completing the following steps:
    a. Click the File tab and then click the Print tab.
    b. At the Print tab Backstage view, click the first gallery in the *Settings* category, and then make sure a check mark displays before the *Print Markup* option that displays below the drop-down list box. (If the *Print Markup* option is not preceded by a check mark, click the option.)
    c. Click the Print button.

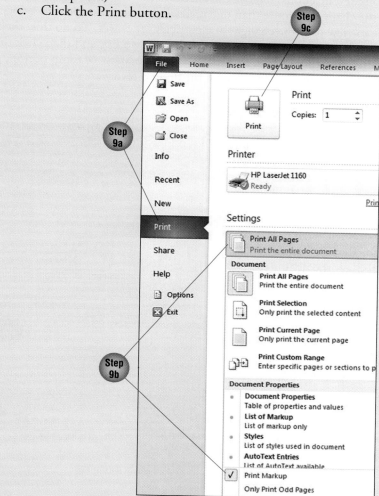

10. Save **C20-E02-BldgAgrmnt.docx**.

Displaying for Review

By default, Word displays all tracked changes and comments in a document. You can change this default setting at the Display for Review button drop-down list. If you change the default setting *Final: Show Markup* to *Final*, the document displays with all changes incorporated in it. If you select *Original: Show markup*, the original document displays with the changes tracked. Select *Original*, and the original document displays without any changes. These four options at the Display for Review button drop-down list allow you to view a document at various stages in the editing process.

Display for Review

Showing Markup

Show Markup

You can customize which tracked changes display in a document with options at the Show Markup button drop-down list. If you want to show only one particular type of tracked change, remove the check marks before all options except the desired one. For example, if you want to view only formatting changes and not other types of changes such as insertions and deletions, remove the check mark before each option except *Formatting*. If the changes of more than one reviewer have been tracked in a document, you can choose to view only the changes of a particular reviewer. To do this, click the Show Markup button, point to *Reviewers* at the drop-down list, and then click the *All Reviewers* check box to remove the check mark. Click the Show Markup button, point to *Reviewers*, and then click the check box of the desired reviewer.

Exercise 20.2C — Changing the Display for Review and Showing Markup — Part 3 of 5

1. With **C20-E02-BldgAgrmnt.docx** open, change the display for review by completing the following steps:
   a. If necessary, click the Review tab.
   b. Click the Display for Review button and then click *Final*. (This displays the document with the changes included.)
   c. Click the Display for Review button and then click *Original*. (This displays the original document before any changes were made.)
   d. Click the Display for Review button and then click *Final: Show Markup*.

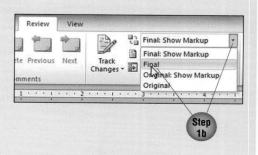

2. Display only those changes made by Lorrie Carter by completing the following steps:
   a. Click the Show Markup button in the Tracking group and then point to *Reviewers*.
   b. Click the *All Reviewers* check box to remove the check mark. (This also removes the drop-down list.)
   c. Click the Show Markup button, point to *Reviewers*, and then click *Lorrie Carter*.
   d. Scroll through the document and observe that only changes made by Lorrie Carter display in the document.
   e. Return the display to all reviewers by clicking the Show Markup button, pointing to *Reviewers*, and then clicking *All Reviewers*.
3. Save **C20-E02-BldgAgrmnt.docx**.

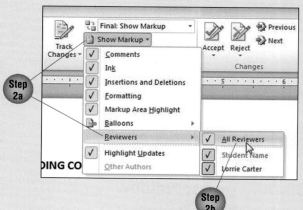

Customizing Track Changes Options

Default settings determine how tracked changes display in a document. For example, inserted text displays in red type with an underline below the text, and deleted text displays in red type with strikethrough characters. Text that has been moved displays both in the original location in green type with double-strikethrough characters and in the new location in green type with a double underline below the text. You can customize these options and others at the Track Changes Options dialog box, shown in Figure 20.4. With options at this dialog box, you can customize the display of markup text, moved text, table cell highlighting, formatting, and balloons. Display this dialog box by clicking the Track Changes button arrow and then clicking *Change Tracking Options* at the drop-down list.

Figure 20.4 Track Changes Options Dialog Box

Change how markup displays with options in this section.

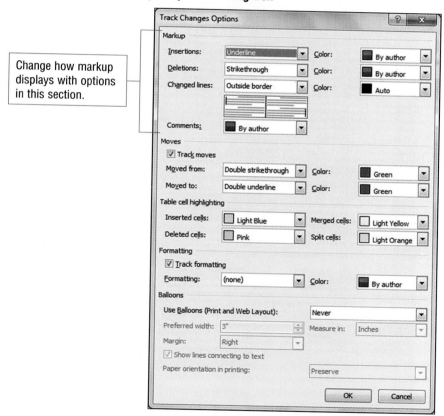

1. With **C20-E02-BldgAgrmnt.docx** open, customize track changes options by completing the following steps:

    a. If necessary, click the Review tab.

    b. Click the Track Changes button arrow and then click *Change Tracking Options*.

    c. At the Track Changes Options dialog box, click the down-pointing arrow at the right of the *Insertions* option and then click *Double underline* at the drop-down list.

    d. Click the down-pointing arrow at the right of the *Insertions* color option box and then click *Green* at the drop-down list. (You will need to scroll down the list to display this color.)

    e. Click the down-pointing arrow at the right of the *Moved from* color option box and then click *Dark Blue* at the drop-down list.

    f. Click the down-pointing arrow at the right of the *Moved to* color option box and then click *Violet* at the drop-down list. (You will need to scroll down the list to display this color.)

    g. Click OK to close the dialog box.

2. Save **C20-E02-BldgAgrmnt.docx**.

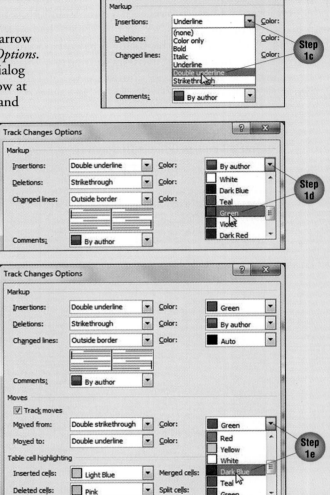

Navigating to Revisions

Next   Previous

Earlier in this chapter, you learned to use the Next and Previous buttons in the Comments group in the Review tab to navigate between comments inserted in a document. Similarly, you can use the Next and Previous buttons in the Changes group in the Review tab to navigate to revisions in a document. Click the Next button, and Word selects the next revision in the document. Click the Previous button to select the preceding revision. If you turn on Track Changes and then move text, revision balloons that contain a small Go button in the lower right corner display identifying the deleted (cut) text and the inserted (pasted) text. Click the Go button in either of the balloons to move the insertion point to the other balloon.

Accepting and Rejecting Revisions

You can accept or reject changes made to a document. Click the Accept button to accept the change and move to the next change. Click the Reject button to reject the change and move to the next. Click the Reject button arrow, and a drop-down list displays with options to reject the change and move to the next change, reject the change, reject all changes shown, or reject all changes in the document. Similar options are available at the Accept button arrow drop-down list.

Accept   Reject

Exercise 20.2E Accepting and Rejecting Changes   Part 5 of 5

1. With **C20-E02-BldgAgrmnt.docx** open, display all tracked changes *except* formatting changes by completing the following steps:
   a. Click the Show Markup button and then click *Formatting* at the drop-down list.
   b. Scroll through the document and notice that the vertical line at the left side of the formatting locations has been removed.
   c. Click the Show Markup button and then click *Formatting* at the drop-down list. (This inserts a check mark in the check box.)
2. Navigate to tracked changes by completing the following steps:
   a. Press Ctrl + Home to move the insertion point to the beginning of the document.
   b. Click the Next button in the Changes group to select the first change.
   c. Click the Next button again to select the second change.
   d. Click the Previous button to select the first change.
3. Navigate between the original location of the moved text and the new location by completing the following steps:
   a. Press Ctrl + Home to move the insertion point to the beginning of the document.
   b. Click the Show Markup button, point to *Balloons*, and then click *Show Revisions in Balloons*.
   c. If necessary, scroll to the right to display the right edge of the balloons and then click the Go button that displays in the lower right corner of the Moved balloon. (This selects the text in the Moved up balloon.)
   d. Click the Go button in the lower right corner of the Moved up balloon. (This selects the text in the Moved balloon.)
   e. Click the Show Markup button, point to *Balloons*, and then click *Show All Revisions Inline*.
4. Press Ctrl + Home to move the insertion point to the beginning of the document.

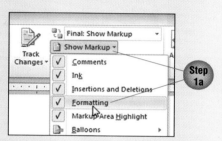

Step 1a

Step 2b

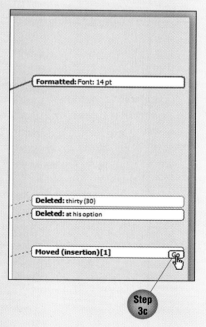

Formatted: Font: 14 pt

Deleted: thirty (30)
Deleted: at his option

Moved (insertion)[1]   Go

Step 3c

5. Display and then accept only formatting changes by completing the following steps:
   a. Click the Show Markup button in the Tracking group and then click *Comments* at the drop-down list. (This removes the check mark and the drop-down list.)
   b. Click the Show Markup button and then click *Ink*.
   c. Click the Show Markup button and then click *Insertions and Deletions*.
   d. Click the Show Markup button and then click *Markup Area Highlight* (Formatting is now the only option in the first section of the drop-down list containing a check mark.)
   e. Click the Accept button arrow and then click *Accept All Changes Shown* at the drop-down list. (This accepts only the formatting changes in the document because those are the only changes showing.)

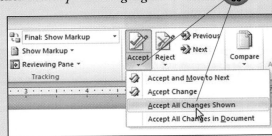

6. Display all changes by completing the following steps:
   a. Click the Show Markup button and then click *Comments* at the drop-down list.
   b. Click the Show Markup button and then click *Ink*.
   c. Click the Show Markup button and then click *Insertions and Deletions*.
   d. Click the Show Markup button and then click *Markup Area Highlight*.
7. Press Ctrl + Home to move the insertion point to the beginning of the document.
8. Reject the change inserting the word *BUILDING* by clicking the Next button in the Changes group and then clicking the Reject button. (This rejects the change and moves to the next revision in the document.)
9. Click the Accept button to accept the change deleting *thirty (30)*.
10. Click the Accept button to accept the change inserting *sixty (60)*.
11. Click the Reject button to reject the change deleting the words *at his option*.
12. Accept all remaining changes by clicking the Accept button arrow and then clicking *Accept All Changes in Document* at the drop-down list.
13. Return Track Changes options to the default settings by completing the following steps:
    a. If necessary, click the Review tab.
    b. Click the Track Changes button arrow and then click *Change Tracking Options*.
    c. At the Track Changes Options dialog box, click the down-pointing arrow at the right of the *Insertions* option and then click *Underline* at the drop-down list.
    d. Click the down-pointing arrow at the right of the *Insertions* color option box and then click *By author* at the drop-down list. (You will need to scroll up the list to display this color.)
    e. Click the down-pointing arrow at the right of the *Moved from* color option box and then click *Green* at the drop-down list. (You may need to scroll down the list to display this color.)
    f. Click the down-pointing arrow at the right of the *Moved to* color option box and then click *Green* at the drop-down list.
    g. Click OK to close the dialog box.
14. Check to make sure all tracked changes are accepted or rejected by completing the following steps:
    a. Click the Reviewing Pane button in the Tracking group.
    b. Check the summary information that displays at the top of the Reviewing pane and make sure that a zero follows all of the options.
    c. Close the Reviewing pane.
15. Save, print, and then close **C20-E02-BldgAgrmnt.docx**.

Comparing Documents

Word contains a legal blackline option that you can use to compare two documents and display the differences as tracked changes in a third document. To use this option, click the Review tab, click the Compare button in the Compare group, and then click *Compare* at the drop-down list. This displays the Compare Documents dialog box, shown in Figure 20.5. At this dialog box, click the Browse for Original button. At the Open dialog box, navigate to the folder that contains the first of the two documents you want to compare and then double-click the document. Click the Browse for Revised button in the Compare Documents dialog box, navigate to the folder containing the second of the two documents you want to compare, and then double-click the document. Click OK to close the dialog box and the compared document displays with track changes.

Compare

Figure 20.5 Compare Documents Dialog Box

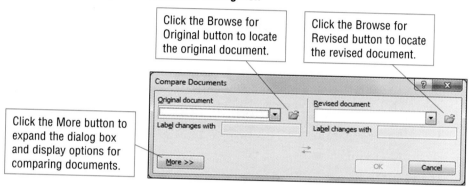

Viewing Compared Documents

When you click OK at the Compare Documents dialog box, the compared document displays with the changes tracked. Other windows may also display depending on the option selected at the Show Source Documents side menu. Display this side menu by clicking the Compare button and then pointing to *Show Source Documents*. You may see just the compared document, or you may see the compared document plus the Reviewing pane, original document, and/or revised document.

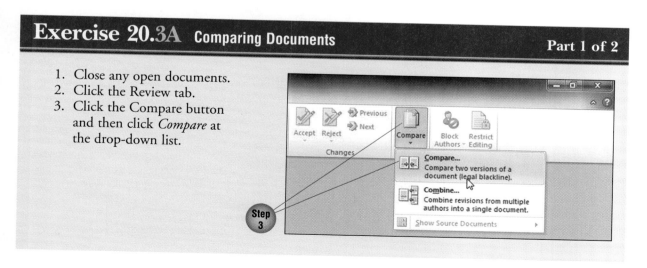

Exercise 20.3A Comparing Documents

Part 1 of 2

1. Close any open documents.
2. Click the Review tab.
3. Click the Compare button and then click *Compare* at the drop-down list.

4. At the Compare Documents dialog box, click the Browse for Original button.
5. At the Open dialog box, navigate to the Chapter20 folder on your storage medium and then double-click **ComAgrmnt.docx**.
6. At the Compare Documents dialog box, click the Browse for Revised button.

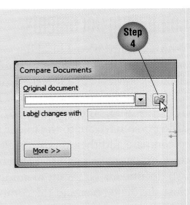

7. At the Open dialog box, double-click **EditedComAgrmnt.docx**.
8. Click the OK button. (If the original and revised documents display along with the compared document, click the Compare button, point to *Show Source Documents* at the drop-down list, and then click *Hide Source Documents* at the side menu.)
9. With the compared document active, print the document showing markups.
10. Click the File tab and then click *Close*. At the message asking if you want to save changes, click the Don't Save button.

Customizing Compare Options

By default, Word compares the original document with the revised document and displays the differences as tracked changes in a third document. You can change this default setting along with others by expanding the Compare Documents dialog box. Expand the dialog box by clicking the More button, and additional options display, as shown in Figure 20.6.

Figure 20.6 Expanded Compare Documents Dialog Box

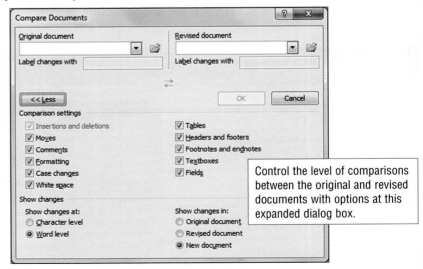

Control the level of comparisons between the original and revised documents with options at this expanded dialog box.

Control the level of comparisons that Word makes between the original and revised documents with options in the *Comparison settings* section of the dialog box. The *Show changes at* option in the *Show changes* section of the dialog box has a default setting of *Word level*. At this setting, Word shows changes to whole words rather than individual characters within the word. For example, if you deleted the letters *ed* from the end of a word, Word would display the entire word as a change rather than just the *ed*. If you want to show changes by character, click the *Character level* option. By default, Word displays differences between compared documents in a new document. With options in the *Show changes in* section, you can change this to *Original document* or *Revised document*. If you change options in the expanded Compare Documents dialog box, the selected options will be the defaults the next time you open the dialog box.

Exercise 20.3B Customizing Compare Options and Comparing Documents   Part 2 of 2

1. Close any open documents.
2. Click the Review tab.
3. Click the Compare button and then click *Compare* at the drop-down list.
4. At the Compare Documents dialog box, click the Browse for Original button.
5. At the Open dialog box, navigate to the Chapter20 folder on your storage medium and then double-click **ComAgrmnt.docx**.
6. At the Compare Documents dialog box, click the Browse for Revised button.
7. At the Open dialog box, double-click **EditedComAgrmnt.docx**.
8. At the Compare Documents dialog box, click the More button. (Skip this step if the dialog box displays expanded and a Less button displays above the *Comparison settings* section.)
9. Click the *Moves* check box and then click the *Formatting* check box to remove the check marks.

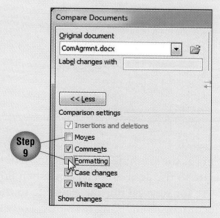

Step 9

10. Click the OK button.
11. Print the document showing markups.
12. Close the document without saving it.
13. Return the options to the default settings by completing the following steps:
    a. Close any open documents.
    b. Click the Review tab.
    c. Click the Compare button and then click *Compare* at the drop-down list.

   d.   At the Compare Documents dialog box, click the Browse for Original button.

   e.   At the Open dialog box, double-click **ComAgrmnt.docx**.

   f.   At the Compare Documents dialog box, click the Browse for Revised button.

   g.   At the Open dialog box, double-click **EditedComAgrmnt.docx**.

   h.   At the Compare Documents dialog box, click the More button and then click the *Moves* check box to insert a check mark and then click the *Formatting* check box to insert a check mark.

   i.   Click the Less button.

   j.   Click the OK button.

14. At the new document, accept all of the changes.

15. Print and then close the document without saving the changes.

Combining Documents

If you send a document to several people for review, you can insert each person's changes into the original document by combining each document with the original until you have incorporated all of the changes. To do this, click the Compare button in the Review tab and then click *Combine* at the drop-down list. This displays the Combine Documents dialog box, shown in Figure 20.7. The Combine Documents dialog box contains many of the same options that are available in the Compare Documents dialog box.

Figure 20.7 Combine Documents Dialog Box

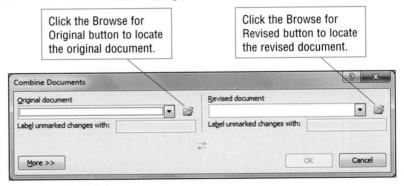

To combine documents at the Combine Documents dialog box, click the Browse for Original button, navigate to the desired folder, and then double-click the original document. Click the Browse for Revised button, navigate to the desired folder, and then double-click one of the documents containing revisions. You can also click the down-pointing arrow at the right of the *Original document* text box or the *Revised document* text box to display a drop-down list of the most recently selected documents.

Combining and Merging Documents

Control how changes are combined with options in the expanded Combine Documents dialog box. By default, Word merges the changes in the revised document into the original document. You can change this default setting with options in the *Show changes in* section. You can choose to merge changes into the revised document or to merge changes into a new document.

1. Close all open documents.
2. Click the Review tab.
3. Click the Compare button in the Compare group and then click *Combine* at the drop-down list.

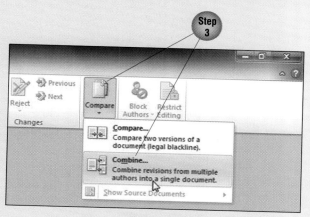

4. At the Combine Documents dialog box, click the More button to expand the Combine Documents dialog box.
5. Click the *Original Document* option in the *Show changes in* section.
6. Click the Browse for Original button.
7. At the Open dialog box, navigate to the Chapter20 folder on your storage medium and then double-click **OriginalLease.docx**.

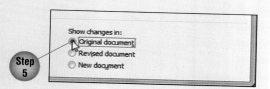

8. At the Combine Documents dialog box, click the Browse for Revised button.
9. At the Open dialog box, double-click **LeaseReviewer1.docx**.
10. Click the OK button.
11. Save the document with Save As and name it **C20-E04-CombinedLease**.

Showing Source Documents

With options in the Show Source Documents side menu, you can specify which source documents to display. Display this side menu by clicking the Compare button and then pointing to *Show Source Documents*. Four options display at the side menu including *Hide Source Documents*, *Show Original*, *Show Revised*, and *Show Both*. With the *Hide Source Documents* option selected, the original and revised documents do not display on the screen; only the combined document displays. If you choose the *Show Original* option, the original document displays in a side pane at the right side of the document. Synchronous scrolling is selected, so scrolling in the combined document results in scrolling in the other. Choose the *Show Revised* option, and the revised document displays in the panel at the right. Choose the *Show Both* option to display the original document in a panel at the right side of the screen and the revised document in a panel below the original document panel.

1. With **C20-E04-CombinedLease.docx** open, click the Compare button, point to *Show Source Documents*, and then, if necessary, click *Hide Source Documents* at the side menu. (This displays the original document with the combined document changes shown as tracked changes.)

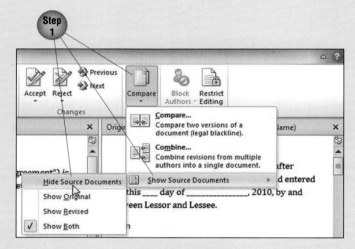

2. Click the Compare button, point to *Show Source Documents*, and then click *Show Original* at the side menu. (This displays the original document at the right and the original document with tracked changes in the middle.)
3. Click the Compare button, point to *Show Source Documents*, and then click *Show Revised*.
4. Click the Compare button, point to *Show Source Documents*, and then click *Show Both*. Scroll in the combined document and notice that the original document and the revised document also scroll simultaneously.
5. Click the Compare button, point to *Show Source Documents*, and then click *Hide Source Documents*.
6. Click the Review tab, click the Compare button, and then click *Combine* at the drop-down list.
7. If the Reviewing pane displays, close it.
8. At the Combine Documents dialog box, click the Browse for Original button.
9. At the Open dialog box, double-click **C20-E04-CombinedLease.docx**.
10. At the Combine Documents dialog box, click the Browse for Revised button.
11. At the Open dialog box, double-click **LeaseReviewer2.docx**.
12. At the Combine Documents dialog box, click the OK button.
13. Save **C20-E04-CombinedLease.docx**.
14. Print the document showing markups.
15. Accept all changes to the document. (Look through the document and notice that the *Rent* heading displays in blue. Select *Rent* and then change the font color to dark red.)
16. Save, print, and then close **C20-E04-CombinedLease.docx**.

Chapter Summary

➤ Insert a comment in a document by clicking the New Comment button in the Comments group in the Review tab. When you click the New Comment button, a comment balloon displays at the right margin. If any previous settings have been applied, the Reviewing pane, rather than a comment balloon, may display.

➤ Turn the display of the Reviewing pane on and off with the Reviewing Pane button in the Tracking group in the Review tab.

➤ You can insert comments in the Reviewing pane or in comment balloons. Insert a comment in a balloon by clicking the Show Markup button in the Tracking group in the Review tab, pointing to *Balloons*, and then clicking *Show Only Comments and Formatting in Balloons* at the side menu.

➤ Navigate through comments using the Previous and Next buttons in the Comments group in the Review tab.

➤ Edit a comment in the Reviewing pane by displaying the pane and then making desired changes to the comment. Edit a comment in a comment balloon by turning on the display of balloons, clicking in the desired comment balloon, and then making desired changes.

➤ Display information about tracked changes, such as author's name, date, time, and the type of change, by positioning the mouse pointer on a change. After approximately one second, a box displays with the information. You can also display information on tracked changes by displaying the Reviewing pane.

➤ If changes are made to a document by another person with different user information, the changes display in a different color. Change user name and initials at the Word Options dialog box with *General* selected.

➤ Print a document along with the inserted comments or choose to print just the comments and not the document.

➤ Delete a comment by clicking the Next button in the Comments group in the Review tab until the desired comment is selected and then clicking the Delete button in the Comments group.

➤ Use the Track Changes feature when more than one person is reviewing a document and making editing changes to it. Turn on tracking by clicking the Track Changes button in the Tracking group in the Review tab.

➤ Control how editing markings display in a document with the Display for Review button in the Tracking group in the Review tab. Control the marking changes that Word displays in a document with options at the Show Markup button drop-down list.

➤ Change Track Changes default settings with options at the Track Changes Options dialog box. Display this dialog box by clicking the Track Changes button arrow in the Tracking group and then clicking *Change Tracking Options* at the drop-down list.

➤ Move to the next change in a document by clicking the Next button in the Changes group in the Review tab or click the Previous button to move to the previous change.

➤ Use the Accept and Reject buttons in the Changes group in the Review tab to accept or reject revisions made in a document.

➤ Use the Compare button in the Compare group in the Review tab to compare two documents and display the differences between the documents as tracked changes.

➤ Customize options for comparing documents at the expanded Compare Documents dialog box. Click the More button to expand the dialog box.

➤ If you send a document to several people for review, you can combine changes made by each person with the original document until all changes are incorporated in the original document. Combine documents with options at the Combine Documents dialog box.

➤ Customize options for combining documents at the expanded Combine Documents dialog box. Click the More button to expand the dialog box.

➤ Specify which source documents to display by clicking the Compare button in the Compare group in the Review tab, pointing to *Show Source Documents*, and then clicking the desired option at the side menu.

Commands Review

FEATURE	RIBBON TAB, GROUP	BUTTON, OPTION	KEYBOARD SHORTCUT
Comment	Review, Comments		
Reviewing pane	Review, Tracking		
Balloons	Review, Tracking	, Balloons	
Delete comment	Review, Comments		
Next comment	Review, Comments		
Previous comment	Review, Comments		
Track changes	Review, Tracking		Ctrl + Shift + E
Display for review	Review, Tracking	Final: Show Markup	
Show markup	Review, Tracking		
Track Changes Options dialog box	Review, Tracking	, Change Tracking Options	
Next revision	Review, Changes		
Previous revision	Review, Changes		
Accept changes	Review, Changes		
Reject changes	Review, Changes		
Compare Documents dialog box	Review, Compare	, Compare	
Combine Documents dialog box	Review, Compare	, Combine	
Show source documents	Review, Compare	, Show Source Documents	

Key Points Review

Completion: In the space provided at the right, indicate the correct term, command, or number.

1. Insert a comment into a document by clicking this button in the Comments group in the Review tab.
2. Navigate between comments by using these two buttons in the Comments group in the Review tab.
3. If a document contains comments, print only the comments by displaying the Print tab Backstage view, clicking the first gallery in the Settings category, clicking this option, and then clicking the Print button.
4. Display information on tracked changes in this pane.
5. Change user information with options at this dialog box.
6. Turn on the tracking feature by clicking the Track Changes button in this group in the Review tab.
7. This is the keyboard shortcut to turn on tracking.
8. This is the default setting for the Display for Review button.
9. With track changes on, moved text, by default, displays in this color.
10. Customize tracking options at this dialog box.
11. Click the *Combine* option at the Compare button drop-down list and this dialog box displays.
12. Specify which source document to display by clicking the Compare button, pointing to this option, and then clicking the desired option at the side menu.

Chapter Assessments

Applying Your Skills

Demonstrate your knowledge of features learned in this chapter by completing the following assessments.

Assessment 20.1 Insert Comments and Track Changes in a Computer Virus and Security Report

1. Open **CompChapters.docx** and save the document with the name **C20-A01-CompChapters**.
2. Insert a comment at the end of the paragraph in the *TYPES OF VIRUSES* section. To do this, type the word Update, select it, and then create a comment with the following text: *Insert information on the latest virus.*
3. Insert a comment at the end of the last paragraph in the *METHODS OF VIRUS OPERATION* section. To do this, type the words Company Example, select the words, and then create a comment with the following text: *Include information on the latest virus to affect our company.*
4. Insert a comment at the end of the last paragraph in the document. To do this, type the word Information, select it, and then create a comment with the following text: *Include information about laws related to copying software.*

5. Turn on tracking and then make the following changes:
   a. Edit the first sentence in the document so it reads *The computer virus is one of the most familiar forms of risk to computer security.*
   b. Type the word computer's between *the* and *motherboard* in the last sentence in the first paragraph of the document.
   c. Delete the word *real* in the second sentence of the *TYPES OF VIRUSES* section and then type significant.
   d. Select and then delete the last sentence in the *Methods of Virus Operation* section (the sentence that begins *A well-known example of a logic bomb was the . . .*). (Do not delete the comment.)
   e. Turn off tracking.
6. Display the Word Options dialog box with *General* selected and then change the *User name* to Stacey Phillips and the *Initials* to SP.
7. Turn on tracking and then make the following changes:
   a. Delete the words *or cracker* located in the seventh sentence in the *TYPES OF VIRUSES* section.
   b. Delete the word *garner* in the first sentence in the CHAPTER 2: SECURITY RISKS section and then type generate.
   c. Select and then move the *EMPLOYEE THEFT* section below the *CRACKING SOFTWARE FOR COPYING* section.
   d. Turn off tracking.
8. Display the Word Options dialog box with *General* selected and then change the *User name* back to the original name and *Initials* back to the original initials.
9. Print the document showing markups.
10. Accept all of the changes in the document *except* the change moving the *EMPLOYEE THEFT* section below the *CRACKING SOFTWARE FOR COPYING* section.
11. Save, print, and then close **C20-A01-CompChapters.docx**.

Assessment 20.2   Compare Documents

1. Compare **Security.docx** with **EditedSecurity.docx** and insert the changes into a new document. ***Hint: Choose*** **New document** ***at the expanded Compare Documents dialog box.***
2. Save the compared document and name it **C20-A02-Security.docx**.
3. Print the list of markups only (not the document).
4. Reject the changes made to the bulleted text and the changes made to the last paragraph in the *DISASTER RECOVERY PLAN* section and accept all other changes.
5. Number the pages at the bottom center of each page.
6. Save, print, and then close **C20-A02-Security.docx**.

Assessment 20.3   Combine Documents

1. Open **LegalSummons.docx** and save the document with the name **C20-A03-LegalSummons**.
2. Close **C20-A03-LegalSummons.docx**.
3. At a blank screen, combine **C20-A03-LegalSummons** (the original document) with **Review1-LegalSummons.docx** (the revised document) into the original document. ***Hint: Choose*** **Original document** ***at the Combine Documents expanded dialog box.***
4. Accept all changes to the document.
5. Save and then close **C20-A03-LegalSummons.docx**.
6. At a blank screen, combine **C20-A03-LegalSummons.docx** (the original document) with **Review2-LegalSummons.docx** (the revised document) into the original document.
7. Print only the list of markups.
8. Accept all changes to the document.
9. Save, print, and then close **C20-A03-LegalSummons.docx**.

Expanding Your Skills

Explore additional feature options or use Help to learn a new skill in creating these documents.

Assessment 20.4   Change Tracking Options and Track Changes Made to a Table

1. Open **MBPSales.docx** and save the document with the name **C20-A04-MBPSales**.
2. You can track changes made to a table and customize the track changes options for the table. Display the Track Changes Options dialog box and experiment with the options in the *Table cell highlighting* section and then make the following changes:
    a. Change the color for inserted cells to *Light Purple*.
    b. Change the color for deleted cells to *Light Green*.
3. Turn on Track Changes and then make the following changes:
    a. Insert a new row at the beginning of the table.
    b. Merge the cells in the new row. (At the message telling you the action will not be marked as a change, click OK.)
    c. Type Mobile Bay Products in the merged cell.
    d. Delete the *Barclay, Kurt* row.
    e. Insert a new row below *Tanaka, Diana* and then type Caswell, Martin in the first cell, $495,678 in the second cell, and $475,850 in the third cell.
    f. Turn off tracking.
4. Save and then print the document with markups.
5. Accept all of the changes.
6. Display the Track Changes Options dialog box and then return the inserted cells color back to *Light Blue* and the deleted cells color back to *Pink*.
7. Save, print, and then close **C20-A04-MBPSales.docx**.

Assessment 20.5   Insert Comments and Track Changes in a Travel Document

1. Open **BTAdventure.docx** and save the document with the name **C20-A05-BTAdventure**.
2. Display the Track Changes Options dialog box, change the *Use Balloons (Print and Web Layout)* option to *Always*, and then make the following changes:
    a. Change the balloon width to 2 inches.
    b. Display balloons at the left margin.
    c. Change the paper orientation to *Force Landscape*.
3. Insert the following comments:
    a. Type the text Country names at the end of the paragraph in the *African Study Adventure* section, select the text, and then insert the comment Ask Jan if she wants to include specific country names.
    b. Type the word Examples at the end of the paragraph in the *Custom Groups* section, select the word, and then insert the comment Please provide custom program examples.
4. Turn on tracking and then make the following changes:
    a. Insert the word *Travel* between *Comprehensive* and *Itineraries* in the *Comprehensive Itineraries* heading.
    b. Change the number *25* in the *Small Groups* section to *20*.
    c. Delete the words *make sure* in the *Accommodations and Meals* section and then type ensure.
    d. Turn off tracking.
5. Save the document and then print the list of markups only (not the document).
6. Accept the changes.
7. Return the options at the Track Changes Option dialog box back to the default settings.
8. Save the document, print only the document, and then close the document.

Achieving Signature Status

Take your skills to the next level by completing this more challenging assessment.

Assessment 20.6   Track Changes in an Employee Performance Document

1. Open **NSSEmpPerf.docx** and then save the document and name it **C20-A06-NSSEmpPerf**.
2. Turn on track changes and then make the changes shown in Figure 20.8. (Make the editing changes before you move the Employment Records information below the Performance Evaluation information.)
3. Turn off track changes and then print only the list of markups.
4. Accept all changes to the document.
5. Save, print, and then close **C20-A06-NSSEmpPerf.docx**.
6. At a blank screen, combine **C20-A06-NSSEmpPerf.docx** (the original document) with **EditedNSSEmpPerf.docx** (the revised document) into the original document.
7. Accept all changes to the document.
8. Save, print, and then close **C20-A06-NSSEmpPerf.docx**.

Figure 20.8 Assessment 20.6

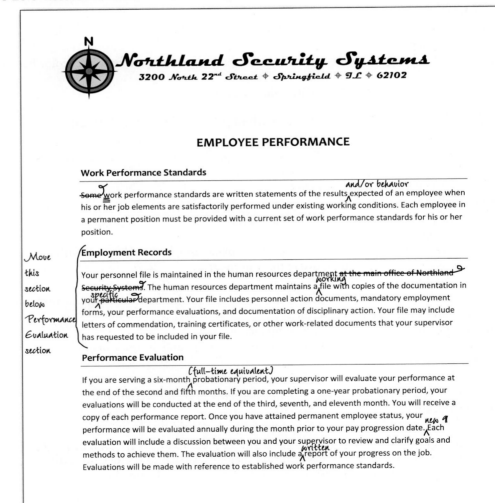

Performance Assessments

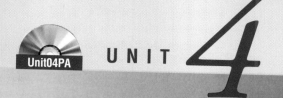

Managing Data

ASSESSING PROFICIENCIES

In this unit, you have learned to prepare customized letters, envelopes, labels, and directories and to sort text in paragraphs, columns, tables, and data source files. You learned how to select specific records from a data source file and merge the specific records with a main document. You also learned how to customize bullets, numbers, and lists; insert and customize headers and footers; insert comments; and track changes.

Note: Before beginning computer assessments, copy to your storage medium the Unit04PA folder from the CD that accompanies this textbook and then make Unit04PA the active folder.

Assessment U4.1   Use Mail Merge to Create Letters to Customers

1. Look at the information shown in Figure U4.1 and Figure U4.2.
2. Use the Mail Merge feature to prepare six letters using the information shown in the figures. (Before typing the letter, click the No Spacing style in the Styles group in the Home tab.)
3. Name the data source file **U4-PA01-MA-DS**, name the main document **U4-PA01-MA-MD**, and name the merged letters document **U4-PA01-MALtrs**.
4. Print and then close **U4-PA01-MALtrs.docx**.
5. Save and then close **U4-PA01-MA-MD.docx**.

Figure U4.1 Assessment U4.1

Mr. Roy Heitzman
5043 Pleasant Street
Grand Rapids, MI 49518

Ms. Julia Quintero
905 Randall Road
Kentwood, MI 49509

Ms. Lola Rose-Simmons
3312 South Meridian
Grand Rapids, MI 49510

Mr. and Mrs. Lawrence Nesbitt
11023 South 32nd Street
Kentwood, MI 49506

Mr. Darren Butler
23103 East Avenue
Grand Rapids, MI 49523

Mr. Samuel McClelland
660 Grove Street
Grand Rapids, MI 49507

Figure U4.2 Assessment U4.1

September 10, 2012

«AddressBlock»

«GreetingLine»

Because you are a valued customer of Motorway Autos, we are offering you a free oil change with your next 15,000-, 36,000-, or 60,000-mile car service appointment. Mention the free offer the next time you schedule a service appointment and the oil change is on us!

For the entire month of October, we are offering fantastic deals on new 2012 models. If you buy a new car from us, we will offer you top trade-in dollars for your used car. Along with our low, low prices, we are also offering low-interest and, in some cases, no-interest loans. Come in and talk with one of our sales representatives to see if you qualify for these special loans.

Please come down to visit our showroom and check out the best-priced automobiles in the region. We are open for your convenience Monday through Friday from 8:00 a.m. to 8:00 p.m., Saturday from 9:00 a.m. to 6:00 p.m., and Sunday from 9:00 a.m. to 5:00 p.m.

Sincerely,

Dusty Powell
Director of Sales

XX
U4-PA01-MA-MD.docx

Assessment U4.2   Use Mail Merge to Create Envelopes

1. Use the Mail Merge feature to prepare envelopes for the letters you created in Assessment U4.1.
2. Specify **U4-PA01-MA-DS.mdb** as the data source document.
3. Save the merged envelope document with the name **U4-PA02-MAEnvs**.
4. Print and then close **U4-PA02-MAEnvs.docx**. (Check with your instructor before printing.)
5. Close the envelope main document without saving it.

Assessment U4.3   Edit Data Source and Main Document and Merge Letters

1. Open **U4-PA01-MA-MD.docx** (at the SQL message, click Yes) and then save the main document with the name **U4-PA03-MA-MD**.
2. Edit the **U4-PA01-MA-DS.mdb** data source file by making the following changes:
   a. Display the record for Mr. Darren Butler and then change the street address from *23103 East Avenue* to *715 South Fifth Street*.
   b. Add *and Mrs.* in the title for Mr. Samuel McClelland. (The title field should display as *Mr. and Mrs.*).
   c. Delete the record for Ms. Lola Rose-Simmons.
   d. Insert a new record with the following information:

   > Ms. Glenda Jefferson
   > 5048 Burton Street
   > Grand Rapids, MI 49503

3. At the main document, add the sentence shown in Figure U4.3 to the end of the third paragraph in the body of the letter and include fill-in fields as shown in parentheses in the figure.
4. Save **U4-PA03-MA-MD.docx**.
5. Merge the records to a new document. At the dialog boxes asking for the number of automobiles and the percents, type the following:

Record 1:	Number = two automobiles	Percent = 2%
Record 2:	Number = one automobile	Percent = 1%
Record 3:	Number = one automobile	Percent = 1%
Record 4:	Number = three automobiles	Percent = 3%
Record 5:	Number = two automobiles	Percent = 2%
Record 6:	Number = one automobile	Percent = 1%

6. Save the merged document with the name **U4-PA03-MALtrs**.
7. Print and then close **U4-PA03-MALtrs.docx**.
8. Save and then close **U4-PA03-MA-MD.mdb**.

Figure U4.3 Assessment U4.3

According to our records, you have purchased (Number) from us. This qualifies you for a special bonus of up to (Percent) off the purchase of a new automobile.

Assessment U4.4   Use Mail Merge to Create Labels

1. Use the Mail Merge feature to create mailing labels with the Avery US Letter 5360 Mailing Labels label product. Use the existing data source **U4-PA01-MA-DS.mdb** for the labels.
2. Display the Mail Merge Recipients dialog box, display the Filter and Sort dialog box with the Filter Records tab selected, and then select only those customers living in Grand Rapids.
3. Complete the merge and then save the labels document with the name **U4-PA04-MALbls**.
4. Print and then close **U4-PA04-MALbls.docx**.
5. Close the labels main document without saving it.

Assessment U4.5   Use Mail Merge to Create a Directory

1. Use the Mail Merge feature to create a directory that uses the records in the **U4-PA01-MA-DS.mdb** data source file to print the customer title, and first and last names at the left margin, the street address at a tab stop, and the city, state and ZIP code at another tab stop. Create a heading for each column.
2. After merging the records in the directory, select the information and then convert the text to a table. Apply formatting to enhance the visual appeal of the table.
3. Save the document and name it **U4-PA05-MADirectory**.
4. Print and then close **U4-PA05-MADirectory.docx**.
5. Close the directory main document without saving it.

Assessment U4.6   Sort Data in Columns and a Table

1. Open **Sort.docx** and save the document with the name **U4-PA06-Sort**.
2. Sort the columns of text below the *CONTACTS* title in ascending order by last name.
3. Sort the amounts in the *Home Equity Loans* column in the table in descending order.
4. Save, print, and then close **U4-PA06-Sort.docx**.

Assessment U4.7   Create and Apply Custom Bullets and a Multilevel List

1. Open **MBPStockAwards.docx** and save the document with the name **U4-PA07-MBPStockAwards**.
2. Apply the Title style to the title *Mobile Bay Products*.
3. Apply the Heading 1 style to the headings *Stock Awards* and *Employee Stock Plan*.
4. Change the style set to Traditional.
5. Select the bulleted paragraphs of text and then define a new picture bullet of your choosing.
6. Select the lines of text below the *Employee Stock Plan* heading and then apply a multilevel list (the middle option in the top row of the *List Library* section of the Multilevel List button drop-down gallery).
7. With the text still selected, define a new multilevel list that inserts capital letters followed by a period (A., B., C.) for level 2 and inserts Arabic numbers followed by a period (1., 2., 3.) for level 3. (Make sure the new multilevel list applies to the selected text.)
8. Save, print, and then close **U4-PA07-MBPStockAwards.docx**.

Assessment U4.8   Keep Text Together and Insert Footers in a Report

1. Open **CompEthics.docx** and save the document with the name **U4-PA08-CompEthics**.
2. Select the entire document and then change the line spacing to 2.0.
3. Change the top margin to 1.5 inches.
4. Apply the Heading 1 style to the two titles in the document *FUTURE OF COMPUTER ETHICS* and *REFERENCES*.
5. Apply the Heading 2 style to the five headings in the document.
6. Hang indent the paragraphs of text below the title *REFERENCES*.
7. Change the style set to Modern.
8. Change the theme to Civic.
9. Keep the heading *SELF-REPLICATING ROBOTS* together with the paragraph of text that follows it.

10. Keep the heading *REFERENCES* together with the paragraph of text that follows it.

11. Create an odd page footer that prints the document title at the left margin and the page number at the right margin and create an even page footer that prints the page number at the left margin and the document title at the right margin.

12. Save, print, and then close **U4-PA08-CompEthics.docx**.

Assessment U4.9   Keep Text Together and Insert Footers in Different Sections of a Document

1. Open **CompSoftware.docx** and then save the document with the name **U4-PA09-CompSoftware**.

2. Change the top margin to 1.5 inches.

3. Insert a section break that begins a new page at the title *SOFTWARE PRICING* (located on page two).

4. Apply the Title style to the two titles in the document *SOFTWARE DELIVERY* and *SOFTWARE PRICING* and apply the Heading 1 style to the six headings in the document.

5. Change the style set to Simple.

6. Apply the Hardcover theme and change the theme fonts to *Origin*.

7. Keep the heading *The Cost of Software in the Cloud* (located at the bottom of page three) together with the paragraph of text that follows it.

8. Create a header that prints the current date at the right margin in both sections in the document.

9. Create a footer for the first section in the document that prints *Software Delivery* at the left margin, the page number in the middle, and your first and last names at the right margin.

10. Edit the footer for the second section so it prints *Software Pricing* instead of *Software Delivery*. **Hint: Make sure you click the Link to Previous button in the Header & Footer Tools Design tab to turn off linking.**

11. Save, print, and then close **U4-PA09-CompSoftware.docx**.

Assessment U4.10   Insert Comments and Track Changes in a Report

1. Open **OnlineShop.docx** and save the document with the name **U4-PA10-OnlineShop**.

2. Type the word Source at the end of the first paragraph in the report, select the word, and then insert the comment Include the source where you found this definition.

3. Type the word Examples at the end of the first paragraph in the *Online Shopping Venues* section, select the word, and then insert the comment Include at least two of the most popular online shopping stores.

4. Turn on tracking and then make the following changes:
   a. Delete the words *and most are eliminating paper tickets altogether* (including the comma that displays before *and*) that display at the end of the last sentence in the second paragraph.
   b. Edit the heading *ADVANTAGES OF ONLINE SHOPPING* so it displays as *ONLINE SHOPPING ADVANTAGES*.
   c. Bold the first sentence of each of the bulleted paragraphs on the first page.
   d. Turn off tracking.

5. Display the Word Options dialog box with *General* selected and then change the *User name* to Colleen Burton and the *Initials* to CB.

6. Turn on tracking and then make the following changes:
    a. Delete the words *the following* in the first paragraph in the *ONLINE SHOPPING ADVANTAGES* section.
    b. Insert the following bulleted text between the third and fourth bulleted paragraphs on the second page: Keep thorough records of all transactions.
    c. Turn off tracking.
7. Display the Word Options dialog box with *General* selected and then change the *User name* back to the original name and *Initials* back to the original initials.
8. Accept all of the changes in the document *except* the change deleting the words *and most are eliminating paper tickets altogether.*
9. Save, print, and then close **U4-PA10-OnlineShop.docx**.

Assessment U4.11   Combine Documents

1. Open **Software.docx** and save the document with the name **U4-PA11-Software**.
2. Close **U4-PA11-Software.docx**.
3. At a blank document, combine **U4-PA11-Software.docx** (the original document) with **Software-CL.docx** (the revised document) into the original document.
4. Save **U4-PA11-Software.docx**.
5. Print the document showing markups.
6. Accept all changes to the document.
7. Make the following changes to the document:
    a. Change the style set to Modern.
    b. Apply the Concourse theme.
    c. Apply the *Elemental* theme colors.
    d. Insert the Mod (Odd Page) footer.
    e. Insert the *SAMPLE 1* watermark in the document.
8. Save, print, and then close **U4-PA11-Software.docx**.

CREATING ORIGINAL DOCUMENTS

The activity in Assessment U4.12 gives you the opportunity to practice your writing skills as well as demonstrate your mastery of some of the important Word features presented in this unit. When you compose the document, use correct grammar, precise word choices, and clear sentence construction.

Assessment U4.12   Use Mail Merge to Create Letters to Volunteers

Situation: You are a volunteer coordinator for the Kentwood School District, and you have been asked to write a letter to the new reading volunteers listed on the next page, thanking them for their interest in volunteering for the reading literacy program and inviting them to an orientation on Tuesday, September 25, 2012, from 7:00 to 8:30 p.m. In the letter, explain that during this orientation volunteers will learn more about the reading program, including the program goals, which students will be served by the program, what reading levels are included in the program, the time commitment required of volunteers, and the materials needed for the program. Use the Mail Merge feature to compose the main document letter and create a data source file with the names and addresses below. Save the data source file with the name **U4-PA12-KSD-DS.mdb** and the letter main document with the name **U4-PA12-KSD-MD.docx**. Merge the main document with the records in the data source file and name the merged document **U4-PA12-VolLtrs**. Print and then close **U4-PA12-VolLtrs.docx** and then save and close **U4-PA12-KSD-MD.docx**.

Ms. Karen Lyons
9023 South 42nd Street
Kentwood, MI 48933

Mr. Bryan Hamilton
11023 12th Northeast
Kentwood, MI 48920

Mr. Richard Ulrich
453 Silverdale Road
Kentwood, MI 48930

Mrs. Lindsay Childers
8931 133rd Place Northwest
Kentwood, MI 48933

Mr. Juan Nunez
8329 Branchwood Drive
Kentwood, MI 48933

Ms. Lisa Taua
1129 Military Road South
Kentwood, MI 48930

Unit 5

Customizing Documents and Features

Chapter 21   Inserting and Customizing Quick Parts

Chapter 22   Customizing AutoCorrect and Word Options

Chapter 23   Customizing Themes

Chapter 24   Creating and Managing Styles

Chapter 25   Protecting and Preparing Documents

Unit 5   Performance Assessments

Chapter 21

SNAP TUTORIALS

Tutorial 21.1
Inserting and Sorting Building
Blocks
Tutorial 21.2
Saving Building Block Content
Tutorial 21.3
Editing Building Block
Properties
Tutorial 21.4
Inserting Custom Building
Blocks
Tutorial 21.5
Managing Document Properties
Tutorial 21.6
Inserting Document Properties
Tutorial 21.7
Inserting and Updating Fields
from Quick Parts

Inserting and Customizing Quick Parts

Performance Objectives

Upon successful completion of Chapter 21, you will be able to:

- Sort and insert building blocks
- Create, edit, and modify building blocks
- Delete building blocks
- Insert fields from Quick Parts
- Update fields

Word offers a number of features to help you streamline the formatting of documents. In this chapter, you will learn how to use predesigned building blocks to build a document. You will also learn how to create, save, and edit your own building blocks as well as how to insert fields in a document and update them.

Note: Before beginning computer exercises for this chapter, copy to your storage medium the Chapter21 folder from the CD that accompanies this textbook and then make Chapter21 the active folder.

In this chapter, students will produce the following documents:

Exercise 21.1. C21-E01-CompChapters.docx
Exercise 21.2. C21-E02-PSLtr.docx
Exercise 21.3. C21-E03-PSLtr.docx
Exercise 21.4. C21-E04-SEBetaAgrmnt.docx
Exercise 21.4. C21-E04-SETestAgrmnt.docx

Model answers for these exercises are shown on the following pages.

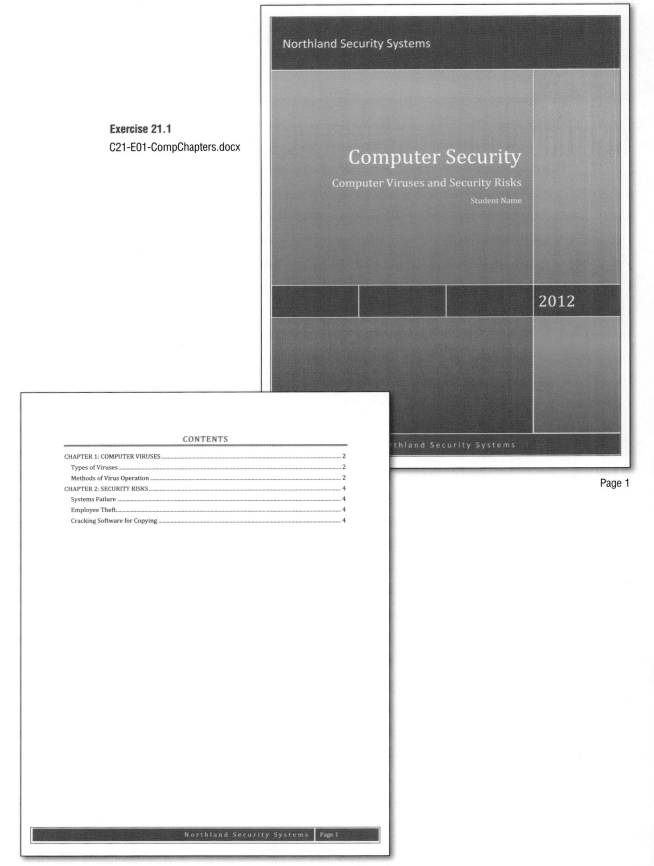

Exercise 21.1

C21-E01-CompChapters.docx

Northland Security Systems

Computer Security

Computer Viruses and Security Risks

Student Name

2012

Northland Security Systems

Page 1

CONTENTS

CHAPTER 1: COMPUTER VIRUSES...2
Types of Viruses..2
Methods of Virus Operation..2
CHAPTER 2: SECURITY RISKS..4
Systems Failure...4
Employee Theft..4
Cracking Software for Copying...4

Northland Security Systems | Page 1

Page 2

Page 3

CHAPTER 1: COMPUTER VIRUSES

One of the most familiar forms of risk to computer security is the computer virus. A computer virus is a program written by a hacker or a cracker, designed to perform some kind of trick upon an unsuspecting victim's computer. In some cases, the trick performed is mild, such as drawing an offensive image on the victim's screen or changing all of the characters in a document to another language. Sometimes the trick is much more severe, such as reformatting the hard drive and erasing all the data or damaging the motherboard so that it cannot operate properly.

TYPES OF VIRUS

Viruses can be categorized by t
which include being a nuisance,
data, facilitating espionage, and
hardware. A nuisance virus usu
real damage but is an inconveni
most difficult part of a compute
the data on the hard drive. The
programs, documents, database
emails form the heart of a perso
A data-destructive virus is desig
destroy this data. Some viruses
to create a backdoor into a syste
security. Called espionage virus
damage but allow a hacker or cr
the system later for the purpose
data or spying on the work of th
Very rarely, a virus is created to
hardware of the computer syste
Called hardware-destructive vir
bits of programming can weake
chips, drives, and other compon

METHODS OF VIRUS OPERATION

Viruses operate and are transmitted in a variety of ways. An email virus is normally transmitted as an attachment to a message sent over the Internet. Email viruses require the victim to click on the attachment, which causes the virus to execute. Another common mode of virus transmission is via a macro, a small subprogram that allows users to customize and automate certain functions. A macro virus is written for a specific program, which then becomes infected when it opens a file with the virus stored in its macros. The

Page 4

ability to attack in several different ways. They may first infect the boot sector and then later act like a Trojan horse virus by infecting a disk file. These viruses are more sophisticated and therefore more difficult to guard against. Another type of virus is the logic bomb, which generally sits quietly dormant waiting for a specific event or set of conditions to occur. A well-known example of a logic bomb was the widely publicized Michelangelo virus, which infected personal computers and caused them to display a message on the artist's birthday.

Page 5

CHAPTER 2: SECURITY RISKS

Although hackers, crackers, and viruses garner the most attention as security risks, companies face a variety of other dangers to their hardware and software systems. Principally, these risks involve types of system failure, employee theft, and the cracking of software for copying.

SYSTEMS FAILURE

A fundamental element in making sure that computer systems operate properly is protecting the electrical power that runs them. Power interruptions such as blackouts and brownouts have very adverse effects on computers. An inexpensive type of power strip called a surge protector can guard against power fluctuations and can also serve as an extension cord and splitter. A much more vigorous power protection system is an uninterruptible power supply (UPS), which provides a battery backup. Similar in nature to a power strip but much bulkier and a bit more expensive, a UPS provides steady, spike-free power and keeps a computer running during a blackout.

EMPLOYEE THEFT

Although accurate estimates are difficult to pinpoint, businesses certainly lose millions of dollars a year in stolen computer hardware and software. In large organizations, such theft often goes unnoticed or unreported. Someone takes a hard drive or a scanner home for legitimate use, then leaves the job sometime later and keeps the machine. Sometimes, employees take components to add to their home PC systems, or thieves break into businesses and haul away computers. Such thefts cost far more than the price of the stolen computers because they also involve the cost of replacing the lost data, the cost of time lost while the machines are gone, and the cost of installing new machines and training people to use them.

CRACKING SOFTWARE FOR COPYING

A common goal of hackers is to crack a software protection scheme. A crack is a method of circumventing a security scheme that prevents a user from copying a program. A common protection scheme for software is to require the installation CD to be resident in the drive whenever the program runs. Making copies of the CD with a burner, however, easily fools this protection scheme. Some game companies are taking an extra step to make duplication difficult by scrambling some of the data on the original CDs, which CD burners will automatically correct when copying. When the copied and corrected CD is used, the software checks for the scrambled track information. If the error is not found, the software will not run.

Exercise 21.2

C21-E02-PSLtr.docx

WORLD WIDE TRAVEL

2400 International Drive ⊕ Las Vegas, NV 77534 ⊕ 1-800-555-3445
www.emcp.net/worldwide

(current date)

Mrs. Jody Lancaster
Pacific Sky Cruise Lines
120 Montgomery Boulevard
Los Angeles, CA 97032

Dear Jody:

Your colorful brochures have made quite an impression on our clients, and consequently, we have given away our entire stock. Please send us an additional box of brochures as well as information and fact sheets about the various specialized cruises coming up.

Are you planning to offer the "Northern Lights" cruise next year? The cruise has been very popular with our clients, and I have had three inquiries in the past three weeks regarding the cruise. As soon as you know the dates of the cruise and stateroom prices, please let me know.

Sincerely,

Student Name
Travel Consultant

XX
C21-E02-PSLtr.docx

> Visit our website at www.emcp.net/worldwide to learn about our weekly vacation specials!

"Making your travel dreams a reality"

WORLD WIDE TRAVEL

2400 International Drive ⊕ Las Vegas, NV 77534 ⊕ 1-800-555-3445
www.emcp.net/worldwide

(Current date)

Mrs. Jody Lancaster
Pacific Sky Cruise Lines
120 Montgomery Boulevard
Los Angeles, CA 97032

Dear Jody:

I imagine you are extremely busy finalizing the preparations for the Pacific Sky Cruise Line's inaugural trip to the Alaska Inside Passage. The promotional literature you provided our company has been very effective in enticing our clients to sign up. This letter is a confirmation of the thirty staterooms that we have reserved for our clients for the inaugural cruise. We have reserved ten each of the following staterooms:

- Category H: Inside stateroom with two lower beds
- Category D: Deluxe ocean-view stateroom with window, sitting area, and two lower beds
- Category B: Superior deluxe ocean-view stateroom with window, sitting area, and two lower beds
- Category S: Superior deluxe suite with ocean view, private balcony, sitting area, and two lower beds

With only a few weeks to go before the cruise, I want to make sure our clients' bookings are finalized so they can enjoy the eight-day, seven-night cruise to the Alaska Inside Passage. Please confirm the stateroom reservations, and send me a fax or email with the confirmation numbers.

Sincerely,

Student Name
Senior Travel Consultant

XX
C21-E03-PSLtr.docx

"Making your travel dreams a reality"

Exercise 21.3

C21-E03-PSLtr.docx

BETA TESTING AGREEMENT

THIS AGREEMENT is made by and between Stylus Software Enterprises, and _____ ("Licensee") having a principal place of business located at _____.

In consideration of the mutual covenants and premises herein contained, the parties hereto agree as follows:

Stylus Software Enterprises grants to Licensee a non-exclusive, non-transferable license to use the Software on a single computer at Licensee's business location solely for beta testing and internal use until _____, 20__ at which time the Software and all copies shall be returned to Stylus Software Enterprises.

In consideration for receiving a copy of the Software for testing, Licensee agrees to serve as a beta testing site for the Software and will notify Stylus Software Enterprises of all problems and ideas for enhancements which come to Licensee's attention during the period of this Agreement, and hereby assigns to Stylus Software Enterprises all right, title and interest to such enhancements and all property rights therein including without limitation all patent, copyright, trade secret, mask work, trademark, moral right or other intellectual property rights.

This Agreement shall be governed, construed, and enforced in accordance with the laws of the United States of America and of the State of California. Any notice required by this Agreement shall be given by prepaid, first class, certified mail, return receipt requested.

Stylus Software Enterprises: Licensee:

_____   _____
Name   Name

First Draft
C21-E04-SEBetaAgrmnt.docx
4/2/2010 1:56:00 PM

Exercise 21.4A

C21-E04-SEBetaAgrmnt.docx

BETA TESTING AGREEMENT

THIS AGREEMENT is made by and between Stylus Software Enterprises, and _____ ("Licensee") having a principal place of business located at _____.

In consideration of the mutual covenants and premises herein contained, the parties hereto agree as follows:

Stylus Software Enterprises grants to Licensee a non-exclusive, non-transferable license to use the Software on a single computer at Licensee's business location solely for beta testing and internal use until _____, 20__ at which time the Software and all copies shall be returned to Stylus Software Enterprises.

In consideration for receiving a copy of the Software for testing, Licensee agrees to serve as a beta testing site for the Software and will notify Stylus Software Enterprises of all problems and ideas for enhancements which come to Licensee's attention during the period of this Agreement, and hereby assigns to Stylus Software Enterprises all right, title and interest to such enhancements and all property rights therein including without limitation all patent, copyright, trade secret, mask work, trademark, moral right or other intellectual property rights.

This Agreement shall be governed, construed, and enforced in accordance with the laws of the United States of America and of the State of California. Any notice required by this Agreement shall be given by prepaid, first class, certified mail, return receipt requested.

Stylus Software Enterprises: Licensee:

_____   _____
Name   Name

First Draft
C21-E04-SETestAgrmnt.docx
6/23/2010 1:09:00 PM

Exercise 21.4C

C21-E04-SETestAgrmnt.docx

Inserting Quick Parts

Quick Parts

Word includes a variety of tools you can use to insert data such as text, fields, objects, or other items in a document to help build it. To view some of the tools available, click the Quick Parts button in the Text group in the Insert tab. Clicking the Quick Parts button displays a drop-down list of options for inserting document properties, fields, and predesigned building blocks. The drop-down list also includes options for saving selected data to the AutoText or the Quick Part gallery.

Inserting Building Blocks

Building blocks are tools you can use to develop or "build" a document. Word provides a number of these reusable pieces of content that you can insert in a document. You can also create your own and save them for future use. To insert one of the predesigned building blocks into a Word document, click the Insert tab, click the Quick Parts button in the Text group, and then click *Building Blocks Organizer* at the drop-down list. This displays the Building Blocks Organizer dialog box, shown in Figure 21.1. On the left, the dialog box displays four columns of information about the building blocks: the building block name, the gallery to which the building block belongs, the building block's category, and the template in which the building block is stored. When you click the name of a building block, the dialog box also displays a preview of the building block, its name, and a brief description of the building block.

QUICK STEPS

Insert Building Block
1. Click Insert tab.
2. Click Quick Parts button.
3. Click *Building Blocks Organizer.*
4. Click desired building block.
5. Click Insert button.

Figure 21.1 Building Blocks Organizer Dialog Box

Click the desired building block in the list box and then preview it in this preview area.

Click a column heading to sort column entries alphabetically.

Building Blocks Organizer

Building blocks:

Click a building block to see its preview

Name	Gallery	Category	Template
Student Na...	AutoText	General	Normal.dotm
SN	AutoText	General	Normal.dotm
Bibliography	Bibliograp...	Built-In	Built-In Buil...
Works Cited	Bibliograp...	Built-In	Built-In Buil...
Sideline	Cover Pages	Built-In	Built-In Buil...
Annual	Cover Pages	Built-In	Built-In Buil...
Mod	Cover Pages	Built-In	Built-In Buil...
Conservative	Cover Pages	Built-In	Built-In Buil...
Stacks	Cover Pages	Built-In	Built-In Buil...
Austere	Cover Pages	Built-In	Built-In Buil...
Transcend	Cover Pages	Built-In	Built-In Buil...
Alphabet	Cover Pages	Built-In	Built-In Buil...
Tiles	Cover Pages	Built-In	Built-In Buil...
Motion	Cover Pages	Built-In	Built-In Buil...
Exposure	Cover Pages	Built-In	Built-In Buil...
Contrast	Cover Pages	Built-In	Built-In Buil...
Puzzle	Cover Pages	Built-In	Built-In Buil...
Cubicles	Cover Pages	Built-In	Built-In Buil...
Pinstripes	Cover Pages	Built-In	Built-In Buil...
Quadratic F...	Equations	Built-In	Built-In Buil...
Taylor Expa...	Equations	Built-In	Built-In Buil...

Student Name

Edit Properties...   Delete   Insert

Close

The Building Blocks Organizer dialog box provides a single location where you can view all of the predesigned building blocks available in Word. You used building blocks in previous chapters when you inserted elements such as predesigned cover pages, headers, footers, page numbering, and watermarks into a document. You used various buttons in the Insert tab to insert these elements. Other galleries of predesigned building blocks include bibliographies, equations, table of contents, tables, and text boxes. At the Building Blocks Organizer dialog box, you can conveniently view and insert all available building blocks.

QUICK STEPS

Sort Building Blocks
1. Click Insert tab.
2. Click Quick Parts button.
3. Click *Building Blocks Organizer.*
4. Click desired column heading.

Sorting Building Blocks

When you open the Building Blocks Organizer dialog box, the building blocks display in a list box sorted by the Gallery column. You can sort the building blocks by other columns by clicking the column heading. For example, to sort building blocks alphabetically by name, click the Name column heading.

Exercise 21.1 Inserting Predesigned Building Blocks   Part 1 of 1

1. Open **CompChapters.docx** and save the document with the name **C21-E01-CompChapters**.
2. Make the following changes to the document:
   a. Insert a continuous section break at the beginning of the first paragraph below the title CHAPTER 1: COMPUTER VIRUSES.
   b. Insert a section break that begins a new page at the beginning of the title CHAPTER 2: SECURITY RISKS located in the middle of the second page.
   c. Insert a continuous section break at the beginning of the first paragraph below the title CHAPTER 2: SECURITY RISKS.
   d. Change the line spacing to 1.15 for the entire document.
   e. Format the section below the first title CHAPTER 1: COMPUTER VIRUSES into two equally spaced columns.
   f. Balance the columns of text on the second page.
   g. Format the section below the second title CHAPTER 2: SECURITY RISKS into two equally spaced and balanced columns.
3. Sort the building blocks and then insert a table of contents building block by completing the following steps:
   a. Press Ctrl + Home, press Ctrl + Enter to insert a page break, and then press Ctrl + Home again.
   b. With the insertion point positioned at the beginning of the new page (first page), click the Insert tab.
   c. Click the Quick Parts button in the Text group and then click *Building Blocks Organizer* at the drop-down list.

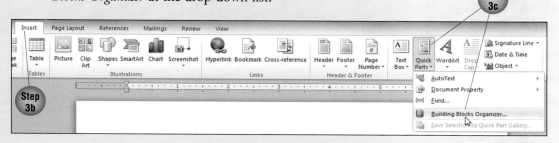

d. At the Building Blocks Organizer dialog box, notice how the building blocks are arranged in the list box. (More than likely, the building blocks are organized alphabetically by Gallery.)

e. Click the Name column heading. (This sorts the building blocks alphabetically by name; however, some blank building blocks may display at the beginning of the list box.)

f. Scroll down the list box and then click *Automatic Table 1*. (You may see only a portion of the name. Click the name, and the full name as well as a description of the building block display in the dialog box below the preview.)

g. Click the Insert button that displays toward the bottom of the dialog box. (This inserts a Contents page at the beginning of the page and uses the titles and headings in the document to create the table of contents.)

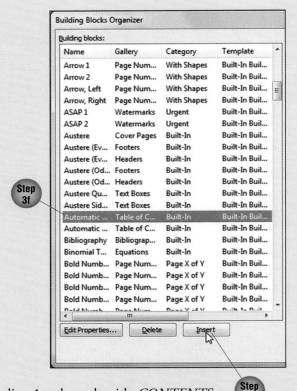

4. Apply the Heading 1 style to the title *CONTENTS* by completing the following steps:
   a. Click on any character in the title *CONTENTS*.
   b. Click the Home tab.
   c. Click the Heading 1 style in the Styles group.

5. Insert a sidebar building block by completing the following steps:
   a. Position the insertion point at the beginning of the title CHAPTER 1: COMPUTER VIRUSES in the document (not the Table of Contents).
   b. Click the Insert tab.
   c. Click the Quick Parts button in the Text group.

d. Click *Building Blocks Organizer* at the drop-down list.
e. At the Building Blocks Organizer dialog box, scroll down the list box and then click *Tiles Sidebar* in the Name column. (This displays the sidebar in the preview section of the dialog box.)

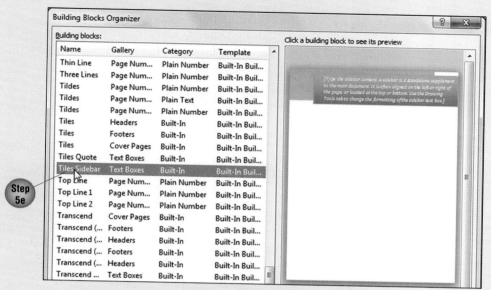

f. Click the Insert button that displays toward the bottom of the dialog box.
g. With the pull quote placeholder text selected, type "Although accurate estimates are difficult to pinpoint, businesses certainly lose millions of dollars a year in stolen computer hardware and software."
h. Select the text you just typed, change the font size to 14 points, and then deselect the text.

6. Insert a footer building block by completing the following steps:
a. Click the Insert tab, click the Quick Parts button, and then click *Building Blocks Organizer*.
b. Scroll down the Building Blocks Organizer list box, click the *Tiles* footer, and then click the Insert button.
c. Click the placeholder text *[Type the company address]* and then type Northland Security Systems.

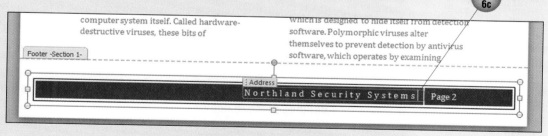

d. Double-click in the document.

7. Insert a cover page building block by completing the following steps:
a. Press Ctrl + Home to move the insertion point to the beginning of the document.
b. Click the Insert tab, click the Quick Parts button, and then click *Building Blocks Organizer*.
c. Scroll down the Building Blocks Organizer list box, click the *Tiles* cover page, and then click the Insert button.
d. Click the placeholder text *[TYPE THE COMPANY NAME]* and then type Northland Security Systems.

e.	Click the placeholder text *[Type the document title]* and then type Computer Security.

f.	Click the placeholder text *[Type the document subtitle]* and then type Computer Viruses and Security Risks.

g.	If a name displays below the document subtitle in the Author placeholder, select the name and then type your first and last names.

h.	Click the placeholder text *[Year]* and then type the current year.

8.	Scroll through the document and look at each page. The sidebar, footer, and cover page building blocks you inserted have similar formatting and are part of the *Tiles* group. Using building blocks from the same group provides consistency in a document and gives a document a polished and professional appearance.

9.	Save, print, and then close **C21-E01-CompChapters.docx**.

QUICK STEPS

Save Content to Text Box Gallery
1. Select content box.
2. Click Insert tab.
3. Click Text Box button.
4. Click *Save Selection to Text Box Gallery*.

Save Content to Header Gallery
1. Select content.
2. Click Insert tab.
3. Click Header button.
4. Click *Save Selection to Header Gallery*.

Save Content to Footer Gallery
1. Select content.
2. Click Insert tab.
3. Click Footer button.
4. Click *Save Selection to Footer Gallery*.

Saving Building Block Content

The Building Blocks Organizer dialog box contains reusable pieces of content organized by galleries such as AutoText, Cover Pages, Headers, Footers, and Quick Part. If you find yourself typing and formatting the same data regularly, consider saving the data as a building block. Saving frequently created data as a building block saves you time and reduces the potential for errors that might occur each time you type data or apply formatting.

Saving Content as a Building Block

You can save content as a building block in a specific gallery. For example, you can save a text box in the Text Box gallery, save content in the Header gallery, save content in the Footer gallery, and so on. To save content in a specific gallery, use the button for the desired gallery. For example, to save a text box in the Text Box gallery, use the Text Box button. To do this, select the text box, click the Insert tab, click the Text Box button, and then click the *Save Selection to Text Box Gallery* option at the drop-down gallery. At the Create New Building Block dialog box that displays, as shown in Figure 21.2, type a name for the text box building block, type a description if desired, and then click OK.

To save content in the Header gallery, select the content, click the Insert tab, click the Header button, and then click the *Save Selection to Header Gallery* option at the drop-down gallery. This displays the Create New Building Block dialog box as shown in Figure 21.2 except *Header* displays in the *Gallery* option box. Complete similar steps to save content to the Footer gallery or the Cover Page gallery.

Figure 21.2 Create New Building Block Dialog Box

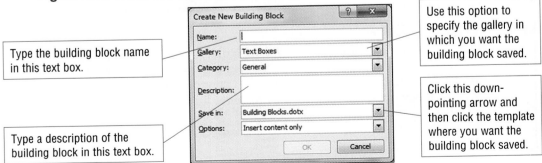

Type the building block name in this text box.

Type a description of the building block in this text box.

Use this option to specify the gallery in which you want the building block saved.

Click this down-pointing arrow and then click the template where you want the building block saved.

By default, content you save as a building block is saved in either the Building Block.dotx template or the Normal.dotm template depending on the gallery in which you save the building block. A building block saved in either of these templates is available each time you open a new blank document in Word. In a public environment such as a school, you may not be able to save data to one of these templates. In some of the exercises in this chapter, you will create and save building blocks to a template in the Chapter21 folder on your storage medium. To specify the template where you want a building block saved, click the down-pointing arrow at the right side of the *Save in* option in the Create New Building Block dialog box and then click the desired template. You must open a document based on a template for the template name to display in the drop-down list.

Saving Content to the AutoText Gallery

You can save content as a building block in the AutoText gallery and the building block can be easily inserted in a document by clicking the Insert tab, clicking the Quick Parts button, pointing to *AutoText*, and then clicking the desired AutoText building bock at the side menu. To save content in the AutoText gallery, type and format the desired content and then select the content. Click the Insert tab, click the Quick Parts button, point to *AutoText*, and then click the *Save Selection to AutoText Gallery* option at the side menu. You can also press Alt + F3 to display the dialog box. At the Create New Building Block dialog box, type a name for the building block, type a description if desired, and then click OK.

Saving Content to the Quick Part Gallery

In addition to saving content in the AutoText gallery, you can save selected content in the Quick Part gallery. To do this, select the desired content, click the Insert tab, click the Quick Parts button, and then click the *Save Selection to Quick Part Gallery* option at the drop-down gallery. This displays the Create New Building Block dialog box with *Quick Parts* specified in the *Gallery* option box and *Building Blocks.dotx* specified in the *Save in* option box. Type a name for the building block, type a description if desired, and then click OK.

QUICK STEPS

Save Content to AutoText Gallery
1. Select content.
2. Click Insert tab.
3. Click Quick Parts button.
4. Point to *AutoText*.
5. Click *Save Selection to AutoText Gallery*.

Save Content to Quick Part Gallery
1. Select content.
2. Click Insert tab.
3. Click Quick Parts button.
4. Click *Save Selection to Quick Part Gallery*.

Exercise 21.2A — Saving Content to the Text Box, Footer, AutoText, and Quick Part Galleries — Part 1 of 3

1. Press Ctrl + N to display a blank document and then save the document as a template by completing the following steps:
   a. Click the File tab and then click Save As.
   b. At the Save As dialog box, click the down-pointing arrow at the right side of the *Save as type* option box and then click *Word Template (*.dotx)* at the drop-down list.
   c. Select the text in the *File name* text box and then type C21-WWTTemplate.
   d. Make sure the Chapter21 folder on your storage medium is the active folder.
   e. Click the Save button.
2. Close the **C21-WWTTemplate.dotx** template.
3. Create a document based on the C21-WWTTemplate.dotx template by completing the following steps:
   a. Click the File tab and then click the New tab.
   b. At the New tab Backstage view, click the New from existing option.

c. At the New from Existing Document dialog box, navigate to the Chapter21 folder on your storage medium and then double-click **C21-WWTTemplate.dotx**.

4. Insert **WWTContent.docx** into the current document. (Do this with the Object button arrow in the Insert tab. This document is located in the Chapter21 folder on your storage medium.)

5. Save the text box as a building block in the Text Box gallery by completing the following steps:

   a. Select the text box by clicking the text box and then clicking the text box border.

   b. Click the Insert tab, click the Text Box button, and then click *Save Selection to Text Box Gallery* at the drop-down gallery.

   c. At the Create New Building Block dialog box, type **WWTTextBox** in the *Name* text box.

   d. Click the down-pointing arrow at the right side of the *Save in* option box and then click *C21-WWTTemplate.dotx* at the drop-down list. (This saves the building block in the C21-WWTTemplate.dotx rather than the default Building Block.dotx template.)

   e. Click OK to close the Create New Building Block dialog box.

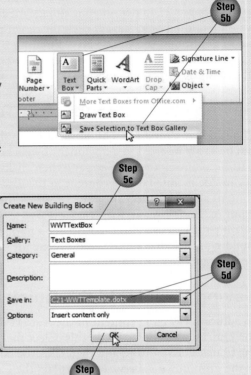

6. Save content as a building block in the Footer gallery by completing the following steps:

   a. Select the text *"Making your travel dreams a reality"* located below the text box.

   b. Click the Footer button in the Insert tab and then click *Save Selection to Footer Gallery* at the drop-down gallery.

   c. At the Create New Building Block dialog box, type **WWTFooter** in the *Name text box*.

   d. Click the down-pointing arrow at the right side of the *Save in* option box and then click *C21-WWTTemplate.dotx* at the drop-down list.

   e. Click OK to close the Create New Building Block dialog box.

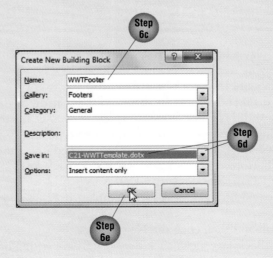

7. Save the company name *Pacific Sky Cruise Lines* and the address below it as a building block in the AutoText gallery by completing the following steps:

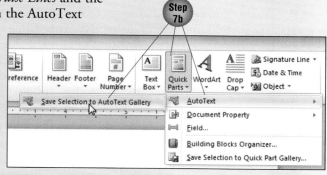

a. Select the company name and the address (the two lines below the company name). (Make sure you include the paragraph mark at the end of the last line of the address.)

b. Click the Quick Parts button in the Insert tab, point to *AutoText*, and then click *Save Selection to AutoText Gallery* at the side menu.

c. At the Create New Building Block dialog box, type **PacificSky**.

d. Click the down-pointing arrow at the right side of the *Save in* option box and then click *C21-WWTTemplate.dotx* at the drop-down list.

e. Click OK to close the Create New Building Block dialog box.

8. Type your name and company title and then save the text as a building block in the AutoText gallery by completing the following steps:

a. Move the insertion point to a blank line a double space below the Pacific Sky Cruise Lines address.

b. Type your first and last names.

c. Press the Enter key and then type **Travel Consultant**.

d. Select your first and last names and the title *Travel Consultant*.

e. Press Alt + F3.

f. At the Create New Building Block dialog box, type **Title**.

g. Click the down-pointing arrow at the right side of the *Save in* option box and then click *C21-WWTTemplate.dotx* at the drop-down list.

h. Click OK to close the Create New Building Block dialog box

9. Save the letterhead as a building block in the Quick Part gallery by completing the following steps:

a. Select the letterhead text (from *WORLD WIDE TRAVEL* through *www.emcp.net/worldwide*).

b. Click the Quick Parts button in the Insert tab and then click *Save Selection to Quick Part Gallery* at the drop-down list.

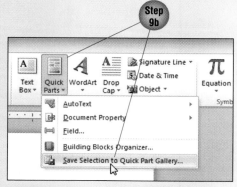

c. At the Create New Building Block dialog box, type **WWT**.

d. Click the down-pointing arrow at the right side of the *Save in* option box and then click *C21-WWTTemplate.dotx* at the drop-down list.

e. Click OK to close the Create New Building Block dialog box

10. Close the document without saving it.

11. At the message that displays telling you that you have modified styles, building blocks, or other content that is stored in C21-WWTTemplate.dotx and asking if you want to save changes, click the Save button.

Edit Building Block
1. Click Insert tab.
2. Click Quick Parts button.
3. Click *Building Blocks Organizer*.
4. Click desired building block.
5. Click Edit Properties button.
6. Make desired changes.
7. Click OK.
OR
1. Click desired button.
2. Right-click custom building block.
3. Click *Edit Properties*.
4. Make desired changes.
5. Click OK.

Editing Building Block Properties

You can make changes to the properties of a building block with options at the Modify Building Blocks dialog box. This dialog box contains the same options that are available at the Create New Building Block dialog box. Display the Modify Building Blocks dialog box by opening the Building Blocks Organizer dialog box, clicking the desired building block in the list box, and then clicking the Edit Properties button. Make desired changes to the Modify Building Block dialog box and then click OK. At the message asking if you want to redefine the building block entry, click Yes.

You can also display this dialog box for a custom building block in a button drop-down gallery, by clicking the button, right-clicking the custom building block, and then clicking the *Edit Properties* option at the shortcut menu. For example, to modify a custom text box building block, click the Insert tab, click the Text Box button, and then scroll down the drop-down gallery to display the custom text box building block. Right-click the building block and then click *Edit Properties* at the shortcut menu.

Exercise 21.2B Editing Building Block Properties

Part 2 of 3

1. Open a blank document based on the WWTTemplate.dotx by completing the following steps:
   a. Click the File tab and then click the New tab.
   b. At the New tab Backstage view, click the New from existing button.
   c. At the New from Existing Document dialog box, navigate to the Chapter21 folder on your storage medium and then double-click **C21-WWTTemplate.dotx**.
2. Edit the *WWT* building block by completing the following steps:
   a. Click the Insert tab.
   b. Click the Quick Parts button, right-click the *WWT* letterhead building block and then click *Edit Properties* at the shortcut menu.

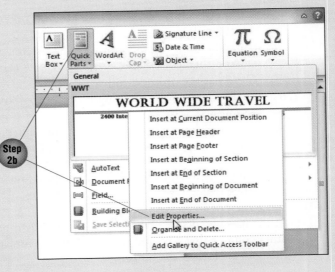

c. At the Modify Building Block dialog box, click in the *Name* text box and then add *Letterhead* to the end of the name.

d. Click in the *Description* text box and then type *Inserts the World Wide Travel letterhead including the company name and address.*

e. Click OK to close the dialog box.

f. At the message asking if you want to redefine the building block entry, click Yes.

3. Edit the *PacificSky* building block by completing the following steps:

a. Click the Insert tab, click the Quick Parts button, and then click *Building Blocks Organizer* at the drop-down list.

b. At the Building Blocks Organizer dialog box, click the Gallery heading to sort the building blocks by gallery. (This displays the AutoText galleries at the beginning of the list.)

c. Using the horizontal scroll bar that displays at the bottom of the *Building blocks* list box, scroll to the right and notice that the *PacificSky* building block does not contain a description.

d. Click the *PacificSky* building block in the list box.

e. Click the Edit Properties button located at the bottom of the dialog box.

f. At the Modify Building Block dialog box, click in the *Name* text box and then add *Address* to the end of the name.

g. Click in the *Description* text box and then type **Inserts the Pacific Sky name and address.**

h. Click OK to close the dialog box.

i. At the message asking if you want to redefine the building block entry, click Yes.

j. Close the Building Blocks Organizer dialog box.

4. Close the document.

5. At the message that displays telling you that you have modified styles, building blocks, or other content that is stored in C21-WWTTemplate.dotx and asking if you want to save changes, click the Save button.

Inserting Custom Building Blocks

Any content you save as a building block can be inserted in a document at the Building Blocks Organizer dialog box. Some content also can be inserted at specific drop-down galleries. For example, insert a custom text box building block by clicking the Text Box button in the Insert tab and then clicking the desired text box at the drop-down gallery. Insert a custom header at the Header button drop-down gallery, a custom footer at the Footer button drop-down gallery, a custom cover page at the Cover Page button drop-down gallery, and so on.

You can specify where you want custom building block content inserted in a document at the button drop-down gallery. To do this, display the button drop-down gallery, right-click the custom building block, and then click the desired location at the shortcut menu. For example, if you click the Insert tab, click the Quick Parts button, and then right-click the *WWTLetterhead* building block, a shortcut menu displays as shown in Figure 21.3.

Figure 21.3 Quick Parts Button Drop-down List Shortcut Menu

Right-click the desired building block at the Quick Parts drop-down gallery and then click the location for inserting the building block at the shortcut menu.

Exercise 21.2C   Inserting Custom Building Blocks   Part 3 of 3

1. Open a blank document based on the WWTTemplate.dotx by completing the following steps:
   a. Click the File tab and then click the New tab.
   b. At the New tab Backstage view, click the New from existing button.
   c. At the New from Existing Document dialog box, navigate to the Chapter21 folder on your storage medium and then double-click **C21-WWTTemplate.dotx**.
2. Click the No Spacing style and then change the font to 11-point Candara.
3. Insert the letterhead building block as a header by completing the following steps:
   a. Click the Insert tab.

b. Click the Quick Parts button,
       right-click **WWTLetterhead**, and
       then click the *Insert at Page Header*
       option at the shortcut menu.
4. Press the Enter key twice, type the
   current date, and then press the Enter
   key four times.
5. Type Mrs. Jody Lancaster and then
   press the Enter key.
6. Insert the Pacific Sky Cruise Lines name
   and address building block by clicking
   the Quick Parts button, pointing
   to *AutoText*, and then clicking the
   PacificSkyAddress building block at
   the side menu.

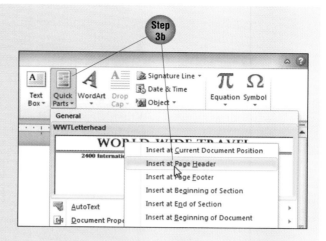

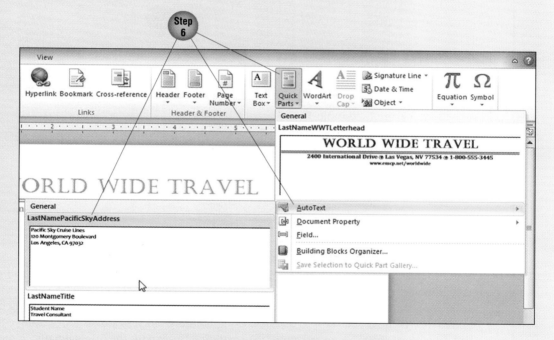

7. Press the Enter key once and then insert a letter document by completing the following steps:
   a. Click the Object button arrow in the Insert tab and then click *Text from File* at the
       drop-down list.
   b. At the Insert File dialog box, navigate to the Chapter21 folder on your storage medium
       and then double-click **PacificSkyLetter01.docx**.
8. With the Insertion point positioned a double space below the last paragraph of text in the
   body of the letter, type Sincerely, and then press the Enter key four times.
9. Insert your name and title building block by clicking the Quick Parts button, pointing to
   AutoText, and then clicking your name and title at the side menu.
10. Press the Enter key, type your initials, press the Enter key, and then type
    C21-E02-PSLtr.docx.

11. Press the Enter key three times and then insert the custom text box you saved as a building block by completing the following steps:
    a. Click the Insert tab.
    b. Click the Text Box button.
    c. Scroll to the end of the drop-down gallery and then click the WWTTextBox text box. (Your custom text box will display in the *General* section of the drop-down gallery.)
    d. Click in the document to deselect the text box.

12. Insert the custom footer you created by completing the following steps:
    a. Click the Insert tab.
    b. Click the Footer button.
    c. Scroll to the end of the drop-down gallery and then click the WWTFooter footer. (Your custom footer will display in the *General* section of the drop-down gallery.)
    d. Close the footer pane by double-clicking in the document.

13. Save the completed letter and name it **C21-E02-PSLtr**.

14. Print and then close **C21-E02-PSLtr.docx**.

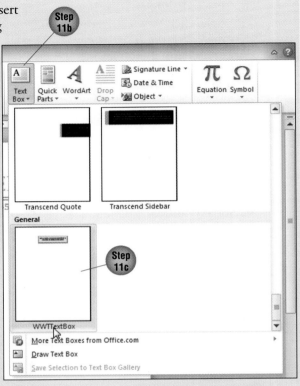

Modifying Building Blocks

You can insert a building block in a document, make corrections or changes to it, and then save it with the same name or a different name. Save a building block with the same name when you want to update the building block to reflect any changes. Save the building block with a new name if you want to use an existing building block as a basis for creating a new building block. When you save a modified building block with the original name, a message displays asking if you want to redefine the building block entry. At this message, click Yes.

Inserting a Building Block Gallery as a Button on the Quick Access Toolbar

If you want to make building blocks more accessible, you can insert a building block gallery as a button on the Quick Access toolbar. To do this, click the desired button, right-click an existing building block, and then click the *Add Gallery to Quick Access Toolbar* option at the shortcut menu. For example, to add the Quick Part gallery to the Quick Access toolbar, click the Quick Parts button in the Insert tab, right-click a building block at the drop-down gallery, and then click *Add Gallery to Quick Access Toolbar*.

To remove a button from the Quick Access toolbar, right-click the button and then click *Remove from Quick Access Toolbar* at the shortcut menu. Removing a button containing a building block gallery does not delete the building blocks.

1. Open a blank document based on the WWTTemplate.dotx by completing the following steps:
   a. Click the File tab and then click the New tab.
   b. At the New tab Backstage view, click the New from existing button.
   c. At the New from Existing Document dialog box, navigate to the Chapter21 folder on your storage medium and then double-click **C21-WWTTemplate.dotx**.

2. At World Wide Travel, you have been promoted from travel consultant to senior travel consultant. You decide to modify your name and title building block by completing the following steps:
   a. At the blank document, click the Insert tab, click the Quick Parts button, point to *AutoText*, and then click your name and title building block at the side menu.
   b. Edit your title so it displays as *Senior Travel Consultant*.
   c. Select your name and title, click the Quick Parts button, point to *AutoText*, and then click *Save Selection to AutoText Gallery* at the side menu.
   d. At the Create New Building Block dialog box, type **Title** (the original name) in the *Name* text box.
   e. Click the down-pointing arrow at the right side of the *Save in* option box and then click *C21-WWTTemplate.dotx* at the drop-down list.
   f. Click OK to close the Create New Building Block dialog box.
   g. At the message asking if you want to redefine the building block entry, click Yes.

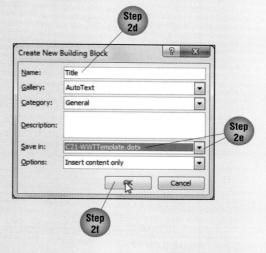

3. Because most of the correspondence you send to Pacific Sky Cruise Lines is addressed to Jody Lancaster, you decide to include her name before the company name and address by completing the following steps:
   a. Click the Quick Parts button, point to *AutoText*, and then click the *PacificSkyAddress* building block at the side menu.
   b. Position the insertion point at the beginning of the company name *Pacific Sky Cruise Lines*, type **Mrs. Jody Lancaster**, and then press the Enter key.
   c. Select the name, company name, and address.
   d. Click the Quick Parts button, point to *AutoText*, and then click *Save Selection to AutoText Gallery* at the side menu.
   e. At the Create New Building Block dialog box, type **PacificSkyAddress** (the original name) in the *Name* text box.
   f. Click the down-pointing arrow at the right side of the *Save in* option box and then click *C21-WWTTemplate.dotx* at the drop-down list.
   g. Click OK to close the Create New Building Block dialog box.

    h.   At the message asking if you want to redefine the building block entry, click Yes.

4. You decide that you want the WWT footer available in the Quick Part gallery. Save the WWT footer in the Quick Part gallery by completing the following steps:

    a.   Click the Footer button in the Insert tab, scroll down the drop-down gallery, and then click the *WWTFooter c*ustom footer building block.

    b.   Press Ctrl + A to select the footer.

    c.   Click the Insert tab, click the Quick Parts button, and then click *Save Selection to Quick Part Gallery*.

    d.   At the Create New Building Block dialog box, type **WWTFooter** in the *Name* text box.

    e.   Click the down-pointing arrow at the right side of the *Save in* option box and then click *C21-WWTTemplate.dotx* at the drop-down list.

    f.   Click OK to close the Create New Building Block dialog box. (You now have the footer saved in the Footer gallery and the Quick Part gallery.)

    g.   Double-click in the document.

5. Insert the Quick Part gallery building blocks as a Quick Parts button on the Quick Access toolbar by completing the following steps:

    a.   Click the Quick Parts button and then right-click one of your custom building blocks.

    b.   At the shortcut menu that displays, click the *Add Gallery to Quick Access Toolbar* option. (Notice the Quick Parts button that appears at the right side of the Quick Access toolbar.)

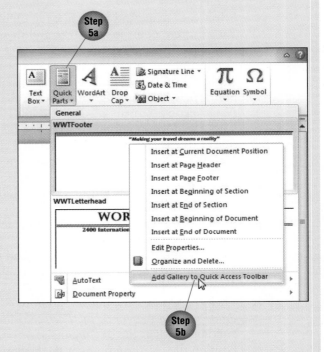

6. Insert the AutoText gallery building blocks as a button on the Quick Access toolbar by completing the following steps:

    a.   Click the Quick Parts button, point to *AutoText*, and then right-click one of your custom building blocks.

    b.   At the shortcut menu that displays, click the *Add Gallery to Quick Access Toolbar* option. (Notice the AutoText button that appears at the right side of the Quick Access toolbar.)

7. Close the document without saving it.

8. At the message that displays telling you that you have modified styles, building blocks, or other content that is stored in C21-WWTTemplate.dotx and asking if you want to save changes, click the Save button.

9. Open a blank document based on the WWTTemplate.dotx by completing the following steps:

    a.   Click the File tab and then click the New tab.

    b.   At the New tab Backstage view, click the New from existing button.

    c.   At the New from Existing Document dialog box, navigate to the Chapter21 folder on your storage medium and then double-click **C21-WWTTemplate.dotx**.

10. Insert the World Wide Travel letterhead building block by clicking the Quick Parts button on the Quick Access toolbar and then clicking the *WWTLetterhead* building block at the drop-down list.

11. Click the *No Spacing* style in the Styles group in the Home tab.

12. Change the font to 11-point Candara.

13. Press the Enter key twice, type today's date, and then press the Enter key four times.

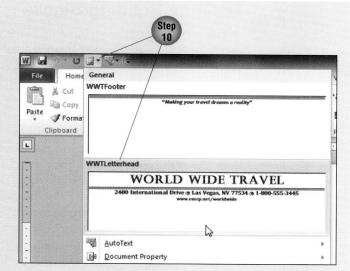

14. Insert the building block that includes Jody Lancaster's name as well as the cruise line name and address by clicking the AutoText button on the Quick Access toolbar and then clicking the building block at the drop-down list.

15. Press the Enter key and then insert the file named **PacificSkyLetter02.docx** located in the Chapter21 folder on your storage medium. *Hint: Do this with the Object button in the Text group in the Insert tab.*

16. Type Sincerely, and then press the Enter key four times.

17. Click the AutoText button on the Quick Access toolbar and then click the building block that inserts your name and title.

18. Press the Enter key and then type your initials.

19. Press the Enter key and then type C21-E03-PSLtr.docx.

20. Insert the footer building block you created by clicking the Quick Parts button on the Quick Access toolbar, right-clicking the footer building block, and then clicking *Insert at Page Footer* in the shortcut menu.

21. Save the completed letter and name it **C21-E03-PSLtr**.

22. Print and then close **C21-E03-PSLtr.docx**.

23. Open a blank document based on the **C21-WWTTemplate.dotx** template.

24. Click the AutoText button on the Quick Access toolbar, press the Print Screen button on your keyboard, and then click in the document to remove the drop-down list.

25. At the blank document, click the Paste button. (This pastes the screen capture in your document.)

26. Print the document and then close it without saving it.

27. Remove the Quick Parts button you added to the Quick Access toolbar by right-clicking the Quick Parts button and then clicking *Remove from Quick Access Toolbar* at the shortcut menu. Complete similar steps to remove the AutoText button from the Quick Access toolbar.

Deleting Building Blocks

QUICK STEPS

Delete Building Block
1. Display Building Blocks Organizer dialog box.
2. Click desired building block.
3. Click Delete button.
4. Click Yes.
5. Close dialog box.
OR
1. Display desired button drop-down gallery.
2. Right-click desired building block.
3. Click *Organize and Delete* option.
4. Click Delete button.
5. Click Yes.
6. Close dialog box.

When you no longer use a building block you created, consider deleting it. To do this, display the Building Blocks Organizer dialog box, click the building block you want to delete, and then click the Delete button. At the message asking if you are sure you want to delete the selected building block, click Yes.

You can also delete a custom building block by right-clicking the building block at the drop-down gallery and then clicking the *Organize and Delete* option at the shortcut menu. This displays the Building Blocks Organizer dialog box with the building block selected. Click the Delete button that displays at the bottom of the dialog box and then click Yes at the confirmation question. For example, to delete a custom footer, click the Insert tab, click the Footer button, scroll down the drop-down gallery, right-click the custom footer, and then click *Organize and Delete*. This displays the Building Blocks Organizer dialog box with the custom footer building block selected. Click the Delete button and then click Yes at the confirmation question.

To delete building blocks from a specific template, open a document based on the template and then complete the steps to delete the building blocks. Close the document without saving it and when the message displays telling you that you have modified building blocks and asking if you want to save the changes, click the Save button.

Exercise 21.3B Deleting Building Blocks   Part 2 of 2

1. Open a blank document based on the **C21-WWTTemplate.dotx** template.
2. Delete the WWTLetterhead building block by completing the following steps:
   a. Click the Insert tab and then click the Quick Parts button.
   b. Right-click the WWTLetterhead building block and then click *Organize and Delete* at the shortcut menu.
   c. At the Building Blocks Organizer dialog box with the building block selected, click the Delete button.
   d. At the message that displays asking if you are sure you want to delete the selected building block, click Yes.
   e. Close the Building Blocks Organizer dialog box.
3. Complete steps similar to those in Step 2 to delete the WWTFooter building block.

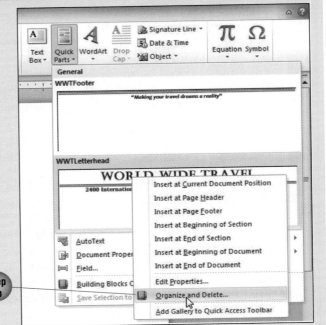

4. Delete the PacificSkyAddress building block by completing the following steps:
   a. Click the Quick Parts button, point to *AutoText*, and then right-click the PacificSkyAddress building block.
   b. Click *Organize and Delete* at the shortcut menu.
   c. At the Building Blocks Organizer dialog box with the building block selected, click the Delete button.
   d. At the message asking if you are sure you want to delete the selected building block, click Yes.
   e. Close the Building Blocks Organizer dialog box.
5. Complete steps similar to those in Step 4 to delete the Title building block.
6. Delete the custom footer (located in the Footer gallery) building block by completing the following steps:
   a. Click the Footer button in the Insert tab.
   b. Scroll down the drop-down gallery to display your custom footer.
   c. Right-click your footer and then click *Organize and Delete* at the shortcut menu.
   d. At the Building Blocks Organizer dialog box with the building block selected, click the Delete button.
   e. At the message asking if you are sure you want to delete the selected building block, click Yes.
   f. Close the Building Blocks Organizer dialog box.
7. Delete the custom text box (located in the Text Box gallery) by completing the following steps:
   a. Click the Text Box button in the Insert tab.
   b. Scroll down the drop-down gallery to display your custom text box.
   c. Right-click your text box and then click *Organize and Delete* at the shortcut menu.

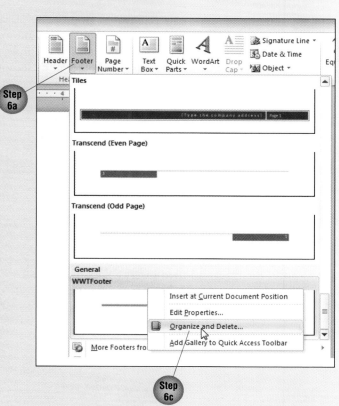

d. At the Building Blocks Organizer dialog box with the building block selected, click the Delete button.

e. At the message asking if you are sure you want to delete the selected building block, click Yes.

f. Close the Building Blocks Organizer dialog box.

8. Close the document.

9. At the message that displays telling you that you have modified styles, building blocks, or other content and asking if you want to save the changes, click the Save button.

Inserting Document Properties

If you click the Quick Parts button in the Insert tab and then point to *Document Property* at the drop-down list, a side menu displays with document property options. Click an option at this side menu and a document property placeholder is inserted in the document. Type the desired text in the placeholder.

When you click the File tab, the Info tab Backstage view displays containing information about the document. At the right side of the Info tab Backstage view, a thumbnail of your document displays along with document properties such as the document size, number of pages, title, and comments. Some document properties that you insert with the Quick Parts button will display at the Info tab Backstage view.

If you insert a document property placeholder in multiple locations in a document, updating one of the placeholders will automatically update all occurrences of that placeholder in the document. For example, in Exercise 21.4A you will insert a Company document property placeholder in six locations in a document. You will then update the first occurrence of the placeholder and the remaining placeholders will update to reflect the change.

Exercise 21.4A Inserting Document Property Placeholders   Part 1 of 3

1. Open **SEBetaAgrmnt.docx** and save the document with the name **C21-E04-SEBetaAgrmnt**.

2. Select the first occurrence of *SE* in the document (located in the first line of text after the title) and then insert a document property placeholder by completing the following steps:

a. Click the Insert tab.

b. Click the Quick Parts button, point to *Document Property*, and then click *Company* at the side menu.

c. Click the Company placeholder tab and then type Stylus Enterprises.

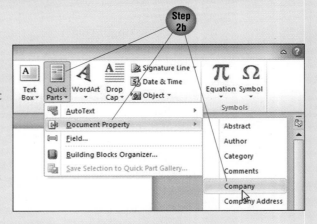

d.   Press the Right Arrow key to move the insertion point outside the Company placeholder.

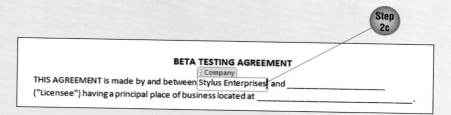

Step
2c

3. Select each of the remaining occurrences of *SE* in the document (SE appears five more times in the document) and insert the Company document property placeholder.

4. Press Ctrl + End to move the insertion point to the end of the document and then insert a Comments document property placeholder by completing the following steps:

   a.   Click the Quick Parts button, point to *Document Property*, and then click *Comments* at the side menu.

   b.   Click the Comments placeholder tab and then type First Draft.

   c.   Press the Right Arrow key.

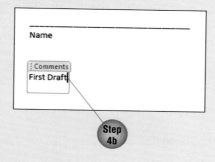

Step
4b

   d.   Press Shift + Enter.

5. Click the File tab, make sure the Info tab is selected, and then notice that the comment you typed in the Comments document property placeholder displays at the right below the document thumbnail. Click the File tab again to display the document.

6. Save and then print **C21-E04-SEBetaAgrmnt.docx**.

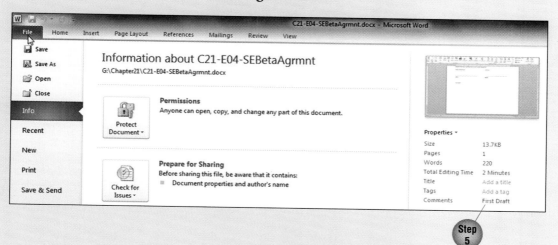

Step
5

7. Click in the first occurrence of the company name *Stylus Enterprises*. (This selects the Company document property placeholder.)
8. Click the Company placeholder tab and then type Stylus Software Enterprises and then press the Right Arrow key. (Notice that the other occurrences of the Company document property placeholder are automatically updated to reflect the new name.)
9. Save **C21-E04-SEBetaAgrmnt.docx**.

QUICK STEPS

Insert Field
1. Click Insert tab.
2. Click Quick Parts button.
3. Click *Field* at drop-down list.
4. Click desired field.
5. Click OK.

Inserting Fields

Fields are placeholders for data that change and thus need to be updated and for data that change when a main document is merged with a data source file. You inserted fields in documents when you merged main documents with data source files, inserted the date and time in a document, and inserted page numbering in a document. Word provides buttons for inserting many of the types of fields you may want to enter into a document. You can also insert a field in a document with options at the Field dialog box shown in Figure 21.4. This dialog box contains a list of all available fields. Just as the Building Blocks Organizer dialog box is a single location for accessing all building blocks, the Field dialog box is a single location for accessing fields. To display the Field dialog box, click the Insert tab, click the Quick Parts button in the Text group, and then click *Field* at the drop-down list. At the Field dialog box, click the desired field in the *Field names* list box and then click OK.

Figure 21.4 Field Dialog Box

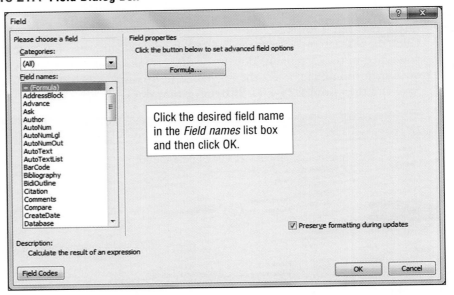

1. With **C21-E04-SEBetaAgrmnt.docx** open, press Ctrl + End to move the insertion point to the end of the document.

2. Insert a field for the current file name by completing the following steps:
   a. Click the Insert tab.
   b. Click the Quick Parts button and then click *Field* at the drop-down list.
   c. At the Field dialog box, scroll down the *Field names* list box and then double-click *FileName*. (This inserts the current file name in the document and closes the Field dialog box.)

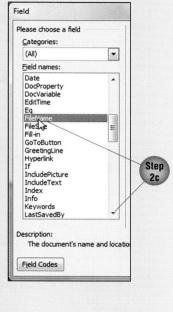

3. Insert a field that inserts the date the file is printed by completing the following steps:
   a. Press Shift + Enter.
   b. Click the Quick Parts button and then click *Field* at the drop-down list.
   c. At the Field dialog box, scroll down the *Field names* list box and then double-click *PrintDate*. (The date and time will display with zeros. The correct date and time may not display until you send the document to the printer.)

4. Insert a header and then insert a field in the header by completing the following steps:
   a. Click the Header button in the Header & Footer group and then click *Edit Header* at the drop-down list.
   b. At the header pane, press the Tab key twice. (This moves the insertion point to the right tab at the right margin.)
   c. Click the Insert tab.
   d. Click the Quick Parts button and then click *Field* at the drop-down list.
   e. At the Field dialog box, scroll down the *Field names* list box and then click *Date*.
   f. Click the date in the *Date formats* list box that will insert the date in figures followed by the time (hours and minutes).
   g. Click OK to close the dialog box.
   h. Double-click in the document.

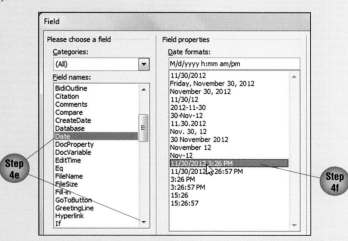

5. Save and then print **C21-E04-SEBetaAgrmnt.docx**.

Update a Field
1. Click field.
2. Click Update tab.
OR
1. Click field.
2. Press F9.
OR
1. Right-click field.
2. Click *Update* at shortcut menu.

Word automatically updates the fields in a document when you open the document. For example, open **C21-E04-ComAgrmnt.docx**, and the time in the header is automatically updated. You can manually update a field three ways: by clicking the field and then clicking the Update tab; by clicking the field and then pressing F9; or by right-clicking the field and then clicking *Update* at the shortcut menu. You can also update all fields in a document except headers, footers, and text boxes by pressing Ctrl + A to select the document and then pressing F9.

Exercise 21.4C Updating Fields   Part 3 of 3

1. With **C21-E04-SEBetaAgrmnt.docx** open, update the time in the header by completing the following steps:
   a. Double-click the header.
   b. Click the date and time and then click the Update tab.

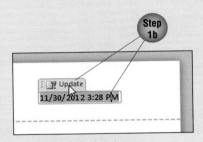

   c. Double-click in the document.
2. Save the document with Save As and name it **C21-E04-SETestAgrmnt**.
3. Press Ctrl + A to select the entire document and then press F9.
4. Save, print, and then close **C21-E04-SETestAgrmnt.docx**.

Chapter *Summary*

➤ Word provides a number of predesigned building blocks you can use to help build a document.

➤ Insert building blocks at the Building Blocks Organizer dialog box. Display this dialog box by clicking the Quick Parts button in the Insert tab and then clicking *Building Blocks Organizer* at the drop-down list.

➤ The Building Blocks Organizer dialog box provides a single location where you can view all available predesigned and custom designed building blocks.

➤ Sort building blocks at the Building Blocks Organizer dialog box by clicking the desired column heading.

➤ You can save content as a building block to specific galleries such as the Text Box, Header, Footer, and Cover Page galleries. To save content to a specific gallery, select the content, click the desired button, and then click the option at the drop-down gallery specifying that you want to save the selection to the specific gallery. At the Create New Building Blocks dialog box, specify a name and make any other desired changes and then click OK.

➤ Save content to the AutoText gallery by selecting the content, clicking the Insert tab, clicking the Quick Parts button, pointing to *AutoText*, and then clicking the *Save Selection to AutoText Gallery* option. This displays the Create New Building Blocks dialog box.

➤ Save content to the Quick Part gallery by selecting the content, clicking the Insert tab, clicking the Quick Parts button, and then clicking *Save Selection to Quick Part Gallery* at the drop-down gallery. This displays the Create New Building Blocks dialog box.

➤ Insert a building block at the Building Blocks Organizer dialog box by displaying the dialog box, clicking the desired building block in the *Building blocks* list box, and then clicking the Insert button.

➤ Insert a custom building block from a gallery using a button by clicking the specific button (such as the Text Box, Header, Footer, or Cover Page button), scrolling down the drop-down gallery, and then clicking the custom building block that displays toward the end of the drop-down gallery.

➤ Insert a custom building block saved to the AutoText gallery by clicking the Insert tab, clicking the Quick Parts button, pointing to *AutoText*, and then clicking the desired building block at the side menu.

➤ Insert a custom building block saved to the Quick Part gallery by clicking the Insert tab, clicking the Quick Parts button, and then clicking the desired building block at the drop-down list.

➤ Edit a building block with options at the Modify Building Block dialog box. Display this dialog box by displaying the Building Blocks Organizer dialog box, clicking the desired building block, and then clicking the Edit Properties button. You can also display this dialog box by right-clicking a building block at a button drop-down gallery and then clicking the *Edit Properties* option at the shortcut menu.

➤ You can insert a building block gallery as a button on the Quick Access toolbar by clicking the desired button, right-clicking an existing building block, and then clicking the *Add Gallery to Quick Access Toolbar* option at the shortcut menu.

➤ Delete a building block at the Building Blocks Organizer dialog box by clicking the building block in the *Building blocks* list box, clicking the Delete key, and then clicking Yes at the confirmation question.

➤ Another method for deleting a building block is the click the button containing the desired building blocks gallery, right-clicking the building block, and then clicking the *Organize and Delete* option at the shortcut menu. This displays the Building Blocks Organizer dialog box with the building block selected. Click the Delete key and then click Yes at the confirmation question.

➤ Insert a document property placeholder by clicking the Insert tab, clicking the Quick Parts button, pointing to *Document Property*, and then clicking the desired option at the side menu. If a document property placeholder appears in more than one location in a document, editing one placeholder automatically updates other placeholders in the document.

➤ Fields are placeholders for data that you can insert with options at the Field dialog box, which provides a single location for accessing all fields provided by Word. Display the Field dialog box by clicking the Quick Parts button and then clicking *Field* at the drop-down list.

➤ Fields in a document are updated automatically when you open the document. You can update a field manually by clicking the field and then clicking the Update tab, pressing F9, or right-clicking the field and then clicking *Update*.

Commands Review

FEATURE	RIBBON TAB, GROUP	BUTTON, OPTION	KEYBOARD SHORTCUT
Building Blocks Organizer dialog box	Insert, Text	, Building Blocks Organizer	
Create New Building Block dialog box (AutoText gallery)	Insert, Text	Select text, , AutoText, Save Selection to AutoText Gallery	Alt + F3
Create New Building Block dialog box (Quick Part gallery)	Insert, Text	Select text, , Save Selection to Quick Part Gallery	
Document Property side menu	Insert, Text	, Document Property	
Field dialog box	Insert, Text	, Field	

Key Points Review

Completion: In the space provided at the right, indicate the correct term, symbol, or command.

1. The Quick Parts button is located in this tab. _____

2. This dialog box provides a single location where you can view all of the predesigned and custom building blocks. _____

3. With the Quick Parts button, you can save a custom building block in the AutoText gallery or this gallery. _____

4. Make changes to the properties of a building block with options at this dialog box. _____

5. You can view custom building blocks you saved to the AutoText gallery by clicking this button in the Insert tab and then pointing to *AutoText*. _____

6. Insert custom building blocks in the Footer gallery in a button on the Quick Access toolbar by clicking the Insert tab, clicking the Footer button, doing this to a custom building block, and then clicking *Add Gallery to Quick Access Toolbar*. _____

7. Delete a building block at this dialog box. _____

8. Insert a document property placeholder by clicking the Quick Parts button in the Insert tab, pointing to this option, and then clicking the desired option at the side menu. _____

9. Complete these steps to display the Field dialog box. _____

10. You can manually update a field by pressing this key on the keyboard. _____

Chapter *Assessments*

Applying Your Skills

Demonstrate your knowledge of features learned in this chapter by completing the following assessments.

Assessment 21.1   Insert Building Blocks and Fields in a Report

1. Open **PropProIssues.docx** and save the document with the name **C21-A01-PropProIssues**.
2. Make the following changes to the document:
   a. Select the entire document and then change the spacing after paragraphs to 6 points.
   b. Press Ctrl + Home to move the insertion point to the beginning of the document and then press Ctrl + Enter to insert a page break.
   c. Apply the Heading 1 style to the two titles *PROPERTY PROTECTION ISSUES* and *REFERENCES*.
   d. Apply the Heading 2 style to the three headings in the document.
   e. Change the style set to Formal.
   f. Change the theme to Flow.
   g. Change the theme colors to Foundry.
   h. Apply a hanging indent to the paragraphs of text below the title *REFERENCES*.
   i. Indent the second paragraph in the *Fair Use* section 0.5 inch from the left and right margins.
3. Press Ctrl + Home to move the insertion point to the beginning of the document and then insert the *Automatic Table 2* table of contents building block.
4. Insert the *Pinstripes* header building block, make sure the *Title* placeholder is selected, and then type Barrington & Gates.
5. Double-click in the document.
6. Insert the *Pinstripes* footer building block, click the *[Type text]* placeholder, and then type Property Protection Issues.
7. Double-click in the document.
8. Press Ctrl + Home and then insert the *Pinstripes* cover page building block with the following specifications:
   a. At the cover page, click the *[Type the document subtitle]* placeholder and then type Property Protection Issues.
   b. Click the *[Pick the date]* placeholder and then insert today's date.
   c. Click the *[Type the company name]* placeholder and then type Barrington & Gates.

d.   Click the Author placeholder tab (if a name displays below the company name, click in the name and then click the Author placeholder tab) and then type your first and last name.

9.   Press Ctrl + End to move the insertion point to the end of the document, press the Enter key, and then insert a field that will insert the file name.

10.   Save, print, and then close **C21-A01-PropProIssues.docx**.

Assessment 21.2   Create Building Blocks and Prepare an Agreement

1.   Press Ctrl + N to display a blank document and then save the document as a template named **C21-BGRRTemplate.dotx**. *Hint: At the Save As dialog box, change the* **Save as type** *option to* **Word Template (*.dotx)**.

2.   Close the **C21-BGRRTemplate.dotx** template.

3.   Create a document based on the C21-BGRRTemplate.dotx template. *Hint: Do this with the* **New from existing option at the New tab Backstage view.**

4.   Insert the **BGRRFooter.docx** document into the current document. (Do this with the Object button arrow in the Insert tab. This document is located in the Chapter21 folder on your storage medium.)

5.   Select the footer text and then save the selected text as a custom building block in the Footer gallery. (Use the Footer button to save the content to the Footer gallery.) Name the building block *BGRRFooter* and change the *Save in* option to *C21-BGRRTemplate.dotx*.

6.   Click the Undo button on the Quick Access toolbar to remove the BGRRFooter document. (You may need to click the Undo button more than once.)

7.   Insert the **BGRRHeading.docx** document into the current document. (Do this with the Object button arrow in the Insert tab. This document is located in the Chapter21 folder on your storage medium.)

8.   Select the entire document and then save the selected text as a custom building block in the Quick Part gallery. Name the building block *BGRRHeading* and change the *Save in* option to *C21-BGRRTemplate.dotx*.

9.   Click the Undo button on the Quick Access toolbar to remove the BGRRHeading document. (You may need to click the Undo button more than once.)

10.   Type the following paragraph of text:

Fees: My hourly rate is $350, billed in one-tenth (1/10th) of an hour increments. All time spent on work performed, including meetings, telephone calls, correspondences, and emails, will be billed at the hourly rate set forth in this paragraph. Additional expenses such as out-of-pocket expenses for postage, courier fees, photocopying charges, long distance telephone charges, and search fees, will be charged at the hourly rate set forth in this paragraph.

11.   Select the entire document and then save the selected text as a custom building block in the AutoText gallery. Name the building block *BGRRFeesPara* and change the *Save in* option to *C21-BGRRTemplate.dotx*.

12.   Insert the Quick Part gallery as a Quick Parts button on the Quick Access toolbar.

13.   Insert the AutoText gallery as an AutoText button on the Quick Access toolbar.

14.   Close the document without saving it. At the message that displays telling you that you have modified styles, building blocks, or other content and asking if you want to save the changes, click the Save button.

15.   Create a document based on the C21-BGRRTemplate.dotx template. *Hint: Do this with the* **New from existing button at the New tab Backstage view.**

16.   Create the agreement shown in Figure 21.5 with the following specifications:

a.   Insert the custom building block that is named with your initials followed by *BGRRHeading*. *Hint: Do this with the* **Quick Parts button on the Quick Access toolbar.**

b.   Insert the custom building block that is named with your initials followed by *BGRRFeesPara*. *Hint: Do this with the* **AutoText button on the Quick Access toolbar.**

c.   Insert the file named BGRepAgrmnt.docx located in Chapter21 on your storage medium. *Hint: Use the* **Text from File** *option from the Object button arrow drop-down list.*

    d. Insert the footer custom building block that is named with your initials followed by *BGRRFooter*. **Hint: Do this with the Footer button.**

17. Save the completed agreement and name it **C21-A02-BGRRAgrmnt**.
18. Print and then close **C21-A02-BGRRAgmnt.docx**.
19. Open a blank document based on the **C21-BGRRTemplate.dotx** template.
20. Click the AutoText button on the Quick Access toolbar, press the Print Screen button on your keyboard, and then click in the document to remove the drop-down list.
21. At the blank document, click the Paste button. (This pastes the screen capture in your document.)
22. Print the document and then close it without saving it.
23. Remove the Quick Parts button and AutoText button you added to the Quick Access toolbar.

Figure 21.5 Assessment 21.2

REPRESENTATION AGREEMENT
Rachel Rasmussen, Attorney at Law

Fees: My hourly rate is $350, billed in one-tenth (1/10th) of an hour increments. All time spent on work performed, including meetings, telephone calls, correspondences, and emails, will be billed at the hourly rate set forth in this paragraph. Additional expenses such as out-of-pocket expenses for postage, courier fees, photocopying charges, long distance telephone charges, and search fees, will be charged at the hourly rate set forth in this paragraph.

Retainer: I reserve the right to require a retainer for legal services. The retainer funds will be deposited in the Barrington & Gates law firm trust account and will be applied against fees and other charges as incurred. Any unused retainer funds will be returned to you immediately upon the conclusion of my legal representation of you.

Payment: Invoices are prepared for all services rendered through the last day of the month. All payments are due within thirty (30) days of the date of the invoice. If you fail to pay any invoice within this time period, I reserve the right to terminate my representation of you and to pursue other remedies available under law.

Terms: This Representation Agreement sets forth all of the terms, conditions, and understandings pertaining to my representation. This Agreement does not obligate you to use me or the firm of Barrington & Gates for all of your legal matters, and you may refer matters to another attorney at any time or withdraw from this Agreement at any time. If you withdraw, you will remain obligated to pay the full amount of all fees and expenses outstanding.

Your signature constitutes your agreement to enter into this contract as permitted under Texas Statutes. If the terms in this Agreement are acceptable to you, please date and sign below, and print your name on the line indicated.

Dated: _____

_____   Printed name: _____
Signature

200 TENTH STREET ◆ SUITE 100 ◆ AUSTIN, TX 73341 ◆ 512-555-2355

Expanding Your Skills

Explore additional feature options or use Help to learn a new skill in creating this document.

Assessment 21.3   Insert Document Properties and Fields in a Report

1. In this chapter, you learned to insert fields in a document from the Field dialog box. Display the Field dialog box by clicking the Insert tab, clicking the Quick Parts button, and then clicking *Field* at the drop-down list.
2. Experiment with the various options at the Field dialog box. Click the down-pointing arrow at the right of the *Categories* option box and notice how you can choose to display only fields in a specific category. Experiment with the other options in the dialog box such as clicking on a field and reading the information that displays about the field in the dialog box and turning on/off field codes.
3. Open **C21-A01-PropProIssues.docx** and then save the document with the name **C21-A03-PropProIssues**.
4. Move the insertion point to the end of the document, position the insertion point on a blank line below the file name field, and then insert fields by completing the following steps:
    a. Display the Field dialog box.
    b. At the dialog box, change the *Categories* option to *Date and Time*.
    c. Click the *Date* field in the *Field names* list box.
    d. Click the option in the *Field properties* section of the dialog box that will insert the date as numbers followed by the time (hours and minutes) and AM or PM (depending on the time of day).
    e. Click OK.
    f. At the document, press Shift + Enter, type File size: and then press the spacebar once.
    g. Display the Field dialog box and then change the *Categories* option to *Document Information*.
    h. Click the *FileSize* field in the *Field names* list box and then click OK.
    i. At the document, press Shift + Enter, type Number of words: and then press the spacebar once.
    j. Display the Field dialog box, make sure the *Categories* option is *Document Information*, and then click the *NumWords* field in the *Field names* list box.
    k. Click OK.
5. Print only the last page in the document.
6. Select and then delete the third reference in the *REFERENCES* section (the reference that begins with *Patterson, M. & . . .*).
7. Move the insertion point to the end of the document, click in the numbers that display after *File size:* and press F9. (This updates the file size numbers.)
8. Click in the numbers that display after *Number of words:* and then press F9.
9. Print only the last page of the document.
10. Save and then close **C21-A03-PropProIssues.docx**.

Assessment 21.4 Insert an Equation Building Block

1. The Building Blocks Organizer dialog box contains a number of predesigned equations you can insert in a document. Display the Building Blocks Organizer dialog box and then insert one of the predesigned equations.
2. Select the equation and then click the Equation Tools Design tab. Notice the groups of commands available for editing an equation.
3. Delete the equation and then type the steps you followed to insert the equation and type a list of the groups available in the Equation Tools Design tab.
4. Save the document and name it **C21-A04-Equations**. Print and then close the document.

Achieving Signature Status

Take your skills to the next level by completing this more challenging assessment.

Assessment 21.5 Create Custom Building Blocks

1. Open a blank document based on the C21-BRGGTemplate.dotx template you created in Assessment 2. (Hint: Do this with the New from existing button at the New tab Backstage view).
2. Insert the **BGRRLtrhd.docx** document into the current document. (Do this with the Object button arrow in the Insert tab. This document is located in the Chapter21 folder on your storage medium.)
3. Select the entire document and then save the selected text as a custom building block in the Quick Part gallery. Name the building block *BGRRLetterhead* and change the *Save in* option to *C21-BGRRTemplate.dotx*.
4. Click the Undo button on the Quick Access toolbar to remove the BGRRLtrhd document. (You may need to click the Undo button more than once.)
5. Click the *No Spacing* style in the Styles group in the Home tab.
6. Type **Very truly yours,** and then press the Enter key twice.
7. Type **BARRINGTON & GATES** and then press the Enter key four times.
8. Type **Rachel Rasmussen** and then press the Enter key.
9. Type **Attorney at Law** and then press the Enter key.
10. Press Ctrl + A to select the entire document and then save the selected text as a custom building block in the AutoText gallery. Name the building block *BGRRClose* and change the *Save in* option to *C21-BGRRTemplate.dotx*.
11. With the entire document selected, press the Delete key.
12. Click the *No Spacing* style in the Styles group in the Home tab and then type the following paragraph of text:

    Thank you for your interest in hiring me as your attorney and the firm of Barrington & Gates to represent you. At Barrington & Gates, we pride ourselves on providing the highest-quality legal counsel and advice for our clients. Please read the enclosed *Representation Agreement*, sign in the appropriate location, and then return the agreement to me by fax, as an email attachment, or send it to me at the address listed below.

13. Select the entire document and then save the selected text as a custom building block in the AutoText gallery. Name the building block *BGRRIntroPara* and change the *Save in* option to *C21-BGRRTemplate.dotx*.
14. Close the document without saving it. At the message that displays telling you that you have modified styles, building blocks, or other content and asking if you want to save the changes, click the Save button.
15. Open a blank document based on the C21-BGRRTemplate.dotx template. ***Hint: Do this with the New from existing option at the New tab Backstage view***.
16. Click the *No Spacing* style in the Styles group in the Home tab and then create the business letter shown in Figure 21.6. Use the building blocks you created to insert the letterhead, footer, first paragraph of text, and the complimentary close (the text that begins *Very truly yours,*). Type the additional text shown in the figure. (Type your initials in place of the XX located toward the end of the letter.)
17. Save the completed letter and name it **C21-A05-ClientLtr**.
18. Print and then close **C21-A05-ClientLtr.docx**.
19. Open a blank document based on the C21-BGRRTemplate.dotx template.
20. Click the Insert tab, click the Quick Parts button, point to *AutoText* (to display the side menu with your custom building block), press the Print Screen button on your keyboard, and then click in the document to remove the side menu.
21. Press Ctrl + N to open a new blank document and then click the Paste button. (This pastes the screen capture of your document with the AutoText side menu displayed.)

22. Click the Word button on the Taskbar and then click the thumbnail representing the first blank document.
23. Click the Quick Parts button and then press the Print Screen key on your keyboard.
24. Click the Word button on the Taskbar and then click the thumbnail representing the document containing the AutoText side menu screen capture.
25. Press Ctrl + End, press the Enter key twice, and then click the Paste button. (This pastes the second screen capture in your document.) Make sure both screen captures display on the first page. If not, delete any space above, between, or below the screen captures to ensure that they fit on one page.
26. Print the document and then close it without saving it.
27. Close the blank document based on the **C21-BGRRTemplate.dotx** template.

Figure 21.6 Assessment 21.5

BARRINGTON & GATES

Rachel Rasmussen, Associate

(Current date)

Mr. Evan Markham
3410 South 44th Street
Austin, TX 73348

Dear Mr. Markham:

Thank you for your interest in hiring me as your attorney and the firm of Barrington & Gates to represent you. At Barrington & Gates, we pride ourselves on providing the highest-quality legal counsel and advice for our clients. Please read the enclosed *Representation Agreement*, sign in the appropriate location, and then return the agreement to me by fax, as an email attachment, or send it to me at the address listed below.

As I mentioned during our telephone conversation, I will review the information you are faxing and then send my responses, suggestions, and questions to you in an email. After reading my email, please call me so we can schedule a meeting to discuss further your legal concerns.

Very truly yours,

BARRINGTON & GATES

Rachel Rasmussen
Attorney at Law

XX
C21-A05-ClientLtr.docx

Enclosure

200 TENTH STREET • SUITE 100 • AUSTIN, TX 73341 • 512-555-2355

Chapter 22

Tutorial 22.1
Using the AutoCorrect Feature
Tutorial 22.2
Customizing AutoCorrect and
Auto Formatting
Tutorial 22.3
Customizing the Quick Access
Toolbar
Tutorial 22.4
Customizing the Ribbon
Tutorial 22.5
Customizing Word Options

Customizing AutoCorrect and Word Options

Performance Objectives

Upon successful completion of Chapter 22, you will be able to:

- Add words to and delete words from the AutoCorrect dialog box
- Insert symbols in the AutoCorrect dialog box
- Use the AutoCorrect Options button
- Customize the Quick Access toolbar and ribbon
- Customize Word options

Word offers a number of features to help you customize documents as well as streamline their formatting. In this chapter, you will learn how to customize the AutoCorrect feature by inserting and deleting characters at the AutoCorrect dialog box. You will also learn how to use the AutoCorrect Options button, customize the Quick Access toolbar and ribbon, and customize Word options.

Note: Before beginning computer exercises for this chapter, copy to your storage medium the Chapter22 folder from the CD that accompanies this textbook and then make Chapter22 the active folder.

In this chapter, students will produce the following documents:

Exercise 22.1. C22-E01-BT-FAV.docx
Exercise 22.2. C22-E02-Computers.docx
Exercise 22.3. C22-E03-BTAdventures.docx

Model answers for these exercises are shown on the following pages.

Bayside Travel

CHINA, KYRGYZSTAN, TAJIKISTAN, UZBEKISTAN

Old Silk Road Adventure

Bayside Travel is partnering with Family Adventure Vacations to provide adventurous and thrilling family vacations. Our first joint adventure is an exotic trip along the Old Silk Road that includes stunning landscapes in China, Kyrgyzstan, Tajikistan, and Uzbekistan. The Old Silk Road is one of the most fascinating destinations in Asia. Sign up for the Old Silk Road Adventure and experience delicious food, comfortable facilities, cultural interactions, abundant wildlife, and a wide variety of activities of interest to people of all ages.

During the twenty-day trip, you and your family will travel across Kyrgyzstan through majestic mountains and open plains. You will drive the Old Silk Road of Tash Rabat through one of the most spectacular regions of Tien Shan. You will travel through parts of China, Tajikistan, and Uzbekistan visiting museums and local bazaars, witness the Tien Shan Mountains at their most beautiful, and experience the sights of Samarkand and sleepy Bukhara.

Contact one of our college travel adventure consultants to learn more about the newest Student Travel package titled "STudent STyle" that offers a variety of student discounts, rebates, and free travel accessories for qualifying participants.

Through the sponsorship of Ameria Resorts®, we are able to offer you a ➔15 percent discount← for groups of twenty or more people.

Individual price:
$3,299 (US)
£1,999 (UK)

Individual price for groups of ten or more:
$3,099 (US)
£1,599 (UK)

For additional information on the Old Silk Road Adventure as well as other exciting vacation specials, please visit our website at www.emcp.net/bayside or visit www.emcp.net/famadvac to read about other joint ventures between Bayside Travel and Family Adventure Vacations.

5530 Bayside Drive ◆ San Francisco CA 94320 ◆ 1-888-555-8890 ◆ www.emcp.net/bayside

Exercise 22.1 C22-E01-BT-FAV.docx

THE COMPUTER ADVANTAGE

Before the early 1980s, computers were unknown to the average person. Many people had never even seen a computer, let alone used one. The few computers that existed were relatively large, bulky devices confined to secure computer centers in corporate or government facilities. Referred to as mainframes, these computers were maintenance intensive, requiring special climate-controlled conditions and several full-time operators for each machine. Because early mainframes were expensive and difficult to operate, usage was restricted to computer programmers and scientists, who used them to perform complex operations, such as processing payrolls and designing sophisticated military weaponry.

Beginning in the early 1980s, the computer world changed dramatically with the introduction of microcomputers, also called personal computers (PCs). These relatively small computers were considerably more affordable and much easier to use than their mainframe ancestors. Within a few years, ownership of personal computers became widespread in the workplace, and today, the personal computer is a standard appliance in homes and schools.

Today's computers come in a variety of shapes and sizes and differ significantly in computing capability, price, and speed. Whatever their size, cost, or power, all computers offer advantages over manual technologies in the areas of speed, accuracy, versatility, storage capabilities, and communications capabilities.

Student Name   Page 1

Exercise 22.2 C22-E02-Computers.docx   Page 1

SPEED

Computers operate with lightening-like speed, and processing speeds are increasing as computer manufacturers introduce new and improved models. Contemporary personal computers are capable of executing billions of program instructions in one second. Some larger computers, such as supercomputers, can execute trillions of instructions per second, a rate important for processing huge amounts of data involved in forecasting weather, monitoring space shuttle flights, and managing other data-intensive applications.

ACCURACY

People sometimes blame human errors on a computer. In truth, if a computer user enters correct data and uses accurate programs, computers are extremely accurate. A popular expression among computers professionals is "garbage in—garbage out" (GIGO), which means that if inaccurate programs and/or data are entered into a computer for processing, the resulting output will also be inaccurate. The computer user is responsible for entering data correctly and making certain that programs are correct.

VERSATILITY

Computers are perhaps the most versatile of all machines or devices. They can perform a variety of personal, business, and scientific applications. Families use computers for entertainment, communications, budgeting, online shopping, completing homework assignments, playing games, and listening to music. Banks conduct money transfers, account withdrawals, and the payment of checks via computer. Retailers use computers to process sales transactions and to check on the availability of products. Manufacturers can manage their entire production, warehousing, and selling processes with

Student Name   Page 2

Page 2

computerized systems. Schools access computers for keeping records, conducting distance learning classes, scheduling events, and analyzing budgets. Universities, government agencies, hospitals, and scientific organizations conduct life-enhancing research using computers. Perhaps the most ambitious such computer-based scientific research of all time is the Human Genome Project. Completed in April of 2003, this program was more than two years ahead of schedule and at a cost considerably lower than originally forecast. This project represented an international effort to sequence three billion DNA (deoxyribonucleic acid) letters in the human genome, which is the collection of gene types that comprise every person. Scientists from all over the world can now access the genome database and use the information to research ways to improve human health and fight disease.

STORAGE

Storage is a defining computer characteristic and is one of the features that revolutionized early computing, for it made computers incredibly flexible. A computer is capable of accepting and storing programs and data. Once stored in the computer, a user can access a program again and again to process different data. Computers can store huge amounts of data in comparably tiny physical spaces. For example, one compact disk can store about 109,000 pages of magazine text, and the capacities of internal storage devices are many times larger.

COMMUNICATIONS

Most modern computers contain special equipment and programs that allow them to communicate with other computers through telephone lines, cable connections, and satellites. A structure in which computers are linked together using special programs and equipment is a network. Newer communications technologies allow users to exchange information over wireless networks using

Exercise 22.2 C22-E02-Computers.docx   Page 3

wireless devices such as personal digital assistants (PDAs), notebook computers, cell phones, and pagers.

A network can be relatively small or quite large. A local area network (LAN) is one confined to a relatively small geographical area, such as a building, factory, or college campus. A wide area network (WAN) spans a large geographical area and might connect a company's manufacturing plants dispersed throughout North America. Constant, quick connections along with other computer technologies have helped boost productivity for manufacturers.

Page 4

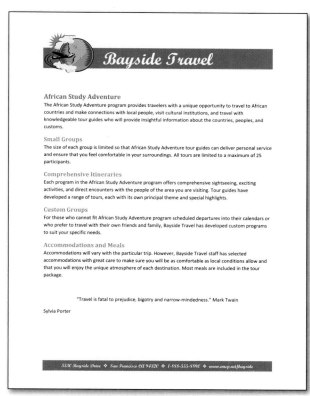

Exercise 22.3 C22-E03-BTAdventure.docx

Customizing AutoCorrect

The AutoCorrect feature in Word corrects certain text automatically as you type. You can control what types of corrections are made with options at the AutoCorrect dialog box with the AutoCorrect tab selected as shown in Figure 22.1. At this dialog box, you can turn an autocorrect feature on or off by inserting or removing check marks from the check boxes, specify autocorrect exceptions, replace frequently misspelled words with the correct spelling, and add frequently used words and specify keys to quickly insert the words in a document.

Figure 22.1 AutoCorrect Dialog Box with AutoCorrect Tab Selected

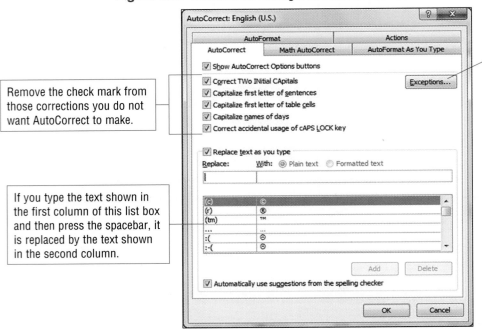

Click this button to display a dialog box with AutoCorrect exceptions and where you can add your own exceptions.

Remove the check mark from those corrections you do not want AutoCorrect to make.

If you type the text shown in the first column of this list box and then press the spacebar, it is replaced by the text shown in the second column.

QUICK STEPS

Display the AutoCorrect Exceptions Dialog Box
1. Click File tab, Options button.
2. Click *Proofing*.
3. Click AutoCorrect Options button.
4. Click AutoCorrect tab.
5. Click Exceptions button.

Specifying AutoCorrect Exceptions

The check box options at the AutoCorrect dialog box with the AutoCorrect tab selected identify the types of corrections made by AutoCorrect. You can make exceptions to the corrections with options at the AutoCorrect Exceptions dialog box shown in Figure 22.2. Display this dialog box by clicking the Exceptions button at the AutoCorrect dialog box with the AutoCorrect tab selected.

AutoCorrect will usually capitalize words that come after an abbreviation ending in a period since a period usually ends a sentence. Exceptions to this display in the AutoCorrect Exceptions dialog box with the First Letter tab selected. Many exceptions already display in the dialog box but you can add additional exceptions by typing the desired exception in the *Don't capitalize after* text box and then clicking the Add button. By default, AutoCorrect will correct two initial capital letters in a word. If you do not want AutoCorrect to correct the capitalizing of two initial capitals in a word, display the AutoCorrect Exceptions dialog box with the INitial CAps tab selected and then type the exception text in the *Don't correct* text box. At the AutoCorrect Exceptions dialog box with the Other Corrections tab selected, type text that you do not want corrected in the *Don't correct* text box. You can delete exceptions from the dialog box with any of the tabs selected, by clicking the desired text in the list box and then clicking the Delete button.

Figure 22.2 AutoCorrect Exceptions Dialog Box

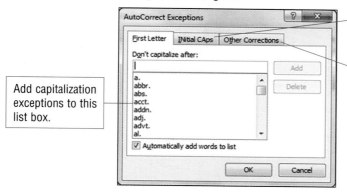

Click this tab to display a list box where you can add exceptions to two initial caps corrections.

Click this tab to display a list box where you can add any other exceptions to corrections.

Add capitalization exceptions to this list box.

Adding Words to AutoCorrect

You can add commonly misspelled words or frequently made typographical errors to AutoCorrect. For example, if you consistently type *relavent* instead of *relevant*, you can add *relavent* to AutoCorrect and tell AutoCorrect to correct it as *relevant*. You can also add an abbreviation to AutoCorrect that, when typed, AutoCorrect will replace with the entire word (or words). For example, in Exercise 22.1A, you will add *fav* and the replacement text *Family Adventure Vacations* to AutoCorrect. Subsequently, when you type *fav* and then press the spacebar, AutoCorrect will insert *Family Adventure Vacations*. You can also control the capitalization of the word (or words) AutoCorrect inserts by controlling the capitalization of the abbreviation. For example, in Exercise 22.1A, you will add *Ky* to AutoCorrect. When you type *Ky* and then press the spacebar, AutoCorrect will insert *Kyrgyzstan*. If you want to insert KYRGYZSTAN in the document, you type KY and then press the spacebar.

QUICK STEPS

Add Word(s) to AutoCorrect
1. Click File tab, Options button.
2. Click *Proofing*.
3. Click AutoCorrect Options button.
4. Click AutoCorrect tab.
5. Type misspelled or abbreviated word.
6. Press Tab.
7. Type correctly spelled word or complete word(s).
8. Click Add button.
9. Click OK.

Exercise 22.1A Adding Exceptions and Text to AutoCorrect   Part 1 of 4

1. At a blank document, click the File tab and then click the Options button.
2. At the Word Options dialog box, click *Proofing* in the left panel.
3. Click the AutoCorrect Options button in the *AutoCorrect options* section.
4. At the AutoCorrect dialog box with the AutoCorrect tab selected, add an exception to AutoCorrect by completing the following steps:
   a. Click the Exceptions button.
   b. At the AutoCorrect Exceptions dialog box, click the INitial CAps tab.
   c. Type STudent in the *Don't correct* text box and then click the Add button.
   d. Click in the *Don't correct* text box, type STyle, and then click the Add button.
   e. Click the OK button.
5. At the AutoCorrect dialog box with the AutoCorrect tab selected, click in the *Replace* text box.

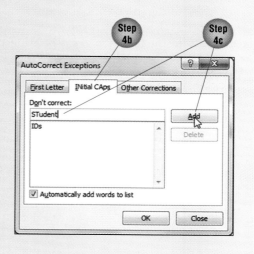

Step 4b

Step 4c

---

6. Type fav.
7. Press the Tab key (this moves the insertion point to the *With* text box) and then type Family Adventure Vacations.
8. Click the Add button. (This adds *fav* and *Family Adventure Vacations* to AutoCorrect and also selects *fav* in the *Replace* text box.)

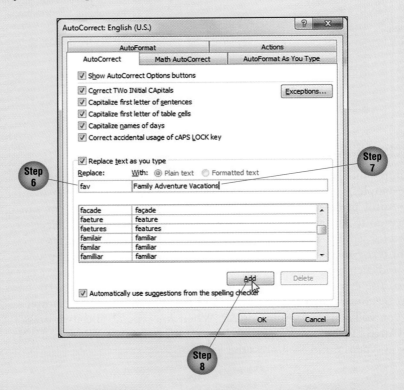

9. Type Ky in the *Replace* text box. (The text *fav* is removed automatically when you begin typing *Ky*.)
10. Press the Tab key, type Kyrgyzstan, and then click the Add button.
11. With the insertion point positioned in the *Replace* text box, type Tj.
12. Press the Tab key, type Tajikistan, and then click the Add button.
13. With the insertion point positioned in the *Replace* text box, type Uz.
14. Press the Tab key, type Uzbekistan, and then click the Add button.
15. With the insertion point positioned in the *Replace* text box, type bt.
16. Press the Tab key, type Bayside Travel, and then click the Add button.
17. With the insertion point positioned in the *Replace* text box, type osr.
18. Press the Tab key, type Old Silk Road, and then click the Add button.
19. Click OK to close the AutoCorrect dialog box and then click OK to close the Word Options dialog box.
20. Open **BTLtrhd.docx** and save the document with the name **C22-E01-BT-FAV**.
21. Type the text shown in Figure 22.3. Type the text exactly as shown. AutoCorrect will correct words as you type and not correct the words *STudent* and *STyle*.
22. Save **C22-E01-BT-FAV.docx**.

Figure 22.3 Exercise 22.1A

CHINA, KY, TJ, UZ

osr Adventure

bt is partnering with fav to provide adventurous and thrilling family vacations. Our first joint adventure is an exotic trip along the osr that includes stunning landscapes in China, Ky, Tj, and Uz. The osr is one of the most fascinating destinations in Asia. Sign up for the osr Adventure and experience delicious food, comfortable facilities, cultural interactions, abundant wildlife, and a wide variety of activities of interest to people of all ages.

During the twenty-day trip, you and your family will travel across Ky through majestic mountains and open plains. You will drive the osr of Tash Rabat through one of the most spectacular regions of Tien Shan. You will travel through parts of China, Tj, and Uz visiting museums and local bazaars, witness the Tien Shan Mountains at their most beautiful, and experience the sights of Samarkand and sleepy Bukhara.

Contact one of our college travel adventure consultants to learn more about the newest Student Travel package titled "STudent STyle" that offers a variety of student discounts, rebates, and free travel accessories for qualifying participants.

bt and fav are offering a 15 percent discount if you sign up for this once-in-a-lifetime trip to travel the osr. This exciting adventure is limited to thirty people so don't wait to sign up!

Using the AutoCorrect Options Button

If you rest the mouse pointer near text that AutoCorrect has just corrected, a small blue box displays below the text. Move the mouse pointer to this blue box, and the AutoCorrect Options button displays. Click this button, and a drop-down list displays with three options. You can choose to change the corrected text back to the original spelling, tell AutoCorrect to stop automatically correcting occurrences of that specific text, or display the AutoCorrect dialog box. If the AutoCorrect Options button does not display, you will need to turn the feature on. To do this, display the AutoCorrect dialog box with the AutoCorrect tab selected, click the *Show AutoCorrect Options buttons* check box to insert a check mark, and then click OK to close the dialog box.

AutoCorrect
Options

Exercise 22.1B   Using the AutoCorrect Options Button   Part 2 of 4

1. With **C22-E01-BT-FAV.docx** open, select and then delete the last paragraph.
2. Type the following text (AutoCorrect will automatically change *Ameria* to *America*, which you will change in the next step): Through the sponsorship of Ameria Resorts, we are able to offer you a 15 percent discount for groups of twenty or more people.

3. Change the spelling of *America* back to *Ameria* by completing the following steps:
   a. Position the mouse pointer over *America* until a blue box displays below the word.
   b. Position the mouse pointer on the blue box until the AutoCorrect Options button displays.
   c. Click the AutoCorrect Options button and then click the *Change back to "Ameria"* option.

Step 3c

Through the sponsorship of America Resorts, we are able to offer you a 15 percent discount for groups of twenty or more people.

🔁 Change back to "Ameria"

Stop Automatically Correcting "Ameria"

🔁 Control AutoCorrect Options...

4. Save and then print **C22-E01-BT-FAV.docx**.

QUICK
STEPS

Insert Symbol to AutoCorrect
1. Click Insert tab.
2. Click Symbol button, *More Symbols*.
3. Click desired symbol.
4. Click AutoCorrect button.
5. Type text used to insert symbol.
6. Click Add button.
7. Click OK.
8. Click Close button.

Inserting Symbols Automatically

AutoCorrect recognizes and replaces symbols as well as text. Several symbols included in AutoCorrect display in the AutoCorrect dialog box, listed first in the *Replace* text box. Table 22.1 lists these symbols along with the characters you type to insert them.

Along with the symbols provided by Word, you can insert other symbols in the AutoCorrect dialog box with the AutoCorrect button in the Symbol dialog box. To insert a symbol in the AutoCorrect dialog box, click the Insert tab, click the Symbol button in the Symbols group, and then click *More Symbols* at the drop-down list. At the Symbol dialog box, click the desired symbol and then click the AutoCorrect button that displays in the lower left corner of the dialog box. This displays the AutoCorrect dialog box with the symbol inserted in the *With* text box and the insertion point positioned

Table 22.1 AutoCorrect Symbols Available at the AutoCorrect Dialog Box

Type	To Insert
(c)	©
(r)	®
(tm)	TM
...	. . .
:) or :-)	☺
:| or :-|	😐
:(or :-(	☹
-->	→
<--	←
==>	→
<==	←
<=>	⇔

in the *Replace* text box. Type the text you will use to insert the symbol, click the Add button, and then click OK to close the AutoCorrect dialog box. Click the Close button to close the Symbol dialog box.

Exercise 22.1C Inserting Symbols Using AutoCorrect Part 3 of 4

1. With **C22-E01-BT-FAV.docx** open, move the insertion point so it is positioned immediately right of the last *s* in *Resorts* and then type (r). (This inserts the registered trademark.)
2. Move the insertion point immediately left of the *1* in *15* and then type ==>. (This inserts the → symbol.)
3. Move the insertion point immediately right of the *t* in *discount* and then type <==. (This inserts the ← symbol.)
4. Insert the pound currency unit symbol (£) in AutoCorrect by completing the following steps:
   a. Click the Insert tab.
   b. Click the Symbol button and then click *More Symbols* at the drop-down list.
   c. At the Symbol dialog box, make sure that *(normal text)* displays in the *Font* option box. If it does not, click the down-pointing arrow at the right of the *Font* option box and then click *(normal text)* at the drop-down list (first option in the list).
   d. Scroll down the list of symbols and then click the pound currency unit symbol £ (located in approximately the sixth or seventh row).
   e. Click the AutoCorrect button located in the lower left corner of the dialog box.
   f. At the AutoCorrect dialog box, type pcu in the *Replace* text box and then click the Add button.
   g. Click OK to close the AutoCorrect dialog box and then the Close button to close the Symbol dialog box.
5. Press Ctrl + End to move the insertion point to the end of the document and then press the Enter key twice. (The insertion point should be positioned a double space below the last paragraph of text.)
6. Type the text shown in Figure 22.4. Create the pound currency unit symbol by typing pcu and then pressing the spacebar. Press the Backspace key once and then type 1,999. (Complete similar steps when typing £1,599 (UK).)
7. Save **C22-E01-BT-FAV.docx**.

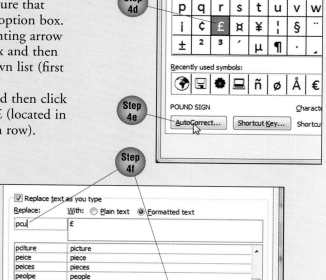

Figure 22.4 Exercise 22.1C

Individual price:
$3,299 (US)
£1,999 (UK)

Individual price for groups of ten or more:
$3,099 (US)
£1,599 (UK)

Customizing AutoFormatting

When you type text, Word provides options to automatically apply some formatting such as changing a fraction to a fraction character (such as changing 1/2 to ½), changing numbers to ordinals (such as changing 1st to 1st), changing an Internet or network path to a hyperlink (such as changing www.emcp.net to www.emcp.net), and applying bullets or numbers to text (you learned about this feature in Chapter 3). The autoformatting options display in the AutoCorrect dialog box with the AutoFormat As You Type tab selected as shown in Figure 22.5. Display this dialog box by clicking the File tab and then clicking the Options button. At the Word Options dialog box, click *Proofing* in the left panel and then click the AutoCorrect Options button. At the AutoCorrect dialog box, click the AutoFormat As You Type tab. At the AutoCorrect dialog box with the AutoFormat As You Type tab selected, remove the check mark from those options you want to turn off and insert a check mark for those options you want Word to automatically format.

Figure 22.5 AutoCorrect Dialog Box with AutoFormat As You Type Tab Selected

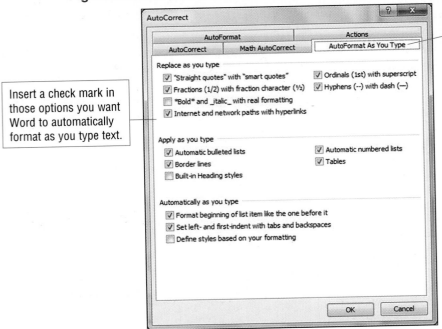

Click this tab to display options that Word automatically formats as you type text.

Insert a check mark in those options you want Word to automatically format as you type text.

Deleting AutoCorrect Text

You can delete text from the AutoCorrect dialog box. To do this, display the dialog box, click the desired word or words in the list box, and then click the Delete button. Complete similar steps to delete text from the AutoCorrect Exceptions dialog box.

Exercise 22.1D · Changing AutoFormatting and Deleting Text from AutoCorrect · Part 4 of 4

1. Make sure **C22-E01-BT-FAV.docx** is open.
2. You need to add a couple of web addresses to the document and you do not want the addresses automatically formatted as hyperlinks (since you are sending the document as hard copy rather than electronically). Turn off the autoformatting of web addresses by completing the following steps:
   a. Click the File tab and then click the Options button.
   b. At the Word Options dialog box, click *Proofing* in the left panel.
   c. Click the AutoCorrect Options button.
   d. At the AutoCorrect dialog box, click the AutoFormat As You Type tab.
   e. Click the *Internet and network paths with hyperlinks* check box to remove the check mark.
   f. Click OK to close the AutoCorrect dialog box.
   g. Click OK to close the Word Options dialog box.
3. Press Ctrl + End to move the insertion point to the end of the document and then press the Enter key twice.
4. Type the text shown in Figure 22.6.
5. Turn on the autoformat feature you turned off in Step 2 by completing Steps 2a through 2g (except in step 2e you are inserting the check mark rather than removing it).
6. Delete *bt* from AutoCorrect by completing the following steps:
   a. Click the File tab and then click the Options button.
   b. At the Word Options dialog box, click *Proofing* in the left panel.
   c. Click the AutoCorrect Options button in the *AutoCorrect options* section.
   d. At the AutoCorrect dialog box, click the AutoCorrect tab.
   e. At the AutoCorrect dialog box, type bt in the *Replace* text box. (This selects the entry in the list box.)
   f. Click the Delete button.

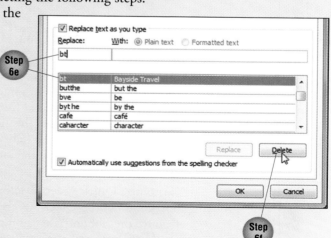

7. Complete steps similar to those in Step 6 to delete the following AutoCorrect entries: *fav*, *Ky*, *osr*, *pcu*, *Tj*, and *Uz*.
8. Delete the exceptions you added to the AutoCorrect Exceptions dialog box by completing the following steps:
    a. At the AutoCorrect dialog box with the AutoCorrect tab selected, click the Exceptions button.
    b. At the AutoCorrect Exceptions dialog box, click the INitial CAps tab.
    c. Click STudent in the list box and then click the Delete button.
    d. Click STyle in the list box and then click the Delete button.
    e. Click OK to close the AutoCorrect Exceptions dialog box.
9. Click OK to close the AutoCorrect dialog box.
10. Click OK to close the Word Options dialog box.
11. Save, print, and then close **C22-E01-BT-FAV.docx**.

Figure 22.6 Exercise 22.1D

For additional information on the osr Adventure as well as other exciting vacation specials, please visit our website at www.emcp.net/bayside, or visit www.emcp.net/famadvac to read about other joint ventures between bt and fav.

Minimizing the Ribbon

Minimize the Ribbon

The Word ribbon displays toward the top of the screen and displays tabs and commands divided into groups. If you want to free up some room on the screen, you can minimize the ribbon by clicking the Minimize the Ribbon button that displays immediately left of the Microsoft Word Help button that displays in the upper right corner of the screen. You can also minimize the ribbon with the keyboard shortcut Ctrl + F1. Click the Minimize the Ribbon button or press Ctrl + F1 and the ribbon is reduced to tabs. To redisplay the ribbon, click the Expand the Ribbon button (previously the Minimize the Ribbon button), press Ctrl + F1, or double-click one of the tabs.

Customize Quick Access Toolbar
1. Click Customize Quick Access Toolbar button.
2. Insert check mark before desired button(s).
3. Remove check mark before undesired button(s).

Customize Quick Access Toolbar

Customizing the Quick Access Toolbar

As its name implies, the Quick Access toolbar provides quick access to buttons for some of the most commonly performed tasks. By default, it contains the Save, Undo, and Redo buttons. You can easily add or remove buttons for basic functions to and from the Quick Access toolbar with options at the Customize Quick Access Toolbar drop-down list, shown in Figure 22.7. Display this list by clicking the Customize Quick Access Toolbar button that displays at the right of the toolbar. Insert a check mark for the commands you want displayed on the toolbar and remove the check mark from those you do not want to appear.

The Customize Quick Access Toolbar button drop-down list includes an option for moving the location of the Quick Access toolbar. By default, the Quick Access toolbar is positioned above the ribbon. You can move the toolbar below the ribbon by clicking the *Show Below the Ribbon* option at the drop-down list.

Figure 22.7 Customize Quick Access Toolbar Button Drop-down List

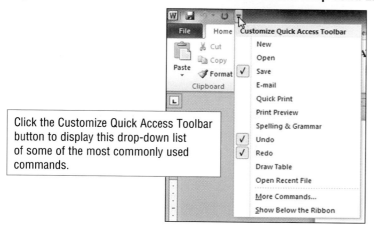

Click the Customize Quick Access Toolbar button to display this drop-down list of some of the most commonly used commands.

QUICK STEPS

Add Buttons to Quick Access Toolbar from Tabs
1. Right-click desired button in tab.
2. Click Add to Quick Access Toolbar at shortcut menu.

Adding Buttons from Tabs

You can add buttons or commands from a tab to the Quick Access toolbar. To do this, click the tab, right-click on the desired button or command, and then click *Add to Quick Access Toolbar* at the shortcut menu.

Exercise 22.2A Minimizing the Ribbon and Customizing the Quick Access Toolbar   **Part 1 of 4**

1. Open **Computers.docx** and then save the document with the name **C22-E02-Computers**.
2. Make the following changes to the document:
   a. Apply the Heading 1 style to the title and the Heading 2 style to the five headings.
   b. Change the style set to *Formal*.
   c. Insert page numbering by clicking the Insert tab, clicking the Page Number button, pointing to *Bottom of Page*, and then clicking the *Accent Bar 2* option. (You will need to scroll down the list to display this option.)
   d. Double-click in the document.
3. Minimize the ribbon by clicking the Minimize the Ribbon button that displays immediately left of the Microsoft Word Help button located in the upper right corner of the screen.
4. Add a New button to the Quick Access toolbar by clicking the Customize Quick Access Toolbar button that displays at the right of the toolbar and then clicking *New* at the drop-down list.
5. Add an Open button to the Quick Access toolbar by clicking the Customize Quick Access Toolbar button that displays at the right of the toolbar and then clicking *Open* at the drop-down list.
6. Click the New button on the Quick Access toolbar. (This displays a new blank document.)

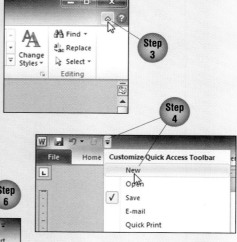

7. Close the document without saving it.
8. Click the Open button on the Quick Access toolbar to display the Open dialog box.
9. Close the Open dialog box.
10. Redisplay the ribbon by double-clicking one of the tabs. (You can also redisplay the ribbon by clicking the Expand the Ribbon button or by pressing Ctrl + F1.)
11. Move the Quick Access toolbar by clicking the Customize Quick Access Toolbar button and then clicking *Show Below the Ribbon* at the drop-down list.
12. Move the Quick Access toolbar back to the default position by clicking the Customize Quick Access Toolbar button and then clicking *Show Above the Ribbon* at the drop-down list.
13. Add the Margins and Themes buttons to the Quick Access toolbar by completing the following steps:
    a. Click the Page Layout tab.
    b. Right-click the Margins button in the Page Setup group and then click *Add to Quick Access Toolbar* at the shortcut menu.
    c. Right-click the Themes button in the Themes group and then click *Add to Quick Access Toolbar* at the shortcut menu.

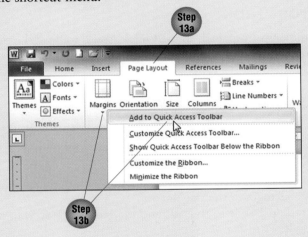

14. Change the top margin by completing the following steps:
    a. Click the Margins button on the Quick Access toolbar and then click *Custom Margins* at the drop-down list.
    b. At the Page Setup dialog box, change the top margin measurement to 1.5 inches and then click OK.
15. Change the theme by clicking the Themes button on the Quick Access toolbar and then clicking *Module* at the drop-down list. (You will need to scroll down the list to display this theme.)
16. Create a screenshot of the Quick Access toolbar by completing the following steps:
    a. Click the New button on the Quick Access toolbar. (This displays a new blank document.)
    b. Click the Insert tab, click the Screenshot button in the Illustrations group, and then click *Screen Clipping* at the drop-down list.
    c. In a few moments, the C22-E02-Computers.docx document displays in a dimmed manner. Using the mouse, drag from the upper left corner of the screen down and to the right to capture the Quick Access toolbar, and then release the mouse.
    d. With the screenshot image inserted in the document, print the document and then close it without saving it.
17. Save **C22-E02-Computers.docx**.

Customizing with Options at the Word Options Dialog Box

The Customize Quick Access Toolbar button drop-down list contains eleven of the most commonly used commands. You can, however, insert many other commands on the toolbar. To display the available commands, click the Customize Quick Access Toolbar button and then click *More Commands* at the drop-down list. This displays the Word Options dialog box with *Quick Access Toolbar* selected in the left panel, as shown in Figure 22.8. You can also display this dialog box by clicking the File tab, clicking the Options button, and then clicking *Quick Access Toolbar* in the left panel of the Word Options dialog box.

Figure 22.8 Word Options Dialog Box with Quick Access Toolbar Selected

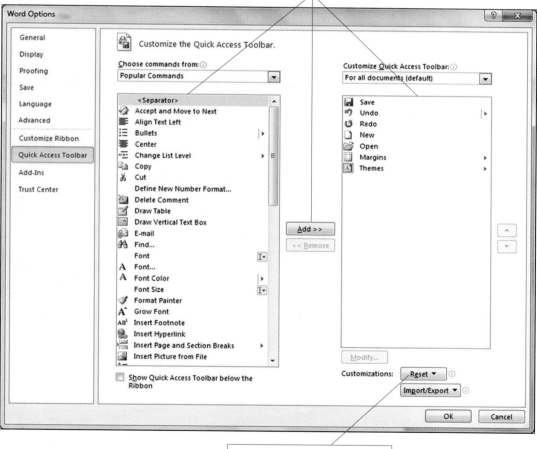

Click the desired command in the list box at the left, click the Add button, and the command displays in the list box at the right.

Click the Reset button to reset the Quick Access toolbar to the default buttons.

To reset the Quick Access toolbar to the default (Save, Undo, and Redo buttons), click the Reset button that displays toward the bottom of the dialog box. At the message

**Add Buttons to
Quick Access
Toolbar from Word
Options Dialog Box**
1. Click Customize
   Quick Access
   Toolbar button.
2. Click *More
   Commands* at
   drop-down list.
3. Click desired
   command at left list
   box.
4. Click Add button.
5. Click OK.

asking if you are sure you want to restore the Quick Access toolbar shared between all documents to its default contents, click Yes.

You can customize the Quick Access toolbar for all documents or for a specific document. To customize the toolbar for the currently open document, display the Word Options dialog box with *Quick Access Toolbar* selected, click the down-pointing arrow at the right of the Customize Quick Access Toolbar option, and then click the *For (document name)* option where the name of the currently open document displays.

The *Choose commands from* option at the Word Options dialog box has a default setting of *Popular Commands*. At this setting, the list box below the option displays only a portion of all of the commands available to insert as a button on the Quick Access toolbar. To display all of the commands available, click the down-pointing arrow at the right of the *Choose commands from* option box and then click *All Commands*. The drop-down list also contains options for specifying commands that are not currently available on the ribbon, as well as commands in the File tab and various other tabs.

To add a button, click the desired command in the list box at the left side of the commands list box and then click the Add button that displays between the two list boxes. Continue adding all desired buttons and then click OK to close the dialog box.

Exercise 22.2B   **Inserting and Removing Buttons from the Quick Access Toolbar**   Part 2 of 4

1. With **C22-E02-Computers.docx** open, reset the Quick Access toolbar by completing the following steps:
   a. Click the Customize Quick Access Toolbar button that displays at the right of the Quick Access toolbar and then click *More Commands* at the drop-down list.
   b. At the Word Options dialog box, click the Reset button that displays toward the bottom of the dialog box, and then click *Reset only Quick Access Toolbar* at the drop-down list.
   c. At the message asking if you are sure you want to restore the Quick Access toolbar shared between all documents to its default contents, click Yes.
   d. Click OK to close the dialog box.

2. Insert buttons on the Quick Access toolbar for the currently open document by completing the following steps:
   a. Click the Customize Quick Access Toolbar button and then click *More Commands*.
   b. At the Word Options dialog box, click the down-pointing arrow at the right of the Customize Quick Access Toolbar option and then click *For C22-E02-Computers.docx* at the drop-down list.

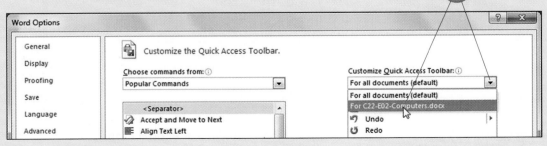

  c. Click the down-pointing arrow at the right of the *Choose commands from* option box and then click *All Commands*.

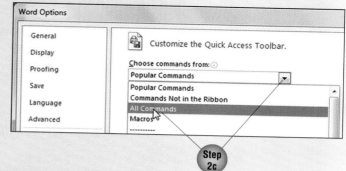

  d. Scroll down the list box and then click the second *Close* command (the option preceded by a close icon). (Commands are listed in alphabetical order.)

  e. Click the Add button that displays between the two list boxes.

  f. Scroll down the list box and then click *Footer*.

  g. Click the Add button.

  h. Click OK to close the dialog box.

  i. Check the Quick Access toolbar and notice the two buttons now display along with the default buttons.

3. Remove page numbering from the document by completing the following steps:

  a. Click the Insert tab.

  b. Click the Page Number button in the Header & Footer group.

  c. Click *Remove Page Numbers* at the drop-down list.

4. Insert a footer by completing the following steps:

  a. Click the Footer button on the Quick Access toolbar.

  b. Click *Alphabet* at the drop-down list.

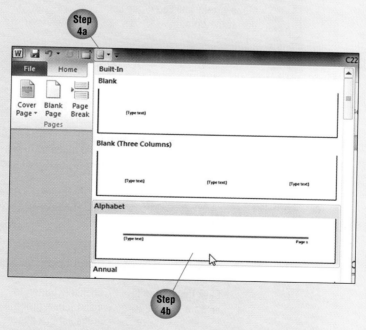

  c. Click in the *[Type text]* placeholder and then type your first and last names.

  d. Double-click in the document.

5. Save and then print **C22-E02-Computers.docx**.

6. Close **C22-E02-Computers.docx** by clicking the Close button on the Quick Access toolbar.

Customizing the Ribbon

In addition to customizing the Quick Access toolbar, you can also customize the ribbon by creating a new tab and inserting groups with buttons in the new tab. To customize the ribbon, click the File tab and then click the Options button. At the Word Options dialog box, click *Customize Ribbon* in the left panel and the dialog box displays as shown in Figure 22.9.

Figure 22.9 Word Options Dialog Box with Customize Ribbon Selected

Click this down-pointing arrow to display a drop-down list with options for specifying what commands you want to display in the list box below.

Click this down-pointing arrow to display a drop-down list with options for customizing all tabs, only the main tabs, or only tool tabs.

Click this to display options for customizing the ribbon.

Click a command in the list box at the left and click the Add button and the command is added to the tab or group selected in the list box at the right.

To remove a command, click the command in the list box at the right and then click the Remove button.

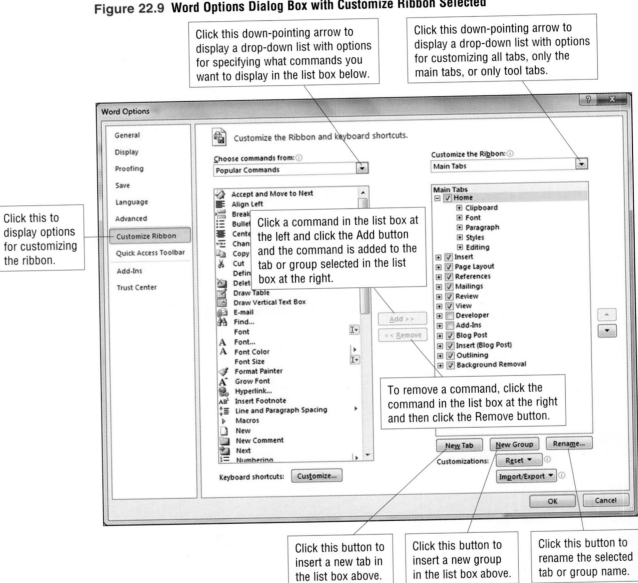

Click this button to insert a new tab in the list box above.

Click this button to insert a new group in the list box above.

Click this button to rename the selected tab or group name.

At the *Choose commands from* drop-down list, you can choose to display only popular commands, which is the default, or choose to display all commands, commands not on the ribbon, and all tabs or commands in the File tab, main tabs, and tool tabs. The commands in the list box vary depending on the option you select at the *Choose commands from* option drop-down list. Click the down-pointing arrow at the right of the Customize the

Ribbon option and a drop-down list displays with options for customizing all tabs, only the main tabs, or only tool tabs. By default, *Main Tabs* is selected.

Creating a New Tab

You can choose to add a command to an existing tab or create a new tab and then add commands in groups in the new tab. To create a new tab, click the tab name in the list box at the right side of the dialog box that you want to precede the new tab and then click the New Tab button that displays at the bottom of the list box. This inserts a new tab in the list box along with a new group below the new tab as shown in Figure 22.10. You can move the new tab up or down the list box by clicking the new tab and then clicking the Move Up or the Move Down buttons that display at the right of the list box.

Figure 22.10 Word Options Dialog Box with New Tab Inserted

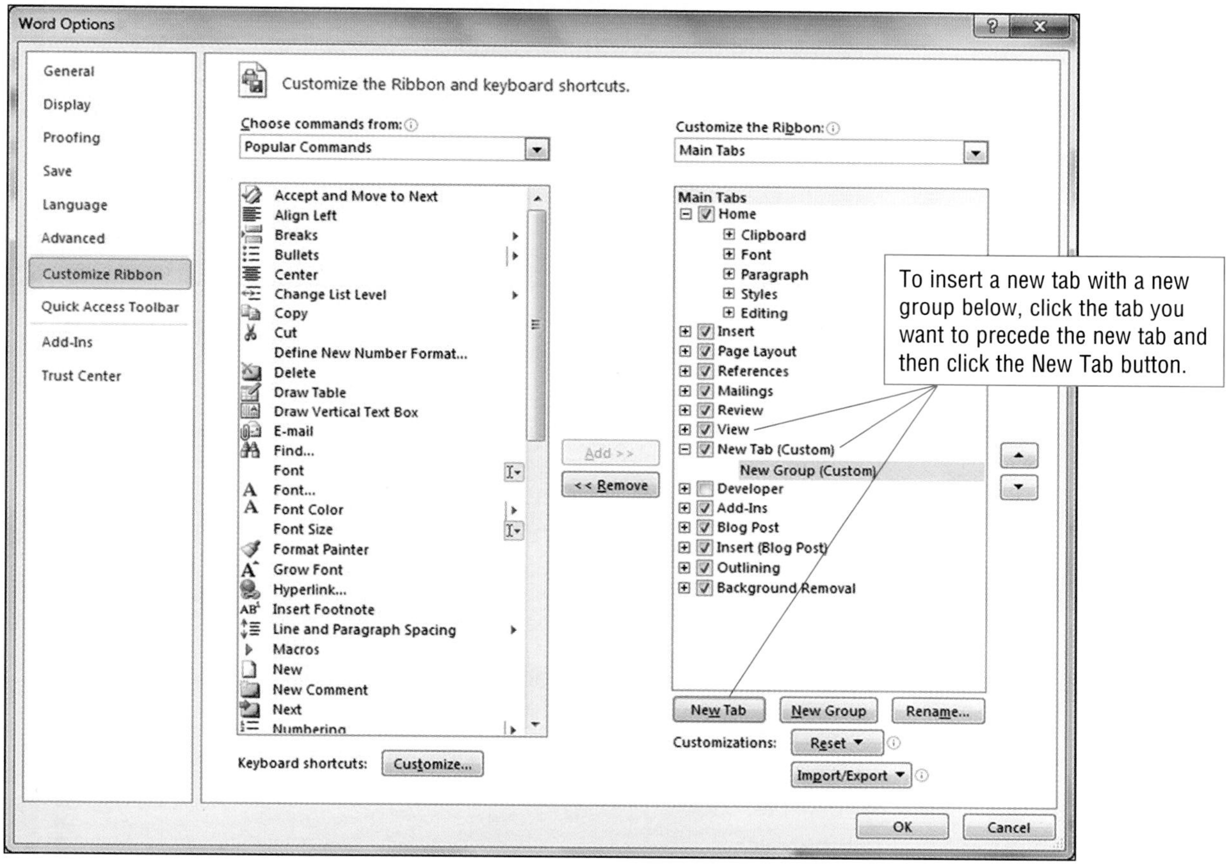

Renaming a Tab and Group

You can rename a tab by clicking the tab in the list box and then clicking the Rename button that displays below the list box at the right. At the Rename dialog box, type the desired name for the tab and then click OK. You can also display the Rename dialog box by right-clicking the tab name and then clicking *Rename* at the shortcut menu.

Complete similar steps to rename the group name. When you click the group name and then click the Rename button (or right-click the group name and then click *Rename* at the shortcut menu), a Rename dialog box displays that contains a variety of symbols. Use the symbols to identify new buttons in the group rather than the group name.

Adding Commands to a Tab Group

Add commands to a tab by clicking the group name within the tab, clicking the desired command in the list box at the left, and then clicking the Add button that displays between the two list boxes. Remove commands in a similar manner. Click the command you want to remove from the tab group and then click the Remove button that displays between the two list boxes.

Resetting the Ribbon

If you customize the ribbon by adding tabs and groups, you can remove all customizations and return to the original ribbon by clicking the Reset button that displays below the list box at the right side of the dialog box. When you click the Reset button, a drop-down list displays with two options—*Reset only selected Ribbon tab* and *Reset all customizations*. If you click the *Reset all customizations* option, a message displays asking if you want to delete all ribbon and Quick Access toolbar customizations for this program. At this message, click Yes.

Exercise 22.2C Customizing the Ribbon   Part 3 of 4

1. Open **C22-E02-Computers.docx**.
2. Add a new tab and group by completing the following steps:
   a. Click the File tab and then click the Options button.
   b. At the Word Options dialog box, click *Customize Ribbon* in the left panel.
   c. Click the View tab that displays in the list box at the right side of the dialog box.
   d. Click the New Tab button located below the list box. (This inserts a new tab below the View tab.)
   e. With *New Group (Custom)* selected below the new tab, click the New Group button that displays below the list box. (This inserts another new group below the new tab.)
3. Rename the tab and the groups by completing the following steps:
   a. Click the *New Tab (Custom)* tab.
   b. Click the Rename button that displays below the list box.

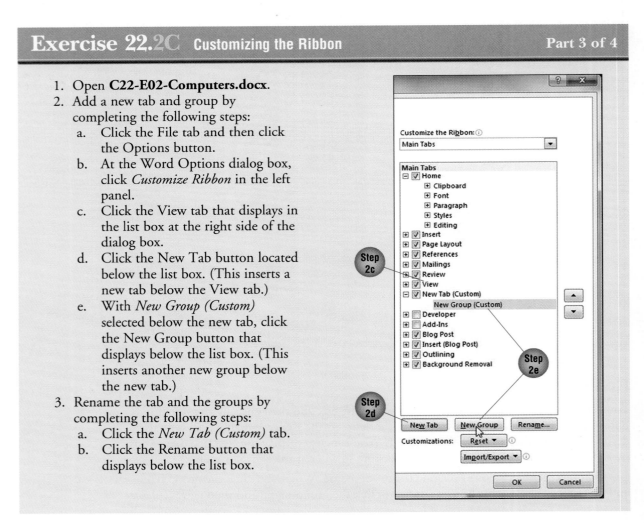

c. At the Rename dialog box, type your initials and then click OK.

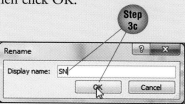

Step
3c

d. Click the *New Group (Custom)* group name that displays below your initials tab.
e. Click the Rename button.
f. At the Rename dialog box, type IP Movement (use IP to indicate insertion point) and then click OK.

Step
3f

g. Click the *New Group (Custom)* group name that displays below the IP Movement (Custom) group and then click the Rename button.
h. At the Rename dialog box, type Image Editing and then click OK.
4. Add buttons to the *IP Movement (Custom)* group by completing the following steps:
   a. Click the *IP Movement (Custom)* group in the list box at the right side.
   b. Click the down-pointing arrow at the right of the *Choose commands from* option box and then click *Commands Not in the Ribbon* at the drop-down list.
   c. Scroll down the list box at the left side of the dialog box (the list displays alphabetically), click the *End of Document* command, and then click the Add button that displays between the two list boxes. (This inserts the command below the *IP Movement (Custom)* group name.)

Step
4b

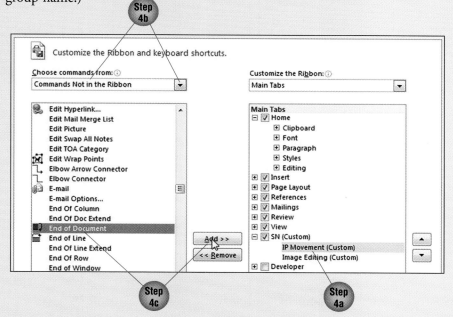

Step
4c

Step
4a

d. With the *End of Line* command selected in the list box at the left side of the dialog box, click the Add button.
e. Scroll down the list box at the left side of the dialog box, click the *Page Down* command, and then click the Add button.
f. Click the *Page Up* command in the list box and then click the Add button.

g. Scroll down the list box, click the *Start of Document* command, and then click the Add button.

h. Click the *Start of Line* command and then click the Add button.

5. Add buttons to the *Image Editing (Custom)* group by completing the following steps:

   a. Click the *Image Editing (Custom)* group (below the *IP Movement (Custom)* group).

   b. Click the down-pointing arrow at the right of the *Choose commands from* option box and then click *All Commands* at the drop-down list.

   c. Scroll down the list box at the left side of the dialog box, click the *Clip Art* command in the list box, and then click the Add button.

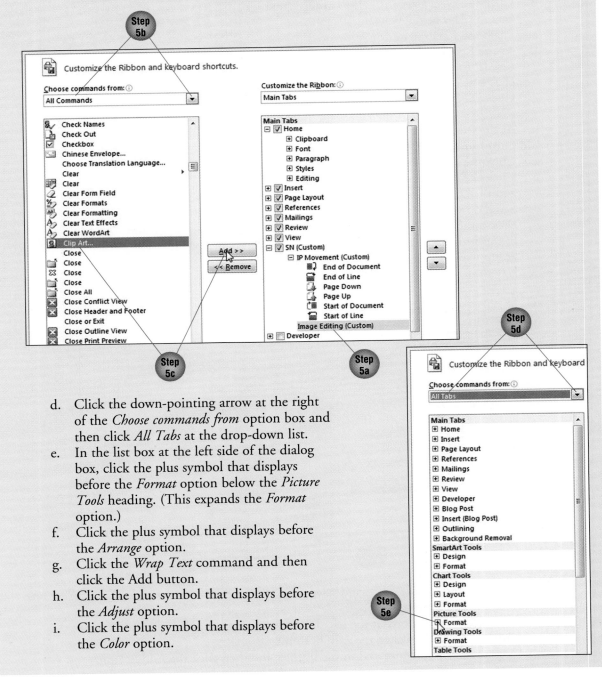

d. Click the down-pointing arrow at the right of the *Choose commands from* option box and then click *All Tabs* at the drop-down list.

e. In the list box at the left side of the dialog box, click the plus symbol that displays before the *Format* option below the *Picture Tools* heading. (This expands the *Format* option.)

f. Click the plus symbol that displays before the *Arrange* option.

g. Click the *Wrap Text* command and then click the Add button.

h. Click the plus symbol that displays before the *Adjust* option.

i. Click the plus symbol that displays before the *Color* option.

j. Click the *Recolor* command and then click the Add button.
k. Click the *Set Transparent Color* command and then click the Add button.
6. Click OK to close the Word Options dialog box.
7. Move the insertion point in the document by completing the following steps:
    a. Click the tab containing your initials.
    b. Click the End of Document button in the IP Movement group in the tab.
    c. Click the Start of Document button in the IP Movement group.
    d. Click the End of Line button.
    e. Click the Start of Line button.

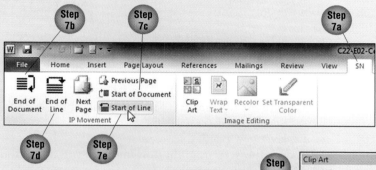

8. Insert a clip art image and then recolor the image by completing the following steps:
    a. Click the Clip Art button in the Image Editing group in the tab containing your initials.
    b. At the Clip Art task pane, type computer in the *Search for* text box and then press the Enter key.
    c. Click the computer image shown at the right.
    d. With the clip art image selected, click the tab containing your initials.
    e. Click the Wrap Text button in the Image Editing group in the new tab and then click *Tight* at the drop-down list.

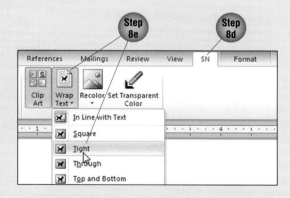

f. Click the Set Transparent Color button in the Image Editing group and then click anywhere in the lighter lime green color in the clip art.

g. Click the Recolor button in the Image Editing group and then click the third option in the second row (the *Aqua, Accent color 2 Dark* option) at the drop-down list.

h. Use the sizing handles to decrease the size of the clip art image so it is approximately 1.5 inches in height and width.

i. Drag the image so it is positioned at the left margin in the middle of the first paragraph of text in the document.

j. Close the Clip Art task pane.

9. Create a screenshot of the ribbon with the tab containing your initials the active tab by completing the following steps:

a. Click the tab containing your initials.

b. Click the clip art image in the document. (This makes all of the buttons active in the Edit Imaging group in the new tab.)

c. Press Ctrl + N to display a new blank document.

d. Click the Insert tab, click the Screenshot button in the Illustrations group, and then click *Screen Clipping* at the drop-down list.

e. In a few moments, the C22-E02-Computers.docx document displays in a dimmed manner. Using the mouse, drag from the upper left corner of the screen down and to the right to capture the Quick Access toolbar and the buttons in the tab containing your initials, and then release the mouse.

f. With the screenshot image inserted in the document, print the document and then close it without saving it.

10. Save **C22-E02-Computers.docx**.

Importing/Exporting Customizations

If you make customizations to the ribbon and/or Quick Access toolbar, you can export the customizations to a file and then use that file on other computers. To export the customized ribbon and/or Quick Access toolbar, display the Word Options dialog box with *Customize Ribbon* or *Quick Access Toolbar* selected in the left panel, click the Import/Export button that displays below the list box at the right side of the dialog box, and then click *Export all customizations* at the drop-down list. At the File Save dialog box that displays, navigate to the desired folder, type a name for the file in the *File name* text box, and then press the Enter key or click the Save button. By default, Word saves the file as *Exported Office UI file (*.exportedUI)* with the *.exportedUI* file extension.

To import a ribbon and Quick Access toolbar customization file, display the Word Options dialog box with *Customize Ribbon* or *Quick Access Toolbar* selected in the left panel, click the Import/Export button, and then click *Import customization file* at the drop-down list. At the File Open dialog box, navigate to the folder containing the customization file and then double-click the file. (The file name will display with the *.exportedUI* file extension.) At the message that displays asking if you want to replace all existing ribbon and Quick Access toolbar customizations for this program, click Yes.

1. With **C22-E02-Computers.docx** open, export your ribbon and Quick Access toolbar customizations to a file by completing the following steps:
    a. Click the File tab and then click the Options button.
    b. Click *Customize Ribbon* in the left panel at the Word Options dialog box.
    c. Click the Import/Export button that displays below the list box at the right side of the dialog box and then click *Export all customizations* at the drop-down list.

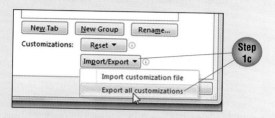

    d. At the File Save dialog box, navigate to the Chapter22 folder on your storage medium.
    e. Click in the *File name* text box (this selects the file name).
    f. Type **CustomRibbon&QA** and then press the Enter key.
2. Reset the Quick Access toolbar and the ribbon by completing the following steps:
    a. Click the Reset button that displays below the list box at the right side of the dialog box and then click *Reset all customizations* at the drop-down list.

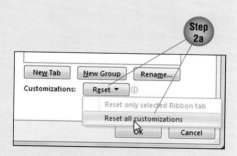

    b. At the message asking if you want to delete all ribbon and Quick Access toolbar customizations, click Yes.
    c. Click OK to close the Word Options dialog box.
3. Keep the heading *Speed* together with the paragraph that follows it.
4. Save, print, and then close **C22-E02-Computers.docx**.

Customize Word Options
1. Click File tab.
2. Click Options button.
3. Click desired option in left panel.
4. Make desired customization choices.
5. Click OK to close Word Options dialog box.

Customizing Word Options

Throughout the chapters in this book, you have made changes to some of the options available at the Word Options dialog box. By default, the Word Options dialog box displays with *General* selected in the left panel, as shown in Figure 22.11. With options at this dialog box, you can customize options for working with Word, including turning the Mini toolbar on or off, turning the display of live galleries on or off, and changing user information. By default, an attachment to an email will open in Print Layout view. If you want an attachment to open in Full Screen Reading view, insert a check mark in the *Open e-mail attachments in Full Screen Reading view* check box.

Figure 22.11 Word Options Dialog Box with General Selected

Click each of the options in this panel to display customization features and commands.

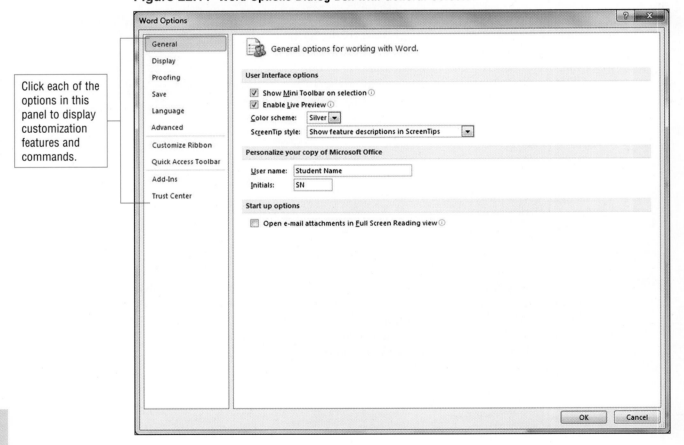

The Word Options dialog box, like many other dialog boxes in Word, contains a Help button in the upper right corner. Click this Help button, and the Word Help window displays with information about the options in the dialog box.

1. Open **BTAdventure.docx** and save the document with the name **C22-E03-BTAdventure**.
2. Customize Word options by completing the following steps:
   a. Click the File tab and then click the Options button.
   b. At the Word Options dialog box with *General* selected in the left panel, click the *Show Mini Toolbar on selection* check box to remove the check mark.
   c. Click the *Enable Live Preview* check box to remove the check mark.
   d. Click the *Open e-mail attachments in Full Screen Reading view* check box to insert a check mark.
   e. Select the current name in the *User name* text box and then type Sylvia Porter.
   f. Select the current initials in the *Initials* text box and then type SP.
   g. Click OK to close the dialog box.

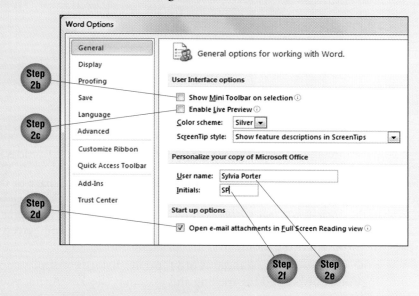

3. Select text in the document and notice that the Mini toolbar does not display because you turned off the feature.
4. With the text still selected, click the Font button arrow and then hover the mouse pointer over the font options that display at the drop-down gallery. Because you turned off the live gallery feature, the text in your document does not display the font over which your mouse pointer is hovering.
5. Change to Full Screen Reading view by completing the following steps:
   a. Click the Full Screen Reading button in the view area on the Status bar.
   b. In the Full Screen Reading view, click the View Options button that displays in the upper right corner of the dialog box and notice that the top option *Don't Open Attachments in Full Screen* does not contain a check mark because you removed the check mark from the *Open e-mail attachments in Full Screen Reading view* check box in the Word Options dialog box.

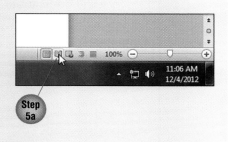

   c.   Click the Close button that displays in the upper right corner of the screen.

6. Insert a user name field by completing the following steps:

   a.   Press Ctrl + End to move the insertion point to the end of the document.

   b.   Click the Insert tab.

   c.   Click the Quick Parts button in the Text group and then click *Field* at the drop-down list.

   d.   At the Field dialog box, scroll to the bottom of the *Field names* list box and then double-click *UserName*.

7. Save **C22-E03-BTAdventure.docx**.

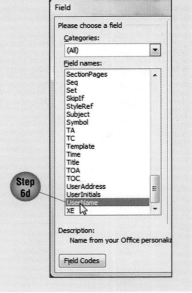

Click the *Display* option, and the Word Options dialog box displays options for specifying how document content appears on the screen and when it is printed. In a previous chapter, you learned how to turn on and off the display of white space that separates pages in Print Layout view by double-clicking the white space or the line separating the pages. You can also turn on or off the display of white space between pages with the *Show white space between pages in Print Layout view* option at the dialog box. Likewise, you can turn on or off the display of highlighting and ScreenTips that display when you hover the mouse over an option or button.

Click the *Proofing* option, and the Word Options dialog box displays options for customizing AutoCorrect and the spelling and grammar checker. Again, you used some of these options in previous chapters.

Click the *Save* option, and the Word Options dialog box displays options for customizing how documents are saved. You can change the format in which files are saved from the default *Word Document (*.docx)* to other formats, such as a previous version of Word, Word template, web page, plain text, or previous versions of Microsoft Works. These save options are also available with the Save as type button at the Save As dialog box. The difference is that changing the file save format with the *Save files in this format* option at the Word Options dialog box with *Save* selected changes the default for all future documents saved.

1. With **C22-E03-BTAdventure.docx** open, click the File tab and then click the Options button.
2. At the Word Options dialog box, click the *Display* option in the left panel and then look at the options available.
3. Click the *Proofing* option that displays in the left panel and then look at the options available.
4. Click the *Save* option that displays in the left panel.
5. Change the default file location by completing the following steps:
   a. Make a note of the current default file location.
   b. Click the Browse button that displays at the right of the *Default file location* option box.

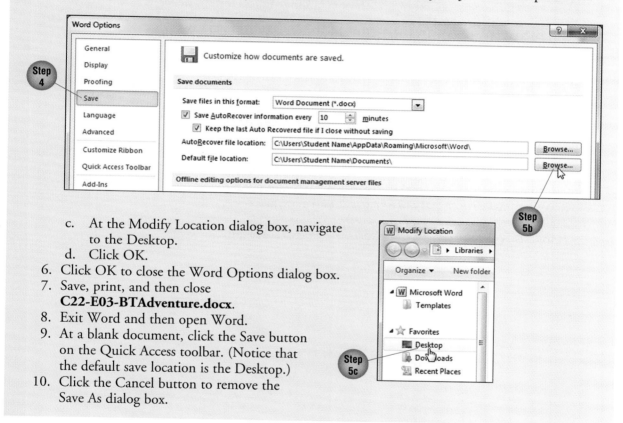

   c. At the Modify Location dialog box, navigate to the Desktop.
   d. Click OK.
6. Click OK to close the Word Options dialog box.
7. Save, print, and then close **C22-E03-BTAdventure.docx**.
8. Exit Word and then open Word.
9. At a blank document, click the Save button on the Quick Access toolbar. (Notice that the default save location is the Desktop.)
10. Click the Cancel button to remove the Save As dialog box.

With the *Advanced* option selected, the Word Options dialog box displays a number of sections for customizing Word, including a section for changing editing options, a section for specifying how you want text pasted in a document, a section for specifying what document content to show, a section for customizing the display and printing of a document, as well as a number of other sections.

Click the *Add-Ins* option, and the Word Options dialog box displays add-ins, which are supplemental options that add custom commands and specialized features to Office 2010 applications.

With the *Trust Center* option selected in the left panel of the Word Options dialog box, hyperlinks display providing navigation to privacy and security information, including the Word privacy statement, the Office.com privacy statement, the Customer Experience Improvement Program, and the Windows security center.

1. At a blank document, click the File tab and then click the Options button.
2. At the Word Options dialog box with *General* selected in the left panel, click the *Show Mini Toolbar on selection* check box to insert a check mark.
3. Click the *Enable Live Preview* check box to insert a check mark.
4. Click the *Open e-mail attachments in Full Screen Reading view* to remove the check mark.
5. Select the current name in the *User name* text box and then type the original name.
6. Select the current initials in the *Initials* text box and then type the original initials.
7. Change the default file location back to the original setting by completing the following steps:
   a. Click the *Save* option in the left panel of the Word Options dialog box.
   b. Click the Browse button that displays at the right of the *Default file location* option box.
   c. At the Modify Location dialog box, navigate to the original location.
   d. Click OK.
8. Close the Word Options dialog box.

Chapter *Summary*

➤ You can add words to AutoCorrect while you spell check a document or at the AutoCorrect dialog box.

➤ Display the AutoCorrect dialog box by clicking the File tab, clicking the Options button, clicking *Proofing*, and then clicking the AutoCorrect Options button.

➤ Display the AutoCorrect Exceptions dialog box by clicking the Exceptions button at the AutoCorrect dialog box with the AutoCorrect tab selected. Specify autocorrect exceptions at this dialog box.

➤ Use the AutoCorrect Options button that displays when you hover the mouse over corrected text to change corrected text back to the original spelling, stop the automatic correction of specific text, or display the AutoCorrect dialog box.

➤ The AutoCorrect dialog box contains several symbols you can insert in a document by typing specific text or characters.

➤ You can insert a symbol from the Symbol dialog box into the AutoCorrect dialog box. To do this, display the Symbol dialog box, click the desired symbol, and then click the AutoCorrect button.

➤ When typing text, control what Word automatically formats with options at the AutoCorrect dialog box with the AutoFormat As You Type tab selected.

➤ Customize the Quick Access toolbar with options from the Customize Quick Access Toolbar button drop-down list.

➤ With options at the Customize Quick Access Toolbar button drop-down list, you can change the location of the Quick Access toolbar.

➤ Add a button or command to the Quick Access toolbar by right-clicking the desired button or command and then clicking *Add to Quick Access Toolbar* at the shortcut menu.

➤ Minimize the ribbon by clicking the Minimize the Ribbon button that displays immediately left of the Microsoft Word Help button or with the keyboard shortcut Ctrl + F1. Maximize the ribbon by clicking the Expand the Ribbon button (previously the Minimize the Ribbon button), with the keyboard shortcut Ctrl + F1, or by double-clicking one of the tabs.

➤ You can customize the Quick Access toolbar with options at the Word Options dialog box with *Quick Access Toolbar* selected.

➤ Reset the Quick Access toolbar to the default by clicking the Reset button at the Word Options dialog box with Quick Access Toolbar selected and then clicking Yes at the message that displays.

➤ You can customize the Quick Access toolbar for all documents or for a specific document.

➤ The *Choose commands from* option at the Word Options dialog box with *Quick Access Toolbar* selected has a default setting of *Popular Commands*. Change this option to *All Commands* to display all buttons and options available for adding to the Quick Access toolbar.

➤ Customize the ribbon with options at the Word Options dialog box with *Customize Ribbon* selected.

➤ At the Word Options dialog box with *Customize Ribbon* selected, add a new tab by clicking the tab name in the list box at the right side of the dialog box that you want to precede the new tab and then clicking the New Tab button. Adding a new tab also adds a new group.

➤ Rename a tab or group at the Word options dialog box with *Customize Ribbon* selected by clicking the tab or group, clicking the Rename button, typing the new name in the Rename dialog box, and then clicking OK.

➤ Add a command to a new tab group by clicking the desired tab group in the list box at the right side of the Word Options dialog with *Customize Ribbon* selected, clicking the desired command in the list box at the left, and then clicking the Add button.

- To remove a command from a tab group at the Word Options dialog box with *Customize Ribbon* selected, click the command and then click the Remove button that displays between the two list boxes.
- Reset the ribbon by clicking the Reset button at the Word Options dialog box with *Customize Ribbon* selected and then clicking either *Reset only selected Ribbon tab* or *Reset all customizations.*
- Export a customization file containing customizations to the ribbon and/or Quick Access toolbar with the Import/Export button at the Word Options dialog box with *Customize Ribbon* or *Quick Access Toolbar* selected.
- Customize Word options at the Word Options dialog box.

Commands Review

FEATURE	RIBBON TAB, GROUP	BUTTON, OPTION	KEYBOARD SHORTCUT
AutoCorrect dialog box	File	Options, Proofing, AutoCorrect Options	
Symbol dialog box	Insert, Symbols	Ω, More Symbols	
Minimize the ribbon			Ctrl + F1
Word Options dialog box	File	Options	

Key Points Review

Completion: In the space provided at the right, indicate the correct term, symbol, or command.

1. This feature corrects certain words automatically as you type them.

2. Use this button, which displays when you hover the mouse over corrected text, to change corrected text back to the original spelling.

3. Type these characters to insert the ☺ symbol in a document.

4. Type these characters to insert the ➜ symbol.

5. When typing text, control what Word automatically formats with options at the AutoCorrect dialog box with this tab selected.

6. Add or remove some basic buttons to and from the Quick Access toolbar with options at this drop-down list.

7. Add a button to the Quick Access toolbar by right-clicking the desired button and then clicking this option at the shortcut menu.

8. Minimize the ribbon by clicking the Minimize the Ribbon button or with this keyboard shortcut.

9. Click the Customize Quick Access Toolbar button and then click *More Commands* and this dialog box displays.

_____

10. This is the default setting for the *Choose commands from* option at the Word Options dialog box.

_____

11. At the Word Options dialog box with this option selected in the left panel, add a new tab by clicking the tab name in the list box that you want to precede the new tab and then clicking the New Tab button.

_____

12. Export a customization file containing customizations to the ribbon and/or Quick Access toolbar with this button in the Word Options dialog box with *Customize Ribbon* or *Quick Access Toolbar* selected.

_____

13. Change user name and initials at the Word Options dialog box with this option selected in the left panel.

_____

14. Change the default file location at the Word Options dialog box with this option selected in the left panel.

_____

Chapter Assessments

Applying Your Skills

Demonstrate your knowledge of features learned in this chapter by completing the following assessments.

Assessment 22.1   Insert and Format Text in a Medical Plan Document

1. Open **KLHPlan.docx** and save the document with the name **C22-A01-KLHPlan**.
2. Add the following text to AutoCorrect:
   a. Insert *kl* in the *Replace* text box and insert *Key Life Health Plan* in the *With* text box.
   b. Insert *m* in the *Replace* text box and insert *medical* in the *With* text box.
3. With the insertion point positioned at the beginning of the document, type the text shown in Figure 22.12.
4. Make the following changes to the document:
   a. Apply the Heading 1 style to the title.
   b. Apply the Heading 2 style to the four headings in the document.
   c. Change the style set to Formal.
   d. Change the theme to Black Tie.
   e. Apply the Relaxed paragraph spacing style. ***Hint: Do this with the Change Styles button in the Home tab.***
5. Insert the Puzzle (Odd Page) footer building block, click the *[Type the company name]* placeholder, type kl, and then press the spacebar. (This inserts *Key Life Health Plan* in the placeholder.)
6. Delete the text *Confidential* that displays in the footer.
7. Double-click in the document.
8. Press Ctrl + End to move the insertion point to the end of the document, press the Enter key twice, and then insert the *FileName* field.
9. Press Shift + Enter and then insert the *PrintDate* field. (You choose the date format.)
10. Save and then print **C22-A01-KLHPlan.docx**.
11. Delete the two entries you made at the AutoCorrect dialog box.
12. Close **C22-A01-KLHPlan.docx**.

Figure 22.12 Assessment 22.1

kl

How the Plan Works

When you enroll in kl, you and each eligible family member selects a plan option. A kl option includes a main m clinic, any affiliated satellite clinics, and designated hospitals. Family members may choose different m plan options and can easily change options.

Some m plan options do not require you to choose a primary care physician. This means a member may self-refer for specialty care within that m plan option. However, kl encourages members to establish an ongoing relationship with a primary care physician and develop a valuable partnership in the management of their m care.

kl provides coverage for emergency m services outside the service area. If the m emergency is not life threatening, call your primary care physician to arrange for care before going to an emergency facility. If you have a life-threatening emergency, go directly to the nearest appropriate facility. Any follow-up care to emergency m services must be coordinated within your plan option.

Assessment 22.2 Create a Vacation Document with AutoCorrect and Special Symbols

1. At a blank document, add the following text to AutoCorrect:
   a. Insert *Pt* in the *Replace* text box and insert *Patagonia* in the *With* text box.
   b. Insert *Ft* in the *Replace* text box and insert *Futaleufu* in the *With* text box.
   c. Insert the Euro currency symbol (€) in the *With* text box (do this through the Symbol dialog box) and type eu in the *Replace* text box. (The Euro currency symbol is located toward the bottom of the Symbol dialog box list box with (normal text) selected.)
2. Type the text shown in Figure 22.13. Create the smiley face icon by typing :) and then pressing the spacebar. (To insert the Euro currency symbol, type eu and then press the spacebar. Press the Backspace key once and then type the amount.)
3. Save the document with the name **C22-A02-FAV**.
4. Print and then close **C22-A02-FAV.docx**.
5. Delete the *eu*, *Ft*, and *Pt* AutoCorrect entries.

Figure 22.13 Assessment 22.2

LUXURY FAMILY ADVENTURE VACATIONS

Sign up today for one of our exciting luxury family adventure vacations, created for families who enjoy a multitude of outdoor activities and a bit of luxury. Our Chile luxury vacation combines whitewater rafting, hiking, kayaking, and horseback riding into one fun-filled week of adventure travel in beautiful Pt, Chile.

More than a family rafting trip, we'll make sure you are exposed to all that the Ft Valley has to offer including whitewater rafting on the Ft River, which contains sections for all levels of ability and experience; hiking up some of the beautiful tributaries of the Ft River; and horseback riding across beautiful valleys at the base of snow-peaked mountains.

Pt, Chile, provides a wide variety of opportunities for active travel that the whole family can enjoy. You can feel confident that we will take care of all of the details so that your experience is a mix of fun, comfort, and relaxation. ☺

Price for single occupancy:
$2,899
€2,675

Price for double occupancy:
$2,699
€2,450

Price for triple occupancy:
$2,499
€2,100

Assessment 22.3   Create a Custom Tab and Group

1. At the blank screen, create a new tab with the following specifications:
   a.   Insert the new tab after the View tab in the list box at the Word Options dialog box with *Customize Ribbon* selected.
   b.   Rename the tab *C22* followed by your initials.
   c.   Rename the custom group below your new tab to *File Management*.
   d.   Change the *Choose commands from* option to *File Tab*.
   e.   From the list box at the left side of the dialog box, add the following commands to the *File Management* group in the new tab: *Close, Open, Open Recent File, Quick Print, Save As,* and *Save As Other Format*.
   f.   Change the *Choose commands from* option to *Popular Commands*.
   g.   From the list box at the left side of the dialog box, add the New command.
   h.   Click OK to close the Word Options dialog box.

2. At the blank screen, click your new tab (the one that begins with *C22* and is followed by your initials).
3. Click the Open Recent File button in the File Management group in your new tab.
4. At the Recent tab Backstage view, click **C22-A02-FAV.docx** that displays at the beginning of the Recent Documents list.
5. With **C22-A02-FAV.docx** open, save the document in the Word 97-2003 format by completing the following steps:
   a. Click the new tab that begins with *C22* and is followed by your initials.
   b. Click the Save As button arrow (this is the second Save As button in the File Management group in your new tab).
   c. Click *Word 97-2003 Document* at the drop-down list.
   d. At the Save As dialog box with *Word 97-2003 Document (*.doc)* selected in the *Save as type* option box, type C22-A03-FAV-Word97-2003Format and then press the Enter key.
   e. Close **C22-A03-FAV-Word97-2003Format.doc** by clicking the Close button in the File Management group in the new tab.
6. Click the Open Recent File button in the new tab and then click **C22-A02-FAV.docx** in the Recent Documents list.
7. Send the document to the printer by clicking your new tab (the tab that begins with *C22* and is followed by your initials) and then clicking the Quick Print button in the File Management group.
8. Close the document by clicking the Close button in the File Management group in the new tab.
9. Click the New Blank Document button in the File Management group in the new tab.
10. At the blank document, click your new tab (the tab that begins with *C22* and is followed by your initials) and then click the New Blank Document button. (You now have two blank documents open.)
11. Click the Insert tab, click the Screenshot button, and then click *Screen Clipping* at the drop-down list.
12. When the first blank document displays in a dimmed manner, use the mouse to select the Quick Access toolbar and the ribbon including the new tab you created with the File Management group buttons.
13. Print the document containing the screen clipping and then close the document without saving it.
14. Display the Word Options dialog box with *Customize Ribbon* selected and then reset the ribbon back to the default.

Expanding Your Skills

Explore additional feature options or use Help to learn a new skill in creating this document.

Assessment 22.4   Create a Report on Word Options and Customization Features

1. Display the Word Options dialog box and determine how to do the following:
   a. Change the color scheme. (General)
   b. Change the number of minutes for saving AutoRecover information. (Save)
   c. Change the number of recent documents that display at the Recent tab Backstage view. (Advanced)
2. At a blank document, create a report that describes how to do the following:
   a. Steps to change the color scheme to Black.
   b. Steps to change the minutes for saving AutoRecover information to 5 minutes.
   c. Steps to change the number of recent documents that display at the Recent tab Backstage view to 15.

3. Use the Help feature to learn how to customize the Status bar and then add to your report steps that describe how to add track changes and caps lock notification in the Status bar.
4. Format your document to improve its visual appeal.
5. Save the document with the name **C22-A04-Options**.
6. Print and then close **C22-A04-Options.docx**.

Achieving Signature Status

Take your skills to the next level by completing this more challenging assessment.

Assessment 22.5   Create a Resume Document with AutoCorrect Text

1. At a blank document, create the document shown in Figure 22.14 with the following specifications:
   a. Create AutoCorrect entries for *chronological resume*, *functional resume*, and *hybrid resume*. You determine the replace text. **Hint: When typing the headings, type the replace text in all caps and Word will insert the AutoCorrect text in all capital letters.**
   b. Set the body text in 11-point Constantia and the title in 26-point Constantia. Change the font color to dark blue.
   c. Insert the page border, paragraph border, and paragraph shading as shown in Figure 22.14. Make sure you change the paragraph and page border color to dark blue.
   d. Insert the clip art shown in the figure **Hint: Look for this clip art image by typing document *in the* Search for *text box in the Clip Art task pane. If this clip art image is not available, choose a similar image.***
   e. Format the clip art by changing the text wrapping to *Tight*, flipping the image horizontally, and changing the color to *Blue, Accent color 1 Light*. (If you did not use the clip art image shown in Figure 22.14, choose your own formatting for the clip art image you insert in the document.) Size and position the clip art image as shown in the figure.
   f. Insert the five symbols at the end of the document as shown in the figure.
2. Save the completed document and name it **C22-A05-ResumeStyles**.
3. Print and then close **C22-A05-ResumeStyles.docx**.
4. Open a blank document, display the AutoCorrect dialog box, and then display the first entry you made for *chronological resume*. Hold down the Alt key and then press the Print Screen button. Close the dialog box, close the Word Options dialog box, and then click the Paste button at the blank document. (This inserts an image of the AutoCorrect dialog box.)
5. Press Ctrl + End and then press the Enter key.
6. Complete steps similar to those in Step 4 to make a screen capture of the AutoCorrect dialog box with the *functional resume* entry displayed and insert the screen capture image in the document (below the first screen capture image).
7. Press Ctrl + End and then press the Enter key.
8. Complete steps similar to those in Step 4 to make a screen capture of the AutoCorrect dialog box with the *hybrid resume* entry displayed and insert the screen capture image in the document (below the second screen capture image).
9. Decrease the size of each of the screen capture images to make them all fit on one page.
10. Save the document and name it **C22-A05-ScreenCaps**.
11. Print and then close **C22-A05-ScreenCaps.docx**.

Figure 22.14 Assessment 22.5

RESUME STYLES

You can write a resume in a variety of ways since different approaches work for different people. The three most popular resume styles include: chronological resume, functional resume, and hybrid resume.

CHRONOLOGICAL RESUME

The chronological resume is the one many people use without thinking. It lists your training and jobs in order of the dates you started each of them. Typically, people list their most recent training or jobs first and proceed backwards to the first things they did in the past. This is called "reverse chronological" order. The components of this resume include:

- Personal contact information
- Employment history, including employers, dates of employment, positions held, and achievements
- Educational qualifications
- Professional development

FUNCTIONAL RESUME

The functional resume emphasizes the skills of the individual and his or her achievements. It is often used when the applicant lacks formal education, or his or her educational qualifications are judged obsolete or irrelevant. If you have had many different jobs with no clear pattern or progression, or a lot of gaps in your work history, some people recommend this approach.

HYBRID RESUME

The hybrid resume is an increasingly popular resume style that combines the best of both the chronological resume and the functional resume. A hybrid resume retains much of the fixed order of the chronological resume, but more emphasis is placed on skills and achievements—sometimes in a separate section. The hybrid resume is the one that we recommend to most people, in that it produces an excellent clear structure but requires the person to really think hard about his or her achievements and what he or she has to offer. If you decide to use a hybrid resume, you may wish to leave out the detailed responsibilities section and just emphasize the skills, knowledge, and abilities you have.

Chapter 23

Customizing Themes

SNAP TUTORIALS

Tutorial 23.1
Creating custom theme colors
and theme fonts
Tutorial 23.2
Applying theme effects

Performance Objectives

Upon successful completion of Chapter 23, you will be able to:

- Create custom theme colors and theme fonts, and apply theme effects
- Save a custom theme
- Apply, edit, and delete custom themes
- Reset to the template theme

The Microsoft Office suite offers themes to help you maintain consistent formatting both within and across documents, creating a professional and polished look. You can use the themes provided by Office or create your own custom themes. In this chapter, you will learn how to customize theme colors and fonts and save custom themes. You will also learn how to edit and delete custom themes and then reset options to the default template theme.

Note: Before beginning computer exercises for this chapter, copy to your storage medium the Chapter23 folder from the CD that accompanies this textbook and then make Chapter23 the active folder.

In this chapter, students will produce the following documents:

Exercise 23.1. C23-E01-Viruses.docx
Exercise 23.2. C23-E02-NSSServices.docx
Exercise 23.3. C23-E03-NSSSecurity.docx

Model answers for these exercises are shown on the following pages.

"Viruses can create effects that range from minor and annoying to highly destructive..."

COMPUTER VIRUSES

One of the most familiar forms of risk to computer security is the computer virus. A computer virus is a program written by a hacker or a cracker, designed to perform some kind of trick upon an unsuspecting victim's computer. In some cases, the trick performed is mild, such as drawing an offensive image on the victim's screen or changing all of the characters in a document to another language. Sometimes the trick is much more severe, such as reformatting the hard drive and erasing all the data or damaging the motherboard so that it cannot operate properly.

TYPES OF VIRUSES

Viruses can be categorized by their effects, which include being a nuisance, destroying data, facilitating espionage, and destroying hardware. A nuisance virus usually does no real damage but is an inconvenience. The most difficult part of a computer to replace is the data on the hard drive. The installed programs, documents, databases, and saved emails form the heart of a personal computer. A data-destructive virus is designed to destroy this data. Some viruses are designed to create a backdoor into a system to bypass security. Called espionage viruses, they do no damage but allow a hacker or cracker to enter the system later for the purpose of stealing data or spying on the work of the competitor. Very rarely, a virus is created to damage the hardware of the computer system itself. Called hardware-destructive viruses, these bits of programming can weaken or destroy chips, drives, and other components.

METHODS OF VIRUS OPERATION

Viruses operate and are transmitted in a variety of ways. An email virus is normally transmitted as an attachment to a message sent over the Internet. Email viruses require the victim to click on the attachment, which causes the virus to execute. Another common form of virus transmission is via a macro, a small subprogram that allows users to customize and automate certain functions. A macro virus is written specifically for one program, which then becomes infected when it opens a file with the virus stored in its macros. The boot sector of a floppy disk or hard disk contains a variety of information, including how the disk is organized and whether it is capable of loading an operating system. When a disk is left in a drive and the computer reboots, the operating system automatically reads the boot sector to learn about that disk and to attempt to start any operating system on it. A boot sector virus is designed to alter the boot sector of a disk so that whenever the operating system reads the boot sector, the computer will automatically become infected.

Other types of viruses and methods of infection include the Trojan horse virus, which hides inside another legitimate program or data file, and the stealth virus, which is designed to hide itself from detection software. Polymorphic viruses alter themselves to prevent detection by antivirus software, which operates by examining familiar patterns. Polymorphic viruses alter themselves randomly as they move from computer to computer, making detection more difficult. Multipartite viruses alter their form of attack. Their name reflects their ability to attack in several different ~~boot sector and then later act like a Trojan horse type by infecting a~~

Exercise 23.1

C23-E01-Viruses.docx

Northland Security Systems

Northland Security Systems Mission
We are a full-service computer information security management and consulting firm offering a comprehensive range of services to help businesses protect electronic data.

Security Services
Northland Security Systems is dedicated to helping business, private and public, protect vital company data through on-site consultation, product installation and training, and 24-hour telephone support services. We show you how computer systems can be compromised, and we walk you through the steps you can take to protect your company's computer system.

Security Software
We offer a range of security management software to protect your business against viruses, spyware, adware, intrusion, spam, and policy abuse.

Exercise 23.2

C23-E02-NSSServices.docx

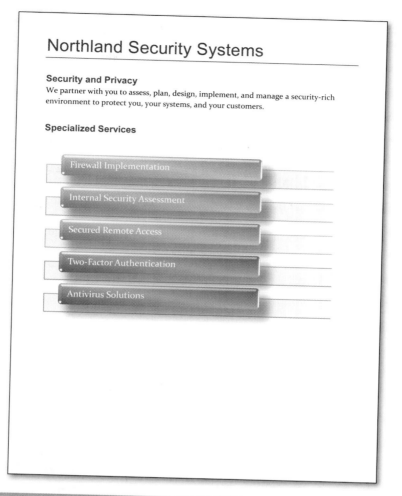

Creating Themes

As you learned in Chapter 1, documents you create in Word are based on a template called the Normal.dotm template. This template provides default layout and formatting instructions and specifies the themes and styles that Word applies to your documents. This default template includes a number of built-in or predesigned themes, some of which you have been using throughout the chapters of this textbook, to apply color, change fonts, and add effects to content in documents. The built-in themes that are available in Microsoft Word are also available in Excel, PowerPoint, and Outlook. Having these themes available across applications allows you to "brand" business files, such as documents, workbooks, and presentations, with a consistent and uniform appearance.

A theme is a combination of colors, fonts, and effects. Within a theme, you can change one or all of these elements with the buttons in the Themes group in the Page Layout tab. You can use the default theme, named Office, change to one of the other built-in themes, or create your own custom theme. A theme that you create displays in the Themes drop-down gallery under the *Custom* section. To create a custom theme, change the color, font, and/or effects of a predesigned theme.

Themes

Theme   Theme
Colors   Fonts

The buttons in the Themes group in the Page Layout tab display a visual representation of the current theme. For example, the Themes button displays an uppercase and lowercase *A* with a row of small colored squares below them. If you change the theme colors, the change is reflected in these squares on the Themes button and in the four squares on the Theme Colors button. If you change theme fonts, the *As* on the Themes button and the uppercase *A* on the Theme Fonts button reflect the change.

QUICK STEPS

Create Custom Theme Colors
1. Click Page Layout tab.
2. Click Theme Colors button.
3. Click *Create New Theme Colors*.
4. Select new background, accent, or hyperlink colors.
5. Type name for custom color theme.
6. Click Save button.

Creating Custom Theme Colors

To create custom theme colors, click the Page Layout tab, click the Theme Colors button, and then click *Create New Theme Colors* at the drop-down gallery. This displays the Create New Theme Colors dialog box, shown in Figure 23.1. A color theme includes four text and background colors, six accent colors, and two hyperlink colors, as shown in the *Theme colors* section of the dialog box. Change a color in the list box by clicking the color button at the right side of the color option and then clicking the desired color in the color palette.

Figure 23.1 Create New Theme Colors Dialog Box

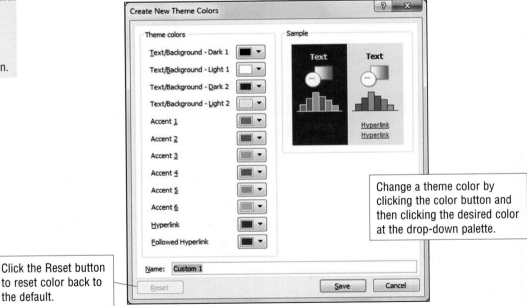

Click the Reset button to reset color back to the default.

Change a theme color by clicking the color button and then clicking the desired color at the drop-down palette.

After you have made all desired changes to the theme colors, click in the *Name* text box, type a name for the custom theme colors, and then click the Save button. This saves the custom theme colors and also applies the color changes to the currently open document. Display the custom theme colors by clicking the Theme Colors button in the Themes group in the Page Layout tab. Your custom theme colors will display toward the top of the drop-down gallery in the *Custom* section, as shown in Figure 23.2.

Figure 23.2 Theme Colors Drop-down Gallery with Custom Theme

Custom theme colors display at the top of the drop-down gallery in the *Custom* section.

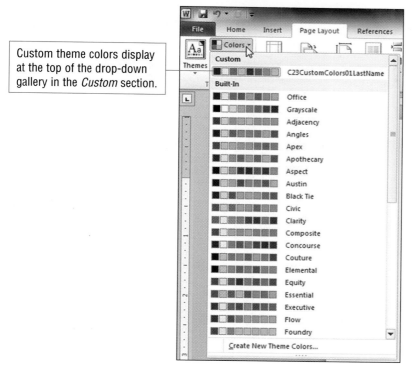

Resetting Custom Colors

If you change the colors at the Create New Theme Colors dialog box and then decide you do not like the changes, click the Reset button located in the lower left corner of the dialog box. Clicking this button resets the colors back to the default Office theme colors.

Exercise 23.1A   Creating Custom Theme Colors   Part 1 of 3

Note: If you are running Word 2010 on a computer connected to a network in a public environment such as a school, you may not be able to save themes to the hard drive. Before beginning Exercise 23.1A, check with your instructor.

1. At a blank document, create custom theme colors by completing the following steps:
   a. Click the Page Layout tab.
   b. Click the Theme Colors button in the Themes group and then click the *Create New Theme Colors* option at the drop-down gallery.

c. At the Create New Theme Colors dialog box, click the color button that displays at the right of the *Text/Background - Light 1* option and then click Dark Red in the color palette (the first color from the left in the *Standard Colors* section).

d. Click the color button that displays at the right of the *Accent 1* option and then click Yellow in the color palette (the fourth color from the left in the *Standard Colors* section).

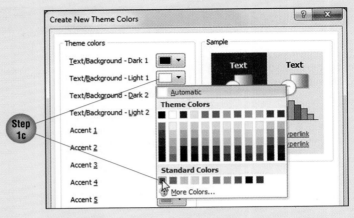

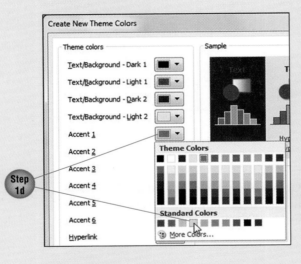

2. After viewing the colors you have chosen in the *Sample* section at the right side of the dialog box, start over by completing the following steps:

a. Click the Reset button located in the lower left corner of the dialog box.

b. Click the color button that displays at the right of the *Text/Background - Dark 1* option and then click *Aqua, Accent 5, Lighter 40%* in the color palette.

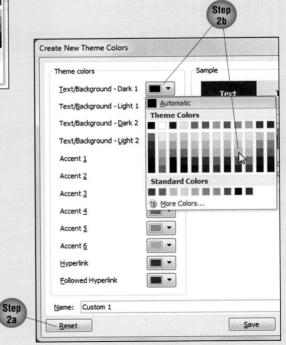

c. Click the color button that displays at the right of the *Text/Background - Light 2* option and then click *Purple, Accent 4, Lighter 80%* in the color palette.

d. Click the color button that displays at the right of the *Accent 2* option and then click *Aqua, Accent 5, Lighter 40%* in the color palette.

3. Save the custom colors by completing the following steps:

a. Select the current text in the *Name* text box.

b. Type C23CustomColors01 and then type your last name.

c. Click the Save button.

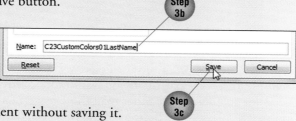

4. Close the document without saving it.

Applying Custom Theme Colors

After you create custom theme colors, you can apply them to your document by clicking the Theme Colors button in the Themes group in the Page Layout tab and then clicking the custom theme colors that display toward the top of the drop-down gallery in the *Custom* section.

Exercise 23.1B   **Applying Custom Theme Colors**   **Part 2 of 3**

1. Open **Viruses.docx** and save the document with the name **C23-E01-Viruses**.
2. Apply the Heading 1 style to the title and the Heading 2 style to the two headings.
3. Change the style set to Formal.
4. Insert a pull quote by completing the following steps:
    a. Click the Insert tab.
    b. Click the Quick Parts button and then click *Building Blocks Organizer*.
    c. At the Building Blocks Organizer dialog box, click the *Name* column heading to alphabetize the building blocks by name.
    d. Scroll down the list box and then click *Contrast Sidebar*.
    e. Click the Insert button.
    f. With the insertion point positioned in the pull quote text box, type "Viruses can create effects that range from minor and annoying to highly destructive . . . ".
    g. Select the quote text you just typed and then change the font size to 12.
    h. Click the Drawing Tools Format tab, click in the Shape Height measurement box, type 1.3, and then press the Enter key.

5. Apply your custom theme colors by completing the following steps:
   a. Click the Page Layout tab.
   b. Click the Theme Colors button in the Themes group.
   c. Click the custom theme colors named *C23CustomColors01LastName* that displays toward the top of the drop-down gallery in the *Custom* group.
6. Save **C23-E01-Viruses.docx**.
7. Print page 1 of **C23-E01-Viruses.docx** and then close the document.

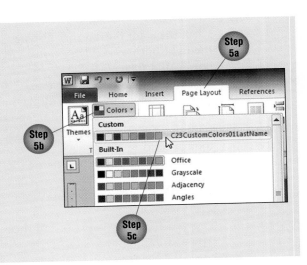

Choosing Colors at the Colors Dialog Box

When you click a color button in the Create New Theme Colors dialog box, color sets display in columns in a color palette. If you want more control over colors (i.e., you want to use a color at a percentage other than those listed in a column), click the *More Colors* option that displays at the bottom of the color palette. This displays the Colors dialog box, which contains two tabs, a Standard tab and a Custom tab. With the Standard tab selected, click the desired color option that displays in the honeycomb. With the Custom tab selected, click the desired color in the color square and fine-tune the color by dragging the slider button (left-pointing arrow) on the vertical slider bar that displays at the right side of the color square. You can also enter numbers in the *Red*, *Green*, and *Blue* text boxes in the dialog box.

Exercise 23.1C   Choosing Custom Colors   Part 3 of 3

1. At a blank document, create custom theme colors by completing the following steps:
   a. Click the Page Layout tab.
   b. Click the Theme Colors button in the Themes group and then click the *Create New Theme Colors* option at the drop-down gallery.
   c. At the Create New Theme Colors dialog box, change the *Text/Background - Dark 1* color by completing the following steps:
      1) Click the color button that displays at the right of the *Text/Background - Dark 1* option and then click the *More Colors* option at the bottom of the color palette.
      2) At the Colors dialog box, click the Standard tab if necessary.
      3) Click the dark green color at the left edge of the honeycomb, as shown at the right.
      4) Click OK to close the Colors dialog box.

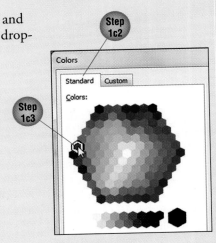

d. Change the *Text/Background - Light 2* color by completing the following steps:
1) Click the *Text/Background - Light 2* color button and then click the *More Colors* option.
2) At the Colors dialog box, click the Standard tab if necessary.
3) Click the yellow color in the lower portion of the honeycomb, as shown below.
4) Click OK to close the Colors dialog box.

e. Change the *Accent 2* color by completing the following steps:
1) Click the *Accent 2* color button and then click the *More Colors* option.
2) At the Colors dialog box, click the Custom tab if necessary.
3) Select the number in the *Red* text box and then type 0.
4) Select the number in the *Green* text box and then type 168.
5) Select the number in the *Blue* text box and then type 0.
6) Click OK to close the Colors dialog box.

2. Save the custom theme colors by completing the following steps:
a. Select the text in the *Name* text box.
b. Type C23CustomColors02 and then type your last name.
c. Click the Save button.
3. Close the document without saving it.
4. Open **C23-E01-Viruses.docx**.
5. Apply the custom theme colors by completing the following steps:
a. Click the Page Layout tab.
b. Click the Theme Colors button in the Themes group.
c. Click the theme colors option that you saved in Step 2 (*C23CustomColors02LastName*) that displays toward the top of the drop-down gallery in the *Custom* group.
6. Save **C23-E01-Viruses.docx**.
7. Print page 1 of **C23-E01-Viruses.docx** and then close the document.

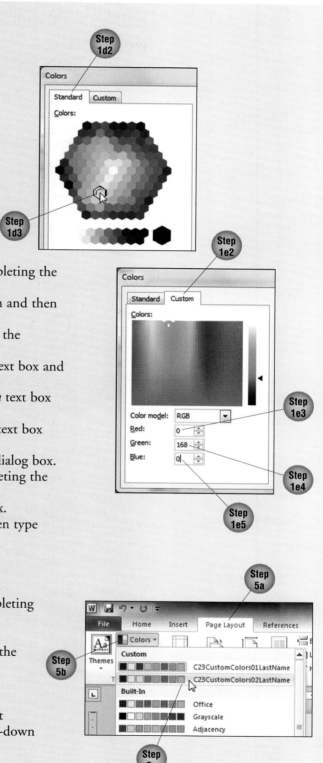

Creating Custom Theme Fonts

To create custom theme fonts, click the Page Layout tab, click the Theme Fonts button, and then click *Create New Theme Fonts* at the drop-down gallery. This displays the Create New Theme Fonts dialog box, shown in Figure 23.3. At this dialog box, choose a heading font and a body font. Type a name for the custom theme fonts in the *Name* box and then click the Save button.

Create Custom Theme Fonts
1. Click Page Layout tab.
2. Click Theme Fonts button.
3. Click *Create New Theme Fonts*.
4. Choose desired fonts.
5. Type name for custom theme fonts.
6. Click Save button.

Figure 23.3 Create New Theme Fonts Dialog Box

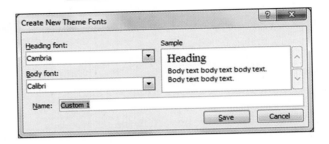

Choose a heading font and body font, type a new name for the theme in the *Name* text box, and then click Save.

Exercise 23.2A Creating Custom Theme Fonts   Part 1 of 3

1. At a blank document, create custom theme fonts by completing the following steps:
   a. Click the Page Layout tab.
   b. Click the Theme Fonts button in the Themes group and then click the *Create New Theme Fonts* option at the drop-down gallery.
   c. At the Create New Theme Fonts dialog box, click the down-pointing arrow at the right of the *Heading font* option box, scroll up the drop-down list, and then click *Arial*.
   d. Click the down-pointing arrow at the right of the *Body font* option box, scroll down the drop-down list, and then click *Times New Roman*.
2. Save the custom fonts by completing the following steps:
   a. Select the text in the *Name* text box.
   b. Type C23CustomFonts01 and then type your last name.
   c. Click the Save button.
3. Close the document without saving it.

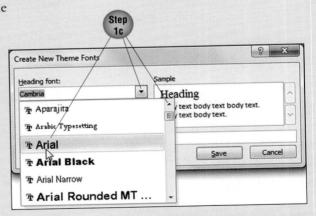

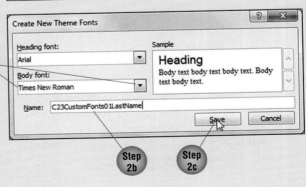

Applying Theme Effects

With options in the Theme Effects button drop-down gallery, you can apply line sets and fill effects to graphics in a document. You cannot create your own theme effects, but you can apply a theme effect and then save the formatting as your own document theme.

Theme Effects

Saving a Document Theme

When you have customized theme colors and fonts and applied theme effects to a document, you can save these in a custom document theme. To do this, click the Themes button in the Themes group in the Page Layout tab and then click *Save Current Theme* at the drop-down gallery. This displays the Save Current Theme dialog box, which has many of the same options that are available in the Save As dialog box. Type a name for your custom document theme in the *File name* text box and then click the Save button.

Save a Document Theme
1. Click Page Layout tab.
2. Click Themes button.
3. Click *Save Current Theme*.
4. Type name for custom theme.
5. Click Save button.

Exercise 23.2B Applying Theme Effects and Saving a Document Theme   Part 2 of 3

1. At a blank document, create custom theme colors by completing the following steps:
   a. Click the Page Layout tab.
   b. Click the Theme Colors button and then click *Create New Theme Colors* at the bottom of the drop-down gallery.
   c. At the Create New Theme Colors dialog box, click the *Text/Background - Dark 2* color button and then click Blue in the color palette (the third color from the right in the *Standard Colors* section).

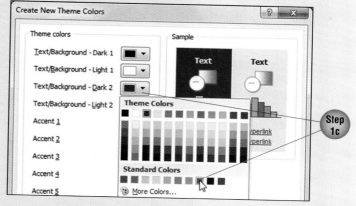

   d. Change the *Accent 1* color by completing the following steps:
      1) Click the color button that displays at the right of the *Accent 1* option.
      2) Click the *More Colors* option at the bottom of the color palette.
      3) At the Colors dialog box, click the Standard tab if necessary.
      4) Click the dark green color at the left of the honeycomb, as shown at the right.
      5) Click OK to close the dialog box.

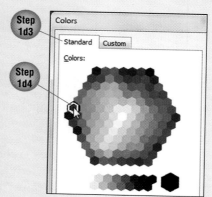

e. Save the custom colors with the name *C23CustomColors03LastName*.
2. Close the document without saving it.
3. Open **NSSServices.docx** and save the document with the name **C23-E02-NSSServices**.
4. Make the following changes to the document:
   a. Apply the Title style to the company name, *Northland Security Systems*.
   b. Apply the Heading 1 style to the heading *Northland Security Systems Mission*.
   c. Apply the Heading 2 style to the headings *Security Services* and *Security Software*.
5. Apply the custom theme colors you saved by completing the following steps:
   a. Click the Page Layout tab.
   b. Click the Theme Colors button in the Themes group.
   c. Click the *C23CustomColors03LastName* option that displays toward the top of the drop-down gallery in the *Custom* group.

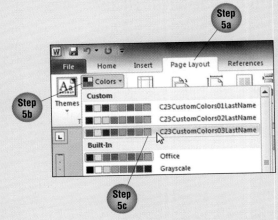

6. Apply the custom theme fonts you saved by clicking the Theme Fonts button in the Themes group and then clicking the *C23CustomFonts01LastName* option that displays toward the top of the drop-down gallery in the *Custom* group.

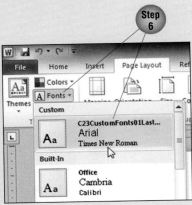

7. Apply a theme effect by clicking the Theme Effects button in the Themes group and then clicking *Concourse* at the drop-down gallery.
8. Make the following changes to the SmartArt diagram:
   a. Click near the diagram to select it. (When the diagram is selected, a light gray border displays around it.)
   b. Click the SmartArt Tools Design tab.
   c. Click the Change Colors button and then click the third color option from the left in the *Colorful* section (*Colorful Range - Accent Colors 3 to 4*).
   d. Click the More button at the right of the SmartArt Styles group and then click the third option from the left in the top row in the *3-D* section (*Cartoon*).
   e. Click outside the diagram to deselect it.

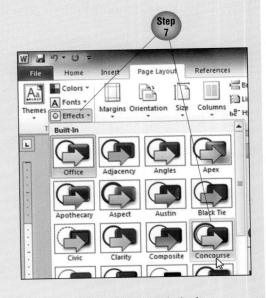

9. Save the custom theme colors and fonts as well as the Concourse theme effect into a custom document theme by completing the following steps:
   a. Click the Page Layout tab.
   b. Click the Themes button in the Themes group.
   c. Click the *Save Current Theme* option that displays at the bottom of the drop-down gallery.
   d. At the Save Current Theme dialog box, type C23CustomTheme01 and then type your last name in the *File name* text box.
   e. Click the Save button.

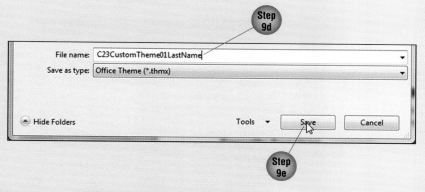

10. Save and then print **C23-E02-NSSServices.docx**.

Editing Custom Themes

You can edit custom theme colors and custom theme fonts. To edit custom theme colors, click the Page Layout tab and then click the Theme Colors button in the Themes group. At the drop-down gallery of custom and built-in themes, right-click your custom theme and then click *Edit* at the shortcut menu. This displays the Edit Theme Colors dialog box, which contains the same options that are available at the Create New Theme Colors dialog box, shown in Figure 23.1. Make the desired changes to theme colors and then click the Save button.

To edit custom theme fonts, click the Theme Fonts button in the Themes group in the Page Layout tab, right-click your custom theme fonts, and then click *Edit* at the shortcut menu. This displays the Edit Theme Fonts dialog box, which contains the same options that are available at the Create New Theme Fonts dialog box, shown in Figure 23.3. Make the desired changes and then click the Save button.

QUICK STEPS

Edit Custom Theme Colors
1. Click Page Layout tab.
2. Click Theme Colors button.
3. Right-click desired custom theme.
4. Click *Edit*.
5. Make desired changes.
6. Click Save button.

Edit Custom Theme Fonts
1. Click Page Layout tab.
2. Click Theme Fonts button.
3. Right-click desired custom theme.
4. Click *Edit*.
5. Make desired changes.
6. Click Save button.

1. With **C23-E02-NSSServices.docx** open, edit the custom theme colors by completing the following steps:
   a. Click the Page Layout tab.
   b. Click the Theme Colors button.
   c. Right-click the *C23CustomColors03LastName* theme and then click *Edit* at the shortcut menu.

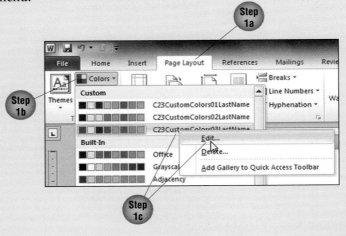

Step 1a

Step 1b

Step 1c

Step 1f

Step 1g

   d. At the Edit Theme Colors dialog box, click the *Text/Background - Dark 2* color button.
   e. Click *More Colors* at the color palette.
   f. At the Colors dialog box, click the Standard tab if necessary.
   g. Click the dark green color at the left edge of the honeycomb, as shown at the right.
   h. Click OK to close the dialog box.
   i. Click the Save button.
2. Edit the custom theme fonts by completing the following steps:
   a. Click the Theme Fonts button in the Themes group.
   b. Right-click the *C23CustomFonts01LastName* theme and then click *Edit* at the shortcut menu.
   c. At the Edit Theme Fonts dialog box, click the down-pointing arrow at the right of the *Body font* option box, scroll up the drop-down list, and then click *Constantia*.
   d. Click the Save button.
3. Apply a different theme effect by clicking the Theme Effects button in the Themes group and then clicking *Apex* at the drop-down gallery. (This effect applies a shadow behind the shapes.)
4. Save the changes to the custom theme by completing the following steps:
   a. Click the Themes button and then click *Save Current Theme* at the drop-down gallery.
   b. At the Save Current Theme dialog box, click the *C23CustomTheme01LastName.thmx* theme document.
   c. Click the Save button.
   d. At the replace question, click Yes.
5. Save, print, and then close **C23-E02-NSSServices.docx**.

If you apply a built-in theme other than the Office default or if you apply a custom theme, you can reset the theme back to the template default. To do this, click the Themes button and then click the *Reset to Theme from Template* at the drop-down gallery. If you are working in the default template provided by Word, clicking this option resets the theme to Office.

Reset Template Theme
1. Click Page Layout tab.
2. Click Themes button.
3. Click *Reset to Theme from Template.*

Exercise 23.3A **Applying Themes and Resetting to the Template Themes** Part 1 of 2

1. Open **NSSSecurity.docx** and save the document with the name **C23-E03-NSSSecurity**.
2. Apply the Title style to the company name and the Heading 1 style to the two headings in the document.
3. Apply your custom theme by completing the following steps:
   a. Click the Page Layout tab.
   b. Click the Themes button.
   c. Click the *C23CustomTheme01LastName* custom theme that displays at the top of the drop-down gallery in the *Custom* section.
4. Save and then print **C23-E03-NSSSecurity.docx**.
5. Reset the theme to the Office default by clicking the Themes button and then clicking *Reset to Theme from Template* at the drop-down gallery. (This returns the theme to the Office default.)

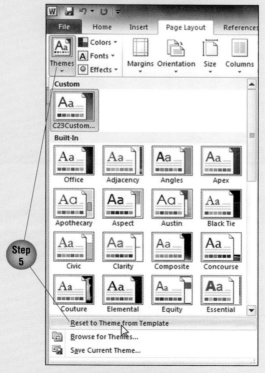

6. Save and then close **C23-E03-NSSSecurity.docx**.

Deleting Custom Themes

You can delete custom theme colors from the Theme Colors button drop-down gallery, custom theme fonts from the Theme Fonts drop-down gallery, and custom themes from the Save Current Theme dialog box.

To delete custom theme colors, click the Theme Colors button, right-click the theme you want to delete, and then click *Delete* at the shortcut menu. At the message asking if you want to delete the theme colors, click Yes. To delete custom theme fonts, click the Theme Fonts button, right-click the theme you want to delete, and then click *Delete* at the shortcut menu. At the message asking if you want to delete the theme fonts, click Yes.

Delete a custom theme (which includes custom colors, fonts, and effects) at the Save Current Theme dialog box. To display this dialog box, click the Themes button and then click *Save Current Theme* at the drop-down gallery. At the dialog box, click the custom theme document name, click the Organize button on the toolbar, and then click *Delete* at the drop-down list. At the message asking if you are sure you want to send the theme document to the Recycle Bin, click Yes.

Delete Custom Theme Colors
1. Click Page Layout tab.
2. Click Theme Colors button.
3. Right-click desired custom theme.
4. Click *Delete*.
5. Click Yes.

Delete Custom Theme Fonts
1. Click Page Layout tab.
2. Click Theme Fonts button.
3. Right-click desired custom theme.
4. Click *Delete*.
5. Click Yes.

Delete Custom Theme
1. Click Page Layout tab.
2. Click Themes button.
3. Click *Save Current Theme*.
4. Click custom theme.
5. Click Organize button.
6. Click *Delete*.
7. Click Yes.

Exercise 23.3B   Applying and Deleting Custom Themes   Part 2 of 2

1. At a blank document, delete the custom theme colors by completing the following steps:
   a. Click the Page Layout tab.
   b. Click the Theme Colors button in the Themes group.
   c. Right-click the *C23CustomColors01LastName* custom theme colors.
   d. Click *Delete* at the shortcut menu.
   e. At the question asking if you want to delete the theme colors, click Yes.

2. Complete steps similar to those in Step 1 to delete the *C23CustomColors02LastName* custom theme colors and the *C23CustomColors03LastName* custom theme colors.
3. Delete the custom theme fonts by completing the following steps:
   a. Click the Theme Fonts button in the Themes group.
   b. Right-click the *C23CustomFonts01LastName* custom theme fonts.
   c. Click *Delete* at the shortcut menu.
   d. At the question asking if you want to delete the theme fonts, click Yes.
4. Delete the custom theme by completing the following steps:
   a. Click the Themes button.
   b. Click *Save Current Theme* located toward the bottom of the drop-down gallery.
   c. At the Save Current Theme dialog box, click the *C23CustomTheme01LastName.thmx* theme document in the list box.
   d. Click the Organize button on the toolbar and then click *Delete* at the drop-down list.

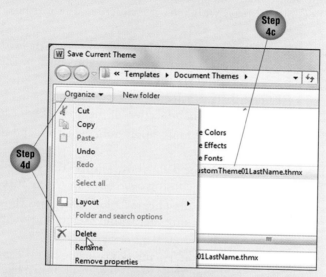

   e. At the message asking if you are sure you want to send the theme to the Recycle Bin, click Yes.
   f. Click the Cancel button to close the dialog box.
5. Close the document without saving it.

Chapter *Summary*

➤ Create custom theme colors with options at the Create New Theme Colors dialog box.

➤ Click the Reset button in the Create New Theme Colors dialog box to reset colors back to the default Office template colors.

➤ Apply custom theme colors by clicking the Page Layout tab, clicking the Theme Colors button, and then clicking the custom theme colors in the *Custom* section of the drop-down gallery.

➤ Additional color options are available at the Colors dialog box with the Standard tab or the Custom tab selected. Display this dialog box by clicking a color button in the Create New Theme Colors dialog box and then clicking the *More Colors* option.

➤ The Colors dialog box with the Standard tab selected contains a honeycomb of colors. Click the Custom tab, and a square of color displays with a vertical slider bar and text boxes for specifying percentages of red, green, and blue.

➤ Create custom theme fonts with options at the Create New Theme Fonts dialog box. Display this dialog box by clicking the Page Layout tab, clicking the Theme Fonts button, and then clicking the *Create New Theme Fonts* option at the drop-down gallery.

➤ Apply custom theme fonts by clicking the Page Layout tab, clicking the Theme Fonts button, and then clicking the custom theme fonts in the *Custom* section of the drop-down gallery.

➤ Create custom theme colors and custom theme fonts, apply a theme effect, and then save the changes in a custom theme.

➤ Save a custom theme at the Save Current Theme dialog box. Display this dialog box by clicking the Themes button in the Themes group and then clicking *Save Current Theme* at the drop-down gallery.

➤ Edit custom theme colors with options at the Edit Theme Colors dialog box. Display this dialog box by clicking the Theme Colors button, right-clicking the custom theme, and then clicking the *Edit* option.

➤ Edit custom theme fonts with options at the Edit Theme Fonts dialog box. Display this dialog box by clicking the Theme Fonts button, right-clicking the custom theme, and then clicking the *Edit* option.

➤ Click the *Reset to Theme from Template* at the Themes button drop-down gallery to reset the theme to the default template.

➤ Delete custom theme colors by clicking the Theme Colors button, right-clicking the custom theme, and then clicking the *Delete* option.

➤ Delete custom theme fonts by clicking the Theme Fonts button, right-clicking the custom theme, and then clicking the *Delete* option.

➤ Delete a custom theme at the Save Current Theme dialog box. Display this dialog box by clicking the Themes button and then clicking *Save Current Theme* at the drop-down gallery. Click the custom theme document name, click the Organize button, and then click *Delete* at the drop-down list.

Commands *Review*

FEATURE	RIBBON TAB, GROUP	BUTTON, OPTION
Create New Theme Colors dialog box	Page Layout, Themes	▣ , Create New Theme Colors
Create New Theme Fonts dialog box	Page Layout, Themes	A , Create New Theme Fonts
Theme effects	Page Layout, Themes	◎
Save Current Theme dialog box	Page Layout, Themes	Aa , Save Current Theme

Key Points *Review*

Completion: In the space provided at the right, indicate the correct term, symbol, or command.

1. The Themes button is located in this tab.
2. This is the name of the default theme.
3. Create custom theme colors with options at this dialog box.
4. Custom theme colors you create display in this section of the Theme Colors button drop-down gallery.
5. The Colors dialog box with this tab selected displays a honeycomb of color options.
6. The Colors dialog box with this tab selected displays the *Red*, *Green*, and *Blue* text boxes.
7. Create custom theme fonts with options at this dialog box.
8. To edit custom theme fonts, click the Theme Fonts button, do this to the custom theme, and then click *Edit* at the shortcut menu.
9. Click this option at the Themes button drop-down gallery to set the theme back to the default template.
10. Delete custom themes at this dialog box.

Chapter Assessments

Applying Your Skills

Demonstrate your knowledge of features learned in this chapter by completing the following assessments.

Assessment 23.1 Create and Apply Custom Themes to a Medical Plans Document

1. At a blank document, create custom theme colors named *C23CustomColors01* followed by your initials that makes the following color changes:
   a. Change the *Accent 2* color to *Dark Blue* (the second option from the right in the *Standard Colors* section).
   b. Change the *Accent 5* color to *Olive Green, Accent 3, Darker 50%* (the bottom option in the seventh column in the *Theme Colors* section).
2. Click the Theme Effects button and then click *Paper* at the drop-down gallery.
3. Save the custom theme and name it *C23CustomTheme01* followed by your initials. **Hint: Do this with the Save Current Theme *option at the* Themes *drop-down gallery.***
4. Close the document without saving the changes.
5. Open **KLHPlan.docx** and save the document with the name **C23-A01-KLHPlan**.
6. Make the following changes to the document:
   a. Change the style set to Formal.
   b. With the insertion point positioned at the beginning of the document, type the title Key Life Health Plan.
   c. Apply the Heading 1 style to the title.
   d. Apply the Heading 2 style to the three headings in the document.
7. Move the insertion point to the end of the document and then insert the document **KLHPDiagram.docx**. **Hint: Do this with the Object button in the Insert tab.**
8. Apply the custom theme you created by clicking the Page Layout tab, clicking the Themes button, and then clicking the custom theme named *C23CustomTheme* followed by your initials.
9. Save, print, and then close **C23-A01-KLHPlan.docx**.

Assessment 23.2 Create and Apply Custom Themes to a Real Photography Document

1. At a blank document, create custom theme colors named *C23CustomColors02* followed by your initials that makes the following color changes:
   a. Change the *Text/Background - Dark 2* color to *Orange, Accent 6, Darker 50%*.
   b. Change the *Accent 1* color to a custom color at the Colors dialog box with the Custom tab selected. Type 0 in the *Red* text box, 140 in the *Green* text box, and 0 in the Blue text box.
2. Create custom theme fonts named *C23CustomFonts01* followed by your initials that changes the Heading font to Harrington.
3. Click the Theme Effects button and then click *Verve* at the drop-down gallery.
4. Save the custom theme and name it *C23CustomTheme02* followed by your initials. **Hint: Do this with the Save Current Theme *option at the* Themes *drop-down gallery.***
5. Close the document without saving the changes.
6. Open **RPServices.docx** and save the document with the name **C23-A02-RPServices**.
7. Apply your *C23CustomTheme02(initials)* theme to the document.
8. Save, print, and then close **C23-A02-RPServices.docx**.

Expanding Your Skills

Explore additional feature options or use Help to learn a new skill in creating this document.

Assessment 23.3 Explore and Apply Office.com Themes

1. Open **DevelopSoftware.docx** and save the document with the name **C23-A03-DevelopSoftware**.

2. Additional themes are available from Office.com and should display at the bottom of the Themes button drop-down gallery. To view the Office.com themes, click the Page Layout tab, click the Themes button in the Themes group, and then scroll down to the bottom of the drop-down gallery. You should see themes with names such as *Decatur*, *Mylar*, *Sketchbook*, and *SOHO*. (If you do not have any Office.com themes available, connect to the Internet and then go to the Office.com website and explore the site to determine if you can download themes.)

3. Hover the mouse over the Office.com themes in the Themes button drop-down gallery to see how the theme changes the document formatting. Apply one of the Office.com themes to the document.

4. Determine the heading font and body font used by the theme by clicking on any character in the title *Application Software*, clicking the Home tab, and then clicking the Font button arrow. The heading font and body font are listed at the beginning of the drop-down list. Make a note of these fonts.

5. With the insertion point positioned on the title *Application Software*, determine the font color by clicking the Font Color button arrow and then checking the color palette to determine which color option is selected (surrounded by an orange border). If no color option is selected, click the *More Colors* option at the bottom of the drop-down gallery. At the Colors dialog box with the Custom tab selected, make a note of the numbers after the *Red*, *Green*, and *Blue* options.

6. Position the insertion point on the heading *Developing Software* and then determine the font color.

7. After determining the Office.com heading and body fonts and font colors, make the following changes:
   a. Press Ctrl + End to move the insertion point to the end of the document.
   b. Type Theme name:, press the spacebar, and then type the name of the theme you applied.
   c. Press Shift + Enter to move the insertion point to the next line.
   d. Type Heading font:, press the spacebar, type the name of the font, type a comma, press the spacebar, and then type the font color name (or type *Red*, *Green*, and *Blue* followed by the specific numbers).
   e. Press Shift + Enter.
   f. Type Body font:, press the spacebar, type the name of the font, type a comma, press the spacebar, and then type the font color name (or type *Red*, *Green*, and *Blue* followed by the specific numbers).

8. Save and then print **C23-A03-DevelopSoftware.docx**.

9. Apply a different Office.com theme to the document and then determine the heading font and font color and the body font and font color. Change the information that displays at the bottom of the document to reflect the new theme.

10. Save, print, and then close **C23-A03-DevelopSoftware.docx**.

Achieving Signature Status

Take your skills to the next level by completing this more challenging assessment.

Assessment 23.4 Create and Apply a Custom Theme

1. Open **TECRevenues.docx** and save the document and name it **C23-A04-TECRevenues**.
2. Apply a theme of your choosing.
3. Create custom theme colors named *C23ColorsTEC* followed by your initials (you determine the custom colors).
4. Create custom theme fonts named *C23FontsTEC* followed by your initials (you determine the fonts).
5. Apply the *Verve* theme effect to the SmartArt graphic image. ***Hint: Do this with the Theme Effects button in the Themes group in the Page Layout tab.***
6. Save the custom theme colors and fonts as well as the *Verve* theme effect into a custom document theme named *C23ThemeTEC* followed by your initials.
7. Save, print, and then close **C23-A04-TECRevenues.docx**.
8. Open **TECCorporate.docx** and save the document with the name **C23-A04-TECCorporate**.
9. Apply the *C23ThemeTEC* (followed by your initials) custom theme to the document.
10. Save, print, and then close **C23-A04-TECCorporate.docx**.
11. At a blank document, use the Print Screen button to make a screen capture of the Theme Colors drop-down gallery (make sure your custom theme colors display), a screen capture of the Theme Fonts drop-down gallery (make sure your custom theme fonts display), and a screen capture of the Save Current Theme dialog box (make sure your custom themes are visible). Insert all three screen capture images on the same page. (You will need to size the images.)
12. Save the document and name it **C23-A04-ScreenImages**.
13. Print and then close **C23-A04-ScreenImages.docx**.
14. At a blank document, delete the custom color theme you created, the custom font theme, as well as the custom themes.

Chapter 24

Tutorial 24.1
Changing the Quick Styles Set
Default
Tutorial 24.2
Creating and Modifying Styles
Tutorial 24.3
Creating and Deleting Custom
Quick Styles Sets
Tutorial 24.4
Creating a Table Style
Tutorial 24.5
Creating a Multilevel List Style
Tutorial 24.6
Managing Styles

Creating and Managing Styles

Performance Objectives

Upon successful completion of Chapter 24, you will be able to:

- Change the Quick Styles set default
- Apply styles
- Create new styles
- Create styles from existing formatting
- Create styles from existing styles
- Modify styles
- Save and delete a custom Quick Styles set
- Manage and organize styles

Along with the themes you learned about in Chapter 23, Word provides a number of predesigned styles, grouped into Quick Styles sets, that you can use to apply consistent formatting to text in documents. If none of these predesigned styles apply the formatting you want, you can create your own styles. In this chapter, you will learn how to apply, create, modify, delete, manage, and organize styles as well as how to save and delete a custom Quick Styles set.

Note: Before beginning computer exercises for this chapter, copy to your storage medium the Chapter24 folder from the CD that accompanies this textbook and then make Chapter24 the active folder.

In this chapter, students will produce the following documents:

Exercise 24.1. C24-E01-AfricanAdventure.docx
Exercise 24.2. C24-E02-BTZenith.docx
Exercise 24.3. C24-E03-BTTours.docx
Exercise 24.3. C24-E03-BTTables.docx
Exercise 24.3. C24-E03-BTTablesModified.docx
Exercise 24.3. C24-E03-BTZenith.docx
Exercise 24.3. C24-E03-BTEastAdventures.docx

Model answers for these exercises are shown on the following pages.

African Study Adventure

The African Study Adventure program provide travelers with a unique opportunity to travel to African countries and make connections with local people, visit cultural institutions, and travel with knowledgeable tour guides who will provide insightful information about the countries, peoples, and customs.

Small Groups

The size of each group is limited so that African Study Adventure tour guides can deliver personal service and ensure that you feel comfortable in your surroundings. All tours are limited to a maximum of 25 participants.

Comprehensive Itineraries

Each program in the African Study Adventure program offers comprehensive sightseeing, exciting activities, and direct encounters with the people of the area you are visiting. Tour guides have developed a range of tours, each with its own principal theme and special highlights.

Custom Groups

For those who cannot fit African Study Adventure program scheduled departures into their calendars or who prefer to travel with their own friends and family, Bayside Travel has developed custom programs to suit your specific needs.

Accommodations and Meals

Accommodations will vary with the particular trip. However, Bayside Travel staff has selected accommodations with great care to make sure you will be as comfortable as local conditions allow and that you will enjoy the unique atmosphere of each destination. Most meals are included in the tour package.

"Travel is fatal to prejudice, bigotry and narrow-mindedness." Mark Twain

Exercise 24.1 C24-E01-AfricanAdventure.docx

Bayside Travel

Extreme Adventures

We are excited to announce that First Choice Travel has teamed with Zenith Adventures to provide our clients with thrilling, adrenaline-producing, extreme outdoor adventures. You can choose from a variety of exciting adventures including Antarctic expedition cruises, tall-ship sailing, and bicycling tours. Many of our trips are appropriate for beginners, so get out and enjoy an amazing outdoor adventure with family and friends!

Antarctic Adventures

Travel with our Antarctic experts, cruise on our state-of-the-art ships, and experience Antarctica in all of its grandeur. We use ice-rated expedition ships custom designed for your comfort and safety. Each ship can carry up to 100 passengers, provides excellent viewing for watching whales, seabirds, and icebergs, and includes facilities for educational presentations by our Antarctic experts. For our more adventurous clients, we offer additional activities such as snowshoeing, sea-kayaking, and camping on the Antarctic ice. Plan on a shore excursion where you can view penguin rookeries, seal colonies, and places of historical and scientific interest. To carry you to the Antarctic shore, we use inflatable boats that can carry 12 to 15 people. After a thrilling day on shore, we will take you back to the ship where you can enjoy a delicious meal prepared by our gourmet chefs. Our Antarctic travel experts are naturalists, historians, and adventurers committed to providing you with a fabulous Antarctic adventure.

- ANTARCTIC EXPLORATION, $4399
- WEDDELL SEA ADVENTURE, $6899
- FALKLAND ISLANDS JOURNEY, $7699
- SAILING SPECTACULAR, $8999

Tall-Ship Adventures

Visit exotic and spectacular locations in the South Pacific aboard the Laura Devon, a luxurious tall ship. On your tall-ship adventure, seek out the hidden Pacific by sailing the trade winds to discover the undisturbed cultures and beauty of remote islands and communities. Our tall-ship sailing adventure combines exotic exploration and timeless romance. You can sign on for the challenge of an ocean voyage with blue water sailing or a more leisurely island voyage sailing through tropical paradises. For

many, tall-ship sailing is the ultimate in escapist adventuring. Sailing on the magnificent Laura Devon, combined with the sparkling beauty of the South Pacific, makes for the adventure of a lifetime.

- VANUATU EXPLORATION, $1599
- TAHITI TO COOK ISLANDS, $2899
- FIJI TO VANUATU, $2999
- TONGA TO FIJI, $3999

Bicycling Adventures

A bicycle is the perfect form of transportation for a travel adventure. Sign up for one of our bicycle tours and travel at your own pace, interact with village residents, stay healthy and fit, and know that your adventure has a minimal effect on the environment. We offer bicycle tours ranging from a leisurely trip through the Loire Valley of France to a mountain-bike expedition in the Atlas Mountains in Morocco. Our Zenith Adventure bicycle guides provide you with historical and educational information about the region in which you are traveling. They also take care of luggage and transportation needs and maintain your bicycle. We are confident that we can provide the bicycle adventure of a lifetime!

- LOIRE VALLEY TOUR, $2399
- TUSCAN VILLAGE TOUR, $2499
- ATLAS TREK EXTREME, $2899
- GREAT WALL OF CHINA, $3299

Volunteer Adventures

Beginning next year, Zenith Adventures, together with First Choice Travel, will offer volunteer vacation opportunities. Tentative volunteer adventures include building village and mountain paths, building homes, and helping the families of trail porters improve village facilities. Our volunteer adventures will provide you with an exciting vacation and a rewarding volunteer experience. The group size will be limited to a maximum of 15, and participants will be required to raise a minimum amount of money to contribute to the program and local charities. All charities have been carefully screened to ensure that funds are well managed and distributed fairly. Look for more information in our next newsletter and consider a rewarding volunteer adventure.

Exercise 24.2 C24-E02-BTZenith.docx   Page 1   Page 2

A) African Study Adventure

* Small groups

* Comprehensive itineraries

* Custom groups

* Accommodations and meals

* Rates

    ✓ Single-occupancy rate:

    ✓ Double-occupancy rate

B) Southwest Sun Adventure

* Small group

* Guided day trips

* Grand Canyon vistas

* Bilingual tour guides

* Rates

    ✓ Single-occupancy rate:

    ✓ Double-occupancy rate

Exercise 2.3

C24-E03-BTTours.docx

Antarctic Adventures

Adventure	Duration	Price
Antarctic Exploration	8 days, 7 nights	$4,399
Weddell Sea Adventure	10 days, 9 nights	$6,899
Falkland Islands Journey	14 days, 13 nights	$7,699
Sailing Spectacular	14 days, 13 nights	$8,999

Tall-Ship Adventures

Adventure	Duration	Price
Vanuatu Exploration	5 days, 4 nights	$1,599
Tahiti to Cook Islands	7 days, 6 nights	$2,899
Fiji to Vanuatu	7 days, 6 nights	$2,999
Tonga to Fiji	10 day	

Bicycling Adven

Adventure	Duratio
Loire Valley Tour	6 days,
Tuscan Village Tour	7 days,
Atlas Trek Extreme	7 days,
Great Wall of China	10 days,

Exercise 2.3

C24-E03-BTTables.docx

Antarctic Adventures

Adventure	Duration	Price
Antarctic Exploration	8 days, 7 nights	$4,399
Weddell Sea Adventure	10 days, 9 nights	$6,899
Falkland Islands Journey	14 days, 13 nights	$7,699
Sailing Spectacular	14 days, 13 nights	$8,999

Tall-Ship Adventures

Adventure	Duration	Price
Vanuatu Exploration	5 days, 4 nights	$1,599
Tahiti to Cook Islands	7 days, 6 nights	$2,899
Fiji to Vanuatu	7 days, 6 nights	$2,999
Tonga to Fiji	10 days, 9 nights	$3,999

Bicycling Adventures

Adventure	Duration	Price
Loire Valley Tour	6 days, 5 nights	$2,399
Tuscan Village Tour	7 days, 6 nights	$2,499
Atlas Trek Extreme	7 days, 6 nights	$2,899
Great Wall of China	10 days, 9 nights	$3,299

Exercise 2.3

C24-E03-BTTablesModified.docx

Exercise 24.3

C24-E03-BTZenith.docx

Extreme Adventures

We are excited to announce that *First Choice Travel* has teamed with *Zenith Adventures* to provide our clients with thrilling, adrenaline-producing, extreme outdoor adventures. You can choose from a variety of exciting adventures including Antarctic expedition cruises, tall-ship sailing, and bicycling tours. Many of our trips are appropriate for beginners, so get out and enjoy an amazing outdoor adventure with family and friends!

Antarctic Adventures

Travel with our Antarctic experts, cruise on our state-of-the-art ships, and experience Antarctica in all of its grandeur. We use ice-rated expedition ships custom designed for your comfort and safety. Each ship can carry up to 100 passengers, provides excellent viewing for watching whales, seabirds, and icebergs, and includes facilities for educational presentations by our Antarctic experts. For our more adventurous clients, we offer additional activities such as snowshoeing, sea-kayaking, and camping on the Antarctic ice. Plan on a shore excursion where you can view penguin rookeries, seal colonies, and places of historical and scientific interest. To carry you to the Antarctic shore, we use inflatable boats that can carry 12 to 15 people. After a thrilling day on shore, we will take you back to the ship where you can enjoy a delicious meal prepared by our gourmet chefs. Our Antarctic travel experts are naturalists, historians, and adventurers committed to providing you with a fabulous Antarctic adventure.

Antarctic Exploration, $4399

Weddell Sea Adventure, $6899

Falkland Islands Journey, $7699

Sailing Spectacular, $8999

Tall-Ship Adventures

...ons in the South Pacific aboard the Laura Devon, a luxurious tall ship. ...out the hidden Pacific by sailing the trade winds to discover the ...of remote islands and communities. Our tall-ship sailing adventure ...imeless romance. You can sign on for the challenge of an ocean

voyage with blue water sailing or a more leisurely island voyage sailing through tropical paradises. For many, tall-ship sailing is the ultimate in escapist adventuring. Sailing on the magnificent Laura Devon, combined with the sparkling beauty of the South Pacific, makes for the adventure of a lifetime.

Vanuatu Exploration, $1599

Tahiti to Cook Islands, $2899

Fiji to Vanuatu, $2999

Tonga to Fiji, $3999

Bicycling Adventures

A bicycle is the perfect form of transportation for a travel adventure. Sign up for one of our bicycle tours and travel at your own pace, interact with village residents, stay healthy and fit, and know that your adventure has a minimal effect on the environment. We offer bicycle tours ranging from a leisurely trip through the Loire Valley of France to a mountain-bike expedition in the Atlas Mountains in Morocco. Our Zenith Adventure bicycle guides provide you with historical and educational information about the region in which you are traveling. They also take care of luggage and transportation needs and maintain your bicycle. We are confident that we can provide the bicycle adventure of a lifetime!

Loire Valley Tour, $2399

Tuscan Village Tour, $2499

Atlas Trek Extreme, $2899

Great Wall of China, $3299

Volunteer Adventures

Beginning next year, *Zenith Adventures*, together with *First Choice Travel*, will offer volunteer vacation opportunities. Tentative volunteer adventures include building village and mountain paths, building homes, and helping the families of trail porters improve village facilities. Our volunteer adventures will provide you with an exciting vacation and a rewarding volunteer experience. The group size will be limited to a maximum of 15, and participants will be required to raise a minimum amount of money to contribute to the program and local charities. All charities have been carefully screened to ensure that funds are well managed and distributed fairly. Look for more information in our next newsletter and consider a rewarding volunteer adventure.

Bayside Travel

Eastern Adventures

Join **Bayside Travel** in a joint adventure with *Lifetime Tours* in experiencing the beauty and splendor of the East. Upcoming adventure tours include the beauty and majesty of Japan and the cultural and natural marvels of China.

Japan Adventures

Japan is a country of unique contrasts from the neon lights and bustling activity of Tokyo to the sweeping vistas of the Japanese Alps. Join Bayside Travel in a joint adventure with Maruyama Tours in experiencing the beauty and splendor of Japan. Choose from one of three adventure tours to experience the sights and sounds of Japan from the urban centers of Tokyo and Kyoto to the breathtaking views of Japan's mountain ranges and coastlines.

Adventure	Duration	Price
Japan Extravaganza	14 days, 13 nights	$9,799
Treasures of Japan	12 days, 11 nights	$8,299
Northern Exploration	10 days, 9 nights	$7,599

China Adventures

The 2008 Olympics hosted by China provided the world the opportunity to see a nation of ancient riches complemented by amazing modern marvels of architecture and engineering. China is a land of natural and cultural beauty from the Great Wall of China and the Forbidden City of Beijing to the Xi'an's Terracotta Army, Suzhou gardens, and the majestic peaks of Huangshan.

Adventure	Duration	Price
Cultural China	14 days, 13 nights	$11,359
China & Yangtze Experience	14 days, 13 nights	$10,759
China Village Experience	10 days, 9 nights	$8,299

Exercise 24.3

C24-E03-BTEastAdventures.docx

Model Answers

Formatting with Styles

A style is a set of formatting instructions that you can apply to text. Word provides a number of predesigned styles and groups those that apply similar formatting into sets called Quick Styles sets. Whereas a theme changes the overall colors, fonts, and effects used in a document, a Quick Styles set changes how the colors, fonts, and effects are combined and which color, font, and effect are dominant. Using the styles within a Quick Styles set, you can apply formatting that gives your document a uniform and professional appearance.

Displaying Styles in a Quick Styles Set

The default Quick Styles set is named *Word 2010,* and the styles in this set are available in the Quick Style list in the Styles group in the Home tab. Several styles display as *thumbnails,* or miniature representations in the Quick Style list in the Styles group. Generally, these style thumbnails include the Normal, No Spacing, Heading 1, Heading 2, and Title styles. (Depending on your monitor and screen resolution, you may see more or fewer style thumbnails in the Styles group.) The styles change to reflect the styles that have been applied to the active document. Click the More button to the right of the style thumbnails in the Quick Style list, and a drop-down gallery displays containing all of the styles available in the default set. Hover your mouse over a style in the Quick Style list drop-down gallery to see how the style will format text in your document.

You can also display the styles available in a Quick Styles set by clicking either the down-pointing arrow or up-pointing arrow to the right of the style thumbnails. Clicking the down-pointing arrow scrolls down the style set, displaying the next styles. Clicking the up-pointing arrow scrolls up the set of styles.

Change Quick Styles Set Default

1. Change desired Quick Styles set colors, fonts, and paragraph spacing.
2. Click Change Styles button.
3. Click *Set as Default*.

AA

Change Styles

Changing the Quick Styles Set Default

Along with the default Quick Styles set, Word provides a number of other Quick Styles sets. You have used some of these sets in previous chapters to apply formatting to your documents. To view all available Quick Styles sets, click the Change Styles button in the Styles group and then point to *Style Set*. Each Quick Styles set has a name, such as *Distinctive*, *Formal*, or *Thatch*, that provides a general description of the type of formatting the styles apply.

The styles in a Quick Styles set apply formatting that includes colors and fonts. You can change the colors or fonts applied by styles in a set with the *Colors* and *Fonts* options at the Change Styles drop-down list. However, because the styles in a set are designed to complement one another, in most situations you will not change them. To change style set colors, click the Change Styles button, point to *Colors,* and then click the desired theme colors. The theme colors available with the *Colors* option are the same as those available with the Themes button and Theme Colors button. Change style set fonts by clicking the Change Styles button, pointing to *Fonts,* and then clicking the desired theme fonts. The theme fonts available with the *Fonts* option are the same as those available with the Themes button and Theme Fonts button. Customize the paragraph spacing in a document with styles at the Paragraph Spacing side menu. Display the paragraph spacing styles by clicking the Change Styles button and then pointing to *Paragraph Spacing*.

Word 2010 is the Quick Styles set default and is available when you open a blank Word document. If you consistently format your documents with a different Quick Styles set, you may want to make that set the default. To do this, change to the Quick Styles set that you want as the default and make any desired changes to the set colors, fonts, and paragraph spacing. Click the Change Styles button and then click *Set as Default* at the drop-down list. The new default Quick Styles set applies to new documents you create, but it is not the default for any existing documents.

Exercise 24.1A   **Change the Quick Styles Default**   Part 1 of 2

Note: If you are running Word 2010 on a computer connected to a network in a public environment such as a school, you may not be able to save styles to the hard drive. Before beginning Exercise 24.1A, check with your instructor.

1. Suppose you format many of your documents with the *Thatch* Quick Styles set using the *Flow* colors and the *Paper* fonts with relaxed paragraph spacing, and you want to make it the default. To do this, complete the following steps:
    a. At a blank document, click the Change Styles button, point to *Style Set*, and then click *Thatch* at the drop-down gallery.
    b. Click the Change Styles button, point to *Colors*, and then click *Flow* at the drop-down gallery.

c. Click the Change Styles button, point to *Fonts*, scroll down the fonts drop-down gallery, and then click *Paper*.

d. Click the Change Styles button, point to *Paragraph Spacing*, and then click *Relaxed* at the side menu.

e. Click the Change Styles button and then click *Set as Default*.

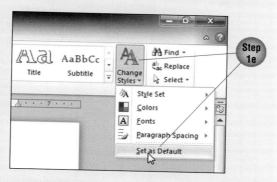

2. Close the document without saving it.

3. Press Ctrl + N to display a blank document.

4. At the blank document, notice the thumbnails in the Quick Style list in the Styles group. The formatting reflects the default Quick Styles set, colors, font, and paragraph spacing.

5. Click the Change Styles button and then point to *Paragraph Spacing* and then notice that the Relaxed style is selected.

6. Click the Page Layout tab and then notice the Themes group buttons. They reflect the colors and fonts of the default Quick Styles set.

7. Suppose you want a previously created document formatted with the styles in the *Word 2010* Quick Styles set to display with the new default styles applied. To do this, you must insert the file in the current document (rather than open it) by completing the following steps:

   a. Click the Insert tab.

   b. Click the Object button arrow and then click *Text from File*.

   c. Navigate to the Chapter24 folder on your storage medium and then double-click **AfricanAdventure.docx**. (Notice that the new default Quick Styles set formatting is applied to the document.)

8. Save the document with the name **C24-E01-AfricanAdventure**.

Applying Styles

You can use a variety of methods to apply styles to text in a document. You can apply a style by clicking the style thumbnail in the Quick Style list in the Styles group or by clicking the More button and then clicking the style at the drop-down gallery. The Styles task pane provides another method for applying a style. Display the Styles task pane, shown in Figure 24.1, by clicking the Styles group dialog box launcher or by pressing Alt + Ctrl + Shift + S. The styles in the currently selected Quick Styles set display in the task pane followed by a paragraph symbol (¶), indicating that the style applies paragraph formatting, or a character symbol (**a**), indicating that the style applies character formatting. If both characters display to the right of a style, the style applies both paragraph and character formatting. In addition to displaying styles that apply formatting, the Styles task pane also displays a *Clear All* style that clears all formatting from the selected text.

Figure 24.1 Styles Task Pane

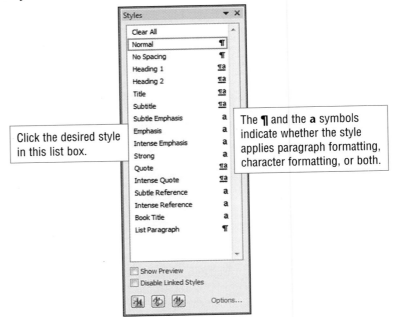

Click the desired style in this list box.

The ¶ and the **a** symbols indicate whether the style applies paragraph formatting, character formatting, or both.

Apply Style
Click style in Quick Style list in Styles group.
OR
1. Click More button in Quick Style list in Styles group.
2. Click desired style.
OR
1. Display Styles task pane.
2. Click desired style in task pane.
OR
1. Click More button in Quick Style list in Styles group.
2. Click *Apply Styles* at drop-down gallery.
3. Click down-pointing arrow at right of *Style Name* option box.
4. Click desired style at drop-down list.

If you hover the mouse pointer on a style in the Styles task pane, a ScreenTip displays with information about the formatting applied by the style. Apply a style in the Styles task pane by clicking the style. Close the Styles task pane by clicking the Close button located in the upper right corner of the task pane.

You can also apply styles at the Apply Styles window, shown in Figure 24.2. Display this window by clicking the More button at the right of the thumbnails in the Quick Style list in the Styles group and then clicking *Apply Styles* at the drop-down gallery. You can also display the Apply Styles window by pressing Ctrl + Shift + S. Like the Styles task pane, the Apply Styles window contains the styles of the currently selected Quick Styles set. Click the down-pointing arrow at the right of the *Style Name* option box and then click the desired style at the drop-down list. You can also type the name of the style in the *Style Name* option box and then press the Enter key.

Figure 24.2 Apply Styles Window

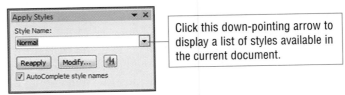

Click this down-pointing arrow to display a list of styles available in the current document.

1. With **C24-E01-AfricanAdventure.docx** open, apply styles using the Styles task pane by completing the following steps:
   a. Select the heading text *SMALL GROUPS*.
   b. Click the Home tab and then click the Styles group dialog box launcher. (This displays the Styles task pane.)
   c. Click the *Subtle Emphasis* style in the Styles task pane. (Notice that the style is followed by the character symbol (**a**) indicating that the style applies character formatting.)

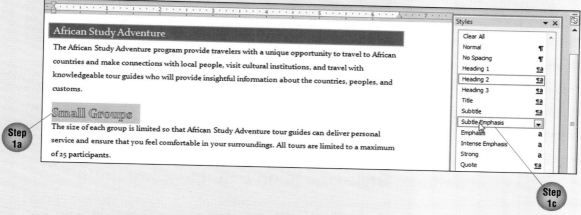

Step 1a

Step 1c

   d. Select the heading text *COMPREHENSIVE ITINERARIES*.
   e. Click the *Subtle Emphasis* style in the Styles task pane.
   f. Complete steps similar to those in Step 1d and 1e to apply the Subtitle Emphasis style to the remaining headings (*CUSTOM GROUPS* and *ACCOMMODATIONS AND MEALS*).
   g. Select the last line of text in the document (the Mark Twain quote) and then click the *Quote* style in the Styles task pane.
   h. After noticing the formatting of the quote, remove it by making sure the text is selected and then clicking the *Clear All* style located toward the top of the Styles task pane.
   i. Click anywhere in the heading *SMALL GROUPS* and notice that the Subtle Emphasis style is selected in the Styles task pane. Hover the mouse pointer over the Subtle Emphasis style and read the information in the ScreenTip about the formatting applied by the style.
   j. Close the Styles task pane by clicking the Close button located in the upper right corner of the task pane.
2. Display the Apply Styles window by clicking the More button at the right of the style thumbnails in the Quick Style list in the Styles group and then clicking *Apply Styles* at the drop-down gallery.

3. Select the quote text located at the end of the document, click the down-pointing arrow at the right of the *Style Name* option box, and then click *Intense Quote* at the drop-down list. (You will need to scroll down the list box to display this option.)

4. Close the Apply Styles window by clicking the Close button located in the upper right corner of the window.

5. Center the title *African Study Adventure.*

6. Save, print, and then close **C24-E01-AfricanAdventure.docx**.

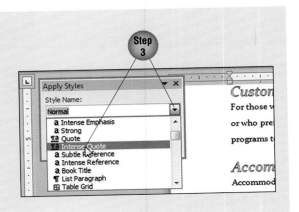

Creating Styles

QUICK STEPS

Create Style Based on Existing Formatting
1. Apply desired formatting to text.
2. Select text.
3. Click More button in Styles group.
4. Click *Save Selection as a New Quick Style.*
5. Type name for new style.
6. Click OK.

Create Style Based on Existing Style
1. Apply style to text.
2. Make desired formatting changes.
3. Select text.
4. Click More button in Styles group.
5. Click *Save Selection as a New Quick Style.*
6. Type name for new style.
7. Click OK.

If none of the predesigned styles provided by Word contain the formatting you desire, you can create your own style. You can create a style based on existing formatting, create a new style and apply all formatting, or modify an existing style.

Creating a Style Based on Existing Formatting

To create a style based on existing formatting, apply the desired formatting to text in a document and then select the text. Click the More button at the right of the thumbnails in the Quick Style list in the Styles group and then click *Save Selection as a New Quick Style* at the drop-down gallery. At the Create New Style from Formatting dialog box, shown in Figure 24.3, type a name for the new style in the *Name* text box and then click OK. The style is inserted in the Quick Styles gallery and is available for the current document.

Creating a Style Based on an Existing Style

To create a style based on an existing style, apply the style to text, make the desired formatting changes, and then select the text. Click the More button at the right of the thumbnails in the Quick Style list in the Styles group and then click *Save Selection as a New Quick Style* at the drop-down gallery. At the Create New Style from Formatting dialog box, type a name for the new style in the *Name* text box and then click OK.

Figure 24.3 Create New Style from Formatting Dialog Box

Type a new name for the style in this text box.

1. Open **BTStyles.docx** and save the document with the name **C24-E02-BTStyles**.
2. Create a style based on the formatting of the *CustomTitle* text by completing the following steps:
   a. Click the Show/Hide ¶ button in the Paragraph group in the Home tab to turn on the display of nonprinting characters.
   b. Select the text *CustomTitle*. (Make sure you select the paragraph mark (¶) after *Title*.
   c. Click the More button at the right of the thumbnails in the Quick Style list in the Styles group.
   d. Click *Save Selection as a New Quick Style*.
   e. At the Create New Style from Formatting dialog box, type your initials followed by CustomTitle.
   f. Click OK.
   g. Click the Show/Hide ¶ button to turn off the display of nonprinting characters.
3. Save **C24-E02-BTStyles.docx**.

Creating a New Style

You can create a style without first applying formatting to text. To do this, click the More button at the right of the thumbnails in the Styles group and then click *Save Selection as a New Quick Style* at the drop-down gallery. At the Create New Style from Formatting dialog box, click the Modify button. This displays an expanded Create New Style from Formatting dialog box, shown in Figure 24.4. At this dialog box, type a new name for the style in the *Name* text box and then use the *Style type* option box to specify the type of style you are creating. Click the down-pointing arrow at the right of the option and a drop-down list displays with options for creating a paragraph style, a character style, a linked style (both a paragraph and character style), a table style, or a list style. Choose the option that identifies the type of style you are creating.

The *Style based on* option has a default setting of ¶ *Normal*. You can base a new style on an existing style. To do this, click the down-pointing arrow at the right of the *Style based on* option box and then click the desired style at the drop-down list. For example, you can base the new style on a predesigned style such as the Heading 1 style. Click the *Heading 1* style at the drop-down list, and the formatting settings of Heading 1 display in the Create New Style from Formatting dialog box. Apply additional formatting at the dialog box to modify the formatting of the Heading 1 style. If a predesigned style contains some of the formatting you desire for your new style, choosing the predesigned style at the *Style based on* option drop-down list saves you formatting time.

Use the *Style for following paragraph* option to tell Word what style to use for the next paragraph in the document when you press the Enter key. For example, you can create a style that formats a caption heading and have it followed by a style that applies paragraph formatting to the text that follows the caption heading (such as italic formatting or a specific font and font size). In this situation, you would create the style that applies the desired paragraph formatting to the text that follows a caption heading. You would then create the caption heading style and then use the

Create New Style
1. Click More button in Styles group.
2. Click *Save Selection as a New Quick Style*.
3. Click Modify button.
4. Type new name for style.
5. Apply desired formatting.
6. Click OK.

Figure 24.4 Expanded Create New Style from Formatting Dialog Box

Type a name for the style in this text box.

Click this button to display a list of formatting options.

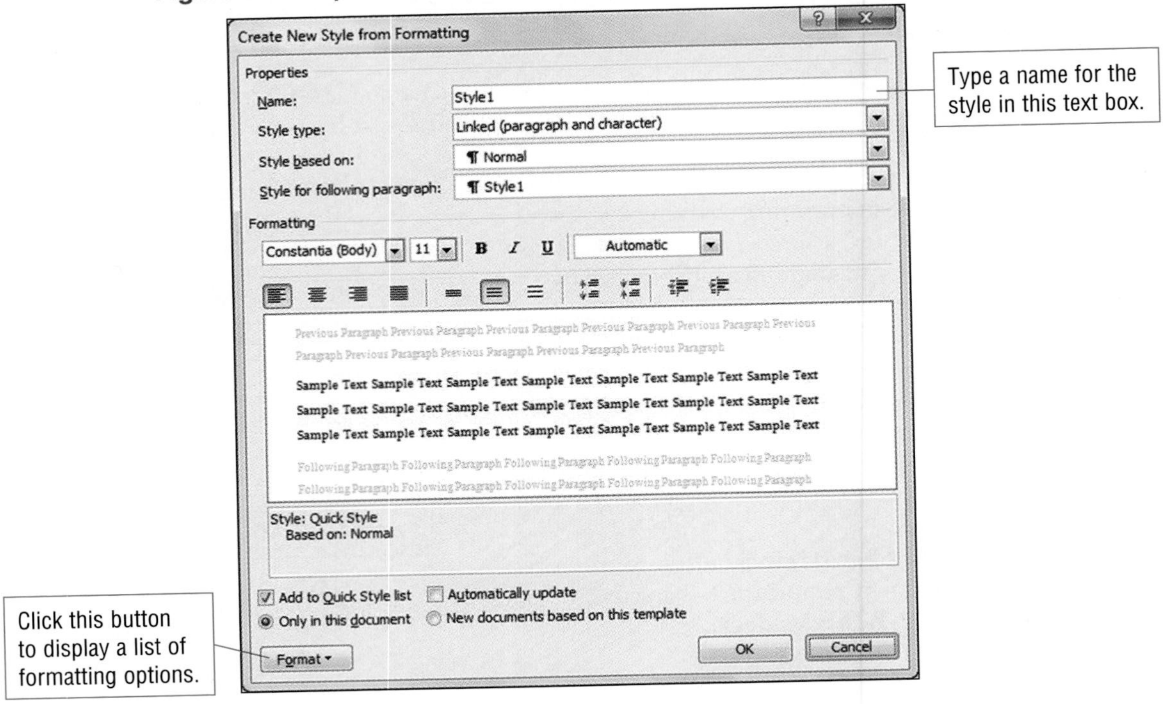

Style for following paragraph option to specify that the paragraph style you created is applied when you press the Enter key after applying the caption heading style.

The Create New Style from Formatting dialog box contains a number of options for specifying formatting for the new style. Use options in the *Formatting* section to apply character and paragraph formatting such as changing the font, font size, font color, and font effects and changing paragraph alignment, spacing, and indenting. Click the Format button that displays in the lower left corner of the dialog box and a drop-down menu displays with a number of formatting options. With options at this drop-down list, you can specify formatting for the style with options in dialog boxes such as the Font, Paragraph, Tabs, Borders, Language, and Frame dialog boxes.

Unless the Create New Style from Formatting dialog has been customized, the *Add to Quick Style list* check box located in the lower left corner of the dialog box contains a check mark. With this option active, the style you create will display in the Quick Style list, which is the list of styles available in the Styles group in the Home tab. Additionally, the *Only in this document* option is active. With this option active, the style is saved only with the current document. If you want the style available for new documents based on the Normal template (or any other template on which the current document is based), click the *New documents based on this template* option. The *Automatically update* check box is empty by default. Insert a check mark in this option if you want every change you make to text with a style applied to update that style. Keep this option inactive if you want the style's formatting to remain as you defined it. When you have made all desired formatting choices, click OK to close the dialog box.

1. With **C24-E02-BTStyles.docx** open, press Ctrl + End to move the insertion point to the end of the document.
2. Click the More button at the right of the thumbnails in the Quick Style list in the Styles group.
3. Click *Save Selection as a New Quick Style*.
4. At the Create New Style from Formatting dialog box, type your initials followed by CustomEmphasis.
5. Click the Modify button.
6. At the Create New Style from Formatting expanded dialog box, make the following changes:

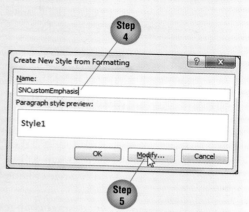

   a. Click the down-pointing arrow at the right of the Font Size button and then click *12*.
   b. Click the down-pointing arrow at the right of the Font Color button.
   c. Click the dark blue color in the *Standard Colors* section.
   d. Click the Format button located toward the bottom of the Create New Style from Formatting dialog box and then click *Font* at the drop-down list.

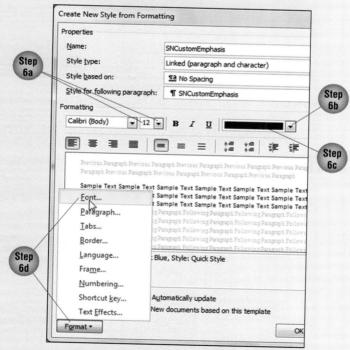

   e. At the Font dialog box, click the *Small Caps* check box to insert a check mark and then click OK to close the dialog box.
   f. Click the Format button and then click *Paragraph* at the drop-down list.
   g. At the Paragraph dialog box with the Indents and Spacing tab selected, click the up-pointing arrow at the right of the *Left* measurement box in the *Indentation* section until *0.3″* displays.

h. Select the current measurement in the *After* measurement box in the *Spacing* section and then type 3.
i. Click OK to close the Paragraph dialog box.
j. Click OK to close the Create New Style from Formatting dialog box.
7. Save **C24-E02-BTStyles.docx**.

QUICK STEPS

Modify a Style
1. Right-click desired style in Styles group or Quick Styles drop-down gallery.
2. Click *Modify*.
3. Type new name for style.
4. Make desired changes.
5. Click OK.

Modifying a Style

If a predesigned style contains most of the formatting you want, you can modify it to create a new style. To do this, right-click the style in the Styles group or the Quick Styles drop-down gallery and then click *Modify* at the shortcut menu. This displays the Modify Styles dialog box, which contains the same options that are available at the Create New Style from Formatting dialog box. Type a new name in the *Name* text box, make the desired changes, and then click OK.

Exercise 24.2C Modifying an Existing Style   Part 3 of 7

1. With **C24-E02-BTStyles.docx** open, modify the Heading 2 style by completing the following steps:
   a. Click the More button at the right of the thumbnails in the Quick Style list in the Styles group.
   b. Right-click the Heading 2 style in the Styles group and then click *Modify* at the shortcut menu.

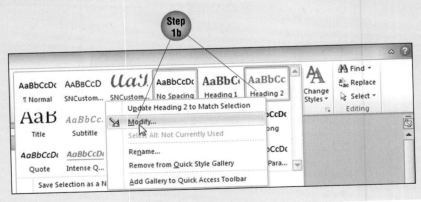

c. At the Modify Style dialog box, type your initials followed by CustomHeading in the *Name* text box.

d. Click the down-pointing arrow at the right of the Font button and then click *Candara* at the drop-down list.

e. Click the Italic button.

f. Click the down-pointing arrow at the right of the Font Color button, and then click *Dark Blue* (the second color from the right in the *Standard Colors* section).

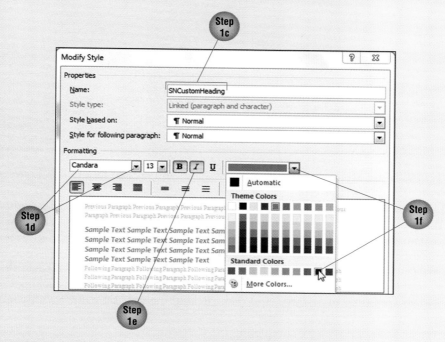

g. Click the Format button located toward the bottom of the dialog box and then click *Paragraph* at the drop-down list.

h. At the Paragraph dialog box with the Indents and Spacing tab selected, click the current measurement in the *After* measurement box in the *Spacing* section and then type 6.

i. Click OK to close the Paragraph dialog box.

j. Click the Format button located toward the bottom of the dialog box and then click *Border* at the drop-down list.

k. At the Borders and Shading dialog box, click the Shading tab.

l. Click the down-pointing arrow at the right of the *Fill* option and then click the *Blue, Accent 1, Lighter 80%* color at the drop-down list (located in the fifth column).

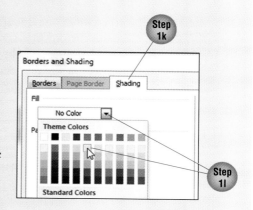

m. Click OK to close the Borders and Shading dialog box.

n. Click OK to close the Modify Style dialog box.

2. Save **C24-E02-BTStyles.docx**.

**Save a Custom
Quick Styles Set**
1. Click Change Styles
   button.
2. Point to *Style Set*.
3. Click *Save as Quick
   Style Set.*
4. Type name for
   Quick Styles set.
5. Click Save button.

Saving a Custom Quick Styles Set

If you want a style that you have created or modified available to apply in other documents, save the style as a custom Quick Styles set. To do this, click the Change Styles button, point to *Style Set*, and then click *Save as Quick Style Set*. At the Save Quick Style Set dialog box, type a name for your Quick Styles set and then click the Save button.

Exercise 24.2D **Saving a Custom Quick Styles Set and Applying** **Part 4 of 7**
Custom Styles

1. With **C24-E02-BTStyles.docx** open, save the styles you created as a Quick Styles set by completing the following steps:
   a. Click the Change Styles button, point to *Style Set*, and then click *Save as Quick Style Set*.
   b. At the Save Quick Style Set dialog box, type your first and last names and then click the Save button.
2. Save and then close **C24-E02-BTStyles.docx**.
3. Open **BTZenith.docx** and save the document with the name **C24-E02-BTZenith**.
4. Change to the Quick Styles set named with your first and last names by clicking the Change Styles button, pointing to *Style Set*, and then clicking the style set named with your first and last names.
5. Apply the custom title style by completing the following steps:
   a. Click anywhere in the text *Extreme Adventures*.
   b. Click the custom title style (style that begins with your initials followed by *Custom Title*) in the Styles group.
   c. Scroll to the end of the document, click anywhere in the text *Volunteer Adventures*, and then click the custom title style.
6. Apply the custom heading style by completing the following steps:
   a. Click anywhere in the text *Antarctic Adventures*.
   b. Click the More button at the right of the thumbnails in the Quick Style list in the Styles group.
   c. Click the custom heading style (style that begins with Heading2, followed by your initials, and then *CustomHeading*).
   d. Apply the custom heading style to the text *Tall-Ship Adventures* and *Bicycling Adventures*.
7. Apply the custom emphasis style by completing the following steps:
   a. Select the lines of text in the *Antarctic Adventures* section that contain money amounts.
   b. Click the More button at the right of the thumbnails in the Quick Style list in the Styles group and then click the custom emphasis style (style that begins with your initials followed by *CustomEmphasis*).
   c. Apply the custom emphasis style to the lines of text in the *Tall-Ship Adventures* section containing money amounts.
   d. Apply the custom emphasis style to the lines of text in the *Bicycling Adventures* section containing money amounts.
8. Save **C24-E02-BTZenith.docx**.

Modifying an Applied Style

One of the advantages of applying styles in a document is that if you modify the style formatting, all the text in the document to which that style has been applied is automatically updated. Using styles streamlines formatting and maintains consistency in your documents.

1. With **C24-E02-BTZenith.docx** open, edit the style to change the font in the custom title style by completing the following steps:
   a. Right-click the custom title style in the Quick Style list (style that begins with your initials followed by *CustomTitle*) and then click *Modify* at the shortcut menu.
   b. At the Modify Style dialog box, change the font size to *22*.
   c. Click the Align Text Left button that displays in the *Formatting* section.

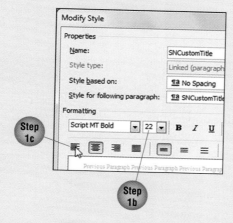

   d. Click OK to close the Modify Style dialog box.
2. Scroll through the document and notice the custom title style applied to both titles in the document.
3. Save **C24-E02-BTZenith.docx**.

Displaying All Styles

Each Quick Styles set contains a title style, body text style, a number of heading level styles, and other styles that are designed to work together in a single document. Only the styles for the currently selected Quick Styles set display in the Quick Styles drop-down gallery or the Styles task pane. You can display all styles with options at the Style Pane Options dialog box, shown in Figure 24.5. Display this dialog box by clicking the Styles group dialog box launcher and then clicking the Options hyperlink that displays in the lower right corner of the Styles task pane.

Figure 24.5 Style Pane Options Dialog Box

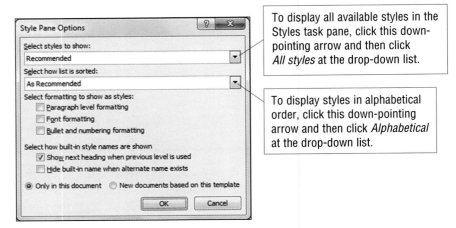

To display all available styles in the Styles task pane, click this down-pointing arrow and then click *All styles* at the drop-down list.

To display styles in alphabetical order, click this down-pointing arrow and then click *Alphabetical* at the drop-down list.

To display all styles, click the down-pointing arrow at the right of the *Select styles to show* option box and then click *All styles* at the drop-down list. Specify how you want the styles sorted in the Styles task pane with the *Select how list is sorted* option.

Exercise 24.2F Displaying and Selecting Styles

Part 6 of 7

1. With **C24-E02-BTZenith.docx** open, display all styles in the Styles task pane by completing the following steps:
   a. Click the Styles group dialog box launcher.
   b. Click the <u>Options</u> hyperlink that displays in the lower right corner of the Styles task pane.
   c. At the Style Pane Options dialog box, click the down-pointing arrow at the right of the *Select styles to show* option and then click *All styles* at the drop-down list.
   d. Click the down-pointing arrow at the right of the *Select how list is sorted* option and then click *Alphabetical* at the drop-down list.
   e. Click OK to close the dialog box.
2. Apply styles by completing the following steps:
   a. Select the lines of text in the *Antarctic Adventures* section that contain money amounts.
   b. Click the *Clear All* style that displays at the top of the task pane list box.
   c. Click the *Body Text 2* style to see how the style affects the selected text.
   d. Click the *Body Text Indent* style.
   e. Click the *Book Title* style.
   f. Apply the Body Text Indent and the Book Title styles to the other two occurrences of lines of text containing money amounts.
3. Save and then print **C24-E02-BTZenith.docx**.

Revealing Style Formatting

As you learned earlier, if you hover the mouse over a style in the Styles task pane, a ScreenTip displays with information about the formatting applied by the style. The styles in the Quick Styles gallery display with a visual representation of the formatting applied by the style. You can also display a visual representation of styles by clicking the *Show Preview* check box in the Styles task pane. Another method for displaying the formatting applied by a style is to display the Reveal Formatting task pane by pressing Shift + F1.

Deleting a Custom Quick Styles Set

If you create a custom Quick Styles set and save it in the Save Quick Style Set dialog box, the style set will be available in the Normal template, on which all documents are based. If you no longer need the custom style set, delete it. Do this by clicking the Change Styles button, pointing to *Style Set*, and then clicking *Save as Quick Style Set*. At the Save Quick Style Set dialog box, click the name of the style set you want to delete, click the Organize button on the toolbar, and then click *Delete* at the drop-down list. At the message asking if you are sure you want to send the document to the Recycle Bin, click Yes.

If you create a new Quick Styles set and then make it the default set by clicking the Change Styles button and then clicking *Set as Default*, it becomes the default for the current and all future documents you create. This is because changing the default, changes the default settings in the Normal.dotm template on which documents are based. If you click the Change Styles button, point to Style Set, and then click the *Reset to Quick Styles from Template* option, your Quick Styles set will still be in effect since that set has been identified as the default in the Normal.dotm template. If you want to return to the Word 2010 default Quick Styles set, you need to reapply the Word 2010 Quick Styles set, change the color to *Office*, change the font to *Office* and then specify these settings as the default. Another method for returning to the original Quick Styles set is to open a previous document that was created with the original Quick Styles set, clicking the Change Styles button, and then clicking *Set as Default*.

If you click the Change Styles button and then point to *Style Set*, the side menu contains another option, *Reset Document Quick Styles*. Use this option in a situation where you open a document, make changes to the Quick Styles set, decide you do not want the changes, and want to return to the original Quick Styles set applied to the document. This keeps you from having to return to the original document Quick Styles set by clicking the Undo button several times or having to apply styles in place of other styles.

QUICK STEPS

Delete Custom Quick Styles Set
1. Click Change Styles button.
2. Point to *Style Set*.
3. Click *Save as Quick Style Set*.
4. Click desired style set name.
5. Click Organize button.
6. Click *Delete*.
7. Click Yes.

Exercise 24.2G Deleting a Quick Styles Set

Part 7 of 7

1. With **C24-E02-BTZenith.docx** open, view styles in the Styles task pane by completing the following steps:
   a. With the Styles task pane open, click the *Show Preview* check box to insert a check mark.
   b. Scroll through the list box to see how styles display with the preview feature turned on.
   c. Click the *Show Preview* check box to remove the check mark.
   d. Close the Styles task pane by clicking the Close button in the upper right corner of the task pane.

2. Display style formatting in the Reveal Formatting task pane by completing the following steps:

   a. Press Shift + F1 to turn on the display of the Reveal Formatting task pane.

   b. Click the *Distinguish style source* check box to insert a check mark.

   c. Click anywhere in the title *Extreme Adventures* and notice in the Reveal Formatting task pane the formatting applied by the style.

   d. Click anywhere in the heading *Antarctic Adventures* and notice in the Reveal Formatting task pane the formatting applied by the style.

   e. Click other text in the document and view the formatting.

   f. Click the *Distinguish style source* check box to remove the check mark.

   g. Press Shift + F1 to turn off the display of the Reveal Formatting task pane.

3. Save and then close **C24-E02-BTZenith.docx**.

4. Delete the custom Quick Styles set you created by completing the following steps:

   a. At a blank document, click the Change Styles button, point to *Style Set*, and then click *Save as Quick Style Set*.

   b. At the Save Quick Style Set dialog box, click the style set named with your first and last names.

   c. Click the Organize button on the toolbar and then click *Delete* at the drop-down list.

   d. At the message asking if you are sure you want to send the document to the Recycle Bin, click Yes.

   e. Click the Cancel button to close the Save Quick Style Set dialog box.

5. Close the document without saving it.

6. Change to the original default Quick Styles set, colors, fonts, and paragraph spacing by completing the following steps:

   a. Open **KMReport.docx**. (This document was created with the original Quick Styles set.)

   b. Click the Change Styles button and then click *Set as Default* at the drop-down list.

7. Close **KMReport.docx** without saving it.

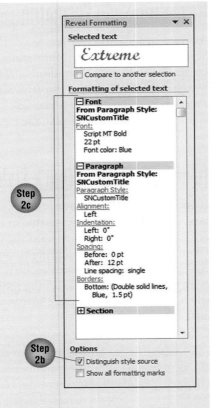

Creating Multilevel List and Table Styles

In this chapter, you have learned how to create styles that are available in the Styles group in the Home tab and also how to save styles in a custom Quick Styles set. You can save character and paragraph styles in the Styles group as well as a custom Quick Styles set but not list styles and table styles. You can save list styles and table styles in the current document or in a template document.

In a home or business setting, you may want to create multilevel list styles and table styles and save them in the Normal.dotm template (this is the template on which all documents are based unless you select a different template). Or, you might want to create a new template in the default Templates folder and then save multilevel list and table styles in the template. However, in a school or other public environment, you may not be able to save styles to the Normal.dotm template. Or, if you save styles to the

Normal.dotm template, those styles may be deleted if the computers at your school (or other public facility) are reset on a regular basis. Resetting computers would also delete any templates you create in the default Templates folder.

In this chapter, you will be instructed to create a new template document and save the template to your storage medium. You will then create and save a multilevel list style and a table style in the template and then use that template as a basis for future documents. Save a document as a template by displaying the Save As dialog box, changing the *Save as type* option to *Word Template (*.dotx)*, and then typing a name for the template. You can also save a document as a template by displaying the Save & Send tab Backstage view, clicking the Change File Type option in the File Types section, clicking the *Template. (*.dotx)* option, and then clicking the Save As button. Type a name for the template at the Save As dialog box and then press Enter. You want to save the document as a template so that you do not overwrite or change the template and you want to use the template as a basis for creating future documents.

To use the template, display the New tab Backstage view, and then click the New from existing button in the Available Templates section. At the New from Existing Document dialog box, navigate to the desired folder and then double-click the template.

Creating a Multilevel List Style

Word contains a number of predesigned list styles that you can apply to text in a document. These styles are generally paragraph styles that apply formatting to text such as paragraph indenting and spacing. These list styles apply formatting to one level of the list only. If you want to create a multilevel list style that applies formatting to more than one level of a list, create the style at the Define New List Style dialog box shown in Figure 24.6. Display this dialog box by clicking the Multilevel List button in the Paragraph group in the Home tab and then clicking *Define New List Style* at the drop-down list. You can also create a multilevel list style at the Create New Style from Formatting dialog box by changing the *Style type* to *List*.

Figure 24.6 Define New List Style Dialog Box

Use options in this section to format the list level.

Preview the list-level formatting in this preview section.

This section displays the applied formatting.

Click this button to display a drop-down list of formatting options.

Click this down-pointing arrow and then choose the list level you want to format.

Click this option if you want to save the style in the template attached to the document.

The Define New List Style dialog box (and the Create New Style from Formatting dialog box with *List* selected in the *Style type* option) contains the same options as the Create New Style from Formatting dialog box with *Paragraph*, *Character*, or *Linked (paragraph and character)* selected along with some additional options such as the *Start at* and the *Apply formatting to* option. By default, the *Apply formatting to* option is set at *1st level*. With this option selected, apply the desired formatting for the letter, number, or symbol that begins the first level of your list. (The formatting you apply affects the letter, number, or symbol only—not the following text.)

After specifying formatting for the first level, click the down-pointing arrow at the right of the *Apply formatting to* option box, click *2nd level*, and then apply the desired formatting for the second level. Continue in this manner until you have specified formatting for the desired number of levels.

Updating a Template in an Existing Document

If you open a document based on a template and then create a style, you can specify that you want the style saved in the template and available for any future documents created with the template. This is because a document based on a template is attached to the template. To save a style in a template, open a document based on the template, create a style, and then click the *New documents based on this template* option at the Create New Style dialog box. When you save the document, a message displays asking if you want to update the attached document template. At this message, click Yes.

Exercise 24.3A **Saving a Document as a Template and Creating and** **Part 1 of 6**
Applying a Multilevel List Style

1. Open **BTListTableTemplate.docx** and then save it as a template by completing the following steps:
   a. Click the File tab and then click Save As.
   b. At the Save As dialog box, click the *Save as type* option box and then click *Word Template (*.dotx)* at the drop-down list.
   c. Click in the *File name* text box, type C24-BTListTableTemplate and then press the Enter key.
   d. Close **C24-BTListTableTemplate.dotx**.
2. Open a document based on the template by completing the following steps:
   a. Click the File tab and then click the New tab.
   b. At the New tab Backstage view, click the New from existing button in the *Available Templates* section.

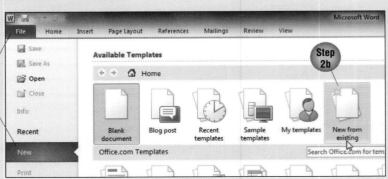

---

c. At the New from Existing Document dialog box, navigate to the Chapter24 folder on your storage medium and then double-click ***C24-BTListTableTemplate.dotx***.

3. At the blank document based on the C24-BTListTableTemplate.dotx template, create a multilevel list style by completing the following steps:

a. Press Ctrl + End and then click the Multilevel List button in the Paragraph group in the Home tab.

b. Click the *Define New List Style* option that displays at the bottom of the drop-down list.

c. At the Define New List Style dialog box, type your initials and then type MultilevelList in the *Name* text box.

d. Click the down-pointing arrow at the right of the option box containing the text *1, 2, 3, …* and then click *A, B, C, …* at the drop-down list.

e. Click the down-pointing arrow at the right of the Font Color button and then click *Orange, Accent 6, Darker 25%* (last column).

Step 3c

Define New List Style ? X

Properties

Name: SNMultilevelList

Style type: List

Formatting

Start at: 1

Apply formatting to: 1st level

Step 3f

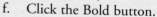
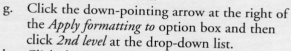

B *I* U

A, B, C, ... Ω

A)

Step 3d **Step 3e**

f. Click the Bold button.

g. Click the down-pointing arrow at the right of the *Apply formatting to* option box and then click *2nd level* at the drop-down list.

h. Click the Symbol button that displays below the Font Color button.

i. At the Symbol dialog box, change the font to Wingdings, scroll to the end of the list box, click the sun symbol (✹), which is located in approximately the fifth row from the bottom of the list box, and then click OK. (At the Define New List Style dialog box, make sure the font color is black. If not, click the Font Color button arrow and then click the Automatic color option at the top of the color palette.)

j. At the Define New List Style dialog box, click the Bold button.

k. Click the down-pointing arrow at the right of the *Apply formatting to* option box and then click *3rd level* at the drop-down list.

l. Click the Symbol button.

m. At the Symbol dialog box, make sure Wingdings is selected as the font, scroll to the end of the list box, click the check mark symbol (✓), which is located in approximately the last row, and then click OK.

n. At the Define New List Style dialog box, click the Bold button.

o. Click the *New documents based on the template* option located toward the bottom of the dialog box.

p. Click OK to close the Define New List Style dialog box.

4. Close the document without saving it. At the message that displays asking if you want to update the attached document template, click Yes.

5. Open a document based on the template by completing the following steps:

a. Click the File tab and then click the New tab.

b. At the New tab Backstage view, click the New from existing button in the *Available Templates* section.

c. At the New from Existing Document dialog box, navigate to the Chapter24 folder on your storage medium and then double-click ***C24-BTListTableTemplate.dotx***.

6. Insert a document into the current document by completing the following steps:
   a. Press Ctrl + End and then click the Insert tab.
   b. Click the Object button arrow and then click *Text from File* at the drop-down list.
   c. Navigate to the Chapter24 folder on your storage medium and then double-click **BTTourList.docx**.
7. Apply the multilevel style you created by completing the following steps:
   a. Select the text you just inserted.
   b. Click the Home tab and then click the Multilevel List button in the Paragraph group.
   c. Scroll down the drop-down list and then click the multilevel list style you created (located in the *List Styles* section). (Hover your mouse over the multilevel list and a ScreenTip will display with the style name.) 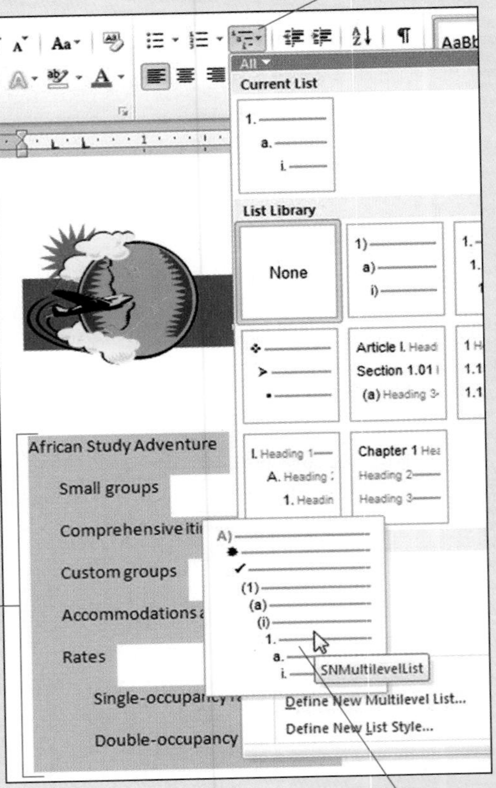
8. Add the text shown in Figure 24.7 to the document by completing the following steps:
   a. Move the insertion point so it is positioned immediately right of the text *Double-occupancy rate: $2,755* and then press the Enter key. (This moves the insertion point down to the next line and inserts a check mark bullet.)
   b. Press Shift + Tab twice to move the insertion point to the left margin. (This inserts *B)* in the document.)
   c. Type the text shown in Figure 24.7. (When typing the text, press the Tab key to move the insertion point to the next level or press Shift + Tab to move the insertion point to the previous level.)
9. Click the Change Styles button in the Styles group in the Home tab, point to *Paragraph Spacing*, and then click *Double* at the side menu.
10. Save, print, and then close **C24-E03-BTTours.docx**.

Figure 24.7 Exercise 24.3A

Southwest Sun Adventure

   Small groups

   Guided day trips

   Grand Canyon vistas

   Bilingual tour guides

   Rates

      Single-occupancy rate: $1,450

      Double-occupancy rate: $1,249

Creating a Table Style

The Table Tools Design tab contains a number of predesigned styles you can apply to a table. If none of these styles applies the desired formatting to a table, create your own table style. You can create a table style at the Create New Style from Formatting dialog box with *Table* selected in the *Style type* option box as shown in Figure 24.8. You can display this dialog box by clicking the More button at the right of the thumbnails in the Quick Style list in the Styles group in the Home tab and then clicking *Save Selection as a New Quick Style*. At the Create New Style from Formatting dialog box, click the Modify button. Click the down-pointing arrow at the right of the *Style type* option and then click *Table* at the drop-down list. You can also display this dialog box by inserting a table in the document, clicking the More button that displays at the right of the thumbnails in the Table Styles group in the Table Tools Design tab, and then clicking *New Table Style* at the drop-down list.

The Create New Style from Formatting dialog box with *Table* selected as the style type contains options for formatting the entire table or specific portions of a table. By default *Whole table* is selected in the *Apply formatting to* option. With this option selected, any formatting options you choose will affect the entire table. To format a specific portion of the table, click the down-pointing arrow at the right of the *Apply formatting to* option and then click the desired option at the drop-down list. With options at this drop-down list, you can specify that you want to apply formatting to sections in the table such as the header row, total row, first column, last column, odd banded rows, even banded rows, and so on.

Figure 24.8 Create New Style from Formatting Dialog Box with the Table Style Type Selected

Use options in this section to format the whole table or specific portions of the table.

Click this down-pointing arrow and then choose the portion of the table you want to format.

Preview the table formatting in this preview section.

This section displays the applied formatting.

Click this button to display a drop-down list of formatting options.

1. Open **C24-BTListTableTemplate.dotx**. (Open the template as a normal document at the Open dialog box [not through the New tab Backstage view].)
2. Create a table style by completing the following steps:
   a. Click the More button at the right of the thumbnails in the Quick Style list in the Styles group in the Home tab and then click *Save Selection as a New Quick Style* at the drop-down list.
   b. At the Create New Style from Formatting dialog box, type your initials in the *Name* text box and then type BTTable.
   c. Click the Modify button.
   d. At the Create New Style from Formatting dialog box, click the down-pointing arrow at the right of the *Style type* option box and then click *Table* at the drop-down list.
   e. Make sure *Whole Table* is selected in the *Apply formatting to* option.
   f. Click the down-pointing arrow at the right of the Font option and then click *Constantia* at the drop-down list.
   g. Click the down-pointing arrow at the right of the Font Size option and then click *12* at the drop-down list.
   h. Click the down-pointing arrow at the right of the Font Color option and then click the Dark Blue color in the *Standard Colors* section.
   i. Click the Border button arrow and then click *All Borders* at the drop-down list. (See image below to locate the button.)
   j. Click the down-pointing arrow at the right of the Border Color option and then click the blue color in the *Standard Colors* section.

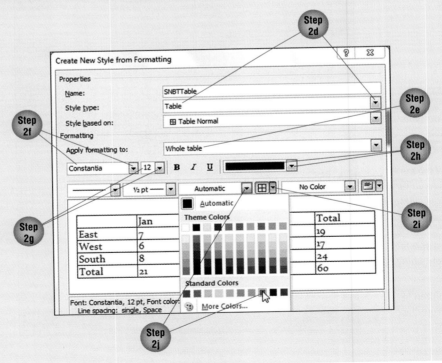

k. Click the down-pointing arrow at the right of the *Apply formatting to* option and then click *Header row* at the drop-down list.

l. Click the down-pointing arrow at the right of the Font Size option and then click *14* at the drop-down list.

m. Click the Bold button.

n. Click the down-pointing arrow at the right of the Fill Color option and then click *Orange, Accent 6, Lighter 40%* (located in the last column).

o. Click the Alignment button arrow located immediately right of the Fill Color option and then click *Align Center* at the drop-down list.

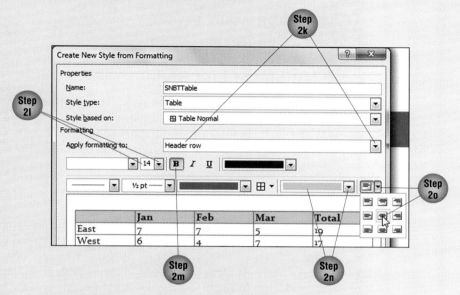

p. Click the down-pointing arrow at the right of the *Apply formatting to* option and then click *Even banded rows* at the drop-down list.

q. Click the Fill Color option and then click *Orange, Accent 6, Lighter 60%* (last column).

r. Click OK to close the Create New Style from Formatting dialog box.

3. At the template, click the Save button on the Quick Access toolbar and then close the template.

4. Open a document based on the template by completing the following steps:
   a. Click the File tab and then click the New tab.
   b. At the New tab Backstage view, click the New from existing button in the *Available Templates* section.
   c. At the New from Existing Document dialog box, navigate to the Chapter24 folder on your storage medium and then double-click *C24-BTListTableTemplate.dotx*.
   d. Save the document with Save As and name it **C24-E03-BTTables**.

5. Insert a document into the current document by completing the following steps:
   a. Press Ctrl + End and then press the Enter key three times.
   b. Click the Insert tab.
   c. Click the Object button arrow and then click *Text from File* at the drop-down list.
   d. Navigate to the Chapter24 folder on your storage medium and then double-click **BTAdvTables.docx**.

6. Apply the table style you created by completing the following steps:
   a. Click in any cell in the top table.
   b. Click the Table Tools Design tab.

c. In the Table Styles group, click the table style you created. (Your table style should be the first thumbnail in the group. If it is not, click the More button at the right of the thumbnails and then click your table style at the drop-down gallery. To find your table style, hover the mouse pointer over a table and wait for the ScreenTip to display the style name.)

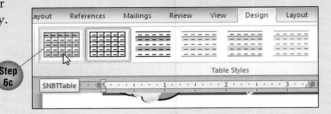

7. Apply your table style to the two other tables in the document.
8. Save, print, and then close **C24-E03-BTTables.docx**.

Modifying a Multilevel List Style

Like other styles, you can modify a multilevel list style. To do this, click the Multilevel List button, scroll down the drop-down list to display the style you want to modify, right-click the style, and then click *Modify* at the shortcut menu. This displays the Modify Style dialog box that contains the same formatting options as the Create New Style from Formatting dialog box.

Modifying a Table Style

You can modify a table style that you created or modify one of the predesigned table styles. To modify a table style, open the document containing the desired table style you want to modify. Click in a table with the table style applied or insert a new table in the document. Click the Table Tools Design tab, right-click the table style, and then click *Modify Table Style* at the shortcut menu. (If the desired table style is not visible, click the More button that displays at the right of the table styles.) This displays the Modify Style dialog box that contains the same formatting options as the Create New Style from Formatting dialog box.

Exercise 24.3C Modifying a Table Style   Part 3 of 6

1. Open **C24-E03-BTTables.docx** and then save the document with the name **C24-E03-BTTablesModified**.
2. Modify the table style you created by completing the following steps:
   a. Click in any cell in the top table.
   b. Click the Table Tools Design tab.
   c. Your table style should be the first thumbnail in the Table Styles group. (If your table style is not visible, click the More button at the right of the thumbnails and then locate your table style.)
   d. Right-click your table style and then click *Modify Table Style* at the shortcut menu.

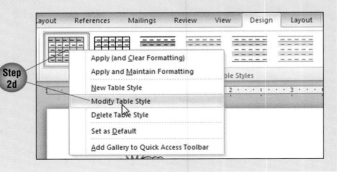

e. At the Modify Style dialog box, click the Format button that displays in the lower left corner of the dialog box and then click *Table Properties* at the drop-down list.

f. At the Table Properties dialog box with the Table tab selected, click the *Center* option in the *Alignment* section.

g. Click OK to close the Table Properties dialog box.

h. Click the down-pointing arrow at the right of the *Apply formatting to* option and then click *Odd banded rows* at the drop-down list.

i. Click the Fill Color option and then click *Dark Blue, Text 2, Lighter 80%* (in the fourth column).

j. Click OK to close the Modify Style dialog box. (Notice that the formatting changes for the three tables in the document because each table has the table style applied.)

3. Select the second row in the top table in the document, press Ctrl + B to turn on bold and then press Ctrl + E to center text in the cells.

4. Apply bold and center formatting to the second row in the middle table and the second row in the bottom table.

5. Save, print, and then close **C24-E03-BTTablesModified.docx**.

Using the Style Inspector

As you continue working with styles and creating and applying styles to documents, situations may arise where you have multiple styles applied to text. If multiple styles are applied to text and the formatting applied is not what you intended, you can investigate the document styles using the Style Inspector. Turn on the Style Inspector by clicking the Styles group dialog box launcher to display the Styles task pane and then clicking the Style Inspector button that displays at the bottom of the task pane. The Style Inspector displays paragraph and text-level formatting for the paragraph where the insertion point is positioned. Figure 24.9 displays the Style Inspector with the insertion point positioned in the title in the **C24-E03-BTZenith.docx** document.

Figure 24.9 Style Inspector

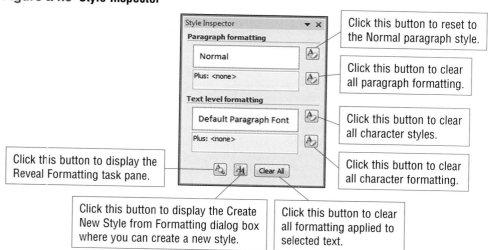

The *Paragraph formatting* option box and the *Text level formatting* option box display style formatting applied to the selected text or the character where the insertion point is positioned. A box displays below each option that contains the word *Plus:* followed by any additional formatting that is not specific to the style formatting.

Hover the mouse over the *Paragraph formatting* option box or the *Text level formatting* option box and a down-pointing arrow displays. Click the arrow and a drop-down list displays with options for clearing formatting applied to the text, applying a new style, and displaying the Reveal Formatting task pane. Click the New Style button that displays to the right of the Reveal Formatting button and the Create New Style from Formatting dialog box displays.

Use the buttons that display at the right of the *Paragraph formatting* option box to return the paragraph style back to the Normal style and clear any paragraph formatting applied to the text. With the buttons at the right of the *Text level formatting* option box you can clear character formatting applied to text.

Exercise 24.3D Using the Style Inspector

1. Open **C24-E02-BTZenith.docx** and then save the document with the name **C24-E03-BTZenith**.
2. Click anywhere in the title *Extreme Adventures*.
3. Click the Styles group dialog box launcher. (This displays the Styles task pane.)
4. Turn on the Style Inspector by clicking the Style Inspector button that displays at the bottom of the Styles task pane.
5. At the Style Inspector, hover the mouse pointer over the *Paragraph formatting* option box and then look at the information about your custom title style that displays in the ScreenTip.
6. Click anywhere in the heading *Antarctic Adventures*.
7. Hover the mouse pointer over the *Paragraph formatting* option and then look at the information that displays about the custom heading.
8. Remove paragraph and character styles, and apply a style to text in the document by completing the following steps:
   a. Select the lines of text in the *Antarctic Adventures* section that contain money amounts.
   b. Remove the paragraph style from the text by clicking the Reset to Normal Paragraph Style button that displays at the right of the *Paragraph formatting* option box.
   c. Remove the character style from the text by clicking the Clear Character Style button that displays at the right of the *Text level formatting* option box.

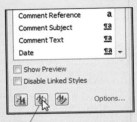

Step 4

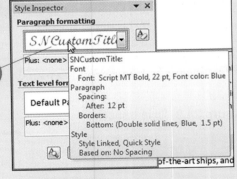

Step 5

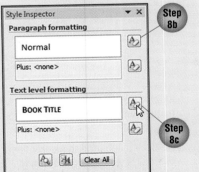

Step 8b

Step 8c

d.   Click the *Block Text* style that displays in the Styles task pane.
9.   Select the lines of text in the *Tall-Ship Adventures* section that contain money amounts and then complete steps 8b through 8d to remove styles and apply a style.
10. Select the lines of text in the *Bicycling Adventures* section that contain money amounts and then complete steps 8b through 8d to remove styles and apply a style.
11. Close the Style Inspector by clicking the Close button that displays in the upper right corner of the Style Inspector.
12. Save **C24-E03-BTZenith.docx**.

Managing Styles

The Manage Styles dialog box provides one location for managing your styles. Display this dialog box, shown in Figure 24.10 by clicking the Manage Styles button that displays at the bottom of the Styles task pane. You can also display the Manage Styles dialog box by clicking the Change Styles button in the Styles group in the Home tab, pointing to *Paragraph Spacing*, and then clicking *Custom Paragraph Spacing* at the side menu.

Figure 24.10 Manage Styles Dialog Box

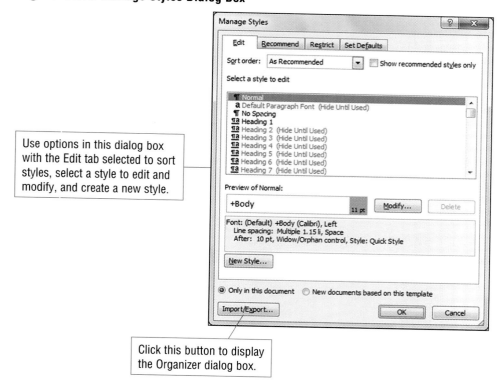

Use options in this dialog box with the Edit tab selected to sort styles, select a style to edit and modify, and create a new style.

Click this button to display the Organizer dialog box.

Use options in the Manage Styles dialog box with the Edit tab selected to sort styles, select a style to edit and modify, and create a new style.

Click the Recommend tab, and options display for specifying which styles you want to display in the Styles pane and in what order. With the Recommend tab selected, styles display in the list box preceded by a priority number. Styles display in ascending order with the styles preceded by the lowest numbers displaying first. You can change the priority of a style by clicking the style in the list box and then clicking the Move Up button, Move Down button, Move Last button, or assign a value number with the Assign Value button.

With the Restrict tab selected, you can permit or restrict access to styles. This allows you to control which styles a person can apply or modify in a document.

Click the Set Defaults tab to display character and formatting options. You can specify whether changes made in this dialog box will affect the current document or documents based on the current document. If you are using the default document, changes will affect the Normal.dotm template.

Exercise 24.3E Managing Styles

Part 5 of 6

1. With **C24-E03-BTZenith.docx** open, make sure the Styles task pane displays. (If not, click the Styles group dialog box launcher.)
2. Click anywhere in the first paragraph of text. (Do not click a title or heading.)
3. Click the Manage Styles button that displays at the bottom of the Styles task pane.
4. At the Manage Styles dialog box, make sure the Edit tab is active. (If not, click the Edit tab.)
5. Click the *Show recommended styles only* check box to insert a check mark. (This causes only the styles recommended by Word [along with your custom styles] to display in the *Select a style to edit* list box.)
6. Make sure *As Recommended* is selected in the *Sort order* option box. If it is not, click the down-pointing arrow at the right of the *Sort order* option box and then click *As Recommended* at the drop-down list.
7. Create a new style by completing the following steps:
   a. Click the New Style button that displays toward the lower left corner of the dialog box.

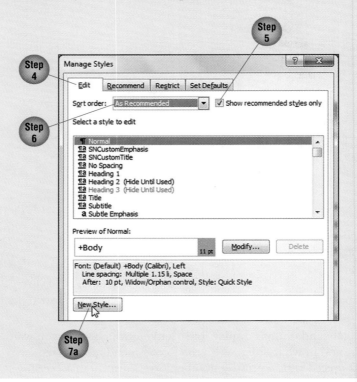

b. At the Create New Style from Formatting dialog box, type your initials in the *Name* text box followed by CoNameEmphasis.

c. Click the down-pointing arrow at the right of the *Style type* list box and then click *Character* at the drop-down list.

d. Click the Bold button in the *Formatting* section of the dialog box.

e. Click the Italic button.

f. Click the down-pointing arrow at the right of the Font Color button and then click the dark blue color in the *Standard Colors* section.

g. Click the *Add to Quick Style list* check box located toward the lower left corner of the dialog box to insert a check mark. (Skip this step if the check box already contains a check mark.)

h. Click OK to close the Create New Style from Formatting dialog box.

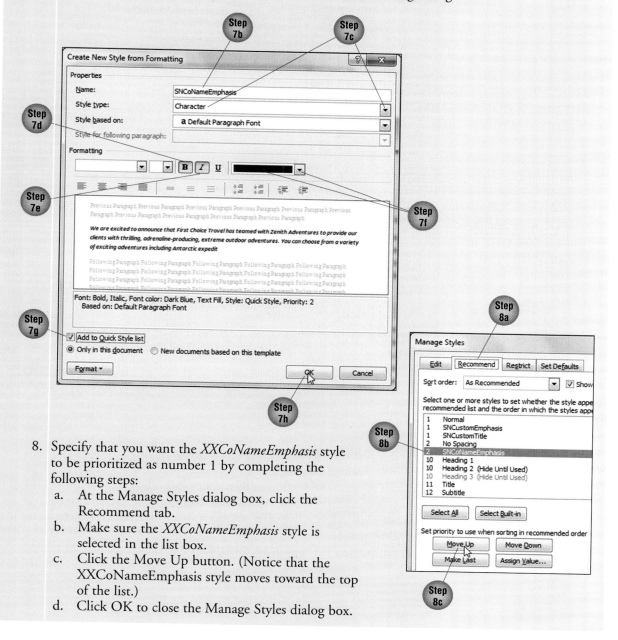

8. Specify that you want the *XXCoNameEmphasis* style to be prioritized as number 1 by completing the following steps:

a. At the Manage Styles dialog box, click the Recommend tab.

b. Make sure the *XXCoNameEmphasis* style is selected in the list box.

c. Click the Move Up button. (Notice that the XXCoNameEmphasis style moves toward the top of the list.)

d. Click OK to close the Manage Styles dialog box.

9. Select the company name *First Choice Travel* in the first paragraph in the document and then apply the *XXCoNameEmphasis* style (where *XX* represents your initials).
10. Select the company name *Zenith Adventures* and then apply the *XXCoNameEmphasis* style.
11. Apply the XXCoNameEmphasis style to the company name *Zenith Adventures* and also *First Choice Travel* located in the last paragraph in the document.
12. Save and then print **C24-E03-BTZenith.docx**.

If you create a style (or styles) for a specific document and then decide that you want to copy the style to the default template, Normal.dotm, copy the style to the template using the Organizer dialog box with the Styles tab selected as shown in Figure 24.11. Display this dialog box by clicking the Import/Export button at the Manage Styles dialog box.

Figure 24.11 Organizer Dialog Box

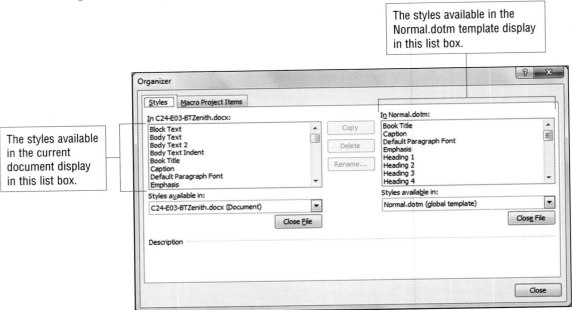

The styles available in the Normal.dotm template display in this list box.

The styles available in the current document display in this list box.

At the Organizer dialog box with the Styles tab selected, you can copy a style to a template, copy a style from a template into a document, and delete and rename styles. To copy a style from the current document into a template, click the style in the list box at the left and then click the Copy button that displays between the two list boxes. Complete similar steps to delete a style. To rename a style, click the desired style in the list box and then click the Rename button that displays between the two list boxes. At the Rename dialog box, type the new name and then press the Enter key.

1. When you created the custom heading style in Exercise 24.2C, you modified the default Heading 2 style. If you copied your custom heading style to the Normal.dotm template, it will overwrite the original Heading 2 style. You do not want to overwrite the original style so you will create a new custom heading style by completing the following steps:

   a. With **C24-E03-BTZenith.docx** open, click anywhere in the heading *Antarctic Adventures*.

   b. Click the More button at the right of the thumbnails in the Quick Style list in the Styles group in the Home tab and then click *Save Selection as a New Quick Style*.

   c. At the Create New Style from Formatting dialog box, type your initials followed by *NewCustomHeading*.

   d. Click OK to close the dialog box.

2. You have created styles for Bayside Travel that are located in a template document and other documents. You decide to consolidate them and save them to the Normal.dotm template so you can use them in other documents by completing the following steps:

   a. Make sure the Styles task pane displays.

   b. Click the Manage Styles button located at the bottom of the Styles task pane.

   c. At the Manage Styles dialog box, click the Import/Export button located in the lower left corner of the dialog box.

   d. At the Organizer dialog box, click the style named *XXCoNameEmphasis* (where the XX represents your initials) in the list box at the left and then click the Copy button that displays between the two list boxes.

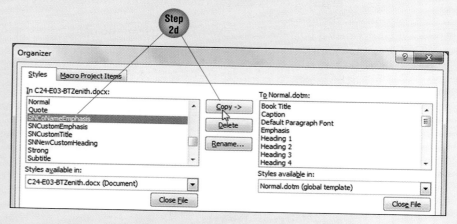

   e. Click the *XXCustomTitle* style (where *XX* represents your initials) in the list box at the left and then click the Copy button.

   f. Click the *XXNewCustomHeading* style (where *XX* represents your initials) in the list box at the left and then click the Copy button.

   g. Click the Close button to close the Organizer dialog box.

   h. Save and then close **C24-E03-BTZenith.docx**.

   i. Open **C24-E03-BTTablesModified.docx**.

   j. Make sure the Styles task pane is visible and then click the Manage Styles button that displays at the bottom of the task pane.

   k. At the Manage Styles dialog box, click the Import/Export button.

l.   At the Organizer dialog box, click the *XXBTTable* style (where *XX* represents your initials) in the list box at the left and then click the Copy button.

m.   Click the Close button to close the Organizer dialog box.

n.   Close **C24-E03-BTTablesModified.docx**.

o.   Close the Styles task pane.

3.   Press Ctrl + N to display a blank document.

4.   Click the Insert tab, click the Object button arrow, and then click *Text from File* at the drop-down list.

5.   At the Insert File dialog box, navigate to the Chapter24 folder on your storage medium and then double-click **BTEastAdventures.docx**. (The styles you copied to the Normal.dotm template are available for future documents you create, not existing documents. You inserted the existing document, **BTEastAdventures.docx**, into a new blank document to make available the styles you copied to the Normal.dotm template.)

6.   Save the new document and name it **C24-E03-BTEastAdventures**.

7.   Apply the following styles to the document (where the *XX* represents your initials):

a.   Apply the XXCustomTitle style to the title *Eastern Adventures*.

b.   Apply the XXNewCustomHeading style to the two headings in the document.

c.   Apply the XXCoNameEmphasis style to *Bayside Travel* and *Lifetime Tours* in the first paragraph in the document.

d.   Apply the XXBTTables style to the two tables in the document.

8.   Save, print, and then close **C24-E03-BTEastAdventures.docx**.

9.   Display a blank document and then delete your styles from the Normal.dotm template by completing the following steps:

a.   Click the Styles group dialog box launcher.

b.   Click the Manage Styles button located at the bottom of the Styles task pane.

c.   At the Manage Styles dialog box, click the Import/Export button that displays in the lower left corner of the dialog box.

d.   At the Organizer dialog box, click the *XXBTTable* style in the right list box and then click the Delete button that displays between the list boxes.

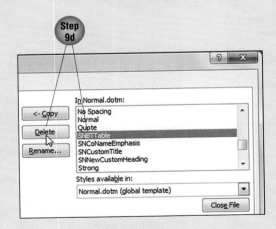

e.   At the message asking if you want to delete the style, click Yes.

f.   Complete steps similar to those in Steps 9d and 9e to delete the XXCoNameEmphasis style, the XXCustomTitle style, and the XXNewCustomHeading style.

g.   Click the Close button to close the Organizer dialog box.

10.   Close the Styles task pane and then close the blank document without saving it.

Chapter Summary

➤ Styles within the currently selected Quick Styles set are available in the Styles group in the Home tab.

➤ To change the Quick Styles set, click the Change Styles button in the Styles group in the Home tab, point to *Style Set*, and then click the desired style set at the drop-down gallery.

➤ You can change the colors, fonts, and paragraph spacing applied by styles in a style set.

➤ *Word 2010* is the default Quick Styles set. To change this default, change to the Quick Styles set you want as the default, click the Change Styles button again, and then click *Set as Default*.

➤ Apply styles in four ways: click the style thumbnail in the Quick Style list in the Styles group, click the More button at the right of the thumbnails in the Quick Style list in the Styles group and then click the style at the drop-down gallery, use options at the Styles task pane, or use options at the Apply Styles window.

➤ Click the Styles group dialog box launcher to display the Styles task pane.

➤ Display the Apply Styles window by clicking the More button at the right of the thumbnails in the Quick Style list in the Styles group and then clicking *Apply Style* at the drop-down gallery.

➤ You can create a style based on existing formatting or on style formatting or by modifying an existing style. You can also create a new style without first applying formatting to text.

➤ Create a style at the Create New Style from Formatting dialog box. Display this dialog box by clicking the More button at the right of the thumbnails in the Quick Style list in the Styles group in the Home tab, and then clicking *Save Selection as a New Quick Style* at the drop-down gallery.

➤ Use options at the expanded Create New Style from Formatting dialog box to name the style and specify the style type and style formatting.

➤ Save styles you create as a custom Quick Styles set with options at the Save Quick Style Set dialog box.

➤ An advantage of applying styles is that when you modify a style, all text in the document to which that style has been applied is automatically updated.

➤ Display all available styles in the Styles task pane by changing the *Select styles to show* option at the Style Pane Options dialog box to *All styles*.

➤ Reveal style formatting by hovering the mouse over a style in the Styles task pane, clicking the *Show Preview* check box in the Styles task pane, or by turning on the display of the Reveal Formatting task pane.

➤ Delete a custom Quick Styles set at the Save Quick Style Set dialog box.

➤ Create a multilevel list style at the Define New List Style dialog box. Display this dialog box by clicking the Multilevel List button in the Paragraph group in the Home tab and then clicking *Define New Style List*.

➤ You can also create a multilevel list style at the Create New Style from Formatting dialog box with the *Style type* option changed to *List*. Specify formatting for each desired level in the list.

➤ A multilevel list style displays in the *List Styles* section of the Multilevel List button drop-down list.

➤ Create a table style at the Create New Style from Formatting dialog box with *Table* selected in the *Style type* option box. Specify formatting for the entire table as well as specific portions of the table.

➤ A table style you create displays in the Table Styles group in the Table Tools Design tab.

➤ Modify a multilevel list style by clicking the Multilevel List button, right-clicking the desired style, and then clicking *Modify* at the shortcut menu. This displays the Modify Style dialog box where you can specify the desired changes.

- Modify a table style by clicking in a table, clicking the Table Tools Design tab, right-clicking the desired table style, and then clicking *Modify Table Style* at the shortcut menu. This displays the Modify Style dialog box where you specify the desired changes.
- Use the Style Inspector to investigate the styles applied to text in a document. Display the Style Inspector by displaying the Styles task pane and then clicking the Style Inspector button that displays at the bottom of the task pane.
- The Manage Styles dialog box provides one location for managing styles. Display the dialog box by clicking the Manage Styles button that displays at the bottom of the Styles task pane.
- If you create styles for a specific document and then decide to make the styles available for all future documents, copy the styles to the Normal.dotm template at the Organizer dialog box. Display this dialog box by clicking the Import/Export button that displays in the bottom left corner of the Manage Styles dialog box. You can also delete and rename styles at the Organizer dialog box.

Commands *Review*

FEATURE	RIBBON TAB, GROUP	BUTTON, OPTION	KEYBOARD SHORTCUT
Styles task pane	Home, Styles	▣	Alt + Ctrl + Shift + S
Apply Styles window	Home, Styles	▾, Apply Styles	Ctrl + Shift + S
Create New Style from Formatting dialog box	Home, Styles	▾, Save Selection as a New Quick Style	
Styles Pane Options dialog box	Home, Styles	▣, Options	
Reveal Formatting task pane			Shift + F1
Style Inspector	Home, Styles	▣, ⊞	
Manage Styles dialog box	Home, Styles	▣, ⊞	
Organizer dialog box	Home, Styles	▣, ⊞, Import/Export...	

Key Points *Review*

Completion: In the space provided at the right, indicate the correct term, symbol, or command.

1. This is the name of the default Quick Styles set.

2. To view available Quick Styles sets, click the Change Styles button and then point to this option.

3. To set a Quick Styles set as the default, change to the desired Quick Styles set, make any desired changes, click the Change Styles button, and then click this option.

4. Click this button to display the Styles task pane.

5. If you hover the mouse pointer over a style in the Styles task pane, this displays with information about the formatting applied.

6. To create a style based on text with existing formatting, select the text, click the More button, and then click this option at the drop-down gallery.

7. To modify an existing style, do this to the style in the Styles group and then click *Modify* at the shortcut menu.

8. Display all styles in the Styles task pane by changing the *Select styles to show* option to *All styles* at this dialog box.

9. Press these keys on the keyboard to display the Reveal Formatting task pane.

10. Create a multilevel list style with options at the Create New Style from Formatting dialog box with the *Style type* changed to *List* or with options at this dialog box.

11. To modify a table style, click in a table, click the Table Tools Design tab, right-click the table style, and then click this option at the shortcut menu.

12. Use this feature to investigate the styles applied to text in a document.

13. Use options at the Manage Styles dialog box with this tab selected to sort styles, select a style to edit and modify, and create a new style.

14. Copy a style to the Normal.dotm template at this dialog box.

Chapter Assessments

Applying Your Skills

Demonstrate your knowledge of features learned in this chapter by completing the following assessments.

Assessment 24.1   Create and Apply Styles to a Committee Report

1. Open **KMStyles.docx** and save the document with the name **C24-A01-KMStyles**.
2. Create a style based on the formatting of the *KodiakTitle* text and name it with your initials followed by *KodiakTitle*. (Make sure you select the paragraph symbol.)
3. Press Ctrl + End to move the insertion point to the end of the document and then create a new style at the Create New Style from Formatting dialog box. Name it with your initials followed by *KodiakQuote*. Apply the following formatting at the Create New Style from Formatting expanded dialog box:
   a. Change the left and right indent to 0.5 inch and the spacing after to 12 points. *Hint: Display these formatting options by clicking the Format button in the lower left corner of the dialog box and then clicking Paragraph.*
   b. Click the Italic button.
   c. Change the font color to dark blue.
   d. Insert a blue, single-line, top border and a blue, single-line, bottom border. *Hint: Display these formatting options by clicking the Format button and then clicking Border.*
4. At the document, press the Up Arrow key once and then create a style and name it with your initials followed by *KodiakHeading* and apply the following formatting:
   a. Change the font to 11-point Copperplate Gothic Bold.
   b. Change the font color to blue.
5. Save the styles you created as a Quick Styles set named with your initials followed by *Kodiak*.
6. Save and then close **C24-A01-KMStyles.docx**.
7. Open **KMReport.docx** and save the document with the name **C24-A01-KMReport**.
8. Change to the Quick Styles set named with your initials followed by *Kodiak*.
9. Apply the XXKodiakTitle style (where XX represents your initials) to the two titles in the document, *Audit Committee Report* and *Compensation Committee Report*.
10. Apply the XXKodiakHeading style (where XX represents your initials) to the four headings in the report: *Committee Responsibilities*, *Fees to Independent Auditor*, *Compensation Philosophy*, and *Competitive Compensation*.
11. Apply the XXKodiakQuote style (where XX represents your initials) to the second paragraph of text in the document (the paragraph that begins *Assist the company's board of directors...*).
12. Edit the XXKodiakTitle style (where XX represents your initials) by changing the font color to dark blue and underlining text.
13. Edit the XXKodiakHeading style (where XX represents your initials) by changing the font color to dark blue.
14. Turn on the display of the Styles task pane and then display all styles in alphabetical order. *Hint: Do this at the Style Pane Options dialog box.*
15. Select the bulleted text in the *Committee Responsibilities* section and then apply the Block Text style. With the text still selected, click the Font Color button in the Home tab, and then click the dark blue color.
16. Select the bulleted text in the *Compensation Philosophy* section, apply the Block Text style, and then change the font color to dark blue.
17. Save the modified styles as a Quick Styles set with the same name (your initials followed by *Kodiak*). (At the Save Quick Style Set dialog box, click your style set name in the list box and then click the Save button. At the message asking if you want to replace the existing file, click Yes.)

18. Insert a page break at the beginning of the title *Compensation Committee Report* (located on the second page).
19. Save, print, and then close **C24-A01-KMReport.docx**.

Assessment 24.2   Create and Apply Multilevel List and Table Styles

1. Open **KMListTableTemplate.docx** and save the document as a template with the name **C24-A02-KMListTableTemplate.dotx**.
2. Press Ctrl + End, click the Multilevel List button in the Paragraph group in the Home tab, click *Define New List Style*, and then create a style named with your initials followed by *KMList*. Apply the following formatting at the Define New List Style dialog box:
   a. For the first level numbering, change the font to Cambria, turn on bold, and change the font color to dark blue.
   b. For the second level numbering, specify the snowflake symbol (❆) as the bullet, turn on bold, and change the font color to dark blue. ***Note: The snowflake symbol is located in approximately the third or fourth row in the Symbol dialog box with the Wingdings font selected.***
3. At the document, click the *1)* that displays and then click the Numbering button to turn off numbering (and remove the *1)* from the document).
4. Save the **C24-A02-KMListTableTemplate.dotx** template.
5. Save the template as a normal document with the name **C24-A02-KMAgendas**.
6. Insert the document named **KMAgendas.docx** into the current document.
7. Change to the Quick Styles set named with your initials followed by *Kodiak*.
8. Apply the XXKodiakTitle style (where XX represents your initials) to the title *Kodiak Annual Meeting*.
9. Apply the XXKodiakHeading style (where XX represents your initials) to the two headings in the document: *Finance Department Agenda* and *Research Department Agenda*.
10. Select the text below the *Finance Department Agenda* heading and then apply the XXKMList multilevel list style (where XX represents your initials). ***Hint: Do this with the Multilevel List button in the Paragraph group in the Home tab.***
11. Select the text below the *Research Department Agenda* heading and then apply the XXKMList multilevel list style (where XX represents your initials).
12. Save, print, and then close **C24-A02-KMAgendas.docx**.
13. Open the template **C24-A02-KMListTableTemplate.dotx**.
14. Press Ctrl + End and then create a table style at the Create New Style from Formatting dialog box with the following specifications:
    a. Type your initials in the *Name* text box and then type KMTable.
    b. At the expanded Create New Style from Formatting dialog box, change the *Style type* to *Table*.
    c. For the whole table, change the font to 12-point Cambria in dark blue color, click the Border button arrow and then click *All Borders*, and then change the border color to blue.
    d. For the header row, change the font size to 14, turn on bold, change the font color to white, and apply a fill color of *Blue, Accent 1, Darker 25%*.
    e. For the odd banded rows, apply a fill color of *Blue, Accent 1, Lighter 80%*.
15. Save the template **C24-A02-KMListTableTemplate.dotx**.
16. Save the template as a normal document with the name **C24-A02-KMTables**.
17. Press Ctrl + End and then insert the document named **KMTables.docx** into the current document.
18. Change to the Quick Styles set named with your initials followed by *Kodiak*.
19. Apply the XXKodiakHeading style (where XX represents your initials) to the four headings in the document: *Finance Department, Research Department, Human Resources Department*, and *Production Department*.
20. Apply the table style you created to each of the tables in the document.

21. Save and then print **C24-A02-KMTables.docx**.
22. Modify the XXKMTable style by changing the font for the entire table to Candara and apply a shading of *Olive Green, Accent 3, Lighter 80%* to even banded rows.
23. Move the insertion point to the beginning of the heading *Finance Department*, insert a continuous section break, and then change the left margin to 2.4 inches.
24. Make sure the text and tables fit on one page. If not, press Ctrl + End to move the insertion point to the end of the document and then press the Backspace key once.
25. Delete the *Kodiak* Quick Styles set you created that is preceded by your initials.
26. Save, print, and then close **C24-A02-KMTables.docx**.

Assessment 24.3   Organize Styles

1. Open the **C24-A01-KMStyles.docx** document.
2. Display the Organizer dialog box. *Hint: Click the Styles group dialog box launcher, click the Manage Styles button, and then click the Import/Export button.*
3. Copy the XXKodiakTitle and XXKodiakHeading styles (where XX represents your initials) from the left list box of the Organizer dialog box to the right list box.
4. Close **C24-A01-KMStyles.docx**.
5. Open the **C24-A02-KMTables.docx** document.
6. Display the Organizer dialog box and then copy the XXKMTable style (where XX represents your initials) from the left list box to the right list box.
7. Close **C24-A02-KMTables.docx**.
8. At a blank document, insert the file named **KMSales.docx** and then save the document with the name **C24-A03-KMSales**.
9. Apply the XXKodiakTitle style (where XX represents your initials) to the title *Quarterly Sales*. (This style will apply blue font color instead of dark blue color since you previously edited the style that was saved in the Quick Styles set, not the original style.)
10. Apply the XXKodiakHeading style (where XX represents your initials) to the four headings in the document. (This style will apply blue font color instead of dark blue color.)
11. Apply the XXKMTable style (where XX represents your initials) to the four tables in the document.
12. Save and then print **C24-A03-KMSales.docx**.
13. Display the Organizer dialog box and then delete the following styles from the right list box: XXKodiakTitle, XXKodiakHeading, and XXKMTables (where XX represents your initials).
14. Close **C24-A03-KMSales.docx**.

Expanding Your Skills

Explore additional feature options or use Help to learn a new skill in creating this document.

Assessment 24.4   Modify a Predesigned Table Style

1. In this chapter, you learned how to create a table style and apply all formatting to the style. You can also create a style based on an existing predesigned table style. At a blank document, insert a table with a couple of rows and columns and then figure out how to modify an existing table style. After experimenting with modifying a table style, close the document without saving it.
2. Open **NSSTables.docx** and save the document with the name **C24-A04-NSSTables**.
3. Click in any cell in the top table and then click the Table Tools Design tab.
4. Modify the Light List – Accent 1 table style by changing the name to *XXNSSTable* (where XX represents your initials) and then apply the following formatting:
   a. For the whole table, change the font to Candara and change the alignment to *Align Center*. *Hint: The alignment button is located to the right of the Fill Color button.*
   b. For the whole table, change the table alignment to *Center*. *Hint: Do this at the Table Properties dialog box with the Table tab selected. Display this dialog box by clicking the Format button and then clicking Table Properties.*

   c. For the header row, change the fill color to blue.

   d. For the first column, change the alignment to *Align Center Left* and turn off bold.

   e. For odd banded rows, change the fill color to *Olive Green, Accent 3, Lighter 60%*.

   f. For even banded rows, change the fill color to *Dark Blue, Text 2, Lighter 80%*.

5. After modifying the table style, apply the table style to the four tables in the document.

6. Save, print, and then close **C24-A04-NSSTables.docx**.

Achieving Signature Status

Take your skills to the next level by completing this more challenging assessment.

Assessment 24.5   Design, Apply, and Organize Styles

1. Open **RPLtrhd.docx** and save the document with the name **C24-A05-RPStyles**.

2. Looking at the letterhead font and colors, create a title style, a heading style, and a quote style. You determine the formatting and names of the styles.

3. Save the styles in a Quick Styles set (you determine the name of the new Quick Styles set).

4. Save and then close **C24-A05-RPStyles.docx**.

5. Open **RPReport.docx** and save the document with the name **C24-A05-RPReport**.

6. Apply the title style you created to the text *Photography, Camera Basics,* and *Digital Cameras*.

7. Apply the heading style you created to the text *Pixels, Aspect Ratio,* and *White Balance*.

8. Apply the quote style you created to the first paragraph in the document and the last paragraph.

9. Save, print, and then close **C24-A05-RPReport.docx**.

10. At a blank document, write a note to your instructor that describes the three styles you created including the name of the styles, the name of the Quick Styles set, and the formatting you applied to each style. Save the completed document and name it **C24-A05-NotetoInstructor**. Print and then close **C24-A05-NotetoInstructor.docx**.

11. At a blank document, create a table style for Real Photography (you determine the name and formatting). After creating the table style, display the Organizer dialog box and then copy the table style to the Normal.dotm template. Save the document and name it **C24-A05-TableStyle**. Close the document.

12. Open **C24-A05-RPStyles.docx**, display the Organizer dialog box, copy to the Normal.dotm template the title style and the heading style you created for Real Photography, and then close the document.

13. At a blank document, insert (use the Object button arrow) the document named **RPTables.docx**.

14. Apply your title style to the text *July Weekly Invoices*, apply your heading style to the four headings, and apply your table style to the four tables.

15. Save the document and name it **C24-A05-RPTables**.

16. Make sure all of the tables display on one page. If not, press Ctrl + End to move the insertion point to the end of the document and then press the Backspace key once.

17. Print and then close **C24-A05-RPTables.docx**.

18. At a blank document, delete the Quick Styles set you created, display the Organizer dialog box, and then delete the title, heading, and table styles you created from the Normal.dotm template.

Chapter 25

SNAP TUTORIALS

Protecting and Preparing Documents

Performance Objectives

Upon successful completion of Chapter 25, you will be able to:

- Restrict formatting and editing in a document and allow exceptions to restrictions
- Protect a document with a password
- Open a document in different views
- Modify document properties
- Inspect and encrypt a document
- Restrict permission to a document
- Create and apply a digital signature
- Insert a signature line
- Mark a document as final
- Check a document for accessibility and compatibility issues
- Manage versions

Tutorial 25.1
Restricting formatting and editing in a document
Tutorial 25.2
Modifying document properties and running the compatibility checker
Tutorial 25.3
Protecting a Document with a Password and Identifying a Document as Read-only
Tutorial 25.4
Inspecting and encrypting a document
Tutorial 25.5
Creating a digital signature and inserting a signature line
Tutorial 25.6
Checking the Accessibility of a Document

In Chapter 20, you learned to perform workgroup activities such as inserting comments into a document, tracking changes made by other users, comparing documents, and combining documents from multiple users. In this chapter, you will learn how to protect the integrity of shared documents, limit the formatting or editing changes that other users can make, and prepare documents for distribution.

Note: Before beginning computer exercises for this chapter, copy to your storage medium the Chapter25 folder from the CD that accompanies this textbook and then make Chapter25 the active folder.

In this chapter, students will produce the following documents:

Exercise 25.1. C25-E01-TECAnnualReport.docx
Exercise 25.3. C25-E03-REAgrmnt .docx
Exercise 25.4. C25-E04-Lease.docx
Exercise 25.5. C25-E05-PremPro.docx

Model answers for these exercises are shown on the following pages.

Exercise 25.1

C25-E01-TECAnnualReport.docx

TERRA ENERGY CORPORATION

OVERVIEW

Terra Energy Corporation is a development stage company that was incorporated on May 1, 2009. The corporation and its subsidiary (collectively referred to as the "Company") designs, develops, configures, and offers for sale power systems that provide highly reliable, high-quality, environmentally friendly power. The Company has segmented the potential markets for its products into three broad categories: high-energy, high-power, uninterruptible power system (UPS), and high-power distributed generation and utility power-grid energy storage system. We have available for sale several high-energy products that deliver a low level of power over a long period of time (typically measured in hours). These products are tailored to the telecommunications, cable systems, computer networks, and Internet markets.

We are developing a new high-energy product for potential applications in the renewable energy market for both photovoltaic and wind turbine uses. As part of exploring these markets, we have committed to invest $2 million in Clear Sun Energies and we have purchased the inverter electronics technology of Technology Pacific[SN1].

We have taken significant actions over the last eighteen months to reduce our expenditures for product development, infrastructure and production readiness. Our headcount, development spending, and capital expenditures have been significantly reduced. We have continued the preliminary design and development of potential products for markets under consideration and with specific approval by the Company's board of directors.

RESEARCH AND DEVELOPMENT

We believe that our research and development efforts are essential to our ability to successfully design and deliver our products to our targeted customers, as well as to modify and improve them to reflect the evolution of markets and customer needs. Our research and development team has worked closely with potential customers to define product features and performance to address specific needs. Our research and development expenses, including engineering expenses, were approximately $8,250,000 in 2011, $15,525,000 in 2010, and $7,675,000 in 2009. We expect research and development expenses in 2009 to be lower than in 2008. As we determine market opportunities, we may need to make significant levels of research and development expenditures in the future. As of December 31, 2011, we employed twenty-five engineers and technicians who were engaged in research and development.

MANUFACTURING

Historically, our manufacturing has consisted of the welding and assembly of our products. We have previously contracted out the manufacture of our high-energy flywheel components, using our design drawings and processes to facilitate more rapid growth by taking advantage of third-party installed manufacturing capacity. For a limited number of non-proprietary components, we generate performance specifications and obtain either standard or custom components.

Page 1

C25-E01-TECAnnualReport.docx

Main document changes and comments

Page 1: Comment [SN1]	Student Name	3/28/2010 11:10:00 AM

Include additional information on the impact of this purchase.

Header and footer changes

Text Box changes

Header and footer text box changes

Footnote changes

Endnote changes

Comments

Exercise 25.3

C25-E03-REAgrmnt.docx

REAL ESTATE SALE AGREEMENT

The Buyer, BUYER, and Seller, SELLER, hereby agree that SELLER will sell and BUYER will buy the following property, with such improvements as are located thereon, and is described as follows: All that tract of land lying and being in Land Lot _____ of the _____ District, Section _____ of _____ County, and being known as Address: _____
City:_____ State: _____ Zip:_____, together with all light fixtures, electrical, mechanical, plumbing, air-conditioning, and any other systems or fixtures as are attached thereto; all plants, trees, and shrubbery now a part thereof, together with all the improvements thereon, and all appurtenances thereto, all being hereinafter collectively referred to as the "Property." The full legal description of said Property is the same as is recorded with the Clerk of the Superior Court of the County in which the Property is located and is made a part of this Agreement by reference.

SELLER will sell and BUYER will buy upon the following terms and conditions, as completed or marked. On any conflict of terms or conditions, that which is added will supersede that which is printed or marked. It is understood that the Property will be bought by Warranty Deed, with covenants, restrictions, and easements of record.

Financing: The balance due to SELLER will be evidenced by a negotiable Promissory Note of Borrower, secured by a Mortgage or Deed to Secure Debt on the Property and delivered by BUYER to SELLER dated the date of closing.

New financing: If BUYER does not obtain the required financing, the earnest money deposit shall be forfeited to SELLER as liquidated damages. BUYER will make application for financing within five days of the date of acceptance of the Agreement and in a timely manner furnish any and all credit, employment, financial and other information required by the lender.

Closing costs: BUYER will pay all closing costs to include; Recording Fees, Intangibles Tax, Credit Reports, Funding Fees, Loan Origination Fee, Document Preparation Fee, Loan Insurance Premium, Title Insurance Policy, Attorney's Fees, Courier Fees, Overnight Fee, Appraisal Fee, Survey, Transfer Tax, Satisfaction and Recording Fees, Wood Destroying Organism Report and any other costs associated with the funding or closing of this Agreement.

Prorations: All taxes, rentals, condominium or association fees, monthly mortgage insurance premiums and interest on loans will be prorated as of the date of closing.

Title insurance: Within five (5) days of this Agreement SELLER will deliver to BUYER or closing attorney: Title insurance commitment for an owner's policy in the amount of the purchase price. Any expense of securing title, including but not limited to legal fees, discharge of liens and recording fees will be paid by SELLER.

C25-E03-REAgrmnt.docx

Model Answers

LEASE AGREEMENT

THIS LEASE AGREEMENT (hereinafter referred to as the "Agreement") made and entered into this DAY of MONTH, YEAR, by and between Lessor and Lessee.

WITNESSETH:

WHEREAS, Lessor is the owner of real property and is desirous of leasing the Premises to Lessee upon the terms and conditions as contained herein.

NOW, THEREFORE, for and in consideration of the covenants and obligations contained herein and other good and valuable consideration, the receipt and sufficiency of which is hereby acknowledged, the parties hereto agree as follows:

1. TERM. Lessor leases to Lessee and Lessee leases from Lessor the described Premises.
2. RENT. The total rent for the premise is RENT due on the fifteenth day of each month less any set off for approved repairs.
3. DAMAGE DEPOSIT. Upon the due execution of this Agreement, Lessee shall deposit with Lessor the sum of DEPOSIT receipt of which is hereby acknowledged by Lessor, as security for any damage caused to the Premises during the term hereof. Such deposit shall be returned to Lessee, without interest, and less any set off for damages to the Premises upon the termination of this Agreement.
4. USE OF PREMISES. The Premises shall be used and occupied by Lessee and Lessee's immediate family, exclusively, as a private single family dwelling, and no part of the Premises shall be used at any time during the term of this Agreement by Lessee for the purpose of carrying on any business, profession, or trade of any kind, or for any purpose other than as a private single family dwelling. Lessee shall not allow any other person, other than Lessee's immediate family, to occupy the Premises.
5. CONDITION OF PREMISES. Lessee stipulates, represents, and warrants that Lessee has examined the Premises, and that they are in good order, repair, and in a safe, clean and tenantable condition.
6. ALTERATIONS AND IMPROVEMENTS. Lessee shall make no alterations or improvements on the Premises or construct any building or make any other improvements on the Premises without the prior written consent of Lessor.
7. NON-DELIVERY OF POSSESSION. In the event Lessor cannot deliver possession of the Premises to Lessee upon the commencement of the term, through no fault of Lessor or its agents, then Lessor or its agents shall have no liability, but the rental herein provided shall abate until possession is given. Lessor or its agents shall have thirty (30) days in which to give possession, and if possession is tendered within such time, Lessee agrees to accept the demised Premises and pay the rental herein provided from that date. In the event possession cannot be delivered within such time, through no fault of Lessor or its agents, then this Agreement and all rights hereunder shall terminate.

Lease Agreement

Page 1

Exercise 25.4 C25-E04-Lease.docx

---

8. UTILITIES. Lessee shall be responsible for arranging for and paying for all utility services required on the Premises.

IN WITNESS WHEREOF the parties have reviewed the information above and certify, to the best of their knowledge, that the information provided by the signatory is true and accurate.

5/5/2012

X Student Name
_____
Student Name
Assistant Manager
Signed by: Student Name

X
_____
Jaden Cowell
Lessee

Lease Agreement

Page 2

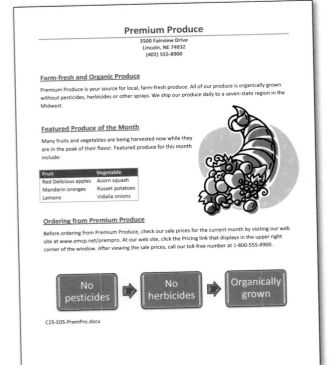

Premium Produce

3500 Fairview Drive
Lincoln, NE 74932
(402) 555-8900

Farm-fresh and Organic Produce

Premium Produce is your source for local, farm-fresh produce. All of our produce is organically grown without pesticides, herbicides or other sprays. We ship our produce daily to a seven-state region in the Midwest.

Featured Produce of the Month

Many fruits and vegetables are being harvested now while they are in the peak of their flavor. Featured produce for this month include:

Fruit	Vegetable
Red Delicious apples	Acorn squash
Mandarin oranges	Russet potatoes
Lemons	Vidalia onions

Ordering from Premium Produce

Before ordering from Premium Produce, check our sale prices for the current month by visiting our web site at www.emcp.net/prempro. At our web site, click the Pricing link that displays in the upper right corner of the window. After viewing the sale prices, call our toll-free number at 1-800-555-8900.

No pesticides → No herbicides → Organically grown

C25-E05-PremPro.docx

Exercise 25.4 C25-E05-PremPro.docx

Protecting Documents

In a company or organization, you may want to distribute copies of documents you create among members of your workgroup. In some situations, you may want to protect a document and limit the changes that can be made to it. If you create a document that contains sensitive, restricted, or private information, consider protecting it by saving it as a read-only document or securing it with a password.

You can limit the formatting and editing that other users can do in a document with options at the Restrict Formatting and Editing task pane. Limiting formatting and editing changes can be especially useful when a number of people in an organization will be reviewing and editing the same document. For example, suppose you are responsible for preparing the yearly corporate report for your company. This report integrates information from a variety of departments, such as finance, human resources, and sales and marketing. You can prepare the report and then specify the portion of it that a given individual is allowed to edit. For example, you can specify that a person from the finance department is able to edit only financial information and a person from human resources is able to edit only data pertinent to the human resources department. In this way, you can protect the integrity of the document.

To protect a document, display the Restrict Formatting and Editing task pane, shown in Figure 25.1, by clicking the Review tab and then clicking the Restrict Editing button in the Protect group. Use options in the *Formatting restrictions* section to limit formatting to specific styles and use options in the *Editing restrictions* section to specify the type of editing allowed in the document.

Restrict Editing

Figure 25.1 Restrict Formatting and Editing Task Pane

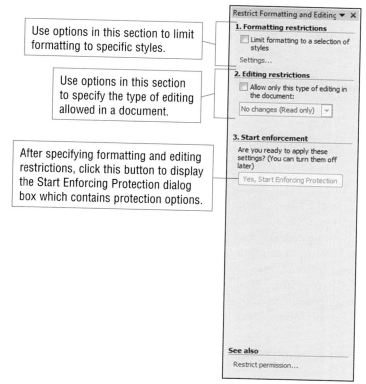

Use options in this section to limit formatting to specific styles.

Use options in this section to specify the type of editing allowed in a document.

After specifying formatting and editing restrictions, click this button to display the Start Enforcing Protection dialog box which contains protection options.

Note: The Protect group in the Review tab contains a Block Authors button. This button is available only when a document is saved to a Microsoft SharePoint Foundation 2010 site that supports Workspaces. If the button is active, select the portion of the document you want to block from editing and then click the Block Authors button. To unblock authors, click in the locked section of the document, and then click the Block Authors button.

Restricting Formatting

QUICK STEPS

Display Formatting Restrictions Dialog Box
1. Click Review tab.
2. Click Restrict Editing button.
3. Click the Settings hyperlink in Restrict Formatting and Editing task pane.

With options in the *Formatting restrictions* section of the Restrict Formatting and Editing task pane, you can lock specific styles used in a document, thus allowing the use of only those styles and prohibiting a user from making other formatting changes. Click the Settings hyperlink in the *Formatting restrictions* section, and the Formatting Restrictions dialog box displays, as shown in Figure 25.2.

Figure 25.2 Formatting Restrictions Dialog Box

Insert a check mark in the check boxes preceding those styles you want to allow and remove the check mark from the check boxes preceding styles you do not want to allow.

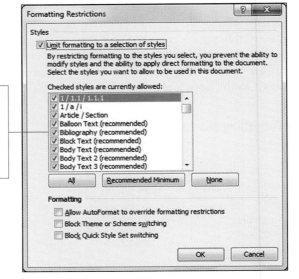

If you insert a check mark in the *Limit formatting to a selection of styles* check box, a list of styles becomes available in the *Checked styles are currently allowed* list box. In this list box, insert check marks in the check boxes that precede styles you want to allow and remove check marks in the check boxes that precede styles you do not want to allow. You can limit formatting to a minimum number of styles by clicking the Recommended Minimum button. Clicking this button allows formatting with styles that Word uses for certain features such as bulleted or numbered lists. Click the None button to remove all check marks and allow no styles to be used in the document. Click the All button to insert a check mark in all the check boxes and allow all styles to be used in the document.

With options in the *Formatting* section of the dialog box, you can allow or not allow AutoFormat to make changes in a document and allow or not allow users to switch themes or Quick Styles sets.

1. Open **TECAnnualReport.docx** and save the document with the name **C25-E01-TECAnnualReport**.
2. Restrict formatting to recommended styles and the Heading 1 and Heading 2 styles by completing the following steps:
    a. Click the Review tab.
    b. Click the Restrict Editing button in the Protect group.

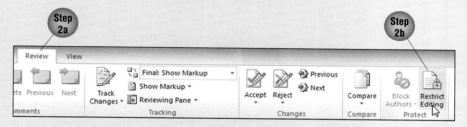

    c. At the Restrict Formatting and Editing task pane, click the *Limit formatting to a selection of styles* check box to insert a check mark. (Skip this step if the check box already contains a check mark.)
    d. Click the <u>Settings</u> hyperlink.
    e. At the Formatting Restrictions dialog box, click the None button.
    f. Scroll down the list box and then insert a check mark in the *Heading 1* check box and also the *Heading 2* check box.

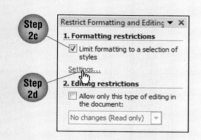

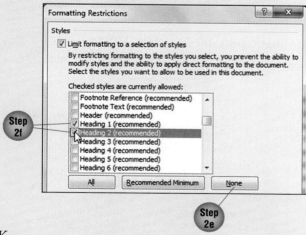

    g. Click OK.
    h. At the message telling you that the document may contain formatting or styles that are not allowed and asking if you want to remove them, click Yes.
3. Save **C25-E01-TECAnnualReport.docx**.

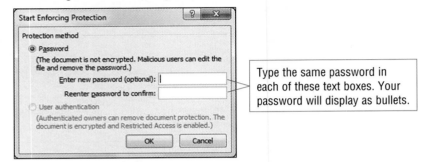

QUICK STEPS

Display Start Enforcing Protection Dialog Box

1. Click Review tab.
2. Click Restrict Editing button.
3. Specify formatting and/or editing options.
4. Click Yes, Start Enforcing Protection button.

Enforcing Restrictions

Specifying formatting and editing restrictions and any exceptions to those restrictions is the first step to protecting your document. The next step is to start the enforcement of the restrictions you have specified. Click the Yes, Start Enforcing Protection button in the task pane to display the Start Enforcing Protection dialog box, shown in Figure 25.3.

Figure 25.3 Start Enforcing Protection Dialog Box

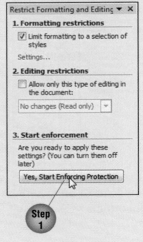

Type the same password in each of these text boxes. Your password will display as bullets.

At the Start Enforcing Protection dialog box, the *Password* option is selected automatically. To add a password, type what you want to use as the password in the *Enter new password (optional)* text box. Click in the *Reenter password to confirm* text box and then type the same password again. Choose the *User authentication* option if you want to encrypt the password and use SSL-secured authentication to prevent any unauthorized changes.

Exercise 25.1B   Protecting a Document   Part 2 of 3

1. With **C25-E01-TECAnnualReport.docx** open, click the Yes, Start Enforcing Protection button (located toward the bottom of the Restrict Formatting and Editing task pane).

Restrict Formatting and Editing

1. Formatting restrictions
☑ Limit formatting to a selection of styles
Settings...

2. Editing restrictions
☐ Allow only this type of editing in the document:
No changes (Read only)

3. Start enforcement
Are you ready to apply these settings? (You can turn them off later)
Yes, Start Enforcing Protection

Step 1

2. At the Start Enforcing Protection dialog box, type formatting in the *Enter new password (optional)* text box. (Bullets will display in the text box rather than the letters you type.)

3. Press the Tab key (this moves the insertion point to the *Reenter password to confirm* text box) and then type formatting. (Bullets will display in the text box rather than the letters you type.)
4. Click OK to close the dialog box.
5. Close the Restrict Formatting and Editing task pane by clicking the Close button in the upper right corner of the task pane.
6. Save and then close **C25-E01-TECAnnualReport.docx**.
7. Open **C25-E01-TECAnnualReport.docx**.
8. Display the Restrict Formatting and Editing task pane by clicking the Review tab and then clicking the Restrict Editing button.
9. Read the information that displays in the task pane telling you that the document is protected, special restrictions are in effect, and you may format text with certain styles only. Click the <u>Available styles</u> hyperlink. (This displays the Styles task pane with only four styles in the *Pick formatting to apply* list box: *Clear All, Normal, Heading 1,* and *Heading 2.*)
10. Apply the Heading 1 style to the title TERRA ENERGY CORPORATION and apply the Heading 2 style to the following headings: *Overview, Research and Development, Manufacturing,* and *Sales and Marketing.*
11. Close the Styles task pane.
12. Change the style set to Formal.
13. At the message indicating that some of the Quick Styles could not be updated, click OK.
14. Save the document.
15. Remove the password protection from the document by completing the following steps:
    a. Click the Stop Protection button located toward the bottom of the task pane.
    b. At the Unprotect Document dialog box, type formatting in the text box.
    c. Click OK.
16. Save **C25-E01-TECAnnualReport.docx**.

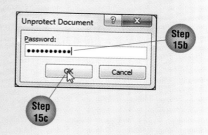

Restricting Editing

Use the *Editing restrictions* option at the Restrict Formatting and Editing task pane to limit the types of changes a user can make to a document. Insert a check mark in the *Allow only this type of editing in the document* option, and the drop-down list below the option becomes active. Click the down-pointing arrow at the right of the option box, and these options are available: *Tracked changes, Comments, Filling in forms,* and *No changes (Read only).*

If you do not want a user to be able to make any changes to a document, choose the *No changes (Read only)* option. If you want the user to be able to make changes that are tracked in the document, choose the *Tracked changes* option. Choose the *Comments* option if you want the user to be able to make comments in a document. The *Tracked Changes* and *Comments* options are useful in a workgroup environment where a document is routed to various members of a group for review. If you choose the *Filling in forms* option, a user will be able to fill in fields in a form but will not be able to make any other editing changes.

1. With **C25-E01-TECAnnualReport.docx** open, restrict editing to comments only by completing the following steps:
   a. Make sure the Restrict Formatting and Editing task pane displays.
   b. Click the *Allow only this type of editing in the document* check box to insert a check mark.
   c. Click the down-pointing arrow at the right of the option box below the *Allow only this type of editing in the document* and then click *Comments* at the drop-down list.

2. Click the Yes, Start Enforcing Protection button located toward the bottom of the task pane.

3. At the Start Enforcing Protection dialog box, click OK. (Adding a password is optional.)

4. Read the information in the task pane that tells you the document is protected and you may only insert comments.

5. Click each of the ribbon tabs and notice the buttons and options that are dimmed and unavailable.

6. Insert a comment by completing the following steps:
   a. Move the insertion point immediately right of the period that ends the last sentence in the second paragraph of the *Overview* section.
   b. Click the Review tab (if necessary), click the Show Markup button in the Tracking group, point to *Balloons*, and then click the *Show All Revisions Inline* option.
   c. If necessary, click the Reviewing Pane button to turn on the display of the Reviewing pane.
   d. Click the New Comment button in the Comments group.
   e. Type the following in the Reviewing pane: Include additional information on the impact of this purchase.

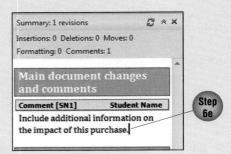

   f. Close the Reviewing pane.
   g. Click the Stop Protection button located toward the bottom of the Restrict Formatting and Editing task pane.
   h. Close the Restrict Formatting and Editing task pane.

7. Save the document and then print only page 1.

8. Print only the comment. (To do this, display the Print tab Backstage view, click the first gallery in the *Settings* category, click the *List of Markup* option, and then click the Print button.)

9. Close **C25-E01-TECAnnualReport.docx**.

Protecting a Document with a Password

Add a Password to a Document
1. Click File tab, *Save As*.
2. Click Tools button, *General Options*.
3. Type a password in the *Password to open* text box.
4. Press Enter.
5. Type the same password again.
6. Press Enter.

In a previous section of this chapter, you learned how to protect a document with a password by using options at the Start Enforcing Protection dialog box. You can also protect a document with a password by using options at the General Options dialog box, shown in Figure 25.4. To display this dialog box, click the File tab and then click Save As. At the Save As dialog box, click the Tools button located toward the bottom of the dialog box next to the Save button and then click *General Options* at the drop-down list.

At the General Options dialog box, you can assign a password to open the document, modify the document, or both. To insert a password to open the document, click in the *Password to open* text box and then type the password. A password should be at least eight characters in length, can contain up to 15 characters, and is case sensitive. Consider combining uppercase letters, lowercase letters, numbers, and symbols in your password to make it more secure. Use the *Password to modify* option to create a password that a person must enter before being able to make edits to the document.

At the General Options dialog box, insert a check mark in the *Read-only recommended* check box to save a document as a read-only document. If you open a document that is saved as a read-only document and then make changes to it, you have to save the document with a new name. Use this option if you do not want the contents of the original document changed.

Figure 25.4 General Options Dialog Box

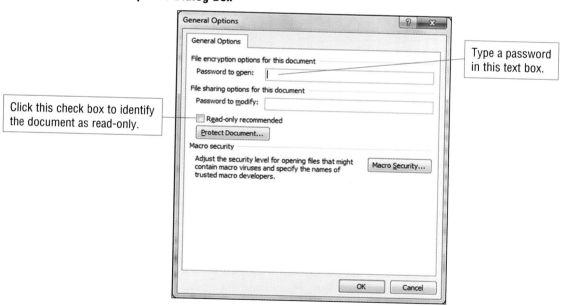

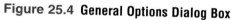

1. Open **TECContract.docx**.
2. Save the document and protect it with a password by completing the following steps:
    a. Click the File tab and then click *Save As*.
    b. At the Save As dialog box, click the Tools button located toward the bottom of the dialog box (next to the Save button) and then click *General Options* at the drop-down list.
    c. At the General Options dialog box, type your first name in the *Password to open* text box. (If it is longer than 15 characters, abbreviate it. You will not see your name; Word displays bullets.)
    d. After typing your name, press the Enter key.
    e. At the Confirm Password dialog box, type your name again (be sure to type it exactly as you did in the *Password to open* text box, including upper or lowercase letters), and then press the Enter key.

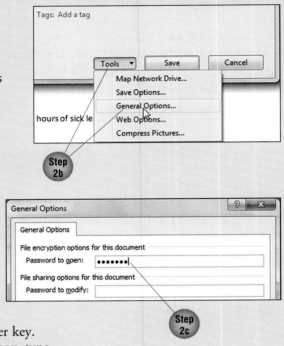

3. Select the current name in the *File name* text box, type **C25-E02-TECContract** and then click the Save button.
4. Close **C25-E02-TECContract.docx**.
5. Open **C25-E02-TECContract.docx** and type your password when prompted.
6. Close **C25-E02-TECContract.docx**.

Opening a Document in Different Views

Open Document in Different Views
1. Display Open dialog box.
2. Click desired document name.
3. Click Open button arrow.
4. Click desired open option at drop-down list.

With the Open button in the Open dialog box, you can open a document in different views. At the Open dialog box, click the Open button arrow and a drop-down list of options displays. Click the *Open Read-Only* option and the document opens in read-only mode. In this mode, you can make changes to the document but you cannot save the document with the same name. Click the *Open as Copy* option and a copy of the document opens and the text *Copy (1)* displays at the beginning of the document name in the Title bar. If you click the *Open in Protected View* option, the document opens and the text *(Protected View)* displays after the document name in the Title bar. Also, a message bar displays telling you that the file was opened in Protected View. If you want to edit the document, click the Enable Editing button in the message bar. You can open a document with the *Open and Repair* option and Word will open a new version of the document in which it will repair any issues with the document.

1. Open **TECTraining.docx** and then save the document and name it **C25-E02-TECTraining**.
2. Close **C25-E02-TECTraining.docx**.
3. Open a document as a read-only document by completing the following steps:
   a. Display the Open dialog box with the Chapter25 folder on your storage medium the active folder.
   b. Click once on the document name **C25-E02-TECTraining.docx**.
   c. Click the Open button arrow (located toward the bottom right corner of the dialog box) and then click *Open Read-Only* at the drop-down list. (Notice that the text *Read Only* displays after the name in the Title bar.)

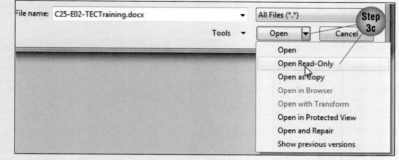

   d. Close the document.
4. Open a document in protected view by completing the following steps:
   a. Display the Open dialog box.
   b. Click once on the document name **PremPro.docx**.
   c. Click the Open button arrow and then click *Open in Protected View* at the drop-down list. (Notice that the text *(Protected View)* displays after the name in the Title bar and the message bar displays telling you that the file was opened in Protected View.)
   d. Click each of the tabs and notice that most formatting options are dimmed.
   e. Click in the document and then click the Enable Editing button in the message bar. (This removes *(Protected View)* after the document name in the Title bar and makes available the options in the tabs.)

   f. Close the document.

Managing Document Properties

Each document you create has properties associated with it such as the type of document, its location, and when it was created, modified, and accessed. You can view and modify document properties at the Info tab Backstage view and modify document properties at the document information panel. Display information about the document by clicking the File tab and then clicking the Info tab. The Info tab Backstage view displays information about the document in the pane at the right side as shown in Figure 25.5.

Figure 25.5 Info tab Backstage view

Click this button to display a
drop-down list of options for
protecting your document.

Document thumbnail

Document information

Click this button to display
options for inspecting and
checking the compatibility
and accessibility of your
document.

Click this button to recover
unsaved versions of a
document.

Click this hyperlink to display
additional document properties.

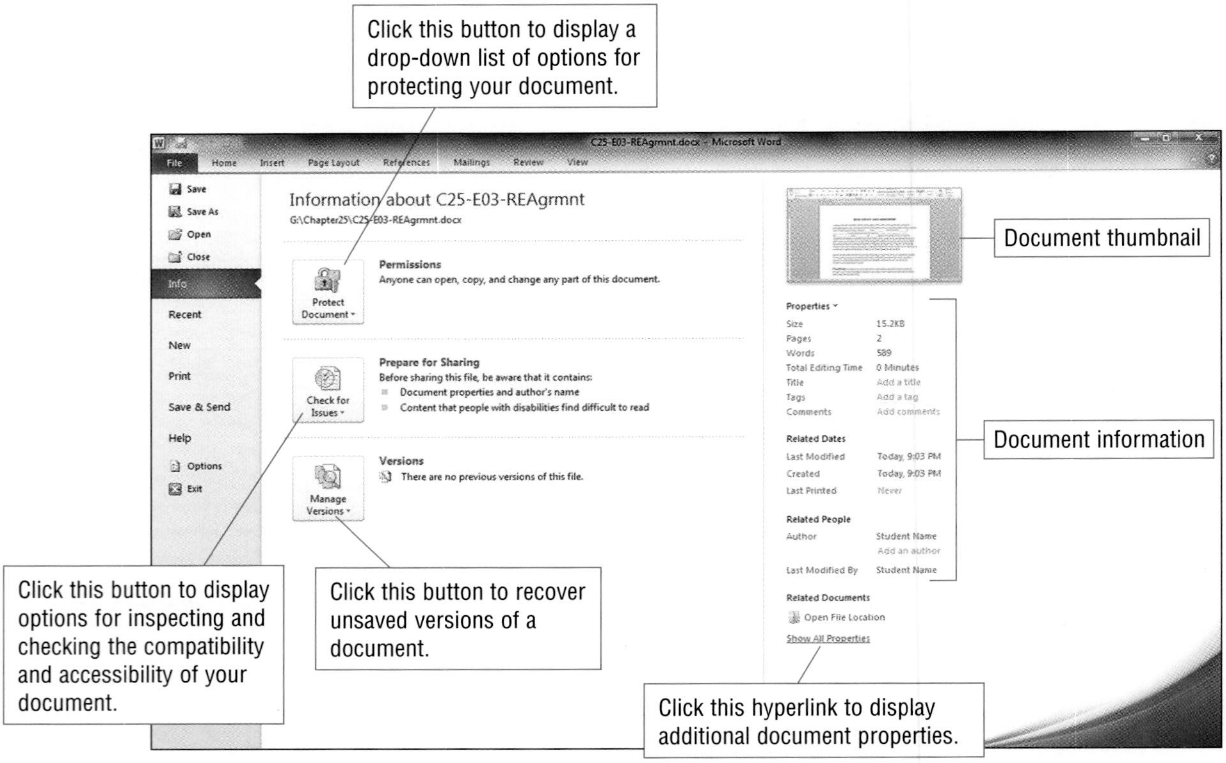

The document property information that displays in the pane at the right includes the file size, number of pages and words, total editing time, and any tags or comments you added. You can add or update a document property by hovering your mouse over the information that displays at the right of the property (a rectangle text box with a light yellow border displays), clicking in the text box, and then typing the desired information. In the *Related Dates* section, dates display for when the document was created and when it was last modified and printed. The *Related People* section displays the name of the author of the document and also contains options for adding additional author names. Display additional document properties by clicking the Show All Properties hyperlink.

You also can add information to a document's properties at the document information panel shown in Figure 25.6. Display this panel by clicking the Properties button that displays below the document thumbnail in the Info tab Backstage view and then clicking *Show Document Panel* at the drop-down list.

Figure 25.6 Document Information Panel

Type document information in the text
boxes in the document information panel.

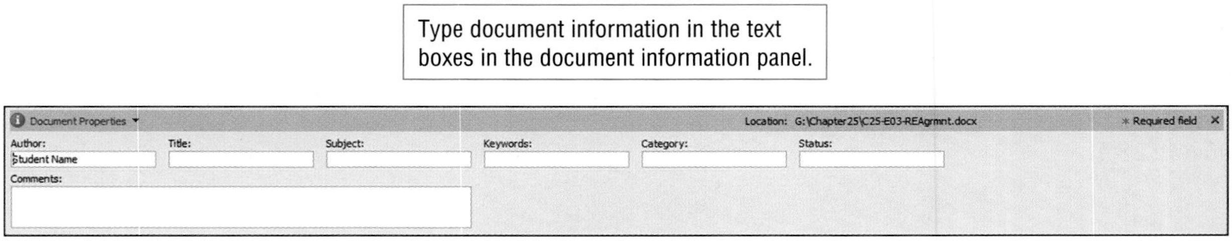

By typing specific information in each of the text boxes in the document information panel, you can describe a document. Inserting text in some of the text boxes can help you organize and identify your documents. For example, insert specific words contained in the document in the *Keywords* text box, and you can search for all documents containing the specific keywords. Text you type in the document information panel is saved with the document. You can print the document properties for a document by displaying the Print tab Backstage view, clicking the first gallery in the *Settings* category, clicking *Document Properties* at the drop-down list, and then clicking the Print button.

In addition to inserting information about a document in the document information panel, you can insert specific information with options at the Properties dialog box shown in Figure 25.7. The name of the dialog box reflects the currently open document. Display this dialog box by clicking the Document Properties button that displays in the upper left corner of the document information panel and then clicking *Advanced Properties* at the drop-down list. You can also display this dialog box by displaying the Info tab Backstage view, clicking the Properties button, and then clicking *Advanced Properties* at the drop-down list. Another method for displaying the Properties dialog box is to display the Open dialog box, click the desired document, click the Organize button, and then click *Properties* at the drop-down list. You can also right-click on the desired file name, and then click *Properties* at the shortcut menu.

Display Document Information Panel
1. Click File tab.
2. Click Properties button at Info tab Backstage view.
3. Click *Show Document Panel*.

Figure 25.7 Properties Dialog Box with General Tab Selected

The Properties dialog box displays information about the document. Click each of the tabs to display additional document information.

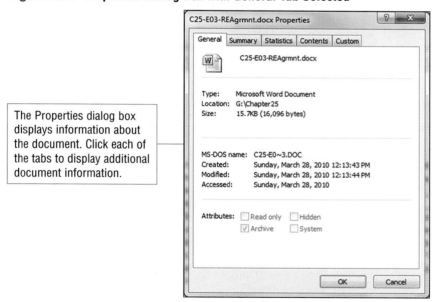

The Properties dialog box with the General tab selected displays information about the document type, size, and location. Click the Summary tab and fields display such as title, subject, author, company, category, keywords, and comments. Some fields may contain data and others may be blank. You can insert, edit, or delete text in the fields. With the Statistics tab selected, information displays such as the number of pages, paragraphs, lines, words, and characters. You can view the document without opening it by clicking the Contents tab. This displays a portion of the document in the viewing window. Click the Custom tab and the Properties dialog box displays as shown in Figure 25.8.

Display Properties Dialog Box
1. Click File tab.
2. Click Properties button at Info tab Backstage view.
3. Click *Advanced Properties*.

Figure 25.8 **Properties Dialog Box with Custom Tab Selected**

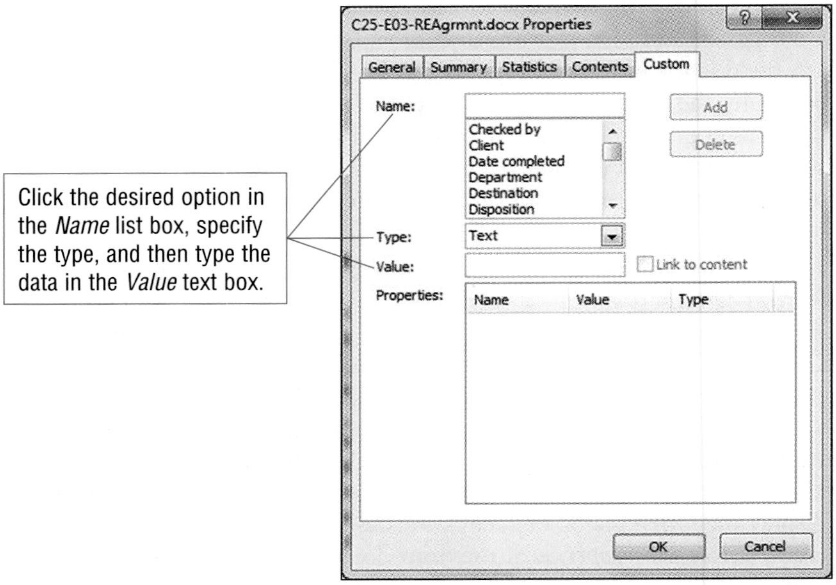

Click the desired option in the *Name* list box, specify the type, and then type the data in the *Value* text box.

Use the options at the Properties dialog box with the Custom tab selected to add custom properties to the document. For example, you can add a property that displays the date the document was completed, information on the department in which the document was created, and much more. The list box below the *Name* option box displays the predesigned properties provided by Word. You can choose a predesigned property or create your own.

To choose a predesigned property, select the desired property in the list box, specify what type of property it is (value, date, number, yes/no), and then type a value. For example, to specify the department in which the document was created, you would click *Department* in the list box, make sure the *Type* displays as *Text*, click in the *Value* text box, and then type the name of the department.

Exercise 25.3A   Inserting Document Properties   Part 1 of 3

1. Open **REAgrmnt.dox** and save the document with the name **C25-E03-REAgrmnt**.
2. Make the following changes to the document:
   a. Search for all occurrences of dark red, 14-point Tahoma bold text and replace with black, 12-point Calibri bold.
   b. Insert page numbers that print at the top of each page at the right margin.
   c. Insert a footer that prints the document name centered on each page. (Use the *Top of Page* option at the Page Number button drop-down list.)
3. Insert document properties by completing the following steps:
   a. Click the File tab. (Make sure the Info tab is selected.)

b. Hover your mouse over the text *Add a title* that displays at the right of the *Title* document property, click in the text box that displays, and then type Real Estate Sale Agreement.

c. Display the document information panel by clicking the Properties button that displays below the document thumbnail, and then clicking *Show Document Panel* at the drop-down list.

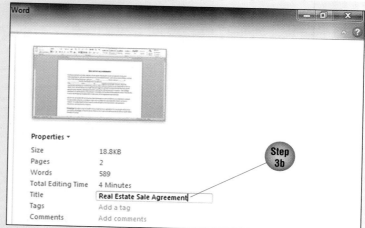

d. Select any text that appears in the *Author* text box and then type your first and last names.

e. Press the Tab key twice (this makes the *Subject* text box active) and then type Real Estate Sale Agreement.

f. Press the Tab key and then type the following words in the *Keywords* text box: real estate, agreement, contract, purchasing.

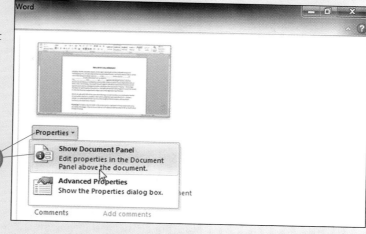

g. Press the Tab key and then type Agreement in the *Category* text box.

h. Press the Tab key twice and then type the following text in the *Comments* text box: This is a real estate sale agreement between two parties.

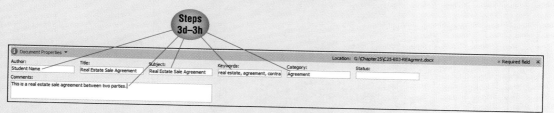

4. Add custom information by completing the following steps:
   a. Click the Document Properties button that displays in the upper left corner of the document information panel and then click *Advanced Properties* at the drop-down list.

b. At the Properties dialog box, click the Summary tab, select the current title in the *Title* text box, and then type C25-E03-REAgrmnt.docx.

c. Click the Custom tab.

d. Click *Checked by* in the *Name* list box.

e. Make sure *Text* displays in the *Type* list box.

f. Click in the *Value* text box and then type your first and last name.

g. Click the Add button.

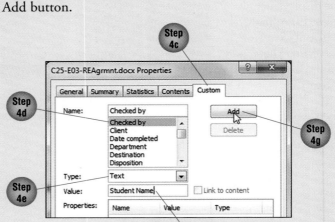

h. Click *Date completed* in the *Name* list box.

i. Click the down-pointing arrow at the right of the *Type* option box and then click *Date*.

j. Click in the *Value* text box and then type today's date in figure (##/##/####).

k. Click the Add button.

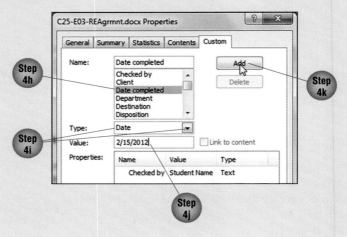

l. Click *Status* in the *Name* list box. (You will need to scroll down the list to display this option.)

m. Click the down-pointing arrow at the right of the *Type* option box and then click *Text*.

n. Click in the *Value* text box and then type First Draft.

o. Click the Add button.

p. Click OK to close the Properties dialog box.

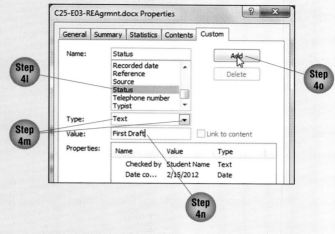

5. Click the Close button that displays in the upper right corner of the document information panel.

6. Save **C25-E03-REAgrmnt.docx** and then print only the document properties by completing the following steps:

a. Click the File tab and then click the Print tab.

b. At the Print tab Backstage view, click the first gallery in the *Settings* category and then click *Document Properties* at the drop-down list.

c. Click the Print button.

7. Save **C25-E03-REAgrmnt.docx**.

Mark a Document as Final
1. Click File tab.
2. Click Protect Document button at Info tab Backstage view.
3. Click *Mark as Final*.

Restricting Documents

The middle panel in the Info tab Backstage view contains buttons for protecting a document, checking for issues in a document, and managing versions of a document. Click the Protect Document button in the middle panel and a drop-down list displays with the following options: *Mark as Final*, *Encrypt with Password*, *Restrict Editing*, *Restrict Permission by People*, and *Add a Digital Signature*.

Marking a Document as Final

Click the *Mark as Final* option to save the document as a read-only document. When you click this option, a message displays telling you that the document will be marked and then saved. At this message, click OK. This displays another message telling you that the document has been marked as final to indicate that editing is complete and that it is the final version of the document. The message further indicates that when a document is marked as final, the status property is set to "Final," typing, editing commands, and proofing marks are turned off, and that the document can be identified by the Mark as Final icon, which displays toward the left side of the Status bar. At this message, click OK. After a document is marked as final, the message "This document has been marked as final to discourage editing." displays to the right of the Protect Document button in the Info tab Backstage view.

Exercise 25.3B   Marking a Document as Final   Part 2 of 3

---

1. With **C25-E03-REAgrmnt.docx** open, mark the document as final by completing the following steps:
   a. Click the File tab.
   b. Click the Protect Document button at the Info tab Backstage view and then click *Mark as Final* at the drop-down list.
   c. At the message telling you the document will be marked and saved, click OK.
   d. At the next message that displays, click OK. (Notice the message that displays to the right of the Protect Document button.)
   e. Click the File tab to return to the document.
2. At the document, notice the message bar that displays above the Ruler and then close the document.
3. Open **C25-E03-REAgrmnt.docx** and then click the Edit Anyway button on the yellow message bar.
4. Save **C25-E03-REAgrmnt.docx**.

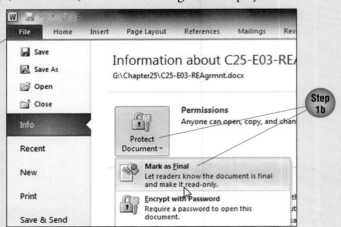

Encrypting a Document

Word provides a number of methods for protecting a document with a password. Previously in this chapter, you learned how to protect a document with a password using options at the Start Enforcing Protection dialog box and how to protect a document with a password using options at the General Options dialog box. In addition to these two methods, you can protect a document with a password by clicking the Protect Document button at the Info tab Backstage view and then clicking the *Encrypt with Password* option at the drop-down list. At the Encrypt Document dialog box that displays, type your password in the text box (the text will display as round bullets) and then press the Enter key (or click OK). At the Confirm Password dialog box, type your password again (the text will display as round bullets) and then press the Enter key (or click OK). When you apply a password, the message "A password is required to open this document." displays to the right of the Protect Document button.

Exercise 25.3C   Encrypting a Document with a Password   Part 3 of 3

1. With **C25-E03-REAgrmnt.docx** open, encrypt the document with a password by completing the following steps:
   a. Click the File tab, click the Protect Document button at the Info tab Backstage view, and then click *Encrypt with Password* at the drop-down list.
   b. At the Encrypt Document dialog box, type your initials in uppercase letters (your text will display as round bullets).

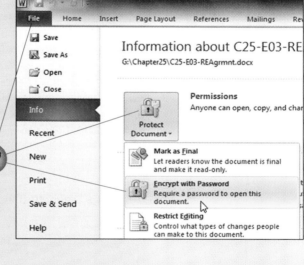

   c. Press the Enter key.
   d. At the Confirm Password dialog box, type your initials again in uppercase letters (your text will display as bullets) and then press the Enter key.
2. Click the File tab to return to the document.
3. Save and then close **C25-E03-REAgrmnt.docx**.
4. Open **C25-E03-REAgrmnt.docx**. At the Password dialog box, type your initials in uppercase letters and then press the Enter key.
5. Save, print, and then close **C25-E03-REAgrmnt.docx**.

Restricting Editing

Click the Protect Document button at the Info tab Backstage view and then click the *Restrict Editing* option at the drop-down list and the document displays with the Restrict Formatting and Editing task pane. This is the same task pane you learned about previously in this chapter. In addition to restricting access to a document with the Restrict Formatting and Editing task pane, you can use Information Rights Management (IRM). With IRM, you can restrict access to Word documents, Excel workbooks, and PowerPoint presentations, and you can prevent sensitive information from being printed or copied by unauthorized people. To use IRM, subscribe to the free trial provided by Microsoft. After you have subscribed, you can use IRM to restrict access to an open document by clicking the Protect Document button at the Info tab Backstage view, pointing to *Restriction Permission by People*, and then clicking *Restricted Access*. Check with your instructor to determine if this software is available for you to use.

Adding a Digital Signature

Create a Digital Signature
1. Click File tab.
2. Click Protect Document button at Info tab Backstage view.
3. Click *Add a Digital Signature*.
4. Click OK.
5. Click *Create your own digital ID*.
6. Click OK.
7. Type information at Create a Digital ID dialog box.
8. Click Create button.
9. Type purpose at Sign dialog box.
10. Click Sign button.
11. Click OK.

You can add a digital signature to a document to authenticate it and indicate that you agree with its contents. When you add a digital signature, the document is locked so that it cannot be edited or changed unless you remove the digital signature. A digital signature is an electronic stamp that vouches for a document's authenticity. Before adding a digital signature, you must obtain one. You can obtain a digital signature from a commercial certification authority, or you can create your own digital signature. When you create a digital signature, it is saved on the hard drive or the network. Depending on how your system is set up, you might be prevented from using a digital signature.

To add a digital signature, click the Protect Document button at the Info tab Backstage view and then click the *Add a Digital Signature* option at the drop-down list. At the Microsoft Word digital signature information message, click OK. At the Get a Digital ID dialog box, click the *Create your own digital ID* option and then click OK. At the Create a Digital ID dialog box, shown in Figure 25.9, insert information and then click Create.

Figure 25.9 Create a Digital ID Dialog Box

Insert information in the text boxes to identify your digital signature.

1. Open **Lease.docx** and save the document with the name **C25-E04-Lease**.
2. Create and add a digital signature by completing the following steps:
   a. Click the File tab, click the Protect Document button at the Info tab Backstage view, and then click *Add a Digital Signature* at the drop-down list.
   b. At the Microsoft Word digital signature information message, click OK.
   c. At the Get a Digital ID dialog box, click the *Create your own digital ID* option and then click OK. (If this dialog box does not display, skip to Step 2e.)

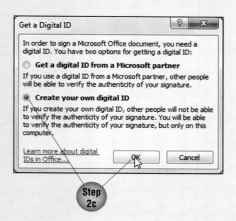

Step 2c

   d. At the Create a Digital ID dialog box, insert the following information:
      1) Type your name in the *Name* text box.
      2) Type your actual email address or a fictitious email address in the *E-mail address* text box.
      3) Type your school's name in the *Organization* text box.
      4) Type the city in which your school is located in the *Location* text box.
      5) Click the Create button.

Step 2e

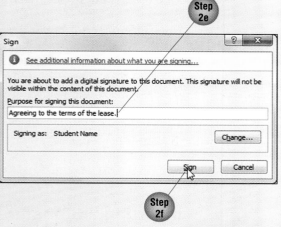

   e. At the Sign dialog box, type Agreeing to the terms of the lease. in the *Purpose for signing this document* text box.
   f. Click the Sign button.
   g. At the message saying your signature has been successfully saved, click OK.

Step 2f

3. Click the File tab to return to the document and then click each of the ribbon tabs and notice the commands and buttons that are inactive or dimmed.
4. Click the Signatures button located toward the left side of the Status bar. (This displays the Signatures task pane at the right side of the screen.)

Step 4

5. View the invisible digital signature details by hovering the mouse pointer over your name in the Signatures task pane, clicking the down-pointing arrow that displays to the right of your name, and then clicking *Signature Details* at the drop-down list.
6. Notice the signature details, including the information on the inserted digital signature and the purpose of the signature.
7. Click the Close button to close the Signature Details dialog box.
8. Close the Signatures task pane by clicking the Close button located in the upper right corner of the task pane.

Removing a Digital Signature

QUICK STEPS

Remove a Digital Signature
1. Click Signatures button on Status bar.
2. Hover mouse pointer over name in Signatures task pane, click down-pointing arrow.
3. Click *Remove Signature.*
4. Click Yes.
5. Click OK.

You can remove a digital signature from a document. When you remove the signature, the document is no longer authenticated, and it is available for formatting and editing. Remove the digital signature at the Signatures task pane. Display the Signatures task pane by clicking the Signatures button that displays toward the left side of the Status bar. This button indicates that a digital signature has been applied to the document. Remove the signature by hovering the mouse pointer over the name in the Signatures task pane, clicking the down-pointing arrow at the right of the name, and then clicking *Remove Signature* at the drop-down list. At the message asking if you want to permanently remove the signature, click Yes and then click OK at the message telling you that the signature has been removed.

Exercise 25.4B   Removing a Digital Signature   Part 2 of 5

1. With **C25-E04-Lease.docx** open, remove the digital signature by completing the following steps:
   a. Click the Signatures button located toward the left side of the Status bar.
   b. Hover the mouse pointer over your name in the Signatures task pane and then click the down-pointing arrow that displays to the right of your name.
   c. Click *Remove Signature* at the drop-down list.
   d. At the message asking if you want to permanently remove the signature, click Yes.
   e. At the message telling you the signature has been removed and the document has been saved, click OK.
2. Close the Signatures task pane.

Inserting a Signature Line

QUICK STEPS

Insert a Signature Line
1. Click Insert tab.
2. Click Signature Line button.
3. At Microsoft Word dialog box, click OK.
4. Type desired signature information.
5. Click OK.

You can insert a signature line in a document that specifies who should sign it. The signature line can include information about the intended signer, such as the person's name, title, and email address. It can also provide instructions for the intended signer. If you send an electronic copy of the document to the intended signer, the person sees the signature line as well as the instructions.

To add a signature line in a document, position the insertion point where you want the signature line to display, click the Insert tab, and then click the Signature Line button in the Text group. At the Signature Setup dialog box, shown in Figure 25.10, type the desired information about the intended signer and then click OK to close the dialog box.

Signature Line

Figure 25.10 Signature Setup Dialog Box

Insert information in this dialog box to insert the signature signer's name and title and to provide instructions to the signer.

Exercise 25.4C Inserting a Signature Line

Part 3 of 5

1. With **C25-E04-Lease.docx** open, insert a signature line at the end of the document by completing the following steps:
   a. Press Ctrl + End to move the insertion point to the end of the document and then press the Enter key.
   b. Click the Insert tab.
   c. Click the Signature Line button in the Text group.

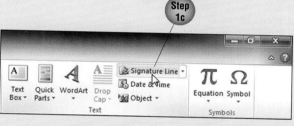

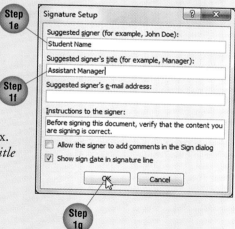

   d. At the Microsoft Word digital signature information message, click OK.
   e. At the Signature Setup dialog box, type your first and last names in the *Suggested signer* text box.
   f. Type Assistant Manager in the *Suggested signer's title* text box.
   g. Click OK.
2. Insert a second signature line for a lessee to sign by completing the following steps:
   a. Press the Enter key.
   b. If necessary, click the Insert tab.
   c. Click the Signature Line button in the Text group.
   d. At the Microsoft Word digital signature information message, click OK.
   e. At the Signature Setup dialog box, type Jaden Cowell in the *Suggested signer* text box and then press the Tab key.
   f. Type Lessee in the *Suggested signer's title* text box.
   g. Click OK.
3. Save **C25-E04-Lease.docx**.

Inserting a Signature on a Signature Line

When you insert a signature line, the signer can type his or her name on the line, select a digital image of his or her signature, or write a signature using a tablet PC. When the signer signs the document, a digital signature is added simultaneously that authenticates the identity of the signer. When the document is signed, it becomes a read-only document.

Exercise 25.4D Inserting a Signature   Part 4 of 5

1. With **C25-E04-Lease.docx** open, double-click the top signature line.
2. At the Microsoft Word digital signature information message, click OK.
3. At the Sign dialog box, type your first and last names in the text box following the *X*.
4. Click the Sign button.
5. At the message telling you that your signature has been successfully saved, click OK.

Sign

ⓘ See additional information about what you are signing...

Before signing this document, verify that the content you are signing is correct.

Type your name below, or click Select Image to select a picture to use as your signature:

X | Student Name | Select Image...

Student Name
Assistant Manager

Signing as: Student Name   Change...

Sign   Cancel

Step 3

Step 4

Inspecting a Document

Use options from the Check for Issues button drop-down list at the Info tab Backstage view to inspect a document for personal and hidden data and to check a document for compatibility and accessibility issues. When you click the Check for Issues button a drop-down list displays with the following options: *Inspect Document*, *Check Accessibility*, and *Check Compatibility*.

Using the Document Inspector

Word includes a document inspector that you can use to inspect your document for personal data, hidden data, and metadata. Metadata is data that describes other data, such as document properties. You may want to remove some personal or hidden data before you share a document with other people. To check your document for personal or hidden data, click the File tab, click the Check for Issues button at the Info tab Backstage view, and then click the *Inspect Document* option at the drop-down list. This displays the Document Inspector dialog box shown in Figure 25.11.

Inspect a Document
1. Click File tab.
2. Click Check for Issues button at Info tab Backstage view.
3. Click *Inspect Document*.
4. Remove check mark from items you do not want to inspect.
5. Click Inspect.

Figure 25.11 Document Inspector Dialog Box

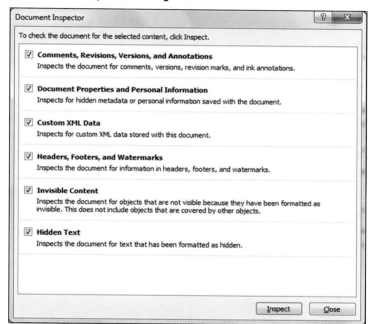

Remove the check mark from those options that you do not want the document inspector to check.

By default, the document inspector checks all of the items listed in the dialog box. If you do not want the inspector to check a specific item in your document, remove the check mark preceding the item. For example, if you know your document has headers and footers that you do not need to check, click the *Headers, Footers, and Watermarks* check box to remove the check mark. Click the Inspect button located toward the bottom of the dialog box, and the document inspector scans the document to identify information.

When the inspection is complete, the results display in the dialog box. A check mark before an option indicates that the inspector did not find the specific items. If an exclamation point is inserted before an option, the inspector found items and displays a list of the items. If you want to remove the found items, click the Remove All button that displays at the right of the desired option. Click the Reinspect button to ensure that the specific items were removed and then click the Close button.

1. With **C25-E04-Lease.docx** open, remove your signature by completing the following steps:
   a. Click the Edit Anyway button that displays in the yellow message bar located toward the top of the screen.
   b. At the message asking if you want to remove the signature, click Yes.
   c. At the message indicating the signature has been removed and the document has been saved, click OK.
2. Press Ctrl + Home and then make the following changes to the document:
   a. Turn on Track Changes.
   b. Select the title *LEASE AGREEMENT* and then change the font size to 14 points.
   c. Delete the text *first* that displays in the second numbered paragraph (the *RENT* paragraph) and then type fifteenth.
   d. Move the insertion point to the beginning of the text *IN WITNESS WHEREOF* (located on page two) and then press the Tab key.
   e. Turn off Track Changes.
3. Hide text by completing the following steps:
   a. Move the insertion point to the end of the first paragraph of text in the document (one space after the period at the end of the sentence).
   b. Type The entire legal description of the property is required for this agreement to be valid.
   c. Select the text you just typed.
   d. Click the Home tab.
   e. Click the Font group dialog box launcher.
   f. At the Font dialog box, click the *Hidden* option in the *Effects* section.
   g. Click OK to close the dialog box.
4. Click the Save button on the Quick Access toolbar.
5. Inspect the document by completing the following steps:
   a. Click the File tab.
   b. Click the Check for Issues button at the Info tab Backstage view and then click *Inspect Document* at the drop-down list.

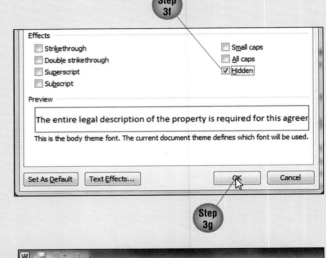

Step 3f

Step 3g

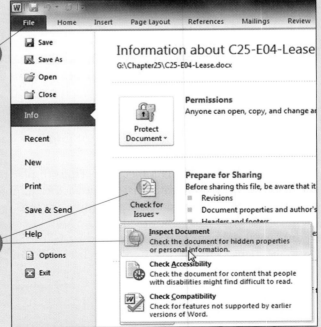

Step 5a

Step 5b

c. At the Document Inspector dialog box, tell the document inspector not to check the document for XML data by clicking the *Custom XML Data* check box to remove the check mark.

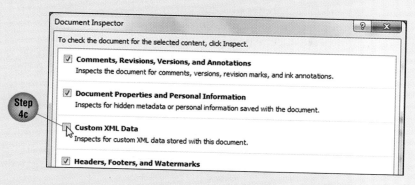

d. Click the Inspect button.
e. Read through the inspection results and then remove all hidden text by clicking the Remove All button that displays at the right side of the *Hidden Text* section. (Make sure a message displays below *Hidden Text* indicating that the text was successfully removed.)

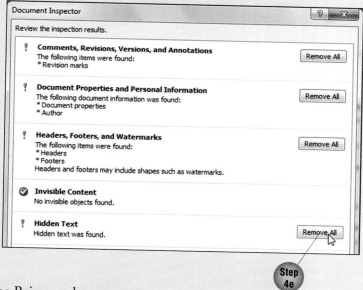

f. Click the Reinspect button.
g. To keep the header and footer text in the document, click the *Headers, Footers, and Watermarks* check box to remove the check mark.
h. Click the Inspect button.
i. Read through the inspection results and then remove all revisions by clicking the Remove All button that displays at the right side of the *Comments, Revisions, Versions, and Annotations* section.
j. Click the Reinspect button.
k. To leave the remaining items in the document, click the Close button.
6. Click the File tab to return to the document and then save the document.
7. Insert your signature in the top signature line (located toward the bottom of the document) by completing steps similar to those in Project 25.4D.
8. Print and then close **C25-E04-Lease.docx**.

Checking the Accessibility of a Document

Word 2010 includes the accessibility checker feature, which checks a document for content that a person with disabilities, such as a visual impairment, might find difficult to read. Check the accessibility of a document by clicking the Check for Issues button at the Info tab Backstage view and then clicking *Check Accessibility*. The accessibility checker examines the document for the most common accessibility problems in Word documents and groups them into three categories: errors—content that is unreadable to a person who is blind; warnings—content that is difficult to read; tips—content that may or may not be difficult to read. The accessibility checker examines the document, closes the Info tab Backstage view, and displays the Accessibility Checker task pane. At the Accessibility Checker task pane, unreadable errors are grouped in the *Errors* section, content that is difficult to read is grouped in the *Warnings* section, and content that may or may not be difficult to read is grouped in the *Tips* section. Select an issue in one of the sections, and an explanation of how to fix the issue and why displays at the bottom of the task pane.

In Word 2010, the accessibility checker examines a document for issues in each of the three categories as shown in Table 25.1:

Table 25.1 Accessibility Checker Issues

Errors	*Warnings*	*Tips*
Alt text	Heading spacing	Layout table reading order
Table headers	Blank table cells	Image watermarks
IRM Access	2D tables structure	Heading ordering
Document structure	Meaningful link text	
	Heading length	
	Floating objects	
	Repeated whitespace	

The first item in the Errors column, *Alt text*, refers to a text-based representation of an image. For example, if your document contains a picture, you may want to include alternate text that describes the picture. To create alternate text for an image, right-click the image in the document and then click *Format Picture* at the shortcut menu. At the Format Picture dialog box, click the *Alt Text* option in the panel at the left. Type a title for the picture in the *Title* text box and type a description for the picture in the *Description* text box. The alternate text you create for an image will display when you use a screen reader to view the document or save the document in a file format such as HTML or DAISY (Digital Accessible Information System).

To resolve an error or warning issue, click the issue in the Accessibility Checker task pane and then read the information that displays at the bottom of the task pane explaining how to fix the issue. When you are finished, close the Accessibility Checker task pane.

1. Open **PremPro.docx** and save the document with the name **C25-E05-PremPro**.
2. Complete an accessibility check by completing the following steps:
   a. Click the File tab.
   b. At the Info tab Backstage view, click the Check for Issues button and then click *Check Accessibility* at the drop-down list.

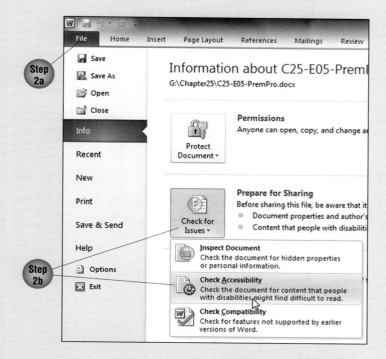

   c. Notice the Accessibility Checker task pane that displays at the right side of the screen. The task pane displays an *Errors* section and a *Warnings* section. Click *Picture 4* in the *Errors* section and then read the information that displays toward the bottom of the task pane describing why you should fix the error and how to fix it.
3. Add alternate text (which is a text-based representation of the clip art image) to the clip art by completing the following steps:
   a. Right-click on the clip art image in the document and then click *Format Picture* at the shortcut menu.

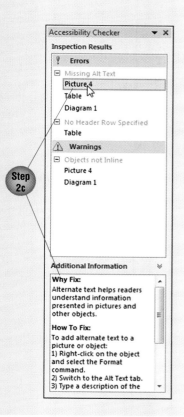

b. At the Format Picture dialog box, click the *Alt Text* option located at the bottom of the left panel.

c. Click in the *Title* text box and then type Cornucopia.

d. Select and then delete any text that displays in the *Description* text box and then type Clip art image of a cornucopia of fruits and vegetables representing Premium Produce.

e. Click the Close button.

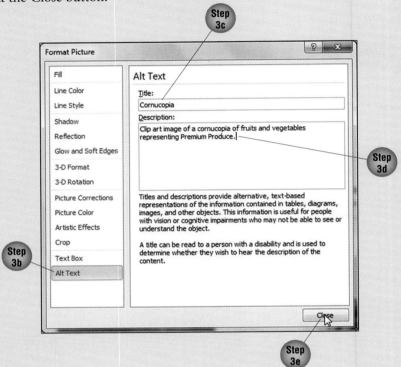

4. Click the first *Table* entry in the *Errors* section and then read the information that displays toward the bottom of the task pane explaining about creating alternate text for a table. Since the table contains text that is easily interpreted, you do not need to include alternate text.

5. Click the *Diagram 1* entry in the *Errors* section and then read the information about alternate text. Since this diagram contains text that is easily interpreted, you do not need to include alternate text.

6. Click the second *Table* entry in the *Errors* section and then read the information that displays toward the bottom of the task pane explaining about header rows. Since the table in the document does not span across pages you can ignore this information.

7. Click *Picture 4* in the *Warning* section and then read the information about objects that are not inline with text. If you made the change suggested, the clip art would move to a different location on the page so do not make the change suggested.

8. Click *Diagram 1* in the *Warning* section and notice it is the same information about objects that are not inline.

9. Close the Accessibility Checker task pane by clicking the Close button located in the upper right corner of the task pane.

10. Save **C25-E05-PremPro.docx**.

Checking the Compatibility of a Document

Word includes a compatibility checker that checks your document to identify elements that either are not supported or will act differently in previous versions of Word from Word 97 through Word 2007. Some features not supported by versions prior to Word 2007 include building blocks, citations and bibliographies, tracked moves, and SmartArt. For example, if you save a Word 2010 document containing a SmartArt diagram as a Word 2003 document, the diagram will be converted into a single object that cannot be edited.

To run the compatibility checker, open the desired document, click the File tab, click the Check for Issues button at the Info tab Backstage view, and then click *Check Compatibility* at the drop-down list. This displays the Microsoft Word Compatibility Checker dialog box shown in Figure 25.12. The dialog box displays a summary of the elements in the document that are not compatible with previous versions of Word and indicates what will happen when the document is saved and then opened in a previous version.

Check Compatibility
1. Click File tab.
2. Click Check for Issues button at Info tab Backstage view.
3. Click *Check Compatibility.*
4. At Microsoft Word Compatibility Checker dialog box, click OK.

Figure 25.12 Microsoft Word Compatibility Checker Dialog Box

This dialog box displays information on what will happen to text or elements in a document that is saved in a previous version of Word.

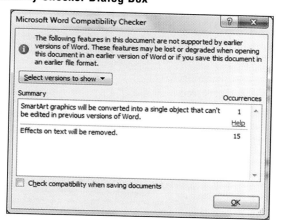

Click the Select versions to show button and a drop-down list displays with two options: *Word 97-2003* and *Word 2007*. If you are sending the document to someone who will be opening it in Word 2007, click the *Word 97-2003* option at the drop-down list to remove the check mark. This displays only compatibility issues in the dialog box between Word 2010 and Word 2007. If you want to check compatibility issues with version 97 through 2003, click *Word 2007* to remove the check mark. If you want the compatibility checker to check a document each time you save a document, insert a check mark in the *Check compatibility when saving documents* check box.

1. With **C25-E05-PremPro.docx** open, check the compatibility of elements in the document by completing the following steps:

   a. Click the File tab, click the Check for Issues button at the Info tab and Backstage view, and then click *Check Compatibility* at the drop-down list.

   b. At the Microsoft Word Compatibility Checker dialog box, read the information that displays in the *Summary* list box.

   c. Click the Select versions to show button and then click *Word 97-2003* at the drop-down list. Notice that the information about SmartArt graphics being converted to a static object disappears from the *Summary* list box. This is because Word 2007 supports SmartArt graphics.

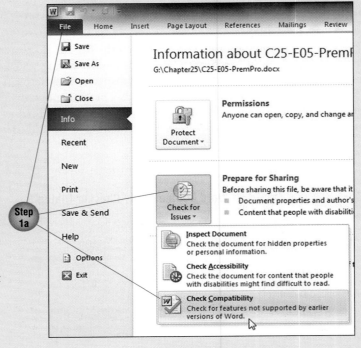

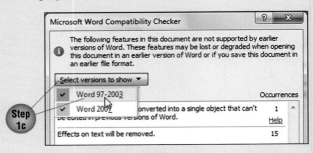

   d. Click OK to close the dialog box.

2. Save the document in Word 2003 format by completing the following steps:

   a. Click the File tab and then click Save As.

   b. At the Save As dialog box, click the *Save as type* option box and then click *Word 97-2003 Document (*.doc)* at the drop-down list.

   c. Select the text in the *File name* text box and then type C25-E05-PremPro-2003format.

   d. Click the Save button.

   e. Scroll through the document and notice the changes.

3. Close **C25-E05-PremPro-2003format.doc**.

Managing Versions

As you are working in a document, Word is automatically saving your document every 10 minutes. This automatic backup feature can be very helpful if you accidentally close your document without saving it, or if the power to your computer is disrupted. As Word is automatically saving a backup of your currently open document, the saved documents are listed to the right of the Manage Versions button in the Info tab Backstage view as shown in Figure 25.13. Each autosave document displays with *Today*, followed by the time and *(autosave)*. When you save and then close your document, the autosave backup documents are deleted.

Figure 25.13 Autosave Documents in Info Tab Backstage View

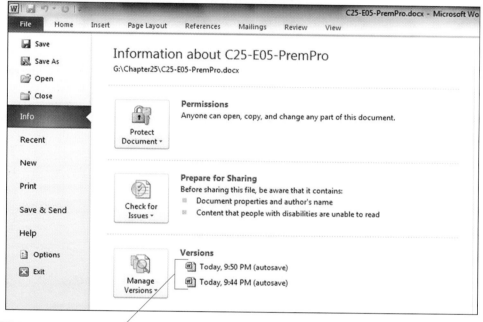

Word automatically creates backups of your document. The backup documents are deleted when you save the document. To open a backup, click the desired version.

To open an autosave backup document, click the File tab, and then click the backup document you want to open that displays to the right of the Manage Versions button. The document opens as a read-only document, and a yellow message bar displays with a Compare button and a Restore button. Click the Compare button and the autosave document is compared to the original document. You can then decide which changes you want to accept or reject. Click the Restore button and a message displays indicating that you are about to overwrite the last saved version with the selected version. At this message, click OK.

Open Autosave Backup Document
1. Click File tab.
2. At Info tab Backstage view, click document name at right of Manage Versions button.

QUICK STEPS

Display UnsavedFiles Folder
1. Click File tab.
2. Click Manage Versions button.
3. Click *Recover Unsaved Documents.*
OR
1. Click File tab.
2. Click Recent tab.
3. Click Recover Unsaved Documents button.

Change AutoRecover Time
1. Click File tab.
2. Click Options button.
3. Click *Save.*
4. Type desired minutes in *Save AutoRecover information every* option box.
5. Click OK.

When you save a document, the autosave backup documents are deleted. However, if you are working in a document that you close without saving (after 10 minutes) or the power is disrupted, Word keeps the backup file in the *UnsavedFiles* folder on the hard drive. You can access this folder by clicking the Manage Versions button in the Info tab Backstage view and then clicking *Recover Unsaved Documents.* At the Open dialog box that displays, double-click the desired backup file you want to open. You can also display the *UnsavedFiles* folder by clicking the File tab, clicking the Recent tab, and then clicking the Recover Unsaved Documents button that displays toward the bottom of the screen.

You can manage the backup files by right-clicking a backup file. At the shortcut menu that displays, click the *Open Version* option to open the backup file, click the *Delete This Version* option to delete the backup file, or click the *Compare with Current* option to compare the backup file with the currently open file. If you want to delete all unsaved files, open a blank document, click the File tab, click the Manage Versions button and then click the *Delete All Unsaved Document* option. At the message asking if you are sure you want to delete the unsaved documents, click Yes.

As mentioned previously, by default, Word automatically saves a backup of your unsaved document every 10 minutes. To change this default setting, click the File tab and then click the Options button below the Help tab. At the Word Options dialog box, click *Save* in the left panel. Notice that the *Save AutoRecover information every* option is set at 10 minutes. To change this number, click the up-pointing arrow to the right of *10* to increase the number of minutes between autosaves or click the down-pointing arrow to decrease the amount of time between autosaves.

Delete Backup File
1. Click File tab.
2. Right-click backup file.
3. Click *Delete This Version* at shortcut menu.

Delete All Unsaved Versions
1. Open blank document.
2. Click File tab.
3. Click Manage Versions button.
4. Click *Delete All Unsaved Documents.*
5. Click yes.

Exercise 25.5C   **Opening an Autosave Document**   Part 3 of 3

1. At a blank document, decrease the autosave time by completing the following steps:
   a. Click the File tab and then click the Options button that displays below the Help tab.
   b. At the Word Options dialog box, click *Save* in the left panel.
   c. Click the down-pointing arrow at the right of the *Save AutoRecover information every* option box until *2* displays.

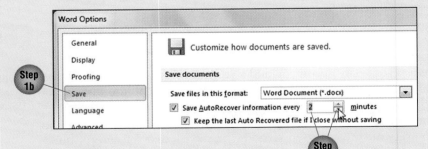

   d. Click OK to close the dialog box.
   e. Close the blank document.

2. Open **C25-E05-PremPro.docx**.
3. Press Ctrl + End to move the insertion point to the end of the document and then insert the file name as a field by completing the following steps:
   a. Click the Insert tab.
   b. Click the Quick Parts button and then click *Field* at the drop-down list.
   c. At the Field dialog box, scroll down the list box and then double-click the *FileName* field.
4. Leave the document open for over two minutes without making any changes. After a couple of minutes have passed, click the File tab and then check to see if an autosave document displays to the right of the Manage Versions button. (If not, click the File tab to return to the document and wait a few more minutes.)

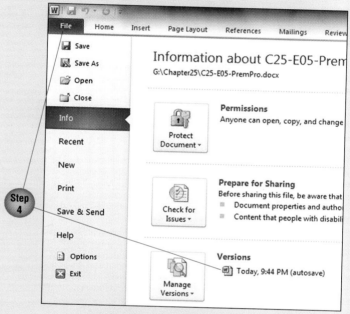

5. When an autosave document displays in the Info tab Backstage view, click the File tab to return to the document.
6. Scroll to the end of the document, select the SmartArt and then delete the SmartArt.
7. Click the File tab and then click the autosave document that displays to the right of the Manage Versions button. If more than one autosave document displays, click the one at the top of the list. This opens the autosave document as read-only.

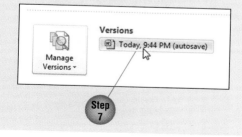

8. Restore the document to the autosave document by clicking the Restore button that displays in the yellow message bar.

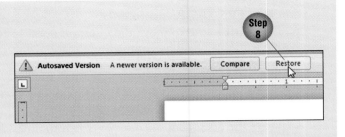

9. At the message that displays indicating you are about to overwrite the last saved version with the selected version, click OK. (This saves the document with the SmartArt.)

10. Check to see what versions of previous documents Word has saved by completing the following steps:

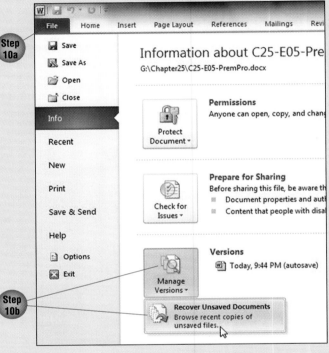

   a. Click the File tab.
   b. Click the Manage Versions button and then click *Recover Unsaved Documents* at the drop-down list.
   c. At the Open dialog box that displays draft documents in the *UnsavedFiles* folder on your hard drive, check the documents that display in the list box.
   d. Click the Cancel button to close the Open dialog box.

11. Delete the backup files by completing the following steps:
   a. Click the File tab.
   b. Right-click the first autosave backup file name that displays to the right of the Manage Versions button.
   c. Click *Delete This Version* at the shortcut menu.
   d. Complete similar steps to delete any other autosave backup files.

12. Return the autosave time back to 10 minutes by completing the following steps:
   a. Click the File tab and then click the Options button that displays below the Help tab.
   b. At the Word Options dialog box, click *Save* in the left panel.
   c. Click the up-pointing arrow at the right of the *Save AutoRecover information every* option box until *10* displays.
   d. Click OK to close the dialog box.

13. Save, print, and then close **C25-E05-PremPro.docx**.

14. Delete all unsaved backup files by completing the following steps:
   a. Press Ctrl + N to display a blank document.
   b. Click the File tab.
   c. Click the Manage Versions button and then click *Delete All Unsaved Documents*.
   d. At the message that displays, click Yes.

15. Click the File tab to return to the blank document.

Chapter Summary

➤ Restrict formatting and editing in a document and apply a password to it with options at the Restrict Formatting and Editing task pane. Display this task pane by clicking the Review tab and then clicking the Restrict Editing button in the Protect group.

➤ Restrict formatting by specifying styles that are allowed and not allowed in a document. Do this at the Formatting Restrictions dialog box. Display this dialog box by clicking the Settings hyperlink in the Restrict Formatting and Editing task pane.

➤ To restrict editing in a document, click the *Allow only this type of editing in the document* option at the Restrict Formatting and Editing task pane, click the down-pointing arrow at the right of the options box, and then click the desired option.

➤ Enforce editing and formatting restrictions by clicking the Yes, Start Enforcing Protection button in the Restrict Formatting and Editing task pane and make changes to what is allowed at the Start Enforcing Protection dialog box.

➤ Protect a document with a password by using options at the Start Enforcing Protection dialog box or by using options at the General Options dialog box.

➤ Open a document in different views with options at the Open button drop-down list in the Open dialog box.

➤ The Info tab Backstage view displays document properties information.

➤ Display the document information panel by clicking the Properties button at the Info tab Backstage view and then clicking *Show Document Panel* at the drop-down list. Type information in the text boxes at the document information panel to describe the document.

➤ In addition to the document information panel, you can insert document information at the Properties dialog box. Display this dialog box by clicking the Properties button at the Info tab Backstage view and then clicking *Advanced Properties* or by clicking the Document Properties button at the document information panel and then clicking *Advanced Properties*.

➤ Mark a document as final, and the document is saved as a read-only document. Mark a document as final by clicking the Protect Document button at the Info tab Backstage view and then clicking *Mark as Final* at the drop-down list. Typing, editing commands, and proofing marks are turned off when a document is marked as final.

➤ Protect a document with a password by clicking the Protect Document button at the Info tab Backstage view and then clicking *Encrypt with Password*. At the Encrypt Document dialog box, type the password and then press the Enter key. Type the password again at the Confirm Password dialog box and then press the Enter key.

➤ Another method for displaying the Restrict Formatting and Editing task pane is to click the Protect Document button at the Info tab Backstage view and then click *Restrict Editing* at the drop-down list.

➤ Add a digital signature to a document to authenticate it and indicate that you agree with its contents. Adding a digital signature locks the document so it cannot be edited or changed unless the digital signature is removed. You can obtain a digital signature from a commercial certification authority or create your own. Create your own digital signature by clicking the Protect Document button at the Info tab Backstage view and then clicking *Add a Digital Signature* at the drop-down list.

➤ Remove a digital signature by clicking the Signatures button on the Status bar to display the Signatures task pane, hovering the mouse over the name, clicking the down-pointing arrow at the right of the name, and then clicking *Remove Signature* at the drop-down list.

➤ Insert a signature line in a document to specify who should sign it. To insert a signature line, click the Insert tab and then click the Signature Line button in the Text group. At the Signature Setup dialog box, type the desired information and then click OK.

➤ Inspect a document for personal data, hidden data, and metadata with options at the Document Inspector dialog box. Display this dialog box by clicking the Check for Issues button at the Info tab Backstage view and then clicking *Inspect Document* at the drop-down list.

➤ The accessibility checker checks a document for content that a person with disabilities might find difficult to read. Run the accessibility checker by clicking the Check for Issues button at the Info tab Backstage view and then clicking *Check Accessibility* at the drop-down list.

➤ Run the compatibility checker to check your document and identify elements that are not supported or will act differently in previous versions of Word. To determine the compatibility of the features in your document, click the Check for Issues button at the Info tab Backstage view and then click *Check Compatibility* at the drop-down list.

➤ By default, Word automatically saves a backup of your unsaved document every 10 minutes, and the backup document displays to the right of the Manage Versions button at the Info tab Backstage view. Click the document name to open the backup document.

➤ When you save a document, Word automatically deletes the backup documents. However, if you close a document without saving it, or if the power to your computer is disrupted, Word keeps the backup document in the *UnsavedFiles* folder on the hard drive. Display this folder by clicking the Manage Versions button at the Info tab Backstage view and then clicking *Recover Unsaved Documents* at the drop-down list.

➤ Delete an autosave backup file by displaying the Info tab Backstage view, right-clicking the desired autosave backup file, and then clicking *Delete This Version* at the shortcut menu. Delete all unsaved documents by displaying a blank document, clicking the File tab, clicking the Manage Versions button and then clicking *Delete All Unsaved Documents*.

➤ By default, Word automatically saves a backup of your unsaved document every 10 minutes. You can change this default setting with the *Save AutoRecover information every* option at the Options dialog box with *Save* selected. Display this dialog box by clicking the File tab, clicking the Options button, and then clicking *Save* in the left panel.

Commands Review

FEATURE	RIBBON TAB, GROUP	BUTTON, OPTION
Restrict Formatting and Editing task pane	Review, Protect	
Formatting Restrictions dialog box	Review, Protect	, Settings
General Options dialog box	File	Save As, Tools, General Options
Document information panel	File	Properties ▾ , Show Document Panel
Properties dialog box	File	Properties ▾ , Advanced Properties
Encrypt Document dialog box	File	, Encrypt with Password
Digital signature	File	, Add a Digital Signature
Signature Setup dialog box	Insert, Text	

FEATURE	RIBBON TAB, GROUP	BUTTON, OPTION
Document Inspector dialog box	File	, Inspect Document
Accessibility checker	File	, Check Accessibility
Compatibility checker	File	, Check Compatibility
UnsavedFiles folder	File	, Recover Unsaved Documents

Key Points *Review*

Completion: In the space provided at the right, indicate the correct term, command, or number.

1. Limit the formatting users can apply to text in a document with options in this section of the Restrict Formatting and Editing task pane.

2. Use options in this section of the Restrict Formatting and Editing task pane to limit the types of changes a user can make to a document.

3. Protect a document with a password using options at the Start Enforcing Protection dialog box or with options at this dialog box.

4. Click this button in the Restrict Formatting and Editing task pane to display the Start Enforcing Protection dialog box.

5. You can add additional information to a document's properties at this panel.

6. Display the Properties dialog box by clicking the Properties button at the Info tab Backstage view and then clicking this option at the drop-down list.

7. Mark a document as final by clicking this button at the Info tab Backstage view and then clicking *Mark as Final* at the drop-down list.

8. Add this type of signature to a document to vouch for the authenticity of the document.

9. Insert a signature line in a document by clicking this tab and then clicking the Signature Line button in the Text group.

10. Use this feature to inspect your document for personal data, hidden data, and metadata.

11. This feature checks a document for content that a person with disabilities might find difficult to read.

12. Use this feature to check your document and identify elements that are not supported in previous versions of Word.

13. By default, Word automatically saves a document after this number of minutes.

14. Word keeps backup files of unsaved documents in this folder on the hard drive.

Chapter Assessments

Applying Your Skills

Demonstrate your knowledge of features learned in this chapter by completing the following assessments.

Assessment 25.1   Restrict Formatting in a Computer Report

1. Open **Computers.docx** and save the document with the name **C25-A01-Computers**.
2. Display the Restrict Formatting and Editing task pane and then restrict formatting to Heading 2 and Heading 3 styles.
3. Enforce the protection and include the password *computers*.
4. Click the <u>Available styles</u> hyperlink in the Restrict Formatting and Editing task pane.
5. Apply the Heading 2 style to the title *THE COMPUTER ADVANTAGE*. (The Heading 3 style may not display until you apply the Heading 2 style to the first title.)
6. Apply the Heading 3 style to the five headings in the document.
7. Close the Styles task pane and then close the Restrict Formatting and Editing task pane.
8. Save the document and then print only page one.
9. Close **C25-A01-Computers.docx**.

Assessment 25.2   Restrict Editing to Comments in a Software Life Cycle Document

1. Open **SoftwareCycle.docx** and save the document with the name **C25-A02-SoftwareCycle**.
2. Display the Restrict Formatting and Editing task pane, restrict editing to only comments, and then start enforcing the protection (do not include a password).
3. Insert the comment Create a SmartArt graphic that illustrates the software life cycle. at the end of the first paragraph of text in the document.
4. Insert the comment Include the problem-solving steps. at the end of the paragraph in the *Design* section.
5. Insert the comment Describe a typical beta testing cycle. at the end of the paragraph in the *Testing* section.
6. Close the Reviewing pane and the Restrict Formatting and Editing task pane.
7. Print only the comments.
8. Save and then close **C25-A02-SoftwareCycle.docx**.

Assessment 25.3   Insert Document Properties, Check Compatibility, and Save a Presentation Document in a Different Format

1. Open **Presentation.docx** and save the document with the name **C25-A03-Presentation**.
2. Make the following changes to the document:
   a. Apply the Heading 1 style to the title *Delivering a How-To Presentation*.
   b. Apply the Heading 2 style to the three headings in the document.
   c. Change the style set to Thatch.
   d. Apply the Flow theme and change the theme colors to Clarity.
   e. Center the title.
   f. Change the color of the clip art image to *Gray-50%, Accent color 1 Light*.
   g. Change the color of the SmartArt (located at the end of the document) to *Colorful Range – Accent Colors 3 to 4* and apply the *White Outline* SmartArt style.

3. Display the document information panel and then type the following in the specified text boxes:
   a. Author = (type your first and last names)
   b. Title = Delivering a How-To Presentation
   c. Subject = Presentations
   d. Keywords = presentation, how-to, delivering, topics
   e. Comments = This document describes the three steps involved in developing a how-to presentation.
4. Display the Properties dialog box (click the Document Properties button in the upper left corner of the document information panel and then click *Advanced Properties*) and then create the following custom properties (with the Custom tab selected):
   a. Click *Checked by* in the *Name* list box, leave the *Type* option set at *Text*, type your first and last name in the *Value* text box, and then click the Add button.
   b. Click *Date completed* in the *Name* list box, change the *Type* to *Date*, type today's date in the *Value* text box, and then click the Add button.
   c. Click *Project* in the *Name* list box, change the *Type* option to *Text*, type Preparing and Delivering Presentations in the *Value* text box, and then click the Add button.
   d. With the Properties dialog box open, press the Print Screen button on your keyboard to capture an image of your screen.
   e. Click OK to close the Properties dialog box.
5. At the document, complete the following steps:
   a. Close the document information panel.
   b. Press Ctrl + N to open a blank document.
   c. Click the Paste button to insert the screen capture image.
   d. Print the document.
   e. Close the document without saving it.
6. Save **C25-A03-Presentation.docx** and then print only the document properties. (The custom properties do not print.)
7. Run the accessibility checker on the document and then create alternate text for the clip art image. Type the text Presentation clip art image for the title and type Clip art image representing a person giving a presentation. for the description. Close the accessibility checker.
8. Save and then print **C25-A03-Presentation.docx**.
9. Run the compatibility checker to determine what features are not supported by earlier versions of Word.
10. Save the document in the *Word 97-2003 Document (*.doc)* format and name it **C25-A03-Presentation-2003format**.
11. Save, print, and then close **C25-A03-Presentation-2003format.doc**.

Expanding Your Skills

Explore additional feature options or use Help to learn a new skill in creating this document.

Assessment 25.4   Explore Commercial Digital Signatures

1. As you learned in this chapter, you can add a digital signature to a document to authenticate it and indicate that you agree with the contents. Before using a digital signature, you must obtain one by creating your own or through a commercial certification authority (third-party vendor). You created your own digital signature in this chapter, but now you want to learn how to obtain a commercial certification from a third-party vendor. To research vendors, visit the Office Marketplace at office.microsoft.en-us/marketplace. At the Office Marketplace website, click the Digital Signing hyperlink. (Look for this hyperlink in a section on browsing Office Marketplace). At the Digital Signing Web page, learn about three companies that provide digital signatures.

2. At a Word blank document, write a memo to your instructor that provides the following information:
   - Steps you took to get to the Office Marketplace website.
   - What you clicked at Office Marketplace to display information about companies that offer digital signatures.
   - Three companies that offer digital signatures, and include the company name, with what products the digital signature will work, and the star rating of the company.
   - Any other information you found interesting about the Office Marketplace website.
3. Save the completed memo and name it **C25-A04-DigitalSigMemo**.
4. Save, print, and then close **C25-A04-DigitalSigMemo.docx**.

Achieving Signature Status

Take your skills to the next level by completing this more challenging assessment.

Assessment 25.5   Format, Insert Document Properties, Check Compatibility, and Save a Document in a Different Format

1. Open **InfoSystem.docx** and save the document with the name **C25-A05-InfoSystem**.
2. Format the document so it appears as shown in Figure 25.14 with the following specifications:
   a. Apply the Paper theme and change the theme colors to Hardcover.
   b. Insert the DRAFT 1 watermark.
   c. Insert page numbers that print in the upper right corner of the page.
   d. Insert the Puzzle (Odd Page) footer. (Click the *[Type the company name]* placeholder and then type your first and last names.)
   e. Insert the SmartArt Continuous Cycle diagram and change the colors to *Colorful – Accent Colors* and apply the Metallic Scene style.
   f. Recolor the clip art image as shown in the figure.
   g. Make any other changes so your document displays as shown in Figure 25.14.
3. Display the document information panel and then type the following in the specified text boxes:
   a. Author = (type your first and last names)
   b. Title = Developing an Information System
   c. Subject = Software Development
   d. Keywords = software, design, plan
   e. Category = Software
   f. Status = Draft
   g. Comments = This document describes the four steps involved in developing an information system.
4. Display the Properties dialog box with the Custom tab selected and then add the following properties:
   a. Add the *Client* property with the text Stylus Enterprises.
   b. Add the *Department* property with the text Development Department.
   c. Add the *Document number* property with the number 24.
   d. Press the Print Screen key to make a capture of your screen.
   e. Close the Properties dialog box.
   f. At the document, close the document information panel, press Ctrl + N to insert a blank document, and then paste your screen capture image. Print the document and then close it without saving it.
5. At the **C25-A05-InfoSystem.docx** document, save the document and then print only the document properties.

6. Inspect the document and remove any hidden text.
7. Run the accessibility checker and then create alternate text for the clip art image.
8. Run the compatibility checker to determine what features are not supported by earlier versions of Word.
9. Save the document in the *Word 97-2003 Document (*.doc)* format and name it **C25-A05-InfoSystem-2003format**.
10. Save, print, and then close **C25-A05-InfoSystem-2003format.docx**.

Figure 25.14 Assessment 25.5

DEVELOPING AN INFORMATION SYSTEM

Identifying and assembling a team of employees with the required skills and expertise is a necessary first step in developing a new in-house information system. A management group may be involved in answering questions and providing information in the early planning phases of the project, but programmers and/or software engineers handle the design and implementation of any new system.

Programmers specialize in the development of new software, while software engineers are highly skilled professionals with programming and teamwork training. Their organized, professional application of the software development process is called software engineering.

PROJECT TEAM

Because of their large size, information systems require the creation of a project team. A project team usually includes a project manager, who acts as the team leader. Sometimes the project manager also functions as a systems analyst, responsible for completing the systems analysis and making design recommendations. Other project team members include software engineers and technicians. The software engineers deal with programming software, while technicians handle hardware issues. The comprehensive process software engineers initiate is called the system development life cycle (SDLC), a series of steps culminating in a completed information system.

PROJECT PLAN

The first step in the system development life cycle is planning. The planning step involves preparing a needs analysis and conducting feasibility studies. During this step, a company usually establishes a project team, and the team creates a project plan. The project plan includes an estimate of how long the project will take to complete, an outline of the steps involved, and a list of deliverables. Deliverables are documents, services, hardware, and software that must be finished and delivered by a certain time and date.

DESIGNING THE SYSTEM

...o the design stage once the project team has approved the plan, ...ign process begins with the writing of the documentation, which ...specifications. In most cases, the project team creates the functional ...t the system must be able to do.

Student Name | Confidential

1

IMPLEMENTATION

The project can move into the next phase, implementation, once the development team and the systems house develop the design specification and approve the plans. This step is where the actual work of putting the system together is completed, including creating a prototype and completing the programming. In most cases, implementing the new system is the longest, most difficult step in the process.

SUPPORT STAGE

A system goes into the support stage after it has been accepted and approved. A support contract normally allows users to contact the systems house for technical support, training, and sometimes on-site troubleshooting. Even if the system was designed in-house, the responsible department often operates as an independent entity—sometimes even charging the department acquiring the system. The support stage continues until a new information system is proposed and developed, usually years later. At that point, the existing system is retired and no longer used.

Student Name | Confidential

2

Chapter Twenty-Five

Performance Assessments

U N I T 5

Customizing Documents and Features

ASSESSING PROFICIENCIES

In this unit, you have learned how to insert, modify, and delete building blocks and how to customize AutoCorrect, Word options, themes, and Quick Styles sets. You also learned how to create, edit, and modify styles, apply styles to text in documents, and protect and prepare a document for distribution.

Note: Before beginning computer assessments, copy to your storage medium the Unit05PA folder from the CD that accompanies this textbook and then make Unit05PA the active folder.

Assessment U5.1   Format and Insert Fields in a Computer Report

1. Open **CompSecurity.docx** and save the document with the name **U5-PA01-CompSecurity**.
2. With the insertion point positioned at the beginning of the document, press Ctrl + Enter to insert a page break.
3. Apply the Heading 1 style to the two titles in the document *SECTION 1: UNAUTHORIZED ACCESS* and *SECTION 2: INFORMATION THEFT*.
4. Apply the Heading 2 style to the six headings in the document.
5. Change the style set to Traditional and change the paragraph spacing to *Open*.
6. Apply the Elemental theme.
7. Insert the Transcend (Even Page) footer building block.
8. Double-click in the document, press Ctrl + Home to move the insertion point to the beginning of the document, and then insert the *Automatic Table 1* table of contents building block.
9. Press Ctrl + End to move the insertion point to the end of the document, press the Backspace key, press the Enter key, and then insert a field that will insert the file name.
10. Press Shift + Enter and then insert a field that will insert the current date and time.
11. Save, print, and then close **U5-PA01-CompSecurity.docx**.

Assessment U5.2   Create Building Blocks and Prepare a Business Letter

1. Open **TRC-CBFooter.docx**.
2. Select the entire document, save the selected text in a custom building block in the Quick Part gallery, and name the building block with your initials followed by *TRC-CBFooter*.
3. Close **TRC-CBFooter.docx**.
4. Open **TRC-CBLtrhd.docx**.
5. Select the entire document, save the selected text in a custom building block in the Quick Part gallery, and name the building block with your initials followed by *TRC-CBLtrhd*.
6. Close **TRC-CBLtrhd.docx**.

7. At a blank document, click the *No Spacing* style in the Styles group in the Home tab and then type the following paragraph of text:

We carry a variety of earth-moving equipment for heavy construction including backhoes, dozers, excavators (including hydraulic excavators and mini-excavators), skid-steer loaders (including compact skid-steer, track skid-steer, and wheeled skid-steer loaders), tractors, cable locators, trenchers (including ride-on and walk-behind trenchers), and wheel loaders.

8. Select the entire document, save the selected text in a custom building block in the Quick Part gallery, and name the building block with your initials followed by *TRC-CBEquipPara*.
9. Save the custom building blocks in the Quick Part gallery as a Quick Parts button on the Quick Access toolbar.
10. Close the document without saving it.
11. At a blank document, click the *No Spacing* style, and then create the business letter shown in Figure U5.1 with the following specifications:
    a. Insert as a page header the custom building block that is named with your initials followed by *TRC-CBLtrhd*. **Hint: To do this, click the Quick Parts button on the Quick Access toolbar,** right-click *the custom building block, and then click the* **Insert at Page Header** *option.*
    b. Type the date, inside address, and first paragraph of text as shown in Figure U5.1.
    c. Insert the custom building block that is named with your initials followed by *TRC-CBEquipPara*.
    d. Type the remaining text in the letter.
    e. Insert as a page footer the custom building block that is named with your initials followed by *TRCC-CBFooter*. **Hint: Refer to Step 11a**.
12. Save the completed letter and name it **U5-PA02-TRC-CBLtr**.
13. Print and then close **U5-PA02-TRC-CBLtr.docx**.
14. Press Ctrl + N to open a new blank document.
15. Click the Quick Parts button on the Quick Access toolbar, press the Print Screen button on your keyboard, and then click in the document.
16. At the blank document, click the Paste button. (This pastes the screen capture in your document.)
17. Print the document and then close it without saving it.
18. Remove the Quick Parts button from the Quick Access toolbar and delete your custom building blocks.

Assessment U5.3   Create and Apply Custom Themes and AutoCorrect Entries to a Rental Form

1. At a blank document, create custom theme colors named with your initials that make the following color changes:
   a. Change the *Text/Background - Dark 2* color to *Tan, Text 2, Darker 75%*.
   b. Change the *Accent 1* color to *Olive Green, Accent 3, Darker 50%*.
2. Create custom theme fonts named with your initials that apply Verdana to headings and Cambria to body text.
3. Save the custom theme and name it with your initials. **Hint: Do this with the Save Current Theme** *option at the Themes drop-down gallery.*
4. Close the document without saving the changes.
5. Open **TRCRentalForm.docx** and save the document with the name **U5-PA03-TRCRentalForm**.

Tennison Rental Company

Council Bluffs Location

(current date)

Mr. Harold Nesbitt
Nesbitt Construction
3102 South 32nd Street
Council Bluffs, IA 51053

Dear Mr. Nesbitt:

Thank you for your interest in renting equipment from our company, Tennison Rental Company. We pride ourselves on maintaining the most extensive and well-maintained equipment in the greater Nebraska-Iowa region.

We carry a variety of earth-moving equipment for heavy construction including backhoes, dozers, excavators (including hydraulic excavators and mini-excavators), skid-steer loaders (including compact skid-steer, track skid-steer, and wheeled skid-steer loaders), tractors, cable locators, trenchers (including ride-on and walk-behind trenchers), and wheel loaders.

Come to our Council Bluffs site or visit our Omaha location and check out our inventory of earth-moving equipment. We are confident that we have the machinery you need.

Sincerely,

Kelsey Sanderson
General Manager

XX
U5-PA02-TRC-CBLtr.docx

4410 West Broadway ✕ Council Bluffs, IA 51052 ✕ 712.555.8800

6. Search for all occurrences of trc and replace with Tennison Rental Company.
7. Add the following text to AutoCorrect:
   a. Insert *trc* in the *Replace* text box and insert *Tennison Rental Company* in the *With* text box.
   b. Insert *cera* in the *Replace* text box and insert *Construction Equipment Rental Agreement* in the *With* text box.
8. Move the insertion point to the blank line above the heading *Further Assurances* (located on the third page) and then type the text shown in Figure U5.2. Use the Numbering feature to number the paragraphs with the lowercase letter

followed by the right parenthesis. (If the AutoCorrect feature capitalizes the first word after the letter and right parenthesis, use the AutoCorrect Options button to return the letter to lowercase.)

9. Apply the Heading 1 style to the title *Construction Equipment Rental Agreement* and apply the Heading 2 style to the headings in the document (*Lease, Rent, Use and Operation of Equipment, Insurance, Risk of Loss, Maintenance, Return of Equipment, Warranties of Lessee, Default*, and *Further Assurances*).
10. Apply your custom theme to the document.
11. Insert a building block that inserts the word *SAMPLE* as a watermark.
12. Insert the Conservative footer.
13. Center the title and change the spacing after the title to *12 pt.*
14. Save, print, and then close **U5-PA03-TRCRentalForm.docx**.
15. At a blank screen, complete the following steps:
    a. Click the Page Layout tab, click the Themes button, and then click *Save Current Theme*.
    b. With the Save Current Theme dialog box open, press the Print Screen key on your keyboard.
    c. Click the Cancel button to close the dialog box.
    d. At the blank document, click the Home tab and then click the Paste button. (This pastes the screen capture in the document.)
    e. Print and then close the document without saving it.
16. At a blank screen, delete your custom theme, custom theme colors, and custom theme fonts. Delete the *trc* and *cera* AutoCorrect entries.

Figure U5.2 **Assessment U5.3**

Default

Upon the occurrence of default, trc may without any further notice exercise any one or more of the following remedies:

a) declare all unpaid Rentals under this cera to be immediately due and payable;

b) terminate this cera as to any or all items of Equipment;

c) take possession of the Equipment, and for this purpose enter upon any premises of Lessee and remove the Equipment, without any liability, suit, action, or other proceeding by Lessee;

d) cause Lessee at his/her expense to promptly return the Equipment to trc in the condition set forth in this cera;

e) use, hold, sell, lease, or otherwise dispose of the Equipment or any item of it on the premises of Lessee or any other location without affecting the obligations of Lessee as provided in this cera;

f) proceed by appropriate action either at law or in equity to enforce performance by Lessee of the applicable covenants of this cera or to recover damages for the breach of them; or

g) exercise any other rights accruing to trc under any applicable law upon a default by a lessee.

Create and Apply Building Blocks and Styles to a Business Conduct Report

1. Open **TRCStyles.docx**.
2. Select the clip art image, the text *Tennison Rental Company*, and the text *Omaha Location*, save the selected text in a custom building block in the Quick Part gallery, and name the building block with your initials followed by *TRCHeader*.
3. Select the horizontal line and the address and telephone number below, save the selected text in a custom building block in the Quick Part gallery, and name the building block with your initials followed by *TRCFooter*.
4. Insert the custom building blocks in the Quick Part gallery as a Quick Parts button on the Quick Access toolbar.
5. Select the *Title* text (including the paragraph mark after the text) and then create a style named with your initials followed by *TRCTitle*. **Hint: Make sure you create a style and not a building block.**
6. Select the *Heading 1* text and then create a style named with your initials followed by *TRCHeading1*.
7. Select the *Heading 2* text and then create a style named with your initials followed by *TRCHeading2*.
8. Save the styles you created as a Quick Styles set named with your initials followed by *Tennison*.
9. Close **TRCStyles.docx** without saving the changes.
10. Open **TRCBusCode.docx** and save the document with the name **U5-PA04-TRCBusCode**.
11. Change to the Quick Styles set named *Tennison* (preceded by your initials).
12. Apply your custom title style to the title *Business Conduct Code*; apply your custom heading 1 style to the headings in all uppercase letters; and apply your custom heading 2 style to the headings with only the first letter in uppercase.
13. Insert the TRCHeader building block (preceded by your initials) as a header.
14. Insert the TRCFooter building block (preceded by your initials) as a footer.
15. Save, print, and then close **U5-PA04-TRCBusCode.docx**.
16. Make screen captures by completing the following steps:
    a. Press Ctrl + N to display a blank document.
    b. Click the Change Styles button, point to *Style Set*, and then press the Print Screen key on your keyoard.
    c. Click in the document to remove the side menu and then click the Paste button.
    d. Click the Quick Parts button on the Quick Access toolbar.
    e. Press the Print Screen key on your keyboard.
    f. Click in the document and then press Ctrl + End.
    g. Press the Enter key once and then click the Paste button.
    h. Make sure the two screen captures display on one page. If necessary, decrease the size of the screen captures.
    i. Print the document and then close it without saving it.
17. Delete the building blocks you created and remove the Quick Parts button from the Quick Access toolbar.
18. Delete the custom Quick Styles set you created that is named *Tennison* (preceded by your initials).

1. At a blank screen, create a new tab with the following specifications:
   a. Insert the new tab after the View tab in the list box in the Word Options dialog box with *Customize Ribbon* selected.
   b. Rename the tab *NSS* followed by your initials.
   c. Rename the custom group below your new tab to *Building Blocks*.
   d. Change the *Choose commands from* option to *All Commands*.
   e. From the list box at the left side of the dialog box, add the following commands to the *Building Blocks* group in the new tab: *Building Blocks Organizer*, *Document Property*, *Field*, and *Organizer*.
   f. Click OK to close the Word Options dialog box.
2. Close the document without saving it.
3. Open the document named **NSSStyles.docx**.
4. Copy styles by completing the following steps:
   a. Click your new NSS tab (the one that begins with NSS followed by your initials).
   b. Click the Organizer button in the Building Blocks group.
   c. Copy from the left list box to the right list box the following styles: *NSSHeading1*, *NSSTable*, and *NSSTitle*.
   d. Close the Organizer.
5. Close **NSSStyles.docx**.
6. Press Ctrl + N to display a blank document and then insert **NSSWebRpt.docx** into the current document. (Make sure you use the Object button arrow in the Insert group.)
7. Save the document and name it **U5-PA05-NSSWebRpt**.
8. Apply the following styles:
   a. Apply the NSSTitle style to the title *Navigating and Searching the Web*.
   b. Apply the NSSHeading1 style to the three headings in the document.
   c. Apply the NSSTable style to the three tables in the document. **Hint: Do this at the Table Tools Design tab.**
9. Insert a document property by completing the following steps:
   a. Move the insertion point to the end of the document.
   b. Click the Document Property button in the Building Blocks group in your tab and then click *Title* at the drop-down list.
   c. Type Navigating and Searching the Web in the Title placeholder and then press the Right Arrow key to deselect the placeholder.
   d. Press Shift + Enter and then insert the Author document property.
   e. Select the name that appears in the Author placeholder, type your first and last names, and then press the Right Arrow key to deselect the placeholder.
10. Insert a footer by completing the following steps:
    a. Click the Building Blocks Organizer button in the Building Blocks group in your tab.
    b. At the Building Blocks Organizer, click the *Name* column heading to sort the building blocks by name.
    c. Insert the *Blank* footer. (Make sure you insert the *Blank* footer and not the *Blank (Three Columns)* footer.)
    d. Delete the [Type text] placeholder by clicking in the placeholder, clicking the placeholder tab that displays at the side of the placeholder, and then pressing the Delete key.
    e. Insert the *Title* document property. (When you insert the document property it automatically inserts the title you typed earlier.)
    f. Double-click in the document to make it active.

11. Save and then print **U5-PA05-NSSWebRpt.docx**.
12. Make the following modifications to the styles:
    a. Modify the font color of the NSSHeading1 style to dark blue.
    b. Modify the NSSTable style so it aligns the table at the left and applies *Blue, Accent 1, Lighter 80%* shading to the even banded rows.
13. Save, print, and then close **U5-PA05-NSSWebRpt.docx**.
14. Press Ctrl + N to display a blank document and then delete styles from the Normal.dotm template by completing the following steps:
    a. Click the Organizer button in the Building Blocks group in your new tab.
    b. At the Organizer dialog box, click *NSSHeading1* in the right list box and then click the Delete button that displays between the two list boxes.
    c. At the message asking if you wish to delete the style, click Yes.
    d. Complete similar steps to delete the *NSSTable* style and the *NSSTitle* style from the right list box.
    e. Close the Organizer.
15. At the blank document, reset your ribbon. ***Hint: Do this at the Word Options dialog box with* Customize Ribbon *selected in the left panel*.
16. Close the document without saving it.

Assessment U5.6   Restrict Formatting in a Report

1. Open **InterfaceApps.docx** and save the document with the name **U5-PA06-InterfaceApps**.
2. Display the Restrict Formatting and Editing task pane and then restrict formatting to Heading 1 and Heading 2 styles.
3. Enforce the protection and include the password *report*.
4. Save and then close **U5-PA06-InterfaceApps.docx**.
5. Open **U5-PA06-InterfaceApps.docx**.
6. Make sure the Restrict Formatting and Editing task pane displays and then click the Available styles hyperlink.
7. Apply the Heading 1 style to the title of the report and apply the Heading 2 style to the four headings in the report.
8. Close the Styles task pane.
9. Close the Restrict Formatting and Editing task pane.
10. Save the document and then print only page one.
11. Close **U5-PA06-InterfaceApps.docx**.

Assessment U5.7   Insert Document Properties and Save a Document in a Previous Version of Word

1. Open **KLHPHighlights.docx** and save the document with the name **U5-PA07-KLHPHighlights**.
2. Make the following changes to the document:
    a. Apply the Heading 1 style to the three headings in the document (*Plan Highlights*, *Quality Assessment*, and *Provider Network*).
    b. Change the style set to Modern.
    c. Apply *Foundry* theme colors.
3. Move the insertion point to the end of the document and then insert the document named **KLHPDiagram.docx**.
4. Display the document information panel and then type the following information in the specified text boxes:
    a. Title   =   Key Life Health Plan
    b. Subject   =   Company Health Plan

     c.   Keywords   =   health, plan, network

     d.   Category   =   Health Plan

     e.   Comments   =   This document describes highlights of the Key Life Health Plan.

     f.   Close the document information panel.

5. Save the document and then print only the document properties.

6. Inspect the document and remove any hidden text.

7. Save and then print **U5-PA07-KLHPHighlights.docx**.

8. Assume that the document will be read by a colleague with Word 2003 and run the compatibility checker to determine what features are not supported by earlier versions of Word.

9. Save the document in the *Word 97-2003 Document (*.doc)* format and name it **U5-PA07-KLHPHighlights-2003format**.

10. Save, print, and then close **U5-PA07-KLHPHighlights-2003format.doc**.

CREATING ORIGINAL DOCUMENTS

The activity in Assessment U5.8 gives you the opportunity to practice your writing skills as well as demonstrate your mastery of some of the important Word features presented in this unit. When you compose the document, use correct grammar, precise word choices, and clear sentence construction.

Assessment U5.8   Design and Apply Building Blocks

Situation: You have been hired as the office manager for Highland Construction Company. The address of the company is 9025 Palmer Park Boulevard, Colorado Springs, CO 80904, and the telephone number is (719) 555-4575. You are responsible for designing business documents that maintain a common appearance and formatting. You decide your first task is to create a letterhead document using the company name, address, telephone number, and a clip art image or other elements to add visual interest. Save the completed letterhead document with the name **HCCLetterhead**. Using the text and elements in the letterhead document, create a building block and name it with your initials followed by *HCCLetterhead*. Save, print, and then close **HCCLetterhead.docx**.

Create the following additional building blocks for your company (you choose the building block names, but use your initials in each):

- Create a building block footer that contains a border line (in a color matching the colors in the letterhead) and the company slogan "Building Dreams Since 1985."

- Create the following complimentary close building block:

    Sincerely,

    Your Name
    Office Manager

- Create the following company name and address building block:

    Mr. Eric Rashad
    Roswell Industries
    1020 Wasatch Street
    Colorado Springs, CO 80902

- Create the following company name and address building block:

  > Ms. Claudia Sanborn
  > S & S Supplies
  > 537 Constitution Avenue
  > Colorado Springs, CO 80911

At a blank document, create a letter to Eric Rashad by inserting the company letterhead (the building block that begins with your initials followed by *HCCLetterhead*). (Refer to Appendix D for the formatting of a business letter using the default Microsoft spacing.) Type today's date, press the Enter key twice, and then insert the Eric Rashad building block. Press the Enter key twice, type Dear Mr. Rashad:, and then press the Enter key twice. Insert the file named **HCCLetter01.docx** and then insert your complimentary close building block. Finally, insert the footer building block you created for the company. Save the letter with the name **U5-PA08-HCCLtr01**. Print and then close the letter. Complete similar steps to create a letter to Claudia Sanborn. Save the completed letter with the name **U5-PA08-HCCLtr02**. Print and then close the letter.

Assessment U5.9   Create AutoCorrect Entries and Format an Agreement Document

Situation: As the office manager at Highland Construction Company, you are responsible for preparing construction agreements. Create an AutoCorrect entry that will replace hcc with Highland Construction Company and bca with Building Construction Agreement. Open **HCCAgreement.docx** and then type the text shown in Figure U5.3 at the beginning of the document.

Insert the following in the document:

- Insert at the end of the document a date printed field and a file name field.
- Insert your footer building block as a footer
- Insert a cover page

Add or apply any other enhancements to improve the visual appeal of the document and then save the document with the name **U5-PA09-HCCAgreement.docx**. Print and then close the document.

Delete the building blocks you created and then delete the AutoCorrect entries *hcc* and *bca*.

Figure U5.3 Assessment U5.9

> ### bca
>
> **THIS bca** made this ___day of _____, 2012, by and between hcc and _____, hereinafter referred to as "owner," for the considerations hereinafter named, hcc and owner agree as follows:
>
> **Financing Arrangements:** The Owner will obtain a construction loan to finance construction under this bca. If adequate financing has not been arranged within thirty days of the date of this bca, or the owner cannot provide evidence to hcc of other financial ability to pay the full amount, then hcc may treat this bca as null and void and retain the down payment made on the execution of this bca.

Unit 6

Referencing Data

Chapter 26 Inserting Endnotes, Footnotes, and References

Chapter 27 Creating Indexes

Chapter 28 Creating Specialized Tables

Chapter 29 Creating Forms

Chapter 30 Using Outline View and Formatting with Macros

Unit 6 Performance Assessments

Chapter 26

TUTORIALS

Tutorial 26.1
Inserting Footnotes and Endnotes
Tutorial 26.2
Choosing a Citation Style
Tutorial 26.3
Formatting the First Page of a Research Paper or Report
Tutorial 26.4
Inserting and Modifying Sources and Citations
Tutorial 26.5
Inserting and Modifying Bibliographies

Inserting Endnotes, Footnotes, and References

Performance Objectives

Upon successful completion of Chapter 26, you will be able to:

- Create footnotes
- Create endnotes
- Insert and modify sources and citations
- Insert, modify, and format bibliographies and works cited

When you write a research paper or report, you may need to include references to identify the sources of information you used. Word provides a variety of methods for citing references including footnotes, endnotes, citations, and bibliographies. You will learn how to cite documents with these reference features as well as how to edit, modify, and delete references.

Note: Before beginning computer exercises for this chapter, copy to your storage medium the Chapter26 folder from the CD that accompanies this textbook and then make Chapter26 the active folder.

In this chapter, students will produce the following documents:

Exercise 26.1. C26-E01-InternetFuture.docx
Exercise 26.1. C26-E01-InterfaceApps.docx
Exercise 26.2. C26-E02-DevelopDTP.docx

Model answers for these exercises are shown on the following pages.

NATURAL INTERFACE APPLICATIONS

Creating a more natural interface between human and machine is the goal in a major area of artificial intelligence. Currently, computer users are restricted in most instances to using a mouse and keyboard for input. For output, they must gaze at a fairly static, two-dimensional screen. Speakers are used for sound, and a printer for hard copy. The user interface consists of typing, pointing, and clicking. New speech recognition and natural-language technologies promise to change that soon.[1]

Speech Recognition

One of the most immediately applicable improvements in technology comes in the area of speech recognition. Rather than typing information in the computer, users can direct the computer with voice commands.

actions is a real step forward in c

developed rather slowly, mainly

capacity until very recently.[2]

Natural-Language Interface

Computers that are able

hundreds of other languages cur

Computers, in the not-so-distant

understand many human langua

better all the time.

Programmers can look fo

interfaces, programmers may be

---

[1] Curtis, Ray, *Artificial Intelligence*, H
[2] Clemens, Heather, and Reyes, Nico
2011, 12-14.

Page 1

rather than writing programs in the highly restrictive and rather alien programming languages in use today. Natural-language interfaces are an area of artificial intelligence that is broader in scope than simple speech recognition. The goal is to have a machine that can read a set of news articles on any topic and understand what it has read. Ideally, it could then write its own report summarizing what it has learned.[3]

Virtual Reality

Virtual reality (VR) describes the concept of creating a realistic world within the computer. Online games with thousands of interacting players already exist. In these games people can take on a persona and move about a virtual landscape, adventuring and chatting with other players. The quality of a virtual reality system is typically characterized in terms of its *immersiveness*, which measures users accept the simulated world systems are able to provide incre escapism," VR is becoming incre

Mental Interface

Although still in the expe than VR, and they don't require interfaces use sensors mounted Thinking of the color blue could number seven could move it to t a command, eliminating the nee

---

[3] Glenovich, Daniel, "Language Inte

Page 2

While this technology has obvious applications for assisting people with disabilities, military researchers are also using it to produce a superior form of interface for pilots.[4]

---

[4] Beal, Kathleen, "Challenges of Artificial Intelligence," *Interface Designs*, Apr. 2012, 16-22.

Page 3

Exercise 26.1

C26-E01-InternetFuture.docx

FUTURE OF THE INTERNET

The Internet is having trouble keeping up with the rapid increase in users and the increased workload created by the popularity of bandwidth-intensive applications such as music and video files. The broadband connections needed to enjoy these new applications are not evenly distributed. Several ongoing projects promise to provide solutions for these problems in the future. Once these connectivity problems are dealt with, people around the world will be able to enjoy the new web services that are only a few short years away.[1]

Satellite Internet Connections

Many people living in remote or sparsely populated areas are not served by broadband Internet connections. Cable or optical fiber networks are very expensive to install and maintain, and ISPs are not interested in providing service to areas or individuals unless they think it will be profitable. One hope for people without broadband connections is provided by satellite TV networks. Remote ISPs connect to the satellite network using antennae attached to their servers. Data is relayed to and from ISP servers to satellites, which are in turn connected to an Internet backbone access point. While the connection speeds might not be as fast as those offered by regular land-based broadband access, they are faster than the service twisted-pair cable can offer and much better than no access at all.[2]

Second Internet

A remedy for the traffic clogging the information highway is **Internet2**, a revolutionary new type of Internet currently under development. When fully operational, Internet2 will enable large research universities in the United States to collaborate and share huge amounts of complex scientific information at amazing speeds. Led by over 170 universities working in partnership with industry and government, the Internet2 consortium is developing and deploying advanced network technologies and applications.

Internet2 is a testing ground for universities to work together and develop advanced Internet technologies such as telemedicine, digital libraries, and virtual laboratories. Internet2 universities ~~will~~ ... high-speed network called the Abilene backbone. Each university will ... to take advantage of transfer speeds provided by the network.

...ds in Computing, Gleason-Rutherford Publishing, 2012, 5-9.
...obison Publishing House, 2012, 15-38.

Internet Services for a Fee

Industry observers predict that large portals such as AOL, MSN, and Yahoo! will soon determine effective structures and marketing strategies to get consumers to pay for Internet services. This new market, called bring-your-own-access (BYOA), will combine essential *content*, for example, news and weather, with *services*, such as search, directory, email, IM, and online shopping, into a new product with monthly access charges. But to entice current and potential customers into the BYOA market, ISP and telecom companies must offer improvements in the area of security, privacy, and ease-of-use. Additionally, they are expected to develop new ways to personalize content and add value to the current range of Internet services.[3]

Internet in 2030

Ray Kurzweil, a computer futurist, has looked ahead to the year 2030 and visualized a Web that offers no clear distinctions between real and simulated environments and people. Among the applications he sees as very possible are computerized displays in eyeglasses that could offer simultaneous translations of foreign language conversations, nanobots (microscopic robots) that would work with our brains to extend our mental capabilities, and more sophisticated avatars (simulated persons on-screen) that people will interact with online. Technologies that allow people to protect their feelings as well as their images and voices may usher in a period when people could "be" with another person even though they are physically hundreds or even thousands of miles apart.

---
[3] Fuzak, Jolene, "Fee-Based Internet Services," *Connections*, Mar./Apr. 2012, 2-6.

Page 2

Inserting Endnotes, Footnotes, and References **913**

Exercise 26.2

C26-E02-DevelopDTP.docx

Page 1

Last Name 1

Student Name

Instructor Name

Course Title

(current date)

Development of Desktop Publishing

Since the 1970s, microcomputers have been an integral part of the business environment. Businesses use microcomputers and software packages to perform a variety of tasks. In the 1980s, the three most popular types of software purchased for microcomputers were word processing, spreadsheets, and databases (Schueller).

During the early 1990s, [a] new type of software, generally called desktop publishing, gained popularity among mic[...] and its ability to produce high[...] fastest growing microcompu[...] today (Wesson).

Until the mid-1980s, [...] professionals. However, desk[...] into the office and home. Fas[...] supply of clip art, increased s[...] desktop publishing (Nakamu[...] created, and produced at a co[...]

In traditional publishi[...] publication project, which ma[...] desktop publishing software, [...]

Page 2

Last Name 2

complete a project, greatly reducing the costs of publishing documents (Nakamura). The two approaches have a great deal in common. "Both approaches involve setting goals, planning and organizing content, analyzing layout and design, arranging design elements, typesetting, printing, and distributing the project" (Corsini 28).

Page 3

Last Name 3

Works Cited

Corsini, Elena. Computers in the Education World. Houston: Rio Grande Publishing, 2012.

Nakamura, Janet. "Computer Applications and Publishing." Current Technology Times 6
    (2011): 20-28.

Schueller, Barbara. The Past, Present and Future of Desktop Publishing. 18 April 2011. 29
    March 2012 <www.emcp.org/publishing>.

Wesson, Scott. "The History of Popular Computer Software." Computer Education (2012):
    10-18.

Creating Footnotes and Endnotes

Research papers and reports generally contain information from a variety of sources. To acknowledge and credit these sources, you can insert footnotes or endnotes in a document. A footnote is an explanatory note or reference that is placed at the bottom of the page on which a source is referenced. An endnote is also an explanatory note or reference, but it is placed at the end of a document.

Two steps are involved in creating a footnote or an endnote. The first step is to insert a reference number for the footnote or endnote in the document where the source is referenced. The second step is to type the bibliographic information about the source. In Word, you create footnotes and endnotes in a similar manner. To create a footnote, position the insertion point where you want the reference number to appear, click the References tab, and then click the Insert Footnote button in the Footnotes group. This inserts a superscript number in the document and also inserts a separator line at the bottom of the page with a superscript number below. With the insertion point positioned immediately right of the superscript number beneath the separator line, type the footnote entry text. Word automatically numbers footnotes with superscript Arabic numbers and endnotes with superscript lowercase Roman numerals.

QUICK STEPS

Insert Footnote
1. Click References tab.
2. Click Insert Footnote button.
3. Type footnote text.

Insert Endnote
1. Click References tab.
2. Click Insert Endnote button.
3. Type endnote text.

Insert Footnote   Insert Endnote

Exercise 26.1A   Creating Footnotes   Part 1 of 3

1. Open **InterfaceApps.docx** and save the document with the name **C26-E01-InterfaceApps**.
2. Create the first footnote shown in Figure 26.1 by completing the following steps:
   a. Position the insertion point at the end of the first paragraph of text in the document.
   b. Click the References tab.
   c. Click the Insert Footnote button in the Footnotes group.
   d. With the insertion point positioned at the bottom of the page immediately following the superscript number, type the first footnote shown in Figure 26.1.

Step 2b

Step 2c

today. Natural-language interfaces are an area of artificial intelligence that is broader in scope than

simple speech recognition. The goal is to have a machine that can read a set of news articles on any

_____

[1] Curtis, Ray, *Artificial Intelligence*, Home Town Publishing, 2012, 45-51.

Step 2d

3. Move the insertion point to the end of the paragraph in the *Speech Recognition* section and then create the second footnote shown in Figure 26.1.
4. Move the insertion point to the end of the second paragraph in the *Natural-Language Interface* section and then create the third footnote shown in Figure 26.1.
5. Move the insertion point to the end of the paragraph in the *Virtual Reality* section and then create the fourth footnote shown in Figure 26.1.

6. Move the insertion point to the end of the last paragraph in the document and then create the fifth footnote shown in Figure 26.1.
7. Save and then close **C26-E01-InterfaceApps.docx**.

Figure 26.1 Exercise 26.1A

Curtis, Ray, *Artificial Intelligence*, Home Town Publishing, 2012, 45-51.

Clemens, Heather, and Reyes, Nicolas, "Integrating Speech Recognition," *Design Technologies*, Jan./Feb. 2011, 12-14.

Glenovich, Daniel, "Language Interfaces," *Corporate Computing*, Nov. 2011, 8-14.

Novak, William, *Virtual Reality Worlds*, Lilly-Harris Publishers, 2012, 46-58.

Beal, Kathleen, "Challenges of Artificial Intelligence," *Interface Designs*, Apr. 2012, 16-22.

Printing Footnotes and Endnotes

When you print a document that contains footnotes, Word automatically reduces the number of text lines on a page by the number of lines in the footnote(s) plus the line separating the footnotes from the document text. (Word separates footnotes from document text with a 2-inch separator line that begins at the left margin.) If the page does not contain enough space, the footnote numbers and bibliographic text are moved to the next page. When you create endnotes in a document, Word prints all endnote references at the end of the document, separated from the text by a 2-inch separator line.

Exercise 26.1B Creating Endnotes   Part 2 of 3

1. Open **InternetFuture.docx** and save the document with the name **C26-E01-InternetFuture**.
2. Change the style set to Simple and change the paragraph spacing to *Relaxed*.
3. Create the first endnote shown in Figure 26.2 by completing the following steps:
   a. Position the insertion point at the end of the first paragraph of text in the document.
   b. Click the References tab.
   c. Click the Insert Endnote button.
   d. Type the first endnote shown in Figure 26.2.

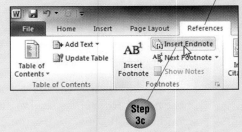

4. Move the insertion point to the end of the paragraph in the *Satellite Internet Connections* section and then create the second endnote shown in Figure 26.2.
5. Move the insertion point to the end of the second paragraph in the *Second Internet* section and then create the third endnote shown in Figure 26.2.
6. Move the insertion point to the end of the paragraph in the *Internet Services for a Fee* section and then create the fourth endnote shown in Figure 26.2.
7. Save **C26-E01-InternetFuture.docx**.

Figure 26.2 Exercise 26.1B

Abrahamson, Joshua, *Future Trends in Computing*, Gleason-Rutherford Publishing, 2012, 8-12.

Dossa, Aileen, *Satellite Systems*, Robison Publishing House, 2012, 15-38.

Ventrella, Terry, "Future of the Internet," *Computing Today*, Oct. 2012, 33-44.

Fuzak, Jolene, "Fee-Based Internet Services," *Connections*, Mar./Apr. 2012, 2-6.

Viewing and Editing Footnotes and Endnotes

To view footnotes in a document, click the Next Footnote button in the Footnotes group in the References tab. This moves the insertion point to the location of the footnote reference number. To view an endnote in a document, click the Next Footnote button arrow and then click *Next Endnote* at the drop-down list. With other options at the Next Footnote button drop-down list, you can view the next footnote, previous footnote, or previous endnote. You can move the insertion point to specific footnote text with the Show Notes button. Click the Next Footnote button to move the insertion point to the next footnote reference number and then click the Show Notes button. This moves the insertion point to the specific footnote text at the bottom of the page. Click the Show Notes button again and the insertion point is moved back to the footnote reference number.

Next Footnote

Show Notes

When you move, copy, or delete footnote or endnote reference numbers all remaining footnotes or endnotes are automatically renumbered. To move a footnote or endnote, select the reference number and then click the Cut button in the Clipboard group in the Home tab. Position the insertion point at the location where you want the footnote or endnote inserted and then click the Paste button. To delete a footnote or endnote, select the reference number and then press the Delete key. This deletes the reference number as well as the footnote or endnote text.

Click the Footnotes group dialog box launcher and the Footnote and Endnote dialog box displays. At this dialog box, you can convert footnotes to endnotes and endnotes to footnotes; change the location of footnotes or endnotes; change the number formatting; start footnote or endnote numbering with a specific number, letter, or symbol; or change numbering within sections in a document.

Exercise 26.1C Formatting Endnotes and Converting Endnotes to Footnotes   Part 3 of 3

1. With **C26-E01-InternetFuture.docx** open, edit the endnotes by completing the following steps:
   a. Click the References tab.
   b. Click the Next Footnote button arrow and then click *Next Endnote* at the drop-down list.
   c. Click the Show Notes button. (This displays the endnote text.)
   d. Change the page numbers for the Joshua Abrahamson entry from *8-12* to *5-9*.

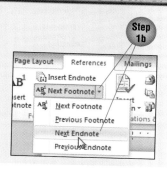

e. Click the Show Notes button again to return to the reference number in the document.

2. Press Ctrl + A to select the document (this does not select the endnote reference text) and then change the font to Constantia.

3. Change the font for the endnotes by completing the following steps:
   a. Press Ctrl + End to move the insertion point to the end of the document.
   b. Click on any endnote entry and then press Ctrl + A to select all of the endnote entries.
   c. Change the font to Constantia.
   d. Press Ctrl + Home.

4. Convert the endnotes to footnotes by completing the following steps:
   a. Click the References tab and then click the Footnotes group dialog box launcher.
   b. At the Footnote and Endnote dialog box, click the Convert button.
   c. At the Convert Notes dialog box with the *Convert all endnotes to footnotes* option selected, click OK.
   d. Click the Close button to close the dialog box.

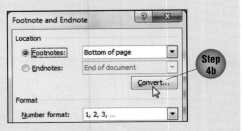

5. Change footnote numbers by completing the following steps:
   a. Click the Footnotes group dialog box launcher.
   b. At the Footnote and Endnote dialog box, click the *Footnotes* option in the *Location* section.
   c. Click the down-pointing arrow at the right side of the *Number format* option box and then click *a, b, c, …* at the drop-down list.
   d. Change the starting number (letter) by clicking the up-pointing arrow at the right side of the *Start at* option until *d* displays in the option box.
   e. Click the Apply button and then scroll through the document and notice the footnotes.

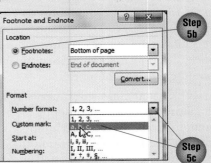

6. Change the footnote number format back to Arabic numbers by completing the following steps:
   a. With the References tab active, click the Footnotes group dialog box launcher.
   b. At the Footnote and Endnote dialog box, click the *Footnotes* option in the *Location* section.
   c. Click the down-pointing arrow at the right side of the *Number Format* option box and then click *1, 2, 3, …* at the drop-down list.
   d. Change the starting number back to 1 by clicking the down-pointing arrow at the right side of the *Start at* option until *1* displays in the option box.
   e. Click the Apply button.

7. Delete the third footnote by completing the following steps:
   a. Press Ctrl + Home.
   b. Make sure the References tab is active and then click three times on the Next Footnote button in the Footnotes group.
   c. Select the third footnote reference number (superscript number) and then press the Delete key.

8. Save, print, and then close **C26-E01-InternetFuture.docx**.

Creating Citations and Bibliographies

In addition to using footnotes and endnotes to credit sources in a research paper or manuscript, consider inserting in-text citations and a works cited page to identify sources of quotations, ideas, and borrowed or summarized material. An in-text citation acknowledges that you are borrowing information from a source rather than plagiarizing (stealing) the words or ideas of another.

Word provides three commonly used editorial styles for citing references in research papers and reports: the American Psychological Association (APA) reference style, which is generally used in the social sciences and research fields; the Modern Language Association (MLA) style, which is generally used in the humanities and English composition; and the Chicago Manual of Style (CMS), which is used both in the humanities and social sciences and is considered more complex than either the APA or MLA style.

If you prepare a research paper or report in APA or MLA style, format your document according to the following general guidelines. Use standard-sized paper (8.5 × 11 inches); set one-inch top, bottom, left, and right margins; set text in a 12-point serif typeface (such as Cambria or Times New Roman); double-space text; indent the first line of each paragraph one-half inch; and insert page numbers in the upper right corner of pages.

Formatting the First Page of a Research Paper or Report

When formatting a research paper or report in MLA or APA standards, you will need to follow certain guidelines for properly formatting the first page of the document. With the MLA style, in the upper left corner of the first page of the document, you will need to insert your name, your instructor's name, the course title, and the current date, all double-spaced. Type the title of the document a double-space below the current date, and then center the document title. You will then need a double-space between the title and the first line of the text. Insert a header located in the upper right corner of the document that includes your last name followed by the current page number.

When using APA style, the title page is located on a separate page from the body of the document. On the title page, you need to include the title of your paper, your name, and your school's name, all double-spaced, centered, and located in the upper half of the title page. The title page also needs to include a header with the text *Running Head:* followed by the title of your paper in uppercase letters at the left margin, and the page number at the right margin.

Exercise 26.2A **Formatting the First Page of a Research Paper** **Part 1 of 8**

1. Open **DevelopDTP.docx** and save the document with the name **C26-E02-DevelopDTP**.
2. Format the first page of the document by completing the following steps:
   a. Press Ctrl + A to select the entire document.
   b. Change the font to Cambria and the font size to 12 point.
   c. Change the line spacing to 2.0.
   d. Remove spacing after paragraphs by clicking the Page Layout tab, clicking in the *After* text box in the *Spacing* section, typing 0, and then pressing the Enter key.

---

e. Press Ctrl + Home to position the insertion point at the beginning of the document, type your first and last names, and then press the Enter key.
f. Type your instructor's name and then press the Enter key.
g. Type the title of your course and then press the Enter key.
h. Type the current date and then press the Enter key.
i. Type the document title Development of Desktop Publishing and then center the title.

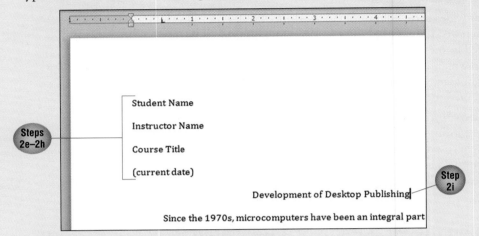

3. Insert a header in the document by completing the following steps:
   a. Click the Insert tab.
   b. Click the Header button in the Header & Footer group and then click *Edit Header* at the drop-down list.
   c. Press the Tab key twice to move the insertion point to the right margin in the Header pane.
   d. Type your last name and then press the spacebar.
   e. Click the Page Number button in the Header & Footer group in the Header & Footer Tools Design tab, point to *Current Position*, and then click the *Plain Number* option.

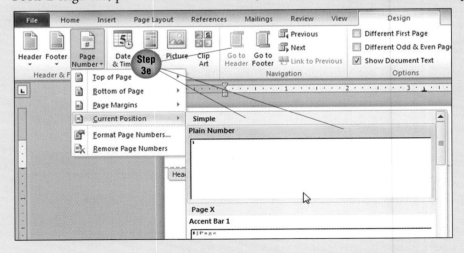

   f. Select the header text and change the font to 12-point Cambria.
   g. Double-click in the body of the document.
4. Save **C26-E02-DevelopDTP.docx**.

Inserting Sources and Citations

When you create an in-text citation, Word requires you to enter information about the source in required fields at the Create Source dialog box. To insert a citation in a Word document, click the References tab, click the Insert Citation button in the Citations & Bibliography group, and then click *Add New Source* at the drop-down list. At the Create Source dialog box, shown in Figure 26.3, select the type of reference you want to cite, such as a book, journal article, or report, and then type the bibliographic information in the required fields. If you want to include more information than required in the displayed fields, click the *Show All Bibliography Fields* check box to insert a check mark and then type additional bibliographic information in the extra fields. After filling in the necessary source information, click OK. The citation is automatically inserted in the document at the location of the insertion point.

Insert New Citation
1. Click References tab.
2. Click Insert Citation button.
3. Click *Add New Source* at drop-down list.
4. Type necessary source information.
5. Click OK.

Insert Citation

Figure 26.3 Create Source Dialog Box

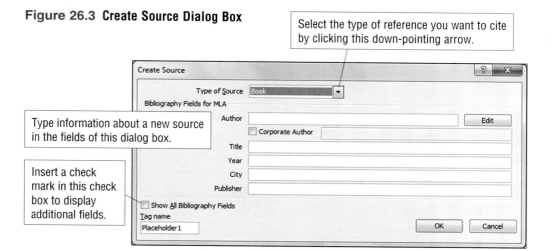

> Select the type of reference you want to cite by clicking this down-pointing arrow.

> Type information about a new source in the fields of this dialog box.

> Insert a check mark in this check box to display additional fields.

Exercise 26.2B   Inserting Sources and Citations   Part 2 of 8

1. With **C26-E02-DevelopDTP.docx** open, press Ctrl + End to move the insertion point to the end of the document and then type the text shown in Figure 26.4 up to the first citation (the text *(Weston)*). To insert the citation, complete these steps:
   a. Press the spacebar once after typing the text *today*.
   b. Click the References tab.
   c. Make sure the Style option is set at MLA Sixth Edition. If not, click the down-pointing arrow at the right of the *Style* option and then click *MLA Sixth Edition* at the drop-down list.
   d. Click the Insert Citation button in the Citations & Bibliography group and then click *Add New Source* at the drop-down list.

e. At the Create Source dialog box, click the down-pointing arrow at the right of the *Type of Source* option and then click *Journal Article* at the drop-down list.

f. Click in the *Author* text box, type Scott Weston, and then press the Tab key three times.

g. Type The History of Popular Computer Software in the *Title* text box and then press the Tab key.

h. Type Computer Education in the *Journal Name* text box and then press the Tab key.

i. Type 2012 in the *Year* text box and then press the Tab key.

j. Type 10-18 in the *Pages* text box.

k. Click OK.

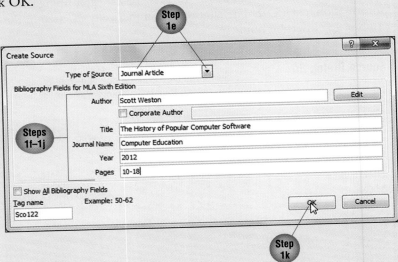

l. Type the period to end the sentence.

2. Continue typing the text up to the next citation (the text *(Prasad)*) and insert the following source information from a book (click the down-pointing arrow at the right of the *Type of Source* option and then click *Book* at the drop-down list):

    Author = Allen Prasad
    Title = Desktop Publishing in Education
    Year = 2012
    City = Chicago
    Publisher = Great Lakes Publishing House

3. Continue typing the text up to the next citation (the text *(Nakamura)*) and insert the following source information from a journal article (make sure you change the *Type of Source* to *Journal Article*):

    Author = Janet Nakamura
    Title = Computer Applications and Publishing
    Journal Name = Current Technology Times
    Year = 2011
    Pages = 20-28
    Volume = 6 (Display the *Volume* field by clicking the *Show All Bibliography Fields* check box and then scroll down the options list.)

4. Type the remaining text in Figure 26.4.

5. Save **C26-E02-DevelopDTP.docx**.

Figure 26.4 Exercise 26.2B

During the early 1990s, another type of software program called desktop publishing gained popularity among microcomputer users. With the introduction of the laser printer and its ability to produce high quality documents, desktop publishing software became the fastest growing microcomputer application of the 1990s, and its widespread use continues today (Weston). Desktop publishing involves using desktop publishing software or word processing software with desktop publishing capabilities, a computer system, and a printer to produce professional-looking documents (Prasad).

Until the mid-1980s, graphic design depended almost exclusively on design professionals. However, desktop publishing changed all that by bringing graphic design into the office and home. Faster microprocessors, improved printer capabilities, increased supply of clip art, increased storage capacity, and the like continue to expand the role of desktop publishing (Nakamura). Everything from a flyer to a newsletter can be designed, created, and produced at a computer.

Inserting a Citation with an Existing Source

Once you insert source information at the Create Source dialog box, Word automatically saves it. To insert a citation in a document for source information that has already been saved, click the Insert Citation button in the Citations & Bibliography group and then click the desired source at the drop-down list.

Insert Citation with Existing Source
1. Click References tab.
2. Click Insert Citation button.
3. Click desired source at drop-down list.

1. With **C26-E02-DevelopDTP.docx** open, press Ctrl + End to move the insertion point to the end of the document and then press the Enter key once.
2. Type the text in Figure 26.5 up to the citation text *(Weston)* and insert a citation from an existing source by completing the following steps:
   a. If necessary, click the References tab.
   b. Click the Insert Citation button in the Citations & Bibliography group.
   c. Click the Scott Weston reference at the drop-down list.

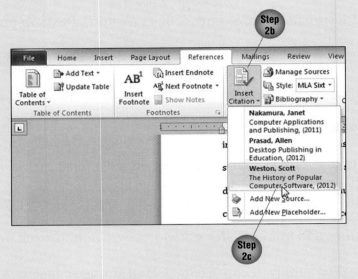

3. Type the remaining text in Figure 26.5 and complete steps similar to those in Step 2 to insert a citation for the existing source by Janet Nakamura.
4. Save and then print **C26-E02-DevelopDTP.docx**.

Figure 26.5 Exercise 26.2C

In traditional publishing, several people may be involved in completing the publication project, which may be costly and time-consuming (Weston). With the use of desktop publishing software, one person may be performing all of the tasks necessary to complete a project, greatly reducing the costs of publishing documents (Nakamura). The two approaches have a great deal in common.

Modifying Sources

After you have inserted information about a source into a document, you may need to modify the citation to correct errors or change data. To modify source information, click the References tab and then click the Manage Sources button in the Citations & Bibliography group. This displays the Source Manager dialog box, shown in Figure 26.6. In the *Master List* section, the Source Manager dialog box displays all of the citations you have created in Word. The *Current List* section of the dialog box displays all of the citations included in the currently open document. At the Source Manager dialog box, click the desired source in the *Current List* section. Click the Edit button that displays between the list boxes and then make any desired changes at the Edit Source dialog box. The Edit Source dialog box contains the same options that are available at the Create Source dialog box. You can also edit a source by clicking the desired citation in the document to select the citation placeholder, clicking the Citation Options arrow, and then clicking *Edit Source* at the drop-down list.

Modify Sources
1. Click References tab.
2. Click Manage Sources button.
3. Edit, add, and/or delete sources.
4. Click Close.

Manage Sources

Figure 26.6 Source Manager Dialog Box

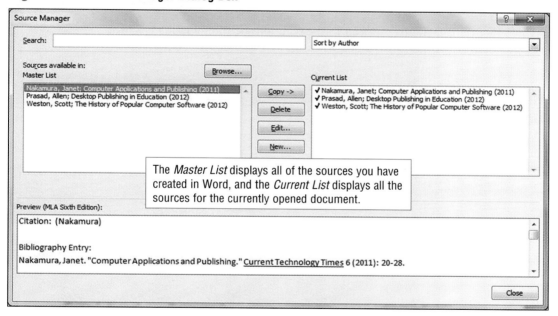

You may also want to add new sources or delete existing sources in a document. To insert a new source, click the New button at the Source Manager dialog box and then insert the source information in the required fields. To delete a source from a document, click the source you wish to delete in the *Current List* section and then click the Delete button.

Inserting Page Numbers in a Citation

**Insert Page
Number in Citation**
1. Click citation to
   display placeholder.
2. Click Citation
   Options arrow.
3. Click *Edit Citation*.
4. Type page
   number(s).
5. Click OK.

If you include a direct quote from a source, you will want to include quotation marks around all of the text borrowed from that source and insert, in the citation the page number(s) of the quoted material. To insert specific page numbers into a citation, click the citation in the document to select the citation placeholder. Click the Citation Options arrow and then click *Edit Citation* at the drop-down list. At the Edit Citation dialog box, type in the page or page numbers of the source where the quote was borrowed then click OK.

Exercise 26.2D Modifying Sources   Part 4 of 8

1. With **C26-E02-DevelopDTP.docx** open, edit a source by completing the following steps:
   a. Click the References tab.
   b. Click the Manage Sources button in the Citations & Bibliography group.
   c. At the Source Manager dialog box, click the source entry for Scott Weston in the *Master List* section.
   d. Click the Edit button.

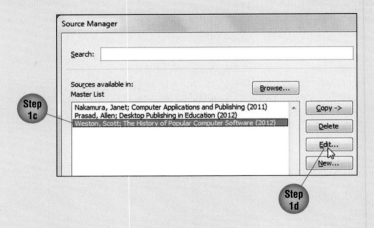

   e. At the Edit Source dialog box, delete the text in the *Author* text box and then type Scott Wesson.
   f. Click OK to close the Edit Source dialog box.
   g. At the message asking if you want to update both the master list and the current list with the changes, click Yes.
   h. Click the Close button to close the Source Manager dialog box. (Notice the last name changed in both of the Wesson citations to reflect the edit.)
2. Delete a source by completing the following steps:
   a. Select and then delete the last sentence in the second paragraph in the document, including the citation (the sentence that begins *Desktop publishing involves using . . .*).
   b. Click the Manage Sources button in the Citations & Bibliography group in the References tab.

c. At the Source Manager dialog box, click the Allen Prasad entry in the *Current List* section. (This entry in the list will not contain a check mark because you deleted the citation from the document.)

d. Click the Delete button.

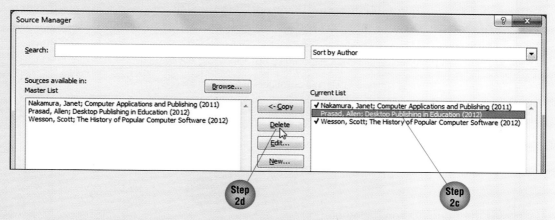

Step 2d

Step 2c

e. Click the Close button to close the Source Manager dialog box.

3. Create and insert a new source in the document by completing the following steps:

a. Click the Manage Sources button in the Citations & Bibliography group in the References tab.

b. Click the New button in the Source Manager dialog box.

c. Type the following book information in the Create Source dialog box (change the *Type of Source* option to *Book*):

Author = Elena Corsini
Title = Computers in the Education World
Year = 2012
City = Houston
Publisher = Rio Grande Publishing

d. Click OK to close the Create Source dialog box.

e. Click the Close button to close the Source Manager dialog box.

f. Position the insertion point one space after the period that ends the last sentence in the document and then type the sentence, "Both approaches involve setting goals, planning and organizing content, analyzing layout and design, arranging design elements, typesetting, printing, and distributing the project" (press the spacebar once after typing the quotation mark after *project*.)

g. Insert a citation at the end of the sentence for Elena Corsini by clicking the Insert Citation button in the Citations & Bibliography group and then clicking the Elena Corsini reference at the drop-down list.

h. Type the period to end the sentence.

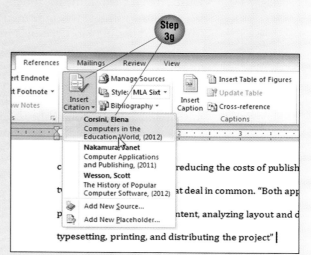

Step 3g

4. Because you inserted a direct quote from Elena Corsini, you will need to include the page number of the book where you found the quote. Insert the page number within the citation by completing the following steps:

   a. Click anywhere in the Corsini citation. (This displays the citation placeholder.)

   b. Click the Citation Options arrow that displays at the right of the citation placeholder and then click *Edit Citation* at the drop-down list.

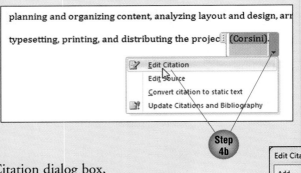

   c. At the Edit Citation dialog box, type 28 in the *Pages* text box.

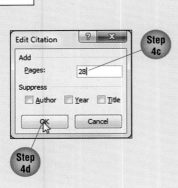

   d. Click OK.

5. Save **C26-E02-DevelopDTP.docx**.

Insert Works Cited Page or Bibliography

1. Insert new page at end of document.
2. Click References tab.
3. Click Bibliography button.
4. Click desired predesigned works cited or bibliography option.

Bibliography

Inserting a Works Cited Page or Bibliography

If you include citations in a report or research paper, you need to insert as a separate page a works cited page or bibliography at the end of the document. A works cited page or bibliography is an alphabetic list of the books, journal articles, reports, or other sources referenced in the document. When you type source information for citations, Word automatically saves information from all of the fields into a bibliography and works cited list, alphabetized by author's last name or the title of the work.

Insert a works cited page for a document formatted in the MLA style and insert a bibliography for a document formatted in the APA style. To insert a works cited page, move the insertion point to the end of the document and then insert a new page. Click the References tab and make sure the Style option is set at *MLA Sixth Edition*. Click the Bibliography button in the Citations & Bibliography group and then click the predesigned works cited option. Complete similar steps to insert a bibliography in an APA-style document except click the predesigned bibliography option.

1. With **C26-E02-DevelopDTP.docx** open, insert a works cited page at the end of the document by completing these steps:
   a. Press Ctrl + End to move the insertion point to the end of the document.
   b. Press Ctrl + Enter to insert a page break.
   c. Click the References tab.
   d. Click the Bibliography button in the Citations & Bibliography group.
   e. Click the *Works Cited* option in the *Built-In* section of the drop-down list.

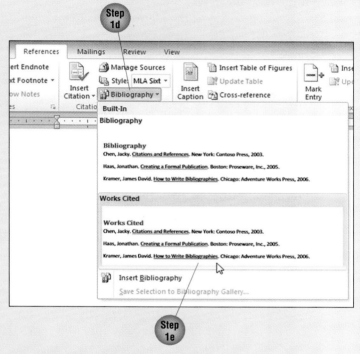

Step 1d

Step 1e

2. Save and then print **C26-E02-DevelopDTP.docx**.

Modifying and Updating a Works Cited Page or Bibliography

If you insert a new source at the Source Manager dialog box or modify an existing source, Word automatically inserts the source information in the works cited page or bibliography. If you insert a new citation, which requires you to add a new source, Word will not automatically update the works cited page or bibliography. To update the works cited page or bibliography, click anywhere in the works cited page or bibliography and then click the Update Citations and Bibliography tab. The updated works cited page or bibliography will reflect any changes made to the citations and source information in the document.

Update Works Cited Page or Bibliography
1. Click anywhere in the works cited page or bibliography.
2. Click Update Citations and Bibliography tab.

1. With **C26-E02-DevelopDTP.docx** open, create a new source and citation by completing the following steps:
   a. Position the insertion point immediately left of the period that ends the last sentence in the first paragraph of the document.
   b. Press the spacebar once.
   c. Click the References tab.
   d. Click the Insert Citation button in the Citations & Bibliography group and then click *Add New Source* at the drop-down list.
   e. At the Create Source dialog box, type the following source information from a website:
      Author = Barbara Schueller
      Name of Web Page = The Past, Present and Future of Desktop Publishing
      Year = 2011
      Month = April
      Day = 18
      Year Accessed = (type current year in numbers)
      Month Accessed = (type current month in letters)
      Day Accessed = (type current day in numbers)
      URL = www.emcp.org/publishing
   f. Click OK to close the Create Source dialog box.
2. Update the works cited page to include the new source by completing the following steps:
   a. Click anywhere in the bibliography text.
   b. Click the Update Citations and Bibliography tab. (Notice that the updated bibliography includes the Schueller reference.)
3. Save **C26-E02-DevelopDTP.docx**.

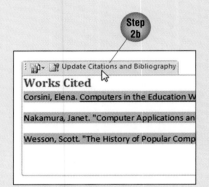

Step 2b

Formatting a Works Cited Page or Bibliography

Reference styles have specific formatting guidelines. The formatting applied by Word to the works cited page or bibliography may need to be changed to meet specific guidelines of the MLA, APA, or Chicago style. For example, MLA and APA styles require the following formatting guidelines for the works cited page or bibliography:

- Begin work cited or bibliography on a separate page after the text of the report.
- Include the title "Work Cited" or "Bibliography" and center the title.
- Double space between and within entries.
- Begin each entry at the left margin and hang indent second and subsequent lines in each entry.
- Alphabetize the entries.

The general formatting requirements for the Chicago style are similar except entries are single spaced within and double spaced between.

1. With **C26-E02-DevelopDTP.docx** open, make the following formatting changes to the works cited page:
   a. Select the *Works Cited* heading and the entries below the heading.
   b. Click the *No Spacing* style in the Styles group in the Home tab.
   c. With the text still selected, change the font to Cambria, the font size to 12, and the line spacing to 2.0.

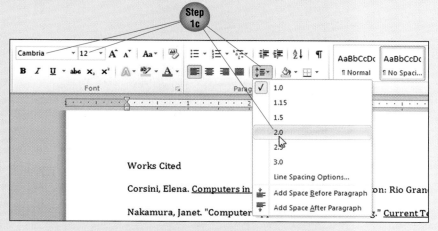

   d. Click anywhere in the title *Works Cited* and then click the Center button in the Paragraph group.
   e. Select only the works cited entries and then press Ctrl + T. (This hang indents the entries.)
2. Press Ctrl + Home to move the insertion point to the beginning of the document.
3. Save and then print **C26-E02-DevelopDTP.docx**.

Choosing a Citation Style

Instructors or professors may require different forms of citation or reference styles. You can change the citation or reference style before beginning a new document or in an existing document. To do this, click the References tab, click the down-pointing arrow at the right of the *Style* option, and then click the desired style at the drop-down list.

Change Citation Style
1. Click References tab.
2. Click down-pointing arrow at right of *Style* option.
3. Click desired style.

1. With **C26-E02-DevelopDTP.docx** open, change the document and the works cited page from MLA style to APA style by completing the following steps:
   a. With the insertion point positioned at the beginning of the document, click the References tab.
   b. Click the down-pointing arrow at the right of the *Style* option in the Citations & Bibliography group and then click *APA Fifth Edition* at the drop-down list.

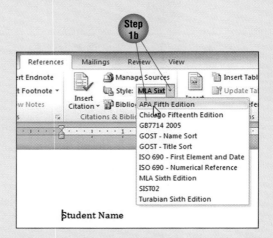

   c. Scroll through the document and notice the changes in the style of the citations and the works cited page.
2. Save **C26-E02-DevelopDTP.docx** and then print only the works cited page.
3. Change the citation and bibliography style to Chicago by clicking the down-pointing arrow at the right of the *Style* option and then clicking *Chicago Fifteenth Edition* at the drop-down list.
4. Scroll through the document and notice the changes in the style of the citations and the works cited page.
5. Print page three of **C26-E02-DevelopDTP.docx**.
6. Save and then close the document.
7. Display a blank document, click the References tab, change the style to *MLA Sixth Edition,* and then close the document without saving it.

Chapter *Summary*

➤ Footnotes and endnotes are explanatory notes or references. Footnotes are inserted and printed at the bottom of the page, and endnotes are printed at the end of the document. Type bibliographic text for footnotes or endnotes at the footnote or endnote pane.

➤ By default, Word numbers footnotes with Arabic numbers and endnotes with lowercase Roman numerals.

➤ If you move, copy, or delete a reference number in a document, all other footnotes or endnotes are automatically renumbered.

➤ Delete a footnote or endnote by selecting the reference number and then pressing the Delete key.

➤ Consider using in-text citations to acknowledge sources in a paper. Commonly used citation and reference styles include American Psychological Association (APA), Modern Language Association (MLA), and Chicago Manual of Style (CMS).

➤ Use the Insert Citation button in the Citations & Bibliography group in the References tab to insert a citation. Specify source information at the Create Source dialog box.

➤ Modify a source by clicking the References tab, clicking the Manage Sources button, clicking the source you want to modify in the Source Manager dialog box, clicking the Edit button, and then making any desired changes at the Edit Source dialog box.

➤ To insert a new source, click the New button at the Source Manager dialog box and then insert the information in the required fields. To delete a source, click the source in the *Current List* section in the Source Manager dialog box and then click the Delete button.

➤ After including citations in a report or paper, insert a works cited page or bibliography at the end of the document on a separate page. Insert a works cited page or bibliography with the Bibliography button in the Citations & Bibliography group in the References tab.

➤ To update a works cited page or bibliography, click anywhere in the works cited page or bibliography and then click the Update Citations and Bibliography tab.

➤ Change the reference style with the Style option in the Citations & Bibliography group in the References tab.

Commands *Review*

FEATURE	RIBBON TAB, GROUP	BUTTON	KEYBOARD SHORTCUT
Footnote	References, Footnotes	AB^1	Alt + Ctrl + F
Endnote	References, Footnotes		Alt + Ctrl + D
Next Footnote	References, Footnotes	AB^1	
Show Notes	References, Footnotes		
Create Source dialog box	References, Citations & Bibliography		
Source Manager dialog box	References, Citations & Bibliography		

FEATURE	RIBBON TAB, GROUP	BUTTON	KEYBOARD SHORTCUT
Bibliography	References, Citations & Bibliography		
Style	References, Citations & Bibliography		

Key Points *Review*

Completion: In the space provided at the right, indicate the correct term, symbol, or command.

1. Footnotes are inserted at the end of a page while endnotes are inserted here.

2. Word numbers footnotes with this type of number.

3. Word numbers endnotes with this type of number.

4. View footnotes in a document by clicking this button in the Footnotes group.

5. Two of the most popular styles for preparing a report are APA (American Psychological Association) and this.

6. Click this tab to display the Citations & Bibliography group.

7. Create a new source for a document with options at this dialog box.

8. To modify a source, click this button in the Citations & Bibliography group.

9. To update a works cited page, click anywhere in the works cited page and then click this tab.

10. Change citation and reference styles with this option.

Chapter *Assessments*

Applying Your Skills

Demonstrate your knowledge of features learned in this chapter by completing the following assessments.

Assessment 26.1 Insert Footnotes in a Designing Newsletter Report

1. Open **DesignNwsltr.docx** and save the document with the name **C26-A01-DesignNwsltr**.
2. Create the first footnote shown in Figure 26.7 at the end of the first paragraph in the *Applying Guidelines* section.
3. Create the second footnote shown in Figure 26.7 at the end of the third paragraph in the *Applying Guidelines* section.
4. Create the third footnote shown in Figure 26.7 at the end of the last paragraph in the *Applying Guidelines* section.
5. Create the fourth footnote shown in Figure 26.7 at the end of the only paragraph in the *Choose Paper Size and Type* section.

6. Create the fifth footnote shown in Figure 26.7 at the end of the only paragraph in the *Choosing Paper Weight* section.
7. Save and then print **C26-A01-DesignNwsltr.docx**.
8. Select the entire document and then change the font to Constantia.
9. Select all of the footnotes and change the font to Constantia.
10. Delete the third footnote.
11. Save, print, and then close **C26-A01-DesignNwsltr.docx**.

Figure 26.7 Assessment 26.1

Habermann, James, "Designing a Newsletter," *Desktop Designs*, Jan./Feb. 2012, 23-29.

Pilante, Shirley G., "Adding Pizzazz to Your Newsletter," *Desktop Publisher*, Sept. 2011, 32-39.

Maddock, Arlita G., "Guidelines for a Better Newsletter," *Business Computing*, June 2012, 9-14.

Alverso, Monica, "Paper Styles for Newsletters," *Design Technologies*, Mar. 14, 2011, 45-51.

Sutton, Keith, "Choosing Paper Styles," *Design Techniques*, Mar./Apr., 2011, 8-11.

Assessment 26.2 Insert Sources and Citations in a Privacy Rights Report

1. Open **PrivRights.docx** and save the document with the name **C26-A02-PrivRights**.
2. Make sure the MLA style is selected in the Citations & Bibliography group in the References tab.
3. Format the title page to meet MLA requirements with the following changes:
   a. Select the entire document, change the font to 12-point Cambria, the line spacing to 2.0, and remove the spacing after paragraphs.
   b. Move the insertion point to the beginning of the document, type your name, press the Enter key, type your instructor's name, press the Enter key, type the title of your course, press the Enter key, type the current date, and then press the Enter key.
   c. Type the title Privacy Rights and then center the title.
   d. Insert a header that displays your last name and the page number at the right margin and change the font to 12-point Cambria.
4. Press Ctrl + End to move the insertion point to the end of the document and then type the text shown in Figure 26.8 up to the first citation (the text *(Hartley)*). Insert the source information from a journal article written by Kenneth Hartley using the following information:
   Author = Kenneth Hartley
   Title = Privacy Laws
   Journal Name = Business World
   Year = 2011
   Pages = 24-46
   Volume = 12
5. Continue typing the text up to the next citation (the text *(Ferraro)*) and insert the following source information from a book:
   Author = Ramona Ferraro
   Title = Business Employee Rights
   Year = 2012
   City = Tallahassee
   Publisher = Everglades Publishing House

6. Continue typing the text up to the next citation (the text *(Aldrich)*) and insert the following information from an article in a periodical:

    Author = Kelly Aldrich
    Title = What Rights Do Employees Have?
    Periodical Title = Great Plains Times
    Year = 2010
    Month = May
    Day = 6
    Pages = 18-22

7. Insert the page number in the Kelly Aldrich citation using the Edit Citation dialog box.

8. Type the remaining text in Figure 26.8.

9. Edit the Kenneth Hartley source title to read *Small Business Privacy Laws* in the *Master List* section of the Source Manager dialog box.

10. Select and delete the last two sentences in the second paragraph and then delete the Ramona Ferraro source in the *Current List* section of the Source Manager dialog box.

11. Insert a works cited page at the end of the document on a separate page.

12. Create a new source in the document using the Source Manager dialog box and include the following source information from a website:

    Author = Harold Jefferson
    Name of Web Page = Small Business Policies and Procedures
    Year = 2011
    Month = December
    Day = 12
    Year Accessed = (type current year)
    Month Accessed = (type current month)
    Day Accessed = (type current day)
    URL = www.emcp.net/policies

13. Insert a citation for Harold Jefferson at the end of the last sentence in the first paragraph.

14. Update the works cited page.

15. Format the works cited page to meet MLA requirements with the following changes:
    a. Select the *Works Cited* heading and all the entries and click the *No Spacing* style.
    b. Change the font to 12-point Cambria and change the spacing to 2.0.
    c. Center the title *Works Cited*.
    d. Hang indent the works cited entries.

16. Save and then print **C26-A02-PrivRights.docx**.

17. Change the document and works cited page from MLA to APA style.

18. Save, print page two, and then close **C26-A02-PrivRights.docx**.

Figure 26.8 Assessment 26.2

An exception to the ability of companies to monitor their employees does exist. If the company has pledged to respect any aspect of employee privacy, it must keep that pledge. For example, if a business states that it will not monitor employee email or phone calls, by law, it must follow this stated policy (Hartley). However, no legal requirement exists mandating that companies notify their employees when and if monitoring takes place (Ferraro). Therefore, employees should assume they are always monitored and act accordingly.

Privacy advocates are calling for this situation to change. "They acknowledge that employers have the right to ensure that their employees are doing their jobs, but they question the need to monitor employees without warning and without limit" (Aldrich 20). The American Civil Liberties Union has, in fact, proposed a Fair Electronic Monitoring Policy to prevent abuses of employee privacy.

Expanding Your Skills

Explore additional feature options or use Help to learn a new skill in creating this document.

Assessment 26.3   Customize Footnotes/Endnotes

1. As you learned in this chapter, you can convert endnotes to footnotes. You can also convert footnotes to endnotes. Open **C26-E01-InterfaceApps.docx** and then save the document and name it **C26-A03-InterfaceApps**.
2. Using options at the Footnote and Endnote dialog box, make the following changes:
   a. Convert the footnotes to endnotes.
   b. Change the number format to Arabic numbers (1, 2, 3, …).
   c. Change the starting number to 5.
3. Select the entire document and then change the line spacing to 1.5. (Do this only to decrease the number of pages for printing.)
4. Save, print, and then close **C26-A03-InterfaceApps.docx**.

Achieving Signature Status

Take your skills to the next level by completing this more challenging assessment.

Assessment 26.4   Format a Report in MLA Style

1. Open **DevelopSystem.docx** and save the document with the name **C26-A04-DevelopSystem**.
2. Format the document so it displays as shown in Figure 26.9 with the following specifications:
   a. Change the document font to 12-point Cambria.
   b. Use the information from the works cited page when inserting citations into the document. The Janowski citation is from a journal article, the Mendoza citation is from a book, and the Yamashita citation is from a website.
   c. Format the works cited page to meet MLA requirements.
3. Save, print, and then close **C26-A04-DevelopSystem.docx**.

Figure 26.9 Assessment 26.4

Last Name 1

Student Name

Instructor Name

Course Title

(current date)

Developing an Information System

Identifying and assembling a team of employees with the required skills and expertise is a necessary first step in developing a new in-house information system. A management group may be involved in answering questions and providing information in the early planning phases of the project, but programmers and/or software engineers handle the design and implementation of any new system. Programmers specialize in the development of new software, while software engineers are highly skilled professionals with programming and teamwork training (Janowski).

Because of their large size, information systems require the creation of a project team. A project team usually includes a project manager, who acts as the team leader. Sometimes the project manager also functions as a systems analyst, responsible for completing the systems analysis and making design recommendations. Other project team members include software engineers and technicians. The software engineers deal with programming software, while technicians handle hardware issues. The comprehensive process software engineers initiate is called the system development life cycle (SDLC), a series of steps culminating in a completed information system.

The first step in the system development life cycle is planning. The planning step involves preparing a needs analysis and conducting feasibility studies. During this step, a company usually establishes a project team, and the team creates a project plan. "The

Page 1

Figure 26.9 Assessment 26.4 (continued)

project plan includes an estimate of how long the project will take to complete, an outline of the steps involved, and a list of deliverables" (Mendoza 42). Deliverables are documents, services, hardware, and software that must be finished and delivered by a certain time and date.

A project is ready to move into the design stage once the project team has approved the plan, including the budget. The design process begins with the writing of the documentation, which covers functional and design specifications. In most cases, the project team creates the functional specifications, describing what the system must be able to do (Yamashita).

The project can move into the next phase, implementation, once the development team and the systems house develop the design specification and approve the plans. This step is where the actual work of putting the system together is completed, including creating a prototype and completing the programming. In most cases, implementing the new system is the longest, most difficult step in the process.

A system goes into the support stage after it has been accepted and approved. A support contract normally allows users to contact the systems house for technical support, training, and sometimes on-site troubleshooting. Even if the system was designed in-house, the responsible department often operates as an independent entity—sometimes even charging the department acquiring the system. The support stage continues until a new information system is proposed and developed, usually years later. At that point, the existing system is retired and no longer used.

Page 2

Figure 26.9 Assessment 26.4 (continued)

Last Name 3

Works Cited

Janowski, Robert. "Information System Management." Technology: Computer Networking (2011): 35-41.

Mendoza, Carla. Building Computer Networks. Oklahoma City: Blue Field Publishing House, 2012.

Yamashita, Paul. How is an Information System Designed? 23 October 2010. 20 February 2012 <www.emcp.net/systemdesign>.

Page 3

Chapter 27

SNAP TUTORIALS

Tutorial 27.1
Marking index entries and
inserting an index
Tutorial 27.2
Creating a concordance file
Tutorial 27.3
Updating and deleting an index

Creating Indexes

Performance Objectives

Upon successful completion of Chapter 27, you will be able to:

- Create an index
- Mark entries for an index
- Insert an index
- Mark text for an index entry that spans a range of pages
- Mark an index entry as a cross-reference
- Create a concordance file
- Update and delete an index

An index is a list of topics contained in a publication and the pages on which those topics are discussed. Creating an index manually can be tedious. With Word, you can automate the process. In this chapter, you will learn the steps to mark text for inclusion in an index and the steps to insert, update, and delete an index.

Note: Before beginning computer exercises for this chapter, copy to your storage medium the Chapter27 folder from the CD that accompanies this textbook and then make Chapter27 the active folder.

In this chapter, students will produce the following documents:

Exercise 27.1. C27-E01-DTP.docx
Exercise 27.2. C27-E02-Computers.docx
Exercise 27.3. C27-E03-PlanNwsltr.docx

Model answers for these exercises are shown on the following pages.

INDEX

design ---------------- **1, 2, 3**
message----------------- **2, 3**
printer ------------------ **1, 2**
   laser ------------------- *1*
publication------------- **1, 2**
   content-------------- *1, 2, 3*

   creating ------------------*2*
   intended audience -----*2, 3*
   planning------------------*1, 2*
publishing----------- **1, 2, 3**
   desktop --------------*1, 2, 3*
   traditional ----------------*1*

software -------------------**1**
   database ------------------ *1*
   spreadsheets -------------- *1*
   word processing----------- *1*

3

Exercise 27.1

C27-E01-DTP.docx
Page 3

INDEX

A

Accuracy 2

C

Communications...3–4
computers.. 1, 2, 3

D

DNA 3

G

GIGO 2

H

Human Genome Project 3

L

LAN.............................. *See* local area network
local area network.. 3

M

microcomputers.......... *See* personal computers

P

personal computers 1

S

Speed..1–2
Storage... 3
supercomputers.. 2

V

Versatility..2–3

W

WAN............................. *See* wide area network
wide area network 4
wireless devices 3
   cell phones.. 3
   notebook computers 3
   personal digital assistants 3

Exercise 27.2

C27-E02-Computers.docx
Page 5

INDEX

C

Communication · 1

D

Design
   consistency · 1

E

Elements · 1, 3
   body copy · 2
   byline · 2
   folio · 2
   graphics images · 2
   headlines · 2
   logo · 1
   nameplate · 1

   subheads · 2
   subtitle · 2

N

Newsletters · 1, 2, 3
   audience · 2, 3
   focal point · 3
   purpose · 1, 2, 3

P

Printers · 1
   laser · 1

S

Software · 1
   desktop publishing · 1
   word processing · 1

Exercise 27.3
C27-E03-PlanNwsltr.docx
Page 4

Creating an Index

Word automates the process of creating an index and, as you will learn in the next chapter, a table of contents, both in a similar manner. Although Word automates the process, creating an index still takes thought and consideration. The author of a book, manuscript, or report must determine which topics should be listed as main entries and which should be listed as subentries under a main entry. An index may include such items as the main idea of a document, the main subject of a chapter or section, variations of a heading or subheading, and abbreviations. Figure 27.1 shows an example of an index.

Marking Text for an Index

When you create an index in Word, you electronically mark the words that you want to include as entries. Before marking the words though, you need to determine what main entries and subentries you want to include. You mark text as an index entry at the Mark Index Entry dialog box.

    To mark text for inclusion in an index, select the word or words, click the References tab, and then click the Mark Entry button in the Index group. You can also press Alt + Shift + X. At the Mark Index Entry dialog box, shown in Figure 27.2, the selected word(s) appears in the *Main entry* text box. If you want the text to be listed as a main entry, leave it as displayed and then click the Mark button. This turns on the display of nonprinting characters in the document and inserts a field code immediately

QUICK STEPS

Mark Text for an Index
1. Select text.
2. Click References tab.
3. Click Mark Entry button.
4. Make desired changes.
5. Click Mark button.
6. Click Close button.
OR
1. Select text.
2. Press Alt + Shift + X.
3. Make desired changes.
4. Click Mark button.
5. Click Close button.

Mark Entry

Figure 27.1 Sample Index

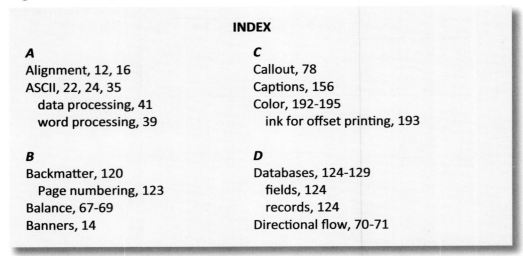

INDEX

A
Alignment, 12, 16
ASCII, 22, 24, 35
  data processing, 41
  word processing, 39

B
Backmatter, 120
  Page numbering, 123
Balance, 67-69
Banners, 14

C
Callout, 78
Captions, 156
Color, 192-195
  ink for offset printing, 193

D
Databases, 124-129
  fields, 124
  records, 124
Directional flow, 70-71

after the selected text. When you mark the word *software* in Exercise 27.1A for inclusion in an index, Word inserts the code *{XE "software"}* immediately after the word. When you mark the words *word processing* as a subentry and *software* as the main entry, Word inserts the code *{XE "software:word processing"}* immediately after the words. Click the Close button to close the Mark Index Entry dialog box.

Figure 27.2 Mark Index Entry Dialog Box

Specify text as a main entry or subentry in an index with these two options.

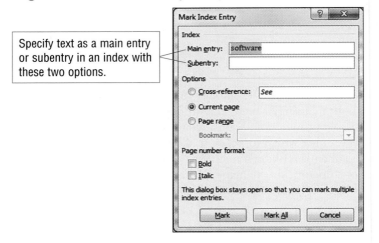

If you want the text that you selected to be listed as a subentry, you will have to make the following changes at the Mark Index Entry dialog box: type the main entry in the *Main entry* text box, click in the *Subentry* text box, and then type the selected text. For example, suppose a publication includes the terms *Page layout* and *Portrait*. The words *Page layout* are to be marked as a main entry for the index and *Portrait* is to be marked as a subentry below *Page layout*. To mark these words for inclusion in an index, you would complete the following steps:

1. Select *Page layout*.
2. Click the References tab and then click the Mark Entry button or press Alt + Shift + X.

3. At the Mark Index Entry dialog box, click the Mark button or the Mark All button. (This turns on the display of nonprinting symbols.)

4. With the Mark Index Entry dialog box still displayed on the screen, click in the document to make the document active, and then select *Portrait*.

5. Click the Mark Index Entry dialog box title bar to make it active.

6. Select *Portrait* in the *Main entry* text box and then type Page layout.

7. Click in the *Subentry* text box and then type Portrait.

8. Click the Mark button.

9. Click the Close button.

The main entry and subentry do not have to be the same as the selected text. You can select text for an index, type the text you want to display in the *Main entry* or *Subentry* text box, and then click the Mark button. At the Mark Index Entry dialog box, you can apply bold and/or italic formatting to the page numbers that will appear in the index. To apply formatting, click *Bold* and/or *Italic* to insert a check mark in the check box.

The *Options* section of the Mark Index Entry dialog box contains three options, and the *Current page* option is the default. At this setting, the current page number will be listed in the index for the main entry or subentry displayed. Click the *Cross-reference* option if you want to cross-reference the main entry or subentry. Type the text you want to use as a cross-reference for that entry in the *Cross-reference* text box. For example, you could mark the word *Serif* and cross reference it to *Typefaces*.

Click the Mark All button at the Mark Index Entry dialog box to mark all occurrences of the text in the document as index entries. Word marks occurrences of the text only if the uppercase and lowercase letters exactly match the index entry.

Exercise 27.1A   Marking Words for an Index   Part 1 of 2

1. Open **DTP.docx** and save the document with the name **C27-E01-DTP**.

2. Number pages at the bottom center of each page.

3. Mark the word *software* in the first paragraph for the index as a main entry and mark *word processing* in the first paragraph as a subentry below *software* by completing the following steps:
   a. Select *software* (located in the second sentence of the first paragraph).
   b. Click the References tab and then click the Mark Entry button in the Index group.
   c. At the Mark Index Entry dialog box, click the Mark All button. (This turns on the display of nonprinting symbols.)

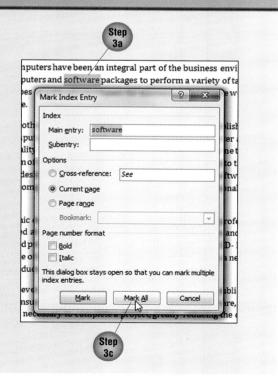

d. With the Mark Index Entry dialog box still displayed, click in the document to make the document active and then select *word processing*, located in the last sentence of the first paragraph. (You may want to drag the dialog box down the screen so more of the document text is visible.)

e. Click the Mark Index Entry dialog box title bar to make the dialog box active.

f. Select *word processing* in the *Main entry* text box and then type software.

g. Click in the *Subentry* text box and then type word processing.

h. Click the Mark All button.

i. With the Mark Index Entry dialog box still displayed, complete steps similar to those in 3d through 3h to mark the *first* occurrence of the following words as main entries or subentries for the index:

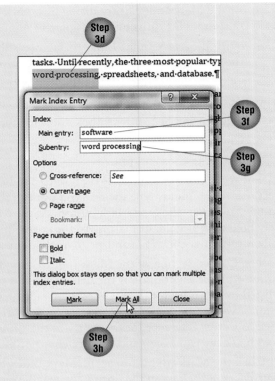

In the first paragraph in the Defining Desktop Publishing section:

spreadsheets	=	subentry (main entry = *software*)
database	=	subentry (main entry = *software*)

In the second paragraph in the Defining Desktop Publishing section:

publishing	=	main entry
desktop	=	subentry (main entry = *publishing*)
printer	=	main entry
laser	=	subentry (main entry = *printer*)

In the third paragraph in the Defining Desktop Publishing section:

design	=	main entry

In the fourth paragraph in the Defining Desktop Publishing section:

traditional	=	subentry (main entry = *publishing*)

In the first paragraph in the Initiating the Process section:

publication	=	main entry
planning	=	subentry (main entry = *publication*)
creating	=	subentry (main entry = *publication*)
content	=	subentry (main entry = *publication*)
intended audience	=	subentry (main entry = *publication*)

In the third paragraph in the Planning the Publication section:

message	=	main entry

j. Click Close to close the Mark Index Entry dialog box.

4. Turn off the display of nonprinting characters.

5. Save **C27-E01-DTP.docx**.

Inserting an Index

After you have marked all of the words that you want to include in an index as either main entries or subentries, the next step is to insert the index in the document. An index should appear at the end of a document, generally beginning on a separate page. To insert the index, position the insertion point at the end of the document and then insert a page break. With the insertion point positioned below the page break, type INDEX and then press the Enter key. With the insertion point positioned at the left margin, click the References tab and then click the Insert Index button in the Index group. At the Index dialog box, shown in Figure 27.3, select any desired formatting and then click OK. Word inserts the index, with the formatting you selected at the Index dialog box, at the location of the insertion point. Word also inserts a section break above and below the index text.

Insert an Index
1. Click References tab.
2. Click Insert Index button.
3. Select desired format.
4. Click OK.

Insert Index

Figure 27.3 Index Dialog Box

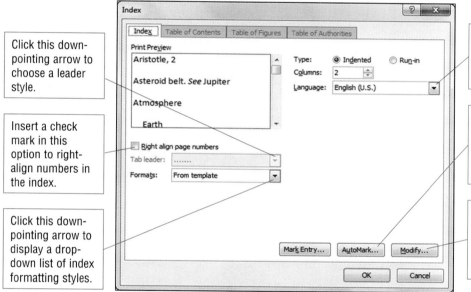

Click this down-pointing arrow to choose a leader style.

Insert a check mark in this option to right-align numbers in the index.

Click this down-pointing arrow to display a drop-down list of index formatting styles.

Click this down-pointing arrow to display a drop-down list of indexing languages.

Click this button and the Open Index Automark File dialog box displays where you can specify a concordance file.

Click this button to display the Style dialog box where you can select an index style and then modify the formatting of the style.

At the Index dialog box, you can customize the format of the index, specifying how the entries will appear. The *Print Preview* section shows how the index will display in the document. If you want numbers right-aligned in the index, insert a check mark in the *Right align page numbers* check box. (This makes the Tab leader option active.) Click the down-pointing arrow at the right side of the *Formats* option and a drop-down list of formatting choices displays. Click the *Formal* option and the *Tab leader* option becomes available. The default tab leader character is a period. To change to a different character, click the down-pointing arrow at the right side of the *Tab leader* option box and then click the desired character at the drop-down list.

In the *Type* section, the *Indented* option is the default, which means subentries appear indented below main entries. If you click *Run-in*, subentries display on the same line as main entries. By default, Word inserts an index in two columns. You can increase or decrease the number of columns in an index with the *Columns* option. If your document contains text in Spanish rather than English, you can create an Index using the Spanish alphabet, which includes additional letters such as *rr* and *ll*. To choose Spanish for the index, click the down-pointing arrow at the right side of the *Language* option and then click *Spanish (International Sort)* at the drop-down list.

You can create a concordance file for an index (you will learn how to create a concordance file later in this chapter) and then identify the file by clicking the AutoMark button and then double-clicking the file name in the Open Index Automark File dialog box. You can modify the formatting of an index style by clicking the Modify button. At the Style dialog box that displays, click the index style in the *Styles* list box that you want to modify and then click the Modify button. At the Modify Style dialog box, apply the desired formatting and then click OK. The Modify Style dialog box that displays is the same dialog box you used to modify styles in Chapter 24.

Exercise 27.1B Inserting an Index
Part 2 of 2

1. With **C27-E01-DTP.docx** open, position the insertion point at the end of the document and then press Ctrl + Enter to insert a page break.
2. Press Ctrl + E, type **INDEX**, press the Enter key, and then press Ctrl + L.
3. Click the References tab and then click the Insert Index button in the Index group.
4. At the Index dialog box, click the Modify button that displays in the lower right corner of the dialog box.
5. At the Style dialog box with *Index 1* selected in the *Styles* list box, click the Modify button.
6. At the Modify Style dialog box, click the Bold button.
7. Click OK to close the Modify Style dialog box.
8. At the Style dialog box, click *Index 2* in the *Styles* list box and then click the Modify button.
9. At the Modify Style dialog box, click the Italic button and then click OK.
10. Click OK at the Style dialog box.
11. At the Index dialog box, click the up-pointing arrow at the right of the *Columns* option to change the number to *3*.
12. Click the *Right align page numbers* check box to insert a check mark. (This makes the *Tab leader* option active.)
13. Click the down-pointing arrow at the right side of the *Tab leader* option box and then click the hyphen leader at the drop-down list.

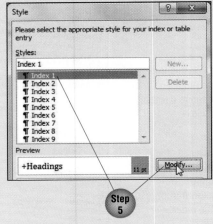

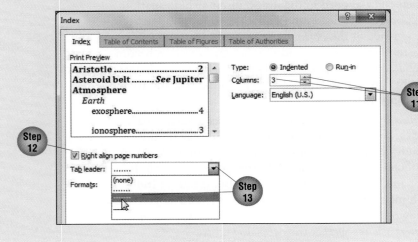

14. Click OK to close the Index dialog box.
15. Apply the Heading 1 style to the title *INDEX*.
16. Save and then print the last page (the index page) of the document.
17. Close **C27-E01-DTP.docx**.

Marking Text that Spans a Range of Pages

If you want to use more than a few words as a single index entry, consider identifying the text as a bookmark and then marking the bookmark as the index entry. This option is especially useful when the text for an entry spans a range of pages. To mark text that you have identified as a bookmark, position the insertion point at the end of the text, click the References tab, and then click the Mark Entry button in the Index group. At the Mark Index Entry dialog box, type the index entry for the text and then click the *Page range* option in the *Options* section. Click the down-pointing arrow at the right of the *Bookmark* option box and then click the bookmark name at the drop-down list. Click the Mark button to mark the bookmark text and close the dialog box.

Marking an Entry as a Cross-Reference

In some situations, you may want to mark for inclusion in an index text that refers the reader to another entry. For example, if you use the initials MIS in a document to refer to *Management Information Systems*, you can mark MIS as an index entry that refers the reader to the entry for Management Information Systems. To do this, you would select MIS, click the References tab, and then click the Mark Entry button in the Index group. At the Mark Index Entry dialog box, you would click *Cross-reference* in the *Options* section of the dialog box (to move the insertion point inside the text box), type Management Information Systems, and then click the Mark button.

Exercise 27.2 Marking Entries and Inserting an Index   Part 1 of 1

1. Open **Computers.docx** and save the document with the name **C27-E02-Computers**.
2. Make the following changes to the document:
   a. Apply the Title style to the title *THE COMPUTER ADVANTAGE*.
   b. Apply the Heading 2 style to the five headings in the document (*Speed*, *Accuracy*, *Versatility*, *Storage*, and *Communications*).
   c. Change the style set to Formal.
   d. Change the theme fonts to Foundry.
3. Create a bookmark for the *Speed* section of the document by completing the following steps:
   a. Select text from the beginning of the heading *Speed* through the paragraph of text that follows the heading.
   b. Click the Insert tab.
   c. Click the Bookmark button in the Links group.
   d. At the Bookmark dialog box, type Speed in the *Bookmark name* text box.
   e. Click the Add button.

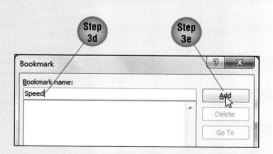

4. Complete steps similar to those in Step 3 to create the following bookmarks:
   a. Select text from the beginning of the *Accuracy* heading through the paragraph of text that follows the heading and then create a bookmark named *Accuracy*.
   b. Select text from the beginning of the *Versatility* heading through the paragraph of text that follows the heading and then create a bookmark named *Versatility*.
   c. Select text from the beginning of the *Storage* heading through the paragraph of text that follows the heading and then create a bookmark named *Storage*.
   d. Select text from the beginning of the *Communications* heading through the two paragraphs of text that follow the heading and then create a bookmark named *Communications*.

5. Mark the *Speed* bookmark as an index entry that spans pages by completing the following steps:

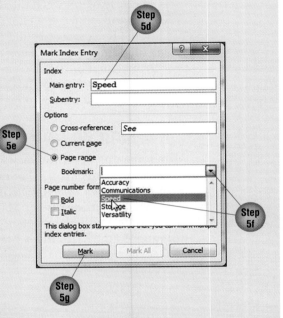

   a. Move the insertion point so it is positioned immediately following the only paragraph of text in the *Speed* section.
   b. Click the References tab.
   c. Click the Mark Entry button in the Index group.
   d. At the Mark Index Entry dialog box, type Speed in the *Main entry* text box.
   e. Click the *Page range* option.
   f. Click the down-pointing arrow at the right of the *Bookmark* option box and then click *Speed* at the drop-down list.
   g. Click the Mark button.

6. Complete steps similar to those in Step 5 to mark the following bookmarks as index entries: *Accuracy, Versatility, Storage,* and *Communications*.

7. With the Mark Index Entry dialog box open, mark the *first* occurrence of the following words (click the Mark All button) as main entries or subentries for the index:
   a. Mark *computers* located in the first sentence of the first paragraph of text in the document as a main entry.
   b. Mark *personal computers* in the second paragraph of text in the document as a main entry.
   c. Mark *supercomputers* in the *Speed* section of the document as a main entry.
   d. Mark *GIGO* in the *Accuracy* section of the document as a main entry.
   e. Mark the following text located in the *Versatility* section:

Human Genome Project	=	main entry
DNA	=	main entry

   f. Mark the following text located in the *Communications* section:

wireless devices	=	main entry
personal digital assistants	=	subentry (main entry = *wireless devices*)
notebook computers	=	subentry (main entry = *wireless devices*)
cell phones	=	subentry (main entry = *wireless devices*)
local area network	=	main entry
wide area network	=	main entry

   g. Click the Close button to close the Mark Index Entry dialog box.

8. Mark *microcomputers* as a cross-reference by completing the following steps:

   a. Press Ctrl + Home to move the insertion point to the beginning of the document.

   b. Select the word *microcomputers* that is located in the first sentence of the second paragraph of text.

   c. If necessary, click the References tab.

   d. Click the Mark Entry button in the Index group.

   e. At the Mark Index Entry dialog box, click the *Cross-reference* option in the *Options* section and then type personal computers.

   f. Click the Mark button.

   g. Click the Close button to close the Mark Index Entry dialog box.

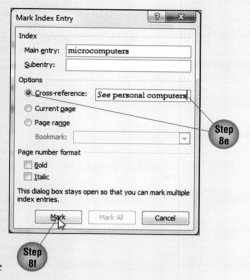

9. Complete steps similar to those in Step 8 to mark the following text as cross references:

   a. Select LAN in the second paragraph of text in the *Communications* section and cross reference it to *local area network*.

   b. Select WAN in the second paragraph of text in the *Communications* section and cross reference it to *wide area network*.

10. Close the Mark Index Entry dialog box and then turn off the display of nonprinting characters.

11. Insert the index in the document by completing the following steps:

    a. Position the insertion point at the end of the document.

    b. Insert a page break.

    c. With the insertion point positioned below the page break, press Ctrl + E and then type INDEX.

    d. Press the Enter key and then change the paragraph alignment back to left.

    e. Click the References tab.

    f. Click the Insert Index button in the Index group.

    g. At the Index dialog box, click the down-pointing arrow at the right of the *Formats* option box, scroll down the drop-down list, and then click *Formal*.

    h. Click OK to close the dialog box.

    i. Select the title *INDEX* and then apply the Heading 1 style.

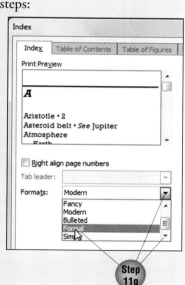

12. Save and then print the last page (the index page) of the document.

13. Close **C27-E02-Computers.docx**.

QUICK
STEPS

**Create a
Concordance File**
1. Click Insert tab.
2. Click Table button
   and drag to create
   table.
3. In first column,
   type words you
   want in index.
4. In second column,
   type the main
   entry and subentry
   (separated by a
   colon).
5. Save document.

Creating a Concordance File

You can save words that appear frequently in a document as a concordance file. Doing this saves you from having to mark references in a document. A concordance file is a Word document that contains a single, two-column table and no text outside the table. In the first column of the table, you enter words you want to index. In the second column, you enter the main entry and subentry that should appear in the index. To create a subentry, separate each main entry from a subentry with a colon. Figure 27.4 shows an example of a completed concordance file.

In Figure 27.4, the first column of the concordance file lists words as they appear in the document (for example, *World War I*, *technology*, and *television*). The second column lists the text as it should appear in the index, specifying whether it is a main entry or subentry. For example, the text *motion pictures* listed in the first column will appear in the index as a subentry under the main entry *Technology*.

After you have created a concordance file, you can use it to quickly mark text in a document for inclusion in an index. To do this, open the document containing text that you want marked for an index, display the Index dialog box, and then click the AutoMark button. At the Open Index AutoMark File dialog box, double-click the concordance file name in the list box. When you double-click the file name, Word turns on the display of nonprinting symbols, searches through the document for text that matches the text in the first column of the concordance file, and then marks it as specified in the second column. After marking text for the index, you can insert the index in the document as described earlier.

Figure 27.4 Concordance File

World War I	World War I
technology	Technology
teletypewriters	Technology: teletypewriters
motion pictures	Technology: motion pictures
television	Technology: television
Radio Corporation of America	Radio Corporation of America
coaxial cable	Coaxial cable
telephone	Technology: telephone
Communications Act of 1934	Communications Act of 1934
World War II	World War II
radar system	Technology: radar system
computer	Computer
Atanasoff Berry Computer	Computer: Atanasoff Berry Computer
Korean War	Korean War
Columbia Broadcasting System	Columbia Broadcasting System
Cold War	Cold War
Vietnam	Vietnam
artificial satellite	Technology: artificial satellite
Communications Satellite Act of 1962	Communications Satellite Act of 1962

As you create the concordance file in Exercise 27.3A, the AutoCorrect feature in Word will automatically capitalize the first letter of the first word entered in each cell. In Figure 27.4, you can see that several of the first words in the first column do not begin with a capital letter. Before you begin the exercise, consider turning off this AutoCorrect capitalization feature. To do this, click the File tab and then click the Options button. At the Word Options dialog box, click *Proofing* at the left side of the dialog box and then click the AutoCorrect Options button. At the AutoCorrect dialog box with the AutoCorrect tab selected, click the *Capitalize first letter of table cells* check box to remove the check mark. Click OK to close the dialog box and then click OK to close the Word Options dialog box.

Exercise 27.3A   Creating a Concordance File   Part 1 of 3

1. At a blank document, create the text shown in Figure 27.5 as a concordance file by completing the following steps:
   a. Click the Insert tab.
   b. Click the Table button in the Tables group.
   c. Drag down and to the right until *2 × 1 Table* displays at the top of the grid and then click the left mouse button.

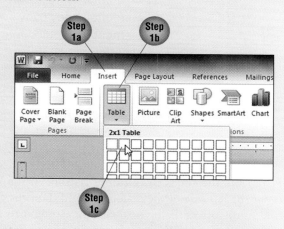

   d. Type the text in the cells as shown in Figure 27.5. Press the Tab key to move to the next cell. (If you did not remove the check mark before the *Capitalize first letter of table cells* option at the AutoCorrect dialog box, the *n* in the first word in the first cell *newsletters* is automatically capitalized. Hover the mouse over the capital N until the blue rectangle displays, click the AutoCorrect Options button that displays, and then click *Stop Auto-capitalizing First Letter of Table Cells* at the drop-down list.)
2. Save the document with the name **C27-E03-CFile**.
3. Close **C27-E03-CFile.docx**.

Figure 27.5 Exercise 27.3A

newsletters	Newsletters
software	Software
desktop publishing	Software: desktop publishing
word processing	Software: word processing
printers	Printers
laser	Printers: laser
design	Design
communication	Communication
consistency	Design: consistency
elements	Elements
Nameplate	Elements: nameplate
Logo	Elements: logo
Subtitle	Elements: subtitle
Folio	Elements: folio
Headlines	Elements: headlines
Subheads	Elements: subheads
Byline	Elements: byline
Body Copy	Elements: body copy
Graphics Images	Elements: graphics images
audience	Newsletters: audience
purpose	Newsletters: purpose
focal point	Newsletters: focal point

If you removed the check mark before the *Capitalize first letter of table cells* option at the AutoCorrect dialog box, you may need to turn this feature back on. To do this, click the File tab and then click the Options button. At the Word Options dialog box, click *Proofing* at the left side of the dialog box and then click the AutoCorrect Options button. At the AutoCorrect dialog box with the AutoCorrect tab selected, click the *Capitalize first letter of table cells* check box to insert the check mark. Click OK to close the dialog box and then click OK to close the Word Options dialog box.

Exercise 27.3B Inserting an Index Using a Concordance File   Part 2 of 3

1. Open **PlanNwsltr.docx** and save the document with the name **C27-E03-PlanNwsltr**.
2. Mark text to include in the index using the concordance file by completing the following steps:
   a. Click the References tab.

b. Click the Insert Index button in the Index group.

c. At the Index dialog box, click the AutoMark button.

d. At the Open Index AutoMark File dialog box, click the file type button to the right of the *File name* text box and then click *All Files (*.*)* at the drop-down list.

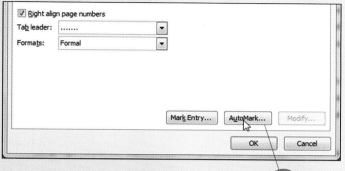

Step 2c

e. Double-click **C27-E03-CFile.docx** in the Content pane. (This turns on the display of the nonprinting symbols.)

3. Insert the index in the document by completing the following steps:
   a. Position the insertion point at the end of the document.
   b. Insert a page break.
   c. Type INDEX.
   d. Press the Enter key.
   e. Click the Insert Index button in the Index group.
   f. At the Index dialog box, click the down-pointing arrow at the right of the *Formats* option box and then click *Modern* at the drop-down list.
   g. Click OK to close the dialog box.
4. Apply the Heading 1 style to the *INDEX* title and then center INDEX.
5. Turn off the display of nonprinting characters.
6. Save **C27-E03-PlanNwsltr.docx** and then print only the index page.

Updating and Deleting an Index

If you make changes to a document after you have inserted an index, update the index. To do this, click anywhere within the index and then click the Update Index button in the Index group or press F9. To delete an index, select the entire index using either the mouse or the keyboard and then press the Delete key.

Update Index

Exercise 27.3C **Updating an Index** **Part 3 of 3**

1. With **C27-E03-PlanNwsltr. docx** open, insert a page break at the beginning of the title *PLANNING A NEWSLETTER*.

2. Update the index by clicking anywhere in the index, clicking the References tab, and then clicking the Update Index button in the Index group.

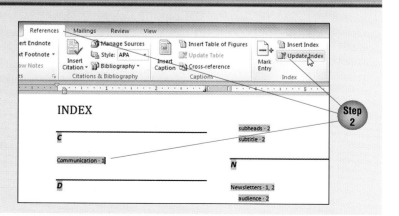

Step 2

3. Save **C27-E03-PlanNwsltr.docx** and then print only the index page.
4. Close **C27-E03-PlanNwsltr.docx**.

Chapter *Summary*

➤ An index is a list of topics contained in a publication and the pages on which those topics are discussed. Word automates the process of creating an index. Mark text for inclusion in an index at the Mark Index Entry dialog box. Display this dialog box by clicking the Mark Entry button in the References tab or pressing Alt + Shift + X.

➤ At the Mark Index Entry dialog box, specify whether the selected text is a main entry or a subentry.

➤ The main entry and subentry do not have to be the same as the selected text.

➤ Click the Mark button at the Mark Index Entry dialog box to mark the currently selected text or click the Mark All button to mark all occurrences in the document.

➤ After all necessary text has been marked as a main entry or a subentry for the index, insert the index, placing it at the end of the document beginning on a separate page.

➤ Apply formatting and customize the appearance of an index with options at the Index dialog box.

➤ Word provides seven formatting choices for an index at the *Formats* option box in the Index dialog box.

➤ You can identify text as a bookmark and then mark the bookmark as an index entry. Doing this is especially useful when text for an entry spans a range of pages.

➤ Mark text for the index as a cross-reference if you want the text to refer the reader to another index entry.

➤ Words that appear frequently in a document can be saved as a concordance file so you do not need to mark each reference. A concordance file is a Word document that contains a single, two-column table.

➤ Use a concordance file to mark text by displaying the Index dialog box and then clicking the AutoMark button. At the Open Index AutoMark File dialog box, double-click the concordance file name.

➤ Update an index by clicking the index and then clicking the Update Index button in the Index group or pressing F9.

Commands *Review*

FEATURE	RIBBON TAB, GROUP	BUTTON, OPTION	KEYBOARD SHORTCUT
Mark Index Entry dialog box	References, Index		Alt + Shift + X
Index dialog box	References, Index		
Open Index AutoMark File dialog box	References, Index	, AutoMark	
Update index	References, Index		F9

Key Points Review

Completion: In the space provided at the right, indicate the correct term, symbol, or command.

1. An index generally appears at this location in the document.

2. The Mark Entry button is located in the Index group in this tab.

3. This is the keyboard shortcut to display the Mark Index Entry dialog box.

4. When you mark a word for the index, the selected word displays in this text box in the Mark Index Entry dialog box.

5. Click this button at the Mark Index Entry dialog box to mark all of the occurrences of the text in the document as index entries.

6. If you want to mark more than a few words or a phrase for an index entry, consider identifying the text as this.

7. Mark text for the index as this if you want the text to refer the reader to another index entry.

8. Create this type of file and then use it to save time when marking text for an index.

9. Click this button at the Index dialog box to display the Open Index AutoMark File dialog box.

10. This is the keyboard shortcut to update an index.

Chapter Assessments

Applying Your Skills

Demonstrate your knowledge of features learned in this chapter by completing the following assessments.

Assessment 27.1   Create an Index for a Natural Interface Report

1. Open **InterfaceApps.docx** and save the document with the name **C27-A01-InterfaceApps**.
2. Make the following changes to the document:
   a. Apply the Heading 1 style to the title *NATURAL INTERFACE APPLICATIONS*.
   b. Apply the Heading 2 style to the four headings in the document.
   c. Change the style set to Modern.
3. Create the following bookmarks:
   a. Create a bookmark for the *SPEECH RECOGNITION* section and name the bookmark *Speech*.
   b. Create a bookmark for the *NATURAL-LANGUAGE INTERFACE* section and name the bookmark *NLInterface*.
   c. Create a bookmark for the *VIRTUAL REALITY* section and name the bookmark *VReality*.
   d. Create a bookmark for the *MENTAL INTERFACE* section and name the bookmark *MInterface*.

4. Mark the following bookmarks as index entries that span pages:
   a. Mark the *Speech* bookmark as an index entry that spans pages and type Speech recognition in the *Main entry* text box.
   b. Mark the *NLInterface* bookmark as an index entry that spans pages and type Natural-language interface in the *Main entry* text box.
   c. Mark the *VReality* bookmark as an index entry that spans pages and type Virtual reality in the *Main entry* text box.
   d. Mark the *MInterface* bookmark as an index entry that spans pages and type Mental interface in the *Main entry* text box.
5. Mark *VR* (located in the *VIRTUAL REALITY* section) as an index entry and cross reference *VR* to *Virtual reality*.
6. Mark the first occurrence of the following words as main entries or subentries for the index:
   a. Mark *artificial intelligence* located in the first sentence of the first paragraph of text in the document as a main entry.
   b. Mark the following text located in the *SPEECH RECOGNITION* section:

computer	=	main entry
voice commands	=	main entry
speed	=	subentry (main entry = *computer*)
capacity	=	subentry (main entry = *computer*)

   c. Mark the following text located in the *NATURAL-LANGUAGE INTERFACE* section:

languages	=	main entry
translators	=	subentry (main entry = *languages*)

7. Insert the index at the end of the document on a separate page and change the *Formats* option at the Index dialog box to *Modern*.
8. Apply the Heading 1 style to the Index heading.
9. Center the two titles in the document *NATURAL INTERFACE APPLICATIONS* and *INDEX*.
10. Save and then print the last page of the document.
11. Close **C27-A01-InterfaceApps.docx**.

Assessment 27.2   Create an Index Using a Concordance File

1. At a blank document, create the text shown in Figure 27.6 as a concordance file.
2. Save the document with the name **C27-A02-CFile**.
3. Print and then close **C27-A02-CFile.docx**.
4. Open **DesignNwsltr.docx** and save the document with the name **C27-A02-DesignNwsltr**.
5. Make the following changes to the document:
   a. Mark text for an index using the concordance file **C27-A02-CFile.docx**.
   b. Insert the index at the end of the document. (Use the default settings at the Index dialog box.)
   c. Apply the Heading 1 style to the *Index* title and center the title.
6. Number the pages at the bottom center of each page.
7. Change the paragraph spacing to *Double* using the Change Styles button in the Home tab.
8. Insert a page break at the beginning of the title *CREATING NEWSLETTER LAYOUT*.
9. Update the index.
10. Save the document again, print the index, and then close **C27-A02-DesignNwsltr.docx**.

Figure 27.6 Assessment 27.2

NEWSLETTER	Newsletter
newsletter	Newsletter
consistency	Newsletter: consistency
element	Elements
margins	Elements: margins
column layout	Elements: column layout
nameplate	Elements: nameplate
location	Elements: location
logos	Elements: logo
color	Elements: color
ruled lines	Elements: ruled lines
Focus	Elements: focus
balance	Elements: balance
graphics images	Graphics images
photos	Photos
Headlines	Newsletter: headlines
subheads	Newsletter: subheads
White space	White space
directional flow	Newsletter: directional flow
paper	Paper
size	Paper: size
type	Paper: type
weight	Paper: weight
stock	Paper: stock
margin size	Newsletter: margin size

Expanding Your Skills

Explore additional feature options or use Help to learn a new skill in creating this document.

Assessment 27.3 Customize an Index

1. You can customize an index with options at the Index dialog box. At a blank document, display this dialog box by clicking the References tab and then clicking the Insert Index button in the Index group. Look at the options offered by the dialog box and determine how to change leaders and number of columns. Close the blank document.
2. Open **C27-A02-DesignNwsltr.docx** and then save the document with the name **C27-A03-DesignNwsltr**.
3. Apply the Adjacency theme.
4. Remove the page break that you inserted before the title *CREATING NEWSLETTER LAYOUT*. ***Hint: Do this by positioning the insertion point after the period that ends the paragraph that displays* before *the title and then press the Delete key two times.***
5. Make the following changes to the index:
   a. Display the Index dialog box for the index.
   b. Change to a format that contains leaders.

    c. Change the leaders to hyphens (rather than periods).

    d. Specify three columns.

    e. Close the Index dialog box. When asked if you want to replace the selected Index, click OK.

6. Save **C27-A03-DesignNwsltr.docx**.

7. Print only the index and then close the document.

Assessment 27.4   Create an Index for a Spanish Document

Note: Before completing the assessment, check to make sure the *Spanish (International Sort)* language option is available at the Index dialog box. If it is not available, install the language. To do this, click the Review tab, click the Language button in the Language group, and then click *Language Preferences* at the drop-down list. At the Word Options dialog box with *Language* selected in the left panel, click the down-pointing arrow at the right side of the *[Add additional editing languages]* option box, scroll down the drop-down list, and then click *Spanish (International Sort)*. Click the Add button located to the right of the *[Add additional editing languages]* option box and then click OK to close the Word Options dialog box. (You will be instructed to restart Office.)

1. With the *Language* option in the Index dialog box, you can create an index for a document written in Spanish. The steps for creating an index for a document written in Spanish are the same as the steps for creating a document written in English except you need to change the *Language* option to *Spanish (International Sort)*. Open the document named **SpanishDoc.docx** and then save the document with the name **C27-A04-SpanishDoc.docx**.

2. Mark text to include in the index using the concordance file named **SpanishCFile.docx** by completing the following steps:

    a. Click the References tab and then click the Insert Index button in the Index group.

    b. At the Index dialog box, click the AutoMark button.

    c. At the Open Index AutoMark File dialog box, make sure Chapter27 on your storage medium is the active folder and then double-click **SpanishCFile.docx** in the Content pane. (This turns on the display of the nonprinting symbols.)

3. Insert the index in the document by completing the following steps:

    a. Position the insertion point at the end of the document and then insert a page break.

    b. Type **INDEX** and then press the Enter key.

    c. Click the Insert Index button in the Index group.

    d. At the Index dialog box, click the down-pointing arrow at the right of the *Language* option box and then click *Spanish (International Sort)* at the drop-down list.

    e. Click the down-pointing arrow at the right of the *Formats* option box and then click *Formal* at the drop-down list.

    f. Click OK to close the dialog box.

4. Apply the Heading 1 style to the *INDEX* title.

5. Turn off the display of nonprinting characters.

6. Save **C27-A04-SpanishDoc.docx** and then print only the index page.

Achieving Signature Status

Take your skills to the next level by completing this more challenging assessment.

Assessment 27.5   Format a Report and Create an Index

1. At a blank document, type the text in a table as shown in Figure 27.7. (You will use this information as a concordance file to create an index for a report.) After typing the text, open **CompSystems.docx** (you may want to print the document), determine at least five additional entries for the index, and then type the entries in the table. After determining at least five index entries, close **CompSystems.docx**.

2. Save the table document and name it **C27-A05-CFile**.

3. Print and then close **C27-A05-CFile.docx**.
4. Open **BMCStyles.docx**.
5. Display the Organizer dialog box. *Hint: Click the Styles group dialog box launcher, click the Manage Styles button, and then click the Import/Export button.*
6. Copy the *BMCHeading*, *BMCTable*, and *BMCTitle* from the left list box of the Organizer dialog box to the right list box.
7. Close **BMCStyles.docx**.
8. At a blank document, insert the file named **CompSystems.docx** and then save the document with the name **C27-A05-CompSystems**. (Make sure you insert the file using the Object button arrow.)
9. Format the document so it appears as shown in Figure 27.8 with the following specifications:
   a. Apply the BMCTitle style to the two titles in the document.
   b. Apply the BMCHeading style to the headings in the document.
   c. Apply the table style to the two tables in the document.
   d. Modify the table style so it appears as shown in Figure 27.8.
   e. Change the paragraph spacing to relaxed.
   f. Insert bullets, a header, and a footer as shown in the figure. (Change the font color for the header and footer text to dark blue.)
   g. Insert an index at the end of the document (you determine the formatting of the index) using the **C27-A05-CFile.docx** concordance file.
10. Save and then print **C27-A05-CompSystems.docx**.
11. Display the Organizer dialog box and then delete the following styles from the right list box: *BMCHeading*, *BMCTable*, and *BMCTitle*.
12. Close **C27-A05-CompSystems.docx**.

Figure 27.7 Assessment 27.5

network	Network
communications	Communications
medium	Communications: medium
wireless signal	Communications: wireless signal
internal	Network: internal
global	Network: global
sharing	Network: sharing
functionality	Network: functionality
hardware	Communications: hardware
transmission	Communications: transmission
relay systems	Communications: relay systems
protocols	Network: protocols
transmission	Transmission
speeds	Transmission: speeds
binary	Binary
converter	Converter
television	Television

Figure 27.8 Assessment 27.5

Page 1

1

Computer Networks

A computer network consists of two or more computing or other devices connected by a communications medium, such as a wireless signal or a cable. A computer network provides a way to connect with others and share files and resources such as printers or an Internet connection.

In business settings, networks allow you to communicate with employees, suppliers, vendors, customers, and government agencies. Many companies have their own network, called an intranet, which is essentially a private Internet within the company's corporate "walls." Some companies also offer an extension of their internal network, called an extranet, to suppliers and customers. For example, a supplier might be allowed to access inventory information on a company's internal network to make sure the company does not run short of a vital part for its manufacturing process. In your home, networks are useful for sharing resources among members of your family. For example, using a home network, you might share one printer or fax machine among three or four computers.

The Internet is a global network made up of several networks linked together. If you consider all the applications, services, and tools the Internet allows you to access, you can begin to understand the power of networking and how it opens up a new world of sharing and functionality.

Communications Systems

A computer network is one kind of communications system. This system includes sending and receiving hardware, transmission and relay systems, common sets of standards so all the equipment can "talk" to each other, and communications software.

You use such a networked communications system whenever you send/receive IM or email messages, pay a bill online, shop at an Internet store, send a document to a shared printer at work or at home, or download a file.

The world of computer network communications systems is made up of:

- Transmission media upon which the data travels to/from its destination.
- A set of standards and network protocols (rules for how data is handled as it travels along a communications channel). Devices use these to send and receive data to and from each other.

Blue Mountain Computer Services and Training

Page 1

Page 2

2

- Hardware and software to connect to a communications pathway from the sending and receiving ends.

The first step in understanding a communications system is to learn the basics about transmission signals and transmission speeds when communicating over a network.

Types of Signals

Two types of signals are used to transmit voices and other sounds over a computer network: analog and digital. An analog signal is formed by continuous sound waves that fluctuate from high to low. Your voice is transmitted as an analog signal over traditional telephone lines at a certain frequency. A digital signal uses a discrete signal that is either high or low. In computer terms, high represents the digital bit 1, and low represents the digital bit 0. These are the only two states for digital data.

Telephone lines carry your voice using an analog signal. However, computers don't "speak" analog; rather, they use a binary system of 1s and 0s to turn analog data into digital signals. If you send data between computers using an analog medium such as a phone line, the signal has to be transformed from digital to analog (modulated) and back again to digital (demodulated) to be understood by the computer on the receiving end. The piece of hardware that sends and receives data from a transmission source such as your telephone line or cable television connection is a modem. The word modem comes from the combination of the words *modulate* and *demodulate*.

Today, most new communications technologies simply use a digital signal, saving the trouble of converting transmissions. An example of this trend is the demise in 2009 of analog television transmissions as the industry switched to digital signals. Many people were sent scrambling to either buy a more recent television set or buy a converter to convert digital transmissions back to analog to work with their older equipment. More recent computer networks, too, use a pure digital signal method of sending and receiving data over a network.

Transmission Speed

If you've ever been frustrated with how long it takes to download a file from a website, you are familiar with the fact that, in a communications system, data moves from one computer to another at different speeds. The speed of transmission is determined by a few key factors.

The first factor is the speed at which a signal can change from high to low, which is called frequency. A signal sent at a faster frequency provides faster transmission (Figure 1). The other factor contributing to

Blue Mountain Computer Services and Training

Page 2

Page 3

3

the speed of data transmission is bandwidth. On a computer network, the term bandwidth refers to the number of bits (pieces of data) per second that can be transmitted over a communications medium. Think of bandwidth as being like a highway. At rush hour, with the same amount of cars, a two-lane highway accommodates less traffic and everybody moves at a slower speed than on a four-lane highway, where much more traffic can travel at a faster speed.

Figure 1: Bandwidth Measurements

Term	Abbreviation	Meaning
1 kilobit per second	1 Kbps	1 thousand bits per second
1 megabit per second	1 Mbps	1 million bits per second
1 gigabit per second	1 Gbps	1 billion bits per second
1 terabit per second	1 Tbps	1 trillion bits per second
1 petabit per second	1 Pbps	1 quadrillion bits per second

If you have plenty of bandwidth and your data is transmitted at a high frequency, you get faster transmission speeds. Any communications medium that is capable of carrying a large amount of data at a fast speed is known as broadband.

Though transmission speeds at any moment in time may vary depending on network traffic and other factors, each of the common communications media has a typical speed (Figure 2). These speeds are constantly being improved upon. In fact, some very high-powered connections provide transmission speeds of as much as 100 gigabits (one billion bits) per second, which allows you to download a high-definition DVD movie in two seconds.

Figure 2: Average Network Connection Speeds

Type of Connection	Typical Speed
56 K dial-up	56 Kbps
satellite	1.5 Mbps
DSL	7 Mbps
fiber-optic	25 Mbps
cable TV	50 Mbps

Blue Mountain Computer Services and Training

Page 3

Page 4

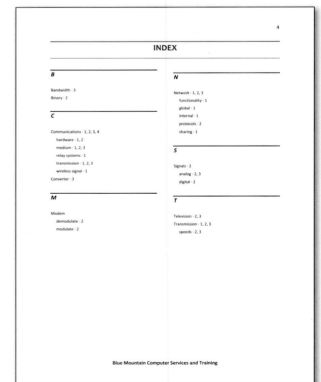

4

INDEX

B

Bandwidth · 3
Binary · 2

C

Communications · 1, 2, 3, 4
  hardware · 1, 2
  medium · 1, 2, 3
  relay systems · 1
  transmission · 1, 2, 3
  wireless signal · 1
Converter · 3

M

Modem
  demodulate · 2
  modulate · 2

N

Network · 1, 2, 3
  functionality · 1
  global · 1
  internal · 1
  protocols · 2
  sharing · 1

S

Signals · 2
  analog · 2, 3
  digital · 2

T

Television · 2, 3
Transmission · 1, 2, 3
  speeds · 2, 3

Blue Mountain Computer Services and Training

Page 4

Chapter Twenty-Seven

Chapter 28

Tutorial 28.1
Creating a Table of Contents
Tutorial 28.2
Customizing and Updating a
Table of Contents
Tutorial 28.3
Assigning Levels to Table
of Contents Entries
Tutorial 28.4
Creating captions
Tutorial 28.5
Creating a Table of Figures
Tutorial 28.6
Creating and updating a Table
of Authorities

Creating Specialized Tables

Performance Objectives

Upon successful completion of Chapter 28, you will be able to:

- Create, insert, and update a table of contents
- Create, insert, and update a table of figures
- Create, insert, and update a table of authorities

Books, textbooks, reports, and manuscripts often include specialized tables, such as a table of contents, table of figures, or table of authorities. Creating these tables manually can be tedious. With Word, the steps and tasks required, like those required to create an index, can be automated, allowing you to create specialized tables quickly and easily. In this chapter, you will learn the steps to mark text for inclusion in a table of contents, table of figures, or table of authorities and steps to insert the table or list.

Note: Before beginning computer exercises for this chapter, copy to your storage medium the Chapter28 folder from the CD that accompanies this textbook and then make Chapter28 the active folder.

In this chapter, students will produce the following documents:

Exercise 28.1. C28-E01-Robots.docx
Exercise 28.2. C28-E02-InternetFuture.docx
Exercise 28.3. C28-E03-OutputDevices.docx
Exercise 28.4. C28-E04-LarsenBrief.docx

Model answers for these exercises are shown on the following pages.

CONTENTS

ROBOTS AS ANDROIDS _____ 1

   VISUAL PERCEPTION _____ 1
   AUDIO PERCEPTION _____ 1
   TACTILE PERCEPTION _____ 1
   LOCOMOTION _____ 2
   NAVIGATION _____ 2

INTERNET COMMUNITY ISSUES _____ 2

   FLAMING _____ 2
   NETIQUETTE _____ 2
   MODERATED ENVIRONMENTS _____ 3

Exercise 28.1 C28-E01-Robots.docx   Page 1

ROBOTS AS ANDROIDS

Robotic factories are increasingly commonplace, especially in heavy manufacturing, where tolerance of repetitive movements, great strength, and untiring precision are more important than flexibility. Robots are especially useful for hazardous work, such as defusing bombs or handling radioactive materials. They also excel in constructing tiny components like those found inside notebook computers, which are often too small for humans to assemble.

Most people think of robots in science fiction terms, which generally depict them as androids, or simulated humans. Real robots today do not look human at all, and, judged by human standards, they are not very intelligent. The task of creating a humanlike body has proved incredibly difficult. Many technological advances in visual perception, audio perception, touch, dexterity, locomotion, and navigation need to occur before robots that look and act like human beings will live and work among us.

VISUAL PERCEPTION

Visual perception is an area of great complexity. A large percentage of the human brain is dedicated to processing stimuli coming from the eyes. As our most powerful sense, sight is the primary means through which we understand the world around us. A single camera is not good enough to simulate the eye. Two camera are needed to give stereoscopic vision, which allows depth and movement perception. Even with two cameras, visual perception still requires understanding what the cameras are seeing. Processing the image is the difficult part. In order for a robot to move through a room full of furniture it must build a mental map of that room, complete with obstacles. The robot must judge distances and the size of objects before it can figure out how to move around them.

AUDIO PERCEPTION

Audio perception is less complex than visual perception but no less important. People respond to audible cues about their surroundings and the people they are with without even thinking about it. Listeners can determine someone's emotional state just by hearing the person's voice. A car starting up prompts someone crossing the street to glance in that direction to check for danger. Identifying a single voice and interpreting what it is saying amid accompanying background noise is a task that is among the most important for human beings—and the most difficult.

TACTILE PERCEPTION

Tactile perception, or touch, is another critical sense. Because robots are made of steel and motors, they can be built with any level of strength. But, how does a robot capable of lifting a car pick up an egg in the dark without dropping it or crushing it? The answer is through a sense of touch. The robot must not only be able to feel an object but also be able to sense how much pressure it is applying to that object. With this feedback, the robot can properly judge how hard it should squeeze. This is a very difficult area, and it may prove that simulating the human hand is even more difficult than simulating the human mind.

Related to touch is the skill of dexterity, or hand-eye coordination. The challenge is to create a robot that can perform small actions, such as soldering tiny joints or placing chips at precise spots in a circuit board, within half a millimeter.

Page 2

LOCOMOTION

Locomotion includes broad movements such as walking. Getting a robot to move around is not easy. This area of science is challenging, as it requires balance within an endlessly changing set of variables. How does the program adjust for walking up a hill, or down a set of stairs? What if the wind is blowing hard or a foot slips? Currently, most mobile robots work with wheels or treads, which limit their mobility in some circumstances but make them much easier to control.

NAVIGATION

Related to perception, navigation deals with the science of moving a mobile robot through an environment. Navigation is not an isolated area of artificial intelligence; it must work closely with a visual system or some other kind of perception system. Sonar, radar, mechanical "feelers," and other systems have been subjects of experimentation. A robot can plot a course to a location using an internal "map" built up by a navigational perception system. If the course is blocked or too difficult, the robot must be smart enough to backtrack so it can try another plan.

INTERNET COMMUNITY ISSUES

Internet users around the world form a community and, like any social organization, the community exhibits the entire range of behavior, from considerate and creative to insulting and damaging. Unfortunately, the anonymous nature of Internet interaction tends to bring out the worst in some people. The fear of embarrassment or shame that governs behavior in face-to-face encounters is lessened when people meet on the Internet. This means that some individuals act very differently than they would if they were in a public forum, ruining the Internet experience for many people.

Flaming is one of the most frequently encountered examples of rude Internet behavior. Guidelines for good Internet behavior, called netiquette, have been developed to encourage people to interact productively. Moderated environments are another solution to inappropriate behavior. They allow a moderator to police behavior in certain settings such as chat rooms, mailing lists, and message boards.

FLAMING

Flaming is the Internet equivalent of insulting someone in a face-to-face setting. Flaming often occurs in public forums, such as emails, message boards, or chat rooms. Taking advantage of their anonymity, some people seem to take a perverse joy in being as rude as possible, to the point that they drive people away. Flame wars are flames that are traded back and forth, often among multiple parties. The best policy is to ignore flames. Anyone using a public Internet forum should be aware of the basic rules of behavior to avoid doing anything that might provoke flaming.

NETIQUETTE

The term netiquette is a result of combining the words Net and etiquette. Netiquette exists to address behavior problems such as flaming and sending rude or hurtful email messages. Most netiquette is based on the Golden Rule, which stipulates that people should treat others as they would like others to treat them. Some netiquette deals with certain Internet conventions that need to be learned in order not to inadvertently offend other users. For example, newcomers commonly type messages in all capital letters without realizing that, by convention, this is

2

Page 3

---

commonly understood to mean that the writer is shouting. Without intending it, an email writer using all capital letters will make people uncomfortable or angry.

MODERATED ENVIRONMENTS

Moderated environments are the answer for many people who want to avoid the seedy side of the Internet. Many chat rooms, message boards, and mailing lists have a moderator, an individual with the power to filter messages and ban people who break the rules. Rules violations can be anything from hurling insults to simply straying off-topic. A moderator running a chat room on travel, for example, might ban people for excessively discussing their favorite movies. Usually, a moderator has complete power over the situation and can ban people in any way he or she sees fit. If a moderator is too harsh, people might switch to another group.

3

Page 4

Exercise 28.2 C28-E02-InternetFuture.docx

Page 1

TABLE OF CONTENTS

FUTURE OF THE INTERNET 1

   Satellite Internet Connections 1

   Second Internet 1

   Internet Services for a Fee 1

   Internet in 2030 2

INTERNET COMMUNITY ISSUES 2

   Flaming 2

   Netiquette 2

   Moderated Environments 3

Page 2

FUTURE OF THE INTERNET

The Internet is having trouble keeping up with the rapid increase in users and the increased workload created by the popularity of bandwidth-intensive applications such as music and video files. The broadband connections needed to enjoy these new applications are not evenly distributed. Several ongoing projects promise to provide solutions for these problems in the future. Once these connectivity problems are dealt with, people around the world will be able to enjoy the new Web services that are only a few short years away.

Satellite Internet Connections

Many people living in remote or sparsely populated areas are not served by broadband Internet connections. Cable or optical fiber networks are very expensive to install and maintain, and ISPs are not interested in providing service to areas or individuals unless they think it will be profitable. One hope for people without broadband connections is provided by satellite TV networks. Remote ISPs connect to the satellite network using antennae attached to their servers. Data is relayed to and from ISP servers to satellites, which are in turn connected to an Internet backbone access point. While the connection speeds might not be as fast as those offered by regular land-based broadband access, they are faster than the service twisted-pair cable can offer and much better than no access at all.

Second Internet

A remedy for the traffic clogging the information highway is Internet2, a revolutionary new type of Internet currently under development. When fully operational, Internet2 will enable large research universities in the United States to collaborate and share huge amounts of complex scientific information at amazing speeds. Led by over 170 universities working in partnership with industry and government, the Internet2 consortium is developing and deploying advanced network technologies and applications.

Internet2 is a testing ground for universities to work together and develop advanced Internet technologies such as telemedicine, digital libraries, and virtual laboratories. Internet2 universities will be connected to an ultrahigh-speed network called the Abilene backbone. Each university will use state-of-the-art equipment to take advantage of transfer speeds provided by the network.

Internet Services for a Fee

Industry observers predict that large portals such as AOL, MSN, and Yahoo! will soon determine effective structures and marketing strategies to get consumers to pay for Internet services. This new market, called bring-your-own-access (BYOA), will combine essential *content*, for example, news and weather, with *services*, such as search, directory, email, IM, and online shopping, into a new product with monthly access charges. But to entice current and potential customers into the BYOA market, ISP and telecom companies must offer improvements in the area of security, privacy, and ease-of-use. Additionally, they are expected to develop new ways to personalize content and add value to the current range of Internet services.

Page 3

Internet in 2030

Ray Kurzweil, a computer futurist, has looked ahead to the year 2030 and visualized a Web that offers no clear distinctions between real and simulated environments and people. Among the applications he sees as very possible are computerized displays in eyeglasses that could offer simultaneous translations of foreign language conversations, nanobots (microscopic robots) that would work with our brains to extend our mental capabilities, and more sophisticated avatars (simulated persons-on-screen) that people will interact with online. Technologies that allow people to protect their feelings as well as their images and voices may usher in a period when people could "be" with another person even though they are physically hundreds or even thousands of miles apart.

INTERNET COMMUNITY ISSUES

Internet users around the world form a community and, like any social organization, the community exhibits the entire range of behavior, from considerate and creative to insulting and damaging. Unfortunately, the anonymous nature of Internet interaction tends to bring out the worst in some people. The fear of embarrassment or shame that governs behavior in face-to-face encounters is lessened when people meet on the Internet. This means that some individuals act very differently than they would if they were in a public forum, ruining the Internet experience for many people.

Flaming is one of the most frequently encountered examples of rude Internet behavior. Guidelines for good Internet behavior, called *netiquette*, have been developed to encourage people to interact productively. Moderated environments are another solution to inappropriate behavior. They allow a moderator to police behavior in certain settings such as chat rooms, mailing lists, and message boards.

Flaming

Flaming is the Internet equivalent of insulting someone in a face-to-face setting. Flaming often occurs in public forums, such as emails, message boards, or chat rooms. Taking advantage of their anonymity, some people seem to take a perverse joy in being as rude as possible, to the point that they drive people away. Flame wars are flames that are traded back and forth, often among multiple parties. The best policy is to ignore flames. Anyone using a public Internet forum should be aware of the basic rules of behavior to avoid doing anything that might provoke flaming.

Netiquette

The term netiquette is a result of combining the words *Net* and *etiquette*. Netiquette exists to address behavior problems such as flaming and sending rude or hurtful email messages. Most netiquette is based on the Golden Rule, which stipulates that people should treat others as they would like others to treat them. Some netiquette deals with certain Internet conventions that need to be learned in order not to inadvertently offend other users. For example, newcomers commonly type messages in all capital letters without realizing that, by convention, this is commonly understood to mean that the writer is shouting. Without intending it, an email writer using all capital letters will make people uncomfortable or angry.

Page 4

Moderated Environments

Moderated environments are the answer for many people who want to avoid the seedy side of the Internet. Many chat rooms, message boards, and mailing lists have a moderator, an individual with the power to filter messages and ban people who break the rules. Rules violations can be anything from hurling insults to simply straying off-topic. A moderator running a chat room on travel, for example, might ban people for excessively discussing their favorite movies. Usually, a moderator has complete power over the situation and can ban people in any way he or she sees fit. If a moderator is too harsh, people might switch to another group.

TABLE OF FIGURES

FIGURE 1 CRT MONITOR 1
FIGURE 2 FLAT-PANEL MONITOR 1
FIGURE 3 INK-JET PRINTER 1
FIGURE 4 LASER PRINTER 1

Exercise 28.3

C28-E03-OutputDevices.docx

Page 1

COMPUTER OUTPUT DEVICES

An output device is any hardware device that makes information from a computer available to the user. A computer produces output using the combination of output devices, media, and software available with a particular system. Some output devices include monitors and printers.

MONITORS

A monitor is a fundamental component of a computer system and is the most common soft copy output mechanism for displaying text, images, graphics, and video on a screen. Available in a variety of shapes, sizes, costs, and capabilities, monitors allow users to view information temporarily.

CRT MONITOR

An early type of monitor for desktop computers was the cathode ray tube (CRT) monitor (see Figure 1). A CRT is a large, sealed glass tube housed in a plastic case. The front of the tube is the screen. A cable at... into a graphics adapter board on... system unit. An electric cord on... electrical outlet. CRT monitors u... technology used in television set... bulky.

Figure 2 Flat-Panel Monitor

FLA...

A fla...
thin...
bene...
pow...
use l...
cryst...
shee...
caus...
allo...
scre...

PRINTERS

A printer is the most common ty...
medium, such as paper or transp...
portrait or landscape format. In...
format is usually used for letters...

Page 2

page is wider than it is tall. Landscape format is best suited for financial spreadsheets and other types of tabular reports. Two types of printers include ink-jet printers and laser printers.

INK-JET PRINTER

An ink-jet printer is a nonimpact printer that forms characters and images by spraying thousands of tiny droplets of electrically charged ink onto a sheet of paper as the sheet passes through the printer (see Figure 3). Most ink-jet printers use two or more ink cartridges, one for black print and one or more for color printing. Each cartridge has multiple holes, called nozzles. During printing, combinations of tiny ink droplets are propelled through the nozzles by heat and pressure onto the paper, forming characters and images.

Figure 3 Ink-Jet Printer

LASER PRINTER

A laser printer is a nonimpact printer that produces output of exceptional quality using a technology similar to that of a photocopy machine. Laser printers are used for any printing application, including those requiring output of printing-press quality material (see Figure 4). Their speed and ability to produce clear, crisp text and images have made them the fastest growing segment of the printer market. A laser printer creates text and graphics on a rotating metal drum using a laser beam. During printing, components inside the printer read characters and relay them to a printer device called a laser mechanism. A laser beam produces characters and images on a rotating drum inside the printer by altering the electrical charge wherever the beam strikes the drum. The charges produce tiny magnetic fields (dots) on the drum, forming characters. As the drum rotates, it picks up an ink-like powder called toner, similar to copy machine toner. The sensitive dots on the drum are then deposited onto the paper. Using heat and pressure, a set of rollers fuses the toner onto the paper, forming the printed image.

Figure 4 Laser Printer

2

Page 3

TABLE OF AUTHORITIES

Cases

State v. Bertelli, 63 W.2d 77, 542 P.2d 751 (1971) --2

State v. Connors, 73 W.2d 743, 430 P.2d 199 (1974)---2, 3

State v. Landers, 103 W.2d 432, 893 P.2d 2 (1984) ---2, 3

Statutes

RCW 7.42A.429(1)--2

RCW 7.53.443 --2

RCW 7.72A.432(2)---2

RCW 7.89.321 --2

i

Exercise 28.4

C28-E04-LarsenBrief.docx

Creating a Table of Contents

A table of contents appears at the beginning of a book, manuscript, or report and contains headings and subheadings with page numbers. In a previous chapter, you created a table of contents using the Quick Parts button in the Text group in the Insert tab. You can also create a table of contents using the Table of Contents button in the Table of Contents group in the References tab. You can identify text to be included in the table by applying built-in or custom heading styles, assigning levels, or marking text.

Applying Styles

To create a table of contents by applying built-in or custom styles, open the document and then apply the styles you want to use. Word uses text with the Heading 1 style applied as the first level of the table of contents text, Heading 2 text for the second level, and so on. Apply the built-in or custom styles with options in the Styles group in the Home tab.

Inserting a Table of Contents

After you have applied styles to the headings in a document, insert the table of contents. To do this, position the insertion point where you want the table to appear in the document, click the References tab, click the Table of Contents button, and then click the desired option at the drop-down list.

Insert a Table of Contents

1. Apply heading styles.
2. Click References tab.
3. Click Table of Contents button.
4. Click desired options at drop-down list.

Table of Contents

Numbering Table of Contents Pages

Number Table of Contents Page
1. Click Insert tab.
2. Click Page Number button.
3. Click *Format Page Numbers* at drop-down list.
4. Change number format to lowercase Roman numerals.
5. Click OK.

Page Number

Generally, the pages in a table of contents are numbered with lowercase Roman numerals (*i, ii, iii*). You can change the page number format to lowercase Roman numerals at the Page Number Format dialog box, shown in Figure 28.1. Display this dialog box by clicking the Insert tab, clicking the Page Number button in the Header & Footer group, and then clicking *Format Page Numbers* at the drop-down list. Numbering on the first page of the document, excluding the table of contents page(s), should begin with number 1. To insert two page numbering formats, separate the table of contents from the beginning of the document with a section break that begins a new page.

Figure 28.1 Page Number Format Dialog Box

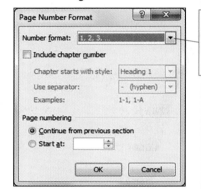

Change the number format to lowercase Roman numerals when numbering table of contents pages.

Navigating using a Table of Contents

When you insert a table of contents in a document, you can use the table of contents headings to navigate in a document. Table of contents headings are hyperlinks that are connected to the heading in the document. To navigate in a document using table of contents headings, click in the table of contents to select it. Position the mouse pointer over the desired heading and a box will display with the path and file name as well as the text *Ctrl+Click to follow link*. Hold down the Ctrl key and then click the left mouse button and the insertion point is positioned in the document at the location of the heading.

1. Open **Robots.docx** and save the document with the name **C28-E01-Robots**.

2. With the insertion point positioned immediately left of the *R* in *ROBOTS AS ANDROIDS*, insert a section break by completing the following steps:

   a. Click the Page Layout tab.
   b. Click the Breaks button in the Page Setup group.
   c. Click the *Next Page* option in the *Section Breaks* section.

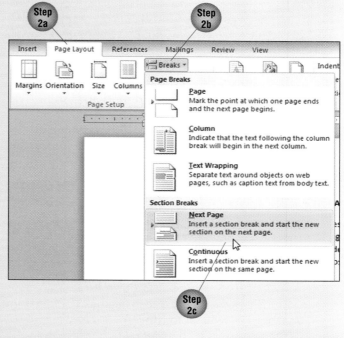

3. With the insertion point positioned below the section break, insert page numbering and change the beginning number to 1 by completing the following steps:

   a. Click the Insert tab.
   b. Click the Page Number button in the Header & Footer group, point to *Bottom of Page*, and then click *Plain Number 2*.
   c. Click the Page Number button in the Header & Footer group in the Header & Footer Tools Design tab and then click *Format Page Numbers* at the drop-down list.

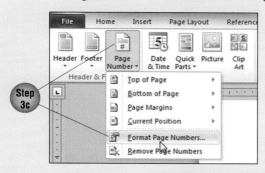

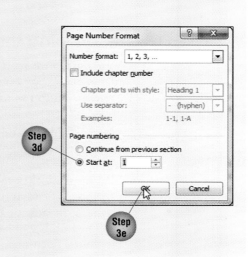

   d. At the Page Number Format dialog box, click *Start at* in the *Page numbering* section. (This inserts a **1** in the *Start at* text box.)
   e. Click OK to close the Page Number Format dialog box.
   f. Double-click in the document to make it active.

4. Apply the Heading 1 style to the title *ROBOTS AS ANDROIDS*.

5. Apply the Heading 2 style to the five headings in the document (*Visual Perception*, *Audio Perception*, *Tactile Perception*, *Locomotion*, and *Navigation*).

6. Insert a table of contents at the beginning of the document by completing the following steps:

   a. Press Ctrl + Home to move the insertion point to the blank page at the beginning of the document.

   b. Click the References tab.

   c. Click the Table of Contents button and then click the *Automatic Table 1* option in the *Built-In* section of the drop-down list.

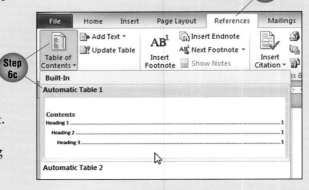

7. Insert page numbering on the table of contents page by completing the following steps:

   a. With the insertion point positioned on any character in the table, click the Insert tab.

   b. Click the Page Number button and then click *Format Page Numbers* at the drop-down list.

   c. At the Page Number Format dialog box, click the down-pointing arrow at the right of the *Number format* option box and then click *i, ii, iii, …* at the drop-down list.

   d. Click OK to close the dialog box.

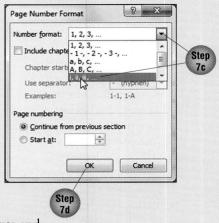

8. Change the style set to Modern.

9. Change the theme fonts to *Solstice*.

10. Navigate in the document using the table of contents by completing the following steps:

    a. Click on any character in the table of contents.

    b. Move the mouse pointer outside the table of contents and then move the mouse pointer back inside the table of contents.

    c. Position the mouse pointer on the *Locomotion* heading, hold down the Ctrl key, click the left mouse button, and then release the Ctrl key. (This moves the insertion point to the beginning of the *Locomotion* heading in the document.)

    d. Press Ctrl + Home to move the insertion point to the beginning of the document.

11. Save **C28-E01-Robots.docx** and then print only the table of contents page.

Customizing the Table of Contents

You can customize a table of contents in a document with options at the Table of Contents dialog box, shown in Figure 28.2. Display this dialog box by clicking the Table of Contents button in the References tab and then clicking *Insert Table of Contents* at the drop-down list.

At the Table of Contents dialog box, a sample table displays in the *Print Preview* section. You can change the format of the table by clicking the down-pointing arrow at the right of the *Formats* option box (located in the *General* section). At the drop-down list that displays, click the format you want to apply. When you select a different format, that format displays in the *Print Preview* section. Page numbers in a table of contents display after the text or aligned at the right margin depending on which options you select. The number of levels that display depends on the number of heading levels you specify in the document.

Figure 28.2 Table of Contents Dialog Box

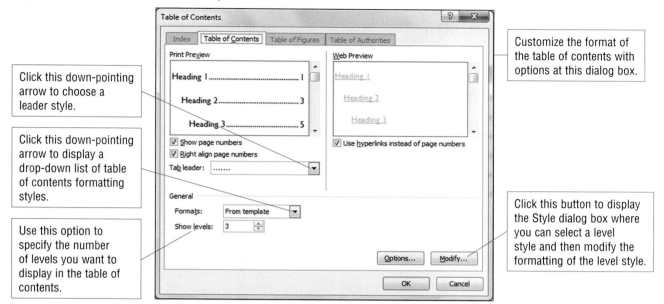

Click this down-pointing arrow to choose a leader style.

Click this down-pointing arrow to display a drop-down list of table of contents formatting styles.

Use this option to specify the number of levels you want to display in the table of contents.

Customize the format of the table of contents with options at this dialog box.

Click this button to display the Style dialog box where you can select a level style and then modify the formatting of the level style.

Tab leaders help guide a reader's eyes from headings in the table to the page numbers. The default tab leader is a period. To choose a different leader, click the down-pointing arrow at the right of the *Tab leader* text box and then click the leader character that you want to use from the drop-down list.

Word automatically identifies headings in a table of contents as hyperlinks and inserts page numbers. You can use these hyperlinks to move the insertion point to a specific location in the document. To move the insertion point to a specific heading, position the mouse pointer on the corresponding heading in the table of contents, hold down the Ctrl key (the mouse pointer turns into a hand), and then click the left mouse button. If you are going to post your document to the Web, consider removing the page numbers because the reader will need only to click the hyperlink to view a specific page. Use the Show levels option to specify the number of levels you want to display in the table of contents.

You can modify the formatting of a level style by clicking the Modify button. At the Style dialog box that displays, click the level in the *Styles* list box that you want to modify and then click the Modify button. At the Modify Style dialog box, apply the desired formatting and then click OK. The Modify Style dialog box that displays is the same dialog box you used to modify styles in Chapter 24.

If you change options at the Table of Contents dialog box and then click OK, a message will display asking if you want to replace the selected table of contents. At this message, click Yes.

Updating a Table of Contents

If you add, delete, move, or edit headings or other text in a document after you have inserted a table of contents, update the table. To do this, click anywhere in the table and then click the Update Table button or press F9 (the Update Field key). At the Update Table of Contents dialog box, shown in Figure 28.3, click *Update page numbers only* if the changes you made were to the page numbers only, or click *Update entire table* if you made changes to headings or subheadings within the document. Click OK or press the Enter key to close the dialog box.

Update Table of Contents
1. Click anywhere in table of contents.
2. Click References tab.
3. Click Update Table button.
4. Select *Update page numbers only* or *Update entire table* at Update Table of Contents dialog box.
5. Click OK.

Update Table

Figure 28.3 Update Table of Contents Dialog Box

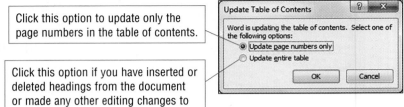

Click this option to update only the page numbers in the table of contents.

Click this option if you have inserted or deleted headings from the document or made any other editing changes to the table of contents text.

Remove Table of Contents
1. Click References tab.
2. Click Table of Contents button.
3. Click *Remove Table of Contents* at drop-down list.
OR
1. Click on any character in table of contents.
2. Click the Table of Contents tab.
3. Click *Remove Table of Contents* at drop-down list.

Removing a Table of Contents

You can remove a table of contents from a document by clicking the Table of Contents button in the References tab and then clicking *Remove Table of Contents* at the drop-down list. You can also remove a contents table by clicking on any character in the table, clicking the Table of Contents tab located in the upper left corner of the table of contents (immediately left of the Update Table tab), and then clicking *Remove Table of Contents* at the drop-down list.

Exercise 28.1B Modifying, Customizing, and Updating the Table of Contents   **Part 2 of 2**

1. With **C28-E01-Robots.docx** open, press Ctrl + End to move the insertion point to the end of the document and then insert the document named **InternetIssues.docx**. (Do this with the Object button arrow in the Text group in the Insert tab.)
2. Apply the Heading 1 style to the title *INTERNET COMMUNITY ISSUES* and apply the Heading 2 style to the three headings *Flaming, Netiquette*, and *Moderated Environments*. Select each heading individually and then apply bold formatting.
3. Press Ctrl + Home and then modify the level 1 and level 2 styles by completing the following steps:
    a. Click the References tab, click the Table of Contents button, and then click *Insert Table of Contents* at the drop-down list.
    b. At the Table of Contents dialog box, click the Modify button that displays in the lower right corner of the dialog box.
    c. At the Style dialog box with *TOC 1* selected in the *Styles* list box, click the Modify button.

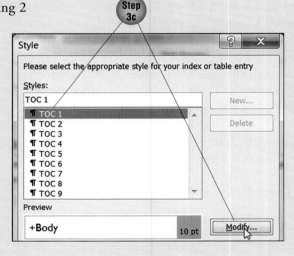

Step 3c

---

d. At the Modify Style dialog box, change the font size to 12 and then click the Italic button.
e. Click OK to close the Modify Style dialog box.
f. At the Style dialog box, click *TOC 2* in the *Styles* list box and then click the Modify button.
g. At the Modify Style dialog box, change the font size to 11, click the Italic button, and then click OK.
h. Click OK at the Style dialog box.
i. At the Table of Contents dialog box, click the down-pointing arrow at the right side of the *Show levels* option box until *1* displays.
j. Click OK to close the Table of Contents dialog box.
k. At the message asking if you want to replace the selected table of contents, click Yes.

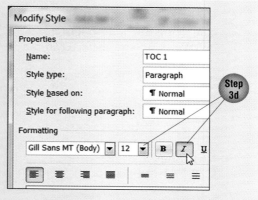

4. After looking at the modified table of contents, you decide to apply a different formatting style and display two levels of the table of contents. With the insertion point positioned in the table of contents, complete the following steps:
a. With the References tab selected, click the Table of Contents button and then click *Insert Table of Contents* at the drop-down list.
b. At the Table of Contents dialog box, click the down-pointing arrow at the right of the *Formats* option in the *General* section and then click *Formal* at the drop-down list.
c. Click the down-pointing arrow at the right of the *Tab leader* option box and then click the solid line option (bottom option) at the drop-down list.
d. Click the up-pointing arrow at the right side of the *Show Levels* option box to display *2* in the option box.
e. Click OK to close the dialog box.
f. At the message asking if you want to replace the selected table of contents, click Yes.

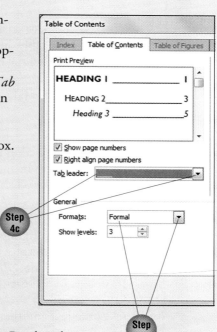

5. Insert a command to keep lines of text together by completing the following steps:
a. Move the insertion point so it is positioned at the beginning of the *LOCOMOTION* heading (in the body of the document, not in the table of contents).
b. Click the Home tab.
c. Click the Paragraph group dialog box launcher.
d. At the Paragraph dialog box, click the Line and Page Breaks tab.
e. Click the *Keep with next* check box to insert a check mark.
f. Click OK to close the dialog box.

6. Update the table of contents by completing the following steps:
   a. Click on any character in the table.
   b. Click the Update Table tab.
   c. At the Update Table of Contents dialog box, make sure *Update page numbers only* is selected and then click OK.
7. Save, print, and then close **C28-E01-Robots.docx**.

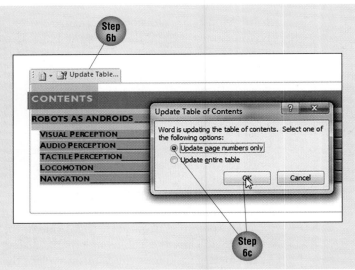

Assigning Levels to Table of Contents Entries

Add Text

Another method for creating a table of contents is to assign a level to text to be included using the Add Text button in the Table of Contents group in the References tab. Click this button, and a drop-down list of level options displays. Click a level option to assign it to text you have selected. After you have specified levels for all the text you want to include in the table, insert the table of contents by clicking the Table of Contents button and then clicking the desired option at the drop-down list.

Marking Table of Contents Entries as Fields

When you apply styles to text, you apply specific formatting. If you want to identify titles or headings to use in a table of contents, but you do not want heading style formatting applied in the document, mark the text as a field entry. To do this, select the text you want to include in the table of contents and then press Alt + Shift + O. This displays the Mark Table of Contents Entry dialog box, shown in Figure 28.4.

The text you selected displays in the *Entry* text box. Specify the level for the selected text with the *Level* option, and then click the Mark button. This turns on the display of nonprinting characters in the document and inserts a field code immediately after the selected text. As you will see in Exercise 28.2A, when you select the first title, Word inserts the following code immediately after the title: { TC "FUTURE OF THE INTERNET" \f C \l " 1 " }. The Mark Table of Contents Entry dialog box also remains open. To mark the next entry for the table of contents, select the text and then click the title bar of the Mark Table of Contents Entry dialog

Figure 28.4 Mark Table of Contents Entry Dialog Box

Click the Mark button to identify the text in the *Entry* text box as a table of contents field.

box. Specify the level and then click the Mark button. Continue in this manner until you have marked all table of contents entries.

If you mark table of contents entries as fields, you will need to activate the *Table entry fields* option when you insert the table in the document. To do this, display the Table of Contents dialog box and then click the Options button. At the Table of Contents Options dialog box, shown in Figure 28.5, click the *Table entry fields* check box to insert a check mark and then click OK.

Figure 28.5 Table of Contents Options Dialog Box

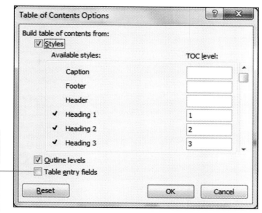

Insert a check mark in this check box if you marked table of content entries as fields.

Exercise 28.2A   Marking Headings as Fields   Part 1 of 2

1. Open **InternetFuture.docx** and save the document with the name **C28-E02-InternetFuture**.
2. With the insertion point positioned immediately left of the *F* in the title *FUTURE OF THE INTERNET*, insert a section break that begins a new page. ***Hint: Refer to Exercise 28.1A, Step 2.***
3. Mark the titles and headings as fields for insertion in a table of contents by completing the following steps:
   a. Select the title *FUTURE OF THE INTERNET*.
   b. Press Alt + Shift + O.
   c. At the Mark Table of Contents Entry dialog box, make sure the *Level* is set at *1* and then click the Mark button. (This turns on the display of nonprinting characters.)

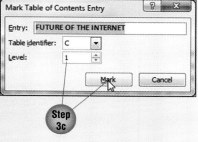

Step 3c

   d. Click in the document and then select the heading *Satellite Internet Connections*.

Step 3d

   e. Click the up-pointing arrow at the right of the *Level* text box in the Mark Table of Contents Entry dialog box until *2* displays.
   f. Click the Mark button.

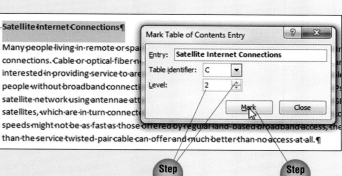

Step 3e   Step 3f

   g. Mark the following headings as level 2:
      Second Internet
      Internet Services for a Fee
      Internet 2030
   h. Click the Close button to close the Mark Table of Contents Entry dialog box.
4. With the insertion point positioned below the section break, insert page numbering at the bottom center of each page of the section and change the starting number to 1. ***Hint: Refer to Exercise 28.1A, Step 3.***

5. Insert a table of contents at the beginning of the document by completing the following steps:
   a. Position the insertion point at the beginning of the document (on the new page).
   b. Type the title *TABLE OF CONTENTS*, centered and bolded, and then press the Enter key. (The insertion point may not move down to the next line.)
   c. Click the References tab.
   d. Click the Table of Contents button and then click *Insert Table of Contents* at the drop-down list.
   e. At the Table of Contents dialog box, click the Options button.
   f. At the Table of Contents Options dialog box, click *Table entry fields* to insert a check mark in the check box. (This option is located in the bottom left corner of the dialog box.)
   g. Click OK to close the Table of Contents Options dialog box.
   h. Click OK to close the Table of Contents dialog box.
6. Insert lowercase Roman numeral page numbering on the table of contents page. ***Hint: Refer to Exercise 28.1A, Step 7.***
7. Turn off the display of nonprinting characters.
8. Save **C28-E02-InternetFuture.docx** and then print only the table of contents page.

You can insert additional information in a document and update the table. To do this, insert the text and then mark the text with options at the Mark Table of Contents Entry dialog box. Click anywhere in the table of contents and then click the Update Table tab. At the Update Table of Contents dialog box, click the *Update entire table* option and then click OK.

Exercise 28.2B Updating the Entire Table of Contents   Part 2 of 2

1. With **C28-E02-InternetFuture.docx** open, insert a file into the document by completing the following steps:
   a. Press Ctrl + End to move the insertion point to the end of the document.
   b. Click the Insert tab.
   c. Click the Object button arrow in the Text group and then click *Text from File* at the drop-down list.
   d. At the Insert File dialog box, navigate to the Chapter28 folder on your storage medium and then double-click ***InternetIssues.docx***.
2. Select and then mark text for inclusion in the table of contents by completing the following steps:
   a. Select the title *INTERNET COMMUNITY ISSUES*.
   b. Press Alt + Shift + O.
   c. At the Mark Table of Contents Entry dialog box, make sure the *Level* is set at *1* and then click the Mark button.
3. Select and then mark as level 2 entries the three headings in the document.

4. Update the table of contents by completing the following steps:
   a. Select the entire table of contents text (excluding the title).
   b. Click the References tab.
   c. Click the Update Table button in the Table of Contents group.
   d. At the Update Table of Contents dialog box, click the *Update entire table* option.
   e. Click OK.

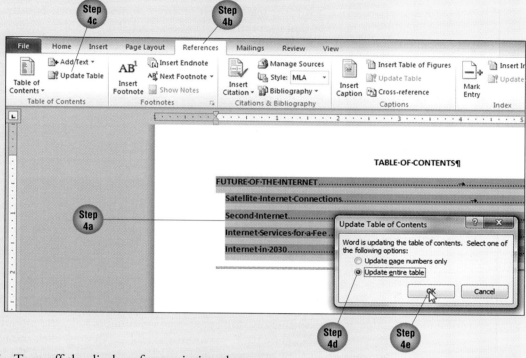

5. Turn off the display of nonprinting characters.
6. Save, print, and then close **C28-E02-InternetFuture.docx**.

Creating a Table of Figures

A document that contains figures should include a list (table) of figures so a reader can quickly locate a specific figure. Figure 28.6 shows an example of a table of figures. You can create a table of figures by marking figures or images as captions and then using the caption names to create the table of figures.

Figure 28.6 Table of Figures

TABLE OF FIGURES

FIGURE 1 SCANNED LINE ART 3
FIGURE 2 DIGITAL HALFTONE 8
FIGURE 3 BAR 12
FIGURE 4 LINE CHARTS 15
FIGURE 5 DETAIL VS. WEIGHT 18

Creating Captions

Create a Caption
1. Select text or image.
2. Click References tab.
3. Click Insert Caption button.
4. Type caption name.
5. Click OK.

A caption is text that describes a figure or picture, which generally displays below the element. You can create a caption by selecting the figure text or image, clicking the References tab, and then clicking the Insert Caption button in the Captions group. This displays the Caption dialog box, shown in Figure 28.7. At the dialog box, make sure *Figure 1* displays in the *Caption* text box and the insertion point is positioned after *Figure 1*. Type a name for the caption, and then press the Enter key. Word inserts *Figure 1 (caption name)* below the selected text or image. Click the down-pointing arrow at the right of the *Label* option to specify the caption label. The default is *Figure*, which you can change to *Equation* or *Table*.

Insert Caption

Figure 28.7 Caption Dialog Box

Type a caption in this text box after *Figure 1*.

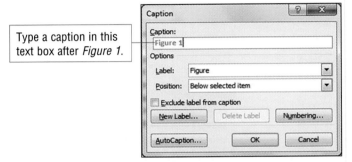

Insert a Table of Figures
1. Click References tab.
2. Click Insert Table of Figures button.
3. Select desired format.
4. Click OK.

Inserting a Table of Figures

After you have marked the figure text or image in a document as captions, insert the table of figures. A table of figures generally displays at the beginning of a document, after the table of contents and on a separate page. To insert the table of figures, click the Insert Table of Figures button in the Captions group in the References tab. At the Table of Figures dialog box, shown in Figure 28.8, make any necessary changes and then click OK.

Insert Table of Figures

Figure 28.8 Table of Figures Dialog Box

Customize the format of the table of figures with options at this dialog box.

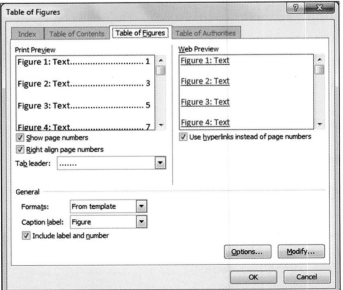

The options available at the Table of Figures dialog box are similar to those available at the Table of Contents dialog box. For example, you can choose a format for the table of figures from the drop-down list at the *Formats* option box, change the alignment of the page numbers, or add leaders before page numbers.

1. Open **OutputDevices.docx** and save the document with the name **C28-E03-OutputDevices**.
2. Add the caption *Figure 1 CRT Monitor* to the CRT monitor image by completing the following steps:
   a. Click the image of the CRT monitor (as shown below).
   b. Click the References tab.
   c. Click the Insert Caption button in the Captions group.
   d. At the Caption dialog box, press the spacebar once and then type CRT Monitor.
   e. Click OK or press the Enter key.

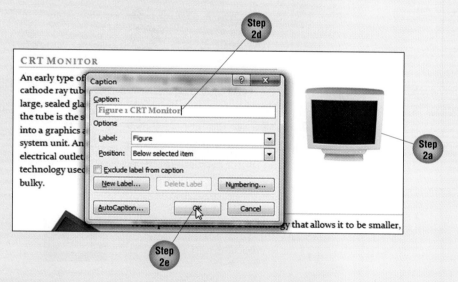

3. Complete steps similar to those in Step 2 to create the caption *Figure 2 Flat-Panel Monitor* for the flat-panel display image.
4. Complete steps similar to those in Step 2 to create the caption *Figure 3 Ink-Jet Printer* for the ink-jet printer image.
5. Complete steps similar to those in Step 2 to create the caption *Figure 4 Laser Printer*.
6. Move the insertion point to the beginning of the title *Computer Output Devices* and then insert a section break that begins a new page.
7. Press Ctrl + Home to move the insertion point to the beginning of the document and then insert a table of figures by completing the following steps:
   a. Type Table of Figures and then press the Enter key. (The insertion point may not move down to the next line.)
   b. Click the References tab.
   c. Click the Insert Table of Figures button in the Captions group.

d. At the Table of Figures dialog box, click the down-pointing arrow at the right of the *Formats* option box and then click *Formal* at the drop-down list.

e. Click OK.

8. Apply the Heading 1 style to the title *Table of Figures*.

9. Center the figure text by clicking the *Figure 1 CRT Monitor* text box and then clicking the Center button in the Paragraph group in the Home tab.

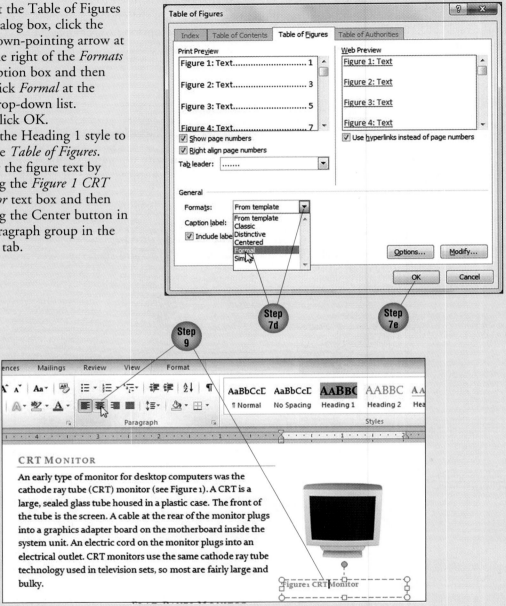

Step 7d

Step 7e

Step 9

CRT MONITOR

An early type of monitor for desktop computers was the cathode ray tube (CRT) monitor (see Figure 1). A CRT is a large, sealed glass tube housed in a plastic case. The front of the tube is the screen. A cable at the rear of the monitor plugs into a graphics adapter board on the motherboard inside the system unit. An electric cord on the monitor plugs into an electrical outlet. CRT monitors use the same cathode ray tube technology used in television sets, so most are fairly large and bulky.

Figure 1 CRT Monitor

10. Center the figure text in the three remaining figure text boxes.

11. Move the insertion point to the title *Computer Output Devices* and then insert page numbering by completing the following steps:

a. Click the Insert tab.

b. Click the Page Number button in the Header & Footer group, point to *Bottom of Page*, and then click *Plain Number 2*.

c. Click the Page Number button in the Header & Footer group in the Header & Footer Tools Design tab and then click *Format Page Numbers* at the drop-down list.

d. At the Page Number Format dialog box, Click *Start at* in the *Page numbering* section. (This inserts *1* in the *Start at* text box.)

e. Click OK to close the dialog box.

f. Double-click in the document to make it active.

12. Move the insertion point to the title *Table of Figures* and then insert page numbering by completing the following steps:
    a. Click the Insert tab.
    b. Click the Page Number button and then click *Format Page Numbers* at the drop-down list.
    c. At the Page Number Format dialog box, click the down-pointing arrow at the right of the *Number format* option box and then click *i, ii, iii, ...* at the drop-down list.
    d. Click OK to close the dialog box.
13. Save **C28-E03-OutputDevices.docx**.

Updating or Deleting a Table of Figures

If you make changes to a document after you have inserted a table of figures, update the table. To do this, click anywhere within the table and then click the Update Table button in the Captions group in the References tab or press F9. At the Update Table of Figures dialog box, click *Update page numbers only* if the changes you made were to the page numbers only, or click *Update entire table* if you made changes to the caption text. Click OK or press the Enter key to close the dialog box. To delete a table of figures, select the entire table using either the mouse or the keyboard and then press the Delete key.

QUICK STEPS

Update Table of Figures
1. Click anywhere in table of figures.
2. Click References tab.
3. Click Update Table button or press F9.
4. Click OK at the Update Table of Figures dialog box.

Delete Table of Figures
1. Select entire table of figures.
2. Press Delete key.

Update Table

Exercise 28.3B **Updating the Table of Figures** **Part 2 of 2**

1. With **C28-E03-OutputDevices.docx** open, update the table of figures by completing the following steps:
   a. Click on any character in the table of figures.
   b. Press F9.
   c. At the Update Table of Figures dialog box, click OK.
2. Save, print, and then close **C28-E03-OutputDevices.docx**.

Creating a Table of Authorities

A table of authorities is a list of citations that appears in a legal brief or other legal document and the page numbers on which the citations appear. Word provides many common categories under which citations can be organized: Cases, Statutes, Other

Authorities, Rules, Treatises, Regulations, and Constitutional Provisions. Within each category, Word alphabetizes the citations. Figure 28.9 shows an example of a table of authorities.

Figure 28.9 **Table of Authorities**

TABLE OF AUTHORITIES

<u>CASES</u>

<u>Mansfield v. Rydell</u>, 72 Wn.2d 200, 433 P.2d 723 (1993) 3
<u>State v. Fletcher</u>, 73 Wn.2d 332, 124 P.2d 503 (1999) 5
<u>Yang v. Buchwald</u>, 21 Wn.2d 385, 233 P.2d 609 (2002) 7

<u>STATUTES</u>

RCW 8.12.230(2) 4
RCW 6.23.590 7
RCW 5.23.103(3) 10

QUICK STEPS

Mark Citation for a Table of Authorities
1. Select first occurrence of citation.
2. Press Alt + Shift + I.
3. At Mark Citation dialog box, edit and format text.
4. Specify the category.
5. Click Mark All button.

Mark Citation

Creating a table of authorities requires thought and planning. Before you mark any text in a legal document for inclusion in such a table, you need to determine what section headings you want to use and what listings should be contained in each section. When you mark text for the table, you need to find the first occurrence of each citation, mark it as a full citation with the complete name, and then specify a short citation. To mark a citation for a table of authorities, complete the following steps:

1. Select the first occurrence of the citation.
2. Click the References tab and then click the Mark Citation button or press Alt + Shift + I.
3. At the Mark Citation dialog box, shown in Figure 28.10, edit and format the text in the *Selected text* box as you want it to appear in the table of authorities. Edit and format the text in the *Short citation* text box so it matches the short citation you want Word to search for in the document.
4. Click the down-pointing arrow at the right of the *Category* text box and then click the category from the drop-down list that applies to the citation.
5. Click the Mark button to mark the selected citation or click the Mark All button if you want Word to mark all long and short citations in the document that match those displayed in the Mark Citation dialog box.
6. The Mark Citation dialog box remains open so you can mark other citations. To find the next citation in a document, click the Next Citation button. (This prompts Word to search through the document for the next occurrence of text commonly found in a citation such as *in re* or *v.*)
7. Select the text for the next citation and then complete Steps 3 through 5.
8. After marking all citations, click the Close button to close the Mark Citations dialog box.

Figure 28.10 Mark Citation Dialog Box

Edit and format text in this text box as you want it to appear in the table of authorities.

Edit and format text in this text box so it matches the short citation you want Word to search for in the document.

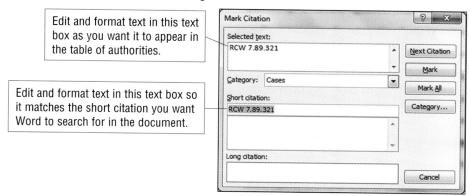

Inserting a Table of Authorities

Once you have marked the citations in a document, you can insert the table of authorities. A table of authorities is inserted in a document in a manner similar to that used to insert a table of contents or figures. A table of authorities generally displays at the beginning of a document. To insert a table of authorities in a document that contains text marked as citations, click the References tab and then click the Insert Table of Authorities button. This displays the Table of Authorities dialog box, shown in Figure 28.11. At this dialog box, make any necessary changes and then click OK to close the dialog box.

QUICK STEPS

Insert a Table of Authorities
1. Click References tab.
2. Click Insert Table of Authorities button.
3. Select desired format.
4. Click OK.

Insert Table of Authorities

Figure 28.11 Table of Authorities Dialog Box

Click this down-pointing arrow to choose a leader style.

Click this down-pointing arrow to display a drop-down list of table of authorities formatting styles.

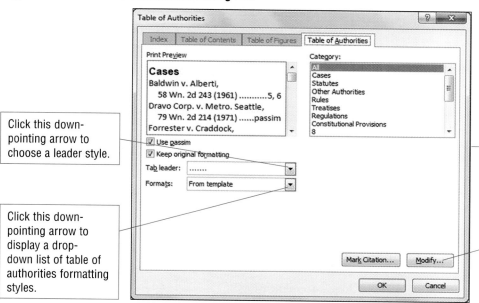

Customize the format of the table of authorities with options at this dialog box.

Click this button to display the Style dialog box where you can select a level style and then modify the formatting of the level style.

Like the Table of Contents dialog box and the Table of Figures dialog box, the Table of Authorities dialog box contains options for formatting a table of authorities. The *Use passim* option is active by default (the check box contains a check mark), which tells Word to replace five or more page references to the same authority with *passim*. With the *Keep original formatting* check box active, Word retains the formatting of

Update a Table of Authorities

1. Click anywhere in table of authorities.
2. Click References tab.
3. Click Update Table of Authorities button or press F9.

Update Table

the citation as it appears in the document. Click the *Tab leader* option if you want to change the leader character. When you insert a table of authorities, Word includes a heading for each of the seven categories by default. If you want to insert citations for a specific category only, select that category at the *Category* drop-down list. Like a table of contents, you can modify the formatting of a level style for a table of authorities. To do this, click the Modify button in the Table of Authorities dialog box, click *Table of Authorities* in the *Styles* list box, and then click the Modify button. At the Modify Style dialog box, apply the desired formatting and then click OK.

Updating or Deleting a Table of Authorities

If you make changes to a document after you have inserted a table of authorities, update the table. To do this, click anywhere within the table and then click the Update Table of Authorities button or press F9. If you need to edit a citation, edit it in the document and not in the table of authorities. If you edit a citation in the table of authorities, your changes will be lost the next time you update the table. To delete a table of authorities, select the entire table of authorities using either the mouse or the keyboard and then press the Delete key.

Exercise 28.4   Inserting a Table of Authorities   Part 1 of 1

1. Open **LarsenBrief.docx** and save the document with the name **C28-E04-LarsenBrief**.
2. Mark *RCW 7.89.321* as a statute citation by completing the following steps:
   a. Select *RCW 7.89.321*. (This citation is located toward the middle of the second page.)
      Hint: Use the Find feature to help you locate this citation.
   b. Click the References tab.
   c. Click the Mark Citation button in the Table of Authorities group.
   d. At the Mark Citation dialog box, click the down-pointing arrow at the right of the *Category* text box and then click *Statutes* at the drop-down list.
   e. Click the Mark All button. (This turns on the display of nonprinting characters.)
   f. Click the Close button to close the Mark Citation dialog box.

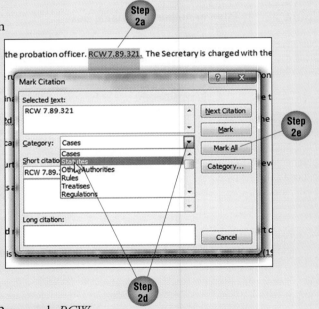

3. Complete steps similar to those in Step 2 to mark *RCW 7.53.443* as a statute citation. (This citation is located toward the middle of the second page.)
4. Complete steps similar to those in Step 2 to mark *RCW 7.72A.432(2)* as a statute citation. (This citation is located toward the bottom of the second page.)
5. Complete steps similar to those in Step 2 to mark *RCW 7.42A.429(1)* as a statute citation. (This citation is located toward the bottom of the second page.)

6. Mark *State v. Connors, 73 W.2d 743, 430 P.2d 199 (1974)* as a case citation by completing the following steps:

   a. Select *State v. Connors, 73 W.2d 743, 430 P.2d 199 (1974)*. (This citation is located toward the middle of the second page.) ***Hint: Use the Find feature to help you locate this citation.***

   b. Press Alt + Shift + I.

   c. At the Mark Citation dialog box, type State v. Connors in the *Short citation* text box.

   d. Click the down-pointing arrow at the right of the *Category* text box and then click *Cases* at the drop-down list.

   e. Click the Mark All button.

   f. Click the Close button to close the Mark Citation dialog box.

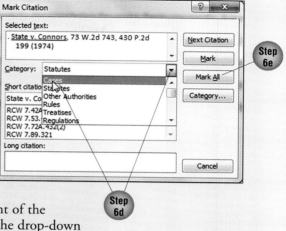

7. Complete steps similar to those in Step 6 to mark *State v. Bertelli, 63 W.2d 77, 542 P.2d 751 (1971)*. Enter State v. Bertelli as the short citation. (This citation is located toward the middle of the second page.)

8. Complete steps similar to those in Step 6 to mark *State v. Landers, 103 W.2d 432, 893 P.2d 2 (1984)*. Enter State v. Landers as the short citation. (This citation is located toward the bottom of the second page.)

9. Insert page numbering by completing the following steps:

   a. Position the insertion point at the beginning of the document and then press the Enter key once.

   b. Position the insertion point immediately left of the *S* in *STATEMENT OF CASE* and then insert a section break that begins a new page.

   c. With the insertion point positioned below the section break, insert page numbering at the bottom center of each page and change the starting number to 1.

10. Double-click in the document to make it active, press Ctrl + Home to move the insertion point to the beginning of the document, and then type TABLE OF AUTHORITIES centered and bolded.

11. Press the Enter key, turn off bold, and then change the paragraph alignment back to left.

12. Modify and insert the table of authorities by completing the following steps:

    a. Click the References tab.

    b. Click the Insert Table of Authorities button in the Table of Authorities group.

    c. At the Table of Authorities dialog box, make sure *All* is selected in the *Categories* list box and then click the Modify button.

    d. At the Style dialog box, click *Table of Authorities* in the *Styles* list box and then click the Modify button.

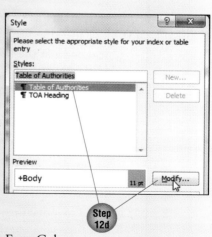

    e. At the Modify Style dialog box, click the Italic button.

    f. Click the down-pointing arrow at the right side of the Font Color option box and then click the Dark Blue color at the drop-down color palette (second color from the right in the bottom row).

g. Click OK to close the Modify Style dialog box, click OK to close the Style dialog box, and click OK to close the Table of Authorities dialog box.

13. Apply different formatting to the table of authorities by completing the following steps:

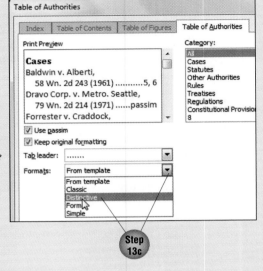

a. Click the Undo button in the Quick Access toolbar to remove the table of authorities. (If this does not remove the table of authorities, select the Cases entries and the Statutes entries and then press the Delete key.)
b. Click the Insert Table of Authorities button.
c. At the Table of Authorities dialog box, click the down-pointing arrow at the right of the *Formats* option box and then click *Distinctive* at the drop-down list.
d. Click the down-pointing arrow at the right side of the *Tab leader* option box and then click the hyphens at the drop-down list (second option from the bottom of the list).
e. Click OK to close the Table of Authorities dialog box.

14. With the insertion point positioned anywhere in the table of authorities, change the numbering format to lowercase Roman numerals.
15. Turn off the display of nonprinting characters.
16. Save **C28-E04-LarsenBrief.docx** and then print the table of authorities page.
17. Close **C28-E04-LarsenBrief.docx**.

Chapter Summary

➤ Word provides options for automating the creation of a table of contents, table of figures, and table of authorities.

➤ Text to be included in a table of contents can be identified three ways: by applying a heading style, assigning a level, or marking text as a field entry.

➤ Mark text as a field entry at the Mark Table of Contents dialog box. Display this dialog box by pressing Alt + Shift + O.

➤ Creating a table of contents involves two steps: applying the appropriate styles to or marking text that will be included and inserting the table of contents in the document.

➤ To insert a table of contents, position the insertion point where you want the table to appear, click the References tab, click the Table of Contents button, and then click the desired option at the drop-down list.

➤ If you want the table of contents to print on a page separate from the document text, insert a section break that begins a new page between the table of contents and the title of the document.

➤ If you make changes to a document after inserting a table of contents, update the table by clicking anywhere in it and then clicking the Update Table button in the References tab or pressing F9. Update a table of figures or table of authorities in a similar manner.

➤ Remove a table of contents by clicking the Table of Contents button in the References tab and then clicking *Remove Table of Contents* at the drop-down list.

- Create a table of figures by marking specific text or images as captions and then using the caption names to create the table. Mark captions at the Caption dialog box. Display this dialog box by clicking the Insert Caption button in the References tab.

- Insert a table of figures in a document in a manner similar to that used to insert a table of contents. A table of figures generally displays at the beginning of a document, after the table of contents.

- A table of authorities is a list of the citations in a legal brief or other legal document and pages on which the citations appear.

- When you mark text for a table of authorities, find the first occurrence of a citation, mark it as a full citation with the complete name, and then specify a short citation at the Mark Citation dialog box. Display this dialog box by clicking the Mark Citation button on the References tab or pressing Alt + Shift + I.

- Insert a table of authorities in a document in a manner similar to that used to insert a table of contents or figures. A table of authorities generally displays at the beginning of a document.

- Delete a table of figures or a table of authorities by selecting the entire table and then pressing the Delete key.

Commands Review

FEATURE	RIBBON TAB, GROUP	BUTTON, OPTION	KEYBOARD SHORTCUT
Page Number Format dialog box	Insert, Header & Footer	, Format Page Numbers	
Table of Contents dialog box	References, Table of Contents	, Insert Table of Contents	
Update Table of Contents Update Table of Figures	References, Table of Contents		F9
Mark Table of Contents Entry dialog box			Alt + Shift + O
Table of Contents Options dialog box	References, Table of Contents	, Insert Table of Contents, Options	
Caption dialog box	References, Captions		
Table of Figures dialog box	References, Captions		
Mark Citation dialog box	References, Table of Authorities		Alt + Shift + I
Table of Authorities dialog box	References, Table of Authorities		
Update Table of Authorities	References, Table of Authorities		

Key Points Review

Completion: In the space provided at the right, indicate the correct term, symbol, or command.

1. In a built-in table of contents, Word uses text with this heading applied to it as the first level. _____

2. A table of contents generally appears in this location in the document. _____

3. A table of contents is generally numbered with this type of numbers. _____

4. This is the keyboard shortcut to update a table of contents. _____

5. Delete a table of contents by clicking the Table of Contents button in the References tab and then clicking this option. _____

6. This is the keyboard shortcut to display the Mark Table of Contents Entry dialog box. _____

7. If you mark table of contents entries as fields, you will need to activate this option at the Table of Contents Options dialog box. _____

8. Create a table of figures by marking figure names as these. _____

9. This is a list identifying the pages on which citations appear in a legal brief or other legal document. _____

10. This is the keyboard shortcut to display the Mark Citation dialog box. _____

Chapter Assessments

Applying Your Skills

Demonstrate your knowledge of features learned in this chapter by completing the following assessments.

Assessment 28.1   Insert a Table of Contents in a Computer Report

1. Open **CompComm.docx** and save the document with the name **C28-A01-CompComm**.
2. With the insertion point positioned at the beginning of the document, press Ctrl + Enter to insert a page break.
3. Apply the Heading 1 style to the three titles in the document and apply the Heading 2 style to the five headings.
4. Change the style set to Distinctive.
5. Hang indent the paragraphs of text below the *REFERENCES* title.
6. Insert a continuous section break at the beginning of the title *COMPUTERS IN COMMUNICATIONS*.
7. With the insertion point positioned below the section break, insert page numbering at the bottom center of each page and change the starting number to 1.
8. Insert a table of contents at the beginning of the document with the *Automatic Table 2* option.
9. In the table of contents page, change the page numbering style to lowercase Roman numerals.
10. Save **C28-A01-CompComm.docx** and then print only the table of contents page.

11. Insert a page break at the beginning of the title *COMPUTERS IN ENTERTAINMENT*.
12. Update the table of contents.
13. Save, print, and then close **C28-A01-CompComm.docx**.

Assessment 28.2 Insert a Table of Contents in a Computer Viruses Report

1. At a blank document, press the Enter key once and then press Ctrl + Enter to insert a page break.
2. Insert **VirusesSecurity.docx**. *Hint: Use the Object button arrow in the Insert tab.*
3. Insert a continuous section break at the beginning of the first title (*CHAPTER 1: COMPUTER VIRUSES*).
4. With the insertion point positioned below the section break, insert page numbering at the bottom center of each page and change the starting number to 1.
5. Insert a table of contents at the beginning of the document with the *Automatic Table 1* option.
6. In the table of contents page, change the page numbering style to lowercase Roman numerals.
7. Change the style set to Formal.
8. Save the document with the name **C28-A02-VirusesSecurity**.
9. Print only the table of contents page.
10. Insert a page break at the beginning of the chapter 2 and the chapter 3 titles.
11. Update the table of contents.
12. Save, print, and then close **C28-A02-VirusesSecurity.docx**.

Assessment 28.3 Insert Captions and a Table of Figures in a Report

1. Open **InputDevices.docx** and save the document with the name **C28-A03-InputDevices**.
2. Insert a caption for each of the three images in the document. (You determine the name of each caption.)
3. Move the insertion point to the beginning of the title *Computer Input Devices* and then insert a section break that begins a new page.
4. Press Ctrl + Home and then insert a table of figures with the title *Table of Figures*.
5. Apply the Heading 1 style to the title *Table of Figures*.
6. Center the figure text in each figure text box.
7. Move the insertion point to the title *Computer Input Devices* and then insert page numbering and change the starting number to 1.
8. Move the insertion point to the title *Table of Figures* and then change the page numbering style to lowercase Roman numerals.
9. Update the table of figures.
10. Save, print, and then close **C28-A03-InputDevices.docx**.

Assessment 28.4 Create a Table of Authorities for a Brief

1. Open **SilversBrief.docx** and save the document with the name **C28-A04-SilversBrief**.
2. Mark the following as case citations with the specified short citations: *Hint: Use the find feature to help you locate each citation.*
   a. *Richmond Newspapers, Inc. v. Virginia*, 448 U.S. 555 (1980)
      Short citation: Richmond Newspapers, Inc. v. Virginia
   b. *Globe Newspaper Co. v. Superior Court*, 457 U.S. 596 (1982)
      Short citation: Globe Newspaper Co. v. Superior Court
   c. *Naucke v. City of Park Hills*, 284 F.3d 923, 927 (2d Cir. 2002)
      Short citation: Naucke v. City of Park Hills
   d. *Singer v. Fulton County Sheriff*, 63 F. 3d 110, 120 (2d Cir. 1995)
      Short citation: Singer v. Fulton County Sheriff
   e. *Bowden v. Keane*, 237 F.3d 125, 129 (2d Cir. 2001)
      Short citation: Bowden v. Keane
   f. *Cf. Guzman v. Scully*, 80 F3d 772, 775-76 (2d Cir. 1996)
      Short citation: Cf. Guzman v. Scully

3. Press Ctrl + Home to move to the beginning of the document and then press the Enter key once.
4. Position the insertion point at the beginning of *STATEMENT OF CASE* and then insert a section break that begins a new page.
5. With the insertion point positioned below the section break, insert page numbering at the bottom center of each page and change the starting number to 1.
6. Move the insertion point to the beginning of the document and then type TABLE OF AUTHORITIES centered and bolded.
7. Press the Enter key, turn off bold, and change the paragraph alignment back to left.
8. Insert a table of authorities (you determine the format style).
9. With the insertion point positioned anywhere in the table of authorities, change the numbering format to lowercase Roman numerals.
10. Update the table of authorities.
11. Save, print, and then close **C28-A04-SilversBrief.docx**.

Expanding Your Skills

Explore additional feature options or use Help to learn a new skill in creating this document.

Assessment 28.5 Create a Table of Contents, and a Table of Figures

1. Open **NavigateWeb.docx** and save the document with the name **C28-A05-NavigateWeb**.
2. Move the insertion point to the beginning of the title *NAVIGATING THE WEB* and then insert a section break that begins a new page.
3. With the insertion point below the section break, number pages at the bottom right of each page and change the starting number to 1.
4. Move the insertion point to the blank line above the first table in the document and then use the caption feature to create the caption *Table A: Common Top-Level Domain Suffixes*. ***Hint: At the Caption dialog box, determine how to change the caption label from* Figure *to* Table. *Click the Numbering button and then, at the Caption Numbering dialog box, figure out how to change the numbering style to uppercase letters.***
5. Move the insertion point to the blank line above the second table and then create the caption *Table B: Common Search Tools*.
6. Move the insertion point to the blank line above the third table and then create the caption *Table C: Advanced Search Parameters*.
7. Move the insertion point to the beginning of the document and then insert the *Automatic Table 2* table of contents.
8. Press Ctrl + Enter to insert a page break.
9. Type Table of Figures, press the Enter key, and then insert the table of figures using the *Formal* format with dashed (---) leaders.
10. Apply the Heading 1 style to the title *Table of Figures*.
11. Move the insertion point to the beginning of the document and then change the numbering format to lowercase Roman numerals.
12. Check the page breaks in the document and if a heading displays at the bottom of a page and the paragraph of text that follows displays at the top of the next page, format the heading so it stays with the paragraph of text that follows. ***Hint: Do this at the Paragraph dialog box with the Line and Page Breaks tab selected.***
13. If necessary, update the entire table of contents and then update the table of figures.
14. Save, print, and then close **C28-A05-NavigateWeb.docx**.

Achieving Signature Status

Take your skills to the next level by completing this more challenging assessment.

Assessment 28.6   Create a Table of Contents, Figures, and Tables

1. Open **Networks.docx** and save the document with the name **C28-A06-Networks**.
2. Format the document so it appears as shown in Figure 28.12 with the following specifications:
   a. Apply the *Medium Shading 2 – Accent 2* table style to the two tables and remove the check mark from the *First Column* check box.
   b. Insert the captions for the figures and the tables as shown in Figure 28.12.
   c. Insert the table of contents as shown in Figure 28.12.
   d. Insert the figures and tables as shown on the second page. (You will need to create two different tables of figures—one for the figures and one for the tables.)
   e. Insert page numbering as shown. (Change the page numbering format to lowercase Roman numerals for the table of contents page and the figures and tables page.)
   f. Apply any other formatting so your document appears as shown in Figure 28.12.
3. Save, print, and then close **C28-A06-Networks.docx**.

Figure 28.12 Assessment 28.6

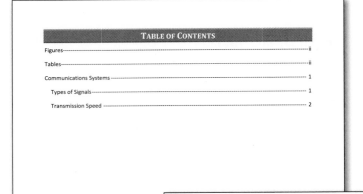

TABLE OF CONTENTS

Figures--ii

Tables---ii

Communications Systems --- 1

    Types of Signals-- 1

    Transmission Speed --- 2

FIGURES

Figure 1: Wireless Network Base 1

Figure 2: Computer Modem 1

TABLES

Table 1: Bandwidth 2

Table 2: Average Network Connection Speeds...3

COMMUNICATIONS SYSTEMS

A computer network is one kind of communications system. This system includes sending and receiving hardware, transmission and relay systems, common sets of standards so all the equipment can "talk" to each other; and communications software.

You use such a networked communications system whenever you send/receive IM or email messages, pay a bill online, shop at an Internet store, send a document to a shared printer at work or at home, or download a file.

The world of computer network communications systems is made up of:

- Transmission media upon which the data travels to/from its destination.
- A set of standards and network protocols (rules for how data is handled as it travels along a communications channel). Devices use these to send and receive data to and from each other.
- Hardware and software to connect to a communications pathway from the sending and receiving ends.

Figure 1: Wireless Network Base

The first step in understanding a communications system is to learn the basics about transmission signals and transmission speeds when communicating over a network.

TYPES OF SIGNALS

Two types of signals are used to transmit voices and other sounds over a computer network: analog and digital. An analog signal is formed by continuous sound waves that fluctuate from high to low. Your voice is transmitted as an analog signal over traditional telephone lines at a certain frequency. A digital signal uses a discrete signal that is either high or low. In computer terms, high represents the digital bit 1, and low represents the digital bit 0. These are the only two states for digital data.

Telephone lines carry your voice using an analog signal. However, computers don't "speak" analog; rather, they use a binary system of 1s and 0s to turn analog data into digital signals. If you send data between computers using an analog medium such as a phone line, the signal has to be transformed from digital to analog (modulated) and back again to digital (demodulated) to be understood by the computer on the receiving end. The piece of hardware that sends and receives

Figure 2: Computer Modem

1

Figure 28.12 Assessment 28.6 (continued)

data from a transmission source such as your telephone line or cable television connection is a modem. The word modem comes from the combination of the words *modulate* and *demodulate*.

Today, most new communications technologies simply use a digital signal, saving the trouble of converting transmissions. An example of this trend is the demise in 2009 of analog television transmissions as the industry switched to digital signals. Many people were sent scrambling to either buy a more recent television set or buy a converter to convert digital transmissions back to analog to work with their older equipment. More recent computer networks, too, use a pure digital signal method of sending and receiving data over a network.

TRANSMISSION SPEED

If you've ever been frustrated with how long it takes to download a file from a website, you are familiar with the fact that, in a communications system, data moves from one computer to another at different speeds. The speed of transmission is determined by a few key factors.

The first factor is the speed at which a signal can change from high to low, which is called frequency. A signal sent at a faster frequency provides faster transmission (Figure 1). The other factor contributing to the speed of data transmission is bandwidth. On a computer network, the term bandwidth refers to the number of bits (pieces of data) per second that can be transmitted over a communications medium. Think of bandwidth as being like a highway. At rush hour, with the same amount of cars, a two-lane highway accommodates less traffic and everybody moves at a slower speed than on a four-lane highway, where much more traffic can travel at a faster speed.

Table 1: Bandwidth

Term	Abbreviation	Meaning
1 kilobit per second	1 Kbps	1 thousand bits per second
1 megabit per second	1 Mbps	1 million bits per second
1 gigabit per second	1 Gbps	1 billion bits per second
1 terabit per second	1 Tbps	1 trillion bits per second
1 petabit per second	1 Pbps	1 quadrillion bits per second

If you have plenty of bandwidth and your data is transmitted at a high frequency, you get faster transmission speeds. Any communications medium that is capable of carrying a large amount of data at a fast speed is known as broadband.

Though transmission speeds at any moment in time may vary depending on network traffic and other factors, each of the common communications media has a typical speed (Figure 2). These speeds are

2

constantly being improved upon. In fact, some very high-powered connections provide transmission speeds of as much as 100 gigabits (one billion bits) per second, which allows you to download a high-definition DVD movie in two seconds.

Table 2: Average Network Connection Speeds

Type of Connection	Typical Speed
56 K dial-up	56 Kbps
satellite	1.5 Mbps
DSL	7 Mbps
fiber-optic	25 Mbps
cable TV	50 Mbps

3

Chapter 29

 TUTORIALS

Tutorial 29.1
Creating a Form
Tutorial 29.2
Editing a Form Template
Tutorial 29.3
Creating Forms Using Tables
Tutorial 29.4
Creating Drop-down Lists
Tutorial 29.5
Creating a Form with Legacy Tools
Tutorial 29.6
Printing a Form
Tutorial 29.7
Filling in a form

Creating Forms

Performance Objectives

Upon successful completion of Chapter 29, you will be able to:

- Design a form
- Create, protect, edit and customize a form template
- Insert and customize text, picture, date picker, and drop-down list content controls
- Insert instructional text
- Fill in a form
- Insert text, check box, and drop-down list form fields
- Customize form field options
- Print a form and print only the data in the form

Many businesses use preprinted forms that generally are filled in by hand or by using a computer. Preprinted forms cost a company money to print and space for storage. With Word 2010, you can create your own forms and eliminate the need to buy and store preprinted forms. In this chapter you will learn how to use ***content controls***, including plain text, picture, date picker, and drop-down list content controls, to create basic forms. You will also learn how to create forms with legacy tools, including text, check box, and drop-down list form fields. You will save forms as protected documents, create documents from the forms, and enter the requested information.

Note: Before beginning computer exercises for this chapter, copy to your storage medium the Chapter29 folder from the CD that accompanies this textbook and then make Chapter29 the active folder.

In this chapter, students will produce the following documents:

Exercise 29.1. C29-E01-DesmondML.docx
Exercise 29.1. C29-E01-PierobonML.docx
Exercise 29.2. C29-E02-SBFax.docx
Exercise 29.3. C29-E03-SBSurvey.docx
Exercise 29.4. C29-E04-TrevierApp.docx
Exercise 29.5. C29-E05-ReynoldsApp.docx
Exercise 29.6. C29-E06-MurciaApp.docx

Model answers for these exercises are shown on the following pages.

STORYTELLER BOOKS
Mailing List Request

First Name: Holly   **Last Name:** Desmond

Address: 1542 Windett Lane

City: Geneva   **State:** IL   **ZIP Code:** 60123

Telephone: 630-555-1443

All information provided will be used by Storyteller Books only to provide you with information regarding upcoming sales and events.

Exercise 29.1 C29-E01-DesmondML.docx

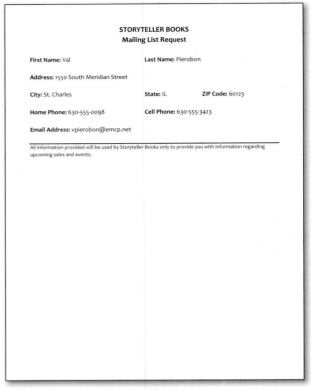

STORYTELLER BOOKS
Mailing List Request

First Name: Val   **Last Name:** Pierobon

Address: 1550 South Meridian Street

City: St. Charles   **State:** IL   **ZIP Code:** 60123

Home Phone: 630-555-0098   **Cell Phone:** 630-555-3423

Email Address: vpierobon@emcp.net

All information provided will be used by Storyteller Books only to provide you with information regarding upcoming sales and events.

Exercise 29.1 C29-E01-PierobonML.docx

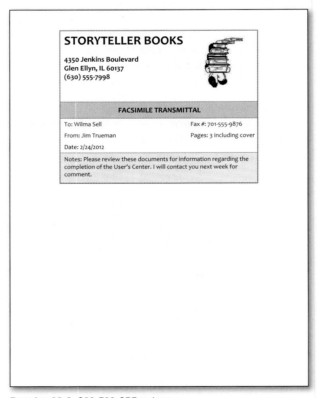

STORYTELLER BOOKS

4350 Jenkins Boulevard
Glen Ellyn, IL 60137
(630) 555-7998

FACSIMILE TRANSMITTAL	
To: Wilma Sell	Fax #: 701-555-9876
From: Jim Trueman	Pages: 3 including cover
Date: 2/24/2012	

Notes: Please review these documents for information regarding the completion of the User's Center. I will contact you next week for comment.

Exercise 29.2 C29-E02-SBFax.docx

Exercise 29.3

C29-E03-SBSurvey.docx

STORYTELLER BOOKS

4350 Jenkins Boulevard
Glen Ellyn, IL 60137
(630) 555-7998

READER SURVEY	
To help us serve you better, please take a moment to complete this survey.	
Today's date	February 24, 2012
How often do you read?	Daily
Do you read for work?	Yes
Do you read for pleasure or entertainment?	Yes
What do you prefer to read for work?	Trade publications
What do you prefer to read for entertainment?	Books
Where do you prefer to shop?	In store
Comments: I do most of my shopping in the store, but I am going to start ordering online in the near future.	

LIFETIME ANNUITY COMPANY

3310 CUSHMAN STREET ❖ FAIRBANKS, AK 99705 ❖ 907-555-8875

INSURANCE APPLICATION

FIRST APPLICANT	**SECOND APPLICANT**
Name: Sara Trevier	Name: Chris Trevier
Address: 17612 210th Ave. E., Fairbanks, AK 99702	Address: 17612 210th Ave. E., Fairbanks, AK 99702
Date of Birth: 03/28/1978	Date of Birth: 10/02/1977
Occupation: Engineer Technician	Occupation: Police Officer

1. During the past three years, have you for any reason consulted a doctor or been hospitalized?

   First Applicant: Second Applicant:
   Yes ☐   No ☒   Yes ☐   No ☒

2. Have you ever been treated for or advised that you have any of the following: heart, lung, kidney, or liver disorder; high blood pressure; drug abuse, including alcohol; cancer or tumor; diabetes; or any disorder of your immune system?

   First Applicant: Second Applicant:
   Yes ☒   No ☐   Yes ☐   No ☒

3. During the past three years, have you for any reason been denied life insurance by any other insurance company?

   First Applicant: Second Applicant:
   Yes ☐   No ☒   Yes ☐   No ☒

   FIRST APPLICANT'S SIGNATURE   SECOND APPLICANT'S SIGNATURE

   _____   _____

Exercise 29.4

C29-E04-TrevierApp.docx

Exercise 29.5

C29-E05-ReynoldsApp.docx

LIFETIME ANNUITY COMPANY
3310 Cushman Street ❖ Fairbanks, AK 99705 ❖ 907-555-8875

PREFERRED INSURANCE APPLICATION

Name: Jennifer Reynolds		Date: 02/24/2012

Address: 2309 North Ridge Drive, Fairbanks, AK 99708

Date of Birth: 12/18/1971	Client #: 210-322	Gender: Female ☒ Male ☐

Nonprofit Employer: Public School	Premium Payments: Quarterly

1. Will this insurance replace any existing insurance or annuity?
   Yes ☒   No ☐

2. Within the past three years has your driver's license been suspended or revoked, or have you been convicted for driving under the influence of alcohol or drugs?
   Yes ☐   No ☒

3. Do you have any intention of traveling or residing outside the United States or Canada within the next twelve months?
   Yes ☐   No ☒

APPLICANT'S SIGNATURE: DATE:

_____   _____

LIFETIME ANNUITY COMPANY
3310 Cushman Street ❖ Fairbanks, AK 99705 ❖ 907-555-8875

APPLICATION FOR BENEFITS CHANGE

Date: 02/24/2012	Policy #: 411-38	Type of Program: Family

First Name: Chad	Middle Name: Richard	Last Name: Murcia

Address: 512 South 142nd Street	City: Fairbanks	State: AK	Zip Code: 99702

Method of Payment:
☐ Direct Payment
☒ Monthly Deduction

Payment Period:
☐ Monthly   ☐ Semi-Annually
☒ Quarterly   ☐ Annually

1. Are you currently working?
   Yes ☒   No ☐

2. Do you work full time?
   Yes ☒   No ☐

3. Do you wish to add the total disability income provision?   Yes ☐   No ☒

4. In which program are you currently enrolled? Premium

5. In which program do you want to enroll? Platinum

SIGNATURE: DATE:

_____   _____

Exercise 29.6

C29-E06-MurciaApp.docx

Creating a Form

In Word, a ***form*** is a protected document that includes user-defined sections into which a respondent enters information. These user-defined sections are made up of ***content controls*** and ***form fields.*** Content controls limit response options to ensure the collection of desired data. Three types of content controls are available: drop-down boxes, check boxes, or date pickers. Form fields are spaces allotted for a respondent to enter specific text.

The Developer tab, shown in Figure 29.1, contains options for inserting content controls. The Developer tab also contains options that allow you to create forms with legacy tools, which are tools for developing forms that were available in previous versions of Word. They, too, include options called ***form fields.***

Figure 29.1 Developer Tab

Designing a Form

The goal in creating a form is twofold: to gather all the information necessary to meet your objective and to gather information that is useful and accurate. Thus, the first step in creating a form is to determine the form's purpose. Make a list of all of the information you need to meet your objective. Be careful not to include unnecessary or redundant information, which will frustrate the person who is completing the form and clutter the form's appearance.

The next step is to plan the layout of the form. The simplest way to design a form is to find an existing form that requests similar information or serves a similar purpose and mimic it. Finding a similar form is not always easy, however, and much of the time you will need to design your form from scratch. If you need to design your form from scratch, you should first sketch your form out on paper. This will give you a guide to follow as you create the form in Word. Some points to consider when designing your form include the following:

- Group like items together in the form. This makes providing complete and accurate information easier for the person filling in the form.

- Place the most important information at the top of the form to increase the likelihood of obtaining the information you desire most. Often a person who is filling in a form fails to complete it entirely before submitting it.

- Use fonts, colors, lines, and graphics purposefully and sparingly. Overuses of such design elements tend to clutter a form and make it difficult to read.

- Use white space, lines, and shading to separate sections of the form. Each section should be clearly defined.

Create a Form Template
1. Click File tab.
2. Click New tab.
3. Click My templates button.
4. Click Blank Document template.
5. Click *Template* option in *Create New* section.
6. Click OK.

Display Developer Tab
1. Click File tab.
2. Click Options button.
3. Click *Customize Ribbon*.
4. Click Developer tab check box to insert check mark.
5. Click OK.

Protect a Template
1. Click Developer tab.
2. Click Restrict Editing button.
3. Click *Allow only this type of editing in the document* check box.
4. Click *Filling in forms* at drop-down list in *Editing Restrictions* section.
5. Click Yes, Start Enforcing Protection button.

Creating a Form Template

A form is created as a template so a respondent who fills in the form is working on a copy of the form rather than the original. The original is the form template document that is saved as a protected document. In this way, a form can be used over and over again without changing the original. When a form is created from a protected form template document, information can be typed only into the fields designated when the form was created.

Figure 29.2 shows an example of a form template document created with the form feature. (You will create this form in Exercise 29.1A.) You can create forms that contain data fields for text, such as the fields *First Name:*, *Last Name:*, *Address:*, and so on. You can also create forms that contain drop-down lists, date pickers, or pictures.

To create a new form template, click the File tab and then click the New tab. At the New tab Backstage view, click the My templates button in the *Available Templates* section. At the New dialog box, click the Blank Document template in the list box. Click the *Template* option in the *Create New* section of the dialog box and then click OK. This displays the new form template document where you can type the form and specify data fields.

Displaying the Developer Tab

To display the Developer tab, click the File tab and then click the Options button. At the Word Options dialog box, click *Customize Ribbon* in the left panel. In the list box at the right, click the Developer tab check box to insert a check mark and then click OK to close the dialog box. The Developer tab is positioned to the right of the View tab.

Protecting a Template

If you want users to enter information in a template but not edit the template itself, protect the template. To do this, click the Restrict Editing button in the Protect group in the Developer tab. This displays the Restrict Formatting and Editing task pane, shown in Figure 29.3. At this task pane, click in the *Allow only this type of editing in the document* check box to insert a check mark. Click the down-pointing arrow at the right

Figure 29.2 Exercise 29.1A

STORYTELLER BOOKS
Mailing List Request

First Name: Click here to enter text.   **Last Name:** Click here to enter text.

Address: Click here to enter text.

City: Click here to enter text.   **State:** Click here to enter text. **Zip Code:** Click here to enter text.

Telephone: Click here to enter text.   **Birthday:** Click here to enter text.

All information provided will be used by Storyteller Books only to provide you with information regarding upcoming sales and events.

of the option box in the *Editing restrictions* section and then click *Filling in forms* at the drop-down list. Click the Yes, Start Enforcing Protection button in the task pane. At the Start Enforcing Protection dialog box, type a password, confirm the password, and then close the dialog box. A password is not required to protect a form. If you do not want to password-protect the template, click OK at the Start Enforcing Protection dialog box without entering a password.

Figure 29.3 Restrict Formatting and Editing Task Pane

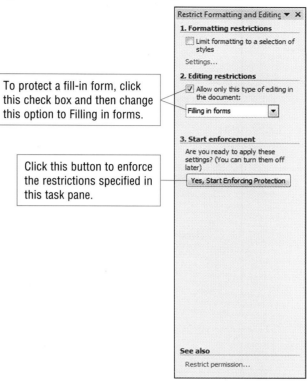

To protect a fill-in form, click this check box and then change this option to Filling in forms.

Click this button to enforce the restrictions specified in this task pane.

Exercise 29.1A   **Creating a Mailing List Form Template**   **Part 1 of 4**

1. Display the Developer tab by completing the following steps:
   a. Click the File tab and then click the Options button.
   b. At the Word Options dialog box, click *Customize Ribbon* in the left panel.
   c. Click the Developer tab check box in the list box at the right to insert a check mark.

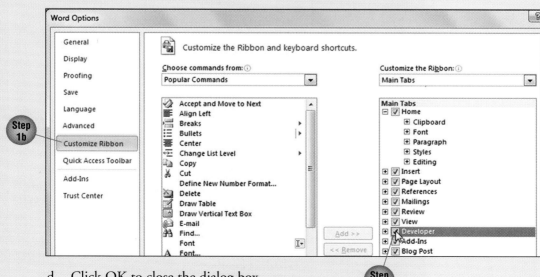

   d. Click OK to close the dialog box.

2. Create the form shown in Figure 29.2 (on page 1000). To begin, create a template by completing the following steps:
   a. Click the File tab and then click the New tab.
   b. At the New tab Backstage view, click the My templates button in the *Available Templates* section.

   c. At the New dialog box, if necessary, click the Blank Document template in the list box.
   d. Click the *Template* option in the *Create New* section of the dialog box and then click OK.

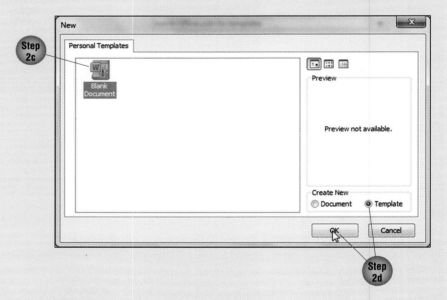

3. At the new template, type the beginning portion of the form shown in Figure 29.2 up to the colon after *First Name:* by completing the following steps:
   a. Click the Page Layout tab and then click the down-pointing arrow at the right of the *Spacing After* option in the Paragraph group until *0 pt* displays in the measurement box.
   b. Click the Home tab, turn on bold, and then change the font to Candara and the font size to 14 points.
   c. Click the Center button in the Paragraph group, type STORYTELLER BOOKS, and then press the Enter key.
   d. Type Mailing List Request and then press the Enter key twice.

   e.   Click the Align Text Left button in the Paragraph group and change the font size to 12 points.

   f.   Set left tabs at the 3-inch mark and the 4.5-inch mark on the Ruler.

   g.   Type First Name: and then turn off bold.

   h.   Press the spacebar once.

4. Insert a text content control by completing the following steps:

   a.   Click the Developer tab.

   b.   Click the Plain Text Content Control button in the Controls group. (This inserts a plain text content control in the document.)

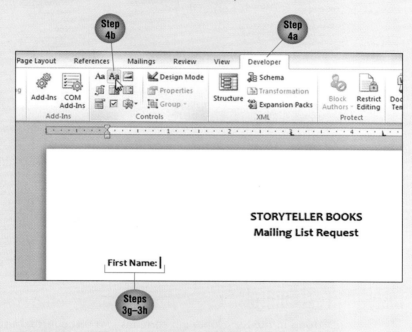

   c.   Press the Right Arrow key to deselect the control.

5. Press the Tab key to move the insertion point to the tab at the 3-inch mark.

6. Turn on bold, type Last Name:, and then turn off bold.

7. Press the spacebar once and then click the Plain Text Content Control button in the Controls group.

8. Press the Right Arrow key to deselect the control.

9. Press the Enter key twice.

10. Continue to enter the text and content controls as displayed in Figure 29.2. Remember to turn off bold before inserting the plain text content control. (When you enter the line that contains *City:*, *State:*, and *ZIP Code:*, press Tab to align each item at the tab settings. As you type, content controls and text appear crowded and wrap to the next line. The content controls will not print when you create a document from this template.)

11. Position the insertion point a double space below the last line of the form.

12. Insert the horizontal line by pressing Shift + - (the hyphen key) three times and then pressing the Enter key. (AutoFormat will automatically change the hyphens to a vertical line.)

13. Change the font to 10-point Candara and then type the paragraph of text below the horizontal line as shown in Figure 29.2.

14. Protect the template by completing the following steps:

   a.   Click the Developer tab.

   b.   Click the Restrict Editing button in the Protect group.

c. Click the *Allow only this type of editing in the document* check box in the Restrict Formatting and Editing task pane.
d. Click the down-pointing arrow at the right of the option box in the *Editing restrictions* section of the task pane and then click *Filling in forms* at the drop-down list.
e. Click the Yes, Start Enforcing Protection button.
f. At the Start Enforcing Protection dialog box, click OK. (Creating a password is optional.)
g. Close the Restrict Formatting and Editing task pane.

15. Save the template by completing the following steps:
a. Click the Save button on the Quick Access toolbar.
b. At the Save As dialog box with the Templates folder active, type XXXMailingListTemplate in the *File name* text box. (Use your initials in place of the *XXX*.)
c. Press the Enter key or click the Save button. (This saves your template with the *.dotx* file extension.)

16. Close **XXXMailingListTemplate.dotx**.

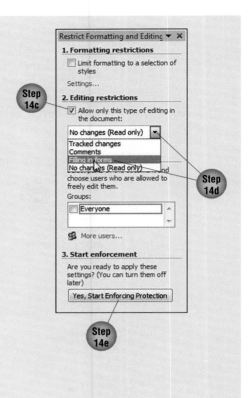

Step 14c

Step 14d

Step 14e

Inserting Text Controls

The Controls group in the Developer tab contains two text control buttons, the Rich Text Content Control and the Plain Text Content Control. The Plain Text Content Control button inserts a control that takes on the format of the text that surrounds it. The Rich Text Content Control button inserts a control that allows users to apply formatting to text and type multiple paragraphs of text. In this chapter, you will use only plain text content controls.

Plain Text
Content Control

Filling in a Form Document

After you create, protect, and save a template form document, you can use the template to create a personalized document that provides for easy data entry. To fill in a form, open the protected form template document by clicking the File tab and then clicking the New tab. At the New tab Backstage view, click the My templates button in the *Available Templates* section. At the New dialog box, click the desired template in the list box, make sure *Document* is selected in the *Create New* section, and then click OK.

When you open a protected form template document, the insertion point is automatically inserted in the first data field. To fill in the form, type the information for that data field and then press the Tab key to move the insertion point to the next data field or press Shift + Tab to move the insertion point to the preceding data field.

1. Create a form document from the **XXXMailingListTemplate** template. To begin, click the File tab and then click the New tab.
2. At the New tab Backstage view, click the My templates button.
3. At the New dialog box, click **XXXMailingListTemplate.dotx**, make sure *Document* is selected in the *Create New* section, and then click OK.
4. With the first text content control selected (the one that displays after *First Name:*), type Holly.
5. Press Tab to advance to the next data field and continue entering the information as displayed in Figure 29.4. Make sure the labels are bold and the data field text is not.
6. Save the document by completing the following steps:
   a. Click the Save button on the Quick Access toolbar.
   b. At the Save As dialog box, navigate to the Chapter29 folder on your storage medium.
   c. Type C29-E01-DesmondML in the *File name* text box and then press the Enter key.
7. Print and then close **C29-E01-DesmondML.docx**.

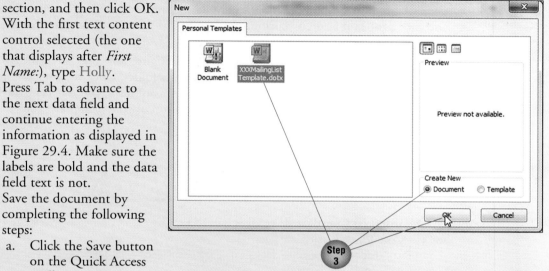

Figure 29.4 Exercise 29.1B

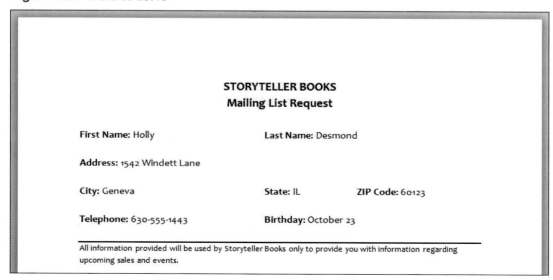

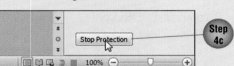

Editing a Form Template

When you create and then protect a form template, the text in the template cannot be changed. If you need to make changes to a form template, you must open the template document, turn off the protection, and then make the changes. After making the changes, protect the template again before you save it.

To turn off the protection of a template document, click the Restrict Editing button in the Protect group in the Developer tab. At the Restrict Formatting and Editing task pane, click the Stop Protection button. Make any necessary changes to the document and then protect it again by clicking the Yes, Start Enforcing Protection button.

Word, by default, saves a template document in the Templates folder. The location of this folder varies depending on your system configuration. The Navigation pane in the Open dialog box should contain the Templates folder. Click the folder name to display the Templates folder. If your template does not display in the Templates folder, check with your instructor to determine the location of your Templates folder.

Edit a Form Template
1. Click Developer tab.
2. Click Restrict Editing button.
3. Click Stop Protection button in Restrict Formatting and Editing task pane.
4. Make desired changes.
5. Click Yes, Start Enforcing Protection button.

Exercise 29.1C Editing the Mailing List Form Template Part 3 of 4

1. Edit the **XXXMailingListTemplate.dotx** as shown in Figure 29.5. To begin, click the File tab and then click the Open button.
2. Click the Templates folder in the Navigation pane located at the left side of the Open dialog box.
3. Double-click **XXXMailingListTemplate.dotx** in the dialog box list box.
4. Unprotect the template by completing the following steps:
   a. Click the Developer tab.
   b. Click the Restrict Editing button in the Protect group.
   c. At the Restrict Formatting and Editing task pane, click the Stop Protection button located toward the bottom of the task pane.

   d. Close the Restrict Formatting and Editing task pane.
5. Delete, edit, and insert a content control by completing the following steps:
   a. Select the word *Birthday*, the colon, and the content control *Click here to enter text.*, and then press the Delete key.
   b. Edit the word *Telephone* so it displays as *Home Phone*.
   c. Move the insertion point to the right of the Home Phone text content control.
   d. Press the Tab key.
   e. Turn on bold, type Cell Phone:, turn off bold, and then press the spacebar.
   f. Click the Plain Text Content Control button in the Controls group.

g. Move the insertion point so it is positioned at the right side of the *Cell Phone:* content control.
h. Press the Enter key twice.
i. Turn on bold, type Email Address:, turn off bold, and then press the spacebar.
j. Click the Plain Text Content Control button in the Controls group.
6. Protect the document by completing the following steps:
   a. With the Developer tab selected, click the Restrict Editing button in the Protect group.
   b. Click the Yes, Start Enforcing Protection button.
   c. At the Start Enforcing Protection dialog box, click OK.
   d. Close the Restrict Formatting and Editing task pane.
7. Save and then close **XXXMailingListTemplate.dotx**.

Figure 29.5 Exercise 29.1C

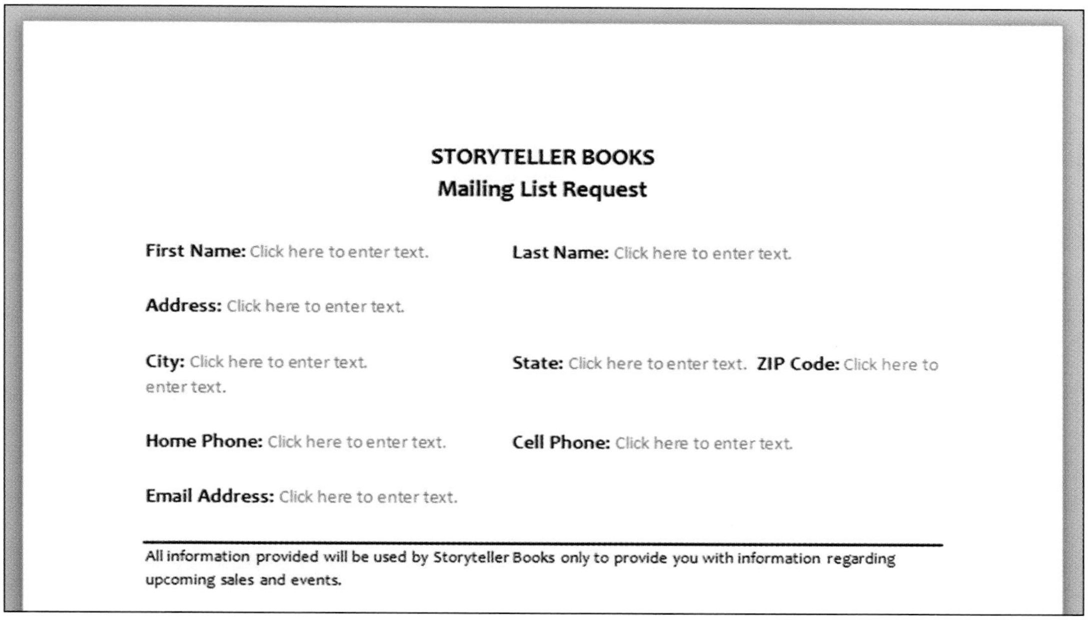

STORYTELLER BOOKS
Mailing List Request

First Name: Click here to enter text.   **Last Name:** Click here to enter text.

Address: Click here to enter text.

City: Click here to enter text.   **State:** Click here to enter text.   **ZIP Code:** Click here to enter text.

Home Phone: Click here to enter text.   **Cell Phone:** Click here to enter text.

Email Address: Click here to enter text.

All information provided will be used by Storyteller Books only to provide you with information regarding upcoming sales and events.

Exercise 29.1D   Filling in the Edited Mailing List Form   **Part 4 of 4**

1. Create a form document from the **XXXMailingListTemplate.dotx** template by completing the following steps:
   a. Click the File tab and then click the New tab.
   b. At the New tab Backstage view, click the My templates button.
   c. At the New dialog box, click **XXXMailingListTemplate.dotx**, make sure *Document* is selected in the *Create New* section, and then click OK.

d. Type the following text in the specified data fields:
   First Name: Val
   Last Name: Pierobon
   Address: 1550 South Meridian Street
   City: St. Charles
   State: IL
   ZIP: 60123
   Home Phone: 630-555-0098
   Cell Phone: 630-555-3423
   Email Address: vpierobon@emcp.net

STORYTELLER BOOKS
Mailing List Request

First Name: Val   **Last Name:** Pierobon

Address: 1550 South Meridian Street

City: St. Charles   **State:** IL   **ZIP Code:** 60123

Home Phone: 630-555-0098   **Cell Phone:** 630-555-3423

Email Address: vpierobon@emcp.net

All information provided will be used by Storyteller Books only to provide you with information regarding upcoming sales and events.

Step 1d

2. Save the document in the Chapter29 folder on your storage medium with the name **C29-E01-PierobonML**.
3. Print and then close **C29-E01-PierobonML.docx**.

Insert Instructional Text
1. Type instructions.
2. Select text.
3. Click Developer tab.
4. Click Plain Text Content Control button.

Plain Text Content Control

Inserting Instructional Text

Providing instructional text for respondents who are filling in a form can aid in obtaining accurate information. When you create a form, you can add text to each data field, providing specific directions on what information to enter. The instructional text is replaced with the data entered by the respondent.

To insert instructional text, type the instructions at the location where you will insert the text content control. Select the text and then click the Plain Text Content Control button in the Controls group in the Developer tab. The instructions are selected and become part of the data field.

Creating Forms Using Tables

The Table feature in Word is an efficient tool for designing and creating forms. Using tables allows you to set up the framework for your form and provides spaces to enter data fields. Using tables also allows for easy alignment and placement of the elements of the form.

1. Open **SBFax.docx** and then save it as a template by completing the following:
   a. Click the File tab and then click the Save & Send tab.
   b. At the Save & Send tab Backstage view, click the Change File Type option in the File Types section.
   c. Click the *Template (*.dotx)* option in the Change File Type section and then click the Save As button.
   d. At the Save As dialog box, make sure the Chapter29 folder on your storage medium is the active folder, type **XXXFaxTemplate** in the *File name* text box (type your initials in place of the *XXX*), and then press Enter.
2. If the table does not contain blue dashed gridlines between the two cells in the first row (and between other cells and rows in the table), turn on the display of nonprinting table gridlines by completing the following steps:
   a. Click in any cell in the table.
   b. Click the Table Tools Design tab.
   c. Click the Borders button arrow and then click *View Gridlines* at the drop-down list.
3. Insert in the *To:* cell instructional text and a text content control by completing the following steps:
   a. Click the Developer tab.
   b. Click in the *To:* text box and position the insertion point one space to the right of the colon.
   c. Type Receiver's name.
   d. Select *Receiver's name* and then click the Plain Text Content Control button in the Controls group.

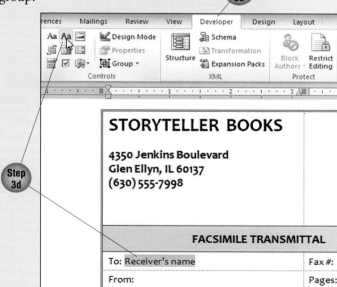

4. Complete steps similar to those in Step 3 to insert the instructional text and text content control in the *Fax #:*, *From:*, *Pages:*, and *Notes:* cells as shown in Figure 29.6 on page 1010.
5. Click the Save button on the Quick Access toolbar to save the template.

Figure 29.6 Exercises 29.2A and 29.2B

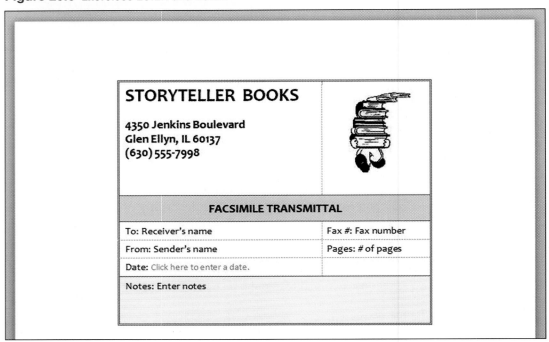

<table>
<tr><td>**QUICK STEPS**</td></tr>
</table>

Insert a Picture
1. Click Developer tab.
2. Click Picture Content Control button.
3. Click picture icon.
4. Navigate to desired folder and double-click desired picture file.

Insert a Date Content Control
1. Click Developer tab.
2. Click Date Picker Content Control button.

Inserting Pictures

You can insert a picture content control that displays a picture, clip art image, drawing, shape, chart, table, or SmartArt diagram. Insert a picture or other visual element in a form using the Picture Content Control button in the Controls group in the Developer tab. Click this button, and a picture frame containing a picture icon is inserted where the insertion point is located. Click the picture icon, and the Insert Picture dialog box displays. At this dialog box, navigate to the folder containing the picture you want to insert and then double-click the picture file. The picture image fills the picture content control.

Using the Date Picker

You can insert a date picker content control that displays a calendar when a user clicks the down-pointing arrow at the right of the control. The user can navigate to the desired month and year and then click the date. To insert a date picker content control, click the Date Picker Content Control button in the Controls group in the Developer tab.

Picture Content Control   Date Picker Content Control

1. With **XXXFaxTemplate.dotx** open, insert a picture content control by completing the following steps:
   a. Click in the upper right corner of the table (this moves the insertion point to the right cell in the first row).
   b. If necessary, click the Developer tab.
   c. Click the Picture Content Control button in the Controls group.
   d. Click the picture icon that displays in the middle of the picture content control in the cell.
   e. At the Insert Picture dialog box, navigate to the Chapter29 folder on your storage medium and then double-click **Books.jpg**.

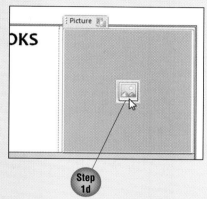

2. Insert a date picker content control by completing the following steps:
   a. Click in the *Date:* cell and then position the insertion point one space to the right of the colon.
   b. Click the Date Picker Content Control button in the Controls group.
3. Protect the template and only allow filling in of the form. (Refer to Exercise 29.1A, Step 14.)
4. Save and then close **XXXFaxTemplate.dotx**.

---

1. Create a form document from the **XXXFaxTemplate.dotx** template by completing the following steps:
   a. Click the File tab and then click the New tab.
   b. At the New tab Backstage view, click the New from existing button.
   c. At the New from Existing Document dialog box, navigate to the Chapter29 folder on your storage medium and then double-click **XXXFaxTemplate.dotx** (where your initials display in place of the *XXX*).
   d. Click on the word *To:*. (This selects the *To:* content control.)
   e. Type Wilma Sell and then press the Tab key.
   f. Type 701-555-9876 and then press the Tab key.
   g. Type Jim Trueman and then press the Tab key.
   h. Type 3 including cover and then press the Tab key.
   i. With the *Date:* content control text selected, click the down-pointing arrow at the right of the content control and then click the Today button that displays below the calendar.
   j. Press the Tab key.
   k. Type Please review these documents for information regarding the completion of the User's Center. I will contact you next week for comment.

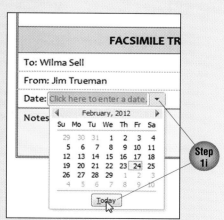

2. Save the document in the Chapter29 folder on your storage medium and name it **C29-E02-SBFax**.
3. Print and then close **C29-E02-SBFax.docx**.

QUICK STEPS

Create a Drop-Down List
1. Create a template form document.
2. Type field label.
3. Click Developer tab.
4. Click Drop-Down List Content Control button.

Specify Drop-Down List Properties
1. Select drop-down list content control.
2. Click Developer tab.
3. Click Properties button.
4. Click Add button.
5. Type desired choice.
6. Click OK.
7. Continue clicking Add and typing desired choices.
8. Click OK to close Content Control Properties dialog box.

Drop-Down List Content Control

Content Control Properties

Creating Drop-Down Lists

When you create a form, you may want the respondent to choose from specific options rather than type data into the data field. To make only specific options available, create a data field with a drop-down list. To create a drop-down list, create a form template document, type the field label, and then click the Drop-Down List Content Control button in the Controls group in the Developer tab.

Setting Properties for Content Controls

You can customize a content control with options at a properties dialog box. The options at the dialog box vary depending on the selected content control. For example, you can add a list of items for a drop-down content control, lock a picture content control, and specify formatting for inserting a date with a date picker content control.

Specifying Drop-Down List Properties

To create the list of items from which a respondent will choose, select the control and then click the Properties button in the Controls group in the Developer tab. This displays the Content Control Properties dialog box, shown in Figure 29.7. Each content control includes properties you can change with options at the Content Control Properties dialog box. The content of the dialog box varies depending on the control selected.

Figure 29.7 Content Control Properties Dialog Box for Drop-Down List Content Control

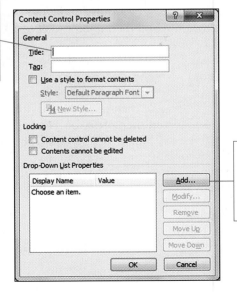

Type text in this text box that you want to display in the drop-down list content control tab.

To insert drop-down list choices, click the Add button and then type the desired text at the Add Choice dialog box.

To add drop-down list choices, click the Add button in the dialog box. At the Add Choice dialog box, type the first choice in the *Display Name* text box and then click OK. At the Content Control Properties dialog box, click the Add button and then continue until you have entered all choices.

Create a title for the drop-down list content control with the Title option in the Content Control Properties dialog box. Type the desired text in the *Title* text box and the text you type displays in the content control tab at the template. A content control title is not necessary, but it can provide additional information for the person filling in the form.

You can modify the list by clicking the desired option in the *Drop-Down List Properties* section and then clicking the Modify button. You can also rearrange the position of an item in the list by selecting the desired item and then clicking either the Move Up or the Move Down button. You can remove an item from the list by selecting the item and then clicking the Remove button.

To fill in a form with a drop-down list data field, select the drop-down list content control, click the down-pointing arrow at the right of the data field, and then click the desired option. You can also hold down the Alt key, press the Down Arrow key until the desired option is selected, and then press the Enter key.

Word also provides the Combo Box Content Control button in the Controls group in the Developer tab. A combo box is similar to a drop-down list but allows the respondent to edit or change the choices in the list.

Exercise 29.3A   Inserting Controls in a Survey Template   Part 1 of 3

1. Open **SBSurvey.docx** and then save it as a template by completing the following:
   a. Click the File tab and then click the Save & Send tab.
   b. At the Save & Send tab Backstage view, click the *Change File Type* option in the File Types section.
   c. Click the *Template (*.dotx)* option in the Change File Type section and then click the Save As button.
   d. At the Save As dialog box, make sure the Chapter29 folder on your storage medium is the active folder, type XXXSurveyTemplate in the *File name* text box (type your initials in place of the *XXX*), and then press Enter.
2. Click in the cell immediately right of the *How often do you read?* cell and then insert a drop-down list by completing the following steps:
   a. Click the Developer tab.
   b. Click the Drop-Down List Content Control button in the Controls group.
   c. With the content control selected, click the Properties button in the Controls group.

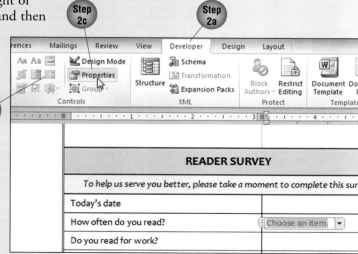

   d.   At the Content Control Properties dialog box, click the Add button.

   e.   At the Add Choice dialog box, type Daily in the *Display Name* text box and then click OK.

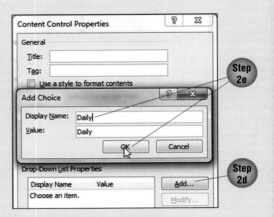

3. Complete steps similar to those in Steps 2d and 2e to insert the remaining drop-down list choices:

     Weekly

     Monthly

     I don't read.

4. Click in the *Title* text box and then type Frequency.

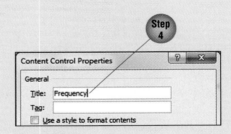

5. Click OK to close the Content Control Properties dialog box.

6. Click in the cell immediately right of the *Do you read for work?* cell and then insert a drop-down list with the following choices:

     Yes

     No

     Sometimes

7. Click in the cell immediately right of the *Do you read for pleasure or entertainment?* cell and then insert a drop-down list with the following choices:

     Yes

     No

     Sometimes

8. Click in the cell immediately right of the *What do you prefer to read for work?* cell and then click the Combo Box Content Control button in the Controls group. With the content control selected, click the Properties button and then add the following choices (make sure you use the Combo Box Content Control button and not the Drop-Down List Content Control button:

     Manuals

     Journals

     Textbooks

9. Click in the cell immediately right of the *What do you prefer to read for entertainment?* cell and then insert a combo box content control with the following choices (make sure you use the Combo Box Content Control button):

   > Books
   > Magazines
   > Newspapers

10. Click in the cell immediately right of the *Where do you prefer to shop?* cell and then insert a drop-down list with the following choices:

    > In store
    > Online

11. Insert a content control in the *Comments:* cell by completing the following steps:

    a. Click in the *Comments:* cell and then position the insertion point one space to the right of the colon.

    b. Type Type comments here.

    c. Select *Type comments here.* and then click the Plain Text Content Control button in the Controls group.

    d. Click in a different cell to deselect the content control.

12. Click the Save button on the Quick Access toolbar to save the template.

Customizing Picture Content Control Properties

When you use a picture control in a form template, consider locking the picture. With the picture locked, the insertion point does not stop at the picture data field when the respondent presses the Tab key to move to the next data field. Lock a picture by selecting the picture data field and then clicking the Properties button in the Controls group in the Developer tab. At the Content Control Properties dialog box, shown in Figure 29.8, insert a check mark in the *Contents cannot be edited* check box. If you do not want the picture content control to be deleted, insert a check mark in the *Content control cannot be deleted* check box.

Lock Picture Control
1. Select picture data field.
2. Click Developer tab.
3. Click Properties button.
4. Insert check mark in *Contents cannot be edited* check box.
5. Click OK.

Figure 29.8 Content Control Properties Dialog Box for Picture Content Control

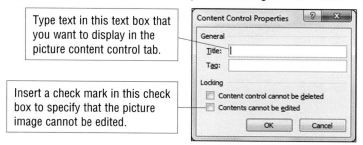

Type text in this text box that you want to display in the picture content control tab.

Insert a check mark in this check box to specify that the picture image cannot be edited.

Customizing Date Picker Content Control Properties

The date picker content control has a default format of *m/d/yyyy* for inserting the date. You can customize the date format with options at the Content Control Properties dialog box, shown in Figure 29.9. Choose the desired date format in the list box in the *Date Picker Properties* section of the dialog box and then click OK.

Figure 29.9 Content Control Properties Dialog Box for Date Picker Content Control

Type text in this text box that you want to display in the date picker content control tab.

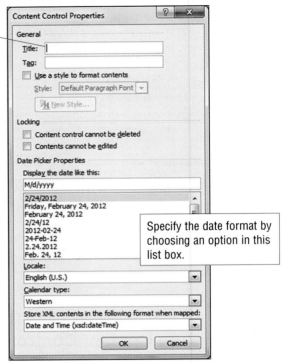

Specify the date format by choosing an option in this list box.

Exercise 29.3B Customizing Picture and Date Picker Content Control Properties   Part 2 of 3

1. With **XXXSurveyTemplate.dotx** open, insert a picture content control and lock the control by completing the following steps:
   a. Click in the cell in the upper right corner of the table.
   b. If necessary, click the Developer tab.
   c. Click the Picture Content Control button in the Controls group.
   d. Click the picture icon that displays in the middle of the picture content control in the cell.
   e. At the Insert Picture dialog box, navigate to the Chapter29 folder on your storage medium and then double-click ***Books.jpg***.
   f. Click the Properties button in the Controls group.
   g. At the Content Control Properties dialog box, type Books Image in the *Title* text box.
   h. Click the *Contents cannot be edited* check box to insert a check mark.
   i. Click OK to close the dialog box.

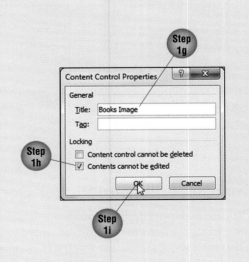

2. Insert a date picker content control and customize the control by completing the following steps:
   a. Click in the cell immediately right of the *Today's date* cell.
   b. If necessary, click the Developer tab.
   c. Click the Date Picker Content Control button in the Controls group.
   d. Click the Properties button in the Controls group.
   e. Type Date in the *Title* text box.
   f. Click the third option from the top in the list box in the *Date Picker Properties* section of the Content Control Properties dialog box.
   g. Click OK to close the dialog box.
3. Protect the template and only allow filling in of the form. (Refer to Exercise 29.1A, Step 14.)
4. Save and then close **XXXSurveyTemplate.dotx**.

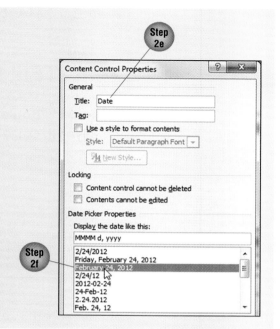

Step 2e

Step 2f

Exercise 29.3C Filling in the Survey Form   Part 3 of 3

1. Create a form document from the **XXXSurveyTemplate.dotx** template by completing the following steps:
   a. Click the File tab and then click the New tab.
   b. At the New tab Backstage view, click the New from existing button.
   c. At the New from Existing Document dialog box, navigate to the Chapter29 folder on your storage medium and then double-click **XXXSurveyTemplate.dotx** (where your initials display in place of the *XXX*).
2. With the *Date:* content control text selected, click the down-pointing arrow at the right of the content control and then click the Today button that displays below the calendar.
3. Press the Tab key. (This selects the drop-down list content control in the cell immediately right of *How often do you read?*)
4. Choose an option from the drop-down list by clicking the down-pointing arrow at the right of the drop-down list content control and then clicking *Daily*.

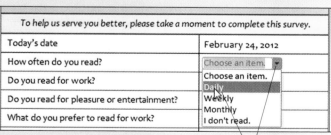

Step 4

5. Continue filling in the form with options as shown in Figure 29.10. Since the combo box for *What do you prefer to read for work?* does not contain the option *Trade publications*, type the entry in the content control.
6. Save the document in the Chapter29 folder on your storage medium with the name **C29-E03-SBSurvey**.
7. Print and then close **C29-E03-SBSurvey.docx**.

Figure 29.10 Exercise 29.3C

STORYTELLER BOOKS

4350 Jenkins Boulevard
Glen Ellyn, IL 60137
(630) 555-7998

READER SURVEY	
To help us serve you better, please take a moment to complete this survey.	
Today's date	February 24, 2010
How often do you read?	Daily
Do you read for work?	Yes
Do you read for pleasure or entertainment?	Yes
What do you prefer to read for work?	Trade publications
What do you prefer to read for entertainment?	Books
Where do you prefer to shop?	In store
Comments: I do most of my shopping in the store, but I am going to start ordering online in the near future.	

Creating a Form with Legacy Tools

Legacy Tools

Click the Legacy Tools button in the Controls group in the Developer tab, and a drop-down list displays with a number of form fields you can insert in a form. You can insert a text, check box, or drop-down list form field.

Inserting a Text Form Field

The text form field in the Legacy Tools drop-down list is similar to the plain text content control. To insert a text form field, position the insertion point in the desired location, click the Legacy Tools button in the Controls group in the Developer tab, and then click the Text Form Field button. This inserts a gray shaded box in the form. This shaded box is the location where data is entered when a person fills in the form. (If the form is printed, the shading does not print.) You can turn off the gray shading by clicking the Form Field Shading button in the Legacy Tools drop-down list. If gray shading is turned off, click the button again to turn it back on.

1. Open **LAApp01.docx** and then save it as a template by completing the following:
   a. Click the File tab and then click the Save & Send tab.
   b. At the Save & Send tab Backstage view, click the Change File Type option in the File Types section.
   c. Click the *Template (*.dotx)* option in the Change File Type section and then click the Save As button.
   d. At the Save As dialog box, make sure the Chapter29 folder on your storage medium is the active folder, type **XXXLAApp01Template** in the *File name* text box (type your initials in place of the *XXX*), and then press Enter.
2. Insert a text form field (Figure 29.11, on page 1020, shows the filled-in form) by completing the following steps:
   a. Click the Developer tab.
   b. Position the insertion point one space to the right of the colon after *Name:* below *FIRST APPLICANT*.
   c. Click the Legacy Tools button in the Controls group in the Developer tab and then click the Text Form Field button.
3. Complete steps similar to those in Steps 2b and 2c to insert text form fields one space to the right of the colon in the following data fields in the FIRST APPLICANT section and the SECOND APPLICANT section: *Name:*, *Address:*, *Date of Birth:*, and *Occupation:*.
4. Click the Save button on the Quick Access toolbar to save the template.

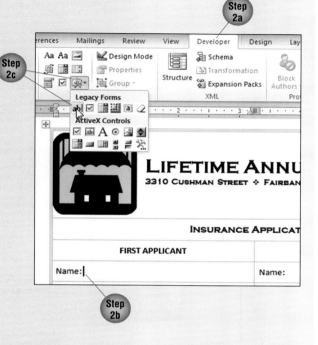

Inserting a Check Box Form Field

You can insert a check box form field where you want the person entering information to insert a check mark or leave the check box blank. Check boxes are useful in forms for indicating *Yes* and *No* and for inserting options where the respondent inserts a check mark for specific options. To insert a check box form field, click the Legacy Tools button in the Controls group in the Developer tab and then click the Check Box Form Field button at the drop-down list. To insert a check mark when filling in the form, make the check box active and then press the spacebar.

Insert a Check Box Form Field
1. Click Developer tab.
2. Click Legacy Tools button.
3. Click Check Box Form Field button.

1. With **XXXLAApp01Template.dotx** open, insert a check box by completing the following steps:
   a. Move the insertion point so it is positioned two spaces to the right of the *Yes* below *First Applicant* below the first question.
   b. Make sure the Developer tab is active.
   c. Click the Legacy Tools button in the Controls group.
   d. Click the Check Box Form Field button at the drop-down list.
2. Complete steps similar to those in Step 1c and 1d to insert the remaining check boxes after *Yes* and *No* below questions 1, 2, and 3 (refer to Figure 29.11).
3. Protect the template and only allow filling in of the form. (Refer to Exercise 29.1A, Step 14.)
4. Save and then close **XXXLAApp01Template.dotx**.

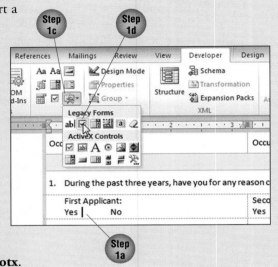

Figure 29.11 **Exercises 29.4B and 29.4C**

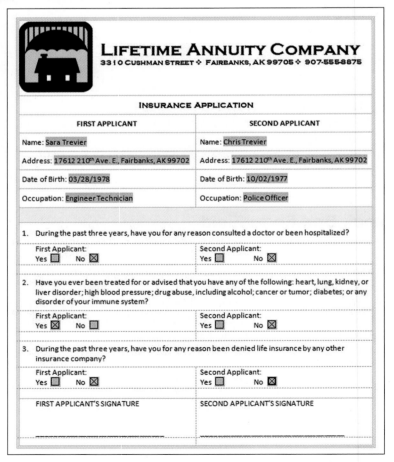

Fill in a form with text and check box form fields in the same manner as filling in a form with content controls. To fill in the form, open the form template document, type the information in the data field, and then press the Tab key to move to the next field or press Shift + Tab to move to the previous field. You can also click in the desired data field and then type the information. To insert a check mark in a check box, press the spacebar or, using the mouse, click in the desired field.

1. Create a form document from the **XXXLAApp01Template.dotx** template as shown in Figure 29.11. To begin, click the File tab and then click the New tab.
2. At the New tab Backstage view, click the New from existing button.
3. At the New from Existing Document dialog box, navigate to the Chapter29 folder on your storage medium and then double-click ***XXXLAApp01Template.dotx***.

4. Word displays the form document with the insertion point positioned in the first form field after *Name:*. Type the name Sara Trevier as shown in Figure 29.11.
5. Press the Tab key to move to the next form field.
6. Fill in the remaining text and check box form fields as shown in Figure 29.11. Press the Tab key to move to the next data field or press Shift + Tab to move to the previous data field. To insert an *X* in a check box, make the check box active and then press the spacebar.
7. When the form is completed, save the document in the Chapter29 folder on your storage medium with the name **C29-E04-TrevierApp**.
8. Print **C29-E04-TrevierApp.docx**.

Printing a Form

After filling in a form document, you can print the document in the normal manner. In some situations, you may want to print just the data (not the entire form) or print the form and not the filled-in data. If you are using a preprinted form that is inserted in the printer, you will want to print just the data. Word will print the data in the same location on the page as it appears in the form document. To print just the data in a form, display the Word Options dialog box and then click the *Advanced* option in the left panel. Scroll down the dialog box and then click the *Print only the data from a form* option in the *When printing this document* section.

When you print the form data in Exercise 29.4C, the table gridlines will print as well as the shading and clip art image. If you do not want these elements to print, you need to remove them from the form.

1. With **C29-E04-TrevierApp.docx** open, specify that you want to print only the data by completing the following steps:
   a. Click the File tab and then click the Options button.
   b. At the Word Options dialog box, click *Advanced* in the left panel.
   c. Scroll down the dialog box to the *When printing this document* section and then click the *Print only the data from a form* option.
   d. Click OK to close the Word Options dialog box.
   e. Click the File tab, click the Print tab, and then click the Print button at the Print tab Backstage view.
2. Remove the check mark from the *Print only the data from a form* option by completing the following steps:
   a. Click the File tab and then click the Options button.
   b. At the Word Options dialog box, click *Advanced* in the left panel.
   c. Scroll down the dialog box to the *When printing this document* section and then click the *Print only the data from a form* option to remove the check mark.
   d. Click OK to close the Word Options dialog box.
3. Save and then close **C29-E04-TrevierApp.docx**.

Customizing Form Field Options

A text form field contains default settings, and you can change some of these defaults with options at the Text Form Field Options dialog box. You can also change some of the default settings for a check box form field with options at the Check Box Form Field Options dialog box. Previously in this chapter, you learned how to insert a drop-down list content control. You can also insert a drop-down list form field and then change default settings with options at the Drop-Down Form Field Options dialog box.

Creating a Drop-Down List Form Field

Properties

If you want a field to provide a number of options from which a person chooses when filling in the form, insert a drop-down list form field. To do this, click the Legacy Tools button in the Controls group in the Developer tab and then click the Drop-Down Form Field button at the drop-down list. To insert the choices, click the Properties button in the Controls group. This displays the Drop-Down Form Field Options dialog box, shown in Figure 29.12.

Figure 29.12 Drop-Down Form Field Options Dialog Box

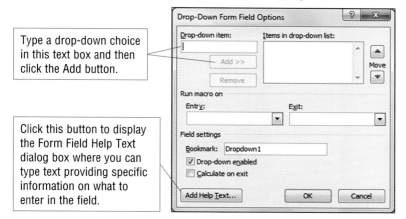

Type a drop-down choice in this text box and then click the Add button.

Click this button to display the Form Field Help Text dialog box where you can type text providing specific information on what to enter in the field.

QUICK STEPS

Create a Drop-Down Form Field
1. Click Developer tab.
2. Click Legacy Tools button.
3. Click Drop-Down Form Field button.
4. Click Properties button.
5. Type first list option.
6. Click Add button.
7. Continue typing desired choices and clicking the Add button.
8. Click OK.

At the dialog box, type the first option in the *Drop-down item* text box and then click the Add button. This inserts the item in the *Items in drop-down list* list box. Continue in this manner until you have inserted all drop-down list items. You can remove drop-down list items from the *Items in drop-down list* list box by clicking the item and then clicking the Remove button. When all items you want to include display in the list box, click OK to close the dialog box.

If you want to provide instructional text for respondents who are filling in the form, click the Add Help Text button located in the lower left corner of the Drop-Down Form Field Options dialog box. This displays the Form Field Help Text dialog box with the Status Bar tab selected. At the dialog box, click the *Type your own* option and then type the text you want to display when the field is active. The text you type displays in the Status bar when the respondent is filling in the form.

To fill in a drop-down list form field, click the down-pointing arrow at the right of the field and then click the desired option at the drop-down list. You can also display the drop-down list by pressing F4 or by holding down the Alt key and then pressing the Down Arrow key.

Exercise 29.5 Inserting Drop-Down Form Fields and Filling in a Form   Part 1 of 1

1. Open **LAApp02.docx** and then save the document as a template named **XXXLAApp02Template.dotx** in the Chapter 29 folder on your storage medium.
2. Insert a drop-down form field (Figure 29.13 shows the filled-in form) by completing the following steps:
   a. Position the insertion point one space to the right of the colon after *Nonprofit Employer:*.
   b. Click the Developer tab.
   c. Click the Legacy Tools button in the Controls group in the Developer tab and then click the Drop-Down Form Field button.

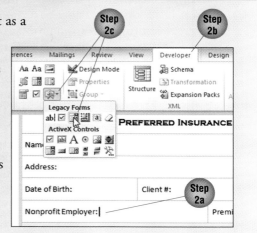

3. Insert the drop-down list choices and create help text by completing the following steps:
    a. With the insertion point positioned immediately right of the drop-down form field, click the Properties button in the Controls group in the Developer tab.
    b. At the Drop-Down Form Field Options dialog box, type College in the *Drop-down item* text box.
    c. Click the Add button.
    d. Type Public School in the *Drop-down item* text box.
    e. Click the Add button.
    f. Type Private School in the *Drop-down item* text box.
    g. Click the Add button.
    h. Click the Add Help Text button that displays in the lower left corner of the dialog box.
    i. At the Form Field Help Text dialog box with the Status Bar tab selected, click the *Type your own* option.
    j. Type the text Click the down-pointing arrow at the right side of the Nonprofit Employer form field and then click the employer at the drop-down list. in the text box.
    k. Click OK to close the Form Field Help Text dialog box.

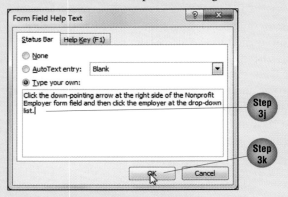

    l. Click OK to close the Drop-Down Form Field Options dialog box.
4. Insert a drop-down form field one space after the colon that follows *Premium Payments:* and complete steps similar to those in Step 3 to insert the following items at the Drop-Down Form Field Options dialog box: *Annually*, *Semiannually*, and *Quarterly*.
5. Insert text form fields (using the Text Form Field button from the Legacy Tools drop-down list) one space following the colon after *Name:*, *Date:*, *Address:*, *Date of Birth:*, and *Client #:*.
6. Insert check box form fields two spaces to the right of each *Yes* and *No* in the form and to the right of *Female* and *Male* following *Gender:*.
7. Protect the template and allow filling in of the form. (Refer to Exercise 29.1A, Step 14.)
8. Save and then close **XXXLAApp02Template.dotx**.
9. Create a form document from the **XXXLAApp02Template.dotx** template and fill in the form as shown in Figure 29.13. To begin, click the File tab and then click the New tab.
10. At the New tab Backstage view, click the New from existing button.
11. At the New from Existing Document dialog box, navigate to the Chapter29 folder on your storage medium and then double-click ***XXXLAApp02Template.dotx***.

12. Enter the data in the data fields as shown in Figure 29.13. (To insert *Public School* in the *Nonprofit Employer* drop-down form field, click the down-pointing arrow at the right of the field and then click *Public School* at the drop-down list. [Notice the help text that displays in the Status bar.] Complete similar steps to insert *Quarterly* in the *Premium Payments* drop-down form field.)

13. When the form is completed, save the document with the name **C29-E05-ReynoldsApp**.

14. Print and then close **C29-E05-ReynoldsApp.docx**.

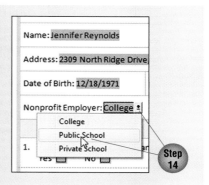

Figure 29.13 Exercise 29.5

Customizing Check Box Form Field Options

You can change check box form field options at the Check Box Form Field Options dialog box. Display this dialog box by selecting a check box form field and then clicking the Properties button in the Controls group in the Developer tab. By default, Word inserts a check box in a form template document in the same size as the adjacent text. You can change the default setting of *Auto* to *Exactly* and then type the desired point measurement in the text box. A check box form field is empty by default. If you want the check box checked by default, click the *Checked* option in the *Default value* section of the dialog box. You can also select and then apply formatting to a check box.

1. Open **LAApp03.docx** and then save the document as a template named **XXXLAApp03Template.dotx**.
2. Insert a check box that contains a check mark (Figure 29.14 shows the filled-in form) by completing the following steps:
   a. Position the insertion point two spaces to the right of the *Yes* located below the *Are you currently working?* question.
   b. Click the Developer tab, click the Legacy Tools button in the Controls group and then click the Check Box Form Field button at the drop-down list.
   c. With the insertion point positioned immediately right of the check box form field, click the Properties button in the Controls group.
   d. At the Check Box Form Field Options dialog box, click the *Checked* option in the *Default value* section.
   e. Click OK.

Step 2d

Step 2e

3. Complete steps similar to those in Step 2 to insert to the right of *Yes* below the *Do you work full time?* question a check box that contains a check mark.
4. Insert the remaining check boxes for questions 1, 2, and 3 (without check marks).
5. Insert a drop-down field two spaces after the question mark that ends question 4 and insert the following items at the Drop-Down Form Field Options dialog box: *Standard*, *Premium*, *Gold*, and *Platinum*.
6. Insert a drop-down field two spaces after the question mark that ends question 5 and insert the following items at the Drop-Down Form Field Options dialog box: *Standard*, *Premium*, *Gold*, and *Platinum*.
7. Save the template.

Customizing Text Form Fields

To change options for a text form field, select the form field (or position the insertion point immediately right of the form field) and then click the Properties button in the Controls group in the Developer tab. This displays the Text Form Field Options dialog box. At this dialog box, you can change the type of text you want inserted in the field. The default setting at the *Type* option box is *Regular text*. You can change this to *Number*, *Date*, *Current date*, *Current time*, or *Calculation*.

If you change the *Type* option, Word displays an error message if the correct type of information is not entered in the form field. For example, if you change the *Type* option to *Number*, a person filling in the form can only enter a number. If the person tries to enter something other than a number, Word displays an error message and selects the entry, and the insertion point stays in the form field until a number is entered. If a particular text form field will generally require the same information, type that information in the *Default text* box. This default text will display in the form field. When the form is filled in, the respondent can leave the default text in the form field or type over the existing text. With the *Maximum length* option at the dialog box, you can specify an exact number of characters for the form field. This option has a default setting of *Unlimited*.

You can apply formatting to text in a form field with options in the *Text format* option box. For example, if you want to display text in all uppercase letters, click the down-pointing arrow at the right of the *Text format* option box and then click *Uppercase* at the drop-down list. When text is typed in the form field as the form is filled in, the text is automatically converted to uppercase letters as soon as the respondent presses the Tab key or the Enter key. The *Text format* options vary depending on what is selected in the *Type* option box. You can also select a form field, apply formatting, and then use Format Painter to apply the same formatting to other form fields.

Exercise 29.6B Customizing Text Form Fields   Part 2 of 2

1. With **XXXLAApp03Template.dotx** open, create a custom text form field by completing the following steps:
    a. Position the insertion point one space to the right of the colon after *Type of Program:*.
    b. Insert a text box form field by clicking the Legacy Tools button in the Controls group and then clicking the Text Form Field button at the drop-down list.
    c. To reflect that most employees are enrolled in a Family program, make *Family* the default setting for the text form field. To do this, make sure the insertion point is positioned immediately right of the text form field and then click the Properties button.
    d. At the Text Form Field Options dialog box, type Family in the *Default text* box.
    e. Click OK to close the dialog box.

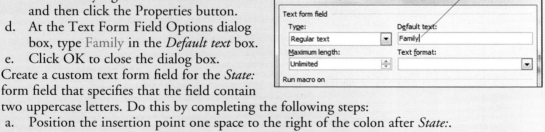

2. Create a custom text form field for the *State:* form field that specifies that the field contain two uppercase letters. Do this by completing the following steps:
    a. Position the insertion point one space to the right of the colon after *State:*.
    b. Insert a text box form field by clicking the Legacy Tools button in the Controls group and then clicking the Text Form Field button at the drop-down list.
    c. Click the Properties button.
    d. At the Text Form Field Options dialog box, click the up-pointing arrow at the right of the *Maximum length* option box until *2* displays.
    e. Click the down-pointing arrow at the right of the *Text format* option box and then click *Uppercase*.

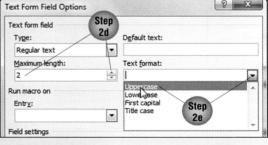

f. Click OK to close the Text Form Field Options dialog box.

3. Complete steps similar to those in Step 2 to create a custom text form field for the *Zip Code:* form field that specifies a maximum length of 5 characters for the field.

4. Complete steps similar to those in Step 2 to create a custom text form field for the *Policy #:* form field that specifies a maximum length of 6 characters for the field.

5. Protect the template and only allow filling in of the form.

6. Save and then close **XXXLAApp03Template.dotx**.

7. Create a form document from the **XXXLAApp03Template.dotx** template and fill in the form as shown in Figure 29.14.

8. Type ak in the *State:* data field and then press the Tab key. This changes the text to uppercase letters.

9. When the form is completed, save the document with the name **C29-E06-MurciaApp**.

10. Print and then close **C29-E06-MurciaApp.docx**.

Figure 29.14 Exercise 29.6B

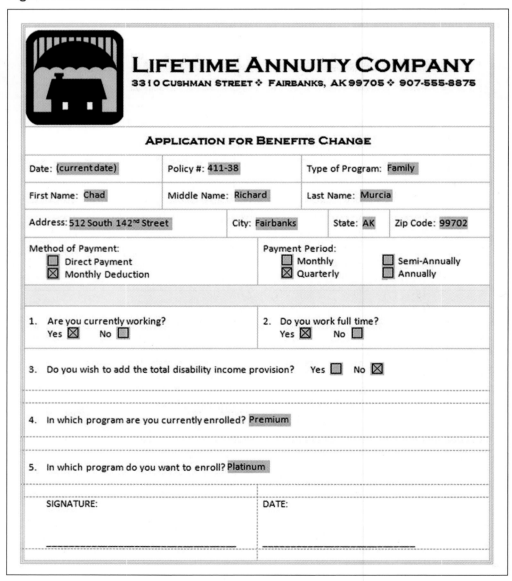

Chapter *Summary*

- ➤ A form is created as a template document with data fields that can be filled in with different information each time the template document is used.

- ➤ Three basic steps are involved in creating a form: 1) designing the form document based on a template and building the structure of the form; 2) inserting data fields where information is to be entered with the keyboard; and 3) saving the form as a protected document.

- ➤ Create a new template at the New dialog box. Display this dialog box by clicking the File tab, clicking the New tab, and then clicking the My templates button.

- ➤ Insert content controls with buttons in the Developer tab. Display this tab by clicking the File tab and then clicking the Options button. At the Word Options dialog box, click *Customize Ribbon* in the left panel, click the Developer tab check box in the list box at the right, and then click OK.

- ➤ The Plain Text Content Control button in the Developer tab inserts a control that takes on the format of the text that surrounds it.

- ➤ Use options at the Restrict Formatting and Editing task pane to protect a template. You can protect a template so a respondent can enter information in the form but cannot edit the form. Display the task pane by clicking the Restrict Editing button in the Protect group in the Developer tab.

- ➤ To open a template document, display the New tab Backstage view and then click the My templates button (if you want to open a template document from the *Templates* folder) or click the New from existing button (if you want to open a template document from your storage medium).

- ➤ Open a template for editing from the Templates folder. Display the folder contents by clicking the *Templates* folder in the navigation pane in the Open dialog box.

- ➤ To edit a form template, first stop protection of the template, make any desired changes, and then protect the template.

- ➤ Include instructional text in a content control by typing the instructional text, selecting the text, and then clicking the Plain Text Content Control button in the Developer tab.

- ➤ Use the Picture Content Control button in the Developer tab to insert a picture content control in a form, use the Date Picker Content Control button to insert a date picker content control, and use the Drop-Down List Content Control button to insert a drop-down list of choices for a data field.

- ➤ Insert a combo box content control if you want to provide a drop-down list of choices as well as let respondents enter their own data.

- ➤ Click the Properties button in the Developer tab to change the properties of the selected content control. This displays the Content Control Properties dialog box. The contents of this dialog box vary depending on what content control is selected.

- ➤ The Legacy Tools button in the Controls group in the Developer tab contains buttons for inserting text, check box, and drop-down list form fields into a form.

- ➤ A text form field is similar to a plain text content control. Insert a text form field by clicking the Legacy Tools button in the Developer tab and then clicking the Text Form Field button at the drop-down list.

- ➤ Insert a check box form field in a form where you want the person entering information to choose an option by inserting an *X* in the check box.

- ➤ You can print a filled-in form in the normal manner or you can print the data only. To print only the data, display the Word Options dialog box with *Advanced* selected and then insert a check mark in the *Print only the data from a form* check box in the *When printing this document* section.

- ➤ Create a drop-down list of choices by inserting a drop-down list form field and then typing choices in the Drop-Down Form Field Options dialog box. Display this dialog box by inserting a drop-down list form field and then clicking the Properties button in the Developer tab.

- ➤ When you fill in a form with a drop-down list form field, click the down-pointing arrow at the right of the form field, and then click the desired option at the drop-down list. You can also display the drop-down list by pressing the F4 function key or holding down the Alt key and pressing the Down Arrow key.

- ➤ Customize check box form field options at the Check Box Form Field Options dialog box. Display this dialog box by inserting a check box form field and then clicking the Properties button in the Developer tab.

- ➤ Customize text form field options at the Text Form Field Options dialog box. Display this dialog box by inserting a text form field and then clicking the Properties button in the Developer tab.

Commands *Review*

FEATURE	RIBBON TAB, GROUP	BUTTON, OPTION	KEYBOARD SHORTCUT
Plain Text Content Control	Developer, Controls		
Restrict Formatting and Editing task pane	Developer, Protect		
Next data field			Tab
New dialog box	File	New, My templates	
Previous data field			Shift + Tab
Templates folder	File	Open, Templates	
Picture Content Control	Developer, Controls		
Date Picker Content Control	Developer, Controls		
Drop-Down List Content Control	Developer, Controls		
Content Control Properties	Developer, Controls		
Legacy Tools drop-down list	Developer, Controls		
Word Options dialog box	File	Options	
Text Form Field	Developer, Controls	, Text Form Field	
Text Form Field Options dialog box	Developer, Controls	, Text Form Field, Properties	
Drop-Down List Form Field	Developer, Controls	, Drop-Down Form Field	
Drop-Down List Form Field Options dialog box	Developer, Controls	, Drop-Down Form Field, Properties	

FEATURE	RIBBON TAB, GROUP	BUTTON, OPTION	KEYBOARD SHORTCUT
Check Box Form Field	Developer, Controls	, Check Box Form Field	
Check Box Form Field Options dialog box	Developer, Controls	, Check Box Form Field, Properties	

Key Points Review

Completion: In the space provided at the right, indicate the correct term, symbol, or command.

1. This group in the Developer tab contains content control buttons. _____

2. Click the Restrict Editing button in the Developer tab, and this task pane displays. _____

3. When filling in a form, press this key to move to the next data field. _____

4. Click this button in the Developer tab to insert a picture frame containing a picture icon. _____

5. Click this button in the Developer tab to insert a date content control. _____

6. Insert this type of control in a form if you want the respondent to choose from a specific list of options. _____

7. Customize a date picker content control with options at this dialog box. _____

8. The Legacy Tools button is located in this group in the Developer tab. _____

9. Insert a text form field, and this is inserted in the form. _____

10. Insert this type of form field if you want the person filling in the form to choose an option by inserting an X. _____

11. To open a template document from your storage medium, display the New tab Backstage view, click the New from existing button, and then double-click the template at this dialog box. _____

12. To print the form data only, display the Word Options dialog box with this option selected and then insert a check mark in the *Print only the data from a form* check box. _____

13. If you want the person filling in the form to insert data in a data field by choosing from a list, insert this type of form field. _____

14. To display a check box in a form with an *X* automatically inserted in the form field, click this option at the Check Box Form Field Options dialog box. _____

15. With the insertion point positioned immediately right of a text form field, click this button in the Developer tab to display the Text Form Field Options dialog box. _____

Chapter Assessments

Applying Your Skills

Demonstrate your knowledge of features learned in this chapter by completing the following assessments.

Assessment 29.1   Create and Fill in a Book Order Form

1. Create the form shown in Figure 29.15 with the following specifications:
   a. Create the form as a template and save it in the Chapter29 folder on your storage medium and name it **XXXBookRequestTemplate**.
   b. At the template, click the *No Spacing* style in the Styles group in the Home tab.
   c. Insert the ***Books.jpg*** image using the Picture button in the Insert tab. Size and move the image so it displays as shown in Figure 29.15. Change the text wrapping of the image to *Behind Text*.
   d. Set the company name STORYTELLER BOOKS in 22-point Candara bold and set the remainder of the text in 11-point Candara bold. Insert the book symbol at the Symbol dialog box with the *Wingdings* font selected. (The book symbol is in the first row of the symbol list box.)
   e. Insert plain text content controls one space after the colon in each of the following: *Name:*, *Book Title:*, *Author:*, *Email:*, *Telephone:*, and *Notes:*.
   f. Insert the horizontal line by holding down the Shift key, pressing the hyphen key three times, and then pressing the Enter key.
2. Protect the template and only allow filling in of the form (you do not need to enter a password).
3. Save and then close **XXXBookRequestTemplate.dotx**.
4. Create a form document from the **XXXBookRequestTemplate** template by completing the following steps:
   a. Click the File tab and then click the New tab. At the New tab Backstage view, click the New from existing button. At the New from Existing Document dialog box, navigate to the Chapter29 folder on your storage medium and then double-click ***XXXBookRequestTemplate.dotx***.

Figure 29.15 Assessment 29.1

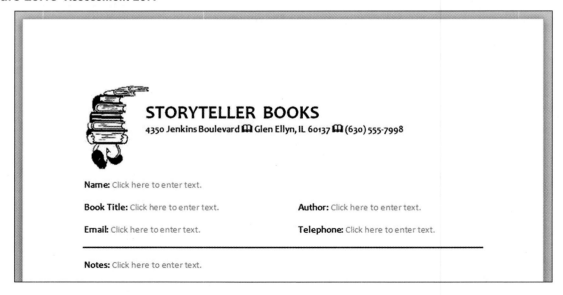

b. Insert the following data in the specified fields:

> Name: Chris Felder
> Book Title: I Know Why the Caged Bird Sings
> Author: Maya Angelou
> Email: cfelder@emcp.net
> Telephone: (630) 555-8965
> Notes: I am interested in purchasing a paperback version either new or used.

6. Save the document with the name **C29-A01-SBRequest**.
7. Print and then close **C29-A01-SBRequest.docx**.

Assessment 29.2   Create and Fill in a Catalog Request Form

1. Open **SBCatRequest.docx** and then save the document as a template in the Chapter29 folder on your storage medium and name the template **XXXCatalogRequestTemplate.dotx**.
2. Create the form shown in Figure 29.16 with the following specifications:
   a. Insert a picture content control in the cell in the upper right corner of the table and then insert the image named ***Books.jpg***. (Specify that the picture content cannot be edited.)
   b. Insert plain text content controls for *Name:*, *Address:*, *City:*, *State:*, *Zip Code:*, *Email:*, and *Telephone:*.
   c. Insert a date picker content control for *Date:* that inserts the date with the month spelled out followed by the day and year in numbers.
   d. Insert a drop-down list content control for *Preferred Shipping Method:* with the following choices: *USPS Standard*, *USPS Priority*, *FedEx Standard*, and *FedEx Overnight*.
3. Protect the template (you do not need to enter a password).
4. Save and then close **XXXCatalogRequestTemplate.dotx**.
5. Create a form document from the **XXXCatalogRequestTemplate** template and insert the following data in the specified fields:

> Name: Donna Hendrix
> Date: *Insert the current date.*
> Address: 2123 North Myers

Figure 29.16 Assessment 29.2

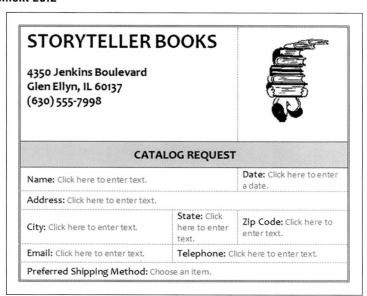

City: St. Charles
State: IL
Zip Code: 60125
Email: dhendrix@emcp.net
Telephone: (630) 555-3204
Preferred Shipping Method: *Choose* USPS Priority *from the drop-down list.*

6. Save the document with the name **C29-A02-SBHendrixCatReq**.
7. Print and then close **C29-A02-SBHendrixCatReq.docx**.

Assessment 29.3   Create and Fill in an Application Form

1. Open **ERCFundingApp.docx** and then save the document as a template in the Chapter29 folder on your storage medium and name the template **XXXERCFundAppTemplate.dotx**.
2. Enter the data in the appropriate cells and insert Legacy tools text and check box form fields in the template form as shown in Figure 29.17.
3. Protect the template and only allow filling in of the form (you do not need to enter a password).
4. Save and then close **XXXERCFundAppTemplate.dotx**.
5. Create a form document from the **XXXERCFundAppTemplate.dotx** template and insert the following data in the specified fields:
   Project Title: Quality Improvement Project
   Date: (*Insert current date*)
   Targeted Department: Pediatrics
   Department Manager: Angela Gilmore

Figure 29.17 Assessment 29.3

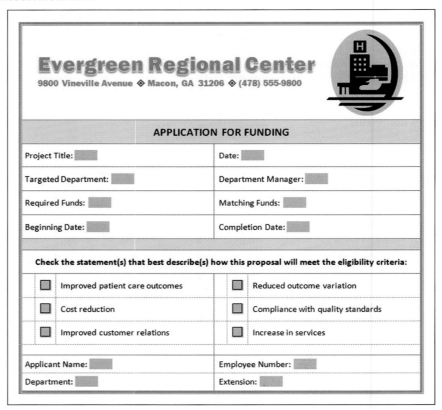

Required Funds: $50,000
Matching Funds: $25,000
Beginning Date: 07/01/2012
Completion Date: 06/30/2013
Insert an "X" in each of the check boxes except *Cost reduction*
Applicant Name: Maria Alvarez
Employee Number: 321-4890
Department: Pediatrics
Extension: 4539

6. Save the document with the name **C29-A03-FundApp**.
7. Print and then close **C29-A03-FundApp.docx**.

Assessment 29.4   Create and Fill in a Patient Update Form

1. Open **WCDSForm.docx** and then save the document as a template in the Chapter29 folder on your storage medium and name the template **XXXWCDSFormTemplate.dotx**.
2. Enter the data in the appropriate cells and insert the Legacy tools form fields in the form as shown in Figure 29.18 with the following specifications:
   a. Insert a text form field for *Patient Number:* that specifies a maximum length of 4.
   b. Insert a text form field for *State:* that specifies a maximum length of 2 characters and a text format of *Uppercase*.
   c. Insert a text form field for *Zip Code:* that specifies a maximum length of 5.

Figure 29.18 Assessment 29.4

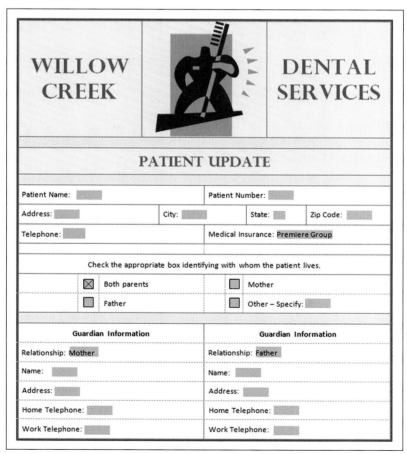

     d.   Insert a text form field for *Medical Insurance:* that specifies *Premiere Group* as the default text.

     e.   Insert a check box form field in the cell immediately left of *Both parents* that is checked by default.

     f.   Insert a text form field for the first *Relationship:* data field that specifies *Mother* as the default text.

     g.   Insert a text form field for the second *Relationship:* data field that specifies *Father* as the default text.

     h.   Insert the remaining text and check box form fields as shown in Figure 29.18.

3. Protect the template and only allow filling in of the form.
4. Save and then close **XXXWCDSFormTemplate.dotx**.
5. Create a form document from the **XXXWCDSFormTemplate.dotx** template and insert the following data in the specified fields:
          Patient Name: Ethan Mark Springer
          Patient Number: 4221
          Address: 345 Jackson Court
          City: Bismarck
          State: nd (This text will change to uppercase when you press Tab.)
          Zip Code: 58506
          Telephone: (701) 555-3481
          Medical Insurance: (*Leave the default* Premiere Group.)
          (*Leave the check mark in the* Both parents *check box.*)
          Relationship: (*Leave the default* Mother.)
          Relationship: (*Leave the default* Father.)
          Name: Elizabeth Springer
          Name: Chris Springer
          Address: 345 Jackson Court, Bismarck, ND 58506
          Address: 345 Jackson Court, Bismarck, ND 58506
          Home Telephone: (701) 555-3481
          Home Telephone: (701) 555-3481
          Work Telephone: (701) 555-8711
          Work Telephone: (701) 555-0075
6. Save the document with the name **C29-A04-ESpringer**.
7. Print and then close **C29-A04-ESpringer.docx**.

Expanding Your Skills

Explore additional feature options or use Help to learn a new skill in creating this document.

Assessment 29.5   Create a Client Information Form that Includes Building Block Gallery Content Controls

1. The Controls group in the Developer tab contains additional buttons you can use when creating a form. In addition to the Legacy Tools check box form field, you can insert a check box with the Check Box Content Control. Use the Building Block Gallery Content Control button to insert a content control for inserting building blocks in a form. Experiment with the Check Box Content Control and the Building Block Gallery Content Control buttons to determine how to use them in a form and then open **BGBuildingBlocks.docx** and create the following building blocks:

     a.   Select the name *Barrington & Gates*, the line below, and the text *Rachel Rasmussen, Associate* and then save the selected text in a custom building block in the Quick Part gallery named with your initials followed by *BGRR*.

   b. Select the text that begins *200 TENTH STREET…* and the line above (the text and line that display below Rachel Rasmussen) and then save the selected text in a custom building block in the Quick Part gallery named with your initials followed by *BGRRFooter*.

   c. Select the name *Barrington & Gates*, the line below, and the text *Gerald Castello, Associate* and then save the selected text in a custom building block in the Quick Part gallery named with your initials followed by *BGGC*.

   d. Select the text that begins *200 TENTH STREET…* and the line above (the text and line that display below Gerald Castello) and then save the selected text in a custom building block in the Quick Part gallery named with your initials followed by *BGGCFooter*.

   e. Close **BGBuildingBlocks.docx**.

2. Open **BGClientInfo.docx** and then save the document as a template in the Chapter29 folder on your storage medium and name the template **XXXBGClientInfo.dotx**.

3. Add the following form fields to the form:

   a. Make the top cell active and then insert the building block gallery content control.

   b. Make the bottom cell active and then insert the building block gallery content control.

   c. Insert check boxes (using the Check Box Content Control button) in the cell immediately left of the following cell entries: *Employee*, *Friend*, *Lawyer referral service*, *Yellow Pages*, *Internet*, and *Other*.

4. Since your template contains the building block gallery content control, you cannot protect the template and only allow filling in the form. Doing this would keep you from being able to use the building block content control. Save and then close **XXXBGClientInfo.dotx**.

5. Create a form document from the **XXXBGClientInfo.dotx** template with the following specifications:

   a. Click the building block content control in the top cell, click the Quick Parts button that displays at the right of the content control tab, and then click the *BGGC* building block that is preceded by your initials.

   b. Click the building block gallery content control in the bottom cell, click the Quick Parts button that displays at the right of the content control tab, and then click the *BGGCFooter* building block that is preceded by your initials.

   c. Fill in each of the text content controls by clicking the text *Click here to enter text* and then typing text of your choosing. Click only one of the check box content controls in the *Referred by* section.

6. Save the completed form document with the name **C29-A05-GC-Client**.

7. Print and then close **C29-A05-GC-Client.docx**.

8. Create a form document from the **XXXBGClientInfo.dotx** template with the following specifications:

   a. Click the building block content control in the top cell, click the Quick Parts button that displays at the right of the content control tab, and then click the *BGRR* building block that is preceded by your initials.

   b. Click the building block gallery content control in the bottom cell, click the Quick Parts button that displays at the right of the content control tab, and then click the *BGRRFooter* building block that is preceded by your initials.

   c. Fill in each of the text content controls by clicking the text *Click here to enter text* and then typing text of your choosing. Click only one of the check box content controls in the *Referred by* section.

9. Save the completed form document with the name **C29-A05-RR-Client**.

10. Print and then close **C29-A05-RR-Client.docx**.

Achieving Signature Status

Take your skills to the next level by completing these more challenging assessments.

Assessment 29.6   Create and Fill in an Application Form

1. Create the form shown in Figure 29.19 as a template and use the Table feature to create the columns and rows. Apply border and shading formatting as shown in the figure. Set the company name in Magneto and set the remaining text in Candara.
2. Insert a picture content control and insert the ***SSAviation.jpg*** image. Insert a date picker content control as well as plain text content controls in the appropriate cells. Insert drop-down list content controls for the two bottom rows in the table. Add the following choices for the *Desired license:* drop-down list content control: *Private, Commercial, Instrument,* and *Certified Flight Instructor.* Add the following choices for the *How did you hear about South Sound Aviation?* drop-down list content control: *Internet, Business card, Referral, Brochure,* or *Other.*
3. Save the document as a template in the Chapter29 folder on your storage medium and name the template **XXXApplicationTemplate.dotx**.
4. Protect the template and only allow filling in of the form.
5. Save and then close **XXXApplicationTemplate.dotx**.
6. Create a form document from the **XXXApplicationTemplate** template. You determine the data to enter in each data field.
7. Save the document with the name **C29-A06-FlightApp**.
8. Print and then close **C29-A06-FlightApp.docx**.

Figure 29.19 Assessment 29.6

Name:		Date:	
Address:			
City:	State:	Zip Code:	
Email:	Home Phone:	Cell Phone:	
Desired license:			
How did you hear about South Sound Aviation?			

Assessment 29.7   Create and Fill in a Secondary Payer Form

1. Create the form template and form fields shown in Figure 29.20 with the following specifications:
   a. Consider using **ERCFundingApp.docx** to help you create the form shown in Figure 29.20. (Make sure gridlines display.)
   b. Create data fields, cells, shading, and other formatting as shown in Figure 29.20.
   c. Consider specifying text form field options for the *State:* and *Zip Code:* data fields.
2. Save the document as a template in the Chapter29 folder on your storage medium and name the template **XXXERCInsFormTemplate.dotx**.
3. Protect the template and only allow filling in of the form.
4. Save and then close **XXXERCInsFormTemplate.dotx**.
5. Create a form document from the **XXXERCInsFormTemplate.dotx** template and insert data of your choosing in each of the data fields.
6. Save the document with the name **C29-A07-InsForm**.
7. Print and then close **C29-A07-InsForm.docx**.

Figure 29.20 Assessment 29.7

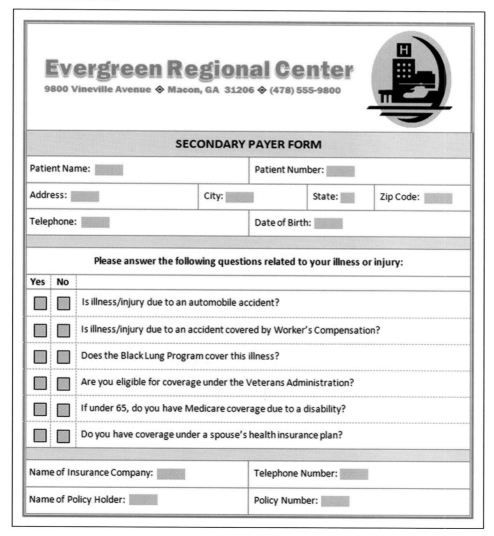

 **TUTORIALS**

Tutorial 30.1
Creating and Organizing an
Outline
Tutorial 30.2
Creating a Master Document
and Subdocuments
Tutorial 30.3
Recording and Running Macros

Using Outline View and Formatting with Macros

Performance Objectives

Upon successful completion of Chapter 30, you will be able to:

- Display a document in Outline view
- Assign levels in an outline
- Collapse and expand outline headings
- Create a master document and subdocuments
- Expand, collapse, open, close, rearrange, split, and delete subdocuments

- Record, run, pause, and delete macros
- Assign a macro to a keyboard command
- Assign a macro to the Quick Access toolbar
- Record and run a macro with Fill-in fields

Use the outline feature in Word to view specific titles, headings, and body text in a document. With the outline feature you can quickly see an overview of a document by collapsing parts of a document so that only specific titles and headings display. With titles and headings collapsed, you can perform such editing functions as moving or deleting sections of a document. For some documents, such as a book or procedures manual, consider creating a master document. A master document contains a number of separate documents called subdocuments.

Word includes a time-saving feature called *macros* that automates the formatting of a document. The word *macro* was coined by computer programmers for a collection of commands used to make a large programming job easier and save time. Two basic steps are involved in working with macros—recording a macro and running a macro. When you record a macro, all of the keys pressed and the menus and dialog boxes displayed are recorded and become part of the macro. After a macro is recorded, you can run the macro to apply the macro formatting.

Note: Before beginning computer exercises, copy to your storage medium the Chapter30 folder located on the CD that accompanies this textbook and then make Chapter30 the active folder.

In this chapter, students will produce the following documents:

Exercise 30.1 C30-E01-InternetSecurity.docx
Exercise 30.2 C30-E02-CompViruses.docx
Exercise 30.3A (Step 3) C30-E03-Newsletters.docx
Exercise 30.3B (Step 6) C30-E03-Newsletters.docx
Exercise 30.4 C30-E04-ResumeStandards.docx

Exercise 30.4 C30-E04-WriteResume.docx
Exercise 30.5 C30-E05-GSHLtr.docx
Exercise 30.6 C30-E06-TofC.docx
Exercise 30.7 C30-E07-Affidavit.docx

Model answers for these exercises are shown on the following pages.

UNAUTHORIZED ACCESS
    User IDs and Passwords
    System Backdoors
    Spyware
INFORMATION THEFT
    Device Security
    Data Browsing

Exercise 30.1

C30-E01-InternetSecurity.docx

HARDWARE AND SOFTWARE SECURITY RISKS
    Cracking Software for Copying
    Systems Failure
COMPUTER VIRUSES
    Types of Viruses
    Methods of Virus Operation

Exercise 30.2

C30-E02-CompViruses.docx

Exercise 30.3A (Step 3)
C30-E03-Newsletters.docx

SECTION A: NEWSLETTERS
Preparing a newsletter requires a number of preliminary steps. Before determining the contents of the newsletter, determine the basic elements to be included in the newsletter, study newsletter design, and determine the purpose of the newsletter.

G:\Chapter30\MODULE 1.docx

G:\Chapter30\MODULE 2.docx

G:\Chapter30\MODULE 4.docx

G:\Chapter30\MODULE 3.docx

SECTION A: NEWSLETTERS
Preparing a newsletter requires a number of preliminary steps. Before determining the contents of the newsletter, determine the basic elements to be included in the newsletter, study newsletter design, and determine the purpose of the newsletter.

G:\Chapter30\MODULE 1.docx

G:\Chapter30\MODULE 5.docx

G:\Chapter30\MODULE 2.docx

G:\Chapter30\MODULE 4.docx

Exercise 30.3B (Step 6)
C30-E03-Newsletters.docx

RESUME PRESENTATION STANDARDS

Presentation focuses on the way your resume looks. It relates to the fonts you use, the paper you print it on, any graphics you might include, and how many pages your resume should be.

Typestyle

Use a typestyle (font) that is clean, conservative, and easy to read. Stay away from anything that is too fancy, glitzy, curly, and the like. Your goal is to create a competitive-distinctive document and, to achieve that, we recommend an alternative typestyle. Your choice of typestyle should be dictated by the content, format, and length of your resume. Some fonts look better than others at smaller or larger sizes; some have "bolder" boldface type; some require more white space to make them readable. Once you have written your resume, experiment with a few different typestyles to see which one best enhances your document.

Type Size

Readability is everything! If the type size is too small, your resume will be difficult to read and difficult to skim for essential information. Interestingly, a too-large type size, particularly for senior-level professionals, can also give a negative impression by conveying a juvenile or unprofessional image. As a general rule, select type from 10 to 12 points in size. However, there is no hard-and-fast rule, and a lot depends on the typestyle you choose.

Type Enhancements

Bold, italics, underlining, and capitalization are ideal to highlight certain words, phrases, achievements, projects, numbers, and other information to which you want to draw special attention. However, do not overuse these enhancements. If your resume becomes too cluttered with special formatting, nothing stands out.

Page Length

For most industries and professions, the "one- to to-page rule" for resume writing still holds true. Keep it short and succinct, giving just enough information to pique your reader's interest. However, there are many instances when a resume can be longer than two pages.

You have an extensive list of technical qualifications that are relevant to the position for which you are applying.

You have extensive educational training and numerous credential/certifications, all of which are important to include.

You have an extensive list of special projects, task forces, and committees to include that are important to your current career objectives.

Exercise 30.4 C30-E04-Resume.docx

You have an extensive list of professional honors, awards, and commendations.

Paper Color

Be conservative with your paper color choice. White, ivory, and light gray are ideal. Other "flashier" colors are inappropriate for most individuals unless you are in a highly creative industry and your paper choice is part of the overall design and presentation of a creative resume.

Graphics

An attractive, relevant graphic can really enhance your resume. Just be sure not to get carried away; be tasteful and relatively conservative.

White Space

Readability in a resume is everything. If people have to struggle to read your resume, they simply won't make the effort. Therefore, be sure to leave plenty of white space. It really does make a difference.

Resume Strategies

Following are core strategies for writing an effective and successful resume:

1. Who are you and how do you want to be perceived?
2. Sell it to me ... don't tell it to me.
3. Use keywords.
4. Use the "big" and save the "little."
5. Make your resume "interviewable."
6. Eliminate confusion with structure and content.
7. Use function to demonstrate achievement.
8. Remain in the realm of reality.
9. Be confident.

Writing Style

Always write in the first person, dropping the word "I" from the front of each sentence. This style gives your resume a more aggressive and more professional tone than the passive, third-person voice. Here are some examples:

First Person:

Manage 22-person team responsible for design and marketing of a new portfolio of PC-based applications for Landmark's consumer-sales division.

Third Person:

Ms. Sanderson manages a 22-person team responsible for design and marketing of a new portfolio of PC-based application for Landmark's consumer-sales division.

Phrases to Avoid

Try not to use phrases such as "responsible for" and "duties included." These words create a passive tone and style. Instead, use active verbs to describe what you did. Compare these two ways of conveying the same information:

Responsible for all marketing and special events for the store, including direct mailing, in-store fashion shows, and new-product introductions and promotions.

Orchestrated a series of marketing and special-event programs for McGregor's, one of the company's largest and most profitable operating locations. Managed direct-mail campaigns, in-store fashion shows, and new-product introductions and promotions.

Exercise 30.4 C30-E04-WriteResume.docx

ST. FRANCIS HOSPITAL

May 12, 2010

Mr. Victor Durham
Good Samaritan Hospital
1201 James Street
St. Louis, MO 62033

Dear Victor:

Congratulations on obtaining eight new registered nurse positions at your hospital. The attached registered nurse job description is generic. Depending on the specialty, you may want to include additional responsibilities:

Procedural

- Uses the nursing process to prescribe, coordinate, and delegate patient care from admission through discharge.
- Analyzes the patient's condition and reports changes to the appropriate health care provider.
- Observes patient for signs and symptoms, collects data on patient, and reports and documents results.

Teaching

- Teaches patient, family, staff, and students.
- Assumes responsibility for patient and family teaching and discharge planning.
- Participates in orientation of new staff and/or acts as preceptor.

I am interested in hearing about your recruitment plan. We are hiring additional medical personnel in the fall at St. Francis, and I need to begin formulating a recruitment plan.

Sincerely,

Marcus Knowles

XX
C30-E05-GSHLtr.docx

3500 MEEKER BOULEVARD ☙ REDFIELD, NE 68304 ☙ 308-555-5000

Exercise 30.5 30-E05-GSHLtr.docx

Exercise 30.6

C30-E06-TofC.docx

COMPUTER CONCEPTS

Computer Hardware..3

    Types of Computers 4

    Hardware Components 8

Computer Software..14

    Operating Systems...16

    Application Software 20

Networking...25

    Types of Networks...27

    Uses of Networks 30

    Network Topologies...34

AFFIDAVIT OF TRUST

1. The name of the currently acting Trustee is LOREN HOUSTON.

2. The address of the currently acting Trustee is 102 Marine Drive, Los Angeles, CA.

3. The trust is currently in full force and effect.

4. Attached to this Affidavit and incorporated in it are selected provisions of the trust evidencing the following:
   a. Article One: Creation of the trust and initial Trustee
   b. Article Four: Statement of revocability of the trust
   c. Article Fifteen: Successor Trustees
   d. Article Seventeen: Powers of the Trustee

5. The trust provisions, which are not attached to this Affidavit, are of a personal nature and set forth the distribution of trust property. They do not modify the powers of the Trustee.

6. The signatory of this Affidavit is currently the acting Trustee of the trust and declares that the foregoing statements and the attached trust provisions are true and correct, under penalty of perjury.

_____
LOREN HOUSTON

STATE OF CALIFORNIA   )
) ss.
COUNTY OF LOS ANGELES)

      On this day personally appeared before me LOREN HOUSTON, known to me to be the individual described in and who executed the aforesaid instrument, and acknowledged that he/she signed as his/her free and voluntary act and deed for the uses and purposes therein mentioned.
      Given under my hand and official seal this 8th day of March, 2012.

_____
NOTARY PUBLIC in and for the State of California
My appointment expires 12/31/2013

Exercise 30.7

C30-E07-Affidavit.docx

Creating an Outline

To create an outline, you identify particular titles, headings, and subheadings within a document as certain levels. Use Outline view to assign particular levels to text. You can also enter text and edit text while working in Outline view. To switch to Outline view, click the View tab and then click the Outline button in the Document Views group. Figure 30.1 shows a document in Outline view with levels assigned to the title and headings. The figure also identifies the Outlining tab that contains options and buttons for working in Outline view.

Figure 30.1 Document in Outline View

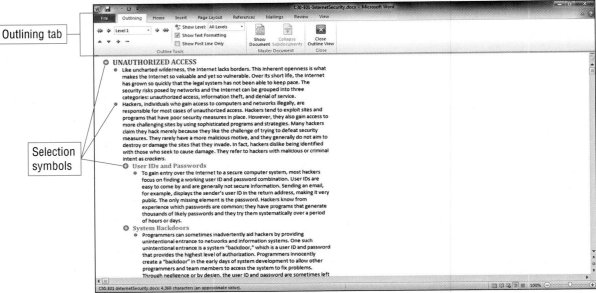

In Figure 30.1, the title *UNAUTHORIZED ACCESS* is identified as a level 1 heading, the heading *User IDs and Passwords* is identified as a level 2 heading, and the paragraph following is identified as body text. The title and headings shown in Figure 30.1 display preceded by a selection symbol (round button containing a plus symbol). Click this symbol to select text in that particular heading.

Assigning Headings

If a title or heading style has not been applied to the title and headings in a document, all text in the document is identified as body text in Outline view. In Outline view, you can assign levels to text in a document using buttons in the Outline Tools group in the Outlining tab. These buttons are described in Table 30.1.

Table 30.1 Outlining Tab Buttons

Button	Name	Action
◄◄	Promote to Heading 1	Promotes text to highest level of the outline.
◄	Promote	Promotes heading (and its body text) by one level; promotes body text to the heading level of the preceding heading.
Level 1 ▼	Outline Level	Assigns and displays current level of text.
►	Demote	Demotes heading by one level; demotes body text to the heading level below the preceding heading.
►►	Demote to Body Text	Demotes heading to body text.
▲	Move Up	Move selected item up within the outline.
▼	Move Down	Move selected item down within the outline.
＋	Expand	Expands first heading level below currently selected heading.
－	Collapse	Collapses body text into heading and then collapses lowest heading levels into higher heading levels.
Show Level: All Levels ▼	Show Level	Displays all headings through lowest level chosen.
☑ Show Text Formatting	Show Text Formatting	Displays outline with or without character formatting.
☐ Show First Line Only	Show First Line Only	Switches between displaying all body text or only first line of each paragraph.

To change a heading that is identified as normal text to a level 1 heading, position the insertion point on any character in the heading and then click the Promote to Heading 1 button in the Outline Tools group in the Outlining tab. This applies the Heading 1 style to the heading. To change a paragraph to a level 2 heading, position the insertion point anywhere within the text and then click the Demote button. This applies the Heading 2 style to the text.

1. Open **InternetSecurity.docx** and save the document with the name **C30-E01-InternetSecurity**.
2. Change to Outline view by clicking the View tab and then clicking the Outline button in the Document Views group.

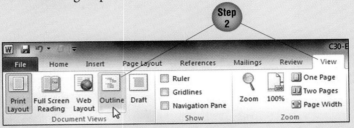

Step 2

3. Promote and demote heading levels by completing the following steps:
   a. Position the insertion point anywhere in the title *UNAUTHORIZED ACCESS* and then click the Promote to Heading 1 button in the Outline Tools group in the Outlining tab. (This displays *Level 1* in the Outline Level button.)
   b. Position the insertion point anywhere in the heading *User IDs and Passwords* and then click the Demote button in the Outline Tools group. (This displays *Level 2* in the Outline Level button.)
   c. Position the insertion point anywhere in the heading *System Backdoors* and then click the Promote button in the Outline Tools group.
   d. Position the insertion point anywhere in the heading *Spoofing* and then click the Promote button in the Outline Tools group.
   e. Position the insertion point anywhere in the heading *Spyware* and then click the Promote button.
4. Save **C30-E01-InternetSecurity.docx**.

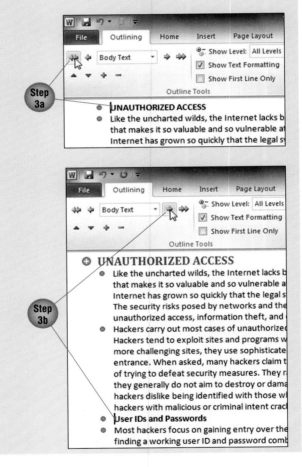

Step 3a

Step 3b

You can also promote or demote a heading in the Outline view by dragging the selection symbol that displays before the heading to the left or right 0.5 inch. The selection symbol for a level heading displays as a circle containing a plus symbol, and the selection symbol for body text displays as a circle. For example, to demote text identified as level 1 to level 2, position the arrow pointer on the selection symbol (circle containing a plus symbol) that displays before the level 1 text until the pointer turns into a four-headed arrow. Hold down the left mouse button, drag the mouse to the right until a gray vertical line displays down the screen, and then release the mouse button. Complete similar steps to promote a heading. You can also promote a heading with the keyboard shortcut Alt + Shift + Left Arrow key, and demote a heading with Alt + Shift + Right Arrow key.

Exercise 30.1B Promoting and Demoting Headings in a Document Part 2 of 3

1. With **C30-E01-InternetSecurity.docx** open and displayed in Outline view, promote the section 2 title to level 1 by completing the following steps:
   a. Position the mouse pointer on the selection symbol (small, gray circle) that displays before the title *INFORMATION THEFT* until the mouse pointer turns into a four-headed arrow.
   b. Hold down the left mouse button, drag the mouse to the left until a gray vertical line displays toward the left side of the page as shown in the image below, and then release the mouse button. (Check to make sure *Level 1* displays in the Outline Level button.)

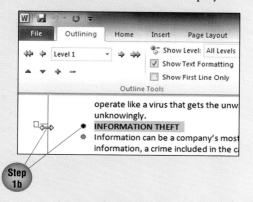

2. Promote the *Device Security* heading to level 2 by completing the following steps:
   a. Position the mouse pointer on the selection symbol (small, gray circle) that displays before the *Device Security* heading until the mouse pointer turns into a four-headed arrow.
   b. Hold down the left mouse button, drag the mouse to the right until a gray vertical line displays as shown in the image at the right, and then release the mouse button. (Check to make sure *Level 2* displays in the Outline Level button.)

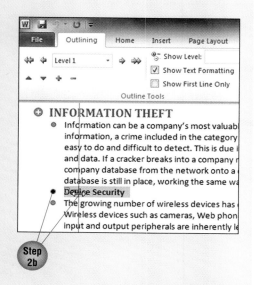

3. Promote the heading *Data Browsing* to level 2 by positioning the insertion point anywhere in the heading and then pressing Alt + Shift + Left Arrow key.

4. Save **C30-E01-InternetSecurity.docx**.

Collapsing and Expanding a Document

One of the major benefits of working in Outline view is the ability to see a condensed outline of your document without all of the text in between titles, headings, or subheadings. Word lets you collapse a level in an outline so any text or subsequent lower levels disappear temporarily. When you collapse levels, viewing the outline of a document is much easier. For example, when an outline is collapsed, you can see an overview of the entire document and move easily to different locations in the document. You can also move titles and headings and their subordinate headings to new locations in the outline.

The ability to collapse and expand headings in an outline provides flexibility in using the outline feature. One popular use of this capability is to move quickly from one portion of a document to another. For example, if you are working at the beginning of a lengthy document and want to move to a particular section, but you cannot remember the name of the heading in that section or the page number on which it is located, switch to Outline view, collapse the entire outline, position the insertion point in the desired heading, and then expand the outline.

Another popular use of the collapse and expand feature is in maintaining consistency between various headings. While creating a particular heading, you may need to refer to the previous heading. To do this, switch to Outline view, collapse the outline, and the previous heading is visible.

To collapse the entire document, click the down-pointing arrow at the right of the Show Level button in the Outline Tools group in the Outlining tab and then click the level desired at the drop-down list. For example, if the document contains three levels, click *Level 3* at the drop-down list. Figure 30.2 shows the **C30-E01-InternetSecurity. docx** document collapsed so only titles and headings display. When a title or heading containing text below it is collapsed, a gray horizontal line displays beneath the heading (as shown in Figure 30.2).

Figure 30.2 Collapsed Document

1. With **C30-E01-InternetSecurity.docx** open, make sure the document displays in Outline view and then press Ctrl + Home to move the insertion point to the beginning of the document.
2. Click the down-pointing arrow at the right of the Show Level button in the Outline Tools group and then click *Level 2* at the drop-down list.

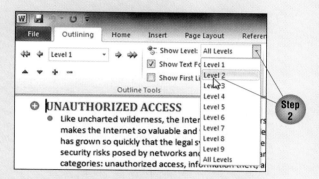

3. With the outline collapsed, click the selection symbol that displays before *Spoofing* and then press the Delete key. (This deletes the heading and text below the heading.)
4. Save and then print **C30-E01-InternetSecurity.docx**. (This will print the collapsed outline, not the entire document.)
5. Click the Close Outline View button.
6. Close **C30-E01-InternetSecurity.docx**.

To collapse all of the text beneath a particular heading (including the text following any subsequent headings), position the insertion point within the heading, and then click the Collapse button in the Outline Tools group in the Outlining tab. To make the text appear again, click the Expand button in the Outline Tools group.

1. Open **CompViruses.docx** and save the document with the name **C30-E02-CompViruses**.
2. Click the View tab and then click the Outline button in the Document Views group.
3. Promote and demote the headings in the document.
   a. Promote the title *COMPUTER VIRUSES* to level 1.
   b. Demote the heading *Types of Viruses* to level 2.
   c. Promote the heading *Methods of Virus Operation* to level 2.
   d. Promote the title *HARDWARE AND SOFTWARE SECURITY RISKS* to level 1.
   e. Demote the heading *Systems Failure* to level 2.
   f. Promote the heading *Employee Theft* to level 2.
   g. Promote the heading *Cracking Software for Copying* to level 2.

4. Collapse and expand the document by completing the following steps:
   a. Position the insertion point anywhere in the title *COMPUTER VIRUSES* and then click the Collapse button in the Outline Tools group in the Outlining tab. (This collapses the text in the first section so only the title and headings display.)

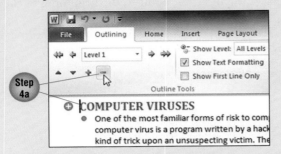

   b. Click the Expand button to expand the display of the text in the first section.
   c. With the insertion point still positioned anywhere in the title *COMPUTER VIRUSES*, click the down-pointing arrow at the right of the Show Level button and then click *Level 1* at the drop-down list. (This displays only the two titles.)

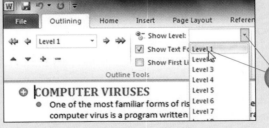

   d. Click the down-pointing arrow at the right of the Show Level button and then click *Level 2* at the drop-down list. (This displays the titles and headings.)
   e. Click the Expand button in the Outline Tools group.
   f. Click the *Show First Line Only* check box in the Outline Tools group to insert a check mark. (This displays only the level headings and the first line of each paragraph in the document.)
   g. Click the *Show First Line Only* check box to remove the check mark.
   h. Click the down-pointing arrow at the right of the Show Level button and then click *Level 2* at the drop-down list. (This displays the titles and headings.)

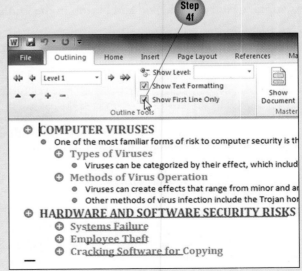

i. Click the selection symbol that precedes *Employee Theft*.
j. With the heading selected, press the Delete key. (This deletes the heading and all text below the heading.)
k. Save and then print **C30-E02-CompViruses.docx**. (This will print the collapsed outline, not the entire document.)
l. Click the down-pointing arrow at the right of the Show Level button and then click *All Levels* at the drop-down list. (This displays the entire document.)
5. Save **C30-E02-CompViruses.docx**.

Organizing an Outline

Collapsing and expanding headings within an outline is only part of the versatility the outline feature offers. It also offers you the ability to rearrange an entire document by reorganizing the outline. Whole sections of a document can quickly be rearranged by moving the headings at the beginning of those sections. The text that is collapsed beneath the headings is moved at the same time.

For example, to move a level 2 heading below other level 2 headings, you would collapse the outline, select the level 2 heading to be moved, and then click the Move Down button in the Outline Tools group until the level 2 heading is in the desired position.

If headings are collapsed, you only need to select the heading and move it to the desired location. Any subsequent text that is hidden is moved automatically. You can also move headings in a document by positioning the mouse pointer on the selection symbol that displays before the desired heading until the pointer turns into a four-headed arrow. Hold down the mouse, drag the heading to the desired location, and then release the mouse button. As you drag the mouse, a gray horizontal line displays in the document with an arrow attached. Use this horizontal line to help you move the heading to the desired location.

Exercise 30.2B   **Moving Headings in a Document**   **Part 2 of 2**

1. With **C30-E02-CompViruses.docx** open, make sure the document displays in Outline view, and then press Ctrl + Home to move the insertion point to the beginning of the document.
2. Click the down-pointing arrow at the right of the Show Level button and then click *Level 1* at the drop-down list.
3. Move the *HARDWARE AND SOFTWARE SECURITY RISKS* section to the beginning of the document by completing the following steps:
   a. Click any character in the title *HARDWARE AND SOFTWARE SECURITY RISKS*.
   b. Click the Move Up button in the Outline Tools group in the Outlining tab.

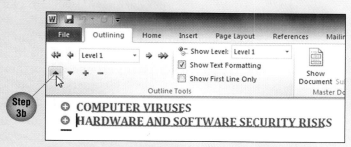

4. Move the heading *Systems Failure* below *Cracking Software* by completing the following steps:
   a. Click the down-pointing arrow at the right of the Show Level button and then click *Level 2* at the drop-down list.
   b. Position the mouse pointer on the selection symbol that precedes the heading *Systems Failure* until the pointer turns into a four-headed arrow.
   c. Hold down the left mouse button, drag the mouse down until the gray horizontal line with the arrow attached is positioned below *Cracking Software for Copying*, and then release the mouse button.
   d. Deselect the text.

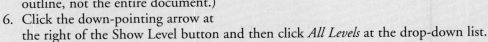

5. Save and then print **C30-E02-CompViruses.docx**. (This will print the collapsed outline, not the entire document.)
6. Click the down-pointing arrow at the right of the Show Level button and then click *All Levels* at the drop-down list.
7. Click the Close Outline View button.
8. Delete the blank line above the heading *Systems Failure*.
9. Save and then close **C30-E02-CompViruses.docx**.

Creating a Master Document and Subdocuments

For projects containing a variety of parts or sections, such as a reference guide or book, consider using a *master document*. A master document contains a number of separate documents referred to as *subdocuments*. A master document might be useful in a situation where several people are working on one project. Each person prepares a document for his or her part of the project and then the documents are included in a master document. A master document allows for easier editing of subdocuments. Rather than opening a large document for editing, you can open a subdocument, make changes, and those changes are reflected in the master document. Create a new master document or format an existing document as a master document with buttons in the Master Document group in the Outlining tab.

Creating a Master Document

To create a master document, switch to Outline view, assign heading levels to titles and headings in the document, and then click the Show Document button in the Master Document group. Select the headings and text to be divided into a subdocument and then click the Create button in the Master Document group. Text specified as a subdocument displays surrounded by a thin, gray line border and a subdocument icon displays in the upper left corner of the border.

Word creates a subdocument for each heading at the top level within the selected text. For example, if selected text begins with Heading 1 text, Word creates a new subdocument at each Heading 1 in the selected text. Save the master document in the same manner as a normal document. Word automatically assigns a document name to each subdocument using the first characters in the subdocument heading.

Opening and Closing a Master Document and its Subdocuments

Open a master document at the Open dialog box in the same manner as a normal document. Subdocuments in a master document display collapsed in the master document as shown in Figure 30.3. This figure displays the master document named **C30-E03-Newsletters.docx** that you will create in Exercise 30.3A. Notice that Word automatically converts subdocument names into hyperlinks. To open a subdocument, hold down the Ctrl key and then click the subdocument hyperlink.

Figure 30.3 C30-E03-Newsletters.docx

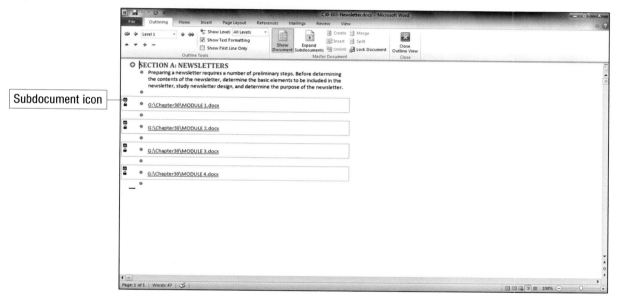

Close a subdocument in the normal manner and, if you made any changes, you will be asked if you want to save the changes. Closing a subdocument redisplays the master document and the subdocument hyperlink displays in a different color (identifying that the hyperlink has been used).

Expanding/Collapsing Subdocuments

Open a master document, and its subdocuments are automatically collapsed. To expand subdocuments, click the Expand Subdocuments button in the Master Document group in the Outlining tab. This expands the subdocuments and also changes the Expand Subdocuments button to the Collapse Subdocuments button.

1. At a blank document, type the text shown in Figure 30.4. (Press the Enter key after typing the text.)
2. With the insertion point positioned at the end of the document, insert the document named **NewsletterElements.docx**. (Do this with the Object button in the Insert tab.)
3. With the insertion point positioned at the end of the document, insert the document named **NewsletterDesign.docx**. (Do this with the Object button in the Insert tab.)
4. Move the insertion point to the beginning of the document.
5. Change to Outline view.
6. Promote or demote the headings in the document as identified below:

SECTION A: NEWSLETTERS	=	Level 1
MODULE 1: DEFINING NEWSLETTER ELEMENTS	=	Level 2
Designing a Newsletter	=	Level 3
Defining Basic Newsletter Elements	=	Level 3
MODULE 2: PLANNING A NEWSLETTER	=	Level 2
Defining the Purpose of a Newsletter	=	Level 3
MODULE 3: DESIGNING A NEWSLETTER	=	Level 2
Applying Desktop Publishing Guidelines	=	Level 3
MODULE 4: CREATING NEWSLETTER LAYOUT	=	Level 2
Choosing Paper Size and Type	=	Level 3
Choosing Paper Weight	=	Level 3
Creating Margins for Newsletters	=	Level 3

7. Save the document and name it **C30-E03-Newsletters**.
8. Create subdocuments with the module text by completing the following steps:

   a. Position the mouse pointer on the selection symbol that displays immediately left of the heading *MODULE 1: DEFINING NEWSLETTER ELEMENTS* until the pointer turns into a four-headed arrow and then click the left mouse button.

   b. Scroll through the document until the *MODULE 4: CREATING NEWSLETTER LAYOUT* heading displays.

   c. Hold down the Shift key, position the mouse pointer on the selection symbol immediately left of the heading until the pointer turns into a four-headed arrow, and then click the left mouse button. (This selects all of the text in modules 1, 2, 3, and 4.)

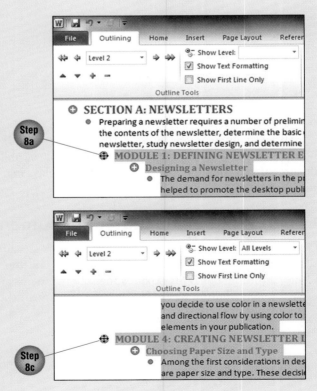

d. With the text selected, click the Show Document button in the Master Document group in the Outlining tab.

e. Click the Create button in the Master Document group.

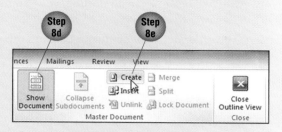

Step 8d   Step 8e

9. Save and then close **C30-E03-Newsletters.docx**.

10. Open **C30-E03-Newsletters.docx**.

11. Print **C30-E03-Newsletters.docx**. At the question asking if you want to open the subdocuments, click No. (The document will print collapsed, as displayed on-screen.)

12. Edit the MODULE 1 subdocument by completing the following steps:

a. Hold down the Ctrl key and then click the G:\Chapter30\MODULE 1.docx hyperlink.

b. With the **MODULE 1.docx** document displayed, edit the title so it reads *MODULE 1: DEFINING ELEMENTS*.

c. Change the heading *Designing a Newsletter* so it displays as *Designing*.

d. Change the heading *Defining Basic Newsletter Elements* so it displays as *Defining Basic Elements*.

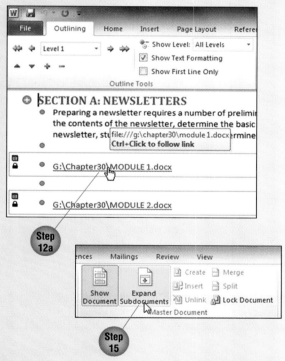

Step 12a

Step 15

13. Save the subdocument by clicking the Save button on the Quick Access toolbar.

14. Close the subdocument.

15. Expand the subdocuments by clicking the Expand Subdocuments button in the Master Document group in the Outlining tab.

16. Print page one of the master document.

17. Collapse the subdocuments by clicking the Collapse Subdocuments button in the Master Document group in the Outlining tab.

18. Save and then close **C30-E03-Newsletters.docx**.

Figure 30.4 Exercise 30.3A

SECTION A: NEWSLETTERS

Preparing a newsletter requires a number of preliminary steps. Before determining the contents of the newsletter, determine the basic elements to be included in the newsletter, study newsletter design, and determine the purpose of the newsletter.

Rearranging Subdocuments

Many of the features of a master document are similar to an outline. For example, expanding and collapsing an outline is very similar to expanding and collapsing subdocuments. Also, like headings in an outline, you can move or rearrange subdocuments in a master document.

To rearrange the order of a subdocument, collapse the subdocuments. Position the mouse pointer on the subdocument icon, hold down the left mouse button (mouse pointer turns into a four-headed arrow), drag to the desired location, and then release the mouse button. As you drag with the mouse, a dark gray, horizontal line displays identifying where the subdocument will be inserted.

When moving a collapsed subdocument, the dark gray, horizontal line must be positioned above the gray circle that displays above a subdocument. If you position the dark gray, horizontal line between the gray circle and the top border of a collapsed subdocument, Word will display a message telling you that you cannot change a locked subdocument or master document. With the dark gray, horizontal line positioned immediately above the subdocument border, Word assumes you want to insert the selected subdocument into the subdocument. Word will not allow this because subdocuments are locked.

Splitting or Combining Subdocuments

You can split a subdocument into smaller subdocuments or combine subdocuments into one. To split a subdocument, first expand subdocuments, select the specific text within the subdocument, and then click the Split button in the Master Document group in the Outlining tab. Word assigns a document name based on the first characters in the subdocument heading.

To combine subdocuments, first expand subdocuments and then click the subdocument icon of the first subdocument to be combined. Hold down the Shift key and then click the subdocument icon of the last subdocument (subdocuments must be adjacent). With the subdocuments selected, click the Merge button in the Master Document group. Word saves the combined subdocuments with the name of the first subdocument.

Exercise 30.3B Rearranging and Splitting Subdocuments   Part 2 of 2

1. Open **C30-E03-Newsletters.docx**.
2. Move the Module 4 subdocument above the Module 3 subdocument by completing the following steps:
   a. Position the arrow pointer on the subdocument icon that displays to the left of the G:\Chapter30\MODULE 4.docx subdocument. (The pointer turns into an arrow pointing up and to the right.)

b. Hold down the left mouse button, drag up so the dark gray, horizontal line displays between the MODULE 2 and MODULE 3 subdocuments (above the gray circle between the modules), and then release the mouse button.

3. Print **C30-E03-Newsletters.docx**. (At the prompt asking if you want to open the subdocuments, click No.)
4. Delete the G:\Chapter30\MODULE 3.docx subdocument by completing the following steps:
   a. Click the subdocument icon that displays to the left of the G:\Chapter30\MODULE 3.docx subdocument.
   b. Press the Delete key.
5. Split the MODULE 1 subdocument by completing the following steps:
   a. Click the Expand Subdocuments button in the Master Document group in the Outlining tab.
   b. Move the insertion point to the MODULE 1 subdocument.
   c. In the MODULE 1 subdocument, edit the heading *Defining Basic Elements* so it displays as *MODULE 2: DEFINING BASIC ELEMENTS*. (You may need to scroll down the document to display this heading.)
   d. Change the level of the heading *MODULE 2: DEFINING BASIC ELEMENTS* from level 3 to level 2.
   e. Position the mouse pointer on the selection symbol that displays immediately left of the heading *MODULE 2: DEFINING BASIC ELEMENTS* until the pointer turns into a four-headed arrow and then click the left mouse button.

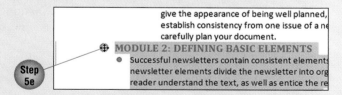

   f. With the text selected, click the Split button in the Master Document group in the Outlining tab.
   g. Click the Collapse Subdocuments button in the Master Document group. At the question asking if you want to save the changes to the master document, click OK.

6. Save and then print **C30-E03-Newsletters.docx**. (The master document will print with the subdocuments collapsed.)
7. Close **C30-E03-Newsletters.docx**.

Recording a Macro

Recording a macro involves turning on the macro recorder, performing the steps to be recorded, and then turning off the recorder. Both the View tab and the Developer tab contain buttons for recording a macro. If the Developer tab does not appear in the Ribbon, turn on the display by opening the Word Options dialog box, inserting a check mark in the *Developer* check box in the list box at the right, and then clicking OK to close the dialog box.

To record a macro, click the Record Macro button in the Code group in the Developer tab. You can also click the View tab, click the Macros button arrow in the Macros group, and then click *Record Macro* at the drop-down list. This displays the Record Macro dialog box shown in Figure 30.5. At the Record Macro dialog box, type a name for the macro in the *Macro name* text box. A macro name must begin with a letter and can contain only letters and numbers. Type a description for the macro in the *Description* text box located at the bottom of the dialog box. A macro description can contain a maximum of 255 characters and may include spaces.

By default, Word stores a macro in the Normal template. Macros stored in this template are available for any document based on the Normal template. In a company or school setting where computers may be networked, consider storing macros in personalized documents or templates. Specify the location for macros with the *Store macro in* option at the Record Macro dialog box (refer to Figure 30.5).

After typing the macro name, specifying where the macro is to be stored, and typing a description, click OK or press the Enter key to close the Record Macro dialog box. At the open document, a Macro icon displays toward the left side of the Status bar, and the mouse displays with a Cassette icon attached. In the document, perform the actions to be recorded, and when the steps are complete, click the Stop Recording button (previously the Record Macro button) located in the Code group in the Developer tab or click the Macro icon that displays toward the left side of the Status bar.

When you record macros in exercises, you will be instructed to name the macros beginning with your initials. An exercise step may instruct you, for example, to "record a macro named XXXInd01." Insert your initials in the macro name instead of the *XXX*. Recorded macros are stored in the Normal template document by default and display at the Macros dialog box. If the computer you are using is networked, macros recorded by other students will also display at the Macros dialog box. Naming a macro with your initials will enable you to distinguish your macros from the macros of other users.

Figure 30.5 Record Macro Dialog Box

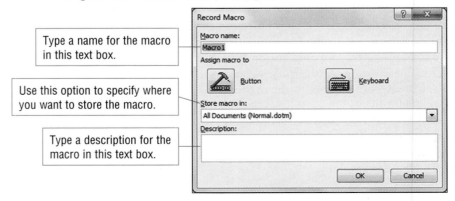

Type a name for the macro in this text box.

Use this option to specify where you want to store the macro.

Type a description for the macro in this text box.

1. Turn on the display of the Developer tab by completing the following steps (skip these steps if the Developer tab is visible.)
   a. Click the File tab and then click the Options button.
   b. At the Word Options dialog box, click *Customize Ribbon* in the left panel.
   c. In the list box at the right, click the *Developer* check box to insert a check mark.

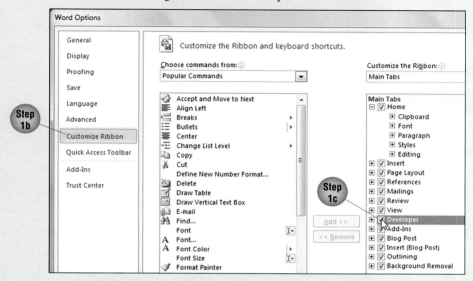

   d. Click OK to close the dialog box.
2. Record a macro that selects text and then indents a paragraph of text and applies italic formatting by completing the following steps:
   a. Open **MacroText.docx** and then position the insertion point at the left margin of the paragraph that begins with *This is text to use for creating macros.*
   b. Click the Developer tab.
   c. Click the Record Macro button in the Code group in the Developer tab.

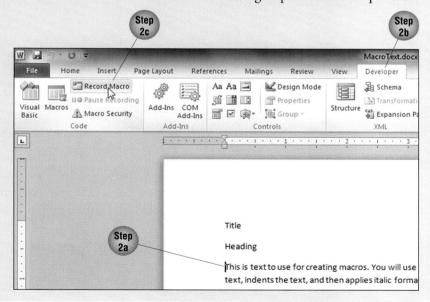

d. At the Record Macro dialog box, type XXXIndentItalics in the *Macro name* text box (type your initials in place of the *XXX*).

e. Click inside the *Description* text box and then type Select text, indent text, and apply italic formatting. (If text displays in the *Description* text box, select the text first, and then type the description.)

f. Click OK.

g. At the document, press F8 to turn on the Extend mode.

h. Hold down the Shift key, the Ctrl key, and then press the Down Arrow key. (Shift + Ctrl + Down Arrow is the keyboard shortcut to select a paragraph.)

i. Click the Home tab.

j. Click the Paragraph group dialog box launcher.

k. At the Paragraph dialog box, click the up-pointing arrow at the right of the *Left* option until *0.5"* displays.

l. Click the up-pointing arrow at the right of the *Right* option until *0.5"* displays.

m. Click OK.

n. Press Ctrl + I to apply italic formatting.

o. Press the Esc key on the keyboard and then press the Left Arrow key. (This deselects the text.)

p. Click the Macro icon on the Status bar to turn off the macro recording.

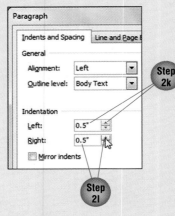

3. Record a macro that applies formatting to a heading by completing the following steps:

a. Move the insertion to the beginning of the text *Heading*.

b. Click the Developer tab and then click the Record Macro button in the Code group.

c. At the Record Macro dialog box, type XXXHeading in the *Macro name* text box (type your initials in place of the *XXX*).

d. Click inside the *Description* text box and then type Select text, change font size, turn on bold and italic, and insert bottom border line. (If text displays in the *Description* text box, select the text first, and then type the description.)

e. Click OK.

f. At the document, press F8 and then press the End key.

g. Click the Home tab.

h. Click the Bold button in the Font group.

i. Click the Italic button in the Font group.

j. Click the Font Size button arrow and then click *12* at the drop-down gallery.
k. Click the Border button arrow and then click *Bottom Border* at the drop-down list.
l. Press the Home key. (This moves the insertion point back to the beginning of the heading and deselects the text.)
m. Click the Macro icon on the Status bar to turn off the macro recording.
4. Close the document without saving it.

Running a Macro

To run a recorded macro, click the Macros button in the Code group in the Developer tab or click the Macros button in the View tab. This displays the Macros dialog box shown in Figure 30.6. At this dialog box, double-click the desired macro in the list box or click the macro and then click the Run button.

Figure 30.6 Macros Dialog Box

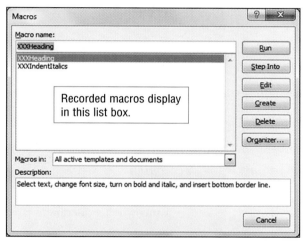

Exercise 30.4B   **Running Macros**   **Part 2 of 4**

1. Open **WriteResume.docx** and save the document with the name **C30-E04-WriteResume**.
2. With the insertion point positioned at the beginning of the heading *Resume Strategies*, run the XXXHeading macro by completing the following steps:
   a. Click the View tab.
   b. Click the Macros button in the Macros group.

c. At the Macros dialog box, click *XXXHeading* in the list box.

d. Click the Run button.

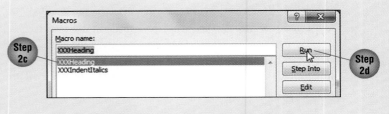

3. Complete steps similar to those in Steps 2a through 2d to run the macro for the two other headings in the document: *Writing Style* and *Phrases to Avoid*.

4. With the insertion point positioned at the left margin of the paragraph below **First Person:**, complete the following steps to run the XXXIndentItalics macro:

   a. Click the Developer tab.

   b. Click the Macros button in the Code group.

   c. At the Macros dialog box, double-click *XXXIndentItalics* in the list box.

5. Complete steps similar to those in Step 4a through 4c to run the XXXIndentItalics macro for the paragraph below **Third Person:**, the paragraph that begins *Responsible for all marketing and special events …*, and the paragraph that begins *Orchestrated a series of marketing and special-event programs …*.

6. Save, print, and then close **C30-E04-WriteResume.docx**.

Running a Macro Automatically

You can create a macro that starts automatically when you perform a certain action such as opening, closing, or exiting Word. To use a macro that starts automatically, it must be saved in the Normal template and it must contain one of the names listed below.

Automatic Macro Name	*Action*
AutoExec	Runs when Word is opened
AutoOpen	Runs when a document is opened
AutoNew	Runs when a new document is opened
AutoClose	Runs when a document is closed
AutoExit	Runs when Word is exited

To create a macro that runs automatically, display the Record Macro dialog box, type the desired macro name from the list above in the *Macro name* text box, and then click OK. Complete the desired steps for the macro and then end the recording.

Exercise 30.4C Running a Macro Automatically   Part 3 of 4

1. At a blank document, create a macro that changes the font and the view and runs automatically when you open a new document by completing the following steps:

   a. Click the View tab.

   b. Click the Macros button arrow in the Macros group and then click *Record Macro* at the drop-down list.

c. At the Record Macro dialog box, type **AutoNew** in the *Macro name* text box.

d. Click inside the *Description* text box and then type **Runs automatically when a new document is opened and changes the font and document view.** (If text displays in the *Description* text box, select the text first and then type the description.)

e. Click OK.

f. Click the Home tab, click the Font button arrow, and then click *Constantia* at the drop-down gallery.

g. Click the View tab and then click the Draft button in the Document Views group.

h. Press the spacebar and then press the Backspace key. (To save the document in Draft view, an action must appear in the Undo drop-down list. Pressing the spacebar and then pressing the Backspace key will create the action in the Undo list.)

i. Click the Macro icon on the Status bar to turn off the macro recording.

2. Close the document without saving it and then exit Word.

3. Open Word and notice that the blank document contains the original default settings (11-point Calibri, Normal view, and so on.)

4. Press Ctrl + N to open a new document. (This opens a new blank document and also runs the AutoNew macro.)

5. Insert into the current document the document named **ResumeStandards.docx** located in the Chapter30 folder your storage medium. (Do this with the Object button arrow in the Insert tab.)

6. Position the insertion point at the beginning of the heading *Typestyle* and then run the *XXXHeading* macro.

7. Position the insertion point at the beginning of each of the remaining headings and run the *XXXHeading* macro. (The remaining headings include *Type Size*, *Type Enhancements*, *Page Length*, *Paper Color*, *Graphics*, and *White Space*.)

8. Select the second through fifth paragraphs in the *Page Length* section and then run the *XXXIndentItalics* macro. (Do not select the paragraph symbol after the last word in the fifth paragraph.)

9. Save the document and name it **C30-E04-ResumeStandards**.

10. Print and then close **C30-E04-ResumeStandards.docx**.

Pausing and Resuming a Macro

When recording a macro, you can temporarily suspend the recording, perform actions that are not recorded, and then resume recording the macro. To pause the recording of a macro, click the Pause Recording button in the Code group in the Developer tab. To resume recording the macro, click the Resume Recorder button (previously the Pause Recording button).

Deleting a Macro

If you no longer need a macro that has been recorded, it can be deleted. To delete a macro, display the Macros dialog box, click the macro name in the list box, and then click the Delete button. At the message asking if you want to delete the macro, click Yes. Click the Close button to close the Macros dialog box.

1. At a blank document, delete the XXXIndentItalics macro by completing the following steps:
   a. Click the Developer tab and then click the Macros button in the Code group.
   b. At the Macros dialog box, click *XXXIndentItalics* in the list box.
   c. Click the Delete button.
   d. At the message asking if you want to delete the macro, click Yes.
   e. Click the Close button to close the Macros dialog box.
2. Complete steps similar to those in Step 1 to delete the AutoNew macro.
3. Close the document without saving it.

Assigning a Macro

Consider assigning macros you use regularly either to a keyboard command or to a toolbar. To run a macro that has been assigned to a keyboard command, just press the assigned keys. To run a macro assigned to a toolbar, just click the button.

Assigning a Macro to a Keyboard Command

A macro can be assigned to a keyboard command with a letter plus Alt + Ctrl or Alt + Shift. Word already uses many combinations for Word functions. For example, pressing Alt + Ctrl + C inserts the copyright symbol. With the Alt + Ctrl combination, the following letters are available for assigning a macro: *A, B, G, J, Q, W,* and *X.* With the Alt + Shift combination, the following letters are available for assigning a macro: *B, G, H, J, Q, S, V, W, Y,* and *Z.*

Figure 30.7 Customize Keyboard Dialog Box

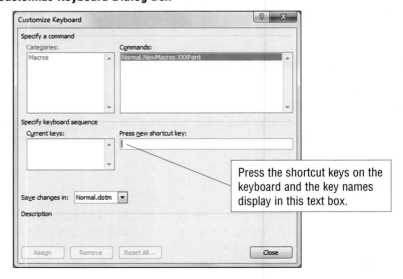

Press the shortcut keys on the keyboard and the key names display in this text box.

Assign a macro to a keyboard command at the Customize Keyboard dialog box shown in Figure 30.7. In Exercise 30.5 you will record a macro and then assign the macro to a keyboard command. If you delete the macro, the keyboard command is also deleted. This allows you to use the key combination again.

Exercise 30.5 Assigning a Macro to a Keyboard Command   Part 1 of 1

1. Record a macro named XXXFont that selects text and applies font formatting and assign it the keyboard command Alt + Ctrl + A by completing the following steps:

   a. At a blank document, click the Developer tab and then click the Record Macro button in the Code group.

   b. At the Record Macro dialog box, type XXXFont in the *Macro name* text box.

   c. Click inside the *Description* text box and then type Select text and change the font and font color.

   d. Click the Keyboard button.

   e. At the Customize Keyboard dialog box with the insertion point positioned in the *Press new shortcut key* text box, press Alt + Ctrl + A.

   f. Click the Assign button.

   g. Click the Close button.

   h. At the document, click the Home tab.

   i. Press Ctrl + A.

   j. Click the Font group dialog box launcher.

   k. At the Font dialog box, click *Cambria* in the *Font* list box and change the *Font color* to Dark Blue.

   l. Click OK to close the Font dialog box.

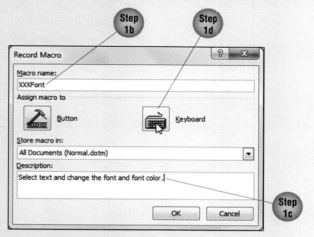

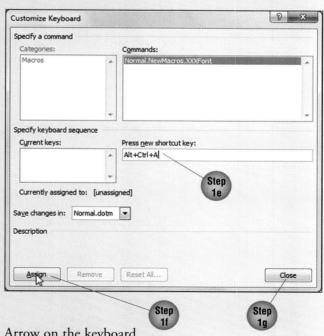

   m. At the document, press the Down Arrow on the keyboard.

   n. Click the Macro icon on the Status bar to turn off the macro recording.

2. Close the document without saving it.

3. Open **GSHLtr.docx** and save the document with the name **C30-E05-GSHLtr**.

4. Run the XXXFont macro by pressing Alt + Ctrl + A.

5. Run the XXXHeading macro for the heading *Procedural* and the heading *Teaching*.

6. Save, print, and then close **C30-E05-GSHLtr.docx**.

Assigning a Macro to the Quick Access Toolbar

A macro that you use regularly can be added to the Quick Access toolbar. To run a macro from the Quick Access toolbar, just click the button. To assign a macro to the toolbar, click the Button button at the Record Macro dialog box. This displays the Word Options dialog box with the *Quick Access Toolbar* option selected in the left panel. Click the macro name in the left list box and then click the Add button that displays between the two list boxes. This adds the macro name in the right list box. Specify a button icon by clicking the Modify button, clicking the desired icon at the Modify Button dialog box, and then clicking OK. Click OK to close the Word Options dialog box, and a Macro button is inserted on the Quick Access toolbar. To remove a Macro button from the Quick Access toolbar, right-click the button on the toolbar and then click *Remove from Quick Access Toolbar* at the shortcut menu.

Exercise 30.6   Assigning a Macro to the Quick Access Toolbar   Part 1 of 1

1. At a blank document, create a macro named XXXTab and assign it to the Quick Access toolbar by completing the following steps:
   a. Click the Macro icon on the Status bar.
   b. At the Record Macro dialog box, type XXXTab in the *Macro name* text box.
   c. Click in the *Description* text box and then type Set left tabs at 0.5 and 1.0 and right tab with leaders at 5.5.
   d. Click the Button button.
   e. At the Word Options dialog box, click the macro named *Normal.NewMacros.XXXTab* in the left list box.
   f. Click the Add button located between the two list boxes.

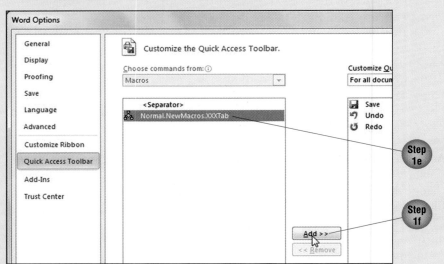

   g. Click the Modify button located in the lower right corner of the dialog box.
   h. At the Modify Button dialog box, click the fourth button from the left in the top row.

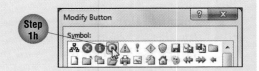

i.   Click OK to close the Modify Button dialog box.
j.   Click OK to close the Word Options dialog box.
k.   At the blank document, click the Home tab and then click the Paragraph group dialog box launcher.
l.   At the Paragraph dialog box, click the Tabs button located in the lower left corner of the dialog box.
m.   At the Tabs dialog box, type 0.5 and then click the Set button.
n.   Type 1 and then click the Set button.
o.   Type 5.5, click the *Right* option in the *Alignment* section, click *2 ....* in the *Leader* section, and then click the Set button.
p.   Click OK to close the dialog box.
q.   At the blank document, click the Macro icon on the Status bar to turn off recording.

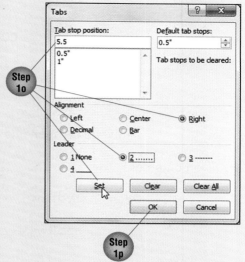

2.   Close the document without saving it.
3.   At a blank document, create the document shown in Figure 30.8 by completing the following steps:
a.   Click the Macro button on the Quick Access toolbar.
b.   Type the text as shown in Figure 30.8. (Type the first column of text at the first tab stop, not the left margin.)

4.   After typing the text, run the XXXFont macro by pressing Alt + Ctrl + A.
5.   Select the title *COMPUTER CONCEPTS* and then turn on bold.
6.   Save the document and name it **C30-E06-TofC**.
7.   Print and then close **C30-E06-TofC.docx**.
8.   Remove the Macro button from the Quick Access toolbar by right-clicking the button and then clicking *Remove from Quick Access Toolbar* at the shortcut menu.

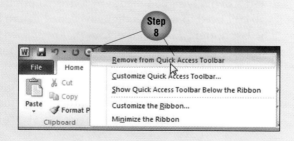

Figure 30.8 Exercise 30.6

COMPUTER CONCEPTS

Computer Hardware 3

    Types of Computers 4

    Hardware Components 8

Computer Software 14

    Operating Systems 16

    Application Software...20

Networking 25

    Types of Networks 27

    Uses of Networks...30

    Network Topologies 34

Specifying Macro Security Settings

Some macros can be a potential security risk and can introduce and spread a virus on your computer or network. For this reason, Microsoft Word provides macro security settings you can use to specify what action you want to occur with macros in a document. To display the macro security settings, click the Developer tab and then click the Macro Security button in the Code group. This displays the Trust Center with *Macro Settings* selected in the left panel as shown in Figure 30.9.

Choose the first option, *Disable all macros without notification*, and all macros and security alerts are disabled. The second option, *Disable all macros with notification,* is the default setting. At this setting, a security alert appears if a macro is present and you can choose to enable the macro. Choose the third option, *Disable all macros except digitally signed macros,* and a digitally signed macro by a trusted publisher will automatically run, but you will still need to enable a digitally signed macro by a publisher that is not trusted. The last option, *Enable all macros (not recommended; potentially dangerous code can run),* will allow all macros to run but, as the option implies, this is not recommended.

Changes you make to the macro security settings in Word only apply to Word. The macro security settings are not changed in the other programs in the Office suite.

Figure 30.9 Trust Center

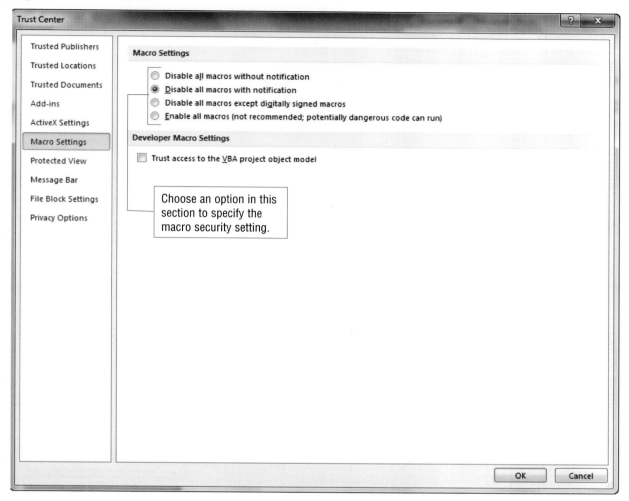

Saving a Macro-Enabled Document or Template

By default, macros you create are saved in the *Normal.dotm* template. The extension *.dotm* identifies the template as "macro-enabled." A template or document must be macro-enabled for a macro to be saved in it. In addition to the *Normal.dotm* template, you can save macros in a specific document or template to make them available when you open the document or template. To specify a location for saving a macro, display the Record Macro dialog box, click the down-pointing arrow at the right side of the *Store macro in* option box and then click the desired document or template.

Save a document containing macros as a macro-enabled document. To do this, display the Save As dialog box and then change the *Save as type* option to *Word Macro-Enabled Document (*.docm)*. Save a template containing macros as a macro-enabled template by changing the *Save as Type* option at the Save As dialog box to *Word Macro-Enabled Template (*.dotm)*.

If you are using Microsoft Word in a public setting such as a school, you may not be able to change macro security settings. If that is the case, skip to Step 4.

1. Open **Affidavit.docx** located in the Chapter30 folder on your storage medium.
2. Change macro security settings by completing the following steps:
   a. Click the Developer tab and then click the Macro Security button in the Code group.
   b. At the Trust Center, click the *Disable all macros without notification* option.
   c. Click OK.
3. Change the macro security setting by completing the following steps:
   a. Click the Macro Security button in the Code group.
   b. At the Trust Center, click the *Disable all macros with notification* option.
   c. Click OK.

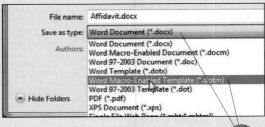

4. Save the document as a macro-enabled template by completing the following steps:
   a. Click the File tab and then click Save As.
   b. At the Save As dialog box, click the down-pointing arrow at the right side of the *Save as type* option box and then click *Word Macro-Enabled Template (*.dotm)* at the drop-down list.
   c. Select the text in the *File name* text box and then type **C30-AffidavitTemplate**.
   d. Make sure the Chapter30 folder on your storage medium is the active folder.
   e. Click the Save button.
5. Close **C30-AffidavitTemplate.dotm**.

Recording a Macro with Fill-in Fields

In Chapter 16, you inserted a Fill-in field in a document that prompted the operator to insert information at the keyboard during a merge. You can also insert a Fill-in field in a macro that requires input from the keyboard. To insert a Fill-in field in a macro, begin the recording of the macro. At the point where the Fill-in field is to be inserted, click the Insert tab, click the Quick Parts button in the Text group, and then click *Field* at the drop-down list. At the Field dialog box with *(All)* selected in the *Categories* list box as shown in Figure 30.10, scroll down the *Field names* and then click the *Fill-in* field. Add information telling the operator what text to enter at the keyboard by clicking in the *Prompt:* text box and then typing the desired message. When you run the macro, type the desired text specified by the prompt message.

Figure 30.10 Field Dialog Box

Type the desired prompt message in this text box.

Click *Fill-in* in this list box.

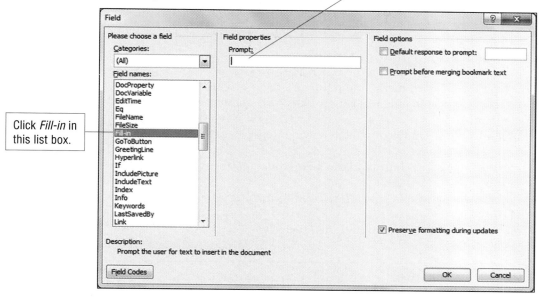

Exercise 30.7B   Recording a Macro with Fill-in Fields   Part 2 of 3

1. Create a document based on the *C30-AffidavitTemplate.dotm* template by completing the following steps:
   a. Click the File tab and then click the New tab.
   b. At the New tab Backstage view, click the New from existing button.
   c. At the New from Existing Document dialog box, navigate to the Chapter30 folder on your storage medium and then double-click **C30-AffidavitTemplate.dotm**.
2. Press Ctrl + End to move the insertion point to the end of the document.
3. Create a macro that is saved in the template document. Begin by clicking the View tab, clicking the Macros button arrow, and then clicking *Record Macro* at the drop-down list.
4. At the Record Macro dialog box, type **XXXNotary** in the *Macro name* text box.
5. Click the down-pointing arrow at the right side of the *Store macro in* option box and then click *Documents Based On C30-AffidavitTemplate.dotm* at the drop-down list.
6. Click in the *Description* text box and then type Notary signature information.
7. Click the Keyboard button.
8. At the Customize Keyboard dialog box with the insertion point positioned in the *Press new shortcut key* text box, press Alt + Shift + S.
9. Click the Assign button.
10. Click the Close button.

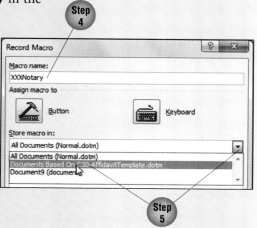

11. At the blank document, click the Home tab and then click the *No Spacing* heading in the Styles group.
12. Set three left tabs by completing the following steps:
    a. Make sure the alignment button at the left side of the Ruler displays with the Left Tab icon.
    b. Click on the 0.5-inch mark on the Ruler.
    c. Click on the 2-inch mark on the Ruler.
    d. Click on the 2.5-inch mark on the Ruler.
13. Type the text shown in Figure 30.11 up to the text *(name of person)*. (Do not type the text *(name of person)*.)
14. Insert a Fill-in field by completing the following steps:
    a. Click the Insert tab.
    b. Click the Quick Parts button in the Text group and then click *Field* at the drop-down list.
    c. At the Field dialog box with *(All)* selected in the *Categories* list box, scroll down the list and then click *Fill-in*.
    d. Click in the *Prompt:* text box and then type Type name of person signing.
    e. Click the OK button.

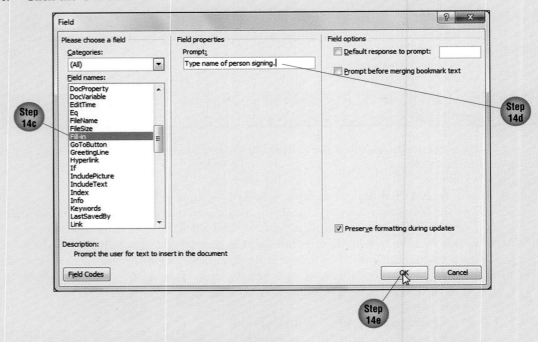

    f. At the Microsoft Word dialog box, type (name of person) in the text box and then click OK.

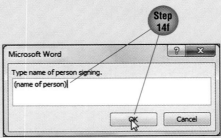

15. Continue typing the notary signature information shown in Figure 30.11 up to the text *(day)* and then insert a Fill-in field, by completing steps similar to those in Step 14, that prompts the operator to type the current day.
16. Continue typing the notary signature information shown in Figure 30.11 up to the text *(month)* and then insert a Fill-in field, by completing steps similar to those in Step 14, that prompts the operator to type the current month.
17. Continue typing the notary signature information shown in Figure 30.11 up to the text *(expiration date)* and then insert a Fill-in field, by completing steps similar to those in Step 14, that prompts the operator to type the expiration date.
18. After inserting the expiration date information, press the Enter key once.
19. End the recording by clicking the Macro icon on the Status bar.
20. Save the document and name it **C30-Affidavit-01**.
21. At the message asking if you want to save changes to the document template, click Yes.
22. Close **C30-Affidavit-01.docx**.

Figure 30.11 Exercise 30.7B

STATE OF CALIFORNIA   )
) ss.
COUNTY OF LOS ANGELES   )

On this day personally appeared before me (name of person), known to me to be the individual described in and who executed the aforesaid instrument, and acknowledged that he/she signed as his/her free and voluntary act and deed for the uses and purposes therein mentioned.

Given under my hand and official seal this (day) day of (month), 2012.

_____

NOTARY PUBLIC in and for the State of California
My appointment expires (expiration date)

Exercise 30.7C Running a Macro with Fill-in Fields   Part 3 of 3

1. Open a document based on the *C30-AffidavitTemplate.dotm* template by completing the following steps:
   a. Click the File tab and then click the New tab.
   b. At the New tab Backstage view, click the New from existing button.
   c. At the New from Existing Document dialog box, navigate to the Chapter30 folder on your storage medium and then double-click **C30-AffidavitTemplate.dotm**.
   d. Click the Enable Content button in the yellow message bar that displays above the Ruler.
2. Save the document with Save As and name it **C30-E07-Affidavit**.
3. Complete the following find and replaces:
   a. Find all occurrences of *NAME* and replace with *LOREN HOUSTON*. (Be sure to replace only the occurrences of *NAME* in all uppercase letters.) **Hint: Expand the Find and Replace dialog box and insert a check mark in the Match case option.**

b. Find the one occurrence of *ADDRESS* and replace with *102 Marine Drive, Los Angeles, CA.* (Be sure to replace only the occurrence of *ADDRESS* in all uppercase letters.)

4. Move the insertion point to the end of the document a double space below the text and then run the XXXNotary macro by completing the following steps:

   a. Press Alt + Shift + S.
   b. When the macro stops and prompts you for the name of person, type LOREN HOUSTON and then click OK.
   c. When the macro stops and prompts you for the day, type 8th and then click OK.
   d. When the macro stops and prompts you for the month, type March and then click OK.
   e. When the macro stops and prompts you for the expiration date, type 12/31/2013 and then click OK.

5. Save, print, and then close **C30-E07-Affidavit.docx**.

Chapter *Summary*

➤ Use the outline feature in Word to format headings within a document, view formatted titles, headings, and body text in a document, and edit text.

➤ Display a document in Outline view by clicking the View tab and then clicking the Outline button in the Document Views group.

➤ In Outline view, identify particular titles, headings, and subheadings within a document as certain levels.

➤ When a document displays in Outline view, the Outlining tab contains buttons for assigning levels and expanding and collapsing an outline.

➤ When a paragraph is identified as a level 1 heading, the Heading 1 style is applied to that paragraph. The Heading 2 style is applied to a paragraph identified as a level 2 heading.

➤ You can promote or demote a heading in Outline view by dragging the selection symbol that displays before a title or heading.

➤ The advantage of working in Outline view is the ability to see a condensed outline of your document without all of the text in between titles, headings, or subheadings. Another benefit of working in Outline view is in maintaining consistency between various titles and headings.

➤ To collapse all text beneath a particular heading, click the Collapse button in the Outline Tools group in the Outlining tab. Click the Expand button to display all text.

➤ In Outline view, you can rearrange the contents of a document. To move a heading and the body text below the heading, select the heading and then click the Move Down or Move Up button in the Outline Tools group. You can also move a heading and the body text below it by dragging the selection symbol that displays before the heading to the desired position.

➤ A master document contains a number of separate documents called subdocuments. Create a master document or format an existing document as a master document in Outline view.

➤ The Outlining tab in Outline view contains buttons for working with master documents and subdocuments. Clicking the Show Document button and then clicking the Create button both located in the Master Document group in the Outlining tab causes Word to create a subdocument for each heading at the top level within the selected text.

- Save a master document in the normal manner. Word automatically assigns a document name to each subdocument using the first characters in the subdocument heading.
- You can rearrange subdocuments in a master document by dragging the subdocument icon to the desired position.
- Use buttons in the Master Document group in the Outlining tab to create, expand, collapse, merge, and split subdocuments.
- Use the macro feature to execute a series of commands or apply formatting.
- Recording a macro involves turning on the macro recorder, performing the steps to be recorded, and then turning off the recorder.
- Run a macro by displaying the Macros dialog box and then double-clicking the desired macro name.
- You can create a macro that starts automatically when Word opens, when a document opens, when a new document opens, when a document is closed, or when Word is exited.
- You can temporarily suspend the recording of a macro by clicking the Pause Recording button in the Code group in the Developer tab.
- Delete a macro by displaying the Macros dialog box, clicking the macro name to be deleted, and then clicking the Delete button.
- Assign a macro to a keyboard command at the Record Macro dialog box.
- To run a macro that has been assigned a keyboard command, press the keys assigned to the macro.
- You can add a macro to the Quick Access toolbar and then run the macro by clicking the Macro button on the toolbar.
- Specify macro security settings at the Trust Center with *Macro Settings* selected in the left panel. Display the Trust Center by clicking the Macro Security button in the Code group in the Developer tab.
- Save a document as a macro-enabled document or a template as a macro-enabled template with the *Save as type* option at the Save As dialog box.
- Insert a Fill-in field in a macro that requires keyboard entry while running the macro.

Commands Review

FEATURE	RIBBON TAB, GROUP	BUTTON, OPTION	KEYBOARD SHORTCUT
Outline view	View, Document Views		Alt + Ctrl + O
Collapse outline	Outlining, Outline Tools		Alt + Shift + _
Expand outline	Outlining, Outline Tools		Alt + Shift + +
Move up outline level	Outlining, Outline Tools		Alt + Shift + Up
Move down outline level	Outlining, Outline Tools		Alt + Shift + Down
Master Document	Outlining, Master Document		
Collapse subdocuments	Outlining, Master Document		
Expand subdocuments	Outlining, Master Document		

FEATURE	RIBBON TAB, GROUP	BUTTON, OPTION	KEYBOARD SHORTCUT
Macros dialog box	Developer, Code OR View, Macros		Alt + F8
Record Macro dialog box	Developer, Code OR View, Macros		
Field dialog box	Insert, Text	, Field	
Trust Center	Developer, Code		

Key Points *Review*

Completion: In the space provided at the right, indicate the correct term, command, or number.

1. The Outline button is located in this tab.

2. Click this button to promote a title or heading to level 1.

3. Use this button in the Outlining tab to switch between displaying all headings through the lowest level chosen.

4. You can promote or demote a heading in Outline view by dragging this symbol that displays before a heading.

5. Click this button in the Outlining tab to collapse all of the text beneath a particular heading.

6. To move a level 1 heading below other level 1 headings, select the level 1 heading to be moved and then click this button until the heading is in the desired position.

7. The Show Document button is located in this group in the Outlining tab.

8. Click the Expand Subdocuments button and the name of the button changes to this.

9. This tab contains the Record Macro button in the Code group.

10. A macro name must begin with a letter and can contain only letters and these.

11. When macro recording is turned on, a Macro icon displays on this.

12. Delete a macro at this dialog box.

13. Assign a macro to a keyboard command at this dialog box.

14. You can add a button to this toolbar to run a recorded macro.

15. Insert this field in a macro that requires input from the keyboard.

Chapter *Assessments*

Applying Your Skills

Demonstrate your knowledge of features learned in this chapter by completing the following assessments.

Assessment 30.1 Assign Levels in Outline View

1. Open **CompComm.docx** and save the document with the name **C30-A01-CompComm**.
2. Change to Outline view and then promote or demote titles and headings as identified below:

COMPUTERS IN COMMUNICATION	=	Level 1
Telecommunications	=	Level 2
Publishing	=	Level 2
News Services	=	Level 2
COMPUTERS IN ENTERTAINMENT	=	Level 1
Television and Film	=	Level 2
Home Entertainment	=	Level 2

3. Collapse the outline so only the two levels display.
4. Save and then print **C30-A01-CompComm.docx**. (This will print the collapsed outline, not the entire document.)

Assessment 30.2 Move and Delete Headings in a Collapsed Outline

1. With **C30-A01-CompComm.docx** open, make sure the document displays in Outline view and then save the document with Save As and name it **C30-A02-CompComm**.
2. Make the following changes:
   a. Change the Show Level button to *Level 1*.
   b. Move the *COMPUTERS IN COMMUNICATIONS* title below the title *COMPUTERS IN ENTERTAINMENT*.
   c. Change the Show Level button to *Level 2*.
   d. Move the heading *Publishing* below the heading *News Services*.
   e. Delete the *Telecommunications* heading.
3. Save and then print **C30-A02-CompComm.docx**.
4. Display the entire document and then close Outline view.
5. Save and then close **C30-A02-CompComm.docx**.

Assessment 30.3 Create and Arrange a Master Document

1. Open **WebContent.docx** and save the document with the name **C30-A03-WebContent**.
2. Change to Outline view.
3. Assign to level 1 the following headings:
   Browsing Web Pages
   Searching Online Content
   Evaluating Web Content
   Intellectual Property
4. Click the Show Document button in the Master Document group in the Outlining tab.
5. Create subdocuments by selecting the entire document and then clicking the Create button in the Master Document group.
6. Save and then close **C30-A03-WebContent.docx**.
7. Open **C30-A03-WebContent.docx** and then print the document. (Subdocuments will be collapsed.)
8. Make the following changes to the document:

a. Move the *Evaluating Web Content* subdocument above the *Searching Online Content* subdocument. (Make sure the dark gray horizontal line is positioned above the gray circle above the *Searching Online Content* subdocument before you release the mouse button.)

b. Delete the *Intellectual Property* subdocument.

9. Save, print, and then close **C30-A03-WebContent.docx**.

Assessment 30.4   Record and Run Formatting Macros

1. Open **MacroText.docx** and then create a macro named XXXTitle with the following specifications:

    a. Position the insertion point at the beginning of the word *Title* and then turn on the macro recorder.

    b. Press the F8 function key and then press the End key.

    c. Click the Center button and then click the Bold button.

    d. Change the font size to *14*.

    e. Click the Shading button arrow and then click *Olive Green, Accent 3, Lighter 40%*.

    f. Click the *Bottom Border* option.

    g. Turn off the macro recorder.

2. Create a macro named XXXDocFont that selects the entire document and then changes the font to Cambria, and assign the macro to the Quick Access toolbar.

3. Close **MacroText.docx** without saving it.

4. Open **CompNetworks.docx** and save the document with the name **C30-A04-CompNetworks**.

5. Click the button on the Quick Access toolbar representing the XXXDocFont macro.

6. With the insertion point positioned at the left margin of the title *Computer Networks*, run the XXXTitle macro.

7. Move the insertion point to the beginning of the title *Communication Systems* and then run the XXXTitle macro.

8. Run the XXXHeading macro (created in Exercise 30.4A) for the two headings in the document: *Types of Signals* and *Transmission Speed*.

9. Save, print, and then close **C30-A04-CompNetworks.docx**.

10. Remove the XXXDocFont button from the Quick Access toolbar.

Assessment 30.5   Record and Run a Macro that Sets Tabs

1. At a blank document, run the XXXTab macro and then create the document shown in Figure 30.12. (Type the text in the first column at the second tab stop [the tab stop at 1 inch], not the left margin.)

2. Save the completed document and name it **C30-A05-PRDept**.

3. Print and then close **C30-A05-PRDept.docx**.

Figure 30.12 Assessment 30.5

McCORMACK FUNDS CORPORATION

Public Relations Department, Extension Numbers

Roger Maldon 129

Kimberly Holland...143

Richard Perez 317

Sharon Rawlins 211

Earl Warnberg 339

Susan Fanning 122

Assessment 30.6 Record and Run a Macro with Fill-in Fields

START From Scratch

1. At a blank document, click the No Spacing style and then record a macro named XXXNotSig that includes the information shown in Figure 30.13. Set left tabs at the 0.5-inch mark, the 1.5-inch mark, and the 3-inch mark on the Ruler. Include Fill-in fields in the macro where you see the text in parentheses. After inserting the *(county)* Fill-in field, press the Enter key and then end the macro recording.
2. Close the document without saving it.
3. Open **Agreement.docx** and save the document with the name **C30-A06-Agreement**.
4. Move the insertion point to the end of the document and then run the XXXNotSig macro and insert the following information when prompted:

(name 1)	=	LLOYD KOVICH
(name 2)	=	JOANNE MILNER
(county)	=	Ramsey County

5. Save, print, and then close **C30-A06-Agreement.docx**.

Figure 30.13 Assessment 30.6

STATE OF MINNESOTA   )
) ss.
COUNTY OF RAMSEY   )

     I certify that I know or have satisfactory evidence that (name 1) and (name 2) are the persons who appeared before me, and said persons acknowledge that they signed the foregoing Contract and acknowledged it to be their free and voluntary act for the uses and purposes therein mentioned.

                           _____

                           NOTARY PUBLIC in and for the State of
                           Minnesota residing in (county)

Expanding Your Skills

Explore additional feature options or use Help to learn a new skill in creating this document.

Assessment 30.7   Create and Run a Macro with Fields

1. Open **SFHMacroText.docx** and then use the document to create the following macros for St. Francis Hospital:
   a. Create a macro named XXXSFHDocFormat that selects the entire document (use Ctrl + A), applies the No Spacing style (click the *No Spacing* style in the Styles group), changes the line spacing to double (press Ctrl + 2), and changes the font to Constantia.
   b. Create a macro named XXXSFHMargins that changes the top margin to 1.5 inch and the left and right margins to 1.25 inch.
   c. Create a macro named XXXSFHTitle that selects a line of text (at the beginning of the line, press F8 and then press the End key), changes the font size to 14, turns on bold, centers text, and then deselects the text.
   d. Create a macro named XXXSFHHeading that selects a line of text, changes the font size to 12, turns on bold, turns on underline, and deselects the text.
2. In this chapter, you learned how to create a macro using a Fill-in field. You can use other fields from the Fields dialog box in a macro. With **SFHMacroText.docx** open, create a macro named XXXSFHEnd that completes the following steps:
   a. Change line spacing to single (press Ctrl + 1).
   b. Insert the FileName field.
   c. Press the Enter key and insert the Date field.
   d. Press the Enter key, type Number of Pages:, press the spacebar, and then insert the NumPages field.
   e. Press the Enter key and then insert a Fill-in field that prompts the user to type his or her name.
3. Close **SFHMacroText.docx** without saving it.
4. Open **EmpComp.docx** and save the document with the name **C30-A07-EmpComp**.
5. Run the XXXSFHDocFormat macro and then run the XXXSFHMargins macro.
6. Run the XXXTitle for the title of the document and run the XXXHeading macro for the five headings in the document (*Rate of Pay*, *Direct Deposit Options*, *Pay Progression*, *Overtime*, and *Longevity Pay*).
7. Press Ctrl + End to move the insertion point to the end of the document and then run the XXXSFHEnd macro. At the prompt asking for your name, type your first and last names.

8. Save, print, and then close **C30-A07-EmpComp.docx**.
9. Open **EmpPerf.docx** and save the document with the name **C30-A07-EmpPerf**.
10. Run macros in the document by completing steps similar to those in Steps 5 through 7.
11. Save, print, and then close **C30-A07-EmpPerf.docx**.

Achieving Signature Status

Take your skills to the next level by completing this more challenging assessment.

Assessment 30.8   Create and Run a Menu Formatting Macro

1. Open **MacroText.docx**.
2. Create a macro with the following specifications:
    a. Name the macro XXXMenu and assign the macro to the Quick Access toolbar. (You determine the description.)
    b. Create a Fill-in field with the prompt *Type the current date*.
    c. Select the entire document and then apply the following formatting:
        • Change the font to 14-point Monotype Corsiva and the font color to *Purple, Accent 4, Darker 25%*.
        • Center the text.
        • Apply *Olive Green, Accent 3, Lighter 60%* paragraph shading.
        • Display the Borders and Shading dialog box with the Borders tab selected, scroll down the *Style* list box and then click the third line option from the end, change the color to *Purple, Accent 4, Darker 25%*, click the Box option in the *Setting* section, and then close the dialog box.
    d. End the recording of the macro.
3. Close **MacroText.docx** without saving it.
4. Open **Menu.docx** and save the document with the name **C30-A08-Menu**.
5. Press the Down Arrow key once and then apply the XXXMenu macro by clicking the button on the Quick Access toolbar that represents the macro. Type the date August 6, 2012 at the fill-in prompt. Your document should appear as shown in Figure 30.14.
6. Save, print, and then close **C30-A08-Menu.docx**.
7. Open **ChefMenu01.docx** and save the document with the name **C30-A08-ChefMenu01**.
8. Press the Down Arrow key once, apply the XXXMenu macro, and type August 11, 2012 at the fill-in prompt.
9. Save, print, and then close **C30-A08-ChefMenu01.docx**.
10. Open **ChefMenu02.docx** and save the document with the name **C30-A08-ChefMenu02**.
11. Press the Down Arrow key once, apply the XXXMenu macro, and type August 12, 2012 at the fill-in prompt.
12. Save, print, and then close **C30-A08-ChefMenu02.docx**.
13. Remove the XXXMenu button from the Quick Access toolbar.

Figure 30.14 Assessment 30.8

August 6, 2012

WEEKLY SPECIALS

Monday – Chicken Marsala, $16.00
Mushrooms, Prosciutto, and Marsala Wine Sauce

Tuesday – Grilled Norwegian Salmon, $21.50
Fresh salmon baked in the chef's sauce of the day

Wednesday – Garlic Chicken, $16.00
Vermicelli, Grilled Asparagus

Thursday – Boneless Pork Chop Cacciatore, $16.50
Vermicelli, Marinara Sauce

Friday – Slow Roasted Prime Rib, $19.50
Onion Straws, Horseradish Cream, Lettuce, and Tomato

Performance Assessments

Referencing Data

ASSESSING PROFICIENCIES

In this unit, you have learned how to reference data with footnotes, endnotes, citations, and bibliographies. You have learned to create an index, table of contents, table of figures, and table of authorities, and you have learned to create forms with content controls and form fields, use the outline view, create a master and subdocument, and format a document with macros. The following assessments address these skills.

Note: Before beginning computer assessments, copy to your storage medium the Unit06PA folder from the CD that accompanies this textbook and then make Unit06PA the active folder.

Assessment U6.1   Insert Footnotes in a Report

1. Open **InterfaceApps.docx** and save the document with the name **U6-PA01-InterfaceApps**.
2. Create the first footnote shown in Figure U6.1 at the end of the first paragraph in the document.
3. Create the second footnote shown in Figure U6.1 at the end of the paragraph in the *Speech Recognition* section.
4. Create the third footnote shown in Figure U6.1 at the end of the paragraph in the *Virtual Reality* section.
5. Create the fourth footnote shown in Figure U6.1 at the end of the last paragraph in the document.
6. Save and then print **U6-PA01-InterfaceApps.docx**.
7. Select the entire document and then change the font to Constantia.
8. Select all of the footnotes and change the font to Constantia.
9. Delete the third footnote.
10. Save, print, and then close **U6-PA01-InterfaceApps.docx**.

Assessment U6.2   Create Citations and Prepare a Works Cited Page for a Report

1. Open **BuildWebsite.docx** and save the document with the name **U6-PA02-BuildWebsite**.
2. Format the title page to meet MLA requirements with the following changes:
    a.   Select the entire document, change the font to 12-point Cambria, the line spacing to 2.0, and remove the spacing after paragraphs.
    b.   Move the insertion point to the beginning of the document, type your name, press the Enter key, type your instructor's name, press the Enter key, type the title of your course, press the Enter key, and then type the current date.
    c.   Insert a header that displays your last name and the page number at the right margin, and change the font to 12-point Cambria.
3. Press Ctrl + End to move the insertion point to the end of the document and then type the text shown in Figure U6.2 (in MLA style) up to the first citation

Raines, C. & Silverstein, S. (2012) *Computers: Natural-language technologies* (pp. 67-72). Newark: Mansfield & Nassen Publishing.

Sutton, T. M. (2011) *Computers and communicating* (pp. 10-14). Los Angeles: Southwest Publishing House.

Chun, J. & Anderson, M. C. (2012) *Natural-language computing*. Cleveland, OH: Hammermaster Publishing.

Castillo, C. (2011) *Computers and the art of virtual reality*. Philadelphia: Old Town Press and Publishing House.

(the text *(Mercado)*). Insert the source information from a journal article written by Claudia Mercado using the following information:

Author	=	Claudia Mercado
Title	=	Connecting a Web Page
Journal Name	=	Connections
Year	=	2012
Pages	=	12-21
Volume	=	5

4. Continue typing the text up to the next citation (the text *(Holmes)*) and insert the following source information from a website:

Author	=	Brent Holmes
Name of Web page	=	Hosting Your Web Page
Year	=	2011
Month	=	September
Day	=	28
Year Accessed	=	(type current year)
Month Accessed	=	(type current month)
Day Accessed	=	(type current day)
URL	=	www.emcp.net/hosting

5. Continue typing the text up to the next citation (the text *(Vukovich)*) and insert the following information from a book:

Author	=	Ivan Vukovich
Title	=	Computer Technology in the Business Environment
Year	=	2011
City	=	San Francisco
Publisher	=	Gold Coast Publishing

6. Insert the page number in the citation by Ivan Vukovich using the Edit Citation dialog box.
7. Type the remaining text in Figure U6.2.
8. Edit the Ivan Vukovich source by changing the last name to *Vulkovich* in the *Master List* section of the Source Manager dialog box.
9. Create a new source in the document using the Source Manager dialog box and include the following source information for a journal article:

Author	=	Sonia Jaquez
Title	=	Organizing a Web Page

$$Journal\ Name\ =\ \text{Design Techniques}$$
$$Year\qquad =\ 2012$$
$$Pages\qquad =\ 32\text{-}44$$
$$Volume\qquad =\ 9$$

10. Type the following sentence at the end of the last paragraph in the document: Browsers look for pages with these names first when a specific file at a website is requested, and index pages display by default if no other page is specified.
11. Insert a citation for Sonia Jaquez at the end of the sentence you just typed.
12. Insert a citation for Claudia Mercado following the second sentence in the first paragraph of the document.
13. Insert a works cited page at the end of the document on a separate page.
14. Format the works cited page to meet MLA requirements with the following changes:
    a. Select the *Works Cited* title and all the entries and click the *No Spacing* style.
    b. Change the font to 12-point Cambria and change the spacing to 2.0.
    c. Center the title *Works Cited*.
    d. Hang indent the works cited entries.
15. Save and then print **U6-PA02-BuildWebsite.docx**.
16. Change the document and works cited page from MLA style to APA style.
17. Save, print page three, and then close **U6-PA02-BuildWebsite.docx**.

Figure U6.2 Assessment U6.2

One of the first tasks in website development is finding a good host for the site.

Essentially, a web host lets you store a copy of your web pages on the hard drive of a

powerful computer connected to the Internet with a fast connection that can handle

thousands of users (Mercado). Hosting your own website is possible but is only feasible if

you own an extra computer that can be dedicated to the role of a web server, have a

high-speed Internet connection, and feel confident about handling the job of network

security and routing (Holmes). Most people's situations do not fit those criteria. Fortunately,

several free and fee-based web hosting services are available.

As you plan a website, decide what types of content you will include and think about

how all of the pages should link together. Most websites have a home page that provides the

starting point for users entering the site. "Like the top of a pyramid or the table of contents of

a book, the home page leads to other web pages via hyperlinks" (Vukovich 26). Most home

pages have the default name of index.html (or sometimes index.htm).

Create an Index and Table of Contents for a Report

1. At a blank document, create the text shown in Figure U6.3 as a concordance file.
2. Save the document with the name **U6-PA03-CFile**.
3. Print and then close **U6-PA03-CFile.docx**.
4. Open **DTPDesign.docx** and save the document with the name **U6-PA03-DTPDesign**.
5. Make the following changes to the document:
   a. Apply the Heading 1 style to the title and apply the Heading 2 style to the two headings in the report.
   b. Change the style set to Simple.
   c. Mark text for an index using the concordance file **U6-PA03-CFile.docx**.
   d. Compile the index at the end of the document.
   e. Apply the Heading 1 style to the title of the index.
   f. Insert a table of contents at the beginning of the document.
   g. Number the table of contents page with a lowercase Roman numeral.
   h. Number the other pages in the report with Arabic numbers and start the numbering with 1 on the page containing the report title.

Figure U6.3 Assessment U6.3

message	Message
publication	Publication
Design	Design
flyer	Flyer
letterhead	Letterhead
newsletter	Newsletter
intent	Design: intent
audience	Design: audience
layout	Design: layout
thumbnail	Thumbnail
principles	Design: principles
Focus	Design: focus
focus	Design: focus
balance	Design: balance
proportion	Design: proportion
contrast	Design: contrast
directional flow	Design: directional flow
consistency	Design: consistency
color	Design: color
White space	White space
white space	White space
Legibility	Legibility
headline	Headline
Subheads	Subheads
subheads	Subheads

6. Make sure the table of contents displays the correct page numbers. If not, update the table of contents.

7. Save, print, and then close **U6-PA03-DTPDesign.docx**.

Assessment U6.4 Create Captions and Insert a Table of Figures in a Report

1. Open **SoftwareCareers.docx** and save the document with the name **U6-PA04-SoftwareCareers**.

2. Move the insertion point to the line above the first table and create the caption *Table 1: Software Development Careers*. (Change the paragraph spacing after to *0 pt.*)

3. Move the insertion point to the line above the second table and create the caption *Table 2: Application Development Careers*. (Change the paragraph spacing after to *0 pt.*)

4. Move the insertion point to the beginning of the document and then insert a section break that begins a new page.

5. With the insertion point below the section break, number pages at the bottom center of each page and change the starting page number to 1.

6. Move the insertion point to the beginning of the document and then insert the *Automatic Table 2* table of contents.

7. Press Ctrl + Enter to insert a page break. (If your insertion point does not move to the new page, continue to Step 8 and the insertion point will move to the new page when you start typing *Tables*.)

8. Type Tables, press the Enter key (your insertion point may not move down to the next line), and then insert the table of figures using the *Formal* format.

9. Apply the Heading 1 style to the title *Tables*.

10. Move the insertion point to the beginning of the document and then change the numbering format to lowercase Roman numerals.

11. Save, print, and then close **U6-A04-SoftwareCareers.docx**.

Assessment U6.5 Create and Fill in a Purchase Order Form

1. Create the form shown in Figure U6.4 as a template and use a table to create the columns and rows. Include the following elements:

   a. Apply border and shading formatting as shown in the figure.

   b. Insert a picture content control, a date picker content control, and plain text content controls in the appropriate cells. Lock the picture content control so it cannot be edited.

   c. Insert a drop-down list content control for *Company Status* with the following choices: *Bronze*, *Silver*, and *Gold*.

2. Protect the template.

3. Save the template with the name **XXXSBPOTemplate**. (Replace the *XXX* with your initials.)

4. Print and then close **XXXSBPOTemplate.dotx**.

5. Create a form document from the **XXXSBPOTemplate** template with the following information:

Company Name:	=	John's Corner Market
Date:	=	(*Insert current date.*)
Company Status:		*Choose the* Gold *option.*
Description:	=	Sales Insight
Quantity:	=	5
Cost:	=	$20.50
Description:	=	Strategic Marketing
Quantity:	=	2

START From Scratch

Cost:	=	$134.50
Description:	=	Advertising
Quantity:	=	3
Cost:	=	$201.00

6. Save the document with the name **U6-PA05-SB-JCM**.
7. Print and then close **U6-PA05-SB-JCM.docx**.

Figure U6.4 **Assessment U6.5**

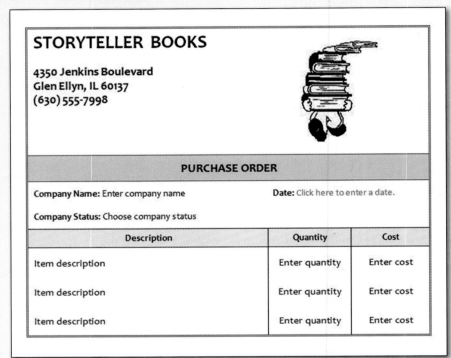

Assessment U6.6   **Create and Fill in an Insurance Application Form**

1. Create a template, insert a file, and then insert form fields in the template as shown in Figure U6.5 with the following specifications:
   a. Create the form as a template.
   b. At the template document, insert the document named **LAApp04.docx**. (Turn on the display of gridlines.)
   c. Insert a text form field for *Client Number:* that specifies a maximum length of 6.
   d. Insert a text form field for *Type of Deduction:* that specifies *Flat* as the default text.
   e. Insert a drop-down list form field for *Deduction Amount:* that includes the following four choices: *None*, *$1,000*, *$2,500*, and *$5,000*.
   f. Insert the four check boxes in the cell in the middle of the form table as shown in Figure U6.5. ***Hint: You can move the insertion point to a tab stop within a cell by pressing Ctrl + Tab.*** Insert a check box form field in the cell immediately left of *AANA* that is checked by default.
   g. Insert the remaining text and check box form fields as shown in Figure U6.5.
2. Protect the template.
3. Save the template with the name **XXXLAProfAppTemplate**.

4. Print and then close **XXXLAProfAppTemplate.dotx**.
5. Create a form document from the **XXXLAProfAppTemplate.dotx** template and then insert the following information in the specified data field:

First Name:	= Rachel
Middle Name:	= Brianne
Last Name:	= Hayward
Address:	= 12091 South 234th Street, Fairbanks, AK 99704
Date of Birth:	= 01/18/1982
Client Number:	= 10-541
Current Date:	= (*Insert the current date.*)
Type of Deduction:	= Flat
Deduction Amount:	= $5,000

(*Leave the check mark in the* AANA *check box and also insert a check mark in the* APTA-PPS *check box.*)

(*Insert a check mark in the* Occupational Therapist *check box.*)

6. Save the document with the name **U6-PA06-ProfAppHayward**.
7. Print and then close **U6-PA06-ProfAppHayward.docx**.

Figure U6.5 **Assessment U6.6**

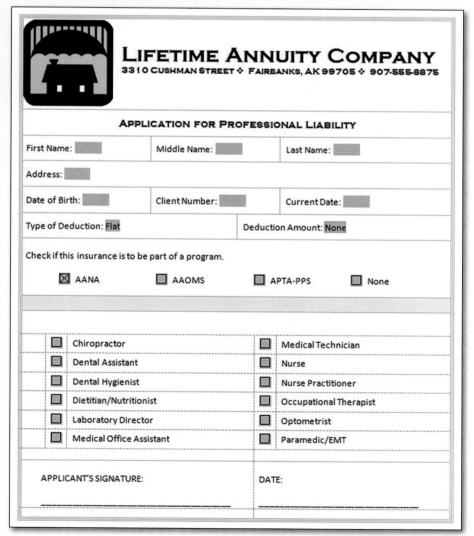

Create Subdocuments

1. Open **CommSoftware.docx** and save the document with the name **U6-PA07-CommSoftware**.
2. Display the document in Outline view and assign to level 1 the following headings:
   Electronic Mail
   Instant Messaging Software
   Groupware
   Web Browsers
   Webconferencing
3. Click the Show Document button in the Master Document group in the Outlining tab.
4. Create subdocuments by selecting the entire document and then clicking the Create button in the Master Document group.
5. Save and then close **U6-PA07-CommSoftware.docx**.
6. Open **U6-PA07-CommSoftware.docx** and then print the document. (The subdocuments will be collapsed.)
7. Make the following changes to the document:
   a. Move the *Web Browsers* subdocument above the *Instant Messaging Software* subdocument. (Make sure the dark gray, horizontal line is positioned above the gray circle above the *Instant Messaging Software* subdocument before you release the mouse button.)
   b. Delete the *Groupware* subdocument.
8. Save, print, and then close **U6-PA07-CommSoftware.docx**.

Create and Run Macros

1. At a blank document, create the following macros:
   a. Create a macro named XXXAPMFormat (use your initials in place of the *XXX*) that selects the entire document, changes the font to Constantia, and changes the font color to dark blue.
   b. Create a macro named XXXAPMTitle that changes the font size to *14*, turns on bold, centers the text, and applies *Blue, Accent 1, Lighter 60%* paragraph shading.
2. At a new blank document, create a macro named XXXAPMInfo that includes the information shown in Figure U6.6. Include the Fill-in fields in the macro where you see the text in parentheses.
3. After recording the macros, close the documents without saving them.
4. Open **Lease.docx** and then save the document and name it **U6-PA08-Lease**.
5. Run the XXXAPMFormat macro.
6. With the insertion point positioned at the beginning of the title *LEASE AGREEMENT*, run the XXXAPMTitle macro.
7. Move the insertion point to the end of the document and then run the XXXAPMInfo macro. Insert the following information when prompted:
   (name)   =   Grace Hillstrand
   (date)   =   May 22, 2012
8. Save, print, and then close **U6-PA08-Lease.docx**.
9. Open **REAgrmnt.docx** and then save the document and name it **U6-PA08-REAgrmnt**.
10. Run the XXXAPMFormat macro.
11. With the insertion point positioned at the beginning of the title *REAL ESTATE SALE AGREEMENT*, run the XXXAPMTitle macro.

12. Move the insertion point to the end of the document and then run the XXXAPMInfo macro. Insert the following information when prompted:

(name) = Grace Hillstrand
(date) = May 29, 2012

13. Save, print, and then close **U6-PA08-REAgrmnt.docx**.

Figure U6.6 Assessment U6.8

This document is the sole property of Azure Property Management and may not be reproduced, copied, or sold without express written consent of a legal representative of Azure Property Management. *(press Enter once)*

Prepared by: (name) *(press Shift + Enter)*
Date: (date)

CREATING ORIGINAL DOCUMENTS

The activities in Assessment U6.9 and Assessment U6.10 give you the opportunity to practice your writing skills as well as demonstrate your mastery of some of the important Word features presented in this unit. When you compose the documents, use correct grammar, precise word choices, and clear sentence construction.

Assessment U6.9   Format an Employee Handbook

Situation: You work in the human resources department at Brennan Distributors where you are responsible for preparing an employee handbook. Open the **BDHandbook. docx** document and save it with the name **U6-PA09-BDHandbook**. Make the following changes to the document:

- Insert page breaks before each of the centered titles (except the first title *Introduction*).
- Apply heading styles to the titles and headings.
- Change to a style set of your choosing.
- Apply a theme that makes the handbook easy to read.
- Insert a table of contents.
- Create a concordance file and then insert an index.
- Insert appropriate page numbering in the document.
- Add any other elements to improve the visual appeal of the document.

Save, print, and then close **U6-PA09-BDHandbook.docx**.

Assessment U6.10   Create a Contact Information Form

Situation: You work for the Evergreen Regional Center where you are responsible for creating fill-in forms for the records department. Your supervisor has asked you to create a fill-in form template. Use **ERCFunding.docx** as a reference (for the clip art image, font face, and colors) and create a form that includes the following specifications (you determine the layout of the form and the types of form fields used):

- Use the information in the first cell in the **ERCFunding.docx** document for the first cell in the template you design.
- Title the form *Contact Information*.
- Include the following fields:
    - Name
    - Birth date
    - Marital status
    - Gender
    - Address
    - Email address
    - Occupation
    - Emergency contact

After creating the form template, save the template document with the name **U6-PA10-ERCContact**. Use the **U6-PA10-ERCContact.dotx** form template to create a filled-in form. You make up the information to insert in the form. Save the completed form document with the name **U6-PA10-ERCContactInfo**. Print and then close **U6-PA10-ERCContactInfo.docx**.

Appendix A

Proofreader Marks

Proofreader Mark		Example	Revised
#	Insert space	letter to the	letter to the
ℐ	Delete	the commands is	the command is
lc /	Lowercase	lc he is Branch Manager	he is branch manager
(cap) or uc ≡	Uppercase	(cap) Margaret simpson	Margaret Simpson
¶	New paragraph	¶ The new product	The new product
no ¶	No paragraph	the meeting.	the meeting. Bring the
		no ¶ Bring the	
∧	Insert	pens, clips	pens, and clips
⊙	Insert period	a global search	a global search.
⊐	Move right	⊐ With the papers	With the papers
⊏	Move left	⊏access the code	access the code
⊐⊏	Center	⊐ Chapter Six ⊏	Chapter Six
∽	Transpose	It is raesonable	It is reasonable
(sp)	Spell out	(sp) 475 Mill (Ave)	475 Mill Avenue
⋯	Stet (do not delete)	I am very pleased	I am very pleased
⌒	Close up	regret fully	regretfully
ss	Single-space	The margin top	The margin top
		ss	is 1 inch.
		is 1 inch.	
ds	Double-space	ds Paper length is set for 11 inches.	Paper length is
			set for 11 inches.
ts	Triple-space	ts The F8 function key turns on Extend	The F8 function
			key turns on Extend
bf	Boldface	bf Boldface type provides emphasis.	**Boldface** type provides emphasis.
(ital)	Italics	(ital) Use italics for terms to be defined.	Use *italics* for terms to be defined.

Appendix B

Formatting a Personal Business Letter

A variety of formatting options are available for formatting a personal business letter (a letter from you as an individual rather than you representing a company) with the ***block style*** being one of the most common. In a block style format, all elements of the letter are aligned at the left margin. You can create a personal business letter with the default Microsoft Word 2010 line and paragraph spacing or remove the spacing and then create the letter.

Formatting with Microsoft Word Default Spacing

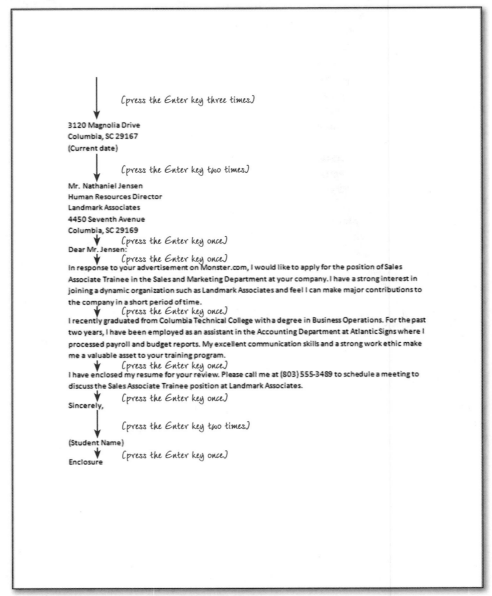

(press the Enter key three times)

3120 Magnolia Drive
Columbia, SC 29167
(Current date)

(press the Enter key two times)

Mr. Nathaniel Jensen
Human Resources Director
Landmark Associates
4450 Seventh Avenue
Columbia, SC 29169

(press the Enter key once)

Dear Mr. Jensen:

(press the Enter key once)

In response to your advertisement on Monster.com, I would like to apply for the position of Sales Associate Trainee in the Sales and Marketing Department at your company. I have a strong interest in joining a dynamic organization such as Landmark Associates and feel I can make major contributions to the company in a short period of time.

(press the Enter key once)

I recently graduated from Columbia Technical College with a degree in Business Operations. For the past two years, I have been employed as an assistant in the Accounting Department at Atlantic Signs where I processed payroll and budget reports. My excellent communication skills and a strong work ethic make me a valuable asset to your training program.

(press the Enter key once)

I have enclosed my resume for your review. Please call me at (803) 555-3489 to schedule a meeting to discuss the Sales Associate Trainee position at Landmark Associates.

(press the Enter key once)

Sincerely,

(press the Enter key two times)

(Student Name)

(press the Enter key once)

Enclosure

The Word default line spacing is 1.15 and the default spacing after paragraphs is 10 points. You can remove this formatting by clicking the *No Spacing* style in the Styles group in the Home tab. Applying this style changes the line spacing to 1 and the spacing after paragraphs to 0 points. To format a personal business letter without the Word default spacing, click the *No Spacing* style and then type the letter as shown below.

Formatting with No Spacing Style Applied

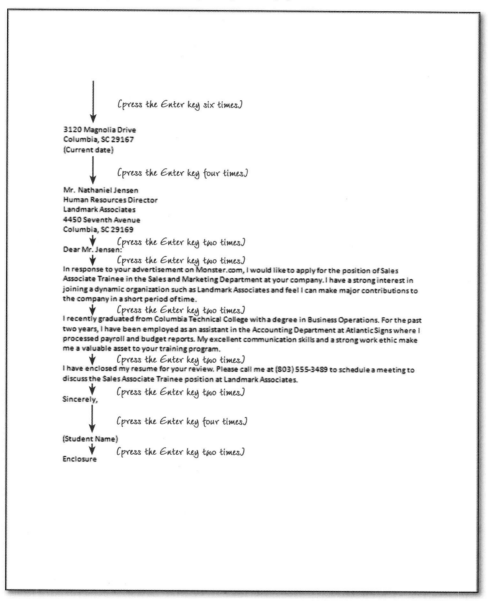

(press the Enter key six times)

3120 Magnolia Drive
Columbia, SC 29167
(Current date)

(press the Enter key four times)

Mr. Nathaniel Jensen
Human Resources Director
Landmark Associates
4450 Seventh Avenue
Columbia, SC 29169

(press the Enter key two times)

Dear Mr. Jensen:

(press the Enter key two times)

In response to your advertisement on Monster.com, I would like to apply for the position of Sales Associate Trainee in the Sales and Marketing Department at your company. I have a strong interest in joining a dynamic organization such as Landmark Associates and feel I can make major contributions to the company in a short period of time.

(press the Enter key two times)

I recently graduated from Columbia Technical College with a degree in Business Operations. For the past two years, I have been employed as an assistant in the Accounting Department at Atlantic Signs where I processed payroll and budget reports. My excellent communication skills and a strong work ethic make me a valuable asset to your training program.

(press the Enter key two times)

I have enclosed my resume for your review. Please call me at (803) 555-3489 to schedule a meeting to discuss the Sales Associate Trainee position at Landmark Associates.

(press the Enter key two times)

Sincerely,

(press the Enter key four times)

(Student Name)

(press the Enter key two times)

Enclosure

Appendix C

Formatting a Memo

The formatting of an interoffice correspondence, referred to as a *memo* (short for *memorandum*) varies from company to company. However, the content of a memo should be brief and to the point, and the format should support quick reading, easy distribution, and efficient filing.

In some of the exercises in this textbook, you will be required to type and format a memo. You can create a memo with the default Microsoft Word 2010 line and paragraph spacing, or remove the spacing and then create the memo. Include your reference initials at the end of the memo as shown in the following (where the *XX* indicates your initials). You can also include the document name below the initials, though this is optional.

In the examples below and on the next page, the reference initials display in uppercase letters. Usually, reference initials are typed in lowercase letters. However, Word automatically formats some text as you type it. When you type a lowercase letter at the beginning of a line, Word automatically corrects it to an uppercase letter. If your instructor wants you to type lowercase initials, you will need to turn off the automatic correction. To do this, complete the following steps.

1. Click the File tab and then click the Options button.
2. At the Word Options dialog box, click *Proofing* in the left panel and then click the AutoCorrect Options button.

Formatting with Microsoft Word Default Spacing

DATE: ——➤ February 14, 2012 *(press the Enter key)*
Tab twice
TO: ——➤ Jim Everson, Resources Coordinator *(press the Enter key)*
Tab twice
FROM: ——➤ Isabelle Brown, Training Coordinator *(press the Enter key)*
Tab twice
SUBJECT: ——➤ Network and Internet Books *(press the Enter key)*
Tab once
While attending the Southern Computer Technology Conference earlier this month, I discovered several excellent network and Internet security reference books. Two of these reference books, *Managing Network Security* by Douglas Baker (published by Evergreen Publishing House) and *Network Management* by Geraldine Kingston (published by Bonari & Jenkins), I would like you to order and make available in the business section of the library. Both books retail for approximately $55. If you have enough in your budget, please order two copies of each book. *(press the Enter key)*

Two other reference books, *Internet Security* by Jeong Pak (published by Meridian Publishers) and *Protecting and Securing Data* by Glenn Rowan (published by Canon Beach Publishing), I would like you to order for the technical support team training that will take place in April. I will need 15 copies of *Internet Security* and 20 copies of *Protecting and Securing Data*. *(press the Enter key)*

XX *(press Shift + the Enter key)*
BookMemo.docx

3. At the AutoCorrect dialog box, click the AutoCorrect tab and then click the *Capitalize first letter of sentences* check box to remove the check mark.

4. Click OK to close the AutoCorrect dialog box and then click OK to close the Word Options dialog box.

After typing your initials, press Shift + Enter (the New Line command) to move the insertion point to the next line without adding paragraph spacing and then type the document name.

The Word default line spacing is 1.15 and the default spacing after paragraphs is 10 points. You can remove this formatting by clicking the *No Spacing* style in the Styles group in the Home tab. Applying this style changes the line spacing to 1 and the spacing after paragraphs to 0 points. To format a memo without the Word default spacing, click the *No Spacing* style and then type the memo as follows.

Formatting with No Spacing Style Applied

DATE: ———▶ February 14, 2012 *(press the Enter key two times)*
   Tab twice
TO: ———▶ Jim Everson, Resources Coordinator *(press the Enter key two times)*
   Tab twice
FROM: ———▶ Isabelle Brown, Training Coordinator *(press the Enter key two times)*
   Tab twice
SUBJECT: ——▶ Network and Internet Books *(press the Enter key three times)*
   Tab once

While attending the Southern Computer Technology Conference earlier this month, I discovered several excellent network and Internet security reference books. Two of these reference books, *Managing Network Security* by Douglas Baker (published by Evergreen Publishing House) and *Network Management* by Geraldine Kingston (published by Bonari & Jenkins), I would like you to order and make available in the business section of the library. Both books retail for approximately $55. If you have enough in your budget, please order two copies of each book. *(press the Enter key twice)*

Two other reference books, *Internet Security* by Jeong Pak (published by Meridian Publishers) and *Protecting and Securing Data* by Glenn Rowan (published by Canon Beach Publishing), I would like you to order for the technical support team training that will take place in April. I will need 15 copies of *Internet Security* and 20 copies of *Protecting and Securing Data*. *(press the Enter key twice)*

XX *(press the Enter key once)*
BookMemo.docx

Formatting a Business Letter

Like a personal business letter, a variety of formatting options are available for formatting a business letter with the ***block style*** being one of the most common. In a block style format, all elements of the letter are aligned at the left margin. You can create a business letter with the default Microsoft Word 2010 line and paragraph spacing, or remove the spacing and then create the letter. Include your reference initials at the end of the letter as shown below (where the *XX* indicates your initials). If you want to type your reference initials in lowercase letters, refer to the information in Appendix C. The business letters on this page and the next page contain standard punctuation, which includes a colon after the salutation (*Dear Mrs. Cardoza:*) and a comma after the complimentary close (*Sincerely,*).

Formatting with Microsoft Word Default Spacing

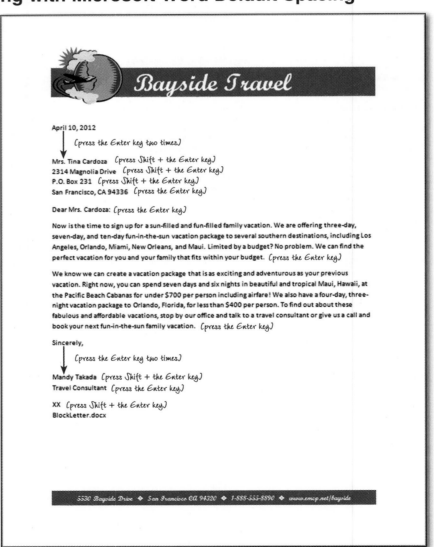

The Word default line spacing is 1.15 and the default spacing after paragraphs is 10 points. You can remove this formatting by clicking the *No Spacing* style in the Styles group in the Home tab. Applying this style changes the line spacing to 1 and the spacing after paragraphs to 0 points. To format a business letter without the Word default spacing, click the *No Spacing* style and then type the letter as shown in the following.

Formatting with No Spacing Style Applied

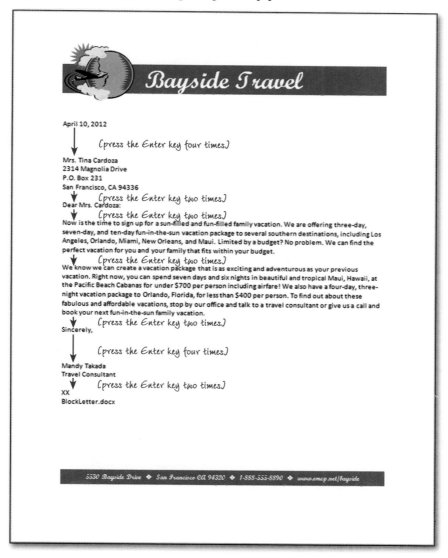

Index

A

Abacus: Chinese, 43
Abbreviations: adding to AutoCorrect, 753
Accept button, 689
Accessibility checker issues, 882
Active document, 310
Add-In options, 777
Address bar
   in Open dialog box, 13, 277
   in Save As dialog box, 9
Address Block button, 544
Addressing envelopes, 324, 326
Add Text button, 974
Alignment. *See also* Margins
   changing cell, 469
   changing paragraph, 64–68
   changing table, 474–475
   deleting tabs from Ruler, 109
   of images, 363–364
   of indexes, 947
   moving tabs on Ruler, 109
   setting tabs on Ruler, 107
   of shapes, 399
   of text in cells, 471
   vertical of text, 235–236
Alignment button on Ruler, 69
Alignment buttons for tabs, 106
Align Text Left button, 64
Alt text, 882
American Psychological Association (APA)
   reference style, 919–920, 928, 930
Antonyms: finding, 147–148
Apply Styles window, 816
Arabic numerals
   changing to other format, 647
   inserting, 220
   removing, 220
Area charts, 496
Arithmetic operations
   default formula, 481
   performing in tables, 481–485
   recalculating formulas, 485
   writing formulas, 484

Arrange All button, 310
Asterisk (*) in document names, 10
Auto Check for Errors button, 547
AutoComplete feature, 8
AutoCorrect
   adding words to, 753
   deleting text, 759
   displaying dialog box, 755
   inserting symbols, 756–757
   specifying exceptions, 752–753
   turning off capitalization, 952, 954
   undoing corrected text, 755
AutoCorrect dialog box
   with AutoCorrect Tab selected, 752
   with AutoFormat As You Type Tab selected,
      78, 758
   symbols available at, 756
AutoCorrect Exceptions dialog box, 753
AutoCorrect feature, 7
AutoCorrect Options button, 755
AutoFit button, 468
AutoFormatting
   customizing, 758
   restricting changes made with, 858
Automatic Grammar Checker feature, 7
Automatic Spell Checker feature, 7
Autosaved backup documents, 887–888
Autosave Documents in Information Tab
   Backstage view, 887
Auto Text gallery: saving content as building block
   to, 723

B

Backslash (\) in document names, 10
Backstage view, 10
Bar charts, 496
Bibliographies
   formatting, 930
   inserting, 928
   modifying, 929
Bibliography button, 928
Blank page: inserting, 217
Blank Page button, 217

Bold button, 37, 40
Bookmark button, 257
Bookmark dialog box, 257
Bookmarks
    turning on, 257
    using to create hyperlinks, 259
    using to navigate in documents, 257–258
Borders
    applying to tables, 447
    changing measurements, 203
    changing spacing options, 103
    customizing, 100–101
    inserting on page, 201–204
    inserting paragraph, 97
Borders and Shading dialog box
    with Borders Tab selected, 100, 447
    with Page Border Tab selected, 201
    with Shading Tab selected, 101
Borders and Shading Options dialog box, 103, 203
Borders button, 447
Borders Button Drop-down List, 97
Break Link button, 409
Breaks: inserting section, 189–190
Breaks button, 189
Breaks Button Drop-down List, 189
Browse button: on Compare Documents dialog box, 691
Browsing in documents, 17
Bubble charts, 496
Building block gallery: inserting as button on Quick Access toolbar, 730
Building blocks
    deleting, 734
    editing properties, 725
    inserting, 718–719
    inserting button on Quick Access toolbar for gallery of, 730
    inserting custom, 727–728
    modifying, 730
    saving content as, 722–723
    saving content as to Auto Text gallery, 723
    saving content as to Quick Part gallery, 723
    sorting, 719
Building Blocks Organizer dialog box, 718
Bulleting paragraphs, 81–82
Bullets
    defining new, 615–621
    inserting custom in lists, 615
Bullets button, 78, 82, 610

Bullets Library, 616
Buttons: adding at Quick Access toolbar, 730, 761

C

Calculations
    default formula, 481
    performing in tables, 481–485
    recalculating formulas, 485
    writing formulas, 484
Capitalization
    controlling using AutoCorrect, 752, 753
    finding irregular, 135
    turning off AutoCorrect, 952, 954
Caption dialog box, 978
Captions
    creating, 978
    described, 978
    inserting, 351
Carpal tunnel syndrome, defined, 41
Case matching, 231
Case sensitive: defined, 588
Cell designation, 438
Cell Margins button, 473
Cell Options dialog box, 473
Cells
    changing alignment in tables, 471
    changing direction, 474
    changing margin measurements, 473
    defined, 41, 438
    entering text in tables, 439
    location designation, 438
    merging in tables, 466
    selecting in table with keyboard commands, 443
    selecting in table with mouse, 442
    splitting in tables, 466
Center button, 64
Change Case button, 37, 42
Change Chart Type button, 499
Change Styles button, 49, 77, 814
Change your view button, 284
Chapters in document
    creating different headers and footers for different, 659
    numbering, 650
    printing specific pages, 661
Characters
    adjusting spacing, 418–419
    creating drop caps, 251
    formatting with WordArt, 418–423

ignoring white-space in searches, 231
inserting special, 249
not allowed in file names, 10
removing formatting, 37
Chart button, 351, 496
Chart Elements button, 503
Charts
    area, 496
    bar, 496
    bubble, 496
    changing design, 499–501
    changing formatting, 508–509
    changing layout and style, 502
    changing location in document, 511
    changing size, 511
    changing type, 499
    column, 496
    creating, 496–497
    creating in Word documents, 496–498
    customizing backgrounds, 507
    doughnut, 496
    formatting layout, 503–508
    inserting elements in, 505
    inserting images in, 505
    inserting in forms, 1010
    inserting text boxes in, 505
    line, 496
    managing data in, 501
    pie, 496
    positioning labels in, 506
    radar, 496
    saving as templates, 499
    scatter, 496
    selecting elements, 503
    stock, 496
    surface, 496
    types, 496
    XY, 496
Chart Title button, 506
Chart Tools Design Tab, 499
Chart Tools Format Tab, 509
Chart Tools Layout Tab, 503
Check box form fields, 1019
    customizing, 1026
Checking and Reporting Errors dialog box, 547
Chicago Manual of Style (CMS), 919
Chinese abacus, 43
Choose a SmartArt Graphic dialog box, 371

Citations
    choosing style, 931
    creating, 919
    creating table of authorities listing, 981–982
    editing, 984
    inserting, 921, 923
    styles for, 919
Clear All button, 120
Clear Formatting button, 37
Click and Type feature, 234
Clip art, 41, 1010
    customizing, 351
    editing individual components of, 369
    formatting, 362
    inserting, 351, 359–361
    inserting in headers and footers, 651–652
    linking to new documents, 261
Clip Art button, 351, 359, 652
Clip Art Task pane, 360, 361
Clipboard: using, 120–122, 276
Clipboard group, 114
    Format Painter, 74
Clipboard Task, 120
Close button, 15, 498
Closing documents, 12, 1055
Collapse button, 1047
Collapsed document example, 1050
Colon (:) in document name, 10
Colors
    changing page, 199
    to distinguish comments of different users, 678
    font, 37
    in Quick Styles Set, 814
    shading, 99, 100–101, 103, 447
    text highlight, 42
Colors dialog box, 99
Color themes, 51, 99
    applying custom, 793
    changing, 52
    choosing at Colors dialog box, 794
    customizing, 790–791
    deleting custom, 802
    editing custom, 799
    resetting custom, 791
Column breaks: inserting, 194
Column charts, 496
Columns
    balancing on page, 195
    changing width and height in tables, 468–469

in concordance files, 952
creating, 191–195
creating with Columns dialog box, 193
creating with section breaks, 192
designation in tables, 438
determining tabs settings, 113
inserting breaks, 194
minimum width, 191
moving in tables, 438
removing, 193
selecting and deleting in tables, 464
sorting at header row, 589
sorting by, 588
sorting text in, 588
Columns button, 191
Columns dialog box, 193
Combine Documents dialog box, 694
Combining
shared documents, 694–695
subdocuments, 1058
Combo Box Content Control button, 1013
Commands
adding to Quick Access toolbar, 761
adding to tabs, 768
creating new, 767
customizing with Quick Access Toolbar button
drop-down list, 763–764
Comment Balloon, 673
Comments in shared documents
deleting, 679
displaying, 685–686
distinguishing those of different users, 678
editing, 677
printing, 678
Compare button, 691
Compare Documents dialog box, 691
Comparison words: inserting during merge, 566–567
Concordance files: creating, 952–955
Condensed option (font), 418
Contact Us button, 25
Content Control Properties button, 1012
Content Control Properties dialog box for Date
Picker Content Control, 1016
Content Control Properties dialog box for Drop-
down List Content Control, 1012
Content Control Properties dialog box for Picture
Content Control, 1015
Content controls
defined, 999

setting properties for, 1012–1016
Content option in Open dialog box, 285
Contextual Alternates (fonts), 422
Contextual ligatures, 420
Continuous section breaks, 189
Convert to Text button, 479
Copy button, 118
Copying
documents to other folders, 281
footnotes and endnotes, 917
shapes, 398
styles to templates, 842
text by pasting, 114
text using Clipboard, 120–122
text using Copy button, 118
text using mouse, 119
Copyright symbol (©), 623, 624
Corrections. *See also* Editing
Auto Check for Errors button, 547
AutoCorrect feature, 7
Eraser button, 451
Cover page: inserting, 217
Cover Page button, 217
Cover Page Drop-down List, 217
Create a Digital ID dialog box, 874
Create button, 13
Create Link button, 409
Create New Building Block dialog box, 722
Create New Style from Formatting dialog box, 818
Create New Theme Colors dialog box, 790
Create New Theme Fonts dialog box, 796
Create Source dialog box, 921
Creating New Style from Formatting dialog box
with Table Style Type selected, 833
Cross-reference button, 264
Cross-reference dialog box, 264
Cross-references
creating, 264
creating in indexes, 945, 949
Custom dictionaries: creating, 144–145
Custom Dictionaries dialog box, 145
Customizations
exporting, 772
importing, 772
Customize Quick Access Toolbar button, 11
customizing, 763–764
Customize Quick Access Toolbar button Drop-
down List, 761
Customize Quick Print button, 11

Customizing. *See also* Documents; Formatting; Text
  AutoCorrect, 752–759
  AutoFormatting, 758
  bullets in lists, 615
  chart backgrounds, 507
  chart formatting, 508
  charts, 503
  check box form field options, 1026
  clip art, 351
  color themes, 790–791, 793
  column width and height, 468–469
  compare options, 692–693
  content control properties for date pickers in forms, 1015–1016
  content control properties for pictures in forms, 1015
  creating custom dictionary, 144–145
  Dialog Box layout, 286
  different headers and footers for different sections, 659
  different headers and footers for odd and even pages, 659
  display of folders and documents in Content pane, 284
  document properties, 868
  envelopes, 540
  first page headers and footers, 659
  form field options, 1022–1027
  Full Screen Reading view, 181
  grammar checking, 141
  headers, 651
  hyperlink Screen Tip, 259
  images, 351, 359, 363
  importing and exporting, 772
  label settings, 327
  layout of images, 363
  line margins, 198
  margins, 187
  numbers in lists, 610
  with Options at Word Options dialog box, 763–764
  page numbers, 647
  paragraph borders and shading, 100–101
  Quick Access toolbar, 760–766
  ribbon, 766–768
  saving custom Quick Styles set, 824
  screenshot images, 391, 392
  shapes, 400
  spell checking, 137
  table of contents, 970–971
  tables, 450
  tables with Table Tools Design tab, 454
  text boxes, 404, 407, 415
  text form fields, 1026–1027
  theme fonts, 796
  themes, 789, 799, 802
  track changes displayed in document, 686–687
  Word Options dialog box, 774, 776–777
Cut button, 114
Cutting. *See* Deleting
Cutting, copying and pasting, 114

D
Database functions
  finding records, 598
  selecting records, 596–599
  sorting records in data source, 592–596
  sorting text, 585–592
Data source files
  creating, 541–542
  defined, 541
  editing, 555–557
  merging, 565-570
  selecting specific records for merge, 596–598
Date
  inserting, 252
  inserting in headers and footers, 652
  sorting type, 586
Date and Time dialog box, 252
Date Picker Content Control button, 1012
Date pickers
  customizing content control properties of in forms, 1015–1016
  inserting in forms, 1012
Date & Time button, 252, 652
Default autosave, 888
Default dictionary, 144, 145
Default document formats, 8
Default document view, 177
Default footer position, 654
Default formatting, 35
Default header position, 654
Default margins, 177
Default margins of cells, 473
Default numbers, 647
Default sorting option, 585
Default styles in Quick Styles Set, 813–814, 827

Default templates, 789, 801
Define New Bullet dialog box, 615
Define New List Style dialog box, 829
Define New Multilevel List dialog box, 620
Define New Number Format dialog box, 613
Delete button, 679
Delete button in Table Tools Layout Tab, 464
Deleting
    AutoCorrect text, 759
    building blocks, 734
    character formatting, 37
    column formatting, 193
    columns in tables, 464
    comments, 679
    custom color themes, 802
    custom style in Quick Styles Set, 827
    custom themes, 802
    dictionaries, 145
    documents, 278–279
    folders, 283
    footers, 224
    footnotes and endnotes, 917
    headers, 224
    indexes, 955
    macros, 1065
    page breaks, 216
    placeholders, 221
    predesigned footers, 224
    predesigned headers, 224
    predesigned page numbers, 220
    to Recycle Bin, 279
    research sources, 925
    rows in tables, 464
    table of authorities, 984
    table of contents, 972
    table of figures, 981
    tabs at Tabs dialog box, 110
    tabs from Ruler, 109
    text, 20, 114
Deletion commands, 20
Demote button, 1047
Demote to Body Text button, 1047
Details options: in Open dialog box, 284
Details pane: in Save As dialog box, 9
Developer Tab, 999
    displaying, 1000
Diagrams. *See* Charts; SmartArt diagrams
Dialog Box: changing layout, 286

Dialog boxes
    changing views, 284–286
    getting Help in, 28
Dictionaries
    creating custom, 144–145
    default, 144
    removing, 145
Digital signatures
    adding, 874
    inserting on signature line, 878
    removing, 876
Directories: merging, 554
Discretionary ligatures, 420
Display for Review button Drop-down List, 685
Display Option, 65–66
Distribute Columns button, 468
Distribute Rows button, 468
Document File Types section, 293
Document icon, 276
Document Information panel, 866
Document in Outline View: example, 1046
Document inspector: using, 879
Document Inspector dialog box, 879
Document management tasks. *See also* Copying;
    Merging documents; Moving; Printing;
    Renaming
    changing dialog box views, 284–286
    copying and moving documents, 281
    creating documents using templates, 299–300
    creating folders, 276
    deleting documents, 278–279
    deleting folders, 283
    displaying document properties, 285
    opening in Read-Only, 283
    opening multiple documents, 283, 310
    renaming documents, 282
    renaming folders, 278
    saving as blog post, 291
    saving in different formats, 292–293, 296
    saving in PDF/XPS format, 297–299
    saving to SharePoint, 290
    saving to SkyDrive, 290
    selecting documents, 278
    sending using e-mail, 290
    sharing documents, 289–299
    using Print Screen, 276
Document properties
    customizing, 868
    displaying, 285

inserting, 736
managing, 865–868
Documents. *See also* Customizing; Formatting; Forms; Shared documents; Text
  accessing most recently opened, 317–318
  adding digital signature to, 874
  arranging, 310, 311
  automatic saving of, 887
  blank screen, 6
  browsing in, 17
  changing chart location in, 511
  changing views, 181–182
  changing zoom, 316
  checking accessibility of, 882
  checking compatibility of, 885
  checking for personal or hidden data, 879
  checking grammar, 135, 136
  checking spelling, 135–137
  closing, 12
  collapsing and expanding, 1050–1051
  combining, 694–695
  copying to other folders, 281
  creating, 6–8
  creating charts in, 496–498
  creating columns in, 191–195
  creating new, 13
  creating using templates, 299–300
  customizing display of Content pane, 284
  customizing how track changes display in, 686
  customizing which track changes display in, 687
  default formats, 8
  deleting, 278–279
  deleting text, 20
  determining which are open, 310
  displaying properties, 285
  editing, 16–24
  editing while spell checking, 136
  encrypting, 873
  example of collapsed, 1050
  hiding white space, 316
  inserting date, 252
  inserting files from other, 253
  inserting hyperlinks, 259–263
  inserting information in, 151
  inserting section breaks in, 189–190
  inserting signature on signature line, 878
  inserting symbols and special characters in, 249
  inserting text, 20
  inserting time in, 252
  inspecting, 878–888
  keyboard commands to navigate in, 182
  limiting access with IRM, 874
  main, 541, 544, 555, 560–563
  managing versions, 887–888
  marking as final, 872
  master and sub, 1041, 1054–1055
  maximizing, 310
  merging, 531–565, 596–598
  minimizing, 310
  moving insertion point with Go To option, 17
  moving insertion point with keyboard, 18
  moving tables in, 474
  naming, 10
  navigating in, 254–258
  numbering chapters in, 650
  opening, 6, 13, 1055
  opening in Read-Only, 283
  opening in different views, 864
  opening multiple, 283, 310
  pinning, 14
  previewing before printing, 319
  printing, 10–11
  printing specific pages, 320
  printing specific sections of, 661
  proofing, 135–154
  protecting with password, 863
  rearranging sections in Outline View, 1053
  recovering unsaved, 318
  redo button, 24
  removing digital signature from, 876
  renaming, 282
  restoring down, 310
  restoring from Recycle Bin, 279
  saving, 9–10
  saving as blog post, 291
  saving as read-only, 857
  saving as template, 829
  saving in different formats, 292–293, 296
  saving in PDF/XPS format, 297–299
  saving themes, 797
  saving to SharePoint, 290
  saving to SkyDrive, 290
  saving with Save As, 15
  seeing overview of, 1041
  selecting text, 20–22, 278
  sharing, 289–298
  showing white space, 316

undo button, 24
updating a template, 830
using New Line command, 8
vertical scroll bar, moving, 16
viewing side by side, 313–314
Document structure checks, 882
Doughnut charts, 496
Draft button, 181
Draft button on Status bar, 181
Draft view, 181
section breaks in, 189
Drawings. *See* Images; Pictures
Drawing Tools Format Tab, 369, 394
Draw Table button, 449
Draw Text button, 505
Drop Cap button, 251
Drop caps: creating, 251
Drop-Down Form Field Options dialog box, 1022
Drop-Down List Content Control button, 1012
Drop-down lists
creating, 1012
creating form field for, 1022–1023
specifying properties, 1012–1013

E

Edit Data button, 501
Edit Data Source dialog box, 557
Editing. *See also* AutoCorrect
advantages of Outline View, 1050
applied styles, 825
bibliographies, 929
building block properties, 725
building blocks with Quick Parts, 730
checking spelling while, 136
citations, 984
by copying and pasting, 114
custom color themes, 799
custom themes, 799
by cutting, 114
data in charts, 501
data source files, 555–557
documents, 16–24
drop-down list properties, 1013
fields in data source file, 557
form templates, 1006
with Go To option, 17
images, 369
limiting with IRM, 874

main documents, 555
moving insertion point with buttons, 17
moving insertion point with Go To option, 17
moving insertion point with keyboard, 18
moving text with mouse, 114
multilevel list styles, 836
predesigned headers and footers, 221–225
predesigned styles, 822
records in data source files, 557
redo button, 24
research sources, 925
restricting to protect templates, 1000–1001
shapes, 400
styles, 822, 825
table styles, 836
undo button, 24
using Paste Options button, 116–117
vertical scroll bar, moving, 16
works cited pages, 929
Editing shared documents
accepting revisions, 689
combining, 694–695
comments, 687
comparing, 691–693, 692–693
concurrently, 669
customizing compare options, 692–693
deleting comments, 679
displaying comments, 685–686
distinguishing comments of different users, 678
inserting comments, 673
inserting comments in Reviewing pane, 675
limiting by others, 857
navigating between comments, 677
navigating to revisions, 688
rejecting revisions, 689
restricting to certain changes, 861
showing source, 695
tracking changes to, 675–677, 682–683, 688
viewing compared, 691
Edit Recipient List button, 555
Edit shape button, 400
Effects theme, 51
applying, 797
changing, 52
Else fields, 561–562
E-mail: sending documents using, 290
Email addresses: using hyperlinks with, 261
Em dashes, 625

Enclosed shapes: drawing, 396–398. *See also* Shapes

Encrypting documents, 873

En dashes, 625

Endnotes
   copying, 917
   creating, 915
   deleting, 917
   moving, 917
   numbering, 915, 917
   printing, 916
   viewing and showing, 917

End-of-cell Marker, 438

End-of-row Marker, 438

Envelopes
   creating and printing, 324–326
   customizing, 550
   merging, 550

Envelopes and Labels dialog box
   with Envelopes tab selected, 324
   with Labels Tab selected, 327

Envelopes button, 324

Envelope Options dialog box, 550

Eraser button, 450

Excel
   editing data in, 501
   entering data in, 497
   inserting and formatting, 452
   using Word with, 493, 497–498

Exceptions button (AutoCorrect dialog box with AutoCorrect Tab selected), 752

Exit button, 15

Exiting Word, 15

Expand button, 1047

Expanded Compare Documents dialog box, 692

Expanded Create New Style from Formatting dialog box, 820

Expanded Find and Replace dialog box, 230–231

Expanded option (font), 418

Exporting customizations, 772

Extend mode (in cells), 443

F

Field dialog box, 738, 1073

Fields
   check box form, 1019, 1026
   in data source file, 541, 542
   editing in data source file, 557
   fill-in, 560, 1072–1073

form, 999
   inserting, 738
   inserting additional in main document, 560
   inserting comparison during merge, 561–562
   inserting date or time as, 252
   in main document, 541
   marking table of contents entries as, 974–975
   selecting specific for merging, 596–598
   separating for sorting, 587–588
   sorting on more than one, 585, 589–590
   text form, 1018, 1026–1027
   updating, 740

File names: characters not allowed in, 10

Files
   concordance, 952–955
   inserting, 253
   using hyperlinks to link to files in multiple documents, 261

File Tab, 6, 7, 9, 13

Filing systems, 273

Fill-in dialog box, 561

Fill-in fields
   inserting in main documents, 560
   recording macro with, 1072–1073

Filter and Sort dialog box
   with Filter Records Tab selected, 596
   with Sort Records Tab selected, 595

Final documents, 872

Find and Replace dialog box
   Expanded, 230–231
   with Replace Tab selected, 229

Find button, 17

Find Entry dialog box, 547

Finding and replacing
   special characters, 627
   text, 226–227, 229–230

Finding personal or hidden text, 879

Find Recipient button, 546

Finish & Merge button, 547

First Line Indent marker, 69

First page: creating different header or footer, 656

First Record button, 546

Flesch-Kincaid Grade Level, 143

Flesch Reading Ease score, 143

Folder icon, 276

Folders
   copying documents to other, 281
   creating, 276
   customizing display of Content pane, 284

deleting, 283

in Open dialog box, 276–277

renaming, 278

Font button, 37, 38

Font Button Drop-down Gallery, 38

Font Color button, 37, 42

Font dialog box, 46

with Advanced tab selected, 418

changing fonts at, 45

Font effects

applying, 42

choosing, 42

Font Group buttons, 37, 42

Fonts

changing, 37–46, 38

changing at Font dialog box, 45

changing at Symbol dialog box, 249

character spacing, 418–422

choosing effects, 42

choosing typestyles, 40

default, 37

default proportional spacing, 420

default tabular spacing, 420

keyboard shortcuts, 42

previewing formatting, 38

in Quick Styles Set, 814

stylistic sets, 421

type size, 38

Font Size button, 37, 38

Font themes, 51

changing, 52

customizing, 796

Footer button, 224, 651

Footers

creating custom, 651

creating different for different sections, 659

creating different for first page, 656

creating different for odd and even pages, 657

editing, 225

inserting elements in, 652

inserting predesigned, 221–222, 224

navigating in, 653

positioning, 654

removing predesigned, 224

saving content as building block, 722

Footnotes

copying, 917

creating, 915

deleting, 917

moving, 917

numbering, 915, 917

printing, 916

viewing and editing, 917

Format, 35

Format Painter: formatting with, 74

Format Painter button, 74

Format Picture dialog box, 363

Format Selection button, 503

Format Text Effects dialog box, 423

Formatting. *See also* Customizing; Documents; Text; Themes

advantages of using styles, 825

applying styles from Quick Styles Set, 49

applying themes, 51–52

bibliographies, 930

changing chart, 508–511

changing chart layout, 499

changing default, 177

changing fonts, 37–46

changing page color, 199

characters with WordArt, 418–423

chart layout, 503–508

clip art, 362

columns, 191–195

comparing, 84

cover page, 217

creating columns, 191–195

creating new style based on existing, 818

customizing AutoFormatting, 758

customizing chart, 508

finding and replacing, 232

first page of research paper, 919

hyphenating words, 196

images, 351–352, 362–365

indexes, 947

inserting blank pages, 217

inserting line numbers, 197–198

inserting page border, 201–204

inserting page breaks, 215–216

inserting predesigned headers and footers, 221–225

inserting predesigned page numbering, 220

inserting watermarking, 199

limiting by others in shared documents, 857

page numbers in table of contents, 968

previewing fonts, 38

removing character, 37

removing column, 193

restricting to certain styles in shared documents, 858

revealing, 83–84

revealing style, 827

SmartArt diagrams, 371, 374

with styles, 813–814

table of authorities, 983–984

table of contents, 970–971

table of figures, 977, 978

text in form field, 1027

vertical alignment of text, 235–236

WordArt text, 413

WordArt text box, 415–417

works cited pages, 930

Formatting marks: turning on, 45, 65

Formatting Restrictions dialog box, 858

Form fields

customizing options, 1022–1027

defined, 999

Forms

creating as templates, 1001

creating using tables, 1008

creating with Legacy Tools, 1018–1021

defined, 999

designing, 997

editing templates, 1006

elements of, 997

filling in, 1002, 1021, 1023

inserting charts in, 1010

inserting check box form fields, 1018

inserting date pickers in, 1010

inserting images in, 1010

inserting instructional text in, 1008

inserting shapes in, 1010

inserting SmartArt diagrams in, 1010

inserting tables in, 1010

inserting text controls, 1004

inserting text form fields, 1018

printing, 1021

protecting templates, 1000–1001

Formula button, 479

Formula dialog box, 479

Formulas

default, 479

recalculating, 483

using functions in Formula dialog box, 479

writing own, 482

Forward slash (/) in document names, 10

Full Screen Reading button, 181

Full Screen Reading button on Status bar, 181

Full Screen Reading view, 181–182

Function: defined, 479

G

General Options dialog box, 863

Go to Footer button, 653

Go To Tab, 17

Got To option, 17

Grammar

changing options, 141

checking, 135, 136

checking explanations, 140

not checking, 136

Grammar Checker, automatic, 7

Graphics. *See also* Images

using hyperlinks with, 261

Graphs. *See* Charts

Greater than sign (>) in document names, 10

Greeting Line button, 544

Gridlines, 438

viewing, 471

Groups: renaming, 767–768

Grow Font button, 37

H

Hanging Indent marker, 69

Hanging indents, 70, 71

Hard copy, 10

Hard page breaks, 215–216

Header button, 221, 651

Header Button Drop-down List, 222

Header & Footer Tools Design Tab, 651

Header rows

repeating, 469

sorting at, 589

Headers

creating custom, 651

creating different for different sections, 651

creating different for first page, 656

creating different for odd and even pages, 657

editing, 225

inserting elements in, 652

inserting predesigned, 221–222

navigating in, 653

positioning, 654

removing predesigned, 224

saving content as building block, 722

Headings in outlines: assigning, 1046–1047
Help: using, 25–28
Help button, 25
Help Tab Backstage view, 25–26
Hidden text
    checking for, 879
    displaying, 45
Hide All hyperlink in Help, 25
Historical ligatures, 420
Home Tab, 17
Homophones: searching, 231
Horizontal ruler, 6, 7, 438
Hyperlink button, 259
Hyperlinks
    inserting, 259
    linking files in multiple documents, 261
    linking files in new document, 261
    linking to email addresses, 261
    navigating in document using, 259
    using graphics, 261
Hyphenating words
    automatically, 196
    manually, 196
Hyphenation button, 196
Hyphens
    in customizing numbers, 647
    inserting, 196, 624–625
    in printing commands, 320, 661
    in setting leader tabs, 112
    in writing formulas, 482

I-beam pointer, 6, 7
If fields, 561–562
Images
    formatting, 351–352, 362–365
    inserting Clip Art, 359–362
    inserting in charts, 505
    inserting in forms, 1010
    inserting pictures, 351
    linking to new documents, 261
    moving, 355–356
    rotating, 356
    sizing, 355
    text representing, 882
    ungrouping, 369
    wrapping text around, 364
Importing customizations, 772

Indented index option, 947
Indenting
    examples of, 71
    options, 70
    text in paragraphs, 69–71
Indent markers, 69
Indexes
    deleting, 955
    described, 941
    inserting, 947
    making cross-references, 945, 948
    marking text for, 943–945, 948
    marking text for with concordance file, 952
    types, 947
    updating, 955
Information
    inserting in documents, 151
    researching, 150–151
Information Rights Management (IRM), 874
Information tab Backstage View, 866
Insert Above button in Table Tools Layout Tab, 462
Insert Below button in Table Tools Layout Tab, 462
Insert Caption button, 978
Insert Chart dialog box, 497
Insert Citation button, 921
Insert Endnote button, 915
Insert Footnote button, 915
Insert Hyperlink dialog box, 259
Insert Index button, 947
Inserting
    additional text in table of contents, 976
    bibliographies, 928
    blank page, 217
    border on page, 201–204
    building block gallery as button on Quick Access toolbar, 730
    building blocks, 718–719
    captions, 351
    chart elements, 505
    charts in forms, 1010
    charts in Word documents, 496–498
    check box form fields, 1019
    citations, 921, 923
    Clip Art, 359–361
    column breaks, 194
    comments in shared documents, 673

comments in shared documents in Reviewing pane, 675
comparison words during merge, 561–562
cover page, 217
cross-references, 264
custom building blocks, 727–728
custom bullets in lists, 615
custom numbers in lists, 610
date, 252
date as field, 252
date pickers in forms, 1010
digital signatures, 874
document properties, 736
fields, 738
files, 253
fill-in fields in main documents, 560
footer elements, 652
header elements, 652
hyperlinks, 259–263
hyphens, 624–625
images, 351
images in forms, 1010
indexes, 947
information in documents, 151
instructional text in forms, 1008
intellectual property symbols, 623
labels in charts, 506
line numbers, 197–198
multilevel numbering in lists, 618
nonbreaking spaces, 626
page breaks, 215–216
paragraph borders, 97
paragraph shading, 99
predesigned footers, 221–222, 224
predesigned headers, 221–222
predesigned page numbers, 220
predesigned text boxes, 404
record numbers during merge, 561
Roman numerals, 647
section breaks, 189–190
shapes in forms, 1010
signature line, 876–877
signature on signature line, 878
SmartArt diagrams, 371–372
SmartArt diagrams in forms, 1010
sources, 921–922
symbols and special characters, 249
symbols automatically, 756–757
table of authorities, 983–984

table of contents, 967
table of figures, 978–979
tables in forms, 1008
text, 20
text boxes in charts, 505
text boxes in shapes, 407
text controls in forms, 1004
text during merge, 560–561
text form fields, 1018
text in main document during merge, 560–561
text in shapes, 400
time, 252
time as field, 252
watermark, 199
WordArt, 413–417
works cited pages, 928
Insertion point, 6, 7
movement commands, 18
moving, 17
moving to bookmarks, 257
moving with buttons, 17
moving with Go To option, 17
moving within tables, 439
moving with keyboard, 18
spacing before new paragraph, 8
in split window, 312
using Click and Type feature, 234
Insert Left button in Table Tools Layout Tab, 464
Insert Merge Field button, 544
Insert Right button in Table Tools Layout Tab, 464
Insert Tab Illustrations Group buttons, 351
Insert Table dialog box, 441
Insert Table of Authorities button, 983
Insert Table of Figures button, 978
Insert Word Field
Fill-in dialog box, 561
If dialog box, 562
Intellectual property symbols: inserting, 623
In-text citations, 919
IRM Access, 882
Italic button, 37, 40

K

Kerning, 418, 419
Keyboard commands
aligning paragraphs, 64–65
assigning macros to, 1066
changing line spacing, 76

copying text, 118

creating new document, 13

formatting font with, 42

in Full Screen Reading view, 182

line spacing, 76

moving from one page to another, 182

moving images, 356

moving insertion point, 18

moving insertion point within tables, 439

navigating in documents, 182

printing documents, 10

selecting cells in tables, 443

selecting text, 22

updating date or time, 252

L

Label Options dialog box, 327, 552

Labels

creating and printing, 326–329

merging, 552

positioning in charts, 506

Labels button, 326

Last Record button, 546

Layout. *See* Formatting; Themes

Layout dialog box

with Position Tab selected, 363

with Size Tab selected, 365

with Text Wrapping Tab selected, 364

Leader Tabs, setting, 112

Left Indent marker, 69

Legacy Tools button, 1018

Less than sign (<) in document names, 10

Ligatures, 418, 420–422

Line and Paragraph Spacing button, 76

Line charts, 496

Line drawings, 394, 396

Line Numbers button, 198

Line Numbers dialog box, 198

Lines

changing spacing, 76

numbering, 197–198

selecting to edit, 21

Line Style button, 447

Line Weight button, 447

Lining (numbers) option, 420

Linking

text boxes, 409

using graphics, 261

Link to Previous button, 659

List management

changing list levels, 610

defining multilevel lists, 619–620

defining new bullets, 615–616

defining numbering format, 612–613

inserting custom bullets, 615

inserting custom numbers, 610

inserting hyphens, 624–625

inserting intellectual property symbols, 623

inserting multilevel numbering, 618

inserting nonbreaking spaces, 626

inserting special characters, 623–626

typing multilevel lists, 622

List option in Open dialog box, 284

Lists: creating drop-down, 1012

List styles

creating, 828–830

modifying, 836

Live feature preview, 38

Lowered option (font), 418

M

Macros

about, 1041

assigning to keyboard command, 1066

assigning to Quick Access toolbar, 1068

deleting, 1065

pausing and resuming, 1065

recording, 1060

recording with fill-in fields, 1072–1073

removing to Quick Access toolbar, 1068

running, 1063, 1066

storing, 1060

Macros dialog box, 1060

Mailing labels: creating and printing, 326–329

Mailing Tab, 541

Mail Merge: about, 531

Mail Merge Recipients dialog box, 556, 593

Mail Merge Wizard: using, 570

Main document

defined, 541

inputting text during merge, 560–561

Manage Sources button, 925

Manage Styles dialog box, 839

Manual Hyphenation Box, 196

Margins. *See also* Alignment; Borders; Tabs

changing, 183–184

changing at Page Setup dialog box, 187

changing measurements of cell, 473

default, 177
default of cells, 471
Margins button, 183
Margins Drop-down List, 184
Mark Citation button, 982
Mark Citation dialog box, 983
Mark Entry button, 943
Mark Index Entry dialog box, 944
Mark Table of Contents Entry dialog box, 974
Master documents
    about, 1041, 1053
    closing, 1055
    creating, 1054
    expanding or collapsing subdocuments in, 1055
    opening, 1055
    rearranging subdocuments in, 1058
    splitting or combining subdocuments in, 1058
Maximize button, 310
Merge Cells button in Table Tools Layout Tab, 466
Merge record numbers, 561
Merge to New Document dialog box, 548
Merging documents
    completing, 541–543
    creating data source file, 541–542
    creating main document, 544
    directories, 544
    editing data source files, 555–557
    editing records, 557
    envelopes, 550
    inputting text during, 560–565
    inserting comparison words, 561–562
    inserting record numbers during, 561
    labels, 552
    previewing merge, 546–547
    selecting specific records, 556
    selecting specific records from data source file for, 596–598
    shared documents, 684
    using Mail Merge Wizard, 570
Metadata, 879
Microsoft Excel. *See* Excel
Microsoft Translator, 154
Microsoft Word. *See* Word
Microsoft Word Compatibility Checker dialog box, 885
Minimize button, 310
Minimize the Ribbon button, 760
Mini toolbar
    for editing, 21

formatting with, 42
    turning off, 43
Mini Translator, 154
Modern Language Association (MLA) style, 919–920, 928, 930
Monospaced typefaces, 37, 38
More button, 49
    on Compare Documents dialog box, 691
Mouse
    copying text with, 119
    displaying information about tracked changes with, 683
    dragging images with, 355
    dragging text with, 116
    finding synonyms with, 150
    hovering to learn Screen Tips, 77
    moving document sections with, 1053
    moving tables in documents with, 476
    moving vertical scroll bar with, 16
    pasting with, 119
    positioning in charts with, 506
    selecting cells in tables with, 442
    selecting text with, 21–22
Move down button, 1047
Move Table Column Marker, 438
Move up button, 1047
Moving
    document sections, 1053
    footnotes and endnotes, 917
    images, 355–356
    tables in documents, 476
    text, 114, 116
    vertical scroll bar, 16
Multilevel List Drop-down Gallery, 618
Multilevel lists
    defining, 619–620
    inserting numbering, 618
    typing, 622
Multilevel list styles
    creating, 829–830
    modifying, 836
Multiple documents
    opening, 283, 310
    using hyperlinks to link to files in, 261

N

Naming documents, 10
Navigating
    between comments in shared documents, 677

in footers, 653
in headers, 653
to revisions, 688
using bookmarks, 257–258
using hyperlinks, 259
using keyboard commands, 182
using Navigation pane, 254–255
using table of contents, 968
Navigation pane, 255
   in Open dialog box, 13, 277
   in Save As dialog box, 9
   showing Search Results, 226–227
New Address List dialog box, 542
New button, 13
New Comment button, 673
New Folder button, 276
New Line command, 8
New Tab, 13
New Tab Backstage view, 299
Next button, 17, 653, 677, 688
Next Footnote button, 917
Next Record button, 546
Nonbreaking hyphens, 624–625
Nonbreaking spaces: inserting, 626
Nonprinting characters
   finding and replacing, 627
   formatting and, 65, 626
   in tables, 438
   turning on or off, 45, 624
Nudging, 356
Numbered paragraphs, 78–80
Number Format Drop-down List, 481
Numbering
   applying, 78–80
   chapters in document, 650
   footnotes and endnotes, 915, 917
   lines in document, 197–198
   table of contents pages, 968
   turning off, 79
Numbering button, 78, 610
Numbering format: defining, 612–613
Numbering Gallery, 610
Numbering Library, 612
Numbers
   customizing page, 647
   inserting custom in lists, 610
   inserting multilevel in lists, 618
   inserting predesigned page, 220

lining options, 420–421
removing predesigned page, 220
sorting type, 586
spacing between, 418, 420

O

Object button, 253
Old-style (numbers) option, 420–421
100% button, 316
One Page button, 316
Open button, 13
Open dialog box, 13
   changing layout, 286
   changing views, 284–285
   deleting folders, 283
   folders, 276–277
   opening and moving documents, 281
   opening multiple documents, 283
   renaming documents, 282
Opening documents, 6, 13, 854, 1055
Opening Word, 6
Open Type features: using, 420–422
Optional hyphens, 624
Options button, 8, 25
Organizational charts: creating with SmartArt, 376–378
Organize button, 282
Organizer dialog box, 842
Orientation button, 185
Orphans, 662
Outline button on Status bar, 181
Outline Level button, 1047
Outlines
   assigning headings, 1046–1047
   collapsing and expanding documents, 1050–1051
   rearranging document sections in, 1053
Overtype mode, 20

P

Page Borders button, 201
Page Break button, 215
Page Color button, 199
Page Layout Tab, 51
   applying themes, 51
   changing borders, 203
   changing margins, 183
   changing orientation, 185
   changing page size, 185

Page Number button, 220, 647, 968
Page Number Format dialog box, 647, 968
Page numbers
    customizing, 647
    inserting predesigned, 220
    removing, 220
    in table of contents, 968
Page orientation: changing, 185
Pages. *See also* Footers; Formatting; Headers
    balancing columns on, 195
    changing border measurements, 203
    changing color, 199
    changing margins, 183–184
    changing margins at Page Setup dialog box, 187
    changing size at Page setup dialog box, 188
    controlling widows and orphans, 662
    creating different headers and footers for odd and even, 657
    customizing headers and footers on first, 656
    default format settings, 177
    default margins, 177
    deleting breaks, 216
    editing predesigned footers, 225
    editing predesigned headers, 225
    inserting blank, 217
    inserting borders, 201–204
    inserting cover, 217
    inserting page break, 215–216
    inserting predesigned footers, 221–222, 224
    inserting predesigned headers, 221–222
    inserting predesigned numbers, 220
    inserting watermark, 199
    moving from one to other using keyboard commands, 182
    numbering table of contents, 968
    previewing, 319
    printing specific, 320
    removing predesigned footers, 224
    removing predesigned headers, 224
    removing predesigned numbers, 220
Page setup
    changing margins, 183–184, 187
    changing orientation, 185
    changing page paper size, 185–186
    changing page paper size at Page setup dialog box, 188
Page Setup dialog box
    changing margins, 187

changing page paper size at, 188
    with Layout Tab selected, 236
Page Width button, 316
Panes, 312
Paper size
    changing, 185–186
    changing at Page setup dialog box, 188
Paragraph borders
    changing spacing options, 103
    customizing, 100–101
    inserting, 97
Paragraph dialog box
    alignment changes at, 68
    with Line and Page Breaks Tab selected, 662
Paragraph Group button, 65
Paragraphs
    applying numbering, 78–80
    bulleting, 81–82
    changing alignment, 64–68
    changing spacing, 77
    changing spacing in Quick Styles Set, 814
    changing text alignment at margins, 65
    changing text alignment within, 65
    checking formatting with Style Inspector, 837–838
    controlling widows and orphans, 662
    creating styles, 819–820
    indenting examples, 71
    indenting options, 70
    indenting text in, 69–71
    selecting to edit, 21
    sorting text in, 105, 585–587
    spacing before and after, 8, 73
    turning off numbering, 79
Paragraph shading
    changing spacing options, 103
    customizing, 100–101
    inserting, 99
Paragraph Spacing button, Line and, 76
Passwords
    encrypting, 873
    protecting documents to enforce restrictions on shared documents, 860
    protecting document with, 857, 863
Paste button, 114
Paste Function Drop-down List, 481
Paste Options button, 116
    Drop-down list, 117
Paste Special dialog box, 122

Pasting
    text, 114
    using Clipboard, 120–122
    using Copy button, 118
    using mouse, 119
    using Paste Options button, 116–117
PDF format: saving documents in, 297–299
Pen Color button, 447
Personal text: checking for, 879
Picture button, 351, 505, 652
Picture Content Control button, 1010
Pictures. *See also* Images
    customizing content control properties of in
        forms, 1015
    inserting, 351
    inserting in forms, 1010
Picture Tools Format Tab, 352, 369
Pie charts, 496
Pinning documents, 14
Pipe symbol (|) in document name, 10
Placeholders
    for cover page, 217
    deleting, 221
    for headers and footers, 221–222
    inserting document property, 736
    updating, 736
Plain Text Content Control button, 1008, 1012
Points, 38, 73
Position button, 355, 511
Position option (font), 418
Predesigned footers
    editing, 225
    inserting, 221–222, 224
    removing, 224
Predesigned headers
    editing, 225
    inserting, 221–222
    removing, 224
Predesigned page numbers
    inserting, 220
    removing, 220
Prefixes: search matching, 231
Previewing
    documents before merging, 546–547
    documents before printing, 319
    fonts formatting, 38
    indexes, 947
Preview pane in Open dialog box, 277
Preview Results button, 546

Previous button, 17, 653, 677, 688
Previous Record button, 546
Printing
    comments in shared documents, 678
    data in forms, 1021
    documents, 10–11
    envelopes, 324–326
    footnotes and endnotes, 916
    labels, 326–329
    previewing pages in documents, 319
    specific pages in documents, 320
    specific sections of documents, 661
    text form fields and, 1018
Print Layout button on Status bar, 181
Print Layout view
    changing, 177
    hiding and showing white space, 316
    section breaks in, 189
Print Preview, 11
Print Screen: using, 276
Print Tab Backstage view, 10, 11, 319
Promote button, 1047
Promote to Heading 1 button, 1047
Proofing options, 776
Proofreading documents
    dictionaries, 144–145
    finding synonyms and antonyms, 147–148,
        150
    grammar checking, 135, 136
    grammar checking explanations, 140
    grammar checking options, 141
    spell checking, 135–137
    style checking options, 141
    thesaurus, 147–148
    using Word Options dialog box, 138
    word count display, 147
Properties button, 471, 1022
Properties dialog box, 285
    changing alignment of text in cells, 471
    with Custom Tab selected, 867
    with General Tab selected, 867
Properties setting for content controls,
    1012–1016
Proportional spacing, 420
Proportional typefaces, 37
Punctuation
    ignoring in searches, 231
    spacing, 8

Q

Question mark (?) in document names, 10
Quick Access toolbar, 6, 7
  adding buttons or commands at, 761
  assigning macros to, 1068
  Customize Quick Print button, 11
  customizing, 760–766
  importing and exporting customizations, 772
  inserting building block gallery as button on, 730
  New button, 13
  Open button, 13
  Quick Print button, 11
  removing macros from, 1068
  Save button, 9
  Undo and Redo buttons, 24
Quick Parts
  deleting building blocks, 734
  editing building block properties, 725
  inserting building blocks, 718–719
  inserting custom building blocks, 727–728
  modifying building blocks, 730
  saving content as building block, 722–723
  saving content as building block to Auto Text
    gallery, 723
  saving content as building block to Quick Part
    gallery, 723
  sorting building blocks, 719
Quick Parts button, 718
Quick Parts button Drop-down List Shortcut
    Menu, 728
Quick Print, 319
Quick Print button, 11
Quick Styles Set
  about, 813
  applying styles from, 49
  changing, 814
  default, 813–814
  deleting custom style in, 827
  displaying all, 825
  displaying styles in, 813–814
  restricting changes made with, 858
  returning to default, 827
  saving custom, 824
Quotation mark (") in document names, 10

R

Radar charts, 496
Raised option (font), 418

Readability statistics, 143
Readability Statistics dialog box, 143
Read-Only function, 283
Recent Documents List, 317–318
Recent Tab, 13
  pinning documents, 14
Recent Tab Backstage view, 317
Record Macro dialog box, 1060
Record numbers: inserting during merge, 561
Records
  defined, 541
  editing in data source files, 557
  finding, 599
  finding in databases, 599
  selecting in databases, 596–599
  selecting specific for merging in data source
    files, 596–598
  sorting in data source, 592–596
Recycle Bin
  deleting documents to, 279
  restoring documents from, 279
Recycle Bin button, 279
Redo button, 24
References, citing. See also Endnotes; Footnotes
  choosing style, 931
  creating, 919
  creating table of authorities listing, 982–983
  editing, 984
  inserting, 921, 923
  styles for, 919
Registered trademark symbol (®), 623, 624
Regular hyphens, 624
Reject button, 689
Remove Split button, 312
Removing. See Deleting
Renaming
  documents, 282
  folders, 278
  groups, 767–768
  tabs, 767
Repeating last action, 73
Replacing
  special characters using find and replace, 627
  text using find and replace, 229–230
Research button, 150
Research papers
  creating citations, 919
  creating footnotes and endnotes, 915–918
  deleting sources, 925

formatting first page, 919
    inserting citations, 921, 923
    inserting sources, 921–922
    modifying sources, 925
Research Task pane, 148
Reset button on Word Options dialog box with
    Quick Access Toolbar selected, 763
Reset Window Position button, 314
Resize handles
    changing table size with, 476
    location on table, 438
Restore Down button, 310
Restrict Editing button, 857
Restrict Formatting and Editing Task pane, 857,
    1000–1001
Reveal Formatting Task pane, 83–84
Reviewing Pane
    editing comments in, 677
    inserting comments in, 675
    printing comments in, 678
    tracking changes, 675
Reviewing Pane button, 675
Ribbon, 6, 7
    customizing, 766–768
    importing and exporting customizations, 772
    minimizing, 760
    resetting, 768
Right Indent marker, 69
Roman numerals
    inserting, 647
    in table of contents, 968
Rotating
    cells, 474
    charts, 507, 511
    images, 351, 356, 364
    WordArt text, 413
Rotation handle, 355
Rows
    repeating header, 471
    selecting and deleting in tables, 464
    sorting columns at header, 589
Ruler and Indent Markers, 69
Rulers, 6, 7
    deleting tabs from, 109
    displaying, 69
    manipulating tabs on, 106–109
    moving tabs on, 109
    setting tabs on, 107

Rules button, 560
Run-in index option, 947

S

Sans serif typefaces, 37, 38
Save As button: using, 9
Save As dialog box, 9, 296
Save As Template button, 499
Save button, 9
Save & Send Tab Backstage view, 289
    with Change File Type Option selected, 293
Saving
    automatic, 887
    autosaved backup documents and, 888
    content as building block, 722–723
    content as building block to Auto Text gallery,
        723
    content as building block to Quick Part gallery,
        723
    custom Quick Styles set, 824
    document as template, 829
    documents, 9–10
    documents in different formats, 292–299
    documents PDF/XPS format, 297–299
    documents to SharePoint, 290
    document theme, 797
    file formats, 776
    to SkyDrive, 290
Saving as
    documents, 15
    options, 776
Scale option (font), 418
Scatter charts, 496
Screen Clipping option, 392
Screen features, 7
Screenshot button, 351, 391
Screenshots: creating, 391–392
Screen Tips, learning, 77
Scroll bar, 6
Scrolling: in one document when more are open,
    313
Searching: text, 226–227, 231
Section breaks
    continuous, 189
    creating columns with, 192
    deleting, 189
    inserting, 189–190
Select Browse Object button, 17
Select button in Table Tools Layout Tab, 464

Selecting
 cells, 442–445
 chart elements, 503
 text, 20–22
Select Recipients button, 541
Semicolon (;) in document name, 10
Sentence(s), selecting to edit, 21
Serif typefaces, 37, 38
Shading
 applying to tables, 447
 changing spacing options, 103
 customizing, 100–101
 inserting paragraph, 99
Shading button, 447
Shading Button Drop-down Gallery, 99
Shape Height and Shape Width boxes, 355
Shape Height button, 511
Shapes
 applying styles to charts, 509
 copying, 398
 drawing, 394
 drawing enclosed shapes, 396–398
 drawing lines, 394, 396
 editing, 400
 editing points in, 400
 inserting in charts, 505
 inserting in forms, 1010
 inserting text boxes in, 407
 inserting text in, 400
 selecting and aligning, 399
Shapes button, 351, 394, 505
Shape Width button, 511
Shared documents
 accepting revisions, 689
 combining, 694–695
 comparing, 691–693
 customizing compare options, 692–693
 deleting comments, 679
 displaying comments, 685–686
 distinguishing comments of different users, 678
 editing comments, 677
 editing concurrently, 669
 encrypting, 873
 enforcing restrictions placed on, 860
 inserting comments, 673
 inserting comments in Reviewing pane, 675
 limiting formatting by others in, 857
 locating original, 691
 marking as final, 872

 navigating between comments, 677
 navigating to revisions, 688
 printing comments, 678
 protecting, 857–864
 protecting with IRM, 874
 protecting with password, 863
 rejecting revisions, 689
 restricting editing to certain changes, 861
 restricting formatting to certain styles in, 858
 saving as read-only, 857
 showing source, 695
 tracking changes to, 675–677, 682–683, 688
 viewing compared, 691
SharePoint
 protecting documents, 858
 saving to, 290
SharePoint Server (2010): editing shared
  documents concurrently, 669
Show All hyperlink in Help, 25
Show First Line Only button, 1047
Show/Hide ¶ button, 45, 65
Show Level button, 1047
Show Markup button, 673, 686
Show Notes button, 917
Show Text Formatting button, 1047
Shrink Font button, 37
Signature Line button, 876
Signature lines
 inserting, 876–877
 inserting signature on, 878
Signatures: digital
 adding, 874
 removing, 876
Signature Setup dialog box, 877
Size button, 185
Size Drop-down List, 186
SkyDrive: saving to, 290
SmartArt button, 351, 371
SmartArt diagrams
 creating, 371–378
 creating organizational charts with, 376–378
 formatting, 371, 374
 inserting, 371–372
 inserting in forms, 1010
 inserting text in, 371
 text wrapping style, 374
SmartArt Tools Design Tab, 372
SmartArt Tools Format Tab, 374
Soft copy, 10

Soft page breaks, 215
Sort button, 105, 480, 585
Sorting
    building blocks, 719
    changing options, 587–588
    by columns, 588
    date type, 586
    default option, 585
    at header rows, 589
    on more than one field, 590, 594–595
    number type, 586
    text in columns, 588
    text in paragraphs, 105, 585–587
    text in tables, 480, 590
    text type, 586
    types, 586
Sort Options dialog box, 587
Sort Text dialog box, 105, 586
Source Manager dialog box, 925
Sources (research)
    deleting, 925
    inserting, 921–922
    modifying, 925
Spacing
    adjusting character, 418–419
    after paragraph, 8, 73
    before paragraph, 73
    between numbers, 418, 420
    changing borders options, 103
    changing line, 76
    changing paragraph, 77
    changing shading options, 103
    inserting nonbreaking spaces, 626
    line, 8
    punctuation, 8
Spacing option (font), 418
Spacing punctuation feature, 8
Special Button Pop-up List, 627
Special characters
    finding and replacing, 627
    inserting, 249
    inserting in lists, 623–626
Spell Checker, automatic, 7
Spelling
    changing options, 137
    checking, 135–137
    checking while editing, 136
    without checking grammar, 136
Spelling and Grammar dialog box

buttons on, 137
    changing spell option, 137
    with Grammar Error selected, 136
    with Spelling Error selected, 135
Spelling & Grammar button, 135
Split bar, 312
Split button, 312
Split Cells button in Table Tools Layout Tab, 466
Split Table button in Table Tools Layout Tab, 466
Splitting
    cells in tables, 466
    master documents or subdocuments, 1058
    windows, 312
Standard ligatures, 420
Start button, 6
Start Enforcing Protection dialog box, 860
Start Mail Merge button, 541
Status bar, 6, 7, 181
Stock charts, 496
Strikethrough button, 37, 42
Style Inspector: using, 837–838
Styles
    advantages of using applied, 825
    applying, 815–816
    applying from Quick Styles Set, 49
    applying table, 445
    applying to charts, 509
    applying to create table of contents, 967
    changing chart, 502
    citation, 919–920, 931
    copying to templates, 842
    creating multilevel list, 828–830
    creating new, 819–820
    creating new based on existing formatting, 818
    creating new based on existing style, 818
    creating table, 833
    default, 813–814
    defined, 813
    deleting custom in Quick Styles Set, 827
    displaying all, 825
    displaying in Quick Styles Set, 813–814
    formatting with, 813–814
    managing, 839–840, 842
    modifying applied, 825
    modifying multilevel list, 836
    modifying predesigned, 822
    modifying tables, 836
    option in Word Options dialog box, 141

revealing formatting applied, 827
using Style Inspector, 837–838
Styles Task pane, 816
Stylistic sets (fonts), 421–422
Subdocuments
about, 1041, 1054
automatically created, 1046
closing, 1055
expanding or collapsing, 1055
opening, 1055
rearranging, 1058
splitting or combining, 1058
Subscript button, 37, 42
Suffixes: search matching, 231
SUM part of formula, 479
Superscript button, 37, 42
Surface charts, 496
Symbol button, 249
Symbol dialog box with Symbols Tab selected, 249
Symbols
finding and replacing, 627
inserting, 249
inserting automatically, 756–757
inserting in lists, 623–626
inserting intellectual property, 623
not allowed in document names, 10
Synchronous Scrolling button, 313
Synonyms: finding, 147–148, 150

T

Tab alignment symbols, 106
Tab leaders, 971
Table button, 438
Table Contents button, 967
Table headers, 882
Table Move Handle, 438
Table of authorities
creating, 982–983
deleting, 984
described, 981–982
inserting, 983–984
updating, 984
Table of Authorities dialog box, 983
Table of contents
applying styles to create, 967
assigning levels to entries, 974
customizing, 970–971
described, 967
inserting, 967

inserting additional text in, 976
marking entries as fields, 974–975
navigating using, 968
numbering pages, 968
removing, 972
updating, 971–972
Table of Contents dialog box, 971
Table of Contents Options dialog box, 975
Table of figures
creating captions for, 978
deleting, 981
inserting, 978–979
updating, 981
Table of Figures dialog box, 978
Table Options dialog box, 473
Table Properties dialog box with Table Tab
selected, 475
Tables
applying borders, 447
applying shading, 447
applying styles, 445
changing alignment, 474–475
changing cell alignment, 471
changing cell margin measurements, 473
changing column width and height, 468–471
changing design, 445–450
changing direction of text in cells, 474
changing layout, 464–481
changing size, 476
converting text to, 478
converting to text, 479
creating, 438–441
creating at Insert Table dialog box, 440–441
creating styles, 833
deleting columns, 464
deleting rows, 464
drawing, 450
entering text in cells, 439
inserting columns, 464
inserting in forms, 1010
inserting rows, 464
merging cells, 466
modifying styles, 836
moving in documents, 476
moving insertion point within, 439
performing calculations, 481–485
repeating header rows, 471
selecting cells with mouse, 442
selecting in with Select button, 464

selecting with keyboard commands, 443
sorting text in, 480, 590
splitting cells in, 466
using to create forms, 1008
viewing gridlines, 471
Table Tools Design Tab, 445
Table Tools Layout Tab, 464
Tabs, 6, 7
   adding buttons or commands from to Quick
      Access toolbar, 761
   adding commands to, 768
   alignment buttons for, 106
   clearing at Tabs dialog box, 110
   creating new, 767
   default header and footer, 654
   deleting from Ruler, 109
   determining at Tabs dialog box, 113
   determining settings, 113
   manipulating at Tabs dialog box, 110–113
   manipulating on Ruler, 106–109
   moving on Ruler, 109
   renaming, 767
   setting at Tabs dialog box, 110
   setting leaders at Tabs dialog box, 112
   setting on Ruler, 107
Tabs dialog box, 110
   clearing tabs at, 110
   manipulating tabs at, 110–113
   setting leader tabs at, 112
   setting tabs at, 110
Tab stops: moving insertion in tables to, 439
Tabular spacing, 420
Templates. *See also* Forms
   copying styles to, 842
   creating documents using, 299–300
   creating form, 1000
   default, 789, 801
   default folder for, 1006
   formatting and, 35
   macros and, 1060
   saving charts as, 499
   saving document as, 829
   updating, 830
Text. *See also* Building blocks; Customizing;
      Documents; Formatting
   applying effects, 422–423
   applying effect to in charts, 509
   assigning as headings, 1046–1047
   changing alignment at margins of paragraph, 65

changing alignment in cells, 471
changing alignment within paragraph, 65
changing direction in cells of, 474
checking for personal or hidden, 879
collapsing in outlines, 1050–1051
controlling widows and orphans, 662
converting to tables, 478
copying, 114
copying by pasting, 114
copying using Clipboard, 120–122
copying using Copy button, 118
copying using mouse, 119
creating columns in, 191–195
cutting, copying and pasting, 114
deleting, 114
deleting AutoCorrect, 759
displaying hidden, 45
editing predesigned footers, 225
editing predesigned headers, 225
entering in cells in tables, 439
finding, 226–227
formatting WordArt, 413
indenting in paragraphs, 69–71
inserting additional in table of contents, 976
inserting and deleting, 20
inserting controls in forms, 1004
inserting in shape, 400
inserting instructional in forms, 1008
inserting into SmartArt diagrams, 371
inserting predesigned footers, 221–222, 224
inserting predesigned headers, 221–222
kerning, 418, 419
marking for index, 943–945, 949
marking for index using concordance file, 952
marking in table of contents, 974–975
moving with mouse, 116
pasting, 114, 116–119
pasting using Clipboard, 120–122
pasting using Paste Special dialog box, 121
removing footers, 224
removing headers, 224
representing image, 882
selecting with keyboard, 22
selecting with mouse, 21–22
sorting columns at header row, 589
sorting in columns, 588
sorting in paragraphs, 105, 585–587
sorting in tables, 478, 590
sorting type, 586

tables converting to, 479

translating, 153–154

undoing or stopping AutoCorrect corrections, 755

vertical alignment, 235–236

wrapping around charts, 511

wrapping around images, 364

wrapping style for SmartArt diagrams, 374

Text Box button, 404

Text boxes

drawing, 405

formatting WordArt, 415–417

inserting in charts, 505

inserting in shapes, 407

inserting predesigned, 404

linking, 409

Text Direction button, 474

Text effects: applying, 422–423

Text Effects button, 37, 42, 422

Text form fields

customizing, 1026–1027

inserting, 1018

Text Highlight Color button, 37, 42

Theme colors, 99

applying custom, 793

choosing at Colors dialog box, 794

resetting custom, 791

Theme Colors button, 52

Theme Colors Drop-down Gallery with Custom Theme, 791

Theme Effects button, 797

Theme Font button, 52

Theme fonts: customizing, 796

Themes

applying, 51–52

applying custom colors, 793

applying effects, 797

choosing colors at Colors dialog box, 794

creating, 789–794

creating custom color, 790–791

customizing fonts, 796

default, 789

defined, 789

deleting custom, 802

resetting custom colors, 791

saving document, 797

Themes button, 51, 790

Themes Colors button, 790

Themes Fonts button, 790

Then fields, 561–562

Thesaurus: using, 147–148

Thesaurus button, 147

Thumbnails, 813

Time

inserting, 252

inserting in headers and footers, 652

Title bar, 6, 7

Toolbar

in Open dialog box, 13, 277

in Save As dialog box, 9

Track Changes button, 682

Track Changes Options dialog box, 687

Tracking changes

changing default, 685

customizing options, 687

displaying specific types, 686

Review Pane display, 675

to shared documents, 675–677, 682–683, 688

Trademark symbol (™), 623, 624

Translate button, 154

Translating text, 153–154

Translation Language Options dialog box, 154

Trust Center option, 777

Two Pages, 316

Typeface. *See* Fonts

Type size, 38

Typestyles, choosing, 40

U

Underline button, 37, 40

Undo button, 24

Undoing: text corrected in AutoCorrect, 755

Unlinking text boxes, 409

Unsaved documents: recovering, 318

Update Index button, 955

Updates button, 25

Update Table button, 971, 981, 984

Update Table of Contents dialog box, 972

Updating

automatically, 252

bibliographies, 929

date, 252

fields, 740

indexes, 945

placeholders, 736

table of authorities, 984

table of contents, 971–972

table of figures, 981
time, 252
works cited pages, 929
Use contextual spelling option, 141
User name and initials: changing, 678, 633

V

Vertical Reviewing pane, 675
Vertical ruler, 6, 7
Vertical scroll bar, 6, 7
   using mouse, 16
Viewing
   documents side by side, 313–314
   footnotes and endnotes, 917
View Ruler button, 69
Views
   changing, 181–182
   default, 177
   draft, 181
   Full Screen Reading, 181–182
View Side by Side button, 313

W

Watermark: inserting, 199
Watermark button, 199
Web Layout button on Status bar, 181
White space: hiding and showing, 316
White-space characters: ignoring in searches, 231
Widows, 662
Wildcards: using in search, 231
Windows
   arranging, 310, 311
   splitting, 312
   working with, 310–317
Wizard: using Mail Merge Wizard, 570–571
Word
   checking compatibility of versions, 885
   exiting, 15
   opening, 6
WordArt
   formatting text, 413
   formatting text boxes, 415–417
   inserting, 413–417
WordArt button, 413

WordArt Drop-down List, 413
WordArt styles: applying to charts, 509
Word Count button, 147
Word Count dialog box, 147
Word Options dialog box
   creating Custom Dictionaries, 144
   customizing, 774, 776–777
   with Display option selected, 65–66
   with General selected, 679, 774
   with New Tab Inserted, 767
   with Proofing selected, 138
   with Quick Access Toolbar selected, 763
   readability statistics, 143
   Writing Style option, 141
Words
   adding to AutoCorrect, 753
   finding specific whole, 231
   hyphenating, 196
   search all forms, 231
   search homophones, 231
   undoing or stopping AutoCorrect corrections, 755
Word wrap feature, 7
Works cited pages
   formatting, 930
   inserting, 928
   modifying, 929
Wrap Text button, 355, 511
Writing Style option, 141

X

XPS format: saving documents in, 297–299
XY charts, 496

Z

Zoom: changing document, 316
Zoom button, 316
Zoom In button, 181
Zoom In button on Status bar, 181
Zoom Out button, 181
Zoom Out button on Status bar, 181
Zoom Slider Bar on Status bar, 181

Feature	Ribbon Tab, Group	Button	Option	Quick Access Toolbar	Keyboard Shortcut
Align text center	Home, Paragraph				Ctrl + E
Align text left	Home, Paragraph				Ctrl + L
Align text right	Home, Paragraph				Ctrl + R
AutoCorrect	File	Options	Proofing		
Bibliography	References, Citations & Bibliography				
Bold text	Home, Font	**B**			Ctrl + B
Borders	Home, Paragraph				
Building Blocks Organizer	Insert, Text		Building Blocks Organizer		
Bullets	Home, Paragraph				
Change case of text	Home, Font	Aa			Shift + F3
Change Quick Styles set	Home, Styles				
Chart	Insert, Illustrations				
Clear all formatting	Home, Font				
Clip Art	Insert, Illustrations				
Close document	File	Close			Ctrl + F4
Columns	Page Layout, Page Setup				
Combine Documents	Review, Compare		Combine		
Compare Documents	Review, Compare		Compare		
Copy text	Home, Clipboard				Ctrl + C
Cover page	Insert, Pages				
Cut text	Home, Clipboard				Ctrl + X
Date and time	Insert, Text				
Display nonprinting characters	Home, Paragraph	¶			Ctrl + *
Drop cap	Insert, Text				
Endnote	References, Footnotes				Alt + Ctrl + D
Envelopes	Mailings, Create				
Exit Word	File	Exit			
Font dialog box	Home, Font				Ctrl + Shift + F
Footer	Insert, Header & Footer				
Footnote	References, Footnotes	AB			Alt + Ctrl + F
Format Painter	Home, Clipboard				Ctrl + Shift + C
Grow font	Home, Font	A			Ctrl + >
Header	Insert, Header & Footer				
Help	File	Help			F1
Highlight text	Home, Font				
Hyperlink	Insert, Links				Ctrl + K
Hyphenate	Page Layout, Page Setup				
Index	References, Index				
Insert file	Insert, Text		Text from File		
Italicize text	Home, Font	*I*			Ctrl + I
Justify-align text	Home, Paragraph				Ctrl + J
Labels	Mailings, Create				
Line spacing	Home, Paragraph				Ctrl + 1 (single) Ctrl + 2 (double) Ctrl + 5 (1.5)
Mail Merge	Mailings, Start Mail Merge				
Margins	Page Layout, Page Setup				
Mark Index Entry	References, Index				Alt + Shift + X

Feature	Ribbon Tab, Group	Button	Option	Quick Access Toolbar	Keyboard Shortcut
Mark Table of Contents Entry					Alt + Shift + O
Multilevel List	Home, Paragraph				
Navigation pane	View, Show		Navigation Pane		Ctrl + F
New document	File, New				Ctrl + N
New Line command					Shift + Enter
Nonbreaking space					Ctrl + Shift + Spacebar
Numbering	Home, Paragraph				
Open dialog box	File	Open			Ctrl + O
Orientation	Page Layout, Page Setup				
Page borders	Page Layout, Page Background				
Page break	Insert, Pages				Ctrl + Enter
Page numbering	Insert, Header & Footer				
Page size	Page Layout, Page Setup				
Paste text	Home, Clipboard				Ctrl + V
Picture	Insert, Illustrations				
Print tab Backstage view	File, Print				Ctrl + P
Redo					
Repeat last action					F4 or Ctrl + Y
Replace	Home, Editing				Ctrl + H
Reveal Formatting					Shift + F1
Save	File	Save			Ctrl + S
Save As	File	Save As			F12
Screenshot	Insert, Illustrations				
Shading	Home, Paragraph				
Shapes	Insert, Illustrations				
Shrink font	Home, Font				Ctrl + <
SmartArt	Insert, Illustrations				
Sort text	Home, Paragraph				
Spelling and Grammar	Review, Proofing				F7
Strikethrough text	Home, Font				
Subscript text	Home, Font				Ctrl + =
Superscript text	Home, Font				Ctrl + Shift + +
Symbol dialog box	Insert, Symbols		More Symbols		
Table	Insert, Tables				
Table of Contents	References, Table of Contents		Insert Table of Contents		
Table of Figures	References, Captions				
Tabs	Home, Paragraph		Tabs		
Text box	Insert, Text		Draw Text Box		
Themes	Page Layout, Themes				
Thesaurus	Review, Proofing				Shift + F7
Track changes	Review, Tracking				Ctrl + Shift + E
Underline text	Home, Font				Ctrl + U
Undo					
Watermark	Page Layout, Page Background				
Word Count dialog box	Review, Proofing				
WordArt	Insert, Text				